The Venomous Reptiles of the Western Hemisphere

Comstock Books in Herpetology

THE VENOMOUS REPTILES OF THE WESTERN HEMISPHERE

VOLUME II

JONATHAN A. CAMPBELL
University of Texas at Arlington

WILLIAM W. LAMAR
University of Texas at Tyler

with contributions by

EDMUND D. BRODIE III and EDMUND D. BRODIE JR.
Indiana University and Utah State University

RONALD L. GUTBERLET JR. and MICHAEL B. HARVEY
University of Texas at Tyler and East Tennessee State University

ROBERT NORRIS
Stanford University Medical Center

DAVID A. WARRELL
Centre for Tropical Medicine, University of Oxford

VINÍCIUS XAVIER DA SILVA
Universidade de São Paulo

Comstock Publishing Associates A DIVISION OF CORNELL UNIVERSITY PRESS, ITHACA AND LONDON

First published 2004 by Cornell University Press

Printed in China

Library of Congress Cataloging-in-Publication Data
Campbell, Jonathan A.
    The venomous reptiles of the Western Hemisphere / by Jonathan A.
Campbell and William W. Lamar, with contributions by Edmund D.
Brodie III . . . [et al.].
        p.   cm.—(Comstock books in herpetology)
Includes bibliographical references and index.
    ISBN 0-8014-4141-2 (cloth : alk. paper)
    1. Poisonous snakes—Western Hemisphere.   2. Reptiles—Western
Hemisphere.   I. Lamar, William W., 1950–   II. Brodie, Edmund
D., 1963–   III. Title.   IV. Series.
    QL666.O6C24   2003
    597.96′165′091812—dc21   2003007834

Cornell University Press strives to use environmentally responsible
suppliers and materials to the fullest extent possible in the publishing
of its books. Such materials include vegetable-based, low-VOC inks
and acid-free papers that are recycled, totally chlorine-free, or partly
composed of nonwood fibers. For further information, visit our
website at www.cornellpress.cornell.edu.

Cloth printing   10 9 8 7 6 5 4 3 2 1

We dedicate this book to our wives,
Tanya Dowdey and Nancy Lamar,
who have enthusiastically
supported our research activities.

CONTENTS

VOLUME I

VOLUME II

Color Maps are between pages 44 and 45 (Vol. I)

Color Plates 1–751 are between pages 92 and 93 (Vol. I); 752–1365, pages xvi and 477 (Vol. II); 1366–1500, pages 684 and 685 (Vol. II)

TABLES

VOLUME II

ABBREVIATIONS

AMNH	American Museum of Natural History, New York, New York, USA
ANSP	Academy of Natural Sciences of Philadelphia, Philadelphia, Pennsylvania, USA
BCB	Bryce C. Brown collection (now Strecker Museum), Waco, Texas, USA
BMNH	British Museum of Natural History, London, United Kingdom
BYU	Brigham Young University, Provo, Utah, USA
CAS	California Academy of Sciences, San Francisco, California, USA
CBF	Colección Boliviana de Fauna, La Paz, Bolivia
CIRAD	Centre de Coopération Internationale en Recherche Agronomique pour le Développement, French Guiana
CM	Carnegie Museum, Pittsburgh, Pennsylvania, USA
CP	Coleção Paralela of the Instituto Butantan, São Paulo, Brazil
CSA	Colección Santiago Ayerbe
CVUCG	Coleção da Vertebrados, Universidade Católica de Goiás, Brazil
CVULA	Colección Vertebratos, Universidad de los Andes, Mérida, Venezuela
DMNH	Dallas Museum of Natural History, Dallas, Texas, USA
ENEPI	Escuela Nacional de Estudios Profesionales Iztacala de la Universidad Nacional Autónoma de México, Mexico
ENS	Eric N. Smith collection
FED	Fundação Ezekial Diaz, Belo Horizonte, São Paolo, Brazil
FHGO	Fundación Herpetológica Gustavo Orcés, Quito, Ecuador
FMNH	Field Museum of Natural History, Chicago, Illinois, USA
FUL	Federación Universitaria de Litoral, Argentina
HINIRENA	Herpetología, Instituto de Investigaciones sobre los Recursos Naturales, Universidad Michoacana de San Nicolás de Hidalgo, Michoacán, Mexico
IB	Instituto Butantan, São Paulo, Brazil
INHMT	Instituto de Higiene y Medicina Tropical, Guayaquil, Ecuador
IVB	Instituto Vital Brazil, Rio de Janeiro, Brazil
JAC	Jonathan A. Campbell collection
JMR	Juan Manuel Renjifo collection
KU	Museum of Natural History, University of Kansas, Lawrence, Kansas, USA
LACM	Los Angeles County Museum of Natural History, Los Angeles, California, USA
LJV	Laurie J. Vitt collection
LSUMZ	Louisiana State University Museum of Zoology, Baton Rouge, Louisiana, USA
MCZ	Museum of Comparative Zoology, Harvard University, Cambridge, Massachusetts, USA
MHNG	Muséum d'Histoire Naturelle, Geneva, Switzerland
MHNUC	Museo de Historia Natural, Universidad de Cauca, Cauca, Colombia
MNHN	Muséum National d'Histoire Naturelle, Paris, France
MNRJ	Museu Nacional, Rio de Janeiro, Brazil

MSNM	Museo Civico de Storia Naturale de Milano, Milan, Italy
MUFAL	Museu Universidade Federal de Alagoas, Alagoas, Brazil
MVZ	Museum of Vertebrate Zoology, University of California at Berkeley, Berkeley, California, USA
MZUSP	Museu de Zoologia, Universidade de São Paulo, São Paulo, Brazil
NCMNH	North Carolina Museum of Natural History, Raleigh, North Carolina, USA
NHRM	Naturhistoriska Riksmuseet, Stockholm, Sweden
NMBA	Naturhistorisches Museum, Basel, Switzerland
NMW	Naturhistorisches Museum, Vienna, Austria
NORMAT	Núcleo de Ofiologia Regional de Mato Grosso
PNN	Parque Nacional Natural, Colombia
QCAZ	Museo de Zoología, Pontífica Universidad Católica del Ecuador, Quito, Ecuador
RMNH	Natuurhistorisches Museum, Leiden, Netherlands
RWM	Roy W. McDiarmid collection
SDSNH	San Diego Society of Natural History, San Diego, California, USA
STRI	Smithsonian Tropical Research Institute, Panama
TCWC	Texas Cooperative Wildlife Collection, Texas A&M University, College Station, Texas, USA
UCG	Universidade Católica de Goiás, Goiás, Brazil
UCR	Universidad de Costa Rica, San José, Costa Rica
UFMT	Universidad Federal de Mato Grosso, Mato Grosso, Brazil
UMMZ	University of Michigan Museum of Zoology, Ann Arbor, Michigan, USA
UNAM-LT	Universidad Nacional Autónoma de México, Los Tuxtlas, Veracruz, Mexico
UNAM-NL	Universidad Nacional Autónoma de México, Nuevo León, Mexico
UNESP	Universidad Estadual Paulista, Brazil
USNM	National Museum of Natural History, Washington, D.C., USA
UTA	University of Texas at Arlington, Arlington, Texas, USA
UV	Universidad del Valle, Guatemala City, Guatemala
WTN	Wilfred T. Neill collection
WWL	William W. Lamar collection
ZFMK	Zoologisches Forschungsinstitut und Museum Alexander Koenig, Bonn, Germany
ZIUG	Zoologisches Institut, Universität Göttingen, Göttingen, Germany
ZMB	Universität Humboldt, Zoologisches Museum, Berlin, Germany
ZMUU	Zoological Museum of the Royal University at Uppsala, Sweden
ZSBS	Zoologische Sammlung des bayerischen Staates, Munich, Germany
ZSM	Zoologische Staatssammlung, Munich, Germany
ZUEC	Museu de História Natural, Universidade Estadual de Campinas, Campinas, São Paulo, Brazil

For journal abbreviations, see Literature Cited. For abbreviated terms, see Glossary.

The Venomous Reptiles of the Western Hemisphere

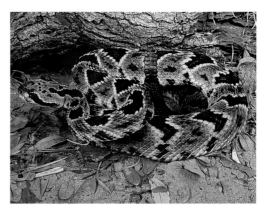

Plate 752. *Crotalus adamanteus*, approximately 150 cm TL. Torreya State Park, Liberty County, Florida, USA. Photo by James H. Carmichael.

Plate 753. *Crotalus adamanteus*. Dade County, Florida, USA. Photo by Louis W. Porras.

Plate 754. *Crotalus adamanteus × horridus*. Jasper County, South Carolina, USA. Photo by Louis W. Porras.

Plate 755. *Crotalus adamanteus*, adult female. Apalachicola National Forest, on Forest Road 136, Liberty County, Florida, USA. Photo by Troy D. Hibbitts.

Plate 756. *Crotalus aquilus*, adult male. La Estanzuela, Hidalgo, Mexico, elevation approximately 3,000 m. Photo by Louis W. Porras at the Dallas Zoo.

Plate 757. *Crotalus aquilus*, female, 58.0 cm TL, UTA R-12598. Parada Santa María, 3.2 km west of Madroño, Querétaro, Mexico.

Plate 758. *Crotalus aquilus*, male, 58.6 cm TL, UTA R-80. Jiquilpán, Michoacán, Mexico.

Plate 759. *Crotalus aquilus*, juvenile, 18.5 cm TL, UTA R-12597. From 20.6 km west of Jiquilpán, Michoacán, Mexico, elevation 2,164 m.

Plate 760. *Crotalus aquilus*. Vicinity of Jacala, Hidalgo, Mexico. Photo by John H. Tashjian.

Plate 761. *Crotalus aquilus*, male, 67.2 cm TL, UTA R-904. La Estanzuela, Hidalgo, Mexico. Photo by David Barker.

Plate 762. *Crotalus aquilus*, male, 54.2 cm TL, UTA R-12594. Los Marmoles, 8.4 km southwest of Durango, Hidalgo, Mexico.

Plate 763. *Crotalus aquilus*, female, 38.5 cm TL, UTA R-12592. Los Marmoles, 8.4 km southwest of Durango, Hidalgo, Mexico.

Plate 764. *Crotalus aquilus*, male, 67.2 cm TL, UTA R-17904. La Estanzuela, Hidalgo, Mexico, elevation approximately 3,000 m.

Plate 765. *Crotalus aquilus*, TCWC 58506. From 33 km west of Xichu, Guanajuato, Mexico. Photo by Robert A. Thomas.

Plate 766. *Crotalus aquilus*, female, 42.0 cm TL, UTA R-12593. Los Marmoles, 8.4 km southwest of Durango, Hidalgo, Mexico, elevation 2,298 m.

Plate 767. *Crotalus aquilus*, female. From 19 km east of San Luis Potosí, San Luis Potosí, Mexico. Photo by David G. Barker.

Plate 768. *Crotalus aquilus*, adult. El Lobo, Querétaro, Mexico. Photo by Louis W. Porras.

Plate 769. *Crotalus aquilus*, adult. El Valle de los Fantasmas, San Luis Potosí, Mexico. Photo by Louis W. Porras.

Plate 770. *Crotalus aquilus*, adult. Álvarez, San Luis Potosí, Mexico. Photo by Louis W. Porras.

Plate 771. *Crotalus aquilus*, male, about 60 cm TL, UTA R-12596. La Estanzuela, Hidalgo, Mexico, elevation 2,835 m.

Plate 772. *Crotalus aquilus*. Mexico. Photo by Paul Freed courtesy of Alan Kardon, San Antonio Zoo.

Plate 773. *Crotalus atrox*, 76.0 cm TL, ENS 10538. Rinconada, Municipio Zentla, Veracruz, Mexico. Photo by Eric N. Smith, courtesy of Robert Mora Gallardo.

Plate 774. *Crotalus atrox*, adult. Isla San Pedro Mártir, Baja California Norte, Mexico. Photo by John H. Tashjian at the California Academy of Sciences, San Francisco.

Plate 775. *Crotalus atrox*, adult. Cuatro Ciénagas, adjacent to Pozo Azul, Coahuila, Mexico. Photo by Robert W. Hansen.

Plate 776. *Crotalus atrox*, male, 190.0 cm TL. Zacatecas, Zacatecas, Mexico. Photo by Eric N. Smith, courtesy of Manuel Varela-Juliá.

Plate 777. *Crotalus atrox*, juvenile. On Chicken Springs Road, 14.4 km northeast of the junction with Alamo Road, Hualupai Mountains, Mohave County, Arizona, USA. Photo by Troy D. Hibbitts.

Plate 778. *Crotalus atrox*, female. Approximately 50 cm TL. Bend, Llano County, Texas, USA.

Plate 779. *Crotalus atrox*, male, 30.1 cm TL, UTA R-1409. From 3 km southeast of Silver, Coke County, Texas, USA. Photo by David G. Barker.

Plate 780. *Crotalus atrox*, adult. McMullen County, Texas, USA. Photo by David G. Barker.

Plate 781. *Crotalus atrox*, melanistic adult male. On Rural Route 2134, 10.2 km north of Millersview, Concho County, Texas, USA. Photo by William B. Montgomery.

Plate 782. *Crotalus atrox*. Val Verde County, Texas, USA. Striped or patternless specimens are not uncommon in some areas of Texas. Photo by Louis W. Porras.

Plate 783. *Crotalus atrox*. Approximately 45 cm TL, Charco Cercado, north of San Luis Potosí, San Luis Potosí, Mexico. Photo by Eric N. Smith, courtesy of Manuel Varela-Juliá.

Plate 784. *Crotalus basiliscus*, male, 190.0 cm TL, ENS 10541. San Blas, Nayarit, Mexico. Photo by Eric N. Smith.

Plate 785. *Crotalus basiliscus*. Colima, Mexico. Photo by Cassano.

Plate 786. *Crotalus basiliscus*. Same as Plate 785.

Plate 787. *Crotalus basiliscus*. Colima, Mexico. Photo by Louis W. Porras.

Plate 788. *Crotalus catalinensis*. Isla de Santa Catalina, Baja California Sur, Mexico. Photo by Louis W. Porras.

Plate 789. *Crotalus catalinensis*. Same as Plate 788. View of tail and vestigial rattle. This species and *C. ruber lorenzoensis* characteristically shed the rattles. Photo by Louis W. Porras.

Plate 790. *Crotalus catalinensis*. Isla de Santa Catalina Baja California Sur, Mexico. Photo by Paul Freed.

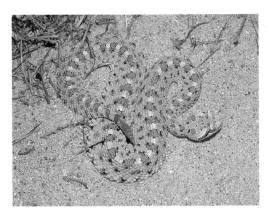

Plate 791. *Crotalus cerastes cerastes*, juvenile. On Redrock-Rands Road, 8.1 km east of the junction with California Highway 14 Kern County, California, USA. Photo by Troy D. Hibbitts.

Plate 792. *Crotalus cerastes cerastes*. Southern Nevada, USA. Photo by Paul Freed.

Plate 793. *Crotalus cerastes cercobombus*, adult. Sandari Road, Tucson, Pima County, Arizona, USA. Photo b Louis W. Porras.

Plate 794. *Crotalus cerastes laterorepens*, adult. Imperial County, California, USA. Photo by Louis W. Porras.

Plate 795. *Crotalus durissus durissus*, 44.1 cm TL, RMNH 23512. Matapica Creek, coastal Suriname. Photo by Albertus Abuys.

Plate 796. *Crotalus durissus durissus*, male, approximately 65 cm TL. Coastal Guyana. Photo by Louis W Porras.

Plate 797. *Crotalus durissus cascavella*. Brazil. Photo by Ludwig Trutnau.

Plate 798. *Crotalus durissus cascavella*, female, approximately 120 cm TL, IB. Brumado, Bahia, Brazil. Photo by Ivan Sazima.

Plate 799. *Crotalus durissus collilineatus*, female, approximately 100 cm TL, IB. Catalão, Goiás, Brazil. Photo b Ivan Sazima.

Plate 800. *Crotalus durissus collilineatus*. Same locality as Plate 799. Photo by Nelson Jorge da Silva.

Plate 801. *Crotalus durissus collilineatus*, adult male. Goiás, Brazil. Photo by Danté Fenolio, courtesy of Nelson Jorge da Silva.

Plate 802. *Crotalus durissus collilineatus*, female, approximately 80 cm TL. Piranhas, Goiás, Brazil. Specimen courtesy of Nelson Jorge da Silva.

Plate 803. *Crotalus durissus cumanensis*, male, 120 cm TL. Huila, Colombia. Photo by Mats Höggren.

Plate 804. *Crotalus durissus cumanensis*, approximately 100 cm TL. Armero, Tolima, Colombia.

Plate 805. *Crotalus durissus cumanensis*, adult. Chiriguaná, César, Colombia. Photo by Juan Manuel Renjifo, courtesy of the Instituto Nacional de Salud, Bogotá.

Plate 806. *Crotalus durissus cumanensis*, adult female. Puerto Borracho (Río Tomo), Vichada, Colombia.

Plate 807. *Crotalus durissus cumanensis*, approximately 120 cm TL. Sabanas de Yaracuy, Yaracuy, Venezuela. Specimen courtesy of El Mundo de las Serpientes, Costa Rica.

Plate 808. *Crotalus durissus cumanensis*, approximately 40 cm TL. Guárico, Venezuela. Populations of *C. durissus* vary considerably in Venezuela. This specimen represents a morph that has been described as *C. pifanorum*.

Plate 809. *Crotalus durissus cumanensis*. Valle de la Pascua, Guárico, Venezuela. Populations of *C. durissus* vary considerably in Venezuela. This specimen represents a morph that has been described as *C. pifanorum*. Photo by César Barrio-Amorós, courtesy of Serpentarium Los Llanos, Venezuela.

Plate 810. *Crotalus durissus marajoensis*, female. Marajó-Mangabal, Ilha de Marajó, Pará, Brazil. Photo by Jack W. Sites Jr., courtesy of the Museu Paraense Emílio Goeldi, Belém, Pará, Brazil.

Plate 811. *Crotalus durissus marajoensis*. Same as Plate 810. Photo by Nelson Jorge da Silva, courtesy of the Museu Paraense Emílio Goeldi, Pará, Brazil.

Plate 812. *Crotalus durissus ruruima*, male. Boa Vista, Roraima, Brazil. Photo by Márcio Martins.

Plate 813. *Crotalus durissus ruruima*, adult. Bomfím, Roraima, Brazil. Photo by Otávio A. V. Marques.

Plate 814. *Crotalus durissus terrificus*, male, 85.6 cm TL ZUEC 810. Carlos Gomes, Campinas, São Paulo, Brazil Photo by Ivan Sazima.

Plate 815. *Crotalus durissus terrificus*, adult female, LJV 2007. Alto de Araguaia, Mato Grosso, Brazil. Photo by Laurie J. Vitt.

Plate 816. *Crotalus durissus terrificus*, female, approximately 100 cm TL. Sandia, Puno, Peru, elevation 1,880 m. Specimen courtesy of the Instituto Nacional de Salud, Lima.

Plate 817. *Crotalus durissus trigonicus*. Rupunun Savanna, Guyana. Photo by Hans Boos.

Plate 818. *Crotalus durissus trigonicus*. Sipaliwini Savanna, district of Sipaliwini, Suriname. Photo by Joep M. Moonen.

Plate 819. *Crotalus durissus unicolor*. Aruba. Photo by Paul Freed.

Plate 820. *Crotalus durissus unicolor*, adult female Aruba. Photo by Louis W. Porras.

Plate 821. *Crotalus durissus unicolor*, adult female. Aruba. Photo by David G. Barker at the Dallas Zoo.

Plate 822. *Crotalus durissus vegrandis*. Las Sabanas de Maturín, Monagas, Venezuela. Photo by Louis W. Porras.

Plate 823. *Crotalus durissus vegrandis*. Las Sabanas d Maturín, Monagas, Venezuela. Photo by Paul Freed.

Plate 824. *Crotalus durissus vegrandis*, neonate. Las Sabanas de Maturín, Monagas, Venezuela. Photo by Paul Freed.

Plate 825. *Crotalus enyo enyo*. Baja California Norte, Mexico. Photo by Ed Cassano.

Plate 826. *Crotalus enyo enyo*, male. Mexico. Photo by David G. Barker.

Plate 827. *Crotalus enyo cerralvensis*. Isla Cerralvo, Baja California Sur, Mexico. Photo by John H. Tashjian at the California Academy of Sciences, San Francisco.

Plate 828. *Crotalus enyo furvus*. Baja California Norte, Mexico. Photo by Louis W. Porras at the Dallas Zoo.

Plate 829. *Crotalus horridus*, female, 109.5 cm TL, UTA R-22358. Italy, Ellis County, Texas, USA. Photo by David G. Barker.

Plate 830. *Crotalus horridus*. Same as Plate 829.

Plate 831. *Crotalus horridus*. Jasper County, South Carolina, USA. Photo by Louis W. Porras.

Plate 832. *Crotalus horridus*, neonate. Rutherford County, North Carolina, USA. Photo by R. Wayne Van Devender.

Plate 833. *Crotalus horridus*, adult. Cherokee National Forest, Monroe County, Tennessee, USA. Photo by Terry Hibbitts.

Plate 834. *Crotalus horridus*. Western Pennsylvania, USA. Black individuals are common, especially along the northeastern portion of the range. Photo by Louis W. Porras.

Plate 835. *Crotalus intermedius intermedius*. North of Perote, Veracruz, Mexico. Photo by Terry Basey, courtesy of James B. Murphy.

Plate 836. *Crotalus intermedius intermedius*, juvenile, 36.1 cm TL, KU 155530. From 1.6 km west of Cacaloapan, Puebla, Mexico, elevation 2,073 m. Photo by John H. Tashjian at the Dallas Zoo.

Plate 837. *Crotalus intermedius gloydi*, female, 42.8 cm TL, UTA R-12569. El Tejocote, Oaxaca, Mexico, elevation 2,377 m.

Plate 838. *Crotalus intermedius omiltemanus*, male, 53.1 cm TL, UTA R-51459. Camino Tlatlalquitepec-Malinaltepec, at km 38.4, Guerrero, Mexico, elevation 2,400 m. Photo by Eric N. Smith.

Plate 839. *Crotalus intermedius omiltemanus*, male, 45.7 cm TL, UTA R-6245. From 1.3 km east of Omilteme, Guerrero, Mexico, elevation 2,073 m. Photo by John Tashjian.

Plate 840. *Crotalus lannomi*, female, preserved specimen, 63.8 cm TL, BYU 23800, holotype. From 2.9 km west of Paso Los Mazos (vicinity of Autlán), or 35.2 km west by road from the Río Tuxcacuescu, a branch of the Río Armeria, on Mexico Highway 80, Jalisco, Mexico. Photo by John H. Tashjian at Brigham Young University, Provo, Utah.

Plate 841. *Crotalus lepidus lepidus*, female, approximately 45 cm TL. Vicinity of Comstock, Val Verde County, Texas, USA.

Plate 842. *Crotalus lepidus lepidus*, male. Indio Mountains Research Center, Hudspeth County, Texas, USA. Photo by Troy D. Hibbitts.

Plate 843. *Crotalus lepidus lepidus*, adult female. Vicinity of Buffalo Trails Boy Scout Camp on Ranch Road 1837, Jeff Davis County, Texas, USA. Photo by Troy D. Hibbitts.

Plate 844. *Crotalus lepidus lepidus*. Val Verde County, Texas, USA. Photo by Louis W. Porras.

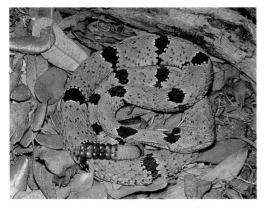

Plate 845. *Crotalus lepidus klauberi*, male. Chihuahua, Mexico. Photo by David G. Barker.

Plate 846. *Crotalus lepidus klauberi*, male. Arroyo Mesteño, Sierra del Nido, Chihuahua, Mexico. Photo by David G. Barker.

Plate 847. *Crotalus lepidus klauberi*, male, approximately 30 cm TL. From 2 km above "Cascada," near Río Baseachic, Chihuahua, Mexico.

Plate 848. *Crotalus lepidus klauberi*, adult male. Franklin Mountains, El Paso County, Texas, USA. Photo by Louis W. Porras.

Plate 849. *Crotalus lepidus klauberi*, adult male. Northeast Organ Mountains, Doña Ana County, New Mexico, USA. Photo by Louis W. Porras.

Plate 850. *Crotalus lepidus klauberi*, adult female. Cathedral Vista Point Canyon, Chiricahua Mountains, Cochise County, Arizona, USA, elevation 1,730 m. Photo by Louis W. Porras.

Plate 851. *Crotalus lepidus klauberi*, adult male. Rancho Santa Barbara, Durango, Mexico. Photo by Louis W. Porras.

Plate 852. *Crotalus lepidus klauberi*. Banderas de Aguila, Durango, Mexico. Photo by Louis W. Porras.

Plate 853. *Crotalus lepidus maculosus*. RWM 1780 at LACM. Vicinity of the Sinaloa-Durango border, 7.6 km east of Santa Rita along Mexico Highway 40, Mexico. Photo by Roy W. McDiarmid.

Plate 854. *Crotalus lepidus maculosus*, male, 78.7 cm TL, UTA R-17836. From 0.8 km west of El Carrizo, Sinaloa, Mexico.

Plate 855. *Crotalus lepidus maculosus*. Los Bancos, west of La Ciudad, Durango, Mexico. Photo by Louis W. Porras.

Plate 856. *Crotalus lepidus morulus*, female, 44.9 cm TL, UTA R-6123. From 10.7 km east of San Antonio de las Alazanas, Coahuila, Mexico, elevation 2,682 m. Photo by David G. Barker at the Dallas Zoo.

Plate 857. *Crotalus lepidus morulus*, adult male. Galeana, Nuevo León, Mexico. Photo by William B. Montgomery.

Plate 858. *Crotalus lepidus morulus*, adult male. Galeana, Nuevo León, Mexico. Photo by William B. Montgomery.

Plate 859. *Crotalus lepidus morulus*, subadult. San Pedro Garza García, Chipinque, Nuevo León, Mexico. This population has been described as *C. l. castaneus*. Photo by William Lamoreaux.

Plate 860. *Crotalus lepidus morulus*, male. From 17.1 km east of San Antonio de las Alazanas, Coahuila, Mexico, elevation 2,682 m. Photo by David G. Barker at the Dallas Zoo.

Plate 861. *Crotalus lepidus morulus*, adult. Rancho Viejo, Gómez Farías, Tamaulipas, Mexico. Photo by Louis W. Porras.

Plate 862. *Crotalus lepidus morulus*, adult female Marcela, Tamaulipas, Mexico. Photo by Paul Freed courtesy of Alan Kardon, San Antonio Zoo.

Plate 863. *Crotalus lepidus morulus*, adult. Marcela, Tamaulipas, Mexico. Photo by Paul Freed, courtesy of Alan Kardon, San Antonio Zoo.

Plate 864. *Crotalus mitchellii mitchellii*, adult. San Bartolo, Baja California Sur, Mexico. Photo by Lee Grismer.

Plate 865. *Crotalus mitchellii mitchellii*, adult. Isla Sa José, Baja California Sur, Mexico. Photo by Lee Grisme

Plate 866. *Crotalus mitchellii angelensis*, subadult. Puerto Refugio, Baja California Norte, Mexico. Photo by Lee Grismer.

Plate 867. *Crotalus mitchellii angelensis*. Isla Ángel de la Guarda, Baja California Norte, Mexico. Photo by John H. Tashjian at the California Academy of Sciences, San Francisco.

Plate 868. *Crotalus mitchellii muertensis*, adult. Isla Muerto, Baja California Norte, Mexico. Photo by Le Grismer.

Plate 869. *Crotalus mitchelli pyrrhus*, juvenile. Washington County, Utah, USA. Photo by Louis W. Porras.

Plate 870. *Crotalus mitchellii pyrrhus*, subadult. Dome Rock Mountains, La Paz County, Arizona, USA. Photo by Troy D. Hibbitts.

Plate 871. *Crotalus mitchellii pyrrhus*, adult. Robl Creek, Camp Pendleton, San Diego County, Californi USA. Photo by Robert W. Hansen.

Plate 872. *Crotalus mitchellii pyrrhus*, subadult. From 9 km south of La Rumarosa, Baja California Norte, Mexico. Photo by Troy D. Hibbitts.

Plate 873. *Crotalus mitchellii stephensi*, adult. Furnace Creek Road, 3.3 km west-northwest of the junction of Mesquite Valley Road and Smith Talc Road, Inyo County, California, USA. Photo by Robert W. Hansen.

Plate 874. *Crotalus mitchellii stephensi*, female. Inyo County, California, USA. Photo by Louis W. Porras.

Plate 875. *Crotalus mitchellii stephensi*, adult. Northwest of Bishop, Mono County, California, USA, elevation 2,027 m. Photo by Robert W. Hansen.

Plate 876. *Crotalus molossus molossus*, female, 59.8 cm TL, UTA R-14511. Seminole Canyon State Park, Val Verde County, Texas, USA.

Plate 877. *Crotalus molossus molossus*, subadult. On Harquahala Peak Road, 8.0 km north of the junction with Eagle Eye Road, Harquahala Mountains, La Paz County, Arizona, USA. Photo by Troy D. Hibbitts.

Plate 878. *Crotalus molossus molossus*, neonate. On Mount Hopkins Road, 2.0 km east of Whipple Observatory Visitor Center, Santa Rita Mountains, Santa Cruz County, Arizona, USA. Photo by Troy D. Hibbitts.

Plate 879. *Crotalus molossus molossus*. Coahuila, Mexico. Photo by Louis W. Porras.

Plate 880. *Crotalus* cf. *molossus*. El Carrizo, Sinaloa, Mexico. Photo by Ed Cassano.

Plate 881. *Crotalus molossus estebanensis*. Isla San Esteban, Sonora, Mexico. Photo by Louis W. Porras.

Plate 882. *Crotalus molossus nigrescens*, male, approximately 213 cm TL. Sierra La Gloria, northeast of El Tuito, Jalisco, Mexico, elevation approximately 1,524 m. Photo by Rick C. West.

Plate 883. *Crotalus molossus nigrescens*, male. Near Dos Aguas, Michoacán, Mexico. Photo by David G. Barker at the Dallas Zoo.

Plate 884. *Crotalus molossus nigrescens*, juvenile. Approximately 20 km east of Tapalpa, Jalisco, Mexico, elevation 2,133 m. Photo by Joe Marek.

Plate 885. *Crotalus molossus oaxacus*, male, 81.0 cm TL, UTA R-25852. El Tejocote, Oaxaca, Mexico, elevation 2,377 m. Photo by David G. Barker.

Plate 886. *Crotalus molossus oaxacus*, male, 81.0 cm TL, UTA R-25852. El Tejocote, Oaxaca, Mexico, elevation 2,377 m.

Plate 887. *Crotalus molossus oaxacus*, juvenile male, 31.7 cm TL, UTA R-25853. El Tejocote, Oaxaca, Mexico, elevation 2,135 m.

Plate 888. *Crotalus molossus oaxacus*, male, 118.2 cm TL, UTA R-12574. From 5.6 km south-southwest of Zapotitlán Salinas, Puebla, Mexico, elevation 1,524 m. Snakes from this population, like those in the extreme northern part of the range, may retain the ringed or banded tail pattern into adulthood.

Plate 889. *Crotalus oreganus oreganus*, female, 33.9 cm TL, UTA R-19412. Washington State, USA. Photo by David G. Barker.

Plate 890. *Crotalus oreganus oreganus*. Same as Plate 889.

Plate 891. *Crotalus oreganus oreganus*, female, 60.2 cm TL, UTA R-31018. Oregon Highway 140, 25.5 km northwest of Harney County line, Klamath County, Oregon, USA. Photo by David G. Barker.

Plate 892. *Crotalus oreganus oreganus*, female, 91.9 cm TL, UTA R-19357. Pine Flat, 40 km east of Fresno, Fresno County, California, USA. Photo by David G. Barker.

Plate 893. *Crotalus oreganus oreganus*, adult. Carrizo Plain, southwest edge of the San Joaquin Valley, Kern County, California, USA. Photo by Louis W. Porras.

Plate 894. *Crotalus oreganus* cf. *abyssus*, adult female. Wide Hollow Reservoir, Garfield County, Utah, USA. Photo by Louis W. Porras.

Plate 895. *Crotalus oreganus* cf. *abyssus*, adult male. Alvey Wash, Kaiparowitz Plateau, Garfield County, Utah, USA. Photo by Louis W. Porras.

Plate 896. *Crotalus oreganus* cf. *abyssus*, subadult female. lvey Wash, Kaiparowitz Plateau, Garfield County, tah, USA. Photo by Louis W. Porras.

Plate 897. *Crotalus oreganus abyssus*, adult. Cottonwood Canyon Road, south of the Cockscomb, Kane County, Utah, USA. Photo by Louis W. Porras.

Plate 898. *Crotalus oreganus* cf. *abyssus*, adult male. Vicinity of Kodachrome Basin State Park, Kane County, Utah, USA. Note the exceptionally long tail. Photo by Louis W. Porras.

ate 899. *Crotalus oreganus* cf. *abyssus*, adult female. om 9.4 km southeast of Cannonville, Kane County, tah, USA. Photo by Louis W. Porras.

Plate 900. *Crotalus oreganus abyssus*, adult. Marble Canyon, Coconino County, Arizona, USA. Photo by Louis W. Porras.

Plate 901. *Crotalus oreganus caliginus*, adult. Isla Coronado, Baja California Norte, Mexico. Photo by John H. Tashjian, courtesy of R. Folsom.

ate 902. *Crotalus oreganus cerberus*, adult male. Pima ounty, Arizona, USA. Photo by Louis W. Porras.

Plate 903. *Crotalus oreganus cerberus*, adult male. Santa Catalina Mountains, Tuscon, Pima County, Arizona, USA. Photo by David L. Hardy.

Plate 904. *Crotalus oreganus cerberus*, adult male. Santa Catalina Mountains, Tuscon, Pima County, Arizona, USA. Photo by David L. Hardy.

ate 905. *Crotalus oreganus concolor*, adult female. Moki nyon, San Juan County, Utah, USA. Photo by Louis Porras.

Plate 906. *Crotalus oreganus concolor*, adult. On Utah Highway 26, 18.8 km east-southeast of Hall's Crossing, San Juan County, Utah, USA. Photo by Louis W. Porras.

Plate 907. *Crotalus oreganus concolor*, juvenile. Firehole Region, Sweetwater County, Wyoming, USA. Photo by Louis W. Porras.

Plate 908. *Crotalus oreganus concolor*, adult male. Escalante Canyon, Delta County, Colorado, USA. Photo by Louis W. Porras.

Plate 909. *Crotalus oreganus helleri*, adult. Palomar Airport, Carlsbad, San Diego County, California, USA. Photo by Troy D. Hibbitts.

Plate 910. *Crotalus oreganus helleri*, adult. From 24 km south of El Arco, Baja California Sur, Mexico. Photo by Louis W. Porras.

Plate 911. *Crotalus oreganus lutosus*, adult. Farmington Canyon, Davis County, Utah, USA. Photo by Louis W. Porras.

Plate 912. *Crotalus oreganus lutosus*, adult. Lone Rock, Skull Valley, Tooele County, Utah, USA. Photo by Louis W. Porras.

Plate 913. *Crotalus oreganus lutosus*, adult male. Gold Hill, Goshute Mountains, Elko County, Nevada, USA. Photo by Louis W. Porras.

Plate 914. *Crotalus oreganus lutosus*, adult male. Hidden Canyon, 3.2 km north of St. George, Washington County, Utah, USA. Photo by Louis W. Porras.

Plate 915. *Crotalus polystictus*, male, approximately 40 cm TL. Mexico. Specimen courtesy of El Mundo de las Serpientes, Costa Rica.

Plate 916. *Crotalus polystictus*, adult male. Llanos de Pasteje, México, Mexico. Photo by Eric N. Smith, courtesy of Manuel Varela-Juliá.

Plate 917. *Crotalus polystictus*, adult male, UTA collection. Southeastern Jalisco, Mexico.

Plate 918. *Crotalus polystictus*, female, 62.9 cm TL, UTA R-12583. From 2.4 km northwest of Tapalpa, Jalisco, Mexico.

Plate 919. *Crotalus pricei pricei*. No locality data. Photo by Ed Cassano.

Plate 920. *Crotalus pricei pricei*, adult male. Vicinity of oyotes, Durango, Mexico. Photo by Ed Cassano.

Plate 921. *Crotalus pricei pricei*, adult female. West of La Ciudad, Durango, Mexico. Photo by John H. Tashjian at the Dallas Zoo.

Plate 922. *Crotalus pricei pricei*, male, 49.2 cm TL, UTA R-6251. Los Bancos, west of La Ciudad, Durango, Mexico. Photo by John H. Tashjian at the Dallas Zoo.

Plate 923. *Crotalus pricei pricei*. Llano Grande, Durango, exico. Photo by John H. Tashjian at the Fort Worth o.

Plate 924. *Crotalus pricei miquihuanus*, neonate. Cerro Peña Nevada, Nuevo León, Mexico. Photo by Paul Freed, courtesy of Alan Kardon, San Antonio Zoo.

Plate 925. *Crotalus pricei miquihuanus*. Vicinity of Galeana, Nuevo León, Mexico. Photo by William B. Montgomery.

Plate 926. *Crotalus pricei miquihuanus*, adult. La antada, above Zaragoza, Nuevo León, Mexico. oto by William B. Montgomery.

Plate 927. *Crotalus pricei* subsp., adult male, UNAM-NL. Vicinity of La Congoja, Municipio de San José de Gracia, Aguascalientes, Mexico, elevation 2,858 m. Photo by David G. Barker, courtesy of David Lascano.

Plate 928. *Crotalus pricei* subsp. Same as Plate 927.

Plate 929. *Crotalus pusillus*, adult, UTA R-7164. Near s Aguas, Michoacán, Mexico. Photo by Louis W. ras.

Plate 930. *Crotalus pusillus*, male, 55.4 cm TL, UTA R-9358. Near Dos Aguas, Michoacán, Mexico. Photo by David G. Barker at the Dallas Zoo.

Plate 931. *Crotalus ravus ravus*, female, 55.5 cm TL, UTA R-12636. Environs of Huitzilac, Morelos, Mexico, elevation 2,743 m. Note the large head plates, unique in *Crotalus*.

Plate 932. *Crotalus ravus ravus.* Vicinity of Zapotitlán Salinas, Puebla, Mexico.

Plate 933. *Crotalus ravus ravus.* Mexico. Photo by David G. Barker at the Dallas Zoo.

Plate 934. *Crotalus ravus ravus*, female, 42.9 cm TL, UT R-12614. From 5.1 km south-southwest of Zapotitlán Salinas, Puebla, Mexico, elevation 1,494 m.

Plate 935. *Crotalus ravus brunneus*, male, 66.3 cm TL, UTA R-12613. From 12.4 km west of Totontepec (Sierra Mixe), Oaxaca, Mexico, elevation 2,524 m.

Plate 936. *Crotalus ravus brunneus*, DMNH 4689. On Mexico Highway 175, 23.8 km north of Mexico Highway 190, Oaxaca, Mexico. Photo by John H. Tashjian at the Dallas Zoo.

Plate 937. *Crotalus ravus exiguus*, paratype, male 57.4 cm TL, UTA R-5663. Ejido San Vicente (east Jazmín), Guerrero, Mexico.

Plate 938. *Crotalus ravus exiguus*, female, 47.7 cm TL, UTA R-10295. From 1.6 km east of Omiltemé, Guerrero, Mexico. Photo by Louis W. Porras.

Plate 939. *Crotalus ravus exiguus*, female, approximately 22 cm TL. Central Guerrero, Mexico, elevation 2,072 m. Photo by John H. Tashjian at the Dallas Zoo.

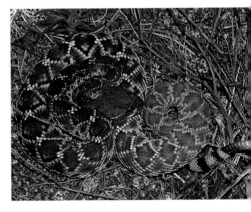

Plate 940. *Crotalus ruber ruber*, adult. Near the junction of California Highway 74 and Carrizo Road, Santa Rosa Mountains, Riverside County, California, USA. Photo by Troy D. Hibbitts.

Plate 941. *Crotalus ruber ruber*, adult. Riverside County, California, USA. Photo by Louis W. Porras.

Plate 942. *Crotalus ruber exsul.* Isla Cedros, Baja California Norte, Mexico. Photo by Louis W. Porras.

Plate 943. *Crotalus ruber exsul.* Isla Cedros, Baja California Norte, Mexico. Photo by Louis W. Porras.

 te 944. *Crotalus ruber exsul*, juvenile. Isla Cedros, Baja
lifornia Norte, Mexico. Photo by Louis W. Porras.

Plate 945. *Crotalus ruber lorenzoensis*, adult. Isla San
Lorenzo Sur, Baja California Norte, Mexico. Photo by
John H. Tashjian at the San Diego Zoo.

Plate 946. *Crotalus ruber lorenzoensis*, adult. Isla San
Lorenzo Sur, Baja California Norte, Mexico. Photo by
John H. Tashjian at the Arizona–Sonora Desert Museum,
Tucson.

te 947. *Crotalus ruber lucasensis*, male. Mexico. Photo
David G. Barker at the Dallas Zoo.

Plate 948. *Crotalus ruber lucasensis*, adult. Bahía San
Ignacio, Baja California Norte, Mexico. Photo by Louis
W. Porras.

Plate 949. *Crotalus scutulatus scutulatus*. Beaver Dam
Slope, Washington County, Utah, USA. Photo by Louis
W. Porras.

te 950. *Crotalus scutulatus scutulatus*, adult male. On
mo Road, 7.0 km southeast of the junction with
;hway 40, Mohave County, Arizona, USA. Photo by
y D. Hibbitts.

Plate 951. *Crotalus scutulatus scutulatus*, adult. River
Road, Brewster County, Texas, USA. Photo by Louis W.
Porras.

Plate 952. *Crotalus scutulatus scutulatus*. Cuencamé,
Durango, Mexico. Photo by Ed Cassano.

te 953. *Crotalus scutulatus scutulatus*, male, approxi-
ely 50 cm TL, UTA R-22367. On Farm-to-Market
d 170, 13.2 km east of Lajitas, Brewster County,
as, USA.

Plate 954. *Crotalus scutulatus salvini*. West-central Veracruz, Mexico. Photo by Saul Friess.

Plate 955. *Crotalus scutulatus salvini*. Same as Plate 954.

Plate 956. *Crotalus simus simus*, male, 165.3 cm TL, UTA R-51456. Santa Ines, Chimalapa, Oaxaca, Mexico. Photo by Eric N. Smith.

Plate 957. *Crotalus simus simus*, male, 130.3 cm TL, UTA R-21911. Vicinity of Huiste, Suchitepéquez, Guatemala. Photo by David G. Barker.

Plate 958. *Crotalus simus simus*, female, 137 cm TL, JA 20787. Aldea El Arenal, San Vicente, Zacapa, Guatemal Photo by Eric N. Smith.

Plate 959. *Crotalus simus simus*, male, approximately 45 cm TL. Parque Nacional Santa Rosa, Guanacaste, Costa Rica.

Plate 960. *Crotalus simus simus*, male, approximately 140 cm TL. Colorado de Abangares, Puntarenas, Costa Rica. Photo by Alejandro Solórzano at the Serpentario Nacional, San José.

Plate 961. *Crotalus simus simus*, female, juveni Chomes, Puntarenas, Costa Rica.

Plate 962. *Crotalus simus culminatus*, adult. Carretera Tierra Colorada–Ayutla (17.1146°N, 99.5108°W), elevation 306 m. Photo by Eric N. Smith.

Plate 963. *Crotalus simus culminatus*, adult. Mexico. Photo by David G. Barker at the Dallas Zoo.

Plate 964. *Crotalus simus culminatus*. Mexico. Photo David G. Barker at the Dallas Zoo.

Plate 965. *Crotalus simus tzabcan*, adult. Yucatán, Mexico. Photo by Louis W. Porras.

Plate 966. *Crotalus simus tzabcan*, adult. From 50 km west-southwest of Belize City, Belize. Photo by Julian C. Lee.

Plate 967. *Crotalus stejnegeri*, male, 59.2 cm TL, UTA 10499. Plomosas, Municipio Rosario, Sinaloa, Mexi Photo by Louis W. Porras.

Plate 968. *Crotalus tigris*, adult male. On Mount opkins Road, 9.4 km east of the junction with Elephant ead Road, Santa Cruz County, Arizona, USA. Photo by oy D. Hibbitts.

Plate 969. *Crotalus tigris*, adult. Pima County, Arizona, USA. Photo by Louis W. Porras.

Plate 970. *Crotalus tortuguensis*. Isla Tortuga, Baja California Sur, Mexico. Photo by John H. Tashjian at the San Diego Zoo.

Plate 971. *Crotalus tortuguensis*, adult female. Isla rtuga, Baja California Sur, Mexico. Photo by David G. rker at the Dallas Zoo.

Plate 972. *Crotalus totonacus*, adult male. Aldama, Tamaulipas, Mexico. Photo by Alan Kardon.

Plate 973. *Crotalus totonacus*, adult. Coastal Tamaulipas, Mexico. Photo by Louis W. Porras.

Plate 974. *Crotalus totonacus*, adult female. Mexico. oto by David G. Barker at the Dallas Zoo.

Plate 975. *Crotalus totonacus*, adult male. West of El Lobo, Querétaro, Mexico. Photo by Ed Cassano.

Plate 976. *Crotalus totonacus*. Same as Plate 975.

Plate 977. *Crotalus totonacus*, juvenile. On the road to La ya, east of Aldama, Tamaulipas, Mexico. Photo by bert W. Hansen.

Plate 978. *Crotalus transversus*. Near Presa Iturbide, Los Tachos, México, Mexico, elevation 3,600 m. Photo by José L. Camarillo.

Plate 979. *Crotalus transversus*. Lagunas de Zempoala, Morelos, Mexico, elevation 2,987 m. Photo by John H. Tashjian, courtesy of Charles Radcliffe.

Plate 980. *Crotalus* sp., female, HINIRENA 308. Cerro Tancítaro, Michoacán, Mexico, elevation 3,300 m. This population appears to be closely allied with *C. transversus*. Photo by Eric N. Smith, courtesy of Javier Alvarado.

Plate 981. *Crotalus triseriatus triseriatus*, adult. Lagunas de Zempoala, Morelos, Mexico. Photo by Eric N. Smith, courtesy of Manuel Varela-Juliá.

Plate 982. *Crotalus triseriatus triseriatus*, male, 57.5 cr TL, UTA R-12599. Near Lagunas de Zempoala, Morelo: Mexico, elevation 2,987 m.

Plate 983. *Crotalus triseriatus triseriatus*, female, 44.8 cm TL, UTA R-12603. Environs of Huitzilac, Morelos, Mexico, elevation 2,743 m.

Plate 984. *Crotalus triseriatus armstrongi*. Rancho San Francisco, 2.4 km northwest of Tapalpa, Jalisco, Mexico, elevation approximately 2,100 m. Photo by Louis W. Porras.

Plate 985. *Crotalus triseriatus armstrongi*, adult mal Rancho San Francisco, 2.4 km northwest of Tapalp: Jalisco, Mexico, elevation approximately 2,100 m. Pho: by John H. Tashjian.

Plate 986. *Crotalus triseriatus armstrongi*, female, 42.5 cm TL, UTA R-12591. Rancho San Francisco, 2.4 km northwest of Tapalpa, Jalisco, Mexico, elevation approximately 2,100 m.

Plate 987. *Crotalus triseriatus armstrongi*. Same as Plate 986.

Plate 988. *Crotalus viridis viridis*, adult male. From 64 k: south of Moab, San Juan County, Utah, USA. Photo b Louis W. Porras.

Plate 989. *Crotalus viridis viridis*, adult. Natural Bridges National Monument, San Juan County, Utah, USA. Photo by Louis W. Porras.

Plate 990. *Crotalus viridis viridis*, adult. Vicinity of Cody, Park County, Wyoming, USA. Photo by Louis W. Porras.

Plate 991. *Crotalus viridis viridis*, male, 91 cm TL. Ne Dillon, Beaverhead County, Montana, USA, elevatic 1,646 m. Photo by John Donovan and Marty Cooksey.

Plate 992. *Crotalus viridis viridis*, male, 96 cm TL. Near illon, Beaverhead County, Montana, USA, elevation 546 m. Photo by John Donovan and Marty Cooksey.

Plate 993. *Crotalus viridis viridis*, female, 84.1 cm TL, UTA R-18255. U.S. Highway 56, between Clayton and Springer, Union County, New Mexico, USA. Photo by David G. Barker.

Plate 994. *Crotalus viridis viridis*. Same as Plate 993.

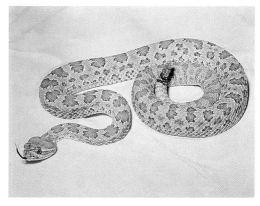

Plate 995. *Crotalus viridis viridis*, adult. Vicinity of oneta, Fremont County, Wyoming, USA. Patternless ecimens have been encountered throughout the range C. viridis. Photo by Louis W. Porras.

Plate 996. *Crotalus viridis viridis*, adult. San Juan County, Utah, USA. Photo by Louis W. Porras.

Plate 997. *Crotalus viridis nuntius*, adult. From 24 km south of Tuba City, Coconino County, Arizona, USA. Photo by John H. Tashjian at the Dallas Zoo.

Plate 998. *Crotalus willardi willardi*, adult male. Sunny-de Canyon, near Sunnyside trailhead, Huachuca ountains, Cochise County, Arizona, USA. Photo by y D. Hibbitts.

Plate 999. *Crotalus willardi willardi*, adult. Huachuca Mountains, Cochise County, Arizona, USA. Photo by David G. Barker at the Dallas Zoo.

Plate 1000. *Crotalus willardi willardi*, adult. Santa Rita Mountains, Pima County, Arizona, USA. Photo by Louis W. Porras.

Plate 1001. *Crotalus willardi amabilis*, adult male. Arroyo steño (Sierra del Nido), Chihuahua, Mexico, eleva- n approximately 2,300 m. Photo by Louis W. Porras.

Plate 1002. *Crotalus willardi amabilis*, adult male. Arroyo Mesteño (Sierra del Nido), Chihuahua, Mexico, eleva-tion approximately 2,300 m. Photo by David G. Barker at the Dallas Zoo.

Plate 1003. *Crotalus willardi meridionalis*, adult. Banderas de Águila (north of Coyotes), Durango, Mexico, eleva-tion 2,440 m. Photo by Saul Friess.

Plate 1004. *Crotalus willardi meridionalis*. Near Coyotes, Durango, Mexico. Photo by Ed Cassano.

Plate 1005. *Crotalus willardi obscurus*, juvenile. Animas Mountains, Hidalgo County, New Mexico, USA. Photo by David G. Barker.

Plate 1006. *Crotalus willardi obscurus*, female, approximately 60 cm TL, Endangered Species Program 2001 Peloncillo Mountains, Hidalgo County, New Mexico USA.

Plate 1007. *Crotalus willardi obscurus*. Same as Plate 1006. Photo by David G. Barker.

Plate 1008. *Crotalus willardi obscurus*, UTA R-17851. Canyon north of Cañón Diablo, Sierra San Luis, Sonora, Mexico, elevation approximately 1,900 m. Photo by David G. Barker.

Plate 1009. *Crotalus willardi silus*, adult male. Arroyo Tinaja, Chihuahua, Mexico. Photo by Louis W. Porras.

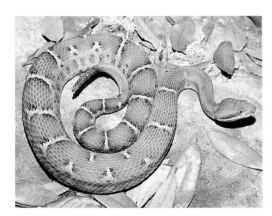

Plate 1010. *Crotalus willardi silus*, adult female. Sierra Nacozari, Sonora, Mexico. Photo by David G. Barker.

Plate 1011. *Sistrurus catenatus catenatus*, adult male. Somerset Center, Hillsdale County, Michigan, USA. Photo by Louis W. Porras.

Plate 1012. *Sistrurus catenatus edwardsi*, adult male. Near Belen, Valencia County, New Mexico, USA. Photo by Troy D. Hibbitts.

Plate 1013. *Sistrurus catenatus edwardsi*, subadult. From 16 km south of Cuatro Ciénegas, Coahuila, Mexico. Photo by George H. Grall.

Plate 1014. *Sistrurus catenatus edwardsi*, adult. Near La Escondida, 16 km west of Aramberri, Nuevo León, Mexico. Photo by John H. Tashjian.

Plate 1015. *Sistrurus catenatus tergeminus*, juvenile. From 19.2 km north of Claflin, Barton County, Kansas USA. Photo by Troy D. Hibbitts.

Plate 1016. *Sistrurus catenatus tergeminus*, female, 3.5 cm TL, UTA R-21923. Benbrook-Aledo Road, Tarrant County, Texas, USA. Photo by David G. Barker.

Plate 1017. *Sistrurus catenatus tergeminus*, male, 76.0 cm TL, UTA R-21924. Benbrook-Aledo Road, Tarrant County, Texas, USA. Photo by David G. Barker.

Plate 1018. *Sistrurus miliarius miliarius*, adult female. Hyde County, North Carolina, USA. Photo by Louis W. Porras.

Plate 1019. *Sistrurus miliarius miliarius*, NCMNH. Crowder's Mountain, Gaston County, North Carolina, USA. Specimens from this part of North Carolina often have an overall reddish ground color. Photo by R. Wayne Van Devender.

Plate 1020. *Sistrurus miliarius barbouri*, adult female. Along Old Tamiami Trail, 28.8 km west of Miami, Dade County, Florida, USA. Photo by Louis W. Porras.

Plate 1021. *Sistrurus miliarius barbouri*, adult. Apalachicola National Forest, Liberty County, Florida, USA. Photo by Troy D. Hibbitts.

Plate 1022. *Sistrurus miliarius streckeri*, adult male. Dallas County, Texas, USA.

Plate 1023. *Sistrurus miliarius streckeri*, male, 39.0 cm TL, UTA R-19315. Sunset, Montague County, Texas, USA. Photo by David G. Barker.

Plate 1024. *Alsophis elegans*, adult. Huampani, Lima, Peru. Photo by Omar Pesantes S.

Plate 1025. *Anilius scytale scytale*. Palmas, Tocantins, Brazil. Photo by Otávio A. V. Marques.

Plate 1026. *Apostolepis assimilis*, female, 54.5 cm TL. Osasco, São Paulo, Brazil. Photo by Otávio A. V. Marques.

Plate 1027. *Apostolepis cearensis*, male, 51.0 cm TL. Feira de Santana, Bahia, Brazil. Photo by Otávio A. V. Marques.

Plate 1028. *Apostolepis dimidiata*, female, 59.3 cm TL, ZUEC 1226. Campinas, São Paulo, Brazil. Photo by Ivan Sazima.

Plate 1029. *Apostolepis flavotorquata*, adult. Serra da Mesa, Goiás, Brazil. Photo by Nelson Jorge da Silva.

Plate 1030. *Apostolepis longicaudata*, adult. Guaraí Tocantins, Brazil. Photo by Otávio A. V. Marques, courtesy of Felipe F. Curcio.

Plate 1031. *Apostolepis polylepis*, adult. Guaraí, Tocantins, Brazil. Photo by Otávio A. V. Marques, courtesy of Felipe F. Curcio.

Plate 1032. *Apostolepis* sp., adult. Serra da Mesa, Goiás, Brazil. Photo by Nelson Jorge da Silva.

Plate 1033. *Apostolepis* sp., adult. Serra da Mesa, Goiás, Brazil. Photo by Nelson Jorge da Silva.

Plate 1034. *Atractus badius*, approximately 20 cm TL. On the road to the Kaw Mountains, Cayenne, French Guiana. Photo by Christian Marty.

Plate 1035. *Atractus elaps*, female, approximately 40 cm TL. Brillo Nuevo, Río Yaguasyacu, Loreto, Peru.

Plate 1036. *Atractus latifrons*, adult, IB. Usin Hidroelétrica Samuel, Rio Jamari, Pôrto Velho Rondônia, Brazil. Photo by Ivan Sazima.

Plate 1037. *Atractus latifrons*, male, approximately 40 cm TL. On the road to Nauta, 25 km south of Iquitos, Loreto, Peru.

Plate 1038. *Atractus maculatus*, juvenile. Juquitiba, São Paulo, Brazil. Photo by Wolfgang Wüster. Courtesy of the Instituto Butantan, São Paulo.

Plate 1039. *Atractus obesus*. Northeast of Popayán Cauca, Colombia. Photo by Martin Carlsson.

Plate 1040. *Atractus trihedrurus*, juvenile, approximately 5 cm TL. Registro, São Paulo, Brazil. Photo by Otávio . V. Marques.

Plate 1041. *Atractus zebrinus*, female, 14.8 cm TL, ZUEC 1283. Parque Estadual, Campos do Jordão, São Paulo, Brazil. Photo by Ivan Sazima.

Plate 1042. *Arizona elegans*. East Texas, USA.

Plate 1043. *Boa constrictor imperator*, juvenile. Bahía ulebra, Guanacaste, Costa Rica.

Plate 1044. *Boa constrictor ortonii*, male, approximately 150 cm TL, FHGO-live 119. Quiniara, Loja, Ecuador, elevation 1,600 m.

Plate 1045. *Boiruna maculata*, juvenile. Rubião Junior, Botucatu, São Paulo, Brazil. Photo by Ivan Sazima.

Plate 1046. *Boiruna maculata*, 89.3 cm TL, ZUEC 946. ubião Junior, Botucatu, São Paulo, Brazil. This specimen is feeding on a lizard. Photo by Ivan Sazima.

Plate 1047. *Cemophora coccinea coccinea*, female, 50.0 cm TL, UTA R-18381. On Farm-to-Market Road 692, 6.4 km northeast of intersection with Texas Highway 63, Newton County, Texas, USA.

Plate 1048. *Chilomeniscus stramineus*. No data. *Chilomeniscus cinctus* was recently placed in the synonymy of this taxon. Photo by R. Wayne Van Devender.

Plate 1049. *Chionactis occipitalis annulata*. Mohawk unes, Yuma County, Arizona, USA. Photo by R. Wayne n Devender.

Plate 1050. *Chionactis palarostris*. Organ Pipe National Monument, Pima County, Arizona, USA. Photo by R. Wayne Van Devender.

Plate 1051. *Chironius carinatus carinatus*, female, 130.5 cm TL, UTA R-15761. Tepoe, Sipaliwini, Suriname.

Plate 1052. *Chironius monticola*, male, 129.8 cm TL, USNM-FS 066645. Vereda de Portachuelo, vicinity of Manzanares, Meta, Colombia, elevation 1,640 m.

Plate 1053. *Chironius scurrulus*, juvenile. Nuevo Perú, Río Yaguasyacu, Loreto, Peru. Photo by Danté Fenolio.

Plate 1054. *Chironius scurrulus*, female, approximately 200 cm TL. Vicinity of Flor de Punga, upper Río Tahuayo, Loreto, Peru.

Plate 1055. *Chironius* sp., female, approximately 50 cm TL. Upper Río Oroza, Loreto, Peru.

Plate 1056. *Clelia bicolor*, female, 68.5 cm TL, ZUEC 598. Fazenda Santa Inês, Poconé, Mato Grosso, Brazil. Photo by Ivan Sazima.

Plate 1057. *Clelia clelia clelia*, female, juvenile. Vicinity of Mazán, Río Mazán, Loreto, Peru. Adults are black dorsally. The specimen on the right is a juvenile *Pseudoboa coronata*.

Plate 1058. *Clelia montana*, juvenile, ZUEC 1379. Parque Estadual, Campos do Jordão, São Paulo, Brazil. Photo by Ivan Sazima.

Plate 1059. *Clelia plumbea*, juvenile. Serra da Mesa, Goiás, Brazil. Photo by Nelson Jorge da Silva.

Plate 1060. *Clelia rustica*, approximately 100 cm TL, UTA R-50359. Vicinity of Entre Ríos, Tarija, Bolivia. Photo by Michael B. Harvey.

Plate 1061. *Clelia scytalina*, male, approximately 120 cm TL. Aguacaliente, Cartago, Costa Rica. Photo by Alejandro Solórzano at the Serpentario Nacional, San José.

Plate 1062. *Coniophanes imperialis imperialis*, adult. Texas, USA. Photo by Paul Freed.

Plate 1063. *Coniophanes imperialis clavatus*, male, 34.3 cm TL, UTA R-44709. Lagartero, Huehuetenango, Guatemala. Photo by Eric N. Smith.

Plate 1064. *Coniophanes piceivittis*, female, approximately 35 cm TL. Parque Nacional Santa Rosa, Guanacaste, Costa Rica.

Plate 1065. *Conophis lineatus*, female, 63.2 cm TL, UTA R-28300. Aldea El Rosario, Zacapa, Guatemala.

Plate 1066. *Corallus annulatus*, male, approximately 76 cm TL. Guayacán de Turrialba, Cartago, Costa Rica.

Plate 1067. *Corallus blombergi*, male, 138.0 cm TL, IGO-live 1074. Charco Vicente, Salto del Bravo, Río Bravo, Esmeraldas, Ecuador.

Plate 1068. *Corallus caninus*, female, approximately 60 cm TL. Napo Province, Ecuador.

Plate 1069. *Corallus cropanii*, adult female, IB 15200. Miracatu, São Paulo, Brazil. Photo by Alphonse Richard Hoge.

Plate 1070. *Corallus hortulanus*, female, approximately 0 cm TL. Puerto Miguel, Río Yarapa, Loreto, Peru.

Plate 1071. *Corallus ruschenbergerii*, male, approximately 150 cm TL. Puerto Porfía, Meta, Colombia.

Plate 1072. *Crisantophis nevermanni*, male, approximately 50 cm TL. Parque Nacional Santa Rosa, Guanacaste, Costa Rica.

Plate 1073. *Cryophis hallbergi*, male, 61.4 cm TL, UTA R-271. From 4.8 km south of Vista Hermosa (north slope the Sierra de Juárez), Oaxaca, Mexico, elevation 22 m.

Plate 1074. *Diadophis dugesi*, male, 37.1 cm TL, UTA R-12274. From 2.4 km northwest of Tapalpa, Jalisco, Mexico.

Plate 1075. *Diadophis punctatus arneyi*, male, 31.2 cm TL, UTA R-11125. Houston Ranch, 12.8 km south of Cherokee on Texas Highway 16, Llano County, Texas, USA.

Plate 1076. *Dipsas albifrons*, female, 54.5 cm TL, ZUEC 962. Joinville, Santa Catarina, Brazil. Photo by Ivan Sazima.

Plate 1077. *Dipsas articulata*, female, approximately 45 cm TL. Guayacán de Siquirres, Limón, Costa Rica.

Plate 1078. *Dipsas catesbyi*, female, approximately 45 cm TL. Río Pindoyacu, tributary of the Río Nanay, Loreto, Peru.

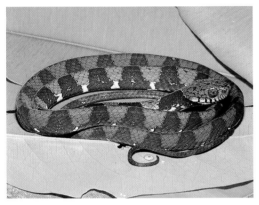

Plate 1079. *Dipsas indica indica*, female, approximately 55 cm TL. San Andrés, Río Momón, Loreto, Peru.

Plate 1080. *Dipsas neivai*. Ilha Bela, São Paulo, Brazil. Photo by Otávio A. V. Marques.

Plate 1081. *Dipsas variegata*. Guatopo, Portuguesa, Venezuela. Photo by James R. Dixon.

Plate 1082. *Dipsas variegata*, female, 65 cm TL, UTA R-15772. Tepoe, Sipaliwini, Suriname.

Plate 1083. *Drepanoides anomalus*, male, approximately 60 cm TL. Near San Andrés, Río Momón, Loreto, Peru.

Plate 1084. *Drymobius chloroticus*, female, 88.2 cm TL, UTA R-20786. Finca El Faro, approximately 4 km north of El Palmar, south slope of Volcán Santa María, Quezaltenango, Guatemala, elevation 1,280 m. Photo by David G. Barker.

Plate 1085. *Drymobius margaritifer*, female, 72.8 cm TL, UTA R-21791. From 5.1 km west-southwest of Puerto Santo Tomás, Montañas del Mico, Izabal, Guatemala.

Plate 1086. *Drymobius melanotropis*, female, approximately 101 cm TL, UCR. Horquetas, Sarapiquí (Rara Avis), Heredia, Costa Rica. Photo by Alejandro Solórzano.

Plate 1087. *Drymobius rhombifer*, male, approximately 90 cm TL, UCR. Horquetas, Sarapiquí (Rara Avis), Heredia, Costa Rica.

Plate 1088. *Drymoluber brazili*, juvenile, MCC 0241. Rio Piranhas, tributary of the Rio Araguaia (16°35′46″N, 4°47′44″W), Goiás, Brazil. Photo by Danté Fenolio, courtesy of Nelson Jorge da Silva.

Plate 1089. *Drymoluber dichrous*, female, juvenile. 28 de Enero, Río Tigre, Loreto, Peru.

Plate 1090. *Elaphe flavirufa*, male, 166.0 cm TL, UTA R-43942. El Arenal, San Vicente Cabañas, Zacapa, Guatemala. Photo by Eric N. Smith.

Plate 1091. *Elaphe guttata guttata*, adult. Jasper County, South Carolina, USA. Photo by Louis W. Porras.

Plate 1092. *Elaphe guttata emoryi*, juvenile female, UTA R-14731. Erath County, Texas, USA. Photo by David G. Barker.

Plate 1093. *Elaphe guttata* subsp., adult. Vicinity of Moab, Grand County, Utah, USA. This race was described as *E. g. intermontana*. Photo by Louis W. Porras.

Plate 1094. *Elaphe obsoleta lindheimeri*, subadult male, UTA R-11151. Benbrook-Aledo Road, just west of the junction with Farm-to-Market Road 2871, Tarrant County, Texas, USA.

Plate 1095. *Elapomorphus assimilis*, male, 52.2 cm TL, ZUEC 951. Cotia, São Paulo, Brazil. Photo by Ivan Sazima.

Plate 1096. *Elapomorphus lepidus*, female, 36.7 cm TL, ZUEC 1377. Serra da Bocaina, Rio de Janeiro, Brazil. Photo by Ivan Sazima.

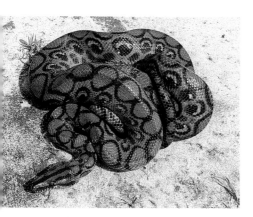

Plate 1097. *Epicrates cenchria cenchria*, female, approximately 200 cm TL. San Andrés, Río Momón, Loreto, Peru.

Plate 1098. *Epicrates cenchria alvarezi*, female, 131.9 cm TL, UTA R-32787. Santiago del Estero region, Argentina. Photo by Paul Freed.

Plate 1099. *Epicrates cenchria crassus*, female, approximately 100 cm TL, CVUCG 8816. Usina Hidroelétrica Corumbá, Goiás, Brazil. Photo by Paul Freed.

Plate 1100. *Erythrolamprus aesculapii aesculapii*, female, 90.1 cm TL, USNM 222354. Explorers' Inn, Tambopata Reserve, 30 km straight-line distance south-southwest of Puerto Maldonado, Río Tambopata, Madre de Dios, Peru. Photo by Roy W. McDiarmid.

Plate 1101. *Erythrolamprus aesculapii aesculapii*, adult. Tepoe, Sipaliwini, Suriname. Photo by Paul Freed.

Plate 1102. *Erythrolamprus aesculapii aesculapii*, adult female, LJV 2011. Alto Rio Araguaia, Mato Grosso, Brazil. Photo by Laurie J. Vitt.

Plate 1103. *Erythrolamprus aesculapii aesculapii*, juvenile female. Quebrada Tamshiyacu, Loreto, Peru.

Plate 1104. *Erythrolamprus aesculapii aesculapii*, adult. Quebrada Blanca, Río Tahuayo, Loreto, Peru. Photo by Charles E. Siegel.

Plate 1105. *Erythrolamprus aesculapii aesculapii*, adult. Usina Hidroelétrica Balbina, Amazonas, Brazil. Photo by Nelson Jorge da Silva.

Plate 1106. *Erythrolamprus aesculapii aesculapii*, adult. Araracuara, Caquetá, Colombia. Photo by Juan Manuel Renjifo, courtesy of the Instituto Nacional de Salud, Bogotá.

Plate 1107. *Erythrolamprus aesculapii aesculapii*, adult female, LJV 6755. Rio Ituxi, Amazonas, Brazil. Photo by Laurie J. Vitt.

Plate 1108. *Erythrolamprus aesculapii aesculapii*, 100.2 cm TL, USNM 321113. Tigüino, Pastaza, Ecuador.

Plate 1109. *Erythrolamprus aesculapii aesculapii*, male, 49.0 cm TL, MVZ 176250. Santa Elena Road, 23.1 km south of turnoff to Kavanayen, Bolívar, Venezuela. Some authorities recognize this population as *E. bauperthuisii*. Photo by John E. Cadle.

Plate 1110. *Erythrolamprus aesculapii venustissimus*, 78.5 cm TL, IB 57350. Juquitiba, São Paulo, Brazil. Photo by Otávio A. V. Marques.

Plate 1111. *Erythrolamprus bizona*, female, approximately 40 cm TL. San Rafael, Heredia, Costa Rica. Photo by Alejandro Solórzano at the Serpentario Nacional, San José.

Plate 1112. *Erythrolamprus guentheri*, female, 55.8 cm TL, USNM 316604. Vicinity of San Antonio (Río Cenepa), Amazonas, Peru, elevation 210 m. Photo by Roy W. McDiarmid.

Plate 1113. *Erythrolamprus guentheri*, male, 60.0 cm TL, USNM 316605. Vicinity of Tujushik entse (between Huampami and Chávez Valdivia), Río Cenepa, Amazonas, Peru, elevation 210 m. Photo by Roy W. McDiarmid.

Plate 1114. *Erythrolamprus mimus micrurus*, adult. Honduras. Photo by Louis W. Porras.

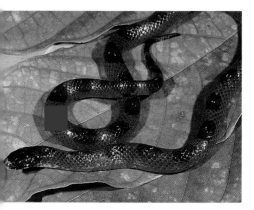

Plate 1115. *Erythrolamprus ocellatus*, approximately ? cm TL. Vicinity of Charlottesville, Tobago, West Indies. Photo by Hans Boos.

Plate 1116. *Erythrolamprus pseudocorallus*, juvenile, CVULA IV-2819. From 7.0 km southeast of La Azulita, Mérida, Venezuela. Photo by Pascual Soriano, courtesy of Enrique LaMarca.

Plate 1117. *Farancia abacura reinwardti*, female, 25.9 cm TL, UTA R-15550. Nacogdoches County, Texas, USA. Photo by David G. Barker.

Plate 1118. *Ficimia streckeri*, adult. Cuatro Ciénagas, Coahuila, Mexico. Photo by William B. Montgomery.

Plate 1119. *Geophis brachycephalus*, approximately 32 cm TL, UCR. Guayacán de Siquirres, Limón, Costa Rica. Photo by Alejandro Solórzano at the Serpentario Nacional, San José.

Plate 1120. *Geophis damiani*, male, 32.7 cm TL, USNM 498356, holotype. From 2.5 km (airline) north-northeast of La Fortuna, Yoro, Honduras, elevation 1,650 m. Photo by J. R. McCranie.

Plate 1121. *Geophis duellmani*, male, 19.2 cm TL, UTA 12333. From 6.8 km south of Vista Hermosa (north slope of the Sierra de Juárez), Oaxaca, Mexico, elevation 1,661 m.

Plate 1122. *Geophis laticinctus*, female, 54.7 cm TL, UTA R-12319. Colonia Rodulfo Figueroa (Cerro Baúl), Oaxaca, Mexico, elevation 1,524 m.

Plate 1123. *Geophis semidoliatus*, female, 31.4 cm TL, UTA R-19910. Parque Moctezuma, Barranca de San Miguel, Cuautlalpan, Veracruz, Mexico.

Plate 1124. *Gomesophis brasiliensis*, male, 45 cm TL, IB. Albertina, Minas Gerais, Brazil. Photo by Ivan Sazima.

Plate 1125. *Gyalopion canum*, male, 22.6 cm TL, UTA R-16129. From 7.6 km north of Aramberri, Nuevo León, Mexico.

Plate 1126. *Gyalopion quadrangulare*. Mexico. Photo by Wayne Van Devender.

Plate 1127. *Helicops angulatus*, female, approximately 50 cm TL. Padrecocha, Río Nanay, Loreto, Peru.

Plate 1128. *Heterodon nasicus nasicus*, UTA R-22284. Mount Selmon, Cherokee County, Texas, USA. Photo by David G. Barker.

Plate 1129. *Heterodon platirhinos*, male, 58.0 cm TL, UTA R-15848. Tyler, on the west side of U.S. Highway 27 near the junction with Loop 323, Smith County, Texas, USA.

Plate 1130. *Heterodon platirhinos*. USA. Photo by Paul Freed.

Plate 1131. *Heterodon simus*. Florida, USA. Photo by Jim Bridges.

Plate 1132. *Hydrodynastes bicinctus*. Serra da Mesa, Goiás, Brazil. Photo by Nelson Jorge da Silva.

Plate 1133. *Hydrodynastes gigas*, juveniles. Asunción, Paraguay.

Plate 1134. *Hydrops martii*, female, approximately 70 cm TL. Mishana, Río Nanay, Loreto, Peru.

Plate 1135. Top row, left to right: *Micrurus surinamensis surinamensis*, *Atractus elaps*, and *Pseudoboa coronata*. Bottom row, left to right: *Hydrops martii* (same as Plate 1134) and *Oxyrhopus petola semifasciatus*.

ate 1136. *Hydrops triangularis bassleri*, female, approximately 75 cm TL. Nuevo Perú, Río Yaguasyacu, Loreto, ru.

Plate 1137. *Hypsiglena torquata jani*, female, approximately 30 cm TL. Near Lajitas on Farm-to-Market Road 21, Brewster County, Texas, USA.

Plate 1138. *Imantodes cenchoa*, juvenile, 46.5 cm TL, UTA R-16023. Las Escobas, 5.1 km west-southwest of Puerto Santo Tomás, Montañas del Mico, Izabal, Guatemala.

ate 1139. *Imantodes gemmistratus*, female, approximately 75 cm TL. Santo Domingo de Heredia, Heredia, sta Rica.

Plate 1140. *Imantodes inornatus*, female, approximately 110 cm TL. Guayacán de Siquirres, Limón, Costa Rica.

Plate 1141. *Imantodes lentiferus*, 60.0 cm TL, USNM 321115. Tigüino, Pastaza, Ecuador.

ate 1142. *Lampropeltis calligaster calligaster*, female, proximately 40 cm TL. 1731 County Road 334, 2.4 km rth of Tyler, Smith County, Texas, USA.

Plate 1143. *Lampropeltis mexicana*. On Mexico Highway 120, 9.6 km west-northwest of Jalpan, Querétaro, Mexico, elevation 1,981 m. Photo by David G. Barker.

Plate 1144. *Lampropeltis mexicana*. Mexico. Photo by Paul Freed.

ate 1145. *Lampropeltis pyromelana knoblochi*, female. m 2 km above the Cascada de Baseachíc, near Río razno, Chihuahua, Mexico.

Plate 1146. *Lampropeltis triangulum abnorma*, female, 37.7 cm TL, UTA R-28382. Biotopo para la Conservación del Quetzal, Baja Verapaz, Guatemala.

Plate 1147. *Lampropeltis triangulum amaura*, male, 101.6 cm TL, UTA R-19568. Vicinity of Monroe, Ouachita County, Louisiana, USA. This race normally has black pigment on top of the head.

Plate 1148. *Lampropeltis triangulum andesiana*, male, approximately 35 cm TL, UTA R-51455. Los Farallones de Cali, Valle del Cauca, Colombia.

Plate 1149. *Lampropeltis triangulum annulata*, adult female. Rancho Viejo, Gómez Farías, Tamaulipas, Mexico. Photo by Ed Cassano.

Plate 1150. *Lampropeltis triangulum blanchardi*, male, approximately 50 cm TL. Mérida, Yucatán, Mexico.

Plate 1151. *Lampropeltis triangulum campbelli*, adult. Zapotitlán Salinas, Puebla, Mexico. Photo by Paul Freed.

Plate 1152. *Lampropeltis triangulum conanti*, adult male. Mexico.

Plate 1153. *Lampropeltis triangulum dixoni*, adult male. Mexico. Photo by David G. Barker.

Plate 1154. *Lampropeltis triangulum elapsoides*, adult. Florida, USA. Photo by Ed Cassano.

Plate 1155. *Lampropeltis triangulum gaigei*, juvenile. Costa Rica. Adults become heavily melanized. Photo by Paul Freed.

Plate 1156. *Lampropeltis triangulum gaigei*, adult, Costa Rica. Adults become heavily melanized. Photo by Paul Freed.

Plate 1157. *Lampropeltis triangulum hondurensis*, adult female. Sula Plain, Honduras. *Micrurus, Lampropeltis*, and other species from the Sula Plain are often orange overall. Photo by Louis W. Porras.

Plate 1158. *Lampropeltis triangulum polyzona*, male, 66.2 cm TL, UTA R-42362. Los Amates, Mariscos, Izabal, Guatemala. Photo by Eric N. Smith.

Plate 1159. *Lampropeltis triangulum sinaloae*. Acaponeta, Nayarit, Mexico. Photo by Charles M. Bogert.

te 1160. *Lampropeltis triangulum sinaloae*, adult. ≥xico. Photo by Ed Cassano.

Plate 1161. *Lampropeltis triangulum stuarti*, female, approximately 100 cm TL. Foothills above Liberia, Guanacaste, Costa Rica.

Plate 1162. *Lampropeltis triangulum syspila*, adult male. Photo by David G. Barker.

te 1163. *Leptodeira annulata annulata*, juvenile, 4 cm TL, KU 220505. Puerto Miguel, Río Yarapa, ₁reto, Peru.

Plate 1164. *Leptodeira annulata annulata*, female, 75.0 cm TL, USNM 321124. Tigüino, Pastaza, Ecuador.

Plate 1165. *Leptodeira annulata ashmeadii*, male, 31.2 cm TL, USNM FS-066653. Finca El Buque, Villavicencio, Meta, Colombia, elevation 490 m.

te 1166. *Leptodeira frenata*, male, 57.0 cm TL, UTA R-₁97. Between kilometer markers 14 and 17 on the road ₁m Tulum to Cobá, Quintana Roo, Mexico.

Plate 1167. *Leptodeira nigrofasciata*, female, approximately 35 cm TL. Parque Nacional Santa Rosa, Guanacaste, Costa Rica.

Plate 1168. *Leptodeira polysticta*, UTA R-25822. El Tejocote, Oaxaca, Mexico.

te 1169. *Leptodeira rubricata*, approximately 60 cm TL, ₁R. Estero de Quepo, Puntarenas, Costa Rica.

Plate 1170. *Leptodeira septentrionalis*, adult. Iturbide, Nuevo León, Mexico. Photo by William B. Montgomery.

Plate 1171. *Leptophis ahaetulla ahaetulla*, male, 107.5 cm TL, UTA R-15864. Tepoe, Sipaliwini, Suriname.

Plate 1172. *Leptophis ahaetulla coeruleodorsus*, female, approximately 100 cm TL. Villavicencio, Meta, Colombia, elevation 490 m.

Plate 1173. *Leptophis ahaetulla praestans*, male, 249.7 cm TL, UTA R-41190. Finca Quebradas, Morales, Río Bobos, Izabal, Guatemala. Photo by Eric N. Smith.

Plate 1174. *Leptophis ahaetulla occidentalis*, male, approximately 150 cm TL. Pacuare de Siquirres, Limón, Costa Rica. Photo by Alejandro Solórzano at the National Serpentarium, San José.

Plate 1175. *Leptophis ahaetulla nigrofasciatus*, male, 101.3 cm TL, KU 220505. Nauta Caño, Río Marañón, Loreto, Peru.

Plate 1176. *Leptophis depressirostris*, female, 96.9 cm TL, UTA R-12905. At the Río Chitaría, 3.0 km northeast of Pavones de Turrialba, Cartago, Costa Rica.

Plate 1177. *Leptophis mexicanus*, male, 106.4 cm TL, UTA R-22178. Near the headquarters of Finca Semuc, Sierra de Santa Cruz, Izabal, Guatemala.

Plate 1178. *Leptophis modestus*, female, 130.1 cm TL, UTA R-42300. Carretera Niño Perdido, La Unión Barrios, Baja Verapaz, Guatemala. Photo by Eric N. Smith.

Plate 1179. *Liophis almadensis*. Serra da Mesa, Goiás, Brazil. Photo by Nelson Jorge da Silva.

Plate 1180. *Liophis breviceps breviceps*, juvenile. Reserva Pacaya-Samiria, Loreto, Peru.

Plate 1181. *Liophis epinephalis juvenalis*, male, approximately 65 cm TL. Cantón de San Carlos, Alajuela, Costa Rica, elevation 1,700 m. Photo by Alejandro Solórzano at the National Serpentarium, San José.

Plate 1182. *Liophis frenatus*, male, 25.2 cm TL, ZUEC 1556. Aguas de São Pedro, São Paulo, Brazil. Photo by Ivan Sazima.

Plate 1183. *Liophis miliaris orinus*, female, 96.1 cm TL, ZUEC 559. Caieiras, São Paulo, Brazil. Photo by Ivan Sazima.

Plate 1184. *Liophis poecilogyrus poecilogyrus*. Niterói, Rio de Janeiro, Rio de Janeiro, Brazil. Photo by Aníbal Melgarejo.

Plate 1185. *Liophis poecilogyrus schotti*. Serra da Mesa, Goiás, Brazil. Photo by Nelson Jorge da Silva.

Plate 1186. *Liophis poecilogyrus* cf. *schotti*, female, 54.1 cm TL, UTA R-18049. Finca Las Mercedes, approximately 22 km south of Villavicencio, Meta, Colombia.

Plate 1187. *Liophis typhlus typhlus*, female, 63.4 cm TL, UTA R-18046. Suriname.

Plate 1188. *Liophis typhlus typhlus*, female, 70.4 cm TL, UTA R-18047. Suriname.

Plate 1189. *Liophis viridis viridis*, ZUEC 629. Floresta, Pernambuco, Brazil. Photo by Ivan Sazima.

Plate 1190. *Lystrophis dorbignyi*, adult. Pôrto Alegre, Rio Grande do Sul, Brazil. The tail is raised defensively to display its red color. Photo by Ivan Sazima.

Plate 1191. *Lystrophis hystricus*. Serra da Mesa, Goiás, Brazil. Photo by Nelson Jorge da Silva.

Plate 1192. *Lystrophis mattogrossensis*, male, 42.0 cm TL, IB 59159. Iturama, Minas Gerais, Brazil. Photo by Otávio A. V. Marques.

Plate 1193. *Lystrophis pulcher*, adult female, IB 58226. No locality data. Photo by Otávio A. V. Marques.

Plate 1194. *Lystrophis semicinctus*. San Rafael, Mendoza, Argentina. Photo by R. Wayne Van Devender.

Plate 1195. *Lystrophis semicinctus*, male, 46.9 cm TL, UTA R-19707. Vicinity of Santa Cruz de la Sierra, Santa Cruz, Bolivia.

Plate 1196. *Mastigodryas bifossatus triseriatus*, female, 186.5 cm TL. Fazenda Santa Inês, Poconé, Mato Grosso, Brazil. Photo by Ivan Sazima.

Plate 1197. *Mastigodryas pulchriceps*, female, juvenile, FHGO-live 267. Parroquía Chongón, Guayas, Ecuador, elevation 300 m.

Plate 1198. *Nerodia cyclopion cyclopion*, male, 77.6 cm T UTA R-17976. Vicinity of Uncertain (Caddo Lake Marion County, Texas, USA.

Plate 1199. *Nerodia erythrogaster erythrogaster*, female, 43.0 cm TL, UTA R-11127. Houston Ranch, 12.8 km south of Cherokee on Texas Highway 16, Llano County, Texas, USA.

Plate 1200. *Nerodia fasciata confluens*, female, 83.7 cm TL, UTA R-14741. Sunset Grove Country Club, near east bank of Adam's Bayou, Orange County, Texas, USA. Photo by David G. Barker.

Plate 1201. *Nerodia rhombifer blanchardi*, female, 93.7 c TL, UTA R-12686. Mexico Highway 105 at Río Venado Hidalgo, Mexico.

Plate 1202. *Ninia sebae*, female, 31.5 cm TL, UTA R-44816. Finca Chiblac Buena Vista, Barillas, Huehuetenango, Guatemala. Photo by Eric N. Smith.

Plate 1203. *Nothopsis rugosus*, male, approximately 40 cm TL. Marenco Biological Station, Osa Peninsula, Puntarenas, Costa Rica.

Plate 1204. *Oxybelis aeneus*, female, 134.0 cm TL, UT R-12386. From 5.6 km south-southwest of Zapotitl. Salinas, Puebla, Mexico.

Plate 1205. *Oxybelis fulgidus*, male, approximately 110 cm TL. Santa Cruz (Río Marañón), Loreto, Peru.

Plate 1206. *Oxyrhopus clathratus*, male. São Bernardo do Campo, São Paulo, Brazil. Photo by Otávio A. V. Marques.

Plate 1207. *Oxyrhopus clathratus*, 110.0 cm TL, CP 22 Riacho Grande, São Paulo, Brazil. Photo by Otávio A. Marques.

Plate 1208. *Oxyrhopus clathratus*, female, 70.0 cm TL. Registro, São Paulo, Brazil. Photo by Otávio A. V. Marques.

Plate 1209. *Oxyrhopus erdisii*, female. Machu Picchu, Cuzco, Peru. Photo by Wilfredo Arizábal.

Plate 1210. *Oxyrhopus formosus*, female, approximately 75 cm TL. Paraiso, Río Tigre, Loreto, Peru.

Plate 1211. *Oxyrhopus formosus*, female, juvenile, approximately 20 cm TL. Vicinity of La Florida, Río Marañón, Loreto, Peru.

Plate 1212. *Oxyrhopus guibei*, female, 113.8 cm TL, ZUEC 2267. Osasco, São Paulo, Brazil. Photo by Ivan Sazima.

Plate 1213. *Oxyrhopus leucomelas*, female, 27.2 cm TL. Vereda de Portachuelo, vicinity of Manzanares, Meta, Colombia, elevation 1,660 m.

Plate 1214. *Oxyrhopus melanogenys*, female, approximately 45 cm TL. Puerto Miguel, Río Yarapa, Loreto, Peru.

Plate 1215. *Oxyrhopus melanogenys*, male, approximately 65 cm TL. From 9 de Octubre, Río Marañón, Loreto, Peru.

Plate 1216. *Oxyrhopus melanogenys*. Bagua Grande, Amazonas, Peru. Photo by James R. Dixon.

Plate 1217. *Oxyrhopus melanogenys*. Bagua Grande, Amazonas, Peru. Photo by James R. Dixon.

Plate 1218. *Oxyrhopus occipitalis*, female, 75.5 cm TL, UTA R-16385. Tepoe, Sipaliwini, Suriname.

Plate 1219. *Oxyrhopus petola digitalis*, male, approximately 75 cm TL. On the Río Marañón, opposite Nauta Caño, Loreto, Peru.

Plate 1220. *Oxyrhopus petola sebae*, adult. Costa Rica. Some authorities refer to this species as *O. petolarius*. Photo by Louis W. Porras, specimen courtesy of the Instituto Clodomiro Picado, San José.

Plate 1221. *Oxyrhopus rhombifer rhombifer*, female, 54.4 cm TL. Itirapina, São Paulo, Brazil. Photo by Otávio A. V. Marques.

Plate 1222. *Oxyrhopus rhombifer inaequifasciatus*, female 73.4 cm TL, ZUEC 1169. Poconé, Mato Grosso, Brazi Photo by Ivan Sazima.

Plate 1223. *Oxyrhopus rhombifer septentrionalis*, female, 77.0 cm TL, CP 2525. Comodoro, Rondônia, Brazil. Photo by Otávio A. V. Marques.

Plate 1224. *Oxyrhopus rhombifer septentrionalis*, adult. Serra da Mesa, Goiás, Brazil. Photo by Nelson Jorge da Silva.

Plate 1225. *Oxyrhopus trigeminus*, adult. Alto Aragua Mato Grosso, Brazil. Photo by Laurie J. Vitt.

Plate 1226. *Oxyrhopus trigeminus*, adult female. Belo Horizonte, Minas Gerais, Brazil. Photo by Donal Boyer.

Plate 1227. *Oxyrhopus* cf. *trigeminus*, male, approximately 75 cm TL. San Andrés, Río Momón, Loreto, Peru.

Plate 1228. *Oxyrhopus doliatus*. El Parque Nacior Henri Pittier, Aragua, Venezuela. Photo by Robe Godshalk.

Plate 1229. *Oxyrhopus petola semifasciatus* (lower left); *Micrurus langsdorffi* (upper left); *Oxyrhopus melanogenys* (right); all from Caucho Caño, Río Momón, Loreto, Peru.

Plate 1230. *Phalotris mertensi*, female, 98.5 cm TL, IB 57467. Paranapanema, São Paulo, Brazil. Photo by Otávio A. V. Marques.

Plate 1231. *Phalotris nasutus*, 39.0 cm TL. Prata, Min Gerais, Brazil. Photo by Otávio A. V. Marques.

Plate 1232. *Phalotris tricolor*, IB collection. Tupi Paulista, São Paulo, Brazil. Photo by Wolfgang Wüster. Courtesy of the Instituto Butantan, São Paulo.

Plate 1233. *Philodryas aestivus aestivus*, adult. Serra da Canastra, Minas Gerais, Brazil. Photo by Otávio A. V. Marques.

Plate 1234. *Philodryas baroni*. Argentina. Photo by Jack W. Sites Jr.

Plate 1235. *Philodryas mattogrossensis*, adult. Alto Araguaia, Mato Grosso, Brazil. Photo by Laurie J. Vitt.

Plate 1236. *Philodryas nattereri*, ZUEC 631. Glória, Bahia, Brazil. Photo by Ivan Sazima.

Plate 1237. *Philodryas olfersi olfersi*, 116.0 cm TL, IB 59063. Espírito Santo do Turvo, São Paulo, Brazil. Photo by Otávio A. V. Marques.

Plate 1238. *Philodryas olfersi olfersi*. Palmas, Tocantins, Brazil. Photo by Otávio A. V. Marques.

Plate 1239. *Philodryas patagoniensis*, juvenile, IB collection. São Paulo, Brazil. Photo by Wolfgang Wüster. Courtesy of the Instituto Butantan, São Paulo.

Plate 1240. *Philodryas viridissimus viridissimus*, female, 145.8 cm TL, UTA R-22246. Tepoe, Sipaliwini, Suriname.

Plate 1241. *Phimophis guianensis*, AMNH. Demerara, Guyana. Photo by Howard York, courtesy of the American Museum of Natural History.

Plate 1242. *Phyllorhynchus browni*, adult. From 20 km north of Mazatlán, Sinaloa, Mexico. Photo by Ed Cassano.

Plate 1243. *Pituophis lineaticollis gibsoni*, female, 95.0 cm TL, UTA R-8792. Summit of Cerro Baúl, Oaxaca, Mexico.

Plate 1244. *Pituophis melanoleucus sayi*, female, 158.4 cm TL, UTA R-14744. From 6.1 km west of the junction of Farm-to-Market Road 2157 and U.S. Highway 377 Loop, Erath County, Texas, USA. Photo by David G. Barker.

Plate 1245. *Pliocercus elapoides*, male, 46.5 cm TL, TCWC 48196. El Salto Falls, San Luis Potosí, Mexico. Many subspecies have been recognized for this species, but these are not well defined. Photo by James R. Dixon.

Plate 1246. *Pliocercus elapoides*, male, 39.5 cm TL, UTA F 25830. Between Metates and Vista Hermosa, Sierr Juárez, Oaxaca, Mexico.

Plate 1247. *Pliocercus elapoides*, female, 34.1 cm TL, UTA R-5774. From 19 km northwest of Rizo de Oro (Cerro Baúl), Oaxaca, Mexico.

Plate 1248. *Pliocercus elapoides*, adult. From 19.6 km south of Kantunilkin, Quintana Roo, Mexico. Photo by Julian C. Lee.

Plate 1249. *Pliocercus elapoides*, male, 50.5 cm TL, UT R-41191. Finca Chiblac Buena Vista (Aldea Buen Aires), Sierra de los Cuchumatanes, Huehuetenang Guatemala. Photo by Eric N. Smith.

Plate 1250. *Pliocercus elapoides*, female, 49.0 cm TL, UTA R-28470. On the trail to Rayo, Finca Chiblac, approximately 22 km northeast of Barillas, Huehuetenango, Guatemala.

Plate 1251. *Pliocercus elapoides*, male, 43.0 cm TL, UTA R-29972. Finca Semuc headquarters, Sierra de Santa Cruz, Izabal, Guatemala.

Plate 1252. *Pliocercus elapoides*, female, 63.0 cm T UTA R-26387. Xiacam, Sierra de Santa Cruz, Izaba Guatemala. Photo by Eric N. Smith.

Plate 1253. *Pliocercus elapoides*, male, 55.0 cm TL, UTA R-21700. Las Escobas, 5.1 km west-southwest of Puerto Santo Tomás, Montañas del Mico, Izabal, Guatemala.

Plate 1254. *Pliocercus elapoides*, male, 33.0 cm TL, KU 187343. From 12.6 km by road west of Puerto Santo Tomás (Montañas del Mico), Izabal, Guatemala, elevation 774 m.

Plate 1255. *Pliocercus elapoides*, male, 52.0 cm TL, UT R-22820. Finca El Faro, 4.0 km north of El Palm south slope of Volcán Santa María, Quezaltenang Guatemala.

Plate 1256. *Pliocercus elapoides*, male, 41.5 cm TL, UTA 22218. Finca El Faro, 4.0 km north of El Palmar, uth slope of Volcán Santa María, Quezaltenango, uatemala.

Plate 1257. *Pliocercus elapoides*, female, 40.0 cm TL, UTA R-21714. Finca El Faro, 4.0 km north of El Palmar, south slope of Volcán Santa María, Quezaltenango, Guatemala, elevation 775 m. Photo by David G. Barker.

Plate 1258. *Pliocercus elapoides*, male, 48.0 cm TL, UTA R-21716. Finca El Faro, 4.0 km north of El Palmar, south slope of Volcán Santa María, Quezaltenango, Guatemala. Photo by David G. Barker.

Plate 1259. *Pliocercus elapoides*, female, 42.0 cm TL, KU 7344. San José El Espinero (southeastern side of Cerro rde), Baja Verapaz, Guatemala, elevation 1,400 m.

Plate 1260. *Pliocercus elapoides*, USNM 339691. From 2.5 km (airline) north-northeast of La Fortuna, Yoro, Honduras, elevation 1,650 m. Photo by J. R. McCranie.

Plate 1261. *Pliocercus elapoides*, female, 39.5 cm TL, UTA R-22819. Finca El Faro, 4.0 km north of El Palmar, south slope of Volcán Santa María, Quezaltenango, Guatemala. The specimen on the right is *Micrurus nigrocinctus zunilensis*, UTA R-22773.

Plate 1262. *Pliocercus elapoides*, male, 51.0 cm TL (tail tip ssing), UTA R-22820 (white rings); and male, 57.5 cm , UTA R-22821 (yellow rings). Finca El Faro, 4.0 km rth of El Palmar, south slope of Volcán Santa María, ezaltenango, Guatemala. Both specimens were col- ted on the same hillside, where they are sympatric h *Micrurus nigrocinctus* and *M. latifasciatus*.

Plate 1263. *Pliocercus elapoides* and *Micrurus nigrocinctus* Same individuals as in Plate 1261.

Plate 1264. *Pliocercus euryzonus*, male, approximately 50 cm TL. Guayacán de Siquirres, Limón, Costa Rica.

Plate 1265. *Pliocercus euryzonus*. Finca La Selva, apiquí, Costa Rica. Some authorities consider this to resent a separate species, *P. dimidiatus*. Photo by chael and Patricia Fogden.

Plate 1266. *Pseudoboa coronata*, female, approximately 90 cm TL. Santa Cruz, Río Marañón, Loreto, Peru.

Plate 1267. *Pseudoboa neuwiedii*. Caracas, Distrito Federal, Venezuela. Photo by Laurie J. Vitt.

Plate 1268. *Pseudoboa nigra*, female, 58.0 cm TL. Fazenda Santa Inês, Poconé, Mato Grosso, Brazil. Photo by Ivan Sazima.

Plate 1269. *Pseudoboa nigra*. Serra da Mesa, Goiás, Brazil. Photo by Nelson Jorge da Silva.

Plate 1270. *Pseudoleptodeira latifasciata*, female, 45.2 cr TL. Mixteca Poblana, Puebla, Mexico. Photo by Eric N Smith.

Plate 1271. *Pseustes poecilonotus polylepis*, male, approximately 40 cm TL. Vicinity of San Andrés, Río Momón, Loreto, Peru.

Plate 1272. *Pseustes sulphureus sulphureus*, male, 278.0 cm TL, UTA R-23647. Tepoe, Sipaliwini, Suriname.

Plate 1273. *Rhinobothryum bovallii*, female, approximately 120 cm TL, UCR. Guayacán de Siquirres, Limón Costa Rica.

Plate 1274. *Rhinobothryum lentiginosum*, LJV 7732. Approximately 90 km north of Nova Mamoré, Parque Estadual Guajará-Mirim, Rondônia, Brazil. Photo by Laurie J. Vitt.

Plate 1275. *Rhinocheilus lecontei antoni*. Carretera Estatal 23, Sinaloa, Mexico. Photo by R. Wayne Van Devender.

Plate 1276. *Rhinocheilus lecontei tessellatus*, male, 74.5 cr TL, UTA R-28831. On Farm-to-Market Road 624 south east of Cotulla, 29.1 km east of the junction with F.M 469, La Salle County, Texas, USA.

Plate 1277. *Scaphiodontophis annulatus*. Los Tuxtlas, Veracruz, Mexico. Photo by R. Wayne Van Devender.

Plate 1278. *Scaphiodontophis annulatus*, male, 71.0 cm TL, UTA R-22191. Finca Semuc, Sierra de Santa Cruz, Izabal, Guatemala.

Plate 1279. *Scaphiodontophis annulatus*, male, 69.5 cm T UTA R-22192. Finca Semuc, Sierra de Santa Cruz, Izaba Guatemala.

ate 1280. *Scaphiodontophis annulatus*, male, 61.5 cm
ail incomplete), UTA R-22193. Finca Semuc, Sierra de
nta Cruz, Izabal, Guatemala.

Plate 1281. On left: *Scaphiodontophis annulatus*, male, 55.1 cm TL, UTA R-22828; on right: *Micrurus nigrocinctus zunilensis*, UTA R-22774. Both from Finca El Faro, 4.0 km north of El Palmar, south slope of Volcán Santa María, Quezaltenango, Guatemala.

Plate 1282. *Scaphiodontophis annulatus*, same as Plate 1281 (upper left). *Pliocercus elapoides*, UTA R-22819 (lower left); *Micrurus nigrocinctus zunilensis*, UTA R-22773 (right). All from Finca El Faro, 4.0 km north of El Palmar, south slope of Volcán Santa María, Quezaltenango, Guatemala.

ate 1283. *Scaphiodontophis annulatus*, male, 69.8 cm
., UCR 15118. Wilson Botanical Gardens, San Vito de
to Brus, Puntarenas, Costa Rica. Photo by Alejandro
lórzano, courtesy of Luis Diego Gómez.

Plate 1284. *Scolecophis atrocinctus*, female, 20.0 cm TL, UTA R-23460. Selcajá, Quiché, Guatemala.

Plate 1285. *Scolecophis atrocinctus*, male, approximately 40 cm TL. Vicinity of San José, Alajuela, Costa Rica.

ate 1286. *Sibon annulata*, female, approximately 55 cm
. Guayacán de Siquirres, Limón, Costa Rica.

Plate 1287. *Sibon anthracops*, female, approximately 45 cm. Pozo Azul de Abengares, Guanacaste, Costa Rica.

Plate 1288. *Sibon dimidiata*, male, 42.0 cm TL, UTA R-29909. Las Escobas, 5.1 km west-southwest of Puerto Santo Tomás, Montañas del Mico, Izabal, Guatemala.

te 1289. *Sibon lamari*, female. Guayacán de Siquirres,
nón, Costa Rica.

Plate 1290. *Sibon longifrenis*, approximately 40 cm TL, UCR, paratype. Guayacán de Siquirres, Limón, Costa Rica.

Plate 1291. *Sibon nebulata grandioculis*, male, 65.5 cm TL, UTA R-21752. Finca Patzulín, south slope of Volcán Santa María, Quezaltenango, Guatemala. Photo by David G. Barker.

Plate 1292. *Sibon sartorii*, male, 49.5 cm TL, UTA R-22843. Finca El Faro, 4.0 km north of El Palmar, south slope of Volcán Santa María, Quezaltenango, Guatemala.

Plate 1293. *Sibon sartorii*, adult. Península de Yucatán, Mexico. Photo by Ed Cassano.

Plate 1294. *Sibynomorphus mikanii*, ZUEC. Sousas Campinas, São Paulo, Brazil. Photo by Ivan Sazima.

Plate 1295. *Sibynomorphus neuwiedi*, 64.0 cm TL, CPIB 1556. Ilha do Cardoso, Cananéia, São Paulo, Brazil. Photo by Otávio A. V. Marques.

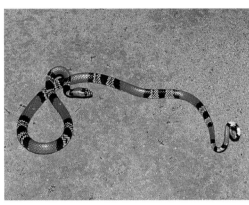

Plate 1296. *Simophis rhinostoma*, female, 77.5 cm TL, ZUEC 684. Fazenda Argentina, Campinas, São Paulo, Brazil. Photo by Ivan Sazima.

Plate 1297. *Siphlophis cervinus*, male, approximatel 60 cm TL. Upper Río Yarapa, Loreto, Peru.

Plate 1298. *Siphlophis compressus*, female, approximately 45 cm TL. Caucho Caño, Río Momón, Loreto, Peru.

Plate 1299. *Siphlophis longicaudatus*, 93.5 cm TL. Ibiúna, São Paulo, Brazil. Photo by Otávio A. V. Marques.

Plate 1300. *Siphlophis pulcher*, ZUEC. Sertão Cambur Ubatuba, São Paulo, Brazil. Photo by Ivan Sazima.

Plate 1301. *Siphlophis worontzowi*, approximately 60 cm TL, IB 53604. Usina Hidroelétrica Samuel, Rio Jamari, Pôrto Velho, Rondônia, Brazil. Photo by Ivan Sazima.

Plate 1302. *Sonora aemula*. Sonora, Mexico. Photo by R. Wayne Van Devender.

Plate 1303. *Sonora aemula*, adult. Approximately 50 k by road north of Culiacán, Sinaloa, Mexico. Photo b Eric N. Smith, courtesy of Manuel Varela-Juliá.

ate 1304. *Sonora michoacanensis*, female, 24.8 cm TL, ▮A R-38146. From Mexico Highway 200, 16 km ▮utheast of the junction with the road to La Unión, ▮errero, Mexico.

Plate 1305. *Sonora semiannulata blanchardi*. Texas, USA. Photo by Paul Freed.

Plate 1306. *Sonora semiannulata blanchardi*. Sproul Ranch, Jeff Davis County, Texas, USA. Photo by David G. Barker.

ate 1307. *Sonora semiannulata blanchardi*. Terlingua, ▮ewster County, Texas, USA. Photo by David G. Barker.

Plate 1308. *Sordellina punctata*, female, 59.1 cm TL, IB 52934. Registro, São Paulo, Brazil. Photo by Ivan Sazima.

Plate 1309. *Stenorrhina freminvillei*, approximately 65 cm TL, UCR. Río Oro de Santa Ana, San José, Costa Rica. Photo by Alejandro Solórzano at the National Serpentarium, San José.

te 1310. *Symphimus mayae*, male, 70.9 cm TL, UTA ▮6870. Between Tulum and Cobá, at km 33, Quintana ▮o, Mexico.

Plate 1311. *Sympholis lippiens*. Mexico Route 3696 (El Fuerte Road), Sinaloa, Mexico. Photo by R. Wayne Van Devender.

Plate 1312. *Tachymenis peruvianus*, 40.0 cm TL. Puno, Puno, Peru. Photo by Pablo Venegas.

te 1313. *Tantilla supracincta*, female, approximately ▮m TL, UCR. Guayacán de Siquirres, Limón, Costa ▮a.

Plate 1314. *Thamnodynastes chaquensis*, female, 44.2 cm TL, ZUEC 1161. Fazenda Santa Inês, Mato Grosso, Brazil. Photo by Ivan Sazima.

Plate 1315. *Thamnodynastes hypoconia*. Ibiúna, São Paulo, Brazil. Photo by Ivan Sazima.

Plate 1316. *Thamnodynastes rutilus*. Usina Hidroelétrica Sérgio Motta, Presidente Epitácio, São Paulo/Anaurilândia, Mato Grosso do Sul, Brazil. Photo by Otávio A. V. Marques.

Plate 1317. *Thamnodynastes strigatus*, female, approximately 56 cm TL, ZUEC 1291. Parque Estadual, Campos do Jordão, São Paulo, Brazil. Photo by Ivan Sazima.

Plate 1318. *Thamnodynastes strigilis*, ZUEC 60 Petrolândia, Pernambuco, Brazil. Photo by Ivan Sazima

Plate 1319. *Thamnodynastes* sp., female, 43.7 cm TL, KU 220506. Puerto Miguel, Río Yarapa, Loreto, Peru.

Plate 1320. *Thamnodynastes* sp., adult female. Uribia, La Guajira, Colombia. This may represent a population of *T. gambotensis*.

Plate 1321. *Thamnophis elegans vagrans*, female, 78.5 c TL, UTA R-16452. From 6.4 km south of U.S. Highwa 30, toward Pegram, Bear Lake County, Idaho, USA.

Plate 1322. *Thamnophis marcianus marcianus*, female, 47.5 cm TL, UTA R-17041. Farm-to-Market Road 624, La Salle County, Texas, USA. Photo by David G. Barker.

Plate 1323. *Thamnophis proximus*, female, 57.0 cm TL, UTA R-37947. Proyecto Geotermico Miravalles, Guayabos de Miravalles, Guanacaste, Costa Rica.

Plate 1324. *Tomodon dorsatus*. Arrededores, São Paul Brazil. Photo by Otávio A. V. Marques.

Plate 1325. *Trachyboa boulengeri*, female, approximately 30 cm TL, FHGO-live 111. Zapayo Grande, Río Cayapas, Esmeraldas, Ecuador.

Plate 1326. *Trachyboa gularis*, adult. Ecuador. Photo by John H. Tashjian.

Plate 1327. *Trimorphodon biscutatus quadruplex*, juveni female. Parque Nacional Santa Rosa, Guanacaste, Cos Rica.

ate 1328. *Trimorphodon lambda vilkinsoni*, female, proximately 65 cm TL, TCWC. Franklin Mountains, El so County, Texas, USA.

Plate 1329. *Trimorphodon tau*, ENEPI 6378. Road between Milpillas and Filo del Caballo, Sierra Madre del Sur, Guerrero, Mexico. Photo by Eric N. Smith.

Plate 1330. *Tropidodryas serra*. Coast of São Paulo, Brazil. Photo by Otávio A. V. Marques.

te 1331. *Tropidodryas striaticeps*, male, 68.3 cm TL, IB 1694. Juquitiba, São Paulo, Brazil. Photo by Otávio V. Marques.

Plate 1332. *Ungaliophis continentalis*, male, 48.8 cm TL, UTA R-25119. From 13.7 km southeast of San Cristóbal de las Casas, Chiapas, Mexico.

Plate 1333. *Ungaliophis panamensis*. Costa Rica. Specimen courtesy of the Houston Zoo.

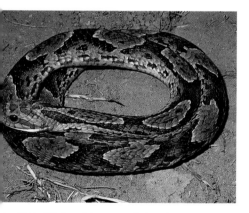

te 1334. *Waglerophis merremii*, female, 69.0 cm TL, A R-37718. Florida, Samaipata, Santa Cruz, Bolivia. oto by Michael B. Harvey.

Plate 1335. *Waglerophis merremii*, approximately 60 cm TL. Serranópolis, Goiás, Brazil.

Plate 1336. *Waglerophis merremii*. Serra da Mesa, Goiás, Brazil. Photo by Nelson Jorge da Silva.

te 1337. *Waglerophis merremii*. Serra da Mesa, Goiás, zil. Photo by Nelson Jorge da Silva.

Plate 1338. *Waglerophis merremii*, 157.4 cm TL, IB 59182. Prata, Minas Gerais, Brazil. Photo by Otávio A. V. Marques.

Plate 1339. *Waglerophis merremii*, female, 80.7 cm TL, ZUEC 551. Rio Atibaia, Jaguariuna, São Paulo, Brazil. Photo by Ivan Sazima.

Plate 1340. *Xenodon guentheri.* Rio Grande do Sul, Brazil. Photo by Otávio A. V. Marques.

Plate 1341. *Xenodon neuwiedi*, male, 67.2 cm TL, ZUEC 800. Brusque, Santa Catarina, Brazil. Photo by Ivan Sazima.

Plate 1342. *Xenodon rabdocephalus*, male, 49.0 cm T UTA R-21788. Finca El Faro, approximately 4.0 k north of El Palmar, south slope of Volcán Santa Mar Quezaltenango, Guatemala, elevation 875 m. Photo b David G. Barker.

Plate 1343. *Xenodon rabdocephalus*, same as Plate 1342. Photo by David G. Barker.

Plate 1344. *Xenodon rabdocephalus*, juvenile, 20.5 cm TL, UTA R-22858. Finca El Faro, approximately 4.0 km north of El Palmar, south slope of Volcán Santa María, Quezaltenango, Guatemala, elevation 875 m.

Plate 1345. *Xenodon rabdocephalus*, female, 50.6 c TL, UTA R-22860. Finca El Faro, approximately 4.0 k north of El Palmar, south slope of Volcán Santa Mar Quezaltenango, Guatemala, elevation 875 m.

Plate 1346. *Xenodon rabdocephalus*, female, 55.5 cm TL, UTA R-22859. Finca El Faro, approximately 4.0 km north of El Palmar, south slope of Volcán Santa María, Quezaltenango, Guatemala, elevation 875 m.

Plate 1347. *Xenodon rabdocephalus*, juvenile, 23.0 cm TL, UTA R-23057. Tikal, near Temple 5, Petén, Guatemala.

Plate 1348. *Xenodon rabdocephalus*, female, 29.7 cm T UTA R-42297. Rancho Alegre, Los Amates, Marisco Izabal, Guatemala. Photo by Eric N. Smith.

Plate 1349. *Xenodon rabdocephalus*, male, approximately 80 cm TL, UCR. Guayacán de Siquirres, Limón, Costa Rica.

Plate 1350. *Xenodon rabdocephalus*, male, approximately 40 cm TL. Finca Las Orquídeas, alto Río Negro, Meta, Colombia.

Plate 1351. *Xenodon rabdocephalus*, adult. Past Province, Ecuador. Photo by Paul Freed.

Plate 1352. *Xenodon rabdocephalus*, female, approximately 70 cm TL. Reserva Paucarillo II, Río Oroza, Loreto, Peru.

Plate 1353. *Xenodon rabdocephalus*, female, approximately 75 cm TL. San Andrés, Río Momón, Loreto, Peru.

Plate 1354. *Xenodon rabdocephalus*, juvenile female. Padre Cocha, Río Nanay, Loreto, Peru.

Plate 1355. *Xenodon rabdocephalus*, adult male, LJV 1596. Campamento Juruá, Rio Xingu, Pará, Brazil. Photo by Laurie J. Vitt.

Plate 1356. *Xenodon severus*, adult. Pastaza Province, Ecuador. Photo by Paul Freed.

Plate 1357. *Xenodon severus*, juvenile, FHGO-live. Comunidad Taisha, Morona-Santiago, Ecuador, elevation 500 m.

Plate 1358. *Xenodon werneri*, female, approximately ? m TL. On the road in the Kaw Mountains, Cayenne, French Guiana. Photo by Christian Marty.

Plate 1359. *Xenopholis scalaris*, adult. Palmas, Tocantins, Brazil. Photo by Otávio A. V. Marques.

Plate 1360. *Xenoxybelis boulengeri*. Cuzco Amazónico, Madre de Dios, Peru. Photo by William E. Duellman.

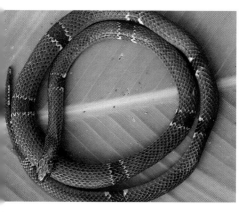

Plate 1361. *Micrurus oligoanellatus*, female, 62.5 cm TL, INUC-HE-00357-Se, holotype. Between El Cocal and Reserva Natural Tambito, Municipio de El Tambo, Cauca, Colombia, elevation 1,300 m. Photo by L. G. Jiménez, courtesy of Santiago Ayerbe.

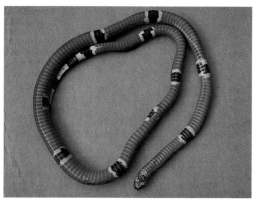

Plate 1362. *Micrurus oligoanellatus*. Same as Plate 1361.

Plate 1363. *Bothrops asper*, 80.0 cm TL. El Caucho, Tumbes, Peru. This is the southernmost locality known for *B. asper*. Photo by Pablo Venegas.

Plate 1364. *Bothrops* sp., 110.0 cm TL. Bagua, Amazonas, Peru. Photo by Pablo Venegas.

Plate 1365. *Bothrops atrox*, 80.0 cm TL. Pucallpa, Ucayali, Peru. Photo by Pablo Venegas.

Pitvipers, Family Viperidae

RATTLESNAKES

Long-lived, slow-reproducing species such as rattlesnakes may, like the endangered California condor, require complete protection from man in order to ensure adequate annual survival for population maintenance.

—Parker and Brown, 1974

Rattlesnakes have perhaps attracted more attention than any other group of snakes. They were subjects of great interest to the early European colonizers of the New World, and a number of illustrations were published during the first half of the seventeenth century, the first perhaps being Hernández's *Rerum medicarum Novae Hispaniae historia* in 1628 (Klauber, 1948). Beaupre and Duvall (1998a) summarized the importance of rattlesnakes as model organisms for diverse studies, including physiological ecology, life history, and behavioral ecology. The 32 species of rattlesnakes currently recognized are placed into two genera. *Sistrurus*, which comprises 2 species, is characterized by the presence of nine large, symmetrical plates on the head. *Crotalus* comprises about 30 species, most of which have numerous small scales on top of the head, especially in the frontal and parietal regions. *Crotalus ravus* was previously placed in the genus *Sistrurus* on the basis of its enlarged head plates (a primitive character), but other anatomical features and recent molecular and morphological studies suggest that it is more properly allocated with *Crotalus*, with which it shares derived skeletal and hemipenial characteristics. As Klauber (1972:265) pointed out, the distinction between *Sistrurus* and *Crotalus* based on the condition of head scalation (nine head plates versus more finely divided scales) is not as sharp as these definitions imply. Many species of *Crotalus* have large head plates on the crown, and conversely, it is not unusual to find specimens of *Sistrurus* with fragmented head scales. Some species of *Crotalus* usually have about four large, rectangular scales in the internasal-prefrontal region (e.g., *C. basiliscus*, *C. durissus*, *C. molossus*, *C. pusillus*, *C. simus*, *C. totonacus*; see Figs. 204, 212); *C. ravus* retains the colubridlike pattern of large head plates typical of *Sistrurus*, but the parietal scales often are partially fragmented. It is also worth noting that in his key to the genera of pitvipers based on skull characters Klauber (1972:136) was unable to distinguish *C. ravus* from other *Crotalus*. The lateral process of the squamosal of both *Sistrurus catenatus* and *S. miliarius* forms a fork having an angle of 80 degrees or less with the longitudinal axis of the main bone. In all species of *Crotalus*, including *C. ravus*, the lateral process of the squamosal may be blunt or pointed, but if it forms a fork with the longi-

tudinal axis of the main bone, the angle formed between them is 90 degrees or more. Further, the squamosal in *C. ravus* is relatively short compared with species of *Sistrurus* and more closely resembles the bone found in certain other montane species of *Crotalus* such as *C. lepidus* and *C. triseriatus* (Brattstrom, 1964).

Although the rattlesnakes are placed in two genera, there is no doubt that all are closely related and form a monophyletic group. Evidence for this argument may be seen in the evolution of a single remarkable and complicated structure not present in any other species of snake—the rattle (see Zimmerman and Pope, 1948, for a discussion of the rattle's development and growth). All species of rattlesnakes have rattles, although several populations are unable to acquire rattle segments during the shedding cycle.

The rattle is used only as a defense mechanism, at least in adults (Greene, 1997). One of the theories regarding the rattle is that it evolved as a protection against being trod upon by large ungulates such as bison (Barbour, 1922, 1926; Hay, 1887a; Klauber, 1940c). Most of the available evidence, however, suggests that the earliest radiation of rattlesnakes may have occurred in the mountainous regions of Mexico (Gloyd, 1940; Smith, 1946b) and that the common ancestor to rattlesnakes was a montane species (Klauber, 1956; Murphy, 1983a, 1983b; Murphy and Ottley, 1984), and therefore probably not subject to being trampled by hooved animals. Most of the species of rattlesnakes that occur today in grassland habitats are not relatively primitive (Greene, 1997). Schuett et al. (1984) suggested that the rattle evolved as a device to enhance caudal luring, although Greene (1997), Tiebout (1997), and Moon (2001) have offered convincing arguments that refute this.

The rattle may have arisen in an area that lacked abundant dry grass or leaves against which a vibrating tail alone would cause a rattling sound, but instead featured rocky outcroppings or talus slopes such as those that serve as a refuge for many species of montane rattlesnakes today (Greene, 1997). Such species as *C. lepidus* and *C. pricei* often sense vibrations caused by humans moving across these rocky habitats and are quick to rattle even before they are discovered and even if they are hidden beneath rocks. This behavior may warn predators such as coatimundis (*Nasua narica*), ringtails (*Bassariscus astutus*), and black bears (*Ursus americanus*) that are known to seek small vertebrates for food (Greene, 1997).

Caudal luring is a slow, intermittent activity that would not require any special physiological modifications, whereas the tail shaker muscles that operate antipredator tail vibration are specialized to sustain fast contractions for prolonged periods (Moon, 2001). Comparisons of the tail shaker and trunk muscles of several species of colubrid snakes, *Agkistrodon contortrix*, and several rattlesnakes revealed that none of the colubrids had muscles with significantly higher respiratory levels, even though one species (*Coluber constrictor*) vibrates its tail. The shaker muscles in both *Agkistrodon contortrix* (a species that also exhibits antipredator tail vibration) and rattlesnakes had a significantly higher respiratory capacity than the trunk muscles (Moon, 2001). Many other imaginative notions about the function of the rattle have been put forth, but these have now been largely discredited. Babcock (1929), for instance, suggested that the rattle served both to decoy insectivorous birds by imitating the sound of crickets and to call the sexes together.

The common belief that rattlesnakes cannot hear their own rattle (e.g., Manning, 1923) may have some basis in fact. Most snakes, including rattlesnakes, hear best in the range of 150–600 Hz and are unable to hear sounds much over 1,000 Hz but typically produce sounds over 3,000 Hz (Young, 1997). Some large individuals of *Crotalus*, however, can produce rattling sounds that have frequencies they can hear (Young and Brown, 1993, 1995). Snakes are sensitive to both airborne and vibratory stimuli. Young and Brown (1993, 1995) found no species-specific acoustic specializations in any of the rattlesnake species they surveyed and concluded that most rattlesnakes produce broadband noise spanning a range from about 2,500 to 19,000 Hz. Pylka et al. (1971) reported a range of 20,000–40,000 Hz, but no subsequent study has found a range that high.

The first comprehensive treatment of the structure, development, and origin of the rattle was undertaken by Garman (1888, 1889), who described the rattle after successive molts and compared it with the tail spine of various species of pitvipers. Rattlesnakes are born with a prebutton that is shed during the first ecdysis, exposing a button that is the first segment of the rattle to be retained (see Fig. 76). A new rattle segment is gained each time the snake sheds. The number of times that a rattlesnake sheds each year is variable and depends on such things as species, age, climate, and amount of food available. Young, rapidly growing snakes may shed four or more times a year, whereas adult snakes usually shed no more than twice a year. In a nine-year study of *C. o. oreganus* in north-central Idaho in which growth was carefully monitored, Diller and Wallace (2002) found that snakes shed two or three times during the first year and usually twice during the second year. Rattles become worn with age, and distal segments frequently break off, so rattlesnakes with long strings of segments are rare. Klauber (1940c) noted that adult rattlesnakes most frequently have 5–9 rattle segments and (Klauber 1971) stated that rattle strings of 7–10 segments are the most effective noisemakers.

Rattles of more than 12 segments are very rarely encountered under natural conditions, although Klauber (1972) reported 16 segments in a specimen of *C. cerastes* and 23 in a *C. atrox*. Rattlesnakes in captivity sometimes acquire unusually long rattles; 29 segments have been recorded for *C. horridus* (Klauber, 1972) and 38 segments for *C. viridis* (Chiszar and Smith, 1994). Berish (1998) showed that the number of rattle segments is positively correlated with SVL in *C. adamanteus* (Fig. 178).

Sound is produced when two or more segments of the rattle strike each other as the tail is vibrated. Klauber (1956), Rowe and Owings (1978), and Pylka et al. (1971) described the sound of the rattle. A number of people have noted that it resembles a sharp hiss (e.g., Conant, 1969; Klauber, 1971, 1972). Kinney et al. (1998), using electronic analysis, found that the rattling sound was acoustically distinct from the hissing sound produced in *C. adamanteus* and *C. atrox*; the rattling sound had a broader frequency (400–4,700 Hz) and higher amplitude (60 dB) than hissing. They hypothesized that hissing is an epiphenomenon of body inflation that is produced only during periods of rapid inhalation. Fenton and Licht (1990) compared the rattling sounds of six species of rattlesnakes and found that the sound produced by all conformed to the same general pattern: medium intensity, broadband sounds with rapid onset and no structural changes in frequency pattern over time. The amount of variation these investigators found between species was comparable to the amount of variation found within a species.

The size of the rattle varies significantly among species (Cook et al., 1994). An aroused large rattlesnake may be heard at a distance of 60 m or more (Klauber, 1940c), whereas the sound produced by certain small species (e.g., *Sistrurus miliarius*, *Crotalus intermedius*, *C. pusillus*, *C. stejnegeri*) may be difficult to detect even when one is practically standing on the snake. When the interspecific differences in SVL are removed by allometric

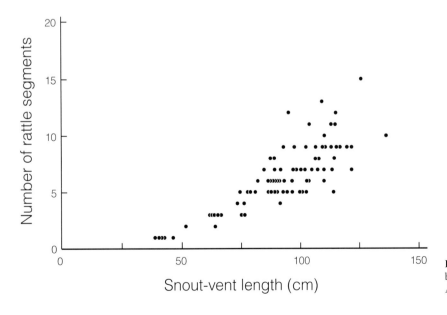

Fig. 178. Number of rattle segments (indicating number of sheds) versus SVL in *Crotalus adamanteus*. Adapted from Berish, 1998:553 (fig. 2).

scaling, however, the rattling sounds of 21 species of rattlesnakes become indistinguishable from one another; only *S. miliarius* produces a comparatively quieter and higher-pitched rattle than the other rattlesnakes (Cook et al., 1994). The acoustics of rattling in *C. oreganus oreganus* were investigated by Young and Brown (1995), who looked at variables including body size, rattle size, rattle segment length, and different environmental conditions. They found that removing the distal rattle segments did not significantly change the dominant, maximum, and minimum frequencies of the sound produced by the rattle and concluded that the size of the proximal rattle segment is the most important feature determining the sound produced by the rattle. Sisk and Jackson (1997) suggested that the ability to retain rattle segments—and thus to evolve a rattle—was contingent on the prior development of the longitudinal bilobing of the terminal scale. They suggested two hypotheses for the initial functional advantage of such bilobing: the luring effectiveness hypothesis, whereby bilobing would enhance visual attractiveness to potential prey; and the dual contact hypothesis, in which aposematic sound quality would be enhanced during tail vibration. When both hypotheses were experimentally tested, the authors could find no support for either although they suggested that other aspects of the dual contact hypothesis should be further investigated.

Kissner et al. (1997) investigated variables including sex, reproductive status, body size, and body temperature in relation to rattling behavior in *Crotalus v. viridis*. Two groups of snakes allowed intruders to come significantly closer before beginning to rattle: gravid females and small snakes. The authors hypothesized that these two groups depend on crypsis to a greater extent than other snakes because they are less able to escape predators and because small snakes may be more cryptic than larger snakes, providing them with an advantage. Most analyses did not seem to show a consistent relationship between body temperature and rattling distance, but cool gravid females did allow intruders to approach more closely than warmer gravid females.

The speed with which rattlesnakes vibrate their tails is temperature dependent (Chadwick and Rahn, 1954; Klauber, 1971; Martin and Bagby, 1972). Chadwick and Rahn (1954) found that the relationship of rattling frequency (measured as cycles per minute) to temperature in *C. v. viridis* was linear between 5 and 40 °C, and Martin and Bagby (1972) found that the relationship between these variables in *C. atrox* was linear between 16 and 32 °C, which corresponds largely to the temperature range at which that snake is active. At temperatures above 34 °C rattling became spasmodic, and between 3 and 15 °C the rattle frequency dropped precipitously. At 15.5 °C rattlesnakes typically have vibration speeds of about 35 cycles per second, but at 35.0 °C the vibration speed increases to about 85 cycles per second (Klauber, 1971).

Six muscles make up what is often referred to as the shaker complex. In a recently skinned rattlesnake these muscles are usually evident because they are a darker red than adjacent skeletal muscle. Studies on *C. horridus*, *C. ruber* (Clark and Schultz, 1980), and *C. atrox* (Shaeffer et al., 1996) determined that tail shaker muscles have large numbers of small myofibrils, large deposits of glycogen, and an extremely high volume of sarcoplasmic reticulum, which together minimize activation, contraction, and relaxation times. A high volume density of mitochondria in this muscle maximizes ATP resynthesis. Shaker muscle differs from other skeletal muscle in that myofibrils do not entirely fill the fibers and the myofibrils are highly

branched, giving the fibers a mottled appearance (Schultz et al., 1980). Conley and Lindstedt (1996) found that the tail shaker muscles have a reduced volume density of myofiber and require minimal ATP for contraction. Thus, the tail shaker muscle is specialized to produce a sustained high-frequency warning sound at a cost that is among the lowest found in striated muscles in vertebrates (Conley and Lindstedt, 1996). The shaker muscles of *C. horridus* and *C. ruber* can contract at a rate of about 50 per second for at least three hours (Clark and Schultz, 1980). Kemper et al. (2001) showed that glycolysis in tail shaker muscles provides a high and sustainable ATP supply along with oxidative phosphorylation without muscle fatigue.

The size and structure of the rattle may vary considerably among populations of the same species and between closely related species. For example, members of the island population of *C. catalinensis* lose the developing rattle segment each time they shed, and thus retain only a shrunken rattle matrix and no rattle or only a single basal segment. *Crotalus ruber lorenzoensis* from Isla San Lorenzo Sur also has this tendency, and about half of the individuals of this population have lost their rattles. In contrast, *C. ruber* individuals, the mainland relatives of *C. catalinensis* and *C. ruber lorenzoensis*, have large, well-formed rattles. The rattle of *Sistrurus catenatus* is large and robust, whereas *S. miliarius* has one of the tiniest rattles found among rattlesnakes. The size of the rattle varies significantly among isolated populations of *Crotalus ravus* (Fig. 179), with the comparatively small rattle of the Guerreran *C. ravus exiguus* being diagnostic for that population (Campbell and Armstrong, 1979).

Besides the rattle, rattlesnakes use hissing, body posture, scent glands, and extended protraction of the tongue as warning signals (Klauber, 1972). A few species may use an open-mouth threat or move the head in a provocative way. *Crotalus molossus* is one of the few rattlesnakes that we have observed to engage in an open-mouth threat, a behavior also noted in this species by Armstrong and Murphy (1979). We have been able to elicit this defense only in a few snakes from southern populations. Armstrong and Murphy (1979) also reported a single specimen of *C. polystictus* that exhibited an open-mouth threat posture. Marchisin (1978) reported observing individuals of *Sistrurus miliarius barbouri* in the field and laboratory bobbing the head vertically while they rattled. He suggested that the bobbing serves as a visual warning signal to potential predators.

In most species of rattlesnakes males grow to greater lengths than females. Several interesting exceptions are the sidewinder, *C. cerastes* (Klauber, 1972), and the pygmy rattlesnake, *Sistrurus miliarius* (Bishop et al., 1996). Porras (pers. comm., 2002) indicated that *Crotalus oreganus concolor* females also exceed males in size (but see Ashton, 2001, for a conflicting view). Klauber (1937) found that males of many species of rattlesnakes were slightly larger (1% of body length) than females at birth, and that the sexual dimorphism in body length increased with age. Klauber (1937) provided information on a sample of 858 *C. viridis* collected from denning sites near Plattesville, Colorado. This series is unusual because of its size and because the snakes were collected with no discrimination for size. Figure 180 summarizes the sizes and sexes represented in this sample. This histogram is strongly bimodal, with juveniles (25.0–34.9 cm) and adults (55.0–79.9 cm) being the most common. The largest size categories are composed entirely of males as a result of sexual dimorphism, and the percentage of males making up the larger size categories is higher for the same reason.

Crotalus atrox is sexually dimorphic in size throughout its range. Beaupre et al. (1998) showed significant sexual size

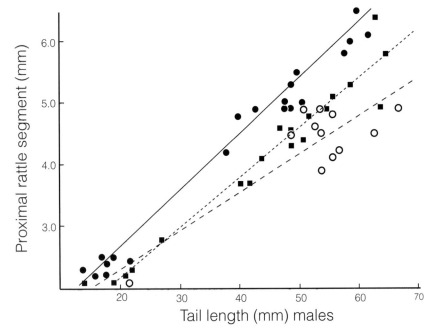

Fig. 179. Regression of dorsoventral width of proximal rattle segment on tail length for males of the three subspecies of *Crotalus ravus*. Closed circles = *ravus*, squares = *brunneus*, open circles = *exiguus*. The slope and elevation of the regression for *ravus* are significantly different (P < 0.001) from those for *brunneus* and *exiguus*, but the regressions of *brunneus* and *exiguus* are not significantly different from each other. Adapted from Campbell and Armstrong, 1979:307 (fig. 3).

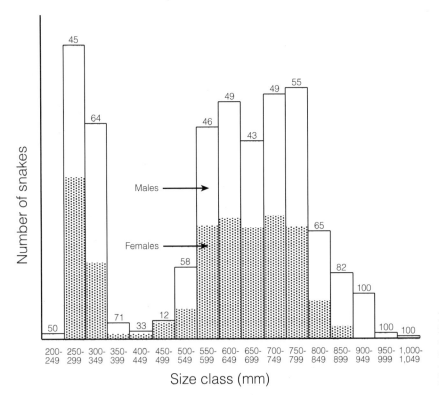

Fig. 180. Size and sex distributions for a sample of 858 individuals (459 males and 399 females) from a snake den population of *Crotalus viridus* near Platteville, Colorado, USA. Figures at the top of columns indicate percentage of males in each size class. Adapted from Klauber, 1937:20 (fig. 4).

dimorphism in a population of *C. atrox* from central Arizona (Fig. 181). There was no significant gender difference in size at birth, and juvenile growth rates were similar. The divergence in size between males and females occured after sexual maturity was achieved.

Certain rattlesnakes aggregate in huge numbers in dens during the fall (Gregory, 1984; Sexton et al., 1992). Hall (1929) found about 50 rattlesnakes around or near a denning site near Ely in eastern Nevada. He identified these as *Crotalus confluentus kellyi* (=*C. scutulatus*), but the geographic locality indicates that they were *C. oreganus lutosus* (L. Porras, pers. comm.). Hall also reported that several persons had reportedly killed 139 rattlesnakes at this site, several days prior to his visit, and the

number of empty gun shells and dead snakes that he found seemed to confirm that figure. When this den was first discovered, during the autumn about five years before Hall's visit, large numbers of rattlesnakes were purportedly seen coiled together into balls around the edge of the entrance.

Graf et al. (1939) reported that 97 *C. oreganus oreganus* were killed in April 1937 and another 27 in 1937 at a denning site on the western side of the Cascade Mountains in Oregon. These authors also reported that more than 100 rattlesnakes were killed by a crew blasting a road through the region.

Bushar et al. (1998) found that individual *C. horridus* from the same denning site usually were more closely related to each other than to snakes from nearby hibernacula. In general,

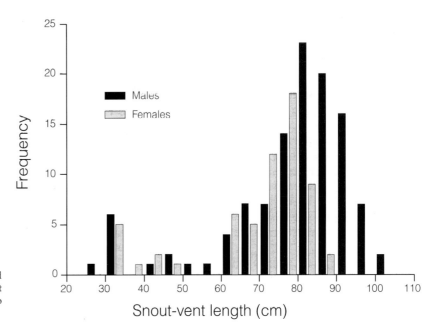

Fig. 181. Size distributions for a sample of male and female *Crotalus atrox* from central Arizona, USA, at first capture. Note that males achieve a larger SVL than do females. Adapted from Beaupre et al., 1998:42 (fig. 1).

genetic distance increased and gene flow decreased as geographic distance increased between hibernacula, although certain structural habitat features such as location of suitable basking locations tended to influence genetic variation in ways not strictly correlated with distance.

A den discovered in Tooele County, Utah, in 1940 was the focus of studies by Woodbury and collaborators (1951). During the course of their studies they marked 930 rattlesnakes and had 1,080 recaptures. No other dens were found within a 3.2-km radius. One marked snake was captured about 2 km from the den. Many more adults than juveniles entered the dens than might be expected if all snakes were equally likely to use the den. Vetas (*in* Woodbury et al., 1951) stated that an air temperature of 60 °F (15.6 °C) adjacent to the entrance of the den was the threshold temperature at which denning *C. oreganus* (*lutosus*) became active and came to the surface. In most of the 11 winter seasons of the study (1939–1950), the number of males coming to the den far exceeded the number of females (Julian, *in* Woodbury et al., 1951). Only in the winter of 1940–1941 did females outnumber males (95 females versus 85 males). Over the total period of the study, 1,179 males and 803 females were recorded from the den. Julian (*in* Woodbury et al., 1951) suggested that sex ratios were about equal for the first three years of life in this population of rattlesnakes but began to diverge at about the time of sexual maturity owing to differential survival rates of the sexes. Glissmeyer (*in* Woodbury et al., 1951) reported that females arrived at the den in the fall with enlarged ovarian eggs on alternate years, suggesting biennial reproduction; 12.5–66.7% of the females were gravid in particular years, with an average of 49% for the 11 seasons. Ovulation occurred in May or June, followed by fertilization, and young were born in August or September. Females carried 2–9 ($\bar{x} = 5.5$) eggs. Hirth (1966b), who also studied snakes from this den, found the smallest mature male to be 65 cm in SVL; the two smallest sexually mature females were 54 and 56 cm in SVL. Heyrend and Call (*in* Woodbury et al., 1951) found that most rattlesnakes shed twice the first full active season after their birth, after which time there was an increasing tendency for snakes to molt only once each season. It was unusual to find more than six to nine rattle segments on a snake.

A follow-up study at this den was undertaken from 1969 to 1973, at which time the population had declined to 12–17 rat-tlesnakes (Parker and Brown, 1974). Overwintering mortality amounted to 3.6% for the four winters, whereas summer mortality averaged 17.8% per year. The overwintering weight losses amounted to 4–9%, with females losing more weight than males. No snakes younger than five years old were found, and the age structure had shifted toward older age groups. Based on a simulated life table and demographic traits of rattlesnakes, Parker and Brown (1974) estimated that this long-studied population was near extinction at the time of their study, and a brush fire in the area on 17 June 1974 may have extirpated the few remaining individuals.

Weight loss during hibernation is no doubt responsible for considerable mortality, especially of juveniles following unfavorable years. Klauber (1972) estimated that adult *C. v. viridis* on average lost about 4% of their weight during hibernation while juveniles lost about 20%. Hirth (1966b) found that weight loss in *C. o. lutosus* from a den in Utah was about 6.3% and 8.8% in adult males and females, respectively, and 25.5% in juveniles (less than 31 cm). The mean number of days spent overwintering in the den was 193 for juveniles and 219 for adults. Hirth estimated the overwintering mortality for rattlesnakes at this site to be about 34% (based on the recapture of 23 of 35 snakes), but some surviving snakes may not have been recaptured, so this figure may be too high.

An estimated 300 *C. oreganus* (*lutosus*) were killed in one den in Tintic Canyon, Juab County, Utah, in about 1937 (Woodbury and Hansen, 1950), but the den was still active in September 1949 when it was encircled by a screen wire fence with several traps to catch snakes coming to it. Five species of snakes used this den, including *Crotalus oreganus lutosus*, *Masticophis taeniatus*, *Pituophis catenifer*, *Lampropeltis triangulum*, and *Thamnophis ordinoides* (=*T. elegans vagrans*, fide L. Porras). Of these, *C. oreganus* accounted for about 54% of the total catch (69 of 127 snakes).

At a den site discovered in 1952 in Tooele County, Utah, Woodbury and Parker (1956) attempted to trap the entire den population. During the spring and fall of 1953 four *C. o. lutosus*, two *Pituophis catenifer*, and 85 *Masticophis taeniatus* were collected.

Parker and Brown (1973) studied a series of snake hibernacula in northern Utah and found that *Coluber constrictor*, *Masti-*

cophis taeniatus, *Pituophis catenifer*, and *Crotalus o. lutosus* overwintered in these dens, but that rattlesnakes were restricted to particular dens. One of these dens had been studied by earlier workers and provided information on long-term changes. A total of 232 *C. oreganus lutosus* were observed at this site in 1950, 55 were seen in 1966, and only 12 were observed in 1972. Killing by humans is almost certainly the primary reason for the precipitous decline.

It has been known for some time that snakes require heat to digest prey. With the advent of the first cold snap of the fall, most snakes appear either to cease feeding or to feed only infrequently thereafter. After returning to dens in the fall, snakes continue for several weeks to emerge on warm days to bask prior to entering the den for a quiescent period of several to many months. It has been suggested that fasting is necessary prior to hibernation to void the gut of food that might putrefy, causing harm or even death to the snake (Gregory, 1982). Macartney's (1989) observation of dried snake scats found in great abundance around the entrances of rattlesnake dens supports the notion that these snakes void most of the digestive tract before cold weather permanently sets in.

Diller and Wallace (1984) found that adult female *C. o. oreganus* from Idaho emerged from hibernation with enlarging ova, ovulated from mid-May to mid-June, and gave birth over about a 30-day period beginning in early September. The mean litter size was 5.5, and the number of young was strongly correlated with female body size. In the several populations studied, the percentage of females reproducing annually varied from 54 to 77%, with the frequency of reproduction primarily influenced by nutrition. These authors found that males longer than 52 cm in SVL and having four or more rattle segments were mature, but most mature females were more than 55 cm in SVL and had five or more rattle segments.

In Sweetwater County, Wyoming, pregnant females moved only a short distance to a rookery after emerging from hibernation, and they remained there throughout gestation without foraging or mating (Ashton and Patton, 2001). In this population offspring were born between 20 August and 18 November, with a mean litter size of 4.7, a mean offspring SVL of 19.3 cm, and a mean offspring mass of 8.0 g; females appeared to reproduce every two or three years (Ashton and Patton, 2001).

A population of *C. v. viridis* near the northern limits of the species' range was active from April to October, and about half of the adult females were gravid each summer (Gannon and Secoy, 1984). Gravid females of this population were significantly more active during all seasons (Gannon and Secoy, 1985). In south-central Wyoming, Duvall et al. (1985) found that female *C. v. viridis* gathered in communal birthing rookeries where they gave birth by early September. Males of this population made lengthy vernal foraging migrations in excess of 5 km from the denning site; both males and females were attracted to sites containing live deer mice (Duvall et al., 1985, 1990). King and Duvall (1990) found that both males and females foraged for food during about the first half of the 3.5-month active period in Wyoming; during the second half of the active season the attention of females continued to be on searching for prey, but males searched for both food and mates (King and Duvall, 1990).

The age at which rattle snakes reach maturity does not appear to be strongly correlated with size or geographic location, although no doubt both factors impose some constraints. *Crotalus horridus*, one of the largest rattlesnakes, requires four to seven years across its range to mature (Brown, 1991). A

moderate-sized rattlesnake, *C. oreganus oreganus*, matures in five to seven years in the northern portion of its range (Macartney et al., 1990) and takes only three years in more southerly regions (Diller and Wallace, 1984; Fitch, 1949b). Most females in a population of *C. o. oreganus* from north-central Idaho reached sexual maturity during their fourth summer, but males in this population matured more quickly, sometimes as early as their second summer (Diller and Wallace, 2002). Most adult females from this Idaho population reproduce biennially, but in some instances may reproduce during two consecutive years, presumably when prey densities provide sufficient energy for annual reproduction (Diller and Wallace, 2002). *Crotalus atrox*, another large snake, achieves maturity in three to four years (Beaupre et al., 1998; Fitch and Pisani, 1993). Secor (1994b) estimated that *C. cerastes* in the eastern Mohave Desert are mature at three years of age. Finally, the relatively small rock rattlesnake, *C. lepidus lepidus*, found in relatively mild climates, requires seven years to reach maturity (Beaupre, 1993).

Females may travel considerable distances from denning sites before giving birth (Duvall et al., 1985; Galligan and Dunson, 1979; Reinert and Kodrich, 1982). How young snakes make their way to the denning site for the first time is not well understood; it is possible that first-year snakes utilize different overwintering sites (Hirth, 1966a; Swanson, 1952; Woodbury and Hansen, 1950). In the case of *C. horridus* and *C. viridis*, which have been relatively well studied, at least some neonates use the same winter refugia as adults use (Duvall et al., 1985; Reinert and Zappalorti, 1988b), raising the question of how these hibernacula are located by neonates. Both laboratory and field observations on *C. horridus* strongly suggest that young *C. horridus* use chemical cues to trail adults to denning sites (Brown and MacLean, 1983; Reinert and Zappalorti, 1988b), and this method seems probable for other denning species as well.

The physiological ecology of rattlesnakes is a very new field, but a few recent studies offer intriguing glimpses into the world of rattlesnakes that have a significant bearing on our understanding of their ecology and evolution. For example, Beaupre (1996) studied metabolic rate and water flux in two populations of mottled rock rattlesnakes (*Crotalus lepidus*) in Big Bend National Park, Texas, and found that one population had an annual energy budget about half the magnitude of that of the other population, indicating a considerable difference in food resources. Not surprisingly, snakes from the low-energy-budget, food-limited population had lower growth rates and attained smaller adult body sizes than snakes from the other population. Snakes from the lower, hotter locality maintained significantly higher body temperatures as a result of environmental thermal constraints (Beaupre, 1995a). In August, the mean body temperature of the hot-locality snakes was about 1 to almost 5 °C higher during different times of the day (Fig. 182).

Body size varies dramatically from species to species. Members of the genus *Sistrurus* and of the species *Crotalus transversus*, *C. intermedius*, *C. triseriatus*, and *C. willardi* usually reach only about 70 cm in TL and weigh less than 0.5 kg, while members of the species *C. atrox*, *C. basiliscus*, *C. durissus*, *C. horridus*, *C. molossus*, and *C. simus* often exceed 150 cm in TL and may weigh in excess of 10 kg. The adult *C. adamanteus* is a truly formidable animal, approaching or exceeding 250 cm in TL and reaching in excess of 30 lbs (13.6 kg), the greatest weight of any venomous snake (Klauber, 1971).

Klauber (1938a), who measured head length in rattlesnakes in relation to SVL, noted that only *C. cerastes* exhibits sexual

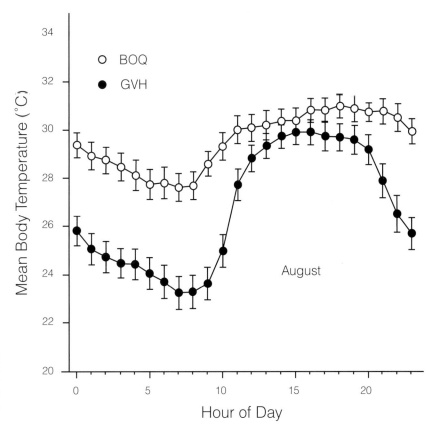

Fig. 182. Daily body temperatures (mean ± 2 SE) of two populations of *Crotalus lepidus* in Big Bend National Park, Texas, USA. The Boquillas Canyon (BOQ) population lives at a relatively low elevation; the Grapevine Hills (GVH) population occurs at a higher elevation. Adapted from Beaupre, 1995a:1660 (fig. 4).

dimorphism, with females having proportionately larger heads than males. Rattlesnakes with relatively large heads include *C. adamanteus*, *C. cerastes*, and *C. triseriatus*; those with relatively small heads include *C. durissus*, *C. mitchellii*, *C. scutulatus*, *C. simus*, and *C. tigris*; those with narrow heads include *C. enyo* and *C. polystictus*; and those with broad heads include *C. cerastes* and *C. mitchellii* (Klauber, 1938a, 1971, 1972).

Recent research has also shown that the quantity of lipids in the epidermis of rattlesnakes is relatively high, and their skins are relatively impermeable as measured by evaporative water loss, a characteristic of xeric-adapted species (Roberts and Lillywhite, 1983). Most species of rattlesnakes do, in fact, occur in xeric or subhumid regions. The southwestern United States and northern Mexico are well known for their high number of rattlesnake species (e.g., Cope, 1896). Ecological studies of species that are broadly sympatric have revealed distinct differences in distributions. For example, the three species of large rattlesnakes that occur in southeastern Arizona are largely segregated from one another. *Crotalus molossus* is found in the mountains (1,494–2,682 m), *C. atrox* is found near the mountains but is mostly confined to mesquite-tarbush associations, and *C. scutulatus* is found in more barren portions of valleys.

The widespread *C. simus* of Mexico and Central America has obviously used tropical deciduous forest and thornforest (sensu Leopold, 1950) and lowland dry forest (sensu Stuart, 1966) to disperse throughout much of the region, but localized populations have become adapted to more mesic habitats, sometimes at moderately high elevations. Likewise, *C. durissus* of South America is adapted primarily to open habitats, especially savannas and other types of grasslands, the cerrado association, and caatinga vegetation, all vegetation types characterized as having a relatively low wet-season potential evapotranspiration (Cochrane and Jones, 1981).

While *Crotalus cerastes* is well adapted to occupy sandy areas of the Mohave Desert, however, some species of rattlesnakes thrive in Mexican cloud forests; two more different habitats can scarcely be imagined. Many species live in relatively flat lowlands or rolling prairies. Some species are found in marshes (*Sistrurus catenatus*) or forests. McCoy (1984) placed *S. catenatus* in his "semiaquatic" ecological category, although it should be noted that this category included species living in marshes, sedge mats, and other habitats peripheral to watercourses and lagunas; this species is certainly not as closely associated with water as the natricines, which are truly semiaquatic. Klauber (1972) voiced the opinion that *C. polystictus* might be somewhat aquatic based on the field notes of Paul Ruthling, who collected this species near Lake Chapala in Jalisco, Mexico. Armstrong and Murphy (1979) suggested that while *C. polystictus* may inhabit lake margins that are subject to flooding after heavy rains, this species is not semiaquatic and is solely an inhabitant of montane meadows, and flatlands. We have most often seen *C. polystictus* in the high, open grassy valleys and the rocky mesquite-grasslands of the southern Mexican Plateau. We have encountered individuals a few meters from slow-moving, meandering steams, but never in what might be considered an aquatic situation. We might be inclined to consider Ruthling's observations aberrant were it not for an even earlier, often overlooked, independent observation, also made near Lake Chapala, that clearly describes the aquatic habits of this species (Beebe, 1905; see the *C. polystictus* account).

The overall ground color of rattlesnakes is often closely associated with their habitats. For example, *Crotalus intermedius* individuals from the deserts of Puebla are pale gray with distinct darker brownish gray blotches, snakes from the open pine-oak forests of Oaxaca and Guerrero have a somewhat darker ground color although the dorsal blotches are still conspicuous, and snakes from the cloud forest of these states are usually dark gray to almost black and dorsal blotches become obfuscated in adults. *Crotalus ravus* specimens from dry habitats in Puebla and Oaxaca likewise have a distinctly pale ground color with well-defined blotches; those in the highlands of Guerrero usually have a somewhat darker ground color; and those in the cloud forest near Totontepec, Oaxaca, and the high-elevation fir-hardwood forest near Huitzilac are mostly dark brown. Several populations of rattlesnakes that live in dark lava fields in the southwestern United States are melanistic, including *C. atrox* from the Pedro Armendariz lava field of New Mexico (Best and James, 1984); *C. mitchellii* from the Pisgah lava flow in southern California (Norris, 1967); and *C. molossus* in New Mexico from the Tularosa malpais (Lewis, 1949), the Afton lava flows (Prieto and Jacobson, 1968), and the Pedro Armendariz lava field (Best and James, 1984).

Rattlesnakes are good swimmers, and some will freely enter water. Dunn (1915b) captured a specimen of *C. horridus* swimming in the Shenandoah River of Virginia, and Frey (1996) observed a *C. lepidus* sitting on a ledge about 50 cm under the water in a small pool of the South Fork of Negrito Creek in Catron County, New Mexico. Frey suggested that the snake may have been foraging for fish, or alternatively that its aquatic behavior was associated with thermoregulation (the air temperature was about 35 °C, while the water temperature was about 16 °C).

Some species of rattlesnakes have no trouble breaching narrow saltwater barriers. Many Atlantic and Gulf coast islands off the southern United States are inhabited by rattlesnakes, especially *C. adamanteus* and *C. atrox*; Catawba and South Bass Islands (Ottawa County) in Lake Erie are known to be populated by *C. horridus* (Walker, 1931); and islands populated by rattlesnakes are especially characteristic of the Gulf of California (Campbell and Lamar, 1989; Grismer, 1999a, 1999b, 2002; Murphy and Ottley, 1984; see Map 92), where some populations have become sufficiently differentiated from their mainland ancestors to be regarded as distinct species. Few islands off the Pacific coast of North America are inhabited by rattlesnakes, undoubtedly because of the cold ocean currents that separate these islands from the mainland; however, rattlesnakes have managed to reach two Pacific islands: Cedros Island (*C. ruber*) and South Coronado Island (*C. oreganus*).

In terms of their elevational distribution, rattlesnakes are among the most successful of the New World snakes, having adapted to climatological conditions ranging from sea level to alpine environments. In California, *C. oreganus helleri* is known from 3,293 m on San Jacinto Peak (Ewan, 1932) and reaches about 3,350 m elsewhere in the state (Klauber, 1936b). A large radiation of small montane species occurred in Mexico and the southwestern United States. One of these species, *C. triseriatus*, is known from 4,573 m (Klauber, 1972), almost at the snow line, on some of the great volcanos of the Transverse Volcanic Cordillera. Although reptile life would seem most unlikely at such high, cold elevations, on sunny days the dark volcanic rocks reach surprisingly high temperatures (Swan, 1952; see Fig. 183). It is no coincidence that montane rattlesnakes are associated with rocky outcroppings, which both provide radiant heat and afford shelter to the snakes' principal prey, lizards of the genus *Sceloporus*. Species that exhibit particularly wide elevational distributions include *C. basiliscus*, *C. horridus*, *C. oreganus*, *C. simus*, and *C. totonacus*. A few species (*C. adamanteus*, *C. transversus*, and the species inhabiting the islands in the Gulf of California) occupy relatively narrow elevational zones.

Rattlesnakes do hybridize in nature, but rarely. Based on morphological evidence, Campbell et al. (1989a) discussed an apparent hybrid between *Crotalus lepidus* and *C. willardi* from the Peloncillo Mountains of New Mexico. This hybrid was similar to *C. lepidus* in the number of scales in the internasal-prefrontal region, the number of loreals per side, the nature of the subocular-supralabial contact, the supralabial pattern, the postocular stripe, and juvenile tail coloration; it resembled *C. willardi* in having an undivided upper preocular; in the number of ventrals, subcaudals, and dorsal scale rows at midbody; and in the body pattern. It was intermediate in many characteristics.

Perkins (1951) reported several instances of hybrid rattlesnakes produced in captive conditions. In one case a male *Crotalus oreganus helleri* mated with a female *C. ruber ruber*, producing 9 viable offspring (Klauber, 1956). Another case involved a female *C. durissus unicolor* that mated with a male *C. scutulatus scutulatus* and produced 4 young. These young eventually reached maturity and bred among themselves, producing a litter that contained 4 viable young. Hybrids between *C. adamanteus* and *C. horridus* have been found in South Carolina and Florida (Pl. 754). We have seen photographs of naturally occurring hybrids between *C. scutulatus* and *C. molossus* in Texas and Arizona, between *C. scutulatus* and *C. atrox* in Texas, and between *C. viridis* and *C. atrox* in Texas.

Based on various venom characteristics, including the presence of Mojave toxins, Glenn and Straight (1990) suggested that hybridization occurs between *C. viridis viridis* and *C. scutulatus scutulatus* in southwestern New Mexico. Murphy and Crabtree

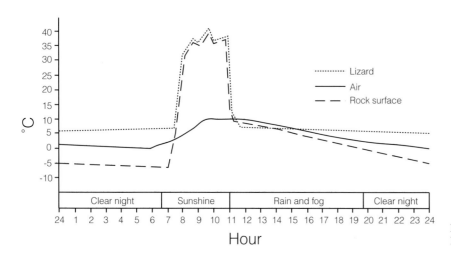

Fig. 183. A typical day at 4,120 m on Volcán Orizaba, Mexico. Adapted from Swan, 1952:109 (fig. 1).

(1988) used allozyme data to identify a hybrid between *Crotalus scutulatus* and *C. viridis viridis* that had been collected in Hudspeth County, Texas. A female *Crotalus scutulatus* from Kern County, California, and a male *C. oreganus oreganus* from Contra Costa County, California, that were maintained together were observed copulating on 10 May 1952. In late September or early October the female gave birth to 12 young. Six of these young had a color pattern similar to *C. scutulatus* with a greenish ground color and blotch borders of unicolored pale scales, 1 individual from this litter closely resembed *C. oreganus oreganus*

in color pattern, and the remaining young were somewhat intermediate between the parental species for color pattern, favoring one or the other. Bailey (1942) reported what he thought was an intergeneric hybrid between *Sistrurus catenatus catenatus* and *Crotalus horridus* from Iowa.

Other terrestrial snakes that are sometimes confused with rattlesnakes include members of the genera *Elaphe* (Pls. 1090–1094), *Heterodon* (Pls. 1127–1131), *Hypsiglena* (Pl. 1137), *Lampropeltis* (Pl. 1142), *Pituophis* (Pls. 1243 and 1244), and *Trimorphodon* (Pls. 1327–1329).

Key to the Species of Rattlesnakes[1]

1. Top of head with fewer than 12 large, symmetrically arranged plates including paired internasals, paired prefrontals, and a single frontal 2

   Top of head with more than 12 smaller, asymmetrically arranged scales, including several in the frontal area and numerous scales in the parietal region 4

2. Canthus angular with lateral edge of canthal scale bearing moderate ridge, not curved downward on side of head; rostral high, truncate at top; body blotches usually as wide as or wider than long 3

   Canthus rounded and lateral edge of canthal scale curving downward on side of head; rostral low, tapering to a point as it curves posteriorly between internasals; body blotches usually longer than wide (Pls. 931–939) . . . . *Crotalus ravus*

3. Upper preocular usually in contact with postnasal, anterior subocular usually contacts supralabials 4 and 5 (Pls. 1011–1017) . . . . *Sistrurus catenatus*

   Upper preocular not in contact with postnasal, anterior subocular usually contacts supralabials 3 and 4 (Pls. 1018–1023) . . . . *Sistrurus miliarius*

4. Lateral edges of supraoculars raised into flat, pointed, hornlike process (Pls. 791–794) . . . . *Crotalus cerastes*

   Lateral edges of supraoculars not extended into pointed, hornlike process 5

5. Fewer than 40 subcaudal scales in males and fewer than 35 in females 6

   More than 40 subcaudal scales in males and more than 35 in females 34

6. Tip of snout and anterior portion of canthus raised into sharp ridge; rostral and mental often with a median vertical pale line (Pls. 998–1010) . . . . *Crotalus willardi*

   Tip of snout and anterior portion of canthus not raised into sharp ridge; rostral and mental not marked with a median vertical pale line 7

7. Prenasals separated from rostral by small, often granular, scales; upper preoculars often divided horizontally or vertically, or both (Pls. 864–875) . . . . *Crotalus mitchellii*

   Prenasals contacting the rostral; upper preoculars usually not divided or, if so, divided only vertically with anterior portion of scale conspicuously higher than posterior section and curved over the canthus in front of the supraocular 8

8. A series of 35 or more crossbands formed of dark dots on a paler background, dorsoventral width of proximal rattle segment less than 2.5 times head length (Pls. 968 and 969) . . . . *Crotalus tigris*

   Dorsal body blotches shaped as diamonds, hexagons, rectangles, ovals, or ellipses, or, if crossbands present, these not made up of conspicuous dots; dorsoventral width of proximal rattle segment more than 2.5 times head length 9

9. Anterior subocular contacts 1 or more (usually 2) supralabials 10

   Anterior subocular not contacting any supralabial[2] 17

10. Supraoculars transversely crossed by a thin, black-bordered pale line; a distinctly outlined round or oval dark blotch below the eye; dorsal body pattern of longitudinal ellipses (Pls. 915–918) . . . . *Crotalus polystictus*

    Supraoculars not transversely crossed by a thin, black-bordered pale line; no distinctly outlined round or oval dark blotch below the eye; dorsal body pattern not of longitudinal ellipses 11

11. Midbody scale rows plus supralabials on both sides total 41 or fewer 12

    Midbody scale rows plus supralabials on both sides total 42 or more 14

12. Loreal in contact with 1 or more supralabials (Pls. 835–839) . . . . *Crotalus intermedius*

    Loreal not in contact with any supralabial 13

13. Lower preocular passes into facial pit and fails to make contact (or only very narrowly so) with the loreal; body pattern of undivided dorsal crossbands (Pls. 978–980) . . . . *Crotalus transversus*

    Lower preocular passes above the facial pit and makes contact with the loreal; body pattern usually of paired spots (some of which may be irregularly connected across the dorsal midline) (Pls. 919–928) . . . . *Crotalus pricei*

14. Only 2 scales in prefrontal area (Pls. 929 and 930) .... *Crotalus pusillus*

    More than 2 scales in prefrontal area 15

15. Upper preocular usually divided vertically, the anterior section being higher than the posterior and curved over the canthus in front of the supraocular; dorsal body botches (fewer than 25) occupy less longitudinal space along midline than interspaces (Pls. 841–863) .... *Crotalus lepidus*

    Upper preocular not divided vertically or, if divided, the anterior section not higher than the posterior and not curved over the canthus in front of the supraocular; dorsal body botches (25 or more) occupy more longitudinal space along midline than interspaces 16

16. Rattle-fringe scales usually 10; rattle relatively large, in snakes exceeding 40 cm in TL the dorsoventral width of the proximal rattle segment is more than 1% of the TL (Pls. 756–772) .... *Crotalus aquilus*

    Rattle-fringe scales usually 8; rattle relatively small, in snakes exceeding 40 cm in TL the dorsoventral width of the proximal rattle segment is less than 1% of the TL (Pls. 981–987) .... *Crotalus triseriatus*

17. More than 2 scales between the nasals in contact with rostral (usually termed internasals) (Pls. 889–914, 988–997) .... *Crotalus oreganus, C. viridis* (see species accounts)

    Two scales (internasals) between nasals in contact with rostral 18

18. Upper preocular usually divided vertically, the anterior section being higher than the posterior and curved over the canthus in front of the supraocular; dorsal body botches occupy less longitudinal space along midline than interspaces (Pls. 841–863) .... *Crotalus lepidus*

    Upper preocular not divided vertically or, if divided, the anterior section not higher than the posterior and not curved over the canthus in front of the supraocular; dorsal body botches occupy more longitudinal space along midline than interspaces 19

19. Ventrals 163 or fewer 20

    Ventrals 164 or more 21

20. Rattle-fringe scales usually 10; rattle relatively large, in snakes exceeding 40 cm in TL the dorsoventral width of the proximal rattle segment is more than 1% of the TL (Pls. 756–772) .... *Crotalus aquilus*

    Rattle-fringe scales usually 8; rattle relatively small, in snakes exceeding 40 cm in TL the dorsoventral width of the proximal rattle segment is less than 1% of the TL (Pls. 981–987) .... *Crotalus triseriatus*

21. Tail rings or bands highly contrasting and conspicuous, alternating white or whitish gray with dark brown or black 22

    Tail black or dark gray; rings or bands, if present, only moderately evident because of lack of contrast between dark rings or bands and ground color 28

22. Rattle matrix shrunken, a single rattle segment present, no loose rattle segments (Pls. 788–790) .... *Crotalus catalinensis*

    Rattle matrix normal, usually several loose rattle segments present (except in very small juveniles, which may have only a button) 23

23. Dark tail rings or bands about equal to or greater than pale interspaces; minimum number of scales between supraoculars rarely less than 4; no flat crescentric scale bordering each supraocular posteriorly 24

    Dark tail rings shorter than pale interspaces; pale postocular stripe, if present, extends posteriorly above rictus; minimum number of scales between supraoculars usually 2; usually a flat crescentric scale bordering each supraocular on the posteromedial side (Pls. 949–955) .... *Crotalus scutulatus*

24. A vertical pale bar on prenasal and first supralabial; postocular pale stripe extending from posterior edge of eye diagonally to a point above or behind angle of mouth (Pls. 752–755) .... *Crotalus adamanteus*

    No vertical pale bar on prenasal and first supralabial; postocular stripe extending from posterior edge of eye diagonally downward to ultimate or penultimate supralabials 25

25. First pair of infralabials usually transversely divided; dorsal blotches not conspicuously marked with black punctations 26

    First pair of infralabials usually not transversely divided; dorsal blotches conspicuously punctated with dark dots 27

26. Usually no intergenial scales; prenasal usually contacting first supralabial; dark tail rings usually not interrupted laterally (Pls. 940, 941, 945–948) .... *Crotalus ruber*

    Intergenial scales usually present; prenasal usually not contacting first supralabial; dark tail rings often interrupted laterally (Cedros Island; Pls. 942–944) .... *Crotalus ruber*

27. Upper preocular usually in contact with postnasal, or such contact prevented by an upper loreal (Pls. 773–783) .... *Crotalus atrox*

    Upper preocular usually not in contact with postnasal, and no upper loreal present (Pls. 970 and 971) .... *Crotalus tortugensis*

28. Pattern on body of black chevron-shaped crossbands (Pls. 829–834) .... *Crotalus horridus*

    Pattern on body of diamond-shaped, squarish, or roundish blotches 29

29. Internasal-prefrontal region covered with 13–25 scales; crown and frontal area covered with mostly rough, ridged, and knobby scales (Pls. 825–828) .... *Crotalus enyo*

Internasal-prefrontal region usually covered with 12 or fewer scales; crown and frontal area covered with mostly flat and smooth scales 30

30. A pair of distinct dorsolateral stripes on the neck 1–3 scales wide, separated by pale middorsal interspace 2–3 scales wide, and extending 1–4 head lengths behind head before reaching the first dorsal blotch 31

No paired dark dorsolateral stripes on neck or, if present, irregular and extending posteriorly less than 1 head length behind head 32

31. Most dorsal diamond-shaped blotches separate along dorsal midline and not extending down sides as cross-bands; paravertebral stripes on neck bordered laterally by a pale scale row that is not conspicuously paler than adjacent area below (Pls. 956–966) .... *Crotalus simus*

Dorsal diamond-shaped blotches mostly in contact along dorsal midline; paravertebral stripes on neck bordered laterally by a pale scale row conspicuously contrasting with next scale row below on sides of neck (Pls. 795–824) .... *Crotalus durissus*

32. A pale-bordered, black or dark brown bar crossing the head between the anterior points of the supraoculars (Pls. 972–977) .... *Crotalus totonacus*

No transverse bar in the prefrontal areas as described 33

33. Tail usually black or very dark brown or gray with pale crossbars rarely in evidence on posterior of tail; rattle matrix usually black (Pls. 876–888) .... *Crotalus molossus*[3]

Tail usually gray with pale gray crossbars in evidence posteriorly; rattle matrix usually gray or brown (Pls. 784–787) .... *Crotalus basiliscus*

34. Minimum number of intersupraoculars 4 or fewer (Pl. 840) .... *Crotalus lannomi*

Minimum number of intersupraoculars 5 or more (Pl. 967) .... *Crotalus stejnegeri*

1. This key is adapted in part from Gloyd, 1940, and several keys presented in Klauber, 1972. We have used many of the same external features that were used by Gloyd (1940) and Klauber (1972) in their identification keys for rattlesnakes. The key presented here, however, departs from previous keys in several significant respects: a single key includes all rattlesnakes rather than being subdivided regionally (eastern and western United States, Mexico); the Mexican species *ravus* is moved to *Crotalus*; a number of new species of *Crotalus* are recognized; and descriptions of many morphological features have been updated where knowledge permits.

2. Several species of small rattlesnakes vary in whether or not the anterior subocular contacts the supralabial series. *Crotalus aquilus*, *C. lepidus*, *C. pusillus*, and *C. triseriatus* all vary in this character. We have followed Klauber (1972) in double-keying these species except for *C. pusillus*, a single specimen of which is known in which the anterior subocular fails to reach the supralabials.

3. Southern populations of *Crotalus molossus* have previously been recognized as an allopatric subspecies of *C. basiliscus*. Campbell and Lamar (1989) were the first to allocate these populations to *C. molossus oaxacus*. Previous confusion of Oaxacan populations with *C. basiliscus* probably arose at least in part because Oaxacan snakes tend to have relatively distinct tail rings; this character appears to vary somewhat clinally as well as ontogenetically.

Clave para las Especies de Serpientes de Cascabel[1]

1. Dorso de la cabeza con menos de 12 placas grandes, distribuidas simétricamente e incluyendo internasales pares, prefrontales pares, y una frontal única 2

Dorso de la cabeza con más de 12 placas de menor tamaño, distribuidas asimétricamente e incluyendo varias en la región frontal y numerosas escamas en la región parietal 4

2. Canto angular con orilla lateral de escama cantal con un filo moderado, no curva hacia abajo al lado de la cabeza; rostral alta, truncado de arriba; manchas corporales usualmente tan anchas o más anchas que largas 3

Canto redondeado con orilla lateral de escama cantal curva hacia abajo al lado de la cabeza; rostral baja, punteando al curvar posteriormente entre las internasales; manchas corporales usualmente más largas que anchas (Pls. 931–939) .... *Crotalus ravus*

3. Preocular superior usualmente en contacto con postnasal, subocular anterior usualmente contacta supralabiales 4 y 5 (Pls. 1011–1017) .... *Sistrurus catenatus*

Preocular superior usualmente no en contacto con postnasal, subocular anterior usualmente contacta supralabiales 3 y 4 (Pls. 1018–1023) .... *Sistrurus miliarius*

4. Orillas laterales de supraoculares elevadas formando procesos planos, puntiagudos y en forma de cuerno (Pls. 791–794) .... *Crotalus cerastes*

Orillas laterales de supraoculares no extendiéndose para formar procesos puntiagudos y en forma de cuerno 5

5. Escamas subcaudales en machos menos de 40 y en hembras menos de 35 6

Escamas subcaudales en machos más de 40 y en hembras más de 35 34

6. Punta del hocico y porción anterior del canto elevado formando un filo agudo; rostral y mental muchas veces con una línea vertical media pálida (Pls. 998–1010) .... *Crotalus willardi*

Punta del hocico y porción anterior del canto no elevado formando un filo agudo; rostral y mental sin una línea vertical media pálida 7

7. Prenasales separadas de rostral por pequeñas escamas, muchas veces granulares; preoculares superiores muchas veces divididas horizontalmente, verticalmente, o de ambas formas (Pls. 864–875) .... *Crotalus mitchellii*

Prenasales contactando rostral; preoculares superiores usualmente no divididas o, si así es, divididas únicamente verticalmente con la porción anterior de la escama conspicuamente más alta que la posterior y curva sobre el canto al frente de la supraocular 8

8. Una serie de 35 o más bandas transversales formadas de puntos oscuros en un fondo más pálido, ancho dorsoventral del segmento proximal del cascabel menos de 2.5 veces en el largo de la cabeza (Pls. 968 y 969).. *Crotalus tigris*

Manchas corporales dorsales en forma de diamantes, hexágonos, rectángulos, óvalos, o elipses, o, si con bandas transversales presentes, estas no formadas por puntos conspicuos, ancho dorsoventral del segmento proximal del cascabel más de 2.5 veces en el largo de la cabeza 9

9. Subocular anterior en contacto con 1 o más (usualmente 2) supralabiales 10

Subocular anterior no en contacto con cualquier supralabial[2] 17

10. Supraoculares atravesadas transversalmente por una línea pálida y delgada bordeada de negro; con una mancha redonda u ovalada bajo el ojo que está delineada distintivamente; patrón dorsal corporal de elipses longitudinales (Pls. 915–918) .... *Crotalus polystictus*

Supraoculares no atravesadas transversalmente por una línea pálida y delgada bordeada de negro; sin una mancha redonda u ovalada bajo el ojo que está delineada distintivamente; patrón dorsal corporal no de elipses longitudinales 11

11. Hileras de escamas a mitad del cuerpo más supralabiales en ambos lados suman 41 o menos 12

Hileras de escamas a mitad del cuerpo más supralabiales en ambos lados suman 42 o más 14

12. Loreal en contacto con 1 o más supralabiales (Pls. 835–839) .... *Crotalus intermedius*

Loreal no en contacto con cualquier supralabial 13

13. Preocular inferior pasa a la fosa facial y no logra hacer contacto (o solamente de forma muy angosta) con la loreal; patrón corporal de bandas transversas dorsales no divididas .... *Crotalus transversus*

Preocular inferior pasa arriba de la fosa facial y hace contacto con la loreal; patrón corporal usualmente de manchas apareadas (algunas de las cuales pueden estar conectadas irregularmente a través de la línea media dorsal) (Pls. 919–928) .... *Crotalus pricei*

14. Solamente 2 escamas en el área prefrontal (Pls. 929 y 930) .... *Crotalus pusillus*

Más de 2 escamas en el área prefrontal 15

15. Preocular superior usualmente dividida verticalmente, la sección anterior siendo más alta que la posterior y curva sobre el canto en frente de la supraocular; manchas dorsales corporales (menos de 25) ocupan menos espacio longitudinal que los espacios entre ellas (Pls. 841–863) .... *Crotalus lepidus*

Preocular superior no dividida verticalmente o, si dividida, la sección anterior no siendo más alta que la posterior y no curva sobre el canto en frente de la supraocular; manchas dorsales corporales (25 o más) ocupan más espacio longitudinal que los espacios entre ellas 16

16. Usualmente 10 escamas bordeando el cascabel; cascabel relativamente grande, en serpientes excediendo los 40 cm de largo total, el ancho dorsoventral del segmento proximal del cascabel es más de 1% del largo total del cuerpo (Pls. 756–772) .... *Crotalus aquilus*

Usualmente 8 escamas bordeando el cascabel; cascabel relativamente pequeño, en serpientes excediendo los 40 cm de largo total, el ancho dorsoventral del segmento proximal del cascabel es menos de 1% del largo total del cuerpo (Pls. 981–987) .... *Crotalus triseriatus*

17. Más de 2 escamas entre las nasales en contacto con rostral (usualmente nombradas internasales) (Pls. 889–914, 988–997) .... *Crotalus oreganus, C. viridis* (ver descripciones)

Dos escamas (internasales) entre nasales en contacto con rostral 8

18. Preocular superior usualmente dividida verticalmente, la sección anterior siendo más alta que la posterior y curva sobre el canto en frente de la supraocular; manchas dorsales corporales ocupando menos espacio longitudinal sobre la línea media que los espacios entre ellas (Pls. 841–863) .... *Crotalus lepidus*

Preocular superior no dividida verticalmente o, si dividida, la sección anterior no siendo más alta que la posterior y no curva sobre el canto en frente de la supraocular; manchas dorsales corporales ocupando más espacio longitudinal sobre la línea media que los espacios entre ellas 19

19. Ventrales 163 o menos 20

Ventrales 164 o más 21

20. Usualmente 10 escamas bordeando el cascabel; cascabel relativamente grande, en serpientes excediendo los 40 cm de largo total, el ancho dorsoventral del segmento proximal del cascabel es más de 1% del largo total del cuerpo (Pls. 756–772) .... *Crotalus aquilus*

Usualmente 8 escamas bordeando el cascabel; cascabel relativamente pequeño, en serpientes excediendo los 40 cm de largo total, el ancho dorsoventral del segmento proximal del cascabel es menos de 1% del largo total del cuerpo (Pls. 981–987) .... *Crotalus triseriatus*

21. Bandas o anillos de la cola fuertemente contrastantes y conspicuos, blanco o gris-blanco alternado con castaño oscuro o negro 22

Cola negra o gris oscura, bandas o anillos, si presentes, solo moderadamente evidentes debido a la falta de contraste entre bandas o anillos oscuros y el fondo 28

22. Matriz del cascabel encogida, un solo segmento de cascabel, sin segmentos sueltos (Pls. 788–790) .... *Crotalus catalinensis*

Matriz del cascabel normal, usualmente varios segmentos de cascabel presentes (excepto en juveniles muy pequeños que pueden tener solamente un botón) 23

23. Anillos o bandas oscuros de la cola como de igual o mayor longitud que los espacios pálidos entre ellos; número mínimo de escamas entre las supraoculares raramente menos de 4; sin escama plana en forma de luna creciente bordeando posteriormente cada supraocular 24

Anillos oscuros de la cola de menor longitud que los espacios pálidos entre ellos; número mínimo de escamas entre las supraoculares raramente usualmente 2; usualmente con 1 escama plana en forma de luna creciente bordeando posteromedialmente cada supraocular (Pls. 949–955) .... *Crotalus scutulatus*

24. Una barra pálida vertical en prenasal y primera supralabial; línea postocular pálida extendiéndose desde el borde posterior del ojo diagonalmente hasta un punto arriba o detrás del ángulo de la boca (Pls. 752–755) .... *Crotalus adamanteus*

Sin barra pálida vertical en prenasal y primera supralabial; línea postocular pálida extendiéndose desde el borde posterior del ojo diagonalmente hacia abajo hasta ultima o penúltima supralabial 25

25. Primer par de infralabiales usualmente divididas transversalmente; manchas dorsales no conspicuamente marcadas con puntos negros 26

Primer par de infralabiales usualmente no divididas transversalmente; manchas dorsales conspicuamente marcadas con puntos oscuros 27

26. Usualmente sin escamas intergeniales; prenasal usualmente contactando primera supralabial; anillos oscuros de la cola usualmente no interrumpidos lateralmente (Pls. 940, 941, 945–948) .... *Crotalus ruber*

Usualmente con escamas intergeniales; prenasal usualmente no en contacto con primera supralabial; anillos oscuros de la cola usualmente interrumpidos lateralmente (Isla Cedros; Pls. 942–944) .... *Crotalus ruber*

27. Preocular superior usualmente en contacto con postnasal o ese contacto impedido por una loreal superior (Pls. 773–783) .... *Crotalus atrox*

Preocular superior usualmente no en contacto con postnasal y sin loreal superior presente (Pls. 970 y 971) .... *Crotalus tortugensis*

28. Patrón corporal de bandas transversales negras en forma de V (Pls. 829–834) .... *Crotalus horridus*

Patrón corporal de manchas en forma de diamantes, cuadros, o redondeadas 29

29. Región internasal-prefrontal de la cabeza cubierta con 13–25 escamas; coronilla y área frontal cubiertas mayormente de escamas ásperas, quilladas, y protuberantes (Pls. 825–828) .... *Crotalus enyo*

Región internasal-prefrontal de la cabeza usualmente cubierta de 12 o menos escamas; coronilla y área frontal cubiertas mayormente de escamas planas y lisas 30

30. Con un par de rayas dorso laterales destacadas en el cuello de 1–3 escamas de ancho, separadas por un espacio pálido medio-dorsal de 2–3 escamas de ancho, y extendiéndose 1–4 largos de la cabeza detrás de la cabeza antes de llegar a la primera mancha dorsal 31

Sin un par de rayas oscuras en el cuello o, si presentes, irregulares y extendiéndose posteriormente menos de un largo de cabeza detrás de la cabeza 32

31. La mayoría de las manchas dorsales en forma de diamante separadas a lo largo de la línea media dorsal y no extendiéndose hacia abajo por los lados como bandas transversales; líneas paravertebrales en el cuello bordeadas lateralmente por una hilera de escamas pálidas que no son conspicuamente más pálidas que el área adyacente inferior (Pls. 956–966) .... *Crotalus simus*

Manchas dorsales en forma de diamante mayormente en contacto a lo largo de la línea media dorsal; líneas paravertebrales en el cuello bordeadas lateralmente por una hilera de escamas pálidas que son conspicuamente más pálidas que las de la hilera adyacente inferior a los lados del cuerpo (Pls. 795–824) ..... *Crotalus durissus*

32. Una barra negra o castaño oscura con borde pálido cruza la cabeza entre los puntos anteriores de las supraoculares (Pls. 972–977) .... *Crotalus totonacus*

Sin barra transversal en las áreas prefrontales como descrita anteriormente 33

33. Cola usualmente negra o castaño muy oscuro o gris con barras transversales pálidas raramente evidentes en parte posterior de la cola; matriz del cascabel usualmente negra (Pls. 876–888) .... *Crotalus molossus*[3]

Cola usualmente gris con barras transversales gris pálidas evidentes en parte posterior; matriz del cascabel usualmente de color gris o castaño (Pls. 784–787) .... *Crotalus basiliscus*

34. Número mínimo de intersupraoculares 4 o menos (Pl. 840) .... *Crotalus lannomi*

Número mínimo de intersupraoculares 5 o más (Pl. 967) .... *Crotalus stejnegeri*

1. Esta clave es adaptada en parte de Gloyd, 1940, y varias claves presentadas en Klauber, 1972. Hemos usado muchas de las mismas características externas que fueron usadas por Gloyd (1940) y Klauber (1972) en sus claves de identificación para serpientes de cascabel. La clave presentada aquí, sin embargo, difiere de las anteriores en varios aspectos significativos: una sola clave incluye todas las serpientes de cascabel, en lugar de estar subdivididas regionalmente (este y oeste de los Estados Unidos, México); la especie Mexicana *ravus* es movida a *Crotalus*; nuevas especies de *Crotalus* son reconocidas; y la variación y condición de muchos caracteres morfológicos han sido puestos al día según lo permite el conocimiento.

2. Varias especies de serpientes de cascabel pequeñas son variables con respecto a tener o no la subocular anterior contactando la serie de supralabiales. *Crotalus aquilus*, *C. lepidus*, *C. pusillus*, y *C. triseriatus* son variables con respecto a este carac-

ter. Hemos seguido a Klauber (1972) en presentar doblemente a estas especies con excepción de *C. pusillus*, en los que un solo ejemplar es conocido por no tener la subocular anterior sin alcanzar las supralabiales.

3. Poblaciones sureñas de *Crotalus molossus* han sido previamente reconocidas como subespecies alopátricas de *C. basiliscus*. Campbell y Lamar (1989) fueron los primeros en identificar estas poblaciones como *Crotalus molossus oaxacus*. Confusión previa de las poblaciones de Oaxaca con *C. basiliscus* probablemente surgió, al menos en parte, porque las serpientes de Oaxaca tienden a tener anillos caudales relativamente destacados; este caracter aparentemente varia un poco clinal y ontogeneticamente.

Rattlesnakes, Genus *Crotalus* Linnaeus, 1758

Crotalus Linnaeus, 1758, *Syst. Nat.*, 10th ed., 824 pp.[214]. Type-species: *Crotalus horridus* Linnaeus, 1758, by subsequent designation of Fitzinger (1843:29). Confirmed and conserved by ICZN, 1926, Opinion 92, *Smithson. Misc. Collect.* 73(4):339. See also ICZN, 1956, Direction 56, Opinions Decls. 1D:337–364[356]; and ICZN, 1956, Direction 57, Opinion Decls. 1D:365–388[374]. The indication in Golay et al., 1993:53, that *Crotalus horridus* is the type-species by subsequent designation of Gray (1825:205) is insupportable and specifically prohibited according to Article 67c (i) of the Code.

Crotalophorus Houttuyn, 1764, *Natuur. Hist.*, 558 pp.[290]. Type-species: *Crotalus horridus* Linnaeus, 1758, by subsequent designation probably by Klauber (1956:29). Recognized as a subgenus by Garman (1884a:110).

Caudisona Laurenti, 1768, *Synops. Rept.*, 214 pp.[92]. Type-species: *Caudisona terrifica* Laurenti, 1768 [=*Crotalus durissus* Linnaeus, 1758], by subsequent designation probably by Klauber (1956:29), who listed *terrificus* by page priority. Gloyd (1940:80) listed *horridus* as the type of *Caudisona*, but this is incorrect because *horridus* was not a species treated by Laurenti.

Crotalinus Rafinesque, 1815, *Analyse Nat.* (Herpetol. section), pp. 73–78[77]. Replacement name or emendation for *Crotalus*. Klauber (1956:29) erroneously treated *Crotalinus* as a new genus erected by Rafinesque (1818:446) for *Crotalinus cyanurus* [=*Crotalus horridus* Linnaeus, 1758].

Crotalurus Rafinesque, 1820, *Ann. Nat.* (Lexington) (22):1–16[5]. Replacement name or emendation for *Crotalinus*.

Crotulurus—Rafinesque, 1820, *Ann. Nat.* (Lexington) (22):1–16[5]. Incorrect subsequent spelling, typographical error for *Crotalurus*.

Uropsophus Wagler, 1830, *Nat. Syst. Amph.*, 354 pp.[176]. Type-species: *Crotalus triseriatus* Wagler, 1830, by monotypy.

Urocrotalon Fitzinger, 1843, *Syst. Rept.*, 106 pp.[29]. Type-species: *Crotalus durissus* Linnaeus, 1758, by original designation and monotypy.

Aploaspis Cope, 1867 [dated 1866], *Proc. Acad. Nat. Sci. Philadelphia* 18:300–314[310]. Type-species: *Caudisona lepida* Kennicott, 1861b, by original designation and monotypy.

Aechmophrys Coues, *in* Wheeler, 1875, *Rep. Geog. Geol. Explor. Surv. West 100th Merid.* 5:585–633[609]. Described as subgenus of *Caudisona* Laurenti, 1768. Type-species: "*Caudisona (Aechmophrys) cerastes* (Hallow.)" [=*Crotalus cerastes* Hallowell, 1854], by original designation and monotypy.

Haploaspis—Cope, 1884 [dated 1883], *Proc. Acad. Nat. Sci. Philadelphia* 35:10–35[13]. Unjustified emendation of *Aploaspis* Cope, 1867.

Paracrotalus Reuss, 1930, *Glasnik Zem. Muz. Bosni Hercegovini* 42:57–114[60, 88]. Type-species: *Caudisona terrifica* Laurenti, 1768 [=*Crotalus durissus* Linnaeus, 1758], by original designation.

The purpose of the rattle of the Crotalidae has exercised the ingenuity of many minds and called forth many conjectures. The old notion that it was intended as a means of preserving man from the bite of the snake does not meet the requirements of the case. The organs of animals and plants are designed for the benefit of their possessors, and not for the benefit of some other organism.

—Hay, 1887a:214

ETYMOLOGY

The genus name is derived from the Greek *krotalon*, meaning "rattle" or "castanet," in reference to the unusual appendage at the end of the tail of these snakes.

The genus *Crotalus* comprises 30 species, with the greatest diversity found on the Mexican Plateau and its fringing mountains. *Crotalus simus* and *C. durissus* range south of the Isthmus of Tehuantepec; *Crotalus simus* occurs through much of Central America to Costa Rica; and *C. durissus* is widespread in South America, reaching northern Argentina. A wide hiatus in these species' distributions occurs in the Isthmus of Panama region. Four species (*C. horridus*, *C. oreganus*, *C. viridis*, and *Sistrurus catenatus*) range as far north as southern Canada. Members of the genus *Crotalus* exist in myriad habitats ranging from the Sonoran Desert of northwestern Mexico to alpine and cloud forest habitats in central and southern Mexico. Species of *Crotalus* occur from below sea level in desert basins in California to about 4,500 m in the Transverse Volcanic Cordillera of central Mexico.

The tropical rattlesnakes that characteristically have a distinct pair of dark stripes on the neck usually have been either recognized under a single name, *C. durissus*, or partitioned into *C. durissus* and two other species represented by small, localized South American populations having derived color patterns (*C. unicolor* and *C. vegrandis*). Campbell and Lamar (1989) preferred not to recognize *C. unicolor* and *C. vegrandis* as valid species.

Based on morphology and historical geology, it makes sense to us to distinguish the populations of Neotropical rattlesnakes occurring in Middle America and South America as separate species. The name that should be applied to the South American species is *Crotalus durissus* Linnaeus (1758), and the earliest available name for the Middle American species is *C. simus* Latreille *in* Sonnini de Manoncourt and Latreille (1801). See the synonymies of these taxa for a history of the names relating to them. Finally, after careful examination of materials related to the northernmost isolated population of Neotropical rattlesnake, we further conclude that the original designation of *C. totonacus* by Gloyd and Kauffeld (1940) is correct and that this well-differentiated population warrants species recognition.

Rattlesnakes of the genus *Crotalus* vary in size from diminutive species that reach only 50–60 cm in TL (*C. intermedius*, *C. pricei*, *C. transversus*) to species that exceed 150 cm (*C. adamanteus*, *C. atrox*, *C. basiliscus*, *C. durissus*, *C. simus*). In general, island populations tend to be smaller than their closest mainland relatives. This is most apparent in two stunted forms,

C. mitchellii muertensis of El Muerto Island in the Gulf of California and *C. oreganus caliginus* of South Coronado Island in the Pacific, both of which are considerably smaller than their mainland relatives. One exception to island dwarfism is *C. mitchellii angelensis* of Ángel de la Guarda Island in the Gulf of Mexico, which reaches a larger size than its conspecifics on the peninsula of Baja California. Small size appears also to characterize some isolated mainland populations with restricted distributions such as *C. viridis* in southeastern Utah (L. Porras, pers. comm.).

The rattle on the end of the tail makes rattlesnakes a very distinctive group, but the rattle is not invariably present. Several island populations, including *C. catalinensis* on Isla Santa Catalina and usually *C. ruber lorenzoensis* on Isla San Lorenzo Sur, have lost the loose rattle segments, and *C. r. lucasensis* and *C. molossus estebanensis* show a tendency for rattle loss (Beaman and Wong, 2001). Some individuals lose the rattle through accident, and Klauber (1972) reported that *C. cerastes, C. horridus,* and *C. pricei* occasionally lack rattles owing to congenital abnormalities. Painter et al. (1999) reported several rattleless individuals of *C. atrox* from near Artesia, Eddy County, New Mexico; and Holycross (2000a) found two rattleless *C. atrox* in the San Simon Valley of Cochise County, Arizona. A rattleless *C. molossus* from Big Bend National Park, Brewster, Texas, had an unusually long tail with a high number of subcaudals, suggesting that its lack of a rattle was not the result of an injury (Smith et al., 1985). Smith (*in* Painter et al., 1999) reported that a rattleless *C. viridis viridis* gave birth to five offspring, one of which was rattleless; and Holycross (2000b) encountered an adult female of this taxon in Nebraska that lacked rattles. Extreme reduction or total loss of the rattle has been observed in eight specimens of *C. willardi* (L. Porras, pers. comm.). These data suggest that a few individuals in natural populations congenitally lack rattles.

Crotalus basiliscus, C. molossus, C. durissus, C. simus, and *C. totonacus* generally have a pair of large, triangular internasals and a pair of large, quadrangular prefrontals in contact medially covering the top of the snout. *Crotalus pusillus* and an occasional specimen of *C. pricei* and *C. triseriatus* also have 4 large scales in the internasal-prefrontal region. In other species of rattlesnakes the internasal-prefrontal region is covered with smaller scales. Species that have the most finely divided snout scales include *C. ruber,* with 7–40; *C. mitchellii,* with 13–51; and *C. willardi,* with 20–40. The number of intersupraoculars may be relatively small, ranging from usually about 2 in *C. scutulatus, C. totonacus,* and some of the smaller montane species to usually 6 or more in *C. ruber* and *C. willardi.*

The rostral is usually wider than high in many of the desert species inhabiting northwestern Mexico and Baja California (*C. cerastes, C. enyo, C. mitchellii, C. tigris*) and in many of the montane species (*C. intermedius, C. lannomi, C. lepidus, C. pricei, C. pusillus, C. transversus,* and usually *C. aquilus* and *C. triseriatus*). In other species this scale may be conspicuously higher than wide. The first supralabial is most often in broad contact with the prenasal; however, a forward extension of prefoveals may partially or completely preclude prenasal-supralabial contact in *C. basiliscus, C. ruber exsul, C. mitchellii, C. molossus, C. oreganus,* and *C. viridis.* The number of loreals varies from 1 to 9, with 1 or 2 most frequently present. The loreal(s) and outer edge of the posterior canthal (often deflected downward) separate the postnasal from the upper preocular in most individuals of most species; a notable exception is *C. atrox,* in which the postnasal usually contacts the upper preocular. Usually in *C.

intermedius, C. pricei, C. pusillus, C. transversus, C. triseriatus,* and often in *C. aquilus* and *C. lepidus,* the anterior subocular touches the supralabial series; in other species 1 or more interoculabials intervene to separate these scales. For specific characters concerning cephalic scalation, refer to Table 45.

All members of the genus have 8–20 supralabials, 8–21 infralabials (the first pair of which is usually transversely divided in *C. ruber* and in *C. simus* from the Yucatán Peninsula), 19–33 midbody dorsal scale rows, 132–206 ventrals, an undivided anal plate, and 14–45 subcaudals that are mostly undivided. Like most snakes, rattlesnakes are sexually dimorphic with regard to the numbers of ventrals and subcaudals, with males tending to have fewer ventrals and more subcaudals than females of the same species (Klauber, 1943; Fig. 184). In general, larger species have more scales. Table 46 summarizes certain external features of rattlesnakes.

The ground color of rattlesnakes often matches their environment and is usually some shade of brown, gray, green, red, pink, or yellow. Most species have a dark pattern consisting of subelliptical, rhombic, or diamond-shaped middorsal blotches and 1–3 series of smaller lateral blotches. In a few species the dorsal markings are relatively short and wide, and they often merge with a lateral series of blotches to form crossbands (*C. tigris, C. transversus,* some populations of *C. lepidus*). Two species tend to have paravertebral blotches rather than a single middorsal series: in *C. polystictus* the paravertebral blotches are large and oval or subelliptical, and in *C. pricei* these blotches are small, usually irregular in outline, and about as wide as long. Some individuals or populations of certain species may become essentially patternless as adults (*C. basiliscus* and *C. intermedius gloydi*) or have a pattern of pale flecks on a darker background (*C. basiliscus, C. durissus, C. molossus*).

The frontal bones have a slightly concave to almost flat dorsal surface, and in the smaller species (e.g., *C. intermedius, C. lepidus, C. polystictus*) these bones are longer than wide (Fig. 185); in larger species (e.g., *C. adamanteus, C. atrox, C. horridus, C. molossus*) they are wider than long (Fig. 186). The postfrontals are relatively large and sometimes contact the frontal, thus excluding the parietals from the dorsal perimeter of the orbit. When the postfrontal fails to contact the frontal, the parietal usually occupies no more than about half of the distance that is occupied by the postfrontal along the orbital perimeter. Posterior to the orbital processes of the parietals, the posterolateral edges of the dorsal surface of the parietals in most larger species form a broad shelf that extends to about the level of the squamosal, and a distinct, broad, raised ridge is present above the squamosal at the juncture of the parietal and pro-otic. No lateral shelf of bone is present posterior to the orbital process in smaller species, but most species have a narrow ridge, and the surface just above the squamosal is slightly convex or angular at the juncture of the parietal and pro-otic, but no distinct ridge is apparent. The anterolateral portion of the ectopterygoid has concave surfaces on the medial and lateral sides to accommodate attachment of the ectopterygoid retractor muscle; the depression on the lateral side is elongated and highly variable among species, ranging from almost flat (e.g., *C. molossus*), to shallow (e.g., *C. lepidus, C. polystictus*), to deep (*C. durissus*). The ectopterygoid is about as long as the expanded, flattened base of the pterygoid (that portion posterior to the ectopterygoid-pterygoid articulation) and has a moderately robust, somewhat compressed shaft that tapers gradually or is relatively narrow throughout. The apex of the choanal process is positioned at a level above the anterior half of the palatine (sometimes only slightly anterior to the

Table 45. Variation in selected cephalic scale characteristics in species of *Crotalus*.

Species	Rostral	Internasals	Prefrontals	Intersupraoculars	Prenasal-supralabial contact	Loreals (per side)	Postnasal-upper preocular contact	Supralabials	Scales in internasal-prefrontal region
C. adamanteus	Higher than wide	2, large	Absent	5–11	Yes	Usually 2	No	12–17, usually 14 or 15	10–21
C. aquilus	Usually higher than wide	2, large	Absent	2–5, usually 3	Yes	1–2, usually 1	No	10–14, usually 11 or 12	5–10
C. atrox	Higher than wide	2, small	Absent	3–7, usually 4–5	Usually	Usually 1	Usually	12–18, usually 15 or 16	11–32
C. basiliscus	Higher than wide	2, large	Present	2–3, usually 2	Variable	1–5, usually 2	Rarely	13–18, usually 5	Usually 4–6, rarely up to 9
C. catalinensis	Higher than wide	2, kidney shaped	Absent	4–5	Yes	Usually 1	No	13–16, usually 14 or 15	More than 8
C. cerastes	Wider than high	2, moderate in size	Absent	4–6	Yes	Usually 1	No	10–15, usually 12 or 13	12–34
C. durissus	Usually slightly higher than wide	2, large	Present	2–5, usually 2	Usually	1–8, usually 1–2	Rarely	11–18, usually 13–16	Usually 4–6, up to 10
C. enyo	Usually wider than high	2, small to moderate	Absent	2–6, usually 4–5	Usually	1–5, usually 2–3	Rarely	12–15, usually 13 or 14	13–25
C. horridus	Usually slightly higher than wide	2, large	Variable	Usually 5–7	Usually	Usually 2, rarely 1	No	10–17, usually 13–15	4–22
C. intermedius	Wider than high	2, large	Usually absent	2–4	Yes	Usually 1	No	8–11, usually 9	4–8
C. lannomi	Wider than high	2, moderate in size	Absent	2	Yes	3	No	14 or 15	7
C. lepidus	Usually wider than high	2, large	Absent	1–4, usually 2	Yes	1–2, usually 1	No	10–15, usually 12 or 13	5–15
C. mitchellii	Usually wider than high	2–4, usually 2, small	Absent	1–8	Variable	0–5, usually 2	No	12–19, usually 15–17	13–51
C. molossus	Usually slightly higher than wide	2, large	Usually present	2–5, usually 2–3	Rarely	1–9, usually 2–4	Rarely	13–20, usually 16–18	4–18, usually ≤6

Species									
C. oreganus	Higher than wide	Usually 4	Absent	4–6	Variable	1–3, usually 1	Rarely	11–18, usually 14–16	7–45
C. polystictus	Higher than wide	2–4, variable in size	Absent	2–5, usually 3	Yes	Usually 2	No	12–15, usually 13 or 14	6–8
C. pricei	Usually wider than high	2, large	Usually absent	2–3	Yes	Usually 1	No	8–10, usually 9	4–11
C. pusillus	Wider than high	2, large	Present	1–4, usually 3	Yes	Usually 1	No	11–13, usually 12	4
C. ravus	About as high as wide	2, large	Present	1	Yes	1	No	9–13, usually 11–12	4
C. ruber	Variable	2, small	Absent	4–10, usually > 6	Usually	1 or 2	Rarely	13–21, usually 16 or 17	8–40
C. scutulatus	Usually higher than wide	2, small	Absent	Usually 2	Yes	Usually 1	Infrequently	12–18, usually 13–15	6–21
C. simus	Usually higher than wide	2, large	Present	2–5	Usually	1–8, usually 2–3	No	11–18, usually 13–15	4–6
C. stejnegeri	About as high as wide	2, large	Absent	5–8	Yes	2–5	No	14–16	10–21
C. tigris	Wider than high	2, small	Absent	3–8	Usually	1–2, usually 1	Rarely	11–16, usually 12–14	11–37
C. tortugensis	Usually higher than wide	2, small	Absent	4–5, usually 4	Yes	Usually 1	Rarely	14–18, usually 15–16	≥8
C. totonacus	Usually higher than wide	2, large	Present	Usually 2	Yes	Usually 2	No	12–15, usually 14	4–6
C. transversus	Wider than high	2, large	Absent	2–3	Yes	1	No	8–10, usually 9	5–6
C. triseriatus	Usually higher than wide	2, large	Absent	2–5, usually 3	Yes	Usually 1	No	10–14, usually 12–13	6–9
C. viridis	Usually higher than wide	1–8, usually 4, small to moderate	Absent	1–9, usually 4–6	Variable	1–3, usually 1	Rarely	10–18, usually 14 or 15	7–45, usually 15–30
C. willardi	Higher than wide	2, small	Absent	6–9	Yes	1–2, usually 2	No	12–17, usually 13–15	20–40

Notes: For additional information, refer to species accounts. Rarely = less than 5% of specimens examined; infrequently = more than 5%, less than 25%; usually = more than 75%.

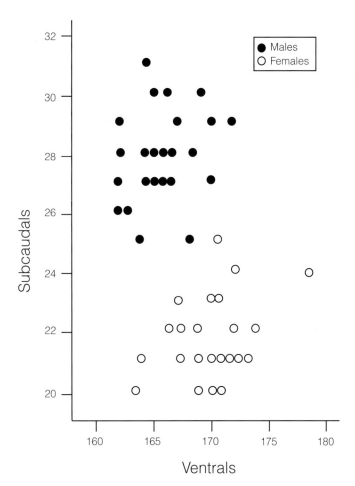

Fig. 184. Number of ventrals and subcaudals present in individuals of *Crotalus durissus vegrandis* showing sexual dimorphism. Adapted from Lancini, 1967:728 (fig. 2).

midline of the bone) and is broadly rounded. The lateral process of the squamosal forms almost a right angle (90°) with the longitudinal axis of the main part of the bone (Klauber, 1972). The dorsal surface of the parietal is elongately triangular or T shaped (sensu Brattstrom, 1964). According to Brattstrom (1964:194) there are 0–4 (usually 3) palatine teeth, 4–11 pterygoid teeth (usually 6–9), and 6–13 dentary teeth (usually 8–10). Several species are unusual in having relatively few teeth: *C. polystictus* has none on the palatine, 7–8 on the pterygoid, and 7–8 on the dentary; and *C. stejnegeri* has none on the palatine, 4–6 on the pterygoid, and 6–9 on the dentary (Fig. 187). The pterygoid teeth extend about three-fourths or more of the way from the anterior tip of the pterygoid to the middle of the junction of the pterygoid with the ectopterygoid. The length of the fang is associated with the size of the head. Species that have small heads in proportion to their bodies have relatively short fangs. Klauber (1939b) demonstrated the correlation between fang length and head length within *C. ruber* (Fig. 188); a similar correlation exists between fang length and body (SVL) length. *Crotalus molossus*, *C. polystictus*, and *C. stejnegeri* have unusually long fangs; whereas *C. aquilus*, *C. lepidus*, *C. triseriatus*, and certain populations of *C. oreganus* and *C. viridis* have relatively short fangs (Klauber, 1939b, 1972; see Fig. 189). The fangs of *C. polystictus* and various populations of Neotropical rattlesnakes are unusual in having relatively slight curvature in comparison with other rattlesnakes (Klauber, 1939b).

Certain anatomical features, including those of soft anatomy, are shared among particular species of *Crotalus* and may be useful diagnostic characters. For example, the presence of rudimentary left lungs in *C. simus*, *C. durissus*, *C. horridus*, *C. molossus*, and *C. basiliscus* may represent a grade character rather than a synapomorphy, but the similarity of this feature and others within these species does suggest a close relationship. The

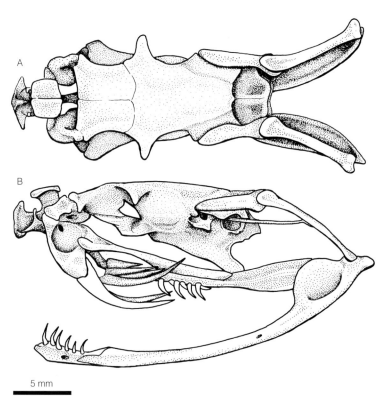

5 mm

Fig. 185. (A) Dorsal and (B) lateral aspects of skull of *Crotalus polystictus* (UTA R-12583), from 2.4 km northwest of Tapalpa, Jalisco, Mexico. Drawing by Paul C. Ustach.

Table 46. Variation in certain characteristics in species of *Crotalus*.

Species	Dorsal scale rows at midbody (mode)	Ventrals Males	Ventrals Females	Subcaudals Males	Subcaudals Females	Body blotches	Maximum size, cm
C. adamanteus	25–31 (29)	165–176	170–187	27–33	20–26	24–35	251.1
C. aquilus	21–25 (23)	140–158	138–156	22–31	19–24	21–41	67.8
C. atrox	23–29 (25)	168–193	174–196	21–32	16–24	24–45	234
C. basiliscus	25–29 (27)	178–201	184–206	26–36	18–30	26–41	204.5
C. catalinensis	25	177–181	182–189	24–28	18–23	34–40	73.1
C. cerastes	19–25 (21 or 23)[a]	132–151	135–154	18–26	14–21	28–47	82.4
C. durissus	25–33 (27)	155–179	163–190	25–32	18–26	18–32	ca. 180
C. enyo	23–27 (25)	157–177	161–181	22–31	18–23	28–42	89.9
C. horridus	21–25 (23)	158–177	163–183	20–30	15–28	15–34	189.2
C. intermedius	21	151–175	157–185	21–29	18–24	38–61	>57.0
C. lannomi	27	—	176	—	37	31	63.8
C. lepidus	21–25 (23)	147–172	149–171	20–33	16–25	13–38	82.8
C. mitchellii	21–27 (23–27)[b]	156–187	163–190	20–28	16–24	26–46	136.7
C. molossus	23–29 (25–29)[c]	164–199	168–199	21–30	16–26	20–43	133.0
C. oreganus	21–29 (25)	161–190	164–196	18–29	15–25	25–52	162.6
C. polystictus	25–29 (27)	161–177	167–187	25–29	17–25	30–47	ca. 100
C. pricei	21–23 (21)	137–162	143–171	21–33	18–27	39–64	66.0
C. pusillus	23–25 (23)	152–162	150–162	28–33	25–29	33–50	68.2
C. ravus	21–25 (21–23)	136–150	138–149	25–30	19–26	22–44	>70
C. ruber	25–33 (27 or 29)[d]	179–203	183–206	21–29	15–25	29–42	162
C. scutulatus	21–29 (25)	165–187	165–192	21–29	15–23	27–44	137.3
C. simus	27–33 (29)	170–188	172–191	25–34	18–26	18–35	ca. 180
C. stejnegeri	25–29 (27)	174–178	171–176	43–45	36–37	32–43	72.4
C. tigris	21–27 (23)	156–172	164–177	23–27	16–21	35–52	88.5
C. tortugensis	25–27 (27)	180–190	183–190	22–25	16–20	32–41	105.8
C. totonacus	25	184–192	192–195	26–29	22–26	27–35	166.5
C. transversus	21	141–145	136–155	25–26	19–22	37–43	46.5
C. triseriatus	21–25 (23)	125–154	137–152	24–33	19–28	30–57	68.3
C. viridis	21–29 (25 or 27)[e]	162–187	169–196	21–31	14–25	33–57	151.5
C. willardi	25–29 (25 or 27)[f]	146–158	147–159	25–36	21–31	18–45	67.0

Sources: Gloyd, 1940; Klauber, 1972; Campbell and Lamar, 1989; and various museum specimens.

Notes: For additional information, refer to species accounts. Rarely = less than 5% of specimens examined; infrequently = more than 5%, less than 25%; usually = more than 75%.

[a] The mode for *C. cerastes cerastes* and *C. c. cercobombus* is 21; for *C. c. laterorepens*, 23.
[b] The mode for *C. m. muertensis* is 23; for *C. m. mitchellii* and *C. m. pyrrhus*, 25; and for *C. m. angelensis*, 27.
[c] The mode for *C. molossus nigrescens* is 25; for *C. m. molossus*, 27.
[d] The mode for *C. ruber lucasensis* is 27; for *C. r. ruber*, 29.
[e] The mode for *C. viridis viridis* is 27; for all other subspecies it is 25.
[f] The mode for *C. willardi willardi* is 25; for all other subspecies it is 27.

hemipenes of *C. adamanteus*, *C. atrox*, *C. ruber*, and *C. tortugensis* are unusually attenuate. *Crotalus tigris* and *C. mitchellii* have relatively similar head proportions. The rattle growth equations are similar for *C. durissus*, *C. simus*, *C. basiliscus*, *C. enyo*, and *C. cerastes*, perhaps suggesting a relationship at least between certain pairs of species within this group. The anterior subocular is in contact with the supralabial series in some of the smaller montane species of rattlesnakes. In *C. aquilus*, *C. triseriatus*, *C. pusillus*, *C. ravus*, and *C. polystictus* supralabials 4 and 5 are contacted, whereas in *C. intermedius* and *C. pricei* contact is made with supralabials 3 and 4. It should be noted that the species of *Sistrurus* are variable in this character, with anterior subocular-supralabial contact being made with supralabials 3 and 4 in *S. miliarius* and with supralabials 4 and 5 in *S. catenatus*. Both *C. horridus* and northern poulations of *C. molossus* have a uniformly dark tail rather than the distinct pattern of pale and dark rings or bands present in many other large species; *C. basiliscus* and southern populations of *C. molossus* are somewhat intermediate for this character, with dark rings that contrast comparatively slightly with a moderately dark background color.

The everted hemipenes are 8–12 subcaudals long in most species of *Crotalus*, although they are often slightly shorter in some individuals of the smaller species (e.g., *C. cerastes*, *C. lepidus*, *C. pricei*, *C. pusillus*, and *C. willardi*). The organ is divided

deeply; the sulcus spermaticus bifurcates at the level of subcaudal 1 or 2, with a branch extending to the apex of each lobe. The lobes are generally subcylindrical but may be slightly to greatly tapered (*C. atrox*, *C. basiliscus*, *C. durissus*; see Fig. 190), somewhat bulbous distally (*C. basiliscus*, *C. triseriatus*), somewhat constricted distally (some *C. molossus*), or greatly compressed mediolaterally (*C. stejnegeri*). The lobes may be straight and thick, straight and slender, or may diverge from one another to varying degrees; in some specimens the lobes of everted hemipenes have a strongly lyriform shape. The crotch tends to be V shaped or U shaped; it is especially broad in *C. scutulatus*, *C. oreganus*, and *C. viridis*.

The number of large basal spines on each lobe (exclusive of smaller spinules) is highly variable: there are more than 100 in *C. polystictus* and *C. stejnegeri*; between 25 and 50 in *C. basiliscus*, *C. cerastes*, *C. molossus*, *C. pricei*, *C. scutulatus*, *C. oreganus*, *C. viridis*, *C. willardi*, and *C. atrox* (sometimes more than 50 in the latter); 15–25 in *C. intermedius*, *C. pusillus*, and *C. triseriatus* (southern populations); and 7–15 in *C. lepidus* and *C. triseriatus* (northern populations). In most species of *Crotalus* the hemipenes have relatively few spines on the base, the microornamentation usually covers most of the lobes, and there is an abrupt transition from the ornamentation on the base to that on the lobes. The basal spines tend to be mostly on the shoulders

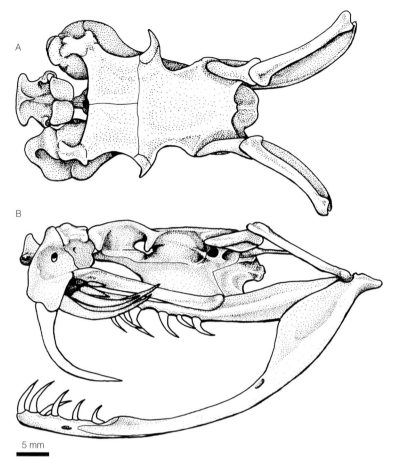

Fig. 186. (A) Dorsal and (B) lateral aspects of skull of *Crotalus molossus* (UTA R-14512) from 6.0 km south of Miltepec, Oaxaca, on Mexico Highway 125. Drawing by Paul C. Ustach.

5 mm

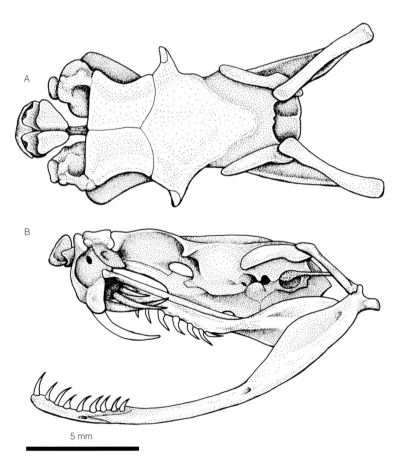

Fig. 187. (A) Dorsal and (B) lateral aspects of skull of *Crotalus stejnegeri* (UTA R-10499), from Plomosas, Municipio Rosario, Sinaloa, Mexico. Drawing by Paul C. Ustach.

5 mm

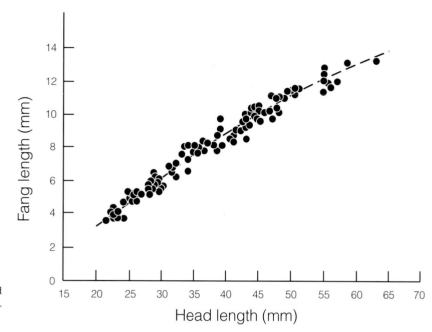

Fig. 188. The relationship between fang length and head length in a sample of 100 *Crotalus ruber* specimens. Adapted from Klauber, 1939b:24 (fig. 35).

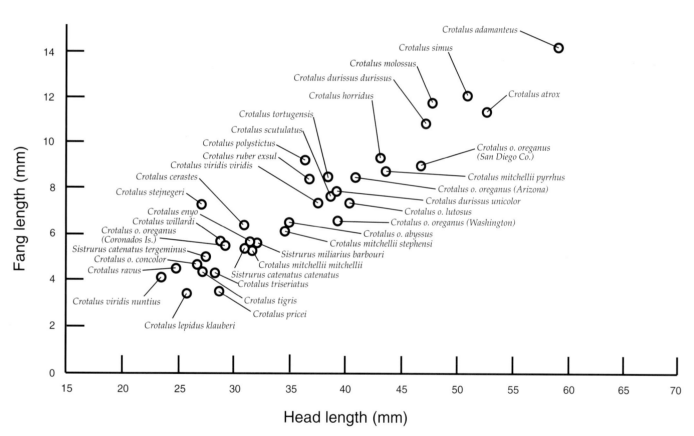

Fig. 189. The relationship between average fang length and head length in various species of rattlesnakes. From Klauber, 1939b:46 (fig. 41).

of the organ, but they may barely extend distally on the proximal third or less of the lobes in many species; in *C. cerastes, C. polystictus,* and *C. stejnegeri* the basal spines extend distally for more than one-third the length of the lobe. Mesial spines may be absent or present. When present, they may be restricted to the asulcomedial surface (*C. scutulatus,* some *C. molossus*); they may be large and well developed (*C. basiliscus, C. cerastes, C. durissus, C. intermedius, C. pricei, C. simus, C. willardi*) or represented by numerous small spines (*C. polystictus, C. stejnegeri*). *Crotalus lepidus* and *C. triseriatus* lack mesial

spines, but the calyces in that region tend to become spinulate. *Crotalus atrox, C. pusillus,* and *C. viridis* usually lack mesial spines.

The distal portion of the lobes is covered by papillate calyces. These calyces often extend further in the region flanking the sulcus than elsewhere. In species lacking mesial spines, calyces often extend to the crotch. In *C. stejnegeri* the proximal calyces are weakly papillate, and distally the calyces are reduced to low, smooth ridges. A few species, including *C. polystictus,* are remarkable in having especially large calyces with low ridges

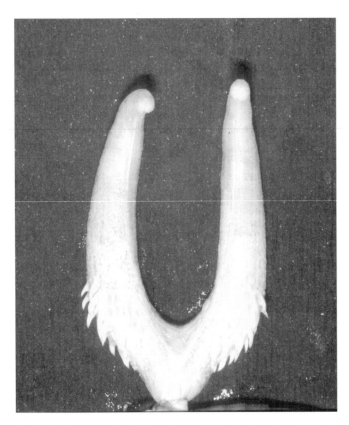

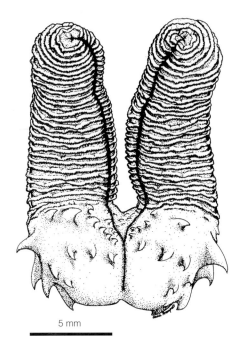

Fig. 191. Sulcate aspect of right hemipenis of *Crotalus ravus* (UTA R-4536). From McCranie, 1988. Published by permission of the Herpetologists' League.

Fig. 190. Sulcate aspect of left hemipenis of *Crotalus simus* from Aldea El Arenal, San Vicente, Zacapa, Guatemala (JAC 20788). Photo by Eric N. Smith.

on the distal asulcate portion of the lobes and a soft papilla on the apex of each lobe.

There usually is a rather sharp boundary between basal spines and calyces; however, in *C. polystictus* and *C. stejnegeri* the spines tend to grade into calyces. The hemipenes of *Crotalus ravus* (a taxon previously allocated to *Sistrurus*) are similar to those of most other *Crotalus* in having a well-defined boundary between spines and calyces (Fig. 191). The organs are divided in this species, with a bifurcate, semicentrifugal sulcus spermaticus that divides slightly below the crotch at about the level of the second subcaudal and sends a branch to the rounded apex of each lobe. The everted organ is 8–10 subcaudals long, and the lobes are slightly tapered distally. The organ is divided at about the level of the third subcaudal. There are about 8–15 large, robust, recurved basal spines per lobe, the largest of which are located on the shoulders of the organ (McCranie, 1988). There are about 12–15 spinules to small spines on the basal portion of each lobe, the smallest of which are near the sulcus. No mesial spines are present and the crotch is mostly naked. There is an abrupt transition from the spines on the base of the organ to the flounces that cover all but a small proximal portion of each lobe (Gloyd, 1940). Distally there is a gradual transition from spinulate flounces to spinulate calyces. There are about 32 rows of papillate fringes or flounces per lobe (McCranie, 1988). In the number of basal spines, the wide crotch, and the abrupt transition from spines to the ornamentation of the lobes *C. ravus* more closely resembles members of the genus *Crotalus* than it does the species of *Sistrurus*, with which it was formerly allied.

Stille (1987) investigated the scale microdermatoglyphics of rattlesnakes and attempted a cladistic analysis using these characters. He was not able to assemble a sufficient number of char-

acters to resolve the problem of rattlesnake phylogeny, and it appears that the characters associated with scale microdermatoglyphics are either too labile or too frequently convergent to be useful at this level of phylogenetic analysis.

Rattlesnakes are not aggressive, and most will make a hasty retreat when threatened. When cornered, however, most species readily defend themselves. The defensive coil of *C. simus* and *C. durissus* is spectacular, with the head and anterior third or more of the body lifted high off the ground, the neck bent like a shepherd's crook, and the head facing the antagonist. *Crotalus basiliscus*, *C. molossus*, *C. scutulatus*, *C. totonacus*, *C. oreganus*, and *C. viridis* display similar postures. *Crotalus scutulatus* is the only rattlesnake known to exhibit a neck-spreading display whereby the head is positioned slightly angled to the ground and the anterior part of the neck is conspicuously flattened, almost cobralike, exposing the pale interstitial skin. This behavior has been documented in both *C. scutulatus scutulatus* (Brown et al., 2000) and *C. scutulatus salvini* (Glenn and Lawler, 1987). Campbell and Armstrong (1979) noted that *Crotalus ravus* from the desert regions of Puebla dorsoventrally compresses the body when defensively coiled.

NATURAL HISTORY

Activity patterns and behavior. Rattlesnakes in temperate regions tend to be diurnal during the spring and fall, and become nocturnal during the hotter parts of the summer (Klauber, 1936b). Klauber (1931a) collected records for various species of snakes—including *C. atrox*, *C. cerastes*, *C. mitchellii*, *C. oreganus*, and *C. ruber*—in San Diego County and found that peak activity periods were May–July for all five species. Gates (1957) reported that near Wickenburg, Arizona, *C. molossus* was active from 21 April until the end of September, *C. atrox* was active from 15 March until November, *C. mitchellii* was active from 28 April until November, and *C. cerastes* was active from May to October. In west Texas, 15 individuals of *C. atrox* were found to be nocturnal or crepuscular from June to early July, but

9 *C. molossus* were found only during the cooler crepuscular hours or on cloudy days, never at night (Axtell, 1959).

Factors other than temperature are also important in determining snake activity. In northeastern Chihuahua, Mexico, Reynolds (1982) found that the activity of *C. atrox*, *C. lepidus*, and *C. scutulatus* was positively correlated with the amount of precipitation. This region experiences the greatest amount of rainfall in July, and the highest snake activity was in August, about one month later, which also coincided with the greatest seed and insect production. Reynolds (1982) concluded that snake activity is also positively correlated with abundance of prey.

During certain times of the year rattlesnakes thermoregulate by basking (Klauber, 1972; Wills and Beaupre, 2000), although the amount of time spent exposed to the sun's rays, especially at midday or on hot days, is very limited. It has long been known that rattlesnakes, and snakes in general, quickly die if they remain in strong sunlight. Mosauer and Lazier (1933) found that adults of two desert-adapted species, *C. cerastes* and *C. atrox*, died within 7–10 minutes when exposed to direct midday sunlight (experiments conducted in the Coachella Valley of California in October) and suggested that these rattlesnakes cannot withstand temperatures above 46°C. Cowles and Bogert (1944) found that *C. atrox* did not become consistently active until ambient temperatures reached 27–30°C. Even at 5,000 feet (1,524 m) in Plumas County, California, a *Crotalus oreganus oreganus* died in 20 minutes when exposed to full sunlight during the late morning in August (Swift, 1933). In another set of experiments a *C. o. oreganus* individual was found to be uninjured when exposed to radiation from different kinds of lights, but when it was subjected to increased heat it died at about 49°C (Blum and Spealman, 1933). Beck (1995) found that the mean activity temperature for *C. atrox*, *C. molossus*, and *C. tigris* in the Sonoran Desert of southeastern Arizona was the same—29.5°C.

Although it is not as dramatic as it is in some lizards, metachrosis has been noted in *C. adamanteus*, *C. atrox*, *C. cerastes*, *C. enyo*, and *C. oreganus*. These species tend to be relatively dark when they are exposed to cold temperatures but become paler with increasing temperatures (Grismer, 2002; Klauber, 1931a, 1944; Neill and Allen, 1955; Rahn, 1942a). Some individuals of *C. o. cerberus* are jet black by day but become brown to gray with dark blotches at night (Lowe et al., 1986).

Home ranges have been determined for a number of rattlesnake species. Some species utilize specific den sites year after year. Less is known about the use of particular refugia over extended periods. Smith (1992) observed a juvenile (60-cm) male *C. adamanteus* at the entrance of a burrow at the base of a decaying tree stump on 17 March 1989. Subsequently, this individual was seen at the same spot on 7 February 1990 and 10 May 1991, after which no further attempts were made to locate it. Thayer (1988) described an individual of *C. atrox* that exhibited considerable fidelity during the summer of 1987 to a particular crevice in a lava cliff at the fringe of the Aden lava flow in southern New Mexico. This snake emerged periodically from the crevice and crawled for about 2 m to a location on a ledge where it would coil, presumably to ambush rodents.

Although rattlesnakes are heavy bodied and adapted to a terrestrial existence, there are abundant records of them climbing into bushes and trees. Linsdale (1927) observed an individual of *C. horridus* on a tree limb about 15 feet (4.6 m) above the ground and found another in a tree about 6 feet (1.8 m) from the ground. Saenz et al. (1996) observed a small female (75.4 cm at

first capture) *C. horridus* in Nacogdoches County, Texas, in vegetation on three occasions. On 10 August 1993 she was found 3.5 m above the ground in an American hornbeam (*Carpinus carolina*), on 5 May 1994 she was discovered 7 m up in a tangle of greenbriar (*Smilax* sp.) growing on a willow oak (*Quercus phellos*), and on 10 May 1994 she was seen again in the same oak tree at a height of 9 m. Sajdak (2001) reported a young adult female *C. horridus* that spent nearly a month moving from tree to bush, sometimes as high as 14 feet (4.5 m) above the ground. In Gage County, Nebraska, the same species was observed on four separate occasions climbing to heights of 1.5–3.0 m above the ground (Fogell et al., 2002c). Sajdak and Bartz (in press) reported an adult *C. horridus* from Iowa that preyed on a yellow-bellied sapsucker 4.5–6 m above the ground in an American elm. During a single afternoon in late May we observed five *C. molossus* in low trees and bushes (1–3 m above the ground) in the Sierra de San Luis, Sonora, Mexico, where they may have been foraging on nestling birds. Allen (1933) also observed *C. molossus* in trees about 2 m above the ground.

Crotalus adamanteus is mostly terrestrial, but Timmerman (1995) recorded an individual climbing into a tree. *Crotalus atrox* has been found resting on top of halophytic rushes and grasses in salt marsh in Matagorda County, Texas (Neill, 1958), and Jackson (1970) found a specimen 3 m up in a pine tree in Arizona. In the Huachuca Mountains of southeastern Arizona a subadult *C. willardi willardi* was observed 46 cm above the ground in a poison oak bush, and a juvenile *C. lepidus klauberi* was seen at a height of 61 cm wedged in the ridges of the bark of a large ponderosa pine (Rossi and Feldner, 1993). McGuire (1991) observed a *C. enyo cerralvensis* repeatedly ascend into the lower branches of shrubs and bushes, once to about 1.5 m above the level of the ground. His observations were made at 0115 on 24 June 1989. Grismer (*in* McGuire, 1991) reported arboreal behavior in another island rattlesnake, *C. catalinensis*. *Crotalus catalinensis* is reported to be quite agile and sometimes climbs in vegetation to heights of 1 m or more (Grismer, 2002). When approached in the field, a *C. ruber lorenzoensis* escaped by ascending into an elephant tree (*Bursera microphylla*) to a height of about 2 m above the ground (Hollingsworth and Mellink, 1996).

In the San Bernardino Mountains of southern California, Cunningham (1955) frequently observed individuals of *Crotalus o. helleri* up to about 1.5 m high in thickets of *Ceanothus cordulatus* (Cunningham, 1955). Juveniles were frequently seen coiled in shrubs and small trees, especially during the fall. One snake was observed coiled on the ground about 1.2 m from the base of a California juniper (*Juniperus californica*). When disturbed, the snake sought refuge in the juniper, coming to rest about 1 m above the ground on a horizontal limb (Cunningham, 1955).

Carr (1940) reported that *Crotalus adamanteus* is mostly nocturnal and is shy and secretive. We have found it to be crepuscular in the Florida panhandle region, however, and L. Porras (pers. comm.) reported it to be diurnal in southeastern Florida. Timmerman (1995) reported that this species moves diurnally from one nocturnal ambush site to another. Although Carr (1940) reported several instances when he was made aware of the presence of *C. adamanteus* because of rattling at a distance of some 6–10 m from him, most frequently these snakes remained unagitated until approached within 1 m.

Timmerman (1995) made 743 observations on 5 males and 3 females of *C. adamanteus* from 3 September 1985 to 21 February 1989. He found that females maintained smaller home ranges (n = 2, $\bar{x}$ = 46.5 ha) than males (n = 4, $\bar{x}$ = 84.3), and that the ranges of both sexes overlapped, suggesting that there is no territoriality in this species. *Crotalus adamanteus* apparently occupies home ranges that remain relatively stable from year to year. Movement practically ceased from December to February, but the snakes remained on the surface 55.4% of the time. Refugia during this period included armadillo (*Dasypus novemcinctus*) and gopher tortoise (*Gopherus polyphemus*) burrows, as well as root channels beneath stands of palmettos.

Brandt et al. (1993) excavated 59 gopher tortoise burrows in Collier Country, Florida, and found only two specimens of *C. adamanteus*. The most active period was from September through November, when snakes moved during the day in excess of 20 m per day. Males traveled longer distances than females, possibly in search of breeding females.

One very large rattlesnake (probably *C. adamanteus*) was discovered in a large clump of vegetation that had floated from the Caloosahatchee River to Sanibel Island during spring floods (Clench, 1925). Clench estimated that the snake must have drifted at least 5 miles (8 km) from the mainland and may have traveled as far as 27 miles (43.2 km). Another individual was found in the middle of the Myakka River, and others have been found in mackerel nets in the Gulf of Mexico several miles from the coast (Carr, 1940). Neill (1958) stated that *C. adamanteus* is more common in salt marsh than any other habitat in some coastal counties of Florida, and he even found this species in patches of dune grass and the debris of the tidal wrack zone.

Trauth et al. (1994) reported that *C. horridus* emerges from hibernation in Arkansas sometime in April. In western Wisconsin, Oldfield and Keyler (1989) encountered 25 *C. horridus* over the course of 42 surveys in 1988, with the earliest observation made on May 1 and the latest on September 11. In southeastern Minnesota, near the northern range limit for *C. horridus*, snakes emerge from denning sites during early to mid-May and return to dens in late September, thus spending 7–7.5 months in overwintering sites (Oldfield and Keyler, 1997). *Crotalus horridus* individuals in a hibernaculum in northeastern New York exhibited body temperatures of 4.3–15.7 °C ($\bar{x}$ = 10.5 °C) from September through May (Brown, 1982).

The Pine Barrens of New Jersey are devoid of rocky outcroppings that might be used as denning sites. Burger (1934) reported that rattlesnakes (*C. horridus*) in this region burrow into sandy banks near springs to a depth of about 2 feet (0.61 m) where they pass the colder months from about late October to mid-April. Although Burger credited the snakes with actively burrowing, it seems probable that they utilize existing mammal burrows.

W. S. Brown et al. (1982) radio-tracked five adult *C. horridus* in northeastern New York as they moved away from a den and followed them throughout the summer. The snakes dispersed an average of 504 m. Gravid females were relatively sedentary, and snakes moved long distances immediately following ecdysis. Factors such as body color, reproductive condition, stage of ecdysis, and feeding all appeared to have an important effect on thermal relationships. Snakes thermoregulated by moving back and forth in and out of rocky crevices or from partially shaded areas in grassy-shrub habitats. Active snakes had an average body temperature of 26.9 °C, but snakes that were above ground on clear days averaged 30.1 °C when the air temperature was 26.0 °C. Snakes that remained underground on these days had body temperatures that averaged 27.8 °C, the same average temperature that was recorded for snakes on cloudy days.

Crotalus horridus individuals from a radius of at least 20 miles (32 km) in Richmond County, Georgia, used the same series of paths to converge on an area of limestone caves where they overwintered (Neill, 1948). Fitch and Shirer (1971) studied *C. horridus* in northeastern Kansas and found that snakes moved an average of 45 m per day (but were inactive on half of the days they were studied). On the days the snakes moved, they most frequently traveled either relatively short (3.5–15 m, 13% of days) or long (31 to more than 150 m, 24% of days) distances. Reinert and Zappalorti (1988a) monitored movements and habitat use by *C. horridus* in the Pine Barrens of New Jersey. Males and nongravid females occupied constantly shifting, nonoverlapping activity areas, with males having the largest activity ranges. Gravid females had smaller, overlapping activity areas and tended to disperse shorter distances from hibernacula. Males and nongravid females were found most frequently in heavily forested habitats with more than 50% canopy closure and heavy, low vegetation, but gravid females were found in more open, and therefore warmer, areas with about 25% canopy closure, about an equal amount of low vegetation and leaf litter, and more fallen logs.

Crotalus molossus may be nocturnal during hot weather or in relatively xeric highland habitats such as southern Puebla, but it is frequently encountered by day as well, especially in the early morning and late afternoon (Campbell and Lamar, 1989). It is generally considered to be a mild-mannered snake, although a few that we have found active during the early morning have been quick to rattle and assume a striking position.

Crotalus atrox individuals often gather in dens during the colder months and become relatively inactive. Dens harboring large numbers of snakes appear to be most prevalent in the northern part of the range and in rocky regions. Snakes occurring in flat areas devoid of rocky outcroppings tend to utilize mammal burrows to escape direct exposure to the extreme temperatures of winter. The activity patterns of this species appear to be more affected by temperature than by light. For example, during the early spring, this snake may be found crawling by day or at dusk and is only rarely found after dark when temperatures are cool. Conversely, during the hot summer months activity seems largely confined to the hours of darkness, although we have seen individuals crawling through thick desert vegetation in the late afternoon during even the hottest days. Specimens have been observed coiled at the entrance of burrows or under brush during the early morning hours (Armstrong and Murphy, 1979). During the hottest part of the day, *C. atrox* will coil in the shade beneath creosote bush and mesquite or retire into burrows (Gates, 1957). In general, mammal burrows are the single most important refuge for most populations of rattlesnakes. Gehlbach (1957) found a *C. atrox* at the mouth of a badger (*Taxidea*) burrow.

Studies of radiotelemetered *C. atrox* in southwestern Oklahoma confirmed that temperature determines the activity of this snake. Activity in the winter occurs during the midday hours, in the spring and fall during early morning and late evening, and in the summer during midnight hours (Fig. 192; Landreth, 1973). Perkins and Lentz (1934) discovered an active denning site for *C. atrox* on Rattlesnake Mountain west of Little Rock, Arkansas, on 18 April 1932. Several snakes were basking near the entrance at about midmorning. During a two-day period they observed 10 *C. atrox*, 8 of which were in pairs. *Crotalus atrox* migrates to and from denning areas in the fall and spring, respectively, often moving distances of 1–2 km between

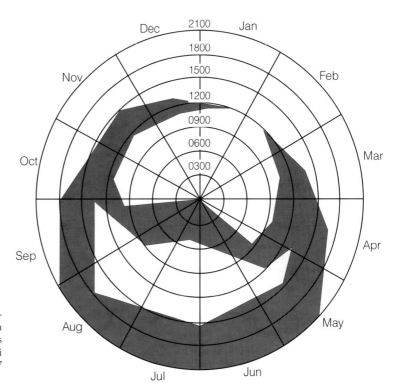

Fig. 192. Daily activity periods of western diamondback rattlesnakes (*Crotalus atrox*) in their natural habitat in southwestern Oklahoma, USA, shown by the darkened area. Concentric circles indicate hours of the day, and the areas between the 12 radii represent months of the year. Adapted from Landreth, 1973:27 (fig. 1).

dens and summer ranges (Landreth, 1973). These snakes apparently do not move randomly and use solar cues to orient themselves.

Crotalus ruber may be encountered during every month of the year but is most active in the late spring (Armstrong and Murphy, 1979). This species may be diurnal during the cooler months, and active individuals have been observed at relatively cool temperatures (18 °C), but most become nocturnal during the late spring and summer. Not surprisingly, *C. ruber* tends to be more nocturnal in the desert foothills, where daytime temperatures may quickly exceed its thermal maximum, than along the Pacific coast of southern California and Baja California, where temperatures tend to be considerably milder.

Crotalus scutulatus was collected as early as 1 April and as late as November near Wickenburg, Arizona (Gates, 1957). In the northern part of its range, *C. scutulatus* is almost always nocturnal (Miller and Stebbins, 1964), although in the spring individuals are sometimes found coiled near the base of a palo verde or creosote bush during the early morning (Armstrong and Murphy, 1979). In the southern part of its range *C. scutulatus* has been collected during the midafternoon basking among the rocks of ancient lava flows (Armstrong and Murphy, 1979). In the Limón Totalco region individuals use *Opuntia* clumps for basking sites (L. Porras, pers. comm.). Plummer (2000) observed a *C. scutulatus* in Arizona during the late morning feeding on a dead squirrel on a dirt road. This snake appeared to become thermally stressed at about the time it had half-swallowed the squirrel, and moved into the shade alongside the road to finish swallowing its prey.

In the temperate climates of the United States and Canada, *C. oreganus* and *C. viridis* individuals often come together in moderate to large numbers in refugia to hibernate. Hibernation often commences in about mid-October, and emergence occurs in about mid-April, but these dates are influenced by latitude. Hibernacula may be in deep rocky fissures or deep burrows such as those found in prairie dog (*Cynomys*) towns. For example, in the Sandhill region of Nebraska, which is devoid

of rocky outcroppings, *C. viridis* individuals use prairie dog (*Cynomys ludovicianus*) towns as denning sites and overwinter deep in the burrows (Holycross, 1995). In more equitable climates, rattlesnakes do not usually hibernate in groups, but rather seek cover individually during the relatively brief periods of harsh weather. In Nebraska, Holycross (1995) found *C. viridis viridis* and recently shed skins at the entrances to prairie dog burrows in the early spring; presumably the snakes had overwintered in the burrows. *Crotalus v. viridis* may remain in the vicinity and use prairie dog burrows during the summer as well (Cunningham et al., 1996).

Ludlow (1981) reported on the activities of *C. v. viridis* in Jefferson County, Colorado: from early January to late March snakes were in hibernation; from late March to late April snakes remained at dens but basked when weather conditions were favorable; from late April to late May snakes began to disperse from den sites to summer ranges (mostly prairie dog towns); from late May to mid-September snakes were actively feeding, breeding, and giving birth on the summer ranges; from mid-September to early October snakes bagan to migrate back to denning sites; from early October to early November snakes finished arriving at denning sites but basked at the entrances when weather was favorable; and from early November to late December snakes were mostly in hibernation. Ludlow (1981) found that *C. v. viridis* sought the shelter of prairie dog burrows during the summer but did not usually overwinter at these sites, instead migrating to den sites in holes or crevices of sedimentary rock outcroppings on the west side of the Dakota Hogback Uplift, where they remained until late spring or early summer.

Linsdale (1940) reported that *C. o. lutosus* is active from about mid-May to early September in Nevada. Diller and Wallace (1996) found that in southwestern Idaho *C. o. lutosus* experiences its peak seasonal activity in late May and early June. During the spring the daily activity pattern is unimodal, with most activity occurring between 0800 and 1400, but during the summer the activity period becomes bimodal, with the primary period of activity early in the day between 0800 and 1400 and a secondary peak between 1700 and 2200. In general, at high elevations where cool temperatures prevail after dark, *C. oreganus* and *C. viridis* appear to be mainly diurnal, but throughout much of the range these species are most commonly active after dark.

Some populations of *Crotalus oreganus* may aggregate prior to shedding, but their reasons for doing so remain obscure (Ashton, 1999; Gregory et al., 1987). Five adult *C. oreganus concolor* in Sweetwater County, Wyoming—including one adult male, one nongravid female, and two gravid females—were found within 2 m of each other on 13 June 1997 (Ashton, 1999). These snakes remained together until 19 June, then began to leave the area once they had shed. During 1997 and 1998 Ashton (1999) discovered 20 premolt snakes, 16 (80%) of which were in aggregations. Ashton (1999) reported that *C. oreganus concolor* denned individually or in small groups in his study area but came together in June and July to shed. L. Porras (pers. comm.), on the other hand, reported that snakes of this species remain close to the den all year. It may be that there are relatively few sites that have thermal and hydric conditions favorable for shedding, or perhaps these aggregation sites offer increased protection from predators during a time when it is thought that snakes in general are most vulnerable.

Vitt (1974), who found denning aggregations of *C. oreganus oreganus* in basaltic slides on western- and southwestern-facing slopes of the Cascade Mountains in Washington, suggested that these aggregations were the result of a shortage of overwintering sites. He found that the body temperatures of these rattlesnakes were higher than the air or substrate temperatures during cooler periods in the fall and early spring and that basking was an important component of the reproductive cycle.

Clarke et al. (1996) tested *C. viridis viridis* under laboratory conditions to determine the effect of moonlight on activity patterns. They found that activity of adults was greatly curtailed in three-quarters and full moonlight, and adults were most active on nights when only starlight was present. Conversely, juveniles showed no significant activity differences during different phases of the moon. These authors suggested that the adults' strategy may reduce predation and may also be influenced by the activity pattern of their main prey—nocturnal rodents. Juveniles feed primarily on nocturnally inactive prey—diurnal lizards and neonate rodents.

Crotalus totonacus has most often been found crawling on lowland roads after dark during light rains. In contrast, we have found that in the highlands this species is often diurnal and associated with rocky outcroppings rather than watercourses. Armstrong and Murphy (1979) offered anecdotal evidence that this snake is usually found along streams in dry lowland areas.

In the savanna regions of southern Guyana, *C. durissus* individuals usually congregate on the rocky knolls that are scattered across the landscape, but during the dry season these snakes most frequently take refuge in burrows that have been excavated by various mammals in huge termite hills (Allen and Neill, 1957). In Uruguay, this species is most frequently found on rocky hillsides (Achával et al., 1978). In Santiago del Estero, Argentina, Abalos and Bucher (1970) found that *C. durissus* activity was very low during the winter and early spring and reached a maximum during the fall (see Fig. 113).

Some of the small Mexican montane rattlesnakes may be found on ledges high on almost vertical cliffs. *Crotalus aquilus*

is mostly diurnal and is generally seen coiled or crawling during the late morning or afternoon, although this species has also been found at night in the vicinity of Durango, Hidalgo (Armstrong and Murphy, 1979). It inhabits a variety of terrains, including open, grassy highland valleys and steep slopes, but is almost always associated with rocky areas.

The activity period of *C. lepidus* varies considerably and is influenced by season, weather, elevation, and latitude. In the arid southwestern United States this species is mostly nocturnal, often being found on roads at night. In trans-Pecos Texas it may be found by day, but usually only during the early morning; as soon as the sun's rays become too direct the snakes quickly disappear. In the isolated mountain ranges scattered from west Texas to Arizona, *C. lepidus* may be found at practically any time during the day, although it generally remains coiled and motionless in some shady retreat during the hotter time of day. We almost never fail to see several individuals each day when walking in the higher parts of the Peloncillo Mountains in New Mexico. During extended dry periods these snakes emerge less frequently and remain underground to retard desiccation. Populations in parts of Mexico at high elevations are probably almost completely diurnal. We found this species abundant near San Antonio de las Alazanas in Coahuila, basking on steep rocky slopes. A stiff, cold wind pervades the valleys and slopes of this region as soon as the sun goes down, and nighttime temperatures fall precipitously, making reptilian activity unlikely.

Beaupre (1995a, 1995b) studied two populations of *C. lepidus* in Big Bend National Park, Texas, that were separated by 40 km. One of the populations occurred in a hotter, drier, and less productive area than the other, and Beaupre found significant differences between the two groups. Snakes from the hotter environment had smaller age-specific body masses and SVLs, lower frequency of surface use, higher average body temperatures, and lower probability of defecation than snakes from the more temperate area. Weather was an important factor in the snakes' movements and activity, but all captures nevertheless occurred between 0700 and 1400 or between 1800 and 2300 (Beaupre, 1995b; Fig. 193). Rain usually increased the number of captures and also extended activity periods later into the day. Night activity tended to be infrequent and was most common in August.

Prival (2000) and Prival et al. (2002) found that male *C. pricei* moved an average of 55 m per week and females moved an average of 24.2 m per week during the rainy season in the Chiricahua Mountains of Arizona. Gravid females in particular moved relatively small distances (3.2 m/week or less) but became much more active following parturition in late August or early September. Overall movements were correlated with home range sizes, which averaged 1.37 ha for 9 males and 0.36 ha for 4 females. Diurnal body temperatures of *C. pricei* collected from July to September averaged 24.5 °C for males (n = 103) and 29.0 for females (n = 57), with relatively slight differences between gravid and nongravid females. When their body temperatures exceeded 33 °C snakes sought cooler retreats. The snakes usually moved to winter retreats by late October, often looking for denning sites in talus slopes but also using other areas. Most snakes passed the winter months in a den by themselves (Prival, 2000; Prival et al., 2002).

Armstrong and Murphy (1979) reported that two *C. pricei* were encountered on a south-facing talus slope at Barfoot (sometimes known as Buena Vista Peak) in the Chiricahua Mountains of Arizona at 1220 on 17 March 1965; snow sur-

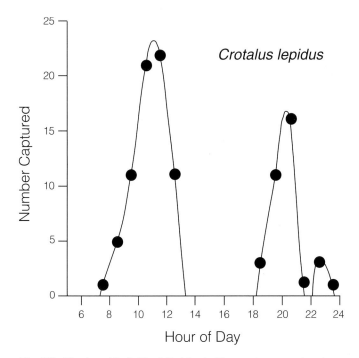

Fig. 193. Number of individual *Crotalus lepidus* specimens captured as a function of time of day. Based on two populations from Big Bend National Park, Texas, USA. Adapted from Beaupre, 1995b:52 (fig. 2).

rounded the talus and the ambient temperature was 11 °C at the time of the encounter.

Crotalus pusillus specimens have been found beneath the bark of fallen trees in oak forest (Armstrong and Murphy, 1979). Our experiences with this species in the Sierra de Coalcomán in Michoacán suggest that on sunny days most activity occurs in mid-to-late morning (0930–1100), with a lesser peak of activity in the afternoon (1600–1700).

Crotalus transversus has been collected by day while basking among huge boulders on steep slopes. We encountered an individual at about 1100 as it crossed the road through the Parque Nacional de Lagunas de Zempoala. This snake has been collected mainly during the summer months when its activity is probably severely curtailed by the frequent cold rains and prevailing cloudy conditions.

Crotalus triseriatus is exclusively diurnal under normal conditions, although at elevations below 2,500 m individuals are occasionally found crawling at night. We observed a specimen on a dirt road at about 2330 during a heavy rainstorm. This specimen apparently had been flooded out of its hiding place and was so cold that it could barely move. Davis and Smith (1953) reported *C. triseriatus* to be fairly common in Morelos in rocky and grassy situations, especially near water. We have frequently found this species basking among volcanic rocks on sunny days. On clear days it seems to be most active during the midmorning and midafternoon hours, whereas on partially overcast days it basks whenever the sun emerges from the clouds, even for a short while.

Most rattlesnakes accomplish forward progress through lateral undulation or rectilinear movement. *Crotalus cerastes*, however, employs a curious type of "horizontal broadside" movement known as sidewinding (Cowles, 1956; Mosauer, 1932a). This type of locomotion has arisen independently in several species of North African vipers (*Cerastes*, *Echis*) that inhabit similar regions of windblown sand and high daily temperatures. Cowles (1957) pointed out that *Crotalus cerastes* can

attain relatively high speeds by sidewinding, and that this speed can be sustained for relatively long intervals, which may be of great advantage when traversing patches of hot sand between shady retreats. Also, sidewinding roughly cuts in half the amount of body surface in contact with the hot substrate compared with more conventional modes of locomotion. This type of efficient and rapid locomotion would be beneficial to species in regions where widely dispersed prey and sparse conspecific populations require extensive movements in search of food or mates that potentially would expose snakes to predation (Cowles, 1957).

Crotalus cerastes is mostly nocturnal and appears to be particularly active during the first several hours after sundown (Moore, 1978). Peak seasonal activity occurs in late May and early June (Armstrong and Murphy, 1979). During the spring and fall this snake is sometimes encountered active during the day. Over a period of 16 years Klauber (1939a) found 151 *C. cerastes* active from February to November (with no records in August). In Yuma County, Arizona, Funk (1965) reported active sidewinders over a similar span of months, including August.

Klauber (1932b) collected several specimens on a road in Clark County, Nevada, on a cold, windy night and remarked that "a more unlikely night for snakes could hardly be imagined." Fowlie (1965) reported that *C. cerastes* was frequently the only snake he encountered crossing roads at night in inclement weather or when there was a full moon, times when most snakes remain sequestered in their hiding places. Cowles and Bogert (1944) and Klauber (1944) found *C. cerastes* active at body temperatures as low as 17.5–19.5 °C. In Riverside County, California, the normal activity range for *C. cerastes laterorepens* was 13.6–40.8 °C, a much broader range than that of the sympatric *C. mitchellii pyrrhus* (18.8–39.3 °C) (Moore, 1978). The preferred body temperatures for these two species as estimated from data taken from April to December were 25.8 °C and 31.2 °C, respectively (Moore, 1978).

In the eastern Mohave Desert, Secor (1994a, 1994b) found that *C. cerastes* emerged from winter retreats as early as mid-March, but only after daytime surface temperatures had reached 31–35 °C for about a week. In the early spring, sidewinders spent most of the day coiled on the surface and sought refuge in rodent burrows at about sunset. As daily temperatures became progressively warmer later in the spring (sometimes above 55 °C on the sand surface), these snakes became more nocturnal, and by summer their activity was restricted to the dark hours. Beginning in September and extending to November, sidewinders began to spend more time on the surface during daylight hours, and by late September they often spent the entire day and night abroad. At about mid-November snakes entered rodent burrows located at the sand-alluvial interface and began to hibernate at depths of 15–75 cm below the surface of the ground. They remained underground through February, with only a few individuals sometimes emerging to the mouth of a burrow on warm, sunny days to bask. Stebbins (1943) observed *C. cerastes* sidewinding across a bare patch of sand in broad daylight at 0930 on 18 October 1941.

Crotalus cerastes specimens are sometimes found "bedded down"—partially or almost wholly buried in the sand. Cowles (1945) described this behavior, whereby the snake forms a tight coil on top of the sand and then proceeds to scoop the sand out from beneath it by rotating the body back and forth, forming a saucer-shaped depression in which the body is about flush with the surrounding surface. The snake becomes covered with sand, either passively by windblown sand or, in some cases, by forming a J with the head and anterior portion of the body and scraping the surrounding sand over itself.

Secor (1994a) found that *C. cerastes* in the eastern Mohave Desert moved an average of 128.3 ± 6.8 m per day. Males tended to move significantly greater distances than females, and subadults traveled greater distances than adults. Movements made in August–September were significantly greater than those made in the spring, a phenomenon also noted by Brown (1970) and Brown and Lillywhite (1992).

In the eastern Mohave Desert adult male *C. cerastes* traveled significantly farther than nongravid females, with most of that movement occurring during the spring and fall mating seasons (Secor, 1994a). Subadult sidewinders that were two to three years old moved greater distances than juveniles (six months to two years old). Tracks left in fine sand indicated that it was not unusual for an individual to move in excess of 1,000 feet (305 m) in a single night (Mosauer, 1933). Sidewinders in general move longer distances during the summer than at any other time of the year. *Crotalus cerastes* has a mean activity range of 23.2 ha, which is among the largest reported for any snake. Activity ranges of individual sidewinders overlap extensively, and there are no significant differences in activity range between sexes or age classes (Secor, 1994a).

Crotalus enyo is mostly nocturnal and is most active during the early fall, a rainy time in its habitat (Armstrong and Murphy, 1979). One specimen (the type of *furvus*) was found at midday coiled at the entrance of a small burrow.

Southern populations of *C. mitchellii* are mostly nocturnal, and individuals are most active during the late summer rainy season; in the north, however, these snakes are most active during the early spring and are often diurnal during the spring and fall, becoming nocturnal during the hot summer months (Armstrong and Murphy, 1979; Moore, 1976). On El Muerto Island this species was collected after sunset on the beach within 3 m of the water as it foraged in beach debris (Armstrong and Murphy, 1979). The differing activity periods of *C. mitchellii* (mostly diurnal in the spring and fall) and *C. cerastes* (mostly nocturnal throughout the year) reduce competition between these rattlesnakes (Moore, 1978).

Conservation and abundance. Rattlesnakes are ruthlessly persecuted wherever they occur, and populations in most areas have severely declined or become extirpated altogether. Apparently some Native American groups deserve credit for being the earliest rattlesnake conservationists. Klauber (1932a) noted that the Hopis seldom harmed snakes, and that at least as early as 1931 the Hopis were noting with regret the indiscrimate destruction of rattlesnakes by whites. Anecdotes abound about the killing of, the former abundance of, and the decline of rattlesnakes within recent decades. Almost 100 years ago Willson (1908) noted, "There can be no doubt that the poisonous snakes, especially the rattlesnakes, are being slowly but surely exterminated." Carr (1940) reported *C. adamanteus* to be "locally common" in Florida in general, and especially abundant in the region northwest of Lake Okeechobee, and in 1930 he found four adults within two blocks of the outskirts of Arcadia in De Soto County. *Crotalus adamanteus* is now in serious decline over most of its range, and especially in Florida, where indiscriminate development is common.

In Massachusetts, the northern part of its range, *C. horridus* was apparently quite common before the region was settled by Europeans (Palmer, 1992). As early as 1680, however, bands of men were organized to kill them (Babcock, 1925). Kimball (1978) reported an overall decline in *C. horridus* populations in New England. *Crotalus horridus* was reported to be relatively common in Ontario, Canada, as well, when the region was first settled, but by 1930 the species had been virtually eliminated (LeRay, 1930). Viable populations of this snake remain in other portions of its range, but for how long? In the George Washington National Forest of Virginia, Uhler et al. (1939) found *C. horridus* to be the most common snake encountered, representing 253 of the 885 (28.6%) snakes collected. Brown (1950) and Werler and Dixon (2000) stated that this species is rare in Texas. Richards (1990) found skeletal remains of *C. horridus* in a number of Indiana sites where the species no longer occurs.

Data from organized rattlesnake hunts in Pennsylvania show that about 84% of the female *C. horridus* collected are gravid (Reinert, 1990), which agrees with Martin's (1993) finding that gestating females are more easily located and captured. Although many of the snake hunters reported that they released their snakes after the hunt, more than one-fourth of the snakes exhibited some sort of injury associated with capture, and many were not released at their capture location. Reinert (1990) concluded that organized rattlesnake hunts have a negative impact on populations and recommended that these events either be strictly regulated or prohibited.

Crotalus horridus was present in the Flint Hills of Kansas prior to 1930, but a survey in 1993 failed to find this snake (Busby and Parmelee, 1996). Although the species may still be in the region, populations appear to have declined. The decline of *C. horridus* in east Texas has been atributed in large part to mortality associated with vehicular traffic, with particularly severe impacts on populations occurring in areas of high road density (Rudolph and Burgdorf, 1997). Platt et al. (1999) reported that *C. horridus* in the piedmont area of western South Carolina has suffered a relatively recent population decline. A bounty was offered for *C. horridus* in Minnesota until 1989, and 28,685 timber rattlesnakes were killed for the reward in one county alone (Oldfield and Keyler, 1997). The steady decrease in numbers of rattlesnakes in Minnesota during the years when bounties were offered is dramatic (Table 47). By 1993, *C. horridus* had received some measure of protection in Ontario, Canada, where it is probably already extirpated, and in 13 of the 32 states in the United States where it occurs (Brown, 1993).

Until the 1980s *Crotalus atrox* was particularly abundant along the rocky, juniper-covered ridge known locally as Cedar Ridge just southwest of Dallas in Dallas County, Texas. We knew the location of several dens where on warm days in winter or early spring some 12–20 snakes could be observed basking at the entrance of rocky outcroppings. Recent development in the area

Table 47. Number of *Crotalus horridus* bountied in selected years in Houston County, Minnesota.

Year	Number of snakes
1939	2,059
1941	5,957
1967	3,787
1970	4,955
1972	1,894
1977	480
1980	819
1987	191

Source: Oldfield and Keyler, 1997.

and unscrupulous collectors have greatly reduced this population, and the den sites now appear to be devoid of snakes. Trapping and collecting, especially during the spring, has virtually eliminated *C. viridis* from certain dens in Colorado (Ludlow, 1981) and South Dakota (Jackey, *in* Klauber, 1972).

As many as 30 individuals of *C. cerastes* could be seen in a single evening of road cruising in the late 1970s (Armstrong and Murphy, 1979), and Fowlie (1965) reported seeing 47 on one moonlit evening between Yuma and Gila Bend, Arizona. Unfortunately, the propensity of these snakes to coil on the road, presumably using the pavement as a source of heat (Brown, 1970), results in high mortality.

Sullivan (2000) compared 1970s and 1990s surveys from one area of California and found that *Crotalus oreganus* had actually increased in the 1990s. It is difficult to duplicate surveys, however, and subtle differences in the collecting methodologies may greatly alter the results. Mendelson and Jennings (1992) compared the relative abundance of snakes in a desert grassland in Arizona and adjacent New Mexico with results from a survey conducted about 30 years previously (Mendelson and Jennings, 1992). The most prominent factor affecting snake distributions in this area over the 30 years was the succession of semidesert grasslands to Chihuahuan Desert scrub. *Crotalus atrox* was found to prefer the scrub habitat while *C. scutulatus* was more abundant in grasslands, so the former species had increased in relative abundance and the latter had declined.

Potential threats to the twin-spotted rattlesnake (*Crotalus pricei*)—and by implication to other montane species of rattlesnakes—were listed by Prival (2000; Prival et al., 2002) as including mining, logging, grazing, recreational and other development, climate change, wildfires, and collecting. Although *C. pricei* has been protected in Arizona since the late 1960s, illegal collecting has continued and probably represents the single greatest threat to the species (Prival, 2000; Prival et al., 2002).

Rattlesnakes exposed to prescribed fires in the Madrean communities of the southwestern United States usually survive low-intensity fires, but intense fires caused by artificially high fuel loads result in high mortality of all reptiles (Smith et al., 2001). Although low-intensity fires are essential to maintain the mosaic of habitats in this ecosystem, high-intensity fires may reduce or eliminate certain rattlesnakes such as *C. willardi obscurus* and their habitat (Smith et al., 2001).

Little information is available for most species of rattlesnakes in Mexico, which harbors the greatest diversity of these animals. They were formerly abundant in many regions, but most species have declined owing to human alteration of habitats. Dugès (1876–1877:23) noted that in San Luis Potosí as many as 700 rattlesnakes were collected in 10 days. He referred to the species taken as *Crotalus rhombifer*; it was probably *C. molossus*. Rattlesnakes in the Valley of Mexico have suffered serious population declines because of urban spawl and habitat destruction. The species inhabiting relatively level meadows or rolling hills—namely, *C. aquilus*, *C. molossus nigrescens*, and *C. polystictus*—were considered vulnerable to extinction by González et al. (1986).

Records of the Instituto Butantan in São Paulo, Brazil, reveal that the institute received 108,001 specimens of *Crotalus durissus* during a period of 43 years, a number surpassed by only one other venomous species, *Bothrops jararaca* (Fonseca, 1949). During the same period the institute received word of 837 rattlesnake bites. In the 1940s there were areas of high ground in the state of Maranhão, Brazil, where collectors could gather about 1,000 *Crotalus durissus* (and 500 *B. atrox*) in only a few days (Fonseca, 1949). Settlers near the El Bagual Ecological Reserve in northeastern Argentina claimed in the 1990s that *C. durissus* was even more abundant in the 1960s than *B. neuwiedi* and *B. alternatus*, species that are common (Yanosky et al., 1996). Yanosky, however, has not seen rattlesnakes on the reserve during 10 years of fieldwork in the area. *Crotalus simus* has disappeared or become very rare in most areas where it was formerly common. In Guatemala, for example, *C. simus* was once abundant on the south coast and it was not unusual to see half a dozen in one morning in the shallow ravines between Cuyotenango and the coast in the region generally referred to as La Máquina. Similarly, rattlesnakes were predictably seen on almost every trip through the dry rain-shadow region between Sanarate and El Rancho, Guatemala. These days they are a rare sight. Other species are suffering population declines owing to habitat degradation and restricted ranges as well. Populations restricted to small islands are particularly vulnerable. The Aruba Island rattlesnake (*C. durissus unicolor*) is threatened by human activities (Greene and Campbell, 1992), but on the positive side, its range on the island is now known to be more extensive than was previously thought (Reinert et al., 2002).

Rattlesnakes that tend to aggregate during the fall to overwinter in dens appear to be especially susceptible to overcollection and eradication. One publication devoted to recreational rattlesnake roundups lists 31–40 towns in Alabama, Georgia, Kansas, New Mexico, Oklahoma, Pennsylvania, and Texas that annually sponsor such events (National *Crotalus* News, 1993a, 1993b, 1994, 1995). Fitzgerald and Painter (2000) determined that five U.S. species (*C. atrox*, *C. adamanteus*, *C. horridus*, *C. molossus*, and *C. viridis*) found mostly in Alabama, Florida, Georgia, Kansas, Oklahoma, New Mexico, Pennsylvania, and Texas are exploited to supply an international trade in skins, meat, gall bladders, and curios.

Crotalus atrox is the main species exploited commercially in the numerous rattlesnake roundups in Texas. Campbell et al. (1989b) discussed the detrimental impact that spraying gasoline into dens, the preferred collection method, had on other species using these refuges and noted that although there had been a general increase over the years in the total number of snakes entered at the Sweetwater Rattlesnake Roundup, this was owing to an increased number of collectors. The removal of gravid females was stated to have a particularly negative impact on *C. atrox* populations. Adams et al. (1994), who noted a general decline in the number of rattlesnakes brought to the major Texas roundups over a nine-year period, recommended the enactment of regulations that would provide annual information on nongame wildlife such as rattlesnakes. Weir (1992) pointed out that an assessment of the environmental impact of rattlesnake hunts such as the one at Sweetwater, Texas, would be difficult owing to a lack of scientific data and suggested that rattlesnake hunts be organized so that these kinds of data could be procured, with particular consideration to the time span and territory covered by hunts. For a summary of rattlesnake roundups and associated activities, see Rubio, 1998, which notes: "It is paradoxical that sponsors promote roundups as a method of eradicating dangerous snakes, and yet, if the snakes were destroyed, they would not be able to maintain an annual cash flow."

A Florida study on the commercialization of rattlesnakes determined that *Crotalus adamanteus* specimens accounted for

84% of the rattlesnakes brought to a skin-processing facility, and *C. horridus* comprised the remaining 16% (Berish, 1998). Berish also found that sex ratios were skewed toward males in both species, suggesting that males are more active than females; and that between 40 and 50% of adult females of both *C. adamanteus* and *C. horridus* were reproductively active at the time of capture.

The only rattlesnake roundup that currently takes place in Kansas was initiated in 1992 in Sharon Springs. The species hunted is *C. viridis* (Fitch, 1998), and about 25% of the snakes captured are gravid females, resulting in a serious depletion in the population. Almost a century ago Strecker (1910) reported this species (as *Crotalus confluentus*) as an inhabitant of prairie dog towns in northwestern Texas and noted that it was being exterminated in the region by humans.

Parker and Brown (1974) listed four reasons why rattlesnake populations may not be able to recover from their contact with humans, regardless of conservation measures: (1) late maturity—a female must survive for four to five years before producing her first litter; (2) biennial reproduction—a mature female produces only one litter every two years; (3) winter aggregation—concentration of the population from a large area at one site leaves it vulnerable to excessive autumn and spring losses; and (4) conspicuous behavior—the rattling response to a disturbance frequently draws attention and results in death to the snake.

Prey. Rattlesnakes generally feed on vertebrates, although numerous invertebrate species have also been recorded in their diets. The smaller species of rattlesnakes feed primarily on lizards. The larger rattlesnakes feed on lizards as juveniles but shift to mostly mammalian prey as adults. Klauber (1936b, 1971, 1972) listed rabbits, ground squirrels, tree squirrels, chipmunks, prairie dogs, gophers, rats, and mice as the most common food items; and birds, snakes, and amphibians as occasionally eaten. Cannibalism has been reported in various species (Polis and Myers, 1985). Studies of the energetics of *C. atrox*, *C. molossus*, and *C. tigris* have led to estimates that rattlesnakes could satisfy their yearly food requirements by consuming prey equivalent to 93% of their body mass, and that energy demand could be met in only two or three large meals (Beck, 1995).

The quantity of venom injected into prey is controlled by the snake, with larger prey generally receiving more venom (Hayes, 1995). The amount of venom injected does not seem to be related to the duration of fang penetration, and different activities elicit different venom flow rates, in some cases even resulting in dry bites (Young, 2001).

Rattlesnakes that feed on rodents usually release the prey immediately after striking and envenomating it. There is evidence that rattlesnakes are able to discriminate among different prey trails to relocate envenomated prey (Lavín-Murcio and Kardong, 1995; Lavín-Murcio et al., 1993).

Several prey species are known to have evolved resistance to the venom of certain species of rattlesnakes. California ground squirrels (*Spermophilus beecheyi*), for example, are 3.3–5.3 times more resistant to the venom of *C. oreganus* than are other species of ground squirrels living in areas devoid of rattlesnakes (Poran et al., 1987). Further, populations of California ground squirrels living in areas with dense rattlesnake populations exhibit more resistance to rattlesnake venom than populations from areas where rattlesnakes are rare or absent (Poran et al., 1987; Biardi et al., 2000). Poran and Coss (1990) discovered that California ground squirrel pups confronted with a snake predator

engaged in adult behaviors such as close-range investigation, substrate throwing, and tail flagging. Pups achieve adult levels of serum resistance at about 30 days of age, or 15 days before their emergence from the burrow.

The LD_{50} for the Mexican ground squirrel (*Spermophilus mexicanus*) for *C. atrox* venom is 53 mg/kg body weight, some 13 times higher than that of laboratory white mice, and these squirrels have an antihemorrhagic factor in their blood that helps neutralize the proteolytic and hemorrhagic activity of *C. atrox* venom (Martinez et al., 1999). Antihemorrhagic factors that provide protection against an important predator, *Crotalus atrox*, have also been isolated in the sera of the southern plains wood rat (*Neotoma micropus*), hispid cotton rat (*Sigmodon hispidus*), and opossum (*Didelphis virginiana*) (García and Pérez, 1984; Pérez et al., 1979). In North America, crude serum from Virginia opossum (*Didelphis virginiana*) was demonstrated to neutralize the hemorrhagic activity of HPLC (high performance liquid chromatography)-fractionated *Crotalus* venoms (Huang and Pérez, 1980; Soto et al., 1988, 1989). *Didelphis virginiana* serum from South American animals has been shown to contain an anti-bothropic complex that affords this species considerable protection against *Bothrops jararaca* (Perales et al., 1994).

Several species of of rattlesnakes have brightly colored yellow or orange tail tips at birth and are known to use caudal luring to attract prey. Kauffeld (1943b) described caudal luring in captive *C. lepidus*, and Starrett and Holycross (2000) observed this behavior in the field in a *C. lepidus* that they judged to be less than two months old. This snake raised its tail about 1 cm above the dorsum and then undulated it at 60–80 cycles per minute for about five minutes. Some *C. willardi* individuals have bright yellow tails at birth (Holycross, 2000c), and it seems likely that this species also employs caudal luring, although only anecdotal reports exist of this behavior (Greene, 1992; Schuett et al., 1984).

Rattlesnakes are often the most important snake predators on rodent populations. In northern Chihuahua, Mexico, Reynolds and Scott (1982) found that three of five snake species that were major rodent predators were rattlesnakes: *C. atrox*, *C. molossus*, and *C. scutulatus*. What sets their study apart from most others is that the investigators attempted to determine which rodent species were present in the area and their densities by trapping for 5,400 trap-nights at 18 sites. Of 351 snakes examined, 153 (43.6%) contained prey items; 22 scats also contained identifiable items. A comparison of the prey contained in individual species of rattlesnakes with the percentages of rodents trapped (Fig. 194) suggested that differences in prey composition are due to distributional differences among rattlesnakes that coincide largely with rodent habitats. *Crotalus atrox* was most abundant in mesquite-grassland, *C. molossus* was found most frequently in the mountain pediment, and *C. scutulatus* was usually encountered in tobosa grassland.

Crotalus adamanteus hunts by positioning itself in a tight coil and ambushing its prey (Timmerman, 1995); snakes may remain at the same hunting location for a day to almost a week. *Crotalus adamanteus* preys on king rails (*Rallus elegans*; Carr, 1940); wood rats (*Neotoma floridana*; Timmerman, 1995); white-footed mice (*Peromyscus* sp.; Carr, 1940, 1973; Timmerman, 1995); hispid cotton rats (*Sigmodon hispidus*; Carr, 1940; Timmerman, 1995); eastern cottontails (*Sylvilagus floridanus*; Funderburg, 1968; Timmerman, 1995); and marsh rabbits (*S. palustris*; Carr, 1940, 1973). Klauber (1972) and Ernst (1992) reported bird prey items to include towhees (*Pipilo*), bobwhite (*Colinus*), turkeys (*Meleagris*), and pileated woodpeckers (*Dryocopus*). In North

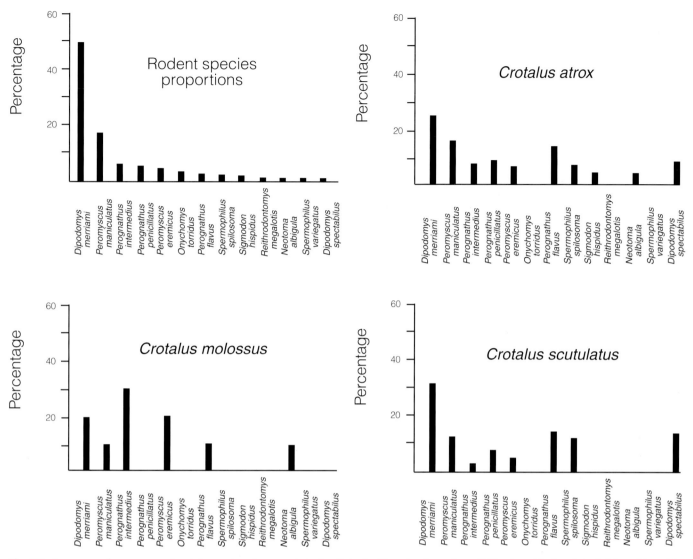

Fig. 194. Frequency of occurrence of certain species of mammals in the diet of rattlesnakes in northern Chihuahua, Mexico. Adapted from Reynolds and Scott, 1982:106–111 (figs. 2–4, 6).

Carolina *C. adamanteus* feeds on rabbits, rodents, and other small mammals (Palmer and Braswell, 1995). Grant (1970) found a rail (probably *Rallus longirostris*) in the stomach of a *C. adamanteus*. DeVault and Krochmal (2002) listed *C. adamanteus* as a scavenger on dead rabbits.

Gates (1957) reported that *Crotalus atrox* feeds on desert spiny lizards (*Sceloporus magister*), ground squirrels, mice, and rabbits. Beavers (1976), who conducted a comprehensive study on the prey of *C. atrox* in Texas, found a wide variety of food items in the gut of these snakes (Table 48), with small mammals the most important group by weight (94.8%) and frequency of occurrence (86.7%). Pocket mice (*Perognathus merriami*), spiny lizards (*Sceloporus* spp.), and banded geckos (*Coleonyx brevis*) were among the prey species removed from the stomachs of Texas *C. atrox* (Milstead et al., 1950). Vorhies (1948) reported an instance of a juvenile *C. atrox* preying on a horned lizard (*Phrynosoma solare*) that terminated fatally for both predator and prey when the horns of the lizard penetrated the esophagus of the snake and locked the two animals together. Beavers (1976) found an unidentified species of *Phrynosoma* that had been successfully ingested by *C. atrox*. Lewis (1950) found a large whiptail lizard (*Cnemidophorus* sp.) in the stomach of a *C. atrox* specimen from east of the Organ Mountains in New Mexico. Best and James

(1984) found food in four New Mexico specimens of *C. atrox*, including a fledgling horned lark (*Eremophila alpestris*), a black-throated sparrow (*Amphispiza bilineata*), an unidentified "sparrow-sized" bird, and a collared lizard (*Crotaphytus collaris*). An Arizona specimen contained a grasshopper mouse (*Onychomys torridus*; Woodin, 1953). Pisani and Stephenson (1991) found a wide variety of mammalian prey in the stomachs of adult *C. atrox* during the fall and early spring in Oklahoma, including prairie dogs (*Cynomys ludovicianus*), kangaroo rats (*Dipodomys ordii*), pocket gophers (*Geomys bursarius, Cratogeomys castanops*), voles (*Microtus ochrogaster*), woodrats (*Neotoma floridana*), pocket mice (*Perognathus hispidus, P. flavescens*), white-footed mice (*Peromyscus leucopus, P. maniculatus*), Old World rats and mice (*Rattus norvegicus, Mus* spp.), harvest mice (*Reithrodontomys megalotus*), fox squirrels (*Sciurus niger*), cotton rats (*Sigmodon hispidus*), ground squirrels (*Spermophilus spilosoma*), rabbits (*Sylvilagus floridanus*), jackrabbits (*Lepus californicus*), an unidentified mole species, and one eastern meadowlark (*Sturnella magna*). Woodbury and Woodbury (1944) found a lizard of the genus *Cnemidophorus* in the stomach of a *C. atrox* specimen from the Tehuantepec region of Oaxaca, Mexico. Grismer (2002) reported a blue-footed booby chick (*Sula nebouxii*), an introduced rat (*Rattus* sp.), and a side-blotched lizard (*Uta palmeri*)

Table 48. Prey recovered from *Crotalus atrox* in Texas.

Prey species	Number of individuals	Percent by frequency of occurrence	Percent by weight
Mammals			
Neotoma sp.	4	4.44	18.28
Sigmodon hispidus	3	3.33	7.47
Peromyscus sp.	6	6.66	4.21
Reithrodontomys sp.	8	8.88	3.63
Microtus mexicanus	1	1.11	1.16
Baiomys taylori	2	2.22	0.49
Perognathus sp.	35	38.88	17.86
Dipodomys sp.	4	4.44	6.64
Sylvilagus sp.	2	2.22	13.71
Geomys bursarius	2	2.22	9.14
Spermophilus variegatus	1	1.11	9.14
Rattus sp.	1	1.11	3.05
Unidentified small rodent	9	10.00	—
Birds			
Pipilo erythrophthalmus	1	1.11	1.31
Melospiza melodia	1	1.11	0.64
Other small sparrows	3	3.33	1.83
Unidentified passerine	2	2.22	—
Reptiles			
Phrynosoma cornutum	2	2.22	0.67
Cnemidophorus sp.	2	2.22	0.64
Eumeces brevilineatus	1	1.11	0.15

Source: Beavers, 1976.

in *C. atrox* from Baja California. DeVault and Krochmal (2002) reported a *C. atrox* scavenging a squirrel.

Grismer (2002) reported black-throated sparrows (*Amphispiza bilineata*), Isla Santa Catalina spiny lizards (*Sceloporus lineatulus*), and Isla Santa Catalina deer mice (*Peromyscus slevini*) as prey species for *C. catalinensis*.

Crotalus cerastes is a classic sit-and-wait predator, and is most often found coiled or partially buried in the sand waiting to ambush prey that happens by. This cryptic, sedentary rattlesnake has a low food intake that is balanced by a low energy expenditure (Secor, 1995; Secor and Nagy, 1994). Fowlie (1965) described the behavior of a kangaroo rat (*Dipodomys* sp.) in Sonora, Mexico, confronting a *C. cerastes*: "On finding his proximity to a buried sidewinder the rat would first tremble and shake and then commence jumping up and down in a very peculiar manner, hopping here and there in front of the snake . . . little attempt was made to flee by the rat which next began this particular and throwing maneuver, finally causing the snake to take refuge in the brush at the base of the clump." A Disney film (*The Living Desert*, 1953) includes a similar sequence of a kangaroo rat kicking sand at a sidewinder with its back legs and eventually driving the snake away (Fowlie, 1965).

Van Denburgh (1922a) found a horned lizard (*Phrynosoma platyrhinos*) in a *C. cerastes*, and Klauber (1932b, 1944) found several mice, a coachwhip (*Masticophis flagellum*), *Callisaurus draconoides*, *Cnemidophorus tigris*, *Uma notata*, *Uta stansburiana*, *Amphispiza bilineata*, California yellow warbler (*Dendroica aestiva*), *Dipodomys* sp., and *Perognathus* sp. An individual from near Borrego Springs, San Diego County, California, was found in the act of consuming a ground squirrel (*Ammospermophilus leucurus*), and several other specimens from California contained *Cnemidophorus tigris* (Cunningham, 1959). Bouskila (1995) studied the interactions between kangaroo rats (*Dipodomys deserti* and *D. merriami*) and sidewinders.

Funk (1965) examined the digestive tracts of 226 *C. cerastes* specimens from Yuma County, Arizona, and recovered food from 171 (76%), including lizards (*Callisaurus draconoides*, *Cnemidophorus tigris*, *Coleonyx variegatus*, *Crotaphytus wislizeni*, *Dipsosaurus dorsalis*, *Phrynosoma mcalli*, *Uma notata*, *Urosaurus ornatus*, and *Uta stansburiana*), snakes (*Arizona elegans*; *Chionactis occipitalis*, *Sonora semiannulata*, and *Crotalus cerastes*), birds (*Amphispiza bilineata*, *Campylorhynchus brunneicapillum*, *Chondestes grammacus*, and *Passer domesticus*), and mammals (*Ammospermophilus harrisi*, *Dipodomys deserti*, *D. merriami*, *Mus musculus*, *Neotoma albigula*, *N. lepida*, *Perognathus baileyi*, *P. longimembris*, *P. penicillatus*, *Peromyscus eremicus*, *P. maniculatus*, *Reithrodontomys megalotis*, *Spermophilus tereticaudus*, *Thomomys bottae*, and *Notiosorex crawfordi*). DeVault and Krochmal (2002) reported scavenging on *Dipodomys*.

Vipers in general are well known for their ability to ingest large prey, and a neonate *C. cerastes* perhaps holds the record among rattlesnakes for ingesting the largest prey item relative to its size. An individual from San Diego County, California, ate a *Cnemidophorus tigris* that weighed 1.72 times its own weight (Mulcahy et al., 2003). This meal may have been sufficiently large to kill the snake, which was found dead with the lizard's tail protruding from its mouth.

Crotalus durissus feeds on teiid lizards (*Ameiva ameiva*; Santos and Germano, 1996), birds, and rodents (Salomão et al., 1995; Vanzolini et al., 1980). A Guyana specimen contained a large spiny rat (Beebe, 1946). Achával et al. (1978) reported that in Uruguay this species feeds on *Cavia pamparum*. Prey species recovered from Brazilian *C. durissus* include *Cavia aperea*, *Rattus norvegicus*, and *Mus* sp. (Salomão et al., 1995). *Crotalus d. vegrandis* is a taxon of smaller snakes that reportedly feed mostly on lizards of the genera *Anolis* and *Tropidurus* (Lancini, 1966; Pifano-C. and Rodríguez-Acosta, 1996), although rodent hair has also been recovered from their gastrointestinal tracts (Pifano-C. and Rodríguez-Acosta, 1996). Smith and Radford

(1989) reported cannibalism in *Crotalus durissus cumanensis* from Colombia.

Crotalus enyo individuals of all sizes feed on smaller rodents, lizards, and centipedes, but smaller snakes feed somewhat more frequently than adults on lizards, and adults feed more frequently than juveniles on rodents (Taylor, 2001). Specific prey items found in stomachs include centipedes (*Scolopendra* spp.), valley pocket gophers (*Thomomys bottae*), pocket mice (*Chaetodipus spinatus, Chaetodipus* spp., and *Peromyscus* spp.), kangaroo rats (*Dipodomys* spp.), desert iguanas (*Dipsosaurus dorsalis*), spiny lizards (*Sceloporus* spp.), common side-blotched lizards (*Uta stansburiana*), and whiptail lizards (*Cnemidophorus* spp.).

We have examined stomachs of *C. intermedius* specimens from Guerrero that contained *Sceloporus formosus* and *S. mucronatus*, and Campbell and Armstrong (1979) reported finding scales of *Sceloporus* sp. in individuals from Guerrero and Oaxaca.

Reinert et al. (1984) reported that *C. horridus* individuals using fallen logs as ambush sites orient the head perpendicular to the long axis of the log, often resting the head on the lateral surface of the log. On four occasions an adult male *C. horridus* was observed placing itself with its head and the anterior part of the body raised in a vertical position against the base of a tree, presumably to ambush arboreal rodents (Brown and Greenberg, 1992).

Crotalus horridus is considered to be among the most arboreal of rattlesnakes (Klauber, 1972). During the course of radio-tracking *C. horridus* over three field seasons in a mixed hardwood forest in Ohio, Coupe (2001) found five of the eight females and two of the nine males that he studied off the ground at some time. Most observations of arboreality were in July and August at heights of about 0.5–5 m. Coupe (2001) suggested that arboreality in this species is associated with ecdysis or foraging for arboreal mammals such as squirrels. Sajdak (2001) reported that a young adult female *C. horridus* in Wisconsin moved from tree to bush, sometimes up to 4 m above the ground, during a period of almost four weeks. An adult *C. horridus* from Iowa was discovered while it was foraging in a tree 4.5–6 m from the ground (Sajdak and Bartz, in press). This snake captured a yellow-bellied sapsucker (*Sphyriacus varius*, Fig. 195).

Crotalus horridus feeds predominantly on small mammals and birds (Savage, 1967; Uhler et al., 1939). Uhler et al. (1939) retrieved food items from 141 specimens from Virginia and West Virginia and found that small mammals constituted 87% of the diet, with birds making up almost all of the remainder. The following species were recorded: *Peromyscus* sp., *Microtus* sp., *Pitymys pinctorum, Evotomys carolinensis, Napaeozapus insignis, Tamias striatus, Sciurus carolinensis, Glaucomys* spp., *Sylvilagus* spp., *Sorex personatus, Blarina brevicauda, Cryptotis parva*, an unidentified species of bat, yellow-billed cuckoo, brown thrasher, wood thrush, cedar waxwing, black-throated blue warbler, ovenbird, towhee, grasshopper sparrow, and remains of unidentified sparrows and warblers. Twelve *C. horridus* specimens collected in August 1946 in Virginia contained white-footed mice (*Peromyscus leucopus, P. maniculatus*), red-backed voles (*Clethrionomys gapperis*), woodland jumping mice (*Napaeozapus insignis*), bog lemmings (*Synaptomys cooperi*), chipmunks (*Tamias striatus*), and masked shrews (*Sorex cinereus*) (Smyth, 1949). Eight Kentucky *C. horridus* specimens contained *C. gapperi, T. striatus, P. maniculatus*, and *N. insignis*; a snail was also found that was almost certainly secondarily ingested (Barbour, 1950). Bush (1959) reported *Peromyscus leucopus, Sciurus carolinensis*, and songbirds from three *C. horridus* from Kentucky.

Fig. 195. *Crotalus horridus* preying on yellow-bellied sapsucker (*Sphyrapicus varius*) in Lansing Township, Allamakee County, Iowa, USA, during summer of 1981. Photograph by Lucille Mitchell.

Huheey and Stupka (1967), Linzey and Linzey (1968), and Savage (1967) identified various prey species in *C. horridus* from the smoky mountains, including mice (*Clethrionomys carolinensis, Napaeozapus insignis, Peromyscus* spp.), voles (*Microtus chrotorrhinus*) chipmunks (*Tamias striatus*), flying squirrels (*Glaucomys volans*), squirrels (*Sciurus carolinensis, Tamiasciurus* sp.), cottontails (*Sylvilagus floridanus*), weasels (*Mustela frenata*), and several species of moles and shrews. Minton (2001) reported *Sciurus niger, S. carolinensis* and an unidentified bird from the stomachs of adult *C. horridus* from Indiana.

Platt et al. (2001) reported a bobwhite (*Colinus virginianus*) and a cotton rat (*Sigmodon hispidus*) in the stomach of an adult *C. horridus* in South Carolina. Clark (1949) found rabbits to be the most common prey in Louisiana, followed closely by rats and quail (*Colinus virginianus*). Dundee and Rossman (1989) reported a fox squirrel (*Sciurus niger*) and a swamp rabbit (*Sylvilagus aquaticus*) in the stomachs of Louisiana snakes. Anderson (1965) reported a specimen from Wayne County, Missouri, that had eaten a cotton rat (*Sigmodon hispidus*) and a big brown bat (*Eptesicus fuscus*). Reinert et al. (1984) identified *Peromyscus leucopus*, *Clethrionomys gapperi*, *Tamias striatus*, *Sylvilagus floridanus*, and an unidentified bird in *C. horridus* specimens from Berks County, Pennsylvania. In southwestern Tennessee and adjacent northwestern Mississippi we have observed numerous *C. horridus* that had preyed on *Sciurus carolinensis*. Klauber (1956, and in personal communications cited in Minton, 2001) reported unusual food items recorded over the range of *C. horridus* as including rabbits, chickens, kittens, young groundhogs, raccoons, minks, turkeys, and ruffed grouse eggs. In Minnesota, Keyler and Oldfield (1992) found thirteen-lined ground squirrels (*Spermophilus tridecemlineatus*) in the diet of *C. horridus*.

Published feeding records for *C. horridus* were summarized by Clark (2002), who assessed geographic variation by comparing snakes from the southern coastal plain and mixed forest with samples from the northern deciduous forest. In the north, voles (*Microtus*), chipmunks (*Tamias*), jumping mice (*Napaeozapus*), and red-backed voles (*Clethrionomys*) formed a significant part of the diet; snakes from the southern part of the range preyed heavily on cotton rats (*Sigmodon*), cottontail rabbits (*Sylvilagus*), golden mice (*Ochrotomys*), and house mice (*Mus*). In the total sample of literature and museum records consisting of 589 instances of predation, mammals were the most frequent prey (91.1%), followed by birds (7.2%), reptiles (1.2%), and amphibians (0.3%).

Crotalus lepidus also preys on a variety of organisms. Grasshoppers, insect larvae, *Syrrhophus marnockii*, *Cnemidophorus gularis*, *Phrynosoma cornutum*, *Urosaurus ornatus*, and *Gyalopion canum* were found in snakes from Terrell County, Texas (Milstead et al., 1950), and a captive specimen ate several *Virginia striatula*. Conant (1955) found an unspecified lizard, a large grasshopper, and a few caterpillars in the stomach of a Texas specimen. Conant (1975) also cited salamanders as being part of the diet, but that report is based on Falck's (1940) report of captive feedings. Dickerman and Painter (2001) reported a *C. lepidus* specimen from Jeff Davis County, Texas, that contained a *Phrynosoma hernandesi*; and Marr (1944) found a *Sceloporus poinsettii* in a snake from the same county. Under captive conditions, *C. lepidus* may sometimes be cannibalistic, with littermates eating each other or a mother consuming her young (Williamson, 1971).

About 70% of the fecal samples of *C. lepidus* that Beaupre (1995b) examined in the Big Bend region of Texas contained reptile remains, and 33% contained evidence of mammalian prey. He identified lizards (*Cnemidophorus* spp., *Cophosaurus texanus*, *Sceloporus merriami*, *Urosaurus ornatus*), rodents (*Perognathus* spp., *Peromyscus* spp., *Dipodomys* spp., *Sigmodon* spp.), and arthropods. In wild-caught specimens of *C. lepidus* from Arizona, B. Campbell (1934) recorded *Sceloporus jarrovi*; Woodin (1953) found a mouse (*Sceloporus jarrovii*) and what was probably a *Sceloporus clarki*. Kauffeld (1943a) found lizard remains in *C. lepidus* feces from the same area. Barker (1991) examined scats from 10 specimens of *C. lepidus* from the Sierra San Luis, Sonora, Mexico, and found lizard scales in 5 and centipede parts in 6 (only 1 specimen had both items). Armstrong and Murphy (1979) reported lizards of the genus *Sceloporus* as the main prey of *C. lepidus*. A *Norops nebulosus* was found in a juvenile *C. l. maculosus* by Bryson et al. (2002a), who also found a large, apparently envenomed *Sceloporus jarrovii* near an adult *C. l. maculosus* and hairs from an unidentified small mammal in the scats of another specimen.

Holycross et al. (2002b) studied the feeding habits of *C. lepidus klauberi* and provided a thorough analysis of the diet of this species. In a sample of *C. l. klauberi* mostly from the northern part of the range, lizards were the most common prey (55.4% by frequency), followed by scolopendromorph centipedes (28.3%), mammals (13.8%), birds (1.9%), and snakes (0.6%). The most common genus of lizard was *Sceloporus* (82.% of lizards overall), with *S. jarrovii* constituting 74.2% of the lizard records.

Crotalus mitchellii apparently feeds on lizards and mammals. Klauber (1972) recorded zebratail lizards (*Callisaurus draconoides*), whiptail lizards (*Cnemidophorus maximus*, *C. tigris*), western skinks (*Eumeces skiltonianus*), chuckwallas (*Sauromalus ater*, *S. hispidus*), spiny lizards (*Sceloporus* spp.), banded rock lizards (*Streptosaurus mearnsi*), and side-blotched lizards (*Uta stansburiana*) from *C. mitchellii*. Mammalian prey included white-footed mice (*Peromyscus crinitus*, *P. maniculatus*, *P. truei*), ground squirrels (*Ammospermophilus leucurus*, *Spermophilus* spp.), kangaroo rats (*Dipodomys agilis*), pocket mice (*Perognathus* spp.), and cottontail rabbits (*Sylvilagus auduboni*). Klauber (1972) also recorded *C. mitchellii* feeding on passerine birds (probably goldfinches, *Spinus tristis*). Scavenging on a ground squirrel was reported by DeVault and Krochmal (2002).

Crotalus molossus is known to prey on Gila monsters (*Heloderma suspectum*; Funk, 1964); white-throated wood rats (*Neotoma albigula*; Klauber, 1972); white-ankled mice (Gehlbach, 1957), including *Peromyscus pectoralis* (Klauber, 1972; Milstead et al., 1950); and western bluebirds (*Sialia mexicana*; Yarrow, 1875).

Crotalus ravus feeds on crickets (*Stenopelmatus* spp.), anurans, lizards (*Barisia imbricata*, *Sceloporus* spp., *Eumeces* spp.), and rodents (Campbell and Armstrong, 1979). Prey species reported by Sánchez-Herrera (1980) include lizards (*Sceloporus grammicus*, *S. megalepidurus*) and mammals (*Microtus mexicanus*, *Mus musculus*).

In northern Idaho, *C. o. oreganus* feeds from mid-April to early October; except for gravid females, which feed from early spring to early August and then again in the fall after parturition (Wallace and Diller, 1990). Juvenile *C. oreganus* feed on a wide variety of lizards while adults feed more frequently on mammals such as mice, rats, squirrels, pocket gophers, and small rabbits (Klauber, 1972). A specimen of *C. o. lutosus* collected in eastern Nevada contained a subadult ground squirrel (*Spermophilus mollis*; Hall, 1929). Johnson (1995) reported that *C. o. oreganus* in Washington feeds on *Microtus*, Merrill's song sparrow, and *Citellus*. Parham (1937) reported an individual of *C. oreganus* that was killed as it was swallowing a woodchuck (*Marmota*), which judging from the photograph was several times larger than the snake's head. Cunningham (1959) reported a number of prey species for *C. oreganus* from California, including *Sceloporus graciosus*, *S. occidentalis*, willow woodpecker (*Dryobates pubescens*), brush rabbit (*Sylvilagus bachmani*), and pika (*Ochotona princeps*); one rattlesnake was encountered while it was eating a California ground squirrel (*Spermophilus beecheyi*) that had been killed on the road. Grismer (2002) observed a *C. o. helleri* in Baja California feeding on a young California ground squirrel (*Spermophilus beecheyi*) and reported another that contained an arboreal salamander (*Aneides lugubris*) in its stomach. On Isla Sur of the Islas de los Coronados, *C. o. caliginus* preys mostly on various species of lizards (Klauber, 1949b; Zweifel, 1952). A neonate *C. o. cerberus* contained an adult spiny lizard (*Sceloporus undulatus*), with a prey/predator mass ratio of 1.138 (Schuett et al., 2002).

Fitch and Twining (1946) investigated the feeding habits of *C. o. oreganus* in Madera County, California, and found that California ground squirrels (*Spermophilus beecheyi*), Heermann's kangaroo rats (*Dipodomys heermanni*), California voles (*Microtus californicus*), dusky-footed woodrats (*Neotoma fuscipes*), white-footed mice (*Peromyscus* spp.), pocket mice (*Perognathus* spp.), valley pocket gophers (*Thomomys bottae*), desert cottontail rabbits (*Sylvilagus auduboni*), brown towhees (*Pipilo fuscus*), California quail (*Lophortyx californica*), side-blotched lizards (*Uta stansburiana*), western fence lizards (*Sceloporus occidentalis*), Colorado checkered whiptails (*Cnemidophorus tesselatus*), and western spadefoot toads (*Spea hammondii*) constituted the diet of that population. Young snakes less than a year old fed more frequently on reptiles and amphibians than did adult snakes but also ate rodents. Squirrels and rabbits constituted about 75% of the prey taken by the largest group of rattlesnakes (72 cm or larger TL). Ground squirrels were the most frequently taken prey and in every instance were immature individuals of the season's brood. Fitch and Twining (1946) observed rattlesnakes on several occasions foraging and feeding by day. On one occasion they saw a rattlesnake seize and retain a California quail, and on several other occasions they saw rattlesnakes strike at ground squirrels. These rattlesnakes appeared to forage frequently in the vicinity of squirrel burrow systems, which also provided a hiding place, and were most successful preying on young, naive squirrels. Snakes with food in the stomach were found from March to November. Fitch and Twining (1946) suggested that a single meal secured in the spring was probably sufficient to maintain the snake in good condition, without its having to feed again, throughout the summer. Females remained mostly underground in burrows from about July onward and must have depended on food taken during the spring.

Cotalus o. oreganus in northern Idaho ate eight species of mammals, one lizard, and one bird (Wallace and Diller, 1990). Voles (*Microtus montanus* and *M. longicaudus*), deer mice (*Peromyscus maniculatus*), and cottontail rabbits (*Sylvilagus nuttallii*) made up about 92% of the biomass ingested (80% of the prey by frequency). Juvenile snakes less than one year of age fed exclusively on shrews (*Sorex vagrans*). Other species taken by *C. o. oreganus* in smaller numbers were *Thomomys talpoides*, *Tamias amoenus*, *Reithrodontomys megalotis*, *Eumeces skiltonianus*, and *Melospiza melodia*.

The diet of a population of *C. o. oreganus* from southern British Columbia, Canada, was studied over a three-year period by Macartney (1989). These snakes were active from late March to early October and fed most frequently during June–August. Rodents (91% by occurrence), shrews (5%), and birds (4%) made up the diet. Gravid females usually did not move about much during the summer and did not feed, thus reducing their exposure to predation and their energy expenditure during gestation. Prey species included northwestern chipmunks (*Tamias amoenus*), yellow-bellied marmots (*Marmota flaviventris*), montane voles (*Microtus montanus*), meadow voles (*M. pennsylvanicus*), bushy-tailed woodrats (*Neotoma cinerea*), Great Basin pocket mice (*Perognathus parvus*), deer mice (*Peromyscus maniculatus*), red squirrels (*Tamiasciurus hudsonicus*), northern pocket gophers (*Thomomys talpoides*), cinereus shrews (*Sorex cinereus*), common bushtits (*Psaltriparus minimus*), European starlings (*Sturnus vulgaris*), dark-eyed juncos (*Junco hyemalis*), and rufous-sided towhees (*Pipilo erythrophthalmus*).

A juvenile *C. o. oreganus* (29.7 cm TL) from Solano County, California, contained a *Sceloporus occidentalis* with a mass about 76% that of the snake (Pauly and Benard, 2002). Although it was still alive, the rattlesnake had recently sustained a mortal body wound. Pauly and Benard suggested that the ingestion of the large meal had rendered the snake incapable of escaping the attack of a predator.

Juvenile Townsend ground squirrels (*Spermophilus townsendi*) constituted 81% of the ingested biomass of *C. oreganus lutosus* in the Snake River Birds of Prey Area of southwestern Idaho (Diller and Johnson, 1988). Other prey ingested, in descending order of biomass, included mountain cottontails (*Sylvilagus nuttallii*), deer mice (*Peromyscus maniculatus*), Ord's kangaroo rats (*Dipodomys ordii*), Great Basin pocket mice (*Perognathus parvus*), montane voles (*Microtus montanus*), and house mice (*Mus musculus*), as well as antelope ground squirrels (*Ammospermophilus leucurus*), desert woodrats (*Neotoma lepida*), western whiptails (*Cnemidophorus tigris*), desert horned lizards (*Phrynosoma platyrhinos*), and Great Basin spadefoot toads (*Spea intermontana*) (Diller and Wallace, 1996). A *C. o. lutosus* was reported to have scavenged a mountain cottontail (*Sylvilagus nuttallii*; DeVault and Krochmal, 2002).

Although California ground squirrels are important in the diet of *C. oreganus*, these squirrels often probe at and otherwise harass rattlesnakes, apparently as an antisnake defense. It is thought that this behavior might facilitate snake species discrimination or might interfere with the snake's hunting activities, thus helping protect young ground squirrels (Coss et al., 1993).

Crotalus pricei feeds on *Sceloporus jarrovii* (Gloyd, 1937; Kauffeld, 1943a, Klauber, 1972; Woodin, 1953) and *S. poinsettii* (Armstrong and Murphy, 1979). Gumbart and Sullivan (1990) observed *C. pricei* feeding on nestlings of the ground-nesting yellow-eyed junco (*Junco phaeonotus*) on several occasions. The most comprehensive studies of the feeding habits of *C. pricei* are Prival, 2000, and Prival et al., 2002. The authors, who studied a population in the Chiricahua Mountains of southeastern Arizona, found that 45% of the males and 23% of the females contained obvious food items in their stomachs during July–September 1998. Prey species, as determined from stomach and fecal samples, included mountain spiny lizards (*Sceloporus jarrovii*), a rattlesnake (a juvenile *C. pricei*), brush mice (probably *Peromyscus boylii*), a woodrat (probably *Neotoma mexicana*), and a bird (probably a canyon wren, *Catherpes mexicanus*). Spiny lizards were present in about three-fourths of the snakes containing identifiable prey, and rodents were present in about one-third, with some snakes containing more than a single food item.

Crotalus pusillus feeds on *Barisia imbricata*, *Sceloporus bulleri*, and *Eptesicus fuscus* (Duellman, 1961). Armstrong and Murphy (1979) reported an orthopteran in the stomach of a *C. pusillus* specimen.

Crotalus ruber feeds on lizards (*Cnemidophorus tigris*, *Ctenosaura hemilopha*), kangaroo rats, woodrats, squirrels, and small rabbits (Grismer, 2002; Klauber, 1972). Tevis (1943) observed the diurnal foraging activities of an adult red rattlesnake in Baja California. The snake slowly investigated antelope squirrel (*Ammospermophilus leucurus*) burrows by inserting its head into the entrance for about 10 seconds and flicking its tongue against the walls. When the snake entered one of the burrows, three squirrels escaped using another exit hole. Eventually the snake coiled near a burrow with its neck positioned in an S-shaped coil and its head facing a hole. When a young squirrel tried to run into the burrow, the snake struck, retaining the animal in its jaws until it died. After swallowing its prey, the snake continued to investigate squirrel burrows, sometimes entering a burrow and remaining underground for five or more minutes. Later in the afternoon (1645) the snake was again seen entering a burrow where it presumably remained all night. When the snake was located at 1115 the next day, its considerably distended body indicated that it had apparently killed and eaten other young squirrels that had been seen in the vicinity the day before.

Adults of *C. simus* in Guatemala feed on rodents, ground-nesting birds, and black iguanas (*Ctenosaura similis*); juveniles feed on lizards, including *Cnemidophorus*, and small mice (Campbell, 1998). Solórzano (2004) reported that *C. simus* feeds principally on rodents and listed *Liomys salvini* and *Sigmodon hispidus* among the prey species.

Crotalus scutulatus scutulatus feeds on ground squirrels (*Spermophilus spilosoma*; Plummer, 2000). In Chihuahua, Mexico, Reynolds and Scott (1982) identified, in descending order of frequency, kangaroo rats (*Dipodomys*), pocket mice (*Perognathus*), white-footed mice (*Peromyscus*), ground squirrels (*Spermophilus*), and rabbits (*Sylvilagus, Lepus*) as prey. Other prey items recorded for this species include centipedes (Reynolds, 1978); *Coleonyx brevis* (Tennant, 1984); and various other lizards, snakes, and amphibians (Ernst, 1992).

Crotalus tigris is known to feed on lizards such as *Cnemidophorus* (Ortenburger and Ortenburger, 1926), but it also feeds on mammals such as kangaroo rats (*Dipodomys*), woodrats (*Neotoma*), pocket mice (*Perognathus*), deer mice (*Peromyscus*), and pocket gophers (*Thomomys*) (Fowlie, 1965; Klauber, 1972; Stebbins, 1954, 1985).

Campbell (1988b) reported on a *C. transversus* specimen that contained an adult *Sceloporus grammicus*, and Klauber (1972) found lizard scales in the stomach of a specimen. In captivity *C. transversus* was induced to eat various species of lizards with which it is sympatric: *Eumeces copei, Sceloporus grammicus, S. mucronatus*, and *S. aeneus* (Camarillo and Campbell, 2002).

Crotalus tortugensis feeds on deer mice (*Peromyscus*; Van Denburgh and Slevin, 1921c; Klauber, 1972).

Crotalus totonacus feeds on rats (*Neotoma* spp.) and squirrels (*Sciurus alleni*; Martin, 1958).

One *C. triseriatus* from Morelos contained a frog, and another had a *Neotomodon alstoni* in its stomach (Davis and Smith, 1953). Klauber (1972) reported lizards, mammals, crickets, and salamanders from this species. Uribe-Peña et al. (1999) found *Sceloporus grammicus microlepidotus* in the stomach of a specimen.

Crotalus viridis eats spadefoot toads (*Scaphiopus* spp.; Stabler, 1948), fence lizards (*Sceloporus undulatus*; Chiszar et al., 1993), and voles (*Microtus montanus*; Genter, 1984). In southwestern South Dakota, *C. viridis* feeds on *Microtus* spp., and *Phrynosoma douglassii* (Hamilton, 1950). Several individuals from Montana contained *Peromyscus maniculatus* (Mosimann and Rabb, 1952). In the Sandhill region of Nebraska *C. viridis* eats black-tailed jackrabbits (*Lepus californicus*), harvest mice (*Reithrodontomys*), pocket gophers (*Geomys*), and ground squirrels (*Spermophilus*), but Ord's kangaroo rats (*Dipodomys ordii*) constitute about 66% of the diet of adult snakes (Holycross, 1995). Genter (1984) reported an incidence of cannibalism in which an adult female (84.2 cm) ingested a juvenile (26.4 cm). Gloyd (1933b) found a *C. viridis* that regurgitated a conspecific that may have been dead when eaten.

Barker (1991) examined the scats from 12 specimens of *C. willardi obscurus* from the Sierra San Luis, Sonora, Mexico, and found lizard scales only in 1 snake, lizard scales and rodent hair

in 1 snake, and rodent hair only in 8 snakes. One of the most thorough summaries of feeding habits available for a small montane rattlesnake is Holycross et al.'s (2002a) report for *C. willardi obscurus*. These authors found that juveniles (less than 35 cm) fed mostly on lizards (57.1% prey frequency) or centipedes (33.3%), whereas adults (35 cm or more) preyed mostly on small mammals (62.3%), lizards (26.4%), and small passerine birds (9.4%) (Fig. 196). Of the mammals consumed, the brush mouse (*Peromyscus boylii*) accounted for 64.9%; spiny lizards (*Sceloporus* spp., especially *S. jarrovii*) were the most common lizards eaten (68.4%). *Crotalus willardi* has also been reported to feed on centipedes (Fowlie, 1965), Wilson's warbler (*Wilsonia pusilla*; Marshall, 1957), and brush mice (*Peromyscus boylii*; Klauber, 1972; Woodin, 1953). Holycross et al. (2002a) reported several instances of predation on southern pocket gophers (*Thomomys umbrinus*) by *C. willardi* in New Mexico and Arizona; and listed centipedes (*Scolopendra* spp.), Townsend's solitaire (*Myadestes townsendi*), an unidentified bird, shrews (*Sorex* spp.), pocket mice (*Perognathus* spp.), white-footed mice (*Peromyscus* spp.), harvest mice (*Reithrodontomys* spp.), spiny lizards (*Sceloporus* spp.), and whiptail lizards (*Cnemidophorus* spp.) in the diet of *C. willardi obscurus*. Other records of *C. willardi* prey include fence lizards (*Sceloporus* spp.) and alligator lizards (*Elgaria kingii*) reported by Klauber (1972), a centipede reported by Fowlie (1965), small rodents (Kauffeld, 1943a; Klauber, 1949c; Van Denburgh, 1922b), a white-footed mouse (*Peromyscus* spp.) reported by Martin (1975a), and a pocket gopher (*Thomomys umbrinus*) reported by Bryson and Holycross (2001).

Venom. Geographic variation in venom composition has been reported for practically every widespread species of rattlesnake on which comparative studies have been made. *Crotalus atrox* venom differs geographically in lethality, protease activity, hemorrhagic activity, and presence of Mojave toxin (Minton and Weinstein, 1986). Venom from snakes in the northeastern part

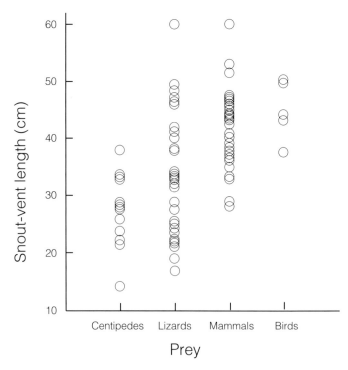

Fig. 196. Prey category versus size for *Crotalus willardi obscurus* (*n* = 95). Adapted from Holycross, et al., 2002a:244 (fig. 1).

of the species' range has the lowest lethality and highest protease activity, whereas venom in the southwestern part of the range has the highest lethality and lowest protease activity. Hemorrhagic activity was slightly higher in the northern samples examined by Minton and Weinstein (1986), and the presence of Mojave toxin was detected only in two samples from Arizona and one from west Texas. Mojave toxin is present in the venom of some populations or subspecies of particular species of *Crotalus* but not others (Glenn and Straight, 1985a). Bober et al. (1988) found the amount of myotoxin *a* in the venoms of rattlesnakes to vary by geographical region.

Because of the extreme variation in adult body size attained by different populations of *C. durissus*, the composition of the diet—and thus the venom—may likewise be predicted to vary. Early studies of the venom of South American rattlesnakes confirmed dramatic differences in venom composition and potency in various populations. Vellard (1938b, 1943) discovered that some of the more southern populations (Argentina, Paraguay, and southeastern Brazil) had highly neurotoxic venom that produced relatively slight necrosis or hemotoxic activity, whereas more northerly populations (northeastern Brazil and Venezuela) had strongly hemotoxic venom capable of doing considerable damage to the blood and producing severe necrosis. A specific toxin is present in the venom of rattlesnakes from southern Brazil and Argentina but absent from snakes from northern and central Brazil (J. M. Gonçalves, 1956; Schenberg, 1959). When the toxicity of the venom from Colombia and Guyana populations was compared with that of rattlesnakes from southeastern Brazil, the latter group was found to be significantly more toxic (Criley, *in* Allen and Neill, 1957). Santoro et al. (1999) found that the specimens of *C. d. cascavella*, *C. d. collilineatus*, and *C. d. terrificus* they examined had quite similar venoms except for minor differences that included a higher clotting activity in *terrificus* and a higher phospholipase A_2 (PLA_2) activity in *cascavella* compared with *collilineatus*. The venom of *C. durissus* in Brazil may be either white or yellow. The yellow venom contains no crotamine, while the white venom of some snakes, but not all, contains this substance. Crotamine-positive venoms appear to be more frequently encountered in the interior of São Paulo State than in the coastal zone of Brazil (Schenberg, 1960). Not all populations of *C. durissus* contain convulxin in their venom (Prado-Franceschi and Brazil, 1981).

Samples of venom from throughout the range of *C. lepidus klauberi* showed extreme variation in lethal toxicity, Mojave toxin content, hemorrhagic and enzyme activities, and electrophoretic profiles (Glenn and Straight, 1987). This taxon is distributed as a series of allopatric montane populations, and the authors suggested that these habitat and diet differences would make this subspecies an excellent model for studying the relationship between environment and venom composition.

Two very different venom types have been identified in *Crotalus scutulatus* in Arizona (Glenn and Straight, 1978). Venom A contains Mojave toxin, which is a phospholipase A_2 complex toxin, but does not have specific proteolytic and hemorrhagic activities. Venom B does have specific proteolytic and hemorrhagic activities but lacks Mojave toxin (Glenn and Straight, 1989; Glenn et al., 1983). The toxicities of these two kinds of venoms are markedly different: the lethal toxicity (i.p. LD_{50}) of venom A in mice is 0.22–0.46 mg/kg, whereas these values are 2.0–6.0 mg/kg for venom B (Glenn et al., 1983). Snakes having venom B are restricted mostly to central Arizona in a region from east and northeast of Phoenix southward to near Tucson (Wilkinson et al., 1991). The two venom types overlap in some

areas, producing a third venom type, venom A + B (Wilkinson et al., 1991). There do not appear to be any morphological features that distinguish individuals of a particular venom race (Glenn et al., 1983). The venom from a female *C. scutulatus scutulatus* from Pima County, Arizona, and her 6 offspring contained hemorrhagic toxin but not Mojave toxin (e.g., they had venom B), but the venom of a female from El Paso County, Texas, contained both hemorrhagic and Mojave toxins (venom A + B), and 5 of 10 of her offspring had venoms with both toxins, 2 had only hemorrhagic toxin, and 3 contained neither toxin.

Juvenile specimens of *C. atrox* from north Texas had more lethal venom than adults from all other samples from throughout the range, but had a low protease activity (Minton and Weinstein, 1986). Within about 15 months venom from these juvenile snakes had declined about fivefold and the protease activity was similar to that of adults. Minton (1975) examined the venom of an individual of *C. atrox* over a 19-year period and found that the toxicity and quantity of venom decreased with age.

Mackessy (1988), who studied ontogenetic differences in the venom of *C. oreganus helleri* and *C. o. oreganus*, found that protease activity increased significantly with size in both taxa, whereas phospholipase A_2 activity and venom toxicity decreased significantly with size. Venom of adult *C. o. oreganus* was about five times higher than that of juveniles in protease (caseinolytic) activity (Mackessy, 1993). The highly toxic venom of juveniles facilitates killing of lizards, their main prey. Snakes in excess of 50 cm feed almost exclusively on mammals, and their venom is less toxic than that of juveniles and has a high protease activity that aids in the digestion of their prey. The venom of adult *C. o. oreganus* has metalloprotease activity that contributes to necrosis, but this protease is absent from the venom of juveniles (Mackessy, 1996).

Juveniles of *C. simus* from Costa Rica produce venom with higher lethality and indirect hemolytic activity than adult snakes, and their venom is devoid of hemorrhagic and edematigenous activities; venom from adults has higher proteolytic, hemorrhagic, and edematigenous activities (Lomonte et al., 1983).

Minton and Weinstein (1984) studied the protease activity and lethal toxicity of several poorly known rattlesnakes. They found that the venom of *C. pricei* has a high lethal potency and produces more serious effects than might be expected from a small rattlesnake; the venoms of *C. pricei* and *C. tigris* lack protease activity; and among rattlesnakes *C. tigris* has the highest and *C. pusillus* the lowest lethal toxicity.

Four *C. horridus* in 66 feeding sequences most frequently directed their strikes to the thoracic region of mice (29%), with the lumbar region (20%) and neck (17%) being the next most frequent sites of venom injection (Minton, 1969).

Rattlesnakes are not completely immune to their own venom (Gloyd and Bevan, 1946), although self-inflicted bites or bites by conspecifics often do not result in death. On the other hand, there is experimental and anecdotal evidence that ophiophagus snakes of the genera *Lampropeltis* and *Drymarchon* are largely immune to the bites of pitvipers, on which they sometimes feed (Keegan and Andrews, 1942).

Swanson (1946) performed a series of experiments to determine the effects of pitviper venoms on conspecifics and other species. Unfortunately, these experiments were not conducted under a rigid protocol and were not standardized with regard to body weight, amount of venom injected, or location of injection, so only a somewhat vague notion of the immunity/susceptibility of snakes to certain venoms can be deduced. He found that 4 of 5 *C. horridus* injected with *C. horridus* venom survived, but *Agkistrodon contortrix* and *Sistrurus catenatus* injected with the venom died. The venom of *A. contortrix* was lethal to *A. piscivorus*, *S. catenatus*, *C. horridus*, and some, but not all, conspecifics. Four of 6 *A. piscivorus* injected with conspecific venom died, and all of the *A. contortrix* tested also died. A single individual each of *A. contortrix* and *S. catenatus* was injected with *S. catenatus* venom, resulting in the death of the former but not the latter. Of the 26 *C. o. lutosus* injected with conspecific venom, 15 died (Sanders, *in* Woodbury et al., 1951).

Because of the powerful toxins they can deliver, venomous snakes in general, and especially rattlesnakes, have long been sources of presumed potent cures and remedies in folk medicine. Minton and Minton (1991) described vendors of dried snake carcasses along the road near Entronque Huizache in San Luis Potosí, Mexico (Fig. 197). The powder made from these dried specimens is used to treat skin and kidney diseases and for the prevention and treatment of cancer. The authors suggested that the practice of selling dried rattlesnakes in the Huizache area may have begun as recently as 1987, but we noticed dried rattlesnakes for sale in the area some 20 years prior to that. The use of rattlesnake products in folk medicine is very widespread in some areas. *Crotalus simus* has been relentlessly persecuted in most of Guatemala (Fig. 198) and has become rare. One-third of the Hispanic patients surveyed in hospitals in El Paso, Texas, admitted that they or a close relative had used rattlesnake powder (*polvo de cascabel*) or some other product from rattlesnakes (Bhatt et al., 1988).

Predators. Humans are the most significant destroyers of rattlesnakes. Other predators include snakes such as kingsnakes (*Lampropeltis*), coachwhips (*Masticophis*), indigo snakes (*Drymarchon*), and racers (*Coluber*); birds such as hawks, eagles, owls, roadrunners, and ravens; and mammals such as coyotes, foxes, wildcats, badgers, skunks, and pigs (Keegan, 1944; Klauber, 1927, 1936b, 1971, 1972). Certain hooved animals such as deer, pronghorns, sheep, goats, horses, and cattle have been observed killing rattlesnakes by stamping them to death (Klauber, 1971). Even bullfrogs (*Rana catesbeiana*), which have

been introduced into the lower Colorado River Valley, have been known to eat juvenile *Crotalus atrox* (Clarkson and DeVos, 1986).

Armstrong and Murphy (1979) described an encounter between *C. totonacus* and an ocelot (*Felis pardalis*) that resulted in severe injuries to the snake. The scat of an ocelot from the state of São Paulo, Brazil, contained remains of *C. durissus* (Wang, 2002). Cunningham (1959) reported that field notes associated with a *C. mitchellii pyrrhus* from California read "bobcat was driven off the still wiggling snake. It apparently consumed the anterior part of the body." Stebbins (1954) reported that a gray fox (*Urocyon cinereoargenteus*) ate a *C. mitchellii*.

Although certain birds of prey apparently feed regularly on rattlesnakes, this behavior is not without risk to the predators. Based on the hemorrhage and gangrenous necrosis present in three dead hawks, as well as their proximity to venomous snakes, Heckel et al. (1994) concluded that the death of these birds was probably attributable to snakebite. Two dead immature red-tailed hawks (*Buteo jamaicensis*) were found next to partially eaten venomous snakes, and a dead adult Cooper's hawk (*Accipiter cooperi*) was adjacent to a den containing a water moccasin (*Agkistrodon piscivorus*) and an eastern diamondback rattlesnake (*Crotalus adamanteus*). Holycross et al. (2001) retrieved a portion of a radio-transmitter-implanted *C. willardi obscurus* in the Animas Mountains of New Mexico that had been killed and partially eaten by probably either a red-tailed hawk (*Buteo jamaicensis*) or a Mexican spotted owl (*Strix occidentalis lucida*).

Graves (1989b) made three separate observations of ants of the genus *Formica* eating small individuals of *C. viridis viridis* and recorded another instance of many ants biting a *C. v. viridis*, with a column of ants traveling between the snake and an ant mound. He concluded that ant predation on small rattlesnakes may not be uncommon, but he did not consider the possibility that these snakes may have been impaired by recent surgeries for the implantation of radio transmitters.

Cobb and Peterson (1999) described injuries sustained by two *C. o. lutosus* that were found dead at entrances to hibernacula. Bushy-tailed woodrats (*Neotoma cinerea*) may have been able to successfully attack the snakes because low temperatures rendered them lethargic. Alternatively, they may have died of

Fig. 197. Children selling wildlife products near Entronque Huizache, San Luis Potosí, Mexico, 9 May 1999. Note dried snake carcasses hanging in the background. Photograph by Eric N. Smith.

Fig. 198. Guatemalan vendors of natural remedies. Dried rattlesnakes are in front of the man holding the *Boa constrictor*, and snake oil is to his right. Photograph taken in Guatemala City, December 1998, by Eric N. Smith.

other causes (they had recently been implanted with radio transmitters) and been scavenged by the rodents. The venom glands of both dead snakes had been selectively targeted for consumption; one snake was missing both glands, and the other was missing one gland. Basey (1988) listed black bears (*Ursus arctos*), common ravens (*Corvus corax*), and red-tailed hawks (*Buteo jamaicensis*) as predators of *C. oreganus*.

Confirmed reptilian predators of *C. cerastes* include other sidewinders (Funk, 1965) and coachwhips (*Masticophis flagellum*; Secor, 1994b). Other predators on *C. cerastes* listed by Secor (1994b) are American kestrels (*Falco sparvarius*), roadrunners (*Geococcyx californicus*), loggerhead shrikes (*Lanius ludovicianus*), possibly red-tailed hawks (*Buteo jamaicensis*), great horned owls (*Bubo virginianus*), ravens (*Corvus corax*), coyotes (*Canis latrans*), and kit foxes (*Vulpes macrotis*). We have seen jabiru (*Jabiru mycteria*, a stork) preying on small *C. durissus* in the Llanos of Colombia. In Guanacaste, Costa Rica, we observed *Drymarchon corais* preying on *C. simus*. Also, we have found headless bodies of *C. simus* that may have been decapitated by birds of prey. The laughing falcon (*Herpetotheres cachinnans*) is common in this region.

Cowles (1938) was apparently the first to report the defense postures assumed by rattlesnakes in response to potential predators. The response of *C. cerastes* and *C. o. oreganus* in the presence of a California kingsnake (*Lampropeltis getula californiae*) was to form a broad loop involving one-fourth to one-third of the body, which was elevated off the ground. At the approach of the kingsnake, the rattlesnake would strike, straightening out the body loop and exerting considerable force. Kingsnakes struck by these blows were often intimidated and retreated from the rattlesnake. Cowles termed this behavior in rattlesnakes the "body blow" response. Species of *Lampropeltis* can effectively neutralize the venoms of many pitvipers, including rattlesnakes, and the ratsnake (*Elaphe guttata*) also shows this ability to a lesser degree (Weinstein et al., 1992).

Various species of rattlesnakes have been shown to be repelled by odors emanating from kingsnakes, from spotted skunks (*Spilogale phenax*), and by human (*Homo sapiens*) body odor (Cowles and Phelan, 1958).

Parasites. Tongue worms, or linguatulids, are found in many wild populations of rattlesnakes. Other common internal parasites include pentastomid worms, tapeworms, and nematodes. Klauber (1956) reported cestodes of the genus *Porocephalus* in rattlesnakes from near Tucson, Arizona. The intermediate hosts of the pentastomid genus *Porocephalus* are rodents. After the rodent is ingested by a snake, the excysted nymphs migrate through the tissues of the rodent into the stomach of the snake and then into the body cavity, where they remain for up to 16 days before penetrating the lumen of the snake's lung (Buckle et al. 1997; Riley, 1981). Rattlesnakes apparently are paratenic (transport) hosts for *Mesocestoides* spp. (Bolette, 1997a) and oligacanthorhynchid cystacanths (Bolette, 1997b). Species of the ascarid genus *Ophidascaris* usually are transmitted through amphibian intermediate hosts (Telford, 1971). Several species of ticks and mites have been taken from rattlesnakes. The mite *Ophionyssus natricis* is mostly found on captive reptiles and may have an Old World origin (Camin, 1953). Chiggers of the genus *Trombicula* may damage the loreal pit and stimulate ecdysis (Loomis, 1951). Particular species of rattlesnakes and the species of parasites reported to inhabit them are listed below.

Crotalus adamanteus: *Isospora dirumpens* (Bovee, 1962); *Kiricephalus coarctatus* (Pentastomida) (Hill, 1935); *Porocephalus crotali* (Pentastomida) (Penn, 1942; Riley and Self, 1979); *Amblyomma dissimile* (tick) (Bishopp and Trembley, 1945).

Crotalus atrox: *Haemogregarina digueti* (Protozoa) (Roudabush and Coatney, 1937); *Sarcocystis* spp. (Apicomplexa) (McAllister et al., 1995); *Porocephalus crotali* (Pentastomida) (Buckle et al., 1997; Penn, 1942; Riley, 1981; Riley and Self, 1979; Stephenson and Pisani, 1991); *Pachysentis canicola* (Acanthocephala) (Bolette, 1997a); tetrathyridia of *Mesocestoides* spp. (Cestoidea) (Bolette, 1997a); *Oochoristica gracewileyi* (Loewen, 1947b); *Entonyssus ewingi* (lung mites, Entonyssidae) (Hubbard, 1939). In southeastern New Mexico *C. atrox* was found to have the following helminths: *Oochoristica osheroffi*, *Mesocestoides* spp., *Hexametra boddaertii*, *Kalicephalus inermis*, larvae of *Physaloptera* spp. and *Physocephalus* spp., and various cystacanths, none of which are unique to *C. atrox* (Goldberg et al., 2002).

Crotalus basiliscus: *Porocephalus crotali* (Pentastomida) (Klauber, 1956); *P. basiliscus* (Riley and Self, 1979).

Crotalus cerastes: *Hexametra boddaertii* (Nematoda) (Bursey et al., 1995); *Thubunacea cnemidophorus* (Nematoda) (Babero and

Emmerson, 1974); hemogregarines (coccidia) (Wozniak et al., 1994). Babero and Emmerson (1974) also found *T. cnemidophorus* in *C. mitchellii* and *C. scutulatus*; this parasite was thought by Goldberg et al. (2002) to be accidental and to have been ingested along with lizard prey.

Crotalus cerastes laterorepens: *Oochoristica crotalicola* (Cestoda) (Alexander and Alexander, 1957).

Crotalus durissus: *Haemogregarina crotali*, *H. romani*, and *H. capsulata* (Protozoa) (Pessôa, 1967); *Trypanosoma cascavelli* (Protozoa) (Pessôa and De Biasi, 1972); *Hepatozoon* spp. (Protozoa) (Pessôa et al., 1974); *Ophidascaris travassosi* and *O. trichuriformis* (Nematoda) (Vaz, 1938); *O. sprenti* (Araujo, 1969); *Ascaridia flexuosa* (Schneider, 1866); *Polydelphis quadrangularis* (Nematoda) (Araujo, 1971); *Hastospiculum oncocercum majus* (Nematoda) (Desportes, 1941); *Porocephalus crotali* (Pentastomida) (Penn, 1942; Rego, 1982b).

Crotalus horridus: *Cryptosporidium serpentis* (Levine, 1980); *Caryospora bigenetica* (Wacha and Christiansen, 1982a, 1982b); *Isospora naiae* (Fanthan and Porter, 1954); *Capillaria* spp. (Nematoda) (Solomon, 1974); *Hexametra leidyi* (Nematoda) (Bowman, 1984); *Porocephalus crotali* (Pentastomida) (Penn, 1942; Riley and Self, 1979); larval *Trombicula* (*Entrombicula*) *alfreddugesi* (chigger) (Wolfenbarger, 1952).

Crotalus lepidus: oligacanthorhynchid acanthocephalans (Goldberg and Bursey, 1999). A nematode (Physalopteridae) that may be an accidental parasite, *Abbreviata terrapenis*, was reported by Goldberg et al. (2002), who suggested that it entered the rattlesnakes along with ingested lizards, the normal host for this worm.

Crotalus mitchellii: *Thubunacea cnemidophorus* (Nematoda) (Babero and Emmerson, 1974); tetrathyridia of *Mesocestoides* spp. (Goldberg and Bursey, 2000a); oligacanthorhynchid acanthocephalan cystacanths (Goldberg and Bursey, 2000a).

Crotalus molossus: *Kalicephalus inermis* (Nematoda) (Prado Vera, *in* Goldberg and Bursey, 1999); tetrathyridia of *Mesocestoides* spp. (Goldberg and Bursey, 1999).

Crotalus molossus nigrescens: *Ophidascaris labiatopapillosa* (Nematoda) (Klauber, 1956).

Crotalus oreganus oreganus: *Mesocestoides variabilis* (Voge, 1953); *Physaloptera obtussima* (Nematoda) (Morgan, 1943).

Crotalus oreganus helleri: *Oochoristica crotalicola* (Cestoda) (Alexander and Alexander, 1957); *Mesocestoides* spp. (Cestoda) (Widmer and Specht, 1992).

Crotalus pricei: tetrathyridia of *Mesocestoides* spp. (Goldberg and Bursey, 1999).

Crotalus ravus: *Haemogregarina digueti* (Protozoa) (Phisalix, 1914).

Crotalus scutulatus scutulatus: *Sarcocystis crotali* (Enzeroth et al., 1985); *Thubunacea cnemidophorus* (Nematoda) (Babero and Emmerson, 1974); oligacanthorhynchid acanthocephalan cystacanths (Bolette, 1997b).

Crotalus simus: *Ophionyssus natricis* (Quintero et al., 1990); *Capillaria crotali* (Nematoda) (Víquez, 1933); *Porocephalus crotali* (Pentastomida) (Penn, 1942); *Amblyomma dissimile* (tick) (Klauber, 1956); *Dermacentor* spp. (tick) (Klauber, 1956).

Crotalus tigris: oligacanthorhynchid acanthocephalans (Goldberg and Bursey, 1999).

Crotalus tortugensis: *Porocephalus crotali* (Pentastomida) (Klauber, 1956); *P. tortugensis* (Riley and Self, 1979; a synonym of *P. crotali*, according to Rego, 1982a); *Raillietiella furcocerca* (Pentastomida) (Klauber, 1956).

Crotalus totonacus: regurgitated "a large number of ascarids" for two weeks following its capture (Armstrong and Murphy, 1979).

Crotalus triseriatus: *Ophionyssus natricis* (Quintero et al., 1990); *Kalicephalus conoidus* (Nematoda) (Comroe, 1948).

Crotalus viridis viridis: *Haemogregarina crotali* (Protozoa) (Laveran, 1902); unidentified hemogregarine (Wood and Wood, 1936); tetrathyridia of *Mesocestoides* spp. (Bolette, 1998; Mankau and Widmer, 1977; Widmer et al., 1995); and *Manodistomum* spp., *Physaloptera* spp., and two species of oligacanthorhynchid acanthocephalan (Bolette, 1998); *Oochoristica osheroffi* (Cestoda);

Kalicephalus inermis and *Physoloptera retusa* (Nematoda) (Pfaffenberger et al., 1989).

Crotalus viridis: *Porocephalus crotali* (Pentastomida) (Klauber, 1956); tetrathyridia of *Mesocestoides* spp. (Bolette, 1998).

Crotalus willardi: tetrathyridia of *Mesocestoides* spp. (Goldberg and Bursey, 2000a); oligacanthorhynchid acanthocephalan cystacanths (Goldberg and Bursey, 2000a).

Crotalus willardi obscurus: *Sarcocystis* spp. (McAllister et al., 1996).

Crotalus sp.: *Polydelphis quadracornis* (Nematoda) (Yamaguti, 1961); *Kalicephalus* spp. (Comroe, 1948; Kreis, 1940; Schad, 1962; Yamaguti, 1961); *Armillifer* spp. (Pentastomida) (Page, 1966); *Entonyssus rileyi* (lung mites, Entonyssidae) (Ewing, 1924).

Sistrurus catenatus: *Caryospora bigenetica* (Wacha and Christiansen, 1982a, 1982b).

Sistrurus miliarius: *Ochetosoma kansense* (Harwood, 1932); *Ochetosoma glandulare* (Byrd and Denton, 1938; Nelson, 1950; Goodman, 1951); *Amblyomma dissimile* (tick) (Bishopp and Trembley, 1945).

Reproduction. The basic life cycle for many Nearctic rattlesnakes has been known for many years. Table 49 summarizes reproduction data for 19 species. Klauber (1936c) pointed out that females undergoing vitellogenesis at the time they enter their third hibernation are about 26 months of age, that the ova of these females are fertilized the ensuing spring, and that young are born the following September or October.

Klauber (1936c) thought that male and female rattlesnakes were born in about equal numbers but found a light to moderate preponderance of males in the preserved samples of rattlesnakes that he examined, with a male : female ratio of 1.1–1.6 : 1.0 for most species. However, in a sample of 56 litters of rattlesnakes representing a total of 463 neonates or embryos of 15 subspecies there were 213 males and 240 females, for a sex ratio of 0.89 : 1.0. Klauber concluded that the apparent disparity among sexes in natural populations was an artifact of collecting. Perhaps males were more exposed to predation and human collecting owing to their activity relating to searching for females in the summer or early fall; or perhaps females, especially when gravid, were simply more secretive and thus less likely to be attacked by predators or to be encountered by human collectors.

Klauber (1936c, 1972) and many others have reported the numbers of young produced by various species of rattlesnakes. As a general trend, small species of rattlesnakes produce a relatively small number (often 5–8) of young that are large relative to the adults, and large species produce more young (15–40 or more) that are smaller relative to adults.

Reproduction in many different species and populations of rattlesnakes has been studied in the last few decades, and the general trend outlined by Klauber (1936c) often holds true, but we now also know that there are many deviations from this typical life cycle. In North America, rattlesnakes usually mate in the spring and young are born in the fall, but owing to the ability of females of some species to store sperm for eight months or more (Schuett, 1992) and the ability of males to store sperm in the vas deferens for at least one year (Aldridge, 1993, 2002), there are several variations on this basic reproductive cycle. All species of temperate North American crotalines undergo spermatogenesis during the summer months (Aldridge and Brown, 1995). In rattlesnakes that employ short-term sperm storage (spring matings) the males store the sperm in the vas deferens, whereas those that have long-term sperm storage (fall matings) store sperm in the female's oviduct. In the species of rattlesnakes known to mate in the summer or fall, the spermatozoa remain viable in the oviduct during the winter and

Table 49. Reproduction in *Crotalus*.

Taxon	Date of birth	No. of young (mean)	TL of young, cm (mean)	Weight of young, g (mean)	Locality of female parent	Authority
C. aquilus	7 June 1974	6	16.8–19.2 (17.8)	5.0–8.8 (6.4)	El Chico, Hidalgo, Mexico	Armstrong and Murphy, 1979
C. aquilus	29 July 1974	7	16.8–19.2 (17.8)	5.0–8.8 (6.4)	El Chico, Hidalgo, Mexico	Armstrong and Murphy, 1979
C. aquilus	29 June 1974	3	16.4–17.1 (16.7)	5.0–6.4 (5.5)	16 km W Jiquilpan, Michoacán, Mexico	Armstrong and Murphy, 1979
C. aquilus[a]	27 July 1977	3[b]	12.0–18.1 (15.0)	4.9–7.8 (6.3)	El Chico, Hidalgo, Mexico	Armstrong and Murphy, 1979
C. atrox*	June–Oct.	6–25[c] (14.3)	—	—	Texas and northern Mexico	Armstrong and Murphy, 1979
C. atrox[j]	Late July–Aug.	2–24 (9)	20.5–33.3	11–12	Arizona	Lowe et al., 1986
C. cerastes[j]	—	7–18	17.7–19.2 (18.5)	(5.4)	Arizona	Lowe et al., 1986
C. durissus unicolor*	23 May 1977	4	28.2[k]	—	Aruba	Carl et al., 1982b
C. durissus unicolor*	13 May 1978	3	26.9–29.0 (27.6)	12.5–15.0 (13.6)	Aruba	Carl et al., 1982b
C. durissus unicolor*	27 Apr. 1978	4	26.0–28.2 (27.1)	13.0–14.0 (13.6)	Aruba	Carl et al., 1982b
C. durissus unicolor*	17 June 1979	2	28.0–29.0 (28.5)	13.0–15.2 (14.1)	Aruba	Carl et al., 1982b
C. durissus unicolor*	16 May 1980	2	23.1–23.9 (23.5)	11.6–12.1 (11.9)	Aruba	Carl et al., 1982b
C. durissus vegrandis*	8 June 1976	2	—	—	Venezuela	Carl et al., 1982a
C. durissus vegrandis*	12 May 1978	3	25.0–27.7 (26.5)	12.0–14.0 (13.2)	Venezuela	Carl et al., 1982a
C. durissus vegrandis*	2 May 1979	6	23.0–28.0 (26.2)	11.5–16.5 (15.1)	Venezuela	Carl et al., 1982a
C. durissus vegrandis*	25 Apr. 1979	8	22.5–26.5 (24.8)	11.9–14.4 (12.9)	Venezuela	Carl et al., 1982a
C. durissus vegrandis*	30 Apr. 1980	8	25.4–27.5 (26.5)	11.6–14.3 (13.2)	Venezuela	Carl et al., 1982a
C. enyo enyo*	21 Nov. 1976	7	21.4–23.5 (22.3)	9.7–11.1 (10.2)	Baja California, Mexico	Tryon, 1977
C. enyo furvus*	26 Aug. 1974	7	20.6–22.2 (21.3)	—	San Quintín Plain, Baja California Norte, Mexico	Armstrong and Murphy, 1979
C. intermedius omiltemanus	28 May 1975	5[d]	19.4–21.2 (20.5)	4.9–5.4 (5.2)	Omilteme, Guerrero, Mexico	Armstrong and Murphy, 1979
C. lepidus klauberi	28 Aug. 1968	3	—	—	Herb Martyr Dam, Chiricahuas, Arizona	Armstrong and Murphy, 1979
C. lepidus klauberi	30 Aug. 1975	4	18.1–19.6 (19.1)	6.3–7.0 (6.6)	4.8 km S Madera, Chihuahua, Mexico	Armstrong and Murphy, 1979
C. lepidus klauberi[j]	July–Aug.	2–8 (4)	15.4–20.5	6–8	Arizona	Lowe et al., 1986
C. lepidus lepidus	1 Aug. 1972	9	14.6–17.8 (16.6)	—	Pablillo, Nuevo León, Mexico	Liner and Chaney, 1986
C. lepidus morulus	5 June 1974	6	16.5–19.0 (17.7)	5.0–5.7 (5.2)	La Ascención, Nuevo León, Mexico	Armstrong and Murphy, 1979
C. lepidus morulus	30 Aug. 1992	10	12.5–14.6 (12.6)	3.1–5.3 (4.2)	Ciénega del Toro, Nuevo León, Mexico	Sánchez et al., 1999
C. mitchellii[j]	Aug.–Sep.	3–8 (5)	23.3–26.7	(12.0)	Arizona	Lowe et al., 1986
C. mitchellii mitchellii*	29 June 1976	1	27.5	17.5	Not given	Armstrong and Murphy, 1979
C. mitchellii muertensis*	13 Sep. 1977	4	14.3–17.9 (16.7)	3.3–7.0 (4.9)	Isla El Muerto, Gulf of California, Mexico	Armstrong and Murphy, 1979
C. molossus molossus[j]	July–Aug.	3–16 (7)	23.3–31.8	11–28	Arizona	Lowe et al., 1986
C. molossus nigrescens	8 July 1934	16[d]	—	—	4 mi W La Colorada, Zacatecas, Mexico	Dunkle and Smith, 1937
C. molossus nigrescens*	9 June 1975	5	29.1–31.6 (30.4)	25.4–27.9 (26.6)	Not given	Armstrong and Murphy, 1979
C. polystictus	13 June 1974	12	21.1–28.7 (22.2)	8.5–11.5 (9.9)	Near Tapalpa, Jalisco, Mexico	Armstrong and Murphy, 1979
C. polystictus	20 June 1974	10	20.0–22.3 (21.1)	6.3–10.9 (7.2)	Near Tapalpa, Jalisco, Mexico	Armstrong and Murphy, 1979
C. polystictus	25 June 1975	7	22.7–23.9 (23.2)	9.5–10.9 (10.2)	Near Tapalpa, Jalisco, Mexico	Armstrong and Murphy, 1979
C. polystictus	26 June 1975	7	19.8–23.2 (21.6)	9.9–10.5 (10.1)	Near Tapalpa, Jalisco, Mexico	Armstrong and Murphy, 1979
C. polystictus	30 June 1975	7	18.2–20.5 (19.7)	9.9–11.1 (10.6)	Near Tapalpa, Jalisco, Mexico	Armstrong and Murphy, 1979
C. polystictus[e]	30 June 1975	5	15.5–20.3 (17.7)	2.4–5.5 (4.0)	Near Tapalpa, Jalisco, Mexico	Armstrong and Murphy, 1979

Table 49—cont.

Taxon	Date of birth	No. of young (mean)	TL of young, cm (mean)	Weight of young, g (mean)	Locality of female parent	Authority
C. polystictus*	21 July 1978	3	20.7–22.3 (21.3)	8.8–10.4 (9.8)	Near Tapalpa, Jalisco, Mexico	Hubbard, 1980
C. pricei pricei*	9 July 1971	4	—	2.4–3.9 (3.0)	Los Bancos, Durango, Mexico	Armstrong and Murphy, 1979
C. pricei pricei	10 July 1977	8	15.7–16.7 (16.4)	4.0–4.2 (4.1)	Llano Grande, Durango, Mexico	Armstrong and Murphy, 1979
C. pricei pricei	14 July 1977	9	15.2–17.3 (16.2)	3.5–4.0 (3.6)	Llano Grande, Durango, Mexico	Armstrong and Murphy, 1979
C. pricei pricei	27 July 1977	6	15.9–16.9 (16.2)	5.1–5.6 (5.3)	Llano Grande, Durango, Mexico	Armstrong and Murphy, 1979
C. pricei pricei	29 July 1977	6	16.0–18.5 (16.8)	3.6–3.9 (3.7)	Llano Grande, Durango, Mexico	Armstrong and Murphy, 1979
C. pricei pricei[j]	July–Aug.	3–9	12.8–20.5	2.6–5.6	Arizona	Lowe et al., 1986
C. pricei pricei	4 Aug. 1995	7	—	5.5–6.4 (5.7)	Chiricahua Mountains, Arizona	Mahaney, 1997a
C. pricei miquihuanus	19 Aug. 1974	5	13.0–14.3 (13.5)	(2.6)[f]	E slope Cerro Potosí, Nuevo León, Mexico	Armstrong and Murphy, 1979
C. pricei miquihuanus	24 July 1985[l]	6	11.4–12.0 (11.6)	—	Near Las Mibres, Nuevo León, Mexico	Chaney and Liner, 1986
C. pusillus	23 Jan. 1974	5[g]	16.5–17.9 (17.1)	3.0–6.1 (4.0)	Dos Aguas, Michoacán, Mexico	Armstrong and Murphy, 1979
C. pusillus*	15 July 1976	3[h]	17.9[h]	6.0	Dos Aguas, Michoacán, Mexico	Armstrong and Murphy, 1979
C. ravus[a]	1 June 1974	7	16.0–20.8 (18.3)	3.9–7.4 (5.4)	Huitzilac, Morelos, Mexico	Armstrong and Murphy, 1979
C. ravus[a]	28 May 1975	9	16.0–20.8 (18.3)	3.9–7.4 (5.4)	Huitzilac, Morelos, Mexico	Armstrong and Murphy, 1979
C. ravus[a]	28 May 1975	3	16.0–20.8 (18.3)	3.9–7.4 (5.4)	Huitzilac, Morelos, Mexico	Armstrong and Murphy, 1979
C. scutulatus scutulatus[j]	July–Aug.	2–13 (8)	23.1–28.2	7–8	Arizona	Lowe et al., 1986
C. scutulatus scutulatus	31 Aug. 1984	17	(21.2)	(10.6)	Near Villa de Ramos, San Luis Potosí, Mexico	Mellink, 1990
C. simus tzabcan*	31 Aug. 1975	21	29.0–35.0 (31.6)	18.4–26.8 (23.4)	Yucatán Peninsula, Mexico	Armstrong and Murphy, 1979
C. tigris[j]	June–Sep.	4–6	21.5–23.6	(9.0)	Arizona	Lowe et al., 1986
C. triseriatus triseriatus	15 July 1970	6[d]	—	—	Nevado de Colima, Jalisco, Mexico	Armstrong and Murphy, 1979
C. triseriatus triseriatus	30 Oct. 1975	4	15.9–17.8 (16.8)	4.8–5.1 (4.9)	Laguna Zempoala, Morelos, Mexico	Armstrong and Murphy, 1979
C. viridis[j]	Aug.–Sep.	3–21	17.9–28.3	—	Arizona	Lowe et al., 1986
C. viridis viridis	—	10.7[i]	—	—	Kansas	Fitch, 1998
C. willardi amabilis	26 July 2000	5	17.3–18.6 (18.2)	6.7–7.1 (7.0)	Sierra del Nido, Chihuahua, Mexico	Bryson and Lazcano, 2001
C. willardi obscurus	13 Aug. 1998	8	(15.9 SVL)	(5.3)	Peloncillo Mountains, New Mexico	Holycross, 2000c
C. willardi silus	28 July–9 Aug. 1993	7	16.5–17.4 (16.9)	7.5–8.5 (8.3)	Near San Juanito, Chihuahua, Mexico	Delgadillo-Espinosa et al., 1999
C. willardi silus	7 Aug. 1970	5	—	—	Sierra de la Púrica, Sonora, Mexico	Armstrong and Murphy, 1979
C. willardi silus	10 Aug. 1978	4	14.6–21.8 (19.0)	4.9–6.9 (6.0)	Sierra de la Púrica, Sonora, Mexico	Armstrong and Murphy, 1979
C. willardi willardi[j]	Aug.–Sep.	2–9, usually 4–6	usually 16.7–19.5, up to 20.3	7	Arizona	Lowe et al., 1986

Note: Asterisk denotes captive breeding.
[a] The variation of TL and weight is a composite for multiple litters.
[b] One of these young was deformed.
[c] Based on nine captive litters.
[d] This litter was encountered in the field, presumably within a day of birth. It is possible that not all of the young were found.
[e] This litter was stillborn, and the neonates probably do not fall within the normal size range of viable offspring for this species.
[f] These neonates were measured to the nearest 0.1 g, and no variation in weight was noted; each individual was 2.6 g (J. B. Murphy, pers. comm.).
[g] Four of the five young were stillborn.
[h] Two of the three young were stillborn and underdeveloped; TL and weight given only for the single live young.
[i] Figure represents mean for multiple litters.
[j] Data for multiple litters.
[k] Only one young measured.
[l] Female died before parturition; young appeared full term.

fertilization ensues the following spring (Ludwig and Rahn, 1943; Rahn, 1942b). Also, in northern latitudes, where climatic conditions are cold over much of the year and the feeding-growing season is short, rattlesnakes may have a biennial reproductive cycle or may reproduce even less frequently. Reproduction of rattlesnakes in central and southern Mexico and the tropics coincides largely with the rainy season, which varies according to geographic location but in general extends from May through October. Females often undergo ecdysis prior to copulation.

Some, and perhaps most or all, male rattlesnakes engage in a ritualized combat dance. During this activity, males raise up and intertwine the anterior parts of their bodies, each endeavoring to topple the opponent. This "dance" may last 15 minutes or more. Male-male combat in viperids has often been mistaken for "courtship" between sexual pairs of snakes. Ritualized combat between males has been reported for *C. aquilus*, *C. atrox* (Armstrong and Murphy, 1979; Shaw, 1948b), *C. basiliscus* (Davis, 1936), *C. cerastes* (Lowe and Norris, 1950), *C. durissus* (Marques et al., 2001), *C. intermedius gloydi*, *C. intermedius omiltemanus* (Armstrong and Murphy, 1979), *C. lepidus* (Carpenter et al., 1976), *C. lepidus klauberi*, *C. pusillus*, *C. ravus* (Armstrong and Murphy, 1979), *C. ruber* (Shaw, 1948b), *C. triseriatus triseriatus* (Armstrong and Murphy, 1979), and *C. viridis* (Gloyd, 1947b; Holycross, 1995). Male *Crotalus ravus* have been observed to engage in combat in captivity, apparently induced by feeding (Lindsey, 1979), and Sutherland (1958) reported that in *C. horridus* male-male combat is often the response when food is introduced.

Among rattlesnakes, the reproductive biology of *C. horridus*, *C. oreganus*, and *C. viridis* has been studied in detail. Spermatogenesis in *C. oreganus* and *C. viridis*, and probably in most rattlesnakes, requires a warm body temperature following a cool, quiescent period, and does not seem to be related to photoperiod (Aldridge, 1975).

Brown (1991) studied reproductive ecology in *C. horridus* in northeastern New York, near the northern limit of the species' range, from 1981 to 1988. He found that the proportion of gravid females varied significantly from year to year, from only 25% in 1985 to 77% in 1988. Most females (57%) reproduced at 3-year intervals (triennially), and many reproduced at 4-year intervals (quadrennially). He could find no evidence for a biennial cycle. Females reproduced for the first time at 7–11 years of age, with most females reproducing at 9–10 years. Females reached maturity at about 84 cm SVL.

Males required 4–6 years to reach sexual maturity (Aldridge and Brown, 1995). Maximum spermatogenesis and seminiferous tubular diameter in this New York population were achieved in July, at which time the mating season started, continuing through September (Brown, 1995). Males were encountered more often than females and suffered a higher death rate on roads than females by a 3.25:1.0 ratio, indicating greater long-range movements for males (Aldridge and Brown, 1995).

Female *C. horridus* in Minnesota require six to eight years to reach sexual maturity, after which time litters of 4–9 young are produced every two or three years (Oldfield and Keyler, 1997). Sealy (1996) observed mating in *C. horridus*, the female having freshly shed. A courtship lasting up to several days often precedes mating, with males courting premolt females. Apparently, copulation is stimulated by the release of phermones at the time of shedding (Brown, 1995). A female killed in Indiana the last week of August contained well-developed embryos (Minton, 2001). Birth dates recorded for six females ranged from Sep-

tember to October, and litter size ranged from 6 to 13 (Minton, 2001). Fitch (1999) found a pair of adults together in Kansas on 25 August, and found neonates in October.

Crotalus horridus gives birth over most of its range from early August to early October. Gravid females tend to utilize rocky, sparsely vegetated areas (Reinert, 1984b). An individual of *C. horridus* found in Warren County, New Jersey, gave birth to 10 young on 8 September 1933 over a period of 4.5 hours (Trapido, 1939). In some instances the fetal membranes ruptured at the time of birth, but in others the neonates took up to 43 minutes to rupture the membranes, which was accomplished by a series of upward thrusts with the snout. On 24 September 1957, a female from Cattaraugus County, New York, gave birth to 12 young (Stewart et al., 1960). These neonates were sexually dimorphic in length and weight, with males being slightly longer and heavier than females (29.6–33.0 cm, $\bar{x}$ = 31.2 cm versus 28.9–30.3, $\bar{x}$ = 29.6 cm; and 14.7–17.6 g, $\bar{x}$ = 16.2 g versus 12.3–15.0 g, $\bar{x}$ = 14.1 g, respectively). A female from South Bass Island in Lake Erie gave birth to 12 young and an underdeveloped embryo on 12 September 1951 (Triplehorn, 1955). Conant (1938) and Ditmars (1936) reported multiple litters of *C. horridus*, presumably from Ohio and New York, respectively, containing 7–12 young that were all born in September. A female from Houston County, Minnesota, gave birth to 7 young on 26 August 1936 that were 31.6–33.4 cm ($\bar{x}$ = 32.3 cm) in TL (Edgren, 1948). Fitch (1999) palpated 13 females carrying eggs and found that they contained 4–14 eggs, with a mean of 8.9 eggs.

The active season of *C. horridus* in the Appalachian Mountains of northwestern Virginia is only 5.3 months, with mating in August and September, ovulation in May and early June the following year, and parturition usually in August–October (Martin, 1993). Females in this population usually require seven to eight years to reach maturity, with gravid and postpartum females being 76–112 cm ($\bar{x}$ = 93 cm) in TL. Several factors, including variation in annual weather cycles and synchronization of female breeding cycles, influence female reproduction, and an estimated 10–75% of mature females are gravid in any given year (Martin, 1993).

Female *C. horridus* in the Aiken, South Carolina, area have a biennial, possibly a triennial, reproductive season (Gibbons, 1972). The mean litter size is 12.5 and is not positively correlated with female size; neonates average 38 cm in SVL and 31 g in body weight. Females are in excess of 100 cm in SVL and 700 g at maturity and probably produce their first litter six years after birth. Males reach a larger size than females, their adult size perhaps associated with selection for male superiority in combat dances, and become reproductively active four years after birth (Gibbons, 1972).

Martin (1996) reported that female *C. horridus* usually remain with their young for 7–10 days after birth. In Virginia and Maryland between the years 1969 and 1990 he found postpartum females with litters from 9 August to 16 October. In 1991, a year in which the growing season was longer, hotter, and drier than normal, he found that parturition occurred as early as 31 July–3 August. In 1992 there was an unusually cool and wet growing season, and births occurred some four to six weeks later than in 1992, with the latest date occurring on about 15 October.

Martin and Wood (1955) collected two female *C. horridus* in Virginia on 14 August 1954. One of the females gave birth to 13 young on 27 August that averaged about 12 inches in TL (30.8 cm), and the other gave birth on 12 September to 7 young averaging 14 inches in TL (35.9 cm). In North Carolina, *C. horridus* gives birth to 1–20 young in late August and September, and the means for neonate TL in 10 individual litters ranged from 31.0 cm to 37.0 cm (Palmer and Braswell, 1995). A female from Arkansas collected in April contained 9 oviductal eggs (Trauth et al., 1994). Berish (1998) found that in Florida the litter size in *C. horridus* varied from 6 to 15 ($\bar{x} = 10.6$); the smallest SVL for a mature female was 109.9 cm. Kelly (1936) reported that 6–14 young are born in Maryland in late August or September; the neonates are about 10 inches (25.4 cm) in TL. In northern Louisiana, Clark (1949) found 7–11 fetuses in three of the gravid females he examined.

Populations of *C. horridus* and *C. viridis* in Kansas both exhibit fairly rapid individual growth, and newly mature adults form a high proportion of the populations (Fitch, 1985b). *Crotalus viridis* has more life history traits that emphasize high reproductive potential and an accelerated life cycle, and *C. horridus* has a lower reproductive potential and higher longevity.

Crotalus o. oreganus from the Pacific slopes and mountains of North America mates in the spring (Fitch, 1949b; Fitch and Glading, 1947; Klauber, 1972), and a similar pattern of reproduction has been suggested for more inland populations in Idaho as well (Diller and Wallace, 1984). Cunningham (1959) reported that several litters containing 2–8 young were born to female *C. o. oreganus* from California from 16 September to 10 October, and one litter containing small, dead embryos was born on 20 December. Neonates from these litters were 25.0–27.5 cm in TL.

In British Columbia, Canada, growth rates in juvenile *Crotalus o. oreganus* are highly variable, but the variability decreases with increasing body size (Macartney et al., 1990). Males grow faster and mature at an earlier age (three to four years) and smaller size (53.5 cm SVL) than females, which reach sexual maturity at five to seven years and 65.0 cm SVL. Growth rates in this species, especially among juveniles, are influenced by latitude, elevation, and annual differences in weather. Rattlesnake dens in British Columbia exhibit a thermal gradient, with increasing temperatures at increasing depths; *C. o. oreganus* maintains a body temperature of 2–7 °C during the winter (Macartney et al., 1989). Charland (1989) collected 115 neonatal *C. o. oreganus* and released this sample to hibernate in two dens. The recapture rate suggested a minimum overwinter survivalship of these neonates of 55%; survivorship was not associated with either weight or condition at birth.

Female *C. oreganus oreganus* in British Colombia attain sexual maturity at five to seven years and produce their first litter at six to seven years (Macartney and Gregory, 1988). Females mate during the late summer and vitellogenesis occurs before they go into hibernation; ovulation occurs the following June, and parturition in September or early October. Females usually do not feed when gravid and have low fat body reserves by the time they give birth. About one-quarter of the females studied regained their body mass during the year after parturition and gave birth in alternate years (biennial reproduction), but the other females required two years or longer to acquire the necessary food reserves for reproduction. In this region *C. o. oreganus* hibernates for seven months and is active only from early April to early October (Macartney, 1985). Within rather wide parameters the amount of food and frequency of feeding apparently have little to do with growth or weight gain in postpartum females.

Charland and Gregory (1989) maintained a group of 30 postpartum female *C. o. oreganus* in outside enclosures under semi-natural conditions. These snakes were divided into two groups, with one group offered food every other day and the other group offered food every other week, and the weights of individual snakes were tracked from May through August. The mean weights of the two groups remained almost identical despite the different feeding regimes. The authors suggested that the similar weights may have been the result of captive conditions. Snakes may have been able to thermoregulate in their enclosures at different levels appropriate to the level of food intake. A lower body temperature would minimize metabolic expenditure and allow for maximum growth when prey is scarce. Nevertheless, with regard to postpartum weight gain, which determines frequency of reproduction, certain abiotic environmental factors such as temperature obviously play a critical role.

Charland and Gregory (1990) also studied thermoregulation in gravid and nongravid female *C. o. oreganus* in an outside enclosure. During the summer all the snakes exhibited a triphasic diel pattern of variation in body temperature. The body temperature rose quickly in the morning, a relatively stable plateau persisted throughout the afternoon (usually between 30 and 35 °C), and the body temperature declined slowly at about sunset. Although the mean body temperatures of gravid and nongravid females did not differ significantly during the afternoon or seasonally, gravid females maintained a significantly less variable body temperature. These differences between gravid and nongravid snakes appear to be the result of the costs and benefits of thermoregulation during gestation.

A population of *C. oreganus concolor* in Sweetwater County, Wyoming, emerged from hibernation in early May, and females moved a short distance (usually no more than 50 m from the den) to the site where they would eventually give birth (Ashton and Patton, 2001). Females in gestation did not usually forage or mate. Parturition occurred between 20 August and 18 September. The number of young per litter was 2–7 ($\bar{x} = 4.7$), and number of young was strongly correlated with the mother's size. The SVLs of neonates were 14.0–22.2 cm ($\bar{x} = 19.3$ cm), and they weighed 3.4–11.1 g ($\bar{x} = 8.0$ g), with no apparent sexual dimorphism in size. Ashton and Patton (2001) suggested that this population reproduces biennially or triennially.

Of 30 adult female *C. o. lutosus* from Juab County, Utah, captured in September as they made their way to a den, 6 were gravid with 6–11 eggs that would be ovulated about the following June (Woodbury and Hansen, 1950). Glissmeyer (1951) stated that the Utah females heading for dens that he examined contained egg clutches that were up to 60% developed.

Klauber (1936c) reported on a sample of 861 individuals of *C. viridis viridis* from the Platteville area of east-central Colorado. The smallest mature female was 58.8 cm in SVL, and the largest female was 86.3 cm. Klauber found that more than half of the females with SVLs above 65 cm were gravid, and almost all females above 75 cm were gravid. He concluded that females in this population reproduced annually and that the number of young was positively correlated with the size of the female. Smaller females tended to have only about 6 young, whereas larger females (80–82 cm) often produced 15–16 young. Klauber's sample included 149 females that contained 1,767 developing eggs, for an average of 11.8 eggs per female. This figure provides some indication of fecundity for that population but is probably slightly higher than the actual number of living young produced because not all of the eggs develop into viable young (Klauber, 1936c). The number of enlarging eggs a particular female contained varied from 4 to 21.

A comparison of the Platteville sample with a series of snakes of the same species from the vicinity of Pierre, South Dakota, revealed only slight differences despite rather dramatic differences in latitude and annual temperature regimes between the two areas. In the Pierre sample, 107 females contained 1,151 developing eggs, for an average of 10.8 young per female. Females contained 4–20 maturing eggs; the smallest female was 68.3 cm in SVL and the largest was 102 cm. Females in the Pierre population were thus larger than those in the Plattesville population but produced slightly fewer young.

Mature female *C. viridis viridis* collected during September from hibernating dens from near Cheyenne, Wyoming, were studied by Ludwig and Rahn (1943), who were able to categorize them as either postpartum females with small ovaries that had given birth to young the previous fall or "ripe" females with large ovaries that had not given birth to young. They dissected females during December or January and found spermatozoa in ripe females only, a fact that Rahn (1942b) attributed to a two-year reproductive cycle for *C. viridis* on the Wyoming Plateau. Sperm was stored only in about a 4-cm-long narrow, posterior, tubular portion of the oviduct, and not in the most posterior enlarged, pouchlike portion.

Wood (1933) observed mating pairs of *C. v. viridis* on two occasions during the first week of August 1931 in central Wyoming. Male *C. v. viridis* were found with females five times from midsummer to early fall in the Sandhill region of Nebraska, and one instance of courtship was observed on 6 April 1991 (Holycross, 1995). Fitch (1998) found that about 80% of the adult female *C. v. viridis* in Kansas produced young every year, and that young matured in about three years.

The female *C. v. viridis* that Graves and Duvall (1993) studied in Wyoming reproduced on a flexible superannual cycle, and follicle number was positively correlated with increasing body size. Females in rookeries maintained a higher body temperature than nonpregnant conspecifics that sought shelter elsewhere. The snakes in Yellowstone National Park, Wyoming, studied by Turner (1955) bred shortly after emerging from hibernation and gave birth to 4–21 young in September (Turner, 1955). Koch and Peterson (1995) reported that young snakes in northeastern Wyoming required several years to reach sexual maturity. Gannon and Secoy (1984) studied *C. viridis* for two years during the active season in Saskatchewan, Canada, and found that about 50% of the adult females were gravid each summer.

Females may remain with their young until the neonates have molted for the first time, which occurs generally within about 10 days after birth (Duvall et al., 1985; Koch and Peterson, 1995). On two occasions on 18 August 1994 Cunningham et al. (1996) discovered adult *C. v. viridis*, which they assumed were females, with a group of young, and in one instance the young remained with the adult for at least one week. Holycross (1995) noted that female *C. viridis* in Nebraska often remained with their young for a short period after birth. These observations suggest some form parental care in this taxon.

In New Mexico *C. viridis* occupies hibernacula from September to April, during which time individuals may emerge to bask on warm days, and is active for about eight months of the year (Jacob and Painter, 1980). Interestingly, New Mexico females were found to produce a significantly greater number of follicles in the right ovary (Aldridge, 1979b).

Berish (1998) found that the litter size in the *C. adamanteus* he studied varied from 7 to 24 ($\bar{x} = 13.8$); the smallest SVL for a mature female was 109.3 cm. Stickel (1952) and Means (1978) reported that the litter size for *C. adamanteus* ranges from 7 to 29; Klauber (1972) gave the number of neonates in a litter as

7–21. Palmer and Braswell (1995) reported a female from North Carolina that contained 21 young at the time she was killed on 15 July. Two other females from Pender Country, North Carolina, gave birth on 25 September and 2 October to 21 and 16 young, respectively. The TLs of neonates from these litters were 38.6–42.4 cm ($\bar{x} = 40.2$ cm) and 38.0–41.1 cm ($\bar{x} = 39.5$ cm), respectively. The average TL of *C. adamanteus* neonates has been reported to be 35.5 cm (Mount, 1975) and 38.8 cm (Dundee and Rossman, 1989). *Crotalus adamanteus* females may give birth in gopher tortoise (*Gopherus polyphemus*) burrows, and neonates may seek shelter in this refuge. Van Hyning (1931) excavated a burrow on 21 August 1925 and found 14 young *C. adamanteus*.

Armstrong and Murphy (1979) described the mating behavior of *C. atrox*; copulation lasted for two to eight hours. In captive pairs copulation occurred between 21 and 26 January. Gates (1957) reported that near Wickenburg, Arizona, the young of *C. atrox* are born in early August. Armstrong and Murphy (1979) reported parturition dates in captivity of 9 litters: 2 in June, 1 in July, 3 in August, 2 in September, and 1 in October; the number of young produced in these litters ranged from 6 to 25. These authors reported that under captive conditions this species may reach sexual maturity in 30–36 months. Wiley (1929) reported the birth of 11 young on 4 June 1925, the result of a captive mating. A female from Oklahoma gave birth to 4 young on 15 August that were 33.9–36.7 cm in TL (Carpenter, 1958). On 31 July 1930 near the mouth of Carr Canyon, Huachuca Mountains, Arizona, Gloyd (1937) discovered a female *C. atrox* with 8 newborn young. When disturbed, these young sought refuge under rocks near the female parent. A female *C. atrox* collected 3 August 1931 near the Dragoon Mountains of Arizona gave birth to young within a day after capture (Gloyd, 1937). Ten gravid female *C. atrox* from Arizona contained 4–9 ($\bar{x} = 5.6$) oviductal ova or young (Rosen and Goldberg, 2003). Twenty-one neonates averaged 32.0 cm in TL and 19.6 g in body mass. Young were born from late July to September. Usually only about half of all adult females reproduce during a particular year in this population, but during years of high rodent abundance up to 73% reproduced, whereas in years of low rodent abundance only 28% were gravid. A California female *C. atrox* 91.4 cm in SVL gave birth to 14 young (Cunningham, 1959). A female *C. atrox* containing 18 almost full-term young was collected 8 August 1930 near Tucson, Arizona, and a copulating pair was observed under a mesquite tree not far from the Santa Rita Mountains on 19 August 1930 (Taylor, 1935). In Riverside County, California, Bogert (1942) observed a pair of mating *C. atrox* on 25 March 1932 in a patch of mesquite at about 1000 hours. A group of *C. atrox* from Riverside County were observed courting and exhibiting male-male combat a few days after their capture on 8 October 1941, suggesting that this was near the peak of their fall mating season (Lowe, 1942).

Tinkle (1962) suggested that female *C. atrox* reproduce biennially in northwestern Texas. Examination of the ovaries of adult females taken from dens in March revealed two different classes: females that had large, yolked follicles ready for ovulation in the spring but lacking corpora lutea, and females without yolked follicles but having corpora lutea, suggesting they had given birth the previous summer. Tinkle estimated that females in that population reached sexual maturity at about three years of age at a SVL of about 90 cm. The reproductive potential of these snake was estimated to be 6–19, with females reproducing for the first time averaging 9.9 offspring, compared with 16.1 in older snakes. In contrast to Tinkle's (1962) findings, Fitch and Pisani (1993) concluded that this species reproduces annually in Oklahoma.

A 155-cm *C. basiliscus* gave birth to 29 young on 7 July 1944; 5 of the neonates ranged in TL from 30.0 to 33.0 cm ($\bar{x} = 31.5$ cm) (Marcy, 1945). After the first molt the ground color of the young was greenish yellow with dark brown dorsal blotches that had paler centers. Several of the young had short paravertebral stripes on the neck. Ramírez-Bautista (1994) reported that *C. basiliscus* gives birth to 24–35 young.

Based on the report of an adult female *C. catalinensis* found in late March that had not ovulated (Cliff, 1954), gravid females found from mid-July to early August, and the appearance of neonates in August and September, Grismer (2002) inferred a spring to early summer breeding season, with birth in the late summer to early fall. There are records of *C. catalinensis* being born in September, and a pair copulated in captivity on 15 January (Armstrong and Murphy, 1979).

Lowe (1942) reported mating activity in *C. cerastes* in southern California between 20 September and 18 October 1941. In several instances tracks left in the sand indicated courtship, and copulation was observed on one occasion. Most activity occurred by day between 0600 and 1000, although one pair of snakes began copulating at about 1230 and continued until 1430. Secor (1994b) reported that *C. cerastes* in the eastern Mohave Desert mates in both the spring and fall, and that females give birth to 5–18 young from about mid-August through September. Neonates are 16.6–18.2 cm in SVL (Brown, 1992; Klauber, 1972; Secor, 1994b). One female *C. cerastes* from the Kelso Dunes of California gave birth to 13 young on 24 September that had a mean TL, SVL, and mass of 18.7 cm, 17.2 cm, and 6.3 g, respectively (Secor, 1994b). Klauber (1944) found a mating pair of *C. cerastes* in the mesquite sandhills east of La Quinta, Riverside County, California, at 0900 on 21 April 1935; he found another mating pair in Fargo Canyon, Little San Bernadino Mountains, Riverside County, California, at 2120 on 6 May 1939. Klauber (1944) reported several litters of *C. cerastes*: a female from Los Angeles County gave birth on 15 October 1939 to 10 young that were 16.1–16.9 ($\bar{x} = 166$) cm in TL, and a female from San Diego County gave birth to 6 young on 4 November 1937. Examination of preserved specimens revealed from 7 to 16 ova (Klauber, 1944).

Carl et al. (1982a) reported that a wild-caught female *C. durissus vegrandis* gave birth to 3 young on 9 July 1970, and that parturition for 5 captive breedings of this taxon occurred between 25 April and 8 June over various years (see Table 49).

Carl (1982b) reported nine captive-born litters of *C. durissus unicolor*; eight of these litters were produced between 27 April and 17 June and contained 2–5 young; one litter containing 5 young was born in early September (see Table 49). Klauber (1972) reported litters of this taxon containing 6, 7, 9, and 15 young. Kauffeld and Gloyd (1939) reported that a wild caught female contained 14 young; she died while giving birth on 7 July.

Leitão de Araujo and Ely (1980) reported litter sizes of 9–14 young for *C. d. terrificus*; the young of one litter had a mean weight of 22.2 g and a mean TL of 33.2 cm. Lira-da-Silva et al. (1994) reported that *C. d. cascavella* in Brazil gives birth from December to February to an average of 15 young that average 40.2 cm in TL. Freitas (1999) reported that in Bahia, Brazil, *C. d. cascavella* gives birth after six months' gestation to about 45 young that are approximately 30 cm in TL. In French Guiana, *C. d. durissus* gives birth to 15–20 young (Starace, 1998). In

Uruguay, *C. durissus* is reported to give birth to young 31–35 cm in TL (Achával et al., 1978).

Female *C. durissus* from Brazil feed particularly heavily before vitellogenesis (during the austral fall and winter) and continue to feed until ovulation (austral spring). The female reproductive tract of *C. d. terrificus* is twisted and convoluted in such a way that it is able to store sperm over the winter season (Almeida-Santos and Salomão, 1997). This taxon has an austral mating season, and females ovulate during the austral spring and give birth following a four- to five-month gestation period (Almeida-Santos and Salomão, 1997).

Armstrong and Murphy (1979) reported that two captive *C. simus tzabcan* copulated on 2 January, and the female gave birth to 21 young (see Table 49). A Honduran *C. s. simus* gave birth to 20 young on 3 August (March, 1928b). Solórzano (2004) and Solórzano and Cerdas (1988c) reported that *C. s. simus* in Costa Rica produces 14–35 (mean number about 23) offspring that are 27.5–43.0 cm and weigh 11.4–46.3 g. Mating occurs from December to February, and parturition from June to August (Fig. 199), which corresponds to the first part of the rainy season. Females reach sexual maturity at a TL exceeding 120 cm.

Marmie et al. (1990) reported two litters of *C. enyo* that each contained 6 neonates. A captive female *C. enyo* gave birth to 7 young on 26 August that were 20.6–22.2 cm ($\bar{x} = 21.3$ cm) in TL (Armstrong and Murphy, 1979). Tryon (1977) reported captive-bred litters of *C. enyo enyo* of 2, 5, 6, and 7 that were born in April, May, April, and November, respectively, with the number of days between the last observed copulation and birth being 242, 176, 299, and 171 days, respectively. Grismer (2002) found neonates from late July to mid-October and suggested that this species mates in the spring and gives birth in the summer or early fall. Taylor (*in* Grismer, 2002) found 1–10 ($\bar{x} = 6.4$) young in the reproductive tracts of preserved museum specimens.

On 28 May 1975 near Omilteme, Guerrero, we collected 5 newborn young and an adult female *C. intermedius* that were basking among the roots of a fallen tree (see Table 49).

Beaupre (1995b) reported that 10 litters of *C. l. lepidus* from the Big Bend region of Texas contained 2–5 ($\bar{x} = 3.6$) offspring, and that neonates appeared as early as 15 July. The smallest gravid female he found was 37.4 cm in SVL. A female collected near Fort Davis, Texas, gave birth to 3 young on 23 August (Minton, 1959). An adult female *C. l. lepidus* collected north of Loma Alta, Val Verde County, Texas, on 17 August 1991 gave birth to 8 young on 17 August that were 19.9–21.6 cm ($\bar{x} = 20.5$ cm) in TL and weighed 8.3–9.7 g ($\bar{x} = 8.8$ g); and a female collected in Presidio County, Texas, on 28 October 1987 gave birth

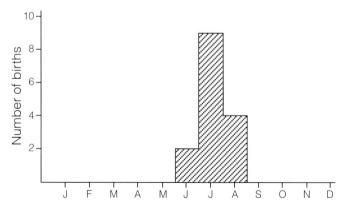

Fig. 199. Birth months for Costa Rican *Crotalus simus*. Adapted from Solórzano and Cerdas, 1988c: 222 (fig. 2).

to 2 young on 18 August 1988 that were 21.9 and 22.0 cm in TL and weighed 11.6 and 11.9 g, respectively (D. Heckard, pers. comm.). A captive pair of C. l. morulus from south of Pablillo, Nuevo León, Mexico, produced 8 young on 8 August 1990 that were 16.6–17.5 cm ($\bar{x}$ = 16.8 cm) in TL and weighed 5.3–6.1 g ($\bar{x}$ = 5.5 g). A photograph showing a litter of 4 C. l. morulus exists (L. Porras, pers. comm.).

Armstrong and Murphy (1979) reported litters of 3–6 for C. lepidus (see Table 49) and a female C. lepidus maculosus found on 10 July with 11 young near her. Williamson (1971) reported that a female C. l. klauberi from the Magdalena Mountains of New Mexico gave birth to 4 young on 29 August 1962. Crotalus l. klauberi in the Chiricahua Mountains of Arizona give birth to an average of 3.7 young (Prival and Schwalbe, 2000). Six young, perhaps constituting an entire brood, were collected in Brown Canyon of the Huachuca Mountains of Arizona on 21 July 1930; these young were 20.7–22.0 cm in TL (Gloyd, 1937).

A mating pair of C. mitchellii encountered in the afternoon on 18 April had the same body temperature as the air temperature, 31.8 °C (Brattstrom, 1965).

Savary (1999) described what appeared to be brood defense in C. molossus molossus in Pima County, Arizona. A female twice approached within about 2–3 m of him while rattling. When he stopped walking, the snake returned to an opening at the base of a rocky outcrop with an large overhang where about 5 newborn young were observed. The young had a bluish cast and opaque pre-buttons, indicating recent birth. At least 2 of the young remained with the female for another day, but four days later neither the adult nor the young were seen. In Arizona, Gates (1957) found a female C. molossus with well-developed embryos on 5 July. Sánchez-Herrera (1980) reported a female C. m. nigrescens that gave birth to 9 young (6 live, 3 stillborn) on 24 June. Greene (1994) reported a pair of mating Crotalus molossus found in a juniper tree.

Crotalus mitchellii in Arizona gives birth during September and October (Gates, 1957). Grismer (2002) observed copulating pairs in Baja California from late April to late May and neonates in late September. Van Denburgh and Slevin (1921b) reported a female with 3 young in September. Because of the disparate sizes attained by individuals of various populations of C. mitchellii, the size of gravid females varies greatly. Klauber (1949b) noted that gravid females of C. m. muertensis ranged in size from 43.1 to 53.3 cm, whereas the smallest gravid female from any mainland population was 67.4 cm.

Goldberg (2000a) found male C. mitchellii with recrudescent testes from March to August, and found also that this species underwent spermiogenesis from April to September. The smallest male containing mature sperm was 51.2 cm in SVL. The vasa deferentia of most males contained sperm from March through September, suggesting that these snakes could breed during these months. There is evidence that C. mitchellii undergoes spermiogenesis mostly in the spring, in contrast to other rattlesnakes, such as C. atrox, C. scutulatus, and C. viridis, that experience spermiogenesis in the summer or fall (Aldridge, 1979a; Goldberg, 1999a; Jacob et al., 1987). Lowe et al. (1986) reported that C. mitchellii in Arizona mates in April and May, and Goldberg (2000a) reported field observations of mating in California during April and June. The smallest reproductively active female examined by Goldberg (2000a) was 55.2 cm in SVL. The number of young produced by this species was reported to be 1–10 by Klauber (1972) and 3–8 by Goldberg (2000a), with the average number of young being about 6. Crotalus mitchellii appears to have a biennial reproductive cycle

with yolk deposition beginning during the summer and ovulation occurring the subsequent year (Goldberg, 2000a). Parturition occurs in September.

Crotalus polystictus gives birth in June or early July (see Table 49). Klauber (1972) reported litters of 3 and 20 offspring for C. polystictus, and Hubbard (1980) reported litters containing 3, 6, and 6 young. A litter of 14 young, purportedly of this species, reported by Cuesta-Terrón (1930b) is probably based on a misidentification because the size given for the young (12 cm) is much smaller than is known for this species.

Crotalus pricei most frequently gives birth from July to early September, usually to 3–9 young. Gravid females are usually encountered basking among rocks in the early morning. Armstrong and Murphy (1979) collected three young C. pricei at Los Bancos, Durango, on 11 July 1973 that had not yet shed, indicating very recent birth. A female obtained at this locality gave birth to 3 young on 24–28 July 1973, and a female from the Chiricahua Mountains of Arizona gave birth to 4 young on 20 May 1967. Other records of birth in this species were provided by Kauffeld (1943a, 1943b), who reported 6 young born on 19 August to a female from the Chiricahuas; Keasey (1969), who reported 8 young born on 23 September 1953; Van Devender and Lowe (1977), who reported 6 young born on 19 July 1971 to a female from Los Leones in Chihuahua; and Lemos-Espinal et al. (2000b), who reported 6 young born on 26 July 1999 to a female from near Creel in Chihuahua that were 16.3–17.5 cm in TL. On 21 August 1931, Gloyd (1937) found 2 newborn snakes that were 19.3 and 20.6 cm in TL in the Chiricahua Mountains. Tanner (1985) found nearly full-term embryos in a snake collected in late August. We collected a female C. pricei from near San Antonio de las Alazanas on 16 July 1976 that gave birth to 4 young the following day. Two captive adult male C. pricei engaged in combat on 10 July 1984, and the successful male subsequently copulated with a female (Mahaney, 1997a), which gave birth to 5 young on 6 June 1985. Another female gave birth in captivity to 7 young on 4 August 1995 and retained another single young that was later surgically removed (Mahaney, 1997b). Other reproductive information for C. pricei is given in Table 49.

In a thorough investigation of male and female reproductive cycles in C. pricei, Goldberg (2000b) found that males underwent recrudescence from June to August and spermiogenesis from June to October. The smallest male containing mature sperm was 33.3 cm in SVL. It was suggested that sperm produced from June to October was stored overwinter in the vasa deferentia and was used during spring mating. The smallest reproductive female was 33.0 cm in SVL. Females gave birth to 3–8 young. Most litters were born from July to September. The proportion of gravid adult females and follicular cycles suggests biennial reproduction for this species.

Prival (2000) and Prival et al. (2002) conducted extensive ecological studies of C. pricei in the Chiricahua Mountains of southeastern Arizona in 1998–1999. Live snakes were palpated to detect embryos. The earliest date that embryos were discovered was 9 June, and the latest was 1 September, with the majority of gravid snakes found during July and August when 16 of 33 (48%) females were gravid, suggesting a biennial reproductive cycle. Gravid females contained 1–6 ($\bar{x}$ = 3.9) embryos and were 36.4–50.0 cm ($\bar{x}$ = 43.2 cm) in SVL. A pair of C. pricei was observed mating on 21 August 1997, and a female gave birth to 4 young in mid-August 1998 that were 16.3–17.3 cm ($\bar{x}$ = 16.9 cm) in SVL and weighed 4.3–4.5 g ($\bar{x}$ = 4.4 g). Another female gave birth to 3 young in late July that were 15.1–16.3 cm in SVL

($\bar{x}$ = 15.5 cm) and weighed 3.8–4.4 g ($\bar{x}$ = 4.1 g). Other radio-telemetered females probably gave birth in late August and late September 1998. The first appearance of neonates in any given year was associated with the date of the beginning of the summer monsoons, with young usually being found some six to eight weeks after the onset of the rains. Gravid females maintained warmer body temperatures than males or nongravid females, probably by basking for longer periods. Mating was usually in August and early September. Females of this species mature in four to five years.

A mating pair of *C. ruber* was observed in Railroad Canyon, just east of Lake Elsimore, California (Armstrong and Murphy, 1979). Courting pairs of *C. ruber* were found in Baja California from March through May, and young have been found from August to December (Grismer, 2002).

In Arizona, Gates (1957) most frequently encountered newborn *C. scutulatus* in late August and September. On 11 August 1958 in Pima County, Arizona, McCoy (1961) observed many recently born *C. scutulatus*, perhaps slightly more than a week old, that still had deeply indented umbilical scars; three of these were 26.5–28.3 cm in TL. Gloyd (1937) captured a juvenile 25.0 cm in TL on 14 August 1930 in Pima County. A female from near Yepómera, Chihuahua, gave birth to 8 young on 18 July that were 20.4–22.1 cm ($\bar{x}$ = 21.8 cm) in SVL (Van Devender and Lowe, 1977). A pair of one-year-old captive-born sibling *C. s. scutulatus* were observed mating on 13 October 1988 (Nevares and Quijada-Mascareñas, 1989), but whether this was precocious sexual behavior or a mating between mature snakes is unknown.

In the northern part of its range, *C. scutulatus* experiences recrudescence from March to July, spermiogenesis occurs from June to September, and sperm is present in the vasa deferentia from March to October (Goldberg and Rosen, 2000). The smallest spermiogenic male Goldberg and Rosen reported was 41.1 cm in SVL. Females give birth from July through September to 5–13 young, with an average number of about 8. The smallest reproductive female measured was 61.1 cm in SVL. Females appear to reproduce biennially, although the proportion of gravid females during any particular year may be related to prey abundance.

Goldberg (1999b), who studied reproduction in *C. tigris*, found that males undergo spermiogenesis in June–October, with sperm present in the vasa deferentia in May–October. Females have a biennial reproductive cycle, with enlarged ovarian follicles present in August–November and ovulation

presumably occurring the following spring. The smallest reproductive male and female were 51.2 cm and 54.1 cm, respectively. Females give birth to 3–6 ($\bar{x}$ = 4.2) young.

Grismer (2002) found gravid *C. tortugensis* in March and neonates of this species in late May.

Two preserved specimens (UCM 513423 and FMNH 100129) of *C. transversus* collected in July and August, respectively, were gravid. Several neonate *C. transversus* were observed on 20 August 1992 near Jiquipilco, México, Mexico (Camarillo and Campbell, 1993); one was 16.4 cm in TL and had a conspicuous umbilical scar. A specimen collected near Jiquipilco on 13 July 1992 gave birth to 4 young a few days later. A biennial reproductive cycle has been suggested for this species (Camarillo and Campbell, 2002).

Ramírez-Bautista et al. (1995) reported that 6–14 ($\bar{x}$ = 10.7) young were produced in three litters of *C. triseriatus triseriatus*. A female captured in Morelos during late July contained 12 embryos; other females captured at this time had already given birth (Davis and Smith, 1953). A juvenile estimated to be probably not more than a week old was found in Morelos on 28 July (Davis and Smith, 1953).

Martin (1975b) collected a gravid female *C. willardi willardi* in the Santa Rita Mountains of Arizona on 3 August 1974 that gave birth to 6 young on 18 August. The young were 18.0–19.5 cm ($\bar{x}$ = 18.9 cm) in TL and weighed 5.43–6.66 g ($\bar{x}$ = 60.8 g). A captive mating of *C. w. willardi* produced 6 young 17.5–20.0 cm in TL and weighing 4.3–6.9 g (Martin, 1975c). Tryon (1978) reported a duration of 15–24 hours for copulation in *C. w. willardi*; gestation in this taxon may be as long as 13 months (Lowe et al., 1986). A gravid female *C. w. amabilis* collected on 21 July 2000 gave birth to 5 young on 26 July 2000 that were 15.6–16.7 cm in SVL and weighed 6.7–7.1 g (Bryson and Lazcano, 2002). A pair of *C. w. amabilis* was found mating under a fallen pine log in the Sierra del Nido on 21 July 2000 at 1521 hours (Bryson and Lazcano, 2002); the copulation lasted for at least 28 hours.

Holycross and Goldberg (2001) found that both sexes in northern populations of *C. willardi* reach reproductive maturity at about 40 cm TL. Spermiogenesis occurs in the summer and early fall, with males containing sperm in the vas deferens from June to September (Fig. 200). Females give birth from late July through August and subsequently remain reproductively inactive prior to hibernation. One or more years after giving birth, females undergo vitellogenesis. The authors suggested that copulation occurs from midsummer to early fall and that ovulation and fertilization occur in the spring, followed by four

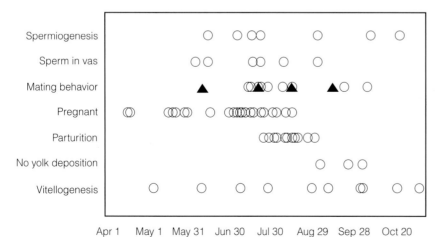

Fig. 200. Phenology of reproduction in northern populations of *Crotalus willardi*. For mating behavior, circles represent dates of copulation and triangles indicate courtship. Adapted from Holycross and Goldberg, 2001:474 (fig. 1).

to five months of gestation. Reproductive frequency appears to be facultative but is usually biennial or longer. The number of young produced is 2–9 ($\bar{x}$ = 5.4), the TL is 15.0–18.2 cm ($\bar{x}$ = 16.7 cm), and the weight of neonates is 5.0–9.0 g ($\bar{x}$ = 6.8 g).

Longevity. There are numerous records of rattlesnakes living in captivity for 15–20 years or even longer. Some of the more impressive longevity records listed by Slavens and Slavens (2000) are *C. adamanteus*, 22 years, 9 months; *C. atrox*, 27 years; *C. cerastes*, 27 years, 4 months; *C. horridus*, 30 years, 2 months; *C. lepidus*, 33 years, 7 months; *C. mitchellii*, 21 years, 3 months; *C. viridis*, 24 years, 1 month; and *C. willardi*, 21 years, 3 months. Cavanaugh (1994) reported a *C. horridus* that survived for 36 years, 7 months, and 27 days in the laboratory. Goodman et al. (1997) documented a captive-born *C. c. cerastes* that was 28 years old and still living at the time of their report. Secor (1994b) suggested that under natural conditions the mean life expectancy for *C. cerastes* is 5–7 years.

Crotalus adamanteus Palisot de Beauvois, 1799
(Map 89, Pls. 752–755)

Crotalus adamanteus Palisot de Beauvois, 1799, *Trans. Am. Philos. Soc.* 4:362–381[368]. Type(s): none designated. Type-locality: not specifically stated in original description; restricted to "Charleston, South Carolina," by Schmidt (1953c:230).

Crotalus rhombifer Latreille, *in* Sonnini de Manoncourt and Latreille, 1801–1802, *Hist. Nat. Rept.* 3:335 pp.[197]. Type(s): "Muséum d'Histoire naturelle de Paris." Not found in the MNHN by Thireau (1991:4). Type-locality: "Amérique." Restricted to "Gainesville" by Schmidt (1953c:230).

Crotalus rhombiferus Brickell, 1805, *Philadelphia Med. Phys. J.* 2:164[164]. Type(s): none designated. Type-locality: not given; probably vicinity of Savannah, Georgia, USA, according to Klauber (1972:31). [Junior primary homonym of *Crotalus rhombifer* Latreille, 1801.]

Crotalus adamanteus var. *adamanteus*—Jan, 1858, *Rev. Mag. Zool.* (Paris) (2)10:148–157[153].

Caudisona adamantea—Cope, 1867 [dated 1866], *Proc. Acad. Nat. Sci. Philadelphia* 18:300–314[307].

Crotalus adamanteus adamanteus—Cope, 1875, *Bull. U.S. Natl. Mus.* 1:104 pp.[33].

Crotalus durissus—Boulenger, 1896b, *Cat. Snakes British Mus.* 3:1–727[578]. [Not of Linnaeus, 1758.]

Crotalus adamanteus pleistofloridensis Brattstrom 1954, *Trans. San Diego Soc. Nat. Hist.* 12:31–46[35]. Holotype: AMNH 6779 (Dept. Vert. Paleon.). Type-locality: "Seminole, Pinellas County, Florida."

Crotalus giganteus Brattstrom, 1954, *Trans. San Diego Soc. Nat. Hist.* 12:31–46[36]. Holotype: AMNH 6772 (Dept. Vert. Paleon.). Type-locality: "Allen Cave, Lecanto, Citrus County, Florida" [USA].

Crotalus adamanteus—Klauber, 1956, *Rattlesnakes*, 1st ed., 1:708 pp.[29, fig. 2.11].

The snake that confronts the imagined man is a moving thing to see. . . . The snake I think forward to is the last in all the pablum agar culture of the purified world. The coils of her body rise and fall in slow spirals, the keen singing of her rattle sounds, and she waits there, testing with the forks of her tongue the whole future of her kind. In my thought the man then stoops with an old urge and picks up a stick. It is almost the only stick left lying in the eastern half of North America, and the man takes it up and moves in closer to the wondering snake. He raises the stick, then somehow lowers it as if in thought, then halfway brings it up again. And then the conjuring fails for me, and the snake song falls away, like the song of cicadas losing heart, one by one. The woods grow dark and fade off into distant times.

—Carr, 1963

Most formidable of the North American poisonous snakes, . . . this huge rattlesnake with its bright and symmetrical markings is a beautiful and terrible creature. Ever bold and alert,

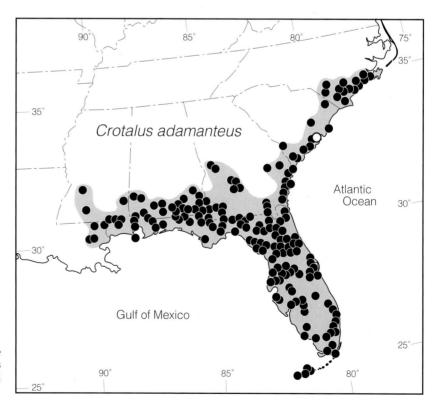

Map 89. Distribution of *Crotalus adamanteus* in the southeastern United States. Unfilled symbol represents type-locality, Charleston, South Carolina, as restricted by Schmidt (1953c:230).

retaining its wild nature when captive, there is awe-inspiring grandeur about the coil of this reptile: the glittering black eyes, the slowly waving tongue, and the incessant rasping note of the rattle. . . . The vibration of a step throws the creature upon guard. Taking a deep inhalation, the snake inflates the rough, scaly body to the tune of a low, rushing sound of air. Shifting the coils to uncover the rattle, this is "sprung" with the abruptness of an electric bell. There is no hysterical striking, but careful watching, and if the opportunity to effect a blow is presented, the result may be mortal.

—Ditmars, 1936

LOCAL NAMES Florida diamondback rattlesnake, water rattlesnake; other common names are listed in Wright and Wright, 1957:936.

ENGLISH NAME Eastern diamondback rattlesnake.

ETYMOLOGY The specific epithet is derived from the Greek *adamant*, meaning "unconquerable," and the Greek suffix *-eus*, meaning "one who is."

DISTRIBUTION In the southeastern United States from Albemarle Sound in North Carolina southward through peninsular Florida and west through southern Alabama and Mississippi to extreme eastern Louisiana (Map 89). This species occurs on a few barrier islands off the coast of Georgia, including Blackbeard, Cumberland, Little Cumberland, Little Saint Simons, Ossabaw, Sapelo, Saint Catherines, and Saint Simons (Behler et al., 1997; Johnson et al., 1974; Martof, 1963); in Chatham County, Georgia, it occurs on Ossabaw Island, which is separated from the mainland by an extensive salt marsh (Ringler, 1977); off South Carolina it occurs on Edisto Island (pers. observ.); on Cudjoy (now called Cudjoe) Key off Key West, Florida (Allen and Slatten, 1945); on Saint Vincent, Saint George, and Dog Islands off the Apalachicola region of Florida (Blaney, 1971); on Cedar Key (pers. observ.); and on Dauphin Island off Alabama (Schroeder, 1979). The diamondback occurs on lowland coastal plains from sea level up to about 500 m.

Distribution records are available for Alabama (Mount, 1975; Schroeder, 1979; Snyder, 1945), Florida (Boulenger, 1896b; Boundy, 1994a; Curran, 1935; Garman, 1884a—in part; Haller, 1971; Loennberg, 1894; Tennant, 1997; Van Hyning, 1933; Wilson and Porras, 1983), Georgia (Behler et al., 1997; Curran, 1935; Gibbons and West, 2000; Hensley, 1959; Jackson, 1983; Jensen and Moulis, 1997, 1999), Florida including the Florida Keys (Allen, 1940; Allen and Slaten, 1945; Ashton, 1978; Ashton and Ashton, 1981; Bartlett and Bartlett, 1999; Carr, 1940; Carr and Goin, 1955; Duellman and Schwartz, 1958; Lazell, 1989; Loennberg, 1894; Means, 1994, 1999; Tennant, 1997), Louisiana (Beyer, 1900; Dundee and Rossman, 1989), Mississippi (Cook, 1943, 1954; Keiser, 1982; Lohoefener and Altig, 1983), North Carolina (Palmer, 1974; Palmer and Braswell, 1995), and South Carolina (Gibbons and West, 2000). The general distribution is discussed in Amaral, 1927g; Conant and Collins, 1998; Garman, 1884b; Gloyd, 1940; Klauber, 1930a, 1971, 1972; McCranie, 1980a; Stejneger, 1895; and Werner, 1922.

HABITAT Upland dry pine forest (Carr, 1940; Dalrymple, 1988), pine-palmetto flatwoods (Ashton and Ashton, 1981; Carr, 1940; Mount, 1975), sandhills, coastal maritime hammocks, longleaf pine–turkey oak associations, grass-sedge bogs, swamp forest, sandy mixed woodlands, mesic hammocks (Carr, 1973; Duellman and Schwartz, 1958; Means, 1994), xeric hammocks, and salt marshes (Neill, 1958); and during dry periods in wet prairies (Timmerman, 1995). *Crotalus adamanteus* is sympatric with *C. horridus* in many regions but favors drier, more upland habitats (Palmer and Braswell, 1995). In many places it appears to utilize gopher burrows (Cook, 1954) or gopher tortoise

burrows (Dundee and Rossman, 1989) for summer retreats and overwintering. This snake is also an accomplished swimmer, regularly crossing rivers and even heading significant distances out to sea (Carr, 1940; Duellman and Schwartz, 1958). A specimen was found floating more than 20 miles (31.5 km) offshore in the Gulf of Mexico (Lazell, 1989), and another was collected on Tortuga Island, West Indies, in the nineteenth century (formerly housed at the MCZ-Harvard; currently at the MZUSP–São Paulo).

DESCRIPTION This heavy-bodied snake is the largest of the rattlesnakes. The maximum sizes reported are 244.0 (Klauber, 1972) and 251.5 cm (Ditmars, 1936). We are aware of a captive specimen that weighed in excess of 12 kg. Owing to a lack of voucher specimens, the stated maximum size for *C. adamanteus* has been called into question (Jones, 1997).

The ground color is brownish, brownish yellow, olive, or brownish gray. The dorsal pattern consists of 24–35 dark brown to black diamonds with slightly paler centers. The dorsal rhombs are outlined by a row of cream or yellowish scales. Posteriorly on the body the dorsal blotches grade into crossbands, followed by 5–10 tail bands. A broad postocular stripe extends from the posterior of the eye downward to the margin of the lip and posteriorly to the rictus. The postocular stripe is bordered anteriorly and posteriorly by distinct white or yellow sripes. The tail is marked with dark bands, and the first band following the vent may be brownish, especially on juveniles and subadults; more posterior bands become blackish, and the proximal rattle segment is black. The venter is yellowish or cream with dark mottling diffused on the lateral portions of ventrals.

In general, individuals from the northern part of the range (the Carolinas) are the most strikingly colored with more contrasting patterns and more yellow. Antonio and Barker (1983) described a number of atypical color patterns in *C. adamanteus* including albinos; amelanistic partial albinos; lacking yellow pigment; dorsal blotches irregularly broken along the midline of the body; a broad, dark middorsal stripe laterally edged with yellow stripes; and fused dorsal botches at midbody.

The rostral is higher than wide. There are 2 internasals in contact with the rostral, about 10–21 scales in the internasal-prefrontal region, and 5–11 (usually 7 or 8) intersupraoculars. The prenasal and first supralabial make broad contact with each other. The posterior canthal is large but is not deflected downward on the side of the head to partially intervene between the upper preocular and postnasal (this area being occupied by an upper loreal). Most frequently, 2 loreals are present on each side (an upper and a lower); these intervene between the preoculars and postnasal. One or 2 interoculabials separate the anterior subocular from the supralabial series. There are 12–17 (usually 14 or 15) supralabials, 15–21 (usually 17 or 18) infralabials (first pair not transversely divided), 25–31 (mode 29) dorsal scale rows at midbody, 165–176 ventrals in males and 170–187 in females, and 27–33 subcaudals in males and 20–26 in females. The population inhabiting the Florida Keys has a relatively high segment count (Christman, 1980).

SIMILAR SPECIES Two other species of rattlesnakes occur within the range of *C. adamanteus*: *C. horridus* and *Sistrurus miliarius*. *Crotalus horridus* has a pattern of blackish crossbands or chevrons, a black tail, and a postocular stripe that is not boldly set off by white stripes on either side; *S. miliarius* is a small snake, usually no more than 60 cm in TL, that has 9 large head plates and a dorsal pattern of small blotches. *Crotalus atrox* is not sympatric with *C. adamanteus*, and the ranges of these species come no closer than about 500 km of each other— *C. adamanteus* extending as far west as southeastern Louisiana and *C. atrox* reaching its eastern limits in north-central Texas and west-central Arkansas. *Crotalus atrox* lacks the distinctive vertical pale stripe on the posterior edges of the prenasals and anterior supralabials, usually has 25 dorsal scale rows at midbody (versus 29), and has a posterior canthal scale that is laterally deflected downward to cover part of the side of the head.

REMARKS   This species has now become extirpated or scarce over most of its range. At one time it was abundant enough over parts of its range to cause problems with livestock. For example, a family living in the Okefenokee area of Georgia was reported to have lost 10–15 pigs in 1910 to bites from *C. adamanteus* (Wright and Bishop, 1915). In the late 1950s we frequently found *C. adamanteus* specimens along the highways around Charleston, South Carolina. Nine road-killed adults were found on a 6-mile (9.5-km) stretch of highway bordering the Ashley River. Today this rattlesnake is an unusual sight in that area.

Crotalus aquilus Klauber, 1952
(Map 90, Pls. 756–772)

Crotalus lugubris—Dugès, 1877, *Naturaleza* (Mexico) 4:1–29[25]. [Not of Jan, 1859, according to Klauber (1952:24).]

Crotalus triseriatus—Cope, 1885, *Proc. Am. Philos. Soc.* 22:379–404[386]. [Not of Wagler, 1830, according to Klauber (1952:24).]

Crotalus triseriatus triseriatus—Klauber, *in* Githens and George, 1931, *Bull. Antivenin Inst. Am.* 5:31–34[33]. [In part; not of Wagler, 1830, according to Klauber (1952:24).]

Crotalus triseriatus triseriatus—Gloyd, 1940, *Chicago Acad. Sci. Spec. Publ.* 4:1–266[84].

Crotalus triseriatus aquilus Klauber, 1952, *Bull. Zool. Soc. San Diego* (26):1–143[24]. Holotype: MCZ R27843. Type-locality: "near Alvarez, San Luis Potosí, Mexico."

Crotalus aquilus—Harris and Simmons, 1978b, *Bull. Maryland Herpetol. Soc.* 14:105–211[107].

Crotalus triseriatus quadrangularis Harris and Simmons, 1978b, *Bull. Maryland Herpetol. Soc.* 14:105–211[126]. Holotype: RS 1233 HSH/RSS (NHSM). Type-locality: "3 mi. SW Jacala, Hidalgo, Mexico, at elevation of 6700 ft."

Crotalus aquilus—Dorcas, 1992, *Biol. Pitvipers*, pp. 71–88[72 (fig. 1), 73 (figs. 2 and 3), 75 (fig. 4), 76 (figs. 5 and 6), 444 (Pl. 9C)].

When [a rattlesnake] is killed suddenly, without its having become irritated, the body lies immobile after the head is cut off. If, on the other hand, it has been angered and has made some resistance, the irritability of the muscular system lasts for a long time after its death. The fat, which in the first instance is employed as an empiric remedy in the country, in the second instance is of no use, for it is alleged that it acquires noxious properties.

—1980 translation of Berlandier's work describing the customs in Mexico during the early 1800s

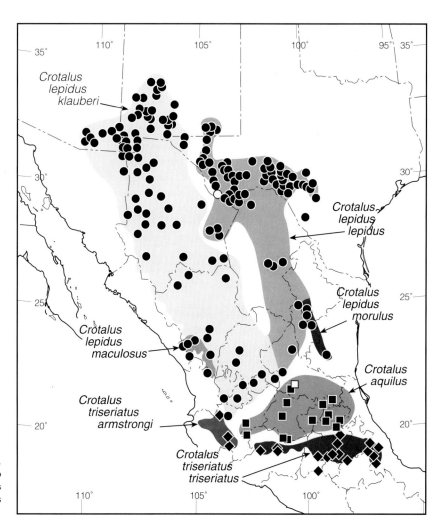

Map 90. Distributions of *Crotalus aquilus* (squares), *C. lepidus* (circles), and *C. triseriatus* (diamonds) in Mexico and the southwestern United States. Unfilled symbols represent type-localities; that for *C. triseriatus* was given simply as Mexico.

LOCAL NAME Víbora de cascabel.

ENGLISH NAME Querétaro dusky rattlesnake.

ETYMOLOGY The species epithet is derived from the Latin *aquilus*, meaning "dark-colored," "dun," or "swarthy," an allusion to the dull, dark pattern noted in the type-series.

DISTRIBUTION The southern portion of the Mexican Plateau from northwestern Veracruz and southern San Luis Potosí southward and westward through northern Hidalgo, Querétaro, Guanajuato, and northwestern Michoacán to the Chapala region of Jalisco (Map 90). This species occurs from about 1,600 to 3,110 m near El Chico in Hidalgo.

Distribution records (sometimes as *C. triseriatus*) are given in Armstrong and Murphy, 1979; Auth et al., 2000; Camarillo and Casas-Andreu, 1998; Cope, 1879; Cuesta-Terrón, 1921b; Dixon et al., 1972; Duellman, 1961, 1965b; Dugès, 1876–1877, 1896a; Dunn, 1936; Gloyd, 1940; Günther, 1895–1902 (in part); Harris and Simmons, 1978b; Klauber, 1952, 1971, 1972; Minton and Minton de Cervantes, 1977; Smith, 1946b; Taylor, 1949; Taylor, 1953b; and Velasco, 1890a.

HABITAT Open grassy and usually rocky habitats north of the Transverse Volcanic Cordillera. We have found this species in pine-oak forest, open karstic areas, grassy montane meadows, and stony mesquite-grassland. It was abundant around La Estanzuela, Hidalgo, in the 1970s beneath cultivated agaves.

DESCRIPTION This heavy-bodied snake reaches a maximum TL of 67.8 cm (Klauber, 1972), but most adults are less than 50 cm.

There is a great amount of intrapopulational and interpopulational variation within this species; further, the ground color of many populations is sexually dimorphic and may be pale to dark brown, gray to gray-green, yellowish green, or pale to reddish brown. Adult males frequently have a greenish or yellowish cast, whereas females are brownish or grayish. A pair of dark brown nape blotches is followed by 21–41 middorsal blotches and 3–8 bands on the tail. The dorsal blotches are usually 5–7 scales wide and frequently are roughly quadrangular, although they may be subcircular or may even form crossbars. Usually a single series of conspicuous lateral blotches is offset from the dorsal series of blotches. Less well defined (sometimes absent) series of dorsolateral and ventrolateral blotches are present in the interspaces between the level of the dorsal and lateral blotches. A well-defined postocular stripe is usually present but may appear faded in some paler specimens. The lower portion of the postocular stripe extends under the eye to the preoculars; posterior to the eye the postocular stripe extends to at least the rictus and usually 4–5 scales beyond. The venter is yellowish, pinkish, or very pale gray with dark brown or gray mottling that becomes more intense posteriorly. The iris is pale yellow, gold, or bronze, finely flecked with dark brown, and usually paler dorsally.

The rostral is usually wider than high but is sometimes about as high as wide. The prenasal curves under the postnasal, and the anterior subocular is usually in contact with supralabials 4 and 5, but it may touch only one of these scales or supralabials 5 and 6, or may be separated by a single interoculabial. The upper preocular is often (in about 40% of specimens) vertically divided. There are 2–3 (usually 2) large internasals, in contact; 1–2 (usually 1) canthals on each side; 0–2 (usually 2) intercanthals; a total of 5–10 scales in the internasal-prefrontal area; 2–5 (usually 3) intersupraoculars; 1–2 loreals (usually 1) on each side separated from the supralabials by foveals and separating the upper preocular from the postnasal; 1–6 (usually 3) prefoveals; 10–14 (mode 12) supralabials; 9–13 (mode 11) infralabials; 21–25 (usually 23) midbody dorsal scale rows; 140–158

ventrals in males and 138–156 in females; 22–31 subcaudals in males and 19–24 in females; and 8–11 (usually 10) rattle-fringe scales.

SIMILAR SPECIES *Crotalus lepidus* and *C. triseriatus* are similar to *C. aquilus* in many respects, although neither species is sympatric with *C. aquilus*. *Crotalus lepidus* has a color pattern that most frequently consists of crossbands rather than blotches, 1–4 tail bands (versus 3–8), an upper preocular that is usually vertically divided (more than 80% versus about 40% in *aquilus*), and usually 12 rattle-fringe scales (versus usually 10). *Crotalus triseriatus* has smaller and more numerous (usually more than 38) dorsal blotches, an upper preocular that is infrequently divided (less than 15% of the time), a prenasal that does not curve under the postnasal, a proportionately longer tail, and a smaller rattle usually fringed with only 8 scales. *Crotalus ravus* occurs to the south of the range of *C. aquilus* and has large head plates and usually 21 dorsal scale rows at midbody. *Crotalus polystictus* may be sympatric with *C. aquilus* in some areas but is easily distinguished by its pattern of horizontally elongated body blotches that are arranged dorsolaterally, at least on the anterior portion of the body.

REMARKS Amaral (1927f, 1927g) confused at least three species (*C. aquilus*, *C. pricei*, and *C. triseriatus*), which he included in a single taxon, *C. triseriatus*. Smith (1946b) recognized *C. pricei* as a separate species, but most authors (e.g., Klauber, 1972) continued to treat *aquilus* as a subspecies of *triseriatus* until Dorcas (1992) demonstrated several distinctive differences between the two taxa. A number of morphological characters suggest that *C. aquilus* may be more closely related to *C. lepidus* than it is to *C. t. triseriatus* or *C. t. armstrongi*, making *C. triseriatus*, as previously recognized, paraphyletic. These characters include the condition of the upper preocular (often vertically divided), shape of the nasal (prenasal curves under postnasal), tendency toward sexual dimorphism in ground color (males greenish or yellowish), osteology (distance between outer edges of frontals comparatively narrow, squamosal more elongate with less prominent posterior processes, foramen in maxillary cavity relatively small), eye size (relatively small), rattle size (relatively large), and hemipenial spines (relatively shorter and stouter). Klauber (1952) suggested that despite the geographical proximity of *C. triseriatus aquilus* (= *C. aquilus*) and *C. triseriatus triseriatus* in Michoacán, there was no evidence of intergradation and these two taxa might actually represent two separate species. Subsequent fieldwork in this region also failed to demonstrate sympatry or intergradation between these populations (Duellman, 1961). After a thorough investigation of the groups' relationship to one another, Dorcas (1992) concluded that *C. aquilus* and *C. triseriatus* should be considered distinct species.

Crotalus atrox Baird and Girard, 1853
(Figs. 201 and 202, Maps 91 and 92, Pls. 773–783)

Crotalus cinereous Le Conte, *in* Hallowell, 1852, *Proc. Acad. Nat. Sci. Philadelphia* 6:177–182[177]. Holotype: present location unknown. Type-locality: "near the Colorado [River]." This name has priority over *atrox*; however, in the interest of conserving widely used names, the ICZN established *atrox* as the accepted name and suppressed *cinereous* (Opinion 365, 16 Nov. 1955).

Crotalus atrox Baird and Girard, 1853, *Cat. N. Am. Rept.* 1:172 pp.[5]. Holotype: USNM 7761. Type-locality: "Indianola," Calhoun County, Texas, USA.

Crotalus adamanteus var. *atrox*—Jan, 1859, *Rev. Mag. Zool.* (Paris) (2)10:148–157[153].

Caudisona atrox var. *atrox*—Kennicott, 1861b, *Proc. Acad. Nat. Sci. Philadelphia* 13:204–208[206].

Caudisona atrox var. *sonoraensis* Kennicott, 1861b, *Proc. Acad. Nat. Sci. Philadelphia* 13:204–208[206]. Type(s): none designated. Type-locality: "Sonora and vicinity."

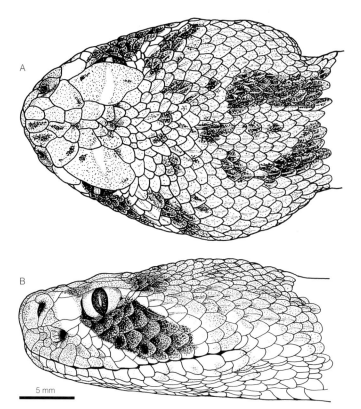

Fig. 201. (A) Dorsal and (B) lateral aspects of head of *Crotalus atrox*, female, 54.5 cm TL (UTA R-12566), from 7.1 km south of Venados, Hidalgo, Puebla, elevation 1,640 m. In this species the interoculabial series is complete, the anterior subocular is separated from the supralabial series by one or more rows of scales, and the upper preocular is usually in contact with the postnasal (or such contact is prevented by an upper loreal). Note that the pale stripe behind the eye extends to slightly in front of the rictus. Drawings by Ty M. Kubin.

Crotalus adamanteus var. *atrox*—Jan, 1863, *Elenco Sist. Ofidi*, 143 pp.[123].

Crotalus adamanteus var. *sonoriensis*—Jan, 1863, *Elenco Sist. Ofidi*, 143 pp.[124]. [Unjustified emendation.]

Caudisona atrox—Cope, 1867 [dated 1866], *Proc. Acad. Nat. Sci. Philadelphia* 18:300–314 [309].

Crotalus adamanteus atrox—Cope, *in* Yarrow, *in* Wheeler, 1875, *Rep. Geog. Geol. Explor. Surv. West 100th Merid.* 5:509–584[536].

Caudisona atrox var. *sonorensis*—Boulenger, 1896b, *Cat. Snakes British Mus.* 3:727 pp.[576]. [Unjustified emendation.]

Crotalus atrox atrox—Cope, 1900 [dated 1898], *Rep. U.S. Natl. Mus.* 1898:153–1270[1164].

Crotalus atrox atrox—Schmidt, 1922, *Bull. Am. Mus. Nat. Hist.* 46:607–707[698].

Crotalus atrox sonoraensis—Amaral, 1929, *Bull. Antivenin Inst. Am.* 3:4–6[5].

Crotalus atrox—Klauber, 1972, *Rattlesnakes*, 2d ed., 1:740 pp.[32, 58 (fig. 2:1), 65 (fig. 2:12)].

Crotalus sonoriensis—Golay et al., 1993, *Endogly. Venom. Snakes World*, 478 pp.[54]. [As cited in the synonymy of *Crotalus atrox*.]

I remember the day my dad's best friend, Rex, got a rattlesnake fang stuck in his leg and he just laughed. His wife begged him to go to the hospital, but Rex just plucked it out, drank a beer, and went to bed. Rex sold ceiling fans for a living, but on the side he was a daredevil snake handler at the Rattlesnake Roundup in Big Spring, Texas, where we lived when I was a kid. Our town, like a handful in Texas and across the U.S., sets aside a few days every spring and throws a party for all the snakes caught by ranchers in their pastures. Thousands of these venomous creatures are thrown into circular pits, and guys like Rex wade through in knee-high boots, poking them, taunting them, picking them up, and kissing them. The kids love it.

—Mealer, 2001

The biggest rattlesnakes known are of the Eastern diamondback species. The largest one officially measured reached a length of eight feet or so. Next in size is the Western diamondback, with an official measurement of seven feet or so. But lots of snakes have been killed when no herpetologist was around to make measurements. The way to make a record in snake-killing is to be off away from tape measures or

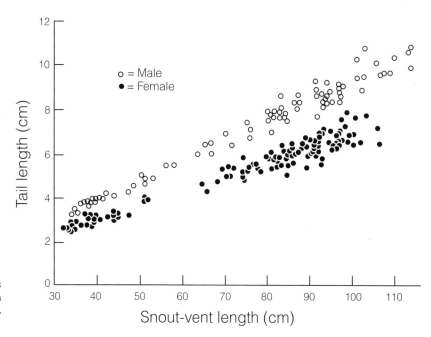

Fig. 202. Tail length versus SVL in a sample of *Crotalus atrox* from the Wichita Mountain Wildlife Refuge in southwestern Oklahoma, USA. Adapted from Boyer, 1957:214 (fig. 1).

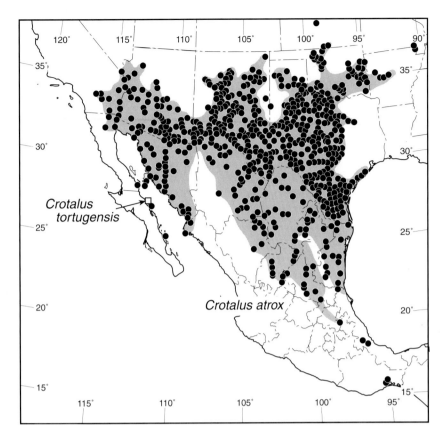

Map 91. Distributions of *Crotalus atrox* (circles) in the southwestern United States and Mexico and of *C. tortugensis* (square), which is restricted to Isla de Tortuga. Unfilled symbol represents type-locality for *C. tortugensis*; that for *C. atrox* too imprecise to plot. *C. atrox* occurs on several islands in the Gulf of California, including (from north to south) Tiburón (shaded), Turner, San Pedro Mártir, Santa María, and Santa Cruz. See text for discussion of two isolated populations in southern Mexico.

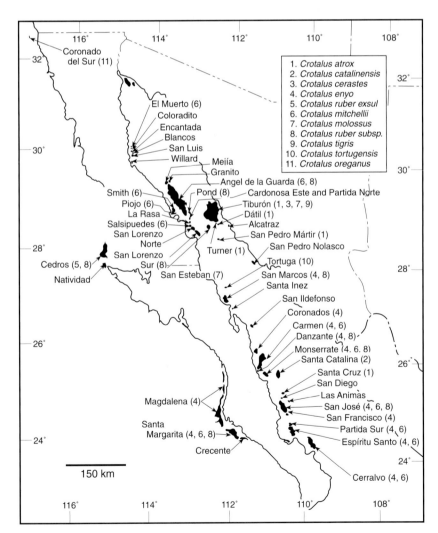

1. *Crotalus atrox*
2. *Crotalus catalinensis*
3. *Crotalus cerastes*
4. *Crotalus enyo*
5. *Crotalus ruber exsul*
6. *Crotalus mitchellii*
7. *Crotalus molossus*
8. *Crotalus ruber subsp.*
9. *Crotalus tigris*
10. *Crotalus tortugensis*
11. *Crotalus oreganus*

Map 92. Species of rattlesnakes inhabiting islands in the Gulf of California and off the Pacific coast. Information taken in part from Campbell and Lamar, 1989; Grismer, 1999a, 2002; Klauber, 1972; and Murphy and Ottley, 1984.

yardsticks or scales and not to have too many witnesses. One way to ruin a good story is to be overcautious on facts.

—Dobie, 1965:8

LOCAL NAMES Coon-tail rattler, víbora de cascabel, víbora serrana.

ENGLISH NAME Western diamondback rattlesnake.

ETYMOLOGY The species epithet comes from the Latin *atrox*, meaning "cruel" or "horrible," an allusion to the danger posed by this snake.

DISTRIBUTION Widely distributed in the western United States and northern Mexico (see Fig. 91). In the United States it occurs from western Arkansas westward through Oklahoma exclusive of the northeastern and north-central parts of the state and the high plains of the panhandle, through Texas exclusive of the northern panhandle and eastern part of the state, and into southern and central New Mexico and Arizona, the extreme southern tip of Nevada, and southeastern California. In California this species occurs on either side of the Chocolate Mountains (Klauber, 1929). It has been reported from extreme southeastern Kansas and from Lyon County, Kansas (Hall and Smith, 1947; Matlack and Rehmeier, 2002), but its presence in these areas is doubtful and the records may be based on introduced snakes. The records from Cowley and Sumner Counties in extreme southern Kansas (Matlack and Rehmeier, 2002) may be based on natural occurrences of the species, and multiple records from near Kanopolis Reservoir in Ellsworth County, Kansas (Matlack and Rehmeier, 2002; Riedle, 1996; Rundquist, 2000), suggest that a viable population may persist in that area. Reports from southeastern and southwestern Missouri are questionable.

In Mexico *C. atrox* ranges westward through most of Nuevo León, Coahuila, and Chihuahua; through much of Sonora to extreme northeastern Baja California del Norte; thence southward to northern Sinaloa and much of the northern plateau region, the Sierra Madre Oriental (exclusive of the higher elevations), and the northern coastal plain of the Gulf of Mexico. The range includes northeastern Durango and Zacatecas, most of San Luis Potosí, and northern Veracruz, Hidalgo, and Querétaro. The presence of this species as far south as the Río Tulancingo (Metztitlán) Valley in east-central Hidalgo has been documented (UTA R-12566) from 7.1 km south of Venados. Of even greater biogeographic interest is the existence of several populations of *C. atrox* isolated far to the south of Hidalgo. Representatives from one such population in the mountains northwest of Tehuantepec, Oaxaca, have been collected on at least a dozen occasions by four collectors; consequently, there appears little doubt that a relictual population of this species was present in the Tehuantepec region as recently as the 1940s, although to our knowledge no specimens have been collected there since then. Perhaps the earliest reference to *C. atrox* in the Tehuantepec region is that of Gadow (1908:197–198), who referred to the species as *Crotalus terrificus* (=*C. simus*). He described a large snake (120 cm) with a distinctly black-barred tail that almost undoubtedly was *C. atrox* rather than *C. simus*, which has a uniformly dark tail. Several specimens collected near the Río Blanco, 20 km west-northwest of Piedras Negras (KU 24129), and from Rinconada, Municipio de Zentla (near 96°50′N, 19°05′W; see Pl. 773), in southern Veracruz are evidence of another isolated population.

Crotalus atrox is also found on San Pedro Mártir, Santa Cruz, Santa María (Sinaloa), Tiburón, and Turner Islands in the Gulf of California (Map 92). Alvarez and Huerta (1974) included an isolated report of this species from the mainland of southeastern Baja California Norte. The vertical distribution is from near sea level (actually below sea level in the Salton Basin of California) to about 2,440 m at Alvarez, San Luis Potosí, Mexico (Klauber, 1972:527); however, over most of its range *C. atrox* does not ascend above the 1,500-m contour.

Distribution records are available for Arizona (Baird, 1859a; Brown, 2000a; Coues, 1875; Fowlie, 1965; Gehlbach, 1957; Gloyd, 1937; Hulse, 1973; Humphrey, 1936; Klauber, 1932a; Little, 1940; Lowe, 1964; Lowe et al., 1986; Nickerson and Mays, 1970; Ortenburger and Ortenburger, 1927; Stejneger, 1902; Taylor, 1935; Vitt and Ohmart, 1978; Woodin, 1953; Yarrow, 1875), Arkansas (Baird, 1859b; Dellinger and Black, 1938; Dowling, 1957; Perkins and Lentz, 1934; Schwardt, 1938; Trauth, 1986; Trauth and Cochran, 1992), California (Cowles, 1941; Glaser, 1970; Klauber, 1927, 1929, 1931a), Missouri (Perkins and Lentz, 1934), Nevada (Linsdale, 1940; Van Denburgh, 1895a), New Mexico (Bogert and Degenhardt, 1961; Degenhardt et al., 1996; Gehlbach, 1965; Lewis, 1950, 1951; Little and Keller, 1937; Mosauer, 1932b; Painter, 1998; Ruthven, 1907; Van Denburgh, 1924; Yarrow, 1875), Oklahoma (Landreth, 1973; Ortenburger, 1929), Texas (Axtell, 1959; Bailey, 1905; Baird, 1859a; A. Brown, 1903a; B. Brown, 1950; Carl, 1980; Cope, 1860a; Crimmins, 1927a, 1927b; Hallowell, 1853; Hambrick, 1975; Hensley, 1959; Jameson and Flury, 1949; Killebrew et al., 1996; McAllister, 1990; Milstead et al., 1950; Minton, 1959; Price, 1998; Rakowitz et al., 1983; Raun and Gehlbach, 1972; Schmidt and Smith, 1944; Shannon and Smith, 1950; Smith, 1947c; Strecker, 1909b, 1922, 1926a, 1926b, 1926d, 1929a, 1930, 1935a, 1935b; Strecker and Johnson, 1935; Strecker and Williams, 1927; Tennant, 1984; Werler, 1964; Yancey, 1996a), Baja California Norte (Alvarez and Huerta, 1974; Cliff, 1954; Curran, 1935; Grismer, 1993, 1994b, 2002; Lindsay, 1966; Linsdale, 1932; R. C. Murphy, 1917; R. W. Murphy, 1983a, 1983b; R. W. Murphy and Ottley, 1984; Savage, 1960; Schmidt, 1922; Soulé and Sloan, 1966), Chihuahua (Cope, 1886; Domínguez et al., 1974; Günther, 1895–1902; Lemos-Espinal et al., 1997, 2000a, 2000b, 2002a, 2002b; Pianka and Smith, 1959; Reynolds, 1982; Smith, 1939; Smith et al., 1963; Tanner, 1985; Williams et al., 1961), Coahuila (Chrapliwy and Fugler, 1955; Dunkle and Smith, 1937; Fugler and Webb, 1956; Garman, 1887a; McCoy, 1984; Schmidt and Owens, 1944), Durango (Williams et al., 1961), Nuevo Léon (Liner, 1964; Velasco-Torres, 1970), Oaxaca (Casas-Andreu et al., 1996; Gadow, 1905, 1908; Hartweg and Oliver, 1940; Woodbury and Woodbury, 1944), Querétaro (Dixon et al., 1972), San Luis Potosí (Taylor, 1952, 1953b), Sinaloa (Dixon et al., 1962; Hardy and McDiarmid, 1969), Sonora (Burger and Hensley, 1949; Cliff, 1954; González-Romero and Alvarez-Cárdenas, 1989; Kennicott, 1861b; Lindsay, 1962—Isla San Pedro Mártir; P. Smith and Hensley, 1958; Taylor, 1938a; Zweifel and Norris, 1955), Tamaulipas (Baker and Webb, 1967; Shannon and Smith, 1950; Smith and Darling, 1952), Veracruz (Pérez-Higareda and Smith, 1991), and Zacatecas (Dugès, 1869). The general Mexican distribution is given in Armstrong and Murphy, 1979; Auth et al., 2000; Cuesta-Terrón, 1920, 1921b, 1931; Campbell and Lamar, 1989; Dugès, 1876–1877, 1896a; Klauber, 1952; Martín del Campo, 1935, 1937a, 1950, 1953; Mocquard, 1908–1909; Nelson, 1922; Smith, 1943a; Smith and Taylor, 1945; and Stejneger and Barbour, 1943. The general distribution is given in Amaral, 1927g; Conant, 1975; Conant and Collins, 1998; Cope, 1900; Cuesta-Terrón, 1920, 1921a, 1931; Garman, 1884a, 1884b; Gloyd, 1940; Haller, 1971; Klauber, 1930a, 1936b, 1971, 1972; Klemmer, 1963; Pickwell, 1972; Pope, 1944–1945; Savage, 1959; Shaw and Campbell, 1974;

Stebbins, 1985; Stejneger, 1895; Van Denburgh, 1922b; Werner, 1922; and Wright and Wright, 1857.

HABITAT Terrain ranging from flat coastal plains to steep, rocky hillsides and canyons and in a variety of vegetation types including mesquite-grassland, desert, desertscrub, sandy creosote areas, and pine-oak forests; along the southern part of its range *C. atrox* occurs in tropical deciduous forest and thornforest. It is most abundant in lowland regions that are xeric or seasonally dry. This snake is sometimes found in the halophilic vegetation along beaches (Taylor, 1938b) and in "low granite and limestone hills surrounded by mixed-grass plains" (Boyer, 1957). Jameson and Flury (1949) reported that *C. atrox* in west Texas was found in creosote bush, catclaw, blackbush, and in salt cedar–mesquite associations. In the 1960s and 1970s we found this species to be especially abundant in the juniper-mesquite association of Cedar Hill in Dallas County, Texas, and in the mesquite-grasslands between Nuevo Laredo and Sabinas Hidalgo in Mexico. On the Stockton Plateau of Texas, Milstead et al. (1950) encountered *C. atrox* in cedar savanna, cedar-ocotillo, persimmon–shin oak, cedar-oak, mesquite-sumac-condalia, walnut–desert willow, live oak, hackberry, and especially mesquite-creosote. In the Sonoran Desert of Arizona this species is found mostly in creosote bush flats, except in the winter, when it switches to rocky slopes (Beck, 1995). Elsewhere in Arizona *C. atrox* occupies open and closed chaparral and piñon-juniper woodland (Jones, 1988).

In west Texas this species is found on floodplains, low lechugilla-covered basalt rubble rills, and streambeds, usually near watercourses, in contrast to *C. molossus*, which inhabits the more xeric uplands of the region (Axtell, 1959). In parts of Arizona *C. atrox* is sympatric with *C. scutulatus* but is more frequently encountered along washes rather than on rocky hillsides (Gates, 1957). Baker and Webb (1967) reported *C. atrox* from the rocky escarpments allong the Río Soto la Marina in Tamaulipas, Mexico.

DESCRIPTION This rattlesnake is exceeded in size only by *C. adamanteus* (eastern diamondback rattlesnake) of the southeastern United States. Specimens of *C. atrox* more than 120 cm long are relatively common, but snakes exceeding 150 cm are infrequently encountered, and those above 180 cm are very rare. Males grow much larger than females (Fig. 181), although this size divergence does not occur until after sexual maturity (Beaupre et al., 1998). The maximum reported length thought to be reliable for this species was given as 213 cm by Klauber (1972). However, two individuals measuring 85 inches (216 cm) and 92 inches (234 cm) in TL were reported collected near Cedar Hill, Dallas County, Texas (Curtis, 1949b); and an individual from northern Tamaulipas was reported to be 7 feet 5 inches (226 cm) in TL exclusive of the rattles (Axtell, 1956). Jones (1997) reported a 92.25-inch (234-cm) specimen and maintained that *C. atrox* is larger than *C. adamanteus*.

The ground color most often is gray-brown with an overall dusty-looking appearance, but it may be pinkish brown, brick red, yellowish, pinkish, or chalky white. The ground color is usually marked by numerous dark brown or black punctations. The 24–45 dorsal body blotches are dark gray-brown to brown. The first body blotch may be a pair of short paravertebral stripes that extend posteriorly from the back of the head and coalesce with each other at their posterior ends. Several of the anteriormost blotches may be somewhat rectangular, but they become roughly hexagonal on the anterior third of the body, and posteriorly they take on a nearly diamond shape. These dorsal blotches are bordered most often with dark brown to black, which is edged partially with white, at least on the anterior two-thirds of the body; dorsal blotches tend to be separated mid-

dorsally by white or pale gray. Several series of small to large, often indistinct dark blotches may be present on the sides. A broad, smoky gray to dark gray-brown postocular stripe extends diagonally from the lower edge of the eye across the side of the head; it is usually bordered below (anteriorly) by a white stripe extending from the upper preocular downward to the supralabials lying directly below or just behind the eye; in some snakes it then runs posteriorly along the upper lip margin. The upper (posterior) white border extends from the upper postocular downward across the temporals to the penultimate or antepenultimate supralabial, where it may merge with the white pigment running along the supralabials, if white is present. The top of the head may be marked irregularly with dark pigment; sometimes a pale transverse line is present across each supraocular.

Perkins and Lentz (1934) reported that *C. atrox* individuals in Arkansas have a slightly greenish ground color and more round dorsal blotches than Texas specimens. Gloyd (1940), Jameson and Flury (1949), and Nickerson and Mays (1969) reported that specimens from southeastern Arizona, southwestern New Mexico, and the Sierra Vieja of west Texas have a pinkish or reddish ground color that becomes more intense on the posterior of the body. Many snakes from southwestern New Mexico, southeastern Arizona, northeastern Sonora, and northern Chihuahua have a decidedly reddish, pinkish gray, or buckskin ground color. The dorsal blotches are only slightly darker than the ground color and often lack the distinctive dark borders; white edging, if present at all, is most prominent at middorsum between the blotches. The dark postocular stripe is ill defined and often does not have white borders. We have seen individuals from near the Red River in Texas with a distinctive brick red ground coloration. Williams et al. (1961) reported three *C. atrox* from Chihuahua that had a reddish ground color and indistinct dorsal blotches.

Snakes from the lava flows of central New Mexico are melanistic. Best and James (1984) and Best et al. (1983) reported that individuals from the population of *C. atrox* living in the Pedro Armendariz lava field of south-central New Mexico have an exceptionally dark ground color. Holmback (1981, 1985) described two specimens from south-central Texas that had a golden brown ground color, either with no pattern or with a dark brown middorsal stripe, and dull yellow stripes in front of each eye; the tails of both snakes were solid black dorsally. Nickerson and Mays (1968) found a *C. atrox* from Pima County, Arizona, that had a pattern of normally colored but elongate or fused blotches on the anterior half of the body that became pale and inconspicuous posteriorly and a narrow middorsal stripe on the tail. Simons (1986) described a litter born to a female from Pinal County, Arizona, that all showed unusual striping on the body and tail. It is probable that the female, collected more than two months prior to parturition, was maintained under environmental conditions that led to developmental abnormalities.

Several albino *C. atrox* have been reported from Texas (Gloyd, 1958), and we have seen several albino, xanthic, and melanistic specimens from near Austin, Waco, and San Antonio. Three individuals from Texas had diffuse melanin uniformly distributed as minute punctations along 4–7 median dorsal scale rows, with no evidence of the typical dorsal blotches (Gloyd, 1958). Other color pattern aberrancies have been reported by Karges (1979b) and Klauber (1972).

The tail has 2–8 (usually 4–6) black bands or rings (these are almost always incomplete ventrally). All of the tail bands are blackish, including the one immediately following the vent. These rings occasionally may be incomplete dorsally or may be staggered so that they do not merge across the midline but instead form vertical bars on each side of the tail. The black rings are usually as long as or slightly longer than the ash white or pale gray interspaces dividing them. The interspaces are decidedly paler than the ground color on the posterior part of the body. The proximal rattle segment is black, at least dorsally.

The mental and anterior infralabials may have a fine dusting of gray pigment, but the gular region and belly are mostly pale (whitish, yellowish, or pinkish) with dark pigment restricted to fine stippling or mottling that is on the lateral portions of the ventrals, often on their anterior edge. Anteriorly, the ventrals are most frequently bright white but become progressively more off-white posteriorly. The pale color of the ventrals extends dorsally to partially cover or to narrowly outline the first 2–3 dorsal scale rows. Except for where the black tail markings encroach ventrally, the subcaudals are pale with a light dusting of gray.

The rostral is higher than wide. There are 2 internasals in contact with the rostral, 11–32 scales in the internasal-prefrontal region, and 3–7 (usually 4 or 5) intersupraoculars. The prenasal and first supralabial usually make contact with each other, although they may be partially separated by the anteriormost prefoveals. The posterior canthal is large and laterally is strongly deflected downward at almost a 90-degree angle to partially intervene between the upper preocular and postnasal, which usually are in contact. A single triangular loreal is usually present on each side; it is situated below the preocular-postnasal suture and partially intervenes between these scales. One or 2 interoculabials separate the anterior subocular from the supralabials. There are 12–18 (usually 15 or 16) supralabials, 14–20 (usually 16 or 17) infralabials (first pair infrequently transversely divided), 23–29 (mode 25) midbody dorsal scale rows, 168–193 ventrals in males and 174–196 in females, and 21–32 subcaudals in males and 16–24 in females.

Boyer (1957) studied the sexual dimorphism in a population of C. atrox from the Wichita Mountain Wildlife Refuge in southwestern Oklahoma. Females slightly outnumbered males (117 to 97), in his sample of 214 snakes, but the sample did not differ significantly from a 1:1 ratio. Males attained greater body lengths and had proportionately longer tails. Males showed no significant changes in ontogenetic differences in tail proportion, but females had marginally significantly shorter tails with increasing body length (Fig. 202). The number of ventrals and subcaudals varied significantly between the sexes. Males had 174–189 ventrals and 24–29 subcaudals, versus 179–193 ventrals and 18–23 subcaudals in females. The number of dorsal scale rows was significantly higher on the anterior of the body (mode 27 in males and 25 in females), but this dimorphism diminished posteriorly. About twice as many males as females had only a single loreal on each side, and there were a few other marginally significant differences in head scalation. The average number of tail rings was higher in males (4–7) than females (3–6), relating to the longer tails of males.

SIMILAR SPECIES The wide-ranging C. atrox is sympatric in portions of its range with many other species of rattlesnakes. Crotalus horridus lacks rings on the tail. The pale and black tail rings of C. scutulatus stand in strong contrast to one another, but the black rings are short relative to the pale rings; 2 (sometimes 3) intersupraoculars are usually present; a crescent-shaped scale borders the posteromedial side of each supraocular; and a white stripe extends from the posterior edge of the eye across the temporal region to a point above the rictus. The range of C. ruber is contiguous with that of C. atrox at the eastern base of the San Jacinto Mountains in California, but no region of sympatry has been discovered. The ground color of C. ruber is reddish brown to pink; usually 29 midbody dorsal scale rows are present; and the first pair of infralabials is usually transversely divided. Crotalus mitchellii can be distinguished from C. atrox by several features: the ground color is usually distinctly speckled with black; the dark tail rings are obscure or, if sharply defined, are not as broad as the pale rings; the prenasals are separated from the rostral by a series of small scales; and the supraoculars are pitted, have deep furrows, or have irregular outer edges. In C. oreganus more than 2 internasals usually are in contact with the rostral, the color of the pale tail rings is the same as the ground color on the posterior of the body, and the pale line extending from the posterior edge of the eye passes above the rictus. Crotalus molossus has a tail that is uniformly dark, or at least the tail rings are indistinctly indicated, and the internasal-prefrontal region usually has 4–6 scales. In C. basiliscus 27 midbody dorsal scale rows are usually present, the internasal-prefrontal region is covered by 4–6 scales, and the tail is mostly dark with tail rings obscure or absent. The dorsal pattern of C. tigris consists of crossbands, the head is proportionately small and the rattles large, and the pale and dark tail rings are not in strong contrast with one another. The midbody blotches on C. simus are usually diamond shaped (rather than hexagonal), the internasal-prefrontal area usually is covered by 4–6 scales, the tail lacks rings and is usually uniformly gray, and a distinctive pair of paravertebral nape stripes extends posteriorly from the parietal region. Rattleshakes of the genus Sistrurus lack tail rings and have enlarged plates on the top of the head.

REMARKS Crotalus atrox has been confused with several taxa over the years. Amaral (1929b) had difficulty distinguishing C. atrox, C. ruber, and C. tortugensis, and suggested that only a single species was involved.

Crotalus atrox has several attributes that make it one of the most medically important snakes in North America: it has a large geographical range, a penchant for quickly defending itself, and large size coupled with relatively potent venom. It is responsible for more human deaths within its range than any other snake. Symptoms usually include an intense, fiery pain at the site of envenomation that eventually radiates in all directions, swelling and edema, discoloration of the tissues, an increase or decrease in pulse rate, changes in blood pressure, and nausea and vomiting. Brown (1950) stated that most ranchers considered stock mortality by C. atrox to be quite extensive.

We have seen several adult C. atrox that were apparently dwarfed. These individuals had unusually long strings of rattles, with 15 or more segments, but were only about 45 cm in TL (Pl. 783). They also had a relatively large head and large, bulging eyes. Unfortunately, these specimens were part of a confiscation, and the locality information associated with them cannot be accepted with absolute certainty. They reportedly came from Charco Cercado, north of San Luis Potosí, San Luis Potosí, Mexico. We have been unable to find this locality on any map.

Crotalus basiliscus (Cope, 1864)
(Map 93, Pls. 784–787)

Caudisona basilisca Cope, 1864, *Proc. Acad. Nat. Sci. Philadelphia* 16:166–181[166]. Holotype: USNM 53586. Type-locality: "Near Colima, Mexico."

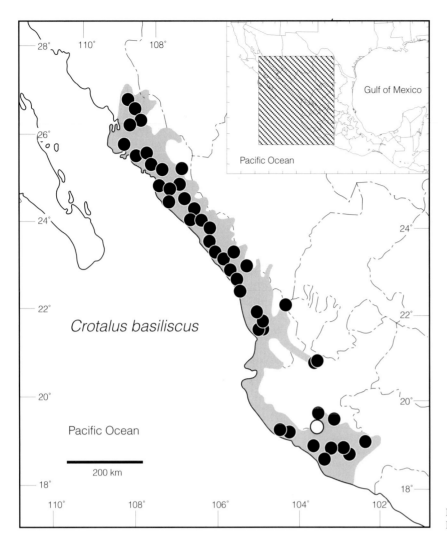

Map 93. Distribution of *Crotalus basiliscus* in western Mexico. Unfilled symbol represents type-locality.

Crotalus basiliscus—Cope, *in* Yarrow, *in* Wheeler, 1875, *Rep. Geog. Geol. Explor. Surv. West 100th Merid.* 5:509–584[532].

Crotalus durissus var. *basiliscus*—Garman, 1884 [dated 1883], *Mem. Mus. Comp. Zool.* 8:1–185[171].

Crotalus terrificus—Boulenger, 1896b, *Cat. Snakes British Mus.* 3:727 pp.[573]. [In part; included *C. durissus.*]

Crotalus terrificus basiliscus—Amaral, 1929, *Bull. Antivenin Inst. Am.* 3:4–6[5].

Crotalus basiliscus basiliscus—Gloyd, 1948b, *Nat. Hist. Misc.* (Chicago) 17:1–4[1].

As soon as possible after the bite is inflicted a pig is caught and, its snout having been cut off, the raw surface is applied to the wound; some of the animal's blood is diluted with warm water and is drunk.

—Hrdlicka, 1908, on a treatment for snakebite used by the Cora Indians of Nayarit

Truly, this is one of the most thrilling experiences imaginable, to hold one of these huge creatures thus, realizing fully its ability to inflict a deadly bite, but knowing that it *will not*! When I succeed thus far in gaining the trust of one of these dangerous pets, it is a "joy beyond the telling"—an ecstasy similar to that experience when one beholds a wonderful sunset, views some grand scenery, or listens to soul-thrilling music. I have at times wondered if Nature doesn't sometimes touch a chord in the being of little dumb creatures, too, so that they come to know that one is a friend!

—Comments made by Grace Olive Wiley (1930) about her pet *C. basiliscus*. This eccentric woman routinely took great risks by freely handling venomous snakes that she thought she could tame. Her untimely end in 1948 followed the bite of an Indian cobra.

LOCAL NAMES Saye (Cora Indians in Nayarit), tepocolcóatl (Nahuatl), teuhtlacozauhqui (Nahuatl), víbora de cascabel.

ENGLISH NAME Mexican west coast rattlesnake.

ETYMOLOGY The species epithet is derived from the Greek *basiliskos*, meaning "king," an allusion to the large size and potent venom of this snake.

DISTRIBUTION Western Mexico, from the Río Fuerte drainage in extreme southern Sonora southward along the coastal plain, foothills, and valleys of Sinaloa, Nayarit, Jalisco, Colima, and northwestern Michoacán, including the middle Río Tepalcatepec Valley (see Fig. 93). In the northern part of its range this species appears to occur mostly below 600 m (see Remarks for *Crotalus molossus*). In the south it ranges from near sea level well up into the Sierra de Coalcomán, Michoacán: UCM 51313 was collected at 2,225 m near Dos Aguas and UTA R-6120 was found at about 2,400 m on Cerro Barolosa.

Distribution records are given in Amaral, 1927c; Armstrong and Murphy, 1979; Campbell and Lamar, 1989; Casas-Andreu, 1981; Cope, 1864, 1885a, 1885b, 1900 (in part); Cuesta-Terrón, 1921b (in part, 1931); Davis and Dixon, 1957; Dixon et al., 1962;

Duellman, 1954, 1958a, 1961, 1965b; Dugès, 1896a (in part); Fouquette and Rossman, 1963; Fugler and Dixon, 1961; García and Ceballos, 1994; Garman, 1884b; Gloyd, 1940; Greene, 1972; Günther, 1895–1902 (in part); Hardy and McDiarmid, 1969; Hoge and Romano, 1971a; Klauber, 1952, 1971, 1972; Martín del Campo, 1935, 1937a, 1950; McCranie, 1981a; Ocaranza, 1930 (in part); Oliver, 1937; Peters, 1954, 1960b; Pope, 1944–1945; Ramírez-Bautista, 1994; Schmidt and Shannon, 1947; Smith, 1943a, 1970; Smith and Taylor, 1945; Smith and Van Gelder, 1955; Spieth, 1950; Taylor, 1938b; Webb, 1984; and Zweifel, 1959b, 1960.

HABITAT Thornforest, tropical deciduous forest, and the ecotonal belt between tropical deciduous forest and pine-oak forest. In the Sierra de Coalcomán this species ranges well up into the pine-oak forest, almost to fir forest, where it is sympatric with *C. simus*.

DESCRIPTION This is among the largest rattlesnakes; specimens exceeding 150 cm are not rare, and the maximum size reported is 204.5 cm (Klauber, 1972), but we have seen several long-term captives that were even larger. Large specimens have a prominent vertebral ridge on the anterior part of the body shaped by high neural spines, but this ridge is not as well developed as in *C. simus* or *C. durissus*.

The ground color of adults is olive green, olive gray, brownish green, or yellowish brown; usually the larger snakes have a more conspicuous greenish cast. Dark punctations are absent from the ground color. Juveniles are reddish brown. The pattern is reminiscent of that of some populations of *C. molossus* in that most individual dorsal scales tend to be unicolored without elements of pattern cutting across them; the major exception is the pale borders of the dorsal blotches, which may consist of scales that are pale only distally. The dorsal pattern consists of 26–41 diamond-shaped blotches; these usually have a pale border and do not coalesce with the lateral series of blotches. The pale border of the dorsal blotches usually involves diagonal series of scales that are pale at least distally. In juveniles and young adults the dorsal blotches are usually reddish brown with paler centers. With age these blotches fade somewhat; in very large or very old specimens they may become indistinguishable from the overall ground color, and the entire dorsum is unicolored except, perhaps, for a few pale and/or dark scales. Pale-bordered, reddish brown ventrolateral blotches offset the lateral points of the dorsal blotches on juveniles. Another series of small lateral blotches may alternate between the primary lateral series and the dorsal series; these usually consist of a small group of reddish brown scales. In many adults, most traces of these lateral markings vanish except for a few dark scales.

The top of the head is pale; an indistinct dark pattern is present on young snakes, but this usually disappears in adults except for a few dark scales. A dark postocular stripe about 3 scales wide extends from behind and below the eye to a point directly above the rictus. The pale borders of the dark postocular stripe are usually not sharply defined, are irregular, and are often discontinuous. Like the other body markings, the postocular stripe becomes obscure with age. The tail is gray with a series of 5–12 darker bands. Anteriorly, the venter is whitish, yellowish, or cream colored with a faint suffusion of gray; the belly becomes darker posteriorly with gray mottling or blotches often in evidence.

The rostral is higher than wide. The internasal-prefrontal region usually does not have more than 4–6 scales, including 2 large, triangular internasals in contact with the rostral; 2 large, quadrangular prefrontals (anterior canthals) in contact with each other medially; and 2 small posterior canthals, each lying behind the upper loreal(s) and interposed between the prefrontal and supraocular. Very rarely, scales in the internasal-prefrontal region are fragmented irregularly, producing up to about 9 scales on the snout. Two or 3 (usually 2) intersupraoculars are present, and the scales in the parietal and occipital regions are small and keeled. The first supralabial may be in broad contact with the prenasal or may be partially or completely separated by the forward extension of prefoveals. Two loreals (an upper and a lower) usually separate the postnasal from the upper preocular. The number of loreals per side may be as low as 1 or as high as 5; occasionally, when only a lower loreal is present, the upper preocular touches the postnasal. One or more small scales (post–upper loreals) often intervene posterior to the upper loreal to partially or completely separate the prefrontal from the upper preocular. One to 3 (usually 2) interoculabials separate the anterior subocular from the supralabials. The first pair of infralabials are not divided transversely. There are 13–18 (usually 15) supralabials, 13–19 (usually 16) infralabials, 24–29 (usually 27) midbody dorsal scale rows, 178–201 ventrals in males and 184–206 in females, and 26–36 subcaudals in males and 18–30 in females. Duellman (1961) and Klauber (1972) remarked that snakes from the southern part of the range in Michoacán usually have fewer ventrals and subcaudals than snakes from north of there.

SIMILAR SPECIES *Crotalus atrox* is sympatric with *C. basiliscus* in southern Sonora and northern Sinaloa but it may be distinguished by a gray-brown ground color heavily punctated with dark brown or black; a pale stripe extending from the upper postocular downward to the lip margin; 2–3 supralabials in front of the rictus; a tail with sharply contrasting, alternating black and ash white rings; more than 9 scales in the internasal-prefrontal region including anterior canthals that are not in contact; and a large posterior canthal on each side that extends over the canthus rostralis to take the place of an upper loreal. *Crotalus simus* is sympatric with *C. basiliscus* in Michoacán but can be distinguished by a ground color that usually does not have a greenish or reddish cast, a sharply defined pair of narrow paravertebral stripes on the neck, dorsal blotches with distinct dark borders, the tail of adults having little or no trace of darker crossbands, and usually 29 or more midbody dorsal scale rows.

A more perplexing problem of identification involves *C. basiliscus* and *C. molossus*. Anyone seeing a large *C. basiliscus* from the coastal lowlands of Sinaloa and an adult *C. molossus* from one of the many rocky canyons of central Durango would have little trouble distinguishing these species from one another; however, these species appear to hybridize freely, creating suture zones wherever they come into contact. Both are found in the lowlands of Alamos, and active hybridization occurs there. A rather broad elevational belt where these species hybridize occurs in eastern Sinaloa and northeastern Nayarit; in most areas this zone of hybridization corresponds roughly to an elevation between 600 and 1,500 m, but in southern Sonora these species may hybridize at lower elevations as well, and specimens of *C. basiliscus* from this area closely resemble *C. molossus* in many scale and hemipenial characters (Bogert and Oliver, 1945). Attempting to determine precise distributional boundaries between these species hardly seems a worthwhile (or possible) endeavor, and range maps should be considered nothing more than approximations based on what are considered the more salient diagnostic features for each. Certain characteristics do distinguish *C. molossus* from *C. basiliscus*: the latter is smaller (*C. molossus* rarely exceeds 120 cm in TL); its dorsal blotches are distinctly darker and have contrasting pale interiors; the pale margins of dorsal blotches are usually made up of scales that are uniformly pale; the dorsal blotches often coalesce with lateral blotches to form crossbands on the body; the top of the head is dark at least anterior to the supraoculars; and the tail of adults is usually uniformly dark without evidence of darker crossbands.

REMARKS This species is most active during the rainy summer months in the lowlands, and most specimens are found crossing roads at night; however, we have encountered a few basking during the early morning.

It is possible that an old report of rattlesnakes from Isla María Magdalena of the Islas Tres Marías (Stejneger, 1899; Van Denburgh and Slevin, 1914) is referable to *C. basiliscus*, although we are not aware of museum specimens. This species has often been confused in the literature with *C. molossus*, and vice versa. Old records for this species from the highlands of the Mexican Plateau are referable to *C. molossus* (e.g., Cuesta-Terrón, 1921b; Dugès, 1888, 1896a; Herrera, 1890). The large rattlesnake inhabiting the highlands of central Oaxaca has often been considered an isolated population of *C. basiliscus*, but Campbell and Lamar (1989) pointed out that this population apparently is more closely related to populations of *C. molossus* on the southern portion of the Mexican Plateau and suggested a new combination, *C. molossus oaxacus*. For a discussion of the distribution and affinities of these snakes, see Remarks in the *C. molossus* account.

The everted hemipenes of *C. basiliscus* are 12–14 subcaudals long and somewhat lyriform. Each lobe tapers slightly toward the distal end, and the tip of each lobe is slightly bulbous. The proximal third of each lobe has 30–40 enlarged spines (including the large mesial spines, which are always present). The hemipenes of *C. basiliscus* and the southern populations of *C. molossus* are quite similar in morphology. The major differences are in the length of the organ (usually 8–10 subcaudals in *C. molossus*) and the greater development of the basal and mesial spines in *C. basiliscus*.

Klauber (*in* Bogert and Oliver, 1945) described the hemipenis of *C. basiliscus* as follows: "(Two specimens said to have come from Colima, type locality of *basiliscus*, but the locality data are uncertain.) The lobes are long and tapering, almost to points. There are many spines in the crotch, in patches facing each other. These spines are smaller than those on the outer shoulders with which they intergrade. There are about 60 to 70 major spines, which are much larger than those in *molossus*, and longer." Klauber (*in* Bogert and Oliver, 1945) described the hemipenis of *C. molossus* as being quite different: "(Specimens from Arizona and New Mexico.) The lobes are very short and blunt. They are only slightly tapering. The spines are short with small points. There are no spines in the crotch; the reticulated areas of the two sides meet in the crotch. About 20 to 30 major spines." Klauber noted that the hemipenes of *C. basiliscus* in the northern part of the range (the Alamos region of Sonora, Mexico) are somewhat intermediate between those of *C. molossus* and *C. basiliscus* to the south but more similar to the latter.

Perkins (*in* Davis, 1936) observed two recently collected *Crotalus basiliscus* engage in courtship in which the male nudged the female and rubbed the side of his head against her body.

Crotalus catalinensis Cliff, 1954
(Map 94, Pls. 788–790)

Crotalus catalinensis Cliff, 1954, *Trans. San Diego Soc. Nat. Hist.* 12:67–98[80]. Holotype: CAS-SU 15631. Type-locality: "Isla Santa Catalina in the Gulf of California, [Baja California Sur] Mexico."

I have seen individuals [of *C. catalinensis*] crawling though the lower branches of Elephant Trees and Palo Verde Trees (*Cercidium microphyllum*) between 0.30 and 4.0 m above the ground. One evening during late July, I found two gravid females 1 m above the ground and approximately 1.5 m away from one another in a large Palo Verde Tree. Four nights later, I found four individuals (three gravid females and one male) in the same tree. . . . All were climbing along the outer edges of the tree rather than on the interior branches. To escape my lantern light, all climbed upward rather than downward toward the interior. . . . I was amazed at the agility with which these snakes climbed, even the gravid females.

—Grismer, 2002

LOCAL NAME Víbora de cascabel.
ENGLISH NAME Santa Catalina rattlesnake.

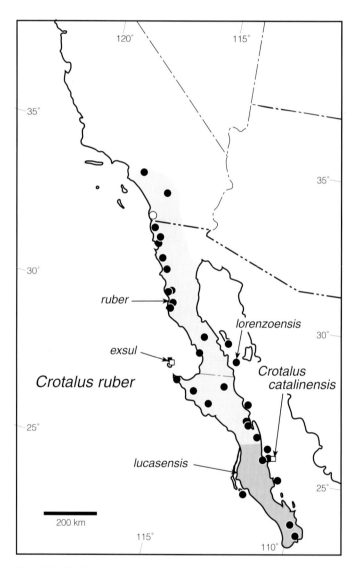

Map 94. Distributions of *Crotalus catalinensis* and *C. ruber*, including subspecies, in the southwestern United States and Baja California Peninsula, Mexico. Unfilled symbols represent type-localities; that for *C. ruber* restricted to "vicinity of San Diego (California, USA)," by Schmidt (1953c).

ETYMOLOGY The species epithet is derived from Isla Santa Catalina, to which this snake is restricted.

DISTRIBUTION Endemic to Isla Santa Catalina off the east coast of Baja California Sur, Mexico, in the Gulf of California (Map 94). References to this species are contained in Armstrong and Murphy, 1979; Campbell and Lamar, 1989; Cliff, 1954; Grismer, 1990, 1999a, 2002; Harris and Simmons, 1977a, 1978b; Hoge and Romano, 1971a; Klauber, 1956, 1971, 1972; Lindsay, 1962, 1964; McPeak, 2000; Murphy, 1975, 1983a, 1983b; Murphy and Crabtree, 1985b; Murphy and Ottley, 1984; Murphy et al., 1989; Orr, 1965, 1982; Radcliffe and Maslin, 1975; Shaw, 1964b, 1964c; Smith and Taylor, 1966; Soulé and Sloan, 1966; and Tremper, 1982.

HABITAT Desert; the terrain of this island is rocky and sparsely covered with brush and cacti.

DESCRIPTION This is a relatively slender, stunted snake; the largest measured specimen is a female 73.1 cm in TL.

The ground color is pale ash gray, gray-brown, tan, or brownish with few dark punctations. There are 34–40 medium brown dorsal body blotches, each with a dark brown to black border about 1 scale wide with cream-colored edging, also about 1 scale in width. Middorsally, 1 or 2 pale scales separate adjacent blotches. On the posterior portion of the body both the pale and the dark margins of blotches become indistinct. Anteriorly the dorsal blotches are longitudinally elongate and may be somewhat quadrangular; at midbody they become roughly hexagonal or diamond shaped. The dorsum of the head is pale gray-brown punctated or irregularly marked with dark brown. The supraoculars have a relatively broad transverse pale streak through their centers. The pale stripes bordering the dark postocular stripe are broad but not sharply defined; the lower (anterior) pale stripe extends from the upper preocular to the supralabials under the eye, and the upper (posterior) pale stripe extends from the upper postocular to near the rictus. Of the 3 series of dark lateral blotches, the series with the largest blotches is below the lateral extensions of the dorsal blotches; the 2 smaller series are situated about halfway between successive lateral blotches, 1 series above and 1 below the large series. The dorsum of the tail has 5 or 6 black rings that encroach on the lateral portions of the subcaudals; the black rings are 4–5 scales wide middorsally but reduced laterally. The ash gray pale interspaces are slightly narrower than the black rings along the dorsal midline and strongly contrast with the ground color on the posterior portion of the body. The proximal rattle segment is brown to black.

A pair of oddly shaped internasals is in contact with the rostral; these internasals are roughly kidney shaped and about 3 times longer than wide. The small anterior canthals touch each other medially, are longer than wide, and partially border the concavity formed by the kidney-shaped internasals. There are more than 8 scales in the internasal-prefrontal regions and 4 or 5 intersupraoculars. On each side the prenasal is in broad contact with supralabial 1. The posterior canthals are large relative to the anterior canthals, and the lateral portion of each scale extends ventrally over the canthus rostralis; together with the single, vertically elongate loreal (in the position of a lower loreal), the lateral portion of the posterior canthal precludes the postnasal from contacting the upper preocular. A single interoculabial separates the anterior subocular from the supralabials. The first pair of infralabials is not transversely divided, and there are no interchinshields or submental. There are 13–16 (usually 14 or 15) supralabials, 13–17 (usually 14 or 15) infralabials, 25 midbody dorsal scale rows, 177–181 ventrals in males

and 182–189 in females, and 24–28 subcaudals in males and 18–23 in females. One of the most distinctive features of this rattlesnake is the absence of any rattles other than the proximal segment. The lobes and grooves of the proximal segment are so poorly developed that a rattle segment is lost every time the snake sheds its skin (in most other rattlesnakes a new segment is added).

SIMILAR SPECIES *Crotalus catalinensis* is the only rattlesnake inhabiting Isla Santa Catalina in the Gulf of California (not to be confused with the Santa Catalina Island off the California coast of the United States, which is inhabited by *C. oreganus helleri*). *Crotalus catalinensis* is readily distinguished from most other rattlesnakes by the single rattle. The first pair of infralabials are usually divided transversely in *C. ruber*, and it is a larger snake; mainland specimens commonly exceed 100 cm in length and usually have at least 27 midbody dorsal scale rows. The black tail rings of *C. scutulatus* are conspicuously narrower than the pale interspaces, only 2 intersupraoculars are usually present, an enlarged crescent-shaped scale often borders the posteromedial side of each supraocular, and the upper (posterior) pale stripe bordering the dark postocular stripe extends posteriorly *above* the rictus.

REMARKS The phylogenetic relationships of *C. catalinensis* have been proposed to be with either *C. ruber* or *C. scutulatus*; most of the morphological, biogeographic, and biochemical data suggest that *C. ruber* is this snake's closest relative. Murphy and Crabtree (1985b) concluded on the basis of allozyme data that *C. catalinensis* shares its most recent ancestor with *C. ruber*, and that *C. catalinensis* is of more recent origin than many of the other reptile species on Isla Santa Catalina.

Crotalus cerastes Hallowell, 1854
(Map 95, Pls. 791–794)

Crotalus cerastes Hallowell, 1854 [dated 1854/55], *Proc. Acad. Nat. Sci. Philadelphia* 7:91–97[95]. Holotype: ANSP 7098. Klauber (1956:30) thought the type was USNM 352, but this notion was not supported by Cochran (1961:169). Type-locality: borders of the Mohave River and in the desert of the Mohave [California].

Caudisona cerastes—Cope, 1867 [dated 1866], *Proc. Acad. Nat. Sci. Philadelphia* 18:300–314 [309].

Caudisona (Aechmophrys) cerastes—Coues, *in* Wheeler, 1875, *Rep. Geog. Geol. Explor. Surv. West 100th Merid.* 5:585–633[609].

Aechmophrys cerastes—Coues, *in* Wheeler, 1875, *Rep. Geog. Geol. Explor. Surv. West 100th Merid.* 5:585–633[609].

Crotalus cerastes—Boulenger, 1896b, *Cat. Snakes British Mus.* 3:727 pp.[583].

Crotalus cerastes cerastes—Klauber, 1944, *Trans. San Diego Soc. Nat. Hist.* 10:91–126[94]. [By fiat.]

Crotalus cerastes laterorepens Klauber, 1944, *Trans. San Diego Soc. Nat. Hist.* 10:91–126[91]. Type(s): SDSNH 34074. Type-locality: "The Narrows, San Diego County, California," USA.

Crotalus cerastes cercobombus Savage and Cliff, 1953, *Nat. Hist. Misc.* (Chicago) 119:1–7[2]. Holotype: CAS-SU 7287. Type-locality: "near Gila Bend, Maricopa County, Arizona," USA.

LOCAL NAMES Awa'ala (Yaqui), chicotera, tl'iish bicho'hi' (Navajo), víbora cornuda, víbora de cascabel.

ENGLISH NAME Sidewinder.

DISTRIBUTION The United States and Mexico. In the United States this species occurs in extreme southwestern Utah, southern Nevada, southeastern California, and western and south-central Arizona, including the Mohave Desert (Stewart, 1994); in Mexico it is found in northwestern Sonora to about the Llanos de San Juan Bautista, which lie southwest of Hermosillo, and in

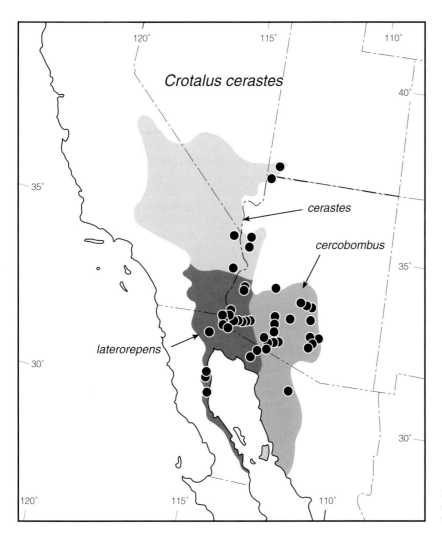

Map 95. Distribution of *Crotalus cerastes*, including sub-species, in the southwestern United States and north-western Mexico. Type-locality too imprecise to plot.

eastern Baja California Norte to the Llano de San Pedro; it also occurs on Isla Tiburón (Map 95). Grismer (2002) reported seeing tracks of this species near San Francisquito. *Crotalus cerastes* occurs from below sea level in desert basins to nearly 1,830 m but usually is found below 1,200 m.

Distribution records are available for Arizona (Boulenger, 1896b; Coues, 1875; Fowlie, 1965; Garman, 1884a; Gloyd, 1937; Klauber, 1932a; Lowe, 1964; Lowe et al., 1986; Smith and Taylor, 1966; Vitt and Ohmart, 1978), California (Baird, 1859a; Boulenger, 1896b; Camp, 1916; Cope, 1860a; Cowles, 1941, 1945, 1953; Cowles and Bogert, 1936; Hallowell, 1854; Jan and Sordelli, 1874; Klauber, 1927, 1930c, 1931a, 1932b; Lowe and Norris, 1950; Meek, 1906; Miller and Stebbins, 1964; Moore, 1976, 1978; Stebbins, 1972; Stejneger, 1895; Tanner, 1966b), Nevada (Boulenger, 1896b; Klauber, 1932b; Linsdale, 1940; Tanner, 1966b; Van Denburgh and Slevin, 1921a), Utah (Boulenger, 1896b; Cox and Tanner, 1995; Tanner, 1927; Woodbury, 1931), the Baja California Peninsula (Brattstrom, 1952; Grismer, 1994b, 2002; Linsdale, 1932; Lowe and Norris, 1954; Malkin, 1962; Meek, 1906; Murphy, 1983a, 1983b; Murphy and Ottley, 1984; Murray, 1955; Savage, 1960; Schmidt, 1922; Soulé and Sloan, 1966), and Sonora (Burger and Hensley, 1949; Croulet, 1963; González-Romero and Alvarez-Cárdenas, 1989; Langebartel and Smith, 1954; P. Smith and Hensley, 1958). For Mexico in general, see Armstrong and Murphy, 1979; Klauber, 1952; Martín del Campo, 1935, 1937a, 1950; and Smith and Taylor, 1945. For the United States, see Cope, 1900; Ditmars, 1907, 1910, 1930, 1936; Pickwell, 1972; Shaw and Campbell, 1974). For the general range, see Garman, 1884b; Gloyd, 1940; Hoge and Romano, 1971a; Klauber, 1944, 1971, 1972; Norris, 1967; Savage and Cliff, 1953; Stebbins, 1985; Stejneger, 1895; Tanner, 1978; Van Denburgh, 1922b; Werner, 1922; and Wright and Wright, 1957. The record from Miñaca, Chihuahua, Mexico, in Cuesta-Terrón, 1931, is almost certainly in error.

HABITAT Desert. This species is often encountered in regions of fine windblown sand, sandy alluvial fans, sand dunes, sandy washes, and the fringes of desert dry lakes. Brown (1970) noted that sidewinders appear to be most common where windblown sand forms small mounds at the bases of creosote bushes, and they are frequently seen coiled under bushes (Miller and Stebbins, 1964). The species is not restricted to sandy habitats, however, and may be encountered in a variety of situations, including "desert flats with scattered brush, and where sand hummocks, crowned with mesquite" (Klauber, 1944:108); hard, rocky terrain (Armstrong and Murphy, 1979); desertscrub; rocky slopes; Joshua tree woodland; and piñon-juniper woodland (Stewart, 1994). In Arizona this species inhabits Mohave desertscrub, mixed riparian scrub, and mesquite-bosque formations (Jones, 1988). The Kelso Dunes region of San Bernardino County, California, where *C. cerastes* is abundant, is dominated by three perennial plants: creosote bush (*Larrea tridentata*), burro weed (*Ambrosia dumosa*), and galleta grass (*Hilaria rigida*), according to Secor (1994a; 1994b). Sidewinders appear to be most abundant where there is sparse vegetation (Dammann, 1961). Armstrong and Murphy (1979) reported finding a snake about 30 cm above the ground in a creosote bush.

DESCRIPTION Most adults are 50–80 cm in TL; the largest specimen recorded measured 82.4 cm (Klauber, 1956). A female *C. cerastes* (SJSU R3216) from near Kelso, San Bernadino County, California, was 63.7 cm in TL (Boundy and Balgooyen, 1988). Unlike most other rattlesnakes, in *C. cerastes* females attain a greater length than males. A spinal ridge is evident, and the dorsal scales are strongly keeled and tuberculate, the vertebral row being the most accentuated.

The ground color is cream, buff, tan, yellowish brown, pink, or ash gray. The 28–47 dorsal body blotches are subrhombic or subelliptical; usually broader than long; and grayish, pale brown, yellowish brown, or occasionally brilliant orange. These blotches have indefinitely and irregularly outlined borders; the middorsal interspace between them is often paler than the overall ground color and may be yellow or orangish. Three series of lateral spots, often indistinct, lie either opposite or alternate to the dorsal blotches. A pale crossbar extends transversely across the supraocular to its distal tip. A few small, irregular dark spots may be present in the parietal region, followed posteriorly by a pair of broad, short occipital blotches. The first 1 or 2 dorsal blotches may be divided into small paravertebral blotches. The dark brown postocular stripe extends from behind the eye to just above the rictus. A small dark spot is often present on the supralabials below the eye. The infralabials may have a fine dusting of brown pigment, but otherwise the infracephalic scales and anterior ventrals are immaculate. The belly is mostly whitish or yellowish; however, some dark markings are present on the ventrals, especially laterally. The distal 2 or 3 of the 2–7 dark tail rings are black or very dark brown. Specimens from Mexico tend to have a black proximal rattle segment, although in those from the southern part of the range the proximal rattle segment may be only partly black.

The rostral is wider than high. There are 2 internasals in contact with the rostral, 12–34 scales in the internasal-prefrontal region, and 4–6 intersupraoculars. The supraoculars are produced into a hornlike process that is greatly upturned and obtusely pointed at the tip. Coues (1875) was so impressed by the raised supraoculars of *C. cerastes* that he erected a separate subgenus, *Aechmophrys*. The prenasal and lacunals are in broad contact with the supralabials, the nasals are usually conjoined above the nostril, a single large loreal broadly separates the upper preocular from the postnasal, and 2 interoculabials usually are found between the anterior subocular and supralabials. There are 10–15 (usually 12 or 13) supralabials, 10–17 infralabials (mode 13), 19–25 midbody dorsal scale rows (snakes from Baja California and the panhandle of extreme northwestern Sonora usually have 23; those from farther east in Sonora usually have 21), 132–151 ventrals in males and 135–154 in females, and 18–26 subcaudals in males and 14–21 in females.

SIMILAR SPECIES The unique hornlike supraoculars of *C. cerastes* should immediately distinguish this species from any of its congeners. The supraoculars may be raised moderately (but do not form projections) in *C. enyo*, which is sympatric with *C. cerastes* only in southeastern Baja California Norte. Furthermore, *C. enyo* has clearly defined, black-edged dorsal blotches; knobby scales in the prefrontal-frontal region; usually 3 or more loreals; and usually 25 or more midbody dorsal scale rows.

REMARKS *Crotalus c. cerastes* (Pls. 791 and 792), which occurs in desert regions of eastern California, southern Nevada, southwestern Utah, and northwestern Arizona, is characterized by a brown proximal rattle lobe in adults, usually 21 dorsal scale rows at midbody, 132–146 ventrals in males and 136–150 in

females, and 19–26 subcaudals in males and 14–20 in females. *Crotalus c. cercobombus* (Pl. 793) inhabits desert regions of south-central Arizona and parts of western Sonora, exclusive of the western panhandle region but including Isla Tiburón, and has a black proximal rattle lobe in adults, usually 21 dorsal scale rows at midbody, 132–144 ventrals in males and 138–148 in females, and 18–24 subcaudals in males and 14–19 in females. *Crotalus c. laterorepens* (Pl. 794), which occupies desert regions of southeastern California, southwestern Arizona, and the western panhandle region of Sonora, has a black proximal rattle lobe in adults, usually 23 dorsal scale rows at midbody, 137–151 ventrals in males and 135–154 in females, and 19–26 subcaudals in females and 14–21 in females.

Sidewinders are mostly nocturnal but may be active diurnally during the early spring and late fall. They often utilize rodent burrows or make their own depressions into sand to escape the heat of the day; some may be encountered resting in the shade at the bases of bushes, especially where windblown sand has accumulated. This species is known to climb in brush (Mertens, 1965).

This snake employs a rather remarkable mode of locomotion known as sidewinding, from which it derives its common name. The biomechanics of sidewinding are extremely complex, but the snake moves essentially in an undulating S by repeatedly throwing a loop of its body in front of its head.

Although there has been much speculation as to the function of the horns or spines over the eyes of various species of vipers, including several desert-dwelling species in the Old World and *Crotalus cerastes*, we have not found any of the suggestions particularly compelling. Cowles (1953) suggested that they are probably just "a whim of evolution." The flexible nature of the raised supraocular scale led Cohen and Myers (1970) to suggest that it is an "eyelid" protecting the eye by being deflected downward over it when the snake crawls through tight spaces that might be abrasive. *Crotalus cerastes* occurs in regions of intense solar radiation and is known to move by day and to rest in relatively open areas, so it is possible that the raised supraocular serves simply as a sunshade over the pupil.

Crotalus cerastes was hypothesized by Foote and MacMahon (1977) to be the sister species of *C. mitchellii* on the basis of venom characteristics, and by Stille (1987) on the basis of scale microdermatoglyphics. Murphy (1983a) suggested that the sister species to *C. mitchellii* is *C. tigris*, not *C. cerastes*.

Crotalus durissus Linnaeus, 1758
(Figs. 203 and 204, Map 96, Pls. 795–824)

Crotalus Dryinas Linnaeus, 1758, *Syst. Nat.*, 10th ed., 1:824 pp.[214]. Holotype: lost; likely sent to the Zoological Museum of the Royal University at Uppsala, Sweden [ZMUU]. Type-locality: "America." Hoge (1966:143) proposed a restriction to Paramaribo, Suriname. Although this name has priority over *terrificus*, Klauber (1941b:89) presented reasons for not adopting it for a South American subspecies; Klauber was unaware of the provenance of the type of *Crotalus durissus*. Linnaeus (1758:214) proposed two different names for the South American rattlesnake on the same page. The Code states (Art. 69b:11) that "all things being equal, preference should be given to the nominal species cited first in the work," which would be *dryinas*. Given the widespread use of the name *durissus*, however, we invoke the Principle of the First Reviser (Art. 24) and propose that the name *durissus* be favored.

Crotalus Durissus Linnaeus, 1758, *Syst. Nat.*, 10th ed., 1:824 pp.[214]. Holotype: apparently lost. Originally in Claudius

Fig. 203. Head of *Crotalus durissus cumanensis* from vicinity of Cartagena, Bolívar, Colombia, showing erect fangs.

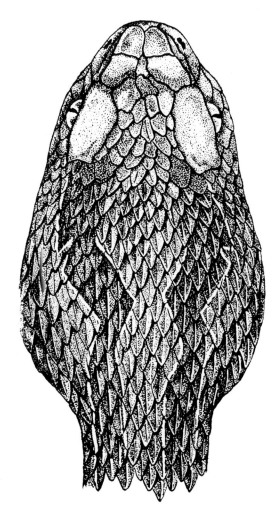

Fig. 204. Dorsal aspect of head of *Crotalus durissus terrificus* from Santiago del Estero, Argentina. From Abalos et al., 1964. Published by permission of the Fundación Miguel Lillo.

Grill Collection (also referred to as the Surinam Collection) and later sent to the Zoological Museum of the Royal University at Uppsala, Sweden (Klauber, 1941b:83). Type-locality: "America." The subsequent restriction to "Jalapa, Veracruz, Mexico," by Smith and Taylor (1950:348) was not supported by Hoge (1966:137) and is extralimital to the range of the species. We propose restriction to Paramaribo, Suriname.

Caudisona terrifica Laurenti, 1768, *Synops. Rept.*, 214 pp.[93]. Type(s): none indicated. Neotype: IB 22997, designated by Hoge (1966:147). Type-locality: originally stated as "America infra gradum elev. 45." Now "Julio de Castilho, Município Taquari, State Rio Grande do Sul, Brasil," by neotype designation by Hoge (1966:147). Klauber (1936b) relegated the name *terrifica* Laurenti (1768) to subspecific status as the name for South American populations. While there is no doubt that the name *durissus* Linnaeus (1758) takes precedence over *terrifica*, as suggested by Klauber (1936b), it is also apparent that the type of *durissus* (unfortunately now lost) almost certainly was South American in origin, contra Klauber, who favored a Mexican provenance based on the number of subcaudals in the type-specimen (24 scales).

Caudisona orientalis Laurenti, 1768, *Synops. Rept.*, 214 pp.[94]. Type(s): based on Pls. 95 (fig. 3) and 96 (fig. 1) in Seba, 1735. Type-locality: "Zeylona" in error; presumably based on two specimens illustrated in Seba, 1735:Pl. 95, fig. 3, Pl. 96, fig. 1, and reported to be from "Ceylon." Gmelin (1788:1081) placed this name in the snynomy of *Crotalus dryinas*, but Klauber (1936b:196) suggested that the description was so poor that there was no certainty that it even pertained to a rattlesnake.

Caudisona Gronovii Laurenti, 1768, *Synops. Rept.*, 214 pp.[94]. Type(s): unlocated. Type-locality: "America." The placement of this name here is based on little more than guesswork; Daudin (1803:305) placed it in the synonymy of *Crotalus durissus* with the comment that it was a poorly described, indeterminable species.

Crotalus exalbidus Boddaert, 1778, *Nova Acta Phys. Med. Acad. Caes. Leop. Carol.* 7:12–27[16]. Type(s): none designated. Type-locality: not given, according to Klauber (1956:33). [Considered a synonym by Klauber (1936b:196) and listed in the synonymy of *Crotalus durissus terrificus* (Klauber, 1956:33).]

Crotalus orientalis—Gmelin, 1788, *Syst. Nat.*, 13th ed., 1:1033–1516[1081].

Crotalus immaculatus Latreille, *in* Sonnini de Manoncourt and Latreille, 1801–1802, *Hist. Nat. Rept.* 3:335 pp.[201]. Type(s): "Muséum d'Histoire naturelle de Paris." Not found in the MNHN, according to Thireau (1991:2). Type-locality: "Indes orientales," obviously in error. [Placed in synonymy by Klauber (1936b:196) and listed in the synonymy of *Crotalus durissus terrificus* (Klauber, 1972:36).]

Crotalus strepitans Daudin, 1803, *Hist. Nat. Gén. Part. Rept.* 5:365 pp.[318]. Type(s): based on Pl. 95 (fig. 3) and Pl. 96 (figs. 1 and 2) in Seba, 1735, and seemingly a specimen in the "museum national d'histoire naturelle." Not in the MNHN, according to Thireau (1991:4). Klauber (1956:33, footnote 6) referred to the "quite unrecognizable figures of Seba" as the types. Type-locality: "continent de l'Amérique." [Listed in the synonymy of *Crotalus durissus terrificus* by Klauber (1956:33).]

Crotalus strepitans var. *dryinas*—Daudin, 1803, *Hist. Nat. Gén. Part. Rept.* 5:365 pp.[320].

Crotalus cumanensis Humboldt, *in* Humboldt and Bonpland, 1813, *Recuil Obs. Zool. Anat. Comp.* 2:1–8[6]. Type(s): none designated, according to Klauber (1972:36). Type-locality: Cumaná, Venezuela, according to Hoge (1966:142). [Placed in the synonymy of *Crotalus durissus terrificus* by Klauber (1936b:196); considered a subspecies by Hoge (1966:139).]

Crotalus loeflingii Humboldt, *in* Humboldt and Bonpland, 1813, *Recuil Obs. Zool. Anat. Comp.* 2:1–8[6]. Type(s): none designated, according to Klauber (1972:36). Type-locality: Cumaná,

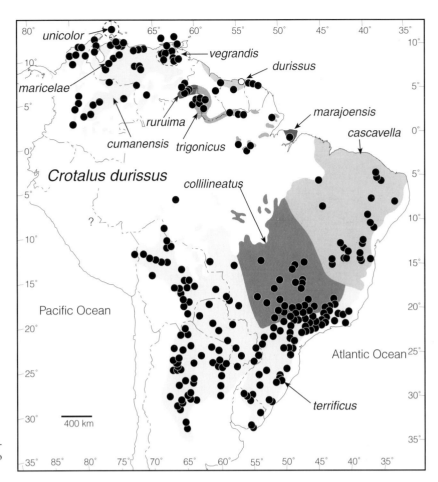

Map 96. Distribution of *Crotalus durissus*, including sub-species, in South America. Type-locality restricted to Paramaribo, Suriname.

Venezuela, according to Klauber (1972:36). [Placed in the synonymy of *Crotalus durissus terrificus* by Klauber (1936b:196) and listed in the synonymy of *Crotalus durissus cumanensis* by Hoge (1966:142).]

Crotalus cascavella Wagler, 1824, *Spec. Nov. Serp. Brasil*, 75 pp.[60, Pl. 24]. Holotype: lost, according to Hoogmoed and Gruber (1983:339). Neotype: IB 23400, designated by Hoge (1966:139). However, Hoogmoed and Gruber (1983:339) correctly pointed out that Hoge's designation was invalid according to Article 75c of the Code (1964). Type-locality: "provinciae Bahia" [Estado da Bahia, Brazil]. Proposed restriction to "Mina Caraiba, Bahia," by Hoge (1966:139).

Urocrotalon durissus—Fitzinger, 1843, *Syst. Rept.*, 106 pp.[29].

Uropsophus durissus—Gray, 1849, *Cat. Spec. Snakes Collect. British Mus.*, 125 pp.[19].

Crotalus durissimus—Troschel, 1855, *Arch. Naturgesch.* 21:411–425[420].

Crotalus horridus—Jan and Sordelli, 1874, *Icon. Gén. Ophid.*, livr. 46, p. 8, Pls. 1–2. [In part, included *C. durissus* and *C. horridus*.]

Crotalus terrificus—Cope, *in* Yarrow, *in* Wheeler, 1875, *Rep. Geog. Geol. Explor. Surv. West 100th Merid.* 5:509–584[532].

Crotalus horridus var. *unicolor* Lidth de Jeude, 1887, *Notes Leyden Mus.* 9:129–139[133]. Holotype: RMNH 613. Type-locality: "Aruba" [Dutch West Indies].

Crotalus terrificus—Boulenger, 1896b, *Cat. Snakes British Mus.* 3:727 pp.[573]. [In part; included *C. basiliscus* and *C. simus*.]

?*Crotalus pulvis* Ditmars, 1905 [dated 1904], *Ninth Ann. Rep. N.Y. Zool. Soc.* 1904(9):197–200[199, Pl.]. Holotype: MCZ R7044. Type-locality: "twenty miles inland from Managua, Nicaragua, in a very dry, sandy district." Placed in the synonymy of *Crotalus terrificus durissus* by Amaral (1930c:243). Gloyd (1936d) considered this name to be a synonym of *C. unicolor* van Lidth de Jeude but did not question the provenance of the type.

Gloyd (1940:140) questioned the provenance of the type and placed the taxon in the synonymy of *Crotalus unicolor*. Klauber (1956:31) included it with a question mark in the synonymy of *C. d. durissus* with the comment that the holotype was "possibly an albino *durissus*, although almost certainly a specimen of *Crotalus unicolor* from Aruba Island." In the same paper, Klauber (1956:44) included it in the synonymy of *C. unicolor*. Hoge (1966:149) commented that this taxon was "probably based on a specimen with erroneous locality." Villa (1981) and Villa and Rivas (1972) reported an albino specimen of *C. simus* from Nicaragua.

Crotalus terrificus var. *terrificus*—Amaral, 1926h, *Rev. Mus. Paulista* 15:89–91[90].

Crotalus terrificus var. *collirhombeatus* Amaral, 1926h, *Rev. Mus. Paulista* 15:89–91[90, Pl. 1]. Syntypes (3): none specifically designated but three specimens illustrated: IB 429 (Piauhy), IB 1464 (Ceará), IB 1610 (Pernambuco). Type-locality: "N.E. do Brasil" [northeastern Brazil]. Proposed restriction to "Mina Caraiba. Bahia, Brasil," by Hoge (1966:139). McDiarmid et al. (1999) questioned the value of this restriction because the locality is not one of the three localities mentioned by Amaral. Placed in the synonymy of *Crotalus durissus terrificus* by Klauber (1936b: 196) and of *Crotalus durissus cascavella* by Hoge (1966:139).

Crotalus terrificus var. *collilineatus* Amaral, 1926h, *Rev. Mus. Paulista* 15:89–91[90, Pl. 2]. Syntypes (3): none specifically designated but three specimens illustrated: IB 2180 (Mato Grosso), IB 1538 (Minas Gerais), IB "s/n" (São Paulo). Lectotype: IB 2180, designated by Hoge (1966:139). Type-locality: "Centro, S.E. e S. do Brasil" [central, southeastern, and southern Brazil]. Restricted by lectotype designation to "State Mato Grosso, Brazil" by Hoge (1966:139). [Placed in the synonymy of *Crotalus durissus terrificus* by Klauber (1936b:196) but recognized as distinct by recent authors.]

Crotalus terrificus terrificus—Amaral, 1929f, *Bull. Antivenin Inst. Am.* 3:4–6[5].

Crotalus terrificus durissus—Amaral, 1929f, *Bull. Antivenin Inst. Am.* 3:4–6[5]. [In part, included *C. durissus* and *C. simus.*]

Crotalus terrificus durissus—Amaral, 1930 [dated 1929], *Mem. Inst. Butantan* 4:129–271 [243]. [In part, included *C. durissus* and *C. simus.*]

Paracrotalus terrificus—Reuss, 1930, *Glasnik Zem. Muz. Bosni Hercegovini* 42:57–114[88].

Crotalus Gronovii—Klauber, 1936, *Trans. San Diego Soc. Nat. Hist.* 8:185–276[196].

Crotalus durissus terrificus—Klauber, 1936, *Occas. Pap. San Diego Soc. Nat. Hist.* 1:2–7[4].

Crotalus unicolor—Klauber, 1936, *Occas. Pap. San Diego Soc. Nat. Hist.* 1:2–7[4].

Crotalus durissus unicolor—Brongersma, 1940, *Stud. Fauna Curaçao, Aruba, Bonaire, Venezuelan Is.* 2:115–137[131, Pl. 12].

Crotalus vegrandis Klauber, 1941, *Trans. San Diego Soc. Nat. Hist.* 9:333–336[334]. Holotype: CM 17384, according to McCoy and Richmond (1966). Type-locality: "Maturín Savannah, near Uracoa, Sotillo District, State of Monagas, Venezuela." [Considered a subspecies by Klauber (1956:34).]

Crotalus durissus vegrandis—Klauber, 1956, *Rattlesnakes*, 1st ed., 1:708 pp.[34, Pl. 2 (fig. 5)].

Crotalus durissus crotaminicus Moura Gonçalves, 1956, *An. Acad. Brasil. Cienc.* 28:365–367[365]. Type(s): none designated, according to Klauber (1972:36). Type-locality: Morro Agudo, Franca, Ituverava, São Paulo, Brazil, according to Klauber (1972:36). Klauber (1972:36) treated this name as a nomen nudum because neither the description nor the diagnosis complies with the requirements of Article 13a(i), Article 45b, and Article 73a of the Code. [Listed in the synonymy of *Crotalus durissus terrificus* by Klauber (1972:36).]

Crotalus durissus cascavella—Hoge, 1966 [dated 1965], *Mem. Inst. Butantan* 32:109–184 [139, Pl. 12].

Crotalus durissus collilineatus—Hoge, 1966 [dated 1965], *Mem. Inst. Butantan* 32:109–184 [139, Pl. 13].

Crotalus durissus cumanensis—Hoge, 1966 [dated 1965], *Mem. Inst. Butantan* 32:109–184 [142].

Crotalus durissus dryinus—Hoge, 1966 [dated 1965], *Mem. Inst. Butantan* 32:109–184[142, Pl. 14].

Crotalus durissus marajoensis Hoge, 1966 [dated 1965], *Mem. Inst. Butantan* 32:109–184[143, Pl. 15]. Holotype: IB 17779. Type-locality: "Tuiuiu, Ilha de Marajó, State Pará, Brasil."

Crotalus durissus ruruima Hoge, 1966 [dated 1965], *Mem. Inst. Butantan* 32:109–184[145, Pl. 16]. Holotype: AMNH 36056. Type-locality: "Paulo Camp, Mt. Roraima, 4,000 ft., Venezuela."

Crotalus durissus terrificus—Hoge, 1966 [dated 1965], *Mem. Inst. Butantan* 32:109–184[147, Pl. 17].

Crotalus (Crotalus) durissus cascavella—Peters and Orejas-Miranda, 1970, *Bull. U.S. Natl. Mus.* 297(1):1–347[75].

Crotalus (Crotalus) durissus collilineatus—Peters and Orejas-Miranda, 1970, *Bull. U.S. Natl. Mus.* 297(1):1–347[76].

Crotalus (Crotalus) durissus cumanensis—Peters and Orejas-Miranda, 1970, *Bull. U.S. Natl. Mus.* 297(1):1–347[76].

Crotalus (Crotalus) durissus dryinus—Peters and Orejas-Miranda, 1970, *Bull. U.S. Natl. Mus.* 297(1):1–347[76].

Crotalus (Crotalus) durissus marajoensis—Peters and Orejas-Miranda, 1970, *Bull. U.S. Natl. Mus.* 297(1):1–347[76].

Crotalus (Crotalus) durissus ruruima—Peters and Orejas-Miranda, 1970, *Bull. U.S. Natl. Mus.* 297(1):1–347[76].

Crotalus (Crotalus) durissus terrificus—Peters and Orejas-Miranda, 1970, *Bull. U.S. Natl. Mus.* 297(1):1–347[76].

Crotalus (Crotalus) durissus unicolor—Peters and Orejas-Miranda, 1970, *Bull. U.S. Natl. Mus.* 297(1):1–347[77].

Crotalus (Crotalus) vegrandis—Peters and Orejas-Miranda, 1970, *Bull. U.S. Natl. Mus.* 297(1):1–347[77].

Crotalus durissus trigonicus Harris and Simmons, 1978 [dated 1976/77], *Mem. Inst. Butantan* 40/41:305–311[306]. Holotype:

"RS 907 HSH/RSS in the authors' collection at the Natural History Society of Maryland." Type-locality: "Rupununi Savanna, of southwestern Guyana."

Crotalus territicus ruruima—Sandner-Montilla, 1980, *Mem. Cient. Ofidiol.* 5:1–12[1].

Crotalus pifanorum Sandner-Montilla, 1980, *Mem. Cient. Ofidiol.* 5:1–12[3]. Holotype: "Serpentario del Instituto Venezolano de Ofidiología (Caracas) Cp No. 1" [live specimen]. Type-locality: "sesenta y ocho kilómetros al S. de la población de Espino, en dirección de Puerto Parmana, Parcelamiento de Agrotécnicos 'Dr. Gonzalo Ladezma,' entre los nacientes de los ríos Otocuao (Este) y Carapa (Oeste), Distrito Infante, Estado Guárico" [Venezuela]. [Tentatively included in the synonymy of *Crotalus durissus cumanensis* by McCranie (1993:577.5), and listed there by Golay et al. (1993:58).

Crotalus vegrandis—McCranie, 1984, *Cat. Am. Amph. Rept.* 1984:350.1–2[350.1].

Crotalus unicolor—McCranie, 1986, *Cat. Am. Amph. Rept.* 1986:389.1–2[389.1].

Crotalus durissus unicolor—Campbell and Lamar, 1989, *Venom. Rept. Latin Am.*, 425 pp.[270 (figs. (344 and 345), 344].

Crotalus durissus vegrandis—Campbell and Lamar, 1989, *Venom. Rept. Latin Am.*, 425 pp.[344].

Crotalus durissus pifanorum—Raw, Guidolin, Higashi, and Kelen, 1991, *Handbk. Nat. Toxins* 5:557–581[557].

Crotalus maricelae García-Pérez, 1995, *Rev. Ecol. Lat. Am.* 3:7–12[8, figs. 1–5]. Holotype: ULABG 3201. Type-locality: "Muchachay (8°29'N, 71°10'W; 2400 msnm), Parque Nacional Sierra Nevada de Mérida, Estado Mérida, Venezuela." [This name represents a nomen nudum according to Esqueda et al., 2001.]

Cuando ella [una Cascabel hembra] ha sido muerta, la Cascabel macho perseguirá al hombre, pero perderá sus huellas más allá del séptimo río. Así cuenta una creencia del Llano de Venezuela.

—Roze, 1970a:153, recounting a common belief about
C. terrificus

O doente fugiu e se pôs a correr pelos campos. Algumas horas mais tarde ele reapareceu, inteiramente calmo, dizendo que tinha sido mordido por uma cascavel e pedindo a presença de um padre. Confessou-se com ele, completamente lúcido. A fedrida causada pela mordida da cobra foi medicada com amoníaco. A partir desse momento cessaram todos os sintomas da hidrofobia, e passado algum tempo a lepra desapareceu completamente.

—Auguste de Saint-Hilaire, 1975, commenting on a man with rabies who was apparently cured by the accidental bite of a
C. durissus terrificus

LOCAL NAMES Cascabel, cascabela, cascavel, víbora de cascabel. Argentina: caiguara, imbarake váe, mba'echiniva, mbaraka, and mboi-mbaraka (Guaraní). Aruba: colebre (Creole). Bolivia: cascabel chonono. Brazil: apát (Caiapó), ayug, boicinim, boicininga, boiçuninga, boicinunga, and boiçununga (Amazonian Brazil), boiquirá (south and central Brazil), boleté (Tupi-Guaraní), cangantí, é pak-ti, pa-ki-ti (Canela), cobra-de-guizo, diago (Xetá), ipócó (Guaná), maikir (Rondônia, Suruí Indians), makha mii (Paumari), maracá, maracabóia (central and Amazonian Brazil), mói-maraká (Guajajara). French Guiana: asakamio, serpent chacha. Guyana: sak-kah-sak (Akawai). Paraguay: mboi-chiní, cascabel. Peru: amaru, pálla, palla carairwa, pálla catári, pallacatari, pall karaiwai, palla katari, sacapáyac (Quechua), cui'tini (Cocama), lloreremo ite, lloreyobai, raidu manorede (Huitoto Murui). Suriname: saka sneki. Venezuela: ma ára, uraiyu (Guajiro), sededetiu (Makiritare), mejiya (Piaroa), yasiito (Guahibo), sedechumu (Ye'kwana).

ENGLISH NAME   South American rattlesnake.

DISTRIBUTION   This most widely distributed rattlesnake ranges discontinuously from Colombia to Argentina (Map 96). *Crotalus durissus* occurs in all mainland countries in South America except Ecuador (see Remarks) and Chile; it was reported by Brongersma (1940) in the Antilles on Morro de la Iguana and Tamarindo (Islas Los Testigos), and on Isla Margarita (Los Frailes). Another population exists on Aruba in thornscrub and desert habitats on the southeastern half of the island but apparently not in the southern or eastern coastal areas (Reinert et al., 2002). It was reported once from the island of Curaçao (Rooij, 1922), but no additional specimens have been forthcoming and this record is almost certainly in error. In Colombia *C. durissus* ranges through the Caribbean lowlands from the Departamento de Córdoba northeastward through the Departamento de la Guajira. In the Río Magdalena Valley this species ranges at least as far south as Garzón in the department of Huila (Pl. 803). East of the Andes *C. durissus* is found throughout the Llanos, primarily north of the Río Guayabero/Guaviare, although we are aware of specimens from the Comisaría del Guaviare, and suitable habitat exists in Guainía as well. Tinoco (1978) claimed that this species occurs at elevations up to 2,000 m in Colombia, but this needs to be confirmed. In Venezuela *C. durissus* is distributed throughout the northern half of the country, with isolated populations in the savannas of southern Anzoátegui and Monagas and in the Guiana highlands of extreme southeastern Bolívar. Additional populations of *C. durissus* probably exist in other areas of suitable habitat in southern Venezuela.

In the Guianas *C. durissus* is found along the coastal lowlands from central Guyana to eastern French Guiana, where it is said to be common in the savannas of the Kourou region (Chippaux et al., 1988). Isolated populations exist in west-central and southwest Guyana and southern Suriname. Beebe (1946) found *C. durissus* to be rare in the forested region around Kartabo, Guyana, finding only three specimens during eight field seasons, but it was common in the open areas around Caripito, Venezuela. A population of *C. durissus* in Território do Amapá, Brazil, may be contiguous with the coastal Guianan population. *Crotalus durissus* can be found throughout much of eastern and southern Brazil. In the northern half of the country it exists in isolated populations in Amazonas, Roraima, Pará, and Amapá, and on Ilha de Marajó. The Roraima and northern Pará populations are associated with the Guiana Massif and occur at the borders of Venezuela, Guyana, and Suriname, respectively. *Crotalus durissus* is distributed more or less continuously from Ceará and Rio Grande do Norte south to Rio Grande do Sul and west into Piauí and Goiás with extensions into Mato Grosso and Rondônia; it appears to be absent from the Atlantic coastal mountains of Brazil.

Crotalus durissus is found only in the extreme north and northeast of Uruguay (Tacuarembó, Artigas, and Maldonado), continuing inland into Argentina, where it occurs as far south as Mendoza, San Luís, and possibly northwestern La Pampa. The range includes all of northern Argentina exclusive of the Andean highlands, and practically all of Paraguay. In Bolivia *C. durissus* is restricted to the eastern lowlands (actually central Bolivia, east of the Andes), and the range continues northward into the upper Ríos Bení–Madre de Dios drainage, including a small portion of adjacent Puno, Peru. Schmidt and Walker (1943a) recorded a specimen from the Selvas de Sandia, Peru, and mentioned verbal reports of the species from the Huánuco region. It is likely that the rumors from the Huánuco region apply to *Bothrop atrox*, often called "cascabel" in Peru. We have seen two specimens from the Sandia region. See Remarks and Plates 795–824 for further information on the geographic races and their distributions.

Orcés (1942, 1943, 1948) listed *C. durissus* among the venomous snakes of Ecuador, but probably based on an erroneous assumption rather than direct observation. Orcés (1942) stated: "La especie parece ser muy rara en el Ecuador," and subsequently wrote, "Mencionamos a *Crotalus terrificus* [=*C. durissus*] como de nuestra fauna porque Afranio de Amaral incluye al Ecuador en el área de distribución" (Orcés, 1948).

Most of the range of *C. durissus* is below 1,000 m in tropical and subtropical lowlands; however, there is a record of this species at 2,040 m from the Sierra Nevada de Santa Marta, Colombia (Ruthven, 1922), and it is reputed to occur in the semiarid highlands of Boyacá at similar elevations. In Venezuela this species was recorded by Lancini (1979) to nearly 2,500 m (Pico Naiguatá, Venezuela), and it may occur as as high as 2,800 m. Esqueda et al. (2001), García-Pérez (1995) and Rodríguez and Rojas-Suárez (1995) reported *C. durissus* from up to 2,000 m in an isolated semiarid patch of forest in the Venezuelan Andes. Carrillo de Espinoza and Icochea (1995) and Pesantes-Segura (2000) recorded *C. durissus* from northeastern Puno and southern Madre de Dios in Peru. In the Sandia region of southern Peru, *C. durissus* has been found at 2,300 m.

General distribution information for this species is given in Barrio, 1961a; Cope, 1860b; Ditmars, 1930; Dixon, 1979; Garman, 1884a, 1884b (in part); Gloyd, 1940; Grzimek, 1975; Harris and Simmons, 1972a, 1972b, 1978b; Hoge, 1966, 1979; Klauber, 1952, 1971, 1972; Klemmer, 1963; Minton et al., 1968; P. Müller, 1973; Peters and Orejas-Miranda, 1970; Rivero-Blanco and Dixon, 1979; and Rosenfeld, 1971. Other distribution information is available for Argentina (Abalos, 1961, 1972, 1977; Abalos and Bucher, 1970; Abalos and Mischis, 1975; Abalos and Pirosky, 1963; Abalos et al., 1964; Acosta et al., 1994; Astort, 1988; Cei, 1979a, 1979b; de la Peña, 1986; Ditmars, 1930; Dunn, 1951; Fernández-Barrán and Freiberg, 1951; Freiberg, 1968, 1984; Gallardo, 1977, 1979; Giraudo and Abranson, 1994; Klappenbach and Orejas-Miranda, 1969; Koslowsky, 1898a; Laurent and Terán, 1981; Sage and Capredoni, 1971; Serié, 1921, 1936; Tada and Villa, 1975; Werner, 1922; Yanosky et al., 1996), Aruba (Amaral, 1944d; Hummelinck, 1940; Jansen et al., 1982; Kauffeld and Gloyd, 1939; Maclean et al., 1977; McCranie, 1986; Meek, 1910; Ruthven, 1923; Tryon, 1986), Bolivia (Boulenger, 1896b; Fugler and Cabot, 1995; Gallardo, 1979; Griffin, 1916; Harvey et al., 2003; Kempff-Mercado, 1975; Miranda et al., 1991; Werner, 1922), Brazil (Alves et al., 1991; Amaral, 1926h, 1926m, 1930b, 1931c, 1934a, 1938, 1944d, 1945, 1948a, 1948b, 1978; Azevedo-Marquez et al., 1985; Borges, 1999; Boulenger, 1886, 1896b; Calleffo, 1999; Cardoso and Brando, 1982; Cordeiro and Hoge, 1974; Cunha and Nascimento, 1982a; Curran, 1935; Fonseca, 1949; Freitas, 1999; Gliesch, 1925; Grantsau, 1991; Günther, 1861—as *horridus*; Hagmann, 1909; Hoge, 1953a, 1953b, 1967; Hoge and Romano, 1973; Hoge and Romano-Hoge, 1981b; Hoge et al., 1975, 1977c, 1981; Hymann, 1909; Ihering, 1911; Jensen, 1900; Koslowsky, 1898b; Lacerda, 1884; Lema, 1971b, 1983; Lema and Fabián-Beurmann, 1977; Lema et al., 1980; Machado, 1945b; Magalhães, 1925; L. Müller, 1927; P. Müller, 1968, 1969a, 1969b, 1971; Nascimento et al., 1991; Rodrigues, 2000; Santos, 1943; Silva et al., 1979; Vanzolini, 1947, 1948; Vanzolini et al., 1980), Colombia (Amaral, 1928a, 1931a, 1931b; Angel-Mejía, 1982, 1987b; Ayerbe, 1995; Daniel, 1949; Dugand, 1975; Dunn, 1944a; Medem, 1969; Nicéforo-María, 1929b, 1930b, 1933, 1942; Pérez-Santos, 1986a, 1986b; Pérez-Santos and Moreno, 1986; Renjifo,

1979; Tinoco, 1978), French Guiana (Chippaux, 1987; Chippaux et al., 1988; Gasc and Rodrigues, 1980; Hoogmoed, 1979; Starace, 1998), the Guianan region (Hoogmoed, 1979, 1983), Guyana (Beebe, 1919, 1946; Harris and Simmons, 1978a; Hoogmoed, 1979; Jan and Sordelli, 1874; Parker, 1935; Quelch, 1898), Paraguay (Amaral, 1925a; Aquino et al., 1996; Bertoni, 1914, 1939; Boulenger, 1894a, 1896b; Canese, 1966; Gallardo, 1979; Gatti, 1955; Migone, 1929; Norman, 1994; Schouten, 1931, 1937; Scott and Lovett, 1975; Talbot, n.d.; Werner, 1922), southern Peru (Carrillo de Espinoza, 1970, 1983; Carrillo de Espinoza and Icochea, 1995; Meneses, 1974a, 1974b; Pesantes-Segura, 2000; Schmidt and Walker, 1943a; Tschudi, 1845; Yarlequé-Chocas, 2000), Suriname (Abuys, 1987d; Brongersma, 1967b; Cope, 1860a; Hoge, 1964; Hoogmoed, 1979; Moonen et al., 1978), Uruguay (Achával, 1976; Achával et al., 1978; Devincenzi, 1925; Vaz-Ferreira and Sierra de Soriano, 1960), and Venezuela (Alemán, 1953; Bisbal, 1990; Boulenger, 1896b; Briceño-Rossi, 1934a; García-López and Sandner-Montilla, 1962; Hoge and Lancini, 1962; Klauber, 1941b; Lancini, 1962c, 1967, 1970, 1979, 1983; Lema and Fabián-Beurmann, 1977; Manzanilla Puppo et al., 1996; Marcuzzi, 1950; Markezich, 2002; McCranie, 1984, 1986; Mijares-Urrutia and Arends R., 2000; Milá de la Roca, 1932; Murphy et al., 1979; Rivero-Blanco and Dixon, 1979; Péfaur, 1992; Péfaur and Rivero, 2000; Rohl, 1949; Roze, 1952, 1964, 1966a, 1970a; Ruthven, 1922; Sandner-Montilla, 1965, 1980, 1985a, 1994; Schargel and García-Pérez, 1999; Shreve, 1947a; Vaz-Ferreira and Sierra de Soriano, 1960; Vellard, 1941, 1943, 1946; Vetencourt-Finol., 1960; Wagler, 1824; Wagner, 1985).

HABITAT Savanna, caatinga, and cerrado. Reported to inhabit littoral xerophilous scrub, psammophilous and halophilous littoral grassland, thorny xerophilous scrub, tropophilous deciduous and semideciduous scrub, and tropophilous semideciduous seasonal forest in northwestern Venezuela (Mijares-Urrutia and Arends R., 2000). Pesantes-Segura (2000) reported C. durissus from selva alta in Peru. Occasionally individuals are found in more mesic situations, but we are unaware of populations in such areas. Böckeler (1988) stated that C. durissus prefers the drier, sandier parts of the Paraguayan Chaco.

DESCRIPTION Crotalus durissus is a large, stout, terrestrial rattlesnake commonly reaching 100 cm or more in length. Large males in some populations may attain lengths of 140–160 cm, and the maximum is probably about 180 cm. Specimens approaching this size have been recorded from northern South America and (questionably) from Uruguay. Barrio and Brazil (1945) gave 140 cm as the maximum TL for this species, and Ihering (1911) gave 180 cm. Some populations are dwarfed, including those in the savannas of northeastern Venezuela, the highlands of southeastern Venezuela, the savannas of southwestern Guyana, and Aruba, where the largest specimens do not exceed 100 cm in TL. Pifano-C. and Rodríguez-Acosta (1996) gave the mean adult TL of C. d. vegrandis as 52 cm for males and 40 cm for females and stated that members of this taxon rarely exceed 60–70 cm. Captive C. d. vegrandis grow considerably larger than do free-living animals.

Like C. simus, this species has a conspicuous spinal ridge, especially evident in large adults; it is most evident on the anterior part of the body because of the height of the neural spines. In adults, the dorsal scales covering the spinal ridge are notable for their prominent, high, tubercular keels; the degree of rugosity found in C. durissus and C. simus is unrivaled by any other species of rattlesnake.

The color pattern is extremely variable. Amaral (1926h) noted the differences in dorsal pattern and ground color in individuals from different regions in Brazil. The ground color may be pale to dark brown, gray-brown, reddish brown, tannish red, pale ash gray, pinkish tan, or almost black. There are usually no dark punctations in the ground color. The ground color of snakes from densely forested regions is often considerably darker than that of snakes from arid regions such as the northern coast of Venezuela or Aruba. Snakes from densely forested Kartabo, Guyana, were described as being pale to deep forest green (Beebe, 1946). The pattern often consists of scales that are nearly all unicolored, at least on the anterior part of the body; however, the scales constituting the pale borders around the dorsal blotches may occasionally be pale distally and have dark bases. Snakes from northeastern Venezuela (C. d. vegrandis) have a gray, tan, or reddish brown ground color with large white flecks that may outline rhombic blotches, a pattern typical of C. durissus, or these flecks may be profuse enough to obliterate the pattern. The rattlesnakes inhabiting the savannas of southern Guyana resemble C. d. vegrandis in having numerous light-tipped scales.

There are 18–32 rhombic or diamond-shaped dorsal body blotches. The dorsal blotches may be too vaguely defined in adults from Aruba to allow an accurate assessment of the number. Middorsally, blotches are separated by 1 or 2 pale scales. The body blotches, at least anteriorly, are reddish brown, dark brown, or black with paler interiors, usually tan to pale gray-brown except in some southern South American snakes. Posteriorly, dorsal blotches tend to become shorter and wider, in some populations coalescing with lateral body blotches and in others remaining discrete. The lateral blotches are below the lateral points of the dorsal series and usually comprise groups of 3–7 dark scales bordered by pale scales. This primary series of lateral blotches frequently engages scale rows 2–5, but in some populations, including those in northern South America, this series may be situated more ventrally and may reach the lateral edges of the ventrals. Another secondary series of lateral blotches alternates between the primary lateral series; this series is usually more diffuse or less dark than the primary series and involves the outer edges of the ventrals.

A transverse dark brown or black bar usually extends across the head, mostly anterior to the supraoculars but including the anterior edges of these scales. Dark spots are usually present immediately behind the supraoculars, and these may be continuous with the paravertebral dark stripes on the neck or with a dark transverse streak in the upper temporal region. A dark postocular stripe, usually about 2 scales wide, extends from the eye to about the rictus; this stripe frequently passes through the eye and merges with the dark transverse bar on the top of the snout. Some snakes lack most dark markings on the head, and individuals of some populations (unicolor and vegrandis) lack even the forward extension of the paravertebral stripes as adults.

The paravertebral stripes are usually 1–4 times longer than the head, but may be shorter in some individuals from east-central Brazil and parts of Venezuela. Each paravertebral stripe is usually 2–3 dorsal scales wide, but stripes are often 4 scales wide in southeast Venezuelan specimens. Each supraocular is marked by a prominent pale transverse crossbar (sometimes connected across the frontal region) or subcircular spot (reported to be triangular in snakes from southwestern Guyana). The tail of adults may be uniformly gray, gray-brown, blackish, or like that of juveniles, in which darker crossbands may be vaguely evident. The proximal rattle segment is dark gray or black in adults and relatively pale in young snakes.

The chin and gular region is usually mostly white or yellowish, although some populations have dark flecking or mottling, especially on the infralabials. The belly is usually whitish, yellowish, or buff, and varies from nearly immaculate to white with pale gray blotches or mottling that becomes progressively darker posteriorly.

Most frequently the internasal-prefrontal region is covered by 4–6 scales, including 2 large, triangular internasals in contact with the rostral, followed by 2 large, quadrangular prefrontals (anterior canthals) in contact with each other along the midline, and sometimes a pair of small posterior canthals. The posterior canthals, if present, are located directly behind the upper loreal and are sometimes considered post–upper loreals. Anteriorly there are 2–5 (usually 2, except in Colombia, where the mode is 3) intersupraoculars. The parietal and occipital regions are covered with small, keeled scales.

The first supralabial usually is in broad contact with the prenasal. The number of prefoveals varies from 3 to 10, with 6–8 most often present. Most frequently the preacunal and sublacunal are separated from the supralabials by a row of foveals. The lateral portions of the prefrontals (anterior canthals) are usually not deflected downward over the canthus rostralis. There are 1–6 loreals (usually 2 or 3) per side; there is usually only 1 lower loreal and 1 or more upper loreals, which preclude postnasal–upper preocular contact. When there is more than a single upper loreal, the extra scales are located posterior to the upper loreal (post–upper loreals) and are between the prefrontal and upper preoculars, usually preventing their contact. One (sometimes 2) interoculabial separates the anterior suboculars from the supralabials. The first pair of infralabials were divided in about half of the specimens of *C. durissus* we examined. Infracephalic scales such as submentals and interchinshields are rarely present.

There are 2–5 intersupraoculars, 11–18 (usually 13–16) supralabials, 12–20 (usually 14–17) infralabials; usually 27 midbody dorsal scale rows; 155–179 ventrals in males and 163–190 in females; and 25–32 subcaudals in males and 18–26 in females, 0–10 (usually 1 or 2) of which are divided.

SIMILAR SPECIES   Throughout its range, *C. durissus* is the only species of rattlesnake present; thus, confusing it with any other rattlesnake is impossible. Species of *Lachesis* have a pattern of bold dorsal rhombs and reach a large size, and therefore might be mistaken for rattlesnakes, but *Lachesis* differs from *Crotalus* in numerous ways, including having a long spine at the end of the tail (versus a rattle), finely divided distal subcaudals (versus undivided scales), 9–15 intersupraoculars (versus 2–5), 200 or more ventrals (versus fewer than 195), and more than 43 subcaudals (versus fewer than 35).

REMARKS   The *Crotalus durissus* complex has been treated by many authors who have often disagreed on the status of certain populations. It appears indisputable that this wide-ranging group of snakes was derived from a North American ancestor and dispersed southward into South America. It seems a reasonable assumption that the common ancestor of *C. simus* and *C. durissus* evolved in North America and subsequently dispersed into Central and South America. It further seems reasonable to assume that this dispersal did not occur prior to the formation of the lower Central American land bridge, generally thought to have been established during the Pliocene, some 3–6 million years ago.

Given the distances and dispersal time involved, and a changing environment, it is likely that the populations at the extremes of the range were already considerably differentiated from one another by the time *C. durissus* entered South America. Subsequent to the South American invasion, rattlesnakes colonized Aruba, probably by successfully traversing the narrow marine barrier between Aruba and the Paraguaná Peninsula, although a land bridge may have existed between the island and the mainland at one time.

Another population became isolated geographically in the Sabanas de Maturín (Venezuela), probably at a time when climatic changes greatly altered the distribution of rattlesnakes in South America. Today, isolated rattlesnake populations exist in open, dry habitats such as savannas all across South America—evidence of their once greater distribution. Because the great forests of South America did not exist until the late Pliocene-Pleistocene, it is possible that that *C. durissus* was present in the region prior to that time and that the vicariance of *C. durissus* resulted when the emerging forests separated populations. The precise timing of the events that isolated *C. d. unicolor* or *C. d. vegrandis* from other populations remains to be ascertained. It appears that a relatively ancient fragmentation of the ancestral range occurred in northern Mexico, followed by a vicariant event in the Isthmus of Panama; relatively recent fragmentations have occurred over much of South America in response to changes in climate and vegetation. We recognize three species in this complex, all of which have available names: *C. totonacus* Gloyd and Kauffeld (1940) in northeastern Mexico, *C. simus* Latreille *in* Sonnini de Manoncourt and Latreille (1801–1802) from Mexico to Costa Rica, and *C. durissus* Linnaeus (1758) in South America. Table 50 summarizes the differences among these species. *Crotalus d. unicolor* and *C. d. vegrandis* have often been accorded full species status. Because both subspecies appear to be comparatively recently derived from an ancestor shared with other northern South American populations of *C. durissus*, but not with populations in Central America and Mexico, recognizing them as full species would make *C. durissus* a paraphyletic species, an untenable situation. In their study of microsatellite genetic markers in rattlesnakes, Bushar et al. (2001) found a close relationship between *C. durissus* populations on Aruba and the South American mainland.

The closest relatives of *C. durissus* appear to be *C. simus* and *C. totonacus*; *C. molossus* and *C. basiliscus* are also in this group.

Crotalus durissus is the most widely distributed rattlesnake, and it is thus not surprising that populations exhibit a considerable amount of geographic variation. However, even adjacent or contiguous populations may be dramatically different from one another. Allen and Neill (1957) described two such populations in southern Guyana that appear to be ecologically separated. A large "bush rattlesnake" with a subdued color pattern, inhabits the forested areas, and a dwarfed "savanna rattlesnake" with a relatively bold color pattern occurrs in the savannas. The bush rattlesnake may reach about 1.5 m in TL, has a dorsal pattern in which the dorsal rhombs often coalesce with the lateral spots, lacks a distinctive head pattern, the paravertebral stripes on the neck are generally rather vaguely indicated and not accented by distinct pale and dark spots, the scales are mostly unicolored, some evidence of crossbands is usually apparent on the tail except in very old specimens, a high spinal ridge is present on the anterior of the body, and the fangs are proportionately shorter than in savanna populations. The savanna rattlesnake reaches no more than about 1 m in TL and has a distinct pattern of dorsal rhombs that are not confluent with the lateral spots; a distinct yellow or white V-shaped marking on the supraoculars; many distinct pale and dark spots on the neck; scales that usually are not uniformly colored but rather are tipped with white, yellow, or pale gray; a tail that is

Table 50. Comparison of selected features of the *Crotalus durissus* group.

Character	*C. totonacus*	*C. simus*	*C. durissus*
Spinal ridge	Poorly developed	Well developed	Well developed
Primary lateral body blotches	Low, on scale rows 1–4, reaching ventrals	High, on scale rows 2–5, not reaching ventrals	Low, on scale rows 1–4, not reaching ventrals
Secondary lateral body blotches	Indistinct or absent	Usually distinct	Usually distinct
Paravertebral stripe length	Usually no more than 1 head length	2–4 times head length	2–4 times head length
Paravertebral stripe width	4 dorsals	1–2 dorsals	2–4 dorsals
Average number of dorsal body blotches	30	24	26
Scales in parietal and occipital region	Often large and flat	Small and keeled	Small and keeled
Prefoveals	Usually 3–4	Usually ≥6	Usually ≥6
Dorsal scale rows at midbody (mode)	25	Usually 29	Usually 27
Ventrals			
Males	184–192	170–188	155–179
Females	193–195	172–191	168–190
Subcaudals			
Males	26–29	22–34	25–32
Females	22–26	18–26	26–29

essentially uniformly black with only a very slight or no trace of crossbands; a low spinal ridge; and proportionately long fangs. The savanna population was reported to be much more docile than the "bush" population and could not be provoked into striking (Allen and Neill, 1957).

We recognize 11 subspecies, which for the most part are distinguished on the basis of pattern, size, color, and to a lesser extent squamation. *Crotalus d. durissus* (Pls. 795 and 796) inhabits the northern coastal portions of Guyana, Suriname, and French Guiana, and the interior of the territory of Amapá, Brazil. The affinities of the Brazilian and French Guianan population are uncertain and they are placed tentatively with *C. d. durissus*.

Crotalus d. cascavella (Pls. 797 and 798) from Brazil is found in the dry caatinga region from southern Maranhão, Piauí, Ceará, and Rio Grande do Norte south through Paraíba, Pernambuco, Alagoas, Sergipe, Bahia, and northeastern Minas Gerais.

Crotalus d. collilineatus (Pls. 799–802) occurs in central and northeastern Brazil, including parts of Rondônia, Mato Grosso, Goiás, southwestern Bahia, western Minas Gerais, São Paulo (where it intergrades with *C. d. terrificus*), and probably extending southward into western Paraná. There is an unsubstantiated report of this subspecies in Bolivia.

Crotalus d. cumanensis (Pls. 803–809) occurs in Colombia and Venezuela and is distributed along the Caribbean coastal plain from the Departamento de Córdoba, Colombia, eastward to extreme eastern Venezuela and perhaps western Guyana. In inter-Andean Colombia this subspecies occurs south to near the headwaters of the Río Magdalena. East and south of the Andes this subspecies is found throughout the Llanos of both countries. There may be an isolated population on the high plains of Boyacá, Colombia. The populations from eastern Colombia appear to be distinguishable from those along the Caribbean coast of Colombia. This race also occurs on the Islas Los Testigos (on Morro de la Iguana and Tamarindo) and on the Islas Los Frailes (Isla de Margarita). *Crotalus pifanorum*, described from Guárico, Venezuela, is tentatively considered to be either a junior synonym of *C. d. cumanensis* or an intergrade.

Crotalus d. maricelae, perhaps indistinguishable from *C. d. cumanensis*, was described from 2,400 m in the "Bolson Arido de Lagunillas," a rainshadow valley in the Parque Nacional Nevada de Mérida of Venezuela. This taxon is purportedly distinguished by having 5 prefrontal scales, a greenish brown ground color, and a small size. Esqueda et al. (2001) suggested that the name *Crotalus maricelae* is a nomen nudem and that this population does not warrant special taxonomic recognition because all of the characters purported to distinguish it fall with the range of *C. durissus cumanensis*.

Crotalus d. marajoensis (Pls. 810 and 811) is restricted to the savannas of Ilha de Marajó in Pará, Brazil.

Crotalus d. ruruima (Pls. 812 and 813) occurs in Venezuela and Brazil and is known from the slopes of Mounts Roraima and Cariman-Perú in the state of Bolívar, Venezuela; a few specimens have been recorded from Território Federal de Roraima, Brazil. This race probably occurs in adjacent Guyana as well.

Crotalus d. terrificus (Pls. 814–816) ranges from the Cordillera de Carabaya in the Puno–Madre de Dios region of Peru southward across central Bolivia, through most of Paraguay, northern Uruguay, northern Argentina, and southeastern Brazil from Rio Grande do Sul and Mato Grosso do Sul north to Minas Gerais.

Crotalus d. trigonicus (Pls. 817 and 818) is known with certainty only from the Rupununi savannas in southwestern Guyana, and probably from the adjacent Território Federal de Roraima, Brazil. There is a single, puzzling report of this subspecies in the savannas of Tiriós, Amapá, Brazil. The validity of this taxon is questionable.

Crotalus d. unicolor (Pls. 819–821) inhabits the island of Aruba off the coast of Venezuela and is a dwarfed snake.

Crotalus d. vegrandis (Pls. 822–824) is restricted to Venezuela. It occurs in southern Anzoátegui and southern Monagas in the Maturín Savanna at elevations of 30–500 m (Lancini, 1967; Roze, 1970a). This dwarfed snake is reported to live mostly in armadillo burrows.

The status of isolated Brazilian populations in the Campos de Humaitá (Amazonas) and the Serra do Cachimbo and Santarém (Pará) is uncertain. *Crotalus durissus* is rumored to occur in the Departamento de Huánuco, Peru, but we are unaware of specimens actually collected there (see the remarks under Distribution, above). Local informants maintain that rattlesnakes occur in southwestern Ecuador and adjacent Peru, where suitable habitat does appear to exist. Again, there are no specimens to substantiate their presence in this region, but we are aware of a pre-Columbian ceramic from western Ecuador with a graphic depiction of a cascabel (J. Boos, pers. comm.).

Linnaeus (1758) listed three species of rattlesnakes: *horridus*, *dryinus*; and *durissus*, and Laurenti (1768) described *terrificus*, but their brief descriptions do not allow a clear distinction to be made between these taxa, resulting in much confusion in the use of these names. Some of the past misallocations of were summarized by Klauber (1941a); the species currently known as *C. horridus* was referred to as *durissus* by Holbrook (1842) and Duméril et al. (1854); *C. adamanteus* was called *durissus* by Boulenger (1896b) and Mocquard (1909); and *C. durissus* from Central America (=*C. simus*) was identified as *horridus* by Duméril et al. (1854) and as *terrificus* by Boulenger (1896b). The type of *Crotalus durissus* is now lost (Loennberg, 1896), but it originally was in the Claudius Grill Collection, also referred to as the Surinam Collection, and later was sent to the Zoological Museum of the Royal University at Uppsala, Sweden (Klauber, 1941a:83).

Crotalus enyo (Cope, 1861)
(Map 97, Pls. 825–828)

Caudisona enyo Cope, 1861, *Proc. Acad. Nat. Sci. Philadelphia* 13:292–306[293]. Holotype: given as "Type 4663. Xant. Coll." by Cope (1861:293), who mentioned that specimens were sent to the Philadelphia Academy and the Smithsonian Institution. Three syntypes are extant: ANSP 7159 (a wet skin) and USNM 5291 (two specimens: one is a juvenile with Xántus number 778; the other is a larger wet skin [records show that three Xántus specimens, numbers 338, 432, and 788, originally were cataloged as USNM 5291]). Klauber (1956:34) indicated that Xántus 4663 is now ANSP 7159, but provided no supporting evidence. Labels associated with ANSP 7159 currently show no indication of a corresponding Xántus number 4663 (J. Cadle, pers. comm.). Lectotype: ANSP 7159, as designated by Beaman and Grismer (1994:589.1). Their designation probably was unnecessary if one accepts Klauber's (1956:34) statement that ANSP 7159 is Xántus 4663. Type-locality: "Inhabits Lower California." Klauber (1956:34, footnote 7) stated: "This specimen [ANSP 7159] was collected at Cape San Lucas, Baja California Sur, which therefore should be considered the type-locality of the species."

Crotalus enyo—Cope, 1875, *Bull. U.S. Natl. Mus.* (1):104 pp.[33].

Crotalus oregonus var. *enyo*—Garman, 1884a [dated 1883], *Mem. Mus. Comp. Zool.* 8:1–185[174].

Crotalus tigris—Boulenger, 1896b, *Cat. Snakes British Mus.* 3:727 pp.[580]. [In part.]

Crotalus confluentus enyo—Amaral, 1929c, *Bull. Antivenin Inst. Am.* 2:86–97[94].

Crotalus enyo enyo—Lowe and Norris, 1954, *Trans. San Diego Soc. Nat. Hist.* 12:47–64[52].

Crotalus enyo furvus Lowe and Norris, 1954, *Trans. San Diego Soc. Nat. Hist.* 12:47–64[52, 63 (pl. 4)]. Holotype: MVZ 55388. Type-locality: "10.9 miles (by road) north of El Rosario, along the main road on the coastwise terrace near the foot of a bold Cretaceous escarpment, Baja California Norte, Mexico." In their review of the species, Beaman and Grismer (1994:589.4) recognized three subspecies but indicated that *Crotalus enyo enyo* and *Crotalus enyo furvus* "should be considered as the binomial *C. enyo*" and that *Crotalus enyo cerralvensis* would best be considered a full species.

Crotalus enyo cerralvensis Cliff, 1954, *Trans. San Diego Soc. Nat. Hist.* 12:67–98[82, 96 (pl. 6, fig. 3)]. Holotype: CAS-SU 14021. Type-locality: "Isla Cerralvo in Gulf of California" [Cerralvo Island, Gulf of California, Mexico].

Crotalus enyo—Beaman and Grismer, 1994, *Cat. Am. Amph. Rept.* 1994:589.1–6[589.1].

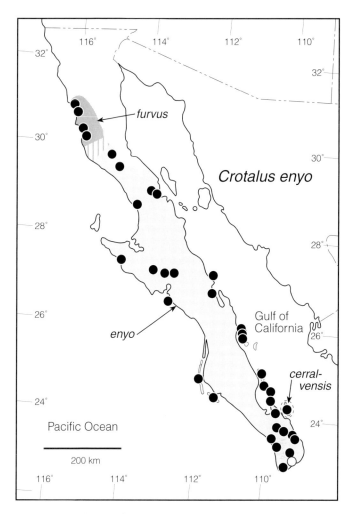

Map 97. Distribution of *Crotalus enyo*, including subspecies, on the Baja California Peninsula, Mexico, and nearby islands. Unfilled symbol represents general area of type-locality (Cape San Lucas).

LOCAL NAME Víbora de cascabel.

ENGLISH NAME Baja California rattlesnake.

DISTRIBUTION Western Mexico. This species occupies the peninsula of Baja California in the north from about Río San Telmo, Baja California Norte, on the Pacific coast, and the mainland opposite Isla Ángel de la Guarda on the Gulf of California southward to Cabo San Lucas (Map 97). It is found on a number of islands, including (from north to south) San Marcos, Arbajos, Coronados, Carmen, Isla Pardo (one of the Islas Los Candeleros), San José, San Francisco, Partida del Sur, Espíritu Santo, and Cerralvo in the Gulf of California; and Magdalena and Santa Margarita in the Pacific (Map 92).

Distribution records are available in Armstrong and Murphy, 1979; Beaman and Grismer, 1994; Banks, 1962 (Cerralvo Island); Bostic, 1971; Cliff, 1954; Cope, 1861, 1900; Cuesta-Terrón, 1920, 1921a, 1931; Etheridge, 1961; Garman, 1884b; Gloyd, 1940; Grismer, 1993, 1994b, 1994c, 2002; Grismer et al., 1994, 1997; Hoge and Romano, 1971a; Klauber, 1931b, 1936b, 1952, 1971, 1972; Leviton and Banta, 1964; Lindsay, 1962; Linsdale, 1932; Lowe and Norris, 1954; Martín del Campo, 1935, 1937a, 1950; Mocquard, 1899, 1908–1909; Murphy, 1983a, 1983b; Murphy and Ottley, 1984; Murray, 1955; Nelson, 1922; Reynoso, 1990; Savage, 1960; Schmidt, 1922; Smith and Taylor, 1945, 1966; Soulé and Sloan, 1966; Stejneger and Barbour, 1943; Van Denburgh, 1895a, 1922b; Van Denburgh and Slevin, 1914, 1921b; Werner, 1922; and Yarrow, 1875, 1883.

HABITAT Usually desert, but also chaparral (coastal sage) in the northwestern part of the range and extending into tropical deciduous forest and pine-oak forest (Sierra de San Lázaro) in the cape region. This snake is often found in rocky areas with cacti and arid thornscrub, and sometimes occurs in sand dunes. It is often found near human habitations in piles of trash (Grismer, 2002).

DESCRIPTION The record TL is 89.8 cm (Klauber, 1972). Murphy and Ottley (1984) reported that two of the three specimens they secured on Isla San Marcos were quite large, exceeding 80 cm in TL. The eyes and rattle are proportionately large, and the head is remarkably small and narrow.

The ground color is tan, pale to dark brown, gray-brown, or silvery gray, and may become paler posteriorly. Snakes in the northern part of the range tend to be darker than those in the south. The ground color is punctated with gray. The 28–42 clearly defined dorsal body blotches are reddish to yellowish brown, black edged, and are subrectangular anteriorly but change to hexagons by midbody. The primary lateral blotches are dark, often black, and frequently coalesce with dorsal blotches, especially on the posterior half of the body, forming crossbands. These lateral blotches often engage the lateral portions of the ventrals. A small, somewhat indistinct series of lateral blotches that alternates with the primary series is sometimes present; these also involve the lateral portions of the ventrals but do not extend up on the sides as high as the primary series.

A distinct pale bar extends across the supraoculars, curving forward medially. A pair of small dark spots is usually present in the anterior parietal area. A pair of longitudinally elongate outer parietal blotches extends from behind the supraoculars to the posterior parietal region, followed by a pair of nape stripes that extends onto the neck and may or may not engage the first dorsal blotch. Often the posterior part of the parietal blotches merges with the anterior portion of the respective nape stripes, forming a pair of large, irregular stripes that extends from the supraocular well onto the body. The postocular stripe extends posteriorly behind the eye to the angle of the jaw, passing above the rictus.

The labials, especially the infralabials, are often suffused with gray. The infralabials and gulars may also be spotted with 1 spot below the pit and another situated 3 or 4 scales anterior to the rictus. The belly is cream colored or buff and heavily mottled or dotted with gray or brown. The tail lacks strongly contrasting pale and dark rings, but has 4–8 brownish tail rings on a ground color heavily suffused with gray. The proximal rattle segment is usually black.

The rostral is usually wider than high. Two internasals are in contact with the rostral; 13–25 scales cover the internasal-prefrontal area, and 2–6 (usually 4 or 5) intersupraoculars are present. The scales in the prefrontal-frontal area tend to be rough and knobby. Laterally, the supraoculars are slanted upward and supraocular sutures are absent. The rostral is in contact with the prenasal, and the prenasal is usually in contact with supralabial 1, but such contact is prevented by anterior prefoveals in an occasional specimen. The lacunals may be in broad contact with the supralabials or may be wholly or partially separated by 1–3 subfoveals. The upper preocular usually is not in contact with the postnasal, such contact prevented by the presence of 1–5 loreals (usually 2 or 3—a lower, an upper, and a post-upper). The lower loreal, if present, is always larger than the upper. There is 1 (sometimes 2) interoculabial between the anterior subocular and supralabials. The first pair of infra-

labials are not transversely divided and there are no interchinshields or submental. There are 12–15 (usually 13 or 14) supralabials, 11–16 (usually 13 or 14) infralabials, 23–27 (usually 25) midbody dorsal scale rows, 157–177 ventrals in males and 161–181 in females (specimens from Isla Cerralvo have a higher average number than individuals from the mainland), and 22–31 subcaudals in males and 18–23 in females (Cerralvo specimens have a higher average number).

SIMILAR SPECIES Three species of rattlesnakes are sympatric with *C. enyo. Crotalus ruber* has contrasting black and ash white bands on the tail, the top of the head has little or no pattern, and usually there are 27 or more midbody dorsal scale rows and 181 or more ventrals. *Crotalus oreganus* has more than 2 internasals in contact with the rostral and dark brown to blackish dorsal blotches with boldly contrasting pale margins. *Crotalus mitchellii* has strongly contrasting black and ash white bands on the tail, prenasals that are usually separated from the rostral by a series of small scales, and upper preoculars that are often divided vertically and/or horizontally.

REMARKS Three subspecies are recognized. *Crotalus e. enyo* (Pls. 825 and 826) ranges from about El Rosario southward through the peninsula of Baja California, including several offshore islands (see Distribution). The SVL of adults is less than 27 times the head length; the ground color is usually tan, fawn, silvery gray, or pale gray; the upper loreal is usually "smaller" than the lower; and there are 157–174 ventrals in males and 161–177 in females, and 22–28 subcaudals in males and 18–23 in females. *Crotalus e. cerralvensis* (Pl. 827) is endemic to Isla Cerralvo. The SVL of adults is 26 or more times the head length, the ground color is pale with distinct dorsal blotches, the upper loreal is usually smaller than the lower, and there are 167–177 ventrals in males and 181 in the single reported female, and 27–31 subcaudals in males and 23 in the female. *Crotalus e. furvus* (Pl. 828) ranges from about Río San Telmo to about El Rosario. The SVL of adults is less than 26 times the head length, the ground color is dark brown or gray-brown, the upper loreal is usually larger than the lower, and there are 159–162 ventrals in males and 165–171 in females, and 26–29 subcaudals in males and 18–26 in females.

Crotalus enyo cerralvensis was described on the basis of its higher number of ventrals and proportionately smaller head (Cliff, 1954). Beaman and Grismer (1994) pointed out that these characters overlap between samples from Isla Cerralvo and the mainland, but they did think that the butterscotch ground color of the island population differed from the gray-brown ground color of the mainland population. On the basis of additional live specimens observed in the field, Grismer (1999a) stated that the purported difference in ground color is also variable and overlaps between populations. Grismer (1999a) proposed that subspecific recognition not be afforded to various populations of *C. enyo*.

Crotalus horridus Linnaeus, 1758
(Map 98, Pls. 829–834)

Crotalus horridus Linnaeus, 1758, *Syst. Nat.*, 10th ed., 1:824 pp.[214]. Type(s): now lost, according to Klauber (1956:35); originally in King Adolph Frideric Collection and later sent to the Royal Zoological State Museum in Stockholm, Sweden [NHRM]. According to Andersson (1899:27), "there are two jars labeled as *Crotalus horridus*, one of which contains a head [NHRM 103] that may be *Lachesis muta* and the other has only a tail of a rattle snake [NHRM 102]." Type-locality: "America." Proposed restriction to the "vicinity of New York City" [USA]

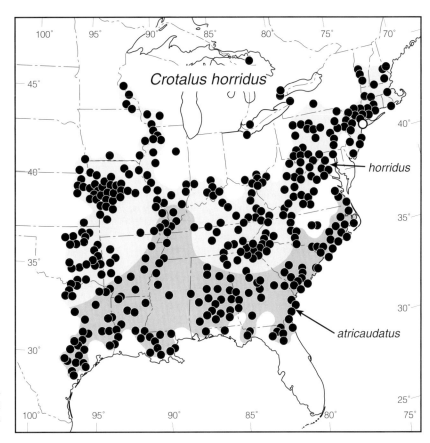

Map 98. Distribution of *Crotalus horridus*, including sub-species, in the eastern United States. Unfilled symbol represents restricted type-locality, "vicinity of New York City" (Schmidt, 1953c).

by Schmidt (1953c:227). The uncertainties regarding the proper allocation of Linnaeus's names to rattlesnake species were discussed by Klauber (1941a:81–95, 1948:1–14).

Crotalus boiquira Lacépède, 1788–1789, *Hist. Nat. Serp.* 2:527 pp.[130, 390, pl. 18 (fig. 1)]. Type(s): none designated, according to Klauber (1956:35). Type-locality: the New World, according to Klauber (1956:35). ICZN, 1987, Opinion 1463, *Bull. Zool. Nomencl.* 44:265–267, ruled that all editions of Lacépède's *Histoire Naturelle des Serpens* are unavailable works.

Crotalus atricaudatus Latreille, *in* Sonnini de Manoncourt and Latreille, 1801–1802, *Hist. Nat. Rept.* 3:335 pp.[209]. Type(s): none designated; none located in MNHN by Thireau (1991:2). Type-locality: "Caroline." Proposed restriction to "Charleston, South Carolina," by Schmidt (1953c:228).

Crotalus zetazomae Brickell, 1805, *Philadelphia Med. Phys. J.* 2:164[164]. Type(s): unlocated. None designated, according to Klauber (1956:35). Type-locality: not given, "probably the vicinity of Savannah, Georgia" [USA], according to Klauber (1956:35).

Crotalinus cyanurus Rafinesque, 1818, *Am. Monthly Mag. Crit. Rev.* 3:445–447[446] and 4:39–42[41]. Type(s): none designated. Type-locality: "the barrens of Kentucky" [USA].

Crotalus catesbaei Hemprich, 1820, *Grundr. Naturgesch.*, 432 pp.[387]. Type(s): none designated. Type-locality: "South America to Carolina." According to Klauber (1956:36, footnote 12), Diesing (1851:431) attributed the specific name *catesbyanum* to Fitzinger. However, Fitzinger (1826b:63) used the name *catesbaei*, which he credited to Hemprich, 1820. Considered a nomen nudum and a synonym of *Crotalus h. atricaudatus* by Klauber (1936b:195).

Crotalurus cyanurus—Rafinesque, 1820, *Ann. Nat.* (Lexington) (22):1–16[5].

Caudisona horrida—Fleming, 1822, *Philos. Zool.* 2:618 pp.[294].

Crotalus durissus var. *concolor* Jan, 1859, *Rev. Mag. Zool.* (Paris) (2)10:148–157[153]. Holotype: "Munich" Museum, now appar-

ently lost, according to a letter from Lorenz Müller that was cited by Gloyd (1940:216, footnote). Type-locality: "Amérique septentrionale." Jan (1863:124) listed "(Monaco) Patria ?" for the same taxon. [Nomen nudum. Listed with a question mark in synonymy by Garman (1884:175). Jan's *concolor* is a senior homonym of *Crotalus concolor* Woodbury, 1929 (=*Crotalus viridis* Rafinesque, 1818) and was suppressed by the ICZN, 1955, Opinion 339, *Opinions Decls.* 10(6):181–200.]

Crotalus durissus var. *melanurus* Jan, 1859a, *Rev. Mag. Zool.* (Paris) (2)11:148–157[153]. Holotype: MNHN 821. Type-locality: "Caroline du Sud" [South Carolina, USA]. [Nomen nudum.]

Crotalus durissus var. *mexicana* Jan, 1863, *Elenco Syst. Ofidi*, 143 pp.[123]. Holotype: RMNH 1574. Type-locality: "Messico, Tejas [Mexico, Texas]." [Nomen nudum.]

Crotalus fasciatus Higgins, 1873, *Ophidians*, 239 pp.[81]. Type(s): none designated. Type-locality: "United States of Columbia."

Crotalus horridus—Jan and Sordelli, 1874, *Icon. Gén. Ophid.*, livr. 46, p. 8, pls. 1–2. [In part, included *C. durissus* and *C. horridus*.] Klauber (1936b:195 and 1956:35, footnote 9) pointed out that there was confusion in the application of the names *horridus* and *durissus* for more than a century, much of it owing to Jan's misapplication of names.

Crotalus durissus concolor—Garman, 1884a [dated 1883], *Mem. Mus. Comp. Zool.* 8:1–185[175]. This name placed here according to Smith (1943).

Crotalus horridus var. *atricaudatus*—Garman, 1884a [dated 1883], *Mem. Mus. Comp. Zool.* 8:1–185[pl. 9, fig. 1].

Crotalus horridus—Boulenger, 1896b, *Cat. Snakes British Mus.* 3:727 pp.[578–580].

Crotalus horridus horridus—Gloyd, 1936a, *Copeia* 1935:175–178[176].

Crotalus horridus atricaudatus—Gloyd, 1936a, *Copeia* 1935:175–178[176].

Crotalus horridus—Collins and Knight, 1980, *Cat. Am. Amph. Rept.* 1980:253.1–2[253.1].

> There is here also, a large and horrible serpent which is called
> a rattlesnake. It has a head like that of a dog, and can bite off
> a man's leg as clear as if it had been hewn down with an ax.
> There are horny joints in their tails which make a noise like
> children's rattles . . . and can be heard at the distance of one
> hundred yards, so that one may put himself on guard."
>
> —Exaggerated comments by Holm (1702) in his description of
> animals in the Pennsylvania region

> A man in Virginia being in yᵉ Woods having a pair of boots
> on was bitt by a RSnake thro' his boots came home to his wife
> & dyed; his Boots were hung up in yᵉ house, & his widdow
> married a second husband, who putt on thos Boots, & by
> riding a Small Journey complain'd with a pain in his Leg &
> likewise dyed, the Boots were hung up again, & yᵉ Woman
> married yᵉ third Husband, who made use of yᵉ same Boots, &
> yᵉ first time of wearing them complained as yᵉ former of a
> small tumor in his legg & likewise died; Upon yᵉ Surgeon cutts
> yᵉ boot in peices & found yᵉ Tooth of yᵉ Rattle Snake that bitt yᵉ
> first Husband, & did all yᵉ Execution since as small as a hair,
> they took it out with a pair of Forceps, & prick'd a dog with it
> that within a few hours dyed, yᵉ Surgeon took yᵉ tooth some
> time after tryed it upon another Dog & it did him no hurt, & it
> was supposed then yᵉ Snake was dead.
>
> —Captain Walduck, account read before the Royal Society on 7
> January 1714, reproduced in Masterson, 1938:215

LOCAL NAMES Banded rattlesnake, canebrake, Seminole rattler (Okefenokee area of Georgia), velvet tail.

ENGLISH NAME Timber rattlesnake.

DISTRIBUTION Eastern United States from southeastern Minnesota and southern Maine southward to east Texas and northern Florida, and southern Ontario, Canada (Map 98). Hurter (1911) discussed a few early records of this species in New Jersey, including a specimen that came down the Delaware River on a raft. Curtis (1949b) reported this snake to range as far west as Dallas County, Texas. It occurs on a few barrier islands, including Saint Catherines off the coast of Georgia (Behler et al., 1997) and Kiawah and Capers Islands off South Carolina (Gaddy, 1982). The species occurred until quite recently, and may still occur, on Catawba and South Bass Islands (Ottawa County) in Lake Erie (Triplehorn, 1955), although it is not known from the adjacent mainland, suggesting that this snake was at one time much more widespread. Perhaps the conditions on these islands remained more equable as environments changed than on the mainland. *Crotalus horridus* apparently is now extirpated from southern Maine (Ernst, 1992; Hunter, 1985; Hunter et al., 1992, 1999) and Ontario, Canada (F. R. Cook, 1984). The elevational distribution is from near sea level to above 2,000 m.

Distribution records are available for Alabama (Gibbons et al., 1990; Haltom, 1931; Mount, 1975), Arkansas (Boulenger, 1896b; Dellinger and Black, 1938; Dowling, 1957; Hurter and Strecker, 1909; Strecker, 1924; Sutton, 1987), Connecticut (DeGraff and Rudis, 1983; Klemens, 1993; Lamson, 1935; Petersen, 1970; Peterson and Fritsch, 1986), Florida (Allen, 1949b; Ashton, 1978; Ashton and Ashton, 1981; Bartlett and Bartlett, 1999; Carr, 1940; Carr and Goin, 1955; Duellman and Schwartz, 1958; Tennant, 1997; Van Hyning, 1933; Wray and Owen, 1999), Georgia (Behler et al., 1997; Gibbons and West, 2000; Jackson, 1983; Jensen, 2001; Jensen and Moulis, 1997, 1999; Martof, 1956; Williamson and Moulis, 1994), Illinois (Estes, 1958; Necker, 1939; Parmalee, 1955; Peters, 1942; Petzing et al., 2000; Phillips et al., 1999; Redmer and Ballard, 1995; Walley, 1963), Indiana (Minton, 1972, 2001; Resetar, 1992), Iowa (Christiansen and Bailey, 1988, 1990;

Guthrie, 1926), Kansas (Collins, 1993; Gloyd, 1928, 1932; Smith, 1956; Taylor, 1929), Kentucky (Barbour, 1950, 1971; Welter and Carr, 1939), Louisiana (Beyer, 1900; Boulenger, 1896b; Dundee, 1994b; Dundee and Rossman, 1989; Fitch, 1949a; Gowanloch, 1934; Gowanloch and Brown, 1943; Himes, 1999; Keiser, 1971; Liner, 1997; Lutterschmidt, 1992; Williams, 2002), Maine (Norton, 1929), Maryland and the District of Columbia (Cooper and Groves, 1959; Harris, 1975; Kelly, 1936; McCauley, 1945; McCauley and East, 1940), Massachusetts (Babbitt and Graham, 1972; Babcock, 1925; Hensley, 1959; Lazell, 1976), Minnesota (Breckenridge, 1944; Hall, 1997; Oldfield and Keyler, 1997; Oldfield and Moriarty, 1994), Mississippi (Cook, 1954; Keiser, 1982; Lohoefener and Altig, 1983), Missouri (Anderson, 1965; Henning, 1938; Johnson, 1979, 1987, 2000; Myers, 1954; Owens, 1949), Nebraska (Hudson, 1942), New Hampshire (DeGraff and Rudis, 1983; Taylor, 1993), New Jersey (Curran, 1935; Fowler, 1907; Schwartz and Golden, 2002; Trapido, 1937), New York (Bishop, 1927; DeGraff and Rudis, 1983; Dekay, 1842; Ditmars, 1905a; Evans, 1947b; Hensley, 1959), North Carolina (Brimley, 1915; Brothers, 1992; Hensley, 1959; Huheey and Stupka, 1967; Martof et al., 1980; Palmer, 1974; Palmer and Braswell, 1995; Stroupe and Dorcas, 2001), Ohio (Conant, 1951; Walker, 1931), Oklahoma (Force, 1930; Lardie, 1979, 1999; Ortenburger, 1925, 1929; Sievert and Sievert, 1988; Webb, 1970), Pennsylvania (Allen, 1992; Bowler, 1974; Hulse et al., 2001; McCoy, 1982; Netting, 1930; Shaffer, 1991; N. Smith, 1958; Surface, 1906), South Carolina (Camper, 2001; Gibbons and West, 2000; Hoy et al., 1953; Jopson, 1940; Martof et al., 1980; Obrecht, 1946), Tennessee (Blanchard, 1922; Gentry, 1941, 1955; Huheey and Stupka, 1967; Redmond et al., 1990; Sinclair, 1965; Snyder, 1972), Texas (Ahlbrandt et al., 2002; Bailey, 1905; Bartlett and Bartlett, 1999; Boulenger, 1896b; A. Brown, 1903a; B. Brown, 1950; Crimmins, 1927b; Dixon, 1987; Guidry, 1953; Karges, 1978; Parks and Cory, 1936; Price, 1998; Raun and Gehlbach, 1972; Saenz et al., 1999; Strecker, 1926c, 1935a; Tennant, 1984, 1985; Werler, 1964), Vermont (Andrews, 1995; Baarslag, 1950; DeGraff and Rudis 1983; Trapido, 1941), Virginia (Brothers, 1992; D'Alessandro and Ernst, 1995; Ernst et al., 1997; Hoffman, 1945; Linzey and Clifford, 1981; Martin et al., 1992; Martof et al., 1980; Mitchell, 1994; Mitchell and Reay, 1999; Smyth, 1949; Tobey, 1985), West Virginia (Bayless, 1979; Green, 1937, 1943; Green and Pauley, 1987; Martin and Wood, 1955; Werler and McCallion, 1951), Wisconsin (Casper, 1996; Cochran and Lyons, 1986; Dickinson, 1949; Messeling, 1953; Oldfield and Keyler, 1989; Vogt, 1981), and Canada (Curran, 1935; Logier, 1958; Logier and Toner, 1955; Mills, 1948). On the general range, see Conant and Collins, 1998; Cope, 1860b, 1900; Garman, 1884a, 1884b; Gloyd, 1940; Harding, 1997; Keyler and Oldfield, 1992; Klauber, 1971, 1972; Pope, 1946; Stejneger, 1895; Werner, 1922; and Wright and Wright, 1957.

HABITAT Usually moist forests in low bottomlands and hilly and mountainous uplands. This species has been found in wiregrass flatwoods in Florida (Carr, 1940), and Barbour (1950) stated that in Kentucky it was most often found in dry, brushy areas but also in beech-birch-maple woodland. Reinert (1984a) discovered that melanistic snakes preferred mature forest with many fallen logs, and nonmelanistic individuals preferred young forest sites with an abundance of leaf litter. In another analysis of Pennsylvania snakes, Reinert (1984b) compared copperheads with *C. horridus* and found that the latter preferred less open areas with less rock density and more surface vegetation. In Crawford County, Arkansas, these snakes regularly occupy caves, taking refuge in the twilight zone or beyond (Briggler and Prather, 2002). In Nebraska *C. horridus* was tracked through agricultural fields, despite available wooded corridors (Fogell et al., 2002b). We have found specimens in hardwood uplands and higher portions of hardwood bottomlands in northwestern Mississippi, Western Tennessee, and east Texas. Hall (1994) found *C. horridus* in similar habitat in South Carolina.

DESCRIPTION The maximum size reported is 189.2 cm (Klauber, 1956). Other records include 189 cm TL (Conant and Collins, 1998) and 188 cm (Ditmars, 1936). Holt (1924) reported a large individual from Montgomery County, Alabama, that was 159 cm in TL and weighed 5.5 pounds (2.5 kg).

The ground color is tan, grayish brown, yellowish, yellow-brown, or pinkish gray. In general the ground color becomes darker on the posterior of the body. Some specimens are melanistic and mostly black, especially in the northern part of the range or at high elevations. There are 15–34 dark brown to black blotches, crossbands, or chevrons on the body. Dorsal body markings are usually irregularly pale edged. On the anterior part of the body the dorsal markings are usually transversely elongate blotches, becoming chevrons or crossbands posteriorly. An orangish, reddish, or reddish brown middorsal stripe is often present in the interspaces between the dorsal crossbands, it is most prominent on the anterior portion of the body. A reddish or dark brown postocular stripe extends from behind the eye to about the angle of the jaw. The top of the head is usually uniformly colored and slightly paler than the ground color on the anterior of the body. The venter is yellowish, grayish, or pinkish with dark flecking, stippling, and/or mottling, and may vary from almost uniformly pale to heavily pigmented and mostly dark. Juveniles have a more distinct pattern, and dark tail bands are usually evident against a slightly paler ground color.

Several xanthic specimens with a pale yellow ground color and dorsal markings that were only slightly darker have been reported (Hensley, 1959; Palmer and Braswell, 1995). Individuals with dorsal blotches modified into middorsal and lateral stripes are rare but have been reported from Pennsylvania (Gloyd, 1934a, 1935b), Illinois (Nickerson and Mays, 1968), and Louisiana (Dundee, 1994a). An amelanistic partial albino was found in Red River County, Texas (Hudson and Carl, 1985). Other color pattern aberrancies were reported by Gloyd (1935b), Neill (1963), and Klauber (1972).

Crotalus horridus shows considerable geographic variation. Gloyd (1936a) diagnosed the southern population (*atricaudatus*) by "its large size, more brilliant markings and differences in scutellation and color pattern. Its dorsal scales are usually in 25 instead of 23 rows. The stripe from the eye to the angle of the mouth stands out very distinctly from the ground color of the head. The black blotches of the anterior fourth of the body are divided in the middle by the bright stripe of reddish brown, and on each side tend to coalesce longitudinally forming a pair of irregular black stripes. An interrupted black streak, midlateral in position, is present between and alternates with the dorsal and lateral series of blotches. The black ventro-lateral spots usually have distinct light centers."

East of the Mississippi River, both pale and dark color phases may occur in certain populations, or sometimes one color phase includes most individuals in a particular population. The dark color phase is most common in mountainous regions, and the pale color phase is generally found in lowlands and piedmonts (Gloyd, 1940; Klauber, 1972). Klauber (1972) thought that dark individuals were most frequently males and that pale snakes were usually females, whereas Gloyd (1940) stated that the color phases were not sex related. Various authors subsequently sided with one opinion or the other, but a careful survey of 157 *C. horridus* from Pennsylvania by Schaefer (1969) revealed no sexual dichromatism.

The rostral is usually slightly higher than wide. There are 4–22 scales in the internasal-prefrontal area including 2 large, triangular internasals in contact with the rostral, followed by 2 large, quadrangular prefrontals (anterior canthals) that may be in contact along the midline or may be separated by many small scales. Only a single canthal is present between the internasal and supraocular. There are 5–7 intersupraoculars. The number of prefoveals varies from 2 to 8. The first supralabial is usually in broad contact with the prenasal, but it is slightly to moderately separated along its posteroventral margin by the anteriormost prefoveals.

The lateral portions of the prefrontals (anterior canthals) are not deflected downward over the canthus rostralis; however, contact between the postnasal and the upper preocular is almost always prevented by the presence of an upper and a lower loreal. One to 3 (usually 2) interoculabials separate the anterior suboculars from the supralabials. The first pair of infralabials are not divided transversely. There are 10–17 supralabials (usually 13–15), 11–19 infralabials (usually 14–16), 21–26 midbody dorsal scale rows (usually 23 in the north, 25 in the south), 158–177 ventrals in males and 163–183 in females, and 20–30 subcaudals in males and 15–26 in females.

SIMILAR SPECIES Few other species of rattlesnakes occur within the range of *C. horridus* in the eastern United States. *Sistrurus miliarius* is a small snake (less than 80 cm in TL) with 9 large plates covering the top of the head; a pair of wavy, elongated blotches extending from the supraoculars to the nape; and a dorsal pattern of relatively small blotches, not black crossbands. *Sistrurus catenatus* is likewise small with 9 large plates on the top of the head and a dorsal pattern of small blotches. *Crotalus adamanteus* and *C. atrox* have a dark postocular stripe extending down to the lip margin (not to above the rictus) that is distinctly pale bordered; a pattern of long, diamond-shaped blotches; and black crossbands on a whitish or pale grayish background on the tail. *Crotalus adamanteus* usually has 29 dorsal scale rows at midbody (versus usually 23–25 in *C. horridus*).

REMARKS Gloyd (1936a) and Klauber (1936b:196) recognized two subspecies, *Crotalus h. horridus* Linnaeus, 1758, and *Crotalus h. atricaudatus* Latreille, 1801, based on size, color pattern, and scutellation. Pisani et al. (1972) analyzed the geographic variation in this species and concluded that no subspecies should be recognized. Conant (1975) rejected the findings of Pisani et al. (1972) and continued to recognize *horridus* and *atricaudatus*. Collins and Knight (1980:253.1) followed Pisani et al. (1972). Brown and Ernst (1986) performed maximum likelihood analysis and stepwise discriminant analysis on the same morphological characters examined by Pisani et al. (1972) plus a few characters relating to color pattern and size and found evidence for retaining the two subspecies. They cautioned that standard morphological characters by themselves would not discriminate between the two subspecies and noted that other features used in combination—including adult size, color pattern, and number of dorsal scale rows and ventral scales—are necessary to distinguish *C. h. horridus* and *C. h. atricaudatus*. Pending a thorough analysis of the species throughout its range, Dundee and Rossman (1989) were inclined to recognize *atricaudatus*. We take no particular stand on the issue of subspecies but have indicated on Map 98 the approximate ranges recognized previously for *C. h. horridus* and *C. h. atricaudatus*.

Crotalus intermedius Troschel, 1865
(Fig. 205, Map 99, Pls. 835–839)

Crotalus intermedius Troschel, *in* Müller, 1865, *Amph., Reisen Ver. Staat., Canada, Mexico* 3:595–619[613]. Holotype: originally in Müller's collection, later in Bonn (ZFMK); destroyed in World War II, according to R. Mertens (pers. comm., *in* Klauber, 1952:10). Type-locality: not given in original description, but "Mexico" is inferred from the title of the paper. Klauber (1952:10) outlined the route of the expedition that collected the holotype.

Crotalus intermedius Fischer, 1881, *Abh. Nat. Ver. Bremen* 7:225–238[230]. Holotype: Bremen (UMB) 435. Type-locality: "aus Mexico." [Junior primary homonym of *Crotalus intermedius* Troschel, 1865.]

Sistrurus intermedius—Garman, 1884b, *Bull. Essex Inst.* 16:1–46[35].

Crotalus omiltemanus Günther, 1895, *Biol. Cent. Am. Rept. Batr.*, 326 pp.[192, pl. 58 (fig. C)]. Syntypes (2): BMNH 1946.1.19.28–29 (both formerly BMNH 93.3.15.11). Type-locality: "Mexico, Omilteme in Guerrero."

Crotalus triseriatus—Boulenger, 1896b, *Cat. Snakes British Mus.* 3:1–727[581]. [In part.]

Crotalus triseriatus omiltemanus—Klauber, 1938b, *Copeia* 1938: 191–197[196].

Crotalus triseriatus omiltemanus—Gloyd, 1940, *Chicago Acad. Sci. Spec. Publ.* 4:1–270[95].

Crotalus triseriatus gloydi Taylor, 1941, *Univ. Kansas Sci. Bull.* 27:105–139[130]. Holotype: UIMNH 25070 (formerly EHT-HMS 23645), according to Smith, Langebartel, and Williams (1964:70). Type-locality: "Cerro San Felipe (elevation 10,000 ft.) near [15 km northeast of] Oaxaca [de Juárez], Oaxaca, Mexico."

Crotalus gloydi lautus Smith, *in* H. M. Smith and Laufe, 1945, *Trans. Kansas Acad. Sci.* 48:325–354[353]. [Nomen nudum.]

Crotalus gloydi—Smith and Taylor, 1945, *Bull. U.S. Natl. Mus.* (187):239 pp.[191].

Crotalus gloydi lautus Smith, 1946b, *Univ. Kansas Sci. Bull.* 31:75–101[75]. Holotype: USNM 110598. Type-locality: "at the lava beds about one kilometer east of El Limón Totalco, Veracruz" [Mexico].

Crotalus gloydi gloydi—Smith, 1946b, *Univ. Kansas Sci. Bull.* 31:75–101[78].

Crotalus intermedius intermedius—Klauber, 1952, *Bull. Zool. Soc. San Diego* (26):1–143[9].

Crotalus intermedius omiltemanus—Klauber, 1952, *Bull. Zool. Soc. San Diego* (26):1–143[14].

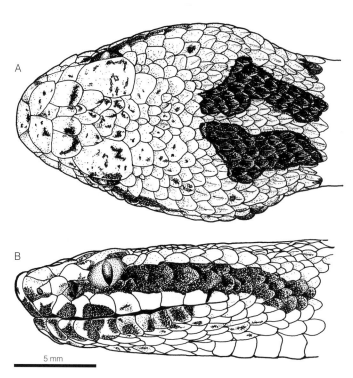

Fig. 205. (A) Dorsal and (B) lateral aspects of head of *Crotalus intermedius gloydi*, male, 34.6 cm TL (UTA R-14214), from Sierra Aloapaneca, 1.0 km west of La Cumbre, Oaxaca, Mexico, elevation 2,719 m. The interoculabial series is incomplete and the anterior subocular is in contact with the supralabial series. Usually no prefoveals are present. Drawings by Ty M. Kubin.

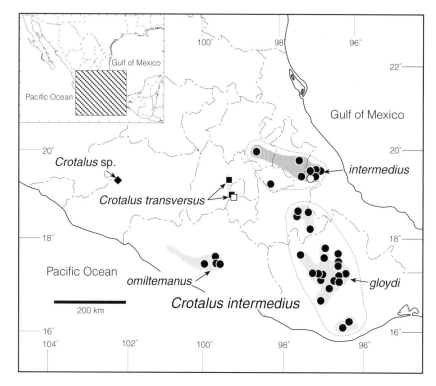

Map 99. Distributions in Mexico of *Crotalus intermedius* (circles), including subspecies, *C. transversus* (squares), and an undescribed species of rattlesnake within this group (diamond). Unfilled symbols represent type-localities; that for *C. intermedius* restricted to El Limón Totalco, Veracruz, Mexico, by Smith and Taylor (1950b).

Crotalus intermedius gloydi—Davis and Dixon, 1957, *Southwest. Nat.* 2:19–27[25].

Crotalus omiltemanus omiltemanus—Shelford, 1963, *Ecol. N. Am.*, 610 pp.[464].

They consider all snakes as omens, and more so the vipers. And it is a worse omen if this snake or viper crosses the road in front of them when they are walking, because, they say, *Coatl onechòhuiltequi,* as if to say, "It cut the thread of my life," and it is to be noted that there are in this land more than ten known kinds of vipers, and the snakes are infinite. Among the snakes they fear the most the one called maçacoatl, which means "snake of beasts," "a snake that can swallow a beast," and it is so because they have been seen seven or more varas long. And among the vipers they fear most is the one called *metlapilcoatl* or *çelcoatl,* for the reason I just mentioned.

—Ruiz de Alarcón, 1629

LOCAL NAMES   Chilladora, colcóatl, víbora de cascabel, víbora sorda (highlands of central Oaxaca; this name may also refer to other species of snakes).

ENGLISH NAME   Mexican small-headed rattlesnake.

ETYMOLOGY   The specific epithet is derived from the Latin *inter,* meaning "between," and *medius,* meaning "middle." The exact meaning intended by Troschel is uncertain; perhaps the name refers to the series of small middorsal blotches.

DISTRIBUTION   Several disjunct populations occur in the central and southern highland regions of Mexico (Map 99). In east-central Mexico the species is known from southeastern Hidalgo, northeastern and central Puebla, southwestern Tlaxcala, and west-central Veracruz; in Oaxaca it is known from the Sierra Juárez, Cerro San Felipe and its associated ridges, the Sierra de Cuatro Venados, the Sierra Madre del Sur, and Sierra de Miahuatlán. It is recorded in Guerrero from several localities west of Chilpancingo including the vicinity of Omilteme, San Vicente, and Filo de Caballo. The vertical distribution is from about 2,000 m to above 3,000 m.

Distribution or locality records for this species are mentioned in Armstrong and Murphy, 1979; Auth et al., 2000; Campbell, 1982a; Campbell and Armstrong, 1979; Casas-Andreu et al., 1996; Cuesta-Terrón, 1921b; Davis and Dixon, 1957, 1959; Fischer, 1881; Gloyd, 1940; Günther, 1895–1902; Klauber, 1938b, 1952, 1956, 1971, 1972; Lynch and Smith, 1965, 1966; Martín del Campo, 1950; Ocaranza, 1930; Pérez-Higareda and Smith, 1991; Pérez-Ramos et al., 2000; Pianka and Smith, 1959; Sánchez-Herrera and López-Ortega, 1987; Smith, 1943a, 1946b, 1970; Smith and Laufe, 1945; Smith and Taylor, 1945, 1966; Taylor, 1941; Troschel, 1866.

HABITAT   Most of this species' range is covered by seasonally dry pine-oak forest; however, we have seen individuals in cloud forest near Omilteme, Guerrero, and in desert near Cacaloapan, Puebla, and Pachuca, Hidalgo.

DESCRIPTION   Large adult males are generally between 50 and 60 cm in TL; females are somewhat smaller. Klauber (1972) gave the maximum TL as 57.0 cm, but captive specimens may exceed that size.

The dorsal ground color is gray, pale blue-gray, or brownish gray with 38–61 medium brown, reddish brown, or dark gray body blotches that are distinctly edged with black and are 3–7 (usually about 5) scales wide and 1.5–3 scales (usually about 2) long. A dark crossbar extends across the top of the head between the anterior portions of the supraoculars, although it may not be particularly evident in Oaxacan specimens. A pair of con-spicuous nape blotches are sometimes fused anteriorly. A broad, dark brown postocular stripe extends from the lower posterior margin of the eye to the angle of the jaw. The pattern may be virtually absent in large, old individuals from Oaxaca. Below this stripe the posterior supralabials tend to be mostly creamy white; anteriorly, black pigment broadly encroaches along the vertical supralabial sutures and margin of the lip. The infralabials and mental are mostly dark but often have pale central spots. The bellies of snakes from the highlands of Guerrero are strongly stippled with gray or black, sometimes so heavily as to be almost uniformly dark. Individuals from central Oaxaca may also have mostly dark ventrals, but more frequently the ventrals are pale with only a moderate amount of gray stippling. The subcaudals are colored similarly to the ventrals, but distally a few may be pale. At San Vicente, Guerrero, we have taken melanistic adult specimens.

The rostral is wider than high. Four large, flat scales—a pair of large internasals and a pair of prefrontals—may cover the anterior portion of the snout, but the prefrontals are most often fragmented into a pair of canthals and smaller intercanthals. The range of scales in the internasal-prefrontal area is 4–8, and there are 2–4 intersupraoculars. The prenasal is in contact with supralabial 1 and extends over the top of the postnasal. A single loreal is usually present on each side, precluding post-nasal–upper preocular contact. The loreal is peculiar in that it contacts the supralabial series. A single prefoveal is usually present directly below the loreal (it is sometimes considered a lower loreal). The supralabials and suboculars make contact below the eye. There are 8–11 (mode 9) supralabials, 8–11 (mode 9) infralabials, 21 midbody dorsal scale rows, 151–175 ventrals in males and 157–185 in females, 21–29 subcaudals in males and 19–24 in females (0–11 may be divided), and 8–10 rattle-fringe scales.

SIMILAR SPECIES   Only two other species of small montane rattlesnakes occur within parts of the range of *C. intermedius. Crotalus triseriatus* has at least 1 lower loreal intervening between the upper loreal and supralabials, and usually at least 23 dorsal scale rows anteriorly and at midbody. The top of the head of *Crotalus ravus* is covered with large, flat plates including a pair of internasals, a pair of prefrontals, a single frontal, and usually a pair of parietals; *C. ravus* usually has fewer ventrals (136–152 versus 151–185) and body blotches (22–44 versus 38–61) than *C. intermedius.*

REMARKS   A record from Cerro Tancítaro in Michoacán reported by many authors (e.g., Duellman, 1961, 1965b; Flores-Villela and Gerez, 1988; Hoge, 1966; Hoge and Romano, 1971a; Klauber, 1972; Klemmer, 1963) is based on a single specimen (FMNH 39115), which, when reexamined, was suggested to be probably either conspecific with or closely related to *C. transversus* rather than *C. intermedius* (Campbell, 1982a).

Klauber (1952) recognized only two subspecies, *C. i. intermedius* and *C. i. omiltemanus,* the former including *C. triseriatus gloydi* Taylor (1941). Davis and Dixon (1957) subsequently recognized *C. i. gloydi.* Recent reviews have recognized three subspecies: *C. i. intermedius, C. i. gloydi,* and *C. i. omiltemanus* (Klauber, 1972:39–40; Campbell and Lamar, 1989:349; McCranie, 1991:519.1–4).

In *C. i. intermedius* (Pls. 835 and 836) from east-central Mexico, the postnasal is in contact with both the first and second supralabials, although contact with the second may be narrow; the loreal usually contacts only the second supralabial; males have 151–161 ventrals and females have 156–165; males have 24–29 subcaudals and females have 20–24; and there are 38–48 dorsal body blotches. In *C. i. gloydi* (Pl. 837) from the highlands of Oaxaca and southern Puebla, the postnasal usually contacts only the first supralabial, the loreal usually contacts both the first and second supralabials, males have 150–165 ventrals and females have 155–171, males have 21–27 subcaudals and females have 18–23, and there are 38–54 dorsal body blotches. *Crotalus i. omiltemanus* (Pls. 838 and 839) from the highlands of Guerrero has a postnasal that contacts both the first and second supralabials, a loreal that contacts the second supralabial only, 167–175 ventrals in males and 172–185 in females, 24–29 subcaudals in males and 19–24 in females, and 45–61 dorsal body blotches. This taxon can be distinguished from the other subspecies by its higher number of ventrals.

This species is infrequently encountered during the dry season. It is diurnal, and on sunny days during the wet season (June–November) individuals may be seen basking or crawling near rocky outcroppings.

Crotalus lannomi Tanner, 1966
(Fig. 206, Map 100, Pl. 840)

Crotalus lannomi Tanner, 1966a, *Herpetologica* 22:298–302[298]. Holotype: BYU 23800. Type-locality: "1.8 miles west of the pass, Puerto Los Mazos, or 22 miles west by road from the Río Tuxcacuesco, a branch of the Río Armeria on Mexican Highway No. 80, Jalisco, Mexico."

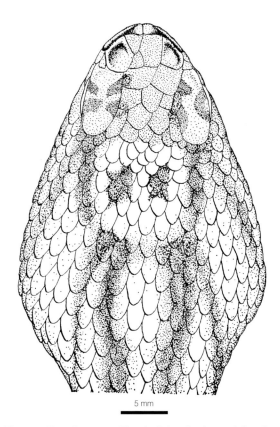

5 mm

Fig. 206. Dorsal aspect of head of *Crotalus lannomi*, female, 63.8 cm TL (BYU 23800), from 1.8 miles (2.9 km) west of the pass, Puerto Los Mazos, or 22 miles (35.2 km) west by road from the Río Tuxcacuesco, a branch of the Río Armeria, on Mexico Highway 80, Jalisco, Mexico. From Tanner, 1966a. Published by permission of the Herpetologists' League.

LOCAL NAME Víbora de cascabel.

ENGLISH NAME Autlán rattlesnake.

ETYMOLOGY The specific epithet is a patronym honoring Joseph R. Lannom Jr., the collector of the type-specimen.

DISTRIBUTION This species is known from a single specimen collected in 1966 about 16 km (by road) southwest of Autlán de Navarro in Jalisco, Mexico (Map 100). The type-locality lies at about 1,000 m on the Pacific slope just below the ridge connecting the Sierra Cacoma with the Sierra Manantlán. It has sometimes been stated or implied that the type-locality is at 1,280 m (McDiarmid et al., 1999; Tanner, 1986) or higher (Campbell and Lamar, 1989), but these elevations refer to the ridge above where the holotype was found. The region is sometimes considered the southwesternmost portion of the Mexican Plateau, but it is effectively isolated from the highlands to the east by the deep entrenchment of the Río Armería and its tributaries.

Since the original description (Tanner, 1966a), references to this species have been made in Armstrong and Murphy, 1979; Campbell and Lamar, 1989; Harris and Simmons, 1978b; Hoge and Romano, 1971a; Klauber, 1972; and Rubio, 1998. No additional specimens have been discovered, and no new information concerning this species has been forthcoming.

HABITAT A transitional zone between tropical deciduous forest and pine-oak forest characterized by an abundant understory of grasses and small bamboos; many rock outcroppings dot the landscape.

DESCRIPTION The single known specimen of *C. lannomi* is a female, presumably an adult, 63.8 cm in TL. The head is 31.6 mm long and constitutes 5.0% of the TL. The long, slender tail is 6.9 cm in length and constitutes 10.8% of the TL. The rattle is relatively small, the dorsoventral width of the proximal rattle being 2.6 mm.

In preservative the ground color is gray and there are 31 dark chocolate brown blotches that are 9–12 scales wide and 3–5 scales long. The middorsal blotches are usually separated narrowly from one another by 1.0–1.5 scales; a few coalesce with each other. The pattern becomes obscure on the posterior third of the body, and the dorsum of the tail is nearly uniformly gray. The dorsal blotches are edged with darker brown or black. Of the 2 series of dark brown lateral spots, 1 alternates with the larger dorsal series. The lower lateral row of blotches sometimes extends to the lateral margins of the ventrals. The belly has 2 highly irregular series of spots near the lateral margin of the ventrals. Spotting on the posterior ventrals is faint and the subcaudals are uniformly colored.

The rostral is wider than high and there are 7 scales in the internasal-prefrontal region. The prenasal is in contact with supralabial 1, there are 4 prefoveals, and 3 loreals per side preclude postnasal–upper preocular contact. The internasals and anterior canthals are slightly raised forming a narrow marginal ridge on the anterodorsal edge of the snout. There are 4 scales across the top of the head between the mid-level of the supraocular. There are 14–15 supralabials, 15–17 infralabials, 27 midbody dorsal scale rows, 176 ventrals, 37 subcaudals, and 8 rattle-fringe scales.

SIMILAR SPECIES *Crotalus lannomi* differs from *C. stejnegeri* in having a rostral that is wider than high, fewer prefoveals (4 versus 7), fewer intersupraoculars (4 versus 7–8), and fewer middorsal body blotches (31 versus 35–43). The body of *C. lannomi* is stouter than that of *C. stejnegeri*, and the head is relatively larger and more lanceolate. *Crotalus lannomi* differs from *C. triseriatus* and *C. pusillus* in having more midbody dorsal scale rows (27 versus 21–25), ventrals (176 versus 162 or fewer), subcaudals (37 versus 34 or fewer), and infralabials (15–17

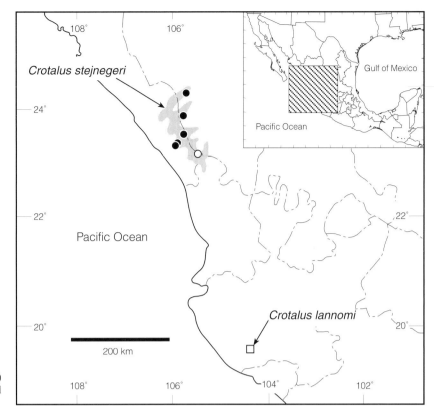

Map 100. Distributions of *Crotalus lannomi* (square) and *C. stejnegeri* (circles) in western Mexico. Unfilled symbols represent type-localities.

versus 9–14). It further differs from *C. pusillus* in having more supralabials (14–15 versus 11–13) and fewer body blotches (31 versus 33–50). *Crotalus lannomi* is most easily distinguished from *C. basiliscus* and *C. simus* by its high number of subcaudals (37 versus 36 or fewer).

REMARKS Tanner (1966a) suggested that the relatively large scales on top of the head and the relatively long tail are primitive characters. Primarily on the basis of these characters, Tanner (1966a) suggested that *C. lannomi* is most closely related to *C. stejnegeri*; however, *C. lannomi* is a much stouter snake with a proportionately stouter head.

Despite intensive collecting near the type-locality of *C. lannomi*, the only rattlesnakes we have encountered in the vicinity have been *C. basiliscus* and *C. triseriatus* (the latter species at a higher locality several kilometers away). The type-locality for *C. lannomi* experiences warm temperatures during the day, and *Heloderma horridum* was not uncommon there during the 1970s.

Crotalus lepidus (Kennicott, 1861)
(Fig. 207, Map 90, Pls. 841–863)

Caudisona lepida Kennicott, 1861b, *Proc. Acad. Nat. Sci. Philadelphia* 13:204–208[206]. Syntypes: ANSP (?) two heads, now lost. Type-locality: "Presidio del Norte and Eagle Pass" [Texas, USA]. Emended to "Presidio (del Norte), Presidio County, Texas," by Smith and Taylor (1950b:362); their proposal was followed by Schmidt (1953c:229).

Aploaspis lepida—Cope, 1867 [dated 1866], *Proc. Acad. Nat. Sci. Philadelphia* 18:300–314 [310].

Crotalus lepidus—Cope, 1884 [dated 1883], *Proc. Acad. Nat. Sci. Philadelphia* 35:10–35[13].

Crotalus tigris var. *palmeri* Garman, 1887a, *Bull. Essex Inst.* 19:119–138[124]. Holotype: MCZ R4578, according to Barbour and Loveridge (1929d:245). Type-locality: "Monclova [Coahuila], Mexico."

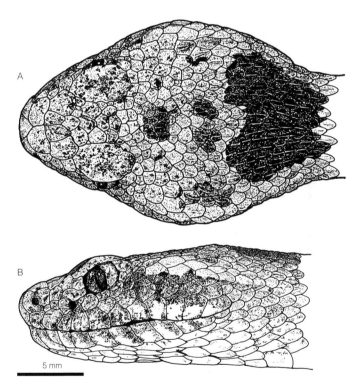

Fig. 207. (A) Dorsal and (B) lateral aspects of head of *Crotalus lepidus klauberi*, male, 41.9 cm TL (UTA R-17833), from Sierra San Luis, Cañón Diablo, Sonora, Mexico, elevation 1,950 m. The upper preocular is divided vertically, and the anterior portion of this scale is higher than the posterior and extends over the edge of the canthus in front of the supraocular. Drawings by Ty M. Kubin.

Crotalus palmeri—Günther, 1895, *Biol. Cent. Am. Rept. Batr.*, 326 pp.[193].

Crotalus lepidus—Boulenger, 1896b, *Cat. Snakes British Mus.* 3:727 pp.[582–583].

Crotalus lepidus lepidus—Gloyd, 1936b, *Occas. Pap. Mus. Zool. Univ. Michigan* (337):1–5[2].

Crotalus lepidus klauberi Gloyd, 1936b, *Occas. Pap. Mus. Zool. Univ. Michigan* (337):1–5[2, pl. 1 (figs. 1 and 2)]. Holotype: UMMZ 79895. Type-locality: "Carr Canyon, Huachuca Mountains, Cochise County, Arizona" [USA].

Crotalus semicornutus Taylor, 1944, *Univ. Kansas Sci. Bull.* 30:47–56[52]. Holotype: UIMNH 25068 (formerly EHT-HMS 23014), according to Smith, Langebartel, and Williams (1964:69). Type-locality: "Mojárachic [near Batopilas], Chihuahua, México."

Crotalus lepidus morulus Klauber, 1952, *Bull. Zool. Soc. San Diego* (26):1–143[52]. Holotype: UMMZ 101376. Type-locality: "10 miles northwest of Gómez Farías on the trail to La Joya de Salas, Tamaulipas, Mexico, at an altitude of about 5,300 ft., in a forested flat."

Crotalus lepidus maculosus Tanner, Dixon, and Harris, 1972, *Great Basin Nat.* 32:16–24[16, figs. 1–3]. Holotype: BYU 33328. Type-locality: "15 miles (24 km) west of La Ciudad, near Highway 40, Durango, Mexico."

Crotalus lepidus castaneus Juliá-Zertuche and Treviño, 1978, *Res. Segundo Congr. Nac. Zool., Monterrey, Mexico*, p. 60. Holotype: none designated, based apparently on multiple specimens ["Los ejemplares que se describen son adultos . . ."]. Type-locality: "Paraje Las Huertas, en la Sierra Madre Oriental, al Sur de Monterrey, N.L," Mexico. [Not a valid publication under the Articles of the Code.]

LOCAL NAMES Cha-cha-mu-ri, chamuré (Tarahumara), víbora, víbora de cascabel, víbora verde de cascabel.

ENGLISH NAME Rock rattlesnake.

ETYMOLOGY The species epithet is derived from the Greek *lepidotos*, meaning "covered with scales."

DISTRIBUTION From southeastern Arizona, southern New Mexico, and southwestern Texas through most of the Sierra Madre Occidental, the northern portion of the Mexican Plateau (Mesa del Norte), and the northern portion of the Sierra Madre Oriental. The eastward extent of the range is limited in Texas by the Balcones Escarpment of the Edwards Plateau, an important natural boundary with environmental conditions markedly different from those of adjacent areas (Smith and Buechner, 1947). The range in Mexico includes eastern Sonora, Chihuahua, Durango, east-central and southeastern Sinaloa, Zacatecas, eastern Nayarit, northern Jalisco, Aguascalientes, western San Luis Potosí, western Nuevo León, Coahuila, and southwestern Tamaulipas (Map 90). The vertical distribution is from about 300 to 3,000 m. Specimens have been found near the city of Chihuahua, Chihuahua, at 915 m; near Villa Ocampo, Durango, at 1,372 m; Sierra de Guatemala, Tamaulipas, at 1,190–1,890 m; and near San Antonio de las Alazanas, Coahuila, at 2,380–2,592 m.

Distribution records throughout the range are given in Gloyd, 1936b, 1940; Klauber, 1952, 1971, 1972; Smith, 1946b; Stejneger and Barbour, 1943; Van Denburgh, 1922b; Werner, 1922; and Wright and Wright, 1957. Distribution records are also available for the United States (Conant and Collins, 1998; Cope, 1900; Stejneger, 1895), Mexico generally (Armstrong and Murphy, 1979; Cuesta-Terrón, 1931; Klauber, 1952; Martín del Campo, 1935, 1937a, 1950, 1953; Mocquard, 1908–1909; Smith, 1943a; Smith and Taylor, 1945), western Mexico (Tanner et al., 1972), Arizona (Fowlie, 1965; Gloyd, 1937; Kauffeld, 1943b; Lowe, 1964; Lowe et al., 1986; Shaw and Campbell, 1974; Stejneger, 1902; Van Denburgh, 1924; Woodin, 1953), New Mexico (Bogert and Degenhardt, 1961; Degenhardt et al., 1996; Jacob and Altenbach, 1977; Shaw and Campbell, 1974), Texas (Axtell, 1959; Bailey, 1905; A. Brown, 1903a; B. Brown, 1950; Boulenger, 1896b; Cope, 1884b; Crimmins, 1927a; Dixon, 1956; Garman, 1884a;

Jameson and Flury, 1949; Milstead et al., 1950; Minton, 1959; Price, 1998; Schmidt and Smith, 1944; Schwartz and Babis, 1949; Smith, 1947c; Strecker, 1909b; Werler, 1964), Aguascalientes (Anderson and Lidicker, 1963; McCranie and Wilson, 1978; Sigala-Rodríguez and Vázquez-Díaz, 1996), Chihuahua (Bryson and Mueller, 2001; Dunkle and Smith, 1937; Jacob and Altenbach, 1977; Klauber, 1952; Lemos-Espinal et al., 2000a, 2000b, 2002a; Morafka, 1977; Reynolds, 1982; Smith and Taylor, 1966; Strecker, 1909b; Tanner, 1985; Van Devender and Lowe, 1977), Coahuila (Garman, 1887a; Gloyd and Smith, 1942; Günther, 1895–1902; McCoy, 1984; Schmidt and Owens, 1944), Durango (Boulenger, 1896b; Drake, 1958; Ponce-Campos et al., 2000; Webb, 1984), Jalisco (Mocquard, 1899a), Nayarit (Mocquard (1899a—as *triseriatus*), Nuevo León (Juliá-Zertuche and Treviño, 1978; Liner and Olson, 1973; Smith, 1944a), San Luis Potosí (Taylor, 1952), Sinaloa (Hardy and McDiarmid, 1969; Webb, 1984; Zweifel, 1954), Sonora (Jacob and Altenbach, 1977), Tamaulipas (Martin, 1955a, 1955b, 1958; Smith and Taylor, 1966), and Zacatecas (Wilson and McCranie, 1979a).

HABITAT A variety of habitats including pine-oak forests, mesquite-grasslands, and desert (only Chihuahuan, not Sonoran). In west Texas, Milstead et al. (1950) and Milstead (1960b) found this snake mostly in persimmon–shin oak associations, Jameson and Flury (1949) found it in a catclaw-grama association, and Axtell (1959) reported it in basalt rubble habitats. In Arizona, Woodin (1953) found *C. lepidus* mostly in south-facing rockslides. *Crotalus lepidus* is often found along rocky streambeds in the Chiricahua and Huachuca Mountains of Arizona and the Sierra del Nido of Chihuahua, and in northern Mexico in desert canyons with rock outcrops and sparse vegetation or open oak forest with grassy savanna-like conditions (Armstrong and Murphy, 1979). Martin (1955a, 1958) encountered this species in pine-oak and cloud forest in the Gómez Farías area of Tamaulipas, Mexico. Near Yepómera, Chihuahua, *C. lepidus* lives in rocky habitats in oak woodland and pine forest (Van Devender and Lowe, 1977). In Durango and Sinaloa it occurs in mixed boreal-tropical forest and tropical deciduous forest (Webb, 1984). In eastern Sinaloa we have found it in the ecotone between pine-oak and tropical deciduous forest.

DESCRIPTION Large adult males are 60–70 cm in TL, with the largest specimens exceeding 80 cm; females are smaller than males. Klauber (1952) recorded a specimen 82.8 cm in TL from Santa Barbara, Chihuahua, Mexico.

A striking amount of interpopulational, ontogenetic, and sexual variation occurs in color and pattern (Table 51). Sexual dichromatism was described by Armstrong and Murphy (1979), Jacob and Altenbach (1977), and Van Devender and Lowe (1977). Males of *C. l. klauberi* often have a greenish or olive ground color, whereas females are grayish; and the interspaces between the crossbands tend to be relatively uniform in males and mottled in females. In other subspecies males and females may have various ground colors, but in adults the mottling usually is less extensive in males.

Snakes from southwestern Texas (exclusive of the El Paso area) and the eastern portion of the Mexican Plateau have 13–24 dark crossbands and a highly variable ground color that may be gray, greenish gray, reddish brown, pale brown, or pinkish. Anteriorly, the crossbands are often only slightly darker than the ground color, but they become more distinct posteriorly. The interspaces between the crossbands usually contain a considerable amount of gray mottling or spotting which sometimes forms 1–3 series of irregular lateral blotches or accessory (secondary) crossbands between the primary ones. The nape blotches are most frequently paired and not in contact with each

Table 51. Variation in subspecies of *Crotalus lepidus.*

Subspecies	Dorsal scale rows	Rattle-fringe scales	Body blotches	Ventral scales males females	Subcaudal scales males females	Average % tail/TL males females	Occipital blotches	Ventral pattern
lepidus	21–25 (23)	—	13–24 (18.6)	150–168 (161.7) 149–168 (161.1)	21–29 (24.6) 17–23 (19.6)	8.6 7.1	Paired	Dark
klauberi	21–25 (23)	10–13 (11.4)	13–21 (~17)	152–172 (~162) 155–170 (~161)	20–29 (~25) 16–24 (~20)	8.1 6.6	Joined	Pale
morulus	23–25 (23)	—	24–34 (29.2)	156–167 (159.9) 160–171 (163.8)	25–30 (28.1) 20–25 (22.1)	9.0 7.2	Paired	Dark
maculosus	23–25 (23)	8–12 (9.9)	23–38 (~31)	159–169 (163.7) 157–173 (165.3)	26–33 (29.6) 20–25 (22.5)	9.4 7.4	Paired	Dark

Sources: Klauber, 1972; Tanner et al., 1972.
Note: Means are in parentheses.

other anywhere along their length. The distal portion of the tail is pinkish, reddish, or yellowish, and the proximal rattle is orangish or buff. The distinctness and amount of ventral mottling are highly variable. A male from Edwards County had a bluish gray ground color with 21 brown dorsal crossbands and 3 secondary blotches between each pair of crossbands (Dixon, 1956). The populations in the Davis Mountains and Big Bend region of Texas have uniformly dark blotches on a pink or buff ground color, whereas the poulations on the Stockton-Edwards Plateau have faded primary blotches and ground colors of various shades of gray (Vincent, 1982). Axtell (1959) described individuals from the Black Gap area of west Texas as having a "pinkish-red hue, with excessive amounts of dark mottling between the regular dark bands." Quinn (1981) reported a pale gray patternless specimen from Val Verde County, Texas.

Snakes from the western portion of the Mexican Plateau, much of the Sierra Madre Occidental, Arizona, southwestern New Mexico, and extreme west Texas have a pattern of 13–21 dark brown to almost black crossbands that are widely and more or less regularly spaced. These crossbands are much wider middorsally than laterally and on northern snakes may extend down the sides to the ventrals; in the south (Durango, Zacatecas, Jalisco) the crossbands or blotches may extend only to the sixth or seventh scale row. The borders of the bands have an irregular outline and are distinctly edged with white. The interspaces between crossbands contain little to moderate amounts of mottling. The postocular stripe is usually vague or absent, but occasionally may be fairly well defined, especially on snakes from the southern portion of the range. The paired nape blotches usually merge across the midline, and the top of the head is without much black pigment. There are 1–6 tail rings, the posterior ones often being vague and hard to count. These snakes are usually strongly sexually dimorphic: the ground color of males has a greenish cast (greenish gray, bluish green, greenish tan), whereas that of females is grayish (pale gray, bluish gray, pinkish gray). The distal portion of the tail, particularly of males, is often reddish or orangish, as is the proximal rattle segment. The amount of mottling on the belly is subject to considerable variation.

The dorsal pattern of snakes from Chihuahua and farther south may be highly variable, as demonstrated by the type of *C. semicornutus* (=*C. lepidus klauberi*). This specimen, described and illustrated by Taylor (1944), had 16 irregular dorsal blotches that alternated with irregular, elongated paravertebral spots. The median dorsal botches on southern snakes are longer than

wide on the anterior of the body but become wider than long posteriorly. The sides of the body are marked with several rows of dark spots, most of which occupy 1–2 scales.

Specimens from near the Sinaloa-Durango border have a series of 22–38 small middorsal spots, often longer than wide; these may be edged irregularly in white, at least on the anterior part of the body, and do not form crossbands except sometimes on the tail. The ground color is brownish gray or dark gray with irregular mottling of dark brown on the sides and dorsum between the primary series of spots. The tail frequently has a reddish gray cast. The postocular stripe is well defined and sometimes white edged above. The venter is heavily pigmented. The top of the head is devoid of conspicuous dark mottling, and the paired nape blotches are small and do not merge. The proximal rattle segment is reddish brown or gray.

Specimens from the Sierra Madre Oriental have 24–34 dark brown body blotches which often have relatively smooth edges. These blotches are usually edged with white, sometimes broadly (1 scale wide). The ground color is pale to dark gray, often with a distinctly orangish cast. Laterally there is considerable mottling. The postocular stripe is well defined and pale bordered above and below. The paired nape blotches usually do not merge at any point, and the top of the head is darkly pigmented, often with a pair of wing-shaped blotches in the parietal–upper temporal region. The proximal rattle segment is dark gray.

Sexual dichromatism is evident from birth. Armstrong and Murphy (1979) reported that the males of a litter of snakes from the Sierra del Nido in Chihuahua (two males and three females) were only slightly mottled with black speckling and had black bands, whereas the females were more amply mottled with gray and had gray bands.

The rostral is usually wider than high, and the prenasal curves under the postnasal. The number of scales in the internasal-prefrontal region varies from 5 to 15 including a large pair of internasals that are in contact medially, a single canthal on each side, and a variable number of intercanthals. There are 1–4 (usually 2) intersupraoculars, 1 or 2 (usually 1) loreals, and 0–6 (usually 2 or 3) prefoveals. The prenasal is in contact with supralabial 1; the postnasal and upper preocular are not in contact. The nasals are usually conjoined above the nostril. One of the most distinctive features of this species is an upper preocular that is vertically divided (in more than 80% of specimens); the anterior portion is situated higher on the head than the portion adjacent to the eye and is curved over the canthus rostralis in front of the supraocular. The population inhabiting the Sierra Madre Oriental is unique in that most specimens do not have divided upper preoculars. Anterior subocular contact with the supralabials is highly variable; in general, snakes from the eastern portion of the Mexican Plateau and the Sierra Madre Oriental have a complete row of interoculabials separating these scales and snakes from the western portion of the plateau and the Sierra Madre Occidental have the anterior subocular and supralabials in contact. There are 10–15 (usually 12 or 13) supralabials, 9–13 (usually 11 or 12) infralabials, 21–25 (usually 23) midbody dorsal scale rows, 147–172 ventrals in males and 149–171 in females, and 20–33 subcaudals in males and 16–25 in females. Most individuals have 10–13 (usually 12) rattle-fringe scales; however, snakes from the Sinaloa-Durango border and the northern portion of the Sierra Madre Oriental have 8–12 (usually 10) rattle-fringe scales and a proportionately smaller rattle.

SIMILAR SPECIES *Crotalus lepidus* is sympatric within parts of its range, or geographically at least closely approaches, four other species of small montane rattlesnakes. *Crotalus pricei* usually has a pattern of 39–64 pairs of paravertebral blotches on a gray ground color; an upper preocular that is not vertically divided; and usually fewer midbody dorsal scale rows, supralabials, and infralabials than *C. lepidus*. *Crotalus stejnegeri* has a distinctive head pattern, the first pair of infralabials are distinctively shaped, the ventrals and subcaudals are more numerous, and the tail is exceptionally slender with a tiny rattle. In the regions where they most closely approach each other *C. aquilus* differs from *C. lepidus* in having 24 or more middorsal body blotches, dorsal body blotches that are longer middorsally than the adjacent interspaces, and an upper preocular that is not divided vertically. *Crotalus willardi* has 6–9 intersupraoculars, usually 25 or 27 midbody dorsal scale rows, an undivided upper preocular, 20 or more scales in the internasal-prefrontal region, and usually a distinctive pattern of white facial stripes. *Crotalus triseriatus* occurs to the southeast of *C. lepidus*, and the two species do not appear to be sympatric anywhere within their ranges.

REMARKS This species mostly inhabits mountains and rugged broken terrain in the vicinity of rocky outcroppings and slides. Within forests it appears to prefer open or relatively barren areas subject to intense sunlight.

Four subspecies are currently recognized. *Crotalus l. lepidus* (Pls. 841–844) ranges from southeastern New Mexico and southwestern Texas (exclusive of the El Paso area) across much of the eastern portion of the Mexican Plateau to San Luis Potosí. There are 147–168 ventrals in males and 149–168 in females; 21–29 subcaudals in males and 17–23 in females; and 13–24 body blotches that are often ill defined on the anterior part of the body but posteriorly grade into narrow, dark crossbands that extend down the sides of the body to the ventrals. The occipital blotches usually are paired and separate from each other, and the venter is usually dark. The ground color is often gray or pinkish gray with an abundant suffusion of darker mottling.

Crotalus l. klauberi (Pls. 845–852) occurs from southeastern Arizona, southwestern New Mexico, and extreme southwestern Texas southward across much of the western portion of the Mexican Plateau to northern Jalisco. There are 152–172 ventrals in males and 155–170 in females, 20–29 subcaudals in males and 16–24 in females, and 13–21 dorsal crossbands on the body that are usually well defined on the anterior of the body; these bands are narrow in the northern part of the range and become more blotchlike in the south. The occipital blotches are usually coalesced and the venter is usually pale. The ground color is often greenish, olive, or pale gray with little or no mottling.

Crotalus l. maculosus (Pls. 853–855) is found on the western slopes of the Sierra Madre Occidental in Durango and Sinaloa. There are 159–169 ventrals in males and 157–173 in females, 26–33 subcaudals in males and 20–25 in females, and 23–38 body blotches that are usually in the form of small spots or transversely elongated blotches that do not extend onto the sides of the body. The occipital blotches are paired and separate, and the venter is usually dark. The ground color is often brown, brownish gray, or purplish gray with little to moderate mottling. We question the veracity of the report of this taxon on Volcán de Tequila (Ponce-Campos et al., 2000) in northern Jalisco for ecological and biogeographic reasons.

Crotalus l. morulus (Pls. 856–863) occupies the Sierra Madre Oriental in southwestern Tamaulipas, central Nuevo León, and southeastern Coahuila. There are 156–167 ventrals in males and 160–171 in females; 25–30 subcaudals in males and 20–25 in females; and 24–24 dorsal markings on body that are usually well defined on the anterior of the body, where they are usually large and blotchlike; posteriorly they form crossbands that often extend to the ventrals. The occipital blotches are paired and usually are not fused, and the venter is usually dark. The ground color is often grayish, gray-brown, or mauve with no to moderate mottling. Males often have a yellowish or orangish middorsum. *Crotalus l. castaneus*, described from the Sierra Madre Oriental south of Monterey, Nuevo León (Juliá-Zertuche and Treviño, 1978), appears to be a junior synonym of *C. l. morulus*.

The identity of a problematic specimen from Santa Teresa, Nayarit, Mexico (USNM 46333), has been a matter of some dispute (Gloyd, 1940; Smith, 1946b). This specimen has characteristics of both *C. lepidus* and *C. triseriatus* with only 22 dorsal crossbands, a dark chin and belly, and an undivided upper preocular. We allocate this specimen to *C. lepidus*, primarily on the basis of the arguments put forth by Smith (1946b) and on subjective biogeographic grounds. Acquisition of additional material from this location to confirm the identity of this population is highly desirable.

Crotalus mitchellii (Cope, 1861)
(Map 101, Pls. 864–875)

Caudisona mitchellii Cope, 1861, *Proc. Acad. Nat. Sci. Philadelphia* 13:292–306[293]. Holotype: USNM 5291½, now lost. Type-locality: "Cape St. Lucas, Lower California," Cabo San Lucas, Baja California Sur, Mexico.

Caudisona pyrrha Cope, 1867 [dated 1866], *Proc. Acad. Nat. Sci. Philadelphia* 18:300–314[308]. Holotype: USNM 6606, according to Cochran (1961:163). Type-locality: not given in original description; given as "Cañon Prieto, a locality near Fort Whipple [Yavapai County], Arizona," by Coues (*in* Wheeler, 1875:608–609), and as "Canyon Prieto, Yavapai County, Arizona" [USA], by Klauber (1956:38).

Crotalus mitchellii—Cope, *in* Yarrow, *in* Wheeler, 1875, *Rep. Geog. Geol. Explor. Surv. West 100th* Merid. 5:509–584[535].

Crotalus pyrrhus—Yarrow, *in* Wheeler, 1875, *Rep. Geog. Geol. Explor. Surv. West 100th Merid.* 5:509–584[532, pl. 22 (figs. 1, 1a)].

Crotalus pyrrhus—Streets, 1877, *Bull. U.S. Natl. Mus.* (7):172 pp.[39].

Crotalus confluentus var. *pyrrhus*—Garman, 1884a [dated 1883], *Mem. Mus. Comp. Zool.* 8:1–185[173].

Crotalus oregonus var. *mitchellii*—Garman, 1884a [dated 1883], *Mem. Mus. Comp. Zool.* 8:1–185[173].

Crotalus mitcheli—Belding, 1887, *West Am. Sci.* 3:97–99[98]. [Unjustified emendation.]

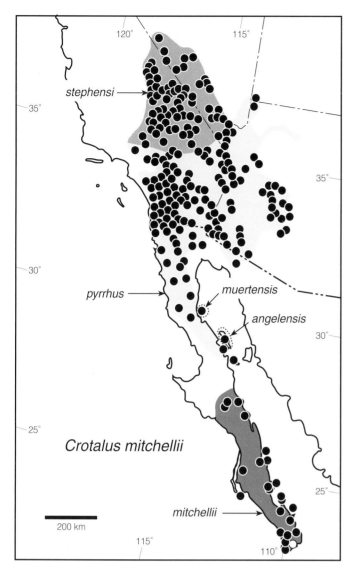

Map 101. Distribution of *Crotalus mitchellii*, including subspecies, in the southwestern United States and Baja California Peninsula, Mexico. Unfilled symbol represents general area of type-locality (Cape San Lucas, Lower California).

Crotalus Mitchellii mitchellii—Stejneger, 1895 [dated 1893], *Ann. Rep. U.S. Natl. Mus.* 1893:337–487[454].

Crotalus Mitchellii pyrrhus—Stejneger, 1895 [dated 1893], *Ann. Rep. U.S. Natl. Mus.* 1893:337–487[456].

Crotalus mitchelli—Boulenger, 1896b, *Cat. Snakes British Mus.* 3:727 pp.[580].

Crotalus goldmani Schmidt, 1922, *Bull. Am. Mus. Nat. Hist.* 46:607–707[701]. Holotype: USNM 37573. Type-locality: "El Piñon, Lower California, 5,300 feet," San Pedro Mártir Mountains, Baja California Norte, Mexico.

Crotalus mitchelli aureus Kallert, 1927, *Bl. Aquar. Terrarienkd. Stuttgart* 38:372[372]. [Nomen nudum.]

Crotalus tigris mitchellii—Amaral, 1929a, *Bull. Antivenin Inst. Am.* 2:82–85[84].

Crotalus confluentus mitchelli—Klauber, 1930b, *Trans. San Diego Soc. Nat. Hist.* 6:95–144[108].

Crotalus confluentus stephensi Klauber, 1930b, *Trans. San Diego Soc. Nat. Hist.* 6:95–144[108]. Holotype: MVZ 6699. Type-locality: "two miles west of Jackass Springs, Panamint Mts., altitude 6,200 ft., Inyo County, California," USA.

Crotalus mitchellii stephensi—Klauber, 1936a, *Trans. San Diego Soc. Nat. Hist.* 8:149–184[162, pl. 20 (fig. 2), text fig. 2].

Crotalus mitchellii pyrrhus—Klauber, 1936a, *Trans. San Diego Soc. Nat. Hist.* 8:149–184[157].

Crotalus mitchellii muertensis Klauber, 1949b, *Trans. San Diego Soc. Nat. Hist.* 11:61–116[97, pl. 6 (fig. 1)]. Holotype: SDSNH 37447 (formerly LMK 37447). Type-locality: "El Muerto Island, Gulf of California, Mexico."

Crotalus mitchelli pyrrhus—Klauber, 1952, *Bull. Zool. Soc. San Diego* (26):1–143[117].

Crotalus mitchelli mitchelli—Klauber, 1952, *Bull. Zool. Soc. San Diego* (26):1–143[123].

Crotalus mitchelli muertensis—Klauber, 1952, *Bull. Zool. Soc. San Diego* (26):1–143[123].

Crotalus mitchelli stephensi—Schmidt, 1953c, *Check List N. Am. Amph. Rept.*, 6th ed., 280 pp.[233].

Crotalus mitchelli angelensis Klauber, 1963, *Trans. San Diego Soc. Nat. Hist.* 13:73–80[73]. Holotype: SDSNH 51994. Type-locality: "about 4 miles southeast of Refugio Bay, at 1,500 feet elevation, Isla Ángel de la Guarda, Gulf of California, México (near 29°29½′N, 113°33′W)."

Crotalus mitchellii angelicus—Hoge, 1966 [dated 1965], *Mem. Inst. Butantan* 32:109–184[152]. [Unjustified emendation for *angelensis*.]

Crotalus mitchellii angelensis—Hoge and Romano-Hoge, 1981a [dated 1978–1979], *Mem. Inst. Butantan* 42/43:179–309[233].

Crotalus mitchellii mitchellii—McCrystal and McCoid, 1986, *Cat. Am. Amph. Rept.* 1986:388.1–4[388.2].

Crotalus mitchellii angelensis—McCrystal and McCoid, 1986, *Cat. Am. Amph. Rept.* 1986:388.1–4[388.2].

Crotalus mitchellii muertensis—McCrystal and McCoid, 1986, *Cat. Am. Amph. Rept.* 1986:388.1–4[388.2].

Crotalus mitchellii pyrrhus—McCrystal and McCoid, 1986, *Cat. Am. Amph. Rept.* 1986:388.1–4[388.2].

Crotalus mitchellii stephensi—McCrystal and McCoid, 1986, *Cat. Am. Amph. Rept.* 1986:388.1–4[388.2].

The species of this genus are of rather sluggish movements, and are not quick to bite, unless trodden on. They throw the body into a coil and sound the rattle, giving a sigmoid flexure to the anterior part of the body, on which the head is poised with open mouth ready for action. At this time drops of the poisonous saliva fall from the fangs, and by a violent expulsion of air from the lungs are thrown at their enemy.

—Cope, 1892:687, writing of *C. mitchellii*

LOCAL NAMES Víbora blanca, víbora de cascabel.

ENGLISH NAME Speckled rattlesnake.

ETYMOLOGY The species epithet is a patronym honoring Silas Weir Mitchell (1829–1914), a medical doctor who conducted research on the venom of rattlesnakes.

DISTRIBUTION Southwestern United States and most of the peninsula of Baja California, Mexico (Map 101). In the United States this species ranges from east-central California, including the Mohave Desert (Stewart, 1994), southwestern Nevada, and extreme southwestern Utah southward through most of southern California and western Arizona. In Mexico it occurs in the northern (Pinacate) portion of the panhandle in northwestern Sonora and throughout the peninsula of Baja California exclusive of the desert region east of the Sierra de Juárez in Baja California Norte and most of the Vizcaíno Desert. It occurs on numerous islands in the Gulf of California, including, from north to south, El Muerto, Ángel de la Guarda, Smith, Piojo, Salsipuedes, Carmen, Monserrate, San José, Espíritu Santo, Partida del Sur, and Cerralvo (see Map 92). In the Pacific it occurs on Isla de Santa Margarita. The vertical distribution is from near sea level to about 2,440 m.

Wong (1997) confirmed the presence of *C. mitchellii* on Isla Santa Margarita but pointed out that no legitimate records exist from Isla Magdalena, despite the fact that Mattison (1996) listed it from that island. Seib (1978) was the first to report *C. mitchellii* from Isla Piojo. Gates (1957) reported finding *C. mitchellii* sympatrically with *C. molossus* and *C. scutulatus* near Morristown, Arizona, at elevations of 518–701 m.

Other distribution records are available for Arizona (Coues, 1875; Fowlie, 1965; Garman, 1884b; Klauber, 1932a; Lowe, 1964; Lowe et al., 1986; Miller et al., 1982; Stejneger, 1893; Vitt and Ohmart, 1978; Woodbury and Hardy, 1947; Yarrow, 1875), California (Amaral, 1927e, 1929a; Camp, 1916; Glaser, 1970; Grinnell and Camp, 1917; Klauber, 1927, 1930c, 1931a, 1932b; Meek, 1906; Miller and Stebbins, 1964; Moore, 1976, 1978; Van Denburgh, 1897, 1912), Nevada (Linsdale, 1940; Tanner, 1966b), Utah (Tanner, 1960), the Baja California Peninsula including various islands (Amaral, 1929a; Banks, 1962; Belding, 1887; Cliff, 1954; Cope, 1861; Cuesta-Terrón, 1931; Etheridge, 1961; Grismer, 1993, 1994b, 2002; Klauber, 1963; Leviton and Banta, 1964; Lindsay, 1962, 1964, 1966; Linsdale, 1932; Mocquard, 1899b, 1908–1909; Meek, 1906; Murphy, 1983a, 1983b; Murphy and Ottley, 1984; Murray, 1955; Orr, 1965; Schmidt, 1922; Smith, 1944c; Smith and Taylor, 1966; Streets, 1877; Van Denburgh, 1894, 1905; Van Denburgh and Slevin, 1914, 1921b; Yarrow, 1883), and Sonora (P. Smith and Hensley, 1958). The overall distribution is given in Amaral, 1927e; Gloyd, 1940; Hoge and Romano, 1971a; Klauber, 1930b, 1936a, 1936b, 1952, 1971, 1972; McCrystal and McCoid, 1986; Pope, 1944–1945; Stebbins, 1985; Tanner, 1978; Van Denburgh, 1894, 1895a, 1922b; and Werner, 1922. For the distribution in United States, see G. B. Pickwell, 1972; Shaw and Campbell, 1974; Stejneger, 1895; Stejneger and Barbour, 1943; Wright and Wright, 1957; and Yarrow, 1883; and for Mexico, see Armstrong and Murphy, 1979; Cuesta-Terrón, 1931; Klauber, 1949b (El Muerto Island); Martín del Campo, 1935, 1937a, 1950; Savage, 1960; and Smith and Taylor, 1945.

HABITAT Desertscrub, Joshua tree woodland, and piñon-juniper woodland; in chaparral in northwestern Baja California Norte; in tropical deciduous forest in the cape region; and in pine-oak forest in the Sierra de Juárez, Sierra San Pedro Mártir, and Sierra de San Lázaro. This species is most frequently found in rugged, rocky terrain, but may sometimes occur in brushy lowland flats, chaparral, or arenicolous washes devoid of rocks (Jones, 1988; Ohmart et al., 1988).

DESCRIPTION Individuals of this species generally do not exceed 100 cm in TL; large adult males are between 90 and 100 cm. The population on Isla Ángel de la Guarda is larger, with a maximum recorded length of 136.7 cm; and individuals of the population on Isla El Muerto are dwarfed, with a maximum known length of 63.7 cm.

The ground color of snakes in the southern half of the peninsula of Baja California is pale gray, tan, or yellowish gray, and the 26–46 dorsal body blotches are dark gray or brown. Snakes from the northern half of the peninsula are extremely variable, with a cream, tan, buff, yellowish, pink, salmon, orange, gray, or pale brown ground color and reddish, orangish, gray, brown, or black blotches. An individual's ground color frequently matches the particular environment (soil, rocks) in which it lives. The number of dorsal blotches ranges from 23 to 46 (the population on Isla Ángel de la Guarda has a higher average number than that on the mainland). Dorsal blotches on the anterior part of the body may be hexagonal or diamond shaped, but posteriorly they coalesce with the lateral series of blotches to form crossbands. The dorsum is punctated liberally with dark pigment, especially within the blotches. The scales comprising

the row that bounds the anterior edge of a dorsal blotch are often dark brown or black tipped distally. Head markings are usually present but often are ill defined. Sometimes there are elongated, paired occipital blotches and upper temporal streaks; the postocular stripe, if present, extends from the posterior edge of the eye to above the rictus. The infracephalic scales, especially the mental and anterior infralabials, are dusted or spotted with black pigment. The belly is pink, pinkish cinnamon, reddish, or orangish and heavily mottled with dark brown. The subcaudals are also heavily mottled. The 3–9 dark tail bands are widely separated, are wider and darker dorsally, and become darker (usually black) distally. The proximal segment of the rattle is black.

The rostral is usually wider than high and contacts 2 (rarely up to 4) small internasals. The 13–51 scales in the internasal-prefrontal region tend to be somewhat knobby, whereas those located more posteriorly on the head are flat and keeled. There are 1–8 intersupraoculars, and the supraoculars may have short, irregular sutures along their outer edges. The rostral is usually separated from the prenasals by the interposition of 1 to several smaller scales. The front edges of the prenasals are often chipped and sutured. The prenasal may or may not be in contact with supralabial 1 (such contact is usually precluded by the forward extension of prefoveals in snakes in the south; in the north, the prenasal often contacts the first supralabial), and the lacunals may or may not be in contact with the supralabials. The number of loreals is highly variable (0–5), but most frequently there are 2; these preclude upper preocular–postnasal contact. The upper preocular is often divided vertically and/or horizontally. Two interoculabials usually separate the anterior subocular and supralabial series. Usually no interchinshields or submentals are present, and the first pair of infralabials are not transversely divided.

The rostral is usually wider than high. There are 12–19 supralabials (usually 15–17 except in snakes from Ángel de la Guarda, which average about 14), 13–19 infralabials (usually 15–17), 21–27 midbody dorsal scale rows (usually 25 on the mainland, 23 on Isla El Muerto, and 27 on Ángel de la Guarda), 156–187 ventrals in males and 163–190 in females (snakes from the southern portion of the peninsula of Baja California average a low number, and snakes from Ángel de la Guarda have a high average), and 20–28 subcaudals in males and 16–24 in females.

SIMILAR SPECIES Specimens of *Crotalus mitchellii* from Mexico usually have two unique characteristics, either one of which should serve to identify this snake: a rostral that is separated from the prenasal by 1 to several intervening scales; and a preocular that is divided, often irregularly, vertically and/or horizontally.

Crotalus atrox, sympatric in Mexico with *C. mitchellii* only in extreme northwestern Sonora, has strongly contrasting black and ash white rings on the tail, a pale stripe that usually extends from the upper postocular downward to the penultimate or antepenultimate supralabial, and a belly that is mostly pale without extensive or heavy dark mottling. *Crotalus cerastes*, sympatric in northwestern Sonora and on the Gulf of California side of Baja California Norte, has supraoculars dramatically elevated into hornlike processes, nasals usually conjoined above the nostril, usually 21–23 midbody dorsal scale rows, and 154 or fewer ventrals. *Crotalus enyo*, broadly sympatric over much of the peninsula of Baja California, has dorsal body blotches clearly defined with black edging, a distinct pale bar on the supraocular that curves forward medially, and a pair of distinct nape stripes that often engages the first dorsal blotch.

Crotalus ruber, sympatric throughout most of Baja California, has a broad, dark postocular stripe that is bordered by narrower pale stripes, dorsal blotches with pale borders, and the first pair of infralabials is transversely divided. *Crotalus scutulatus*, sympatric only in northwestern Sonora, has strongly contrasting dark and pale tail rings; a broad, dark postorbital stripe that is bordered by distinct narrow pale stripes; a nearly immaculate belly with only a slight amount of pigment encroaching on the lateral portions of the ventrals; usually no more than 2 intersupraoculars; and 6–21 scales in the internasal-prefrontal region. *Crotalus tigris*, which is probably not sympatric anywhere in Mexico except possibly in the panhandle of northwestern Sonora, has a proportionately much smaller head than *C. mitchellii*, a pattern of crossbands that extends from the anterior part of the body to the tail, and 23 or fewer midbody dorsal scale rows. *Crotalus oreganus*, sympatric along the Pacific slopes of Baja California Norte, has a pale brownish gray ground color, diamond-shaped blotches that are edged in black and bordered by a single row of pale scales, and 3 or more internasals.

REMARKS Klauber (1972) and McCrystal and McCoid (1986) recognized five subspecies, but this complex appears in need of thorough revision. *Crotalus m. mitchellii* (Pls. 864 and 865) and *C. m. pyrrhus* (Pls. 869–872) occur in the southern and northern halves of the peninsula of Baja California, respectively, with *pyrrhus* extending northward into southern California, western Arizona, and extreme southwestern Utah; *Crotalus m. angelensis* (Pls. 866 and 867) and *C. m. muertensis* (Pl. 868) occur on Islas Ángel de la Guarda and El Muerto, respectively, in the Gulf of California; and *C. m. stephensi* ranges from east-central California to southwestern Nevada. Grismer (2002) treated *angelensis* and *muertensis* as species.

The coloration and lepidosis of the population of *C. mitchellii* on Ángel de la Guarda overlap with these characteristics in populations on the mainland (Klauber, 1963); however, Klauber (1963) stated that the island population differs from mainland populations in attaining a much greater overall size and in having a proportionately smaller rattle. The maximum SVLs for various subspecies given by Klauber (1963) are 63.7 cm for *C. m. muertensis*, 93.9 cm for *C. m. mitchellii*, 94.3 cm for *C. m. stephensi*, 111.4 cm for *C. m. pyrrhus*, and 141.0 cm for *C. m. angelensis*. The girth and length of *C. m. angelensis* make it a particularly impressive snake. Grismer (1999a) considered the population on Ángel de la Guarda (*angelensis*) to be a species distinct from *C. mitchellii* on the basis of differences in body and rattle size.

Crotalus mitchellii muertensis of Isla El Muerto was at one time considered to have distinctive squamation and color patterns and to attain a smaller body size than other subspecies (Klauber, 1949b). As more material from various populations of *C. mitchellii* accumulated, it became apparent that only the latter characteristic is diagnostic, but Grismer (1999a) argued that this is sufficient to allocate full species status.

This species is mostly nocturnal during midsummer but may be diurnal in early spring and late fall. It has a reputation for being nervous and quick to bite.

Crotalus molossus Baird and Girard, 1853
(Map 102, Pls. 876–888)

Crotalus molossus Baird and Girard, 1853, *Cat. N. Am. Rept.* (1):172 pp.[10]. Holotype: USNM 485. Type-locality: "Fort Webster, St. Rita del Cobre, N. Mex." [Fort Webster, Santa Rita del Cobre, Grant County, New Mexico, USA].

Crotalus ornatus Hallowell, 1854, *Proc. Acad. Nat. Sci. Philadelphia* 7:192–193[192]. Holotype: USNM 486. Type-locality: "between El Paso and San Antonio, Pecos River, Texas," USA.

Caudisona molossus—Cope, 1860b, *Smithson. Contrib. Knowl.* 12(6):119–126[124].

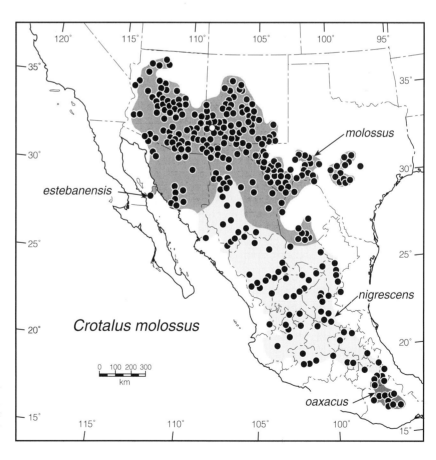

Map 102. Distribution of *Crotalus molossus*, including subspecies, in Mexico and the southwestern United States. Unfilled symbol represents the type-locality, Fort Webster, Santa Rita del Cobre, Grant County, New Mexico, USA.

Caudisona molossa—Cope, 1867 [dated 1866], *Proc. Acad. Nat. Sci. Philadelphia* 18:300–314[307].

Crotalus durissus var. *molossus*—Garman, 1884b [dated 1883], *Mem. Mus. Comp. Zool.* 8:1–185[171].

Crotalus terrificus—Boulenger, 1896b, *Cat. Snakes British Mus.* 3:727 pp.[573]. [In part.]

Crotalus molossus molossus—Gloyd, 1936c, *Occas. Pap. Mus. Zool. Univ. Michigan* 325:1–5[2].

Crotalus molossus nigrescens Gloyd, 1936c, *Occas. Pap. Mus. Zool. Univ. Michigan* 325:1–5[2]. Holotype: UMMZ 77833. Type-locality: "4 miles west of La Colorada, Zacatecas, Mexico."

Crotalus basiliscus oaxacus Gloyd, 1948b, *Nat. Hist. Misc.* (Chicago) 17:1–4[1, figs. 1–3]. Holotype: USNM 46467. Type-locality: "Oaxaca," Mexico; given as "Cerro San Felipe, near Oaxaca, Oaxaca, Mexico, 8,500 ft.," by Cochran (1961:169).

Crotalus molossus estebanensis Klauber, 1949b, *Trans. San Diego Soc. Nat. Hist.* 11:61–116[104, pl. 6 (fig. 2)]. Holotype: SDSNH 26792 (formerly LMK 26792). Type-locality: "San Estéban Island, Gulf of California, Mexico."

Crotalus molossus oaxacus—Campbell and Lamar, 1989, *Venom. Rept. Latin Am.*, 425 pp.[276 (figs. 390 and 391), 356].

LOCAL NAMES Green rattler (New Mexico), palanca, palancacóatl (southern Puebla), sayao, sayawi, sayawi-ri-ra (Tarahumara), tecutlacotzauhqui, tepecolcóatl, teuhtlacotza-uhqui (suggested by Smith, 1970), teuhtlacozauhqui, tleua (Nahuatl derivatives—Valley of Mexico, Guanajuato, Jalisco), víbora, víbora de cascabel, víbora de cascabel de cola negra.

ENGLISH NAME Black-tailed rattlesnake.

ETYMOLOGY The species epithet is derived from the Greek place-name Molossus, a region in Epirus famous for its hounds. The name is perhaps an allusion to the blunt muzzle.

DISTRIBUTION Southwestern United States to southern Mexico (Map 102). In the United States this species ranges from western and northern Arizona southward and eastward through southern Arizona, central and southern New Mexico, and west Texas to the Edwards Plateau of central Texas; and in Mexico from Sonora eastward through most of Chihuahua and Coahuila south to the southern part of the Mexican Plateau and Mesa del Sur in central Oaxaca (Campbell and Lamar, 1989; Casas-Andreu et al., 1996). At one time this species apparently was relatively common in the Valley of Oaxaca and surrounding hillsides, but it has become rare in the southern portion of its range. This snake also inhabits Isla Tiburón and Isla de San Esteban in the Gulf of California. The vertical distribution is from near sea level to about 2,930 m. In the northern part of the distribution it ranges from sea level to 2,592 m in the Chiricahua Mountains of Arizona, and in the south (Puebla and Oaxaca) it occurs mostly between 1,700 and 2,500 m.

Distribution records are available for Arizona (Brown, 2000b; Coues, 1875; Curran, 1935; Fowlie, 1965; Gehlbach, 1957; Gloyd, 1937; Hulse, 1973; Humphrey, 1936; Kauffeld, 1943a; Klauber, 1932a; Koenig and La Grone, 2000; A. Holycross, 2001; D. Holycross and Smith, 2001; Little, 1940; Lowe, 1964; Lowe et al., 1986; McKee and Bogert, 1934; Miller et al., 1982; Nickerson and Mays, 1970; Ortenburger and Ortenburger, 1927; Pough, 1966; Quaintance, 1935; Shaw and Campbell, 1974; Stejneger, 1902; Woodin, 1953; Yarrow, 1875), California (Klauber, 1938b), New Mexico (Baird, 1859a; Bogert and Degenhardt, 1961; Chenoweth, 1950; Christman and Painter, 1998; Degenhardt et al., 1996; Garman, 1884a; Gehlbach, 1957, 1965; Lewis, 1950; Little and Keller, 1937; Mosauer, 1932b; Shaw and Campbell, 1974; Van Denburgh, 1924), Texas (Axtell, 1959; A. Brown, 1903a; B. Brown, 1950; Brown and Mittleman, 1947; Crimmins, 1927a; Curran, 1935; Engelhardt, 1932; Jameson and Flury, 1949; Milstead et al., 1950; Minton, 1959; Price, 1998; Schmidt and

Smith, 1944; Smith, 1947c; Smith and Buechner, 1947; Strecker, 1935b; Stecker and Williams, 1927; Tennant, 1984, 1985; Troschel, 1860; Werler, 1964), Aguascalientes (Anderson and Lidicker, 1963; Sigala-Rodríguez and Vázquez-Díaz, 1996), Baja California Norte (Klauber, 1938b; Lowe and Norris, 1954; Murphy, 1983b; Murphy and Ottley, 1984; Schmidt, 1922; Townsend, 1916), Chihuahua (Domínguez et al., 1974; Lemos-Espinal et al., 1997, 2000a, 2000b, 2002a, 2002b; McCranie and Wilson, 1978; Morafka, 1977; Smith, 1943a; Tanner, 1985; Taylor and Knobloch, 1940; Van Devender and Lowe, 1977), Coahuila (Chrapliwy and Fugler, 1955; Fugler and Webb, 1956; Gloyd and Smith, 1942; Klauber, 1938b; McCoy, 1984; Schmidt and Owens, 1944; Smith, 1943a), the Distrito Federal (Uribe-Peña et al., 1999), Durango (Auth et al., 2000; Drake, 1958; Fouquette and Rossman, 1963; Webb, 1984; Webb and Baker, 1962), Guanajuato (Cuesta-Terrón, 1921b), Jalisco (Cuesta-Terrón, 1921b; Dugès, 1869; Mocquard, 1899a), México (Cuesta-Terrón, 1921b; Dugès, 1896a—as *horridus*; Herrera, 1890—as *basiliscus*, 1891—as *adamanteus* and *basiliscus*?; Mertens, 1930—as *terrificus basiliscus*), Michoacán (Duellman, 1961, 1965b), Nuevo León (Liner, 1964; Smith, 1944a), Oaxaca (Casas-Andreu et al., 1996; Gloyd, 1948b; Smith, 1943a; Smith and Lynch, 1967; Smith and Taylor, 1966; Spengler et al., 1982), Puebla (Ferrari-Perez, 1886; Gehlbach and Collette, 1957), Querétaro (Dixon et al., 1972; Minton and Minton de Cervantes, 1977), San Luis Potosí (Cuesta-Terrón, 1921b; Dixon et al., 1962; Garman, 1887a; Grant and Smith, 1959; Taylor, 1949), Sinaloa (Hardy and McDiarmid, 1969; Webb, 1984), Sonora, including Isla San Esteban and Isla Tiburón (Allen, 1933; Cliff, 1954; Grismer, 2002; Klauber, 1938b, 1949b; Lowe and Norris, 1955; Schmidt, 1922; Soulé and Sloan, 1966; Taylor, 1938a), Tamaulipas (Burchfield et al., 1982; Martin, 1958), Veracruz (Pérez-Higareda and Smith, 1991), Zacatecas (Cuesta-Terrón, 1921b; Dunkle and Smith, 1937; Wilson and McCranie, 1979a), Mexico generally (Armstrong and Murphy, 1979; Cuesta-Terrón, 1921b—in part, 1931—in part, as *basiliscus*; Dugès, 1876–1877—as *rhombifer*; Gloyd, 1936c; Günther, 1895–1902—in part; Klauber, 1938b, 1949b—San Esteban Island, 1952; Martín del Campo, 1935, 1937a, 1950, 1953, 1955; Smith, 1943a; Smith, 1970; Smith and Taylor, 1945; Sumichrast, 1873—as *durissus*), the United States (Conant and Collins, 1998; Curran, 1935; Garman, 1884b; Stejneger and Barbour, 1943; Van Denburgh, 1922b; Wright and Wright, 1957), and the general range (Brown, 1901; Conant, 1975; Cope, 1900; Gloyd, 1940; Hoge and Romano, 1971a; Klauber, 1936b, 1971, 1972; Pope, 1944–1945; Price, 1980; Stebbins, 1985; Yarrow, 1883).

HABITAT Pine-oak forest, pine-fir forest, oak-grass savanna, boreal forest, sweetgum-oak forest, mesquite-grassland, upland Sonoran Desert, chaparral, tropical deciduous forest, de-sertscrub, and probably thornforest. In west Texas this species has been reported from various rocky habitats such as canyons, cliffs, and talus slopes (Axtell, 1959); and from catclaw-grama and catclaw-cedar associations (Jameson and Flury, 1949). Milstead et al. (1950) and Milstead (1960b) found it most frequently in persimmon–shin oak associations on the Stockton Plateau of Texas. Gates (1957) reported that this species occurs to the south and west of the Colorado Plateau in the rocky hills north and east of Wickenburg, Arizona, and that *C. molossus* is sympatric with *C. mitchellii* and *C. scutulatus* at 701 m elevation near Morristown, Arizona, in Sonoran desertscrub. In the Sonoran Desert of Arizona this species is found mostly in rocky areas, but in the late summer and fall it frequents arroyos and creosote bush flats (Beck, 1995). It has also been reported to inhabit chaparral in Arizona (Jones, 1988). Woodin (1953) offered anecdotal evidence that this species ranges up to 9,440 feet (2,877 m) in Arizona. Van Devender and Lowe (1977) reported it to be common in the woodlands and forests around Yepómera, Chihuahua. This ecologically widespread species has even been taken in the sand dunes south of Ciudad Juárez in Chihuahua (Armstrong and Murphy, 1979). In Michoacán, Duellman (1961) found this rattlesnake in pine forests in the Transverse Volcanic Cordillera at elevations of 1,550–2,300 m; and we have collected it in Durango, Zacatecas, Jalisco, and Michoacán at elevations exceeding 2,000 m. Webb (1984) reported it from mesquite-grassland, pine-oak forest, and mixed boreal tropical forest in Durango.

DESCRIPTION Large specimens of this medium-sized rattlesnake usually do not greatly exceed 100 cm in TL. Gloyd (1940) reported a large specimen from Brewster County, Texas, that was 125.0 cm in TL, and Klauber (1972) and Shaw and Campbell (1974) reported slightly larger specimens measuring 125.7 cm and 129.5 cm in TL, respectively. Tennant (1984) reported a specimen from Kerr County, Texas, that was 132.1 cm in TL, and Hardy and Greene (1995) measured an individual from Cochise County, Arizona, that had a TL of 133.0 cm. Snakes of the populations on islands in the Gulf of California are relatively small and are not known to reach 100 cm.

There is considerable north–south and east–west clinal variation for a number of characteristics in this wide-ranging species. Discordant variation in other characters, much individual variation within most populations, and rather striking ontogenetic variations in tail color and pattern further confuse the situation. For the purpose of describing the variation of some traits, it is convenient to broadly bisect the range of this snake into "north" and "south" using about 25 degrees north latitude as the dividing line.

Snakes in the north are usually paler than those to the south and have a greenish gray, steel gray, grayish olive, olive green, yellow-green, sulphur yellow, orange-yellow, rust, or cream ground color. Axtell (1959) described west Texas individuals as having a greenish gray ground color. Werler and Dixon (2000) described Texas snakes as being olive green, olive brown, or gray above and greenish on the sides. Degenhardt et al. (1996) reported that individuals from New Mexico are gray, olive, or greenish yellow; and Lowe et al. (1986) described Arizona snakes as yellowish green. The 20–43 rhombic dorsal blotches are chestnut brown to black; on the anterior one-half to two-thirds of the body the interiors of these blotches tend to contain several pale scales on each side of the midline. The dorsal blotches may be separated from one another by a group of scales on the midline that is considerably paler than the ground color. The first dorsal blotch often extends anteriorly as a pair of paravertebral stripes. On the anterior part of the body the blotches are rhombic to diamond shaped; more posteriorly the dorsal blotches become progressively wider transversely and often coalesce with lateral blotches to form vertical bars that extend downward to the ventrals. The pale margins of the dorsal blotches open laterally to border each side of these vertical bars. The top of the head from the rostral to about the supraoculars is often black; the back of the head is paler (about the same as the general ground color of the body) and may have irregularly scattered dark scales. The tail is dark brown to black; the dark pigment does not extend forward onto the posterior part of the body and terminates rather abruptly at about the level of the vent. The belly is whitish, yellowish, or pale gray with a subtle infusion or indistinct mottling of gray. Members of the Isla San Esteban population tend to resemble snakes from the northern mainland of Mexico but have a high number of dorsal blotches (39–43) and indistinct dark tail rings that remain evident on adults.

Crotalus molossus occurs in the lava beds of the Malpais of the Tularosa Basin of New Mexico. This dull black lava extends in a north–south strip covering about 120 square miles (310 km²). Bradt (1932) and Benson (1932) described the dark pelage of rodents found in this dark lava rock, and Lewis (1949) noted that many of the reptiles occurring in the Malpais area are also dark, including *C. molossus*, which has a dark greenish gray ground color in contrast to the paler greenish or yellow-gray ground color typical of *C. molossus* from the nearby Organ Mountains. The dorsal blotches of Malpais specimens are black rather than dark green, but have paler centers, and the lateral black bars on the sides of the body are 2 scales long rather than 1. The tail and proximal rattle segment are completely black, and the venter is whitish with indistinct gray blotches. Best and James (1984) and Best et al. (1983) reported that individuals in a population of *C. molossus* inhabiting the Pedro Armendariz lava field of south-central New Mexico tend to be strongly melanistic. Prieto and Jacobson (1968) found melanistic *C. molossus* in the Afton lava flows of New Mexico.

The general ground color of southern populations of *C. molossus* may be brownish olive, yellowish olive, or brownish gray. Posteriorly the ground color becomes more darkly suffused with brownish black to black pigment, which extends onto the tail; in most snakes the pattern on the posterior one-third to one-half of the body is completely obscured by the dark pigmentation. Some snakes are essentially totally black, and all elements of the dorsal pattern are obscured except for the pale borders of the blotches. Twenty-four to 34 dark brown or black rhomboidal or diamond-shaped blotches are bordered by yellow or yellowish gray scales, and the pale borders of adjacent blotches are usually in contact at middorsum. A few pale scales may be grouped within each blotch; pale scales are distributed primarily on each side of the midline but sometimes come together across the dorsum. Usually fewer dorsal blotches coalesce with lateral blotches than is the case for northern snakes; however, this is not an infrequent occurrence, especially on the posterior part of the body.

The top of the head of southern snakes, including the parietal-occipital area, is often dark with a few pale longitudinal streaks or groups of scales; alternatively, the head is brown or gray with darker markings that include upper temporal and parietal stripes. Usually a dark postocular stripe is clearly evident; it extends from beneath and behind the eye, where it is about 3–4 scales wide, to a point above the rictus, where it narrows to a single scale. The lower margin of this stripe extends along the scale row above the supralabials. The dark postocular stripe is bordered by pale lines. The lower (anterior) pale line curves from the upper preocular downward under the eye to a point on the lip margin 3–5 supralabials anterior to the rictus, and thence continues to the ultimate supralabial. The upper (posterior) pale line extends diagonally from about the upper posterior corner of the eye to just behind, or just above, the rictus. The belly is cream to pale yellow with a moderate amount of mottling or suffusion of dark pigment laterally; the ventrals become darker on the posterior part of the body.

The ground color includes no dark punctations, and it is not unusual for the dark dorsal body blotches to coalesce on the anterior part of the body. One peculiarity of the pattern is the marked tendency for each dorsal scale to be more or less unicolored; the elements of pattern do not cut across individual scales as is typical of most rattlesnakes. Melanistic specimens are known from regions of dark volcanic rock in the southwestern portion of the Mexican Plateau. In juveniles 4–9 dark crossbands are evident on the tail. Throughout most of the range the tail of adults is uniformly dark, but occasional individuals have a dark gray tail with indistinct black rings. Most members of southern populations in Puebla and Oaxaca retain the tail rings as adults, although they may become somewhat obscure.

The rostral is usually slightly higher than wide. Most frequently there are 6 scales in the internasal-prefrontal area including 2 large, triangular internasals in contact with the rostral, followed by 2 large, quadrangular prefrontals (anterior canthals) in contact along the midline; a pair of small posterior canthals lies posterolaterally to the prefrontals and partially intervenes between this scale and the supraoculars. Sometimes the posterior canthals are absent, leaving only 4 large scales on the dorsum of the snout. Some snakes in the northern part of the range exhibit a good deal of fragmentation of scales in the internasal-prefrontal region, making the total range of variation 4–18 scales. Anteriorly there are 2–5 intersupraoculars, with a tendency for 2 in the south and 3 in the north. Snakes from the south also tend to have larger scales in the parietal region, with a large elongated scale often present behind the posteromedial edge of the supraocular. The number and extent of the prefoveals are highly variable: snakes in the north average about 10, those in the south only 6 or 7. Supralabial 1 may be in broad contact with the prenasal or may be partially separated from it by the anteriormost prefoveals. When the prenasal and first supralabial do make contact, they frequently isolate an anterior prefoveal from the other prefoveals; this isolated foveal has sometimes been called a postrostral.

The lateral portions of the prefrontals (anterior canthals) are usually not deflected downward over the canthus rostralis; however, contact between the postnasal and the upper preocular is almost always prevented by the presence of 1–9 (usually 2–4) loreals. Snakes throughout the range usually have an upper and a lower loreal on each side, but northern snakes feud to have more loreals than southern snakes. One to 3 (usually 2) interoculabials separate the anterior suboculars from the supralabials. Very rarely the interchinshields or the first pair of infralabials are divided transversely. There are 13–20 supralabials (usually 17 or 18 in the north, 16 or 17 in the south); 14–21 infralabials (usually 17 or 18 in the north, 16 or 17 in the south); 23–31 midbody dorsal scale rows (usually 27 in the north, 25 in the south); 164–199 ventrals in males and 168–199 in females (average number higher in the north); and 21–30 subcaudals in males and 16–26 in females, 0–19 (usually 1–3) of which are divided. The average number of subcaudals in males is lower in the central part of the range than at the northern and southern extremes.

SIMILAR SPECIES *Crotalus molossus* can usually be distinguished from other rattlesnakes *in regions of sympatry* by a *combination* of characteristics: (1) a dark tail with dark tail rings obfuscated or only vaguely indicated in adults; (2) usually no more than 6 scales in the internasal-prefrontal area; (3) the interior of the dark dorsal blotches with pale scales, often on each side of the midline; (4) individual dorsal scales tend to be more or less unicolored; and (5) parietal stripes, if present, are obscure and irregular in outline. Some specimens of *Trimorphodon* (Pl. 1328) resemble *C. molossus*.

REMARKS Four subspecies of *C. molossus* are recognized: *C. m. molossus* (Pls. 876–880) from the southwestern United States, much of northern Mexico, and Isla Tiburón; *C. m. estebanensis*

(Pl. 881) from Isla San Esteban in the Gulf of California; *C. m. nigrescens* (Pls. 882–884) from the southern portion of the Mexican Plateau; and *Crotalus molossus oaxacus* (Pls. 885–888) from the highlands of central Oaxaca and Puebla. The Oaxacan population had previously been thought to have its affinities with *C. basiliscus*, primarily on the basis of plesiomorphic color pattern. In a number of characters, however—including a relatively low number of ventrals, a higher average number of labials, a lower average number of body blotches, and hemipenial morphology—these snakes more closely resemble *C. molossus* (Campbell and Lamar, 1989). The banded tail pattern characteristic of juvenile *C. molossus* is retained in many adult Oaxacan specimens; however, the tails of some snakes become uniformly dark, as is typical of snakes to the north.

Crotalus molossus estebanensis of Isla San Esteban often varies from mainland populations in having rattles that are compressed longitudinally and transversely (Klauber, 1949b), in having smaller and paler dorsal blotches that fade out on the posterior of the body, and in lacking a conspicuous darkened internasal-prefrontal area (Campbell and Lamar, 1989). Based on rattle shape and color pattern, Grismer (1999a) elevated this taxon to species level.

Crotalus molossus exhibits obvious clinal differences in hemipenial morphology. The lobes of snakes from northern Mexico and the United States are straight, thick, and stubby. More than 50 relatively small spines are present on the basal part of the organ below each lobe, and these do not or only barely extend onto the lobes. The lobes are covered by papillate calyces, and these calyces extend on the medial surfaces of the lobes down to the crotch; there are no mesial spines. Snakes from the southern portion of the Mexican Plateau, north of the Transverse Volcanic Cordillera, have spines on the shoulders and proximal part of the lobes that are slightly larger than those found on snakes to the north; and the spines are fewer, between 25 and 50. The distal portion of the lobes is covered by papillate calyces, but these do not extend to the crotch. Occasionally there are a few soft spinules in the mesial area, but there are no large spines. The lobes of snakes from Puebla and Oaxaca are relatively slender and often lyriform when everted. The basal spines are much larger than those in snakes from the north. There are 25–40 spines on the shoulders and up to the proximal third of each lobe. In most snakes, large mesial spines encroach on the asulcomedial surface of each lobe; however, in some snakes the spines terminate on the asulcate side of the organ.

In the foothills along the northwestern coast of Mexico, *C. molossus* apparently hybridizes freely with *C. basiliscus*. Most specimens from above about 1,500 m in eastern Sinaloa and western Durango clearly appear to be *C. molossus*, and snakes from below 600 m are allocatable to *C. basiliscus*; however, many specimens from moderate elevations (600–1,500 m) exhibit traits of both species. For a comparison of the hemipenes of *C. molossus* and *C. basiliscus*, see Remarks for *C. basiliscus*.

Crotalus molossus estebanensis is a somewhat stunted subspecies with smaller blotches than mainland specimens (Klauber, 1938b).

Crotalus oreganus Holbrook, 1840
(Fig. 208, Map 103, Pls. 889–914)

Crotalus oreganus Holbrook, 1840, N. Am. Herpetol., 1st ed., 4:126 pp.[115, pl. 29]. [The text states plate 24, but the plate is incorrectly numbered 29; volume 4 has only 28 plates.] Holotype: ANSP 7158, according to Malnate (1971:369). Type-locality:

"banks of the Oregon or Columbia river . . . in the Oregon territory." Restricted to "The Dalles, Wasco County, Oregon," USA, by Smith and Taylor (1950b:360); "confluence of Columbia and Snake rivers, Washington," USA, by Schmidt (1953c:232); and "probably between Walla Walla, Washington, and the Pacific Coast" by Klauber (1956:53).

Crotalus oregonus—Holbrook, 1842, *N. Am. Herpetol.*, 2d ed., 3:128 pp.[1, 21, 23]. [Unjustified emendation in text; correctly spelled *Crotalus oreganus* on plate 3.]

Fig. 208. Frontal view of head of *Crotalus oreganus oreganus*, 58.0 cm TL, UTA R-31018: from 254 km northwest of Harney County line on State Highway 140, Lake County, Oregon, USA. Photograph by David G. Barker.

Crotalus lucifer Baird and Girard, 1852, *Proc. Acad. Nat. Sci. Philadelphia* 6:174–177[177]. Holotype: USNM 7762 (Oregon). Type-locality: "Oregon and California." Yarrow (1875:606) indicated that the type was "originally described from Oregon . . . subsequently found in California." Restricted to "western Oregon" by Schmidt (1953c:232).

Crotalus adamanteus var. *lucifer*—Jan, 1863, *Elenco Sist. Ofidi*, 143 pp.[124].

Caudisona lucifer—Cope, 1867 [dated 1866], *Proc. Acad. Nat. Sci. Philadelphia* 18:300–314 [307].

Crotalus hallowelli Cooper, *in* Cronise, 1868, *Nat. Wealth California*, 483 pp.[483]. A nomen nudum, according to Klauber (1956:48).

Caudisona lucifer var. *cerberus* Coues, *in* Wheeler, 1875, *Rep. Geog. Geol. Explor. Surv. West 100th Merid.* 5:585–633[607]. Syntypes (4): ANSP 7085–88. Malnate (1971:368) listed only ANSP 7085 and ANSP 7088. The two syntypes, ANSP 7086 and 7087, that Klauber (1956:46) indicated might be lost are in the ANSP collection, according to J. Cadle (*in* McDiarmid et al., 1999). Gloyd (1940:214) indicated type specimens as ANSP 7085–89, but Cadle (*in* McDiarmid et al., 1999) stated that ANSP 7089 is not a syntype. Type-locality: "San Francisco Mountains," Coconino County, Arizona, USA.

Crotalus confluentus var. *lucifer*—Cope, 1884 [dated 1883], *Proc. Acad. Nat. Sci. Philadelphia* 35:10–35[11].

Crotalus oregonus var. *lucifer*—Garman, 1884a [dated 1883], *Mem. Mus. Comp. Zool.* 8:1–185[173].

Crotalus oregonus var. *cerberus*—Garman, 1884a [dated 1883], *Mem. Mus. Comp. Zool.* 8:1–185[173].

Crotalus confluentus lucifer—Cope, 1892, *Proc. U.S. Natl. Mus.* 14:589–694[692].

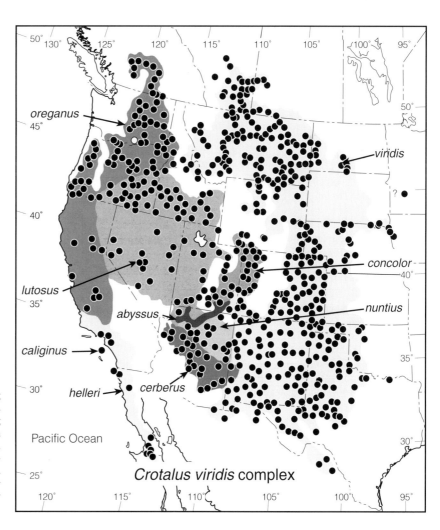

Map 103. Distributions of *Crotalus oreganus*, including subspecies *abyssus*, *caliginus*, *cerberus*, *concolor*, *helleri*, *lutosus*, and *oreganus*; and *Crotalus viridis*, including subspecies *nuntius* and *viridis*, in the southwestern United States and northwestern Mexico. Unfilled symbol represents restricted type-locality of *C. oreganus*, "confluence of Columbia and Snake rivers, Washington" (Schmidt, 1953). Restricted type-locality of *C. viridis* given as Gross, Boyd County, Nebraska, by Smith and Taylor (1950b).

Crotalus oregonus—Van Denburgh, 1898, *Proc. Am. Philos. Soc.* 37:149–141[141].

Crotalus helleri Meek, 1906, *Field Columbian Mus. Zool. Ser.* 7:1–19[17, pl. 2]. Holotype: FMNH 1272. Type-locality: "San Jose, Lower California," San José [lat. 31°N], Baja California del Norte, Mexico, according to Klauber (1956:47).

Crotalus oreganus niger Kallert, 1927, *Bl. Aquar. Terrarienkd. Stuttgart* 38:372[372]. [Nomen nudum.]

Crotalus confluentus oreganus—Amaral, 1929c, *Bull. Antivenin Inst. Am.* 2:86–97[92].

Crotalus concolor Woodbury, 1929, *Bull. Univ. Utah* 20:3 pp. (unnumbered pages) [2, figs. 1 and 2]. Holotype: UU 306. Type-locality: "King's Ranch, Garfield Co., at base of the Henry Mts [Utah]." The ICZN validated *concolor* as the name for this taxon in Opinion 339, dated 17 March 1955, *Opinions Decls.* 10(6):181–200, suppressing *concolor* Jan, 1859, a synonym of *horridus*. *Crotalus v. concolor* Woodbury, 1929, has precedence over *C. v. decolor* Klauber, 1930. The taxonomic controversy surrounding these names was discussed by Woodbury (1958).

Crotalus confluentus lutosus Klauber, 1930, *Trans. San Diego Soc. Nat. Hist.* 6:95–144[100, pl. 10 (fig. 2)]. Holotype: SDSNH 1814 (formerly LMK 1814). Type-locality: "10 miles northwest of Abraham on the road to Joy, Millard County, Utah," USA.

Crotalus confluentus decolor Klauber, 1930, *Trans. San Diego Soc. Nat. Hist.* 6:95–144[111]. Holotype: FMNH 923. Type-locality: "Grand Junction, Mesa County, Colorado," USA. Woodbury (1942) presented arguments why his name, *Crotalus concolor*, should have precedence over Klauber's name.

Crotalus confluentus abyssus Klauber, 1930, *Trans. San Diego Soc. Nat. Hist.* 6:95–144[114, pl. 11 (fig. 1)]. Holotype: SDSNH 2216 (formerly LMK 2216). Type-locality: "Tanner Trail 300 ft. below the south rim of the Grand Canyon, Coconino County, Arizona [USA]; altitude approximately 7,000 ft."

Crotalus confluentus concolor—Woodbury, 1930, *Bull. Antivenin Inst. Am.* 4:23[23].

Crotalus viridis abyssus—Klauber, 1936b, *Trans. San Diego Soc. Nat. Hist.* 8:185–276[191].

Crotalus viridis concolor—Klauber, 1936b, *Trans. San Diego Soc. Nat. Hist.* 8:185–276[191].

Crotalus viridis lutosus—Klauber, 1936b, *Trans. San Diego Soc. Nat. Hist.* 8:185–276[191].

Crotalus viridis oreganus—Klauber, 1936b, *Trans. San Diego Soc. Nat. Hist.* 8:185–276[191].

Crotalus viridis decolor—Gloyd, 1940, *Chicago Acad. Sci. Spec. Publ.* (4):266 pp.[216, pl. 25 (fig. 2)].

Crotalus viridis helleri—Klauber, 1949b, *Trans. San Diego Soc. Nat. Hist.* 11:61–116[77, pl. 4 (fig. 2)].

Crotalus viridis cerberus—Klauber, 1949b, *Trans. San Diego Soc. Nat. Hist.* 11:61–116[83, pl. 5 (fig. 1)].

Crotalus viridis caliginis Klauber, 1949b, *Trans. San Diego Soc. Nat. Hist.* 11:61–116[90, pl. 5 (fig. 2)]. Holotype: SDSNH 2800 (formerly LMK 2800). Type-locality: "South Coronado Island, off the northwest coast of Baja California, Mexico."

Crotalus viridis decolor—Klauber, 1956, *Rattlesnakes*, 1st ed., 1:708 pp.[46, 55 (fig. 2:6), 79 (fig. 2:51)].

Crotalus viridis concolor—Klauber, 1972, *Rattlesnakes*, 2d ed., 1:740 pp.[51, 61 (fig. 2:6), 92 (fig. 2:66). Although the second edition of this important work uses the correct name, it is incorrectly attributed to Klauber instead of Woodbury.

While exploring the Columbia River Valley, he camped on the banks of the Spokane River, at the foot of a high peak on August 22. About 10 p.m. he was drawn away from a roaring fire by the evident alarm of his mule, and by a great rustling on the stream bank. On nearing the river, he beheld by the brilliant moonlight literally hundreds of *Crotalus horridus* [sic; *C. oreganus* occurs in this area] weaving around and across each other at a great pace, emitting an unbearable stench and beating their rattles on the granite rock.

—Wood, 1933, quoting Geyer, 1847

The snake symbolizes much of what is western about the West. It has seen and rattled at the mountain men, the fur trappers, the explorers, the Bunyanesque lumbermen, the cowboys, the farmers, the plainsmen and women plodding beside their wagons on the Oregon trail. Today, in dwindling numbers, its habitats with accelerating pace being destroyed and the object of human predation, it still hangs on, seeking to avoid discovery, defiant when discovered. It may not last long, though its angry buzz is as much a part of the western scene as the screech of a bobcat or the howl of a coyote. Cars run over it; bulldozers root it out; people kill it. Yet, in it remains something of nature and something of beauty.

—Shaw and Campbell, 1974

LOCAL NAME   Víbora de cascabel.

ENGLISH NAME   Western rattlesnake.

ETYMOLOGY   The species name is derived from Oregon, now a state in the northwestern United States, but previously a name encompassing the region from northern California to Alaska (ca. 1818–1846), and the Latin suffix -*anus*, meaning "belonging to." The origin of the name Oregon is not known with certainty, but it may be derived from the Spanish *orejón*, meaning "big ear," a term applied to local Indian tribes.

DISTRIBUTION   Southwestern Canada, much of the western half of the western United States, and as far south as northern Mexico (Map 103). In Canada *C. oreganus* occurs in southern British Columbia; in the western United States it is found in Washington, Oregon, western and southern Idaho, California, Nevada, Utah, Arizona, and probably west-central New Mexico; and in northern Mexico it occurs in western Baja California Norte and extreme northern Baja California Sur. This species has been reported on five islands (Ashton, 2000; Klauber, 1972) throughout its range. Three of these islands are located in freshwater bodies of water: Anaho Island in Pyramid Lake, Washoe County, Nevada; Rattlesnake Island in Clear Lake, Lake County, California; and Morro Rock in San Luis Obispo County, California. Rattlesnakes may no longer occur on Rattlesnake Island, and Morro Rock is now connected to the mainland by a causeway (Ashton, 2000). *Crotalus oreganus* occurs on two Pacific Islands: Santa Catalina Island, one of the Channel Islands about 32 km from the California mainland, and Isla Coronado del Sur, the largest of the four Coronado Islands, about 12 km west of the Mexican mainland. The vertical distribution in Mexico is from about sea level to above 2,500 m. Two subspecies of *C. oreganus* occur in Mexico: *C. o. helleri* along the Pacific coast and in the mountains of about the northern half of the peninsula of Baja California, and *C. o. caliginis* on Isla Coronado del Sur.

Distribution records are available for Arizona (Boundy, 1992; Coues, 1875; Durham, 1956; Eaton, 1935; Fowlie, 1965; Jones et al., 1981; Klauber, 1932a, 1935b; Little, 1940; Lowe et al., 1986; McKee and Bogert, 1934; Miller et al., 1982; Nickerson and Mays, 1970; Quaintance, 1935; K. L. Williams, 1960; Yarrow, 1875), California (Ashton, 2000; Bogert and Degenhardt, 1961; Cope, 1860a; DeLisle et al., 1986; Glaser, 1970; Hayes and Cliff, 1982; Klauber, 1927, 1930c, 1931a, 1932b; Lucas and Vindum, 2000; Meek, 1906; Savage, 1967; Spencer et al., 1998; Stebbins, 1972; Stejneger, 1893; Storer and Usinger, 1966; Van Denburgh, 1912), Colorado (Hammerson, 1982, 1999; Hammerson et al., 1991a—in part; Maslin, 1959), Idaho (Cope, 1884b; Evenden, 1946; Linder and Fichter, 1977; Nussbaum et al., 1983; Slater,

1941; Tanner, 1966b), Nevada (Ashton, 2000; Banta, 1965a, 1965b; Linsdale, 1940; Tanner, 1966b; Taylor, 1912; Van Denburgh and Slevin, 1921a), New Mexico (Degenhardt et al., 1996; Mello, 1978), Oregon (Anderson and Slater, 1941; Baird, 1859b; Cope, 1860a; Curran, 1935; Ferguson, 1952, 1954; Graf et al., 1939; Kozloff, 1976; Nussbaum et al., 1983), Utah (Cooper and Groves, 1859; Cope, 1872; Cox and Tanner, 1995; Eaton, 1935; Hensley, 1959; V. Tanner, 1927, 1930; W. Tanner, 1966b; Van Denburgh and Slevin, 1915; Wauer, 1964; Woodbury, 1931), Washington (Johnson, 1942, 1995; Kozloff, 1976; McAllister, 1995; Nussbaum et al., 1983; Owen, 1940; Slater, 1939; Svihla and Svihla, 1933), Wyoming (Ashton et al., 1997; Baxter and Stone, 1985; Schuett and Kraus, 1982b; Smith, 1963), Baja California and associated islands (Bostic, 1971; Cuesta-Terrón, 1931; Grismer, 1994b; Kauffeld, 1964; Klauber, 1949b; Mocquard, 1899b, 1908–1909; Murray, 1955; Savage, 1960, 1967; Schmidt, 1922; Smith et al., 1971; Van Denburgh, 1905; Van Denburgh and Slevin, 1914), the United States generally (Cope, 1860b; Glenn and Straight, 1982; Shaw and Campbell, 1974; Smith and Brodie, 1982; Stejneger and Barbour, 1943), British Columbia (Carl, 1968; Cowan, 1937; Gregory and Campbell, 1984; Kozloff, 1976; Logier and Toner, 1955; Mills, 1948; Slater, 1939), Mexico (Armstrong and Murphy, 1979; Campbell and Lamar, 1989; Cuesta-Terrón, 1931; Dugès, 1896a—as *lucifer*; Grismer, 1993, 2002; Jones, 1981; Klauber, 1952; Lemos-Espinal et al., 1994, 1997; Linsdale, 1932; Lockington, 1880; Martín del Campo, 1935, 1937a; Meek, 1906; Mosauer, 1936; Murphy, 1983a; Ottley and Hunt, 1981; Schmidt, 1922; Smith and Taylor, 1945; Smith et al., 1971; Starrett, 1993; Streets, 1877; Van Denburgh, 1896), and general distribution (Amaral, 1929c—in part; Boulenger, 1896b—in part; Cope, 1900; Ditmars, 1949; Garman, 1884b; Gloyd, 1940; Klauber, 1930b, 1949b, 1971, 1972; G. B. Pickwell, 1972; Savage, 1959; Stebbins, 1954, 1985; Stejneger, 1895; Van Denburgh, 1922b; Werner, 1922; Wright and Wright, 1957).

HABITAT In Mexico this species inhabits chaparral and desert; it enters pine-oak forest in the mountain ranges of northern Baja California. Basey (1988) found *C. oreganus* at 3,355 m above sea level in the Sierra Nevada of California. Tanner (1966b) found it in low brush and in oak-aspen habitats at elevations up to 9,000 feet (2,743 m), and Nussbaum et al. (1983) reported it from the desert regions of southeastern Oregon and southern Idaho. Jameson and Flury (1949) observed a specimen coiled at the entrance of a prairie dog (*Cynomys ludovicianus*) burrow in a tobosa-grama association. Little (1940) found *C. oreganus* to be common in the chaparral-woodland and pine-fir zones in central Arizona. Jones (1988) found *C. o. cerberus* in chaparral in Arizona. Murray (1955) collected *C. o. helleri* in "flat desert with hard-packed soil and a well developed vegetation of cardon, cirio, copal, ocotillo, *Yucca* and cholla." In southwestern Idaho, Diller and Wallace (1996) found *C. o. lutosus* to be confined almost exclusively to rocky habitats.

DESCRIPTION Snakes from the mainland commonly exceed 100 cm in TL; the maximum TL on record is 162.6 cm (Klauber, 1956). In a sample of 176 males and 143 females from a hibernaculum in north-central Idaho, males had an average length of 88.8 cm, and females averaged 69.2 cm (Diller and Wallace, 2002). Large adults from Isla Coronado del Sur (*C. o. caliginus*) are usually only 60–70 cm in overall length. There is a lot of variation throughout the range, with populations of stunted or very large snakes.

Populations of *C. oreganus* exhibit a considerable amount of ontogenetic variation. In general, juveniles have relatively distinct patterns, but these become progressively faded or obscured with age. The iris color is often similar to the ground color and may be gold, bronze, or various shades of tan, gray, or pink.

Crotalus o. oreganus has a dark brown, olive brown, dark gray, or occasionally black or pale yellowish ground color. There are large, dark, white-edged body blotches with uneven edges, and the blotches are wider than the interspaces between them. The lateral blotches are conspicuous on all but the darkest specimens, and usually are darker than the dorsal blotches. The white-bordered, dark brown postocular stripe is usually boldly indicated and extends from the eye to about the angle of the jaw. The rings on the proximal part of the tail are about the same color as the posterior body blotches, but these become progressively darker, and the distal 2 rings, including the base of the rattle, are usually black. The snout is usually marked with a large, dark brown blotch followed posteriorly by a pale border that forms transverse bars on the supraoculars. In some individuals from the southern part of the range the postocular stripe is ill defined and grades into the ground color on the side of the head (Pl. 892), and the dorsal blotches are large, dark, and have a relatively small pale area in the center. The venter is pale yellow, usually speckled or mottled with brown.

Crotalus o. abyssus has a pinkish, salmon, vermilion, pinkish tan, or pinkish gray ground color. Most specimens are buff to yellowish tan (L. Porras, pers. comm.). The dorsal body blotches are often ill-defined in adults but conspicuous in juveniles. The borders of these blotches are dark, sometimes with black edging or flecking, and the centers are only slightly or not at all darker than the ground color. Some snakes are uniformly colored with scarcely a trace of the dorsal pattern, and others retain juvenile coloration into adulthood. The postocular stripe varies from distinct to inconspicuous; the top of the head is marked with diffuse blotches and a pale transverse supraocular bar, or it may be uniformly colored. Adults reach about 1 m in length.

Crotalus o. caliginus has a pale tan, pale ash gray, dark gray, or olive green ground color with large, chocolate brown dorsal blotches that are darker peripherally. This is a handsome snake with the dorsal blotches standing in sharp contrast against the pale ground color. Posteriorly the blotches form uniformly brown crossbands that continue onto the tail. The distalmost tail bands or rings show no darkening. There is generally a dark brown spot on the muzzle and also several dark spots on the anterior of the supaoculars and prefrontal region (sometimes fused into a crossbar); the top of the head posterior to the pale supraocular crossbar is uniformly dark. Overall, snakes from Isla Coronado del Sur closely resemble those from the adjacent mainland but are more vividly colored.

Crotalus o. cerberus usually has a dark grayish, brownish black, reddish brown, or blackish ground color, but individual specimens may be quite pale with considerable yellow in the pattern (Pl. 904). Individuals may be uniformly dark without evidence of pattern, or with even darker dorsal blotches that are bordered anteriorly and posteriorly with white, cream, or yellow transverse rows of scales. The pale middorsal interspaces between dorsal blotches cover about 1–2 dorsal scales and become increasingly less vivid posteriorly. Dorsal blotches, if evident, are usually rectangular on the anterior and midbody, become subhexagonal more posteriorly, and are modified into crossbands just before the tail. The series of blotches on the sides of the body are only slightly darker than the ground color or may be obfuscated by the dark ground coloration. The postocular stripe is not bold in dark snakes but is quite evident in paler individuals. The sides of the head on almost black specimens are slightly darker than the top of the head, which is uniformly dark. The venter is heavily mottled with black or gray. Dark individuals of *C. o. cerberus* are remarkable for their ability to change their ground color from black to pale grayish tan within a short period (Klauber, 1972; Lowe et al., 1986; Nickerson and Mays, 1970). Adults commonly exceed 1 m in TL.

Crotalus o. concolor may have a pinkish, pale brown, yellow-brown, straw-colored, or reddish yellow-brown ground color with brown elliptical or rectangular dorsal blotches, but most individuals are gray or silvery (L. Porras, pers. comm.). The pattern is distinct in juveniles but usually becomes faded in adults, often becoming only slightly darker than the ground color. The edges of the dorsal blotches may be straight or uneven, and there may be a small amount of white edging around the blotches. Patterned snakes have several series of blotches on the sides of the body—dorsolateral, lateral, and ventrolateral—and over most of the body these tend to be diffuse, round, and discrete; but posteriorly the lateral series usually becomes fused with the dorsal blotches. In older snakes the blotches on the sides of the body become diffuse, and sometimes only the ventrolateral series of blotches is discernible or the sides are entirely unicolored. Usually at least a trace of the postocular stripe is present, and it may be boldly indicated in young snakes; it is 2 scales wide, extending from the eye to the rictus or beyond, and it may be fused with the first lateral body blotch, which is usually horizontally elongated. The top of the head is often marked with 8–12 dark brown symmetrical spots and streaks, or it may be unicolored. The venter is mostly yellow, but the lateral portions of ventrals sometimes have brown flecking or mottling. Schuett and Kraus (1982b) reported four *C. o. concolor* from Sweetwater County, Wyoming, with unusual color patterns that consisted of many coalesced dorsal blotches that often formed a broad stripe on part of the body. Specimens rarely exceed 60 cm in total length.

Crotalus o. helleri has a pale brown, gray-brown, or yellowish ground color with large, dark brown dorsal blotches that may or may not be paler in the center. The postocular stripe is moderately to very conspicuous. The postocular stripe of juveniles is bordered above by a distinct pale stripe, whereas on older, darker specimens it is set off from the head color by drab yellow or brown. Some individuals have a distinct pale crossbar across the supraoculars, posterior to which the head is uniformly dark; in some old, dark snakes the top of the head is mostly dark with only a trace or no hint of a pale supraorbital crossbar. The distal portion of the tail is bright orange in juveniles (Pl. 910), but as the snake matures, the orange is replaced with brown. The basal segment of the rattle and the dark tail band preceding it are brown in adults.

The ground color of juvenile to medium-sized *C. o. helleri* from the Baja California mainland is pale brownish gray. There are 27–43 dark brown, often diamond-shaped blotches that are edged in black and bordered by a single row of pale scales. These dorsal blotches are separated from one another middorsally by 1 or 2 pale scales. Of the 2 series of dark brown lateral blotches, the upper is the largest. The top of the head is brown, and a pale prefrontal bar connects the pale lower (anterior) borders of the dark brown to black postocular stripes on either side of the head; a pale bar extends across the supraoculars and frontal region followed posteriorly by a dark brown bar, and a pale upper temporal streak forms the upper (posterior) border of the postocular stripe and extends to above the angle of the jaw. The pale head markings that are so obvious on young snakes disappear in adults, and the top of the head becomes uniformly dark brown or black; the body of large snakes may

be blackish or very dark with an indistinct body pattern. There are 2–8 dark tail rings. The end of the tail has a long yellow or orange ring that gradually turns gray or black as the snake matures and is 1.5 to more than 2 times as long as the preceding black ring. The basal rattle segment is yellow or orange in juveniles and subadults, becoming black in older snakes. The venter has a moderate to heavy amount of dark mottling.

Crotalus o. lutosus usually has a buff, pale gray, pale brown, olive brown, or yellowish brown ground color and 32–49 dark brown to black subcircular, ellipsoidal, or rectangular dorsal body blotches that are often irregular in shape and wider than long with pale centers. The ground color of some populations is bright yellow or pinkish (L. Porras, pers. comm.). Posteriorly, the blotches merge with the lateral blotches, forming crossbands. The dorsal blotches are usually distinct with a bold black periphery, but larger individuals sometimes have a faded pattern. Alternatively, older specimens may have uniformly black blotches and a black dorsum of the head. The lateral blotches are indistinct or absent on the anterior part of the body but usually become more distinct posteriorly. The ventrolateral series of blotches, the most conspicuous of the series of blotches on the side of the body, is medium to dark brown without dark edging. The tail rings are about the same color as the posterior body blotches but become progessively darker distally. The markings on the side of the head are at best only moderately distinct, with the postocular stripe being 2–4 scales wide and grading into the ground color at about the angle of the jaw; some specimens lack a postocular stripe (Pl. 911). The postocular stripe is usually bordered below by a broad, pale stripe 2–3 scales wide that extends from the snout through the postnasal region to the lip border below the eye and then curves posteriorly along the supralabials to the rictus. A pale, dark-edged bar extends across the head through about the middle of the supraoculars in most snakes, including juveniles, but the top of the head is marked with diffuse or irregular black pigment on some specimens (Pl. 914) and is mostly black on others (Pl. 911). Smart (*in* Woodbury et al., 1951) described the ground color of *C. o. lutosus*, but his comments and comparisons include several distinct races of *C. oreganus*.

The rostral is usually higher than wide. One of the most distinctive features of *C. oreganus* is that it often has 3 or more (mode 4) internasals, a feature it shares with *C. viridis*. There are usually 2 canthals on each side, sometimes 3, rarely 4. The number of scales on the snout in front of a line between the anterior edges of the supraoculars ranges from 7 to 45, but most specimens have between 15 and 30. The number of intersupraoculars is likewise variable, with 4–6 most common. Usually there is a single loreal per side, but sometimes there are 2, or very rarely 3, especially in *C. o. cerberus*. The prenasal may or may not contact supralabial 1. There are 11–18 (usually 14 or 15) supralabials, 12–20 (usually 15 or 16) infralabials, 21–29 midbody dorsal scale rows (usually 25), 161–190 ventrals in males and 164–196 in females, 18–29 subcaudals in males and 15–25 in females, and usually 12 rattle-fringe scales. Specimens rarely exceed 1 m in overall length.

SIMILAR SPECIES A number of species of rattlesnakes having large dorsal blotches and reaching a moderate to large length are sympatric with *C. oreganus* in parts of its range, but all of these normally have only 2 internasals in contact with the rostral. The tail of *Crotalus atrox* has strongly contrasting rings of white and black, and the pale posterior border of the postocular stripe extends to the rictus (not to above the angle of the jaw). *Crotalus scutulatus* also has a tail with strongly contrasting rings of white and black and often has a crescent-shaped scale bordering the posteromedial side of each supraocular. *Crotalus ruber* has a reddish ground color, and the first pair of infralabials are transversely divided. *Crotalus enyo* is beetle-browed, with supraoculars inclined upward toward the lateral sides of the head; the tail lacks strongly contrasting pale and dark rings; and the scales in the prefrontal-frontal region are knobby. *Crotalus molossus* has a uniformly dark tail with no bands or rings evident and 4–6 large, flat scales in the internasal-prefrontal area. *Crotalus mitchellii* has prenasals that are not in contact with the rostral owing to the intervention of a series of small scales, and its pattern is often banded rather than blotched. *Crotalus tigris* has a pattern of 35 or more crossbands on the body, and *Sistrurus catenatus* has 9 large, symmetrical plates on top of the head.

REMARKS Except for the Neotropical rattlesnakes (sensu lato), the *C. viridis* complex has presented perhaps the most difficulties to systematists. Until recently, most followed the taxonomic arrangement presented by Klauber (1956). This scheme recognizes 9 subspecies: *abyssus, caliginus, cerberus, concolor, helleri, lutosus, nuntius, oreganus,* and *viridis.* Recently, however, several groups of researchers have presented data suggesting that some reassignments of taxonomic levels are warranted among these subspecies. Although they have presented different ideas on how to best treat the taxonomy of the *C. viridis* complex, they nevertheless have arrived at many of the same conclusions regarding the phylogeny.

The first to examine molecular variation in *C. viridis* (sensu lato) was Quinn (1987), who presented evidence for a multispecies complex. Murphy and Crabtree (1985a) and Crabtree and Murphy (1984) looked at certain aspects of isozymes, gene loci, and gene expression in a phylogenetic context, but their studies were limited to one population of *C. viridis* from Chouteau County, Montana, in which they addressed intrapopulational variation and variation in maternal-offspring allozymes.

Pook et al. (2000) analyzed mitochondrial DNA sequences from 1,345 base pairs of the genes for cytochrome *b* and NADH dehydrogenase subunit 4 and discovered two main clades, one from east and south of the Rocky Mountains that included populations conventionally placed with *C. v. viridis* and *C. v. nuntius,* and another from west of the Rocky Mountains that contained all of the other subspecies recognized by Klauber (1956). The phylogenetic pattern they obtained for the western clade did not completely correspond to current notions of subspecies, but in it *cerberus* represented the sister taxon to all other western populations. Aside from not recognizing *caliginus,* these authors refrained from making any direct taxonomic recommendations and suggested that further studies be undertaken. Glenn and Straight (1977) and Pook et al. (2000) noted that the venom of *C. v. concolor* is especially toxic. Glenn and Straight (1990) found that the northern Arizona population of *C. v. viridis* contains a "concolor toxin" that is probably attributable to intergradation with *C. v. concolor.*

Ashton and de Queiroz (2001) examined mitochondrial DNA sequence data from the D-loop region and ND2 gene from 26 populations and found that the various populations comprising *C. viridis* form a monophyletic group, but that two strongly divergent clades were present. One clade contained *viridis* and *nuntius* and the other contained all the other taxa. They recommended recognizing as separate species each of the major clades representing the *C. viridis* complex: *C. viridis* in the east and *C. oreganus* in the west. Interestingly, these two clades are divergent in body size variation: members of the western clade (*C. oreganus*) are smaller in cooler and more seasonal areas, whereas

individuals of the eastern clade (*C. viridis*) are larger in cooler and more seasonal environments (Ashton, 2001).

In the most recent and comprehensive study, Douglas et al. (2002) sampled 149 individuals from various populations, using several rapidly evolving mitochondrial DNA genes to analyze 169 base pairs of ATPase 6 and 509 base pairs of ATPase 8. These authors also identified eastern and western clades, with the eastern clade containing *viridis* and *nuntius,* and the western clade containing everything else. According to their analysis, *C. v. cerberus* is the sister taxon to the remainder of the western clade. They recommended that seven of the nine subspecies recognized by Klauber (1972) be elevated to full species status (*viridis, abyssus, cerberus, concolor, helleri, lutosus,* and *oreganus*). Additionally, Grismer (2002) elevated *caliginis* to species status.

There is general agreement among various investigators about the broad phylogenetic pattern of the *C. viridis* complex (Ashton and de Queiroz, 2001; Douglas et al., 2002; Pook et al., 2000). It is worth noting that the same general pattern was found earlier by Quinn (1987), who identified two distinct lineages using morphological and molecular data. Unfortunately, Quinn's dissertation was published only in abstract form. Most of the controversy has arisen in attempting to classify the populations of the *C. viridis* complex. How many of the lineages should be recognized as species? We have taken a semiconservative approach in recognizing the two major clades representing eastern and western populations as separate species. We could be persuaded as well to recognize *C. v. cerberus*—the apparent sister taxon to the western clade—but think it prudent to await further evidence and justification for this action.

As recognized herein, *C. oreganus* comprises seven subspecies. *Crotalus o. oreganus* (Pls. 889–893) has tail rings that are all about of the same length, and the last 1–2 rings (including the base of the rattle) are black; there are 161–190 ventrals in males and 170–189 in females, 18–29 subcaudals in males and 15–24 in females, and 20–41 dorsal body blotches. This subspecies is distributed in British Columbia, Oregon, western Idaho, and California.

Crotalus o. abyssus (Pls. 894–900), occurring in the Colorado River system of northern Arizona and south-central Utah, may have a reddish or pinkish tinge in the ground color, the dorsal body blotches are faded or absent in adults (and sometimes juveniles), and there are 173–185 ventrals in males and 179–191 in females, 23–29 subcaudals in males and 18–24 in females, and 36–48 dorsal body blotches.

Crotalus o. caliginus (Pl. 901), occurring only on Isla Sur of the Islas de los Coronados off Baja California Norte, has little in the way of scutellation or color pattern to distinguish it from the population of *C. oreganus helleri* on the adjacent mainland, but it differs in being a smaller snake (maximum recorded size 68.3 cm TL versus 134.6 cm for *lutosus,* according to Klauber, 1972) and in having a proportionately smaller head (Klauber, 1938a). There are 167–174 ventrals in males and 171–179 in females, 22–28 subcaudals in males and 15–23 in females, and 27–37 dorsal body blotches.

Crotalus o. cerberus (Pls. 902–904) ranges across central and southern Arizona to extreme western New Mexico. The ground color is often very dark, and there are 161–180 ventrals in males and 164–184 in females, 20–26 subcaudals in males and 16–24 in females, and 25–46 dorsal body blotches.

Crotalus o. concolor (Pls. 905–908), from eastern Utah and western Colorado, has blotches that are only faintly indicated or absent in adults and is relatively small (usually less than 65 cm). There are 163–183 ventrals in males and 171–182 in females, 21–29 subcaudals in males and 16–22 in females, and 34–52 dorsal body blotches.

Crotalus o. helleri (Pls. 909 and 910) inhabits the Pacific coast and foothills of southern California and about the northern half of the peninsula of Baja California. The ultimate tail ring is not darker than those on the proximal part of the tail, and usually the last tail ring is at least twice as long as the other tail rings. There are 162–184 ventrals in males and 166–189 in females, 19–29 subcaudals in males and 15–25 in females, and 27–43 body blotches.

Crotalus o. lutosus (Pls. 911–914), of Nevada and adjacent portions of California, Oregon, Idaho, and Utah, usually has a buff or drab ground color (this varies ontogenetically) and interspaces between dorsal blotches about as long as or longer than the length of the dorsal blotches. There are 171–189 ventrals in males and 174–196 in females, 20–29 subcaudals in males and 16–24 in females, and 32–49 dorsal body blotches.

Crotalus polystictus (Cope, 1865)
(Fig. 209, Map 104, Pls. 915–918)

Crotalus lugubris Jan, 1859b, *Rev. Mag. Zool.* (Paris) (2)10: 148–157[153, 156–157]. Syntypes (4): two specimens in the Milan Museum [MSNM], one specimen in the Westphal-Castelnau Collection (Montpellier), and one in the Paris Museum [MNHN]. Klauber (1940a:17) designated the Westphal-Castelnau specimen [=*Crotalus polystictus*] as a paralectotype in order to conserve the name *Crotalus triseriatus*. This same specimen is the holotype, by indication, of *Crotalus lugubris* var. *multimaculata* Jan (1863a) and identified as *Crotalus polystictus* by Klauber (1940a:17). Type-locality: "Mexique."

Crotalus lugubris var. *multimaculata* Jan, 1863a, *Elenco Sist. Ofidi*, 143 pp.[124]. Holotype: based on the specimen from "Coll. Westphal" that was a syntype of *Crotalus lugubris* Jan, 1859; present location unknown. Type-locality: "Messico" [Mexico]. Smith and Taylor (1950b:330) proposed a restriction to "Tupátaro, Guanajuato, Mexico." [A valid description by indication

to the description of the paralectotype of *Crotalus lugubris* Jan, 1859 identified as *Crotalus polystictus*. Suppressed by ICZN, 1955, Opinion 366, *Opinions Decls.* 11(16):231–244, in favor of *polysticta* Cope, 1865.]

Caudisona polysticta Cope, 1865, *Proc. Acad. Nat. Sci. Philadelphia* 17:185–198[191]. Type(s): none designated, according to Klauber (1972:45). Type-locality: "Table Land, Mexico." A proposed restriction to "Tupátaro, Guanajuato, Mexico," was made by Smith and Taylor (1950b:330).

Crotalus lugubris var. *multimaculata*—Jan and Sordelli, 1874, *Icon. Gén. Ophid.*, livr. 46:[index to pl. 3 (fig. 3)]. [Also based on the "Mexique" specimen from the Westphal-Castelnau Collection. Suppressed by ICZN, 1955, Opinion 366, *Opinions Decls.* 11(16):231–244.]

Crotalus polystictus—Cope, *in* Yarrow, *in* Wheeler, 1875, *Rep. Geog. Geol. Explor. Surv. West 100th Merid.* 5:509–584[533].

Crotalus Jimenezii Dugès, 1877, *Naturaleza* (Mexico) 4:1–29[23, 34, pl. 1 (figs. 18–20)]. Syntypes (5): USNM 46508 from Guanajuato, Mexico, is labeled "Duplicate Type" according to Smith and Necker (1944:187) and Cochran (1961:170). Two other specimens (USNM 24448, USNM 26152) from "Guanajuato" may be syntypes, according to Thireau (1991:3). Finally, two specimens (MNHN 1883.284, MNHN 1883.288) from "200 km a l'Est de Guadalajare [*sic*] [Mexico]" also may be syntypes, according to Thireau (1991:3). Type-locality: "Silao [Guanajuato], Colima et Guadalajara [Jalisco]," Mexico. Smith and Taylor (1950b:334) suggested restriction to "Guadalajara, Mexico." Dugès's (1877) description of *Crotalus jimenezii* appeared in a paper that was published over two years and in four entregas, with the index and plate in the fifth. According to Smith's (1942:95–96) review of the dates of publication of *La Naturaleza*, volume 4, entrega 1, pp. 1–16 appeared in 1876, and entregas 2–5, pp. 17–80 in 1877. McDiarmid et al. (1999) detected a discrepancy in the inclusive pages of the entregas as given by Smith (entrega 1 includes pp. 1–8; entrega 2, 9–16; entrega 3, 17–24) but adopted his publication dates for the pages as correct.

Crotalus triseriatus var. *jimenezii*—Garman, 1884a [dated 1883], *Mem. Mus. Comp. Zool.* 8:1–185[176]. Cope (1884a) stated in error that Garman spelled the subspecies epithet as *ximmesii*.

Fig. 209. Newborn *Crotalus polystictus*. Female parent from near Tapalpa, Jalisco, Mexico.

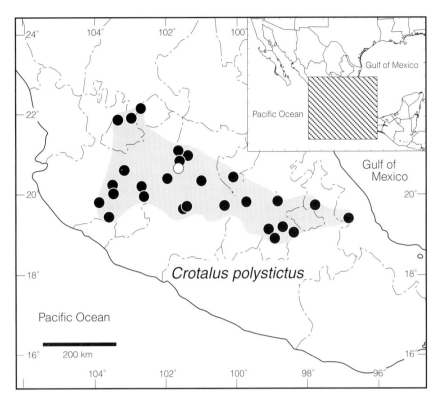

Map 104. Distribution of *Crotalus polystictus* in central Mexico. Unfilled symbol represents type-locality, restricted to Tupátaro, Guanajuato, Mexico, by Smith and Taylor (1950a:330).

Crotalus polystictus—Boulenger, 1896b, *Cat. Snakes British Mus.* 3:727 pp.[582].

Crotalus polystictus—Klauber, 1972, *Rattlesnakes*, 2d ed., 1:740 pp.[44, 63 (fig. 2:8), 82 (fig. 2:46)].

Here we were near the source of the Rio Santiago, where it flows from Lake Chapala. . . . At the great marsh, . . . many ebony rattlesnakes lived a semi-aquatic life, slipping, when disturbed, from the damp mounds, and undulating through the black water, like the moccasins in a Florida cypress swamp.

—Beebe, 1905, describing what probably was *C. polystictus* seen in his travels through Jalisco

The *polystictus* which I collected at the mouth of Rio Lerma, Lake Chapala, Jalisco, Mexico, were extremely abundant among the rushes. . . . This was a flooded swamp land, and the snakes were above the water. They would usually dive into the water when approached, but sometimes they would allow the canoe to come within arm's reach. All specimens were far from land. At the time, I did not realize the value of the find, and thinking them a very common species, did not collect as many as I could have secured.

—Ruthling, *in* Klauber, 1956

LOCAL NAMES   Chiauhcótl, chiáuitl, tlehua (Nahuatl), hocico de puerco, tziripa (Tarascan, according to León, 1889), víbora de cascabel.

ENGLISH NAME   Mexican lance-headed rattlesnake.

ETYMOLOGY   The species epithet is derived from the Greek *poly*, meaning "many," and *sticto*, meaning "spotted," an allusion to the pattern on the skin.

DISTRIBUTION   The southern portion of the Mexican Plateau from west-central Veracruz westward across central Puebla, the Distrito Federal, northern Michoacán, southwestern Querétaro, southern Guanajuato, central and eastern Jalisco, and southern Zacatecas (Map 104). Although not documented by specimens, *C. polystictus* probably occurs or occurred until recently in Colima, Tlaxcala, and Aguascalientes; literature reports exist for

these states and Hidalgo. Most of the range lies within the Mesa Central, but in the northwest this species occurs in the eastern outlying ranges of the southern portion of the Sierra Madre Occidental, and may occur as far north as southern Durango. The vertical distribution is from about 1,450 to 2,600 m.

The following works refer to this species: Armstrong and Murphy, 1979; Beebe, 1905; Boulenger, 1896b; Campbell, 1979b; Cope, 1860a, 1865, 1879, 1884b, 1885a, 1887, 1900; Cuesta-Terrón, 1921b, 1931 (as *triseriatus*, in part); Duellman, 1961, 1965b; Dugès, 1869 (as *lugubris*), 1876–1877, 1888, 1890, 1896a; Garman, 1884b; Gloyd, 1940; Herrera, 1890, 1891; Jan and Sordelli, 1874; Klauber, 1936b, 1938a, 1940a, 1952, 1971, 1972; León, 1889; Martín del Campo, 1935, 1937a, 1940a, 1950; McCranie, 1976; Mocquard, 1908–1909; Pérez-Higareda and Smith, 1991; Sigala-Rodríguez, 1996; Sigala-Rodríguez and Vázquez-Díaz, 1996; Smith, 1943a, 1970; Smith and Necker, 1944; Smith and Pérez-Higareda, 1965; Smith and Smith, 1969; Smith and Taylor, 1945; Troschel, 1866; Velasco, 1890a, 1890b; Werner, 1922; and Wilson and McCranie, 1979a.

HABITAT   The broad valleys, gently rolling plains, and grassy meadows of the highlands of the Mexican Plateau in mesquite-grassland, pine-oak forests, and openings in forests comprised mostly of pine, often in rocky outcroppings or old lava flows. This snake has been extirpated over most of its range but has managed to survive locally, and in a few areas remains abundant. Numerous gopher burrows and/or massive rock walls in certain regions provide retreats helping to ensure its survival. Apparently, some populations living near highland lakes or marshes subject to seasonal flooding were at one time semi-aquatic, but none of these populations is known to be extant.

DESCRIPTION   Adults of this medium-sized rattlesnake usually attain a TL of 70–80 cm, although exceptional specimens may approach 100 cm. The head is particularly slender, its width being less than 60% of its length (most other rattlesnakes have head widths that are 70–80% of the head length).

The ground color is buff, tan, pale brown, pale gray, to almost white, often becoming pale golden or reddish brown middorsally. The dark brown pattern is distinctive and unique among rattlesnakes. A series of 30–47 horizontally elongated, subelliptical or oval body blotches is present; anteriorly, the blotches tend to be arranged in a dorsolateral position, but posteriorly they usually become more circular and may or may not merge across the midline to form individual middorsal blotches. The dorsolateral blotches as well as other blotches are black edged. In addition to the paravertebral blotches, there are 2 series of large lateral blotches and a series of small ventrolateral blotches. The blotches of the uppermost lateral series are usually horizontally elongated anteriorly but become subcircular by midbody; the lower lateral series comprises subcircular or vertically elongated blotches. The blotches of the ventrolateral series tend to be roundish. The tail has 4–7 crossbands; the proximal bands are separated by the ground color of the body, and the distal bands are separated by pale gray pigment.

Markings on the side of the head include a large spot below the pit that extends to the infralabials, a large spot extending from the lower margin of the eye to almost the margin of the upper lip, and a broad postocular stripe that extends from near the posterior edge of the eye to, or over, the rictus. The top of the head is marked with a pair of prefrontal spots, often somewhat triangular; a pair of smaller parietal spots; and a pair of broad upper temporal streaks that extend anteriorly to the supraoculars, and posteriorly usually to a level above the third or fourth supralabial and continuing to the last supralabial. The upper temporal streaks sometimes extend posteriorly past the rictus. The pale color separating the prefrontal spots and upper temporal streaks forms a prominent transverse bar across the center of each supraocular. A large spot is present on the side of the head posterior to the rictus; either the postocular or upper temporal stripe may merge with this spot in some specimens.

There are 2–4 small dark spots and irregular dark brown stippling along the infralabials. On the anterior fifth of the belly the ventrals are mostly white or yellow, but posteriorly they become heavily stippled or mottled with dark brown pigment that is frequently concentrated medially along the anterior margin of each ventral. The subcaudals are yellowish with dark stippling and have irregular large dark spots that fall mostly at levels between the dark crossbands on the dorsum of the tail. The upper third of the iris is yellow or tan, the lower two-thirds is darkly speckled with black. The proximal rattle segment is dark brown to black. The tongue is black.

The rostral is higher than wide. A pair of large internasals may meet at the midline, or, more frequently, a small medial scale or a pair of small medial internasals separates a pair of large, crescent-shaped internasals that lies over the nasals. A single canthal is located on each side; canthals are often separated from one another by 2 elongated intercanthals. The internasal-prefrontal area is thus typically covered by 2–4 internasals, 2 canthals, and 2 intercanthals, for a total of 6–8 scales. There almost always are 3 intersupraoculars between the anterior level of the supraoculars; the range is 2–5. The most lateral internasal is in contact with the upper loreal; the upper preocular is not vertically divided; usually 2 subequal loreals on each side do not reach the supralabials but do intervene to preclude postnasal–upper preocular contact. Usually the anterior subocular is in contact with supralabials 4 and 5. The prenasal is in contact with supralabial 1, and the prenasal is usually indented above by a crescent-shaped lateral internasal (canthal). There are 1–3 prefoveals; 12–15 (usually 13 or 14) supralabials; 11–16 (mode 14) infralabials; 25–29 (usually 27) midbody dorsal scale

rows; 161–177 ventrals in males and 167–187 in females; 25–29 subcaudals in males and 17–25 in females; and usually 10 rattle-fringe scales, the posterior tips of which may be serrated.

SIMILAR SPECIES Other species of rattlesnakes occurring within the range of C. polystictus include C. triseriatus, C. pusillus, and C. aquilus. Crotalus polystictus is easily distinguished from all by its distinct color pattern of elliptical dorsolateral blotches and the large, distinct spot under the eye.

REMARKS We have found this species active by day and at night. It appears to be especially common in rocky regions or areas with numerous gopher burrows in which it may take refuge.

Crotalus pricei Van Denburgh, 1895
(Map 105, Pls. 919–928)

Crotalus pricei Van Denburgh, 1895b, Proc. California Acad. Sci. (2)5:856–857[856]. Holotype: CAS-SU 1702 (formerly SU 1702). Type-locality: "Huachuca Mts. [Cochise Co.], Arizona."

Crotalus triseriatus pricei—Klauber, in Githens and George, 1931, Bull. Antivenin Inst. Am. 5:31–34[33].

Crotalus triseriatus miquihuanus Gloyd, 1940, Chicago Acad. Sci. Spec. Publ. 4:1–266 [102, pl. 10]. Holotype: FMNH 30850. Type-locality: "Cerro Potosí, near Galeana, Nuevo León" [Mexico].

Crotalus pricei pricei—Smith, 1946b, Univ. Kansas Sci. Bull. 31:75–101[79].

Crotalus pricei miquihuanus—Smith, 1946b, Univ. Kansas Sci. Bull. 31:75–101[79].

LOCAL NAMES Mountain sidewinder (Arizona), chachámuri (Tarahumara name fide Conant, 1997), víbora de cascabel (Mexico).

ENGLISH NAME Twin-spotted rattlesnake.

ETYMOLOGY The specific epithet is a patronym honoring W. W. Price, the collector of the holotype.

DISTRIBUTION In the western portion of its range this species occurs from the mountainous regions of southeastern Arizona southward through the Sierra Madre Occidental in Mexico, including northeastern Sonora and western Chihuahua and Durango. In the east this species is known from the Sierra Madre Oriental of southeastern Coahuila, southern Nuevo León, southwestern Tamaulipas, and north-central San Luis Potosí (Map 105). Crotalus pricei is known from at least four mountain ranges in Arizona: Chiricahua, Pinaleño (Graham), Huachuca, and Santa Rita. There is a slight possibility that it occurs in the Peloncillo and Dos Cabezas Mountains of southeastern Arizona as well (see Johnson and Mills, 1982; Pilsbry and Ferriss, 1919), but confirmation is needed. Reports of C. pricei from the Santa Catalina Mountains (Klauber, 1936b; Van Denburgh, 1922b; MVZ specimen) are almost certainly in error (fide Prival, 2000). It has been suggested that C. pricei may occur in eastern Sinaloa and northern Nayarit, but no specimens have been collected there. A record for Aguascalientes was verified by Campbell and Lamar (1989). The elevational distribution is from about 1,850 to at least 3,203 m.

Distribution information or records are available for Arizona (Cope, 1900; Fowlie, 1965; Gloyd, 1937; Kauffeld, 1943b; Leviton, 1953; Lowe, 1964; Lowe et al., 1986; Nickerson and Mays, 1970; Shaw and Campbell, 1974; Stebbins, 1985; Stejneger, 1902; Stejneger and Barbour, 1943; Van Denburgh, 1895b, 1922b; Woodin, 1953), Aguascalientes (Klauber, 1972; Sigala-Rodríguez and Vázquez-Díaz, 1996; Wilson and McCranie, 1979a—as Crotalus sp.), Chihuahua (Conant, 1997; Domínguez et al., 1974; Dunn, 1936; Lemos-Espinal et al., 2000b; Smith, 1939, 1943a;

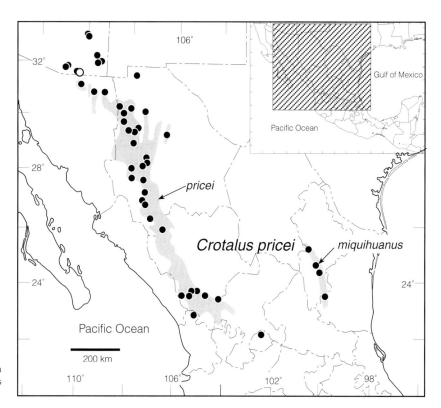

Map 105. Distribution of *Crotalus pricei* in northern Mexico and Arizona, USA. Unfilled symbol represents type-locality.

Tanner, 1985; Taylor and Knobloch, 1940; Van Devender and Lowe, 1977), Coahuila (Axtell and Sabath, 1963), Durango (Auth et al., 2000; Chrapliwy and Fugler, 1955; Drake, 1958; Webb, 1984; Webb and Baker, 1962), Nuevo León (Smith, 1944a), Tamaulipas (Smith, 1946b), Mexico generally (Armstrong and Murphy, 1979; Klauber, 1952; Martín del Campo, 1937a, 1953; Smith and Taylor, 1945), and throughout the range (Gloyd, 1940; Klauber, 1952, 1971, 1972; McCranie, 1980b; Smith, 1946b; Wright and Wright, 1957). Klauber (1934) showed that the record of *C. pricei* for New Mexico reported by Van Denburgh (1924) was actually based on a specimen of *C. viridis* (USNM 52273).

HABITAT Pine-oak forest or woodland, usually in areas of volcanic rock or extensive limestone outcroppings; often in talus slides on south-facing slopes. In Arizona this species occurs in Madrean montane conifer forest and Madrean evergreen woodland (Brown, 1994; Prival et al., 2002). Near Yepómera, Chihuahua, it is found in rocky habitats in woodlands and forests (Van Devender and Lowe, 1977). In Durango, Mexico, *C. pricei* has been found in open grassy meadows and rolling hillsides covered with manzanita and scrub oaks (Armstrong and Murphy, 1979). It has been found among logs, stumps, and piles of dead branches in logged areas (Bryson et al., 2002b).

DESCRIPTION This is a small rattlesnake; adults generally reach a TL of no more than 50–60 cm; the largest specimen known is 66 cm. The largest specimen in a series of 127 snakes from Arizona reported on by Prival et al. (2002) was a male 57.2 cm in TL. Males attain slightly greater lengths than females.

The ground color is gray, bluish gray, brownish gray, or medium to reddish brown, generally with fine brown speckling. The middorsal blotches tend to be divided medially forming a pattern of 39–64 pairs of small, dark brown or gray paravertebral blotches. The dorsal blotches of specimens from the Sierra Madre Oriental and, less frequently, the Sierra Madre Occidental may be undivided medially. Dorsal blotches are often bordered with dark brown or black that is edged with white. There are 5–10 indistinct crossbands on the tail, and the basal segment of the rattle is orange to reddish orange. Laterally, the 3 alternating series of dark spots tend to become obscure in adults. Some specimens lack the contrasting borders of the dorsal spots or, more rarely, lack the blotches altogether. A dark postocular stripe extends from the lower posterior edge of the eye to the angle of the jaw. The labials are white, cream, or pinkish, and heavily stippled with gray or black, especially anteriorly. The throat is usually pale also, but the ventrals become increasingly more suffused with black and posteriorly may be almost entirely black.

The variability of the color pattern is exemplified by four adults captured at Los Bancos in Durango and described by Armstrong and Murphy (1979:40): "One individual had the typical coloration of a slate-gray background with brown dorsal spots. The second example exhibited a blue-gray background with rusty colored spots. The third specimen was overall salmon-pink with tan spotting, and a fourth snake was a completely patternless light tan."

The rostral is usually wider than high. There are 2 large internasals. A single canthal (rarely 2) is usually present on each side, and there are 4–11 scales in the internasal-prefrontal area. Two or 3 scales separate the supraoculars. The prenasal curves over the top of the postnasal, and the first supralabial is in broad contact with both the prenasal and postnasal. One loreal (sometimes 2) is present on each side; the postnasal and upper preocular are not in contact. The upper preocular is not divided vertically, and the anterior subocular touches several supralabials (usually 3 and 4) under the eye. There are 8–10 (usually 9) supralabials, 8–11 (usually 10) infralabials, 19–23 (usually 21) midbody dorsal scale rows, 137–162 ventrals in males and 143–171 in females, and 21–33 subcaudals in males and 18–27 in females.

SIMILAR SPECIES Several other small montane rattlesnakes may occur sympatrically with or geographically close to *C. pricei*. *Crotalus willardi* can be distinguished from *C. pricei* by its sharp canthus rostralis and more numerous midbody dorsal scale rows (25–29), supralabials (12–17), and infralabials (12–16). Many specimens of *C. willardi* have distinctive pale facial stripes that further distinguish them from *C. pricei*. *Crotalus lepidus* usually has a pattern of widely spaced crossbands or large mid-dorsal blotches; specimens from along the Sinaloa-Durango border may have small dorsal spots, but these are not arranged in paravertebral pairs. Unlike *C. pricei*, *C. lepidus* (in the region of sympatry) has an upper preocular that is usually vertically divided and usually has more midbody dorsal scale rows, supralabials, and infralabials (see Table 51). There are 13–38 primary body blotches in *C. lepidus* and 39–64 (usually arranged in pairs) in *C. pricei*. *Crotalus triseriatus* is not known to be sympatric with *C. pricei*, but their ranges are almost parapatric in the vicinity of the Nayarit-Durango border. *Crotalus triseriatus* has unpaired dorsal blotches and usually more midbody dorsal scale rows than *C. pricei*.

REMARKS A specimen (UMMZ 110878) from west of Rincón de Romos in the Sierra Fria, Aguascalientes, was hypothesized either to represent an isolated population of *C. pricei* or to belong to a novel taxon. Additional material (Pl. 927) revealed the former to be correct (Campbell and Lamar, 1989).

Two subspecies of *C. pricei* are recognized: *C. p. pricei* (Pls. 919–923) of the Sierra Madre Occidental and *C. p. miquihuanus* (Pls. 924–926) of the Sierra Madre Oriental. The population inhabiting the Sierra Fria of Aguascalientes (Pls. 927 and 928) has not been allocated to subspecies. The characteristics purported to distinguish *C. p. miquihuanus* from *C. p. pricei* are brown rather than gray ground color, middorsal blotches less frequently divided medially, less subdivision of the head plates, and fewer ventral scales. The latter characteristic is perhaps the most reliable for purposes of identification; there are 137–143 ventrals in *C. p. miquihuanus* and 149–171 in *C. p. pricei*.

Amaral (1927f, 1927g) confused at least three species (*C. aquilus*, *C. pricei*, and *C. triseriatus*), all of which he included in a single taxon, *C. triseriatus*.

Crotalus pusillus Klauber, 1952
(Map 106, Pls. 929 and 930)

Crotalus triseriatus—Gadow, 1908, *Through Southern Mexico*, 527 pp.[513]. [In part.]
Crotalus triseriatus triseriatus—Klauber, 1936b, *Trans. San Diego Soc. Nat. Hist.* 8:185–276[192, 248]. [In part, according to Klauber (1952:34).]
Crotalus pusillus Klauber, 1952, *Bull. Zool. Soc. San Diego* (26):1–143[34]. Holotype: FMNH 39112. Type-locality: "Tancítaro, Michoacán, Mexico, altitude 5000 feet."

LOCAL NAME   Víbora de cascabel.

ENGLISH NAME   Tancitaran dusky rattlesnake.

ETYMOLOGY   The species epithet is derived from the Latin *pusillus*, meaning "very small," an allusion to the size attained by this taxon.

DISTRIBUTION   West-central Mexico in the highlands of the Sierra de Coalcomán in southwestern Michoacán and the western portion of the Transverse Volcanic Cordillera from the Nevado de Colima (and probably the Volcán de Colima) in south-central Jalisco across the Sierra de los Tarascos to near Carápan in Michoacán (Map 106). A major hiatus in the distribution occurs where the Sierra de Coalcomán is separated from the highlands of the Mexican Plateau by the headwaters of the Río Tepalcatepec and the Río Ahuijullo Depression. The vertical distribution is from 1,525 to 2,380 m.

Distribution records are given in Armstrong and Murphy, 1979; Capocaccia, 1961; Duellman, 1961, 1965b; Klauber, 1952, 1971, 1972; McCranie, 1983; Schmidt and Shannon, 1947 (in part, as *triseriatus*); and Smith and Taylor, 1966.

HABITAT   Pine-oak forest, usually in areas of volcanic rock or extensive limestone outcroppings.

DESCRIPTION   Large adult males may exceed 50 cm in TL; females are smaller. The largest specimen known (FMNH 37048) is 68.2 cm in TL.

The ground color is gray-brown or, rarely, fawn. A reddish brown cast may intervene between the 33–50 dark brown mid-

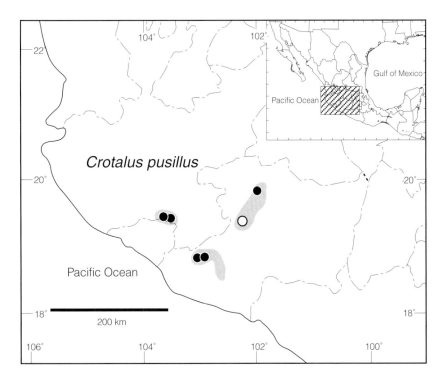

Map 106. Distribution of *Crotalus pusillus* in west-central Mexico. Unfilled symbol represents type-locality.

dorsal body blotches. Duellman (1961) noted that specimens from Cerro Tancítaro tend to have fewer dorsal blotches (33–46) than snakes from the Sierra de Coalcomán (40–50). Dorsal blotches are sometimes bordered with black and narrowly and irregularly edged with white. A dark brown postocular stripe that is distinctly pale bordered above and below extends from the lower posterior edge of the eye to the angle of the jaw; the supralabials below this stripe usually are mostly pale with fine brown peppering, and anteriorly the supralabials become heavily stippled with dark pigment. A distinctive primary series of dark brown lateral blotches is present; each lateral blotch lies opposite a dorsal blotch, from which it is separated by a pale interspace. Two other series of lateral blotches may be present, both lying on a vertical line running between the dorsal blotches, one series above and the other series below the level of the primary series of lateral blotches; however, these accessory series of lateral blotches are indistinct or absent in many specimens. A dark brown subocular spot usually borders the lip margin, and a pair of nape blotches precedes the middorsal series of blotches. Head markings are often present, including a pair of occipital spots, an upper temporal streak on either side, and an ill-defined bar across the top of the snout in front of the eyes. The infralabials are mostly pale with fine brown peppering and clumps of pigment forming spots that often lie along the infralabial sutures. The gular region and anterior ventrals are finely speckled with brown pigment that becomes progressively heavier and darker posteriorly, so that the subcaudals become dark gray to black. The iris is gold to copper above and dark brown below. The proximal rattle segment is dark gray to black.

The rostral is wider than high. The anterior portion of the snout is covered by 4 scales: 2 internasals and 2 prefrontals (canthals). The prefrontals are most often bordered posteriorly by 3 intersupraoculars, but sometimes by 1, 2, or 4 scales. The anterior subocular is in contact with the supralabial series, usually supralabials 4 and 5; the single loreal does not touch the supralabials; there are 1–5 prefoveals; and the prenasal is not in contact with the loreal. There are 11–13 (usually 12) supralabials, 10–13 (usually 11) infralabials, 23–25 (usually 23) midbody dorsal scale rows, 152–162 ventrals in males and 150–162 in females, 28–33 subcaudals in males and 25–29 in females, and usually 8 rattle-fringe scales.

SIMILAR SPECIES *Crotalus pusillus* bears a striking resemblance to *C. triseriatus*, and these species are sympatric in a portion of their ranges. The most salient character that distinguishes them is the presence of 2 more or less symmetrical prefrontals in *C. pusillus*, whereas *C. triseriatus* has 3 or more irregular scales immediately posterior to the internasals. The only other small montane rattlesnake that is sympatric with *C. pusillus* is a population representing a new species on Cerro Tancítaro (see Remarks for *C. transversus*); its members have a poorly defined postocular stripe and 21 dorsal scale rows at midbody (Campbell, 1982a).

REMARKS We have seen this snake active only by day; nighttime temperatures within its range are cool and apparently restrict its activity.

Crotalus ravus Cope, 1865
(Fig. 210, Map 107, Pls. 931–939)

Crotalus ravus Cope, 1865, *Proc. Acad. Nat. Sci. Philadelphia* 17:185–198[191]. Cotypes: USNM 25050, 25051. Type-locality: tableland of Mexico. Smith and Taylor (1950b:351) restricted the type-locality to Totalco, Veracruz.

Caudisona rava—Cope, 1875, *Bull. U.S. Natl. Mus.* (1):104 pp.[33].

Crotalus miliarius var. *ravus*—Garman, 1884a [dated 1883], *Mem. Mus. Comp. Zool.* 8:1–185[120, 177].

Crotalophorus ravus—Cope, 1885b [dated 1884], *Proc. Am. Philos. Soc.* 22:379–404[382].

Sistrurus ravus—Boulenger, 1896b, *Cat. Snakes British Mus.* 3:727 pp.[571].

Crotalus (Sistrurus) ravus—Hoge, 1966 [dated 1965], *Mem. Inst. Butantan* 32:109–184[161].

Sistrurus ravus ravus—Harris and Simmons, 1978b, *Bull. Maryland Herpetol. Soc.* 14:105–211[135].

Sistrurus ravus brunneus Harris and Simmons, 1978b, *Bull. Maryland Herpetol. Soc.* 14:105–211[135]. Holotype: AMNH 102916. Type-locality: "1.7 mi E Ixtlán de Juárez (Vivero Rancho Teja), Oaxaca, Mexico, in pine-oak woodland, at an elevation of 7400 ft."

Sistrurus ravus lutescens Harris and Simmons, 1978b, *Bull. Maryland Herpetol. Soc.* 14:105–211[136]. Holotype: UCM 9124. Type-locality: "Huitzilac, Morelos, Mexico." [Placed in the synonymy of *Sistrurus r. ravus* by Campbell and Armstrong (1979:305).]

Sistrurus ravus exiguus Campbell and Armstrong, 1979, *Herpetologica* 35:304–317[310, figs. 6 and 7]. Holotype: UTA R4533.

Fig. 210. Lateral aspect of head of *Crotalus ravus brunneus*, male, 66.3 cm TL, UTA R-12613: from 12.4 km west of Totontepec, Oaxaca, Mexico, elevation 2,524 m.

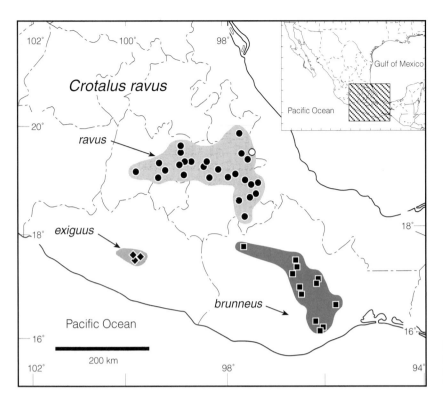

Map 107. Distribution of *Crotalus ravus*, including subspecies, in central and southern Mexico. Unfilled symbol represents the type-locality, El Limón Totalco, Veracruz, Mexico (Smith and Taylor, 1950b).

Type-locality: "1.6 km E Omilteme, Guerrero, elevation 2090 m" [Mexico].

Sistrurus ravus sinaloensis Juliá-Zertuche, 1982, *Res. Sexto Congr. Nac. Zool.*, 1 p. Holotype: none designated. Type-locality: "Sierra de Sinaloa," Sinaloa, Mexico. [Not a valid publication under the Articles of the Code.]

LOCAL NAMES   Colcóatl, cascabel enana, víbora de cascabel, viborita de cascabel.

ENGLISH NAME   Mexican pygmy rattlesnake.

ETYMOLOGY   The species epithet is derived from the Latin *ravus*, meaning "gray" or "grayish yellow," an allusion to the skin color.

DISTRIBUTION   Temperate montane regions of moderate to high elevations across the Mexican Plateau from the Volcán de Toluca (Zinantecatl) in the state of México to the highlands of west-central Veracruz, southward through the Sierra de Acatepec in Puebla and extreme northern Oaxaca; the Mesa del Sur in Oaxaca including the Sierra Juárez, the mountains that extend northward from Cerro San Felipe, and the Sierra Mixe; and the Sierra Madre del Sur in Guerrero (Map 107). The vertical distribution is from about 1,490 m to slightly above 3,000 m.

Distribution records are available for the Distrito Federal (Martín del Campo, 1942; Uribe-Peña et al., 1999), Guerrero (Pérez-Ramos et al., 2000), México (Herrera, 1891—as *Crotalophorus edwardsi*; Martín del Campo, 1955), Morelos (Davis and Smith, 1953; Harris and Simmons, 1978b), Oaxaca (Casas-Andreu et al., 1996; Dugès, 1876–1877—as *Crotalophorus Edwardsii*; Harris and Simmons, 1978b), Puebla (Smith and Laufe, 1945), Tlaxcala (Smith and Laufe, 1945), Veracruz (Boulenger, 1896b; Cuesta-Terrón, 1930b; Sumichrast, 1882), Mexico generally (Armstrong and Murphy, 1979; Garman, 1884a 1884b; Gloyd, 1940; Günther, 1895–1902—as *Crotalophorus miliarius*; Harris and Simmons, 1978b; Klauber, 1952, 1971, 1972; Martín del Campo, 1935; Mocquard, 1908–1909; Smith and Taylor, 1945; Sumichrast, 1873; Werner, 1922), and the "table land of Mexico" (Cope, 1865, 1885b). The report of a specimen

from Sinaloa (Juliá-Zertuche, 1982) must be regarded with extreme skepticism.

HABITAT   Pine-oak forest, cloud forest, boreal forest, high tropical scrub, and upper tropical deciduous forest—zones of considerable ecological diversity. This small rattlesnake is most frequently encountered in open areas such as meadows or regions covered by low vegetation. It appears to be most abundant in relatively flat areas such as plateaus, floodplains, and alluvial fans or basins, but we have taken this wide-ranging species from steep slopes within virgin cloud forest.

DESCRIPTION   This is a moderately stout little rattlesnake; adults generally reach a TL of 40–65 cm, and occasionally exceed 70 cm.

The anterior portion of the top of the head is patternless; posteriorly, a broad pair of nape blotches is usually evident. A postocular stripe is usually absent or only faintly indicated. The labials are yellow or peach colored and may or may not be stippled. The ground color is extremely variable, even within populations; it may be pale grayish brown, dark brown, bluish gray, or pale rust. The 22–44 reddish brown or dark brown body blotches frequently are paler in the center. Except on rust-colored specimens from Guerrero, dorsal blotches tend to have narrow, dark margins. The ground color between dorsal blotches is paler than that on the sides of the body. There are 2–8 dark tail bands. There tends to be a moderate to great amount of stippling or mottling on the ventrals and proximal subcaudals, although some specimens from widely scattered localities have almost immaculate bellies except for the darkened lateral portions of the ventrals. Large specimens tend to be darker than juveniles, and melanistic specimens are known from high elevations along the Transverse Volcanic Cordillera. The iris ranges from gray to copper.

The top of the head usually is covered by 9 symmetrically arranged head plates (Fig. 210); however, the parietal scales frequently are divided transversely in the Guerrero population and occasionally in other populations as well. There are 9–13 supralabials (usually 11 or 12), 9–13 infralabials (generally 11 or

12), 21–25 middorsal scale rows (usually 23 in Oaxacan and Guerreran snakes, 21 in more northerly populations), 136–150 ventrals in males and 138–149 in females, and 25–30 subcaudals in males and 19–26 in females. For other variation in scutellation, see Campbell and Armstrong (1979).

SIMILAR SPECIES This snake can be distinguished from all other Mexican rattlesnakes except *Sistrurus catenatus* by the presence of 9 (or 11 or more if the parietals are divided) large head plates. *Sistrurus catenatus* is known only from two small areas well to the north of where *C. ravus* occurs (see Maps 107 and 112) and has distinct markings on top of the head over and in front of the eyes, a well-defined postocular stripe, cordiform dorsal blotches, an upper preocular that is in contact with the postnasal, and a sharper canthus. *Crotalus pusillus*, which occurs to the west of the range of *C. ravus*, has relatively large anterior dorsal head scales, but the parietal region is covered by small scales, there are 150 or more ventrals, and the postocular stripe is well defined.

REMARKS Campbell and Armstrong (1979), the most recent reviewers, recognized three subspecies. *Crotalus r. ravus* (Pls. 931–934) of the Altiplanicie Meridional has highly variable parietals and normally has 21 dorsal scale rows at midbody, fewer than 3 prefoveals, a relatively large rattle (dorsoventral width of proximal rattle segment usually exceeding 10% of tail length in males and 13% in females), and 2–4 tail bands in both sexes. *Crotalus r. brunneus* (Pls. 935 and 936) from the Oaxacan highlands usually has undivided parietal scales, 23 dorsal scale rows at midbody, 3–6 prefoveals, a relatively small rattle in which the proximal rattle segment is less than 10% of the tail length in males and less than 13% in females, and 5–8 tail bands in males and 4–6 in females. *Crotalus r. exiguus* (Pls. 937–939) from the Sierra Madre del Sur in Guerrero usually has transversely divided parietal scales, 23 dorsal scale rows at midbody, 6 or more prefoveals, a relatively small rattle in which the proximal rattle segment is usually less than 10% of the tail length in males and less than 13% in females, and 3–6 tail bands in males and 2–4 in females.

In parts of its range *C. ravus* may be sympatric with other pitvipers, including *Ophryacus melanurus*, *O. undulatus*, *C. triseriatus*, and *C. intermedius* (Campbell and Armstrong, 1979). This snake is usually diurnal, but Davis and Smith (1953) found a specimen at night in an open field.

Crotalus ruber Cope, 1892
(Map 94, Pls. 940–948)

Caudisona atrox sonoraensis—Cope, 1861, *Proc. Acad. Nat. Sci. Philadelphia* 13:292–306[292]. [In part.]

Crotalus adamanteus atrox—Cope, 1875, *Bull. U.S. Natl. Mus.* (1):104 pp.[33]. [In part.]

Crotalus exsul Garman, 1884a [dated 1883], *Mem. Mus. Comp. Zool.* 8:1–185[114, 174]. Syntypes: MCZ R652 [2 specimens]. Type-locality: "Cedros Island, Lower California."

Crotalus adamanteus ruber Cope, 1892, *Proc. U.S. Natl. Mus.* 14:589–694[690–691]. Holotype: USNM 9209. Type-locality: none given in original description. Smith and Taylor (1950b:356) proposed "Dulzura, San Diego County, California," as a possibility, and Schmidt (1953c:230) designated "vicinity of San Diego, California."

Crotalus ruber—Van Denburgh, 1896, *Proc. California Acad. Sci.* (2)5:1004–1008[1007].

Crotalus atrox ruber—Stejneger, 1895 [dated 1893], *Rep. U.S. Natl. Mus.* 1893:337–487[439].

Crotalus exsul—Grinnell and Camp, 1917, *Univ. California Publ. Zool.* 17:127–298[196].

Crotalus lucasensis Van Denburgh, 1920, *Proc. California Acad. Sci.* (4)10:29–30[29, pl. 3 (fig. 1)]. Holotype: CAS 45888. Type-locality: "Agua Caliente, Cape Region of Lower [Baja] California, Mexico."

Crotalus atrox lucasensis—Schmidt, 1922, *Bull. Am. Mus. Nat. Hist.* 46:607–707[698].

Crotalus atrox elegans Schmidt, 1922, *Bull. Am. Mus. Nat. Hist.* 46:607–707[699]. Holotype: USNM 64452. Type-locality: "Angel de la Guardia Island, Gulf of California," Mexico.

Crotalus exsul ruber—Kallert, 1927, *Bl. Aquar. Terrarienkd. Stuttgart* 38:372[372].

Crotalus ruber ruber—Klauber, 1949a, *Trans. San Diego Soc. Nat. Hist.* 11:57–60[59].

Crotalus ruber lucasensis—Klauber, 1949a, *Trans. San Diego Soc. Nat. Hist.* 11:57–60[59].

Crotalus ruber lorenzoensis Radcliffe and Maslin, 1975, *Copeia* 1975(3):490–493[490, fig. 1B]. Holotype: SDSNH 46009. Type-locality: "San Lorenzo Sur Island in the Gulf of California, Baja California Norte, Mexico."

Crotalus ruber elegans—Harris and Simmons, 1978b, *Bull. Maryland Herpetol. Soc.* 14:105–211[121].

Crotalus ruber monserratensis Harris and Simmons, 1978b, *Bull. Maryland Herpetol. Soc.* 14:105–211[122, fig. 53]. Holotype: RS 1217 HSH/RSS. Type-locality "Isla Monserrate, Gulf of California, Baja Sur, Mexico."

Crotalus exsul exsul—Grismer, 1993, *Herpetol. Nat. Hist.* 1:1–10[4].

Crotalus exsul exsul—Grismer, McGuire, and Hollingsworth, 1994, *S. California Acad. Sci.* 93:45–80[71].

Crotalus exsul lucasensis—Grismer, McGuire, and Hollingsworth, 1994, *S. California Acad. Sci.* 93:45–80[71].

Crotalus exsul lorenzoensis—Grismer, McGuire, and Hollingsworth, 1994, *S. California Acad. Sci.* 93:45–80[71].

LOCAL NAME Víbora de cascabel.

ENGLISH NAME Red diamond rattlesnake.

ETYMOLOGY The species epithet is derived from the Latin *ruber*, meaning "red," an allusion to the ground color.

DISTRIBUTION The southwestern United States and Mexico. This species occupies extreme southwestern California from near Pioneertown and the Morongo Valley of San Bernardino County and southeastern Los Angeles County southward through the peninsula of Baja California, Mexico (exclusive of the desert east of the Sierra de Juárez in northeastern Baja California Norte), to Cabo San Lucas (Map 94). It occurs on either side of the peninsular mountain ranges and on a number of islands in the Gulf of California, including, from north to south, Ángel de la Guarda, Pond, San Lorenzo del Sur, San Marcos, Danzante, Monserrate, and San José. Off the Pacific coast *C. ruber* occurs on Isla de Santa Margarita, Baja California Sur, and Isla Cedros (sometimes called Cerros) of Baja California Norte, Mexico (Map 94); *Crotalus ruber exsul* is the only rattlesnake known from Isla Cedros. The vertical distribution on the mainland is from near sea level to about 1,500 m, but most specimens are encountered below 1,200 m.

Wong (1997) confirmed the presence of *C. ruber* (reported as *C. exsul*) from Isla Santa Margarita but pointed out the lack of a museum record for this species from Isla Magdalena, even though Bostic (1975) listed it as occurring there. Goodrich et al. (1978) reported this species from Isla Danzante (25°47'N, 111°15'W). Additional distribution records are available for California (Cornett, 1979; Glaser, 1970; Grinnell and Camp, 1917; Klauber, 1927, 1929, 1930c, 1931a; Meek, 1906; Savage, 1959; Shaw and Campbell, 1974; Stebbins, 1972) and the Baja California Peninsula and associated islands (Bostic, 1971; Cliff, 1954; Cope, 1861; Cuesta-Terrón, 1931—as *exsul* and *lucasensis*; Garman, 1884a, 1884b; Grismer, 1993, 1994b, 1994c, 2002;

Grismer et al., 1994; Harris and Simmons, 1978b; Hoard, 1939; Leviton and Banta, 1964; Lindsay, 1962, 1964, 1966; Linsdale, 1932; Meek, 1906; Mocquard, 1899b; Mosauer, 1936; Murphy, 1983a; Murphy and Ottley, 1984; Murray, 1955; Nelson, 1922; Osorio Tafall, 1948; Savage, 1967; Schmidt, 1922; Smith, 1944c; Smith and Holland, 1971; Soulé and Sloan, 1966; Tevis, 1943, 1944; Van Denburgh, 1895a, 1896, 1905, 1920; Van Denburgh and Slevin, 1914, 1921b; Yarrow, 1883). The overall distribution of this species is discussed in Cope, 1900; Gloyd, 1940; Klauber, 1930a, 1971, 1972; Pope, 1944–1945; Van Denburgh, 1922b; and Werner, 1922. On the general distribution in the United States, see Brown, 1901; G. B. Pickwell, 1972; Stebbins, 1985; Stejneger, 1895; Stejneger and Barbour, 1943; and Wright and Wright, 1957. On the general distribution in Mexico, see Armstrong and Murphy, 1979; Campbell and Lamar, 1989; Cuesta-Terrón, 1931; Klauber, 1949a; Martín del Campo, 1937a, 1950; Savage, 1960; and Smith and Taylor, 1945.

HABITAT   Desert, chaparral, pine-oak woodland, and tropical deciduous forest. In the southern part of its range this snake is most frequently found in rocky outcroppings or heavy brush (Armstrong and Murphy, 1979). Bostic (1971) collected one individual about 10 yards above the high-tide mark on a cobblestone beach and another beneath an ocotillo in a sandy, dunelike habitat. On Isla Cedros, which may be enshrouded in fog for weeks at a time, *Crotalus r. exsul* occurs mainly in rocky terrain covered with desert vegetation. One specimen of *C. r. exsul* was taken on a gravel fan at the mouth of a canyon, and another was found on a rocky slope of a canyon (Murray, 1955).

DESCRIPTION   *Crotalus ruber* is a moderately large rattlesnake; mainland specimens commonly exceed 100 cm in TL, and large males may exceed 140 cm. Snakes above 150 cm are quite rare, however; the largest specimen reported measured 162 cm (Klauber, 1937). Apparently, some island populations are stunted and do not reach 100 cm in length; the largest specimen known from Isla San Lorenzo Sur is only 87.2 cm in TL, and large adult males of the Isla Cedros population, *C. r. exsul*, usually reach no more than 90 cm, with the largest reported specimen having a TL of 94 cm.

The ground color of specimens from the northern part of the range is pale reddish brown, pale pinkish gray, pale brick red, or tan. The 29–42 rhombic or diamond-shaped dorsal blotches are usually dark reddish brown and uniformly pigmented without pale centers. On the anterior one-half to two-thirds of the body the dorsal blotches are distinctly separated from one another middorsally by white or buff; this pale edging becomes very narrow or incomplete along the lateral margins of the dorsal blotches. The top of the head has little or no pattern and is usually nearly unicolored. A dark brown or reddish brown postocular stripe extends diagonally from the lower edge of the eye to over the posterior part of the mouth; it is bordered anteriorly by a broad stripe about 2 scales wide that extends from the upper preocular to the supralabials lying below the eye and thence usually along the margin of the lip to the rictus. The posterior (upper) pale line bordering the dark postocular stripe is often incomplete, indistinct, or absent; when present it extends diagonally across the temporal region to make contact with one of the last 3 supralabials. The lateral blotches tend to be obscure, consisting of 1–4 dark reddish brown scales.

Snakes from the southern half of the peninsula of Baja California (from about Loreto to the cape) tend to have an olive brown, yellowish brown, or straw-colored ground color. There are 20–42 brown dorsal blotches with dark brown to almost black borders and distinctly paler centers. The yellowish white to buff edging around the dorsal blotches is more prominent than in snakes from the north and tends to completely surround each blotch. The borders of the dorsal blotches are somewhat irregular compared with those of northern snakes. The top of the head has conspicuous dark spots, and the dark postocular stripes are bordered by a pale preocular (anterior or lower) stripe 2–3 or more scales wide and a pale postocular (posterior or upper) stripe that is usually well defined. The 2–3 series of lateral blotches are relatively distinct and usually consist of groups of 2–4 dark brown scales. Gloyd (1935b) described an unusual specimen of *C. r. lucasensis* from the cape region of Baja California in which the ground color and pattern were unusually pale, the body blotches were reduced in size, and the top of the head was mostly unmarked except for 2 small spots on the snout and an occipital streak above the angle of the jaw.

The ground color of *C. r. exsul* is pale reddish gray to pinkish. The 30–37 dorsal blotches are usually reddish brown, are often poorly defined in large adults, have a subcircular or roughly hexagonal shape on the anterior one-half to two-thirds of the body, and may become transversely elongated, forming crossbands on the posterior part of the body. Color and pattern are subject to a considerable amount of ontogenetic change. The dorsal blotches on young snakes are outlined with dark brown, but on adults the blotches are usually nearly uniformly pigmented and become somewhat paler. Dorsal blotches usually have inconspicuous pale edging. In adults this is restricted to a narrow margin along the posterior border of the blotches on the anterior part of the body; it may be particularly evident at midbody. Irregular dark markings are usually present on the dorsum of the head of juveniles; adults exhibit little or no dark marking and the top of the head is more or less uniformly colored. The supraoculars of young snakes have a pale transverse bar, but this disappears in adults. A dark postocular stripe is evident on young snakes, and the pale lines bordering it are similar in their placement to those of *C. r. ruber*, but tend not to be as bright; in many adults the postocular stripe becomes faded and all but a slight trace of the anterior pale border disappears. Lateral blotches are dark on juveniles but become obscure on adults. The tail is marked with strongly contrasting ash gray to whitish and black rings; the 3–5 black rings are as long as or slightly longer than the pale rings separating them and often are broken laterally. The proximal rattle segment is black.

The tail is pale gray with 2–7 black rings that are 2–3 scales in length laterally and conspicuously longer dorsally than the pale interspaces dividing them; the black tail rings infrequently are broken laterally. The belly is immaculate, and many scales in dorsal rows 1–3 are whitish or narrowly edged with white. The subcaudals are black where encroached on by the black tail rings; otherwise they are pale with a heavy suffusion of black peppering. Juveniles have a gray ground color.

The shape of the rostral is highly variable; snakes in the southern portion of the peninsula of Baja California and on Isla Cedros usually have a rostral that is higher than wide, whereas the rostral of more northerly snakes is often wider than high. Two internasals contact the rostral, with more than 8 scales in the internasal-prefrontal region (up to 17–40 in *C. r. exsul*), and 4–10 (usually 6 or more) intersupraoculars. The prenasal touches supralabial 1 in most mainland specimens, but it is not unusual in snakes from Isla Cedros for contact of these scales to be prevented by the intervention of prefoveals that extend forward to the rostral. The posterior canthal is large and angles over the canthus rostralis to intervene partially between the upper preocular and postnasal and to occupy the space of an upper loreal. There may be 1 or 2 loreals; snakes from the southern half of the peninsula and from Isla Cedros typically have 2, those from farther north most frequently have 1. The presence of the loreal(s) and/or the intervening portion of the canthal almost always precludes contact between the upper preocular and postnasal. One to 3 interoculabials separate the anterior subocular from the supralabials. A pair of interchinshields is usually absent. There are 12–19 (usually 15–17) supralabials, 13–21 (usually 16–18) infralabials (first pair usually divided transversely), 25–33 midbody dorsal scale rows (mode 29 in northern snakes, 27 in southern and Isla Cedros snakes, 25 in snakes from Isla San Lorenzo Sur), 179–203 ventrals in males and 183–206 in females, 21–29 subcaudals in males and 15–25 in females, and usually 12–13 rattle-fringe scales.

Crotalus r. ruber and *C. r. lucasensis* of the mainland differ from *C. r. exsul* in having an adult TL that commonly exceeds 100 cm, tail rings that are complete or broken at midline (but usually not laterally), prenasals that are usually in contact with the first pair of supralabials, and in lacking interchinshields.

SIMILAR SPECIES   Five other rattlesnakes may be sympatric with *C. ruber* in certain portions of the range. *Crotalus oreganus* usually has more than 2 internasals contacting the rostral, the black tail rings are conspicuously narrower than the pale interspaces dividing them, and the pale interspaces on the tail are the same color as the ground color on the posterior part of the body. The ground color of *C. mitchellii* is distinctly speckled with black; the dark tail rings are obscure or, if sharply defined, are not as broad as the pale ones; the prenasals are separated from the rostral by a series of small scales; and the supraoculars are pitted, deeply furrowed, or have irregular outer edges. The supraoculars of *C. enyo* are inclined considerably upward toward the lateral side of the head, the tail lacks strongly contrasting pale and dark rings, and the scales in the frontal region are knobby. *Crotalus cerastes* is sympatric with *C. ruber* in northeastern Baja California Norte but can be distinguished by its raised, hornlike supraoculars. *Crotalus atrox* appears to be parapatric with with *C. ruber* in southern California and northeastern Baja California Norte, but its ground color is usually pale gray-brown, the first pair of infralabials usually are not transversely divided, and the postnasal and upper preocular touch each other.

REMARKS   It has been long recognized that *Crotalus ruber* and *C. catalinensis* are closely related. Using allozyme data, Murphy and Crabtree (1985b) obtained results suggesting that these two taxa are sister species.

Amaral (1929b) had difficulty distinguishing among *C. atrox*, *C. ruber*, and *C. tortugensis*, and suggested that only a single species was involved. Klauber (1949a) discussed the close relationships of *ruber* and *lucasensis* and suggested that these taxa should be considered subspecies of *C. ruber*; he continued to argue that *exsul* deserved species status, although he recognized its close relationships with *C. ruber*. Campbell and Lamar (1989) pointed out that the Cedros Island population is poorly differentiated from and might be conspecific with *C. ruber*, in which case the name *C. exsul* would have priority. Grismer (1993) used the trinomial *C. exsul exsul* without comment; Grismer and Mellink (1994) stated that they considered *C. ruber* and *C. exsul* to be conspecific but gave no justification. Grismer et al. (1994:71) considered *C. exsul* and *C. ruber* to represent the same species and recognized two subspecies: *C. e. exsul* Garman, 1884a, and *C. e. lorenzoensis* Radcliffe and Maslin, 1975. Murphy et al. (1995) studied genetic and morphological diversity in *C. exsul* from Isla Cedros and *C. ruber* from the mainland and found insufficient difference between the two populations to

warrant recognizing separate species. Because *C. exsul* Garman (1884a) has priority over *C. ruber* Cope (1892), they recommended that the mainland populations be known as *C. exsul ruber* and the insular population on Isla Cedros be known as *C. e. exsul*, and the insular population on Isla San Lorenzo be known as *C. e. lorensoensis*. Smith and 10 others (1998) prepared a petition requesting the ICZN to validate the name *ruber* over *exsul* because of the long-standing and frequent use of the name *Crotalus ruber*. This action was supported by Minton et al. (1999). The International Commission on Zoological Nomenclature (2000a) ruled in Opinion 1960 that *Crotalus ruber* should have precedence over *C. exsul*.

Recently, Grismer (1999a, 2002) suggested that *C. ruber lorenzoensis* be afforded full species status on the basis of its poorly developed rattle. We adhere to a more conservative approach and recognize four subspecies: *C. r. ruber* (Pls. 940 and 941) in southern California and the northern part of the peninsula of Baja California, *C. r. lucasensis* (Pls. 947 and 948) occupying the southern portion of the peninsula, *C. r. exsul* (Pls. 942–944) on Isla Cedros, and *C. r. lorenzoensis* (Pls. 945 and 946) on Isla San Lorenzo Sur.

Crotalus ruber ruber has a well-developed rattle matrix, and adults usually have a string of segments, a mode of 29 dorsal scale rows at midbody, and 22–29 subcaudals in males and 16–25 in females. *Crotalus r. exsul* has typical rattles, a mode of 27 dorsal scale rows at midbody, 18–26 subcaudals in males and 17–23 in females, and achieves a relatively small size (the largest specimen known was 94 cm in TL). *Crotalus r. lucasensis* also has typical rattles, a mode of 27 dorsal scale rows at midbody, and 22–29 subcaudals in males and 17–23 in females. The population from Isla San Lorenzo del Sur, *C. r. lorenzoensis*, has a rattle matrix that is somewhat shrunken in, and about half of the adults are thus missing a string of rattles. Other characteristics of this population include a low number of scale rows at midbody (mode 25), fewer subcaudal scales (21–23 in males, 15–19 in females), and a relatively small size (the largest specimen on record was 87.2 cm). Murphy and Crabtree (1985b) and Grismer (2002) preferred to recognize *ruber* and *lorenzoensis* as species.

Harris and Simmons (1978b) provided an incomplete preliminary description of the population on Isla Monserrat, designating it *Crotalus ruber monserratensis*. Their justification for this designation was so feeble, however, that their recommendations were not taken seriously by subsequent investigators. McCranie and Wilson (1979) chose not to recognize this taxon, stating that it was a nomen nudum. Murphy and Ottley (1984) agreed with the conclusions of McCranie and Wilson (1979) and considered the name a nomen suspectum. Murphy and Ottley (1984) also suggested that the reasons given by Harris and Simmons for recognizing *C. ruber elegans* from Isla Ángel de la Guarda were inadequate.

Despite its apparently close relationship to the irascible *C. atrox*, *C. ruber* has a reputation for placidity; often a vigorous prod is necessary to elicit a rattle.

Crotalus scutulatus (Kennicott, 1861)
(Fig. 211, Map 108, Pls. 949–955)

Caudisona scutulata Kennicott, 1861b, *Proc. Acad. Nat. Sci. Philadelphia* 13:206–208[207]. Holotype: ANSP 7069 (formerly USNM 5027); see Remarks. Type-locality: none given. Smith and Taylor (1950b:353) proposed "Wickenburg, Maricopa County,

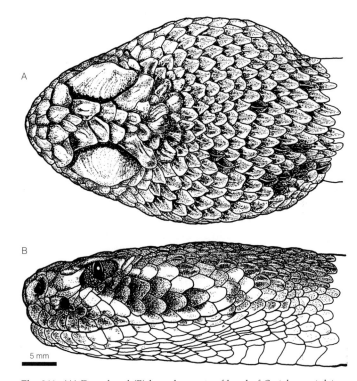

Fig. 211. (A) Dorsal and (B) lateral aspects of head of *Crotalus scutulatus scutulatus*, female, 100.5 cm TL (UTA R-17932), from 10 km southeast of Nuevo Casas Grandes on Highway 10, Chihuahua, Mexico. The supracephalic scales are usually relatively large and have numerous striations, and the pale stripe behind the eye usually extends to about the rictus. Drawings by Ty M. Kubin.

Arizona," USA, and Schmidt (1953c:229) listed the type-locality as "Mojave Desert, California," USA.

Crotalus scutulatus—Cope, *in* Yarrow, *in* Wheeler, 1875, *Rep. Geog. Geol. Explor. Surv. West 100th Merid.* 5:509–584[533].

Crotalus adamanteus scutulatus—Cope, 1875, *Bull. U.S. Natl. Mus.* 1:104 pp.[33].

Crotalus molossus—Garman, 1887a, *Bull. Essex Inst.* 19:119–138[123]. [Not of Baird and Girard; see comments below for *Crotalus salvini* Günther, 1895].

Crotalus salvini Günther, 1895, *Biol. Cent. Am. Rept. Batr.*, 326 pp.[193, pl. 59 (fig. A)]. Syntypes (2): BMNH 1946.1.19.35 (BMNH formerly 1873.1.13.1) from Huamantla and MCZ R4544 from Alvarez, which is Garman's (1887a:123) specimen of *Crotalus molossus*. Lectotype: "Type specimen in British Museum" as designated by Gloyd (1940:201) and as "BM 73.1.13.1" by Klauber (1956:42). Type-locality: "Mexico, Huamantla, alt. 8000 feet" and "Alvarez Mts., near San Luis Potosi." Restricted to "Huamantla, Tlaxcala, Mexico," by lectotype designation of Gloyd.

Crotalus scutulatus—Boulenger, 1896b, *Cat. Snakes British Mus.* 3:727 pp.[575].

Crotalus confluentus kellyi Amaral, 1929c, *Bull. Antivenin Inst. Am.* 2:86–97[91]. Holotype: SDSNH 194 (formerly LMK 194). Type-locality: "Needles, Calif[ornia]." [Amaral's *kellyi* was a composite of *C. viridis lutosus* and *C. s. scutulatus*, but the type was a *scutulatus* according to Klauber (1936b:196).

Crotalus scutulatus scutulatus—Gloyd, 1940, *Chicago Acad. Sci. Spec. Publ.* 4:266 pp.[200, pl. 19 (figs. 1 and 2), 201 (map 15)].

Crotalus scutulatus salvini—Gloyd, 1940, *Chicago Acad. Sci. Spec. Publ.* 4:266 pp.[201 (map 15)].

They reached Zuni Pueblo on September 1. There, Woodhouse encountered a rattlesnake and, hoping to add this large specimen to his collection, broke its back by striking it hard with his ramrod. But he grabbed the still living snake too far

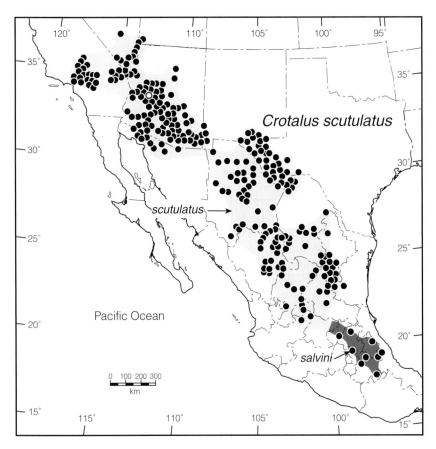

Map 108. Distribution of *Crotalus scutulatus* in Mexico and the southwestern United States. Unfilled symbol represents the restricted type-locality, "Wickenberg, Maricopa County, Arizona, USA (Smith and Taylor, 1950b).

behind its head, and it sank a fang into the index finger of the unfortunate naturalist's left hand. The effect was immediate and terrible pain. For the next several days he treated himself by applying a ligature, lacerating the wound, sucking the poison, drinking ammonia water, taking Dover's powders, applying a poultice of flax-seed meal—and on Kern's advice—getting drunk on whiskey and brandy. Whatever the efficacy of these measures, Woodhouse slowly recovered during the next few weeks.

—From the journal of S. W. Woodhouse; Tomer and Brodhead, 1992

LOCAL NAMES Chiauhcóatl (Nahuatl), víbora de cascabel.

ENGLISH NAME Mohave rattlesnake. The common name in English has been widely employed and is well known, but we use it here somewhat reluctantly because very little of this snake's range lies within the Mohave Desert; its distribution is actually more extensive in the Chihuahuan Desert. We support the spelling "Mohave" for the common name, rather than "Mojave," because the name derives from the Native American term *hamakhava*, as discussed in the regional account of the United States in Volume 1.

ETYMOLOGY The species epithet is derived from the Latin *scutula*, meaning "small plate or shield," and the suffix *-atus*, meaning "provided with," presumably in reference to the scaly skin.

DISTRIBUTION United States and Mexico. In the United States this species occurs from the western edge of the Mohave Desert in southern California (Stewart, 1994), southern Nevada, and southwestern Utah through western and southern Arizona and the extreme southwestern tip of New Mexico to the Chihuahuan Desert of trans-Pecos Texas; in Mexico from northern Sonora eastward through Chihuahua and Coahuila to western Nuevo León, southward through most of Durango and Zacatecas, southern Nuevo León, southwestern Tamaulipas, western San Luis Potosí, northern and eastern Jalisco, most of Aguascalientes, northern Guanajuato, central Querétaro, southern Hidalgo, possibly northeastern México, much of Tlaxcala, northern Puebla, and southwestern Veracruz (Map 108). The vertical distribution is from about sea level to above 2,500 m; in the southern part of the range it is restricted to elevations above 1,800 m.

Distribution records or information have been reported for Arizona (Bogert and Degenhardt, 1961; Coues, 1875; Fowlie, 1965; Gloyd, 1937; Hahn and May, 1972; Hensley, 1950b; Humphrey, 1936; Kauffeld, 1943a; Klauber, 1932a; Lowe, 1964; Lowe et al., 1986; Van Devender and Lowe, 1977; Vitt and Ohmart, 1978; Woodin, 1953), California (Miller and Stebbins, 1964; Stebbins, 1972), Nevada (Klauber, 1932b; Linsdale, 1940; Woodbury, 1947), New Mexico (Cope, 1884b; Degenhardt et al., 1996; Gehlbach, 1957), Texas (Boulenger, 1896b; A. Brown, 1903b; B. Brown, 1950; Jameson and Flury, 1949; Kraus and Schuett, 1980; Minton, 1959; Price, 1998; Raun and Gehlbach, 1972; Smith, 1947c; Werler, 1964), Utah (Nadeau, 1978), Aguascalientes (Banta, 1962; Sigala-Rodríguez and Vázquez-Díaz, 1996), Chihuahua (Bogert and Degenhardt, 1961; Cope, 1886; Dunkle and Smith, 1937; Lemos-Espinal et al., 2000a, 2000b, 2002a, 2002b; Morafka, 1977; Reynolds, 1982; Smith, 1943a; Smith and Mittleman, 1943; Tanner, 1985; Van Devender and Lowe, 1977), Coahuila (Liner, 1964; McCoy, 1984), Durango (Dunkle and Smith, 1937; Webb, 1984), Jalisco (Campbell, 1979a), México (Bravo, 1927), Nuevo León (Liner, 1964; Liner et al., 1976; Reese, 1971), Puebla (Smith, 1943a), Querétaro (Dixon et al., 1972), San Luis Potosí (Cuesta-Terrón, 1921b; Dixon et al., 1962; Liner, 1964; Taylor, 1949), Sonora (Burger and Hensley,

1949; González-Romero and Alvarez-Cárdenas, 1989; Hensley, 1950b; P. Smith and Hensley, 1958), Tlaxcala (Boulenger, 1896b; Cuesta-Terrón, 1921b; Günther, 1895–1902; Sánchez-Herrera and López-Ortega, 1987), Veracruz (Pérez-Higareda and Smith, 1991), Zacatecas (Dugès, 1896a), Mexico generally (Auth et al., 2000; Cuesta-Terrón, 1921b; Klauber, 1952, 1971, 1972; Martín del Campo, 1937a, 1950; Mocquard, 1908–1909; Smith, 1943a; Smith and Taylor, 1945), the northern portion of the range (Conant and Collins, 1998; G. B. Pickwell, 1972; Shaw and Campbell, 1974; Stebbins, 1985; Stejneger and Barbour, 1943; Tanner, 1978; Wright and Wright, 1957), and the general distribution (Armstrong and Murphy, 1979; Cope, 1900; Garman, 1884b; Gloyd, 1940; Hoge and Romano, 1971a; Klauber, 1936b, 1952, 1971, 1972; Pope, 1944–1945; A. H. Price, 1982; Savage, 1959; Werner, 1922).

HABITAT Desertscrub, Joshua tree woodland, piñon-juniper woodland, mesquite-grassland, and, in the southern portion of the range, pine-oak forest. In west Texas, Jameson and Flury (1949) found a specimen in a gopher burrow in a tobosa-grama association. In Arizona, Jones (1988) recorded *C. scutulatus* from Mohave desertscrub, mixed riparian scrub, and mesquite-bosque formations. Gates (1957) reported that *C. scutulatus* is sympatric with *C. atrox* in parts of Arizona, but noted that the former is more frequently encountered on rocky hillsides than in washes. Woodin (1953) reported it to occur "at elevations of not over 4900 feet" (1,494 m) in Arizona. Throughout its range in Mexico this snake occurs mostly in relatively flat terrain such as the bottoms of broad, open valleys or high plains. In the vicinity of Durango, Webb (1984) reported it from mesquite-grassland. In the extreme south this species is often found in rocky habitats such as old lava flows; in the north it may be found in a variety of situations. In the Perote region of Mexico we have collected *C. s. salvini* at elevations above 2,500 m. In Chihuahua *C. scutulatus* occurs in desertscrub, desert-grassland, plains grassland, and oak woodland (Van Devender and Lowe, 1977).

DESCRIPTION Large specimens of this medium-sized rattlesnake usually do not greatly exceed 100 cm in length; the largest specimen on record measured 137.3 cm (Tennant, 1984).

This species exhibits a fair amount of north–south clinal variation in some characters, and it is convenient to refer to southern and northern snakes. In our discussion, this division corresponds roughly to the ranges of the two subspecies (see Remarks); however, some features such as color and pattern are highly discordant.

In northern snakes the ground color is greenish gray, olive green, greenish brown, greenish yellow, brownish, or yellowish. The 27–44 dark dorsal blotches are yellowish olive to dark brown, hexagonal to diamond shaped, and bordered by a single row of pale scales that may be incomplete. A pair of dark occipital blotches is usually present; anteriorly, the dorsum of the head is nearly uniformly colored except for the posterior edges of the supraoculars, which may be dark. The lower (anterior) pale stripe bordering the dark postorbital stripe extends from the upper preocular downward to the lip margin *behind* the posterior edge of the eye, thence along the supralabials to the rictus. The upper (posterior) pale stripe extends diagonally from the upper postocular across a point immediately *above* the ultimate supralabial. The pale tail rings are ash gray and stand in sharp contrast against the ground color on the posterior part of the body. Proximally, the 2–8 dark tail rings may be about the same color as or a little darker than the dorsal blotches, but distally they become considerably darker and may be almost black. The dark tail rings are narrower than the pale interspaces, considerably so in northern populations. The dorsal portion of the proximal rattle segment is black.

Nickerson and Mays (1968) described a specimen from Pima County, Arizona, that had a pair of paravertebral strips just behind the head that extended to about midbody, where they coalesced into a single middorsal stripe that continued posteriorly but became less bold. Another specimen had the first 6–8 dorsal blotches on the anterior one-third of the body forming a broad stripe followed by normal dorsal blotches on the rest of the body. Nickerson and Mays (1968) observed snakes with similar anterior fused blotches in Gila and Maricopa Counties, Arizona, and also reported an essentially patternless specimen from Pima County that had only a hint of darker paravertebral stripes that varied in intensity at different times.

In southern snakes the ground color is pale olive gray to straw colored. Thirty to 35 brownish olive to black subrhombic dorsal blotches are present on the body; no contrasting narrow pale border is evident around the margins of the dorsal blotches. The dorsum of the head may be pale and similar in color to the ground color of the body, irregularly marked with dark pigment, or almost uniformly black. The dark postocular stripe, if present, is very much reduced, extending only 2–4 scales from the lower edge of the eye and not reaching the margin of the lip; it may be black or indistinct. Other than dark postocular and temporal stripes, which may or may not be present, the side of the head is pale and the pale stripes bordering the dark postorbital stripe are broad with irregular margins (Fig. 211). The top of the head may have a pair of occipital blotches, or these may be obscured by heavy pigmentation. The 4–6 dark tail rings distally do not become darker than the dorsal markings. The pale interspaces separating the dark tail rings are about the same color as that on the posterior part of the body. The dorsal portion of the proximal rattle segment is only slightly darkened with brown pigment.

The belly is whitish or yellowish in both populations and nearly immaculate except for a little dark pigment encroaching on the lateral portions of the ventrals in some snakes. The subcaudals are pale with dark gray or black flecking.

The rostral is usually higher than wide. Two internasals contact the rostral. There are 6–21 scales in the internasal-prefrontal region; snakes from the south have 9 or fewer, whereas populations in the north are highly variable but tend to have higher average numbers than those to the south. The number of intersupraoculars is rarely more than 2. The prenasal is in broad contact with supralabial 1. Frequently, a large, crescent-shaped scale borders the posteromedial edge of each supraocular; this scale is divided in some specimens. The posterior canthals are large and their lateral portions extend ventrally over the canthus rostralis to take the place of an upper loreal and to intervene between the upper preocular and postnasal. A posterior canthal along with the single loreal on each side (in the position of a lower loreal) prevent contact between the postnasal and upper preocular. Usually 1 interoculabial separates the anterior subocular from the supralabial series. There are 12–18 supralabials (usually 13–14 in the south, 15 in the north), 12–18 infralabials (usually 14 in the south, 15 or 16 in the north), 21–29 (mode 25) midbody dorsal scale rows, 165–187 ventrals in males and 165–192 in females (the average number for both males and females is lower in the southern part of the range), and 21–29 subcaudals in males and 15–23 in females.

SIMILAR SPECIES *Crotalus scutulatus* has an extensive distribution and might be confused with many other rattlesnakes. In *C. atrox* the upper (posterior) pale line that borders the dark postocular stripe is narrow (less than 1 scale wide) and extends to just in front of the rictus; in regions of sympatry, the dark tail rings are relatively longer, usually 3 or more scales long as opposed to 2 or less; the scales on top of the head are more numerous (usually 4 or more intersupraoculars); and the upper preocular usually contacts the postnasal (Bush and Cardwell, 1999). In *C. viridis* (possibly sympatric with *C. scutulatus* in west Texas in the United States and in northern Coahuila and Chihuahua in Mexico), the pale interspaces separating dark tail rings are about the same color as the ground color on the posterior part of the body, and there are more than 2 internasals. *Crotalus molossus* has 4 (rarely 6) scales in the internasal-prefrontal region, including a large pair of prefrontals in contact medially. In *C. mitchellii* the prenasal is separated from the rostral by a series of small scales, the ground color is heavily punctated with black, and the supraoculars are pitted, have deep furrows, or have irregular outer edges. The dorsal pattern of *C. tigris* consists of crossbands, and the head is proportionately small and the rattles large.

REMARKS The type of *Crotalus scutulatus* has an interesting history, as outlined by McDiarmid et al. (1999). The first person known to refer to USNM 5021 as the type of *C. scutulatus* was Cope (1900:1160). Although not designated as a type-specimen, USNM 5021 was listed twice by Yarrow (1883:76), once as a specimen of *Crotalus adamanteus scutulatus* and once as a specimen of *Crotalus lucifer*. The specimen catalog at the U.S. National Museum provides no information regarding the identity or status of USNM 5021 (Klauber, 1956:42, footnote 21; McDiarmid et al., 1999:294). Examination of USNM 5021 revealed that it consists only of a head, probably that of either *C. oreganus cerberus* or *C. o. helleri* according to Klauber (1956:42, footnote 21); almost certainly this specimen is the record of *C. lucifer* reported by Yarrow (1883:76).

It is possible that Kennicott's designation of USNM 5021 as a type was a misprint for some other number or a simple mix-up of specimens. McDiarmid et al. (1999) noted that USNM 5027 was identified as "*Caudisona lepturus*" on 30 January 1861 in the USNM catalog and comprised two specimens of *Crotalus scutulatus*. It appears likely that one of these specimens was the one referred to by Cope (1900) as the type of *C. scutulatus*. Both USNM 5021 and 5027 came from Fort Buchanan, Arizona, and both were received from the same person. It is possible that Kennicott planned to use at least one of the two specimens cataloged under the number USNM 5027 as the type of the species *Caudisona lepturus*, a name he never got around to publishing.

The possibility of a misprint of USNM 5021 for USNM 5027 was also considered by Klauber (1956), who examined a single specimen of USNM 5027 and noted that the labial counts did not match those given by Kennicott (1861b). Klauber did not know that the second specimen cataloged as USNM 5027 had been sent to the Academy of Natural Sciences in Philadelphia sometime after 1861. This specimen is still extant in the ANSP and apparently is the holotype of *C. scutulatus*.

Cuesta-Terrón (1921b:188) implied that he was describing a new species when he listed *Crotalus salvini* sp. nov. in his treatment of the rattlesnakes of Mexico, but it is obvious that his description was taken from Günther's (1895:193) original description; futhermore, the localities given by Cuesta-Terrón—"Huamantla, Tlax. Montes de Alvarez, cerca de San Luis Potosí"—are the same as those listed for the types of *Crotalus salvini* (Günther, 1895:193). It is worth noting that Cuesta-Terrón (1921b:187) treated *Crotalus omiltemanus* (sp. nov.) in much the same way. Therefore, rather than consider *Crotalus salvini*

Cuesta-Terrón (1921b) as a junior primary homonym of *Crotalus salvini* Günther, 1895, McDiarmid et al. (1999) preferred to treat it as Cuesta-Terrón's peculiar and erroneous way of referring to Günther's species.

Two subspecies are recognized: *C. s. scutulatus* (Pls. 949–953) in the northern part of the range from California eastward to west Texas and south to Querétaro, and *C. s. salvini* (Pls. 954 and 955) from Hidalgo through Tlaxcala and Puebla to southwestern Veracruz. *Crotalus s. scutulatus* can be distinguished from *C. s. salvini* by the row of unicolored scales bordering its dorsal blotches (*C. s. salvini* has no pale border on the dorsal blotches), usually black distal tail bands that are noticeably darker than the posterior body blotches (versus about the same color), and a black upper part of the proximal rattle lobe in adults (versus only slightly darkened, if at all).

At lower elevations this snake is mostly nocturnal during the hotter months. At high elevations and during the cooler months it is frequently active during the daylight hours. This snake has very potent venom. Symptoms of snakebite are reported to include double vision and difficulty in speaking and swallowing water. Saltation as a method of self-defense was described in this species by Bartholomew and Nohavec (1995).

Crotalus simus Latreille, 1801
(Figs. 212 and 213, Map 109, Pls. 956–966)

Crotalus simus Latreille, *in* Sonnini de Manoncourt and Latreille, 1801–1802, *Hist. Nat. Rept.* 3:335 pp.[202]. Type(s): "Muséum national." Not located in MNHN, according to Thireau (1991:4). Type-locality: "Ceylan." Obviously in error. Placed in the synonymy of *Crotalus durissus durissus* by Klauber (1936c:197).
Caudisona durissa—Cope, 1861, *Proc. Acad. Nat. Sci. Philadelphia* 13:292–306[292].

Crotalus terrificus—Cope, *in* Yarrow, *in* Wheeler, 1875, *Rep. Geog. Geol. Explor. Surv. West 100th Merid.* 5:509–584[532].
Crotalus durissus durissus—Klauber, 1936c, *Occas. Pap. San Diego Soc. Nat. Hist.* 1:2–7[4].
Crotalus terrificus copeanus Amaral, 1937 [dated 1935–1936], *Mem. Inst. Butantan* 10:87–162 [162, continued footnote]. Replacement name for the Central American rattlesnake, *Crotalus terrificus durissus* (Linnaeus, 1758). Klauber (1941:91, and 1972:34, footnote 5) suggested that Amaral's name was a nomen nudum for technical reasons (*Rules Zool. Nomen.*, 1926, Art. 25, c), even though the name was intended as a substitute for *C. d. durissus*. McDiarmid et al. (1999) thought it was an incorrect original spelling rather than a nomen nudum. Gloyd (1940:123) included *copeanus* as a synonym of *durissus*, apparently recognizing it as a replacement name rather than as a nomen nudum.
Crotalus durissus culminatus Klauber, 1952, *Bull. Zool. Soc. San Diego* (26):1–143[65]. Holotype: FMNH 126616 (formerly EHT-HMS 5224). Type-locality: "Hacienda . . . El Sabino near Uruapan, Michoacán, Mexico."
Crotalus durissus tzabcan Klauber, 1952, *Bull. Zool. Soc. San Diego* (26):1–143[71]. Holotype: FMNH 36168. Type-locality: "Kantunil, Yucatán, Mexico."
Crotalus (*Crotalus*) *durissus culminatus*—Peters and Orejas-Miranda, 1970, *Bull. U.S. Natl. Mus.* 297(1):1–347[74].
Crotalus (*Crotalus*) *durissus durissus*—Peters and Orejas-Miranda, 1970, *Bull. U.S. Natl. Mus.* 297(1):1–347[75].
Crotalus durissus neoleonensis Juliá-Zertuche and Treviño-Saldaña, 1978, *Res. Segundo Congreso Nacional de Zoología*, 60 pp.[60]. [Nomen nudum.]

Tecuhtlacozauqui—Dicen que es el príncipe o princesa de todas las culebras; es gruesa y larga, tience eslabones en la cola, como víbora; tiene . . . escamas guesas y es de color amarillo, del color de la flor de la calabaza, (y) tiene unas manchas negras como las del tigre; los eslabones tiene pardillos y duros.
—Martín del Campo, 1984, quoting from the ninth volume of the *History of Sahagún*, about a snake thought to be *C. simus*

The *Croatalus horridus* [=*Crotalus simus*] furnished me with a still more striking example of this diffusion of life in the most distant parts of the body. We had caught one of these reptiles, and it had been dead, apparently, for several hours, and we had hung it up for the purpose of skinning it. Morin, who performed this operation, commenced by separating the head from the back bone, after which he undertook to strip off the skin; when the reptile suddenly threw up its tail and wound it closely around his arm. The same vitality was also manifested

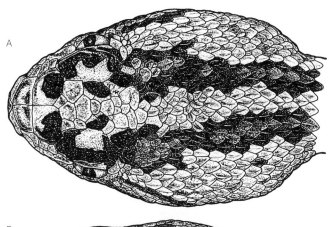

5 mm

Fig. 212. (A) Dorsal and (B) lateral aspects of head of *Crotalus simus simus*, male, 38.5 cm TL (UTA R-12567), from 7.4 km northeast of Tehuantepec, Oaxaca, Mexico, elevation 305 m. Note the large, flat paired internasals and prefrontals; this scale arrangement on the snout is also characteristic of several other large rattlesnakes, including *C. durissus*, *C. basiliscus*, and *C. molossus*. Drawings by Ty M. Kubin.

Fig. 213. Tails and rattles of *Crotalus simus simus* from Aldea El Arenal, San Vicente, Zacapa, Guatemala: (top) an adult (UTA R-51701), and (bottom) a juvenile (UTA R-46721). The pale tail with several dark blotches on the proximal portion characteristic of juveniles will undergo an ontogenetic change; adults have uniformly dark gray or black tails.

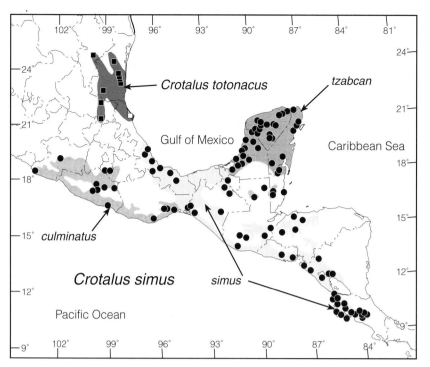

Map 109. Distributions of *Crotalus simus* (circles), including subspecies, and *C. totonacus* (squares) in Mexico and Central America. Isolated populations in northern Guatemala and Belize exhibit morphological characteristics intermediate between *C. s. simus* and *C. s. tzabcan*. Unfilled symbol represents type-locality for *C. totonacus*; that for *C. simus* too imprecise to plot.

in the upper portion of its body; nay more, after its miserable trunk was entirely divested of skin it seemed to as full of life as ever.

—Morelet, 1871, on travels in northern Guatemala

LOCAL NAMES Cascabel, víbora de cascabel, cascabela. Costa Rica: chil-chil. El Salvador: kwechwah (Pipil). Guatemala: quiakxop, sochaj (Mayan). Mexico: ahau-can, ah tsab ti'kkan, sakk ahaw kan (Mayan), shunu (Zapotec, according to Sumichrast, 1880, 1881–1882), teotlacozauhqui, tepocolcóatl, teuhtlacozauhqui (Nahuatl).

ENGLISH NAME Middle American rattlesnake.

ETYMOLOGY The species epithet is derived from the Latin *simus*, meaning "flat nosed," an allusion to the blunt head of this snake in comparison with many other species of lance-headed vipers.

DISTRIBUTION Mexico to Costa Rica (Map 109). This species occurs from southwestern Michoacán southward along the Pacific coastal plain and foothills through Mexico, Guatemala, El Salvador, Honduras, and Nicaragua to the extreme western portion of the Meseta Central, Provincia de San José, in west-central Costa Rica. It crosses over to the Atlantic lowlands in the Isthmus of Tehuantepec region, ranging to central Veracruz and through much of the northern Yucatán Peninsula. Several isolated populations occur in the dry pine forests of Belize, dry savannas of northern Guatemala, and the dry interior valleys of Chiapas, Guatemala, and Honduras. This species has not been recorded from Panama, although it has been alleged to exist in the dry tablelands of Veraguas and Chiriquí (Elton, 1948). We have heard rumors of rattlesnakes in southern Puntarenas Province, Costa Rica, in the Golfito region, near the Panamanian border. This species is usually found at elevations below 1,000 m, but populations at elevations between 1,500 and 2,200 m are known from Mexico in the Sierra de Coalcomán in Michoacán, the Sierra Madre del Sur of Guerrero, near Comitán in Chiapas, and on the steep slopes (Cerro de Oro) bordering the northern side of Lago de Atitlán in Guatemala. In Costa Rica, it occurs up to near 1,000 m on the Meseta Central, and up to 1,600 m in the Cordillera de Guanacaste.

Distribution records are available for Mexico (Alvarez del Toro, 1983; Andrews, 1937; Armstrong and Murphy, 1979; Auth et al., 2000; Barrera, 1963; Blair et al., 1997; Boulenger, 1896b; Casas-Andreu et al., 1996; Cope, 1887; Cuesta-Terrón, 1921b— in part; Davis and Dixon, 1959; Davis and Smith, 1953; Duellman, 1961, 1965a, 1965b; Dugès, 1896a; Dundee et al., 1986; Dunn, 1951; Ferrari-Perez, 1886; Gadow, 1905, 1908; Gaige, 1936; Günther, 1895–1902; Hartweg and Oliver, 1940; I. Kauffeld, 1940; Klauber, 1952; Lee, 1980, 1996; Martín del Campo, 1935, 1937a, 1950, 1984; Mocquard, 1908–1909—in part; Pérez-Higadera [*sic*] et al., 1987; Pérez-Higareda, 1978; Pérez-Higareda and Smith, 1991; Pérez-Ramos et al., 2000; Powell and Parmerlee, 1980; Ramírez-Bautista et al., 1981; Rubio, 1972; Schmidt and Andrews, 1936; Smith, 1938, 1943a; Smith and Taylor, 1945, 1966; Sumichrast, 1873, 1880, 1881–1882, 1882; Taylor, 1950; Velasco, 1895; Werner, 1922; Woodbury and Woodbury, 1944), Belize (Fugler, 1960; Gann and Gann, 1939; Garel and Matola, 1996; Günther, 1895–1902; Henderson and Hoevers, 1975; Hoevers, 1967; Neill, 1960a, 1962, 1965; Neill and Allen, 1959a, 1959b, 1960; Stafford and Meyer, 2000), Guatemala (Campbell, 1998; Campbell and Vannini, 1989; March, 1928b; Rodas, 1938; Stuart, 1935, 1948, 1950, 1954a, 1963, 1966), Honduras (Clark, 1925; Curran, 1935; Ditmars, 1928a; Dunn and Emlen, 1932; George, 1930a, 1930b; March, 1928b; Meyer, 1969; Neill, 1959; Wilson, 1983; Wilson and McCranie, 1979a, 1979b, 1991; Wilson and Meyer, 1985; Wilson et al., 2001), El Salvador (Cope, 1861, 1862; 1887; Dueñas et al., 2001; Mertens, 1952b), Nicaragua (Ditmars, 1905b; Villa, 1962, 1984), Costa Rica (Cope, 1876a; Gutiérrez et al., 1979; Leenders, 2001; Picado T., 1931a; Sasa and Solórzano, 1995; Savage, 1980, 2002; Scott, 1969, 1983b; Scott et al., 1983; Solórzano, 2004; E. Taylor, 1951, 1954; R. Taylor et al., 1974; Trejos, 1937; Wettstein, 1934), and for the general distri-bution (Bolaños, 1971, 1982, 1983, 1984; Bolaños et al., 1981; Clark, 1942; Cope, 1860b, 1861, 1887; Ditmars, 1930; Garman, 1884a, 1884b—in part; Gloyd, 1940; Grzimek, 1975; Harris and Simmons, 1972b, 1978b; Hoge, 1966; Klauber, 1952, 1972; Klemmer, 1963; Minton et al., 1968; and Peters and Orejas-Miranda, 1970).

Flores-Villela et al. (1987) reported *C. simus* from the region of Las Tuxtlas in southern Veracruz. Although this species occurs around the Sierra de los Tuxtlas, we are unaware of any specimens from the slopes of that range.

HABITAT Usually in semiarid regions including dry to very dry tropical forest, arid scrub forest, and thorn woodland, but also in relatively dry, open areas within mesic forests, particularly in limestone outcroppings. Other habitats utilized in various parts of the range include tropical deciduous forest; pine-oak forest; grass (*Trachipogon*), pine, or palm savannas (including those bordered by rainforest); and, rarely, along natural breaks in cloud forest. *Crotalus simus* is encountered infrequently in dense forest and is largely absent from rainforest, as reflected by its distribution. In Belize, Neill (1960a) and Neill and Allen (1959b) found this species in pine parkland associations, and Henderson and Hoevers (1975) reported it from "hilly pine parkland, palm and pine savanna, and sandy coastal pine ridge."

DESCRIPTION *Crotalus simus* is a stout rattlesnake that commonly exceeds 130 cm in TL. Large males in some populations attain TLs of 140–160 cm, and the maximum is at least 180 cm, with males reaching greater lengths than females. Specimens of about this size have been recorded from Mexico, Guatemala, and Costa Rica.

A conspicuous spinal ridge is present, especially in large adults and most evident on the anterior part of the body, owing to the height of the neural spines. In adults, the dorsal scales covering the spinal ridge are notable for their prominent, high, tubercular keels—a degree of rugosity rivaled only by *C. durissus* among other rattlesnakes.

The ground color may be gray-brown, brown, reddish brown, yellowish gray, pale blue-gray, greenish gray, yellowish olive, straw yellow, or orangish. There are no dark punctations in the ground color. As a broad generality (with many exceptions), the ground color of snakes from densely forested regions such as the Pacific lowlands of Guatemala tends to be considerably darker than that of snakes from more arid regions such as the Río Balsas and Río Motagua Valleys in Mexico and Guatemala, respectively. The pattern often consists of scales that are nearly all unicolored, at least on the anterior part of the body; the scales that form the pale borders around the dorsal blotches are occasionally pale distally and have dark bases.

There are 21–32 rhombic or diamond-shaped dorsal body blotches. Middorsally, blotches are separated by 1–2 pale scales. The body blotches, at least anteriorly, are reddish brown, dark brown, or black with paler interiors, usually tan to pale gray-brown. Posteriorly, dorsal blotches tend to become shorter, wider, and more obscure, often coalescing with lateral body blotches. The lateral blotches are below the lateral points of the dorsal series and usually comprise groups of 3–7 dark scales bordered by pale scales. This primary series of lateral blotches frequently engages scale rows 2–5. Another secondary series of lateral blotches alternates between the primary lateral series; this series is usually paler than the primary series and involves the outer edges of the ventrals.

The head pattern is fairly intricate in most populations and usually consists of a transverse dark bar across the anterior portions of the supraoculars, posterior part of the prefrontals, and anterior intersupraoculars (sometimes interrupted medially); a dark streak extending posteriorly from the loreal pit to the upper part of supralabials 6–9; a dark postocular stripe extending from behind the eye to the rictus or angle of the jaw; often a pair of upper temporal stripes extending diagonally from the posterior portion of the supraocular to above the angle of the jaw; and a pair of parietal stripes extending from the posterior portion of the supraocular (where they usually merge with the upper temporal stripe) to the back of the head, where they become narrower and continue onto the body as paravertebral stripes. Some or all of these head markings are pale bordered, but their extent and intensity vary considerably. The paravertebral stripes are usually 2–4 times longer than the head. Throughout most of the range of each paravertebral stripe is usually 1 or 2 dorsal scales wide. Each supraocular is marked by a prominent pale transverse crossbar (sometimes connected across the frontal region) or subcircular spot.

The tail of adults may be uniformly gray, gray-brown, blackish, or like that of juveniles, in which 4–11 darker crossbands may be vaguely evident. The proximal rattle segment is dark gray in adults and tan in young snakes.

The ventral side of the head tends to be uniformly white or yellowish, although some populations bear a few punctations on the mental and anterior infralabials. The belly is usually whitish, yellowish, or buff, and varies from nearly immaculate (the usual condition) to white with pale gray blotches becoming darker posteriorly or encroached by the lateral series of dark blotches or stippled and suffused laterally with yellow, orange, or gray.

Most frequently there are 4–6 scales in the internasal-prefrontal region, including 2 large, triangular internasals in contact with the rostral, followed by 2 large, quadrangular prefrontals (anterior canthals) that contact each other along the midline, and sometimes a pair of small posterior canthals. The posterior canthals, if present, are located directly behind the upper loreal and are sometimes considered post–upper loreals. Snakes from Pacific Mexico north of the isthmus are characterized by a tendency for a relatively greater subdivision of scales in the internasal-prefrontal region; the range for these snakes is 4–10, with the prefrontals being the scales most frequently fragmented into smaller canthals and intercanthals. It is possible to encounter specimens anywhere within the range that have irregularly divided plates on the head. Anteriorly, there are 2–5 (usually 2, except in southwestern Mexico, where the mode is 3) intersupraoculars. The parietal and occipital regions usually are covered with small, keeled scales.

The first supralabial usually is in broad contact with the prenasal; however, in snakes from southwestern Mexico it is not rare (about one specimen in five) for the first supralabial to be separated from the prenasal by a row of foveals. In many Mexican populations, a single small prefoveal (postrostral) is often isolated between the rostral, prenasal, and first supralabial. The number of prefoveals varies from 3 to 11, with 6–8 most often present. Most frequently the pre- and sublacunal are separated from the supralabials by the interposition of a row of foveals, but in about half of the snakes we have examined from southwestern Mexico and the Yucatán Peninsula the lacunals make contact with the supralabials. The lateral portions of the prefrontals (anterior canthals) are usually not deflected downward over the canthus rostralis. There are 1–6 (usually 2–3, except in snakes from southwestern Mexico, which normally have 4–5 and a range of 3–8) per side; there is usually only 1 lower loreal and 1 or more upper loreals, which prevent postnasal–upper preocular contact. When there is more than a single upper loreal, the extra scales are located posterior to the upper loreal (post–upper loreals) and are between the prefrontal and upper preoculars, usually precluding their contact. One or 2 (usually 1) interoculabials separate the anterior suboculars from the supralabials. The first pair of infralabials are most frequently divided in specimens from the Yucatán Peninsula and are commonly divided in snakes from southwestern Mexico. Infracephalic scales such as submentals and interchinshields are rarely present.

There are 2–5 intersupraoculars; 11–18 (usually 13–16) supralabials; 12–20 (usually 14–17) infralabials; 25–33 midbody dorsal scale rows (usually 29); 170–188 ventrals in males and 172–191 in females; and 25–34 subcaudals in males and 18–26 in females, 0–10 (usually 1 or 2) of which are divided.

SIMILAR SPECIES Throughout most of its range *C. simus* is the only species of rattlesnake present; thus, confusing it with any other is out of the question. Only in Mexico north of the Isthmus of Tehuantepec does its range overlap or approach that of other species of rattlesnakes, from which it can be distinguished by its conspicuous, narrow, dark paravertebral stripes.

Crotalus atrox and *C. scutulatus* have tails with strikingly contrasting black (or dark brown) and ash white rings, a dark postocular stripe that is distinctly bordered by narrow pale stripes on either side, and usually at least 8 scales in the internasal-prefrontal area. *Crotalus basiliscus* usually has a ground color with a greenish cast (reddish in juveniles), dorsal blotches that do not have dark borders that sharply contrast with their centers, a gray tail that has darker crossbands plainly evident, and usually 27 midbody dorsal scale rows (usually 29 in *C. simus*).

REMARKS This rattlesnake exhibits a considerable amount of geographic variation across its extensive distribution. We recognize three subspecies. One subspecific name, *C. d. neoleonensis*, is a nomen nudum. *Crotalus simus* has a long and tangled association in the literature with the South American *C. durissus* (sensu stricto) and *C. totonacus* of northeastern Mexico. Making matters worse, *C. simus*, *C. durissus*, and *C. horridus* were frequently confused in much of the early literature (e.g., Jan and Sordelli, 1874).

Crotalus s. simus (Pls. 956–961) ranges from Mexico to Costa Rica, occurring on the Atlantic versant from about central Veracruz, Mexico, to western Honduras, including many interior valleys (Río Grijalva, Río Negro, Río Motagua, Río Uluá-Chamelecón, Río Aguán), and on the Pacific from about the Isthmus of Tehuantepec to south-central Costa Rica. *Crotalus s. culminatus* (Pls. 962–964) inhabits southwestern Mexico from southern Michoacán to about the Isthmus of Tehuantepec. *Crotalus s. tzabcan* (Pls. 965 and 966) occurs in Mexico in the Yucatán Peninsula south to northern Belize and northern Guatemala.

Sánchez-Herrera et al. (1981) suggested that the harmless colubrid *Pituophis lineaticollis* mimics *C. simus*. However, *P. lineaticollis* is a highland species that is only narrowly sympatric with *C. simus* in a few places.

For the most part, the various subspecies of *C. simus* are distinguished on the basis of pattern, size, color, and to a lesser extent squamation. The closest relative of *C. simus* appears to be *C. durissus* of South America, but *C. totonacus*, *C. molossus*, and *C. basiliscus* also appear to be closely related. Ditmars (1930) was one of the first to suggest that *C. molossus* and *C. durissus* (sensu lato) are closely related, based on their high-keeled scales and markings.

An interesting aspect of the distribution of *C. simus* is its apparent absence from Panama, although it occurs on the Pacific side of Costa Rica and the Atlantic side of Colombia. Several reports allege that it occurs in the dry tablelands of Chiriquí and Veraguas Provinces, which appear to have habitat suitable for *C. simus*, and it is possible that the species occurs, or recently occurred, in Panama, although its presence has never been documented.

Elton (1948), chief of the Board of Health Laboratory at the Gorgas Hospital in the Canal Zone, offered an interesting, but perhaps fictitious, account of this species in Panama: "It is alleged to exist in the dry table-lands of the Provinces of Chiriquí and Veraguas, where it is zealously protected by the natives of the Bocas del Toro region. To these Indians the tropical rattler is a religious symbol and an economic asset, for, depending on its venom for obtaining their food, they make up a mixture of liver paste and venom with which to tip their hunting arrows and spears. They allow no white intruders to enter their domain, or to molest their snakes. Explorers in that area . . . are no more welcome than were the conquistadores." Lyman (1949) stated that during his 30-year residence in Panama he never saw a rattlesnake that originated in that country, and that in a snake census of the country not a single rattlesnake was present in a collection of 13,300 snakes. According to Duke (1967), rattles from rattlesnakes have been given to nonscientists on the Azuero Peninsula of Panama, where there appears to be suitable habitat for *C. simus*, and Clark (1942) stated that rattles had been received at the Gorgas Laboratory in Panama from the dry tablelands of Veraguas and Chiriquí. However, Ibáñez and Solís (1993) reported that no evidence existed to document this species in Panama, and to date, no specimen has reached any museum collection.

Crotalus stejnegeri Dunn, 1919
(Fig. 214, Map 99, Pl. 967)

Crotalus tigris—Boulenger, 1896b, *Cat. Snakes British Mus.* 3:727 pp.[580]. [Not of Kennicott.]

Crotalus stejnegeri Dunn, 1919, *Proc. Biol. Soc. Washington* 32:213–216[214]. Holotype: USNM 46586; given as 46486 in original description (typographical error). Type-locality: "Plumosas [Plomosas] Sinaloa, Mexico." [In part.]

LOCAL NAME Víbora de cascabel.

ENGLISH NAME Long-tailed rattlesnake.

ETYMOLOGY The species name is a patronym honoring Leonhard Hess Stejneger (1851–1943), a Norwegian who emigrated to the United States in 1881. He had a long and distinguished association with the National Museum of Natural History (Smithsonian Institution), where he became head curator of biology.

DISTRIBUTION Western Mexico. This snake is found in the rugged canyons and foothills of the western portion of the Sierra Madre Occidental in western Durango and southeastern Sinaloa, Mexico (Map 99). It has been collected within a few kilometers of the Nayarit border and almost certainly occurs in the northern part of that state. The vertical distribution is from about 500 to 1,200 m.

Distribution records are given in Armstrong and Murphy, 1979; Boulenger, 1896b (as *tigris*); Cochran, 1961; Collins, 1993; Coues, 1875; Dunn, 1919; Gloyd, 1940; Hardy and McDiarmid, 1969; Klauber, 1936b, 1940c, 1952, 1971, 1972; Martín del Campo, 1935, 1937a, 1950; McDiarmid et al., 1976; Smith, 1943a; Smith and Taylor, 1945; Tanner, 1966a; Webb, 1984; and Werner, 1922.

HABITAT Tropical deciduous and pine-oak forests. Most of the specimens with which we are familiar have come from the ecotone between these two types of forest.

DESCRIPTION This is a relatively small rattlesnake, usually not exceeding 60 cm in TL; the largest specimen known is 72.4 cm. The tail is slender and proportionately long, in adults constituting 11.0–14.8% of the total length in males and

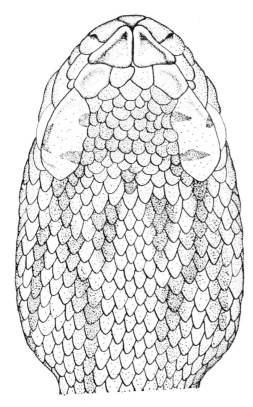

Fig. 214. Dorsal aspect of head of *Crotalus stejnegeri*, female, 59.0 cm TL (USNM 46486—holotype), from Plumosas, Sinaloa, Mexico. From Tanner, 1966a. Published by permission of the Herpetologists' League.

9.8–12.5% in females. The rattle is tiny, and Klauber (1940c) suggested that it is probably inaudible.

The ground color is pale gray-brown or pale buckskin, becoming somewhat darker (usually dark gray) on the posterior part of the body and the tail. The conspicuous dark brown markings on top of the head often include a pair of spots in the prefrontal region, a dark bar between the supraoculars, a pair of small parietal spots bordered by a pair of elongated crescent-shaped blotches, a pair of stripes in the upper temporal region, and a pair of nape stripes that may continue unbroken onto the body. A dark brown postocular stripe extends from the lower posterior border of the eye to the rictus. The nape blotches are followed by 32–43 medium brown, black-edged dorsal body blotches. Three series of lateral body blotches alternate along the side of the body: the larger median series is sometimes bordered by large orange flecks and is offset from the dorsal blotches, sometimes coalescing with these on the posterior of the body; a small upper series on scale rows 6–8 and a small lower series on scale rows 1–3 are located one above the other about halfway between the middorsal blotches. The tail has 8–15 crossbands that become indistinct distally. The infralabials and gular region are white, almost immaculate; the belly is white with irregular, roundish, gray or brown blotches toward the lateral edges of the ventrals and faint brown speckling that becomes heavier posteriorly; the subcaudals are pale gray. The proximal segment of the rattle is dark gray to black. The iris is yellow with fine black peppering, and the tongue is black with white tips.

The rostral is usually about as high as wide; there are 2 large, triangular internasals, and 10–21 scales occupy the internasal-prefrontal region. Five to 8 intersupraoculars, 2–5 loreals, and 1 or 2 canthals are evident on each side between the internasal

and supraocular. Two interoculabials separate the suboculars from the supralabials, except for the anterior subocular, which is generally separated by only 1 scale. The prenasal is in broad contact with supralabial 1, and the postnasal is precluded from contacting the upper preocular by the intervening loreals. The first pair of infralabials are enlarged, extend backward, and are broadly in contact behind the mental; they often partially or completely separate the second pair of infralabials from the chinshields. The posterior ends of the first pair of infralabials are blunt and do not intervene between the chinshields. There are 14–16 supralabials, 14–18 infralabials, 23–29 (mode 27) midbody dorsal scale rows, 174–178 ventrals in males and 171–176 in females, 43–48 subcaudals in males and 36–37 in females (0–7 divided distally), and 7–10 rattle-fringe scales.

SIMILAR SPECIES It would take a vivid imagination to mistake this snake for any other rattlesnake. Of the other small montane rattlesnakes inhabiting the Sierra Madre Occidental, only *C. lepidus* is known to be sympatric with this species; *C. pricei* and *C. willardi* occur at higher elevations in this mountain system. The distinctive head pattern, shape of the first pair of infralabials, high number of ventrals and subcaudals, and slender tail with diminutive rattle distinguish *C. stejnegeri* from these species. A large rattlesnake tentatively considered to be a hybrid between *C. basiliscus* and *C. molossus* (see Remarks for *C. basiliscus*) has been collected on the same slopes as *C. stejnegeri*. It can be distinguished from *C. stejnegeri* by its pale-bordered, diamond-shaped dorsal blotches; a pair of large prefrontals; fewer than 5 intersupraoculars; thick tail with fewer subcaudals; and relatively large size. The rattlesnake that perhaps most closely resembles *C. stejnegeri*, *C. lannomi*, is known only from the type-locality in Jalisco. It differs from *C. stejnegeri* in having a rostral wider than high, fewer prefoveals (4 versus 7), and only 2 intersupraoculars.

REMARKS This rare rattlesnake is known from only about a dozen specimens. Individuals have been found active after dark, but they also bask during the early morning.

Crotalus tigris Kennicott, 1859
(Map 110, Pls. 968 and 969)

Crotalus tigris Kennicott, *in* Baird, *in* Emory, 1859, *Rep. U.S.-Mex. Bound. Surv.* 3:1–35[14, Pl. 4]. Holotype: USNM 471. The original series consisted of three specimens (USNM 471–473), all with the same data. It is not clear which specimen(s) Kennicott examined when he wrote the description. Only a single specimen, "No. 471. Sierra Verde and Pozo Verde," was listed by Baird (1859a:14), and this specimen was called the type by Gloyd (1940:223), Klauber (1956:43), and Cochran (1961:171). USNM 471 and USNM 472 were called "the types" by Cope (1900:1182), with no mention of USNM 473. It seems likely that USNM 473 had been sent to the Academy of Natural Sciences in Philadelphia before Cope's manuscript was completed. Klauber (1930b:106) referred to USNM 471 and USNM 472 as cotypes, and later Klauber (1956:43) stated that USNM 472 and USNM 473 [now ANSP 7160] are cotypes. In contrast, Gloyd (1940:223 and footnote) referred to USNM 472 and USNM 473 as paratypes. Because we may never know what Kennicott saw and because only a single specimen is listed in the original description, McDiarmid et al. (1999) preferred to treat USNM 471 as the holotype rather than as one of three syntypes. If data become available that suggest that Kennicott actually examined multiple specimens, then it would be appropriate to consider the three specimens syntypes, and Gloyd's (1940:223)

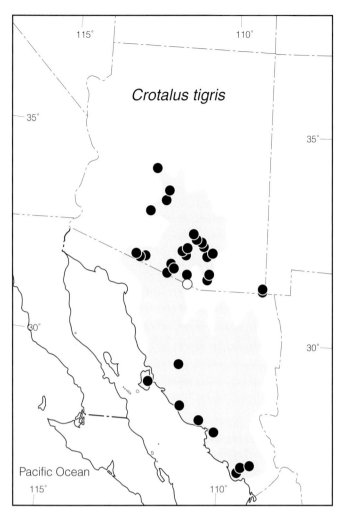

Map 110. Distribution of *Crotalus tigris* in the southwestern United States and northwestern Mexico. Unfilled symbol represents type-locality.

ETYMOLOGY   The species epithet is derived from the Latin *tigris*, meaning "tiger," an allusion to the numerous narrow dorsal crossbands that create a vertically striped pattern.

DISTRIBUTION   Southwestern United States and northwestern Mexico. This species ranges from south-central Arizona in the United States southward through most of Sonora, Mexico, exclusive of the panhandle in the northwest and the high mountains in the eastern portion of that state (Map 110), and on Isla Tiburón in the Gulf of California. The vertical distribution is from near sea level to about 1,465 m; Van Denburgh (1922b) recorded the maximum elevation as 2,440 m, but no recent records confirm this exceptionally high figure.

Range or locality records are available for Arizona (Amaral, 1929a; Badman, 2001; Baird, 1859a; Coues, 1875; Fowlie, 1965; Gehlbach, 1957; Gloyd, 1937; Holycross, 1998; Howland et al., 2002; Humphrey, 1936; Kauffeld, 1943a; Lowe, 1964; Lowe et al., 1986; Ortenburger and Ortenburger, 1927; Painter and Milensky, 1993; Shaw and Campbell, 1974; Troschel, 1860); Sonora, including Isla Tiburón (Allen, 1933; Davis and Dixon, 1957; Dixon et al., 1962; Grismer, 2002; Smith and Chrapliwy, 1958; Taylor, 1938a; Zweifel and Norris, 1955); Mexico generally (Armstrong and Murphy, 1979; Garman, 1884a; Klauber, 1952; Martín del Campo, 1937a, 1950; Murphy and Ottley, 1984; Smith and Taylor, 1945); the United States (Cope, 1900; Stejneger and Barbour, 1943); and throughout the range (Ditmars, 1931; Gloyd, 1940; Hoge and Romano, 1971a; Klauber, 1931b, 1952, 1971, 1972; Mocquard, 1908–1909; Pope, 1944–1945; Stebbins, 1985; Stejneger, 1895; Van Denburgh, 1922b; Werner, 1922; Wright and Wright, 1957). *Crotalus tigris* has been reported frequently in the literature as occurring in California; most of these records are apparently based on *C. mitchellii pyrrhus* or *C. m. stephensi*. The record from near Monclova in Coahuila (Cuesta-Terrón, 1921b) is obviously in error.

HABITAT   Sonoran Desert and mesquite-grassland, barely entering tropical deciduous forest in southern Sonora. This rattlesnake is found almost exclusively in rugged, rocky country. In Arizona, Jones (1988) found *C. tigris* primarily in chaparral. In the Sonoran Desert of Arizona it is found mostly in rocky areas during the winter and spring; during the summer it uses the edges of arroyos (Beck, 1995). Humphrey (1936) reported that the elevational distribution of *C. tigris* in various mountain ranges in Arizona spans that of *C. atrox*, *C. molossus*, and *C. scutulatus*.

DESCRIPTION   This snake is less than 100 cm in TL; the largest measured specimen is 88.5 cm (Klauber, 1956). The rattles are relatively large, and the head is small.

The ground color may be gray, lavender, blue-gray, pink, or buff, usually turning to pink, pale orange, or cream on the sides. The dorsal pattern consists of 35–52 crossbands that are dark gray or brown and consist largely of heavy punctations. The crossbands have vague borders, are wider middorsally than laterally, and are wider at the middorsum than the interspaces; they become more clearly defined and darker on the posterior part of the body. Both the ground color and the crossbands are heavily punctated with dark pigment; the ground color tends to be paler posteriorly, and thus the dark crossbands stand in greater contrast there. A series of small lateral blotches alternates between the crossbands and is located on the first 2–3 scale rows; these blotches are more distinct posteriorly. The head markings are vague and irregular, but the back of the head has a few dark markings that may be arranged as paired occipital blotches and upper temporal streaks. Pale transverse bars are sometimes present on the supraoculars; these bars tend to curve forward medially. An ill-defined dark postocular stripe

action (possibly an earlier one exists) designating USNM 471 as the lectotype should be followed (McDiarmid et al., 1999). Type-locality: "Sierra Verde and Pozo Verde." Pozo Verde is a spring located on the Sonoran side of the U.S.-Mexico border, near Sasabe. It is on the western slope of the southern end of the Sierra Verde, which is also known as the Sierra del Pozo Verde, according to Stejneger (1893:214, footnote), and appears on recent maps of Sonora, Mexico.

Caudisona tigris—Cope, 1867 [dated 1866], *Proc. Acad. Nat. Sci. Philadelphia* 18:300–314[309].
Crotalus tigris—Boulenger, 1896b, *Cat. Snakes British Mus.* 3:727 pp.[580].
Crotalus tigris tigris—Amaral, 1929a, *Bull. Antivenin Inst. Am.* 2:82–85[84, fig. 1].

Venomous snakes bite men not out of an aggressive desire to kill, but because they react to what their instincts interpret as an attack. They bite people who are ignorant, careless, foolish, or sometimes just plain unlucky. They usually bite people who either don't know the habits of venomous snakes or who ignore safety precautions. Not infrequently they bite people who, while handling them, suffer a momentary lapse of concentration, a fateful distraction.
—Shaw and Campbell, 1974

LOCAL NAME   Víbora de cascabel.
ENGLISH NAME   Tiger rattlesnake.

extends from the posterior edge of the eye to above the rictus; it is rarely bordered along its upper margin by a narrow, pale stripe. The tail has 4–10 dark brown, indistinct, speckled crossbands. The caudal crossbands are wider than the adjacent interspaces along the middorsum. The infracephalic scales are mostly pale except for heavy punctations on the mental and infralabials. The belly is straw colored, yellow, or pink, and moderately to heavily mottled or flecked with gray or brown pigment. The proximal rattle segment is tan or brown.

The rostral is wider than high, and 2 internasals are in contact with the rostral. There are 11–37 scales in the internasal-prefrontal area and 3–8 intersupraoculars. The prenasals are in broad contact with the rostral and usually with the first supralabial. There is usually only a single loreal per side, less frequently 2. The contact of the posterior canthal with a loreal usually prevents the upper preocular from touching the postnasal. Most frequently there is 1 interoculabial, but in some specimens the anterior subocular is in contact with the supralabial series. There are 11–16 (usually 12–14) supralabials, 11–16 (usually 13–15) infralabials, 20–27 (usually 23) midbody dorsal scale rows, 156–172 ventrals in males and 164–177 in females, and 23–27 subcaudals in males and 16–21 in females.

SIMILAR SPECIES *Crotalus tigris* can be distinguished from other species of rattlesnakes by the crossbands on the anterior part of its body. Four other species of rattlesnakes occur within the range of *C. tigris*. *Crotalus atrox* has conspicuously contrasting pale and dark tail rings, a pale postocular stripe extending from the upper postocular to a point in front of the rictus, and usually 25 or more midbody dorsal scale rows. *Crotalus cerastes* has supraoculars that form hornlike projections and 154 or fewer ventrals. *Crotalus mitchellii*, sympatric in one limited area in Arizona, has scales separating the rostral from the prenasals and usually 25 or more midbody dorsal scale rows. Though it is believed to be closely related to *C. tigris*, *C. mitchellii* has a proportionately much larger head. In *C. molossus* the ground color and blotches are not punctated with dark pigment, the tail of adults is nearly uniformly dark, usually 2 large prefrontals are in contact with each other medially, and 25 or more midbody dorsal scale rows are present. *Crotalus scutulatus* has conspicuously contrasting pale and dark tail rings; a broad, dark postocular stripe that is bordered above and below by narrow pale stripes; usually 2 intersupraoculars; and usually 25 or more midbody dorsal scale rows.

REMARKS This species may be active any time of the day, but like all rattlesnakes it avoids prolonged exposure to direct sunlight during the hotter hours. It tends to be especially active after summer rains.

Crotalus tortugensis Van Denburgh and Slevin, 1921
(Map 91, Pls. 970 and 971)

Crotalus tortugensis Van Denburgh and Slevin, 1921c, *Proc. California Acad. Sci.* 11:395–398[398]. Holotype: CAS 50515. Type-locality: "Tortuga Island [Baja California Sur], Gulf of California, Mexico."
Crotalus atrox tortugensis—Stejneger and Barbour, 1933, *Check List N. Am. Rept.*, 3d ed., 185 pp.[133].
Crotalus tortuguensis—Hoge and Romano-Hoge, 1971, *Venom. Animals Venoms* 2:211–293[277]. [Unjustified emendation.]
Crotalus atrox tortuguensis—Hoge and Romano-Hoge, 1971, *Venom. Animals Venoms* 2:211–293[277]. [As cited in the synonymy of *Crotalus tortuguensis*; unjustified emendation.]
Crotalus tortugensis—Golay et al., 1993, *Endogly. Venom. Snakes World*, 478 pp.[71].

LOCAL NAME Víbora de cascabel.
ENGLISH NAME Tortuga Island diamond rattlesnake.
ETYMOLOGY The species epithet is derived from Isla Tortuga (Spanish for Turtle Island), to which this snake is restricted.
DISTRIBUTION Endemic to Isla Tortuga off the east coast of Baja California Sur in the Gulf of California, Mexico (Map 91). References to this species on Isla Tortuga are contained in Armstrong and Murphy, 1979; Cliff, 1954; Cuesta-Terrón, 1931; Gloyd, 1940; Grismer, 2002; Klauber, 1930a, 1936b, 1938, 1971, 1972; Lindsay, 1962; Martín del Campo, 1937a, 1950; Murphy, 1983b; Murphy and Ottley, 1984; Schmidt, 1922; Smith and Taylor, 1945; Soulé and Sloan, 1966; Stejneger and Barbour, 1943; Van Denburgh, 1922b; and Van Denburgh and Slevin, 1921c.
HABITAT Desert; rocky, barren terrain covered with sparse brush and cacti.
DESCRIPTION This snake is smaller than its close relative, *C. atrox*. Large males may slightly exceed 100 cm in TL; the largest known specimen measured 105.8 cm in TL (Klauber, 1972). The head length is proportionately smaller relative to body length in *C. tortugensis* than in *C. atrox*; this trait is often considered an indicator of dwarfing, a common characteristic of island populations.

The ground color is gray to gray-brown, sometimes with a slight purplish or pinkish cast. The 32–41 dark brown to purplish brown dorsal blotches are diamond shaped or hexagonal, punctated with black spots, and bordered with irregular black mottling; they tend to have pale interiors on each side of the dorsal midline and become relatively pale and ill defined on the posterior part of the body. On the anterior two-thirds to three-fourths of the body, the dorsal blotches are edged along their middorsal portions with white or buff; this pale edging is usually absent, or at most extremely narrow, on the lateral margins of the dorsal blotches. The dorsum of the head usually has irregular black mottling or speckling. Each supraocular is marked with a transverse pale line. The dark postocular stripe is bordered by a lower (anterior) pale stripe that extends from the upper preocular to the lip margin below the eye and an upper (posterior) pale stripe that extends from the upper postocular to the lip margin near the rictus; overall, these pale lateral head markings are not particularly well defined. The tail has strongly contrasting ash white and black rings; the 3–7 black tail rings are as wide as or wider than the pale rings. The proximal rattle segment is black.

The rostral is usually higher than wide. There are 2 internasals in contact with the rostral, more than 8 scales in the internasal-prefrontal region, and 4–5 (usually 4) intersupraoculars. The prenasal is invariably in contact with the first supralabial. The posterior canthal is large and its lateral portion extends ventrally over the canthus rostralis to partially intervene between the upper preocular and postnasal. A single loreal, the lower, is usually present on each side of the head; it is situated below the canthal, with which it usually makes contact, and thus usually separates the postnasal from the upper preocular. Two or 3 interoculabials separate the anterior subocular from the supralabials. There are 14–18 (usually 15 or 16) supralabials, 14–19 (usually 16 or 17) infralabials (the first pair of which is not transversely divided), 25–27 (usually 27) midbody dorsal scale rows, 180–190 ventrals in males and 183–190 in females, and 22–25 subcaudals in males and 16–20 in females.
SIMILAR SPECIES *Crotalus tortugensis* is the only rattlesnake on Isla Tortuga. *Crotalus atrox* occurs on the Mexican mainland to the northeast of Isla Tortuga and also on at least five islands in the Gulf of California. The dorsal blotches on *C. tortugensis* are

distinctive: the margins are much darker than the inner portions lying on both sides of the midline, which may be about the same color as the ground color. In *C. atrox* the upper preocular usually touches the postnasal; if not, contact is prevented by the presence of an *upper* loreal. *Crotalus ruber*, which occurs on the adjacent peninsula of Baja California, can be distinguished from *C. tortugensis* by having the first pair of infralabials transversely divided and a reddish, reddish brown, or pink ground color.

REMARKS Amaral (1929b) had difficulty distinguishing among *C. atrox*, *C. ruber*, and *C. tortugensis*, and suggested that only a single species was involved. Although Klauber (1972:58), Campbell and Lamar (1989:365), Golay et al. (1993:71), and Grismer (2002) considered this taxon a distinct species, it is not well differentiated from *C. atrox*, and a strong case for conspecificity might be made. Grismer (1994a) treated this population as a subspecies of *C. atrox* and attributed its presence on Isla Tortuga to a recent overwater dispersal from mainland Mexico. More recently, however, Grismer (2002) afforded this population full species status. Hoge and Romano (1971a) treated the population on Isla Tortuga as a subspecies of *C. atrox* but did not provide information justifying this arrangement.

Crotalus tortugensis is reported to be quick to rattle vigorously but is less irritable than mainland *C. atrox*.

Crotalus totonacus Gloyd and Kauffeld, 1940 (Map 109, Pls. 972–977)

Crotalus totonacus Gloyd and Kauffeld, 1940, *Bull. Chicago Acad. Sci.* 6:11–14[12]. Holotype: CA 4469. Type-locality: "Panuco Island, about 75 miles south of Tampico, Veracruz, Mexico, 12 miles inland from Cabo Rojo."
Crotalus durissus totonacus—Smith and Taylor, 1945, *Bull. U.S. Natl. Mus.* 187:239 pp.[190].
Crotalus basiliscus totonacus—Taylor, 1950, *Univ. Kansas Sci. Bull.* 33:519–603[453].
Crotalus (Crotalus) durissus totonacus—Peters and Orejas-Miranda, 1970, *Bull. U.S. Natl. Mus.* 297(1):1–347[74].
Crotalus durissus neoleonensis Juliá-Zertuche and Treviño-Saldaña, 1978, *Res. Segundo Congr. Nac. Zool.*, p. 60[60]. [Nomen nudum.]

LOCAL NAME Víbora de cascabel.

ENGLISH NAME Totonacan rattlesnake.

ETYMOLOGY The specific epithet is named for the Totonac Indians of northeastern Mexico, with the Latin termination *-us* denoting a masculine adjective.

DISTRIBUTION Northeastern Mexico from central Nuevo León through southern Tamaulipas, northern Veracruz, eastern San Luis Potosí, and northern Querétaro (Map 109). This species occurs from near sea level to at least 1,680 m in the Sierra de Guatemala of Tamaulipas.

Distribution records are given in Armstrong and Murphy, 1979; Auth et al., 2000; Dixon et al., 1972; Gloyd, 1940; Gloyd and Kauffeld, 1940; Klauber, 1952, 1971, 1972; Martin, 1955a, 1955b, 1958; Martín del Campo, 1950; Minton and Minton de Cervantes, 1977; Pérez-Higareda and Smith, 1991; and Smith and Taylor, 1945.

HABITAT Lowland tropical thornforest and tropical deciduous forest, in some areas ranging up into pine-oak forest and even to lower cloud forest (Martin, 1955a, 1958).

DESCRIPTION *Crotalus totonacus* is a stout rattlesnake; adults commonly exceed 150 cm in TL, and the maximum known is at least 166.5 cm (Klauber, 1972). A poorly developed spinal ridge is usually evident in large adults on the anterior part of the

body. The dorsal scales covering the spinal ridge are strongly keeled on adults but are not high and tubercular.

The ground color is usually yellowish brown, straw yellow, orange citrine, pale olive brown, or pale gray-brown, but some individuals from high elevations tend to have a dark brown ground color. There are no dark punctations in the ground color. There are 27–35 ($\bar{x}$ = 30) black or dark brown dorsal body blotches; these are often subhexagonal anteriorly, becoming diamond shaped on the midbody and forming crossbars posteriorly. Middorsally, blotches are separated by 1–2 pale scales on the anterior part of the body and by 3–4 scales more posteriorly. The centers of the blotches, at least anteriorly on the body, are medium to dark brown, becoming paler on the posterior of the body. The dorsal blotches are made particularly prominent by the border of a single row of white, cream, or yellow scales. The pattern consists of scales that are nearly all unicolored, at least on the anterior of the body. Posteriorly, dorsal blotches often coalesce with lateral body blotches. The lateral body blotches are below the lateral points of the dorsal series and usually comprise groups of 2–4 dark scales, usually arranged in a more or less vertical row, engaging scale rows 1–4, and set off from the ground color by surrounding white, cream, or yellow scales. A secondary series of lateral blotches is usually not apparent on adults. The venter is cream or yellowish, with the head and gular region immaculate but with clumps of gray or grayish brown pigment on most of the body on either side of the ventral midline and becoming darker on the posterior of the body, where dark ventral blotches may extend to the lateral edges of the ventrals.

The head pattern usually consists of dark pigment along the posterior edges of the prefrontals and along the medial edges of the supraoculars. A dark patch of scales is sometimes present behind the eye, but this does not form a postocular stripe. A dark upper temporal stripe extends diagonally from behind the supraocular to a point well above the angle of the jaw, and a pair of parietal stripes extends from behind the supraoculars (anteriorly these sometimes merge into a spear-shaped point or are separated by 1–2 scales) to the back of the head, where they continue onto the body as poorly defined paravertebral stripes and merge with the first elongated body blotch. The paravertebral blotches usually extend onto the neck for no more than a head length and are 4 scales wide. The tail of adults is dark gray, dark gray-brown, or blackish and may be uniformly colored, but usually there is at least a faint indication of darker crossbands. Patterning on the tail is more conspicuous on juveniles, which may have 6–9 darker crossbands.

Most frequently there are 4 scales in the internasal-prefrontal region, including 2 large internasals in contact with the rostral followed by 2 large, quadrangular prefrontals (anterior canthals) that contact each other along the midline. Irregular fragmention of scales is sometimes present on the snout. There are 2 (rarely 1 or 3) intersupraoculars, and the anterior parietal region is covered with relatively large, unkeeled, but striated scales. The first supralabial is in broad contact with the prenasal, there are 3–4 prefoveals, and the prelacunal and sublacunal may be separated from the supralabials by the interposition of a row of foveals or may be in contact with the supralabials. The lateral portions of the prefrontals (anterior canthals) are not deflected downward over the canthus rostralis. Usually 1 lower and 1 upper loreal are present, precluding postnasal–upper preocular contact. The upper loreal is horizontally elongate (sometimes divided into 2 scales) and is interposed between the prefrontal and upper preocular. Two or 3 (usually 2) interoculabials separate the anterior suboculars from the supralabials. The first pair of infralabials is most frequently not transversely divided, and infracephalic scales such as submentals and interchinshields are not present.

There are 12–15 (usually 14) supralabials, 12–17 (usually 15) infralabials, 25 dorsal scale rows at midbody, 184–192 ventrals in males and 193–195 in females, and 26–29 subcaudals in males and 22–26 in females.

SIMILAR SPECIES *Crotalus totonacus* differs from other members of the *C. durissus* group in a number of morphological aspects (see Table 50). The spinal ridge on the anterior portion of the body is comparatively poorly developed. The average number of dorsal blotches is 30, relatively high for this group, and the lateral body blotches are situated relatively low on the sides of the body (scale rows 1–4) and reach the ventrals. Secondary lateral body blotches are absent. Paravertebral stripes are short, wide, and ill defined, and they are separated from each other by an irregular, broken, pale midvertebral stripe that is 1 to several scales wide along its length. Large, flat, somewhat irregular, vestigial parietals are usually present behind the supraoculars, and there are only 3–4 prefoveals per side.

Some *C. molossus* specimens closely resemble individuals of *C. totonacus*. Indeed, specimens from northeastern Querétaro (TCWC collection) appear to have traits of both *C. totonacus* and *C. molossus* and provide strong evidence of hybridization between the two species. The following traits characterize *C. molossus* and may help distinguish it from *C. totonacus*: (1) paired parietal or occipital stripes may be present, but these are even more obscure and ill defined than in individuals of *C. totonacus* occurring in northeastern Mexico, and they continue only for a short distance onto the neck; (2) the dorsal blotches tend more often to coalesce with the primary lateral series, forming dorsal crossbands; and (3) the dorsum of the head is usually quite dark and without any intricate markings such as a dark prefrontal crossbar or supraocular spots or bars.

Crotalus transversus Taylor, 1944
(Fig. 215, Map 99, Pls. 978–980)

Crotalus triseriatus anahuacus—Martín del Campo, 1940b, *An. Inst. Biol. Univ. México* 11:741–743[742]. [In part.]
Crotalus transversus Taylor, 1944, *Univ. Kansas Sci. Bull.* 30:47–56[47, fig. 1 (Pl. 6)]. Holotype: FMNH 100129 (formerly EHT-HMS 30001). Type-locality: "about 55 km. SW México (city), near Tres Marías (Tres Cumbres), Morelos [Mexico], elevation about 10,000 ft." Davis and Smith (1953:141) gave reasons for considering the type-locality to be "Laguna Zempoala, [state of] México." However, Campbell (1988b:450.1) pointed out that the emended type-locality actually lies in the state of Morelos.

> De los dos ejemplares de víboras de cascabel encontrados en los alrededores de las Lagunas de Cempoala, el más interesante es, sin duda[,] un individuo joven que recolecté en una de las veredas que conducen de la primera a la quinta lagunas.
>
> —Martín del Campo (1940b) describing what he thought was an aberrant *C. triseriatus*, but which was actually an individual of what would become *C. transversus* four years later

LOCAL NAME Víbora de cascabel.
ENGLISH NAME Cross-banded mountain rattlesnake.
ETYMOLOGY The species epithet is derived from the Latin prefix *trans-*, meaning "across," and *versus*, meaning "to

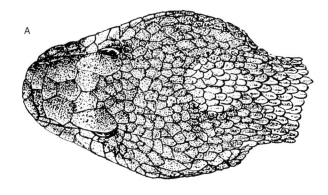

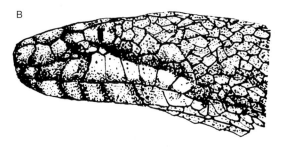

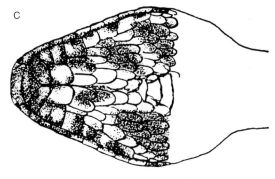

Fig. 215. (A) Dorsal, (B) lateral, and (C) ventral aspects of head of *Crotalus transversus*, adult female, 46.4 cm TL (FMNH 10,0129—holotype); (D) dorsal color pattern of holotype, probably from Lagunas de Zempoala, Morelos, Mexico, elevation 3,048 m, according to Campbell, 1988b. From Taylor, 1944. Published by permission of the Natural History Museum of the University of Kansas.

turn," in reference to the distinctive dark crossbands on the dorsum.

DISTRIBUTION Central Mexico. This rattlesnake is known from a small portion of the Transverse Volcanic Cordillera (Map 99). It occurs in the Sierra Ajusco south of Mexico City, where specimens have been taken from the hillsides surrounding the

Lagunas de Zempoala in extreme northwestern Morelos and adjacent portions of the state of México at elevations of 2,900–3,300 m; the species probably also occurs in an adjacent portion of the Distrito Federal. A disjunct population was recently reported by Camarillo and Campbell (1993, 2002) from the state of México at a locality 12 km east of Jiquipilco at elevations of about 3,000–3,600 m; this locality is on Cerro Cañada Honda, which rises to 3,710 m (the entire range is sometimes referred to as the Sierra de Monte Alto).

Distribution records are available in Armstrong and Murphy, 1979; Camarillo and Campbell, 1993, 2002; Campbell 1988b; Davis and Smith, 1953; Klauber, 1952, 1971, 1972; Martín del Campo, 1940b; Smith, 1946b; Smith and Taylor, 1945; and Taylor, 1944.

HABITAT Steep volcanic slopes in relatively open areas dominated by pine and bunchgrass (*zacatón*), usually on south-facing hillsides (Campbell, 1988b). In some collection sites many species of boad-leaved trees are present, and the habitat has been considered temperate boreal forest (Leopold, 1950).

DESCRIPTION This is a small rattlesnake; the longest specimen known, a female, is only 46.5 cm in TL. The tail length constitutes about 10.5% of the TL in a single adult male and 7.1–7.9% in six adult females (Campbell, 1988b).

There are two different color morphs, and individuals may have an orangish or brownish gray ground color. A pair of short, dark nape blotches is present, and a dark postocular stripe extends from the lower posterior edge of the eye past the rictus to the angle of the jaw. The supralabials tend to be pale with varying amounts of dark mottling, especially anteriorly and along the margin of the lip. There are 37–43 narrow, dark brown to black crossbands on the body and 5–9 on the tail. The mental is dark and the infralabials are heavily mottled. The belly may be pale with scattered dark mottling or may be so heavily mottled as to be almost uniformly black. The basal segment of the rattle is similar in color to the ground color.

The rostral is wider than high. There are 2 large internasals, a single canthal on each side, 4–6 scales in the internasal-prefrontal area, 1–3 intersupraoculars, and a single loreal on each side that usually (but not invariably) fails to contact supralabial 2 owing to the presence of a single large prefoveal. The prenasal is in broad contact with supralabial 1; the postnasal is precluded from contact with the upper preocular by the intervening loreal. Subfoveals and postfoveals are absent. The upper preocular is not vertically divided and the lower preocular may or may not extend forward to make contact with the posterior margin of the loreal. Supralabials 3–5 usually touch the suboculars. There are 8–10 (usually 9) supralabials, 8 or 9 (usually 9) infralabials, 21 midbody dorsal scale rows, 141–145 ventrals in males and 136–155 in females, 25–26 subcaudals in males and 18–22 in females (the distal 3–9 may be divided), and 8 rattle-fringe scales.

SIMILAR SPECIES The only rattlesnake sympatric with *C. transversus* is *C. triseriatus*. These species differ from each other most conspicuously in their dorsal patterns: *C. transversus* has 37–43 narrow crossbands, whereas *C. triseriatus* has 30–57 dark middorsal blotches. *Crotalus triseriatus* also differs from *C. transversus* in having 2 or more prefoveals; in having the posterior edge of the loreal pointed and projecting between the anterior portions of the upper and lower preoculars; and in usually having 3 suboculars—the anteriormost in contact with 2 supralabials (usually the third and fourth), but the posterior 2 separated from the supralabials by a single row of interoculabials. *Crotalus triseriatus* usually has 23 or more midbody dorsal scale rows (versus 21) and more numerous supralabials (9–15 versus

8–10) and infralabials (10–14 versus 8–9) than *C. transversus*. *Crotalus ravus* has been taken within a few kilometers of *C. transversus* but is easily distinguished by its large, symmetrical head plates; distinctive pattern; and usually more numerous labials (10–13 supralabials and 9–13 infralabials).

REMARKS This rattlesnake is known from fewer than 20 specimens. Camarillo and Campbell (1993) reported an adult *C. transversus* that was discovered beneath a small rock and several neonates that were seen crawling in a small rocky, grassy area within a forest. This snake has relatively large eyes and is probably strictly diurnal, especially in view of the cold nighttime temperatures within its habitat.

A single unusual rattlesnake specimen (FMNH 39115) was collected in 1941 on Cerro Tancítaro, Michoacán, and was subsequently mentioned first by Klauber (1952) and then by Duellman (1961), Harris and Simmons (1978b), and Campbell (1982a, 1988b). Most authors have allocated the specimen to *C. intermedius*, although Campbell (1982a) suggested it was closer to *C. transversus* and probably represented an undescribed species. The status of the population represented by this meager material remains uncertain, but as our understanding of the variation and distribution of *C. intermedius*, *C. transversus*, and *C. pricei* has increased, it seems most likely that an undescribed species is present on Cerro Tancítaro.

Campbell (1982a) provided a brief description of the salient features of this specimen: "It is a female 384 mm in body length; the tail is cut off at the ninth subcaudal; three internasals are present, [a large scale] on each side and a small scale medially; there is a small prefoveal on the right side; the first and second supralabials contact the loreal on the left side, while on the right side the second supralabial is excluded by the prefoveal; the loreal does not contact the prenasal or lower preocular; there are 160 ventrals; the dorsal scale rows are disposed in 21-21-17 rows; a narrow postocular stripe, which is poorly defined above, extends from the lower posterior edge of the eye to the angle of the jaw, involving the lower temporal scales and, posteriorly, the upper part of the supralabials; the labials are darkly mottled; and the gular area is light, but the rest of the venter including subcaudals is heavily mottled."

Crotalus triseriatus (Wagler, 1830)
(Figs. 216 and 217, Map 90, Pls. 981–987)

Uropsophus triseriatus Wagler, 1830, *Nat. Syst. Amph.*, 354 pp.[176]. Syntypes (4): ZMB 2908–2911. Type-locality: "Mexico." Proposed restriction to "Alvarez, San Luis Potosí, Mexico," by Smith and Taylor (1950b:342). This restriction is not valid because *C. t. triseriatus*, as presently defined, does not enter San Luis Potosí; Alvarez is the type-locality for *C. t. aquilus* [=*Crotalus aquilus*].

Crotalus triseriatus—Gray, 1831, *Synops. Rept., Animal Kingdom* (Appendix) 9:1–110[78].

Crotalus lugubris Jan, 1859a, *Rev. Mag. Zool.* (Paris) (2)10:148–157[153, 156]. Syntypes (4): two specimens in the Milan Museum [MSNM], one in the Westphal-Castelnau Collection, and one in the Paris Museum [MNHN]. Lectotype: MSNM 1414, designated by Klauber (1940:17), now destroyed according to Klauber (1952:34). Type-locality: "Mexique." [This species originally was a composite; see account for *Crotalus polystictus*.]

Caudisona lugubris—Cope, 1860b, *Smithson. Contrib. Knowl.* 12:119–126[122].

Caudisona triseriata—Cope, 1867 [dated 1866], *Proc. Acad. Nat. Sci. Philadelphia* 18:300–314[309].

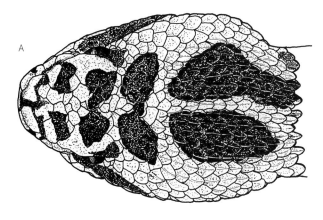

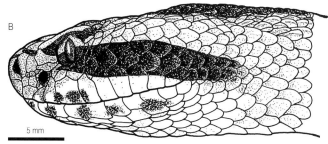

Fig. 216. (A) Dorsal and (B) lateral aspects of head of *Crotalus triseriatus triseriatus*, male, 40.7 cm TL (UTA R-12600), from near Huitzilac, Morelos, Mexico, elevation 2,743 m. The canthals are separated by several scales. Drawings by Ty M. Kubin.

Fig. 217. Lateral aspect of heads of *Crotalus triseriatus armstrongi*: (A) adult male, 48.4 cm TL (UTA R-6258—holotype); (B) adult female 48.5 cm TL (UTA R-6260—paratype); both specimens from 2.4 km northwest of Tapalpa, Jalisco, Mexico, elevation 2,100–2,103 m.

Crotalus pallidus Günther, 1895, *Biol. Cent. Am. Rept. Batr.*, 326 pp.[193]. Holotype: BMNH 1946.1.17.70 (formerly BMNH 1868.4.7.23). Type-locality: "City of Mexico" [Mexico].

Crotalus triseriatus—Boulenger, 1896b, *Cat. Snakes British Mus.* 3:727 pp.[581].

Crotalus triseriatus triseriatus—Klauber, *in* Githens and George, 1931, *Bull. Antivenin Inst. Am.* 5:31–34[33]. [In part, according to Klauber (1952:20).]

Crotalus triseriatus anahuacus Gloyd, 1940, *Chicago Acad. Sci. Spec. Publ.* (4):266 pp.[91]. Holotype: MCZ R33681. Type-locality: "Valley of Mexico." Restricted to "Coyoacán, Distrito Federal, Mexico," by Smith and Taylor (1950b:329).

Crotalus triseriatus armstrongi Campbell, 1979, *Trans. Kansas Acad. Sci.* 81:365–369[365, figs. 1–3]. Holotype: UTA R6258. Type-locality: "Rancho San Francisco, 1.5 mi NW Tapalpa, Jalisco, Mexico, elevation 2,103 m."

Ajusco Peak rises to a height of over 14,000 feet [4,267 m] above sea level. The little rattler . . . was not found on the summit, but somewhere, possibly 1,000 feet below, or roughly at an elevation of about 13,000 feet [3,962 m] above sea level. It was found among patches of snow in spots where the *zacatón* or bunch grass . . . grows profusely. The snake was not in the snow, but . . . at high altitudes when the radiant heat of daytime strikes directly from the sun, it may be very warm, even in the vicinity of snow patches, whereas in the more shady spots nearby, the snow may linger indefinitely.

Another specimen of *Crotalus t. triseriatus* was found under very similar conditions on the slopes of Pico de Orizaba. . . . At the edge of timber line, in a very sparsely vegetated area, rocky but with abundant tufts of *zacatón*, . . . we discovered another of these little rattlers when the sun had warmed up the ground after a slight snowfall the night before. This was at about 3,000 feet below the crater (elevation 18,696 feet [= 5,698 m], I should judge at about 15,000 feet [= 4,572 m] elevation. From there on up, there were no trees, just rocky slides, and plenty of big snow fields.

—Paul D. R. Ruthling, *in* Klauber, 1972

LOCAL NAMES Chiauhcótl, chiáuitl, colcóatl (Nahuatl), chilladora, hocico de puerco, víborita de cascabel.

ENGLISH NAME Mexican dusky rattlesnake.

ETYMOLOGY The species epithet is derived from the Latin prefix *tri-*, meaning "three," and *series*, meaning "row," and the suffix *-atus*, meaning "provided with," an allusion to the pattern of a single dorsal row of spots or blotches with prominent lateral rows on each side.

DISTRIBUTION The highlands of the Transverse Volcanic Cordillera of Mexico from west-central Veracruz westward through parts of Puebla, Tlaxcala, México, Morelos, to western Michoacán (Map 90). The vertical distribution ranges from about 2,500 to 4,572 m, making this the highest-ranging New World snake. Gadow (1905:56) recorded it at 13,000 feet (3,962 m) on Volcán Orizaba (Citlaltepetl), and Ruthling (*in* Klauber, 1972) observed it even higher on that mountain.

Distribution records are available in Auth et al., 2000; Boulenger, 1896b; Campbell, 1979b; Cope, 1864, 1885a, 1885b; Cuesta-Terrón, 1921b, 1931 (as *polystictus*); Davis and Smith, 1953; Duellman, 1961, 1965b; Ferrari-Perez, 1886; Flores-Villela and Hernández-García, 1989; Gadow, 1905, 1908, 1910; Gloyd, 1940; Günther, 1895–1902 (in part); Herrera, 1891 (as *lugubris*); Klauber, 1952; Martín del Campo, 1935, 1937a, 1940a, 1940b, 1950; Mertens, 1930; Pérez-Higareda and Smith, 1991; Pérez-Ramos et al., 2000; Ramírez-Bautista et al., 1995; Schmidt and Shannon, 1947; Smith, 1943a; Smith and Laufe, 1945; Sumichrast, 1882; and Uribe-Peña et al., 1999. On Mexico generally, see Armstrong and Murphy, 1979; Garman, 1884a; Klauber, 1940b, 1952, 1971, 1972; Leviton, 1953; Smith, 1946b; and Smith and Taylor, 1945.

HABITAT Pine-oak forest, boreal forest, coniferous forest, and bunchgrass grasslands above tree line. On Volcán Orizaba, on which *C. triseriatus* occurs at very high elevations, the snow line descends to about 15,000 feet (4,572 m) from June to August, and the maximum elevation at which green plants grow is 15,200 feet (4,633 m) (Swan, 1963). Although *C. triseriatus* occurs up to the level where snow descends and flowering plants ascend, it appears to be most abundant at elevations between about 2,700 and 3,350 m (Armstrong and Murphy, 1979).

DESCRIPTION Large adult males commonly exceed 60 cm in TL; females are somewhat smaller. The largest specimen reported was 68.3 cm in TL (Klauber, 1972).

Specimens from the Transverse Volcanic Cordillera have a medium to gray-brown ground color. The ground color is sometimes darker laterally and paler on the middorsum between the 30–57 dark brown middorsal blotches and 3–10 tail bands. The dark-bordered dorsal blotches are no more than 5 scales wide and are frequently only 3; they may be roundish or subelliptical and frequently have an irregular pale outer edge. The top of the head may be uniformly brown; brown with black flecking; or marked with dark brown blotches in the prefrontal, supraocular, and parietal regions. The postocular stripe and paired nape blotches are dark brown. The lower portion of the postocular stripe extends beneath the eye to the preoculars; posteriorly, the postocular stripe extends to the rictus or slightly beyond. There may be three series of small, dark lateral blotches, often roundish in shape, but these may be reduced, indistinct, or absent. In general, the lateral blotches that offset the dorsal blotches are the most distinct, and the dorsolateral and ventrolateral series of blotches that are in the interspaces between the level of the dorsal and lateral series are diffuse and indistinct. The venter usually has a pinkish, cream, or ivory cast, becoming more intense posteriorly, with heavier brown to black mottling that tends to be concentrated toward the lateral margins of the ventrals. In some individuals the venter is mostly dark. The iris is yellowish, bronze, orange, or tan, usually with the lower two-thirds made darker by dark flecking.

The rostral is usually wider than high but is sometimes about as high as or slightly higher than wide. The prenasal does not curve under the postnasal, and the anterior subocular is usually in contact with supralabials 4 and 5, but it may touch only one of these scales, supralabials 3 and 4, or supralabials 5 and 6, or it may be separated by a single interoculabial. The upper preocular is infrequently (in fewer than 15% of individuals) vertically divided. There are 2–3 (usually 2) large internasals, in contact; 1–2 (usually 1) canthals on each side; 1–3 (usually 2) intercanthals; 6–9 (mode 6) scales in the internasal-prefrontal area; 2–5 (usually 3) intersupraoculars; 1–2 (usually 1) loreals on each side that are separated from the supralabials by foveals and that separate the upper preocular from the postnasal; 1–7 (mode 3) prefoveals; 10–14 (mode 12) supralabials; 9–13 (usually 11 or 12) infralabials; 21–25 (usually 23) midbody dorsal scale rows; 125–154 ventrals in males and 137–152 in females; 24–33 subcaudals in males and 19–28 in females; and 8–10 (usually 8) rattle-fringe scales.

SIMILAR SPECIES The Mexican Plateau is home to many rattlesnake species, some of which might be mistaken for *C. triseriatus*. *Crotalus intermedius* and *C. transversus* have 21 midbody dorsal scale rows (versus usually 23 or more), usually 9 supralabials and infralabials (versus 11 or 12), and 0–1 prefoveals

(versus usually 2–7); *C. polystictus* has at least 25 midbody dorsal scale rows, 162–187 ventrals (versus 136–161), and a dorsal pattern consisting of oval paravertebral blotches; *C. pusillus* has 4 scales in the internasal-prefrontal area (versus a minimum of 6); and *Crotalus ravus* has large, symmetrical head plates, usually 9. *Crotalus t. triseriatus* and *C. t. armstrongi* usually have more numerous (usually more than 38) and smaller dorsal blotches, a smaller rattle, and a proportionately longer tail than *C. aquilus*. Both *C. t. triseriatus* and *C. t. armstrongi* invariably have a well-defined postocular stripe, usually have 8 rattle-fringe scales, and only rarely is the upper preocular vertically divided; *C. aquilus* may or may not have a well-defined postocular stripe, usually has 10 rattle-fringe scales, and the upper preocular is vertically divided with some frequency. *Crotalus t. armstrongi* and most populations of *C. aquilus* are sexually dimorphic for color; *C. t. triseriatus* is not.

REMARKS We recognize two subspecies: *C. t. triseriatus* (Pls. 981–983) with a disjunct distribution across the highlands of the Transverse Volcanic Cordillera from west-central Veracruz to western Michoacán, and *C. t. armstrongi* (Pls. 984–987) in the western part of the Mesa Central and the western portion of the Transverse Volcanic Cordillera. *Crotalus t. armstrongi* can be distinguished from *C. t. triseriatus* on the basis of its sexually dimorphic ground color, less frequently divided upper preocular (ca. 5 versus 15%), and body blotches that are usually as wide as or wider than long. In contrast to the dark snakes found on most of the higher peaks of the eastern Transverse Volcanic Cordillera (*triseriatus*), populations in the western portion of the range (*armstrongi*) usually have paler ground colors of gray-brown to reddish brown. Some individuals of *C. t. armstrongi* have a relatively dark ground color, but these snakes tend to have a highly contrasting pattern in comparison with the dull, dusky appearance of the darker specimens of *C. t. triseriatus*. Overall, *C. t. armstrongi* is more variable in color pattern than *C. t. triseriatus*, which exhibits remarkable uniformity among the various isolated populations. The blotches in *C. t. armstrongi* tend to be more boldly indicated and are 5–7 scales wide. The paired dark nape blotches are usually more lyriform in *armstrongi* than in *triseriatus*.

Two other subspecies of *C. triseriatus* have been described: *C. t. anahuacus* Gloyd (1940) and *C. t. quadrangularis* Harris and Simmons (1978b), but they appear to be junior synonyms of *C. t. triseriatus* and *C. aquilus*, respectively.

Envenomation by this species is reported to cause intense pain, faintness, cold perspiration, and swelling.

Crotalus viridis (Rafinesque, 1818)
(Fig. 218, Map 103, Pls. 988–997)

Crotalinus viridis Rafinesque, 1818, *Am. Monthly Mag. Crit. Rev.* 4:39–42[41]. Type(s): none designated. Type-locality: "the Upper Missouri" Valley, USA. Smith and Taylor (1950b:358) proposed an emendation to "Gross, Boyd County, Nebraska."

Crotalurus viridis—Rafinesque, 1820, *Ann. Nat.* (Lexington) (22):1–16[5].

Crotalus confluentus Say, *in* James, 1823, *Acct. Exped. Pittsburgh Rocky Mountains* 2:442 pp.[48, footnote]. Holotype: "Philadelphia Museum" [ANSP] in original description; the present location is unknown. Type-locality: "vicinity of the Rocky Mountains." Stated to be "Valley of the Arkansa" by Schmidt (1953c:231). After reviewing the itinerary of the expedition for 18 July 1820, Klauber (1956:45, footnote 25) deduced that the type specimen was probably collected in the vicinity of Bell Springs, Colorado.

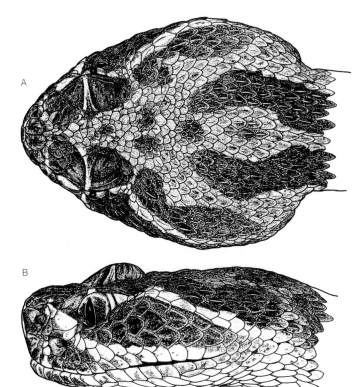

Fig. 218. (A) Dorsal and (B) lateral aspects of head of *Crotalus viridis viridis*, female, 77.5 cm TL (UTA R-18255), from U.S. Highway 56 between Clayton and Springer, Union County, New Mexico, USA. Characteristically, four internasals are present (an additional tiny median scale is present in this specimen). The pale stripe behind the eye usually extends well above the rictus. Drawings by Ty M. Kubin.

Crotalus Lecontei Hallowell, 1852, *Proc. Acad. Nat. Sci. Philadelphia* 6:177–182[180]. Holotype: USNM 4233, now lost according to Stejneger (*in* Amaral, 1929c:87). The holotype was illustrated by Hallowell (1853:139–141, pl. 28). Type-locality: "Cross Timbers . . . near the Colorado." Stejneger (*in* Amaral, 1929c:87) emended the type-locality to "along the North Fork of the Canadian River in Oklahoma in about 36° N. Lat. and 98° 30′ W. Long."

Caudisona confluenta—Cope, 1867 [dated 1866], *Proc. Acad. Nat. Sci. Philadelphia* 18:300–314[307].

Caudisona confluenta var. *confluenta*—Cope, 1867 [dated 1866], *Proc. Acad. Nat. Sci. Philadelphia* 18:300–314[307].

Caudisona confluenta var. *lecontei*—Cope, 1867 [dated 1866], *Proc. Acad. Nat. Sci. Philadelphia* 18:300–314[307].

Crotalus confluentus var. *pulverulentus* Cope, 1883, *Proc. Acad. Nat. Sci. Philadelphia* 35:10–35[11]. Syntypes (2): Klauber (1956:45) listed "type specimen: PANS 10745" and thereby designated a lectotype. Malnate (1971:364) listed ANSP 10745 as the holotype but noted that Cope mentioned two specimens in the original description. The location of the second specimen is unknown. Type-locality: "Lake Valley, New Mexico," Sierra County.

Crotalus confluentus var. *confluentus*—Cope, 1884b [dated 1883], *Proc. Acad. Nat. Sci. Philadelphia* 35:10–35[11].

Crotalus confluentus confluentus—Cope, 1892 [dated 1891], *Proc. U.S. Natl. Mus.* 14:589–694[691].

Crotalus confluentus lucifer—Cope, 1892 [dated 1891], *Proc. U.S. Natl. Mus.* 14:589–694[692].

Crotalus confluentus lecontei—Cope, 1892 [dated 1891], *Proc. U.S. Natl. Mus.* 14:589–694[692].

Crotalus confluentus nuntius Klauber, 1935b, *Trans. San Diego Soc. Nat. Hist.* 8:75–90[78, pl. 8 (fig. 1)]. Holotype: SDSNH 3105

(formerly LMK 3105). Type-locality: "Canyon Diablo, Coconino County, Arizona," USA.

Crotalus viridis viridis—Klauber, 1936, *Trans. San Diego Soc. Nat. Hist.* 8:185–276[191, 241 (figs. 50, 52), 253 (fig. 68), 262 (fig. 85)].

Crotalus viridis nuntius—Klauber, 1936, *Trans. San Diego Soc. Nat. Hist.* 8:185–276[191].

The reptiles which I have observed in this quarter are the Rattlesnake of the species described on the Missouri. They are abundant in every part of the country and are the only poisonous snake which we have met with since we left St. Louis.

—Meriwether Lewis, Walla Walla, Washington, 30 May 1806, *in* Thwaites, 1904–1905, 5:86.

Here at Walpi the great snake dance is performed. For several days before this festival is held the people with great diligence gather snakes from the rocks and sands of the region round about and bring them to the kiva of one of their clans in great numbers, by scores and hundreds. Most of these snakes are quite harmless, but rattlesnakes [*C. viridis*] abound, and they are also caught, for they play the most important rôle in the great snake dance. The medicine men, or priest doctors, are very deft in the management of rattlesnakes. When they bring them to the kiva they herd all the snakes in a great mass of writhing, hissing, rattling serpents. For this purpose they have little wands, to the end of each one of which a bunch of feathers is affixed. If a snake attempts to leave its allotted place in the kiva the medicine man brushes it or tickles it with the feather-armed wand, and the snake turns again to commingle with its fellows.

—Powell, 1895

LOCAL NAME   Víbora de cascabel.

ENGLISH NAME   Prairie rattlesnake.

ETYMOLOGY   The species epithet is derived from the Latin *viridis*, meaning "green," an allusion to the greenish cast of the ground color of many individuals.

DISTRIBUTION   Southern Canada, over much of the Great Plains of the central United States, and as far south as northern Mexico (Map 103). In Canada this snake occurs in southern Alberta and Saskatchewan; in the western United States it is found in North Dakota, South Dakota, Nebraska, Kansas, Oklahoma, Texas, New Mexico, extreme eastern Arizona, Colorado, Wyoming, Montana, and eastern Idaho; and in northern Mexico it occupies northern Coahuila and northwestern Chihuahua. Its vertical distribution in Mexico is from about 100 m near the Rio Grande to above 2,775 m in Wyoming (Klauber, 1972).

Distribution records are available for Arizona (Fowlie, 1965; Lowe et al., 1986; Miller et al., 1982), Colorado (Chiszar and Smith, 1993; Chiszar et al., 1995; Ellis and Henderson, 1913, 1915; Freddy and Kogutt, 1978; Hallowell, 1853; Hammerson et al., 1991a; Hensley, 1959; Holland et al., 1995; Smith et al., 1993), Idaho (Linder and Fichter, 1977; Slater, 1941; Tanner, 1966b), Iowa (Christiansen and Bailey, 1990; Klauber, 1938b), Kansas (Clark, 1959; Hensley, 1959; Irwin, 1979; Taggart, 1992), Minnesota (Klauber, 1938b), Montana (Coues and Yarrow, 1878a; Genter, 1984; Maxell et al., 2003; Mosimann and Rabb, 1952; Rodgers and Jellison, 1942), Nebraska (Cooper and Groves, 1859; Cox and Franklin, 1989; Hudson, 1942; Klauber, 1938b), New Mexico (Bogert and Degenhardt, 1961; Christman et al., 2000; Cope, 1884b; Degenhardt et al., 1996; Gehlbach, 1957, 1965; Klauber, 1934, 1935b; Lewis, 1950; Little and Keller, 1937; Van Denburgh, 1924), North Dakota (Wheeler and Wheeler, 1966), Oregon (Brown et al., 1995), South Dakota (Anderson, 1947;

Gloyd, 1947a; Hensley, 1959; Klauber, 1938b; Over, 1923), Texas (Bailey, 1905; Baird, 1859b; A. Brown, 1903a; B. Brown, 1950; Crimmins, 1927a; Dixon, 1987, 2000; Hibbits et al., 1996; Jameson and Flury, 1949; Killebrew et al., 1996; Minton, 1959; Price, 1998; Schuett and Kraus, 1980a; Smith, 1947c; Smith and Chiszar, 1997; Tennant, 1998; Werler, 1964; Werler and Dixon, 2000; Yancey, 1996b), Utah (Cox and Tanner, 1995; Miller et al., 1982), Washington (Brown et al., 1995; Johnson, 1942; Owen, 1940; Svihla and Svihla, 1933), Wyoming (Ashton et al., 1997; Baxter and Stone, 1985; Koch and Peterson, 1995; Smith, 1963), Alberta (Logier and Toner, 1955; Mills, 1948; Russell and Bauer, 1993), Saskatchewan (Logier and Toner, 1955; Mills, 1948), Mexico (Armstrong and Murphy, 1979; Bogert and Degenhardt, 1961; Campbell and Lamar, 1989; Klauber, 1952; Lemos-Espinal et al., 1994, 1997; Schmidt and Owens, 1944; Smith and Taylor, 1945; Tanner, 1985), the United States (Conant and Collins, 1998; Girard, 1858; Savage, 1959; Shaw and Campbell, 1974; Smith and Brodie, 1982; Stebbins, 1985; Stejneger and Barbour, 1943), and the general distribution (Amaral, 1929c; Boulenger, 1896b; Cope, 1900; Garman, 1884b; Gloyd, 1940; Klauber, 1930b, 1971, 1972; Van Denburgh, 1922b; Werner, 1922; Wright and Wright, 1957). Preston (1982) reported this species in Manitoba, Canada, but its presence there needs to be confirmed.

HABITAT This species occupies a variety of habitats through most of its distribution. Hammerson (1999) stated that C. viridis occurs in practically every terrestrial habitat within its broad range in Colorado, including plains grasslands, sandhills, semi-desert shrubland, mountain shrubland, riparian zones, piñon-juniper woodland, and montane woodland. In the Great Basin region, Tanner (1966b) found it in low brush and in oak-aspen habitats at elevations up to 9,000 feet (2,743 m). In Wyoming, Brown and Duvall (1993) encountered C. viridis in different habits over the active season, including sagebrush (Artemisia tridentata), greasewood (Sarcobatus vermiculatus), and grasslands. These authors found much individual variation. Postfeeding snakes were often associated with greasewood, yet appeared to avoid this bush just prior to shedding. In New Mexico, C. viridis likewise inhabits a wide variety of habitats, including lava flows, shortgrass and saltbrush associations, and the Roughlands Life Belt (Gehlbach, 1965). Jameson and Flury (1949) observed a specimen coiled at the entrance to a prairie dog (Cynomys ludovicianus) burrow in a tobosa-grama association in west Texas. Strecker (1910) reported this species (as Crotalus confluentus) as an inhabitant of prairie dog towns in northwestern Texas. In Mexico, this species inhabits mesquite-grassland and desert (even the dunes near Samalayuca, Chihuahua), and it enters pine-oak forest near the Continental Divide along the northern Sonora-Chihuahua border.

DESCRIPTION Crotalus v. viridis commonly exceeds 100 cm in TL; the largest known specimen measured 151.5 cm (Klauber, 1937). On the other hand, large adults of C. v. nuntius are usually less than 60 cm, with the largest known specimen of this taxon only 73.2 cm in TL (Klauber, 1972). In the northern part of the range (Montana) C. v. viridis individuals occasionally exceed 120 cm in TL (J. Donovan, pers. comm.), and Klauber (1972) indicated that this taxon reaches its greatest size in that region.

In general, populations of C. viridis exhibit a considerable amount of individual and geographic variation. Ontogenetic variation is also present, with relatively distinct patterns evident in juveniles that become progressively obscured with age.

Crotalus v. viridis is highly variable with regard to ground color. Snakes from Colorado have a ground color ranging from pale tan to dark brown to greenish (Ludlow, 1981); individuals

from Kansas have a greenish gray to brown ground color (Collins, 1982); specimens from Texas have a greenish gray, greenish brown, or yellowish ground color (Werler and Dixon, 2000); snakes from New Mexico are pale brown to dusty yellowish tan (Degenhardt et al., 1996); and those from extreme southeastern Arizona are pale green or greenish (Lowe et al., 1986). In general, C. v. nuntius is similar to C. v. viridis but is dwarfed (rarely more than 60 cm in TL) and usually has more distinctly colored dorsal blotches. The ground color of this taxon varies from tan to pale brown, reddish brown, pinkish, or pinkish brown (Lowe et al., 1986). There are 33–57 dorsal blotches that are dark brown peripherally and medium brown in the center. The edges of dorsal blotches may be straight or irregular, but usually they are broader than long and the blotches on the anterior and midbody are indented along their anterior and posterior edges. Over most of the body the dorsal blotches are distinctly white edged, but posteriorly they become somewhat faded, uniformly colored, and lack white edging. Fairly conspicuous to diffuse lateral blotches are present and discrete over most of the body, but may coalesce with the dorsal blotches on the posterior part of the body to form dorsal cross-banding.

A conspicuous, broad (usually 3 or more scales) postocular stripe extends from beneath the eye to the rictus or the angle of the jaw, and is bordered anteriorly and posteriorly by distinctive white stripes that are 1–1.5 scales wide. The anterior white stripe extends downward from the canthus to about supralabials 7–8, and the posterior stripe curves downward from behind the eye and passes above the rictus. There is a pale-edged transverse bar across the supraoculars.

The tail is marked with short, dark rings, most about the same color as the posterior body blotches but becoming progressively darker distally, with the last 1–2 often black. The venter is mostly whitish or pale gray with little mottling.

Snakes from Chihuahua to Coahuila in north-central Mexico have brown dorsal blotches that are narrowly edged (less than 1 scale) with white on a greenish gray, greenish brown, pale brown, or straw yellow ground color. The dorsal blotches are often indented along their anterior and/or posterior margins; however, these indentations are absent from some specimens and the blotches may appear nearly hexagonal or rectangular. The 2–3 series of lateral blotches are not particularly well defined on young snakes and usually are virtually invisible on large adults. A broad postocular stripe curves downward from the eye to the angle of the jaw and is bordered by 2 pale diagonal stripes, one passing in front of the eye from the upper preocular or posterior canthal downward to the lip margin at a point below the posterior edge of the eye, and thence along the supralabials to the rictus; the other extending from the upper postocular to a point above the angle of the jaw. Narrow transverse white stripes are present in the prefrontal and the supraocular-frontal regions; these 2 bars are often connected by a medial white stripe. Large adults usually lack pale dorsal head markings. Of the 4–10 dark tail bands, the ultimate one is usually darker than, but no longer than, the others. The proximal rattle segment is black. The venter has little or no dark mottling.

An adult male from Wheatland County, Montana, had a pale brown dorsum but lacked dorsal and lateral blotches, having only small black spots scattered on the middorsum on the anterior of the body and an irregular black dorsal blotch over the vent (Slowinski and Rasmussen, 1985). A patternless specimen that was essentially uniformly pale tan was reported from

Hamilton County, Kansas (Irwin, 1979). Nickerson and Mays (1968) described a patternless *C. v. viridis* from Prowers County, Colorado, that had an olive green dorsum. Hammerson (1999) reported nearly patternless individuals and striped snakes from southeastern Colorado. A similarly patternless olive gray specimen having a single black band at the base of the rattle was reported from Yuma County, Colorado, by Aird (1984). An albino juvenile male was collected in Lipscomb County, Texas (Killebrew and James, 1983). Other color pattern aberrancies were reported by Chace and Smith (1968), Gloyd (1958), and Klauber (1972). Populations of *C. atrox* and *C. molossus* inhabiting the Pedro Armendariz lava field in south-central New Mexico are melanistic, but *C. v. viridis* individuals living in this area are no darker than conspecifics from surrounding areas (Best and James, 1984).

Rahn (1942a) showed that melanophores in *C. viridis viridis* disperse or concentrate their pigment in response to hormones and temperature. Rattlesnakes from which the pituitary gland was removed became permanently pale. Snakes that were not subjected to hypophysectomy could be induced to exhibit color changes by maintaining them at different temperatures. At 35 °C snakes were extremely pale, at 23 °C snakes assumed coloration typical of an intermediate state, and at 8 °C snakes became maximally darkened.

The rostral is usually higher than wide. One of the most distinctive features of *C. viridis* is that it often has 3 or more internasals, with the mode being 4. There are usually 2 canthals on each side, but sometimes there are 3 or, rarely, 4. The number of scales on the snout in front of a line between the anterior edges of the supraoculars is extremely variable, ranging from 7 to 45, but most specimens have between 15 and 30. The number of intersupraoculars is likewise variable (most frequently 4–6). Usually there is a single loreal per side, but sometimes there are 2 or, very rarely, 3. The prenasal may or may not contact the first supralabial. There are 10–18 (mode 15) supralabials, 11–19 (usually 15 or 16) infralabials, 21–29 midbody dorsal scale rows (usually 25 in *nuntius*, 27 in *viridis*), 162–187 ventrals in males and 169–196 in females, 21–31 subcaudals in males and 14–25 in females, and usually 12 rattle-fringe scales.

SIMILAR SPECIES   A number of species of rattlesnakes having large dorsal blotches and reaching a moderate to large length are sympatric with *C. viridis* in parts of its range; all of these normally have only 2 internasals in contact with the rostral. *Crotalus atrox* has strongly contrasting white and black rings on the tail, and the pale posterior border of the postocular stripe extends to the rictus (not to above the angle of the jaw). *Crotalus scutulatus* also has strongly contrasting white and black tail rings and often has a crescent-shaped scale bordering the posteromedial side of each supraocular. *Crotalus molossus* has a uniformly dark tail with no bands or rings evident and 4–6 large, flat scales in the internasal-prefrontal area. *Sistrurus catenatus* has 9 large, symmetrical plates on top of the head.

REMARKS   This species has a convoluted taxonomic history (see synonymies for *C. viridis* and *C. oreganus* and Remarks under the latter).

Two subspecies are recognized: *C. v. viridis* (Pls. 988–995) has 23–29 (usually 27) dorsal scale rows at midbody, 164–187 ventrals in males and 171–196 in females, 21–31 subcaudals in males and 16–25 in females, 33–57 dorsal body blotches, and usually a ground color with some green, olive green, or brown; *C. v. nuntius* (Pls. 996 and 997) has 21–27 (usually 25) dorsal scale rows at midbody, 162–178 ventrals in males and 169–184 in females, 21–28 subcaudals in males and 14–22 in females, 33–53 dorsal body blotches, and usually a ground color with some red or pink. According to Douglas et al. (2002), *C. v. nuntius* cannot reliably be distinguished from the nominate race.

Crotalus willardi Meek, 1906
(Figs. 219 and 220, Map 111, Pls. 998–1010)

Crotalus willardi Meek, 1906 [dated 1905], *Field Columbian Mus.*, Zool. Ser. 7:1–19[18, Pl. 3]. Holotype: FMNH 902. Type-locality: "Tombstone, Arizona." On the basis of data secured from Frank C. Willard, the original collector, Swarth (1921:83) emended the locality to "the Huachucas [Mountains], . . . a short distance above Hamburg in the middle branch of Ramsey Canyon, . . . at about 7,000 feet altitude."

Crotalus willardi willardi—Klauber, 1949c, *Trans. San Diego Soc. Nat. Hist.* 11:121–140[125, pl. 8 (fig. 1), map].

Crotalus willardi silus Klauber, 1949c, *Trans. San Diego Soc. Nat. Hist.* 11:121–140[128]. Holotype: MVZ 46694. Type-locality: "on the Río Gavilán, 7 miles southwest of Pacheco, Chihuahua, Mexico, altitude 6,200 ft."

Crotalus willardi meridionalis Klauber, 1949c, *Trans. San Diego Soc. Nat. Hist.* 11:121–140[131]. Holotype: SDSNH 6569 (formerly LMK 6569 and FMNH 1493). Type-locality: "Coyotes, Durango, Mexico, at elevation 8,000 ft." This Coyotes is on the railroad to El Salto, according to Klauber (1949c:131).

Crotalus willardi amabilis Anderson, 1962, *Copeia* 1962:160–163[160]. Holotype: MVZ 68896. Type-locality: "Arroyo Mesteño, 8,500 feet, Sierra del Nido, Chihuahua, Mexico."

Crotalus willardi obscurus Harris, 1974, *Natl. Park Conserv. Mag.* 48:22–24[23]. Holotype: not given in original description, but subsequently designated USNM 195546 by Harris and Simmons (1976:5). Type-locality: given as "one canyon in the Animas Mountains," New Mexico, USA, in original description; subsequently given as "upper end Indian Creek Canyon, Animas Mountains, Hidalgo County, New Mexico," by Harris and Simmons (1976:5).

The most striking feature in the world, as the Huichol looks upon it, is the prevalence of serpents. In all ages, and in most religions, serpents have played an important part. The serpent, by shedding its skin, rejuvenates itself, and thus becomes the symbol of health and strength. As it is the only animal that moves on the ground without legs, and swims without fins, it is particularly cunning.

—Lumholtz, [1902] 1987:234, describing the thoughts of the people indigenous to the Sierra Madre Occidental of northwestern Mexico

LOCAL NAME   Víbora de cascabel.

ENGLISH NAME   Ridge-nosed rattlesnake.

ETYMOLOGY   The species name is a patronym honoring Frank C. Willard of Tombstone, Arizona, who collected the type.

DISTRIBUTION   Northern Mexico and the extreme southwestern United States. Most of the range lies within the highlands of the Sierra Madre Occidental and associated ranges of northwestern Mexico. This species occurs in north-central and northeastern Sonora, western Chihuahua, and the Sierra del Nido complex to the east of the main mountain system. In Mexico, it is known from the Sierra de San Luis, Sierra del Tigre, Sierra Púrica, Sierra de Oposura, Sierra Huachinera, Sierra Aconchi, Sierra de los Ajos, Sierra (Cerro) Azul, and Sierra de Cananea. In the south, it occurs from the vicinity of Coyotes, Durango, eastward to the Cerro Candelaria in southwestern Zacatecas; its distribution is probably fragmented by the Río Mezquital

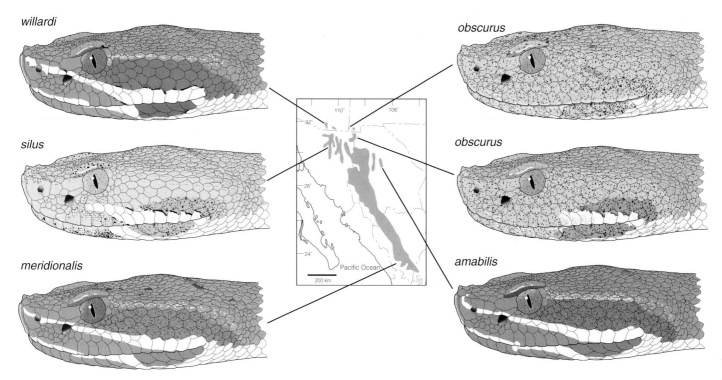

Fig. 219. Variation in face patterns in subspecies of *Crotalus willardi* (head scalation stylized). Pattern for *willardi* based on UTA R-17856 from Sunnyside Canyon on the west side of the Huachuacas, Arizona, USA; for *silus*, based on UTA R-21922 from the Sierra Púrica, Sonora, Mexico; for *meridionalis*, based on UTA R-17849 from Rancho Santa Barbara, Durango, Mexico; for *obscurus*, based on UNM-Esp 2001 from Peloncillo Mountains, New Mexico, USA, and UTA R-17850 from the Sierra de San Luis, Sonora, Mexico; and for *amabilis*, based on UTA R-17847 from the Sierra del Nido, Chihuahua, Mexico. Drawings by David G. Barker.

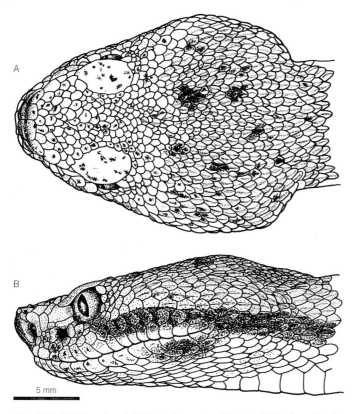

Fig. 220. (A) Dorsal and (B) lateral aspects of head of *Crotalus willardi obscurus*, male, 45.1 cm TL (UTA R-17903), from Sierra San Luis, canyon north of Cañón Diablo, Sonora, Mexico, elevation 1,950 m. Some individuals of this subspecies lack pale facial markings. Drawings by Ty M. Kubin.

Depression. In the United States, it is known only from the Animas and Peloncillo Mountains in southwestern New Mexico and the Huachuca, Patagonia, and Santa Rita Mountains in southeastern Arizona (Map 111). It was recently discovered in the Peloncillo Mountains along the southern border of New Mexico and Arizona (Campbell et al., 1989a; Holycross and Smith, 1997) and the Whetstone Mountains of Arizona (Thirkhill and Starrett, 1992). Perry (1997) listed it for the Canelo Hills of southern Arizona as well, and Fowlie (1965) reported an unconfirmed record for the Empire Mountains in Arizona. McCrystal (*in* Perry, 1997) noted undocumented reports for the species from the Chiricahua Mountains of Arizona. The vertical distribution ranges from about 1,460 m to 2,750 m.

Distribution records are available for Arizona (Fowlie, 1965; Greene, 1994; Hartman, 1911; Kauffeld, 1943a; Lowe, 1964; Lowe et al., 1986; Manion, 1968; Mocquard, 1908–1909; Rado and Rowlands, 1981; Sigala-Rodríguez, 1999; Stejneger and Barbour, 1943; Swarth, 1921; Werner, 1922; Woodin, 1953), New Mexico (Campbell et al., 1989a; Degenhardt et al., 1996; Harris, 1974; Harris and Simmons, 1975), Chihuahua (Anderson, 1962; Greene, 1994; Lemos-Espinal et al., 2000b; Leopold, 1967; McCranie and Wilson, 1978; Smith and Taylor, 1966; Tanner, 1985; Taylor and Knobloch, 1940; Van Devender and Lowe, 1977), Durango (Klauber, 1949c), Sonora (Barker, 1991; Sigala-Rodríguez, 1998), Mexico in general (Armstrong and Murphy, 1979; Campbell and Lamar, 1989; Klauber, 1952, 1971, 1972; Martín del Campo, 1935, 1937a; Smith and Taylor, 1945), the northern portion of the range (Shaw and Campbell, 1974; Wright and Wright, 1957), and the general range (Barker, 1992; Gloyd, 1940; Harris and Simmons, 1976; Klauber, 1936b, 1949c, 1952, 1971, 1972; Van Denburgh, 1922b).

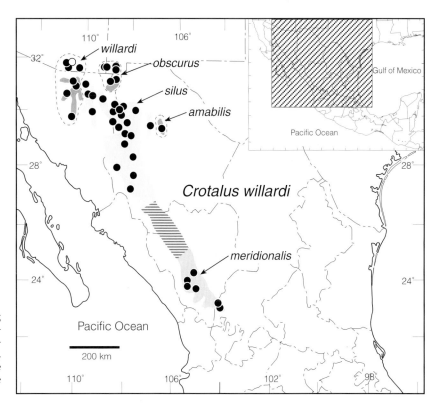

Map 111. Distribution of *Crotalus willardi*, including subspecies, in northwestern Mexico and the southwestern United States. Unfilled symbol represents type-locality, restricted to Huachuca Mountains, Arizona, USA, by Swarth (1921). Parallel lines represent a large hiatus between known localities, but an area of suitable habitat where the species may occur.

HABITAT Pine-oak woodland, oak scrub, pine-fir forest, deciduous woodland, mesquite-grassland, and open grassy meadows within pine-oak forests. This species is more abundant in humid canyon bottoms and less exposed, more mesic slopes. Near Yepómera, Chihuahua, *C. willardi* inhabits rocky habitats in woodland and forest (Van Devender and Lowe, 1977). In the Sierra del Nido of Chihuahua Armstrong and Murphy (1979) found *C. willardi* at the bases of small trees in piles of twigs and leaf litter near streams. Rado and Rowlands (1981) encountered an individual at only 1,600 m in an oak-juniper community.

DESCRIPTION Large adult males may exceed 55 cm; females are usually somewhat smaller. The largest measured specimen, a long-term captive male, is 67.0 cm in TL (see Campbell and Lamar, 1989, fig. 436). Keegan et al. (1999) reported TLs of 66.8, 64.5, 64.9, and 64.9 cm for four adult male *C. willardi obscurus* from the Animas Mountains, Hidalgo County, New Mexico, that were measured in the field.

The ground color is reddish brown, rust colored, yellowish brown, gray-brown, or gray. The 18–45 dorsal blotches are deep chestnut or chocolate brown, usually edged on their anterior and posterior margins with dark brown and/or black pigment; they are more or less subquadrate and tend to merge with the ground color laterally. The interspaces between the dorsal blotches are paler than the lateral ground color and may form distinctive cream-colored, buff, or pale brown crossbands. There may be 3 series of dark brown lateral spots, but these are frequently irregular or vague, and are absent altogether in some specimens. The top of the head is usually marked with a few irregular dark brown or black spots, flecks, or stipples. A post-ocular stripe, only moderately darker than the top of the head, extends from the lower posterior edge of the eye to the angle of the jaw; this stripe may be ill defined or absent in snakes from northwestern Chihuahua and southwestern New Mexico. The proximal portion of the tail has 1–3 blotches or bands, whereas the distal portion is striped or unicolored with gray or brown. The anterior ventrals usually have a yellowish, cream, or pinkish cast and are finely peppered with dark pigment; posteriorly the pigment often, but not invariably, tends to be distributed in clumps and is concentrated toward the lateral margins of the ventrals. The belly becomes progressively darker posteriorly. The subcaudals are pinkish, reddish, or orangish with irregular black markings. The iris is yellowish brown or bronze with heavy black peppering. The basal rattle segment is deep reddish brown, orange, gray-brown, or gray. The tongue is black with gray tips.

The pattern of pale facial stripes is one of the most conspicuous features of this species, but it varies considerably among populations (Fig. 219). The head of *C. w. willardi* from the Huachuca Mountains of Arizona has a deep reddish brown ground color, and a darker reddish brown postorbital stripe extends from the eye to the angle of the jaw. A relatively broad upper facial stripe extends from the prenasal across the top of the loreal pit to the supralabials just behind the level of the eye and then posteriorly to the last supralabial. A pale stripe extends along the lower portion of the anterior 5–6 supralabials, then crosses over to the infralabials and continues for 4–5 infralabials, terminating at a level below the upper facial stripe. A distinct vertical pale stripe is present on the rostral. This head pattern is characteristic of snakes from Arizona and the Sierra de los Ajos and the Sierra Cananea in Mexico.

The reddish brown coloration of the head and pattern of pale facial stripes in snakes from the Sierra del Nido in Chihuahua (*C. w. amabilis*) and from Durango and Zacatecas (*C. w. meridionalis*) are similar in most respects to those of *C. w. willardi*, but the upper and lower facial stripes are slightly narrower (although well defined) in *C. w. amabilis* and *C. w. meridionalis* than in *C. w. willardi* and are usually separated throughout their lengths, not coming into contact at about the level of supralabial/infralabial 9 as they do in *C. w. willardi*. Facial stripes are characteristically expanded into a small, pale spot on *C. w. amabilis* at the level were the lower facial stripe crosses from the supralabials to the infralabials.

Crotalus w. silus from much of the northern portion of the Sierra Madre Occidental southward to the vicinity of Basaseachic has reduced facial patterns in which the upper facial stripe extends from a level below the eye diagonally downward to the supralabials and then posteriorly to the last supralabial. The forward extent of the upper facial stripe is variable and in some specimens extends forward to the loreal pit. The lower facial stripe is absent on the supralabials, but there is a pale streak on about infralabials 8–9 that extends posteromedially. No vertical pale stripe is present on the rostral, and the dorsal ground color of the head is relatively pale brown or grayish brown. This head pattern is found in snakes from the Sierra Púrica, Sierra Opasura, Sierra Aconchi, Sierra del Tigre, and the mountains north of Copper Canyon.

The ground color in snakes from the Animas Mountains, Peloncillo Mountains, and the Sierra de San Luis (*C. w. obscurus*) is gray or brownish gray with scattered dark punctations. Facial stripes may be completely absent. Although the Sierra de San Luis population usually has at least traces of the pale upper facial stripe on the posterior supralabials, there is no pale stripe on the infralabials.

Tail coloration of neonates is variable and may be yellow (Martin, 1975b), dark brown, or gray and is often striped (Quinn, 1977; Wilson, *in* Holycross, 2000c). A litter of *C. willardi obscurus* from the Animas Mountains of New Mexico had mostly black tails (Martin, 1976). Several instances of caudal dichromatism within a single litter have been reported. Martin (1975b) described a litter of *C. willardi willardi* born to captive parents from the Santa Rita Mountains in Arizona in which four neonates had gray striped tails and two had yellow tails. A litter produced by a female from the Peloncillo Mountains contained six neonates with yellow tails and two with solid black tails (Holycross, 2000c).

One of the most distinctive features of *C. willardi* is the facial pattern of pale (usually bright white) stripes; however, there is a considerable amount of variation among the various populations. In snakes from the Sierra del Nido and the states of Durango and Zacatecas, the upper stripe extends posteriorly from the prenasal across the postnasal, lower loreal, (or lower portion, if only 1 loreal) lower preocular, suboculars, usually several interoculabials, and the posterior 7–8 supralabials to the rictus. The lower stripe usually begins on about infralabial 2 or 3 and extends posteriorly along the lip margin 4–7 infralabials before angling ventromedially and continuing along those gulars that are contiguous with the posterior infralabials; thence it turns dorsally and merges with the upper pale stripe at the rictus. The lower stripe may also merge at several points along its length with more medially situated pale markings or stripes on the gular region. Even though the lower stripe does not extend to the anterior tip of the lower jaw, a pale streak along the lip margin of the upper jaw may involve the first 3–5 pairs of supralabials; thus a continuous pale stripe is evident along the anterior portions of the mouth when the jaws are closed. A vertical stripe is usually present on the rostral and mental; that of the mental widens as it extends posteriorly across the medial portions of the first pair of infralabials and chinshields and ultimately merges with the pale coloration of the posterior gulars and anterior ventrals.

Some specimens from northern Sonora and adjacent Arizona lack a pale stripe along the anterior lip margin of the lower jaw. Instead, a pale stripe angles immediately inward toward the ventral midline at about the level of infralabial 8, extends along the gulars parallel to the lip, and then turns dorsally to merge with the upper stripe at the rictus.

This unique pattern of pale facial stripes is less distinct in most snakes from northeastern Sonora and western Chihuahua, in which the upper pale facial stripe does not extend anteriorly past the level of the eye. Snakes from southwestern New Mexico and the Sierra de San Luis on the Chihuahua-Sonora border have no distinct pattern of facial stripes, but the posterior supralabials are generally pale with some dark peppering. The postocular stripe in these snakes is poorly defined. The distal portion of the tail of newborn snakes may be bright yellow, but it becomes grayish or brownish after about the second molt (Lowe et al., 1986).

The rostral is higher than wide. The pair of internasals and 2/2 canthals are relatively large compared with most other scales on the crown. The canthus rostralis and tip of the snout are distinctly raised by the flared-up internasals, anterior canthals, and sometimes the posterior canthals. Other than the internasals and canthals, the scales covering the top of the snout are small; there are 20–40 between the rostral and front edges of the supraoculars. There are 6–9 intersupraoculars. The prenasal is in contact with supralabial 1, and the upper preocular is not vertically divided and is not in contact with the postnasal. Most frequently there are 2 loreals on each side, the upper usually smaller than the lower; however, it is not unusual, particularly in snakes from the south, to find a single vertically elongate scale in the loreal region. The interoculabial series is most frequently reduced to a single scale (rarely 2) between the anterior subocular and supralabials. There are 12–17 (mode 14) supralabials; 12–17 (mode 14) infralabials; 25–29 midbody dorsal scale rows (usually 27, except in snakes from the northern part of the range, where 25 is more common); 146–158 ventrals in males and 147–159 in females; 25–36 subcaudals in males and 21–31 in females; and 8–10 rattle-fringe scales, which are usually sharply pointed.

SIMILAR SPECIES No other rattlesnake has the distinctive white facial stripes and the characteristic sharply raised canthus rostralis found in most populations of *C. willardi*. *Crotalus lepidus* can be further distinguished from *C. willardi* by having 1–4 intersupraoculars, usually 23 midbody dorsal scale rows, an upper preocular that is divided vertically, a single loreal, and usually fewer than 10 scales on top of the snout between the rostral and anterior edge of the supraoculars. *Crotalus pricei* usually has a gray ground color with a series of 39–64 pairs of small, dark brown paravertebral blotches; a single canthal; a single loreal; no more than about 6 or 7 scales on top of the snout between the rostral and anterior edge of the supraoculars; 2 or 3 intersupraoculars; usually 21 midbody dorsal scale rows; and the anterior subocular in contact with several supralabials. *Crotalus cerastes* occurs in xeric habitats to the northwest and west of *C. willardi* and is morphologically quite distinctive. *Crotalus cerastes* usually has 23 or fewer midbody dorsal scale rows, the supraocular is strongly produced into a soft hornlike process, and the outline of the scales along the upper lip margin is distinctly scalloped; furthermore, males and females of *C. cerastes* have fewer subcaudals than their respective sexes in *C. willardi*.

REMARKS Five subspecies of *C. willardi* have been described, and these are most easily distinguished on the basis of facial pattern (Fig. 219). *Crotalus w. willardi* (Pls. 998–1000) occurs in the Huachuca, Patagonia, and Santa Rita Mountains of southeastern Arizona south into the Sierra de los Ajos, Sierra de Cananea, and Sierra Azul of northern Sonora, Mexico. This subspecies tends to have fewer dorsal scale rows at midbody (mode

25), fewer subcaudals (25–30 in males, 21–25 in females), and a correspondingly shorter tail (averages 10.2% of TL in males and 8.0% in females). *Crotalus w. amabilis* (Pls. 1001 and 1002) is known only from several canyons (arroyos) in the Sierra del Nido of north-central Chihuahua and has a distinct facial pattern and more body blotches (36–45) than the other subspecies. *Crotalus w. meridionalis* (Pls. 1003 and 1004) occurs in southern Durango and northwestern Zacatecas, and probably occurs northward in the Sierra Madre Occidental into northwestern Durango; it is distinguished by a distinct facial pattern, scale rows at midbody usually more than 25, subcaudals 30 or more in males and 27 or more in females, and more than 26 dorsal body blotches. *Crotalus w. obscurus* (Pls. 1005–1008) inhabits the Animas and Peloncillo Mountains, New Mexico, and the Sierra de San Luis in extreme northeastern Sonora and northwestern Chihuahua, and characteristically lacks a facial pattern, although some specimens from the Sierra de San Luis may have 6–7 pale posterior supralabials. *Crotalus w. silus* (Pls.

1009 and 1010) occurs in the mountains of northeastern Sonora and western Chihuahua, including the Sierra del Tigre, Sierra de Oposura, Sierra Aconchi, and Sierra Púrica, as well as to the south in the Sierra Madre Occidental. This taxon also lacks a distinct facial pattern except for a white streak usually starting beneath the eye and continuing across the posterior supralabials and a white streak extending posteromedially from about the middle of the infralabials.

Holycross et al. (2002) observed adult *C. willardi obscurus* waiting in ambush near fallen branches or at the base of partially felled trees that were used as runways by brush mice, the main prey of adults. Juveniles were found against sides of rocks or in vertical fissures often frequented by spiny lizards, their primary prey. Juvenile snakes postured the body in a loose S with the head directed upward, and adults adopted a more classical ambush coil.

This species is mainly diurnal and, in our experience, tends to have a mild temperament.

Massasauga and Pygmy Rattlesnake, Genus *Sistrurus* Garman, 1884

Crotalus Linnaeus, 1766, *Syst. Nat.*, 12th ed., 532 pp.[372]. [In part.]

Crotalophorus Gray, 1825, *Ann. Philos.* (2)10:193–217[205]. Type-species: *Crotalophorus miliaris* [*sic*] (Linnaeus, 1766) [=*Sistrurus miliarius* (Linnaeus, 1766)], by monotypy. [Preoccupied by *Crotalophorus* Houttuyn, 1764, a synonym of *Crotalus* Linnaeus, 1758.]

Caudisona Fitzinger, 1826b, *Neue Classif. Rept.*, 66 pp.[34, 63]. Type-species: *Crotalus miliarius* Linnaeus, 1766 [=*Sistrurus miliarius* (Linnaeus, 1766)], by monotypy. [Preoccupied by *Caudisona* Laurenti, 1768, a synonym of *Crotalus* Linnaeus, 1758.]

Sistrurus Garman, 1884a [dated 1883], *Mem. Mus. Comp. Zool.* 8:1–185[110, 118, 176]. Type-species: *Crotalus miliarius* Linnaeus, 1766, by generic substitution. [Replacement name for *Crotalophorus* Gray, 1825 and *Caudisona* Fitzinger, 1826.]

> Structurally, the rattle is of beautiful and intricate design, reinforced at possible points of weakness; for example, there is a fold where a tear might start at the anterior edge, the sides are furrowed for reinforcement, and strengthening webs appear in the transverse grooves.
> —Klauber, 1940c:45–46

ETYMOLOGY

The generic name is derived from the Latin *sistrum* or Greek *seistron*, meaning "rattle," and the Greek *oura*, meaning "tail."

The genus *Sistrurus* comprises two North American species of rattlesnakes. The massasauga (*S. catenatus*) is widely distributed from southeastern Canada across much of the eastern and central United States to southeastern Arizona. In Mexico this species is confined to a few relictual populations occurring in dry habitats, although it is usually found in the vicinity of water. The pygmy rattlesnake (*S. miliarius*) occurs in the southeastern United States from North Carolina through peninsular Florida and west to central Oklahoma and east Texas.

The rostral is high and is rounded above, the canthus rostralis is sharp, and there are usually 9 large, symmetrical plates on top of the head (Fig. 221). There are 8–14 (usually 10–12) supra-

labials; 9–16 (usually 11–13) infralabials; 19–27 (usually 23–25) midbody dorsal scale rows; 122–155 ventrals in males and 123–160 in females; and 25–39 subcaudals in males and 19–35 in females, most or all of which are undivided (Table 52). The middorsal body scales are keeled and the anal plate is undivided. Like rattlesnakes in general, males of this genus tend to reach a larger size than females.

The middorsal body blotches on *S. catenatus* are usually wider than long and occupy more space along the dorsal midline than the interspaces, whereas the blotches are smaller on *S. miliarius*, with most blotches not as long as the intervening spaces. Detailed descriptions of color and pattern follow in the species accounts. Members of the genus *Sistrurus* are small rattlesnakes, usually not exceeding 75 cm in TL, although several species of *Crotalus* are as small or smaller.

The frontal bones have a concave dorsal surface and are longer than wide (Fig. 222). The postfrontals are moderate in size, do not contact the frontal, and constitute about an equal amount of the dorsal perimeter of the orbit as the parietals. The posterolateral edge of the dorsal surface of the parietal posterior to the parietal orbital process forms a distinct raised ridge, and the junction between the parietal and pro-otic forms an obtuse angle. The anterolateral portion of the ectopterygoid has a concave surface on the medial side to accommodate attachment of the ectopterygoid retractor muscle; no such depression is evident on the lateral side. The ectopterygoid is noticeably longer than the expanded, flattened base of the pterygoid (the portion posterior to the ectopterygoid-pterygoid articulation) and has a moderately slender, somewhat compressed shaft that tapers gradually. The apex of the well-developed choanal process is positioned at about midlength on the palatine and is broadly rounded. The lateral hook (process) of the squamosal forms an acute angle (45–80 degrees) with the longitudinal axis of the bone (Klauber, 1972). The dorsal surface of the parietal is trapezoidal (sensu Brattstrom, 1964). According to Brattstrom (1964), there are 1–3 (usually 3) palatine teeth, 5–9 pterygoid teeth (5–7 in *S. miliarius* and 7–9 in *S. catenatus*), and 9–11 dentary teeth (9–10 in *S. miliarius* and 10–11 in *S. catenatus*). The

Fig. 221. Dorsal aspect of heads of (A) *Sistrurus catenatus tergiminus* (Tarrant County, Texas, USA) and (B) *S. miliarius streckeri* (Montague County, Texas, USA) showing characteristic head patterns. Note the relatively small size of the rattle of *S. miliarius*.

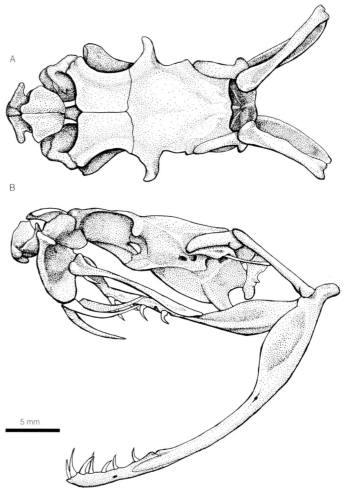

Fig. 222. (A) Dorsal and (B) lateral aspects of the skull of *Sistrurus catenatus* (UTA R-8730), adult male, from 3.2 km west-southwest of Farm-to-Market Road 2376 on U.S. Highway 377, Parker County, Texas, USA. Drawing by Paul C. Ustach.

Table 52. Variation in selected scale characteristics in rattlesnakes of the genus *Sistrurus*.

Character	*S. catenatus*	*S. miliarius*
Supralabials	9–14 (usually 11 or 12)	8–13 (usually 10 or 11)
Infralabials	10–16 (usually 12 or 13)	9–14 (mode = 11)
Ventrals		
Males	129–155	122–144
Females	132–160	123–148
Subcaudals		
Males	25–36	28–39
Females	19–29	25–35
Midbody dorsal scale rows	21–27 (25)[a]	19–25 (23)[b]
Body blotches	21–50	22–45
Pterygoid teeth	5–7	7–9
Average adult tail length[c]		
Males	10.6–11.0	12.0–12.7
Females	8.1–8.4	9.8–11.0
Rattle size	Moderate	Tiny

[a] Mode usually 25 except in western populations (*S. c. edwardsii*), where it is usually 23.

[b] Mode usually 23 except in western populations (*S. m. streckeri*), where it is usually 21.

[c] Range in averages pertains to different subspecies given in Klauber, 1972:191.

pterygoid teeth extend no more than one-half to two-thirds of the way to the middle of the junction of the pterygoid with the ectopterygoid. The maxillary fang is about 1.0–1.3 times longer than the height of the maxilla. The fang at rest extends to the level of supralabials 6 or 7 in *S. miliarius* and to the level of the suture between supralabials 7 and 8 in *S. catenatus*.

The genus *Sistrurus* is characterized by a hemipenis with numerous spines on the base that extend well up on the organ, covering about the proximal half of the lobes, with a relatively subtle transition from spines to the fringes that cover the distal portion of the lobes (Gloyd, 1940; McCranie, 1988). The hemipenes are divided with a bifurcate centrifugal sulcus spermaticus that divides slightly below the crotch at about the level of subcaudal 2 and sends a branch to the apex of each lobe (Fig. 223). The sulcus spermaticus terminates in a short papilla in *S. catenatus*, whereas in *S. miliarius* each branch of the sulcus terminates at the blunt tip of the lobe. The everted organ is between 5 and 10 subcaudals long and the lobes are more or less cylindrical thoughout most of their length, but taper near the apex in *S. catenatus* and are somewhat bulbous in *S. miliarius*. The organ is divided at about the level of subcaudal 3. The base of the organ and proximal portions of the lobes are covered with 60–70 (or more) small to large spines, which gradually diminish in size distally and grade into the spinulate calyces

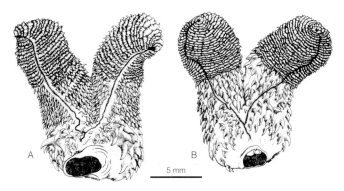

Fig. 223. (A) Sulcate aspect of left hemipenis of *Sistrurus catenatus* (UTA R-6809), and (B) sulcate aspect of right hemipenis of *S. miliarius* (UTA R-18364). From McCranie, 1988. Published by permission of the Herpetologists' League.

that cover about the distal half of each lobe (Gloyd, 1940). In *S. miliarius* the basal spines of the organ are often less robust than in *S. catenatus*, and there are fewer spinules or calyces on the opposing sides of the lobes, which are relatively flat and smooth in some individuals, in contrast with *S. catenatus*, in which the interfaces of opposing lobes have numerous calyces and spinules (Gloyd, 1940).

The hemipenes of *Crotalus ravus* (formerly placed in the genus *Sistrurus*) resemble those of other species of *Crotalus* in that there is an abrupt transition from basal spines to calyces (see description in *Crotalus* generic account).

NATURAL HISTORY

Activity patterns and behavior. Seasonal and daily activities of *Sistrurus catenatus* appear to vary with locality and habitat. In field studies conducted at several widely scattered sites (Arizona, Colorado, and Missouri), *S. catenatus* emerged from hibernation in mid-April and remained active until about late October or sometimes early November, depending on the weather (Hobert, 1997; Johnson, 1987; Lowe et al., 1986; Mackessy, 1998; Seigel, 1986). In the southern part of the range (Texas), snakes may emerge as early as mid-March during warm weather (Greene and Oliver, 1965). Snakes in the Missouri populations studied by Seigel (1986) were active for 193–202 days annually, and in a Pennsylvania population studied by Reinert (1978) they were active for 192 days per year. Casual observations in Indiana also indicate a lengthy activity period (Minton, 2001).

Various authors have reported different months of activity for *S. catenatus*. The differences may in some cases actually represent populational differences in activity but are probably also the result of variations in annual rainfall and weather patterns. In Tarrant and Parker Counties, Texas, during the 1980s we found massasaugas most frequently in late April and early May, whereas Greene and Oliver (1965), reporting on the same area, stated that these snakes were most abundant in May and early June. Likewise, in Throckmorton and Shackleford Counties, about 160 km northwest of Tarrant County, this species was most active in May and early June, but in the northwestern part of the Texas panhandle (Roberts and Lipscomb Counties) Knopf and Tinkle (1961) found specimens in the greatest numbers in August. They are most commonly encountered in Colorado in September and October, according to Hobert (1997). Fowlie (1965) claimed to have found this species in Arizona after light rains (which occur in the summer

months) basking in low, grassy hummocks, sometimes surrounded by water. Conant (1938) also found several individuals on tussocks of grass that they could have reached only by swimming. Seigel (1986) encountered most of his Missouri specimens in April and May, with another smaller peak of activity in October; he found that snakes were least common from July to September, which he attributed to possibly a change in habitat utilization.

Hammerson (1999) and Seigel (1986) reported that the massasaugas they studied in Colorado and Missouri, respectively, were active during the day when cool weather prevailed during the spring and fall, but during the hotter summer months they confined most of their activity to the hours following sunset. Vogt (1981) found that in Wisconsin, activity in this species was "restricted to daylight hours, primarily in the early morning, although they are active throughout the day in warm, humid, overcast weather." He also found them crossing roads on warm August nights. In Missouri, Johnson (1987) observed *S. catenatus* on sunny, warm spring days basking on abandoned ant mounds, grass hummocks, and near the entrance to crayfish burrows, but stated that the species becomes nocturnal during July and August. Minton (2001) reported occasional nocturnal activity for specimens in Indiana. Greene and Oliver (1965) found two active snakes in Chase Country, Kansas, during the morning hours in summer. In Pennsylvania, Reinert (1978) found massaugas to be most active during the day between 0900 and 1500. We have seen practically no diurnal activity in snakes from Tarrant and Parker Counties, Texas, which seem to be mostly nocturnal and are especially active during the first few weeks of late spring when early nighttime temperatures remain above 22 °C. *Sistrurus catenatus* is found abroad only infrequently at any time during the dry summer months (July–September) when nocturnal lows may not fall below 27 °C. Greene and Oliver (1965) noted that snakes from these same counties in Texas were "largely nocturnal" and could be found by driving at night over country roads. Not one of Tennant's (1998) 60 field observations of this snake in Texas was recorded during the day. In Arizona as well this snake is nocturnal (Lowe et al., 1986), with maximum activity occurring during the summer rains in the area. Hobert (1997) reported Colorado snakes to be active at temperatures of 14–30 °C, with most activity occurring between 20 and 26 °C; and in a field study involving radiotelemetry, Mackessy (1998) found most snakes active at air temperatures of 25–30 °C.

Field studies using radiotelemetry have revealed differences in daily activity and range areas, among populations. Reinert and Kodrich (1982) tracked 25 *S. catenatus* individuals by radiotelemetry for up to 50 days (total of 225 snake-days) in Pennsylvania and found a mean activity range area of 0.0098 km^2, a mean maximum range length of 89 m, and an average daily movement of 9.1 m. Although these authors found no significant gender differences in movements or range areas, gravid females had significantly shorter range lengths ($\bar{x} = 40$ m) than nongravid females. Weatherhead and Prior (1992) radio-tracked 12 snakes for periods of 15–59 days (total 419 snake-days) in Ontario, Canada, and estimated the activity ranges to average 0.25 km^2, with females covering significantly smaller areas than males. The mean maximum range length was 1030.4 m. Individuals made daily movements about 60% of the time, with 56 m being the mean distance moved. One snake covered a distance of almost 1.5 km in a single day. The activity range of this species in Colorado was reported to be 0.9–1.2 km^2 (Mackessy, 1998).

Massasaugas hibernate in crayfish burrows in Missouri (Seigel, 1986), and in rocky crevices along the Des Plains River in Illinois (Wright, 1941). Massasaugas hibernate in crayfish burrows, remaining just above the waterline, in Ohio and Wisconsin as well (Maple, 1968; Maple and Orr, 1968; Vogt, 1981). Other winter hibernacula are located in deep rock fissures, mammal burrows, and large rotten logs. In Colorado, Mackessy (1998) found *S. catenatus* hibernating in rodent burrows in areas of firm, loamy soils that were adjacent to the sandy areas the snakes used for feeding. Seasonal movements between various habitats were observed in snakes from western Pennsylvania by Reinert and Kodrich (1982). In Missouri, snakes have been found mostly in cordgrass (*Spartina*) prairie in spring and autumn, but they utilize drier, upland areas such as old fields and deciduous woods in the summer (Seigel, 1986). Gebhard (1853), Atkinson and Netting (1927), and Reinert and Kodrich (1982) noted that in northeastern North America (New York and Pennsylvania) massasaugas return to swampy areas in the fall, where they hibernate and mate the following spring, but during the summer these snakes move into higher ground to drier, sparsely vegetated areas. In Kansas, Smith (1956) found this snake "characteristically . . . in swampy places except in summer when they may move into drier stiuations." It has been suggested that this species is attracted to areas of sandy soils because they support high numbers of rodents and lizards, the snakes' main prey.

Sistrurus catenatus individuals may either remain very still or quickly flee when encountered in grassland prairie or forested situations. When cornered or approached in an open area, however, such as a warm paved road shortly after sunset, these snakes will usually coil and strike repeatedly. Our experiences closely follow the observations of Minton (1972), who stated that massasaugas are "alert, bad tempered snakes, quicker to strike than several species of larger rattlesnakes." Other authors have decribed this snake as having a mild disposition, however, and there probably is a strong geographical component to aggressive behavior. Prior and Weatherhead (1994) reported that in 174 trials in which snakes from Ontario, Canada, were approached to within 0.5 m, not a single snake made a defensive strike, suggesting to them that one practically has to touch the snake to be bitten.

Sistrurus miliarius may be active by day or at night and in many respects exhibits activity patterns similar to those of its close relative, *S. catenatus*. During the cooler days of spring, *S. miliarius* is often found basking in relatively open areas, but during the hot summer months of July and August it is mostly nocturnal (Johnson, 1987). Johnson (1987) reported this snake to be active in Missouri from mid-April to mid-October. Palmer and Braswell (1995) found it active during every month in North Carolina, but found most snakes from July through October, with peak activity occurring in September. In a series of 55 snakes collected in South Carolina, 65% were collected from July through September (Chamberlain, 1935). Chamberlain's earliest seasonal record for activity was on 9 January, and the latest was on 21 November. On Long Pine Key in Everglades National Park, Florida, Dalrymple et al. (1991b) found *S. miliarius* during every month of the year, with peak activity occurring in October (Fig. 224), a time that juveniles were also especially common. In south and central Florida, respectively, Hudnall (1979) and May et al. (1996) found that *S. miliarius barbouri* remained active all year. May et al. (1996) further reported that individuals were found above ground at ambient temperatures of 14–32 °C and that peaks of movement

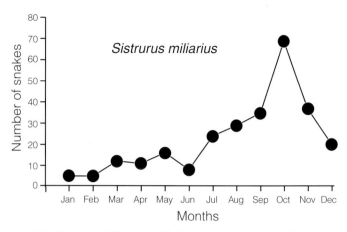

Fig. 224. Number of *Sistrurus miliarius* captured per month from 1984 to 1986: based on a total of 271 captures on Long Pine Key, Everglades National Park, Florida, USA. Adapted from Dalrymple, 1991b:299 (fig. 6).

occurred in the spring and fall. Ashton and Ashton (1981) most often found *S. miliarius* crossing roads at dusk or shortly after dark, especially in the fall. Neill (1947a) observed a specimen of *S. m. miliarius* emerge from what was probably a rodent burrow, in which it apparently had been hibernating, on a mild day in February 1937 to bask in the sun for several minutes.

Sistrurus miliarius was the most common species of snake found in a study of the vertebrate symbionts of gopher tortoise (*Gopherus polyphemus*) burrows in Hernando County, Florida (Witz et al., 1991). These authors excavated 1,019 burrows and discovered 50 snakes of various species, 5 of which were *S. miliarius*. By day pygmy rattlesnakes often hide in clumps of grass or beneath cover (Palmer and Braswell, 1995). In central Florida, Lee (1968) found *S. miliarius* in nests of the round-tailed muskrat (*Neofiber alleni*), in burrows of the old field mouse (*Peromyscus polionotus*), and in burrows of the Florida gopher mouse (*Peromyscus floridanus*). In June 1967 we found *S. m. miliarius* to be abundant on the lowland coastal plain near Charleston, South Carolina, where we observed individuals crawling across moist sandy areas in the early afternoon. Along the Tennessee River in northeastern Mississippi and adjacent Tennessee we found *S. m. streckeri* coiled but alert on shale in secluded willow stands at water's edge. All of our specimens were encountered in June. In August 1980, following a prolonged drought and heat spell, rains brought *S. m. streckeri* onto the roads surrounding Lake Fairfield, Texas, at night. Five specimens were found in less than an hour.

Conservation and abundance. The massasauga previously was locally abundant in many wetlands and prairies, but most populations have vanished or are in danger of disappearing, especially in parts of the range east of the Mississippi and in Canada (Ashton, 1976; Seigel, 1986). Even more than a century ago, describing this snake in Wisconsin, Hoy (1883) stated that "they are becoming rare, but were once abundant." Hay (1892) later wrote that "on the prairies of Illinois, before the country became thickly populated, these reptiles were extremely abundant, and the killing of two or three dozen of them in a season was not an unusual thing for any farmer's boy. Now, in the same region, not one is seen in years." In Ontario, Canada, over 70 years ago *S. catenatus* had been exterminated in most of its former range (LeRay, 1930). In 1986 Seigel reported that viable populations survived at only two sites in New York and five in Missouri.

Strecker (1910) noted that around the turn of the century *S. catenatus* was a common snake in northwestern Texas, with 25–30 often encountered in a single wheat field when shocks were being moved, but during the four or five years prior to his publication these snakes had become rare. A few years later, Strecker (1915) stated that "this species was formerly abundant in the Panhandle district [of Texas], but farmers report that it is getting scarcer every year. Mr. Lutrell of Claude, Armstrong County, informs me that he has often killed from fifty to sixty during one wheat season, but that during the past four or five years he has not seen more than half a dozen in any one year." Greene and Oliver (1965), in contrast, reported that the massasauga was the most commonly encountered snake on roads at night in the prairie just west of Fort Worth. These snakes continued to be extremely abundant in this area through the 1980s, and we found a record number of 43 in one evening during the first week of May 1985. However, housing developments, beginning in the 1990s and continuing to the present, have drastically reduced this population. Knopf and Tinkle (1961) collected 15 *S. catenatus* on the evening of 14 May 1960 over a distance of 16 miles (25.6 km) between Throckmorton and Woodson in Throckmorton County in the Texas panhandle, but extensive night driving on the same road yielded nothing during July and August.

Sistrurus catenatus remains abundant in some parts of southeastern Colorado (Hobert, 1997; Mackessy, 1998), which is mostly devoted to livestock grazing and supports high-quality prairie rangeland in some areas (Hammerson, 1999). In El Paso County, Colorado, it was moderately common until about 1989, after which time the population declined precipitously. This species is now approaching extinction in that general area (Pegler et al., 1995) and is probably threatened in Baca Country as well (Montgomery et al., 1998).

In the 1830s a sizable population of massasaugas inhabited a marshy area that is now part of downtown Milwaukee, and hundreds of these snakes were killed (Olin, 1930). In 1967 a collector found 26 massasaugas in a single morning in Juneau County, Wisconsin, but this population began to seriously decline starting in 1972 (Vogt, 1981). A bounty was placed on massasaugas in Wisconsin until 1975, when a complete reversal in state and federal laws placed them on the endangered species list (Vogt, 1981).

The decline in massasauga populations is almost entirely associated with human activities. The available evidence suggests that this snake is able to recover quickly from periodic natural disasters. Seigel et al. (1998) found that extensive flooding during the summer of 1993, for example, affected the sex ratio, population structure, and body condition—but not the abundance—of a Missouri population of *S. catenatus*. Only two to three years later this population appeared to be recovering. Massasaugas are especially sensitive to changes in adult and juvenile survival, and smaller populations may have a high probability of extinction (Seigel and Sheil, 1999).

Sistrurus miliarius may be common locally (Wright and Wright, 1957). In one mesic habitat near a freshwater marsh in central Florida, Farrell et al. (1995) found a population density of more than 40 individuals per hectare. This snake has been reported to be abundant in some parts of North Carolina during two extremes of weather—after heavy rains and during prolonged drought (Palmer and Williamson, 1971). On the piedmont of South Carolina, however, Platt et al. (1999) reported that *S. miliarius* was uncommon and patchily distributed and suggested further investigations to determine its conservation

status. *Sistrurus miliarius* has become quite rare in Tennessee and is listed by the state as endangered (Jacob, 1981). We have found *S. miliarius* to be locally abundant in several east Texas localities; however, their occurrence appears to be spotty and they are absent from intervening areas.

Prey. *Sistrurus catenatus* feeds on a variety of small vertebrates, including small mammals, lizards, and snakes, as well as certain invertebrates such as centipedes. Rodents and reptiles are the two most important kinds of prey, with juveniles feeding mostly on reptiles (especially lizards in western populations and snakes in eastern populations) and adults eating mostly rodents (Hammerson, 1999; Keenlyne and Beer, 1973b; Seigel, 1986). Many authors (e.g., Anderson, 1965; Ditmars, 1907; Froom, 1964; Hammerson, 1999; Pope, 1926; Schmidt and Davis, 1941) have reported frogs to be part of the diet of *S. catenatus*. In the Michigan specimens Ruthven et al. (1928) examined, frogs formed the bulk of the prey. Klauber (1956) also mentioned that this species feeds more frequently on frogs than any other rattlesnake. Curran (1935) stated that frogs are the chief food item of *S. catenatus* and that captive snakes refused all other prey. However, anurans are a relatively unimportant component of the diet for many populations, and it appears that frog predation is more typical of certain eastern or northern populations. Lowe et al. (1986) found mostly rodents and lizards in Arizona specimens, and our examination of snakes from Tarrant and Parker Counties, Texas, has revealed mostly rodents and reptiles (lizards and snakes) rather than frogs. Fowlie (1965) claimed that he found mostly amphibians in Arizona specimens, but this claim has not been substantiated.

Specific prey records for *S. catenatus* include centipedes, *Scolopendra* spp. (Degenhardt et al., 1996; Hammerson, 1999; Hobert, 1997; Lardie, 1976; McKinney and Ballinger, 1966); crayfish (Evermann and Clark, 1914; Reinert, 1978), plains spadefoot toads, *Spea bombifrons* (Hobert, 1997); spring peepers, *Pseudacris crucifer* (Atkinson and Netting, 1927; Netting, 1932); Rio Grande leopard frogs, *Rana berlandieri* (Greene and Oliver, 1965); green frogs, *Rana clamitans* (Schuett et al., 1984), leopard frogs, *Rana pipiens* (Schuett et al., 1984), wood frogs, *Rana sylvatica* (Schuett et al., 1984), collared lizards, *Crotaphytus collaris* (Webb, 1970); lesser earless lizards, *Holbrookia maculata* (Hobert, 1997; Holycross and Mackessy, 2002); Texas horned lizards, *Phrynosoma cornutum* (Greene and Oliver, 1965); side-blotched lizards, *Uta stansburiana* (McKinney and Ballinger, 1966); Texas spiny lizards, *Sceloporus olivaceus* (Greene and Oliver, 1965); fence lizards, *Sceloporus undulatus* (Holycross and Mackessy, 2002); *Sceloporus* spp. (Holycross and Mackessy, 2002); *Urosaurus ornatus* (Holycross and Mackessy, 2002); *Uta stansburiana* (Holycross and Mackessy, 2002); ground skinks, *Scincella lateralis* (Greene and Oliver, 1965); Great Plains skinks, *Eumeces obsoletus* (Hobert, 1997; Holycross and Mackessy, 2002); unidentified skink (Holycross and Mackessy, 2002); Texas spotted whiptails, *Cnemidophorus gularis* (Greene and Oliver, 1965); six-lined racerunners, *C. sexlineatus* (Hobert, 1997; Holycross and Mackessy, 2002); desert grassland whiptails, *C. uniparens* (Holycross and Mackessy, 2002); *Cnemidophorus* spp. (Holycross and Mackessy, 2002; Klauber, 1972; Loewen, 1947a; Lowe et al., 1986); western hognosed snakes, *Heterodon nasicus* (Greene and Oliver, 1965); smooth green snakes, *Opheodrys vernalis* (Mauger and Wilson, 1999); ground snakes, *Sonora semiannulata* (Greene and Oliver, 1965; Hammerson, 1999); brown snakes, *Storeria dekayi* (Conant, 1951; Mauger and Wilson, 1999; Seigel, 1986) and *S. occipitomaculata* (Reinert, 1978); lined snakes, *Tropidoclonion lineatum* (Greene and Oliver, 1965; Hammerson, 1999;

Holycross and Mackessy, 2002); other massasaugas, *Sistrurus catenatus* (Hallock, 1991; Ruthven, 1911; Ruthven et al., 1928); common gartersnakes, *Thamnophis sirtalis* (Keenlyne and Beer, 1973a; Seigel, 1986); unidentified snakes (Conant, 1951; Greene and Oliver, 1965; Hallock, 1991; Holycross and Mackessy, 2002; Keenlyne and Beer, 1973a; Ruthven et al., 1928); adult warblers (Minton, 1972, 2001); red-winged blackbirds, *Agelaius phoeniceus* (Keenlyne and Beer, 1973a); eggs of northern bobwhites, *Colinus virginianus* (Applegate, 1995); warbler (Minton, 1972), song sparrows, *Melospiza melodia* (Weatherhead and Prior, 1992); eggs of the lark sparrow, *Chondestes grammacus* (Brush and Ferguson, 1986), unspecified sparrows (Best, 1978; Loewen, 1947a; Selous, 1900), unspecified birds (Ditmars, 1907; Hallock, 1991; Holycross and Mackessy, 2002; Netting, 1932), short-tailed shrews, *Blarina brevicauda* (Greene and Oliver, 1965; Reinert, 1978) and *Blarina* spp. (Johnson, 1995); least shrews, *Cryptotis parva* (Holycross and Mackessy, 2002); gray shrews, *Notiosorex crawfordi* (Holycross and Mackessy, 2002); masked shrews, *Sorex cinereus* (Anton, 1993; Keenlyne and Beer, 1973a); *Sorex* spp. (Johnson, 1995; Resetar, 1992); pygmy mice, *Baiomys taylori* (Holycross and Mackessy, 2002); southern red-backed voles, *Cleithrionomys gapperi* (Hallock, 1991); prairie voles, *Microtus ochrogaster* (Seigel, 1986); meadow voles, *Microtus pennsylvanicus* (Atkinson and Netting, 1927; Conant, 1951; Hallock, 1991; Keenlyne and Beer, 1973a; Lyon and Bishop, 1936); *Microtus* spp. (Anton, 1993; Crawford, 1936; Hallock, 1991; Keenlyne and Beer, 1973a; Lyon and Bishop, 1936; Mauger and Wilson, 1999; Wright, 1941); woodland jumping mice, *Napaeozapus insignis* (Hallock, 1991); northern grasshopper mice, *Onychomys leucogaster* (Holycross and Mackessy, 2002); plains pocket mice, *Perognathus flavescens* (Hobert, 1997; Holycross and Mackessy, 2002); hispid pocket mice, *P. hispidus* (Greene and Oliver, 1965); Merriam's pocket mice, *P. merriami* (Greene and Oliver, 1965); *Perognathus* spp. (Holycross and Mackessy, 2002); white-footed mice, *Peromyscus leucopus* (Keenlyne and Beer, 1973a; Reinert, 1978; Wright, 1941); deer mice, *Peromyscus maniculatus* (Hobert, 1997) and *Peromyscus* spp. (Hallock, 1991; Holycross and Mackessy, 2002; Johnson, 1995; Mauger and Wilson, 1999; Seigel, 1986); western harvest mice, *Reithrodontomys megalotis* (Hobert, 1997; Holycross and Mackessy, 2002); plains harvest mice, *R. montanus* (Greene and Oliver, 1965); meadow jumping mice, *Zapus hudsonius* (Bielema, 1973; Johnson, 1995; Keenlyne and Beer, 1973a); and young snowshoe hares, *Lepus americanus* (Weatherhead and Prior, 1992).

The most comprehensive study of the diet of *Sistrurus catenatus* is that of Holycross and Mackessy (2002), who thoroughly summarized previous reports of prey and presented new information. In 165 prey items recovered from *S. c. edwardsii* these authors identified lizards as the most frequent food (58.8%), followed by mammals (30.9%), and centipedes of the genus *Scolopendra* (9.1%), with only single instances of predation on an anuran (*Spea bombifrons*) and a snake (*Tantilla nigriceps*). Juveniles of *S. c. edwardsii*, feed more on lizards and less on mammals than adults. *Sistrurus c. tergeminus* and *S. c. catenatus* tend to feed primarily on small mammals, with juveniles also feeding on snakes and lizards. In Wisconsin, Keenlyne and Beer (1973a) found that meadow mice (*Microtus*) made up 85% of the diet of adult snakes, with other snakes making up the balance.

Massasaugas sometimes feed on carrion (LeRay, 1930; Ruthven, 1911; Schwammer, 1983), including on snakes that have been killed on the road (Greene and Oliver, 1965). We found road-killed specimens in Tarrant County, Texas, during April and May that had fed on *Tropidoclonion* and *Virginia*. Gravid females feed rarely or not at all during gestation (Keenlyne and Beer, 1973a). Schuett et al. (1984) reported that juvenile *S. catenatus* use their brightly colored tails as a lure to attract prey such as lizards.

Sistrurus miliarius feeds on frogs, field mice, insects, and spiders (Wright and Wright, 1957). Specific records of prey include orthopterans (Klauber, 1972; Wright and Bishop, 1915); eastern narrowmouthed toads, *Gastrophryne carolinensis* (Palmer and Braswell, 1995); treefrogs, *Hyla* spp. (Farrell et al., 1995); southern leopard frogs, *Rana utricularia* (Farrell et al., 1995; Palmer and Braswell, 1995); green anoles, *Anolis carolinensis* (Farrell et al., 1995); prairie lizards, *Sceloporus undulatus* (Anderson, 1965); southeastern five-lined skinks, *Eumeces inexpectatus* (Farrell et al., 1995); ground skinks, *Scincella lateralis* (Farrell et al., 1995; Palmer and Braswell, 1995; Wright and Bishop, 1915); six-lined racerunners, *Cnemidophorus sexlineatus* (Palmer and Braswell, 1995); wormsnakes, *Carphophis amoenus* (Palmer and Braswell, 1995); black racers, *Coluber constrictor* (Palmer and Braswell, 1995); and brown snakes, *Storeria dekayi* (Palmer and Braswell, 1995). Jacob (1981) reported a variety of small mammals from the guts of Tennessee specimens, including short-tailed shrews (*Blarina*), long-tailed shrews (*Sorex*), voles (*Microtus*), rice rats (*Oryzomys*), and harvest mice (*Reithrodontomys*).

The presence of prey odor appears to be important in the selection of foraging sites by *S. miliarius*. Roth et al. (1999) established six pairs of parallel transects in western Volusia County, Florida, from September to November. Each pair of transects consisted of an experimental transect along which the investigators sprayed distilled water in which leopard frogs had been kept for the previous 48 hours and a control transect that was sprayed with pure distilled water. They found more pygmy rattlesnakes on the experimental transects at all times, especially 72 hours after spraying.

Sistrurus miliarius is known to use its tail as a lure. The brightly colored tail of juveniles fades with age, and Rabatsky and Farrell (1996) suggested that luring behavior occurs less frequently in adult snakes than in juveniles. They did not observe luring behavior in adults at all, although it was reported by Jackson and Martin (1980). Frogs appear to be attracted to the movements of the tail, which is undulated over the body and the ground (Jackson and Martin, 1980). Rabatsky and Farrell (1996) found that tail luring in *S. miliarius* involved two different movement patterns: lateral undulations of about the distal 1 cm of the tail, and the curving to one side, then straightening, followed by curving to the other side of the distal 0.3 cm of the tail. Under laboratory conditions, these authors found that snakes were immediately stimulated to expose their tails and begin luring by the introduction of prey into their enclosures; the light level had no effect on the frequency of luring. May et al. (1996) studied a central Florida population and reported capture of prey during all months of the year but most frequent feeding during the warmer months.

Parasites. Goldberg et al. (2001) reported finding *Hexametra boddaertii* (ascarid nematode) in the stomach musculature of *Sistrurus catenatus* from Chaves County, New Mexico, These authors also discovered several larval nematodes in the gut contents of *S. catenatus*, namely *Physaloptera* sp. (physalopterid nematode) and *Physocephalus* sp. (spiruroid nematode), but suggested that the presence of these parasites in massasaugas was a result of their predation on lizards. Goldberg et al. (2001)

pointed out that lizards are intermediate hosts for both *Physaloptera* and *Physocephalus* (Anderson, 2000).

Venom. The venom of *Sistrurus* contains proteolytic enzymes, phosphodiesterase, and L-amino acid oxidase (Russell, 1983). The LD_{50} (noted in mg/kg body weight) for *S. catenatus* and *S. miliarius* has been estimated to be 2.91 and 2.85, respectively, for white mice (Russell, 1983). Russell (1983) found dry weight venom yields for *S. catenatus* and *S. miliarius* of 15–45 mg and 12–35 mg, respectively, relatively low for rattlesnakes. In experiments with white mice, the intraperitoneal LD_{50} (mg/kg) for *S. catenatus* was only 0.22, considerably lower than that for *Agkistrodon piscivorus* (6.85), *Crotalus adamanteus* (1.67), or *C. atrox* (8.42) (Minton, 1956). Minton (1956) discovered that the toxicity of the venom of *S. catenatus* was about 20 times greater in mice when administered intraperitoneally rather than subcutaneously. In experiments involving subcutaneous injections of venom into white mice, Minton (1956) found that *S. miliarius* venom produced an area of necrosis about five times greater than *S. catenatus* venom did.

Despite numerous experiments and analyses demonstrating the toxicity of its venom, *Sistrurus catenatus*, perhaps because of its small size, has sometimes been considered incapable of inflicting a dangerous bite. Statements such as Ruthven et al.'s (1928) that "it is doubtful if the bite is sufficiently noxious to kill a healthy adult" abound in the literature. This snake should be treated with respect, however, because it is fully capable of a life-threatening bite. Early experiments at the Antivenin Institute of America suggested that although *S. catenatus* delivered a relatively small amount of venom during a bite, the venom was about five times more toxic than that of the western diamondback rattlesnake, *Crotalus atrox* (LeRay, 1930). More recently, the venom of *S. catenatus* has been called one of the most toxic of rattlesnake venoms, almost equal to that of *C. scutulatus* and about 10 times as toxic as the venom of *C. atrox* (Lowe et al., 1986). Massasauga bites can be extremely painful and may be accompanied by swelling, faintness, nausea, and a cold sweat. Hemolysin and a strong neurotoxic factor are present in this venom, which, according to Smith (1956), "is known to be extremely toxic although only two deaths of human beings, caused by the bite of this species, have been recorded." Minton (1972) noted well-authenticated fatalities from the bite of *S. catenatus*, and Lyon and Bishop (1936) documented a fatality in Indiana. There are two recorded fatalities from *S. catenatus* in Ontario, Canada, according to Froom (1964). One of these was caused by a young massasauga that was seized as it was swimming in Six Mile Lake; the victim died eight days after being bitten. The second instance was that of a 10-year-old girl who stepped on or near a snake that bit her; she died later the same day en route to a hospital.

Allen (1956) reported the bite from an adult *S. c. catenatus* (59 cm) to the right thumb of an adult male. Within an hour the hand had swollen to about 2.5 times its normal size. There was no pain around the bite, but a feeling of general numbness was present; respiration and body temperature of the patient remained normal. A total of 15 cc of North American serum for snakebite was injected, half of this amount in the edematous area surrounding the bite and the other half into the muscle of the upper arm. The following day the hand remained badly swollen but there seemed to be no other effects and the patient was released from the hospital. About a week after the bite, an itchy red rash developed on the victim's right hand. It is thought that this was caused by either the penicillin or the antivenom.

The most detailed description of an untreated snakebite by *S. catenatus* is by Baldwin (1999), who reported an immediate burning sensation following a bite on the middle finger of his left hand. After 5 minutes there was profuse bleeding from the fang punctures and intense throbbing of the finger, and after 15 minutes the bitten finger and hand were noticeably swollen and a dry metallic taste was present in the mouth. The swelling had affected the forearm within an hour. Baldwin experienced intense sweating, uncontrollable shaking with chills, a slight fever (38.3 °C), mild nausea, and lightheadedness within 8 hours after the bite. After 14 hours, a dull pain continued and the forearm was extremely sensitive to the slightest touch and to sunlight. One week after the bite most of the swelling was gone, but the joints and muscles in the left hand, wrist, and forearm remained stiff and sore. Seventeen months later, a dull pain remained in the bitten finger, which was still somewhat inflexible.

LaPointe's (1953) response to a *S. catenatus* bite involved a strong nervous reaction, sweating, a feeling of faintness, and nausea within half an hour following the bite. He was administered antivenom (15 cc anti-crotalid) and spent about one and a half days in the hospital, after which he recovered uneventfully.

With respect to *S. miliarius*, Anderson (1965) stated that "even though no fatalities are known from the bites of these little snakes, they should be treated with caution and respect, as a bite can cause much discomfort." Brimley (1944) stated that "while too small to be really dangerous, the bite of this snake will give the victim quite an unpleasant time for several days." Chamberlain (1935) described several bites from this species, one of which resulted in considerable discomfort and inflammation. As of 1938 the Florida Reptile Institute had recorded 28 *S. m. barbouri* bites, none of which was fatal (Allen, 1938). Allen (1938) also described the bite from this species received by one of his assistants, who suffered severe pain and swelling for about 24 hours. In Florida, Kauffman (1928) treated two young brothers, 8 and 11 years of age, who were bitten by the same snake while they were walking barefoot. Both were administered antivenom and recovered quickly. A small child bitten in Hardin County, Texas, by a *S. miliarius* required several weeks of hospitalization (Guidry, 1953). An early, secondhand account of a fatality by this species exists in the form of handwritten notes made by the eminent herpetologist Edward Hallowell, which state: "Col. McCall informed me that one of the privates attached to his regiment was killed by the bite of a *miliarius*" (Sutcliffe, 1952).

Predators. Predators of *S. catenatus* include the loggerhead shrike, *Lanius ludovicianus* (Chapman and Castro, 1972). Hammerson (1999) listed carnivorous mammals, hawks, raccoons, and coachwhips as possible predators in Colorado; and Vogt (1981) listed skunks and foxes in Wisconsin. Racers (*Coluber constrictor*) are known to feed on *S. catenatus* (Minton, 2001), and hogs, feral and otherwise, have probably eradicated massasaugas from many areas (Minton, 1972). Domestic fowl may also feed on these snakes; Brown (1950) mentioned that "over 30 specimens were collected in one small area using turkeys as detectors where previously only 3 had been known."

Babis (1949) reported that an adult indigo snake (*Drymarchon corais*) from Everglades National Park, Florida, had ingested two *S. miliarius*; and Prentiss (1994) encountered a black racer (*Coluber constrictor*) that was swallowing an adult (41 cm TL) pygmy rattlesnake.

Reproduction. Sistrurus catenatus exhibits considerable geographic variation in reproductive biology. Females reproduce when they reach about 32.5 cm, which is usually achieved in the third or fourth year of life (Keenlyne, 1978; Seigel, 1983, 1986; Wright, 1941). The smallest reproductive male and female observed by Goldberg and Holycross (1999) were 28.0 cm and 32.9 cm in SVL, respectively, suggesting that males may reach sexual maturity at an earlier age than females.

Not all mature female *S. catenatus* reproduce every year; geography and environmental conditions determine which segment of the population is reproductively active. In Pennsylvania, Reinert (1981) found that 58% of adult females were gravid; in Missouri, Seigel (1986) found that 33–71% of adult females reproduced during the individual years of his study; and in Arizona and Colorado, Goldberg and Holycross (1999) found that only a portion of the adult female population reproduced during any particular year, but their samples were too small to establish an accurate estimate of this proportion. Female massasaugas in Missouri potentially produce every year according to Johnson (1987).

Atkinson and Netting (1927) suggested that mating occurs in April or early May in western Pennsylvania. Johnson (1987) observed that in Missouri, courtship and mating may occur during either the spring or the fall. In Colorado, Mackessy (1996) found a pair of *S. catenatus* possibly engaged in courtship on 3 September. In Arizona and Colorado, Goldberg and Holycross (1999) found that spermiogenesis occurred from June through October, suggesting that males are capable of inseminating females throughout this period. Based on captive specimens, Lowe et al. (1986) reported that in Arizona *S. catenatus* mates in the spring and fall.

In Clinton County, Illinois, Jellen et al. (2001) observed mating behavior from 26 July to 23 September, with breeding behavior peaking in late August and early September. Females were accompanied for an average of almost three days by an average of five males, suggesting a polygynous mating system.

Over most of the range, young are born in August and September (Adler, 1960; Anderson, 1965; Anton, 2000; Hay, 1887a; Hobert, 1997; Keenlyne and Beer, 1973b; Mackessy, *in* Hammerson, 1999; Swanson, 1933; Watkins-Colwell, 1995; Wright, 1941), but Atkinson and Netting (1927) suggested that parturition in Pennsylvania may occur slightly earlier, in July and early August. Seigel (1986) found newborn young with conspicuous umbilical scars in Missouri from 17 August to 23 September.

Conant and Bridges (1939) stated that *S. c. catenatus* produces 5–12 young. A sample of 17 gravid *S. catenatus* from Squaw Creek National Wildlife Refuge in Missouri carried litters of 4–10 young ($\bar{x} = 6.4$) (Seigel, 1986). Johnson (1987) also gave figures of 4–10 offspring for Missouri females. In Kansas this snake produces 5–13 offspring (Collins, 1993), and in Colorado and Texas females give birth to 3–11 young (Fitch, 1985a; Gloyd, 1955; Greene and Oliver, 1965; Klauber, 1972). In Wisconsin this species has 6–19 young ($\bar{x} = 11.1$) and reproduces annually (Keenlyne, 1978), whereas in Pennsylvania and Missouri the litter size is smaller (4–10, $\bar{x} = 6.4$–7.2, depending on locality; Atkinson and Netting, 1927; Reinert, 1981; Seigel, 1986; Swanson, 1933). Several studies in Illinois (Wright, 1941; Bielema, 1973) have suggested that these populations are intermediate between those of Wisconsin and Missouri, with litter sizes of 5–14. Tobiasz (1941) reported two litters of 11 young born on 19 and 30 August 1940 to females collected in late June in Du Page County, Illinois. Two females from Ohio each gave

birth to 9 young (Watkins-Colwell, 1995), and another from Champaign County gave birth to 6 living young and 3 underdeveloped embryos on 11 August 1951 (Triplehorn, 1955). Seigel (1986) reported variation in mean litter sizes from 5.3 in Texas to 11.1 in Wisconsin. Goldberg and Holycross (1999) reported that 4–8 ($\bar{x} = 5.8$) young are born in Arizona and 4–5 ($\bar{x} = 4.5$) young are born in Colorado. The greatest number of young known is 20 produced by an Illinois female (Anton, 2000).

Keenlyne and Beer (1973b) reported on 207 *S. catenatus* neonates (107 males and 100 females) from Wisconsin. The males were 18.6–24.9 cm ($\bar{x} = 22.0$ cm) in TL, and the females were 18.1–25.2 cm ($\bar{x} = 22.1$ cm). The weight range for both sexes was 5.1–14.8 g ($\bar{x} = 9.7$ g). Wright (1941) examined six litters from northeastern Illinois in which neonates averaged 22.3 cm in TL. Anton (2000) reported that the neonates in a litter from Illinois were 20.0–22.0 cm ($\bar{x} = 21.2$ cm) in SVL and weighed 10.6–12.0 g ($\bar{x} = 11.5$ g). Adler (1960) reported a litter of 7 young from northern Indiana, with the TL of 6 of these being between 24.2 and 25.7 cm. Two females from Ohio gave birth to young that were 15.4–19.0 cm ($\bar{x} = 18.2$ cm) and 21.5–23.0 cm ($\bar{x} = 22.4$ cm) in SVL and weighed 7–8 g ($\bar{x} = 7.6$ g) and 11–14 g ($\bar{x} = 12.0$ g), respectively (Watkins-Colwell, 1995). In Missouri, the mean size of neonates ranged from 18.2 cm for a litter of 6 born in the laboratory to 25.2 cm for 16 wild-caught individuals, the latter group obviously having grown somewhat since birth (Seigel, 1986). Arizona neonates average about 17.1 cm (Lowe et al., 1986), a somewhat shorter length than is found in eastern populations. Neonates captured in the field in Arizona were 16.2–17.6 cm in SVL and weighed 3.9–5.1 g (Goldberg and Holycross, 1999). Klauber (1972) reported young of the western massasauga to be 17.8–23.5 cm in TL. Greene and Oliver (1965) reported that the offspring in one Texas litter were 21.7–23.4 cm long and weighed 9.5–11.6 g, with a marked sexual dimorphism in the tail length/total length ratio of 10.3–11.0% ($\bar{x} = 10.7\%$) in males and 7.4–9.3% ($\bar{x} = 8.5\%$) in females.

Chiszar et al. (1976) observed courtship behavior in a pair of *S. catenatus tergeminus*. Active courtship lasted for about two hours, followed by a quiescent period when copulation was apparently occurring. The male positioned his body on top of the female's and often rubbed her head and neck with longitudinal strokes of his chin while flexing his entire body and wrapping his tail around the female's tail. The male used his coiled tail to stroke the female from about the level of the vent to the base of the rattle.

Sistrurus miliarius mates in September and October in central Florida (Farrell et al., 1995). In North Carolina, most mating probably occurs in the spring (Palmer and Braswell, 1995). Farrell et al. (1995) found that female *S. miliarius* in central Florida were potentially capable of annual reproduction, although of the 19 females captured during two consecutive years, 6 (32%) were not gravid in either year, 8 (42%) were gravid in one of the two years, and 5 (26%) were gravid in both years. Bishop et al. (1996) found no sexual dimorphism in growth rate or size in a population from Volusia County, Florida, but field observations suggested that larger males may experience greater reproductive success than smaller males. Ritualized combat behavior between two captive males from widely separated localities (Florida and Oklahoma) was observed in November by Carpenter (1979). Lindsey (1979) reported this behavior in two males of *S. m. barbouri* from Alachua County, Florida, that seemed to be induced by the introduction of dead food items into their cage. These snakes became entwined, raised the anterior part of their bodies, and attempted to force each other to the ground, with the larger individual usually winning these bouts.

Sistrurus miliarius usually gives birth from July to September. A female from Montgomery County, Texas, gave birth on 31 July 1958 (Sabath and Worthington, 1959). Two females from east Texas gave birth on 23 August and 24 August (Fleet and Kroll, 1978). Ford et al. (1990) provided data on five litters of *S. miliarius* from east Texas that were born during 2–13 August. A female from Oklahoma gave birth on 6 August 1959 (Carpenter, 1960). Trauth et al. (1994) reported that an Arkansas female gave birth on 9 September. Two litters from Missouri females were born on 31 August and 28 September (Anderson, 1965), and Johnson (1987) stated that in Missouri young are born from August through September. A female from Vernon Parrish, Louisiana, gave birth on 9 July (Clark, 1963), and Dundee and Rossman (1989) reported parturition dates in Louisiana of 12 August and 25 August. Mount (1975) reported that a female from Chilton County, Alabama, gave birth on 15 August.

In Florida, *S. miliarius* gives birth during the late summer (Ashton and Ashton, 1981). Dalrymple et al. (1991b) reported that young were extremely common on Long Pine Key, Florida, in July and August of every year. May et al. (1996) reported that birth occurred in a central Florida population in August, and that young were most frequently encountered during this month and in the winter months. Iverson (1978) reported that two Florida females gave birth on 15 July and 2 August, respectively. In central Florida, 24 of 26 (92%) gravid females gave birth in August, and clutch mass and litter size were significantly correlated with the length of the female (Farrell et al., 1995). Palmer and Braswell (1995) reported that young are born in August and September in North Carolina.

Anderson (1965) reported on a female from Taney County, Missouri, collected on 1 July, that contained 7 embryos, and Hurter (1911) mentioned a female from Stone County collected on 19 August that contained an equal number of embryos. Iverson (1978) reported a female that contained 6 partially developed embryos on 2 July.

Sistrurus miliarius usually gives birth to about 2–18 young, although litters are occasionally larger. Carpenter (1960) reported a litter of 32 born to a female from Oklahoma, the largest litter known. Sabath and Worthington (1959) reported that a female from Montgomery County, Texas, gave birth to 5 young, and Fleet and Kroll (1978) reported that two females from east Texas each gave birth to 5 young. Ford et al. (1990) reported that five litters from east Texas contained 6–9 ($\bar{x} = 7.4$) young. Trauth et al. (1994) reported that litter size for eight gravid females from Arkansas varied from 6 to 14 ($\bar{x} = 10.0$). Litters of 3 and 5 young were born to two Missouri females (Anderson, 1965), and Johnson (1987) stated that 6–14 young are born in Missouri. A female from Vernon Parrish, Louisiana, gave birth to 5 young (Clark, 1963), and Dundee and Rossman (1989) reported that two females from Louisiana gave birth to 4 and 6 offspring, respectively. A female from Chilton County, Alabama, gave birth to 6 young (Mount, 1975). Based on the litters of 17 females and the dissection of 3 gravid females from North Carolina, Palmer and Braswell (1995) determined that the litter size in that region ranges from 3 to 9 ($\bar{x} = 5.3$). This species produces 5–9 young in the Okefenokee area of Georgia (Wright and Bishop, 1915). A female from Silver Springs, Marion County, Florida, gave birth to 8 young (Gloyd, 1940), and Ashton and Ashton (1981) reported that *S. miliarius* gives birth to 7–9 young in Florida. In central Florida, females produce 2–11 young (Farrell et al., 1995).

Sistrurus miliarius neonates usually are between 12 and 18 cm in TL. Sabath and Worthington (1959) reported on a litter of young from Montgomery County, Texas, that were 13.5–14.1 cm ($\bar{x} = 13.9$ cm); and Ford et al. (1990) provided data on five litters of *S. miliarius* from east Texas in which the mean SVL of young from individual litters varied from 13.6 to 16.4 mm, and the mean weight varied from 1.83 to 3.13 g. Fleet and Kroll (1978) reported on two litters from Texas that were 10.2–10.4 cm ($\bar{x} = 10.3$ cm) and 14.1–16.1 cm ($\bar{x} = 15.3$ cm) in TL, respectively. The 17 males and 15 females from a single Oklahoma litter were 13.5–14.8 ($\bar{x} = 14.3$) and 15.5–16.9 ($\bar{x} = 16.5$) cm in TL, respectively, and weighed 2.2–2.9 g (Carpenter, 1960). Young from two litters from Missouri were 12.0–13.0 cm in TL (Anderson, 1965). Based on the litters of 17 females and the dissection of 3 gravid females, Palmer and Braswell (1995) determined that young in North Carolina range in TL from 14.9 to 19.1 cm ($\bar{x} = 17.2$ cm). Two newborn *S. m. miliarius* from an unspecified locality were 14.8 and 17.3 cm in TL (Gloyd, 1940), and the young from a female from Silver Springs, Marion County, Florida, were 15.7–17.3 cm in TL (Gloyd, 1940). Freed (1997) reported 8 young (2 stillborn) born to a long-term captive female from an unspecified locality that ranged from 7.8 to 15.6 ($\bar{x} = 13.9$) cm in TL and weighed 0.8–4.2 ($\bar{x} = 3.0$) g. The smallest of these neonates, 7.8 cm in TL and weighing 0.8 g, was born alive but died within a week.

Longevity. The longest life spans known are 20 years for *S. catenatus* and 16 years and 1 month for *S. miliarius* (Slavens and Slavens, 2000); both animals were captives.

Sistrurus catenatus (Rafinesque, 1818)
(Figs. 221–223, Map 112, Pls. 1011–1017)

Crotalinus catenatus Rafinesque, 1818, *Am. Monthly Mag. Crit. Rev.* 4:39–42[41]. Type(s): none designated. Type-locality: "on the prairies of the Upper Missouri" [Valley, USA]. Schmidt (1953c) proposed the type-locality be restricted to "Kansas City, Missouri."

Crotulurus (Crotalus) catenatus—Rafinesque, 1820, *Ann. Nat.*, pp. 1–16[5].

Crotalus tergeminus Say, *in* Long, 1823, *Acct. Exped. Pittsburgh Rocky Mountains* 1:503 pp.[499]. Syntypes (2): none designated. Type-locality: "between the Mississippi River and the Rocky Mountains." Subsequently, Smith and Taylor (1950b: 358) proposed a restriction to "Winfield, Cowley County, Kansas."

Crotalophorus tergeminus—Gray, 1831, *Synops. Rept., Animal Kingdom* (Appendix) 9:1–110[78].

Crotalus messasaugus Kirtland, *in* Mather, 1838, *Second Ann. Rep. Geol. Surv. Ohio*, pp. 157–200[190, footnote]. Type(s): none designated. Adler (1965:56) suggested USNM 526 as the possible holotype. Type-locality: "Ohio" [USA].

Crotalophorus Kirtlandi Holbrook, 1842, *N. Am. Herpetol.*, 2d ed., 3:128 pp.[31, pl. 6]. [Plate 6 was mislabeled *Crotalophourus Kirtlandi*, incorrect subsequent spelling.] Syntypes (3): none designated in original description, but three specimens were cataloged as syntypes: ANSP 7238, ANSP 7239, and ANSP 16662, according to Malnate (1971:367). Type-locality: "Ohio and Michigan" [USA]. Schmidt (1953c:226) proposed restriction to Trumbull County, Ohio, but Adler (1976:xxxv) noted that the types were more likely to have been collected in an area that today is part of Mahoning County, Ohio.

Crotalophorus consors Baird and Girard, 1853, *Cat. N. Am. Rept.* (1):172 pp.[12]. Holotype: USNM 512. Type-locality: "Indianola" [Texas, USA].

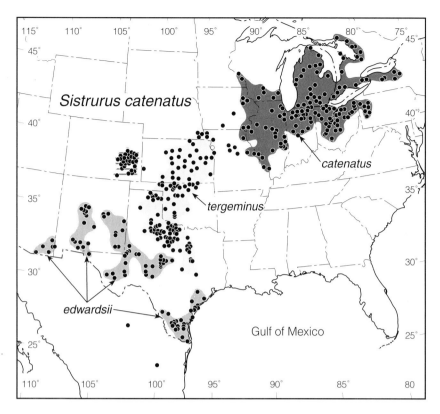

Map 112. Distribution of *Sistrurus catenatus*, including subspecies, in North America. The Colorado, USA, population is morphologically somewhat intermediate between *S. c. tergeminus* and *S. c. edwardsii*. See text for discussion of a few records that represent relictual populations. Unfilled symbol represents the restricted type-locality, Kansas City, Missouri, USA, as proposed by Schmidt (1953c).

Crotalophorus tergeminus—Baird and Girard, 1853, *Cat. N. Am. Rept.* (1):172 pp.[14].

Crotalophorus Edwardsii Baird and Girard, 1853, *Cat. N. Am. Rept.* (1):172 pp.[15]. Syntypes (3 or 4): USNM 506 (Sonora), USNM 507 (Tamaulipas), USNM 508 (Texas [south bank of Rio Grande]), and USNM 509 (Mexico [presumably Tamaulipas]). Lectotype: USNM 509, according to designation by Yarrow (1882:78). Minton (1983b:332.2) listed USNM 507 as the "holotype." Type-locality: "Tamaulipas . . . S. Bank of Rio Grande . . . Sonora."

Crotalophorus Kirtlandii—Baird and Girard, 1853, *Cat. N. Am. Rept.* (1):172 pp.[16].

Crotalophorus massasauga—Baird, 1854, *Serp. New York*, 28 pp.[12]. [Unjustified emendation.]

Crotalus (Crotalophorus) miliarius var. *tergeminus*—Jan, 1863a, *Elenco Sist. Ofidi*, 143 pp.[124].

Crotalus (Crotalophorus) miliarius var. *Edwardsii*—Jan, 1863a, *Elenco Sist. Ofidi*, 143 pp.[124].

Caudisona tergemina—Cope, 1875, *Bull. U.S. Natl. Mus.* (1):104 pp.[34].

Caudisoma edwardsii—Yarrow, *in* Wheeler, 1875, *Rep. Geog. Geol. Explor. Surv. W. 100th Merid.* 5:509–633[531].

Crotalus consors—Coues, *in* Wheeler, 1875, *Rep. Geog. Geol. Explor. Surv. W. 100th Merid.* 5:585–633[610].

Sistrurus catenatus—Garman, 1884a [dated 1883], *Mem. Mus. Comp. Zool.* 8:1–185[118, 176, pl. 9 (fig. 2)].

Sistrurus catenatus var. *consors*—Garman, 1884a [dated 1883], *Mem. Mus. Comp. Zool.* 8:1–185[176].

Sistrurus miliarius var. *edwardsii*—Garman, 1884a [dated 1883], *Mem. Mus. Comp. Zool.* 8:1–185[177].

Crotalophorus catenatus catenatus—Cope, 1892, *Proc. U.S. Natl. Mus.* 14:589–694[685].

Crotalophorus catenatus edwardsii—Cope, 1892, *Proc. U.S. Natl. Mus.* 14:589–694[685].

Sistrurus catenatus consors—Stejneger, 1895 [dated 1893], *Rep. U.S. Natl. Mus.* 1893:337–487[415].

Sistrurus catenatus edwardsii—Stejneger, 1895 [dated 1893], *Rep. U.S. Natl. Mus.* 1893:337–487[416, pl. 6].

Sistrurus catenatus—Boulenger, 1896b, *Cat. Snakes British Mus.* 3:727 pp.[570].

Sistrurus edwardsii—Cockerell, 1896, *Am. Nat.* 30:323–327[326].

Sistrurus catenatus catenatus—Cope, 1900 [dated 1898], *Rep. U.S. Natl. Mus.* 1898:152–1294[1146, fig. 329].

Sistrurus catenatus var. *edwardsii*—Ditmars, 1907, *Rept. Book*, 472 pp.[433, 438, pl. 125 (figs. 3, 5)].

Sistrurus catenatus tergeminus—Klauber, 1936c, *Occas. Pap. San Diego Soc. Nat. Hist.* 1:1–24[6].

Sistrurus catenatus edwardsi—Gloyd, 1955, *Bull. Chicago Acad. Sci.* 10:83–98[84, map].

Crotalus (Sistrurus) catenatus edwardsi—Hoge, 1966 [dated 1965], *Mem. Inst. Butantan* 32:109–184[160].

Most collectors report these snakes as sluggish, inoffensive, and slow to rattle. This has not been my impression of those I have had in captivity. Nearly all have been alert, bad-tempered snakes, quicker to strike than several species of larger rattlesnakes.

—Minton, 2001

LOCAL NAMES Black massasauga, black rattler, black snapper, gray rattlesnake (Iowa, *fide* Guthrie, 1927), little gray rattlesnake (Canada), muck rattler, prairie rattlesnake, pygmy rattler, sauger, spotted rattler, swamp rattler, víbora de cascabel (Mexico).

ENGLISH NAME Massasauga. Kirtland (1838) was one of the first to apply this name to *S. catenatus*; it is derived from the Mississauga Indians and Mississauga River in Ontario, Canada. Apparently the term *mississauga* is derived from several Chippewa Indian words that refer to the delta region of large rivers (meaning "great river mouth"), which presumably have swampy habitats suitable for this snake (Atkinson and Netting, 1927; Ingersoll, 1883).

ETYMOLOGY The specific epithet is derived from the Latin *catena*, meaning "chain," and the suffix *-atus*, meaning "provided with," perhaps in reference to the dorsal pattern or the rattle.

DISTRIBUTION From southeastern Arizona, southern New Mexico, and most of Texas northeastward to central New York and southern Ontario, Canada; several isolated populations occur in Mexico (Map 112). Although the range has often been indicated as a broad, continuous swath cutting diagonally across North America from the southwestern United States to the Great Lakes region, the distribution of this species is disjunct in several places. One such disjunction occurs in Missouri, where an isolated population is found in the north-central part of the state (Anderson, 1965; Evans and Gloyd, 1948; Johnson, 1987; Seigel, 1986) that appears to be separated from other populations to the east and west by distances of about 75 km. Although this snake is often found along wooded edges, the habitat provided by dense, mature forests appears to be an effective natural barrier to dispersal (Bushey, 1978). This species does not occur in Texas east of the Brazos River drainage. Gibbs et al. (1997) found significant genetic differentiation among populations separated by only a few kilometers, suggesting relatively long isolation in localized areas.

The disjunct distribution has been correlated with post glacial relict habitats (Wright, 1941); undoubtedly, recent habitat alteration by human agency has further fragmented the range (Bushey, 1978; Seigel, 1986). Bushey (1978) discussed the fragmentation of the distribution of S. catenatus since European settlement in Illinois and mapped the probable range of this species through time (1834–1975) based on human-induced modifications of vegetation and preferred habitats of the species. Sistrurus catenatus is known from several islands surrounded by fresh water, including Bois Blanc in northern Lake Huron, the Charity Islands, and North Island and Heisterman Island in Saginaw Bay (Gloyd, 1940). Baird and Girard (1853) also reported it from Grosse Isle in the Detroit River. In Texas, this species occurs on several barrier islands, including North Padre Island, Matagorda Island, and San José Island (Brown, 1950). Over most of its range S. catenatus occurs at low elevations, only rarely reaching 1,500 m or slightly higher in a few places. In west Texas, New Mexico, and Arizona, however, this species occurs mostly above 1,000 m.

The western part of the range features a number of isolated populations. Lowe et al. (1986) stated that in Arizona the massasauga occurs only in a few small areas in Cochise County, that it is no longer extant at most historical localities in Cochise County, and that it has been extirpated from Graham County. In Arizona, the elevational distribution in the San Bernardino Valley is 1,341–1,433 m (Lowe et al., 1986). In New Mexico S. catenatus is distributed in isolated populations in the central and southern parts of the state at elevations of 925–2,100 m (Degenhardt et al., 1996). Cockerell (1896) reported S. catenatus in the Mesilla Valley from near Las Cruces, New Mexico.

A disjunct population occurs in southeastern Colorado below 1,675 m (Hammerson, 1999; Maslin, 1965). The first unequivocal evidence of this snake in Colorado is contained in Ellis and Henderson, 1913, which reports a single specimen from Baca Country in the extreme southeastern corner of the state that was collected in 1882 (but see James, 1823, and Dundee, 1996). This specimen, previously cataloged in the University of Northern Colorado (previously Colorado State Normal College) collection as 96-265, is now missing (Mackessy et al., 1996). Maslin (1950) reported an additional six specimens from Kiowa County, Colorado, and subsequently this species has been found in most of the counties in the southeastern part of the state (Hammerson, 1999). Other reports of this snake from

Colorado are contained in Brown et al., 1970; Hammerson, 1982, 1999; Hammerson et al., 1991b; Hobert, 1997; Mackessy, 1998; Mackessy et al., 1996; Maslin, 1959; Montgomery et al., 1998; Pegler et al., 1995; and Smith et al., 1965. One specimen (KU 221506) from western Kansas (Hamilton County: Sec 36, T23S, R42W) may represent a relictual population or may be from an area that until fairly recently constituted the eastern edge of the range for the Colorado population.

A number of works provide information on the general distribution (Conant and Bridges, 1939; Conant and Collins, 1998; Cope, 1860b, 1900; Garman, 1884a 1884b; Gloyd, 1940; Harding, 1997; Klauber, 1971, 1972; Minton, 1983b; Mocquard, 1908–1909; Stejneger, 1895; Werner, 1922; Wright and Wright, 1957). Locality records are also available for Arizona (Coues, 1875; Fowlie, 1965; Gloyd, 1955; Lowe, 1964; Lowe et al., 1986; Stebbins, 1985; Stejneger, 1902; Van Denburgh, 1922b; Woodin, 1953; Yarrow, 1875), Colorado (Hobert et al., 1997; Montgomery et al., 1998), Illinois (Boulenger, 1896b; Peters, 1942; Smith, 1961), Indiana (Minton, 1972, 2001; Resetar, 1992), Iowa (Loomis, 1948), Kansas (Branson, 1904; Collins, 1993; Cope, 1860a; Gloyd, 1928; Smith, 1931, 1956; Woodburne, 1956), Michigan (Creaser, 1927; Roberts and Quarters, 1947; Ruthven et al., 1928), Missouri (Anderson, 1965; Evans and Gloyd, 1948; Jan and Sordelli, 1874), Nebraska (Hudson, 1942), New Mexico (Degenhardt et al., 1996; Holycross and Rubio, 2000; Stebbins, 1985; Stuart and Brown, 1996; Van Denburgh, 1924), New York (Moesel, 1918; Wright, 1919), Ohio (Cope, 1860a; Conant, 1938, 1951; Dexter, 1944; Wood and Duellman, 1947), Pennsylvania (Atkinson and Netting, 1927; Bowler, 1974; McCoy 1982), Oklahoma (Webb, 1970; Woodburne, 1956), Texas (Bailey, 1905; Baird, 1859a; A. Brown, 1903a; B. Brown, 1950; Crimmins, 1927a; Dial and Smith, 1964; Dixon, 1987; Garman, 1892c; Hibbits, 1991; Merkord, 1975; Price, 1998; Rakowitz et al., 1983; Ramsey, 1951; Raun, 1965; Raun and Gehlbach, 1972; Schuett and Kraus, 1980b; Smith and Taylor, 1945; Strecker, 1908a, 1908b, 1935c; Thornton and Smith, 1993; Ward, 1983; Werler, 1964; Werler and Dixon, 2000), Wisconsin (Dickinson, 1949; Hoy, 1883; Pope and Dickinson, 1928; Vogt, 1981), the western United States (Shaw and Campbell, 1974), and Canada (Boulenger, 1896b; Curran, 1935; Logier and Toner, 1955; Mills, 1948). Old records of this species from as far west as Utah (e.g., Hay, 1892) are based on misidentifications of snakes of the genus Crotalus. The presence of S. catenatus in Canada was indicated by Froom (1967) and Logier (1958).

Several old records exist for Mexico, but locality data pertaining to the specimens representing these records and the status of the specimens have been subject to much confusion (see Remarks). It has been suggested that populations of Sistrurus catenatus in Mexico are relicts that were isolated after the advent of drying conditions that followed Pleistocene pluvial periods. All Mexican specimens with precise locality data have come from near permanent streams or marshes. Gloyd (1940:41), Smith and Taylor (1945:199, footnote 10), and Klauber (1952:116) regarded the occurrence of S. catenatus in Mexico as questionable. However, this species is now known with certainty from the Cuatro Ciénegas Basin, Coahuila (McCoy and Minckley, 1969), and from the vicinity of Aramberri, Nuevo León (Campbell and Lamar, 1989). It probably occurs or occurred until fairly recently in northern Tamaulipas (Jan and Sordelli, 1874), northern Chihuahua, and possibly in northeastern Sonora. Given the deep incursion of this species into Mexico as evinced by the Coahuila and Nuevo León records, an unconfirmed report for Durango (Cuesta-Terrón, 1921b) should be given some credulity, although this author sometimes confused various species of rattlesnakes (Martín del Campo, 1935). Cuesta-Terrón (1930b) clearly listed *S. catenatus* as a Mexican species, saying that it occurs in draws, around small lakes, and at the edges of marshes, but he provided no definite localities.

Several confirmed Arizona records are very near the Mexican border, and it is not unreasonable to believe that the species occurred at least until very recently in Sonora. Bogert and Oliver (1945) suggested that the record from Sonora mentioned by Baird and Girard (1853) may have come from what is now Arizona but did not rule out the possibility of this snake occurring in Sonora. Baird's (1859a:15) report originated not long after the Gadsen Purchase of 1853, a time when much of what had become Arizona was still referred to as the Mexican territory of Sonora. Other reports of this species in Mexico have been provided by Martín del Campo (1937a, 1950), McCoy (1984), and Minckley and Rinne (1972).

HABITAT   Mostly open, low-lying areas such as moist bogs, tamarack bogs, marshes, and grassy meadows; rolling plains and prairie lands including tallgrass prairie, shortgrass prairie, and cordgrass (*Spartina*) prairie; grassland–deciduous forest ecotones; rocky hillsides and limestone outcroppings; grasslands including desert grassland, tobosa grassland, and grass- and brush-covered sand dunes; low plains consisting of mesquite, juniper, and overgrazed grassland; the sandhills of west Texas; and high rolling plains of the Texas panhandle. Even those populations occurring in drier habitats are often found near water, and massasaugas are occasionally found swimming (Froom, 1964).

In Ontario, Canada, Weatherhead and Prior (1992) found that radio-tracked *S. catenatus* were stongly associated with wetlands dominated by various tree species and coniferous forest and that these snakes usually avoided open areas, meadows dominated by grasses, and mixed forest. However, these authors found that when they were not using radiotelemetry they most often captured this species in open areas, presumably because individuals were more easily detected by humans in such habitats. *Sistrurus c. catenatus* is said to prefer bogs and swamps in the eastern part of its range but is more frequently found in wet prairie habitats in the west (Conant, 1975).

The preferred habitat in the southwestern United States is desert-grassland. The region about the Cuatro Ciénegas Basin, Coahuila, where this snake has been collected is an area of low, unconsolidated gypsum dunes vegetated with various combinations of creosote bush, chenopods, low mesquite, desert willow, salt grass (*Distichlis*), and numerous cacti (McCoy and Minckley, 1969). The vegetation near Aramberri, Nuevo León, is mostly xerophytic; however, the Río Blanco and several other tributaries of the Río Soto la Marina cut through the countryside near this location and have luxuriant riparian vegetations. Northern Tamaulipas is covered by mesquite-grassland.

DESCRIPTION   This is a relatively small rattlesnake. Adults attain a size of 50–70 cm, with the maximum reported lengths being 95.2 cm (Klauber, 1972) and 100.3 cm (Conant, 1975). Snakes in the eastern part of the range tend to reach greater lengths. The largest specimen of *S. c. edwardsii* reported from Arizona by Lowe et al. (1986) was only 53.9 cm. Holycross (2002) reported two exceptionally large males from Cochise County, Arizona, that were 57.8 and 58.8 cm in TL. Werler and Dixon (2000) gave 88.3 cm as the maximum length for *S. c. tergeminus* in Texas. Wright (1941) reported that males in Illinois reach larger sizes than females. Seigel (1986), working in Missouri, did not detect any sexual dimorphism in SVL but did find that the relative tail length was longer in the males he examined, thus giving them a longer TL.

The dorsal ground color is pale brown, brown, gray, or gray-brown. Specimens in the eastern part of the range are occasionally melanistic. In the Niagara Peninsula of Canada, melanistic specimens are common (Mills, 1948). According to Minton (2001), the offspring of melanistic females are spotted. The snout generally bears irregular markings that extend from the prenasal (or first supralabial) up over the canthus onto the internasals and extend posteriorly across the prefrontals to the anterior part of the frontal and supraoculars and downward across the canthus to include the upper part of the upper preocular. This dark snout marking is continuous with the dark postocular stripe and may be divided in two along the dorsal midline of the snout, or the snout may be entirely dark. An irregular transverse dark bar is often present on the posterior part of the supraoculars and frontal, although the bar is sometimes reduced to an ill-defined spot on the frontal. A single median brown spot is present on the parietals, and a pair of nape blotches form a somewhat lyriform figure that extends from the posterior part of the supraoculars onto the nape. A broad, dark brown postocular stripe extends to the angle of the jaw or slightly beyond onto the side of the neck. The postocular stripe is edged below by a distinct white stripe that extends diagonally from about the postnasal to the rictus. Above, the postocular stripe is narrowly edged in white. There are 21–50 medium to very dark brown middorsal blotches on the body; these are cordiform, subcircular, subovate, or subelliptical and are usually wider than long and separated by 1.0–1.5 scales. In many eastern populations (*S. c. catenatus*) the dorsal blotches and the several series of blotches on the sides of the body are blackish and narrowly edged with white, whereas in more western populations (*S. c. tergeminus* and *S. c. edwardsii*), the dorsal blotches are usually medium to dark brown and are bordered with blackish brown or black and edged narrowly with white or pale ash gray. The middorsal blotches are offset laterally by 3 lateral series of alternating dark spots: dorsolateral, lateral, and ventrolateral. The 3 lateral series of blotches are indistinctly edged with either paler or darker pigment. The dorsolateral blotches are circular and alternate with the dorsal blotches. In eastern populations (*S. c. catenatus*) all 3 series of lateral blotches may be blackish and may be as distinct as the dorsal series. In more western snakes (*S. c. tergeminus* and *S. c. edwardsii*) the blotches of the dorsolateral series contrast less with the dorsal ground color than do the dorsal blotches and are not darkly edged, and the blotches of the lateral series are smaller than those in the dorsolateral series, are arranged opposite the dorsal blotches, and are often darker and may have dark edging. The blotches of the ventrolateral series are very small and usually ill defined or absent posteriorly. The labials are stippled or mottled with brown or gray, and the mental and chinshields are white to pale brown and sometimes immaculate. A pair of irregular dark stripes usually is present, each extending from the anterior infralabials posteriorly onto the gulars, and a median dark stripe is sometimes present from the mental posteriorly along the mental groove. The ventrals are white or cream and lightly to heavily mottled, especially laterally, with gray or brown; some individuals have a wash of orange as well; the ventrals in some specimens from the western part of the range approach a nearly immaculate condition. The tongue is black, and the iris is brown with a suffusion of black ventrally.

Some individuals in the eastern and northern portions of the range (Ohio, Indiana, Michigan, Illinois, Wisconsin) are almost entirely black (Gloyd, 1940; Hay, 1887a, 1892; Higley, 1889;

Holbrook, 1842; Kennicott, 1855; Minton, 1972; Roberts and Quarters, 1947), often with only a pale stripe evident on the side of the head and a slight amount of white mottling on the chin and throat. This melanism is apparently ontogenetic and is found only in adults, juveniles having normal color patterns.

Individuals from around Cuatro Ciénegas, Coahuila, Mexico, have narrow oval dorsal blotches, and the lyriform marking on the head is incomplete (McCoy and Minckley, 1969). The belly is pale with a few dark spots on the lateral edges of the ventrals and rather inconspicuous dark stippling along the midventer.

Juvenile snakes are paler than adults, and their pattern is more distinct; their tail tips are pale yellowish white, yellow, or pink. The venter of newborn snakes often has a decidedly pinkish cast.

Irwin (1979) reported an aberrant individual from Ellsworth County, Kansas, that had a pale brown middorsal stripe running from behind the head for about two-thirds of the length of the dark gray body. A specimen from Ontario, Canada, had many of the dorsal blotches fused to form broad, interrupted, paravertebral stripes over much of the body (Oldham, 1985).

There are 9 large, symmetrical head plates (Fig. 221), 9–14 (usually 11 or 12) supralabials, 10–16 (usually 12 or 13) infralabials, 21–27 (usually 23 or 25) midbody dorsal scale rows, 129–155 ventrals in males and 132–160 in females, and 25–36 subcaudals in males and 19–29 in females. Most of the subcaudals are undivided, but from 0 to 7 of the distal subcaudals may be divided.

SIMILAR SPECIES *Sistrurus catenatus* can be distinguished from all other species of rattlesnakes with which it is sympatric, except *S. miliarius*, by usually having 9 large, symmetrically arranged head plates. *Sistrurus catenatus* and *S. miliarius* are sympatric in small areas of Texas and Oklahoma, but occupy different habitats. Garman (1892c) reported both *S. catenatus* and *S. miliarius* from Deming's Bridge in Matagorda County, Texas. *Sistrurus miliarius* has an upper preocular that does not contact the postnasal (precluded by the intervening loreal scale), the anterior subocular contacts supralabials 3 and 4, and there is usually a reddish middorsal stripe on the body. Several large species of rattlesnakes that coexist with *S. catenatus*, including *Crotalus atrox, C. molossus, C. viridis,* and *C. scutulatus,* have more ventrals (164 or more) and usually have more midbody dorsal scale rows (25 or more), supralabials (14 or more), and infralabials (14 or more) than *S. catenatus. Crotalus lepidus* has a dorsal pattern of 13–24 widely spaced dark crossbands. *Crotalus horridus* has a dorsal pattern of dark chevrons and a dark tail. *Heterodon nasicus* (Pl. 1128), a species not dangerous to humans, bears a strong superficial resemblance to *S. catenatus* but is easily distinguished by its sharp, upturned rostral; divided subcaudals; round pupil; and lack of a rattle. *Arizona elegans* (Pl. 1042), another harmless species, is relatively slender, has divided subcaudals, and lacks a rattle.

REMARKS Three subspecies of *S. catenatus* are recognized. *Sistrurus catenatus catenatus* (Pl. 1011), the eastern massasauga, usually has 25 dorsal scale rows at midbody and a venter that is heavily blotched with gray or black and is sometimes nearly entirely black. *Sistrurus c. tergeminus* (Pls. 1015–1017), the western massasauga, most frequently has 25 dorsal scales rows at midbody and a white or cream venter that is moderately blotched laterally with brown or gray. *Sistrurus c. edwardsii* (Pls. 1012–1014), the desert massasauga, usually has 23 dorsal scale rows at midbody, a relatively pale brown dorsal ground color, and a whitish venter that may be nearly immaculate or may have diffuse, irregular spotting. This taxon is smaller (Werler and Dixon [2000] recorded the maximum size at 53.8 cm, and

Holycross [2002] gave the maximum at 58.8 cm) and slightly more slender than *S. c. tergeminus.*

Some populations are not clearly assignable to subspecies. Knopf and Tinkle (1961) thought that the population of *S. catenatus* inhabiting the high plains of the panhandle of Texas more closely resembled *S. c. edwardsii* than *S. c. tergeminus,* and that intergradation between these two taxa most likely occurred along the Caprock region, an area of intensely eroded terrain extending from Palo Duro Canyon near Amarillo southward to about Midland and Odessa. The isolated population in Colorado was thought to be intermediate between *S. c. tergeminus* and *S. c. edwardsii* by Maslin (1965), but based on a larger sample, Hobert (1997) suggested that this population more closely resembles *S. c. edwardsii.* McCoy and Minckley (1969) described two specimens from Cuatro Ciénegas, Mexico, as having a combination of charateristics of *S. c. tergeminus* and *S. c. edwardsii.*

Baird and Girard (1853:15) listed three individuals as types of *S. c. edwardsii;* these were from "Tamaulipas," "S. Bank of Rio Grande," and "Sonora" collected by Dr. Edwards, General Churchill, and Colonel Graham, respectively. *Sistrurus c. edwardsii* was described in 1853, but specimens in the Smithsonian Institution were not given catalog numbers until 1856. Stejneger (1895:417, footnote) stated that the specimens used in the original description for the taxon were numbered USNM 506–508, and that USNM 507 from Tamaulipas served as the type, and 506 and 508 were paratypes. USNM 506 represented the specimen from Sonora, USNM 507 was from Tamaulipas, and USNM 508 was listed by Stejneger as being from "Texas" rather than the "S. Bank of the Rio Grande" but bore data indicating that it was collected by General Churchill. Gloyd (1955) pointed out that the first published account referring to any of these catalog numbers was that of Baird (1859a:15), which mentions only USNM 506 from Sonora (but credits J. H. Clark as the collector); subsequently, Cope (1900:1146) reported this specimen and listed Colonel Graham as the collector, in agreement with the original description (Baird and Girard, 1853:15). In his examination of material from the Smithsonian Institution, Gloyd (1940:36) was convinced that another specimen, not listed by Stejneger (1895), probably represented the type of *S. c. edwardsii,* namely, USNM 509 from "Mexico" collected by Dr. Edwards. Gloyd (1955:85–86) subsequently reversed himself, stating that USNM 507 from Tamaulipas collected by Dr. Edwards was probably the type. Gloyd had not examined USNM 507 because it was exchanged with the Museo Civico di Milano sometime between 1858 and 1863. This specimen is the one illustrated by Jan and Sordelli (1874:pl. 3, figs. 4 and 6). To further muddle the issue, Yarrow (1883:78) designated 509 as a lectotype (perhaps unaware that USNM 507 was still extant at that time but on another continent); Cochran (1961:168) listed USNM 506 and 509 as cotypes (excluding USNM 508, which may have been exchanged at the same time that USNM 507 was, but its present whereabouts are unknown); and McDiarmid et al. (1999) said there were three or four syntypes, including some combination of USNM 506–509. It seems clear that USNM 507 (cataloged into the Milan Museum) would stand as the holotype of *S. c. edwardsii* had it not been destroyed during World War II (Scortecci, *in* Gloyd, 1955:86). At present, we recognize USNM 506 from Sonora as the neotype. It should be noted that Gloyd (1940:41) assumed that USNM 506 was from Sonora, Sutton County, Texas, based on Cope's (1900:1146) assertion that the specimen was from "Sonora, Texas." However, as he later pointed out (Gloyd, 1955:86), the original tag for the specimen bears only the information "Sonora 145: 26: 23 81/2: 1 1/8," and no specific locality should be inferred. Although the record for Sonora probably refers to the Mexican state, the actual provenance of the specimen may now lie within the borders of the United States. The specimen was collected in 1851, before the Gadsden Purchase, when much of southern Arizona and New Mexico was part of Sonora, Mexico (Stejneger, 1940).

Sistrurus miliarius (Linnaeus, 1766)
(Figs. 221–223, Map 113, Pls. 1018–1023)

Crotalus miliarius Linnaeus, 1766, *Syst. Nat.*, 12th ed., 1:532 pp.[372]. Type(s): deposition unknown, presumed lost. Type-locality: "Carolina." Schmidt (1953c) proposed the type-locality be restricted to "Charleston, South Carolina."

Crotalus miliaris—Palisot de Beauvois, 1799, *Trans. Am. Philos. Soc.* 4:362–381[367]. [Unjustified emendation.]

Crotalophorus miliaris—Gray, 1825, *Ann. Philos.* (2)10:193–217[205]. [Unjustified emendation.]

Caudisona miliaria—Fitzinger, 1826b, *Neue Classif. Rept.*, 66 pp.[63].

Crotalophorus miliarius—Holbrook, 1842, *N. Am. Herpetol.*, 2d ed., 3:128 pp.[25, pl. 4].

Crotalus (Crotalophorus) miliarius—Jan, 1863a, *Elenco Sist. Ofidi*, 143 pp.[124].

Sistrurus miliarius—Garman, 1884a [dated 1883], *Mem. Mus. Comp. Zool.* 8:1–185[177].

Sistrurus miliarius—Boulenger, 1896b, *Cat. Snakes British Mus.* 3:727 pp.[569–570].

Sistrurus miliarius miliarius—Gloyd, 1935d, *Occas. Pap. Mus. Zool. Univ. Michigan* 322:1–7[2].

Sistrurus miliarius barbouri Gloyd, 1935d, *Occas. Pap. Mus. Zool. Univ. Michigan* 322:1–7[2]. Holotype: MCZ R12512. Type-locality: "Royal Palm Hammock, 12 miles west of Homestead, Dade County, Florida" [USA].

Sistrurus miliarius streckeri Gloyd, 1935d, *Occas. Pap. Mus. Zool. Univ. Michigan* 322:1–7[4]. Holotype: UMMZ 76751. Type-locality: "near Imboden, Lawrence County, Arkansas," [USA].

But before long my inexperience and reckless pride did me in. It happened one afternoon when I was cleaning a cage containing several pygmy rattlesnakes, my star attractions. . . .

In a moment of carelessness I moved my left hand too close to one of the coiled rattlers. Like a squirrel sprung from a crossbow, it uncoiled and struck the tip of my index finger. The two fang punctures felt like a bee sting. I knew I was in trouble.

—Wilson, 1994:78, describing a *S. miliarius* bite that he suffered as a teenager

LOCAL NAMES Bastard rattlesnake, dwarf rattlesnake, ground rattler, hog-nosed rattler, alba, ihaanikosi (Alabama tribe), hacolaycí, hacolaycosí (Koasanti), oak-leaf rattler, pigmy ground rattlesnake, southern pigmy rattlesnake, spotted rattlesnake (other names are contained in Wright and Wright, 1957, and Tipton, 2004).

ENGLISH NAME Pygmy rattlesnake.

ETYMOLOGY The specific epithet is taken from the Latin *miliarius*, meaning "warlike," probably in reference to this snake's willingness and ability to defend itself.

DISTRIBUTION Southeastern and south-central United States. This species ranges from the Dismal Swamp area of North Carolina southward through peninsular Florida and westward through the Gulf States to eastern Oklahoma and Texas (Map 113). It occurs as far north as southwestern Kentucky between the Tennessee and Cumberland Rivers at least as far north as the Trigg-Lyon County line and in southern Missouri in the upper White River drainage south of the Ozark Plateau. In Texas, *S. miliarius* ranges as far west as Wise and Montague Counties and as far south as Victoria and Refugio Counties near the Gulf of Mexico (Strecker, 1908a), where it apparently does not range south of the Nueces River (Gloyd, 1944). Cook (1943) reported this species from Deer Island in the Gulf of Mexico off the Mississippi coast, and Blaney (1971) found it on Saint Vincent Island in the Apalachicola area of Florida. Coues and Yarrow (1878b) reported *S. miliarius* on Bogue and Shackleford Banks off the coast of North Carolina, but more recent field investigations have not found it on these islands (Engels, 1952; Palmer, 1971; Palmer and Braswell, 1995). This species ranges from sea level to slightly above 500 m (Wright and Wright, 1957).

Distribution maps or other information on this snake throughout its range can be found in Conant and Collins, 1998;

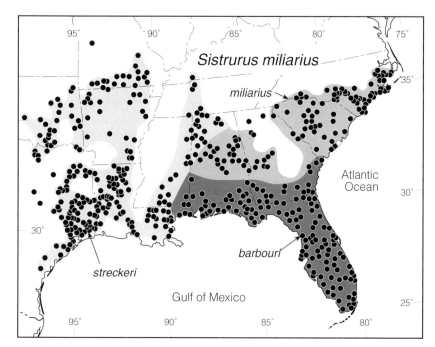

Map 113. Distribution of *Sistrurus miliarius* in the United States. See text for distribution records that represent relictual populations. The westernmost record for this species is central Texas (USNM 494), with the locality given as headwaters of the Colorado River, "at about one hundred and first meridian" (Stejneger, 1895:420), which is west of the area indicated on the map. Unfilled symbol represents the restricted type-locality, Charleston, South Carolina, as proposed by Schmidt (1953c).

Cope, 1860b, 1900; Garman, 1884b; Gloyd, 1935d, 1940; Klauber, 1971, 1972; Palmer, 1978; Stejneger, 1895; and Wright and Wright, 1957; This species has been reported from Alabama (Mount, 1975), Arkansas (Baird, 1859a; Blihovde and Irwin, 2001; Hurter and Strecker, 1909; Strecker, 1924; Trauth, 1987, 1988), Florida (Allen and Neill, 1950; Ashton and Ashton, 1981; Boulenger, 1896b; Boundy, 1994a; Catlin, 1950; Christman et al., 2000; Cope, 1860a; Curran, 1935; Loennberg, 1894; Neill, 1952; Tennant, 1997; Van Hyning, 1933; Wilson and Porras, 1983), Georgia (Gibbons and West, 2000; Herman, 1982; Herman and Baker, 1982; Neill, 1949; Wainberg et al., 2000), Kentucky (Barbour, 1971; Snyder et al., 1967), Louisiana (Boulenger, 1896b; Dundee and Rossman, 1989; Fitch, 1949a; Gowanloch and Brown, 1943; Liner, 1997), Mississippi (Ferguson, 1961), Missouri (Anderson, 1965; Berger, 1974; Johnson, 1987; Paukstis, 1977), North Carolina (Palmer and Braswell, 1995), Oklahoma (Ball, 1975; Webb, 1970), South Carolina (Cope, 1860a; Gibbons and West, 2000; Hoy et al., 1953; Jopson, 1940; Obrecht, 1946), Tennessee (Gentry, 1955, 1956; Jacob, 1981), Texas (Boulenger, 1896b; Boundy, 1994a; A. Brown, 1903a; B. Brown, 1950; Crimmins, 1927a; Garman, 1892c; Guidry, 1953; McCord and Dorcas, 1989; Nelson, 1988; Olson, 1967; Parks and Cory, 1936; Price, 1998; Rakowitz et al., 1983; Raun, 1965; Stecker, 1926a, 1926b, 1926c, 1935a; Tabor, 1985; Werler, 1964; Werler and Dixon, 2000), and generally (Conant and Bridges, 1939; Garman, 1884a).

The westernmost record is in central Texas (USNM 494), with the locality given as headwaters of the Colorado River "at about the one hundred and first meridian" (Stejneger, 1895:420), a locality in Mitchell County (Gloyd, 1940) far removed from the nearest record in east Texas. No other specimens have been taken in this area, suggesting that this specimen represented an isolated population, now probably extirpated, or perhaps that it bore erroneous locality data. Two other isolated western populations have been mentioned by various authors, one in Dallas County (Brown, 1950:223; Curtis, 1949b:12; Gloyd, 1940:73) and the other in McLennan County (Brown, 1950:222; Gloyd, 1940:73; Strecker, 1908b:78, 1915:42), but no recent specimens have been forthcoming, and populations of *S. miliarius* probably no longer exist in these counties. We last saw this species in Dallas County in 1980 (Pl. 1022).

HABITAT Swampy or marshy areas, floodplains, and dry wooded uplands. Usually found near water, open areas of brush and rock, cedar glades, the interface between forests and meadows, pine forest, loblolly/longleaf pine forest, pine flatwoods, palmetto lowlands, mixed hardwood forest, scrub, river-bottom hardwoods, edges of bayous, driftwood along rivers, dense thickets, drier sections of swamps, and wet sawgrass prairie. In Missouri, the preferred habitat is "south-facing, rocky and partially wooded hillsides" (Johnson, 1987), and Jacob (1981) reported that road-killed individuals in Tennessee were usually found near riparian habitats. Carr (1940) reported that when "the Everglades are flooded pigmy rattlers may often be seen in small trees, and lying coiled on cabbage palm leaves eight or ten feet high." In Florida, this species occupies pine flatland, prairies, and wet prairies (Dalrymple, 1988; Dodd and Charest, 1988).

DESCRIPTION This is a small rattlesnake; adults usually attain a TL of 40–60 cm. Klauber (1972) reported a maximum TL of 78.8 cm, a specimen of *S. m. barbouri* measuring 80.3 cm in TL was reported by Snellings and Collins (1997; correcting the earlier report of Snellings and Collins, 1996), but it had been maintained under captive conditions for more than 12 years. The largest specimen of *S. m. barbouri* examined by Gloyd (1940) was a female from St. Petersburg, Pinellas County, Florida, that

was 63.8 cm in TL. Males in some populations may be larger than females (Shine, 1978), but Bishop et al. (1996) found no sexual dimorphism in size, growth rate, or color pattern in a population from Volusia County, Florida. Clark (1963) suggested that Louisiana specimens exhibit sexual dimorphism in color pattern, but his observations were based solely on a litter of five neonates, and no other author has mentioned gender-related differences of color pattern. The body is of medium build, the head is broad and distinct, and the tail is attenuate. *Sistrurus miliarius* has a comparatively tiny rattle compared with most other rattlesnakes, including *S. catenatus*, and the sound it produces is comparatively quieter and higher pitched.

The ground color is usually various shades of gray, pale grayish brown, brownish gray, to almost blackish, sometimes suffused with pink. The ground color is usually stippled or flecked with dark brown or gray, although this may be slight and evident only under magnification. A series of 22–45 reddish brown, dark brown, to almost black middorsal spots or blotches extends the length of the body to the tail, and there are 7–14 spots or crossbands on the tail. These spots usually are narrowly edged with white and may be oval or quadrangular, or may form short, irregular transverse bars. Often a reddish brown to pale orange middorsal stripe extends from the posterior of the parietals or the nape region to the base of the tail in the intervening space (usually 1.5–2.5 scales long) between the dorsal blotches; however, it is not unusual for individuals to lack this middorsal stripe. The interspace between dorsal blotches varies from slightly more than two-thirds of to longer than the length of the dorsal blotches. One or 2 series of dark spots are present on each side of the body, and an additional series of small dark spots is usually present on the lateral portion of the ventrals that extends onto several of the lower dorsal scale rows; elements of this series alternate with a slightly more dorsally situated ventrolateral series of blotches. The spots of the lateral series are usually about 1–2 scales long, are located mostly on scale rows 2–5 (blotches sometimes reduced in size, especially in western populations), and are separated from the dorsal series by about 2 scales. The dorsolateral series of usually indistinct, dark grayish olive spots is infrequently evident; if present, this series is usually more distinct on the posterior of the body, is located on dorsal scale rows 6–9, and alternates with the dorsal and lateral series of spots. The elements of the ventrolateral series of spots are located at a level between the lateral series, are usually about the same size as or slightly smaller than the lateral spots, and are located on dorsal scale rows 1–2 and the lateral edges of the ventrals. A pair of curved, lyre-shaped markings extends from the posterior part of the supraoculars across the lateral portion of the parietals and onto the nape of the neck. A dark bar usually extends across the top of the head at about the level of the prefrontals. A dark brown postocular stripe extends to the angle of the jaw or just past and is bordered below by white or cream that extends from just below the eye to the ultimate supralabial and rictus. Usually there is another broad, dark spot or stripe extending diagonally from just below the eye across the supralabials and onto the infralabials. The venter of the head is cream, lightly to heavily mottled or spotted with dark brown. The venter of the body is whitish, cream, pale gray, or pale brown with dark brown to blackish spots, blotches, or mottling. In some individuals the venter is predominantly pale; in some others it is mostly dark. Juveniles' patterns are similar to those of adults but may be more vividly marked or paler overall, and the tail tip is yellow.

Palmer and Whitehead (1961) were the first to note the reddish ground colorations and bright patterns of *S. miliarius* from Hyde County, North Carolina. These snakes also reach a relatively large size, sometimes exceeding 55.0 cm in TL. The population occurring in the southern Albemarle-Pamlico Peninsula of North Carolina (just south of Hyde County) is also erythristic, having a reddish or pinkish dorsal ground color and varying in several other ways from adjacent populations to the south and west (Palmer, 1971). The venter is white on the anterior part of the body, grading to reddish or pinkish posteriorly. There are conspicuous dark markings along the edges of the scutes and diffuse dark markings over the rest of the venter. The dark postocular stripe is red-brown. Juveniles from this erythristic population are paler and brighter than adults, with a pinkish or orange-brown ground color that becomes darker, often brick red, as the snake matures (Palmer, 1971). Snakes from Carteret and Craven Counties in North Carolina (slightly south of the Albemarle-Pamlico Peninsula) exhibit color pattern characteristics intermediate between the erythristic population to the north and the gray snakes to the south.

The rostral is higher than wide, there are 9 large head plates on top of the head (Fig. 221), 8–13 (usually 10 or 11) supralabials, 9–14 (usually 11) infralabials, 21–25 dorsal scale rows at midbody (usually 23 except in western populations, which have 21), 122–144 ventrals in males and 123–148 in females, and 28–39 subcaudals in males and 25–35 in females.

SIMILAR SPECIES The presence of 9 large head plates and a rattle at the end of the tail distinguishes *S. miliarius* from all other snakes, including rattlesnakes, with which it coexists except *S. catenatus*, which may be sympatric (but occurring in different habitats) in small portions of Texas and Oklahoma. *Sistrurus catenatus* has an upper preocular that extends forward to contact the postnasal, the anterior subocular usually contacts supralabials 4 and 5, the interspace that separates the dorsal blotches is less than half the length of the blotches, and there is never a reddish middorsal stripe on the body. Hognosed snakes (*Heterodon nasicus*, Pl. 1128; *H. platirhinos*, Pls. 1129–1130; and *H. simus*, Pl. 1131) are variable and sometimes have a color pattern that resembles that of *S. miliarius*, but they are easily distinguished by their sharp, upturned rostral; divided subcaudals; round pupil; and lack of a rattle. The kingsnake (*Lampropeltis calligaster*, Pl. 1142) and short-tailed snake (*Stilosoma extenuatum*) have smooth dorsal scales, divided subcaudals, round pupils, and tapering tails that do not end in a rattle.

REMARKS The dorsal spots on the Carolina pygmy rattlesnake, *S. m. miliarius* (Pls. 1018 and 1019), may be rounded or somewhat quadrangular, the venter is cream and lightly to moderately flecked with dark brown or gray, and there usually are 23 dorsal scale rows at midbody. The dusky pygmy rattlesnake, *Sistrurus m. barbouri* (Pls. 1020 and 1021) has dorsal spots that tend to be rounded, usually has a whitish venter that is heavily mottled or flecked with dark brown or black, and usually has 23 dorsal scale rows at midbody. The dorsal spots on the western pygmy rattlesnake, *S. m. streckeri* (Pls. 1022 and 1023), are often reduced to irregular dark crossbands, the venter is whitish and is moderately to heavily mottled with dark brown, and there usually are 21 dorsal scale rows at midbody.

Venomous Snake Mimicry

Edmund D. Brodie III and Edmund D. Brodie Jr.

If it were true, as Thayer asserts, that Crows and Coral Snakes and Heliconiid butterflies are concealingly coloured, then one surely might as well suggest that snails are swift and earthworms heavily armoured.

—Cott 1940:173

Mimicry is one of the most exciting and deeply developed examples of the power of natural selection to affect both major phenotypic shifts and fine-tuned adaptations. The striking color patterns of dangerous or distasteful aposematic prey and the degree to which they are matched by a variety of less well defended taxa capture the imagination of seasoned naturalists and casual observers alike. Probably not a single student makes it through a high school or undergraduate biology class without learning the (somewhat inaccurate) story of monarch butterflies and their viceroy mimics (Brower, 1958a, 1958b; Brower et al., 1972; Brower and Moffitt, 1974; Ritland, 1991; Ritland and Brower, 1991).

But the aesthetic appeal of mimicry is secondary to its power as a tool to understand evolutionary processes and patterns. Mimicry involves such a variety of phenomena that it could be used as an exemplar for virtually every major concept in an evolutionary biology course. Elements of basic population genetics are critical to understanding how color patterns and warning signals evolve (Charlesworth and Charlesworth, 1975, 1976a, 1976b; Sheppard, 1959; Sheppard et al., 1985; Turner, 1967). Frequency dependence rules the basic selection scenario that drives most mimicry systems (Gavrilets and Hastings, 1998; Pfennig et al., 2001; Sasaki et al., 2001). Coevolutionary dynamics, from arms races to geographic mosaics, are fundamental to the evolution of mimetic signals (Mallet and Gilbert, 1995; Thompson, 1994, 1997, 1999a). Phenomena ranging from sensory drive (Yachi and Higashi, 1998) to speciation (Mallet, 1993; Mallet and Barton, 1989; Mallet et al., 1998) to shifting balance (Mallet and Joron, 1999; Mallet and Singer, 1987) all find application in studies of mimicry. The list goes on from here. Moreover, both naturalists and theoreticians have contributed considerably to our understanding of mimicry in exactly the way that science ideally works. Mimicry theory has developed directly from the observations of fieldworkers, beginning with the original formulation of the concept by Henry Bates (1862), the legendary naturalist. Theory in turn has identified new hypotheses that have subsequently been tested by field and laboratory empiricists, whose observations typically open the door for further theoretical development.

Paradoxically for a topic so central to evolutionary biology, this cycle of observation-theory-empiricism has been dominated by work on one group of organisms, Lepidoptera (Joron and Mallet, 1998; Mallet and Singer, 1987; Turner, 1977, 1985). In fact, the vast majority of work on mimicry in natural systems and the related development of theory focuses on mimicry involving a single genus, the *Heliconius* butterflies of Central and South America (Jiggins and McMillan, 1997; Joron et al. 1999; Kapan, 2001; Mallet, 1989, 1993; Mallet and Gilbert, 1995; Sheppard et al., 1985). It is thus ironic that one of the first cases of mimicry described involves South American coralsnakes and similarly colored colubrids (Wallace, 1867, 1870). Despite more than a century of research into the problem of coralsnake mimicry by herpetologists, the topic has not risen to a high enough profile to earn even a mention in recent general reviews of mimicry (Joron and Mallet, 1998; Malcolm, 1990). Although a number of high-quality experimental and comparative treatments of snake mimicry (coralsnakes and others, see below) exist, they seem to be pigeonholed into a special-case category that, while appealing, does not broadly inform our understanding of the more general process of mimicry. Whether or not this opinion is fair is immaterial, the onus is on those who study mimicry involving snakes to extend our work to test and embrace general theory if we wish to move studies of snakes from the cloistered realm of preaching to the choir onto the main stage. Both the success of mimicry theory as a viable explanation of the evolution of groups outside of Lepidoptera and our understanding of the evolution of snake diversity depend on this shift.

The goal of this chapter is to provide a conceptual overview of the general process and theoretical problems of mimicry to help guide future research on the topic in snakes. By explicitly reviewing the process, we hope to identify the kinds of data that are required to test mimicry theory as well as dispel some misconceptions that have mired research on some taxa. In discussing the current conceptual developments in general mimicry theory we hope to point research toward some problems of contemporary interest to the broader community of mimicry researchers. We further examine how mimicry involving snakes may differ from that involving other taxa and, conversely, how these exceptions to the rule might be used to inform the general process. Although we discuss a variety of examples, our goal is not to review the breadth of purported cases of snake mimicry—excellent compendia of this sort are already available (see Campbell and Lamar, 1989; Greene and McDiarmid, 2004). Our review concentrates on protective mimicry, but we also attempt to show how other categories of mimicry apply to snakes.

THE MIMICRY PROCESS

Mimicry in its broadest application is normally considered as a process involving at least three players: two transmit signals while a third receives the signals. Wickler (1968) referred to this as a "tripartite" mimicry system and dubbed the participants signaler 1, signaler 2, and receiver, but these also are often referred to as model, mimic, and operator or dupe (Fig. 225; Pasteur, 1982; Vane-Wright, 1976). In this scenario, two individuals emit signals—be they visual, chemical, auditory, or some other modality—and the third individual uses the signal as the basis for some sort of behavioral action. What separates mimicry from other signal-receiver interactions is the fact that one of the signals the receiver detects is counterfeit and conveys false information. For example, cryptic coloration is generally not considered a form of mimicry because resemblance to the background causes a predator to fail to detect a prey item (Pasteur, 1982). Conversely, crypsis of the form exemplified by

A
Fixed Elements of Mimicry

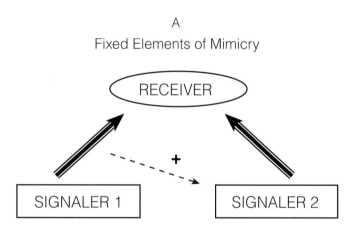

B
Variable Elements of Mimicry

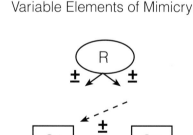

Fig. 225. The tripartite mimicry system as depicted by Vane-Wright (1976). (A) The fixed elements of all mimicry systems include two signalers that produce signals that are indistinguishable to the receiver. The Receiver (R) associates some consequence with the signal produced by Signaler 1 (S1), and Signaler 2 (S2) gains some advantage through the interaction of R and S1. (B) The variable elements of mimicry systems include the biological roles that R plays in relation to each signaler. The roles need not be the same for each signaler and may be positive or negative. The interaction between R and S2, the mimic, can have variable consequences for the model, S1.

walking sticks, vinesnakes, and dead-leaf-mimic katydids is sometimes referred to as special resemblance mimicry (Cott, 1940). Protection in this case occurs because a predator detects the organism but confuses it with an inedible object, thus involving reception of a signal and misinterpretation of the information.

This broad but simple definition of mimicry can cover an astonishing variety of phenomena. Vane-Wright (1976) used this framework to identify 40 unique kinds of mimetic interaction. Each of the three participants in a tripartite mimicry system can have a positive or negative effect on the fitness of each of the other two participants. Depending on the combinations, this leads to eight possible classes of interaction divided into two major groups (Fig. 226). Synergic systems involve positive or neutral influences of the mimic on the model (e.g., anglerfish or snapping turtles with wormlike lures to entice prey), whereas antergic systems involve negative consequences to the model (e.g., brood parasitism by cuckoos, which deposit mimetic eggs in host nests resulting in reduced survivorship of the host species' young). The parties in a tripartite mimicry system may comprise one, two, or three species. The various combinations thereof define a second axis with five possible categories. The disjunct situation wherein all three players are different species is the one most commonly considered. However, partially or completely conjunct situations arise that involve signalers and receivers of the same species. An example is sexual mimicry in which males mimic signals of females of the same species and divert the mating attentions of conspecific males, as observed in some gartersnakes (Mason and Crews, 1985, 1986). Although this system of classification may seem unnecessarily broad (it is true that Vane-Wright [1976] identified only 12 of the possible 40 categories with real world examples), it does highlight some of the essential generalities about mimicry, as well as the distinctions among categories.

CATEGORIES OF MIMICRY INVOLVING SNAKES

The most commonly considered form of mimicry involves situations in which one organism gains protection as a result of its resemblance to a second, undesirable organism. The usual use of the term *mimicry* often implicitly describes this sort of interaction, which is more precisely known as "protective" (or "defensive") mimicry (Pasteur, 1982; Vane-Wright, 1976; Wickler, 1968). The defining element shared by various forms of protective mimicry is that by resembling another organism, the signaler reduces the probability of the receiver having a negative fitness consequence on the signaler. Typically, this is considered in the context of a potential predator that does not attack the mimic because it interprets the mimic's signal as that of the model's. Most cases of mimicry in snakes, either demonstrated or purported, involve protective mimicry. The classic example, of course, is the taxonomically and geographically widespread similarity to elapid coralsnake color patterns (Greene and McDiarmid, 1981, 2004; Pough 1988a, 1988b; Wallace, 1867). Other protective mimicry complexes have been suggested, usually involving venomous snakes, including various vipers and Old World elapids (Greene and McDiarmid, 1981, 2004; Pough 1988a, 1988b).

Protective mimicry has traditionally been divided into at least two groups, Batesian and Müllerian (Pasteur, 1982; Wickler, 1968). The common portrayal of the difference between Batesian and Müllerian mimicry is that it relies on the palat-

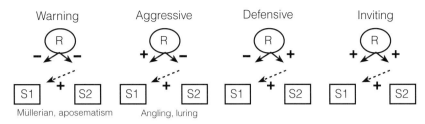

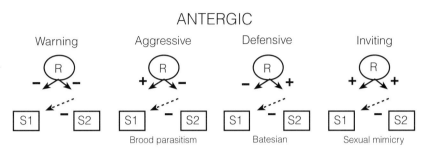

Fig. 226. The eight possible forms of mimetic interactions as depicted by Vane-Wright (1976). Interactions can be synergic if the presence of the mimic (S2) has positive consequences for the model, or antergic if the presence of the mimic (S2) has negative consequences for the model. Within each of these categories there are four possible combinations of biological roles (positive or neutral versus negative) for the Receiver (R). Some of the more common forms of mimicry that correspond to each category are listed below each diagram. These categories depend in part on the species composition of R, S1, and S2.

ability (or more generally, the profitability) of the mimic. If the mimic is palatable, it is considered Batesian, whereas mimics that have their own noxious qualities are typically considered Müllerian mimics. In fact, the real distinction between Batesian and Müllerian mimics has to do with the selective consequences of the mimic for the model (thus Vane-Wright's [1976] classification as synergic and antergic defensive mimicry, respectively). This relationship depends on a number of factors that influence the selective dynamic of mimicry, which we explore below. In short, any encounter between a predator and a palatable (Batesian) mimic can have negative consequences for a similarly signaling model, whereas an encounter with a noxious (Müllerian) mimic can reinforce avoidance and thereby have positive fitness consequences for the model (Mallet and Joron, 1999; Speed and Turner, 1999; Vane-Wright, 1976). Palatability of the mimic correlates roughly with the fitness consequence for the model, which has led to this misrepresentation in the literature. However, the dynamics of selection in mimicry systems depend on many factors, including congenital avoidance, the learning capability and memory of predators, densities and frequencies of models and mimics, and the degree of negative stimulus associated with the signal in question. These influences can create some unexpected fitness interactions between models and mimics and have led recently to a reevaluation of the dichotomous Batesian versus Müllerian classification (Mallet, 2001; Speed and Turner, 1999; see below).

Instead of deterring, mimicry can also be used to attract a receiver. Such is the case in aggressive mimicry (Pasteur, 1982; Vane-Wright, 1976; Wickler, 1968). The comic-book version of aggressive mimicry involves an anglerfish or snapping turtle dangling a "worm" in front of or inside of its mouth, luring a fish within its grasp, and snapping shut on the unsuspecting victim. Many snakes exhibit similar behavior in the form of caudal luring, in which the tip of the tail is twisted about to attract potential prey (Carpenter et al., 1978; Greene and Campbell, 1972; Murphy et al., 1978; Neill, 1960b). Caudal luring in particular, and many forms of aggressive mimicry in general, are probably forms of diffuse mimicry, in which the model imitated is a generalized stimulus pattern (e.g., a small, writhing invertebrate) rather than a single species or object

(Pough 1988a, 1988b; Wickler, 1968). This scenario clearly has a negative effect on the receiver but is advantageous to the mimic in that it gains a meal. The model potentially also benefits through the direct removal of potential predators from the immediate environment (Vane-Wright, 1976).

Mimicry occasionally involves models and mimics of the same species—what Wickler (1968) lumped together as intraspecific mimicry and Vane-Wright (1976) called conjunct mimicry. The most obvious example of this case in snakes is the sexual mimicry exhibited by some gartersnakes mentioned above. On emergence from hibernacula, some *Thamnophis sirtalis* males apparently give off chemical signals that make them attractive to other males, which vigorously court the "she-male" snakes (Mason and Crews, 1985, 1986; Shine et al., 2000b). Repeated attempts to understand the adaptive value of this transgender signal misrepresention have failed to explain why such mimicry occurs. Presumably, she-male snakes divert the attention of other males (the receivers) from receptive females, but this phenomenon has not been observed (Shine, 1977; Shine et al., 2000a, 2000b, 2000c). One suggested benefit to the she-males involves an indirect effect of the courtship behavior of misguided males. The writhing balls of males generate enough heat to raise the body temperature of she-males 3 °C higher than that of an average male (Shine et al., 2001). Being nestled among hot balls of males may thus provide a metabolic advantage over nonmimetic males, but no evidence of a concomitant fitness benefit has been found. Similar phenomena in other taxa include mouth-brooding cichlids with false egg spots on the anal fin that stimulate females to pick up sperm released by the male (Knapp and Sargent, 1989; Strange, 2001; Wickler, 1968). How widespread such sexual mimicry is among snakes remains to be seen.

The label "automimicry" has been applied to two different kinds of intraspecific phenomena. The first, which does not clearly apply to snakes, involves species that are polymorphic for defense abilities. In such cases, palatable or undefended individuals function as mimics of the defended individuals. The known cases (involving Lepidoptera; Brower et al., 1970, 1972) involve defenses derived from host plants, and the polymorphism occurs because of differences in larval host plant use. The second version of automimicry involves mimicry of particular body parts. Many snake species, from ericine boas to coralsnakes (e.g., *Leptomicrurus* [Pl. 15], *Micrurus* sp. [Pls. 199, 202, 219, 222, 223, 241, 259], and *Micruroides* [Pl. 25]), have defensive displays that involve coiling and moving the tail as though it were a head (Gans, 1987; Gehlbach, 1972; Greene, 1973a). Some species—*Charina bottae*, for example—even attempt to "strike" with the tail (Nussbaum and Hoyer, 1974). Such behavioral and morphological features are often referred to as deflection mechanisms because they deflect attack to a less vulnerable body region (Greene, 1988; Wickler, 1968). However, some authors use the label "automimicry," and the phenomenon does fit the general definition of mimicry set out above except that the model and mimic are a single individual.

Special resemblance mimicry (Cott, 1940) generally falls into one of the above categories but deserves mention because it sometimes is referred to as crypsis or camouflage. As mentioned above, the distinction between crypsis and mimicry is that the former operates by causing a detection failure, whereas mimicry involves a detected signal that is counterfeit (Vane-Wright, 1976; Wickler, 1968). Although this seems a clear line, it may be more difficult to determine what function a set of morphological and behavioral features has in practice. Special resemblance mimicry in snakes, for obvious morphological reasons, often involves vine or twig mimicry (Greene, 1988). Both Old and New World lineages of vinesnakes exist (e.g., *Leptophis* [Pls. 1171–1178], *Oxybelis* [Pls. 1204 and 1205], and *Xenoxybelis* [Pl. 1360] in the Americas, and *Ahaetulla* in Asia) that exhibit not only dramatically narrowed and elongated bodies, but also exceptionally slow movement and a behavioral tendency to "sway in the breeze" (Fleischman, 1985; Greene, 1988). In the absence of explicit data, one could argue that this form of mimicry is aggressive because it allows these species to move unrecognized toward prey, or that it is protective because potential predators do not recognize potential prey. Indeed, whether resemblance to a vine actually constitutes mimicry depends on whether receivers detect a snake and interpret it as a vine, or whether resemblance to a vine amid a tangle of vines causes the snake to go undetected. These are difficult details of perception to discern, and they may vary from receiver to receiver.

SENSORY MODALITIES EXPLOITED BY MIMICS

A number of authors, most notably Wickler (1968), use differences in sensory modality as a primary distinction among types of mimicry. The classification system outlined above does not focus on sensory modality, but it does emphasize three basic points about signals. First, models and mimics must utilize similar sensory modalities in their signals. Second, effective mimetic signals must be of a sensory type that is perceived by the receiver. This fact does not imply that the sensory modality of the signal must overlap with the most acute abilities of the receiver, but merely that the perceptive abilities of the receiver are sufficient to detect the signal. Finally, a given signaler may possess several kinds of signals, each of which is relevant in different contexts or to different receivers. For example, a color pattern that serves an aposematic function to diurnal predators with color vision may be ineffective toward nocturnal predators. At night, the prey species may employ olfactory or auditory signals to deliver the same sort of information. The vast majority of identified mimicry

systems involve visual cues—color patterns, shape, or elaborate structures (Wickler, 1968)—perhaps as a result of the sensory bias that humans have as primates with well-developed visual systems and relatively poor olfactory, chemosensory, and auditory abilities. The first mimetic complexes identified, including coralsnakes and their mimics by Wallace (1867), were noticed because of conspicuous and strikingly similar coloration. Since the late 1800s, the amount of research on color pattern mimicry has so outweighed efforts to understand other sensory modalities that it would be easy for someone new to the field to imagine that mimicry occurs only through resemblance of color patterns. The majority of purported mimicry complexes involving snakes operate through visual signals, including not only the famous coralsnake mimicry complexes of the Americas but also a variety of species and color patterns around the world that appear to mimic various vipers and elapids (reviewed by Greene and McDiarmid, 1981, 2004; Pough, 1988a, 1988b). Such mimicry often involves color patterns that are conspicuous to the human eye, such as the bright orange or pink head and tail offset by a dark blue body exhibited by both the elapid *Calliophis bivirgatta* and some harmless reedsnakes of the genus *Calamaria* (Greene and McDiarmid, 2004).

Behavioral displays, too, fall into the realm of visual signals. Throughout the world there are a variety of colubrid groups that adopt behavioral postures, including triangulation of the head, that are suggestive of local viper species. In Latin America, for example, *Xenodon rabdocephalus* (Pl. 1347) flattens its head and neck and triangulates in a posture that accentuates its already striking color pattern resemblance to *Bothrops asper* (Pls. 499–517). Juveniles of *Pseustes poecilonotus* characteristically triangulate the head and rear back in a strike posture when threatened, a behavior not typically observed in adults (Fig. 227), which do not share the heterogeneously blotched *Bothrops*-like pattern of juveniles (pers. observ.; see Rossman and Williams, 1966, for *P. sulphureus*). As evidenced by the number of botanists at La Selva Biological Station in Costa Rica who have reported *Bothrops* striking at them from shrubs in the understory only to have the culprit later identified as *P. poecilonotus*, such behavioral signals have the potential to result in misidentification by at least some receivers. Mimicry of the elevated-tail defensive displays of coralsnakes is also common among their mimics (Marques, 2000; Sazima and Abe, 1991; Yanosky and Chani, 1988), including *Atractus* (Pl. 1035), *Erythrolamprus* (Pl. 1106), *Lystrophis* (Pl. 1190), *Pliocercus*, and *Simophis* (Pl. 1296).

Many snake species utilize auditory signals, primarily as antipredator mechanisms. The rattles of rattlesnakes are the most obvious and best known, but other snake species produce similar sounds when threatened. In the New World, *Pituophis* and other lampropeltines vibrate their tails rapidly, and on some substrates this can generate a surprisingly rattlelike sound (Kardong, 1980a). Saw-scaled vipers in Africa rub their sides together in a continuously moving coil, generating a sustained hiss as specialized scales with protruding knobs flick past each other (Gans and Baic, 1974, 1977). *Dasypeltis*, a harmless colubrid from the same area, reportedly exhibits similar behavior and sound production, though by slightly different mechanical means (Gans and Baic, 1974). *Pituophis melanoleucus* in northwestern North America (the only snake reported to have a vocal cord; Young et al., 1995) is known locally as the "blow snake" for its tendency to emit extended, controlled exhalations that produce a sound interpretable, at least by humans, as a rat-

Fig. 227. The defensive display of *Pseustes poecilonotus* from La Selva, Costa Rica. (A) Juvenile *P. poecilonotus* have broken banded patterns similar to those of some viperids and exhibit head triangulation and the S-shaped strike posture characteristic of pitvipers. (B) Adults grow to more than 2 m in length and thus are larger than many pitvipers. Adults have a generally uniform olive dorsal coloration and yellowish venter, and do not typically exhibit head triangulation. Photographs by E. D. Brodie III.

tlesnake's rattle. *Pituophis* may be an example of a species that employs multiple sensory modes in mimicry, as some populations exhibit behavioral displays similar to rattlesnakes while geographic variations in color pattern closely parallel those of sympatric *Crotalus oreganus/viridis* (Kardong, 1980a; but see Sweet, 1985).

Olfactory or chemosensory signaling modes are widely believed to dominate intraspecific communication in snakes (Ford and Burghardt, 1993), but may be less important as signals to other taxa. This difference highlights the importance of understanding the sensory biases of the signal receiver as well as the signaler. We might expect most snakes to have complex and multidimensional chemical signaling abilities based on their own sensory abilities in this area; however, such signals may be less recognizable to taxa such as avian predators whose chemosensory abilities are less well developed. Similarly, our ability to detect chemosensory mimicry is hampered by our own perception biases. Accordingly, few examples of chemosensory mimicry have been suggested for any taxa, and those that do exist tend to be intraspecific mimicry. One of the best examples is the previously discussed sexual mimicry in *Thamnophis sirtalis*, wherein some males apparently exude a femalelike odor on emergence from hibernacula (Mason and Crews, 1985, 1986).

THE SELECTIVE SCENARIO OF MIMICRY

The power of mimicry as an exemplar of evolution rests on the complicated scenario through which selection in mimicry systems acts. The potential for feedback and indirect effects in a system with three players is enormous, and the complexity of dynamics intimidating. Most "studies" of mimicry in snakes and other taxa do little more than describe similar signals in a pair of (usually sympatric) taxa (reviewed by Greene and McDiarmid, 1981, 2004; Pough, 1988a, 1988b). While necessary, this information is certainly less than sufficient to demonstrate mimicry and provides little in terms of the kinds of data that are useful in further illuminating the general process. A brief review of how selection in mimicry systems operates, with special attention to common misconceptions, will be helpful in guiding future studies of snake mimicry toward more rigorous demonstration of the phenomenon and greater advancement of the theory.

Predator Experience

Selection on models and mimics is generated by the receiver. For a particular species to function as a receiver driving a mimicry system, a single individual must experience both model and mimic. Contrary to common depictions, this does not mean that model and mimic must exist syntopically or even sympatrically (Hecht and Marien, 1956; Poulton, 1908), nor does it mean that model and mimic must overlap phenologically (Brodie, 1981; Waldbauer, 1971, 1988b). What must be true is that individual receivers overlap the combined temporal and spatial distributions of models and mimics. This realization is particularly important when considering systems involving migratory birds, which potentially could learn a signal in one region and retain the response to that signal when they migrate (Hecht and Marien, 1956; Smith, 1980). This mechanism has been suggested as an explanation of the distribution of snakes with coralsnake-like patterns (e.g., *Lampropeltis* spp. in North America; Pfennig et al., 2001) north of the range of true coralsnakes (Smith, 1980). Avoidance of tricolor ringed patterns developed by Neotropical migrant birds during their time in Central and South America may protect similarly patterned snakes in areas inhabited by the migrants in other seasons, though the one empirical test of this hypothesis did not show avoidance in migratory passerines (Smith, 1980). Similarly, seasonal or diel differences in activity periods of potential models and mimics does not preclude mimicry if a receiver is active during both periods. This problem has been investigated in salamanders (Brodie, 1981) and insects (Waldbauer, 1988b), in which models emerge earlier than mimics, thus allowing receivers that are active during both periods to associate the signal with a negative stimulus before the mimic is present.

It is generally assumed that responses to signals are learned in most mimicry systems (Mallet, 2001; Mallet and Joron, 1999; Servedio, 2000; Speed and Turner, 1999; Vane-Wright, 1976; Wickler, 1968). Through experience with models, receivers learn to associate particular positive or negative phenomena with a stimulus. Conversely, experience with a mimic can undo the association between signal and consequence. Thus, selection in learned mimicry systems is a complex function of learning and forgetting by the receiver (Mallet, 2001; Mallet and Joron, 1999; Speed, 1993; Speed and Turner, 1999). The time frame over which a receiver learns and forgets, the number of trials required to acquire or lose a response, and the relationship between learning and the severity of the consequence all play critical roles in determining the dynamics of selection (Huheey, 1988; Mallet, 2001; Mallet and Joron, 1999; Speed, 1993; Speed and Turner, 1999). Recent models (Servedio, 2000) focusing on these factors show that aposematic signals are unlikely to evolve in systems with receivers that are gradual learners. Similarly, warning signals should evolve only if stimuli are extremely negative (i.e., toxic) and signals develop through incremental changes in phenotype. Many of the interesting evolutionary dynamics that accompany mimicry (see below), such as frequency or number dependence, build on this sort of learning process.

Somewhat at odds with the usual depiction of mimicry is the possibility that some receiver responses—in particular, avoidance of some prey types by predators—may be innate (Greene and Pyburn, 1973; Schuler, 1982; Schuler and Hesse, 1985; Smith, 1975, 1977). Because responses to signals are hard-wired in such instances, the usual problems of understanding the psychology of learning and forgetting are suspended. Innate avoidance also obviates one of the major problems associated with venomous snake mimicry. A classic argument against protective mimicry of venomous snakes is that predators cannot learn to avoid that which kills them, rendering it difficult to understand how species that resemble deadly venomous coralsnakes and other taxa could have evolved such patterns through mimicry (Greene and McDiarmid, 1981; Greene and Pyburn, 1973; Pough, 1988a, 1988b). If predators evolve congenital avoidance of coralsnake patterns, then similarly patterned snakes would be protected from those predators without any learning taking place. Using painted dowels and hand-reared, naive subjects, Susan Smith (Smith, 1975, 1977) demonstrated exactly such innate avoidance of coralsnake ringed patterns in two species of potential avian predators. It has also been suggested that a general innate avoidance of snake forms has evolved in many avian and primate predators, leading to very generalized mimicry of snakes by elongate invertebrates, including lepidopteran pupae (Pough, 1988b).

The taxonomic breadth of innate avoidance (or, more generally, responses) is poorly known, in terms of both the species that evolve innate responses and the species and signals that are avoided (Eisner, 1970; Guilford, 1990; Schuler, 1982; Schuler and Hesse, 1985). Considerable effort has been devoted to demonstrating innate avoidance of various banding patterns commonly found in aposematic insects, including Hymenoptera, and some evidence suggests early congenital avoidance of wasplike patterns (Schuler, 1982; Schuler and Hesse, 1985). Although the results are ambiguous, it is at least clear that innate avoidance is not widespread among predator-prey systems that involve distasteful prey. Ground squirrels, which are preyed on by rattlesnakes, appear to have evolved innate antisnake responses that are delivered indiscriminately at any snake species by naive squirrels, but only toward rattlesnakes by adults (Poran et al., 1987). The few examples of innate response appear to be restricted to potentially deadly encounters, such as with venomous snakes or perhaps with stinging insects. This is not surprising given that selection must be strong to drive the evolution of a genetically based avoidance; the cost of passing up a potential prey item must be less than the cost of attacking it. Such inequality is not likely obtained if the cost of attacking is merely an unpleasant experience (Brodie and Brodie, 1999). Reactions of predators to any signals associated with venomous snakes, including not only coralsnake ringed patterns but other pigmentation patterns, behavioral displays such as head triangulation and hood spreading, and auditory signals such as tail rattling and scale buzzing, are therefore good candidates for congenital responses.

One common misconception regarding the predators driving mimicry systems is that they must be a major source of mortality, or at least the primary predator. This opinion is analogous to arguing that phenotypes in general evolve only in response to the largest source of variance in fitness, which is clearly nonsensical. For example, the primary source of mortality in many populations of temperate snakes may be related to overwintering success (Parker and Plummer, 1987). This source of fitness variance would not be expected to covary with color pattern, antipredator mechanisms, mating behaviors, or any number of other traits typically considered to be adaptations. Moreover, many taxa employ a variety of antipredator mechanisms, each effective toward a different kind of predators. One of the clearest examples is the blood-squirting behavior of horned lizards (*Phrynosoma*) exhibited only in response to threats by canid predators, which are not likely to be the major predator on horned lizards (Middendorf and Sherbrooke, 1992; Sherbrooke and Middendorf, 2001). Selection can be defined as a covariance between a trait and fitness, so any source of mortality that covaries with a trait can be a relevant agent of selection (Brodie et al., 1995; Lande and Arnold, 1983). In terms of mimicry, this may be a receiver or class of receivers that, although not the major source of mortality, exerts selection on a particular dimension of the phenotype. Most species have a variety of predators that use different senses to forage; obviously, only visually foraging predators are likely to confuse visual signals and thus drive color pattern mimicry, regardless of whether or not most predation comes from predominantly olfactory foraging predators. Such may be the case in salamander mimicry systems, in which most mortality may result from night-foraging predators, semifossorial salamanders, or snakes, none of which are likely to be duped by color pattern resemblance. Nonetheless, predation by birds appears to be significant enough to drive color pattern resemblance.

Many venomous snakes have fairly specialized interactions with predators that have evolved either physiological or morphological resistance to venoms. Laughing falcons and caracaras, for example, well-known snake predators throughout Latin America, have highly scleratized tarsi that are presumably a defense against snakes in general and the fangs of venomous elapids in particular (Stiles and Skutch, 1989). A few ophiophagus snakes have evolved resistance to the venoms of prey species, including *Lampropeltis getula*, which preys on *Crotalus* spp. in North America (Philpot and Smith, 1950; Philpot et al., 1978). Some mammals are resistant to pitviper venoms, including potential predators, such as opossums (Perales et al., 1986), and prey, such as ground squirrels (Owings et al., 2001; Poran et al., 1987). Well-defended predators may not be deterred by protective resemblance to venomous snake species and therefore may not be important selective agents with regard to mimicry complexes. On the other hand, some resistant predators may have the opportunity to learn to avoid venomous snakes because the effects of envenomation would not necessarily be lethal, in which case they may be critical forces in the evolution of mimicry. The role of specialized predators in the evolution of snake mimicry is largely unexplored, and most avian and mammalian predators of snakes have not been tested for venom resistance.

Interactions between Models and Mimics

Models and mimics also generate indirect selection on one another, and the strength and form of this selection is a complex interaction of the relative deterrence and cost associated with interacting with models and mimics, as well as the relative frequency of encounter with each type of signaler. The receiver is still the agent through which all selection flows, however, so none of these factors is divorced from the aspects of predator psychology and perception mentioned above.

One basic result of many studies of mimicry in both natural and artificial systems is that models with stronger negative stimuli protect a greater range of mimics (Duncan and Sheppard, 1965). Models that are only distasteful typically support only a few types of mimics, and those are generally quite precise in their resemblance to the model (Edmunds, 2000; Greene and McDiarmid, 2004; Pough, 1988b). The reason for this relationship is that the cost to a predator of mistaking a model for an unprotected mimic is proportional to the deterrent, so predators are less likely to take a chance if the consequences are severe (i.e., Layla's paradox; Greene, 1988, 1997; Greene and McDiarmid, 2004).

Related to this pattern is the observation that less accurate mimics are not as well defended as perfect mimics (Brodie, 1993; Sexton, 1960). Although it is difficult to rank the resemblance of mimics to a model because signals like color patterns are rarely simple enough to reduce to a single dimension, experimental studies of mimicry have had some success in demonstrating that predation rates on mimics are inversely proportional to their resemblance to a noxious model (Brodie, 1993; Sexton, 1960). Again, the reason relates to the risk of misinterpreting a signal. Given a particular level of cost associated with a mistake, the likelihood of misinterpretation decreases as resemblance to the model decreases. Both factors interact, so that species with more severe deterrents, such as stinging insects and venomous snakes, are expected to have a large number of mimics, many of which may resemble the model imprecisely (Edmunds, 2000; Greene and McDiarmid, 2004). This pattern is observed in coralsnake mimicry systems, wherein a large number of banded or ringed species are apparently protected through resemblance to venomous snakes (Pough, 1988a, 1988b). In this situation, the cost of mistaking a signal is potentially so severe that even small amounts of risk are not supported. Nevertheless, limits exist to the range of resemblance protected through mimicry of even deadly models. Some species of snakes that apparently mimic venomous models only do so as juveniles. For example, juveniles of *Clelia* spp. are red with tricolor rings on the head and neck, but adults, which grow much larger than coralsnakes, have uniformly drab pigmentation patterns (Pls. 1056–1060). A similar ontogenetic color pattern shift is observed in Costa Rican *Lampropeltis triangulum* (Pls. 1155 and 1156), the adults of which grow to several times the girth and length of local coralsnakes.

The process of learned avoidance in protective mimicry generates a dynamic of selection between models and mimics that is mediated through the predator. Again, the predator's psychology, in terms of how quickly it learns or forgets and how it interprets signals, determines the details of the interaction. So, too, do the relative encounter rates or number of encounters of predators with each type of prey. In the simplest case, avoidance of a signal by a predator increases with each encounter with a model but decreases with each encounter with a mimic. Learned avoidance is reinforced when the predator is nega-

tively stimulated, and "forgetting," or positive reinforcement of the signal, occurs with each encounter with an undefended prey item (Huheey, 1988; Mallet, 2001; Mallet and Joron, 1999). These observations lead to the oversimplified prediction that mimics must be less common (or at least less commonly encountered) than models in most mimicry systems in which models are much better defended than mimics (Greene and McDiarmid, 1981; Pough, 1988a, 1988b). Of course, the nuances of real world systems may have little resemblance to this sort of black-and-white comparison. Different predators may respond differently to the same prey, generating the so-called palatability spectrum—that is, a prey that is distasteful to one predator may be more or less so to another (Brower and Moffitt, 1974; Turner, 1984). Similarly, motivation and nutritional condition of individual predators will also alter the rates at which learning and forgetting take place as well as the relative costs of misinterpreting signals. Learning may be a function of the frequency of encounters with models, the absolute number of models encountered, or the time from last encounter with a model (Huheey, 1988; Mallet, 2001; Mallet and Joron, 1999; Speed and Turner, 1999). Reinforcement may also occur through observation without attack if the receiver interprets a signal as a model, in which case viewing mimics can increase avoidance (Lindström et al., 1999; Speed and Turner, 1999). Each of these scenarios alters the dynamics of selection in subtle ways, and models incorporating each have been developed. Although it is generally true that more models than mimics can be supported, the actual ratio of models and mimics maintained in a mimicry system may be a complex interplay of predator perception, density of prey, relative encounter rates, and relative undesirability (Speed and Turner, 1999).

Models and mimics coevolve in the classic sense of exerting reciprocal selection on one another through their respective effects on receivers' responses to signals. The form of this coevolution is the primary distinction between Batesian and Müllerian mimicry (Speed and Turner, 1999; Vane-Wright, 1976). Batesian mimicry is usually considered to involve a well-defended model and an undefended mimic (Wickler, 1968). Selection via predator confusion causes mimics to converge in signal on the model. As encounters with mimics degrade the aversive response of predators to the signal, however, selection should drive the model's signal away from that of the mimic, generating a chase-away dynamic in the coevolution of mimic and model signals (Gavrilets and Hastings, 1998; Speed and Turner, 1999). Because frequency dependence also operates within the mimic species (the signal becomes less advantageous as the unprotected mimics are more commonly encountered), polymorphism might be expected to occur in Batesian mimics (Joron and Mallet, 1998; Mallet and Joron, 1999).

In many cases, mimics are not undefended, but rather have their own deterrents; coralsnake mimicry complexes are potentially one example. Müller described selection here in terms of the number of individuals that have to die to train predators to avoid a signal (Müller, 1879). If two or more undesirable local species share a common signal, then the proportion of each species that dies during predator training is reduced and both gain an advantage. Reciprocal selection in Müllerian mimicry is expected to drive both species toward a similar signal and to be basically stabilizing around the most common signal. Rare or deviant signal types should also be selected against within populations or species, leading to the prediction that Müllerian mimics should be monomorphic (Joron and Mallet, 1998; Mallet and Joron, 1999).

More recent treatments of mimicry have argued that Müllerian and Batesian mimicry more correctly represent extremes of a spectrum of selective dynamics (Speed, 1993; Speed and Turner, 1999). This argument is based on the observation that species are rarely equal in deterrent value (at least in the perception of some predators), even in apparent Müllerian systems (Brower and Moffitt, 1974; Speed and Turner, 1999; Turner, 1984). If one species is less palatable or more noxious than the other, then opportunities for the sort of parasitic interactions more characteristic of Batesian mimicry occur in groups of taxa that are, on the surface, all well defended. Müller (1879) assumed that predator learning was simply number dependent, which would always generate positive frequency-dependent selection that should lead to mutualistic interactions and a common signal (Mallet, 2001). If predator learning/forgetting is more complex and depends on the same fraction of each prey type consumed at any density, then less palatable species might suffer higher relative mortality than their more palatable partners. The result is a selective dynamic more like the chase-away, which is referred to as "quasi-Batesian" (Mallet, 2001; Mallet and Joron, 1999; Speed and Turner, 1999). These distinctions rely primarily on the psychology of predator learning, about which almost nothing is known in real systems. At present, computer simulations and a few artificial predator-prey systems account for our understanding of quasi-Batesian mimicry, and its existence as a phenomenon distinct from Müllerian mimicry is debatable (Mallet, 2001).

IS SNAKE MIMICRY DIFFERENT?

One fundamental question for snake biologists is whether mimicry involving snakes operates under a different scenario than the general one described above. Pough (1988b) suggested that some of the rules governing snake mimicry are different from those that involve invertebrates, and more recently Greene and McDiarmid (2004) noted a number of macroevolutionary patterns (the Savage-Wallace effects) that may be unique to mimicry involving venomous snakes. An alternative view is that the same underlying processes and paradigms that govern other taxa also govern mimicry in snakes, but that snakes represent the extremes on a set of continuums. Because the bulk of modern mimicry theory and the empiricism that informs it are based on lepidopterans and a few other insects, the possibility that mimicry involving snakes is unique could have profound impacts on the general understanding of mimicry as an evolutionary phenomenon. Below, we examine some of the proposed unique features of snake mimicry.

Mertensian Mimicry

Coralsnake mimicry has been a surprisingly controversial topic over the last century, due primarily to our own ignorance of the habits of both signalers and potential receivers. Much of the controversy was laid to rest with Smith's (1975, 1977) demonstration of innate avoidance of coralsnake ringed patterns by some predators and by Greene and McDiarmid's (1981) masterful dissection of the controversy and assemblage of field observations. One of the most significant products of the controversy, however, was the suggestion of a unique class dubbed Mertensian mimicry by Wickler (1968). One major objection to coralsnake mimicry in the past was the belief that venomous snake models killed predators and therefore prevented the

learned avoidance central to the operation of mimicry. Mertens (1956, 1957b) noted that the assemblage of coralsnake-patterned species in any locality often included some venomous rear-fanged colubrids, such as *Erythrolamprus* (Pls. 1100–1116) and *Pliocercus* (Pls. 1245–1265), which presumably could envenomate a predator without causing death (see Table 53). If these less venomous species functioned as models, then both deadly venomous elapids and harmless colubrids would gain protection from resemblance to the "mildly" venomous taxa. Under this scenario, harmless colubrids are traditional Batesian mimics, but venomous elapids are neither Batesian nor Müllerian mimics of the mildly venomous species and the form of selection on model color patterns with respect to mimics is unclear. As a result, a new form of mimicry, Mertensian, was coined to describe cases in which a deadly species mimics a less noxious species (Wickler 1968). Unfortunately, this description is based simply on the presumed relative deterrence and does not include any aspect of the selective dynamic.

Moreover, there is little direct evidence that Mertensian mimicry as defined is really operating in coralsnake systems. Innate avoidance of coralsnake ringed patterns eliminates the need for alternative models, and some regions with coralsnakes and mimics include no "mildly venomous" species (Greene and McDiarmid, 1981). In most localities in Latin America, a number of species with varying color patterns occur, and attack frequencies on each pattern vary where tested (Brodie, 1993). These observations cannot demonstrate which species truly function as models, but the overall complex seems more consistent with a number of species of varying degrees of noxiousness in a Müllerian or even quasi-Batesian dynamic.

Evolutionary Relationships and Body Plan

Generally speaking, mimicry is expected to involve taxa with similar gross morphology and therefore to involve closely related groups. Where mimicry does span distant evolutionary relationships, it is more likely to involve taxa with simple body plans (Greene and McDiarmid, 2004). Snakes have a relatively rare body plan among vertebrates, so mimicry of and by snakes can be expected to be restricted taxonomically. This is a reasonable expectation, but one limited in several dimensions. First, the available data are primarily anecdotal and presumptive (i.e., many described mimics have not been demonstrated to function as such). Proposed snake mimics include at least eight classes from four phyla and organisms as morphologically diverse as planarians, millipedes, turtles, and birds (Greene and McDiarmid, 2004; Pough, 1988a, 1988b; Vitt, 1992). At face value this list seems an exception to the first point, that mimicry involves related taxa, but supportive of the second, that mimicry involving distant taxa is more likely in simple-body-form organisms like snakes. However, a variety of other mimetic complexes span orders and even kingdoms. Spiders, immature hemipterans, and other arthropods mimic various species of ants (Cushing, 1997; Edmunds, 1978, 1993; Reiskind, 1977). Beetle larvae aggregations have been proposed as bee mimics (Hafernik and Saul-Gershenz, 2000). Special resemblance mimicry is widely distributed across several insect orders, including mantids that mimic plant parts from orchid flowers to branches, orthopterans that mimic dead leaves right down to decay spots and herbivore damage (pers. observ.; Cott, 1940; Edmunds, 1972, 1974, 1990), and lepidopteran larvae and pupae that bear an uncanny resemblance to lizard or bird feces (Cott, 1940). One species of horned lizard has even been pro-

Table 53. Genera of venomous snakes of the Americas and their potential mimics.

Coralsnakes		Potential coralsnake mimics		Pitvipers		Potential pitviper mimics	
Genus	Plates	Genus	Plates	Genus	Plates	Genus	Plates
Leptomicrurus	13–22	*Anilius*	1025	*Agkistrodon*	291–318	*Alsophis*	1024
Micruroides	24, 25	*Apostolepis*	1026–1033	*Atropoides*	319–368	*Arizona*	1042
Micrurus	26–282, 1261, 1263, 1281, 1282, 1361, 1362	*Atractus*	1034–1041	*Bothriechis*	369–426	*Boa*	1042–1044
		Cemophora	1047	*Bothriopsis*	427–453	*Corallus*	1066–1071
		Chilomeniscus	1048	*Bothrocophias*	454–485	*Cryophis*	1073
				Bothrops	486–662, 1363–1365	*Dipsas*	1076, 1079–1082
		Chionactis	1049, 1050				
		Clelia	1057, 1058	*Cerrophidion*	663–680	*Drymobius*	1087
		Dipsas	1077	*Lachesis*	681–701	*Ficimia*	1118
		Drepanoides	1083	*Ophryacus*	702–714	*Gyalopion*	1125
		Drymoluber	1089	*Porthidium*	715–751	*Heterodon*	1128–1131
		Elapomorphus	1095, 1096	*Crotalus*	752–1010	*Hydrodynastes*	1133
		Erythrolamprus	1100–1116	*Sistrurus*	1011–1023	*Hypsiglena*	1137
		Farancia	1117			*Liophis*	1179
		Geophis	1119–1123			*Lystrophis*	1190, 1191
		Gyalopion	1126			*Mastigodryas*	1196, 1197
		Helicops	1127			*Nerodia*	1198–1201
		Hydrodynastes	1132			*Nothopsis*	1203
		Hydrops	1134–1136			*Pituophis*	1243, 1244
		Lampropeltis	1142–1162			*Pseustes*	1271, 1272
		Liophis	1180–1182, 1184			*Sibon*	1286, 1290, 1291
		Lystrophis	1190, 1192–1195			*Sibynomorphus*	1294, 1295
		Ninia	1202			*Siphlophis*	1299
		Oxyrhopus	1206–1229			*Tachymenis*	1312
		Phalotris	1230–1232			*Thamnodynastes*	1314–1320
		Pliocercus	1245–1265			*Tomodon*	1324
		Pseudoboa	1057, 1266–1269			*Trachyboa*	1325
		Rhinobothryum	1273, 1274			*Tropidodryas*	1330, 1331
		Rhinocheilus	1275, 1276			*Ungaliophis*	1332, 1333
		Scaphiodontophis	1277–1283			*Waglerophis*	1334–1337, 1339
		Scolecophis	1284, 1285			*Xenodon*	1340–1356
		Sibon	1287–1290, 1292, 1293				
		Simophis	1296				
		Siphlophis	1297, 1298, 1300, 1301				
		Sonora	1302–1307				
		Stenorrhina	1309				
		Sympholis	1310				
		Tantilla	1313				
		Waglerophis	1338				
		Xenopholis	1359				

posed as a stone mimic (Sherbrooke and Montanucci, 1988). These examples suggest that the required similarity of form may be somewhat subjective, and that mimicry among widely unrelated taxa might be more common than previously thought.

The concept of similar gross morphology is also influenced by our perceptive biases as primates. Visual mimicry requires at least some similarity of body plans, but acoustic and chemical mimicry are completely exempt from that restriction. Chemical mimicry of sexual pheromones allows orchids to attract bees for pollination (Schiestl et al., 2000) and bolas spiders to attract moth prey (Haynes et al., 1996, 2001). With regard to snakes, one of the most striking examples is the acoustic mimicry of rattlesnakes by young burrowing owls. When their burrow is approached, owlets emit a hiss that is easily misinterpreted as a rattlesnake rattle (Garman, 1882). Field observations indicate similar acoustic signatures of both signals as well as similar behavioral responses by ground squirrels (Martin, 1973; Rowe

et al., 1986). On the other hand, a number of other examples of acoustic mimicry of venomous snakes involve other snakes: the growling of king cobras is mimicked by Indian ratsnakes even though the morphologies used to produce the growl are different (Young, 1991; Young et al., 1995); a number of North American colubrids mimic rattlesnake rattles by rapidly vibrating the tail tip on the substrate (Greene, 1988; Pough, 1988a); egg-eating snakes and other taxa mimic the rasping sound produced by saw-scaled vipers by rubbing coils of the body together (Pough, 1988a). These observations suggest that alternative explanations, such as common predators, might be more responsible for the perceived ubiquity of mimicry among closely related taxa than the similarity of body plans.

Abstract Mimicry

Pough (1988b) suggested that a unique aspect of venomous snake mimicry is the degree of abstract mimicry, in which the model cannot be readily identified as a single species or group of species. A number of observations support the interpretation that abstract mimicry of snakes is common, including lepidopteran larvae that mimic generalized snake forms but no single species, resemblance of multiple coralsnake species by a single mimic ("dual mimicry"; Greene and McDiarmid, 1981), and broad generalization of the signal components of models by some predators. These features presumably result from the serious consequences of a receiver failing to recognize a venomous snake. These observations certainly are borne out in snake mimicry, but it is not clear that they are unique to snakes or even to deadly models. In fact, this pattern is expected from the general feature of mimicry that extremely negative stimuli protect a broad range of mimics.

Generalized resemblance to an abstract form is seen in a variety of mimetic systems, and not necessarily only those with deadly models. Many species of rove beetles (Staphylinidae) arch the abdomen and stab it in a stinging motion similar to that exhibited by wasps and other hymenopterans (pers. observ.). Despite the fact that the abdomen of a rove beetle is soft and stingless, this behavior is quite effective against hominid insect collectors and likely against other potential predators as well. One of the most extreme and widespread examples of abstract mimicry involves venomous snakes, but as mimics, not models (as noted in Pough, 1988b). Caudal luring is a behavior widely distributed among snake taxa; it has been observed in numerous viperids and boids, and less commonly in colubrids and elapids (Carpenter et al., 1978; Murphy et al., 1978; Neill, 1960b). Many snakes, especially juveniles, have contrastingly colored tail tips that they wave about near their heads when prey approach. Lizards, frogs, and other taxa approach the lure, sometimes attempting to bite the writhing but nondescript prey item, only to become prey themselves (Greene and Campbell, 1972; Schuett, 1984; Schuett et al., 1984).

Broad generalization of the signal elements important in recognizing undesirable prey is a difficult phenomenon to evaluate objectively. It is virtually impossible to identify the stimulus components that are involved in receiver perception. Outside of experiments that directly test predator response, generalization may not be testable. In lieu of such data, researchers are usually left with their own perceptions and inferences for deciding what might and might not serve as a mimic. Nowhere is this problem more prevalent than in descriptions of coralsnake mimics. Proposed snake mimics of true coralsnakes range in pattern from nearly exact duplications of coralsnake rings, to tricolored bands, to red snakes with a single set of rings near the head, to black- or brown-and-white-banded species (see, e.g., Pough, 1988a; Savage and Slowinski, 1990, 1992). Field experiments in the Atlantic lowlands of Costa Rica suggest that this whole range of patterns may indeed be protected to varying degrees at that locality, but this result probably varies across localities that differ in regard to the number and type of true coralsnakes present (Brodie, 1993). What is more striking is the range of non-snake coralsnake mimics that have been suggested. It is not an overstatement to say that almost anything with red, yellow, and black pigmentation in the Neotropics has been suggested by someone as a potential coralsnake mimic (see Table 53). These range from somewhat believable elongate body forms such as sphingid moth larvae with tricolor rings and various millipedes with banded patterns (Janzen, 1980; Vitt, 1992) to wholly unsnakelike organisms such as atelopid frogs (*Atelopus varius* in Costa Rica), adult geometrid moths (pers. observ.), and even a turtle (*Rhinoclemmys pulcherrima*) with red, yellow, and black

coloration on the underside of the plastron (Janzen, 1980). Generalization of a signal is in the eye of the observer, and without direct tests of receiver responses there is no way to know whether a particular species is even avoided, let alone whether avoidance is due to mimicry of some other signaler (Edmunds, 2000).

Dual mimicry of sympatric coralsnakes was noted by Greene and McDiarmid (1981) for *Pliocercus* spp. and other mimics in Central and South America. The dorsal pigmentation of single individuals of *P. elapoides* from southern Mexico shares major elements of the patterns of sympatric *Micrurus diastema* and *M. elegans*. One species of colubrid (*Lystrophis dorbignyi* [Pl. 1190]; Yanosky and Chani, 1988) has been proposed as a dual mimic of coralsnakes and vipers. Such apparent mimicry of multiple models by single mimicking individuals is thought to be restricted to venomous snake systems, but may in fact be more widespread. Some individuals of the salamander *Desmognathus ocoee*, for example, exhibit both red cheeks and red legs, which mimic different populations of *Plethodon jordani* (Brodie and Howard, 1973). Dual mimicry does not represent broad generalization of signal if different species or individual predators learn different signal components (Edmunds, 2000; Pough, 1988b). It is also possible that individual predators have home ranges that overlap the distribution of multiple models and mimics, thereby allowing them the opportunity to learn avoidance of multiple signals. A mimic that exploits multiple signals could thereby function as a precise mimic of multiple species depending on the perception biases and diversity of relevant receivers.

Overall, it appears that mimicry of venomous snakes represents some extreme aspects of the evolution of mimicry, but that few if any features are unique in the sense that they represent elements of the mimicry process that we do not expect to observe based on general theory. Most of the features of special interest involve the severely noxious negative stimulus of interacting with a potentially deadly model (e.g., broad protection of imprecise mimics, abstract mimicry, and dual mimicry) and are not unexpected in the spectrum of mimicry. The one unique dimension that this does seem to influence is the evolution of innate avoidance of venomous snake signals, but even that is observed in potential predators of insect systems. Innate avoidance potentially changes the rules of mimicry by obviating the learning process and thereby altering the time scale of the selective dynamic between model and mimic. In general, it may be more instructive in the future to consider mimicry of venomous snakes as an extreme along the same continuum as mimicry in other taxa rather than as a unique phenomenon.

SPECIAL TOPICS IN SNAKE MIMICRY

Mimicry involving snakes may not be fundamentally different from mimicry in other taxa, but several phenomena warrant special discussion because of their historical and biological importance. These topics range from the belabored controversy over coralsnake mimicry to the underinvestigated but taxonomically diverse phenomenon of acoustic mimicry in snakes.

Coralsnake Mimicry

The argument over why so many Neotropical snakes resemble the venomous elapids of the genera *Leptomicrurus*, *Micrurus*, and *Micruroides* (see Table 53) is one of the oldest in herpetology. Beginning with Cope's (1860d) and Wallace's (1867) observations of color pattern resemblance, and continuing today with manipulative field experiments and molecular phylogenetic studies, the color pattern convergence of Neotropical snakes on various combinations of red, yellow or white, and black (i.e., tricolor) rings or bands has been the subject of considerable research effort. The controversy over the existence of coralsnake mimicry as a phenomenon once dominated the effort but has given way more recently to specific studies of how coralsnake mimicry operates in nature.

The "coralsnake mimicry problem" was based primarily on the argument, discussed above, that predators cannot learn to avoid a deadly prey item. Therefore, it was argued, the tricolor patterns of coralsnakes are not warning signals, and nontoxic or mildly toxic species of snakes are not likely to benefit from resemblance to true coralsnakes. This argument generated other concerns regarding sometimes nonoverlapping geographic distributions of coralsnakes and purported mimics, the nocturnal habits of coralsnakes, possible alternative functions of tricolor ringed and banded patterns, and, of course, the identity of models and mimics in such a system. In 1981, the history of the controversy was recounted and effectively dispelled in what stands as one of the most elegant manifestations of inductive synthesis in modern science (Greene and McDiarmid, 1981). Rather than repeat the reviews by Greene and McDiarmid (1981, 2004) and Pough (1988a, 1988b), we turn primarily toward the empirical advances offered since the early 1980s.

The early arguments over coralsnake mimicry typically involved the predator learning problem noted earlier. Susan Smith's studies (1975, 1977) of naive motmots and kiskadees obviated this concern by demonstrating that avian predators can exhibit innate prey avoidance and attack behaviors based on color pattern. By presenting dowels painted with various ringed patterns, Smith showed that some Neotropical birds with no previous experience with live prey reacted with alarm to red, yellow, and black arrayed in a ringed pattern. In a different set of experiments she showed that avian predators have an innate tendency to attack potentially dangerous prey on the head or neck region as identified by eyespots or neck constrictions (Smith, 1973, 1976, 1978). These studies lent credence to the notion that many predatory behaviors that could influence not only coralsnake mimicry but other systems as well are genetically based and do not require learning. Research on other systems partially supported this finding for predators of banded Hymenoptera (Schuler, 1982; Schuler and Hesse, 1985). On the other hand, recent studies of wild coatimundis (*Nasua narica*) indicated no aversion to tricolor snakes, so innate avoidance is clearly not uniform among potential predators of coralsnakes (Beckers et al., 1996).

The finding of innate avoidance virtually ended discussion and testing of empathic learning. Several authors have suggested that individual predators might learn to avoid venomous snakes through observing conspecifics or foraging partners (Gans, 1961, 1964; Gehlbach, 1972; Klopfer, 1957), but the only test of empathically learned avoidance of snakes is Gehlbach's (1972) observations of reactions to coralsnake models by captive javelinas and coatis. Gelbach's experiments showed that there may be some social facilitation of avoidance but fell well short of demonstrating empathic learning. Empathic learning has been demonstrated in related contexts for primates (Gans, 1964; Jouventin et al., 1977).

For mimicry to explain the taxonomic diversity of similarly colored snakes, tricolor patterns must function as warning signals. Innate avoidance by some predators in captivity suggests that the patterns are aposematic but does not demonstrate that this is the case in the wild, nor do such observations make the case for all or even most predators. Some authors have questioned whether predators of snakes can see the colors or whether coralsnakes are active during periods of sufficient light to allow the color patterns to function as warning signals (see Greene and McDiarmid, 1981) and have offered other explanations for color pattern convergence in Neotropical snakes. Grobman (1978) suggested that such color patterns are selectively neutral, an idea that has never garnered much support given the conspicuous phylogenetically diverse convergence on similar patterns and later demonstration of their functional significance (Greene and McDiarmid, 1981). Crypsis of tricolor patterns, although seemingly farcical to human observers when they see a coralsnake in a cage or preserving jar, was proposed first by Gadow (1911) and supported by Brattstrom (1955) based on two points. First, transverse rings or bands, although brightly colored, break up the form of an elongate body, generating a disruptive effect. Second, a color pattern in motion can have visual effects different from the same pattern in stasis. Banded patterns at some speeds and to some visual systems blur into a solid color that can appear motionless. Similar effects have been described for striped and blotched natricines (Brodie, 1992; Pough, 1976) and are but one category of effects of moving color patterns.

The aposematic function of (motionless) ringed patterns has been tested in nature in Costa Rica using artificial models. By constructing replica snakes out of precolored plasticine, Brodie (1993) was able to record predation attempts by observing the imprints in the plasticine left by bird bills and mammalian mandibles (Fig. 228). The plasticine paradigm allows the manipulation of variables ranging from color patterns of the replicas to backgrounds. Brodie compared attack rates on tricolor patterns with attacks on brown patterns on both natural and plain white backgrounds to determine if attack frequency differences resulted from failure to detect tricolor patterns or from active avoidance. His results indicated active avoidance of nonmoving tricolor patterns by free-ranging avian predators. Although this experiment demonstrated an aposematic function for coralsnake patterns, it did not rule out crypsis in other behavioral contexts.

The question of who is mimicking whom in coralsnake systems traces back to the early debates and suggestions of Mertensian mimicry (Mertens, 1956, 1957b; Wickler, 1968). In part, the problem here is that no clear data were available on relative avoidance of particular color patterns by any predators, wild or captive. The array of possible model and mimic color patterns in any one locality can be bewildering and often includes more than 100 species (Pough, 1988a). Again using the plasticine paradigm (Fig. 228), Brodie (1993) sampled attack frequencies on the color patterns of true coralsnakes (*Micrurus alleni* [Pl. 32], *M. multifasciatus* [Pls. 207–209], and *M. nigrocinctus* [Pls. 135–137]) and their presumed mimics (juvenile *Clelia clelia*, *Erythrolamprus mimus*, *Lampropeltis triangulum* [Pl. 1155], *Ninia sebae*, *Oxyrhopus petola* [Pl. 1220], *Pliocercus euryzonus* [Pls. 1264 and 1265], and *Scaphiodontophis annulatus*) in a lowland tropical rainforest in Costa Rica. All patterns with ringed or banded patterns were avoided relative to a brown control, and differences were observed among some groups of patterns. Unfortunately, the diversity of the color patterns represented precluded ranking of patterns relative to true coralsnakes. In a follow-up study in another region, Brodie and Janzen (1995)

A

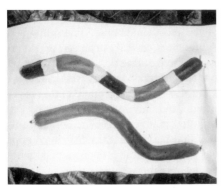
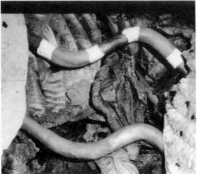

B

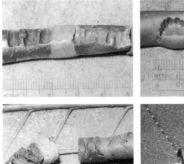
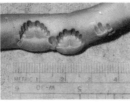
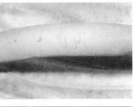

Fig. 228. Plasticine snake replicas used to study coralsnake mimicry. (A) Tricolored (coralsnake) replicas and brown controls shown against plain white background (left) and natural background (right). Experiments conducted in Costa Rica demonstrate that free-ranging avian predators attack coralsnake patterns less often than they attack brown controls regardless of background, showing that coralsnake patterns have an aposematic function. (B) Marks left on plasticine replicas by animals reveal the identity of attackers. Clockwise from upper left: incisor marks left by a large rodent, probably an agouti; dental imprints from an opossum; bill imprints of four different species of birds. Bill imprints are generally matched on opposite sides of the models. Photographs by E. D. Brodie III.

took advantage of a limited community of coralsnakes and presumed mimics to demonstrate that red-and-black-ringed patterns were avoided in an area where tricolor-ringed, but no red-and-black-ringed, snakes occurred. These results were interpreted as evidence that predators generalize avoidance of true coralsnake patterns to similar ringed patterns. Although these results suggest that true coralsnakes may function as a model for novel patterns, they do not preclude the operation of Müllerian or quasi-Batesian selective dynamics in which each color pattern is avoided to some degree.

The clearest evidence to date that true coralsnakes are models in a Batesian or at least quasi-Batesian form of mimicry comes from geographic comparisons of attack frequencies on tricolor plasticine replicas in North America (Pfennig et al., 2001). In eastern North America the kingsnake, *Lampropeltis triangulum elapsoides* (Pl. 1154), is a presumed mimic of the harlequin coralsnake, *Micrurus fulvius* (Pls. 98–100), whereas in southwestern North America the mountain kingsnake, *L. pyromelana* (Pl. 1145), resembles the western coralsnake, *Micruroides euryxanthus* (Pls. 23–25). In both regions only a single coralsnake species is present, and the range of the presumed mimic extends beyond that of the presumed model—in the Southwest, *M. euryxanthus* is less common at higher elevations and is not present above 1,770 m, whereas in the East, *M. fulvius* is not found north of latitude 35.1°N. Pfennig and colleagues (2001) placed plasticine replicas of the local mimic and controls in 16–24 localities across an elevational transect in the Southwest and a latitudinal transect in the East. Attack frequencies on mimics were positively correlated with elevation and latitude, respectively, demonstrating that mimetic patterns were more likely to be avoided where coralsnakes were more frequent. Interestingly, the rela-

tionship was not a step function; that is, some avoidance of mimetic patterns was evident even at localities where true coralsnakes were absent. As such, this is the best evidence to date in any system that the geographic range of individual predators is what drives mimicry, and that sympatry of model and mimic may not be necessary.

An intriguing alternative to coralsnake mimicry is the suggestion that ringed and banded snakes are actually part of a wider mimicry complex that centers on millipedes as models for elongate vertebrates. Vitt (1992) noted that millipedes are inherently banded in appearance due to structure and coloration; are well defended by a variety of extremely noxious chemical compounds; occur syntopically with coralsnakes, presumptive mimics, and other elongate vertebrates; and have existed on Earth during the entire evolution of vertebrates. As such they represent a potential model for mimicry complexes, and Vitt (1992) offered several very convincing cases of resemblance that involve millipedes. Furthermore, the experiments of Smith (1975, 1977) and Brodie (1993; Brodie and Janzen, 1995) used model sizes that might be construed as millipedes rather than snakes. It seems clear from these observations that at least some millipedes are involved in mimetic relationships with coralsnakes, but as with snake taxa, it is difficult to tease apart the selective relationships that define model and mimic or Batesian versus Müllerian mimicry.

Several points suggest that mimicry of millipedes may not be a widespread phenomenon, and in particular may not be the driving force behind coralsnake mimicry. In more plasticine experiments, Brodie and Moore (1995) showed that avian predators in Costa Rica attacked millipede-ringed patterns more often than snake-ringed patterns on a millipede-sized replica, suggesting that millipedes are avoided less than similar snakes, at least in one region. Impressive parallel geographic variation in color pattern between members of the genus *Micrurus* and other Neotropical snakes (Campbell and Lamar, 1989; Greene and McDiarmid, 1981; Marques, 2002; Roze, 1996) strongly suggests selection pressure for close phenotypic resemblance. One striking example is the coralsnake *Micrurus hippocrepis* from Guatemala, which varies in appearance from a full ringed pattern to incomplete black rings that appear as reverse saddles or spots (Pls. 101–115), and *Pliocercus elapoides laticollaris* (Pls. 1253 and 1254), which exhibits comparable polymorphism in the same localities. Other examples exist, but this one is particularly interesting because we are unaware of any millipede with dorsolateral saddles of any color.

Biogeographic and phylogenetic evidence also points against millipedes as a driving force in snake mimicry systems. Ringed or banded millipedes are found throughout the world, but assemblages of Neotropical coralsnakes and other similarly patterned snakes are conspicuous because they are the only groups of snakes with such a high frequency of ringed and banded species (Pough, 1988a). If millipedes were the original model for ringed snake mimicry, then we would expect similar radiations of ringed or banded snakes in the Old World. Moreover, we would expect that radiations of millipede mimics would begin with bicolored ringed patterns, since no tricolored millipedes are known. Molecular phylogenies indicate that the ancestral color pattern of true coralsnakes is tricolor ringed (Slowinski, 1995; Slowinski et al., 2001), as are the majority of extant species, making it difficult to argue that this clade evolved as mimics of a bicolored elongate invertebrate.

Viper Mimicry

If venomous snakes are effective models for mimicry, we should expect to find mimicry complexes that involve a variety of taxa worldwide. Historically, herpetologists interested in mimicry have been preoccupied with coralsnake mimicry, and for the most part descriptions of mimicry involving other venomous taxa have been limited to suggestive accounts based simply on observed phenotypic (usually color pattern) similarity (see Greene and McDiarmid, 2004). Mimicry of vipers stands as an exception; the quality and quantity of observational data make a convincing case for mimicry in at least some systems (Greene and McDiarmid, 2004; Pough, 1988a).

Detecting and demonstrating mimicry in vipers may be more difficult than doing so in elapids because both Old World vipers and New World pitvipers tend to be cryptically patterned. Cryptic coloration is usually considered distinct from aposematic coloration, but as noted above, a single color pattern can have multiple functions, particularly with regard to different behavioral contexts and different predators. Many vipers also exhibit such characteristic behavioral and acoustic warning signals as head triangulation and strike postures, hissing, tail rattling, and scale rubbing, signals that could be exploited by mimics.

One of the earliest described examples of viper mimicry involves egg-eating snakes (*Dasypeltis scabra* and *D. palmarum*) and several genera of African vipers (*Causus, Echis, Bitis,* and *Cerastes*; Gans, 1961, 1964, 1973; Gans and Richmond, 1957; Weale, 1871). Egg-eating snakes are nearly toothless and are considered relatively defenseless against predators, whereas many vipers deliver an exceedingly painful bite along with venom. *Dasypeltis* species have patterns conspicuously similar

to those of sympatric viper taxa, including the prominent V found in the nuchal region of many viperids. *Dasypeltis scabra* has a much broader range than any single species of viper, and geographic variation in its color pattern parallels that found in local viper taxa, at least in the perception of human observers (Gans, 1961, 1973; Pough, 1988a). Mimicry of the night adders *Causus defilippii* and *C. rhombeatus* includes parallel geographic variation in color pattern within both model and mimic species in sub-Saharan Africa. Ontogenetic color pattern changes in *Causus* species, which in some regions become unicolored as they grow older, are not paralleled by *Dasypeltis*. Instead, the relatively lithe *D. scabra* expresses patterns similar to those of *Causus* of comparable girth. Similar parallel geographic variation in pattern is seen where *D. scabra* co-occurs with *Bitis caudalis* (Gans, 1961).

The color pattern resemblance of *Dasypeltis* to vipers is only one component of a multidimensional mimetic phenotype. Even more convincing is the similarity in their warning postures and acoustic signals (Fig. 229). Saw-scaled vipers (*Echis* spp.) form a C-shaped coil that allows specialized scales on the sides of the body to be rubbed together to generate a hissing noise (Gans and Baic, 1974, 1977; Gans and Maderson, 1973; Gans and Richmond, 1957). *Dasypeltis scabra* exhibits a similar C-shaped moving coil when threatened, and keeled scales produce a rasping sound as in *Echis*. The sound-producing scales take different forms in the two taxa, but similar sounds are produced. *Dasypeltis* exaggerates its display by inflating the body, thereby increasing its apparent size and the distinctness of its dorsal patterning (Gans and Richmond, 1957). This inflation may also amplify the hissing sound produced by scale rubbing. Throughout the display, egg-eating snakes spread the posterior quadrates to give the head a more triangular shape (as in vipers) and may strike open-mouthed, but do not bite (Gans, 1961; Gans and Richmond, 1957).

The degree of similarity in pattern, behavior, and acoustic signal combined with parallel geographic variation in color

Fig. 229. The defensive display of the egg-eating snake *Dasypeltis* sp. The characteristic moving C-coil allows the sound-producing scales to rub against each other and generate a hissing sound, and head triangulation increases the snake's resemblance to a viper. In the final stages of the display, *Dasypeltis*, although essentially toothless, performs open-mouthed strikes. Photograph by E. D. Brodie Jr.

pattern makes a strong case for some form of mimicry complex including *Dasypeltis* and local vipers, although no experiments designed to reveal patterns of selection or relative advantage have been conducted that would allow us to deduce what form of mimicry is represented here. Many of the arguments against coralsnake mimicry have also been applied to this system, chief among them the inability of predators to learn to avoid venomous snakes. Gans (1964) suggested that empathic learning might be the most important mechanism leading to avoidance in viper-based mimicry, given that many of the potential mammalian predators such as warthogs and baboons forage in groups. Empathic learning has been demonstrated to be more effective than direct experience in captive mandrills (Jouventin et al., 1977).

Numerous other examples of presumptive viper mimicry have been offered (see Table 53), ranging from geographically parallel variations in the color patterns of colubrids and pitvipers (e.g., *Sibon longifrenis* [Pl. 1290] and *Bothriechis schlegelii* [Pl. 401]; Greene, 1997; see also species accounts) to more abstract forms of general viper mimicry. Behavioral head triangulation, usually produced by spreading the posterior tips of the quadrates, is observed in a wide variety of taxa but is especially common in Neotropical species of the "goo-eater" clade (Cadle and Greene, 1993) that includes *Sibon*, *Dipsas* [Pl. 1076], and *Sibynomorphus*. Similar behavior is especially impressive in *Xenodon rabdocephalus*, which accompanies triangulation with a neck-spreading behavior that exaggerates its resemblance to local *Bothrops asper* in Guatemala (Pls. 1347, 501). In Costa Rica, *Pseustes poecilonotus* displays triangulation and an elevated S-shaped strike posture as a juvenile but rarely as an adult (pers. observ.). Color pattern differences accompany this ontogenetic shift in behavior: juveniles express a contrasting-brown-saddled pattern superficially similar to that of *B. asper*, while adults are uniform olive green (Fig. 227). Few attempts have been made to quantitatively or experimentally address the problem of viper mimicry. One of the most troubling aspects of the problem is that viper patterns appear to be cryptic, leaving examples of parallel geographic variation in viper and colubrid color patterns less than satisfying evidence of mimicry. This issue was tackled directly for the purported mimicry between *Pituophis melanoleucus* and the western rattlesnake, *Crotalus oreganus/viridis*, by Sweet (1985). Both species have conspicuous dark dorsal blotches, and geographic variation in the size, shape, and color of the blotches in some regions is parallel. However, coastal populations of *C. oreganus* and *P. melanoleucus* occur in different microhabitats with different background patterns and do not resemble each other. Inland populations exhibit much greater overlap in habitat usage and share similarly cryptic coloration. Sweet also noted that individuals of both species from inland populations were much more likely to produce acoustic warning signals (rattling for *C. oreganus/viridis*, tail rattling and hissing for *P. melanoleucus*) than were individuals from coastal populations. These data suggest that convergent evolution of locally cryptic coloration may drive pattern similarity of vipers and colubrids and underscore the need for more rigorous tests of presumed mimicry complexes.

Acoustic Mimicry

Mimicry of the acoustic signals produced by venomous snakes is particularly widespread both taxonomically and geo-graphically. The characterization of acoustic signals and tests of mimetic function lag behind those that deal with visual mimicry, but the variety of signals and species involved suggests this may be a productive direction for future study.

The variety of acoustic warning signals produced by venomous snakes is amazing given the relatively simple sound production anatomy that snakes possess. The rattle of rattlesnakes is undoubtedly the most famous of the snake acoustic warnings. Similar broad-spectrum sounds are produced by saw-scaled vipers as described above. Rattlesnakes and some other pitvipers typically emit loud hisses during defensive displays (Greene, 1988), and king cobras (*Ophiophagus hannah*) produce a low-frequency growl when threatened (Young, 1991).

The case for mimicry of such acoustic signals is generally made through observations of similar signals in sympatric but unrelated species. One of the more convincing cases involves the scale-rubbing behavior of *Dasypeltis* described above that produces saw-scaled viper–like signals with an independently derived but unique set of behavioral and morphological traits (Gans, 1961; Gans and Baic, 1974, 1977; Gans and Richmond, 1957). A similar example of convergently evolved signals involves the vocalization of king cobras. Described as a growl, the vocalization is a 600-Hz sound produced by diverticula in the trachea that function as resonating chambers (Young, 1991). Indian ratsnakes emit similar sounds during defensive displays, but the morphological apparatus used to produce the sound is different (Young et al., 1999).

A variety of North American colubrids rapidly vibrate their tail tips when threatened. This behavior can be observed in many taxa but has been specifically suggested as rattlesnake mimicry for foxsnakes (*Elaphe vulpina*) and gophersnakes (*Pituophis melanoleucus*) (Greene and McDiarmid, 2004; Kardong, 1980a). The rapidly vibrating tail tip can produce a rattlelike sound on some substrates (Kuch, 1997b) and adds to the dimensions of presumed mimicry of rattlesnakes by gophersnakes. In addition to tail vibration, gophersnakes in some parts of western North America produce a loud, drawn-out hiss that accompanies an S-shaped strike posture and behavioral head triangulation (Kardong, 1980a).

Acoustic mimicry obviates the necessity for gross morphological resemblance and thus opens the door for mimicry by unrelated taxa. Such a possibility is exemplified by the vocalizations of juvenile burrowing owls, which have been likened to rattlesnake rattles (Garman, 1882; Martin, 1973; Rowe et al., 1986). Burrowing owls nest in burrows similar to those often occupied by rattlesnakes in the arid regions of western North America, and the young emit a hiss when the burrow is approached. Quantitative analyses of sound production show the hisses of burrowing owls to be similar to the broad-spectrum sounds produced by rattlesnake rattles (Martin, 1973), though related owls that do not occupy burrows produce similar sounds as begging calls (Thomsen, 1971). Experiments with ground squirrels (*Spermophilus beecheyi*) have shown that individuals from regions with rattlesnakes treat burrowing owl hisses with caution, whereas squirrels from outside the range of rattlesnakes do not (Rowe et al., 1986). Other phylogenetically diverse species may practice similar acoustic mimicry of venomous snakes. Geckos of the genus *Teratoscincus*, which are sympatric with saw-scaled vipers (*Echis*), produce a hissing sound by moving overlapping scales on the tail against one another (Gans and Maderson, 1973); this sound production may be another example of acoustic mimicry of venomous snakes.

Caudal Luring

The apparent use of the tail tip to lure prey is typically interpreted as a form of abstract mimicry of some unidentified invertebrate prey that dupes the receiver into approaching near enough for the snake to strike. Some anecdotal observations, including actual attacks of tail tips by subsequent prey, have been published supporting such a functional interpretation. However, to date no explicit tests of the function or fitness consequences of caudal luring have been conducted.

Caudal luring typically involves brightly or contrastingly colored tail tips that are wagged either overhead or in front of the head of a coiled snake (Campbell and Lamar, 1989; Greene, 1997; Pough, 1988a). Comparable behaviors have been observed in boids, colubrids, elapids, and viperids, and are particularly widespread through the pitvipers. A scan of the illustrations in this volume will show that many American pitvipers, especially juveniles, have contrastingly colored tail tips, and many are known to practice caudal luring behavior, including the genera *Atropoides* (Pls. 331–333, 335, 366–368), *Bothriechis* (Pls. 378, 393), *Bothrocophias* (Pl. 458), *Bothrops* (Pls. 521–523, 538, 540, 592, 602, 603), *Porthidium* (Pls. 730, 732, 743, 744), and *Crotalus* (Pl. 791). Some adults, notably *Agkistrodon* spp. (Pls. 296–313), *Bothriopsis bilineata* (Pls. 427–430), and *B. oligolepis* (Pls. 436 and 437), also exhibit the brightly colored tail and luring behavior. Most accounts of caudal luring that report foraging success involve frogs or lizards as prey (Greene and Campbell, 1972; Schuett, 1984; Schuett et al., 1984). These observations lead to the prediction that this form of mimicry should be observed in species and life stages that feed primarily on these groups, and do so by ambush foraging.

An interesting parallel to caudal luring has been reported in aquatic gartersnakes in western North America. Adult *Thamnophis atratus* are active foragers that feed on a wide variety of prey, including fish and amphibians, but juveniles are ambush foragers that feed primarily on juvenile salmonids (Lind and Welsh, 1994). Among the suite of ambush foraging behaviors exhibited by juvenile *T. atratus* is a behavior described as lingual luring (Welsh and Lind, 2000), in which the tongue is held out rigid with the tips quivering on the surface. This behavior presumably functions as abstract mimicry of insects in the surface film and attracts young steelhead and Chinook salmon into the snake's strike range. A similar behavior exhibited by juvenile watersnakes (*Nerodia rhombifer* and *N. sipedon*) has been described as "flycasting" for fish (Czaplicki and Porter, 1974).

A FUTURE SO BRIGHT . . .

For all of the tantalizing examples that suggest mimicry involving snakes, the suggestions of different processes for venomous snake mimicry, and the diversity of modes and taxa involved, distressingly little work has gone past the mere description and documentation of mimetic resemblance. A few authors have succeeded in collecting examples and describing patterns of mimicry among taxa (Greene and McDiarmid, 2004; Pough, 1988a, 1988b), but focused experimental work has examined the diversity of forms avoided and the nature of avoidance only in coralsnake mimicry systems (Brodie, 1993; Brodie and Janzen, 1995; Brodie and Moore, 1995; Pfennig et al., 2001; Smith, 1975, 1977, 1980; Smith and Mostrom, 1985). Impressive assemblages

of observations of geographic variation, behavior in the field, and convergent evolution of similar signals make a strong case for mimicry in several groups (Gans, 1961; Gans and Baic, 1974; Greene and McDiarmid, 1981; Pough, 1988a).

Beyond these contributions, virtually nothing is known about the details of the evolutionary process of mimicry in snakes, or how well general theory applies to snake mimicry. Furthermore, many problems in the general understanding of mimicry are being addressed almost solely through the study of a few taxa, and directed research into snake mimicry is needed to allow a broader test of theory and empirical basis for new ideas.

Genetic Architecture

The genetic bases of warning signals and mimetic resemblance can greatly influence their evolutionary potential. Whether a color pattern element is controlled by one or many genes, whether such genes act additively or nonadditively, and whether the genes act zygotically or maternally can all change the sort of selection required for warning signals to evolve (Brodie and Agrawal, 2001; Mallet and Joron, 1999; Sheppard, 1959; Sheppard et al., 1985; Turner, 1977). "Supergenes," in which a few linked regions with strong dominance control multiple signal components, are predicted to evolve in many cases as well as allow for the evolution of polymorphism within mimics (Turner, 1967). One explanation is that a gene of major effect is required to alter a pattern sufficiently to appear similar to a model, but that after its appearance selection can favor the evolution of linked modifiers that refine resemblance to a more precise degree (Charlesworth, 1994; Charlesworth and Charlesworth, 1976a; Turner, 1977). The empirical evidence available on the inheritance of mimetic signals comes from a few groups of butterflies (Clarke et al., 1968; Clarke and Sheppard, 1971; Sheppard, 1959). For example, multiple genes are involved in controlling the color patterns of *Heliconius* spp., but there also appear to be genes of major effect that can switch mimetic patterns on and off in the manner of supergenes (Mallet, 1989; Mallet and Joron, 1999; Sheppard et al., 1985).

Virtually nothing has been published on the genetics underlying natural color pattern variation in snakes, let alone for mimicry systems. An eclectic array of discrete polymorphisms or abnormalities is understood in various taxa (Bechtel, 1978, 1995), but these hardly provide meaningful reference for complex natural color patterns. Undercurrents in the herpetological community suggest that some breeders have amassed sufficient data to test genetic models for a few species, but this information has yet to be published.

Polymorphism

One of the major paradoxes in mimicry is how Müllerian mimicry can generate polymorphism within mimics (Joron and Mallet, 1998; Joron et al., 1999; Mallet, 2001; Mallet and Joron, 1999). True Müllerian mimicry should select for model and mimic to share the same signal, preventing the origin and maintenance of polymorphism. However, presumably Müllerian mimics such as *Heliconius* butterflies exhibit considerable polymorphism, which has led some researchers to consider alternative forms of mimicry (e.g., quasi-Batesian; Speed and Turner, 1999; but see Mallet, 2001), or to develop theory and tests of how polymorphism might arise in the context of Müllerian selection. Leading candidates include the role of geographic or temporally variable selection, the operation of shifting balance dynamics or similar effects of population subdivision, and the existence of predator psychology rules that alter the frequency-dependent relationship between models and mimics (Mallet and Joron, 1999). Particular forms of genetic architecture might also promote (e.g., supergenes) or prevent (e.g., multiple independent loci of small effect) the evolution and maintenance of new signal types (Charlesworth, 1994; Mallet and Joron, 1999).

Coralsnake mimicry complexes may be one of the best (non-lepidopteran) examples of polymorphism in mimicry. Phylogenetic analyses have traced the evolution of color pattern within the true coralsnakes (Slowinski, 1995; Slowinski et al., 2001), and considerable local geographic variation is known in coral-snake color patterns (see this volume; Greene and McDiarmid, 1981). This variation is closely paralleled by some species of mimics (e.g., *Pliocercus elapoides, Scaphiodontophis*; Greene and McDiarmid, 1981; Savage and Slowinski, 1996) but hardly at all by others. Within any single locality in Central or South America, multiple pattern types considered to be mimetic exist (Brodie, 1993; Brodie and Janzen, 1995; Pough, 1988a, 1988b). Polymorphism among multiple species is clearly a different evolutionary phenomenon than polymorphism maintained within the same genome, but some of the selective dynamics are similar. Additionally, some models (e.g., *Micrurus multifasciatus* in Costa Rica, [Pls. 207–209] and *M. hippocrepis* in Guatemala [Pls. 101–115]) and mimics (e.g., *Pliocercus elapoides* [Pls. 1253 and 1254], *P. euryzonus* [Pls. 1264 and 1265], and *Sonora* [Pls. 1305–1307]) are polymorphic within single populations.

The Geographic Mosaic of Coevolution

Mimicry is inherently a coevolutionary process that involves at least three interacting players (Mallet, 1999; Vane-Wright, 1976). Recent conceptual advances emphasize the role of geographic structure in influencing the dynamics and outcomes of coevolution (Thompson, 1994, 1999a, 1999b). Because selection occurs at the population level and is likely to vary in space because of many ecological factors, hotspots of intense reciprocal selection are predicted to arise in some areas and coldspots in others. This mosaic of coevolution can lead to different levels of phenotype matching, maladaptation, and a variety of other phenomena (Gomulkiewicz et al., 2000; Nuismer et al., 2000; Thompson, 1999b). Most work on geographic mosaics has involved relatively simple two-player systems, but the conceptualization applies just as well to mimicry, and the available evidence suggests the presence of all of the important elements of geographic structure.

Again, research on *Heliconius* butterflies comes the closest to filling this bill. Field studies of geographic variation in pattern, mimetic assemblage, and selection suggest the structure necessary for geographic mosaic effects to occur (Joron et al., 1999; Mallet, 1993; Mallet and Gilbert, 1995; Mallet and Joron, 1999; Mallet et al., 1998). For the most part, the results of this work have been interpreted in light of the shifting balance theory, which is based on a similar but more restrictive set of conditions involving geographic subdivision. Several snake mimicry systems, including coralsnake complexes and the resemblance of *Dasypeltis* to various African vipers, appear to have the geographic variation within species necessary to address problems of geographic structure. Differences in predator assemblages, model and mimic communities, alternative prey availability, and habitat structure could each contribute to spatially variable selection and thereby drive a geographic mosaic of mimicry.

Receiver Psychology

Receiver psychology generates the selection that drives mimicry. Theoretical efforts to include predator psychology in conceptual models of mimicry and warning signal evolution have suggested that the rules of signal perception, learning, and forgetting can dramatically alter the selective environment on signals (Servedio, 2000; Speed, 1993; Speed and Turner, 1999; Yachi and Higashi, 1998). The results are nontrivial; depending on predator psychology, warning signals can evolve gradually and slowly or not at all, mimicry may be Batesian or Müllerian, and polymorphism may be maintained or monomorphism may be ubiquitous. At this point, little information is available on which to base models, and the case may be worse for snakes, for which we may not even know some of the major predators.

Nonetheless, predator psychology is obviously a critical component of mimicry, and even a cursory understanding of the process must acknowledge these details. Two coarse-level elements that crop up again and again in discussions of snake mimicry are innate avoidance and empathic learning. The existence of innate avoidance has been demonstrated for only two species of potential predators of snakes worldwide. Whether or not this is a widespread phenomenon, or at least widespread enough to drive mimicry systems in vipers and pitvipers, remains to be seen. Moreover, empathic learning has been invoked for many cases of venomous snake mimicry, yet still awaits a clear demonstration as a feasible mechanism for avoidance of snakes. Other relatively simple issues in psychology include learning rates of predators, signal generalization (Brodie and Janzen, 1995), and even the ways the light environment and visual system influence predators' perception of signals (Endler, 1992, 1993).

Mimicry as a Radiating Force

Mimicry, like other forms of strong ecological selection, may contribute to speciation and adaptive radiation. Because of its strong positive frequency dependence, mimicry may be a particularly strong force selecting against hybrid or intermediate phenotypes and may thereby contribute to the maintenance of species barriers (Jiggins and McMillan, 1997; Mallet, 1993; Mallet and Barton, 1989; Mallet et al., 1990; McMillan et al., 1997). Much of the evidence from Lepidoptera is consistent with this prediction in particular; Müllerian mimics are rarely from the same clade, and related taxa tend to belong to different mimicry complexes (Turner, 1984). Sister taxa often differ with respect to mimetic patterns (Brower, 1994, 1996). While not a definitive test, these patterns suggest that speciation within one clade may allow other clades to follow by opening up new niches, and that exploitation of new model forms allows radiation.

This point was extended by Greene (1997) and Greene and McDiarmid (2004) in reference to snakes when they suggested that the evolution of venoms can contribute to diversity within groups, and in turn can create protected niches for less well defended taxa. The radiation of New World coralsnakes and the diversity of presumed coralsnake mimics would seem to lend credence to this notion. However, as Greene and McDiarmid (2004) pointed out, explicit phylogenetic tests must be conducted to evaluate this prediction, including comparisons of related groups of mimics and nonmimics against null models for symmetrical cladogenesis (Slowinski and Guyer, 1993).

CONCLUSION

The rich natural history foundation of detailed observations of snake phenotypes and geographic variation provides ample evidence that mimicry of venomous snakes takes place in nature and that the diversity of form and function in mimicry is not restricted to the traditional Batesian-Müllerian dichotomy of protective mimicry. Mimicry of snakes involves behavioral and acoustic signals as well as the oft-observed color pattern signals. Other forms of mimetic interaction, including aggressive mimicry and sexual mimicry, may be more widespread than is currently appreciated. Although most of the research attention has been devoted to coralsnakes and their mimics, an amazing taxonomic array of possible model-mimic systems exists around the world.

Mimicry is a complex evolutionary process, however, and it cannot be evaluated or effectively studied by mere descriptions of similar phenotypes. How signals are inherited can alter the evolutionary response of aposematism and mimicry. The perception of these signals by receivers will determine the selection and evolutionary response in such a precise way that small differences in learning curves can change the whole selective dynamic among models and mimics. The synthesis of these elements can lead to different forms of mimicry, some of which may influence macroevolutionary patterns in model and mimic clades. The study of snake mimicry has produced a solid and diverse foundation of examples to work with, as well as a variety of experimental techniques and analytical approaches that might be applied more broadly. To advance our understanding of the role of mimicry in snake evolution, and conversely the role of snakes in mimicry theory, it is time to use our current knowledge of natural history to take the next step and develop empirical research programs focused on general problems in mimicry in snakes.

The Evolution of New World Venomous Snakes

Ronald L. Gutberlet Jr. and Michael B. Harvey

The remarkable diversity of venomous snakes in the Americas poses a challenging, but tractable, riddle. Where did all of these pitvipers and coralsnakes come from, and how did they become so different from one another? A little ridge-nosed rattlesnake, *Crotalus willardi* (Pls. 998–1010), is quite different from a terciopelo, *Bothrops asper* (Pls. 499–517), both of which are very different from a Merendón palm-pitviper, *Bothriechis thalassinus* (Pls. 422–425); and none of these species resembles an ornate coralsnake, *Micrurus ornatissimus* (Pls. 158 and 159). What produced the great diversity of venomous snakes in the Americas? Why are some species arboreal while others are fossorial? Why do some exhibit strikingly bold coloration while others melt imperceptibly into the background? Although these questions might be dismissed with a few words—*evolution, speciation, adaptive radiation*—scientists strive for more definitive answers. Scientists have been examining these and similar questions for more than two centuries, and basic patterns are beginning to emerge. The diversity arose over a period of 15–30 million years from a couple of Old World colonizing species (Parkinson et al., 2002; Slowinski and Keogh, 2000). The purpose of this chapter is to recount the history of venomous snakes in the New World through a review and synthesis of research on their phylogenetic relationships. We begin with an introduction to biological classification and methods of phylogenetic reconstruction, and then discuss the development of knowledge—from 1758 to the present—of the phylogeny, classification, biogeography, and morphological evolution of venomous snakes of the Americas.

PHYLOGENY AND CLASSIFICATION

Charles Darwin's landmark publication *On the Origin of Species* (1859) provided evidence that the biological diversity on Earth has arisen over time through the process of speciation: extant species are the descendants of ancestral species. The implication is that all living things are related to one another through genealogical descent. Past speciation events can be reconstructed using evidence recovered from living species and fossil specimens. We refer to evolutionary relationships among species and other taxonomic groups as phylogeny, and we commonly depict such relationships with branching diagrams called phylogenetic trees such as the one depicted in Figure 230. Since 1859, biologists have attempted to summarize what we know about evolutionary history through the system of biological classification. Thus, for approximately 150 years the classification of life has been directly affected by our growing knowledge of evolutionary history.

An Introduction to the Classification of Life

The process of biological classification in its modern form involves two discrete but related steps: discovery of lineages and assignment of formal names to them. The smallest lineages that maintain their identities independent of other such lineages are known as species (de Queiroz, 1998). Lineages that may include one to many species have been classified (from least to most inclusive) as genera, families, orders, classes, phyla, kingdoms, and domains. The correct identification of lineages is important to many biological disciplines. The naming of lineages, while not as important as discovering them, is essential for effective communication, information retrieval, and summary of knowledge about evolutionary relationships.

A Brief History of Approaches to Classification

Although naturalists had started to catalog life before 1758 (e.g., Seba, 1734–1765; Shaw, 1802), it is Carolus Linnaeus's binomial system and nested categories that are widely used today. The 10th edition of his *Systema Naturae* (1758), by convention and codified by the International Commission on Zoological Nomenclature (ICZN), is the earliest source of valid scientific names. Names introduced before it was published (e.g., *Vipera aquatica* Catesby, 1743, used in reference to the cottonmouth) are not accepted in the current nomenclatural system.

As new discoveries poured into European natural history collections during the eighteenth century, an organized method for cataloging this great diversity was needed. Linnaeus's system of binomial nomenclature, in which each species is assigned a two-word name (genus + specific epithet; e.g., *Agkistrodon contortrix*), provided a standardized approach for this task. This system not only assigns each species to a genus, but includes each genus within a family, each family within an order, and so forth up to the most recently recognized and most inclusive category, called a domain. Although the framework of this Linnaean hierarchy is straightforward, the way it has been used by biologists has varied considerably.

Because the Linnaean system of nomenclature originated more than 100 years before *On the Origin of Species* was published, its early application was not intended to summarize

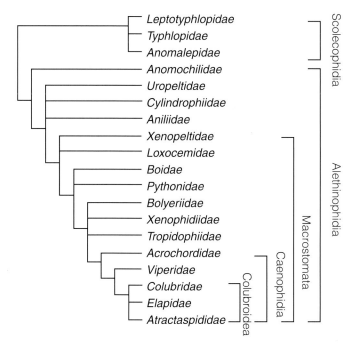

Fig. 230. Phylogenetic relationships among snake families, modified from Pough et al., 2001, and based on results obtained by Cundall et al. (1993), Kluge (1991), Cadle (1988), and Wallach and Günther (1998).

evolutionary history. The system functioned primarily as a sorting tool, a way to organize the rapidly growing knowledge of life's varied forms in a standardized language accessible to all scientists. With the dawn of evolutionary biology, the classification of life took on a new significance. Biologists began to use the classification system to summarize information about the history of life on Earth. For instance, species were placed in the same genus to indicate their close relationship in an evolutionary sense. George A. Boulenger (1920b) was among the first to recognize the importance of such an approach: "The time has come to rid ourselves of the empirical methods which have necessarily prevailed so long in zootaxy, and endeavor to group species as far as possible, according to their phylogenetic relationships." Although branching diagrams (e.g., Haeckel, 1866) were sometimes used, ideas about evolutionary relationships among and within taxa were often expressed by the order in which species, genera, and families were placed in checklists (e.g., Boulenger, 1893, 1894b, 1896b).

Three approaches to classification have dominated taxonomic efforts during the past 100 years. They vary with respect to the types of evolutionary information that are summarized in the classification scheme. The evolutionary taxonomists (e.g., Mayr, 1954; Simpson, 1961) believed that any named group should be the product of evolution; thus they emphasized distinctions between homologous and convergent characters, generally using shared homologous characters as evidence of close relationship. When assigning names, however, evolutionary taxonomists placed greater emphasis on phenotypic similarity than on monophyly (sensu Wiley, 1981). The phenetic school of taxonomy (e.g., Sneath and Sokal, 1973) attempted to develop objective methods of classification based on measures of overall similarity among species. In general, species with the most characters in common were classified into the same groups. The cladistic school of taxonomy (e.g., Hennig, 1966; Wiley, 1981) emphasizes the discovery and naming of true phylogenetic groups. This is accomplished through distinguishing homology

from homoplasy, but also through recognizing that only homologous characters derived within a group (synapomorphies) indicate relationship. Monophyly is emphasized over phenotypic similarity, so not only are named groups natural with respect to being the result of evolution, they are also natural in that they inlude all (not just some) of the descendants of a particular common ancestor. The consensus today is that only monophyletic groups should be assigned formal names so that our classification will provide an accurate description of evolutionary history. With the realization that knowledge of phylogeny and its description through classification are valuable came intensive efforts to develop methods for accurately recovering phylogenetic relationships (see below).

The classification of life is an ongoing process (most extant species have not even been named, much less studied phylogenetically), and our current classification is a conglomerate of taxa that have been distinguished and recognized by different criteria according to a variety of taxonomic philosophies. While the most recent revision of one group may have been undertaken by a cladistic taxonomist, another group may have been revised most recently by an evolutionary taxonomist. The phylogeny of many groups has never been studied at all, and the higher classification of such groups may be based on relatively limited information; thus, not every group currently recognized with a formal name is monophyletic. When paraphyly of a genus or other group is discovered, the classification is revised to achieve monophyly.

Despite the advances that cladistic taxonomy offers with respect to accurately describing nature through classification, not all phylogenetic knowledge can be summarized through use of the Linnaean hierarchy. Relationships within genera and higher categories are not fully recognized through this system, although categories such as subgenus and superorder may be used to identify additional monophyletic groups. A more serious problem with using the Linnaean hierarchy to construct a monophyletic classification is that there is no completely objective criterion for deciding how many monophyletic groups within a larger group ought to be assigned formal names. How inclusive or exclusive should a genus be? A family? An order? Questions about the genus category are especially important because the genus name is part of the species name. Is the Mexican jumping pitviper best known as *Bothrops nummifer*, *Porthidium nummifer*, or *Atropoides nummifer*?

Careful thought has been given to the intended significance of the genus category, and reviews may be found in de Queiroz and Gauthier, 1990, 1992, 1994; Harvey and Pagel, 1991; Mayr, 1982; Simpson, 1961; and Wiley, 1981. In recognizing genera, many authors have implicitly or explicitly used criteria based on convenient numbers of species, estimated divergence times of particular groups, or a sense of morphological or ecological cohesion. All authors acknowledge that there is a subjective element to determining genus boundaries and that this is an unnatural aspect of the category.

Because there is no natural genus boundary to be discovered through scientific method, alternative generic classifications cannot be evaluated objectively: there is more than one way to construct a monophyletic classification using Linnaean ranks. This in turn may lead to nomenclatural instability as alternative generic arrangements are proposed by different authors. There has been a recent proposal (de Queiroz and Gauthier, 1990, 1992, 1994) to discontinue the association of clade names with particular Linnaean ranks. Thus we can recognize the Reptilia for the common ancestor and all descendants of the group including turtles, lepidosaurians, crocodilians, and birds without having to subjectively select the appropriate rank for this group. Some texts have adopted this phylogenetic taxonomy approach in part (e.g., Pough et al., 1999, 2001), but a difficult problem is that the binomial system of naming species would have to change if the genus category were abandoned (Cantino et al., 1999; Graybeal, 1995). A new set of rules for biological nomenclature, called the PhyloCode, is currently being developed (Cantino and de Queiroz, 2000); if instituted, the code will have a major effect on how we classify life. No one has attempted to apply phylogenetic taxonomy to the groups covered in this book, nor has the PhyloCode been adopted at this time; thus Linnaean ranks and binomial nomenclature are retained.

Of What Value Are Phylogenetic Studies and Historically Accurate Classifications?

Despite occasional claims to the contrary, species are real, not artificial human constructs (see de Queiroz, 1998; Frost and Hillis, 1990). As lineages they are direct products of their own unique histories. The scientists who work to discover species and other more inclusive lineages are studying the history of life—an interesting and worthy endeavor in itself. But by indulging their curiosity with respect to life's history, these scientists are providing information that is needed by biologists in general and by many others as well.

Whether a wide-ranging group of organisms represents one species or several matters to anyone (from cell biologists to ecologists, from protein chemists to physiologists) who studies these organisms. Were one to study organisms with separate and distinct evolutionary histories as if they were part of the same (tokogenetic) lineage, interpretation of the results would be compromised.

Accurate species identification and classification are also critical to conservation activities. In order to rank different areas with respect to their biological importance (so that limited conservation funds can be allocated where they are most needed), we need to know how many species occur in these areas and also how much supraspecific variation and endemism there is. Without an accurate classification, there is no objective measure of biodiversity. Many endangered species have not yet been recognized with formal names, and this hidden diversity may be overlooked in the absence of taxonomic recognition (Chippindale et al., 2000; Gifford, 2002; Parkinson et al., 2000; Zamudio and Greene, 1997).

Assigning names to species and more inclusive groups facilitates communication among scientists, conservation workers, physicians, and anyone with an interest (practical or recreational) in natural history. As Klauber (1972:156–157) noted: "Naming things is a matter of definite practical value; it produces a basis whereby knowledge of the animals and their activities is so segregated and unified that different workers may apply their observations to the same creature and hence broaden our understanding of that creature. Matters of a real practical nature may be involved; for example, the several kinds of rattlesnakes differ in the toxicity of their venoms, and a recognition of the kind of rattler involved in a snake-bite accident may be of major importance in determining the best method of treatment to be afforded the victim." Spawls and Branch (1995) drew attention to a similar situation involving the saw-scaled vipers (*Echis*) of the Old World when they noted that "antivenom prepared from Iranian [saw-scaled vipers] is ineffective in treating bites from [saw-scaled] vipers in west Africa."

The development of accurate methods for determining the phylogenetic relationships among species is also of practical importance. Methods of phylogenetic reconstruction have proven to be important tools for epidemiologists; for example, the source of HIV infection of a number of people was verified through phylogenetic analysis (Hillis and Huelsenbeck, 1994). Also, the search for valuable natural products can be narrowed significantly when the nearest relatives of medically useful or economically important species are known. Any biological discipline involving comparisons among species (e.g., comparative physiology, comparative ethology) benefits from, and typically requires, knowledge of the phylogeny of the species being compared. Owing to their shared ancestry at some point in the tree of life, separate species cannot be treated as independent units in statistical analyses; their phylogenetic history must be accounted for if the conclusions from comparative studies are to be interpreted with confidence (Harvey and Pagel, 1991). Modern biogeographic studies also rely on phylogenetic information. Hillis et al. (1996) discussed additional applications of phylogenetic systematics.

Nomenclatural Stability

Anyone with incomplete knowledge of the reasons behind nomenclatural revision may view changing names as inconvenient and annoying—some sort of academic game played at the expense of the layperson who just wants to find a little information about the rattler in the backyard. Even some biologists make complaints of this nature. Stability of nomenclature is clearly an important goal, but if we want a biologically meaningful classification, one that actually describes real entities in nature—and this has been the consensus since 1859—then names will continue to change as knowledge grows.

Classification has been affected by changing taxonomic philosophies, but of even greater impact has been our incomplete knowledge of the planet's biodiversity. It is estimated that 10–100 million different species exist on Earth, yet we have named only about 1.7 million. Recognition of previously unknown species usually occurs in one of two ways: a "new" organism that no scientist has ever documented is discovered (e.g., Campbell, 1976; Harvey, 1994), or careful study of a known group reveals underestimated diversity (e.g., Parkinson et al., 2000; Silva, 2000, this volume; Zamudio and Greene, 1997). Also, as we learn more about relationships, some of the subjective grouping decisions (or decisions based on less data) of the past will be exposed as inconsistent with evolutionary history. Valuable references for tracing name changes of venomous snakes include the abbreviated synonymies in the species accounts in this book; extensive synonymies in McDiarmid et al., 1999; and a useful summary in Wüster et al., 1997a.

Methods for Recovering the Phylogenetic History of Life

Important information about phylogenetic methods and their philosophical underpinnings may be found in Avise et al., 1987; Felsenstein, 1981, 1982, 1988, 1993, 2004; Harvey and Pagel, 1991; Hillis et al., 1993; Lewis, 2001; Swofford et al., 1996; and Wiley, 1981. Freeman and Herron (2001) provide a useful discussion for the uninitiated. Phenetic methods use calculations based on pairwise similarity among taxa to generate a tree (in this case, a branching diagram depicting relative similarity), whereas the currently favored methods of phylogenetic reconstruction compare multiple trees using optimality criteria; the optimal tree based on the criterion used is taken to represent the best estimate for the phylogeny of the group. Additional methods can be employed to assess confidence in the accuracy of relationships depicted in optimal trees. Here we provide an abbreviated introduction to methods of phylogenetic reconstruction as background material for our discussion of venomous snake phylogeny. Instead of reviewing the technical details of these methods, we have provided literature citations for readers who would like to learn more about this complex but engrossing field.

Early Methods and the Development of Optimality Criteria

Many traditional discussions of phylogeny based relationships on certain "key characters" that were given more weight (implicitly or explicitly) by the investigator. Cope (1895) illustrated this approach when in reference to the hemipenes of snakes he stated: "In fact these organs exhibit a variety of ornamentation and armature beyond any part of the anatomy in the Ophidia, and I am satisfied that they furnish more important indication of near affinity than any other part of these reptiles yet examined. No one hereafter can be sure of the place of a serpent in the system until the hemipenis has been examined."

Owing to the phenomena of convergent evolution and evolutionary reversal, this approach to phylogenetic reconstruction led to a variety of errors through the years. Although this relatively simplistic approach has recovered some true phylogenetic groups (e.g., pitvipers as defined by facial pit, rattlesnakes as defined by rattle), a true test of relationships cannot be made by reference to a few characters. This has been known for decades, yet the key character approach has been used recently in pitviper systematics, often obfuscating relationships in the process (e.g., Schätti and Kramer, 1993; Schätti et al., 1990). Simultaneous analysis of multiple characters according to criteria derived from an objective and biologically realistic model of evolution is needed for accurate testing of phylogenetic hypotheses.

Two major advances in the search for evolutionary relationships were formalized in the methods of cladistic analysis (e.g., Farris, 1983; Hennig, 1966; Kluge and Farris, 1969; Wiley, 1981). The idea that only shared derived character states (synapomorphies) indicate evolutionary relationships was emphasized by Hennig (1966), although previous authors (e.g., see Harvey and Pagel, 1991:54) clearly appreciated this point as well. The cladists also developed an objective method for distinguishing homoplasy, a character state that changes more than once, from true synapomorphy, a shared derived character state, by applying the principle of parsimony to phylogenetic analysis. This principle states generally that the simplest explanation for a particular phenomenon is likely to be the correct one. In the context of phylogenetic analysis, the most parsimonious trees are those that require the fewest character state changes to explain the character state distributions among the taxa being studied.

If relationships are to be determined on the basis of synapomorphies, then characters must be polarized—derived states must be distinguished from ancestral ones. Several methods for determining character polarity have been proposed (e.g., ontogenetic criterion, paleontological method), but the most commonly used is outgroup comparison (Bryant, 1991; de Queiroz, 1985; Mabee, 2000; Wiley, 1981). An outgroup is a taxon known to be closely related to but not included within the group of taxa

for which relationships are trying to be determined (the ingroup). Character states present in the outgroup and in some ingroup members are interpreted as ancestral, and character states present in the ingroup but absent from the outgroup are interpreted as having been derived within the ingroup. In practice, phylogenetic software (e.g., PAUP*; Swofford, 1999) first finds the most parsimonious unrooted tree and then roots this tree with the outgroup.

When using maximum parsimony, exhaustive tree searches can be used to assess the tree length for every possible tree topology for the taxa under consideration. Exhaustive searches are not often used because they are too computationally intensive when large numbers of taxa are involved. The branch-and-bound option (Hendy and Penny, 1982) does not search all possible tree topologies but is guaranteed to find the most parsimonious tree or trees. Heuristic tree searches are not guaranteed to find the shortest tree, but they are much more computationally efficient and make possible parsimony analyses of data sets with many taxa.

Maximum likelihood methods in phylogenetic analysis were first attempted by Cavalli-Sforza and Edwards (1967) and were later developed for use with nucleotide sequence data (Felsenstein, 1981, 1993) and amino acid sequence data (Kishino et al., 1990). These methods are generally much more computationally intensive than parsimony methods, and only with recent advances in computer technology has their use become more widespread. Most recent studies of venomous snake phylogeny based on DNA sequence data have employed both maximum parsimony and maximum likelihood methods. Useful reviews of likelihood methods may be found in Huelsenbeck and Crandall, 1997, and Swofford et al., 1996; for discussion of differences between parsimony and likelihood methods, see Felsenstein, 1978; Hendy and Penny, 1989; Huelsenbeck, 1995; and Steel et al., 1993.

Maximum likelihood methods identify phylogenetic trees that have the greatest probability of producing the observed data given a particular model of evolution. In order to be computationally tractable the earliest models (Jukes and Cantor, 1969) had to be simple, but there has been a steady progression in the introduction of more realistic models (Felsenstein, 1981; Hasegawa et al., 1985; Lanave et al., 1984). Bayesian probability calculations are making the application of maximum likelihood much more computationally efficient (Larget and Simon, 1999; Lewis, 2001), but this approach to phylogenetic reconstruction is so new that it has not yet been applied in published studies of venomous snake phylogeny. The maximum likelihood approach has been developed most extensively for nucleotide sequence data, but a few recent studies have applied likelihood methods to the study of morphological evolution (e.g., Pagel, 1999).

When more than one equally optimal tree is found, as is often the case, these can be summarized in a strict consensus tree (Sokal and Rohlf, 1981), which retains all clades held in common among the optimal trees. Branching arrangements that conflict in two or more optimal trees are collapsed into polytomies in strict consensus trees. Fifty percent majority-rule consensus trees depict all relationships recovered in 50% or more of the optimal trees, and may be used to depict the results of nonparametric bootstrap analyses (see below).

Assessing the Accuracy of Phylogenetic Trees

When a particular phylogenetic tree is found to be most parsimonious, or most likely, that does not mean that all branches within that tree are equally well supported by the data, so numerous methods have been developed to help assess confidence in different regions of phylogenetic trees (see Lee, 2000, for a review of many of these methods). Those that have been used in the study of venomous snake phylogeny are the nonparametric bootstrap (Felsenstein, 1985), the decay index (Bremer, 1988), the jackknife monophyly index (Lanyon, 1985; Siddall, 1995), relative likelihood support (Jermiin et al., 1997), functional ingroup-outgroup evaluations (Fu and Murphy, 1997; Murphy et al., 1983; Watrous and Wheeler, 1981), and nodal-specific permutation tail probabilities for character covariation (Fu and Murphy, 1999; Peres-Neto and Marques, 2000). The most commonly used of these methods has been the nonparametric bootstrap, and Hillis and Bull (1993) suggested that clades supported by bootstrap proportions of 70 or greater are likely to be accurate. Use of the g1 statistic was proposed as a means of testing whether a data set contains phylogenetic signal or only random noise (Hillis and Huelsenbeck, 1992).

Data Used in Phylogenetic Analysis

Anatomy provided the main source of evidence in early studies of evolutionary relationships (e.g., Cope, 1895), and it continued to be of primary importance during the early years of cladistic analysis (e.g., Kluge, 1993; Kluge and Farris, 1969). Although phylogenetic studies based on molecular data now greatly outnumber those based on anatomy, anatomical data continue to be a valuable source of information about phylogeny (Hillis, 1987). Examples of recent applications of morphological data in venomous snake phylogenetics include studies by Crother et al. (1992), Gutberlet (1998a), Gutberlet and Harvey (2002), Slowinski (1995), and Werman (1992). Wiens (2000) edited a book addressing the use of morphological data in phylogenetic analysis.

Data from scalation (Campbell and Lamar, 1989; Klauber, 1972), hemipenis morphology (Dowling and Savage, 1960), osteology (Brattstrom, 1964; Kardong, 1990; Klauber, 1972), and color pattern (Campbell and Lamar, 1989; Klauber, 1972) have been used most often is snake systematics, but musculature (Kardong, 1990) and visceral anatomy (Gans and Gaunt, 1998; Klauber, 1972) characters have also been useful. Any morphological character that varies (i.e., has two or more states) among members of the ingroup may be parsimony-informative and can be used to reconstruct relationships (see Smith and Gutberlet, 2001, and references therein). For example, two character states can be defined for the rattle (present or absent); presence of a rattle is a synapomorphy that contributes support for the monophyly of rattlesnakes. Additional information about the rattle (e.g., interspecific variation in its proportions) could be used in a study of relationships within the rattlesnake clade.

The recently acquired ability to amplify and determine the nucleotide sequences for specific genes has had a dramatic impact on phylogenetic systematics. Many studies now use DNA sequences to reconstruct phylogenetic relationships, and some of the most comprehensive studies of venomous snake phylogeny have taken advantage of this technological advance (e.g., Douglas et al., 2002; Murphy et al., 2002; Parkinson et al., 2002; Slowinski and Keogh, 2000; Wüster et al., 2002a).

Other types of data less frequently used in phylogenetic analyses include allozymes (e.g., Barker, 1992); venom proteins (e.g., Minton, 1956); number, shape, and size of chromosomes (e.g., Cole, 1990); and behavior (Halloy et al., 1998). The

microstructure of scale surfaces (known variously as epidermal microstructure, scale microornamentation, or microdermatoglyphics) has proven informative in resolving some relationships within squamate reptiles (e.g., Harvey and Gutberlet, 1995, 2000; Irish et al., 1988; Leydig, 1872; R. M. Price, 1982), including in pitvipers (e.g., Estol, 1981; Gutberlet, 1998b; Hoge and Souza Santos, 1953; Picado T., 1931b; see below).

The collection of varied data and the application of sophisticated analytical methods have greatly enhanced our understanding of the diversity of New World venomous snakes. From rainforests to prairies, from the highest mountains to low deserts, pitvipers and coralsnakes are integral components of American ecosystems; and the history of these snakes—the changes that have made them prominent elements of the New World fauna—is being accurately reconstructed. Systematists today know much more than our predecessors (see also http://tolweb.org/tree), and our confidence in what we know is higher than ever. Yet questions remain, and modern naturalists have ample opportunity for discovery.

PHYLOGENETIC RELATIONSHIPS OF VENOMOUS SNAKES

Five major groups of snakes (including 31 families; McDiarmid et al., 1999) are recognized (see Fig. 230). The Scolecophidia, often known as blindsnakes and wormsnakes, diverged from the ancestor of other snakes (Alethinophidia) very early in serpent history. The venomous snakes are members of the Caenophidia, a derived group within the Macrostomata. The Caenophidia includes the Acrochordidae, Atractaspididae, Colubridae, Elapidae, and Viperidae. The relationships among these five families are partially resolved: the Acrochordidae is basal to all other families, and the Viperidae, which includes the New World pitvipers, is basal to the remaining families, which make up the Colubroidea. Relationships within the Colubroidea, including the phylogenetic position of the Elapidae, are unresolved. Dangerously venomous snakes are found in all caenophidian families other than the Acrochordidae, but the Elapidae and Viperidae are the most notorious for their dangerous venoms.

The venom delivery apparatus of snakes is diverse and has played a prominent role in their classification. It is convenient to refer to snakes as either "front-fanged" or "rear-fanged" depending on whether their fangs are positioned in front of or behind the remaining maxillary teeth. Both types of fangs evolved independently several times among advanced snakes (Cadle, 1988; Heise et al., 1995; Kardong, 1980b; Knight and Mindell, 1994; Vidal et al., 2000). Snakes with enlarged, grooved, posterior maxillary teeth are referred to as opisthoglyphous (Greek *opisthen*, "behind"; *glyphis*, "knife"). Venom produced by Duvernoy's gland evolved early among colubrids in which the opisthoglyphous condition is found. Among the dangerously venomous snakes described in this book, venom is delivered by the first—and usually only—maxillary tooth. Developmental and morphological evidence suggests that this fang represents a rear maxillary tooth whose position has been shifted forward (McDowell, 1968). Coralsnakes and seasnakes have proteroglyphous (Greek *proteros*, "earlier"; *glyphis*, "knife") dentition: their fangs are relatively short and remain in a vertical position when the mouth is closed. Vipers have solenoglyphous (Greek *solen*, "pipe" or "channel"; *glyphis*, "fang") dentition: their fangs are the only teeth on highly mobile maxillae. At rest, the fangs of viperids lie against the roof of the mouth and rotate through about 120 degrees during protraction (Cundall, 1983). Mobile maxillae with folding fangs also evolved independently in stiletto snakes (Atractaspididae). Discussions and useful references on phylogenetic relationships among the snake families may be found in Greene, 1997; McDiarmid et al., 1999; Pough et al., 2001; and Zug et al., 2001.

The Phylogenetic Position of *Pelamis* and New World Coralsnakes within the Elapidae

Most taxonomists believe that the proteroglyphs form a natural group, and all proteroglyphs are usually placed in a single family, the Elapidae; however, elapid monophyly has been challenged in the recent past. In an often-cited dissertation, Savitzky (1978) argued that the New World coralsnakes are more closely related to the South American colubrids *Apostolepis* and *Elapomorphus* than to other elapids. His proposal was later challenged on the basis of immunological (Cadle and Sarich, 1981) and morphological (McCarthy, 1985) data. McDowell (1968) transferred the African genus *Homoroselaps* to the Colubridae. Based on a phylogenetic analysis of morphological data, Underwood and Kochva (1993) returned *Homoroselaps* to the Elapidae and remarked that they considered *Homoroselaps* to be a basal lineage.

Although their close affinities with terrestrial proteroglyphs have not been in question, the classification of seasnakes has long been in a state of flux. The evolution of a marine existence occurred at least twice within the Elapidae, and seasnakes do not form a natural group: *Laticauda* and its relatives (collectively referred to as laticaudines) are not closely related to *Pelamis*, *Hydrophis*, and their relatives (collectively, hydrophiines). In older classifications, the laticaudines and hydrophiines were placed in their own subfamily (the Hydrophiinae of Boulenger, 1896b) or family (the Hydrophidae and Hydrophiidae, respectively, of Cope, 1860a, and Smith, 1926). Although he retained Boulenger's subfamilial classification, Underwood (1967) expressed some skepticism about the monophyly of the Hydrophiinae.

McDowell (1967, 1969, 1970, 1972), who worked with Australo-Papuan species, concluded that elapids fall into two groups: "palatine erectors" and "palatine draggers." So named because the palatine is erected along with the maxilla during protraction of the palate (McDowell, 1969), the palatine erectors include *Laticauda* and the African, American, and Asian elapids (Fig. 231). In the palatine draggers, the palatine acts as an anterior extension of the pterygoid and remains horizontal even when the maxilla is erected. This group includes the hydrophiines and the terrestrial Australo-Papuan elapids. McDowell's conclusions were later formalized by Smith et al. (1977), who retained *Laticauda* in the Elapidae and subdivided the Hydrophiidae into two subfamilies: Hydrophiinae and Oxyuraninae.

With the advent of phylogenetic methods, McDowell's conclusions have been tested empirically (Cadle and Gorman, 1981; Guo et al., 1987; Mao et al., 1977, 1978, 1983; McCarthy, 1986; Minton and da Costa, 1975; Murphy, 1988; Schwaner et al., 1985; Slowinski and Keogh, 2000). These studies support McDowell's recognition of two subdivisions within the Elapidae, but they do not support his contention that *Laticauda* is closely related to the African, Asian, and American species. Seasnakes still do not form a monophyletic group, however. Both laticaudines and hydrophiines are related to Australian palatine draggers (Davidson and Dennis, 1990; Dufton and Hider, 1983; Keogh,

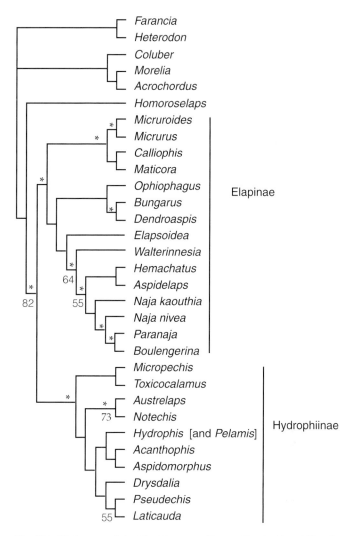

Fig. 231. Phylogeny of the Elapidae according to Slowinski and Keogh (2000). Asterisks indicate clades present in both maximum likelihood and parsimony analyses. Although these authors did not include *Pelamis* in their study, this taxon almost certainly would be placed in the same position as the closely related *Hydrophis*.

1998; Keogh et al., 1998; Slowinski et al., 1997; Slowinski and Keogh, 2000; Tamiya, 1985). A taxonomy consistent with these results is that proposed by Slowinski et al. (1997): Elapidae is divisible into the subfamilies Elapinae Boie, including the terrestrial Asian, African, and American genera; and Hydrophiinae Fitzinger, including all marine genera and the terrestrial Australo-Papuan and Melanesian genera (Fig. 231). To achieve a natural taxonomy, *Homoroselaps* is excluded from the Elapinae. An older taxonomy divides the Elapidae into six subfamilies (McDowell, 1987); however, the monophyly of some of these subfamilies is suspect (David and Ineich, 1999; Heatwole and Cogger, 1993; Saint Girons, 1989).

Phylogenetic Relationships and Classification of the Coralsnakes

Historically, New World coralsnakes were lumped with several Old World species in Schneider's (1801) genus *Elaps*, later defined (Wagler, 1830), among other characters, by the absence of maxillary teeth behind the fang. Günther (1859a) published the first review of these snakes and partitioned *Elaps*, referring Old World species to *Callophis* (=*Calliophis* Gray and also including species now in *Maticora*), *Vermicella*, and *Poecilophis*, and restricting *Elaps* to the New World. *Elaps* was then used exclusively for New World coralsnakes by subsequent nineteenth-century authors such as Giorgio Jan, George A. Boulenger, and Edward D. Cope.

The ultimate fate of the genus *Elaps* reveals much about the conventions of zoological nomenclature. Today, the rules regarding the description of genera are explicit (ICZN, 2000b). A "type-species" is designated for any new genus. If the genus is found to be polyphyletic (i.e., not natural) and is later partitioned, the generic name remains associated with the type-species. In the early 1800s, authors frequently did not designate a type-species. Schneider (1801) applied the genus *Elaps* to a diverse array of snakes including several colubrids, *Micrurus*, and several Old World elapids. The type species of *Elaps* was subsequently designated *Coluber lemniscatus* Linnaeus by the ICZN. However, *Elaps* would be suppressed; *Micrurus* Wagler (1824), with *M. spixii* the type-species by monotypy, is the name currently accepted and is Official Generic Name No. 2144 according to ICZN Opinion 1201. The issue of using *Micrurus* versus *Elaps* was discussed by Amaral (1926a).

Attempts to partition the large genus *Micrurus* began in the early twentieth century. Schmidt (1928a) erected the monotypic genus *Micruroides* for the Sonoran coralsnake on the basis of its solid maxillary teeth positioned behind the fangs. Later (1937), he erected *Leptomicrurus* to accommodate *M. collaris* and *M. narduccii*. At that time, Cope's (1870) *Elaps scutiventris* was considered to be synonymous with *L. narduccii* (Boulenger, 1896b). Initially, both genera were widely accepted, but the validity of *Leptomicrurus* would be questioned by future authors (Campbell and Lamar, 1989; Romano, 1972).

The sister group of New World coralsnakes occurs in eastern Asia and most likely belongs to *Maticora* or *Calliophis* (Fig. 231). Like their relatives in the New World, these Asian snakes are brightly colored; some also have rings, and they are frequently called coralsnakes. Based on morphology McDowell (1968) predicted a close relationship between the Old and New World coralsnakes, and this was later confirmed by molecular data (Keogh, 1998; Slowinski and Keogh, 2000). The Old and New World coralsnakes are so similar to one another that Slowinski and Boundy (unpublished data reported in Slowinski and Keogh, 2000) found no compelling morphological evidence linking *Micruroides* and *Micrurus* to the exclusion of Asian species. However, monophyly of the New World species is supported by molecular characters (Keogh, 1998; Slowinski and Keogh, 2000).

In sharp contrast to the phylogeny of pitvipers, the evolutionary history of New World coralsnakes has received much less attention and remains poorly resolved. Investigators frequently point out that coralsnakes are conservative morphologically and thus provide researchers with few characters for phylogenetic analysis, but this assertion is somewhat exaggerated. Although molecular data show promise for overcoming any dearth of morphological characters, many species are exceedingly rare and live in countries with restrictive laws prohibiting the collection and export of biological materials.

The relationships of coralsnakes have been the subject of four studies (one unpublished). Roze and Bernal-Carlo (1988) provided the first explicit statements about coralsnake relationships. Their phylogenetic hypothesis (Fig. 232A) divides *Micrurus* into four groups: species with rings arrayed in tricolored monads (e.g., Pl. 54), Mexican species with tricolored triads (e.g., Pls. 195–197), Central and South American triadal species

(e.g., Pl. 224), and a *Micrurus mipartitus* group (e.g., Pls. 198–206) are each monophyletic, with the *M. mipartitus* group being the most basal of the four. *Leptomicrurus* is recognized as a distinct sister genus to *Micrurus*, and *Micruroides* is sister to all other New World coralsnakes. Roze and Bernal-Carlo (1988) based their analysis on 27 characters of morphology, immunology, and paleontology, but they did not explicitly describe the methods they used to evaluate these characters.

Slowinski's (1995) analysis (Fig. 232B) used clearly defined methods and also recovered seemingly monophyletic groups of monadal long-tailed and triadal short-tailed coralsnakes. In his hypothesis, however, *Leptomicrurus* is nested within *Micrurus* as a basal lineage of the triadal clade. *Micrurus mipartitus* is sister to the monadal coralsnakes. In addition, some species of Central and South American coralsnakes with a triad pattern appear to belong to the monadal clade. With the exception of *M. surinamensis*, the species of the "triadal" clade have short tails constituting 4.0–10.8% of the total length in males, and the species of the "monadal" clade have long tails constituting 10.0–18.5% of the total length in males (Roze, 1996: table 2). *Micruroides* (6.8–9.1% in males), *Leptomicrurus* (5.5–7.3% in males), and the *M. mipartitus* group (6.5–10.2% in males) also have short tails.

The short-tailed species share a slightly bilobed, stout, and short hemipenis that is fewer than 11 subcaudal scales in length (Roze, 1996). In addition to the species depicted in Figure 232B, Slowinski (1995) suggested that *M. ancoralis*, *M. decoratus*, *M. filiformis*, *M. frontifasciatus* (=*M. serranus* and *M. lemniscatus*), *M. hemprichii*, *M. isozonus*, *M. pyrrhocryptus*, *M. rondonianus* (=*M. hemprichii*), *M. sangilensis*, and *M. tschudii* also belong to this clade because of their similar coloration, short tails, and distribution. However, *M. sangilensis* has a long hemipenis and tail (15.5–18.7% of the total length in males; Roze, 1996), suggesting that its affinities lie with the monadal species. The short-tailed group also contains *M. altirostris*, *M. baliocoryphus*, *M. brasiliensis*, *M. diana* (all considered synonyms or subspecies of *M. frontalis* in 1995), *M. meridensis* (considered a subspecies of *M. dissoleucus* in 1995), and *M. serranus* (undescribed and confused with *M. frontifasciatus* in 1995; Harvey et al., 2003). The short-tailed triadal coralsnakes are restricted to South America and with the exception of *M. tschudii* have cis-Andean distributions.

At first, the placement of *Micrurus surinamensis* in the short-tailed group seems incongruous because the tail of male *M. surinamensis* is 11.2–13.1% of the total length (Roze, 1996). A primitive (based on outgroup comparisons) trait in coralsnakes, a short tail is an adaptation for burrowing; extreme reduction of tail length characterizes exclusively fossorial genera such as *Apostolepis*, *Calamaria*, and *Uropeltis*. The long tail of the monadal coralsnakes accommodates a long hemipenis. Although *M. surinamensis* has a long tail, its short hemipenis establishes its position in the short-tailed group. The long tail of this species evolved independently and may represent an adaptation for aquatic habits.

With the short-tailed triadal species, *Leptomicrurus* shares a slightly bilobed, stout, and short hemipenis (see Fig. 16) and a cis-Andean distribution. The posterior trunk vertebrae of *Leptomicrurus* are longer than those of *Micrurus* and *Micruroides* (Roze and Bernal-Carlo, 1988). The vertebral hypophyses of *Leptomicrurus* and *Micrurus* differ in two ways (Roze and Bernal-Carlo, 1988): the hypophysis is weakly convex and does not extend as far as the posterior condyle in *Leptomicrurus*, whereas the hypophysis is sigmoidal and extends beyond the posterior condyle in *Micrurus*. Savitzky (1978) described the venom gland of *Leptomicrurus* and *M. mipartitus* as being strongly inflected,

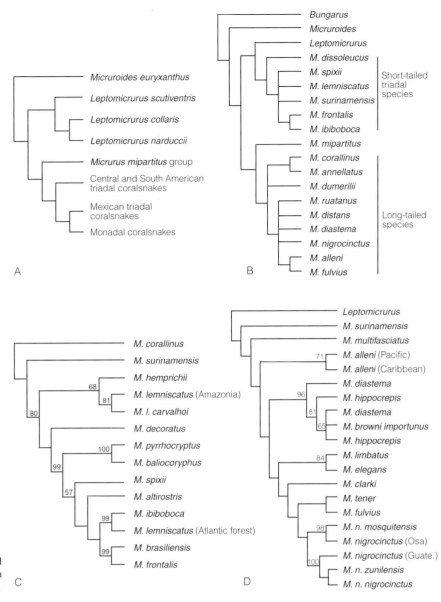

Fig. 232. Phylogenetic hypotheses of (A) Roze and Bernal-Carlo, 1988; (B) Slowinski, 1995; (C) Jorge da Silva and Sites, 2001; and (D) Sasa and Smith, 2001.

an observation confirmed by Roze and Bernal-Carlo (1988). Slowinski (1995), however, argued that the venom gland of *M. mipartitus* is similar to that of other *Micrurus* and that the more strongly inflected venom gland of *Leptomicrurus* is unique to that genus. In *Micrurus*, the first pair of infralabials usually separates the mental from the chinshields. Contact between the mental and chinshields (see Fig. 9) occurs as a polymorphism at low frequencies in several coralsnakes (Harvey et al., 2003; Romano, 1972; Roze and Bernal-Carlo, 1988; Schmidt, 1936a). Nonetheless, fixation (i.e., presence in 100% of specimens) of mental-chinshield contact is a synapomorphy of *Leptomicrurus*.

The clade of long-tailed species is supported by two derived hemipenial characters: presence of a hypertrophied basal pocket and terminal awns on the hemipenial lobes (Slowinski, 1995). Arguably, the long tail is another synapomorphy of the group, and tail length accounts for 10.0–18.5% of the total length of males of these species (Roze, 1996: table 2). Several species of this group extend into Amazonian South America, but the group is most diverse in Central America. To the long-tailed clade Slowinski (1995) assigned *Micrurus albicinctus, M. alleni, M. annellatus, M. averyi, M. bernadi, M. bocourti, M. bogerti, M. browni, M. catamayensis, M. clarki, M. corallinus, M. diastema, M.*

distans, M. dumerilii, M. elegans, M. ephippifer, M. fulvius, M. hippocrepis, M. langsdorffi, M. laticollaris, M. latifasciatus, M. limbatus, M. margaritiferus, M. mertensi, M. nebularis, M. nigrocinctus, M. ornatissimus, M. peruvianus, M. petersi, M. proximans, M. psyches, M. putumayensis, M. ruatanus, M. steindachneri, M. stewarti, M. stuarti, and *M. waehnerorum (=M. albicinctus).* Slowinski (1995) described an everted hemipenis of *M. annellatus* (USNM 193814) that extended for only 4 subcaudals, but as he suspected, the hemipenis of *M. annellatus* is usually longer. In situ, the hemipenis of this species may be 20 subcaudal scales in length (Harvey et al., 2003) and is normally about 17 subcaudals long (Roze, 1996). Not appearing in the list above are several species that were considered in 1995 to be subspecies of *M. psyches* (*M. medemi, M. paraensis,* and *M. remotus*) and *M. fulvius* (*M. tener*). *Micrurus pachecogili,* described recently (Campbell, 2000), also belongs to this group. As we pointed out earlier, *M. sangilensis* was assigned to the short-tailed triadal clade by Slowinski (1995).

Most species in the long-tailed group are tricolored with the rings arrayed in monads; however, triads appear in *M. elegans* and *M. laticollaris* in Mexico and Central America and in *M. bocourti, M. catamayensis, M. circinalis, M. dumerilii,* and *M. sangilensis* in South America. These species differ from the short-tailed triadal species in several important ways: (1) in addition to being longer, their tails are bicolored, whereas the triadal pattern extends onto the tail in the short-tailed species; (2) the accessory rings are often poorly developed; (3) some of these species, such as *M. circinalis* and *M. dumerilii*, are polymorphic for the triadal pattern, with some individuals or populations having monads and others having triads.

The *Micrurus mipartitus* group shares with the long-tailed group a strongly bilobed and slender hemipenis with lobes that are distinct from the base. Unfortunately, several potential synapomorphies of the group are known for only some of the species. Reduction of the lateral fold of the basal pocket is a derived feature of *M. mipartitus*. The venom of *M. multifasciatus* differs chemically from that of other coralsnakes (Stevan and Seligmann, 1970), but characteristics of the venom of other species in this group are unknown. Slowinski (1995) referred to a *Micrurus mipartitus* "group" but did not explicitly assign any species to it. However, Roze and Bernal-Carlo (1988) included *M. mipartitus*, *M. multifasciatus*, *M. multiscutatus*, and *M. spurrelli* in this group. The species of this group are more elongate and slender than most other coralsnakes, and all have a bicolored dorsal pattern and a relatively short tail. Although *M. stewarti* has a similar distribution and is also bicolored, it belongs to the monadal clade because it has a long tail (13.6–15.6% of the total length in male *M. stewarti* versus 6.5–10.2% in males of the other species) and fewer ventral scales (197–207 in males compared with more than 232 in all other species except *M. mipartitus*, which has 197–284).

Slowinski's (1995) hypothesis indicates that recognition of *Leptomicrurus* renders *Micrurus* paraphyletic. If names were assigned to the short- and long-tailed clades, a taxonomy consistent with Slowinski's hypothesis would be achieved. Before any taxonomic revisions are attempted, however, it would be informative to further test this hypothesis by including additional outgroup taxa and additional characters. *Calliophis* and *Maticora* are the sister groups of New World coralsnakes, and consideration of these genera may influence character polarization. Characters of the posterior trunk vertebrae (Roze and Bernal-Carlo, 1988) have been shown to be informative. Also, McDowell (1986) and Roze and Bernal-Carlo (1988) reported interspecific differences in morphology of the *m. levator anguli oris* (terminology of McDowell, 1986; Fig. 233). Fibers of the *m.*

levator anguli oris attach directly to the quadrate in *M. miparti-tus* and *Leptomicrurus*, whereas they arise from the surface of the medialis in other coralsnakes (Roze and Bernal-Carlo, 1988; Roze, 1996). The shared unique morphology for this muscle in *M. mipartitus* and *Leptomicrurus* seems to contradict the placement of these taxa in Slowinski's (1995) phylogeny. Scrocchi (1991) described the osteology of 13 species, including short- and long-tailed species, *M. surinamensis*, and *Leptomicrurus*. Although he found the cranial osteology to be relatively conservative, he nonetheless identified seven potentially informative characters, two of which are multistate. Additional osteological information is summarized in Roze, 1996. Future studies might consider coding variation in scale surface morphology (described in Roze, 1996; and Roze and Bernal-Carlo, 1987), cephalic color pattern, and presence/absence of supracloacal keels. Recent advances in cladistic methodology (e.g., Smith and Gutberlet, 2001) allow researchers to use meristic (e.g., ventral counts), continuous (e.g., tail lengths), and polymorphic (e.g., prefrontal-supralabial contact; Harvey et al., 2003) morphological data. Minimally, a total evidence approach to the phylogeny of coralsnakes should include Roze and Bernal-Carlo's (1988), Scrocchi's (1991), and McDowell's (1986) characters.

Slowinski's (1995) analysis is the only comprehensive phylogenetic treatment of *Micrurus*. Recent studies have clarified relationships among the short-tailed (Jorge da Silva and Sites, 2001) and long-tailed (Sasa and Smith, 2001) clades. Jorge da Silva and Sites (2001) generated a data set of allozymes and mtDNA sequences for 11 species of short-tailed coralsnakes. The monadal species *M. corallinus* was used as an outgroup. Maximum parsimony and maximum likelihood analyses revealed several common patterns about short-tailed coralsnake relationships (Fig. 232C). *Micrurus surinamensis* is the most basal member of the group analyzed, but *M. tschudii*, one of the most divergent species of the group, was not included in the study. It may well occupy a more basal position than *M. surinamensis*. The *M. frontalis* complex (Jorge da Silva and Sites, 1999) is not monophyletic; however, *M. pyrrhocryptus* and *M. baliocoryphus* are sister species, as are *M. frontalis* and *M. brasiliensis*. In all analyses, *M. lemniscatus* appears to be polyphyletic. Populations from the Atlantic coast appear to be closely related to *M. ibiboboca*, whereas *M. lemniscatus* from

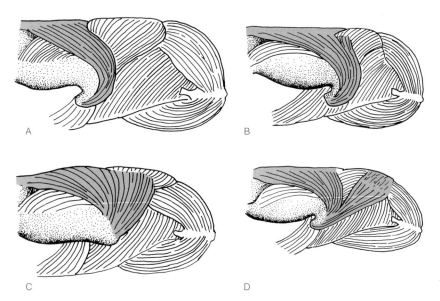

Fig. 233. Pattern of the *m. levator anguli oris* in (A) *Micrurus tschudii*, Medina specimen; (B) *M. bernadi*, AMNH 76432; (C) *M. ibiboboca*, ZMB 3020; and (D) *M. filiformis*, Basel 2318. Adapted from McDowell, 1986:386 (fig. 7).

Amazonia and *M. l. carvalhoi* appear to be closely related to *M. hemprichii*.

A still unpublished study (Sasa and Smith, 2001) of the long-tailed species raises similar questions about the validity of several taxa. Using the ND4 gene, Sasa and Smith (2001) generated a phylogeny of several Central American species and subspecies (Fig. 232D). Some results of their study bear mention. *Micrurus browni* and *M. hippocrepis* are nested within a clade of *M. diastema*, suggesting that these three taxa may all be the same species. The remaining species appear to be monophyletic, including the polytypic *M. nigrocinctus*: its subspecies form a clade and are the sister group of the harlequin and Texas coralsnakes (*M. fulvius* and *M. tener*). Although few South American species were included, the results do not conflict with

Slowinski's conclusions that (1) the long-tailed species are monophyletic; (2) the *M. mipartitus* group, represented by *M. multifasciatus*, is the sister group of the long-tailed coralsnakes; and (3) the short-tailed species, represented by *M. surinamensis*, are the sister group of the *M. mipartitus* group and the long-tailed species. Sasa and Smith (2001) used *Leptomicrurus* to root the tree, and its position in Figure 232D should not be taken as confirmation of Roze and Bernal-Carlo's (1988) hypothesis.

Phylogeny of the Coralsnakes: A Consensus

Relatively few species are common to the four phylogenetic hypotheses discussed above. Figure 234 offers a working hypothesis of coralsnake relationships based on these studies.

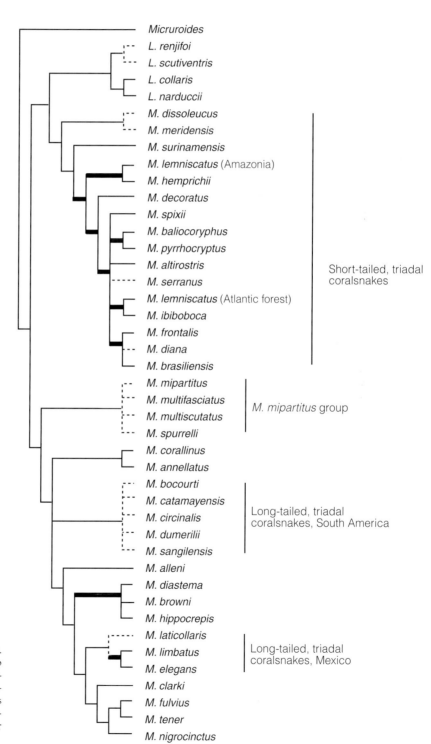

Fig. 234. Our "consensus" phylogeny of coralsnakes. Heavy lines indicate internodes with high bootstrap support. Narrow lines represent branches and internodes recovered in earlier phylogenetic analyses of coralsnakes. Species placed on the phylogeny by dashed lines have not been included in modern phylogenetic analyses; their placement is strictly hypothetical (see text for justification) and requires testing in future analyses.

The phylogenies of Slowinski (1995) and Jorge da Silva and Sites (2001) are not in conflict, and the topology of the clade of short-tailed triadal species is constrained by these studies. Internodes represented by heavy lines have high bootstrap support and were recovered in equally weighted maximum parsimony and maximum likelihood analyses. Narrower lines represent branches and internodes present in the four phylogenetic hypotheses of coralsnakes. We have placed a few species (dashed lines) on the phylogeny based on our best guess about their relationships. Twenty-four species could not be placed on the phylogeny with any degree of confidence.

Separate parsimony and likelihood analyses (Jorge da Silva and Sites, 2001) each completely resolved the large apical polytomy within the short-tailed triadal clade; however, the topologies of these different analyses are largely incongruent. In the consensus phylogeny we collapsed internodes where the parsimony and likelihood analyses are in conflict and retained groups recovered in both analyses. We added two species to this apical polytomy. *Micrurus diana* is closely related to (Jorge da Silva and Sites, 2001), if not synonymous with (Harvey et al., 2003), *M. brasiliensis* and *M. frontalis*. A close relationship between Atlantic Forest *M. lemniscatus* and the *M. frontalis/M. brasiliensis* clade (Jorge da Silva and Sites, 2001) is interesting because Harvey et al. (2003) considered *M. serranus* to be most similar to these species. *Micrurus meridensis* was originally thought to be a subspecies of *M. dissoleucus*, and these species share a seemingly derived character: the single black nape ring. *Micrurus ancoralis*, *M. isozonus*, *M. filiformis*, and *M. tschudii* belong to the short-tailed triadal clade but were left off the tree because it is not clear whether they belong to the apical polytomy or to more basal groups.

The topology of *Leptomicrurus* is that presented by Roze and Bernal-Carlo (1988). These authors did not explain why they thought *L. collaris* and *L. narduccii* are more closely related to one another than either is to *L. scutiventris*. In terms of osteology and coloration, *L. narduccii* seems more similar to *L. scutiventris* (see species accounts, this volume). Although *L. renjifoi* and *L. scutiventris* differ in coloration, they have almost identical patterns of scalation, and Lamar and Sasa (2003) suggested that they are closely related.

Among the long-tailed species, 20 species cannot be placed on the phylogeny. The triadal pattern appears to have evolved three times among coralsnakes. Sasa and Smith (2001) found strong support for a close relationship between *Micrurus elegans* and the bicolored species *M. limbatus*. Slowinski (1995) did not find a close relationship between *M. dumerilii* and the Central American long-tailed species. *Micrurus dumerilii* and 4 other species have mostly trans-Andean distribution patterns in northern and western South America and Trinidad. Aside from the Mexican triadal species, these species are the only other long-tailed species with triads. Based on their distribution and shared triadal pattern, they appear to form a natural group.

Historical Biogeography of the Coralsnakes

Although many branches in our consensus phylogeny of New World coralsnakes are poorly supported, the diversification of coralsnakes can be interpreted as the result of past geologic and climatic events. In the absence of a more robust phylogeny containing most species of coralsnakes, however, any biogeographic interpretations are necessarily tentative.

Several authors have suggested that the New World coralsnakes arose from Old World ancestors in the early Miocene or late Oligocene (Cadle, 1983; Cadle and Sarich, 1981; Mao et al., 1983); the presence of coralsnakes in the New World by the middle Miocene is confirmed by fossil vertebrae from Nebraska (Holman, 1977). An extinct elapid from the middle Miocene of Europe was described as a species of *Micrurus* (*M. gallicus* Rage and Holman, 1984); however, this species is known only from vertebrae. Rage and Holman (1984) did not specify their means of identification; they may not have compared the vertebrae of their new species with vertebrae of Asian genera such as *Calliophis* and *Maticora*.

Distribution patterns of the various clades in the consensus phylogeny (Fig. 234) can be reduced to the area cladogram presented in Figure 235. This cladogram poses an immediate and puzzling question: How is it possible that the sister species of *Micruroides* occurred in South America when *Micruroides* is currently known only from the western United States and northern Mexico? Knowing only that *Micruroides* is the most primitive coralsnake, one might expect an "out of North America" diversification of coralsnakes. Under such a hypothesis, the most basal groups are predicted to be in North America and Central America, and the South American species are predicted to have reached that continent via the Panamanian isthmus. One would expect *M. fulvius* or *M. tener* to be the closest relative of *Micruroides*. However, these two species, in their apical position within the long-tailed clade, are about as distantly related to *Micruroides* as possible. Surprisingly, the phylogeny of coralsnakes seems to support an "out of South America" pattern of diversification.

South America and Central America were "connected" during the late Cretaceous or early Tertiary, about 60–90 million years ago (mya), by a series of volcanic islands. At the beginning of the Tertiary (ca. 80 mya), prior to the arrival of coralsnakes in the late Oligocene and early Miocene, the volcanic islands drifted eastward, severing this link (Zamudio and Greene, 1997). The Panamanian isthmus was not reestablished until the Pliocene, between 3 (Marshall et al., 1979; Webb, 1978) and 5.2 mya (Raven and Axelrod, 1974; Savage, 1974b). The con-

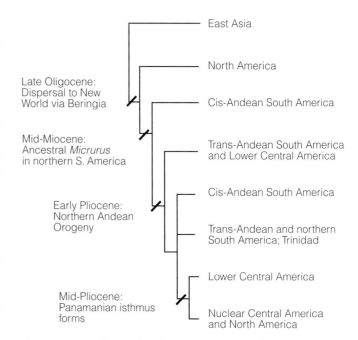

Fig. 235. Area cladogram based on our "consensus" phylogeny showing distribution of major clades of coralsnakes and historical events that may have influenced their evolution.

siderable diversity of coralsnakes and number of basal clades within South America suggests that coralsnakes reached that continent before the isthmian link was reestablished. Thus, dispersal of the ancestral stock of *Micrurus* to South America interrupted gene flow and allowed speciation of the ancestor of all extant *Micrurus*. In the middle Miocene, the New World elapids would have been represented by *Micruroides* in North America and *Micrurus* (including *Leptomicrurus*) in South America.

Several authors, Lillegraven et al. (1979) and Rosen (1976) among them, have proposed the existence of island chains between Central and South America during the Miocene. An island chain might have facilitated dispersal of coralsnakes into South America, or coralsnakes might have reached South America by overwater dispersal. Such a dispersal hypothesis is problematic because currents in the Caribbean flow northwest. In fact, this current pattern explains why the vast majority of Caribbean reptiles and amphibians evolved from South American ancestors (Hedges, 1996). There is scant evidence that land connections via the Caribbean islands existed during this period. The Caribbean fauna is not and never was a cross section of the mainland fauna (Hedges, 1996). Coralsnakes occur on Trinidad and Roatán; and, apparently having reached the islands by recent dispersal from Central America, a single specimen of *M. nigrocinctus* is known from Isla de Providencia off the coast of Nicaragua (Hedges, 1996). Neither extinct (Pregill and Olson, 1981) nor extant species of coralsnakes are known to occur in the Greater Antilles. Thus, there is no easy answer to the question of how coralsnakes reached South America during the Miocene. One possibility is that coralsnakes arrived in the New World earlier than previously thought and reached South America in the Paleocene before the connection between Central and South America was broken.

After reaching South America, the second major event affecting the evolution of *Micrurus* appears to have been the uplift of the northern Andes during the late Miocene and early Pliocene. This vicariant event appears to explain the diversification of *Leptomicrurus* and the short-tailed triadal species east of the Andes and the *M. mipartitus* group and long-tailed species west and north of the Andes. This scenario is supported by the basal position of the long-tailed triadal species of South America but contradicted by the basal position of the cis-Andean species *M. annellatus* and *M. corallinus*. Resolution of the basal polytomy in the clade of long-tailed species would help clarify this hypothesis. If uplift of the Andes was the event that led to the formation of the two main clades of *Micrurus*, *M. annellatus* and the other cis-Andean long-tailed species are predicted to have invaded Amazonia in the Pliocene. Furthermore, the long-tailed species with a cis-Andean distribution would be expected to form a natural group because the Andes create a barrier to dispersal into Amazonia.

Formation of the Panamanian isthmus in the Pliocene allowed the northward dispersal of *Micrurus*. For the most part, speciation in the long-tailed clade appears to have taken place in a series of steps as the group moved north. The most basal member of the Central American clade, *M. alleni*, occurs in lower Central America. Except for *M. clarki*, the remaining species occur in Nuclear Central America and North America. Among the other major clades, the *M. mipartitus* group invaded Central America, extending only as far north as Costa Rica, and the range of *M. dumerilii* extends into Panama.

Future evaluation of the biogeographic scenario suggested by current knowledge of coralsnake relationships will need to address several problems that this hypothesis poses. If the ancestral New World coralsnake extended its range from North America to South America, what caused the extinction of all the populations that would have occurred through at least some parts of Mexico and Central America at that time? Also, some of the Middle American species of *Micrurus* appear to have relictual distributions; a complete hypothesis of coralsnake biogeography must explain how these distributions were established. Finally, if coralsnakes and pitvipers reached the New World at approximately the same time, why do they seem to have such different biogeographic histories? Many species of coralsnakes have never been included in phylogenetic analyses, and additional study is needed before great confidence in coralsnake relationships will be achieved. These future studies will be critical to testing the hypothesis of coralsnake biogeography that is best supported by the currently available data.

Phylogenetic Position of the Crotalinae

Four subfamilies are recognized within the Viperidae (McDiarmid et al., 1999), and recent studies (Groombridge, 1986a; Heise et al., 1995; Knight and Mindell, 1993; Vidal and Lecointre, 1998) support the following relationships among them: (Causinae (Viperinae (Azemiopinae, Crotalinae))). The monophyly of the Crotalinae has been supported in all modern studies (although Cadle [1992] found paraphyly with respect to *Azemiops*) and can be deemed a historical fact (Kraus et al., 1996; Parkinson, 1999; Parkinson et al., 2002; Vidal and Lecointre, 1998).

The Phylogenetic Relationships and Classification of Pitvipers of the Americas

Major Groups of Pitvipers and the Path to the Current Generic Nomenclature

Early History of Pitviper Classification Although 20–22 genera of pitvipers are currently recognized (Gutberlet and Campbell, 2001; McDiarmid et al., 1999; Zhang, 1998; Ziegler et al., 2000), no fewer than 57 generic names have been used to classify these snakes. Fortunately, it is possible to explain the early development of ideas about relationships of pitvipers without dissecting all the intricate details of that nomenclatural history.

In the 10th edition of *Systema Naturae* Linnaeus (1758) provided the first four available scientific names for pitvipers. He allocated three species of rattlesnakes (*horridus*, *durissus*, and *dryinas* [now considered a synonym of *durissus*]) to *Crotalus*, and the common lancehead (now *Bothrops atrox*) to *Coluber*. Linnaeus (1766) later described the South American bushmaster (now in *Lachesis*) as *Crotalus mutus* and the copperhead (now in *Agkistrodon*) as *Boa contortrix*. Laurenti (1768) introduced the name *Coluber nepa* for the snakes we now know as *Hypnale nepa*, and his name *Vipera caerulescens* is probably synonymous with *Bothrops lanceolatus* (McDiarmid et al., 1999). Gmelin (1789) disagreed with Linnaeus's decision to include the South American bushmaster in *Crotalus* and reassigned the species to *Coluber*, but in doing so he used the specific epithet *crotalinus* instead of *mutus*.

Lacépède (1788–89) introduced the names *Coluber lanceolata* (now *Bothrops lanceolatus*), *Coluber brasiliensis* (possibly also referring to *B. lanceolatus*; McDiarmid et al., 1999), and *Crotalus piscivorus* (now *Agkistrodon piscivorus*). Thus, until 1799, all named pitviper species—and in fact all snake species—had been classified among the genera *Boa*, *Coluber*, *Crotalus*, and

Vipera. Palisot de Beauvois (1799) erected the genus *Agkistrodon* for rattleless pitvipers and placed within it the copperhead (under the name *A. mokasen*, a junior synonym of *Boa contortrix* Linnaeus, 1766). Later, Daudin (1803) described the genus *Lachesis* for *Crotalus muta* Linnaeus.

Many new species and genera were described during the 1800s, and their synonymies (this volume; McDiarmid et al., 1999) are invaluable for those who would explore this complex history. Near the beginning of this century, Oppel (1811b) first made the distinction between pitless vipers and pitvipers and introduced the names Crotalini (now Crotalinae, since the ICZN specifies that subfamilial names end in -inae) for the pitvipers and Viperini (now Viperinae) for vipers lacking facial pits. Gray (1825), Fitzinger (1826), and Boie (1827) also made this distinction. Wagler (1824) erected the genus *Bothrops* for *B. lanceolatus*, *B. furia* (=*atrox*), *B. leucostigma* (=*jararaca*), *B. megaera* (=*leucurus*), and *B. neuwiedi*. Schlegel (1837) included in *Trigonocephalus* Oppel (1811) all the rattleless pitvipers except *Lachesis muta*, which he placed with the rattlesnakes in *Crotalus*. Other workers divided the rattleless pitvipers into six (Fitzinger, 1843; Wagler, 1830) to eight genera (Gray, 1849). Three of Gray's genera—*Cenchris* (part of *Agkistrodon*), *Lachesis*, and *Craspedocephalus* (=*Bothrops*)—contained American species.

Numerous workers (e.g., Baird and Girard, 1853; Fitzinger, 1826; Fleming, 1822; Gray, 1825) recognized a generic distinction between the rattlesnakes with plates on their heads (pygmy rattlesnakes or "ground rattlers"; Pls. 931–939, 1011–1023) and those with smaller head scales (e.g., Pls. 773–783), but Garman (1884a) was the first to propose an acceptable name, *Sistrurus*, for the pygmy rattlesnakes. In his discussion of the evolution of the rattle Garman (1889:178), commented on the relationships of several American pitvipers. He proposed that species of *Bothrops*, *Crotalus*, and *Sistrurus* are closely related to *Agkistrodon* and that the "mute rattlesnake," *Lachesis muta*, is closely related to *Crotalus durissus*.

During the latter half of the nineteenth century, Wilhelm Peters and Edward Drinker Cope independently undertook the daunting task of identifying individual lineages within the speciose and confusingly variable pitviper radiation. These authors developed generic classifications for pitvipers based mostly on cranial osteology and squamation, and described five generic names still in current use. In 1859 Peters described the genus *Bothriechis* for *B. nigroviridis*, and in 1861a described *Bothriopsis* for the species now known as *B. taeniata*. Cope (1860a, 1871, 1887, respectively) proposed the names *Calloselasma* (for *rhodostoma*), *Porthidium* (for *lansbergii* and *nasutum*), and *Ophryacus* (for *undulatus*).

Peters (1863b) published a generic classification of the Trigonocephali (pitvipers other than rattlesnakes) based on pitviper skull morphology, especially the morphology of the palatine and ectopterygoid. He recognized 11 genera in six groups, and though some of the names are different from those in current use, their content is largely consistent with current ideas about pitviper relationships. One American group included *Bothriechis* (with representatives of modern *Bothriechis* and *Atropoides*) and *Agkistrodon*, and the other included *Trigonocephalus* (now *Bothrops*) and *Lachesis*. The four Asian groups consisted of (1) *Trimeresurus*, *Tropidolaemus*, *Megaera* (=*Trimeresurus*), and *Atropos* (=*Trimeresurus*); (2) *Halys* (now *Gloydius*); (3) *Hypnale*; and (4) *Tisiphone* (now *Calloselasma*).

Cope's (1860a, 1861, 1868, 1871, 1887) contributions to pitviper taxonomy culminated in "The Classification of the Ophidia" (Cope, 1895), in which he noted that snake classifica-

tion had been based primarily on osteology and dentition and that these character systems had failed to resolve much of the phylogenetic history of snakes. Cope (1895) emphasized features of hemipenial (Cope, 1893) and pulmonary (Cope, 1894) morphology, but he did not discuss any data from these systems in the context of pitviper relationships. In this paper Cope (1895) treated the pitvipers as a family (Crotalidae; Gray, 1825) with two subfamilies, Cophiinae and Crotalinae. The Cophiinae contained 11 genera of rattleless pitvipers, and the 2 genera of rattlesnakes were allocated to the Crotalinae. He distinguished among these genera primarily on the basis of subcaudal condition (divided or undivided), head scale condition (plates, small scales, or a combination thereof), tail condition (prehensile or not), and presence or absence of supraocular horns. Within the Cophiinae Cope recognized one group with divided subcaudals (*Lachesis*, *Cophias*, *Peltopelor*, *Hypnale*, *Trigonocephalus*, and *Calloselasma*) and a second group with undivided subcaudals (*Bothriopsis*, *Bothriechis*, *Ophryacus*, *Teleuraspis*, and *Agkistrodon*), although several members of the latter group (*Ophryacus*, *Bothriopsis*) have divided subcaudals, and some members of *Agkistrodon* (sensu Cope) exhibit a combination of divided and undivided subcaudals. Cope's concept of *Lachesis* was consistent with our current application of this name; in it he included those species with small scales on the top of the head and with four rows of subcaudals at the tip of the tail.

Relationships between Old World and New World Pitvipers Biologists have agreed for years that pitvipers originated in the Old World. The origin and diversification of the New World pitviper fauna, however, has been the subject of much debate. Did a single pitviper species colonize the New World and eventually give rise to all New World species, or did multiple species reach the New World, with each radiating independently? Until recently the majority of herpetologists favored the latter interpretation, although they disagreed regarding the number of colonizing species. Modern phylogenetic studies eventually solved this puzzle.

Boulenger's (1896b) classification distinguished four groups of pitvipers. The two rattlesnake groups (*Crotalus* and *Sistrurus*) are strictly New World, but the other two groups (*Agkistrodon* and *Lachesis* sensu lato) have many species in both Asia and the Americas. Species of *Agkistrodon* (sensu Boulenger) are currently assigned to the genera *Agkistrodon*, *Calloselasma*, *Deinagkistrodon*, *Gloydius*, and *Hypnale*, and are collectively known as the *Agkistrodon* complex (Gloyd and Conant, 1990). These snakes have large plates (internasals, prefrontals, frontal, supraoculars, parietals; see Figs. 84–86, 88) rather than small scales on the surface of the head (though some fragmentation of the anterior plates is characteristic of *Hypnale*). Members of the *Agkistrodon* complex occur primarily in the Northern Hemisphere; Javanese populations of *C. rhodostoma* are the sole representatives of the group south of the equator.

Species of *Lachesis* (sensu Boulenger) typically have many small scales on the surface of the head (see Figs. 164 and 165) and are sometimes known as scale-snouted pitvipers. Species of this group are distributed throughout the Americas and Southeast Asia and are currently assigned to the genera *Atropoides*, *Bothriechis*, *Bothriopsis*, *Bothrocophias*, *Bothrops*, *Cerrophidion*, *Lachesis*, *Ophryacus*, and *Porthidium* in the New World; and *Ermia*, *Ovophis*, *Protobothrops*, *Triceratolepidophis*, *Trimeresurus*, and *Tropidolaemus* in the Old World. With such a bewildering array of diversity, it is no wonder that early attempts to sort the pitvipers were based on a few easily noticed differences. With the unfair advantage of hindsight, it is not surprising that the first approximations were inconsistent with the evolutionary history of these snakes. The development of our knowledge of the phylogenetic relationships between New and Old World members of the *Agkistrodon* complex and the scale-snouted pitvipers is outlined below.

The *Agkistrodon* Complex. Following Boulenger's (1896b) inclusion of all members of the *Agkistrodon* complex in a single genus, new studies of the group began to discern putative lineages and to afford them taxonomic status. Chernov (1957) resurrected *Calloselasma* Cope (1860a), and Gloyd (1977) resurrected *Hypnale* Fitzinger (1843). Gloyd (1979) then placed the hundred-pace viper (*A. acutus*) in the new genus *Deinagkistrodon*. Even with these taxonomic changes, both Old and New World species remained together in *Agkistrodon*, suggesting that the New World pitviper fauna was derived through colonization by at least two Asian pitviper species—one giving rise to New World *Agkistrodon* and at least one more giving rise to the other New World species.

In the years between Chernov's and Gloyd's taxonomic revisions, several publications addressed phylogenetic relationships within the *Agkistrodon* complex. In his major study of pitviper evolution based on comparative osteology, Brattstrom (1964) could find "no major osteological characters to distinguish all Old World from all New World species of *Agkistrodon*." Furthermore, he did not believe that the New World *Agkistrodon* species constituted a single lineage. He proposed instead that the affinities of *Agkistrodon piscivorus* and *A. bilineatus* were to *Deinagkistrodon acutus* and that *A. contortrix* was related to species currently assigned to *Calloselasma*, *Gloydius*, and *Hypnale* (Figs. 236A, 237A). Brattstrom reported that *D. acutus*, *A. bilineatus*, and *A. piscivorus* have 13 of 26 osteological characters in common (his table 10), including square frontals, T-shaped parietals, broader anterior ends to the ectopterygoids, and high processes of the basisphenoid (Fig. 238). Species in the group including *A. contortrix* were reported to have 8 of 14 characters in common, including elongate frontals, triangular parietals, and low processes of the basisphenoid (Fig. 237A). Many of Brattstrom's conclusions about pitviper phylogeny proved to be inaccurate, probably owing to his reliance on a single character system as well as his reference to overall similarity rather than synapomorphic character information.

Tu and Adams (1968) compared the venom proteins of several members of the *Agkistrodon* complex using immunodiffusion and found that venom of *Gloydius blomhoffii* was antigenically as similar to venom of American *Agkistrodon* as it was to venom of *Calloselasma rhodostoma*.

Leslie Burger's (1971) doctoral dissertation, although never formally published, is an invaluable resource for students of pitviper phylogeny. Burger presented many original ideas about the phylogeny of pitvipers, and although several did not hold up under further scrutiny, a few have proven accurate (see below). Using a variety of morphological data, Burger took a unique approach to the *Agkistrodon* complex, allocating the species now known as *Calloselasma rhodostoma* and *Deinagkistrodon acutus* to the genus *Calloselasma*, allocating other Old World species of the *Agkistrodon* complex to *Hypnale*, and restricting the name *Agkistrodon* to the three New World species. Burger noted that species in *Calloselasma*, *Hypnale*, and *Agkistrodon* have large head scales and pterygoids with similar proportions and numbers of teeth. He distinguished *Calloselasma* from the other two genera on the basis of palatine shape and parasubcaudal dimensions (higher than long in *Calloselasma*), and distinguished *Hypnale* from *Agkistrodon* on the basis of number of middorsal scale rows, condition of subcaudals, and various features of the skull.

Burger (1971) treated the pitvipers as a family (Crotalidae) with three subfamilies: Agkistrodontinae (equivalent to the *Agkistrodon* complex), Lachesinae (equivalent to scale-snouted pitvipers), and Crotalinae (for rattlesnakes only). Burger

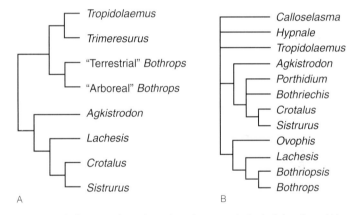

Fig. 236. Phylogenetic hypotheses based on morphological data from (A) Brattstrom, 1964, and (B) Burger, 1971, showing multiple origins of the New World pitvipers.

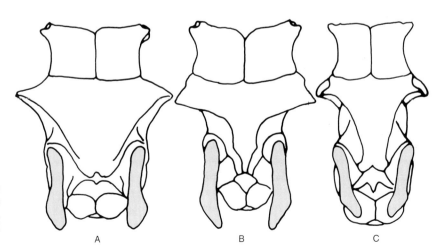

Fig. 237. Differences in skull proportions among (A) *Agkistrodon contortrix*, (B) *A. piscivorus*, and (C) *Gloydius blomhoffii*. The supratemporals are shaded. Adapted from Hoge and Romano-Hoge, 1981a, and Kardong, 1990.

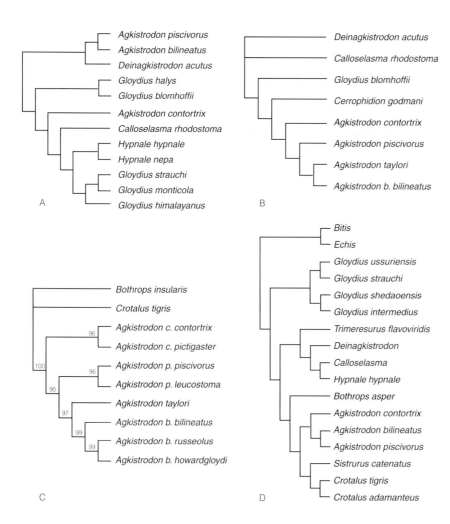

Fig. 238. Phylogeny of the *Agkistrodon* complex and research cycles. (A) Brattstrom, 1964: phylogeny based on phenetic analysis of cranial morphology. (B) Knight et al., 1992: maximum parsimony tree derived from 16s rDNA sequences using an exhaustive search and *C. rhodostoma* and *D. acutus* as outgroups. (C) Parkinson et al., 2000: phylogeny reconstructed with maximum likelihood analysis of mtDNA sequences from three genes (ND4, 12S rRNA, 16S rRNA) and two tRNAs (tRNA-HIS, tRNA-SER), using the F84 model with rate heterogeneity; numbers along branches are nonparametric bootstrap proportions. (D) Parkinson et al., 1997: single most parsimonious tree recovered when 16S rDNA sequence data were analyzed using a heuristic search and with transversions weighted twice as much as transitions.

suggested that a species of *Hypnale* reached the New World and gave rise to *Agkistrodon*. Thus Burger recognized the New World species of *Agkistrodon* as a distinct lineage, but he believed this lineage to be more closely related to genera within the *Agkistrodon* complex than to other American pitvipers (Fig. 237B). Burger's taxonomic arrangement of the *Agkistrodon* complex was not followed by other researchers, probably at least in part because it was never published. As mentioned above, Gloyd (1977, 1979) later proposed a different taxonomy that included a much narrower concept of *Hypnale*, recognition of *Deinagkistrodon acutus* as a distinct lineage, and use of *Agkistrodon* for both Old and New World species.

Hoge and Romano-Hoge (1981a) erected the genus *Gloydius* for the Old World *Agkistrodon* (sensu Gloyd, 1979), leaving only the three New World species in the genus. They distinguished *Gloydius* from *Agkistrodon* on the basis of three characters (condition for *Agkistrodon* in parentheses): a long, narrow cranium (cranium short and broad), parasubcaudals near the tip of the tail not distinctly higher than wide (parasubcaudals higher than wide), and "very short supratemporals not extending posteriorly beyond the braincase" (supratemporals extending posteriorly beyond the braincase; Fig. 237). In their diagnosis of *Agkistrodon* they also mentioned that the anterior subcaudals are single in *Agkistrodon*, which is typically not the case in *Gloydius*.

Because their work is essentially a checklist, Hoge and Romano-Hoge did not discuss details of the phylogenetic relationships among the genera listed, but they did recognize two tribes within Crotalinae: the Agkistrodontini and the Crotalini. Within the Agkistrodontini they included *Agkistrodon*, *Calloselasma*, *Deinagkistrodon*, *Gloydius*, and *Hypnale*—the same genera

included in the *Agkistrodon* complex by Gloyd and Conant (1990)—and suggested that the close relationship of these genera warrants their recognition as a single tribe (Hoge and Romano-Hoge, 1981a:187). Furthermore, they asserted (p. 188) that the three species of *Agkistrodon* are more closely related to *Deinagkistrodon* and *Calloselasma* than to *Gloydius*, but they did not discuss the basis for this conclusion. Although like Burger they restricted *Agkistrodon* to the New World, they did not consider all New World pitvipers to constitute a monophyletic group.

Groombridge (1986b) found that all members of *Agkistrodon* and *Gloydius* that he examined lacked a distinct *m. pterygoideus glandulae*, and he interpreted this character state as the ancestral condition. Also found in *Azemiops* and viperines, this character state cannot be taken as evidence of a close relationship between *Gloydius* and *Agkistrodon*, but this observation is consistent with the view that *Gloydius* and *Agkistrodon* are the least derived pitvipers (Groombridge, 1986b). Kardong's (1990) examination of additional species of the *Agkistrodon* complex supported the conclusions of Groombridge. Earlier studies that commented on the condition of the *m. pterygoideus* in pitvipers include Dullemeijer, 1958, 1959; Kardong, 1973; Kochva, 1958, 1962; and Liem et al., 1971.

A biochemical analysis of skin keratin in 10 species of pitviper and 1 species of viper (Campbell and Whitmore, 1989) suggested that *Gloydius* and *Agkistrodon* may constitute a monophyletic group and that the *Agkistrodon* complex may be monophyletic as well; however, these data suggested paraphyly of *Agkistrodon* (sensu stricto).

Chiasson et al. (1989) examined scale surface microstructure of the *Agkistrodon* complex. Using light microscopy they distinguished five patterns of coarse scale microstructure (sensu Harvey and Gutberlet, 2000): smooth, verrucate, low canaliculate, canaliculate, and canaliculate/cristate. Reticulate and porous patterns of fine microstructure (sensu Harvey and Gutberlet, 2000) were detected in all species examined with scanning electron microscopy. In the verrucate pattern, the scale surface is covered by low, rounded "wartlike" elevations. The canaliculate pattern consists of relatively long ridges, which can be low and indistinct or noticeably higher. Chiasson et al. referred to a pattern of shorter high ridges as cristate (see R. M. Price, 1982, for additional discussion of the terminology for scale surface patterns in snakes). Although they did not attempt to polarize characters of scale morphology, they did detect noteworthy similarities and differences among species in the complex. *Deinagkistrodon acutus* was the only species with a verrucate pattern. *Gloydius h. halys*, *G. h. caraganus*, *G. monticola*, and *G. i. intermedius* lacked coarse microstructure and exhibited a smooth pattern at lower magnifications. *Gloydius intermedius caucasicus*, *G. i. stejnegeri*, *G. saxatilis*, *G. strauchi*, *G. himilayanus*, and *G. caliginosus* (regarded as a synonym of *G. ussuriensis* by McDiarmid et al., 1999) had a low canaliculate pattern. *Gloydius b. blomhoffii*, *G. b. brevicaudus*, *G. ussuriensis*, and the three species of *Hypnale* had higher ridges and were classified as canaliculate. *Agkistrodon bilineatus*, *A. contortrix*, and *A. piscivorus* had the highest ridges but were also classified as canaliculate. Owing to their shorter ridges, the surfaces of *A. piscivorus* scales were classified as canaliculate/cristate. Dorsal scales of most taxa examined by Chiasson et al. exhibited "apical stigmata" (more commonly known as apical pits), but these structures were absent from the species with the smooth pattern of coarse microstructure.

In their definitive treatment of the *Agkistrodon* complex Gloyd and Conant (1990) chose not to recognize *Gloydius*, instead retaining both Old and New World species in *Agkistrodon*. Gloyd and Conant (1990:444) and Van Devender and Conant (1990) believed that the New World *Agkistrodon* species form a monophyletic group and are more closely related to Asian *Agkistrodon* than to any other New World pitvipers. In their section on phylogeny and zoogeography, Gloyd and Conant (1990:435) described variation in 19 different characters of the *Agkistrodon* complex. In a postscript to the *Agkistrodon* monograph (Gloyd and Conant, 1990:461), Roger Conant summarized some of the evidence for retaining both Old and New World species in *Agkistrodon* and stated that "someone else will have to resolve the status of the genus *Gloydius*." Presciently, he continued, "it may be a student of molecular biology who will contribute to eventually settling the matter."

Kardong (1990) studied dentition, osteology, and myology within the *Agkistrodon* complex and summarized important information about these character systems. He agreed with Groombridge (1986b), Gloyd (1979), and Gloyd and Conant (1990) that the species assigned to *Gloydius* by Hoge and Romano-Hoge (1981a) should be retained in *Agkistrodon* along with the three New World species. Kardong based this conclusion in part on two features shared by *Agkistrodon* and *Gloydius*: similar palatine shape and absence of the *m. pterygoideus glandulae*. Kardong also proposed that the differences in skull proportions (see Fig. 237) described by Hoge and Romano-Hoge (1981a) may be attributable simply to differences in body size between *Gloydius* and the larger *Agkistrodon*. Also, Kardong found two different states of the position of the *ligamentum quadrato-glandulare* within *Gloydius*, which suggested to him that *Gloydius* may not be monophyletic. The *l. quadrato-glandulare* lies

next to the *m. adductor mandibulae externus medialis* in *Deinagkistrodon*, *Calloselasma*, *Hypnale*, *Gloydius caliginosus* (=*G. ussuriensis*; McDiarmid et al., 1999), *G. blomhoffii*, and *Agkistrodon* (sensu stricto), but passes through that muscle in the other six species of *Gloydius* examined. Unfortunately, Kardong did not attempt to distinguish between ancestral and derived states when interpreting the variation he observed within these characters. Kardong's conclusions are representative of the persistent problem of recognizing *Agkistrodon* (sensu lato) on the basis of shared ancestral states.

Malnate (1990) reported on variation in hemipenis morphology within the *Agkistrodon* complex. Although he did not draw conclusions about phylogeny from the variation he reported, his diagram summarizing "structural transformations" in the hemipenes within the *Agkistrodon* complex (1990:fig. 2) suggests paraphyly of *Gloydius* (with respect to New World *Agkistrodon* and *Deinagkistrodon*) and even paraphyly of *Gloydius* + *Agkistrodon* (with respect to *Deinagkistrodon*). The branching arrangement was based on Malnate's observation that a dorsal insertion of the *m. retractor penis magnus* is shared by two Old World species (*G. blomhoffii* and *G. caliginosus* [=*G. ussuriensis*]) and the New World species. The retractor muscle inserts at the tips of the hemipenis in the other species of the *Agkistrodon* complex (Malnate, 1990:table 1). Although he did not incorporate these into his diagram, Malnate did note two differences between *Agkistrodon* and *Gloydius*: the hemipenes of *Agkistrodon* are longer and more deeply forked, and the calyces in that genus extend "proximally through the spinous area adjacent to the sulcus walls." Malnate did not attempt to assess which hemipenial conditions are derived.

Using immunoelectrophoresis and radial immunodiffusion, Minton (1990a) studied similarity among plasma proteins in 27 species of snakes (including 9 species of the *Agkistrodon* complex). Minton's protein data appear to support monophyly of both *Agkistrodon* and *Gloydius* as well as a close relationship between these genera. Minton (1992) expanded on his earlier study by using radial immunodiffusion to compare 30 pitviper species, 5 species of *Vipera*, and 32 other snake species. This study supported his earlier findings with regard to the distinction between *Agkistrodon* and *Gloydius*. However, Minton's techniques assess overall similarity and do not provide a means of distinguishing derived forms of a protein from ancestral forms.

To elucidate relationships within the *Agkistrodon* complex, Knight et al. (1992) used venom proteins, mtDNA restriction fragments, and nucleotide sequence data from an approximately 400-base-pair fragment of the 16S rRNA gene. They used maximum parsimony analyses and outgroup rooting in analyses of restriction fragments and sequence data, but they only examined overall similarity (using UPGMA cluster analysis) of venom proteins. New World *Agkistrodon* monophyly was supported by the restriction fragment and nucleotide sequence analyses; furthermore, these analyses indicated that *Agkistrodon* (sensu Gloyd and Conant, 1990) is paraphyletic (Fig. 238B). Venom proteins were most similar among species of New World *Agkistrodon*; *Gloydius saxatilis* shared the fewest venom proteins with the other species studied. Knight et al. (1992) recognized that their data convincingly demonstrated paraphyly of *Agkistrodon* (sensu Gloyd and Conant, 1990) and suggested that "serious consideration must be given to recognition of the genus *Gloydius*." They cautioned, however, that anyone wishing to revise the taxonomy of Gloyd and Conant (1990) should first test the monophyly of *Gloydius* through further study of Asian pitviper phylogeny. Their suggestion was not lost on Golay et al. (1993), who retained the species of *Gloydius* in *Agkistrodon*.

Knight et al.'s (1992) study was extremely important for several reasons. Not only was theirs the first study to apply DNA sequence data to the *Agkistrodon* complex, it was also one of the first to use outgroup comparison to distinguish between ancestral and derived characters. It also generated the surprising conclusion that all rattleless snakes with head plates do not form a monophyletic group—another first, since even those who had allocated American and Asian species to separate genera (Burger, 1971; Hoge and Romano-Hoge, 1981a) still considered all the rattleless species with head plates to be members of a single lineage.

Porter et al. (1994:302–313) determined the chromosomal location of ribosomal RNA genes in a variety of squamate reptiles, including seven species of pitvipers. These genes were found on two pairs of microchromosomes in *Crotalus viridis* (*C. v. viridis* from Texas), *C. atrox*, *Sistrurus catenatus*, and *Calloselasma rhodostoma*; however, the genes were present on only a single pair of microchromosomes in *Gloydius intermedius* and *Agkistrodon piscivorus*. In *A. contortrix*, ribosomal RNA genes were located on the Z chromosomes, a rare condition among vertebrates (Porter et al., 1994). Porter et al. suggested that variation in rRNA gene location may provide useful information about the phylogeny of pitvipers, but the small taxonomic sample for this group hindered interpretation of character state changes. Using colubrids and elapids as outgroups, Porter et al. determined that the presence of rRNA genes on two pairs of microchromosomes may be a derived condition. If that is true, the similarity between *G. intermedius* and *A. piscivorus* would represent a shared ancestral (plesiomorphic) character. These authors also entertained the possibility that this character is derived, in which case it would support a monophyletic *Agkistrodon* (sensu Gloyd and Conant, 1990), and they suggested that study of this character in viperine snakes might allow a more definitive statement about its polarity.

Cullings et al. (1997) analyzed 297–394 base pairs of the mitochondrial cytochrome *b* gene in five species of pitvipers. Using *Calloselasma rhodostoma* as an outgroup, they recovered two different topologies when transitions and transversions were weighted equally: (1) ((*Gloydius halys*, *Lachesis muta*)(*Agkistrodon contortrix*, *Crotalus viridis*)), and (2) (*G. halys* (*L. muta* (*A. contortrix*, *C. viridis*))). The latter reconstruction was also obtained when transversions were weighted twice as much as transitions. The relationship of *A. contortrix* to *C. viridis* was well supported by nonparametric bootstrap proportions of 70–90%. This study is consistent with that of Knight et al. (1992) in suggesting that *Agkistrodon* (sensu Gloyd and Conant, 1990) is paraphyletic, although the limited taxonomic sample precludes any strong recommendation about the appropriate classification for members of the *Agkistrodon* complex.

Two studies based on mitochondrial DNA sequence data (Kraus et al., 1996; Parkinson et al., 1997) finally put questions about the status of *Gloydius* and the *Agkistrodon* complex to rest. Kraus et al. (1996) sequenced a 694-base-pair fragment of the ND4 gene from *Causus rhombeatus*; *Azemiops feae*; and 30 pitviper species, including *Agkistrodon piscivorus*, *A. contortrix*, *Gloydius blomhoffii*, and *G. intermedius*. Among the species studied, the sequence divergence was 5.5–24.4% overall and 13.4–49.1% at third codon positions, indicating that mutational saturation might be a problem for their data. In order to address that problem Kraus et al. conducted separate analyses in which they removed the parts of the data set most likely to be affected by saturation. They used heuristic searches and the maximum parsimony criterion to analyze a data set including all first and second codon position substitutions and third position transversions (their preferred analysis a priori), and a data set consisting of transversions only. The first analysis resulted in recovery of 72 equally parsimonious trees, the strict consensus of which revealed relatively little about intergeneric relationships but detected a number of smaller monophyletic groups. One application of successive weighting using retention indices resulted in a single shortest tree (Fig. 239A). The second analysis recovered only 7 shortest trees, but again intergeneric relationships were largely unresolved. One cycle of successive weighting based on character retention indices was sufficient for recovering a single shortest tree.

After successive weighting, Kraus et al. (1996) recovered a monophyletic *Agkistrodon* (sensu stricto) and a monophyletic *Gloydius*; in no analysis did *Gloydius* and *Agkistrodon* form an exclusive monophyletic group (Fig. 239A). Based on their results and those of Knight et al. (1992), Kraus et al. argued strongly for the recognition of *Gloydius*. They also pointed out that *Agkistrodon* (sensu Gloyd and Conant, 1990) had been defined primarily on the basis of symplesiomorphy and that the Agkistrodontini of Hoge and Romano-Hoge (1981a) is polyphyletic and should not be recognized.

Parkinson et al. (1997) studied nucleotide sequences of a 505-base-pair region of the mitochondrial 16S ribosomal RNA gene in 15 crotaline and 2 viperine species. These authors implemented four alternative maximum parsimony analyses. In three of the analyses transitions and transversions were weighted equally, and in the fourth analysis transversions were assigned twice as much weight as transitions. In the three equal-weighting analyses, gaps were treated as either missing data, a fifth character state, or additional binary characters. All four analyses supported monophyly of New World *Agkistrodon* and the monophyly of *Gloydius*, but in no analysis was the *Agkistrodon* complex recovered as monophyletic (Fig. 238D). Although all shortest trees recovered by the analyses using equal weighting included a monophyletic *Agkistrodon* and a monophyletic *Gloydius*, the relationship of these groups to one another was undetermined in a majority-rule consensus of all those shortest trees. In the analysis using unequal weighting of transitions and tranversions, *Agkistrodon* was part of the clade that included only New World species, and the Old World pitvipers were paraphyletic with respect to the New World species. Many of the relationships depicted in the shortest tree were not well supported, although *Gloydius* monophyly was supported in 98% of the nonparametric bootstrap replications. Based on these results, Parkinson et al. recommended that the genus *Gloydius* be recognized for the Old World species of *Agkistrodon* (sensu Gloyd and Conant, 1990) as originally suggested by Hoge and Romano-Hoge (1981a). Further, they stated that Agkistrodontini (Hoge and Romano-Hoge, 1981a) should not be recognized owing to its putative paraphyly. Finally, though it was not demonstrated conclusively by their study, these authors suggested the possibility that New World pitvipers are monophyletic—quite a surprising development given the long history of contrary opinion.

The single biggest impediment to discovering the paraphyly of the *Agkistrodon* complex was almost certainly the failure to distinguish between derived and primitive characteristics. The head plate arrangement shared by members of the *Agkistrodon* complex is a conveniently obvious and distinctive trait, but it is

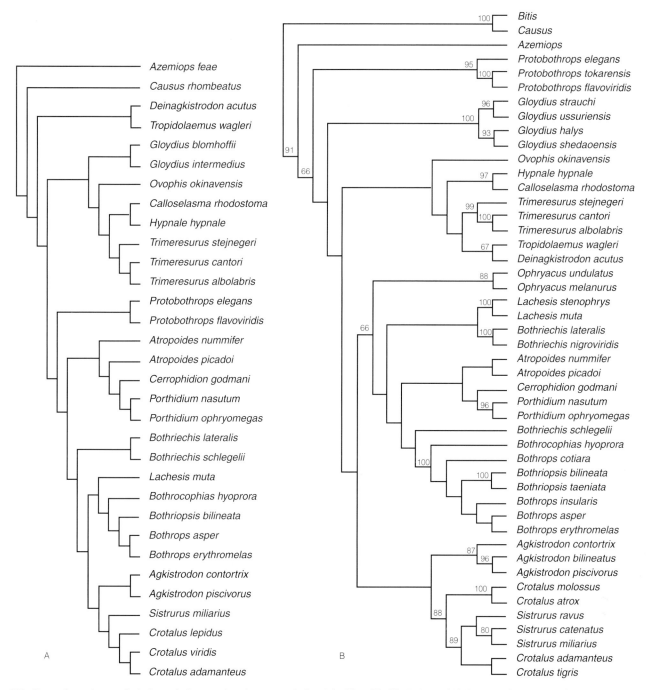

Fig. 239. Recent hypotheses of pitviper phylogeny showing monophyly of the New World pitvipers. (A) Kraus et al., 1996: single most parsimonious tree obtained from successive weighting of molecular characters (ND4 gene sequences) according to their retention indices. (B) Parkinson, 1999: phylogram based on a maximum parsimony analysis of 12S and 16S rDNA sequences with transversions weighted twice as much as transitions. Numbers along branches are nonparametric bootstrap proportions; branches without numbers were supported in fewer than 50% of the bootstrap pseudoreplications.

clearly ancestral based on outgroup comparisons; large head plates occur in *Azemiops*, *Causus*, *Vipera*, and almost all colubrids, elapids, and atractaspidids. As outlined above, many of the less obvious traits shared by species of *Gloydius* and *Agkistrodon* are ancestral and uninformative as well. The appropriate treatment of character polarity and newly available molecular data was especially important in this discovery.

The Scale-Snouted Pitvipers. Numerous conflicting ideas about relationships of Old World and New World scale-snouted pitvipers (*Lachesis* sensu Boulenger) have been proposed. Soon after the publication of Boulenger's classification of snakes,

Mocquard (1905) suggested that the name *Lachesis* be reserved for the bushmasters and that all other species placed in *Lachesis* by Boulenger (1896b) be included in *Trimeresurus*. Then Stejneger (1907), on biogeographic grounds, restricted use of the name *Trimeresurus* to Asian scale-snouted pitvipers, allocating American members of the group to *Bothrops*. Barbour (1912), Oshima (1920), and Wall (1921) used Stejneger's classification, but others (e.g., Amaral, 1922b; Werner, 1922) persisted in using *Lachesis* in the wider sense of Boulenger. Amaral (1925c, 1926c) later embraced the more restricted concept of *Lachesis* (sensu Mocquard, 1905) following the discovery that bushmasters are oviparous (R. R. Mole, *in* Ditmars, 1910). In these papers Amaral referred the other American scale-snouts to *Bothrops* and went on to summarize six differences (including reproductive mode) between *Lachesis* and *Bothrops*. Amaral (1926c) also summarized past use of the generic names *Scytale*, *Trigonocephalus*, *Cophias*, and *Craspedocephalus* for scale-snouted pitvipers and explicitly adopted the three-genus system of Stejneger (1907).

Until recently (e.g., Burger, 1971; Burger, *in* Pérez-Higareda et al., 1985; Campbell and Lamar, 1989) this three-genus approach to the scale-snouted pitvipers was followed by most biologists (e.g., Amaral, 1944e; Dowling and Duellman, 1978; Hoge and Romano, 1971a; Klemmer, 1963; Minton et al., 1968; Peters and Orejas-Miranda, 1970; Stejneger and Barbour, 1940), although practically no character evidence for this arrangement had been presented and biogeographic concerns were the main reasons used to justify the segregation of *Bothrops* and *Trimeresurus*. Given this lack of evidence, some continued to include all scale-snouted pitvipers other than *Lachesis* in *Trimeresurus*: McDowell and Bogert (1954:138), Neill (1964:39), and M. A. Smith (1943:502), for example. Some *Bothrops* were also placed in *Trimeresurus* by Dunn (1939), Pope (1944), Schmidt and Walker (1943a), and H. M. Smith (1941a).

Maslin (1942) listed the morphological characters that he thought distinguished most Old and New World species of scale-snouted pitvipers. One character was the nasal pore, a tiny opening in the scale inside the nostril, the anatomy of which had been studied by Kathariner (1900:415) and Radovanovic (1935:321). Maslin reported the absence of a nasal pore from seven of the eight American species he examined (present in *Bothrops castelnaudi*=*Bothriopsis taeniata*) and its presence in most Asian species. Maslin further reported the absence of the pore from the Asian species *T. wagleri* and *T. philippinensis* (both =*Tropidolaemus wagleri*; the correct spelling of the latter name is *philippensis*; see McDiarmid et al., 1999:351). M. A. Smith (1942) expressed his opinion that the nasal pore is not a taxonomically useful character because it is present in all snakes. More recent observations have shown that neither Maslin nor Smith adequately understood the condition of the nasal pore. Actually it is present in all *Bothrops* (sensu lato) examined thus far and in *T. wagleri*, but its location deeper within the nostril makes it difficult to detect (Burger, 1971). Hoge (1954) reported the nasal pore to be lacking in *B. brazili*, but Burger (1971) questioned the veracity of this claim. The pore does appear to be absent from *Crotalus* and *Sistrurus* (Burger, 1971; Gutberlet and Harvey, 2002). Both Maslin (1942) and Burger (1971) noted the importance of the position of the pore, and this character may hold additional phylogenetic information.

Based on his perception of shared absence of a nasal pore in *wagleri* and most American scale-snouts, Maslin placed *T. wagleri* in *Bothrops* and provided a new definition for *Trimeresurus*, restricting its content to species of Asian scale-snouts other than *T. wagleri*. Maslin reported other characters shared by *wagleri* and several to most species of *Bothrops* and not found in *Trimeresurus*: strongly keeled head scales; wide head with small, triangular snout, neurotoxic venom; and a spinous hemipenis lacking calyces on the distal portion of the lobes. Our much-expanded knowledge of variation among pitvipers reveals that none of the discriminating features proposed by Maslin is definitive for the groups he recognized.

Ruiz (1951) compared the skulls of 31 species of pitvipers, including *Trimeresurus gramineus* and *Tropidolaemus wagleri*. In a key to the pitviper genera he separated these Asian species from *Bothrops* (including *Bothrocophias hyoprora*) on the basis of the shape of the dorsal process of the palatine (forked in *Bothrops*,

rounded in the Asian species; Figs. 240C, 240D) and the shape of the anterolateral margin of the maxillary fossa (in the shape of a simple curve or open semicircle in *Bothrops*, forming two distinct curves in the Asian species; Figs. 240A, 240B).

Although Brattstrom (1964) recognized *Bothrops* and *Trimeresurus* as separate genera, he considered each to be the other's closest relative (Fig. 236A), suggesting that *Trimeresurus* and *Bothrops* share a most recent common ancestor that must have dispersed into the New World. In the figure depicting his proposed biogeographic history of pitvipers, however, Brattstrom (1964:fig. 39) indicated paraphyly of *Trimeresurus* with respect to *Bothrops*. Brattstrom stated that *Bothrops* and *Trimeresurus* are "quite distinct osteologically" and that there are "two relatively exclusive characters." Brattstrom did not elaborate on which characters he used to infer a close relationship between *Bothrops* and *Trimeresurus*. He also hypothesized that the other scale-snouted pitvipers, *Lachesis*, are more closely related to the rattlesnakes and members of the *Agkistrodon* complex.

Burger (1971:150 and his fig. 238) proposed that two Asian pitviper species dispersed into the New World via the Bering land bridge: a representative of the *Agkistrodon* complex (an ancestral species of *Hypnale* sensu Burger; *Gloydius* according to our current classification) and a representative of the scale-snouted pitvipers (an ancestral species of *Trimeresurus*). Burger further indicated that some American scale-snouted pitvipers in addition to the rattlesnakes and *Agkistrodon* (sensu stricto) evolved from the colonizing species of *Hypnale* and that the other American scale-snouts arose from the species of *Trimeresu-*

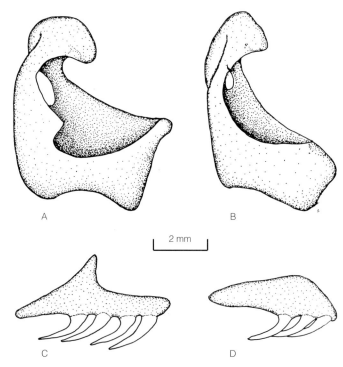

Fig. 240. Two osteological characters described by Peters (1863b) and Ruiz (1951) and used in recent phylogenetic analyses of pitvipers (e.g., Gutberlet and Harvey, 2002; Werman, 1992): shape of the maxilla (A and B) and shape of the palatine (C and D). (A) *Sistrurus catenatus*, showing process on anterolateral margin of the maxilla; (B) *Agkistrodon piscivorus*, showing smooth contour of anterolateral margin of the maxilla; (C) *Bothrops jararaca*, showing an attenuate choanal process ("forked" condition sensu Ruiz, 1951, and Brattstrom, 1964) of the palatine; (D) *Tropidolaemus wagleri*, showing a rounded choanal process of the palatine (after Ruiz, 1951).

rus that entered the New World (Fig. 236B). Thus Burger's interpretations support neither a monophyletic New World pitviper group nor a monophyletic scale-snouted group. Although Burger discussed evidence for many of his phylogenetic hypotheses, he did not do so with respect to relationships between scale-snouts of the Old and New Worlds.

Hoge and Romano-Hoge (1981a) included both Old World (*Trimeresurus, Tropidolaemus, Ovophis*) and New World (*Lachesis, Crotalus, Sistrurus, Bothrops*) pitviper genera within the tribe Crotalini, but did not state any phylogenetic hypothesis for classifying these genera in the same group. This is in accord with previous views that the New World pitvipers are not monophyletic. Hoge and Romano-Hoge included rattlesnake species with head plates in the scale-snouted group rather than in their Agkistrodontini: the rattle, unique in the tree of life, has consistently trumped head plates in matters of taxonomy.

In his doctoral dissertation Carlos Estol examined the epidermal microstructure of dorsal scales of 55 taxa of American (*Bothrops* sensu lato) and 30 taxa of Asian (*Trimeresurus* sensu lato) scale-snouted pitvipers (Estol, 1981:appendixes A and B). In this ambitious and valuable study Estol documented phylogenetically informative characteristics of scale microstructure. Estol was careful to note that these characters should not be used independent of other data, but he did provide some phylogentic interpretations of these characters.

With respect to the question of scale-snouted pitviper monophyly, Estol considered both *Bothrops* and *Trimeresurus* to be polyphyletic and found that some Middle American species assigned to *Bothrops* share microstructural patterns with certain *Trimeresurus*. For example, Estol noted that *B. lansbergi, B. nasutus,* and *B. yucatanicus* (all currently assigned to *Porthidium*) are similar to most *Trimeresurus* and suggested that they should perhaps be placed in that genus. He also reported that *Cerrophidion godmani* exhibits the same microstructural pattern (reticulo-undulate) as *T. chaseni* and *T. monticola* and that *C. barbouri* shares a strio-undulate pattern with *T. jerdoni* and *T. flavoviridis*. Estol noted that the South American *Bothrops* (species currently assigned to *Bothrops, Bothriopsis,* and *Bothrocophias*) exhibit a microstructural pattern ("keel-like surface projections [carinae] and visible oberhautchen cell boundaries" = reticulo-carinate) that easily distinguishes them from all species of *Trimeresurus* examined. He noted that *T. okinavensis* (now assigned to *Ovophis*) is most similar to the South American *Bothrops* in epidermal microstructure but cautioned that this might be the result of convergence rather than recent shared ancestry. "It seems probable," he concluded, "that the genus *Trimeresurus* has representatives in Mexico and Central America, presently classified as species of the genus *Bothrops*" (Estol, 1981:180). Unfortunately, Estol never published his dissertation research, and his numerous micrographs do not fare well in the transfer from microfilm to paper.

Estol (1981:152) quoted Burger to describe the persistent difficulties in scale-snout taxonomy:

> Burger (1971) clearly summarized the reasons for the absence of any attempts in trying to enlighten the taxonomic status of the genera *Trimeresurus* and *Bothrops* by stating that ". . . efforts to resolve the situation in a simple way have failed because of (1) the degree of diversity in the American representatives and in the Asiatic representatives that prevents them from being separated readily according to continent; and (2) the existence of alleged annectant species like *B. castelnaudi,* [=*Bothriopsis taeniata*] connecting otherwise distant groups like Central American arboreal pitvipers with entire subcaudals to the South American arboreal pitvipers with divided subcaudals." The situation is not at all improved when one considers that amount of morphological overlapping added to the somewhat confusing tangle of diversity exhibited by this pitviper complex.

Questions about the affinities of Old and New World scale-snouted pitvipers remained open until several workers were finally able to conduct phylogenetic analyses based on large data sets and broad taxonomic sampling of Old and New World species.

The Monophyly of New World Pitvipers   The determination that the New World pitvipers are monophyletic (Fig. 239), contradicting the long-held notion that they are descendants of at least two Asian pitviper groups (Figs. 236, 237A), is among the most interesting and unexpected discoveries about the history of these snakes. This result has been supported in all recent analyses that included both Old and New World taxa (Kraus et al., 1996; Parkinson, 1999; Parkinson et al., 1997, 2002; Vidal et al., 1997, 1999; Vidal and Lecointre, 1998), and was even suggested by the results of two earlier studies (Knight et al., 1992; Minton, 1992).

Kraus et al. (1996) were the first to include a broad taxonomic sample of Old and New World pitvipers in the same phylogenetic analyses; in fact, with the exception of *Ophryacus* they were able to study at least one representative of each of the 19 pitviper genera recognized at that time. With the application of successive approximations they found support for the monophyly of New World pitvipers in both of their analyses (Fig. 239A); however, without this a posteriori weighting technique, the question of New World pitviper monophyly was unresolved. Kraus et al. (1996) did not use the nonparametric bootstrap or other statistical techniques to assess the strength of support for the relationships suggested in their study, nonetheless American pitviper monophyly is clearly supported under a criterion of maximum parsimony.

The studies of Vidal et al. (1997, 1999) and Vidal and Lecointre (1998), though including many fewer taxa than other recent studies, also support New World pitviper monophyly. Vidal and Lecointre (1998) used data from three mitochondrial genes (cytochrome *b*, ND4, 16S rRNA) to reconstruct relationships among 13 species of pitvipers (*Calloselasma rhodostoma, Deinagkistrodon acutus, Gloydius blomhoffii, Protobothrops tokarensis, Trimeresurus stejnegeri, Tropidolaemus wagleri, Agkistrodon contortrix, Bothriechis schlegelii, Bothriopsis bilineata, Bothrops atrox, Crotalus atrox, Lachesis muta,* and *Porthidium nasutum*). In separate analyses of each gene, Vidal and Lecointre used a variety of viperids, atractaspidids, elapids, and boids as outgroups; in analyses combining all genes in one data set they used *C. rhodostoma* as the outgroup. When the genes were analyzed separately with maximum parsimony, only the ND4 data (collected by Kraus et al., 1996) supported New World pitviper monophyly; however, when all three genes were analyzed together, New World pitviper monophyly was supported under both of the weighting schemes they applied (elimination of third codon position transitions of cyt *b* and ND4 genes with equal weighting of all other substitutions versus elimination of third codon position transitions of ND4 only with equal weighting of all other substitutions). Vidal et al. (1999) analyzed relationships among the same species of pitvipers and reached similar conclusions.

Parkinson (1999) sequenced the 16S and 12S rRNA genes of two outgroups (*Bitis arietans* and *Causus defilippii*), *Azemiops feae,* and 44 pitviper species representing all 19 genera recognized at that time. The broad taxonomic sample and extensive sequence data utilized in this study allowed Parkinson to comment confidently on many aspects of pitviper phylogeny. Parkinson employed three alternative weighting schemes in his maximum parsimony analyses: (1) equal weighting, (2) transversions weighted twice as much as transitions, and (3) transversions weighted four times as much as transitions. In a fourth analysis Parkinson used maximum likelihood with the F84 model. The New World pitvipers were recovered as monophyletic (Fig. 239B) in every analysis, with nonparametric bootstrap support ranging from 50 to 74. Bootstrap support for this clade became more robust as the weight of transversions was increased, suggesting that transitions at some nucleotide positions occurred independently in Old and New World species. Nonetheless, as noted by Parkinson, two unambiguous transitions (both C ↔ T) and two unambiguous transversions (A ↔ C and A ↔ T) support New World pitviper monophyly. Successive weighting using rescaled consistency indices of characters from the initial equal-weighting analysis also supported New World pitviper monophyly. Monophyly of the separate lineages *Gloydius* and *Agkistrodon* (sensu stricto) was strongly supported in all analyses (Fig. 239B).

Parkinson et al. (2002) significantly expanded the scope of the earlier study (Parkinson, 1999) by including two additional genes (cyt *b* and ND4), two more viperid outgroups (*Causus resimus* and *Atheris nitschei*), and 12 more pitviper species. All told, these investigators evaluated 2,341 base pairs of mtDNA sequence for 61 species—the most comprehensive analysis of pitviper relationships to date. They analyzed the data from each gene separately using maximum parsimony and also conducted maximum parsimony and maximum likelihood (using the F84 model) analyses on a data set including all genes. Third codon position transitions in the two protein-coding genes were excluded from most maximum parsimony analyses in order to minimize the effects of mutational saturation, but these transitions were included in one maximum parsimony analysis of the combined data. In one maximum likelihood analysis, rates of change at individual nucleotide sites were not incorporated into the model, whereas in a second analysis they were. In general, Parkinson et al. found relatively little intergeneric resolution in trees recovered by analyses of individual genes, but found well-resolved and well-supported topologies as a result of combined data analyses (Fig. 241A). The monophyly of New World pitvipers was well supported in all combined data analyses

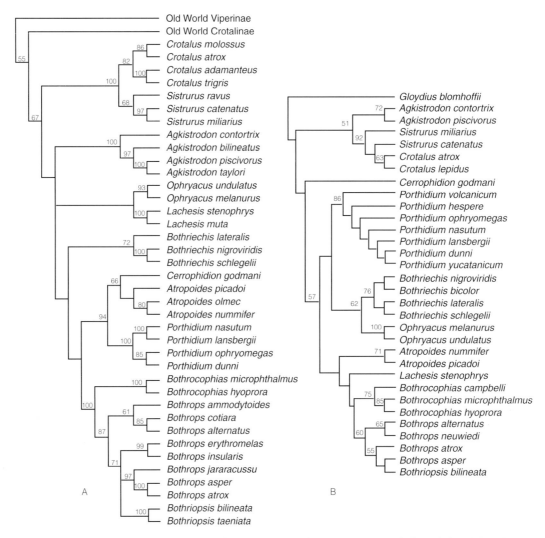

Fig. 241. Phylogenetic relationships of New World pitvipers inferred from (A) molecular and (B) morphological data. (A) Parkinson et al., 2002: strict consensus of four most parsimonious trees generated by weighting all characters (ND4, cytochrome *b*, and 12S and 16S rDNA sequences) equally. (B) Gutberlet and Harvey, 2002: single most parsimonious tree recovered by analysis of morphological characters using a branch-and-bound search, minimum ordering of multistate characters, and generalized frequency coding of meristic characters. Numbers above branches of both phylogenies are nonparametric bootstrap proportions; branches without numbers were supported in fewer than 50% of the bootstrap pseudoreplications.

with nonparametric bootstrap support ranging from 67 to 74 in maximum parsimony analyses and from 92 to 99 in maximum likelihood analyses. Relative likelihood support for this clade was 100 in both maximum likelihood analyses.

In light of the morphological conservatism (e.g., very little division of head scales) of the species now in *Gloydius* and *Agkistrodon* and the amazing similarity between some Asian and American scale-snouted species, it makes sense that molecular data were the first to elucidate the monophyly of New World species. We know of no morphological synapomorphy that is shared by all New World pitvipers yet absent from Old World pitvipers. Most morphological features found in some New World pitvipers can also be found in some Old World pitvipers. For example, palatine shape (Fig. 240), a highly informative character within the New World pitviper radiation, is similar in different groups of Old World pitvipers (Gutberlet and Harvey, 2002; Kardong, 1990). It appears that the independent Asian and American radiations have derived remarkably similar morphological features through convergent evolution, and it seems likely that in some cases ancestral characters have been retained in different lineages. A morphology-based phylogenetic analysis including both New and Old World species is needed to assess character state changes along the branch leading to New World pitvipers.

Although confidence in the monophyly of New World pitvipers is high as a result of recent studies, much less is known about the potential sister group of New World pitvipers. In their preferred analysis Kraus et al. (1996) found that a clade consisting of *Protobothrops elegans* and *P. flavoviridis* was sister to New World pitvipers (Fig. 239A), but *Ovophis okinavensis* occupied this position in their analysis that used transversions only. In all maximum parsimony analyses Parkinson (1999) found support for a sister relationship between a clade consisting of *Calloselasma*, *Hypnale*, *Deinagkistrodon*, *Tropidolaemus*, *Trimeresurus*, and *Ovophis* and the New World pitviper radiation (Fig. 239B). In the maximum likelihood reconstruction, *Ovophis okinavensis* was sister to the New World pitvipers, with the other genera mentioned previously forming the next most proximate clade. In two of their analyses Parkinson et al. (2002) found that a clade containing *Gloydius* and *Ovophis okinavensis* formed a sister group to New World pitvipers, but the authors noted that this relationship was not well supported. In their maximum parsimony analysis that excluded third-position transitions, *Protobothrops* was also included in the sister group to New World pitvipers; and in their maximum likelihood analysis that incorporated nucleotide change rates, *Ovophis monticola* replaced *O. okinavensis* in the sister group.

Among the species he studied with immunoelectrophoresis, Minton (1990a) found *G. blomhoffii* to be most similar to species of *Agkistrodon*. Knight et al. (1992:58) noted the close relationship of *G. blomhoffii* to New World species, as did Gloyd and Conant (1990), Vidal and Lecointre (1998), and Vidal et al. (1999). Although additional data are needed to further test ideas about the sister group of New World pitvipers, it seems tenable that a *Gloydius*-like snake was the aboriginal American pitviper (Parkinson et al., 2002).

Genera of Pitvipers Most taxonomists recognized five genera of New World pitvipers during most of the 1900s: *Agkistrodon*, *Sistrurus*, *Crotalus*, *Lachesis*, and *Bothrops*. Of these genera, *Bothrops* was by far the most speciose; and although many recognized the polyphyletic nature of *Bothrops* (Amaral,

1944e; Brattstrom, 1964; Hoge, 1966; Smith and Taylor, 1945), few attempted to untangle natural groups from this morass of ecological and morphological diversity.

Although he is seldom given credit for this arrangement (perhaps owing to his inclusion of all scale-snouts in a single genus), it is clear from Boulenger's (1896b) nonalphabetic grouping of species within *Lachesis* that he had deciphered some of the groups of New World pitvipers. Boulenger recognized 40 species within *Lachesis*, 22 of which are denizens of the New World. Species currently assigned to *Bothrops* occur together near the beginning of his list (immediately after the first species listed, *Lachesis muta*), and 3 species currently recognized as close relatives within *Bothrops* (*alternatus*, *neuwiedi*, and *ammodytoides*) are even listed together. A representative of *Bothriopsis* (*castelnaudi=taeniata*) is listed immediately after the species of *Bothrops*, and thereafter follow 4 Central American species now assigned to *Atropoides*, *Cerrophidion*, and *Porthidium*, respectively. New World species are interrupted at this point by inclusion of the 18 Old World species, which are grouped quite consistently with current concepts of *Ovophis*, *Protobothrops*, *Trimeresurus*, and *Tropidolaemus*, respectively. Next is a species now known as *Bothriopsis bilineata* (the only drastically misplaced New World species), followed by *undulatus* (now in *Ophryacus*) and then 5 species (*lateralis*, *bicolor*, *schlegelii*, *nigroviridis*, and *aurifer*) currently in *Bothriechis*.

Amaral (1944e) divided *Bothrops* into six provisional subgenera but did not name them:

1. Terrestrial species without a prehensile tail and generally with divided subcaudals—"*alternata, ammodytoides, itapetiningae, neuwiedii, erythromelas, iglesiasi, cotiara, pirajai, neglecta, atrox, jararaca, jararacussu, andiana* (+*barnettii*)*, medusa, xanthogrammus, microphthalma* (+*pleuroxantha*)*, pulchra, barbouri, melanura, picta, e insularis.*"
2. Terrestrial species without a prehensile tail and generally with undivided subcaudals—"*godmanni, nummifera, nasuta, lansbergii, ophryomegas e hyoprora.*"
3. Intermediate species ("forma intermédia"), arboreal with a semiprehensile tail and with both divided and undivided subcaudals—"*castelnaudi.*"
4. Arboreal species with a prehensile tail and with divided subcaudals—"*monticelli, peruviana e undulata.*"
5. Arboreal species with a prehensile tail and with both divided and undivided subcaudals—"*bilineata e chloromelas.*"
6. Arboreal species with a prehensile tail and with undivided subcaudals—"*lateralis, bicolor, schlegelii e nigroviridis.*"

Within *Bothrops* (sensu lato) Brattstrom (1964) recognized an "arboreal" group and a "terrestrial" group (Fig. 236A), but noted that both groups contain arboreal and terrestrial species. Brattstrom stated that at least *Bothrops nummifer* and *B. schlegelii* belong to the arboreal group, noting great similarity between the two in the shapes of their frontals, parietals, lower jaws, palatines, ectopterygoids, and premaxillae. Brattstrom continued, "Both appear to be quite primitive, with *schlegeli* probably the most primitive member of the genus. As noted above, *schlegeli* has several characters in common with the unique *Trimeresurus wagleri*. *Bothrops schlegeli* and *T. wagleri* probably have changed very little since their differentiation from the main lines of evolution of their respective genera." Through reference to their "scutellation and habit," Brattstrom suggested that *B. bicolor*, *B. lateralis*, *B. brachystoma*, *B. dunni*, and *B. nigroviridis* may also belong to the arboreal group. Brattstrom assigned species of the arboreal group to the subgenus *Bothriechis* within the genus *Bothrops*.

Within his terrestrial group Brattstrom recognized two subgroups. One subgroup contained relatively small species that he referred to as "hog-nosed pitvipers," and the other subgroup contained larger species. On the basis of osteological similarity, Brattstrom included *cotiara* and *nasuta* in the small terrestrial subgroup, and suggested including *lansbergi*, *itapetiningae*, and *ophryomegas* as well based on unspecified external characters. In the large terrestrial subgroup Brattstrom placed *B. jararaca*, *B. jararacussu*, *B. atrox*, *B. neuwiedi*, *B. godmani*, *B. alternatus*, *B. bilineatus*, and *B. lanceolatus*. He also mentioned *B. insularis*, *B. castelnaudi*, and *B. picadoi* as potential members of this subgroup on the basis of external characteristics. Brattstrom assigned members of his terrestrial group to the subgenus *Bothrops* within the genus *Bothrops*, but remarked that the small terrestrial species may belong in additional subgenera.

In 1971, for the first time since the pioneering work of Cope and Peters, an attempt was made to assign generic names to lineages of New World scale-snouts (Burger, 1971). Although Burger evaluated a large number of anatomical features, he did not employ an objective criterion (e.g., parsimony, maximum likelihood) for phylogeny reconstruction and apparently resorted to defining groups based on one to a few characters in addition to geographic considerations. Burger partitioned *Bothrops* into five genera: *Bothriechis*, *Bothriopsis*, *Bothrops*, *Ophryacus*, and *Porthidium* (Table 54), and noted that this arrangement is similar in many respects to those of Amaral (1944e), Cope (1895), and Peters (1863b). Burger differed from Amaral in his allocations of *barbouri* and *melanurus* (placed in *Porthidium* by Burger), *castelnaudi* (=*taeniata*) and *medusa* (placed in *Bothriopsis*), and *undulatus* (placed in *Ophryacus*).

Burger's genera continue to be recognized, although the results of subsequent studies have called for some revision of their content as well as recognition of new genera. New World genera that have been recognized since Burger's work are *Atropoides* Werman, 1992; *Cerrophidion* Campbell and Lamar,

1992; and *Bothrocophias* Gutberlet and Campbell, 2001 (all are discussed in more detail below). Burger did not publish his dissertation research, but in their description of *Porthidium olmec* (=*Atropoides olmec*) Pérez-Higareda et al. (1985) published the generic arrangement proposed by him. Burger's classification greatly advanced our understanding of major historical groups of pitvipers and laid the groundwork for modern studies of their phylogeny.

In *The Venomous Reptiles of Latin America*, Campbell and Lamar (1989) adopted the classification proposed by Burger, thus finally disseminating this taxonomic arrangement to a wide audience and presenting much information about the genera outlined by Burger. Campbell and Lamar (1989) recognized that Burger's concept of *Porthidium* would require revision, but their willingness to present the state of knowledge at that time stimulated much phylogenetic research that has since resolved the problem of *Porthidium* polyphyly (see below). Soon after the publication of that book, modern methods of phylogenetic analysis were brought to bear on questions about the evolutionary history of New World pitvipers. We believe that the present volume continues in that tradition, although the problematic genus is now *Bothrops* (see below and introduction to Viperidae in this volume).

The generic classification of Old World pitvipers has also changed considerably since the use of *Trimeresurus* (sensu lato); additional information about the phylogeny and classification of Old World pitvipers may be found in Kraus et al., 1996; Malhotra and Thorpe, 1997, 2000; McDiarmid et al., 1999; and Parkinson et al., 2002. The maximum number of Old World pitviper genera recognized currently is 10, although additional phylogenetic studies are needed to evaluate this classification. These genera are *Calloselasma* Cope (1860a); *Deinagkistrodon* Gloyd (1979); *Ermia* Zhang (1992); *Gloydius* Hoge and Romano-Hoge (1981a); *Hypnale* Fitzinger (1843); *Ovophis* Burger in Hoge and Romano-Hoge (1981a); *Protobothrops* Hoge and

Table 54. Allocation of *Bothrops* (sensu lato) species to five genera by Burger (1971).

Bothriechis	Bothriopsis	Bothrops (atrox group)	Bothrops (neuwiedi, alternata, and ammodytoides groups)	Ophryacus	Porthidium
B. a. aurifer	B. albocarinatus	B. andiana	B. iglesiasi	O. undulatus	P. barbouri
B. a. marchi	B. c. castelnaudi	B. asper	B. itapetiningae		P. g. godmani
B. bicolor	B. c. lichenosus	B. atrox	B. n. neuwiedi		P. g. vulcanicum
B. lateralis	B. c. plorator	B. barnetti	B. n. boliviana		P. hyoprora
B. nigroviridis	B. c. quadriscutatus	B. brazili	B. n. dipora		P. l. lansbergi
B. s. schlegelii	B. medusa	B. caribbaea	B. n. fluminensis		P. l. dunni
B. s. nigroadspersus	B. oligolepis	B. insularis	B. n. goyazensis		P. l. yucatanicum
	B. punctatus	B. jararaca	B. n. lutzi		P. n. nasutum
	B. b. bilineatus	B. jararacussu	B. n. mattogrossensis		P. n. sutum
	B. b. smaragdinus	B. lanceolata	B. n. paranaensis		P. ophryomegas
	B. peruvianus	B. lojana	B. n. pauloensis		P. melanurum
		B. marajoensis	B. n. piauhyensis		P. n. nummifer
		B. moojeni	B. n. pubescens		P. n. mexicanum
		B. picta	B. n. urutu		P. n. occiduum
		B. pifanoi			P. n. picadoi
		B. pirajai	B. alternata		
		B. pradoi	B. cotiara		
		B. pulchra	B. fonsecai		
		B. santaecrucis			
		B. xanthogramma	B. ammodytoides		
			B. m. microphthalma		
			B. m. colombiana		
			B. roedingeri		

Note: Burger's concept of *Porthidium* has been shown to be polyphyletic; see Table 55 for a summary of changes to the content of *Porthidium*. The taxonomy used by Burger has been maintained here.

Romano-Hoge (1983); *Triceratolepidophis* Ziegler, Herrmann, David, Orlov, and Pauwels (2000); *Trimeresurus* Lacépède (1804); and *Tropidolaemus* Wagler (1830).

Phylogenetic Relationships among Pitvipers of the Americas

The symposium volume *Biology of the Pitvipers* (Campbell and Brodie, 1992) heralded the modern era of phylogenetic research with several papers that brought objective analytical techniques to bear on questions of pitviper phylogeny (Barker, 1992; Cadle, 1992; Crother et al., 1992; Dorcas, 1992; Knight et al., 1992; Werman, 1992). Werman (1992) studied 23 New World pitviper species using morphological, isozyme, and allozyme characters in maximum parsimony analyses. Werman's study indicated that the genus *Porthidium* as recognized by Burger was paraphyletic, and as a partial solution to this problem he erected the genus *Atropoides* for three species (*A. nummifer*, *A. olmec*, and *A. picadoi*) that had been included in *Porthidium* (Table 55). The content of *Atropoides* has now been increased to five species with the demonstration that *A. nummifer* was a complex of three distinct species (*A. mexicanus*, *A. nummifer*, and *A. occiduus*; Campbell and Lamar, this volume; Castoe et al., 2003).

Soon after Werman's study was published, Campbell and Lamar (1992) further addressed the paraphyly of *Porthidium* by naming *Cerrophidion* for three other species (*C. barbouri*, *C. godmani*, *C. tzotzilorum*) that had been placed in *Porthidium*. A fourth species, *C. petlalcalensis*, was later discovered and assigned to this genus by López-Luna et al. (1999). Recognition of *Atropoides* and *Cerrophidion* is consistent with the three groups within *Porthidium* recognized by Burger (Table 55). *Atropoides* corresponds to Burger's *Porthidium nummifer* group, although Burger also included *melanurum* as a divergent member of this group; and *Cerrophidion* corresponds to Burger's *Porthidium godmani* group. Burger's *Porthidium lansbergi* group corresponds to species remaining in *Porthidium* (+*hyoprora*). Recognition of these groups is also largely consistent with earlier proposals (Burger, 1950:59; Dunn, 1919:214; Smith, 1940:62).

Gutberlet (1998a) studied 52 anatomical characters in 13 pitviper species, and in four different maximum parsimony analyses found that *Porthidium melanurum* is most closely related to *Ophryacus undulatus* and does not form a clade with the other *Porthidium* species included in the study (*P. nasutum* and *P. ophryomegas*). The *P. melanurum–O. undulatus* clade is supported by nonparametric bootstrap proportions of 97–99. Based on these results, Gutberlet suggested that *melanurum* be placed in *Ophryacus* (Table 55).

Mitochondrial DNA analyses (Kraus et al., 1996; Parkinson, 1999; Parkinson et al., 2002) and anatomical analyses (Gutberlet and Harvey, 2002), indicate that *Porthidium hyoprora* is closely related to species of *Bothrops* and does not form a monophyletic group with other species of *Porthidium*. Based on these findings, McDiarmid et al. (1999) assigned *P. hyoprora* to *Bothrops*, and Gutberlet and Campbell (2001) subsequently erected *Bothrocophias* to accommodate *Bothrops hyoprora*, *B. microphthalmus*, *B. campbelli*, and the newly described

Table 55. Revision of *Porthidium* from 1971 to the present.

Burger, 1971	Campbell and Lamar, 1989	Werman, 1992	Campbell and Lamar, 1992	Gutberlet, 1998a	Gutberlet and Campbell, 2001	Campbell and Lamar, this volume
Porthidium	*Porthidium*	*Porthidium*	*Porthidium*	*Porthidium*	*Porthidium*	*Porthidium*
P. lansbergi group	Hognosed pitvipers					
P. l. dunni	P. dunni	P. dunni	P. dunni	P. dunni	P. dunni	P. dunni
P. l. lansbergi	P. lansbergii	P. lansbergii	P. lansbergii	P. lansbergii	P. lansbergii	P. lansbergii
P. l. yucatanicum	P. yucatanicum	P. yucatanicum	P. yucatanicum	P. yucatanicum	P. yucatanicum	P. yucatanicum
P. nasutum	P. nasutum	P. nasutum	P. nasutum	P. nasutum	P. nasutum	P. nasutum
P. ophryomegas	P. ophryomegas	P. ophryomegas	P. ophryomegas	P. ophryomegas	P. ophryomegas	P. ophryomegas
P. hyoprora	P. hespere	P. hespere	P. hespere	P. hespere	P. hespere	P. hespere
	P. hyoprora	P. hyoprora	P. hyoprora	P. volcanicum	P. volcanicum	P. volcanicum
			P. melanurum	P. hyoprora		P. porrasi
						P. arcosae
P. nummifer group	Jumping pitvipers	*Atropoides*	*Atropoides*	*Atropoides*	*Atropoides*	*Atropoides*
P. n. nummifer	P. n. nummifer	A. n. nummifer	A. n. nummifer	A. n. nummifer	A. n. nummifer	A. nummifer
P. n. mexicanum	P. n. mexicanum	A. n. mexicanum	A. n. mexicanum	A. n. mexicanum	A. n. mexicanum	A. mexicanus
P. n. occiduus	P. n. occiduum	A. n. occiduum	A. n. occiduum	A. n. occiduum	A. n. occiduum	A. occiduus
P. n. picadoi	P. picadoi	A. picadoi	A. picadoi	A. picadoi	A. picadoi	A. picadoi
P. melanurum	P. olmec	A. olmec	A. olmec	A. olmec	A. olmec	A. olmec
P. godmani group	Montane pitvipers		*Cerrophidion*	*Cerrophidion*	*Cerrophidion*	*Cerrophidion*
P. barbouri	P. barbouri	P. barbouri	C. barbouri	C. barbouri	C. barbouri	C. barbouri
P. godmani	P. godmani	P. godmani	C. godmani	C. godmani	C. godmani	C. godmani
	P. tzotzilorum	P. tzotzilorum	C. tzotzilorum	C. tzotzilorum	C. tzotzilorum	C. tzotzilorum
	P. melanurum	P. melanurum			C. petlalcalensis	C. petlalcalensis
					Bothrocophias	*Bothrocophias*
					B. hyoprora	B. hyoprora
				Ophryacus	*Ophryacus*	*Ophryacus*
				O. melanurus	O. melanurus	O. melanurus

Note: Only currently recognized species are listed. The following taxa were described after 1971: *Bothrops hesperis* Campbell (1976); *Bothrops tzotzilorum* Campbell (1985); *Porthidium olmec* Pérez-Higareda, Smith, and Juliá-Zertuche (1985); *Porthidium lansbergii arcosae* Schätti and Kramer (1993); *Porthidium volcanicum* Solórzano (1995a); *Cerrophidion petlalcalensis* López-Luna, Vogt, and Torre-Loranca (1999); and *Porthidium porrasi* Lamar and Sasa (2003). Campbell and Lamar (this volume) elevated *P. l. arcosae*, *A. n. mexicanum*, and *A. n. occiduum* to species status. Burger (1971) listed two subspecies that are no longer recognized: *P. godmani vulcanicum* and *P. nasutum sutum*.

Bothrocophias myersi. A fifth species, *B. colombianus*, is now included in *Bothrocophias* (Campbell and Lamar, this volume).

Several recent studies (Murphy et al., 2002; Parkinson et al., 2002; Stille, 1987) have demonstrated paraphyly of *Sistrurus* with respect to *S. ravus*. This species is now included in *Crotalus* (Campbell and Lamar, this volume; Murphy et al., 2002; Parkinson et al., 2002).

The current generic arrangement for New World pitvipers (Campbell and Lamar, this volume) appears to accurately reflect evolutionary history, although issues regarding the status of *Atropoides* and *Bothrops* remain to be addressed (see below). Relationships among genera have been more difficult to discern. Uncertainty in this area persisted through the early 1990s, but some consensus is finally unfolding.

Among New World pitviper genera, Burger postulated a close relationship between *Agkistrodon*, *Porthidium*, *Crotalus*, and *Sistrurus*, and recognized a separate lineage consisting of *Ophryacus*, *Bothriopsis*, and *Bothrops* (Fig. 236B). Burger was undecided about the phylogenetic affinities of *Bothriechis* and *Lachesis*, although he ventured that *Bothriechis* may be closely related to *Porthidium*. Burger stated that the resemblance between *Lachesis* and *Porthidium nummifer* is probably the result of convergence.

Estol (1981) used his extensive data set on epidermal microstructure to discuss relationships among New World pitvipers. The relationships since supported by additional data are discussed further below, but several other proposals have proven to be inaccurate. Estol grouped *Bothriechis schlegelii* with *Porthidium dunni* and *P. ophryomegas* based on a shared microstructural pattern called reticulo-carinoverrucate. He remarked that the generic name *Teleuraspis* is available for this group, but that additional characters would have to be studied before this genus can be recognized. Estol grouped *Bothriopsis medusa* with *Bothriechis rowleyi* based on a shared pattern called reticulo-pseudocarinate.

Although modern, objective approaches to pitviper phylogeny and classification began in the 1990s, some papers published during this period relied on less objective "key character" approaches and consequently introduced some unsound ideas about pitviper classification. Schätti et al. (1990), for instance, suggested that species assigned to *Bothriechis* and *Bothriopsis* by previous authors (Burger, 1971; Campbell and Lamar, 1989) should be included in *Bothriechis* based on shared presence of a prehensile tail. Campbell and Lamar (1992:3) responded to that suggestion as follows: "In lieu of additional evidence, a prehensile tail might be considered a homologous character uniting Middle American and South American groups of arboreal pitvipers. However, when the preponderance of evidence is considered (summarized by Campbell and Lamar, 1989), it appears more likely that a prehensile tail is convergent in these two groups." Campbell and Lamar (1992:2) also "hypothesize[d] that *Bothriechis* and *Bothriopsis* represent monophyletic groups, whereas the diverse, widespread genus *Bothrops* may be paraphyletic."

Several subsequent phylogenetic studies demonstrated that *Bothriechis* and *Bothriopsis* do not together form a monophyletic group (e.g., Gutberlet and Harvey, 2002; Kraus et al., 1996; Parkinson, 1999; Parkinson et al., 2002; Werman, 1992, 1997). Gutberlet and Harvey (2002) scored 76 characters of scalation, hemipenes, osteology, and color pattern for 32 pitviper species, including representatives of all New World genera; their data even included character states related to arboreality such as presence of a prehensile tail and green dorsal coloration.

Maximum parsimony analyses of these data supported Campbell and Lamar's (1992) hypothesis that the prehensile tail arose through convergent evolution in the two groups, and in no analysis did *Bothriechis* and *Bothriopsis* form an exclusive monophyletic group.

Schätti and Kramer (1993) again referred to few characters in their suggested revision of *Porthidium*, in which they proposed allocation of two species then in *Bothrops* (*B. microphthalmus* and *B. campbelli*; the latter is the correct name for *Porthidum almawebi* named by Schätti and Kramer in that article) to *Porthidium*. It is clear from their taxonomic decision that they noticed the close relationship between *campbelli*, *microphthalmus*, and *hyoprora* (included in *Porthidium* at that time; see Table 55), but their lack of a phylogenetic analysis of relevant species (or at least consideration of all available synapomorphic information) led them to the erroneous conclusion that the two species of *Bothrops* should be added to *Porthidium* when actually *hyoprora* needed to be *removed* from *Porthidium*. The elevated snouts of *hyoprora*, *microphthalmus*, and many species of *Porthidium*, like the prehensile tails of *Bothriechis* and *Bothriopsis*, arose through convergent evolution (Gutberlet and Harvey, 2002). Golay et al. (1993) adopted the classification of *Porthidium* and *Bothriechis* proposed by Schätti and his collaborators and additionally did not recognize *Atropoides* or *Cerrophidion*, but instead included the jumping pitvipers and montane pitvipers in *Porthidium*.

Reporting on his study of albumin divergence in vipers, Cadle (1992), emphasizing the limited value of his data, tentatively suggested monophyly of *Bothrops* sensu lato (all New World genera now recognized except *Agkistrodon*, *Crotalus*, *Sistrurus*, and *Lachesis*). Subsequent studies have not supported this hypothesis (e.g., Gutberlet and Harvey, 2002; Kraus et al., 1996; Parkinson, 1999; Parkinson et al., 1999; Vidal et al., 1997; Werman et al., 1999). In Kraus et al.'s analyses (Fig. 239A), *Bothrops* sensu lato (bothropoid genera sensu Kraus et al., 1996) was found to be paraphyletic with respect to *Agkistrodon*, *Crotalus*, *Sistrurus*, and *Lachesis*. *Bothrops* sensu lato was paraphyletic only with respect to *Lachesis* in the studies by Gutberlet and Harvey (2002), Parkinson (1999), and Parkinson et al. (2002).

Phylogenetic studies of New World pitvipers based on morphology and allozymes (Werman, 1992) and morphology only (Gutberlet, 1998a) suggested a sister relationship between *Porthidium* and the clade containing *Bothrops* and *Bothriopsis*, but this relationship has not been supported by more recent molecular (Kraus et al., 1996; Parkinson, 1999; Parkinson et al., 2002; Werman et al., 1999) and morphological (Gutberlet and Harvey, 2002) studies. Werman (1999) provided a likely explanation for this discrepancy, implicating convergent evolution of various components of the cranium and palatomaxillary arch. The skulls of *Porthidium* and at least some species of *Bothrops* are elongate and relatively narrow compared with skulls of most other New World pitviper groups (Werman, 1999). Species of *Bothrops* and *Porthidium* also share relatively long and narrow ectopterygoids without lateral flanges and relatively long and weakly curved fangs (see Figs. 111 and 169). Uncertainty about the polarity of these character states was also a concern for Werman, although based on more recent evidence these osteological features of *Porthidium* and *Bothrops* can be reasonably interpreted as derived. Werman (1999) went on to note numerous differences in scalation between *Bothrops* and *Porthidium*, which together with the mtDNA evidence would support a hypothesis of convergence for the osteological features. Werman (1992) and Gutberlet (1998a) examined fewer taxa than later researchers did. The study by Gutberlet and Harvey (2002) based exclusively on morphological data did not indicate a close relationship between *Porthidium* and *Bothrops*, so the limited taxonomic sample used in the earlier studies in addition to morphological convergence may have contributed to their failure to detect the independent origin of certain osteological features within *Porthidium* and *Bothrops*. Although these osteological features appear to be convergent at the intergeneric level, they still provide valuable data about the monophyly of *Porthidium* and should be useful in detecting clades within the *Bothrops* radiation as well (see below).

At the time Werman (1999) wrote, the data were somewhat equivocal with respect to the phylogenetic positions of *Bothrops* and *Porthidium*, but subsequent studies (Gutberlet and Harvey, 2002; Parkinson, 1999; Parkinson et al., 2002; Werman et al., 1999) have built a strong case for the independent origin of these groups. There is now at least some support for recognizing two major groups of New World pitvipers: a North American group consisting of *Agkistrodon*, *Crotalus*, and *Sistrurus*; and a Neotropical group consisting of all other New World genera (Gutberlet and Harvey, 2002; Kraus et al., 1996; Parkinson, 1999; Parkinson et al., 2002). Gutberlet and Campbell (2001) further proposed that the Neotropical group may contain two clades: a Middle American group including *Atropoides*, *Bothriechis*, *Cerrophidion*, *Ophryacus*, and *Porthidium*; and a South American group including *Bothriopsis*, *Bothrocophias*, *Bothrops*, and *Lachesis*.

The North American and Neotropical groups were recovered in six of eight analyses conducted by Gutberlet and Harvey (2002) (Fig. 241B), three of four analyses conducted by Parkinson et al. (2002; Fig. 241A), and all analyses conducted by Parkinson (1999; Fig. 239B). Kraus et al.'s (1996) analysis that included transitions (Fig. 239A) recovered a monophyletic North American group nested within the Neotropical group. Although all studies using large taxonomic samples are now recovering these groups, nonparametric bootstrap support has been weak. In two studies, the highest level of bootstrap support for the North American group was 50 (Parkinson, 1999) or 51 (Gutberlet and Harvey, 2002); however, in Parkinson et al.'s (2002) maximum likelihood analysis that accounted for differential rates of substitution among nucleotide sites, monophyly of the North American group was supported by a relative likelihood support score of 82. Nonparametric bootstrap support for the Neotropical group was less than 50 in all of the above studies. Clearly, monophyly of the North American and

Neotropical groups is the best hypothesis, but further testing is desirable.

One clade within the Middle American group (*Atropoides-Cerrophidion-Porthidium*) has been well supported by recent mtDNA studies (Kraus et al., 1996; Parkinson, 1999; Parkinson et al., 2002), but the phylogenetic positions of *Bothriechis* and *Ophryacus* have been less stable in those studies. Studies using morphological data (Crother et al., 1992; Gutberlet and Harvey, 2002; Werman, 1992) have provided compelling evidence for a close relationship between *Ophryacus* and *Bothriechis* but have not recovered the *Atropoides-Cerrophidion-Porthidium* clade (species in this clade were not studied by Crother et al., 1992). Furthermore, owing to the conflicting results obtained by the DNA and morphological studies, no study to date has recovered a monophyletic Middle American group. Obviously, further testing of this hypothesis is necessary.

An alternative hypothesis, proposed here for the first time, is that the Middle American group as delimited by Gutberlet and Campbell (2001) is paraphyletic with respect to the South American group: (*Bothriechis-Ophryacus* (*Atropoides-Cerrophidion-Porthidium*, South American group)). Although in need of additional testing, this hypothesis appears to be most consistent with the evidence currently available (Gutberlet and Harvey, 2002; Parkinson et al., 2002); it is discussed further in the section below on historical biogeography. A third possibility (*Ophryacus* (*Bothriechis* (*Atropoides-Cerrophidion-Porthidium*, South American group))) must also be considered in light of the results of Parkinson (1999) and Parkinson et al. (2002; Figs. 241B, 242A).

The *Atropoides-Cerrophidion-Porthidium* clade was recovered in all analyses conducted by Kraus et al. (1996), Parkinson (1999; nonparametric bootstrap support always less than 50), and Parkinson et al. (2002; nonparametric bootstrap support from 94 to 100; relative likelihood support 100 in both maximum likelihood analyses).

Their numerous shared, derived features of hemipenial morphology, osteology, and scalation (discussed further below) make it difficult to imagine that *Ophryacus* and *Bothriechis* do not form a monophyletic group. As discussed by Crother et al. (1992), a sister relationship between these two genera also makes good geographic sense (see Maps 44–47, 83, 84) and is perfectly consistent with past vicariance across the Isthmus of Tehuantepec. The *Ophryacus-Bothriechis* clade was recovered by Werman (1992; Fig. 242) and in all analyses conducted by

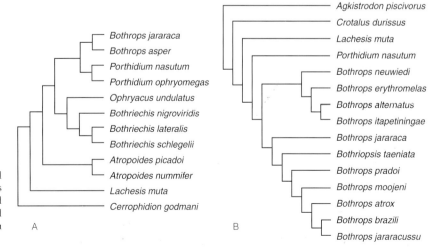

Fig. 242. Phylogenetic relationships of New World pitvipers inferred from maximum parsimony analyses of morphological and biochemical (isozymes and allozymes) data (Werman, 1992). Werman conducted separate analyses focusing on (A) Middle American taxa and (B) South American taxa.

Gutberlet and Harvey (2002; nonparametric bootstrap support from less than 50 to 66; Fig. 241B).

In considering the South American group, monophyly of the *Bothrops-Bothriopsis-Bothrocophias* clade is very well supported by many studies, but the placement of *Lachesis* in this group is more problematic. The *Bothrops-Bothriopsis-Bothrocophias* clade was recovered in one of eight analyses conducted by Gutberlet and Harvey (2002), three of four analyses conducted by Kraus et al. (1996), and all analyses conducted by Parkinson (1999; nonparametric bootstrap support 97–100), Parkinson et al. (2002; nonparametric bootstrap support and relative likelihood support 100 in all analyses), and Wüster et al. (2002a; nonparametric bootstrap support 91–100). *Lachesis* was placed in a South American clade by one analysis of Kraus et al. (1996) and two analyses of Gutberlet and Harvey (2002); *Lachesis* was associated with *Bothrops* or *Bothrocophias* in all analyses conducted by Gutberlet and Harvey (2002). Species of *Bothrops*, *Bothriopsis*, and *Bothrocophias* share a unique pattern of epidermal microstructure that is similar to that found in *Lachesis* (Estol, 1981; Gutberlet, 1998b; Gutberlet and Harvey, unpublished data). Although further testing is required, the available data suggest that *Lachesis* may be the most basal lineage within the South American group (see the section below on historical biogeography).

In order to resolve the remaining questions about intergeneric relationships of New World pitvipers, combined analyses of morphological and molecular data (Gutberlet and Parkinson, in prep.) are needed, as are further taxonomic sampling and the use of new characters from genes (mitochondrial and nuclear) and morphology (musculature, viscera, epidermal microstructure).

Minton (1992:160) appears to have been the first to propose North American and Neotropical groups within the radiation of New World pitvipers: "My serologic data is compatible with monophyletic origin for the American pitvipers perhaps from an *Agkistrodon*-like snake. This stock might have divided early into a southern branch that became *Bothrops* and related Central American genera and a northern branch that gave rise to American *Agkistrodon* and to the rattlesnakes. It is equally possible that *Bothrops* and its allies arose from a different Asian stock." Parkinson (1999) conducted the first rigorous test of this hypothesis.

Based on extensive congruence among the results of recent studies, we now have great confidence in various aspects of the evolutionary history of American pitvipers, and additional study should solve the remaining mysteries of New World pitviper evolution. Below we provide an overview of our best estimate of relationships among genera within each of the three putative clades, among species within each genus, and among currently recognized subspecies in some species.

North American Group   Within the North American group, the rattlesnakes form a clade, and *Agkistrodon* is their sister group: (*Agkistrodon* (*Sistrurus*, *Crotalus*)). These relationships are supported by Gutberlet and Harvey, 2002; Kraus et al., 1996; Parkinson, 1999; Parkinson et al., 2002; Vidal and Lecointre, 1998; and Vidal et al., 1999. Minton (1992) also demonstrated similarity between rattlesnakes and *Agkistrodon*.

Agkistrodon.   Throughout the twentieth century, three species of *Agkistrodon* were recognized in the New World (Campbell and Lamar, 1989; Gloyd and Conant, 1990); but Parkinson et al. (2000), based on a phylogeographic analysis of the genus,

elevated *Agkistrodon bilineatus taylori* to species status; this revision is also supported by the data of Knight et al. (1992:58). Today these four species can be confidently recognized as a monophyletic group. Evidence for the monophyly of *Agkistrodon* sensu stricto has been presented by Gloyd and Conant (1990), Gutberlet and Harvey (2002), Hoge and Romano-Hoge (1981a), Knight et al. (1992), Kraus et al. (1996), Parkinson (1999), and Parkinson et al. (1997, 2002).

Few morphological synapomorphies of *Agkistrodon* have been discerned, and this (together with earlier disregard for character polarity) is probably the primary reason why the uncertainty about this group's monophyly persisted as long as it did. If, as suggested by many workers (e.g., Parkinson et al., 2002), the common ancestor of *Agkistrodon* resembled *Gloydius blomhoffii*, then the following morphological features discussed by Gloyd and Conant (1990) could be interpreted as synapomorphies (though not unique to *Agkistrodon*). Relative to species of *Gloydius*, species of *Agkistrodon* exhibit a higher frequency of abnormalities of the cephalic plates, especially with regard to fragmentation of the parietals. The anterior subcaudals of *Agkistrodon* are undivided and the posterior subcaudals are divided, although the relative proportion of each varies among individuals and populations. The head lacks extensive dorsal markings in *Agkistrodon*, yet such markings are common in *Gloydius*. Also, the small, dark parietal spots present on all *A. contortrix* are rarely observed in juveniles of its congeners. Relative to *Gloydius*, species of *Agkistrodon* have fewer and longer body blotches and are generally larger. Species of *Agkistrodon* have more dentary and pterygoid teeth (Kardong, 1990). Hemipenial lobes are longer in *Agkistrodon* relative to *Gloydius* and have calyces that extend farther proximally along the sulcus spermaticus (Malnate, 1990). Hoge and Romano-Hoge (1981a) also reported longer supratemporal bones (Fig. 237) and parasubcaudals that are higher than wide in *Agkistrodon*. If the higher canaliculate scale microstructure pattern observed by Chiasson et al. (1989) is interpreted as derived, this condition may also be a synapomorphy of *Agkistrodon*. The genus retains many ancestral features (e.g., symmetrical head plates) and does not have any known morphological character (like the rattle) that is unique and unequivocally derived.

Genetic data supporting the monophyly of *Agkistrodon* include mitochondrial DNA restriction fragments (Knight et al., 1992) and nucleotide sequences from the following genes: 16S rRNA (Knight et al., 1992; Parkinson, 1999; Parkinson et al., 1997, 2000, 2002), 12S rRNA (Parkinson, 1999; Parkinson et al., 1997, 2000, 2002), cyt *b* (Parkinson et al., 2002), ND4 (Kraus et al., 1996; Parkinson et al., 2000, 2002), tRNA-HIS and tRNA-SER (Parkinson et al., 2000).

Numerous authors have discussed relationships among the species of *Agkistrodon*, and many alternative scenarios for the evolution of this group have been suggested. As we would expect, most earlier studies did not address the phylogenetic position of *A. taylori*. Campbell and Whitmore (1989) recovered a sister relationship between *A. contortrix* and *A. piscivorus* and also found a sister relationship between *A. bilineatus* and *A. taylori*. Other studies suggest a closer relationship between *A. contortrix* and *A. bilineatus* (Conant, 1986; Gloyd and Conant, 1943; Jones, 1976; Van Devender and Conant, 1990). Gloyd and Conant (1943) reported similarity between *contortrix* and *bilineatus* in numbers of middorsal scale rows and subcaudals, but similarity between *bilineatus* and *piscivorus* in numbers of ventrals and infralabials. Minton (1956) reported that *bilineatus* is intermediate in several venom characters between *contortrix* and *piscivorus*, and the conclusions of Jones (1976) were also based on venom proteins. The phylogenetic tree presented by Van Devender and Conant (1990:fig. 7), based on historical climatic and vegetational changes and some reference to morphological characters, clearly depicts a sister relationship between *contortrix* and extant *bilineatus-taylori*; however, a verbal summary of this diagram in Gloyd and Conant, 1990:447, would seem to suggest a closer relationship between *piscivorus* and *bilineatus-taylori*: "*A. bilineatus* [=common ancestor of all *Agkistrodon* species] disappeared from the northwestern part of its range, and the northeastern population differentiated into *A. contortrix* and adapted to the newly formed, largely deciduous forests. As the northern edge of the range of *bilineatus* [=common ancestor of *bilineatus-taylori* and *piscivorus*] was pushed southward, the populations in the warm, humid southeastern United States differentiated into *A. piscivorus*."

Knight et al.'s (1992) parsimony analysis of restriction fragments recovered a close relationship between *contortrix* and *bilineatus-taylori*, although their analysis of DNA sequence information indicated a closer relationship between *A. piscivorus* and the *A. bilineatus–A. taylori* clade (Fig. 238B). Several earlier studies (Brattstrom, 1964; Minton, 1990a) and every recent molecular study (Parkinson, 1999; Parkinson et al., 1997, 2000, 2002) have presented convincing evidence that *A. piscivorus* is more closely related to *A. bilineatus* and *A. taylori* than it is to *A. contortrix*. Nonparametric bootstrap support for a clade of *A. taylori* (then known as *A. bilineatus*) and *A. piscivorus* ranged from 88 to 96 in Parkinson, 1999 (Fig. 239B), was 90 in Parkinson et al., 1997 (Fig. 238D), and was 95–98 in Parkinson et al., 2000 (Fig. 238C). We have observed the absence of loreals, a state typically regarded as unique to *A. piscivorus*, in some specimens of *A. bilineatus*; use of frequency coding (Smith and Gutberlet, 2001; Wiens, 1993, 1995) will enable inclusion of this synapomorphic information in future morphological analyses.

Van Devender and Conant (1990:fig. 7) proposed the following relationships among subspecies of *Agkistrodon contortrix*: ((*pictigaster*, *laticinctus*) (*phaeogaster* (*mokasen*, *contortrix*))) and provided an extensive discussion of how the geographic distribution of these subspecies may have changed during the Pleistocene. Knight et al. (1992) reported that individuals they studied from throughout the range of *Agkistrodon contortrix* were very similar genetically. In a maximum parsimony analysis of their restriction fragment data they recovered a monophyletic *A. contortrix* with the following relationships among named subspecies: ((*contortrix*, *mokasen*)((*laticinctus*, *pictigaster*) (*phaeogaster*, *contortrix*))). Their *A. c. contortrix* from Mississippi was more closely related to *A. c. phaeogaster* than it was to their *A. c. contortrix* from South Carolina. Knight et al. presented three hypotheses that might explain this discordance between their molecular data and the subspecific classification (which is based mostly on color pattern and to a lesser degree on features of scalation): (1) The phylogeny reconstructed from their molecular data is correct, and morphological similarities among specimens currently referred to *A. c. contortrix* have arisen through convergence. (2) Nuclear DNA introgression may have occurred, creating discord between morphological information (affected by nuclear DNA) and mtDNA information (which would not be affected by nuclear DNA introgression). (3) The subspecific classification is historically accurate, but mtDNA introgression has occurred, obfuscating the true relationships among copperheads as shown by their morphology. Knight et al. (1992) selected the third hypothesis as most probable.

However, given the recent findings of Burbrink et al. (2000 and references therein), perhaps the first hypothesis is correct. Knight et al. did suggest that the morphological similarity of copperheads distributed across the southeastern United States (*A. c. contortrix*) may have resulted from "parallel adaptation to the sandy lowland pinewoods environment rather than inheritance from a common ancestor." A potential problem with this interpretation is that there is much less divergence among *A. contortrix* subspecies than among *A. piscivorus* subspecies (see below). Current habitat preferences and latitudinal distributions of the two species may help to explain these differences: perhaps eastern and western populations of snakes currently referable to *A. c. contortrix* were isolated for a shorter time than eastern and western populations of *A. piscivorus*. A full phylogeographic analysis of *A. contortrix* is warranted in order to test these alternative hypotheses.

Van Devender and Conant (1990:fig. 7) proposed the following relationships among subspecies of *Agkistrodon piscivorus*: (*conanti* (*piscivorus*, *leucostoma*)). Knight et al.'s (1992) maximum parsimony analysis of restriction fragment data suggested paraphyly of *A. piscivorus*, with the western subspecies (*leucostoma*) more closely related to *A. bilineatus* than to the other subspecies of *A. piscivorus*. Knight et al. (1992) reported a high estimated sequence divergence (3.7%) between eastern (*piscivorus* and *conanti*) and western (*leucostoma*) cottonmouths, hypothesizing that during the Pleistocene cottonmouths retreated to separate refugia in Florida and Texas (see Blair, 1958). They suggested further study of the two lineages to determine whether they are actually distinct species. The two eastern subspecies (*piscivorus* and *conanti*) formed a clade in Knight et al.'s analysis of nucleotide sequences.

Van Devender and Conant (1990:fig. 7) noted the distinctiveness of *taylori* relative to currently recognized subspecies of *Agkistrodon bilineatus* and proposed the following relationships within the group: (*taylori* (*bilineatus* (*howardgloydi*, *russeolus*))). Parkinson et al. (2000) presented strong support for this hypothesis based on maximum parsimony and maximum likelihood analyses of mitochondrial DNA (Fig. 238C).

Rattlesnakes. The rattle is so unusual that it would be surprising if rattlesnakes did not form a monophyletic group, although Knight et al.'s (1993) observation that "the only evidence that the rattle evolved once is the complexity of that structure (Klauber, 1972)" was accurate until recently. New evidence from anatomy (Gutberlet and Harvey, 2002) and molecular biology (Kraus et al., 1996; Murphy et al., 2002; Parkinson, 1999; Parkinson et al., 2002) supports this conclusion, and rattlesnake monophyly can now be considered a fact. Garman (1889) presented hypotheses about the origin of the rattle, and Brattstrom (1954) studied fossil rattlesnakes (additional fossil studies listed in Holman, 1995).

In addition to the rattle, the following morphological synapomorphies support rattlesnake monophyly: a moderately (e.g., *Crotalus stejnegeri*, *Sistrurus miliarius*) to extremely short tail, apparent lack of a nasal pore (Burger, 1971; Gutberlet and Harvey, 2002; though not all species have been examined for this trait), position of the facial pit below the naso-ocular line (Burger, 1971; Gutberlet and Harvey, 2002; not all species have been examined for this character, and Burger reported that the pit is above the naso-ocular line in *C. intermedius*), and entire subcaudals (not unique to rattlesnakes). It seems likely that additional synapomorphies will be discovered when a morphology-based phylogenetic analysis of the group is conducted.

Nucleotide sequences from the following mitochondrial genes support the monophyly of the rattlesnakes: 16S rRNA (Knight et al., 1993; Murphy et al., 2002; Parkinson, 1999; Parkinson et al., 2002), 12S rRNA (Knight et al., 1993; Murphy et al., 2002; Parkinson, 1999; Parkinson et al., 2002), cyt *b* (Murphy et al., 2002; Parkinson et al., 2002), ND4 (Kraus et al., 1996; Parkinson et al., 2002), ND5 (Murphy et al., 2002), and tRNA-VAL (Murphy et al., 2002).

Very early in the classification of snakes a distinction was made between the rattlesnakes with head plates and those with smaller head scales (*Crotalus*). After some earlier taxonomic confusion (see Gloyd, 1940, for an excellent summary), Garman (1884a) proposed the name *Sistrurus* for the species with head plates (*catenatus*, *miliarius*, and *ravus*), and until recently they were considered to represent a natural group.

Amaral (1929d) discussed the venom characteristics of several rattlesnake species and presented a branching diagram of relationships for the group based on characters of "size, shape, mutual relation of skull bones, size and shape of lungs, hemipenis and crepitaculum, marking distribution on the body, physiognomy, living habits and geographic distribution, together with the general composition, physiological action and immunological reaction of their venoms." He also noted that he considered the "skin markings" to be one of the "most important characters in phylogeny."

Amaral (1929d) suggested that *Crotalus scutulatus* may be the most basal of the extant rattlesnakes, and that the common ancestor of rattlesnakes gave rise to three main phyletic lines. According to Amaral's hypothesis, one line produced *C. molossus* and subsequently *C. durissus* and *C. basiliscus*; the second line produced *C. atrox* (including *lucasensis* and *tortugensis*), *C. adamanteus*, and *C. exsul*; and the third line produced three major groups. One of these groups included *C. horridus*, *C. lepidus*, *C. viridis*, *C. oreganus*, *C. willardi*, and as a group *C. tigris*, *C. cerastes*, and *C. mitchellii*; the second group consisted of *C. triseriatus*, *C. stejnegeri*, and *C. polystictus*; and the third group included the species of *Sistrurus* recognized at that time (*catenatus*, *miliarius*, and *ravus*).

Githens and Butz (1929) compared the venoms of *Crotalus oreganus*, *C. atrox*, *C. horridus*, *C. mitchellii*, *C. adamanteus*, *C. exsul*, and *C. durissus* and found that the first 6 species were remarkably similar but that they differed substantially from *C. durissus*. Githens and George (1931) compared venoms of 14 rattlesnake species by determining the LD_{50} for pigeons injected with the venom. No major phylogenetic conclusions could be drawn from the results, although Githens and George did diagram rattlesnake relationships according mostly to the findings of Klauber (1930a) and proposed that *C. tigris* is specifically distinct from *C. mitchellii stephensi*. Gloyd (1940:15) did not find evidence from venoms particularly convincing and noted, "No relationships have been indicated on the basis of venom reactions which can not also be demonstrated by means of the other criteria mentioned [structure, color pattern, and geographic position]. At best, venom tests expressed in terms of the amount necessary to cause death in experimental animals seem to be but confirmatory evidence of relationship between otherwise similar forms."

Laurence Klauber conducted extensive research on rattlesnake biology, which culminated in his two-volume monograph (1956) on the group (see Greene, *in* Klauber, 1997). Klauber (1930a) reviewed *Crotalus atrox* and similar species, recognizing *lucasensis*, *tortugensis*, *exsul*, and *ruber* as distinct species. Based on specimens available at that time, Klauber

(1930b) considered *Crotalus m. mitchellii* and *C. m. stephensi* subspecies of *C. viridis* (then known as *C. confluentus*). Klauber (1936a) later recognized *C. mitchellii* as specifically distinct from the *C. viridis* complex and determined that *C. mitchellii* consists of three subspecies (*mitchellii*, *pyrrhus*, and *stephensi*). Klauber (1931b) hypothesized a close relationship between *C. enyo* and *C. tigris*.

Gloyd's (1940) monograph on the rattlesnakes provides a thorough and highly readable summary of taxonomic developments related to these snakes and presents hypotheses about the relationships of several rattlesnake groups based on considerations of scalation, color pattern, and hemipenis morphology. Gloyd continued to recognize *Sistrurus* and also recognized four species groups within *Crotalus*: the *durissus* group (including *durissus*, *terrificus*, *unicolor*, *molossus*, *nigrescens*, *basiliscus*, *totonacus*, *horridus*, and *atricaudatus*), the *triseriatus* group (including *triseriatus*, *pricei*, *omiltemanus*, *lepidus*, *klauberi*, *anahuacus*, and *miquihuanus*), the *viridis* group (including *viridis*, *lutosus*, *oreganus*, *abyssus*, *decolor*, *nuntius*, *mitchellii*, *pyrrhus*, and *stephensi*), and the *atrox* group (including *atrox*, *ruber*, *exsul*, *lucasensis*, *tortugensis*, and *adamanteus*). The names used above are those used by Gloyd; some refer to subspecies while others refer to species. Gloyd recognized *C. scutulatus* as intermediate between the *atrox* and *viridis* groups, calling it a "synthetic" form. Owing to a lack of knowledge about their relationships, Gloyd did not assign *C. tigris*, *C. enyo*, *C. cerastes*, *C. willardi*, *C. polystictus*, and *C. stejnegeri* to any group.

Gloyd (1940) criticized Amaral's (1929d) suggestion of a close relationship between *Sistrurus* and the *triseriatus* group, citing hemipenis and scutellation differences between the two groups. Gloyd further remarked that similarities of color pattern between *Sistrurus* and the *triseriatus* group are a result of parallel evolution. Within *Sistrurus*, Gloyd suggested that the three species diverged separately from a common stock and that *S. ravus* is relictual and probably not closely related to any living species.

Within the *triseriatus* group Gloyd (1940) recognized two species: *C. lepidus* with the subspecies *lepidus* and *klauberi*, and *C. triseriatus* with the other five subspecies in the group. Gloyd suggested that *C. t. triseriatus* gave rise to the other subspecies of *C. triseriatus*, but in his figure 7 did at least recognize a close relationship between *pricei* and *miquihuanus*, which today are both regarded as subspecies of *C. pricei*. Gloyd considered *C. l. klauberi* specialized relative to *C. l. lepidus* but did not make great progress in elucidating relationships within this group. His discussion of relevant characters indicates that he was hampered by the lack of an objective method for sorting conflicting character information.

Within the *durissus* group Gloyd (1940) recognized six species: *C. durissus* with the subspecies *durissus* and *terrificus*; *C. molossus* with the subspecies *molossus* and *nigrescens*; *C. horridus* with the subspecies *horridus* and *atricaudatus*; and the three monotypic species *C. unicolor*, *C. basiliscus*, and *C. totonacus*. Gloyd suggested the relationships within this group to be ((*atricaudatus*, *horridus*) ((*molossus*, *nigrescens*) (*basiliscus* (*unicolor* (*durissus*, *terrificus*))))).

Gloyd did not treat the *atrox* and *viridis* groups in great detail owing to their recent revision by Klauber (1930a and 1936a, respectively), but he did provide the following hypothesis of relationships for the *atrox* group: (*adamanteus* (*atrox* (*tortugensis* (*ruber*, *exsul*, *lucasensis*))))) and offered some commentary relevant to relationships within the *viridis* group (Gloyd, 1940:221–222).

Although Klauber (1940b) provided a very favorable review of Gloyd's (1940) monograph, he did point out some areas of disagreement with respect to rattlesnake phylogeny. He did not agree with Gloyd's hypothesis of a close relationship of *C. horridus* and *C. molossus* with the other members of Gloyd's *durissus* group, and also stated his opinion that *lucasensis* is more closely related to *C. atrox* than *C. ruber* is. Klauber further stated that more importance should have been placed on hemipenial differences between *C. triseriatus* and *C. lepidus*.

Smith (1946b) reviewed the *triseriatus* group, elevating *Crotalus triseriatus pricei* to species status and suggesting that *C. lepidus* and *C. triseriatus* form a clade. He recognized an *omiltemanus* subgroup (equivalent to Klauber's [1952] *intermedius* group), in which he included *C. intermedius* and *C. transversus*.

Klauber (1952) summarized a number of features shared by *C. stejnegeri* and *C. polystictus* (e.g., relatively long heads and tails and lack of palatine teeth; see also Klauber, 1937, 1938a, 1939b). Klauber (1952) suggested a close relationship between *C. intermedius* and *C. transversus* on the basis of similarities in color pattern and scalation, a close relationship between *C. lepidus* and *C. triseriatus*, and a close relationship between *C. mitchellii* and *C. tigris*. He presented a hypothesis of rattlesnake relationships in his classic monograph on the group (Klauber, 1956). His ideas remained unchanged in most respects in the second edition (Klauber, 1972; see below), although he no longer placed *Crotalus catalinensis* as sister to *C. ruber* as he had done in the 1956 work.

Minton (1956), on the basis of similarities in venom proteins, suggested that *C. ruber* and *C. atrox* are more closely related to each other than either is to *C. adamanteus*. He also noted similarities between *C. cerastes* and *C. enyo* and their association with the *viridis* group.

Brattstrom (1964) examined the cranial osteology of 22 rattlesnake species (a total of 35 taxa including all subspecies examined) and used overall similarity in these features in discussing rattlesnake relationships. He continued to recognize *Sistrurus* and the *triseriatus*, *durissus*, *atrox*, and *viridis* groups, but his conclusions varied from Gloyd's (1940) in some respects, and he also attempted to further resolve relationships within some groups. Brattstrom also recognized *C. polystictus* and *C. stejnegeri* as sister species within their own unnamed group. He argued that *Sistrurus* should be treated as a subgenus of *Crotalus* because the differences between *Sistrurus* and *Crotalus* were no greater than the differences among the groups within *Crotalus*. Hoge (1966) followed Brattstrom on this point, but most subsequent authors did not; other authors have been concerned about the status of *Sistrurus* (e.g., see also Foote and McMahon, 1977; Parkinson, 1999; and Stille, 1987).

Unlike Gloyd, Brattstrom included *C. willardi* in the *triseriatus* group along with additional species that had been recognized since Gloyd's study (*C. pusillus*, *C. intermedius*, and *C. transversus*). Brattstrom's concepts of the *durissus* and *atrox* groups were the same as Gloyd's. Brattstrom added *C. cerastes*, *C. enyo*, *C. tigris*, *C. scutulatus*, and the extinct *C. potterensis* to the *viridis* group.

Brattstrom recognized *Sistrurus*, the *triseriatus* group, and the *stejnegeri-polystictus* group as the most basal rattlesnake groups, placing the *triseriatus* group and *Sistrurus* closer to one another in his tree of relationships (1964:fig. 36). He noted the similarity of *Sistrurus* and the *triseriatus* group in 12 of 29 osteological characters. He also stated that the *stejnegeri-polystictus* group probably diverged early in rattlesnake history, soon after the origin of *Sistrurus*, and commented on the close relationship

between the *atrox* and *viridis* groups. Brattstrom did not discuss the relationships among groups any further, but his figure 36 depicts intergroup relationships as follows: (*Sistrurus* (*triseriatus* group ((*polystictus*, *stejnegeri*) (*durissus* group (*atrox* group, *viridis* group))))).

Within *Sistrurus* Brattstrom considered *catenatus* and *miliarius* to be sister species, with *ravus* as the most basal member of the group, and further called *S. ravus* "the most *Crotalus*-like species in its group." Brattstrom recognized three subgroups within the *triseriatus* group: the *triseriatus* subgroup, including (*pricei* (*triseriatus*, *pusillus*)); the *intermedius* subgroup, including *intermedius* and *transversus*; and the *lepidus* subgroup, including *lepidus* and *willardi*. He considered the *intermedius* subgroup the most basal but closely related to the *triseriatus* group; he also suggested a close relationship between the *lepidus* subgroup and the *triseriatus* subgroup, thus: (*intermedius* subgroup (*triseriatus* subgroup, *pusillus* subgroup)).

Brattstrom's osteological data supported the relationships within the *durissus* group as proposed by Gloyd (1940). Within the *atrox* group, he considered *C. tortugensis* a close relative of *C. atrox*, *C. exsul* and *C. catalinensis* close relatives of *C. ruber*, and *C. adamanteus* to be the most basal member of the group. Brattstrom suggested that *C. scutulatus* is the most basal member of the *C. viridis* group and stated that osteologically *C. viridis*, *C. potterensis*, *C. enyo*, and *C. tigris* are very similar. He also suggested that *C. mitchellii* is the least derived member of the *viridis* group, but not the most basal. Despite the osteological similarities discussed, Brattstrom (1964:fig. 36) depicted relationships within the *viridis* group as follows: (*scutulatus* ((*potterensis*, *viridis*) ((*tigris*, *mitchellii*) (*enyo*, *cerastes*)))). In the description of *Crotalus lannomi*, Tanner (1966a) suggested that *C. lannomi*, *C. stejnegeri*, and *C. willardi* are the most basal species of *Crotalus*.

Klauber (1972) summarized rattlesnake phylogeny in a phylogenetic tree (Fig. 243). He based his conclusions on the following morphological characters, which he ranked in order from most informative (most "stable") to least informative (most "plastic"): osteological, visceral (e.g., lungs, hemipenes), head and tail proportions, rattle dimensions, scalation, and color pattern. He supplemented his morphological data with references to venom (see references in Klauber, 1972:157–158), ecology, and geographic distribution, and also referred to the historical biogeography of other sympatric groups. Given the recent debate about the use of polymorphic characters in phylogenetic studies (e.g., Murphy and Doyle, 1998; Smith and Gutberlet, 2001; Wiens, 1995), it is interesting to note that Klauber (1972:157) clearly recognized the utility of such characters: "Species differences are rarely so sharply defined or limited in application that there is little or no overlapping. It is usual that some feature of a characteristic that distinguishes a species will be present in a few specimens of closely related species; the degree of this overlapping will often verify relationships."

Klauber recognized *Sistrurus* at the genus level on the basis of the symplesiomorphic head plate arrangement; he considered *ravus* the most basal species and *miliarius* and *catenatus* more recently derived sister species. In the same work Klauber (1972) recognized a group consisting of *Crotalus durissus*, *basiliscus*, *molossus*, and *horridus*, all of which share a rudimentary left lung. He also noted that *scutulatus* may be closely related to *durissus* based on shared venom characteristics, although he placed these two species some distance apart in his phylogenetic tree (Fig. 243). Klauber suggested a close relationship

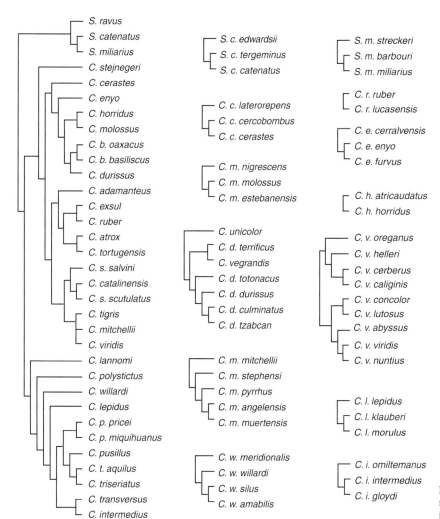

Fig. 243. Klauber's (1972) phylogenetic hypothesis of rattlesnakes based on morphological data. Classification is that of Klauber.

between *durissus* and *basiliscus* based on the shared presence of tuberculate keels, a vertebral ridge, and paravertebral stripes ("almost lost" in *basiliscus*); and he noted the shared presence of a black tail and chevronlike or crossbanded dorsal patterns in *horridus* and *molossus*.

Klauber noted that although *atrox* was once considered a subspecies of *adamanteus*, differences in hemipenes (prominent mesial spines in *adamanteus*), scalation (more scales in frontal and prefrontal region in *adamanteus*), and color pattern (bolder tail pattern in *atrox*) indicate that these two species are not particularly closely related. Klauber also noted a close relationship between *scutulatus* and *catalinensis*, and suggested a possible relationship between *enyo* and *durissus*. Klauber recognized a *Crotalus atrox* group including *atrox, tortugensis, ruber, lucasensis,* and *exsul,* citing similarities in morphology and pattern; and in another group associated with the arid Southwest he included *cerastes, tigris,* and *mitchellii.* Based on the osteological data of Brattstrom (1964), Klauber suggested that the latter group is more closely related to *C. viridis* than to the *C. atrox* group. On his phylogenetic tree, Klauber's depiction of his arid Southwest group is paraphyletic, with *mitchellii* and *tigris* as sister species but with *cerastes* on the branch leading to *enyo* and the *durissus* group (Fig. 243).

Klauber considered the small rattlesnakes occurring in the mountains of central Mexico and the adjacent United States to constitute a montane rattlesnake group consisting of *stejnegeri, lannomi, polystictus, triseriatus, intermedius, transversus, pusillus, lepidus, pricei,* and *willardi.* Of these, Klauber considered *stej-*

negeri, lannomi, polystictus, and *pusillus* to be the most primitive, although again this does not accord perfectly with his phylogenetic tree (Fig. 243).

Using electrophoresis, Foote and MacMahon (1977) compared venom proteins of 18 rattlesnake species, allocating the species they studied to the following groups: *Sistrurus* (*S. miliarius* and *S. catenatus*), the *triseriatus* group (*Crotalus willardi, C. triseriatus, C. pricei, C. lepidus,* and, surprisingly, *S. ravus* and *C. cerastes*), the *durissus* group (*C. durissus, C. horridus, C. molossus, C. mitchellii, C. tigris,* and *C. scutulatus*), the *atrox* group (*adamanteus, atrox, ruber*), and the *viridis* group (*C. viridis* only). These results clearly called into question the validity of *Sistrurus.* Murphy and Crabtree (1985b) found that *Crotalus catalinensis* is more closely related to *C. ruber* as suggested by Brattstrom (1964) than to *C. scutulatus* as suggested by Klauber (1972).

Stille (1987) studied the epidermal microstructure of dorsal scales in 30 rattlesnake species and identified five synapomorphies, three of coarse and two of fine microstructure. These data support an unresolved relationship at the base of the rattlesnake tree among *Crotalus lannomi, C. stejnegeri,* and *C. willardi,* as these species exhibited no synapomorphies. A group including *Sistrurus miliarius, C. pricei, C. cerastes,* and *C. mitchellii* was supported by the shared presence of a foveate coarse microstructure. Within this group, the latter three species share an additional derived feature of coarse microstructure—raised cell borders; and *C. cerastes* and *C. mitchellii* also share a vermiculate fine microstructure. Most of the species Stille studied

(*S. catenatus, S. ravus, C. adamanteus, C. atrox, C. basiliscus, C. catalinensis, C. intermedius, C. lepidus, C. molossus, C. polystictus, C. pusillii, C. ruber, C. scutulatus, C. tigris, C. tortugensis, C. transversus, C. triseriatus, C. viridis, C. durissus, C. d. unicolor, C. d. vegrandis, C. enyo, C. horridus*) shared a derived fine microstructure of linear ridges. *Crotalus horridus* was included in this group on the basis of the next character, but was unique in exhibiting papillae-like rather than linear ridges. Within this group a close relationship among *C. durissus, C. d. unicolor, C. d. vegrandis, C. enyo,* and *C. horridus* was supported by shared presence of a tuberculate coarse microstructure. Of greatest interest in Stille's study was the suggestion of the paraphyly of both *Sistrurus* and *Crotalus*, a significant departure from earlier notions of reciprocal monophyly between the two genera.

McCranie (1988) described the hemipenial morphology of *Sistrurus ravus* (see Fig. 191). Both Gloyd (1940) and Klauber (1972) had noted hemipenial differences between *Crotalus* and *Sistrurus*, but these authors had very little material of *S. ravus* to work with. Whereas the condition in *S. miliarius* and *S. catenatus* is a gradual transition from spines to calyces, the condition in *Crotalus* is an abrupt transition from spines to fringes at the point of bifurcation of the lobes. Gloyd's (1940) examination of one specimen of *S. ravus* suggested a morphology more like that of *Crotalus*. McCranie's (1988) more extensive study confirmed this difference and determined the hemipenes of *S. ravus* to be most similar to those of *C. intermedius, C. pusillus,* and *C. triseriatus*. Knight et al. (1993) noted that the condition of *Crotalus* may be plesiomorphic because it is seen in *Agkistrodon* and other New World groups. Under this interpretation of the polarity, the monophyly of *Sistrurus* sensu lato could not be confirmed or rejected, but the difference between *S. ravus* and its congeners suggested possible paraphyly of *Sistrurus*.

Cadle (1992) reported albumin immunological distances between *Crotalus enyo* and nine other rattlesnake species (*C. mitchellii, C. viridis, C. scutulatus, C. adamanteus, C. durissus, C. horridus, C. cerastes, Sistrurus catenatus,* and *S. miliarius*). These distances were found to be quite low among all the *Crotalus* species examined except *C. horridus*, which differed from *C. enyo* by 13 immunological distance units. Cadle interpreted the great similarity among the majority of *Crotalus* species as indicative of a close relationship among them. The two *Sistrurus* species differed from *C. enyo* by distances of 13 (*S. catenatus*) and 17 (*S. miliarius*) units.

Using radial immunodiffusion, Minton (1992) compared 21 rattlesnake taxa (*Crotalus adamanteus, C. atrox, C. cerastes, C. durissus, C. enyo, C. exsul, C. horridus, C. lepidus, C. m. mitchellii, C. m. pyrrhus, C. molossus, C. polystictus, C. pusillus, C. scutulatus, C. tigris, C. v. viridis, C. v. concolor, C. v. lutosus, Sistrurus catenatus, S. miliarius,* and *S. ravus*). Based on index of deviation values, which estimate the degree of serum albumin divergence from the species chosen for comparison (*Agkistrodon contortrix mokasen* and *Crotalus v. viridis*), Minton concluded that *Crotalus* represents a natural group but that *Sistrurus* probably does not, because serum albumins of species in that genus were determined to be quite divergent.

In order to investigate the potential paraphyly of *Sistrurus*, Knight et al. (1993) studied nucleotide sequences from the 12S and 16S rRNA genes in *Sistrurus ravus, S. catenatus, S. miliarius, Crotalus horridus, C. viridis lutosus, C. aquilus,* and *C. triseriatus*; they used *Agkistrodon bilineatus* as an outgroup. They executed four alternative parsimony analyses and recovered a sister relationship between *S. catenatus* and *S. miliarius* in all of them. *Sistrurus* was recovered as monophyletic in three analyses

(maximum unweighted parsimony; transversion parsimony, W. M. Brown et al., 1982; dynamic weighted parsimony, Williams and Fitch, 1989, 1990), and its status was unresolved in the fourth analysis (EOR-weighted parsimony, Knight and Mindell, 1993). The sister relationship between *S. catenatus* and *S. miliarius* was supported by nonparametric bootstrap proportions of 62–89. Bootstrap support for *Sistrurus* monophyly was weak (less than 50–59) but was still considered the best hypothesis based on the data evaluated. Fu and Murphy (1999) evaluated support for Knight et al.'s (1993) results and found support only for the *S. miliarius–S. catenatus* clade on the basis of significant character covariation.

Kraus et al. (1996) included four rattlesnake species in their phylogenetic analyses based on ND4 sequence data. *Crotalus v. concolor* and *C. adamanteus* were recovered as sisters in all analyses, with *C. lepidus* in a sister relationship to them and *S. miliarius* at the base of this rattlesnake clade (Fig. 239A). Parkinson (1999) included seven rattlesnake species (including all three species of *Sistrurus*) in his study using 12S and 16S rRNA genes. In all analyses, paraphyly of *Crotalus* with respect to *Sistrurus* was indicated (Fig. 239B). In all but one analysis a monophyletic *Sistrurus* was resolved, but never with high nonparametric bootstrap support. *Crotalus adamanteus* and *C. tigris* came out together as sister to *Sistrurus*, and a clade of *C. molossus* and *C. atrox* was sister to that group.

Parkinson et al. (2002) examined the same rattlesnake species as Parkinson (1999), but with the inclusion of sequence data from two additional genes (cyt *b* and ND4) paraphyly of *Crotalus* was no longer indicated, and *Crotalus* monophyly was strongly supported with the nonparametric bootstrap (67–87) and relative likelihood support (98–99; Fig. 241A). In three of four analyses, *Sistrurus ravus* did not form a monophyletic group with the other two *Sistrurus* species (which were always recovered as a strongly supported clade). Instead *S. ravus* was placed at the base of the *Crotalus* clade (nonparametric bootstrap support less than 50–70; relative likelihood support 98). Parkinson et al. (2002), noting the relatively small number of rattlesnake taxa included in their study, were cautious about interpreting these rattlesnake relationships.

Murphy et al. (2002) conducted the most extensive study of rattlesnake relationships to date, including all 3 species of *Sistrurus* and 27 species of *Crotalus*. For a number of *Crotalus* species (e.g., *C. triseriatus, C. horridus*) they even included multiple individuals from different localities, but they were unable to include any samples of two rare Mexican taxa, *C. stejnegeri* and *C. lannomi*. Relationships among the species studied were inferred from maximum parsimony analyses of nucleotide sequence data from the 12S rRNA, 16S rRNA, cytochrome *b*, ND5, and tRNA-VAL genes for a total of 2,945 base pairs, nearly 800 of which were parsimony-informative. The outgroup taxa were *Agkistrodon contortrix, A. piscivorus,* and *Gloydius ussuriensis*. Heuristic searches were used in multiple alternative analyses of the data set (e.g., genes were analyzed separately and also combined in total evidence analyses), though we mostly restrict our discussion here to the preferred analysis of Murphy et al. (2002): all data included, transversions weighted three times greater than transitions (Fig. 244A). The measures of nodal support that we include were calculated based on equal weighting of transitions and transversions; Murphy et al. did not calculate these values for their weighted analysis. When Murphy et al. analyzed their RNA genes separately from the protein-encoding genes (cyt *b* and ND5), they did find a few relationships that conflicted between the two analyses; when all genes

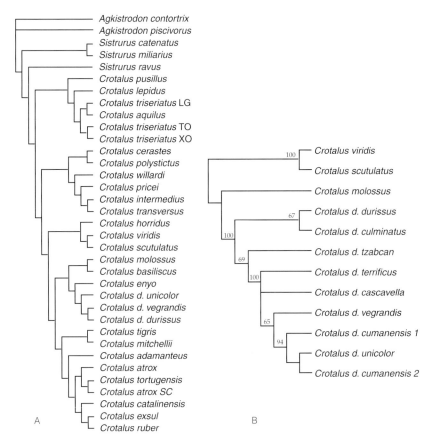

Fig. 244. Phylogenetic relationships of rattlesnakes inferred from maximum parsimony analyses of mtDNA sequence data. (A) Murphy et al., 2002: their preferred tree based on maximum parsimony analysis of sequence data from four genes (cytochrome *b*, ND5, 12S rRNA, and 16S rRNA) and one tRNA (tRNA-VAL) with transversions weighted three times more than transitions and the two species of *Sistrurus* used as a functional outgroup; Murphy et al. determined the relationship of *Sistrurus* to other rattlesnakes in previous analyses. LG = Llano Grande, TO = Toluca, XO = Xochimilco; all localities in Mexico. (B) Wüster et al. 2002a: phylogenetic relationships within the *Crotalus durissus* complex: strict consensus of six most parsimonious trees derived from an analysis of cytochrome *b* sequence data using the branch-and-bound tree-searching algorithm. Numbers above branches are nonparametric bootstrap proportions; branches without numbers were supported in fewer than 50% of the bootstrap pseudoreplications. Numbers 1 and 2 following *Crotalus durissus cumanensis* refer to two different individuals.

were combined, the strongly supported relationships in each separate analysis were retained and the weakly supported conflicting relationships were no longer recovered.

Murphy et al.'s (2002) preferred analysis resulted in a single shortest tree (Fig. 244A), which indicated paraphyly of *Sistrurus*. The sister relationship of *S. catenatus* and *S. miliarius* was strongly supported (decay index 21, jackknife monophyly index 99, nonparametric bootstrap proportion 100), but *S. ravus* was recovered as the sister species to all *Crotalus*. In functional ingroup-outgroup evaluations, this position for *S. ravus* was retained or *S. ravus* was placed within the *C. triseriatus* clade. Based on these findings, Murphy et al. (2002) allocated *S. ravus* to *Crotalus*, thus resolving a long-standing question in pitviper systematics (e.g., Knight et al., 1993; Parkinson, 1999; Stille, 1987). Although the available evidence strongly supports the inclusion of *ravus* in *Crotalus*, the exact position of *ravus* was not well resolved in Murphy et al.'s study. The relationships of this enigmatic species deserve further investigation.

The montane rattlesnakes (the *triseriatus* group, sensu Gloyd, 1940) were found to be paraphyletic with respect to a moderately well supported clade including *Crotalus cerastes* and *C. polystictus* (decay index 4, jackknife monophyly index 76, nonparametric bootstrap proportion 68) and to all the larger rattlesnake species (Fig. 244A), certainly an unexpected relationship based on previous hypotheses. When RNA genes only were analyzed, *C. cerastes* was closely related to *C. enyo*, a relationship that has been suggested by many others on the basis of morphology (e.g., Brattstrom, 1964) and venoms (Minton, 1956). The phylogenetic position of *C. cerastes* deserves additional study. Murphy et al. (2002) suggested that the *triseriatus* group (sensu lato) had been defined primarily on the basis of characters that are plesiomorphic within *Crotalus*. The *C. cerastes–C. polystictus* clade formed the sister group to the clade

including *C. willardi*, *C. pricei*, *C. intermedius*, and *C. transversus*, but the relationship between these two clades was not stable in functional ingroup-outgroup evaluations, nor was inclusion of *C. willardi* in the latter clade a stable arrangement. A clade of *C. pusillus*, *C. lepidus*, *C. triseriatus*, and *C. aquilus* was basal to all rattlesnakes other than *C. ravus*.

Crotalus triseriatus was found to be paraphyletic with respect to *C. aquilus*, and Murphy et al. (2002) suggested that multiple geographically isolated montane species are probably represented under the name *C. triseriatus*. This would not be surprising given that two putatively allopatric subspecies of *C. triseriatus* are already recognized (Campbell, 1979b). These results conflict with the well-supported, morphology-based results of Dorcas (1992), who found a closer relationship between *C. lepidus* and *C. aquilus*. Murphy et al.'s (2002) results placed *C. lepidus* as sister to *C. triseriatus–C. aquilus*, so Dorcas's (1992) concept of the *triseriatus* group is supported. *Crotalus pusillus* was found to be the basal member of this clade. Relationships within the other clade of montane rattlesnakes were as follows: (*C. willardi* (*C. pricei* (*C. intermedius*, *C. transversus*))).

Three major clades were recovered within the radiation of large rattlesnake species. A clade representing a modified *viridis* group (*C. horridus*, *C. scutulatus*, and *C. viridis*) was sister to a clade containing modified *durissus* and *atrox* groups. In functional ingroup-outgroup evaluations, the position of the *viridis* group was sometimes found to be sister to the *atrox* group. Within the *viridis* group, *C. viridis* and *C. scutulatus* were found to be sister taxa, and this relationship was well supported; however, since *C. scutulatus* and *C. viridis* are known to hybridize (Murphy and Crabtree, 1988), Murphy et al. (2002) acknowledged the possibility that mtDNA introgression may account for the genetic similarity observed between these

Table 56. Allocation of *Crotalus* species to seven groups by Murphy et al. (2002).

C. ravus	C. triseriatus	C. polystictus	C. durissus	C. viridis	C. mitchellii	C. atrox
C. ravus	C. triseriatus	C. polystictus	C. durissus	C. viridis	C. mitchellii	C. atrox
	C. aquilus	C. cerastes	C. simus	C. oreganus	C. tigris	C. adamanteus
	C. lepidus	C. willardi	C. totonacus	C. scutulatus		C. catalinensis
	C. pusillus	C. pricei	C. enyo	C. horridus		C. ruber
		C. intermedius	C. basiliscus			C. tortugensis
		C. transversus	C. molossus			

Note: *Crotalus stejnegeri* and *C. lannomi* were not included in Murphy et al.'s (2002) study, so these taxa were listed as incertae sedis by them. We have added *C. simus* and *C. totonacus*, which are recognized by Campbell and Lamar (this volume). Adapted from Murphy et al., 2002: Table 6.

species. The group including *C. durissus* exhibited the following relationships in Murphy et al.'s preferred tree: ((*C. molossus*, *C. basiliscus*) (*C. enyo* (*C. d. unicolor* (*C. d. vegrandis*, *C. durissus*)))). Members of the *atrox* group were related as follows: (*C. adamanteus* ((*C. atrox* (*C. tortugensis*, *C. atrox*)) (*C. catalinensis*, *C. ruber*))). As indicated, *C. atrox* was found to be paraphyletic with respect to *C. tortugensis*. Since *C. atrox* from Isla Santa Cruz was recovered as sister to *C. tortugensis*, and since additional genetic and anatomical differences have been identified (Murphy, unpublished data), Murphy et al. (2002) recommended that the snakes known as *C. atrox* on Isla Santa Cruz be recognized as a separate species. A clade consisting of *C. tigris* and *C. mitchellii* was sister to the *atrox* group, but this position was not well supported. When *C. horridus* was removed from the data set for an additional analysis, the *C. tigris*–*C. mitchellii* clade was placed with the *viridis* group. In summary, Murphy et al. (2002) recognized seven species groups within *Crotalus*: the *ravus*, *triseriatus*, *polystictus*, *durissus*, *viridis*, *mitchellii*, and *atrox* groups, leaving *C. stejnegeri* and *C. lannomi* incertae sedis (Table 56).

Murphy et al. (2002) suggested on the basis of morphological data (e.g., Brattstrom, 1964; Klauber, 1972) that *Crotalus stejnegeri* (not included in their study) may be closely related to *C. polystictus*, but considered the phylogenetic position of *C. lannomi* to be undetermined. The morphological data supporting a close relationship between *C. stejnegeri* and *C. polystictus* is compelling, but additional testing of this hypothesis is needed. Klauber (1972) placed *C. lannomi* as basal to *C. polystictus* on a branch leading to *C. triseriatus* and most other montane rattlesnakes (Fig. 244A). Tanner (1966a) suggested a relationship to *C. stejnegeri*, but this was on the basis of shared ancestral states (relatively long tail and relatively large head scales); Campbell and Lamar (this volume), however, note the stouter body and different head proportions of *C. lannomi* relative to *C. stejnegeri*. The phylogenetic position of *C. lannomi* remains one of the unsolved riddles of American pitviper evolution.

A morphology-based phylogenetic analysis of the rattlesnakes is much needed—both as an independent test of the relationships suggested by mtDNA data and to objectively trace morphological evolution within this unique group. Klauber (1972) listed nine morphological characteristics that may provide a starting point for such an undertaking:

1. Palatine teeth are absent in *Crotalus polystictus* and *C. stejnegeri*.
2. A rudimentary left lung is present in *C. durissus*, *C. basiliscus*, *C. molossus*, and *C. horridus*.
3. Hemipenes are attenuated in *C. adamanteus*, *C. atrox*, *C. ruber*, and *C. tortugensis*.

4. Rattle-growth equations are similar for *C. durissus*, *C. basiliscus*, *C. enyo*, and *C. cerastes*.
5. The head proportions are similar in *C. tigris* and *C. m. mitchellii*.
6. Head plates are present in *C. ravus*, *Sistrurus catenatus*, and *S. miliarius*.
7. The top preocular is divided in 97% of *C. lepidus* examined (300 specimens), ca. 25% of *C. triseriatus aquilus*, and occasionally in *C. pricei*. The scale is also divided in *C. mitchellii*, but Klauber noted the extensive division of other scales in this species, which might suggest that this feature represents a convergence in *C. mitchellii*.
8. The anterior subocular contacts supralabials 4 and 5 in *C. triseriatus*, *C. aquilus*, *C. polystictus*, and *C. pusillus*; and the anterior subocular contacts supralabials 3 and 4 in *C. intermedius* and *C. pricei*. Subocular-supralabial contact "may be present, but is rather unusual in *tigris* and in *lepidus*, especially in the subspecies *klauberi*." The contact occurs in *C. ravus* and *Sistrurus* but is never present in the larger rattlesnake species.
9. There is progressive fragmentation of the head plates from south to north in *C. durissus* (sensu lato), *C. basiliscus*, *C. molossus*, and *C. scutulatus*.

Crotalus. Relationships among most rattlesnake species are reviewed above; in this section we summarize recent studies of small groups and species complexes within *Crotalus*, including several phylogeographic analyses. The species of *Crotalus* are morphologically diverse, and unique morphological synapomorphies supporting the monophyly of this genus are not readily apparent. The synapomorphy of divided head scales is shared by all species except *C. ravus*, but perhaps it is significant that compared with species of *Sistrurus*, *C. ravus* exhibits a higher frequency of irregularities and partial fragmentation of the head plates (Klauber, 1972:159).

The monophyly of *Crotalus* is supported by synapomorphies from the following genes: 12S rRNA (Knight et al., 1993; Murphy et al., 2002; Parkinson et al., 2002), 16S rRNA (Knight et al., 1993; Murphy et al., 2002; Parkinson et al., 2002), cytochrome *b* (Murphy et al., 2002; Parkinson et al., 2002), ND4 (Kraus et al., 1996; Parkinson et al., 2002), ND5 (Murphy et al., 2002), and tRNA-VAL (Murphy et al., 2002). However, in analyses of sequences from 12S and 16S rRNA genes for relatively few rattlesnake taxa, *Crotalus* monophyly was not always supported (see above).

Dorcas (1992) studied relationships among the subspecies of *Crotalus triseriatus* and *C. lepidus* through maximum parsimony analyses of characters of scalation, color pattern, body proportions, hemipenis morphology, and osteology. Of the 50 characters examined, 27 were parsimony-informative. The phylogenetic results of this study were robust to the use of three alternative outgroups (*C. atrox*, *C. pricei*, or a hypothetical ancestor), and also to various partitions of the data (hemipenial characters only; osteological characters only; hemipenial and osteological characters combined; scalation, color pattern, and body proportions; and all characters combined). All analyses showed that *C. t. aquilus* is more closely related to *C. lepidus* than it is to the other subspecies of *C. triseriatus*. In all analyses, *C. t. triseriatus* and *C. t. armstrongi* formed a clade, as did *C. l. lepidus* and *C. l. klauberi*. In most analyses, *C. l. maculosus* was recovered as sister to the *C. l. lepidus–C. l. klauberi* clade. In two analyses based on few characters (hemipenial characters only, and hemipenial and osteological data combined), *C. l. maculosus* was found to be sister to *C. t. aquilus*, but in most analyses *C. t. aquilus* was recovered as sister to the clade including all subspecies of *C. lepidus*. Only data from scalation, color pattern, and body proportions were available for *C. l. morulus*, so this taxon was included in only one analysis, which placed it as sister to the other *C. lepidus* subspecies. Based on these results, Dorcas elevated *C. t. aquilus* to species status and also revised the *triseriatus* group, including within it only *C. triseriatus*, *C. lepidus*, and *C. aquilus*. In the analyses that included all informative characters, 10–12 synapomorphies supported the sister relationship of *C. aquilus* and *C. lepidus*; this relationship can be considered well supported based on these data.

Barker (1992) conducted a phylogeographic analysis of *Crotalus willardi* in which he evaluated 56 morphological characters of scalation, body proportions, and color pattern and 36 allozyme characters. Twenty of the morphological characters and 22 of the allozyme characters were parsimony-informative. For allozyme characters, the locus was treated as the character and the alleles were treated as character states. *Crotalus lepidus* and *Sistrurus catenatus* were used as outgroup taxa. Barker conducted three maximum parsimony analyses, in which he first analyzed the morphological and molecular data separately and then analyzed all the data together. The analysis of allozyme data only generated nine equally parsimonious trees, the strict consensus of which depicted a clade including *C. w. willardi*, *C. w. silus*, and *C. w. obscurus*. The phylogenetic positions of *C. w. meridionalis* and *C. w. amabilis* were unresolved relative to this clade. The morphology only and the combined analyses generated single shortest trees that were topographically identical: *C. w. silus* was sister to *C. w. obscurus*, and these two subspecies were the sister group to a clade of *C. w. amabilis* and *C. w. meridionalis*. The most basal subspecies was *C. w. willardi*. Barker (1992) summarized reasons for considering *C. willardi* one of the more ancient rattlesnake species: its extensive yet disjunct range in the Sierra Madre Occidental (Klauber, 1972), its occurrence in several mountain ranges that are disjunct from the main Sierra Madre Occidental uplift, and its putatively plesiomorphic epidermal microstructure (Stille, 1987).

Within *Crotalus durissus* (sensu lato) Klauber (1972:161) considered the northernmost subspecies to be the most derived, positing an origin for the complex in Middle America, a southward expansion into South America, and subsequent northward expansion in Mexico (Fig. 243). The mtDNA sequence data of Wüster et al. (2002a) do not support this hypothesis. They used 701 base pairs (116 were parsimony-informative) of the cytochrome *b* gene to study the phylogeography of the *Crotalus durissus* complex. They included 15 individuals from 10 localities in Central and South America representing eight of the named subspecies, and they used *C. viridis*, *C. scutulatus*, and *C. molossus* as outgroups. The results of both maximum parsimony and maximum likelihood analyses were consistent with each other (Fig. 244B). The South American subspecies included in the study (*terrificus*, *cascavella*, *vegrandis*, *cumanensis*, and *uni-

color) formed a monophyletic group that was supported by a nonparametric bootstrap proportion of 100. Two Middle American subspecies (*durissus* [=*simus*] and *culminatus*) formed a clade, but the third Middle American subspecies (*tzabcan*) was recovered as the sister to the South American clade.

Sequence divergence was low among the South American populations studied, with a maximum divergence between any two individuals of 1.5%, but divergence among the Middle American lineages was as high as 8.0%. These results suggest a Middle American origin for the *C. durissus* complex and recent dispersal into South America. The genetic divergence among Middle American groups is consistent with the decision of Campbell and Lamar (this volume) to elevate two Middle American lineages (*C. totonacus* and *C. simus*; Map 109) to species status. The name *C. durissus* (Map 96) is restricted to the South American species.

With regard to the *Crotalus viridis* complex, Klauber (1972:164) observed: "It is not impossible that some of the newer methods of blood and venom studies may eventually indicate that the forms which we now consider *viridis* subspecies may really belong to two or more different species, and this despite the confirmatory evidence of the internasals." Early taxonomic revision of the complex was undertaken by Klauber (1930b, 1935b, 1936b, 1949b). Githens and George (1931) found the effects of the venom of *C. v. oreganus* and *C. v. cerberus* to be nearly identical and suggested that these names may be synonyms. Brattstrom (1964) considered relationships within the *C. viridis* complex difficult to determine on the basis of osteology, but did suggest a close relationship between *C. v. concolor* and *C. v. lutosus* and also a close relationship between *C. v. helleri* and *C. v. oreganus*. Brattstrom noted, however, that other characters conflict with this interpretation, showing similarity between *C. v. oreganus* and *C. v. viridis*.

Four studies thus far have used mtDNA to address the phylogeography and taxonomy of the *Crotalus viridis* complex (Ashton and de Queiroz, 2001; Douglas et al., 2002; Pook et al., 2000; Quinn, 1987), and all have verified Klauber's prediction. In an unpublished doctoral dissertation, Quinn (1987) compared several *C. viridis* species using mtDNA and isozymes. Although Quinn did not distinguish between derived and ancestral characters, he still detected distinct lineages in the eastern and western parts of the range, a result that has been consistently supported by more recent studies.

Among 68 specimens from 33 localities (including representatives of all nine subspecies), Pook et al. (2000) found 37 unique cytochrome *b* haplotypes that they used in phylogenetic analyses. Outgroups were *C. scutulatus* and *C. durissus* (sensu lato). They used the results of their cytochrome *b* analysis to choose 19 specimens (representing major groups found in the cytochrome *b* analysis) for ND4 sequencing, and then conducted parsimony and likelihood analyses on the combined data set. The analyses recovered the eastern and western clades (Fig. 245B), and also detected three lineages within the western clade: (1) *C. v. cerberus*; (2) *C. v. lutosus* and *C. v. abyssus*; and (3) *C. v. caliginis*, *C. v. helleri*, *C. v. oreganus*, and *C. v. concolor*. When the cytochrome *b* data were analyzed alone, *C. v. cerberus* was basal to all other *C. viridis*, including the eastern clade; however, the combined analyses supported inclusion of *C. v. cerberus* in the western clade. Pook et al. (2000) did not suggest any taxonomic modifications.

Ashton and de Queiroz (2001) used sequences from the D-loop and ND2 gene from 26 individuals of *Crotalus virdis*, and they used *C. atrox*, *C. cerastes*, *C. enyo*, *C. mitchellii*, and *C. tigris*

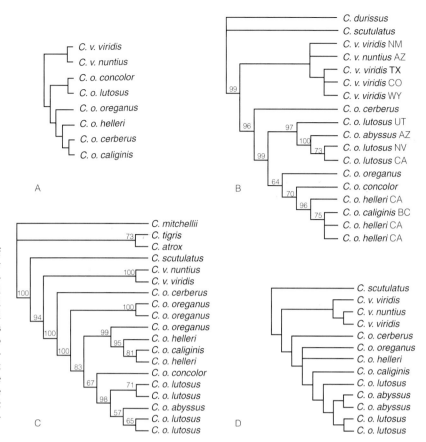

Fig. 245. Phylogenetic relationships among subspecies of the *Crotalus viridis* complex. (A) Klauber, 1972: phylogeny based on morphological data; (B) Pook et al., 2000: consensus of 10 most parsimonious trees from an unweighted branch-and-bound search for 1,345 base pairs of combined cytochrome *b* and ND4 sequence data; (C) Ashton and de Queiroz, 2001: strict consensus of 57 most parsimonious trees based on equal weighting of ND2 and D-loop sequence data; (D) Douglas et al., 2002: maximum likelihood tree of 60 unique haplotypes of the *C. viridis* complex based on analysis of nucleotide sequences of the ATPase 6 and 8 genes. Numbers above branches in B and C are nonparametric bootstrap proportions; branches without numbers were supported in fewer than 50% of the bootstrap pseudoreplications.

as outgroups. The results of their preferred analyses (maximum likelihood and maximum parsimony analyses of their combined data; Fig. 245C) were largely congruent with those of Pook et al. (2000), recognizing the eastern and western clades and supporting inclusion of *C. v. cerbeus* as the most basal member of the western clade. However, the results of Ashton and de Queiroz support a close relationship among *C. v. concolor*, *C. v. lutosus*, and *C. v. abyssus*, whereas the results of Pook et al. place *C. v. concolor* as a closer relative of *C. v. helleri* and *C. v. caliginis*. Based on their findings, Ashton and de Queiroz recommended that the eastern and western clades be afforded species status as *C. virdis* and *C. oreganus*, respectively.

The most thorough study of the *Crotalus viridis* complex to date was undertaken by Douglas et al. (2002), who used 669 base pairs of the relatively rapidly evolving mtDNA genes ATPase 6 and ATPase 8. They sampled all nine subspecies, analyzing 153 individuals, 111 of which were from the Colorado Plateau (an area of potential contact of six of the subspecies). The outgroups were *Agkistrodon contortrix* and *Crotalus scutulatus*. Alternative analyses (weighted and unweighted maximum parsimony, maximum likelihood, and distance analyses) recovered the same well-supported clades (Fig. 245D): (1) an eastern clade (*C. viridis* sensu stricto, nonparametric bootstrap support 100%) within which the monophyly of *C. v. nuntius* was only weakly supported (52%), and (2) a western clade (*C. oreganus*, nonparametric bootstrap support 87%). Within the western clade, the following groups were distinguished: *C. o. cerberus* (88%), *C. o. concolor* (94%), *C. o. lutosus–C. o. abyssus* group (88%) within which *C. o. lutosus* is paraphyletic with respect to a monophyletic *C. o. abyssus* (74%), a paraphyletic *C. o. oreganus*, and a monophyletic *C. o. helleri–C. o. caliginis* group within which *C. o. helleri* is paraphyletic with respect to *C. o. caliginis*. *Crotalus o. cerberus* is the most basal member of *C. oreganus*.

Based on the detection of these lineages and application of the phylogenetic species concept, Douglas et al. (2002) argued for recognition of seven species within the *C. viridis* complex: *C. abyssus*, *C. cerberus*, *C. concolor*, *C. helleri*, *C. lutosus*, *C. oreganus*, and *C. viridis*; but only the well-differentiated eastern and western clades (*C. viridis* and *C. oreganus*) are afforded specific status by Campbell and Lamar in this volume.

Phylogeographic analyses of all widespread rattlesnake species would be of considerable interest. For example, further study of variation in *Crotalus horridus* is warranted (Brown, 1993). Githens and George (1931:32) reported that the venom of western *C. horridus* specimens was much more toxic than that of specimens from New York and Pennsylvania. *Crotalus horridus* may have a history similar to that of the broadly sympatric *Elaphe obsoleta* complex, in which distinct eastern and western lineages can be distinguished (Burbrink, 2001; Burbrink et al., 2000)—this despite the traditional recognition of northern (*C. h. horridus*) and southern (*C. h. atricaudatus*) subspecies.

Sistrurus. The relationships of the two species of *Sistrurus* to other rattlesnakes and the allocation of *S. ravus* to *Crotalus* are discussed above. If the polarity interpretation of Knight et al. (1993) is accurate, the condition of the hemipenis (a gradual transition of spines to calyces from the base to the lobes) may be a synapomorphy of *Sistrurus* (see Figs. 190, 191, 223).

Strong support for the monophyly of *Sistrurus* has been found in sequence data from the following genes: 12S rRNA (Knight et al., 1993; Murphy et al., 2002; Parkinson et al., 2002), 16S rRNA (Knight et al., 1993; Murphy et al., 2002; Parkinson et al., 2002), cytochrome *b* (Murphy et al., 2002; Parkinson et al., 2002), ND4 (Kraus et al., 1996; Parkinson et al., 2002), ND5 (Murphy et al., 2002), and tRNA-VAL (Murphy et al., 2002), and the sister relationship between *S. catenatus* and *S. miliarius* can be considered a fact.

Within *Sistrurus miliarius*, Gloyd (1940) recognized *barbouri* as the most basal subspecies, suggesting that *streckeri* and *miliarius* were derived independently from a *barbouri*-like ancestor. Gloyd (1940) recognized two subspecies within *Sistrurus catenatus* and hypothesized that *tergeminus* gave rise to *catenatus*. Phylogeographic studies of these species might further elucidate the history of the North American fauna.

Middle American Group Two clades of Middle American pitvipers are known: *Atropoides-Cerrophidion-Porthidium* and *Bothriechis-Ophryacus*. Whether these clades together form a single monophyletic group (Gutberlet and Campbell, 2001) is not known. Whereas molecular data provide strong support for recognition of the former group, phylogenetic analyses based on morphology have not resolved this clade. The latter clade is well supported by morphological data but has not been supported by molecular studies.

Atropoides-Cerrophidion-Porthidium clade. Strong support for the monophyly of this group has been found in sequence data from the following genes: 12S rRNA (Parkinson, 1999; Parkinson et al., 2002), 16S rRNA (Parkinson, 1999; Parkinson et al., 2002), cytochrome *b* (Castoe et al., 2003; Parkinson et al., 2002), ND4 (Castoe et al., 2003; Kraus et al., 1996; Parkinson et al., 2002). Morphological synapomorphies include entire subcaudals and absence of a lacunolabial; neither is unique to this group. This is a morphologically diverse group, and a more thorough assessment of morphological synapomorphies must await analyses including both molecular and morphological data (Gutberlet and Parkinson, in prep.).

In the study by Kraus et al. (1996), relationships among the genera in this group were not particularly well supported (Fig. 239A), and the monophyly of *Atropoides* was not supported (see below). Three of four of the analyses presented by Parkinson (1999) supported the relationships (*Atropoides* (*Cerrophidion*, *Porthidium*)); the fourth analysis did not resolve relationships within the group. However, all analyses conducted by Parkinson et al. (2002) supported the relationships (*Porthidium* (*Cerrophidion*, *Atropoides*)). Castoe et al. (2003) conducted a phylogeographic analysis of *Atropoides* based on 1,400 base pairs of mtDNA sequence from cytochrome *b* and ND4. In their ingroup they included multiple individuals of all species of *Atropoides*, multiple individuals of *Cerrophidion godmani*, and four species of *Porthidium*. Three species of *Bothriechis* and both species of *Ophryacus* were included as outgroups. Similar to the results of Kraus et al. (1996), in no analysis was *Atropoides* recovered as monophyletic (Fig. 246A). Parsimony analysis of the total data yielded the relationships (*Atropoides* (*Cerrophidion* (*A. picadoi*, *Porthidium*))), but maximum likelihood analysis of these data supported ((*A. picadoi*, *Porthidium*) (*Cerrophidion*, *Atropoides*)). Castoe et al. (2003) discussed the poor resolution of intergeneric relationships in this group and the problematic placement of *A. picadoi*, and suggested that the difficulty in resolving relationships within the group may be attributable to a rapid radiation soon after its origin. Evidence for alternative relationships within this group must be considered equivocal, but a thorough study to address this problem is already under way (Castoe and Parkinson, pers. comm.).

ATROPOIDES. Monophyly of this genus has been supported by morphological data (Gutberlet and Harvey, 2002; Werman,

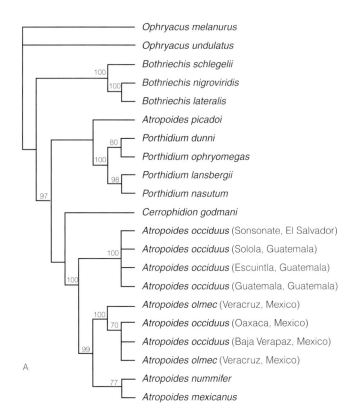

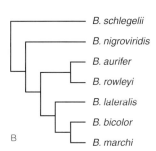

A

B

Fig. 246. (A) Phylogenetic relationships of Middle American pitvipers (Castoe et al., 2003) inferred from 1,401 base pairs of combined mtDNA sequence data (ND4 and cytochrome *b* genes) using a heuristic maximum likelihood search. Numbers above branches are nonparametric bootstrap proportions; branches without numbers were supported in fewer than 50% of the bootstrap pseudoreplications. (B) Phylogeny of *Bothriechis* based on maximum parsimony analysis of morphological data (Crother et al., 1992). An independent analysis of allozyme data resulted in the same tree topology, except that the positions of *B. marchi* and *B. lateralis* were reversed.

1992), allozymes and isozymes (Werman, 1992, 1997), and DNA sequences (Parkinson, 1999; Parkinson et al., 2002). A monophyletic *Atropoides* was not recovered by other analyses of DNA sequence data (Castoe et al., 2003; Kraus et al., 1996). Despite the conflicting results of these studies, the monophyly of *Atropoides* can be considered well supported because those studies including the most data and the most taxa (Gutberlet and Harvey, 2002; Parkinson et al., 2002) found support for this arrangement. The phylogenetic position of *A. picadoi* has been the only source of confusion, and it is worth noting that Dunn (1939) recognized the affinities of *A. picadoi* with the other jumping pitvipers by describing it as a subspecies of *A. nummifer*.

Numerous morphological synapomorphies support the monophyly of *Atropoides*: anteriorly directed posterior portion of the postfrontal and extensive head scale fragmentation (including narrow supraoculars and high numbers of inter-supraoculars, interoculabials, prefoveals, subfoveals, and canthals; see Fig. 18, Pl. 91). Estol (1981) observed a unique microstructure (strio-convex) in *A. nummifer*, *A. occiduus*, and *A. mexicanus*, but he did not examine *A. picadoi* or *A. olmec* (which was undescribed at the time).

The taxonomic history of the species included in *Atropoides* is complex, and Campbell and Lamar (this volume) provide an excellent account of the main issues involved. The only phylogenetic studies to include more than two species of *Atropoides* are Castoe et al., 2003 (all 5 species) and Parkinson et al., 2002 (*A. nummifer* [=*A. mexicanus*], *A. olmec*, and *A. picadoi*). Parkinson et al. (2002) recovered a strongly supported sister relationship between *A. mexicanus* and *A. olmec*, with *A. picadoi* as sister to them. Castoe et al. (2003) could not reject a hypothesis of *Atropoides* monophyly using their data and suggested placing *A. picadoi* as the most basal species in the genus. The other species of *Atropoides* constitute the *nummifer* complex, within which *A. occiduus* was found to be basal with respect to the other three species, thus (*A. picadoi* (*A. occiduus* (*A. olmec* (*A. nummifer*, *A. mexicanus*)))). In this volume Campbell and Lamar, through reference to morphological characters, present a hypothesis of relationships that is largely congruent with that of Castoe et al. (2003): (*A. picadoi* (*A. occiduus* (*A. nummifer* (*A. olmec*, *A. mexicanus*)))). They consider the stout body and associated low ventral scale counts to be synapomorphies of the *nummifer* complex, and consider *A. occiduus* to be unspecialized (e.g., nasorostrals absent or poorly developed, rostral and prenasal in broad contact) relative to other members of this complex. The well-developed nasorostrals and lack of contact between the rostral and prenasal may be synapomorphies linking *A. olmec* and *A. mexicanus*.

CERROPHIDION. Based on the presence of several derived characters the monophyly of *Cerrophidion* seems likely, but this has yet to be tested in a phylogenetic analysis including all species. Thus far, phylogenetic studies of New World pitvipers (e.g., Castoe et al., 2003; Gutberlet and Harvey, 2002; Parkinson et al., 2002) have included only *C. godmani*. Campbell and Lamar (this volume) do note, however, that a close relationship among members of this genus has been suggested for quite some time (Burger, 1971; Campbell, 1985, 1988a; Campbell and Lamar, 1989; Smith, 1941a).

The species of *Cerrophidion* share many characters that are derived relative to *Agkistrodon* and *Gloydius* but appear to be less derived relative to most Neotropical pitvipers. For example, the partially fragmented head plates (see Fig. 156) can easily be interpreted as a synapomorphy of the genus. Genetic synapomorphies of *Cerrophidion* are likely to be detected when sequence data from additional species are collected (T. Castoe and C. Parkinson, pers. comm.).

Relationships within *Cerrophidion* have not been studied in a phylogenetic analysis, but a hypothesis for further testing can be presented here as (*C. godmani* (*C. tzotzilorum* (*C. barbouri*, *C. petlalcalensis*))). *Cerrophidion petlalcalensis* and *C. barbouri* share the derived conditions of low numbers of teeth and low numbers of middorsal scale rows, and tooth numbers in *C. tzotzilorum* are derived relative to *C. godmani*. Campbell (1988a) suggested that *C. barbouri* may be the most basal species in the genus, which would be consistent with the more derived head scale conditions of the other three species (see Figs. 156–158, 160, 161). The section below on historical biogeography also considers issues relevant to *Cerrophidion* phylogeny, such as the possibility that

speciation events in this genus were contemporaneous with speciation in the *Bothriechis-Ophryacus* clade.

Geographic variation in *Cerrophidion godmani* was thoroughly analyzed by Campbell and Solórzano (1992). Castoe and Parkinson (pers. comm.) are conducting an extensive phylo-geographic analysis of *Cerrophidion* that will help to clarify relationships in this widespread genus.

PORTHIDIUM. This genus currently contains 9 species (after removal of species to *Atropoides*, *Cerrophidion*, *Ophryacus*, and *Bothrocophias*; see Table 55). Gutberlet and Harvey (2002) were the first to include all species (except the recently described *P. porrasi* and the recently elevated *P. arcosae*, this volume) in a phylogenetic analysis, providing strong evidence of monophyly as currently recognized (Fig. 241B).

Monophyly of *Porthidium* is supported by numerous morphological synapomorphies, including a rostral scale that is higher than broad (Pls. 731–736), one row of prefoveals between the prelacunal and second supralabial (Fig. 247A), a low number of gulars between the chinshields and the first preven-

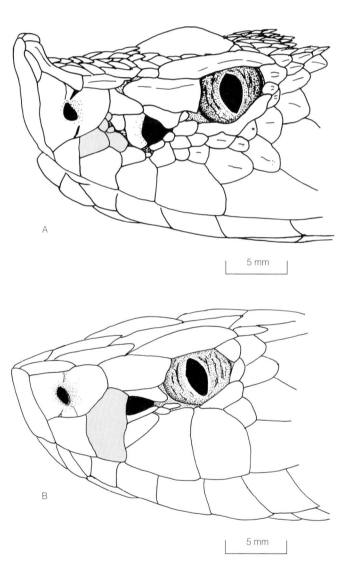

Fig. 247. Selected morphological characters used by Gutberlet and Harvey (2002): differences in number of interoculabials, number of prefoveals (shaded in A, *Porthidium nasutum*, UTA R-25372), condition of the prelacunal (shaded in B, *Agkistrodon piscivorus*, UTA R-28771), and forward extension of suboculars. After Gutberlet and Harvey, 2002.

tral (Fig. 248B), a palatine bone with the choanal process positioned anteriorly, a low number of palatine teeth (usually 2–3), and an apical papilla on the hemipenes (Gutberlet and Harvey, 2002). Werman (1999) summarized synapomorphies from the palatomaxillary arch.

Estol (1981) reported two different microstructural patterns on the dorsal scale surfaces of *Porthidium* species: reticulo-convex in *P. lansbergii*, *P. nasutum*, and *P. yucatanicum*, and reticulo-carinoverrucate in *P. dunni* and *P. ophryomegas*. Estol also reported the latter pattern in *Bothriechis schlegelii*. Although the relative proportions of coarse microstructural features may vary somewhat, we have observed great similarity in the rounded "hillocks" on scale surfaces of all *Porthidium* species (Gutberlet, 1998b; Gutberlet and Harvey, unpublished data), and a uniformly pitted fine microstructure is also characteristic of this genus.

Most studies of pitviper phylogeny based on mtDNA included only two species of *Porthidium*, but Parkinson et al. (2002) included four. At least within this relatively limited taxonomic sample, synapomorphies of *Porthidium* may be found in sequences of the following genes: 12S rRNA (Parkinson, 1999; Parkinson et al., 2002), 16S rRNA (Parkinson, 1999; Parkinson et al., 2002), cytochrome *b* (Parkinson et al., 2002), and ND4 (Kraus et al., 1996; Parkinson et al., 2002; Wüster et al., 2002a). Support for *Porthidium* monophyly has also come from allozymes and isozymes (Werman, 1992, 1997).

The correct identification of species within *Porthidium* initially proved difficult, and the early literature on the group reflects the extensive confusion and debate. Campbell and Lamar (this volume) provide a very useful introduction to the history of *Porthidium* taxonomy. Key references for appreciating this history include Amaral, 1927b, 1929e, 1944a; Dunn, 1928; Picado T., 1931a, 1936; Prado, 1939; and Wilson and Meyer, 1985. Recently available evidence suggests that further taxonomic

work is needed; for example, Wüster et al. (2002a) found that South American *P. nasutum* are more closely related to *P. lansbergii* than to Central American *P. nasutum*. The potential presence of cryptic species within the *Porthidium lansbergii* complex has also been suggested (Campbell and Lamar, this volume; S. Wilks, unpublished data).

Relationships within *Porthidium* have not been extensively investigated in modern phylogenetic analyses. Although Gutberlet and Harvey's (2002) study included seven species in the genus, intrageneric relationships were not resolved (Fig. 241B). In his description of *Porthidium volcanicum*, Solórzano (1995a) noted the similarity between *P. volcanicum* and *P. lansbergii* and suggested that the two species may be closely related. Parkinson et al. (2002) recovered a strongly supported relationship between *P. nasutum* and *P. lansbergii*, on the one hand, and between *P. ophryomegas* and *P. dunni*, on the other, but these were the only four species of *Porthidium* included in their study. *Porthidium porrasi* from the Osa Peninsula of Costa Rica was formerly confused with *P. nasutum*, suggesting a close relationship between the two. Using the same reasoning with respect to *P. arcosae*, we can hypothesize a close relationship between that species and *P. lansbergii*. The species that are primarily restricted to seasonally dry forest (*P. dunni*, *P. hespere*, *P. ophryomegas*, and *P. yucatanicum*) might be expected to form a clade, as suggested by the results of Parkinson et al. (2002). A phylogenetic analysis of this genus will reveal much about the historical biogeography of Middle America.

Bothriechis-Ophryacus Clade. Many morphological synapomorphies support the monophyly of this clade, yet a sister relationship between these two genera has not been supported in any phylogenetic analyses of mtDNA sequence data (Parkinson, 1999; Parkinson et al., 2002). All analyses by Parkinson (1999) recovered a weakly supported relationship between two species

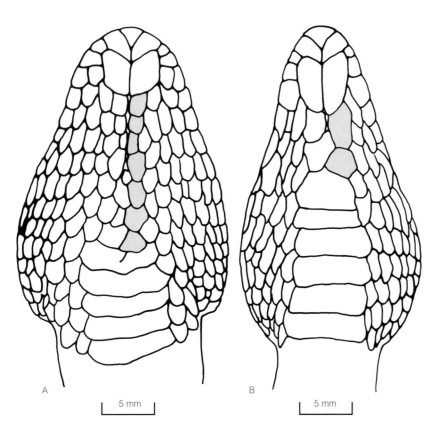

A

| 5 mm |

B

| 5 mm |

Fig. 248. Extremes of variation in number of gular scales between the chinshields and the first preventral in American pitvipers. (A) *Ophryacus melanurus*, UTA R-12554; (B) *Porthidium ophryomegas*, UTA R-39755. After Gutberlet, 1998a.

of *Bothriechis* (*B. lateralis* and *B. nigroviridis*) and *Lachesis*, and the phylogenetic position of *Ophryacus* relative to other Neotropical pitviper clades was either basal or unresolved (Fig. 239B). In the study by Parkinson et al. (2002), three of four analyses suggested a close (albeit weakly supported) relationship between *Ophryacus* and *Lachesis*, and the fourth analysis placed *Lachesis* with *Bothriechis*. In none of these analyses did *Bothriechis* and *Ophryacus* form an exclusive monophyletic group, but it is also noteworthy that none of the relationships indicated was strongly supported (Fig. 241A). The instability of the phylogenetic positions of *Bothriechis*, *Ophryacus*, and *Lachesis* in these DNA studies may stem in part from problems of long-branch attraction (see Kraus et al., 1996). Morphological data strongly suggest a close relationship between *Bothriechis* and *Ophryacus*, most likely a sister relationship.

Among the 49 taxa of New World pitvipers that he examined, Groombridge (1986b) reported that only specimens of *Bothriechis schlegelii*, *B. nigroviridis*, and *Ophryacus undulatus* lacked an *m. pterygoideus glandulae* (his state A). Although this may well represent an ancestral state (this muscle is also absent from *Azemiops*, viperines, and some *Gloydius*), it might be a synapomorphic reversal. Derived characters shared by *Bothriechis* and *Ophryacus* include a large number of canthal scales (sensu Klauber, 1972; canthals + postcanthals of many authors) (see Figs. 97, 167, 168; Pls. 369–426, 702–714), a large number of gular scales between the chinshields and first preventral (Fig. 248A), presence of more than one loreal scale on each side of the head (found in all *O. melanurus*, most *O. undulatus*, and many *B. schlegelii* and *B. nigroviridis*; the loreal is single in *B. lateralis* and *B. bicolor*; the condition has not been examined in other species of *Bothriechis*; Gutberlet, 1998a), lateral projection of loreals in *Ophryacus* and *B. schlegelii* (Gutberlet and Harvey, 2002), relatively few basal and lateral hemipenial spines, and posterolateral projection of the supratemporal in *Ophryacus* and *B. schlegelii*. Initially (Burger, 1971; Gutberlet, 1998a; Gutberlet and Harvey, 2002) the homology of the supraocular horns in *Bothriechis* (*B. schlegelii* and *B. supraciliaris*) and *Ophryacus* was undetermined owing to interspecific differences in these structures and the supraocular plates. The absence of supraocular plates from *Ophryacus* raises the question of whether its horns are constructed at least in part from these "missing" plates. The horns of *B. schlegelii* and *B. supraciliaris* are clearly not made from the supraocular plates because these plates are intact. An aberrant specimen of *O. undulatus* with partial supraocular plates and normally developed horns (Gutberlet and Gutberlet, unpublished data) suggests that horns in *Ophryacus* are not constructed from the supraocular plates and that the horns in the two genera may be homologous.

Several unusual synapomorphies are shared by *Bothriechis schlegelii* and one or the other of the two species of *Ophryacus*. Some canthal scales are elevated into small horns (Pls. 703–714 and 395–414, respectively) in *O. undulatus* and *B. schlegelii* (unique to these taxa; *B. supraciliaris* not examined). The top preocular is divided in *O. melanurus* and *B. schlegelii* (a very rare condition among New World pitvipers). In the few specimens of *Bothriechis* and *O. undulatus* that have been examined, the haemapophyses of the midcaudal vertebrae are in contact distally. Juliá-Zertuche and Varela (1978) endorsed a close relationship between *Bothriechis* and *Ophryacus* by assigning *O. undulatus* to *Bothriechis*.

BOTHRIECHIS. Using *Ophryacus undulatus* as an outgroup, Crother et al. (1992) considered *Bothriechis* to form a monophyletic group on the basis of seven morphological and six or seven allozyme synapomorphies. Other studies that support the monophyly of *Bothriechis* include Gutberlet, 1998a; Gutberlet and Harvey, 2002; Kraus et al., 1996; Parkinson et al., 2002; and Werman, 1992, 1997. As described above, the monophyly of *Bothriechis* was not supported in the study by Parkinson (1999), but the most comprehensive genetic analysis of New World pitvipers (Parkinson et al., 2002) did recover a monophyletic *Bothriechis* (nonparametric bootstrap support 72–87, relative likelihood support 98).

The most noticeable morphological synapomorphies supporting the monophyly of *Bothriechis* are associated with arboreality: the prehensile tail and the usual presence of green dorsal coloration (Pls. 369–426). Although these traits are not unique among New World pitvipers (e.g., they are also found in *Bothriopsis*), the available evidence suggests that they did evolve independently in the line leading to *Bothriechis* (Campbell and Lamar, 1989, 1992; Gutberlet and Harvey, 2002). Gutberlet (1998b) and Gutberlet and Harvey (unpublished data) noted a unique coarse microstructure of attenuate hillocks on dorsal scales of *Bothriechis*, although Estol (1981) described several different types of epidermal microstructure in this genus. Genes that include synapomorphic information supporting the monophyly of *Bothriechis* include 12S rRNA (Parkinson et al., 2002), 16S rRNA (Parkinson et al., 2002), cytochrome *b* (Parkinson et al., 2002), and ND4 (Kraus et al., 1996; Parkinson et al., 2002).

In his description of *Bothriechis rowleyi* Bogert (1968) compared his new species with *B. bicolor* and *B. lateralis*, stating (as quoted in Estol, 1981): "It can scarcely be doubted that *B. rowleyi*, *B. bicolor*, and *B. lateralis* were derived from an ancestral population once more widely distributed. . . . Thus *B. rowleyi* and its relatives are essentially relicts. . . . Presumably they have been isolated for a long period of time, as indicated by the levels of their divergence."

Burger (1971:154) commented on relationships within *Bothriechis* as follows:

> *Bothriechis* evolved through most of the Tertiary isolated in Central America. Most of the species have restricted, disjunct ranges and seem to be relicts of a retreating group. Only *B. schlegeli* has the characteristics of a successful expanding species. It may be postulated that *B. nigroviridis* and *B. aurifer* are the most primitive of existing species—the former with its dark markings, large supraoculars, and few ventrals and subcaudals; the latter with its large frontal, occasional spotting, and relatively few ventrals. *Bothriechis bicolor* and *B. lateralis* are advanced; in these the adult coloration is plain or striped and the ventrals, dorsals, and intericals are numerous. *Bothriechis schlegeli* presents a rather distinctive line combining primitively few ventrals and caudals with many advancements: "eyelashes"; very small, heavily keeled head scales; numerous dorsals and intericals; and color polymorphism. However, its kinship to the others is clear; its ancestral line must have included snakes similar to *B. nigroviridis*.

Phylogenetic analyses of *Bothriechis* were conducted by Crother et al. (1992) and Taggart et al. (2001). Crother et al. used maximum parsimony analyses of 18 allozyme characters and 29 morphological characters to reconstruct relationships of all species of palm-pitvipers recognized at that time. They analyzed the morphological and molecular data separately and then in a combined analysis. Results of the independent analyses were congruent in almost all respects (Fig. 246B). *Bothriechis schlegelii* is the most basal species in the genus, followed by *B. nigroviridis*, which is basal to two clades: (1) *B. aurifer–B. rowleyi* and (2) *B. bicolor–B. lateralis–B. marchi*. Relationships within the latter clade were not well resolved: the morphological data supported a sister relationship between *B. bicolor* and *B. marchi*, whereas the allozyme data indicated that *B. bicolor* and *B. lateralis* are more closely related. Nonparametric bootstrap support for all relationships that were consistently recovered among analyses was high (88–99%). Two most parsimonious trees were generated by the combined analysis, and they were identical with those recovered by the analyses of partitioned data already described.

Taggart et al. (2001) conducted maximum parsimony analyses of 382 base pairs (54 were parsimony-informative) of the 12S rRNA gene from 12 individuals representing nine taxa (*Ophryacus undulatus*, which was used as an outgroup, and all known species of *Bothriechis* except *B. thalassinus*). In the single shortest tree recovered by their analyses of these mtDNA data, a clade consisting of *B. schlegelii* and *B. supraciliaris* was basal to the remaining species of *Bothriechis*, which were divided among a northern clade ((*B. marchi, B. rowleyi*) (*B. bicolor, B. aurifer*)) and a southern clade (*B. lateralis, B. nigroviridis*). Although this arrangement is appealing on biogeographic grounds, Taggart et al. argued that the relationships recovered by Crother et al. (1992) are more likely to be accurate, and that the mtDNA data may be misleading owing to introgression or lineage sorting. The most interesting question raised by this study is the phylogenetic position of *B. lateralis*: is this species allied with the sympatric *B. nigroviridis* as the mtDNA data suggest, or is it more closely related to the northern species as suggested by allozymes and morphology? In combined analyses including the data of Crother et al. (1992) with their DNA sequence data, Taggart et al. recovered five shortest trees, which indicated that *B. lateralis* is more closely related to the northern species. Nevertheless, additional data are needed to test this hypothesis further.

The greatest number of *Bothriechis* species included in other phylogenetic studies is four (Gutberlet, 1998a; Gutberlet and Harvey, 2002) and three (Parkinson, 1999; Parkinson et al., 2002; Werman, 1992). Although the newly described *Bothriechis thalassinus* (Campbell and Smith, 2000) has never been included in a phylogenetic analysis, it may be closely related to *B. bicolor*, the species with which it was previously confused.

OPHRYACUS. Prior to the publication of Gutberlet, 1998a, this genus was considered to be monotypic, containing only the Mexican horned pitviper (*O. undulatus*). In a parsimony analysis of 52 morphological characters, Gutberlet found that *Porthidium melanurum* shared numerous derived morphological features with *O. undulatus*. The two species formed a monophyletic group in all analyses, and this clade was supported by very high bootstrap proportions (97–99%). Parkinson's (1999) mtDNA evidence also supported this finding, as have subsequent studies that included both species (Gutberlet and Harvey, 2002; Parkinson et al., 2002). In the latter three studies, bootstrap support for the *Ophryacus* clade ranged from 73 to 100%.

Synapomorphies from the skull, hemipenes, and scales support the monophyly of *Ophryacus*. Some of the more notable of these include weak development of the choanal process of the palatine bone; relatively wide and flattened dorsal surface of the supratemporal bone; calyces on lateral surfaces of hemipenial lobes that extend to the level of the crotch; and numerous tiny scales on the head as shown by high numbers of intersupraoculars, supralabials, infralabials, canthals, prefoveals, interoculabials, and gulars between the chinshields and first preventral (Fig. 248A). With the exception of some specimens of *Atropoides mexicanus*, the species of *Ophryacus*

are unique among New World pitvipers in completely lacking supraocular plates (see Figs. 167, 168; Pls. 702–714). The supraocular horns, although not identical in the two species, are similar and are probably homologous (Gutberlet and Gutberlet, unpublished data). Estol (1981) and Gutberlet (1998b) noted the derived microstructural pattern (strio-rugulate, sensu Estol) shared by the two species of *Ophryacus*. Estol also reported that the cell boundaries are very noticeable in *O. melanurus* but not in *O. undulatus*.

A more complete list of morphological synapomorphies supporting the monophyly of *Ophryacus* may be found in Gutberlet, 1998a; Gutberlet and Harvey, 2002, describes additional relevant morphological features. Synapomorphies from four mitochondrial genes (12S rRNA, 16S rRNA, ND4, and cytochrome *b*; Parkinson, 1999; Parkinson et al., 2002) also strongly support *Ophryacus* monophyly. The monophyly of this genus can reasonably be considered a fact.

Although the two species of *Ophryacus* are more closely related to each other than to any other species, it is interesting to note that they diverge with respect to multiple characters: the subcaudals of *O. undulatus* are divided, and those of *O. melanurus* are undivided; some canthal scales in *O. undulatus* are raised into small horns, and the canthals in *O. melanurus* are predominantly flat; *O. undulatus* is semiarboreal, and *O. melanurus* is terrestrial; the top preocular is entire in *O. undulatus* and divided (a fairly rare condition among New World pitvipers) in *O. melanurus*; and the palatine bones bear one tooth or none in *O. undulatus* and typically bear three teeth in *O. melanurus*. Gutberlet (1998a) suggested that these marked differences between the two species may have hindered discovery of their close relationship for such a long time. The condition of the subcaudals has long been considered an important taxonomic character, and previous workers may have given undue weight to this feature when assessing the relationships of the Mexican horned pitvipers. Supraocular horns, on the other hand, are known to occur in a variety of distantly related viper species, and previous workers may have been too hasty in judging the horns of these snakes to be products of convergent evolution. Such is the benefit of an objective criterion like maximum parsimony: subjective biases about the importance of particular characters are minimized and the entire weight of the evidence is brought to bear on the problem of reconstructing relationships. For additional examples in which reliance on one to several "key characters" has obscured rather than clarified relationships, see the sections on *Bothriechis, Bothriopsis, Porthidium*, and *Bothrocophias* in this chapter.

Given its disjunct distribution in southern Mexico, a phylogeographic analysis of *Ophryacus undulatus* would be useful for further testing hypotheses about the historical biogeography of Mexico.

South American Group Although several analyses performed by Gutberlet and Harvey (2002) found the *Bothrocophias-Bothrops-Bothriopsis* clade to be paraphyletic with respect to *Lachesis*, other recent studies (Parkinson et al., 2002; Wüster et al., 2002a) strongly support the monophyly of this clade, and it can reasonably be considered a fact. The phylogenetic position of *Lachesis* relative to other Neotropical pitvipers has been far less certain and requires further study, but we tentatively consider it the most basal member of the South American group based on the findings of Gutberlet (1998b) and Gutberlet and Harvey (2002). Whether the South American group originated in southern Central America or northern South America is an interesting question that we deal with below in the section on historical biogeography.

Estol (1981) described a character of dorsal scale microstructure that is a synapomorphy uniting *Bothrops*, *Bothriopsis*, and *Bothrocophias*; and Gutberlet (1998b) noted that the scale microstructure of *Lachesis*, although not identical with that of the other genera, is similar in the presence of short, high ridges over at least some parts of dorsal scales. According to Estol, two species in this group have slightly divergent scale microstructure: *Bothriopsis medusa* exhibits reticulo-pseudocarinate microstructure and *Bothrops pictus* has reticuloconvex-semicarinoverrucate microstructure. Estol (1981:176) commented that the similar microstructures of *Bothrops* and *Bothriopsis* may warrant their inclusion in a single genus. All species of *Bothriopsis*, *Bothrocophias*, and *Bothrops* that have been examined have a uniquely shaped palatine bone. The shape, described as "forked" by Brattstrom (1964; see also Ruiz, 1951; Fig. 240C), results from the anterior curvature and attenuation of the choanal process (Gutberlet, 1998a; Gutberlet and Harvey, 2002; Werman, 1992).

No genetic data positively support the monophyly of the South American group (sensu lato), but synapomorphies from the following genes strongly support the monophyly of the *Bothrocophias-Bothrops-Bothriopsis* clade: 12S rRNA (Parkinson, 1999; Parkinson et al., 2002), 16S rRNA (Parkinson, 1999; Parkinson et al., 2002), ND4 (Kraus et al., 1996; Parkinson et al., 2002; Wüster et al., 2002a), and cytochrome *b* (Parkinson et al., 2002; Wüster et al., 2002a).

Although Wüster et al.'s (2002a) analyses suggested that *Bothrocophias* may be paraphyletic with respect to *Bothrops-Bothriopsis*, this finding was not well supported by the nonparametric bootstrap, and analyses of morphological data have strongly supported *Bothrocophias* monophyly (Gutberlet and Campbell, 2001; Gutberlet and Harvey, 2002; see below). Reports of *Bothrops* paraphyly (with respect to *Bothriopsis*), on the other hand, are very well supported by morphological (Campbell and Lamar, 1992; Gutberlet and Harvey, 2002; Werman, 1992), allozyme (Werman, 1992), and DNA sequence data (Kraus et al., 1996; Parkinson, 1999; Parkinson et al., 2002; Salomão et al., 1997; Wüster et al., 2002a). Recent molecular studies place species of *Bothrocophias* as sister to the *Bothrops-Bothriopsis* clade.

Bothriopsis. Recent studies have shown that Burger's (1971) concept of *Bothriopsis* (see Table 54) was paraphyletic, and Campbell and Lamar (this volume) have revised the content of this genus so that it now includes only six species. Species from the Pacific versant of the Andes (*Bothrops punctatus* and *B. osbornei*) formerly assigned to *Bothriopsis* are now included in *Bothrops* (Campbell and Lamar, this volume). Although *Bothrops*, as now recognized, is paraphyletic with respect to *Bothriopsis*, it is quite likely that *Bothriopsis* itself is monophyletic. This hypothesis has been verified for three species of *Bothriopsis* (Wüster et al., 2002a, nonparametric bootstrap support 88–97), but a phylogenetic analysis including all species in the genus is needed to further test the monophyly of this group.

Although not unique to this genus, morphological synapomorphies of *Bothriopsis* apparently include the prehensile tail and the presence of green coloration on the dorsum. The tail of *B. medusa* was described by Roze (1966a) as not prehensile, but in fact it is prehensile (Campbell and Lamar, this volume; Pls. 434 and 435). Estol (1981:158) reported that *B. medusa* has a scale

microstructure (reticulo-pseudocarinate) that differs from that of other South American pitvipers; this interesting observation deserves further investigation. Genetic synapomorphies (based on analysis of two or three species only) have been identified in the following genes: 12S rRNA (Parkinson, 1999; Parkinson et al., 2002), 16S rRNA (Parkinson, 1999; Parkinson et al., 2002), ND4 (Parkinson et al., 2002; Wüster et al., 2002a), and cytochrome *b* (Parkinson et al., 2002; Salomão et al., 1999; Wüster et al., 2002a).

Early studies that comment on species of *Bothriopsis* include Burger, 1971; Cunha and Nascimento, 1972, 1975a, 1975b; Dunn, 1944a; Peters, 1960a; Shreve, 1934; and Vellard, 1946. Shreve (1934) suggested a close relationship between *B. albocarinata* (=*B. pulchra*) and *B. oligolepis* (=*B. chloromelas*). Vellard (1946) reported that the hemipenial morphology of *B. taeniata* is similar to that of *Bothrops atrox*, *B. jararaca*, and *B. jararacussu*; and Estol (1981:157–158) considered *Bothriopsis oligolepis* (=*chloromelas*) and *B. pulchra* to exhibit a similar hemipenial morphology as well.

Burger (1971) recognized three groups within his *Bothriopsis*: a *bilineata* group for *B. bilineata* and *B. peruviana* (=*oligolepis*); a *castelnaudi* (=*taeniata*) group for *B. pulchra*, *B. taeniata*, and *B. medusa*; and a *punctatus* group for *B. oligolepis* (=*chloromelas*) and *Bothrops punctatus*. Within his *castelnaudi* group Burger (1971:152) considered *B. medusa* to be the most primitive and also suggested that *B. pulchra* is relatively primitive. He considered *B. taeniata* more advanced. He suggested that the *bilineata* group is an "offshoot" of the *castelnaudi* group, with *B. peruviana* primitive relative to *B. bilineata*. Within the *punctatus* group Burger placed *Bothrops punctatus* as derived relative to *Bothriopsis chloromelas*.

No modern phylogenetic analysis has included more than three species of *Bothriopsis* (Wüster et al., 2002a), so relationships within this genus remain unresolved. The study by Wüster et al. (2002a) recovered a sister relationship between *B. pulchra* and *B. bilineata*, and *B. taeniata* was basal to this clade; however, relationships among these three species were not strongly supported. A study of the entire genus is needed to further test the monophyly of this group and increase our knowledge of South American biogeography.

Bothrocophias. Gutberlet and Campbell (2001) recognized four species within this genus, and Campbell and Lamar (this volume) have allocated an additional species, *B. colombianus*, to this group as well. Morphology-based phylogenetic analyses that included *B. hyoprora*, *B. microphthalmus*, and *B. campbelli* (Gutberlet and Harvey, 2002) strongly support the monophyly of this genus (Fig. 241B); and DNA-based studies (e.g., Parkinson et al., 2002) found strong support for the *B. hyoprora–B. microphthalmus* clade (Fig. 241A). The only DNA-based study to include *B. campbelli* (Wüster et al., 2002a) recovered a monophyletic *B. hyoprora–B. microphthalmus* clade, but suggested a sister relationship between *B. campbelli* and the *Bothrops-Bothriopsis* clade (Fig. 249C); this relationship was not supported by the nonparametric bootstrap, however, and we deem the monophyly of *Bothrocophias* well supported. Morphological synapomorphies supporting *Bothrocophias* monophyly include small, usually unkeeled intersupraocular scales, tubercular keels on dorsal scales, and distinctive white spots on infralabial and gular scales (Pls. 454–485). Amaral (1935), Burger (1971), and Prado (1939) believed that *Bothrocophias hyoprora*, with its undivided subcaudals and upturned snout, was allied with species currently assigned to *Porthidium*, but more recent

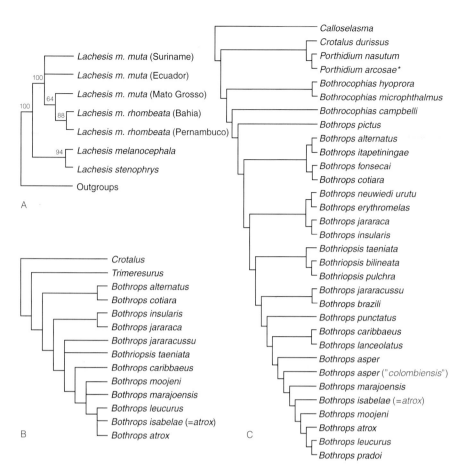

Fig. 249. (A) Strict consensus of three most parsimonious trees showing phylogenetic relationships among bushmasters; based on maximum parsimony analyses of ND4 and cytochrome *b* sequence data (from Zamudio and Greene, 1997). (B) Semistrict consensus of trees obtained in four alternative analyses (maximum parsimony, maximum likelihood, Fitch-Margoliash method, Fitch-Margoliash method with molecular clock assumption) of cytochrome *b* sequence data (from Salomão et al., 1997). (C) Phylogenetic relationships of South American pitvipers (Wüster et al., 2002a) inferred from a maximum likelihood analysis (GTR + I + G model) of mtDNA sequence data (cytochrome *b* and ND4 genes). Numbers above branches in A and C are nonparametric bootstrap proportions; branches without numbers were supported in fewer than 50% of the bootstrap pseudoreplications. * Recognized as *Porthidium lansbergii arcosae* by Wüster et al., 2002a.

studies (e.g., Gutberlet and Harvey, 2002; Parkinson et al., 2002) have demonstrated the convergent evolution of these characters in *Porthidium* and *Bothrocophias*.

In the description of *Bothrocophias myersi*, Gutberlet and Campbell (2001) noted that *B. hyoprora* and *B. microphthalmus* are sister species based on the presence of canthorostrals and absence of a lacunolabial. The sister relationship of *B. hyoprora* and *B. microphthalmus* was also noted by McDiarmid et al. (1999), and these two species share many other genetic synapomorphies (Parkinson et al., 2002; Wüster et al., 2002a). Gutberlet and Campbell (2001) considered the phylogenetic positions of *B. myersi* and *B. campbelli* unresolved relative to the *hyoprora-microphthalmus* clade.

Neither *Bothrocophias myersi* nor *B. colombianus* has been included in a modern phylogenetic analysis. Campbell and Lamar (this volume) refer to several morphological features in proposing alternative hypotheses for relationships within the genus: (1) ((*B. campbelli*, *B. myersi*) (*B. colombianus* (*B. hyoprora*, *B. microphthalmus*))); (2) (*B. campbelli* (*B. myersi* (*B. colombianus* (*B. hyoprora*, *B. microphthalmus*)))); (3) (*B. myersi* (*B. campbelli* (*B. colombianus* (*B. hyoprora*, *B. microphthalmus*)))). The phylogenetic position of *Bothrocophias colombianus* in these hypotheses is based on its derived absence of a lacunolabial shared with *B. hyoprora* and *B. microphthalmus*. Additional study of the anatomy and DNA of *Bothrocophias* is needed to test these alternative hypotheses through phylogenetic analysis.

Bothrops. All the available evidence suggests that *Bothrops* is the only paraphyletic genus of New World pitvipers now recognized. Ongoing phylogenetic studies (e.g., Gutberlet and Parkinson, in prep.) can be expected to better delimit monophyletic groups within this diverse genus.

Selected early contributions relevant to relationships within *Bothrops* include Amaral, 1922b, 1938, 1955a, 1955b; Brattstrom, 1964; Burger, 1971; Estol, 1981; Hoge, 1953d; Hoge and Belloumini, 1959b, 1964; Lazell, 1964; Lema, 1962; Mertens, 1942; Parker, 1938; Schmidt and Walker, 1943a, 1943b; and Vellard, 1946. Vellard (1946) used hemipenis morphology to recognize a southern group of *Bothrops* that included *B. neuwiedi*, *B. alternatus*, and *B. cotiara*; and a northern group with *B. atrox*, *B. jararaca*, and *B. jararacussu* (see Burger, 1971:123, for hemipenial differences between groups). In species of the southern group the hemipenes have short, calyculate lobes that are rounded distally. In species of the northern group the hemipenes are longer with lobes that are slightly tapered. Lema (1962) reported that the hemipenes of *B. ammodytoides* and *B. itapetiningae* are similar to those of Vellard's northern group.

Burger (1971) recognized the *atrox*, *neuwiedi*, *alternata* (=*alternatus*), and *ammodytoides* groups within *Bothrops* (see Table 54). He suggested that a basal split occurred between the *atrox* and *neuwiedi* groups and that the *alternatus* and *ammodytoides* groups were subsequently derived from within the *neuwiedi* group. Burger noted that species of the *atrox* group have a lacunolabial scale, whereas species of the other groups do not. As reported by Burger, the characteristics of the *alternatus* group (*B. alternatus*, *B. cotiara*, *B. fonsecai*) include large size, one internasal on each side of the head, and 9–14 intersupraoculars; and the characteristics of the *ammodytoides* group (*Bothrops ammodytoides*, *B. roedingeri*, *Bothrocophias microphthalmus*, and *B. colombianus*) include small size, two internasals on each side of the head, and 4–9 intersupraoculars. Estol (1981:155) found few differences in the scale surface microstructure of species now assigned to *Bothrops*, but did note that the carinations of *B. alternatus* and *B. ammodytoides* are noticeably shorter than those of most other species.

In an unpublished master's thesis, Pesantes-Segura (1989) used hemipenis morphology and plasma proteins to distinguish the *alternatus*, *atrox*, and *jararaca* groups within *Bothrops*. Pesantes-Segura et al. (unpublished manuscript) expanded this study by analyzing variation in hemipenial morphology in *B. andianus*, *B. ammodytoides*, *B. brazili*, *B. erythromelas*, *B. iglesiasi*, *B. itapetiningae*, *B. lojanus*, *B. marajoensis*, *B. pictus*, and *B. roedingeri*. These authors recognized six groups within *Bothrops* on the basis of a phenetic analysis of 25 hemipenial characters: (1) the *atrox* group (*B. atrox*, *B. moojeni*, *B. pradoi*, *B. marajoensis*), (2) the *jararacussu* group (*B. brazili*, *B. jararacussu*), (3) the *jararaca* group (*B. insularis*, *B. jararaca*), (4) the *alternatus* group (*B. alternatus*, *B. cotiara*, *B. fonsecai*, *B. ammodytoides*, *B. itapetiningae*), (5) the *neuwiedi* group (*B. iglesiasi*, *B. erythromelas*, *B. andianus*, *B. neuwiedi*), and (6) the *pictus* group (*B. pictus*, *B. roedingeri*, *B. lojanus*).

Werman (1992) included 10 species of *Bothrops* and 1 species of *Bothriopsis* in his morphology-, isozyme-, and allozyme-based study of Neotropical pitviper phylogeny. All of his most parsimonious trees depict two clades: (1) *B. pradoi*, *B. atrox*, *B. brazili*, *B. jararacussu*, *B. moojeni*, *B. jararaca*, and *Bothriopsis taeniata*; and (2) *B. neuwiedi*, *B. erythromelas*, *B. alternatus*, and *B. itapetiningae* (Fig. 242B). This was the first cladistic analysis of *Bothrops*, and it provided the first compelling evidence that *Bothrops* is paraphyletic with respect to *Bothriopsis*.

Salomão et al. (1997) used 565 base pairs (142 were variable within the ingroup) of cytochrome *b* to assess relationships among 11 species of *Bothrops* and 1 species of *Bothriopsis* (Fig. 249B). Using *Crotalus durissus* and *Trimeresurus albolabris* for outgroup rooting, they conducted maximum parsimony, maximum likelihood, and Fitch-Margoliash tree searches. All analyses supported a monophyletic group of species bearing a lacunolabial (Fig. 247B; *Bothrops atrox*, *B. leucurus*, *B. isabelae*, *B. moojeni*, *B. marajoensis*, *B. caribbaeus*, *B. jararacussu*, *B. insularis*, *B. jararaca*, and *Bothriopsis taeniata*) and a monophyletic group of species with this scale divided (Fig. 247A; *Bothrops alternatus* and *B. cotiara*). This study also supported the monophyly of a restricted *Bothrops atrox* group defined by Salomão et al. (1997) as *B. atrox*, *B. isabelae*, *B. leucurus*, *B. moojeni*, and *B. marajoensis*. As previously indicated in the study by Pesantes-Segura and Fernandes (1989), a sister relationship between *Bothrops insularis* and *B. jararaca* was supported. Werman's discovery of the paraphyly of *Bothrops* was further supported by these data, and Salomão et al. (1997) suggested that *Bothriopsis* be synonymized with *Bothrops* in order to rectify this situation. With a slightly augmented taxonomic sample, Salomão et al. (1999) reached similar conclusions. They added support for a monophyletic Antillean clade (*B. caribbaeus* + *B. lanceolatus*), and their three samples of *Bothrops atrox* did not represent a single lineage.

Including the most extensive taxonomic sample to date, Wüster et al. (2002a) used mtDNA to assess relationships within *Bothrops*, *Bothriopsis*, and *Bothrocophias*. They used maximum parsimony and maximum likelihood analyses of cytochrome *b* and ND4 sequences (1,401 total base pairs; 491 were parsimony-informative) from 32 species, including *Porthidium nasutum*, *P. arcosae*, *Crotalus durissus*, and *Calloselasma rhodostoma* (as an outgroup). As expected from previous studies, *Bothrops* was found to be paraphyletic with respect to *Bothriopsis* (Fig. 249C). *Bothrops punctatus* (formerly included in *Bothriopsis*) was not recovered as a close relative of the three *Bothriopsis* species included in the study. *Bothrops pictus* was placed as the most basal species of the *Bothrops* studied, but this placement was not strongly sup-

ported by the nonparametric bootstrap. Although four species with divided lacunolabials (*B. alternatus*, *B. itapetiningae*, *B. fonsecai*, and *B. cotiara*) formed a well-supported clade, two other species with this character state (*B. neuwiedi* and *B. erythromelas*) were placed as the sister clade to *B. jararaca*–*B. insularis*; thus the analyses of Wüster et al. suggest that a divided lacunolabial has evolved at least twice within *Bothrops*. A sister relationship between the two Lesser Antillean species (*B. caribbaeus* and *B. lanceolatus*) was strongly supported.

Wüster et al. (1996) studied species limits within three members of the *Bothrops atrox* complex using multivariate analysis of morphological features. Although they found distinct differences between *B. atrox* and *B. moojeni*, their data also suggested the presence of a hybrid zone between these species. They considered *B. marajoensis* to be poorly differentiated from *B. atrox* and recommended further study of its taxonomic status. Wüster et al. (1997b, 1999b) conducted further analysis of morphological variation within the *B. atrox* complex and also used sequence data from the cytochrome *b* gene to compare members of this complex. Their work again supported a distinction between *B. atrox* and *B. moojeni*, but their morphological and genetic data differed with respect to recognition of other species within this complex.

Puorto et al. (2001) used multivariate analyses of morphometric features and phylogeographic analyses of DNA sequence data from the cytochrome *b* and ND4 genes to evaluate the taxonomic status of *Bothrops leucurus* and *B. pradoi*. The authors concluded that these taxa are not specifically distinct and are both referable to *B. leucurus*, which supports the findings of earlier studies by Ripa (1997) and Wüster et al. (1997b). Moro (1996) studied cranial osteology and mandibular musculature in three species of *Bothrops*, polarizing her characters through comparison with *Crotalus durissus*, and found the following relationships: (*alternatus* (*neuwiedi*, *ammodytoides*)).

Several other recent studies have included a few species of *Bothrops* (Gutberlet and Harvey, 2002; Kraus et al., 1996; Parkinson, 1999; Parkinson et al., 2002; Werman, 1997), but numerous species of *Bothrops* have never been included in a phylogenetic analysis. An analysis based on morphological and DNA sequence data for all species in *Bothrops*, *Bothriopsis*, and *Bothrocophias* is needed to delimit the monophyletic groups of South American pitvipers with confidence.

Lachesis. As is the case with the rattlesnakes, the recent nomenclatural history of *Lachesis* has not been intertwined with that of *Bothrops* (sensu lato) owing to the presence of distinctive features of the sort easily noticed by taxonomists (see below). Until recently the monophyly of *Lachesis* could be taken for granted: only a single species was recognized, although four subspecies were included within it (Campbell and Lamar, 1989). Four species of *Lachesis* are now recognized (Zamudio and Greene, 1997; Campbell and Lamar, this volume).

Morphological synapomorphies that support the monophyly of *Lachesis* include the unusually divided scales on the tail tip (unique among pitvipers; see Figs. 76 and 77), the large size (see thorough assessment of this character by Campbell and Lamar in this volume), and high numbers of various types of scales associated with body size (e.g., ventrals, middorsals). The members of *Lachesis* are unique among New World pitvipers (with the possible exception of *Bothrocophias colombianus*; Campbell and Lamar, 1992, this volume) in that they lay eggs rather than giving birth to live young. While the characters mentioned previously are clearly derived and indicate the shared ancestry of the four species of *Lachesis*, the polarity of egg laying is difficult to determine at this time. Some Old World pitvipers are oviparous (e.g., *Deinagkistrodon acutus, Calloselasma rhodostoma*; Gloyd and Conant, 1990). It is possible that the ancestral New World pitviper was oviparous and that this habit has been retained in *Lachesis* but lost in other New World pitviper lineages. Alternatively, oviparity in *Lachesis* may represent an evolutionary reversal, providing further evidence of *Lachesis* monophyly. A strict parsimony interpretation based on current information favors the interpretation that oviparity is an additional synapomorphy for the genus. Evidence from mitochondrial DNA (12S rRNA, 16S rRNA, ND4, and cytochrome *b* genes; Parkinson et al., 2002) also supports the monophyly of *Lachesis*. In all analyses conducted by Parkinson et al., *Lachesis* (represented by *stenophrys* and *muta* in that study) was recovered as monophyletic with nonparametric bootstrap support of 100%. Morphological and molecular data are extensive and are in accord: the monophyly of *Lachesis* can be viewed as fact.

Zamudio and Greene (1997) conducted a phylogeographic analysis of *Lachesis* based on variation in the ND4 and cytochrome *b* genes. Based on compelling evidence from this analysis they recognized three species within the genus: *Lachesis stenophrys, L. melanocephala*, and *L. muta* (including the subspecies *L. m. muta* and *L. m. rhombeata*). Outgroup taxa for the study were *Atropoides nummifer* (=*mexicanus*) and *Agkistrodon contortrix*. Even when several different approaches to weighting nucleotide transitions and transversions were implemented, the results of maximum parsimony and maximum likelihood analyses of the data were the same. The Central American species *L. stenophrys* and *L. melanocephala* are sister taxa, and this clade forms a sister group to *L. m. muta* + *L. m. rhombeata*. Although the analysis supports monophyly of *L. m. rhombeata*, it suggests paraphyly of *L. m. muta* with respect to *L. m. rhombeata*. Thus Zamudio and Greene favored retaining *muta* and *rhombeata* as subspecies of *L. muta*. Bootstrap support was high for most groups recovered in this study (Fig. 249A).

A fourth species, *Lachesis acrochorda* (García, 1896), is now recognized (Campbell and Lamar, this volume; Ripa, 1994a), although its relationships to other species of *Lachesis* remain problematic. Bolaños et al. (1978b) studied *Lachesis* venom using immunoelectrophoresis and found great similarity between the venoms of *L. melanocephala* and *L. acrochorda*. Interpretation of this result is hindered by the inability of this technique to distinguish between derived and ancestral characteristics of the venom. Primarily on the basis of biogeography, and noting the need for further study, Campbell and Lamar (1989) tentatively assigned the populations of *Lachesis* now recognized as *L. acrochorda* to *L. stenophrys*, and McDiarmid et al. (1999) followed this treatment. However, Martínez and Bolaños (1982) referred a specimen of *L. acrochorda* from eastern Panama to *L. m. muta* based on its high number of ventral scales, and Peters and Orejas-Miranda (1970) considered *acrochordus* to be a synonym of *L. m. muta*. Kuch (unpublished data) has also suggested that *L. acrochorda* (which was not represented in Greene and Zamudio's study) is more closely related to *L. muta* than it is to the two Central American species. Based on the information summarized here, Campbell and Lamar (this volume) propose the relationships within *Lachesis* to be ((*L. stenophrys, L. melanocephala*) (*L. acrochorda, L. muta*)). Although the relationships reported by Zamudio and Greene (1997) are very well supported, the phylogenetic position of *L. acrochorda* requires further investigation. A more extensive phylogeographic study

of *L. m. muta* would also be expected to provide interesting information about the history of the Amazon Basin.

HISTORICAL BIOGEOGRAPHY OF NEW WORLD PITVIPERS

The phylogenetic relationships of New World pitvipers are now sufficiently resolved (Figs. 250 and 251) to propose hypotheses that reconcile the cladogenesis summarized in the previous sections with the geological and climatological history of the Americas. Here we provide only a brief overview of important events in the history of American pitvipers; additional phylogenetic analysis of this group will soon make possible a detailed consideration of its biogeography. Some parts of the following account are well supported by data, whereas other parts require further testing through phylogenetic analysis and collection of more data about geology, climate, and rates of molecular evolution.

Harry Greene (1992) provided an enlightening discussion of the origin of pitvipers and characteristics of the common ancestor of all pitvipers. There is now general agreement (based on considerable evidence; e.g., Parkinson et al., 2002) that pitvipers

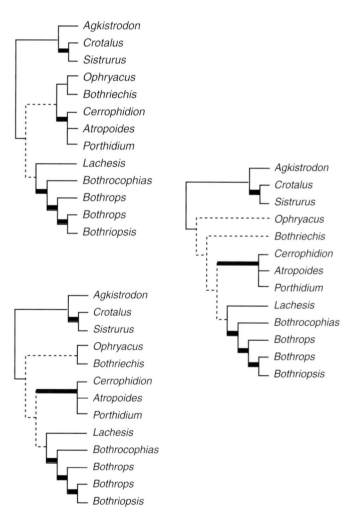

Fig. 250. Three consensus phylogenies depicting alternative hypotheses of intergeneric relationships of New World pitvipers. Heavy lines indicate branches with high bootstrap support. Narrow lines represent branches recovered in earlier phylogenetic analyses of pitvipers. Relationships of genera placed on the trees with dashed lines are uncertain owing to conflicting evidence about their placement.

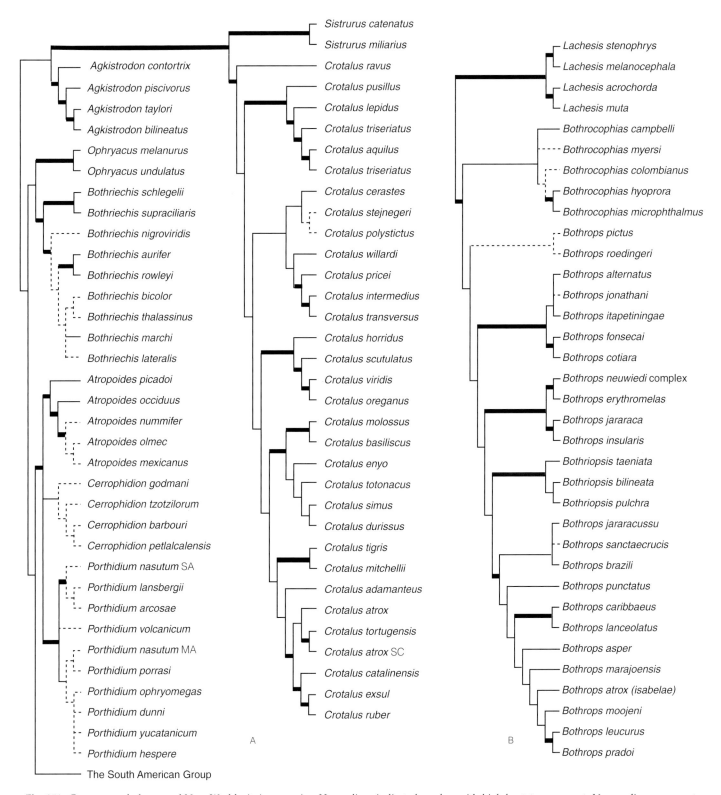

Fig. 251. Consensus phylogeny of New World pitviper species. Heavy lines indicate branches with high bootstrap support. Narrow lines represent branches recovered in earlier phylogenetic analyses of pitvipers. Relationships depicted with dashed lines are uncertain owing to conflicting evidence or the fact that the species concerned have never been included in a phylogenetic analysis. Their placement is strictly hypothetical (see text for justification) and requires testing in future analyses. (A) Relationships within the North and Middle American groups. (B) Relationships within the South American group. SA, South America; MA, Middle America; SC, Isla Santa Cruz, Baja California.

originated in Asia. The monophyly of American pitvipers (Kraus et al., 1996; Parkinson et al., 2002) requires that a single pitviper species of Asian origin was the progenitor of all American species. This founding species dispersed into North America across the Bering land bridge and may have resembled *Gloydius blomhoffii* in many respects (Parkinson et al., 2002; Van Devender and Conant, 1990).

The arrival time of crotalines in the New World has been estimated variously as Paleocene or Eocene (Brattstrom, 1964), middle Oligocene (Kardong, 1986), and late Oligocene or early Miocene (Van Devender and Conant, 1990). Conant (1990) believed that Brattstrom's (1964) estimate is probably too early considering that no American fossil crotalines are available from this period, but Parkinson et al. (2002) and Vidal and

Lecointre (1998) suggested a slightly earlier arrival (late Cretaceous or early Tertiary) than Brattstrom did. The earliest viper fossil (a vertebra, genus and species undetermined) known from the New World was reported from the early Miocene (Holman, 1981).

The first speciation event in the New World would have produced the common ancestor of the North American group (*Agkistrodon*, *Crotalus*, *Sistrurus*), on the one hand, and the common ancestor of the Neotropical group, on the other (Fig. 252). Wüster et al. (2002a) suggested that the split between the North American and Neotropical groups may have occurred as a result of the Tertiary Vicariance II event proposed by Savage (1982), which would have included a southward expansion into Central America of the range of the original American pitviper species followed by a vicariant event that divided this taxon into isolated northern and southern units. Using different molecular clock estimates, Wüster et al. (2002a) suggested that this event may have occurred between 8.5 and 30 mya, but the low end of this range is inconsistent with the ages of several *Agkistrodon* fossils (see below).

North American Diversification

Speciation of the common ancestor of the North American group gave rise to the common ancestor of *Agkistrodon* and the first rattlesnake species. The fossil record indicates that *Agkistrodon* and the rattlesnakes had diverged at least by the late Miocene (ca. 10–12 mya; Conant, 1990), and some workers (see below) have suggested a much earlier date for this divergence. The common ancestor of *Agkistrodon* was probably similar to the original American pitviper, whereas the first rattlesnake would have exhibited obvious modifications such as the rattle and possible loss of the nasal pore. Both founding species of the North American pitviper radiation exhibited the nine-plate arrangement of head scales. While the common ancestor of *Agkistrodon* occupied lowland habitats that were either temperate (Parkinson et al., 2000) or more tropical (Van Devender and Conant, 1990), the first rattlesnake may have been a highland species, in which case altitudinal segregation might have precipitated this initial speciation event after uplift of the Sierra

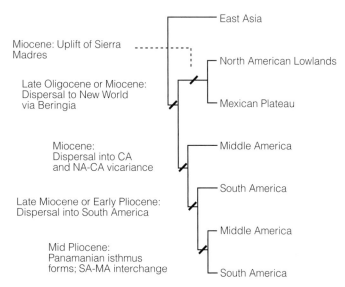

Fig. 252. Area cladogram based on consensus phylogeny showing distribution of major clades of pitvipers and historical events that may have influenced their evolution.

Madre Occidental and Sierra Madre Oriental in the Miocene. Greene (1997) proposed that rattlesnakes originated in talus slopes rather than grasslands (Klauber, 1972), and the basal phylogenetic position of the Mexican montane rattlesnakes (Fig. 244A) is consistent with this hypothesis.

Parkinson et al. (2000) and Van Devender and Conant (1990) provided extensive discussions of the historical biogeography of *Agkistrodon*. Parkinson et al. (2000) suggested that *A. contortrix*, *A. piscivorus*, and *A. taylori* diversified in eastern North America and that the common ancestor of the subspecies of *A. bilineatus* later dispersed to the Pacific lowlands of Middle America across the Isthmus of Tehuantepec. Van Devender and Conant (1990) envisioned a common ancestor of *Agkistrodon* that was widespread across the United States and Mexico. According to their reconstruction, the uplift of the Sierra Madre Occidental and Sierra Madre Oriental during the Miocene would have restricted the distribution of the ancestor of *Agkistrodon* to the United States and the lowlands around the perimeter of the Mexican Plateau. The subsequent uplift of the Rocky Mountains in the western United States affected the climate in the eastern United States, and temperate forests began to form. Van Devender and Conant (1990) suggested that, with these changes, one population of the common ancestor of *Agkistrodon* was isolated in the temperate forest, where it differentiated into *A. contortrix*, and a population isolated in the southeastern United States became *A. piscivorus*. A very dry period during the late Miocene (5–8 mya) may have isolated the population that gave rise to *A. taylori*. The allopatric populations of *A. bilineatus* may have become isolated and differentiated during the Pleistocene.

At the same time that species within *Agkistrodon* were evolving, the rattlesnakes were undergoing their own, more prolific, radiation. Klauber (1972:154) suggested that rattlesnakes had originated and diversified extensively by the Pliocene. Knight et al. (1993:366) suggested a mid-Cenozoic origin for rattlesnakes from 20 to 30 mya based on 12S and 16S rDNA divergence between *Sistrurus* and *Crotalus*. Klauber (1972) provided some discussion of the historical biogeography of rattlesnakes, but his proposed phylogeny for the group (Fig. 243) is different from the best current estimate of rattlesnake relationships (Murphy et al., 2002; Fig. 244A). Barker (1992), Dorcas (1992), and Douglas et al. (2002) implicated Pleistocene events as causative agents of diversification within *Crotalus willardi*, the *C. triseriatus* group, and the *C. viridis* complex.

One member of the North American group (*Agkistrodon bilineatus*) extended its range into Central America, and another member of this group (the ancestor of *C. durissus* sensu stricto) even colonized South America (probably during the Pleistocene, about 1–2.2 mya; Wüster et al., 2002a).

Origin of the Neotropical Group

The following information about the history of Central and South America, summarized by Zamudio and Greene (1997; see also references therein), is critical to any consideration of the biogeographic history of Neotropical pitvipers. A connection between Central and South America in the form of a series of volcanic islands existed during the late Cretaceous or early Tertiary (60–90 mya). At the beginning of the Tertiary (ca. 80 mya) the volcanic islands drifted eastward, leaving a marine gap between South and Central America that persisted for much of the Tertiary. Contact between Central and South America was reestablished during the Pliocene (ca. 3.5 mya) through formation of the isthmian link, which created the solid land connection that persists today between the two continents. Parts of the Andes existed during the Cretaceous, but at much lower elevations than today. During the mid-Miocene (ca. 11–14 mya), uplifting occurred in the northern Andes causing elevations to exceed 1,000 m. More extensive uplifting occurred during the Pliocene and Pleistocene, elevating the mountains to their current heights above 4,000 m. Uplift of the Central American highlands may have occurred from north to south, beginning in the Miocene. The mountains of lower Central America (including the biogeographically important Talamancan highlands) uplifted in the late Miocene or early Pliocene (5–8 mya), eventually resulting in formation of the isthmiam link. During the Pleistocene, climatic fluctuations and associated changes in vegetation may have played important roles in recent diversification among Neotropical pitvipers. Selected contributions that provide an introduction to Neotropical herpetogeography include Cadle, 1985; Cadle and Greene, 1993; Campbell, 1999; Duellman, 1979c; Hedges, 1996, 1999; Parkinson et al., 2000; Savage, 1966, 1982; Vanzolini and Heyer, 1985; Wüster et al., 2002a; and Zamudio and Greene, 1997.

The range of the original New World pitviper species probably extended south at least beyond the Isthmus of Tehuantepec, and the southern populations of this species must have become isolated in Central America, possibly during the Tertiary (Wüster et al., 2002a). Based on the habitat occupied by the most basal Neotropical pitvipers (e.g., *Bothriechis schlegelii*, *Porthidium nasutum*, *Lachesis muta*, *Bothrocophias myersi*), we consider it likely that the common ancestor of the Neotropical group became a denizen of lowland tropical wet forest soon after its isolation in Central America. This ancestor of the Neotropical radiation probably reached Central America after the creation of the marine portal that separated Central and South America.

Middle American Diversification

Although this hypothesis requires additional confirmation, the common ancestor of the Neotropical group may have diverged into a large terrestrial species that resembled *Lachesis* or *Bothrocophias* and a smaller arboreal species that resembled *Bothriechis schlegelii*. The range of the arboreal species eventually expanded northward beyond the Isthmus of Tehuantepec, and subsequent vicariance at the isthmus precipitated the divergence of *Bothriechis* and *Ophryacus* (Crother et al., 1992). Farther south, the large terrestrial species diverged into the ancestors of the South American group and the *Porthidium-Atropoides-Cerrophidion* clade.

The ancestor of the *Porthidium-Atropoides-Cerrophidion* clade may have undergone a relatively rapid radiation (Castoe et al., 2003) after it diverged from the ancestor of the South American group, and this may account for some of the recent uncertainty about *Atropoides* monophyly (Castoe et al., 2003; Kraus et al., 1996). Presumably, during this time a propagule of the Central American–based, common ancestor of the South American group reached South America (see below). Wüster et al. (2002a) estimated the date of this event at 10–23 mya, which was long before the formation of the Panamanian isthmus in the Pliocene. One of the interesting riddles of Neotropical biogeography is the apparent dispersal between Central and South America of multiple groups during this period of purported marine separation (Cadle, 1985; Hanken and Wake, 1982; Zamudio and Greene, 1997).

Crother et al. (1992) hypothesized that the common ancestor of *Ophryacus* and *Bothriechis* became isolated in Middle America between the upper Cretaceous and lower Eocene, because during this time the eastward movement of the proto–Antillean island arc separated South America from Middle America. They also suggested that this was the event that precipitated the divergence between the Middle American and South American groups, but it is possible that pitvipers had not yet reached South America at that time (see above).

Crother et al. (1992) also suggested that the *Ophryacus-Bothriechis* split may have been caused by uplifting of the Sierra Madre del Sur and Sierra Madre Oriental and also possibly by inundation of the Isthmus of Tehuantepec. Uplifting in Central America would have started the process of highland speciation within *Bothriechis*, first yielding one widespread highland species and one lowland species. The highland species then diverged into a southern species (*B. nigroviridis*) and the common ancestor of the northern species + *B. lateralis*, probably as a result of a barrier that formed along the southern border of the Chortis Block and was associated with the Nicaraguan Depression. The split between the two northern clades (*rowleyi-aurifer* and *bicolor-lateralis-marchi*) may have been caused by separation along the Motagua and/or Polochic fault zones. The divergence of *B. rowleyi* and *B. aurifer* in the north and *B. bicolor* and *B. marchi* in the south may have been caused by further highland fragmentation on either side of the Motagua-Polochic fault zones. Crother et al. (1992) attributed the presence of *B. lateralis* in southern Central America to a north-to-south dispersal of this species. If, however, the 12S rRNA sequence data of Taggart et al. (2001) are an accurate indicator of the phylogenetic position of *B. lateralis*, then this species may have originated in the Talamancan highlands where it now occurs. This is an interesting question to be addressed as new data relevant to the phylogeny of *Bothriechis* are collected and analyzed.

The uplift of the Sierra de Talamanca had an easily noticed effect on speciation in Neotropical pitvipers, with the following sister species occurring on either side of this range: *Bothriechis supraciliaris*, *B. schlegelii*; *Porthidium porrasi*, *P. nasutum*; and *Lachesis melanocephala*, *L. stenophrys*. The Sierra de Talamanca itself is an important area of endemism, containing *Bothriechis nigroviridis*, *B. lateralis*, and *Atropoides picadoi*. Members of the Middle American group that occur in South America (see Parkinson, 1999; Wüster et al., 2002a) are *Bothriechis* (*B. schlegelii*) and *Porthidium* (common ancestor of *P. lansbergii* and South American *P. nasutum*).

South American Diversification

The available evidence is equivocal with respect to the geographic origin of the South American group. While the genera *Bothrocophias*, *Bothrops*, and *Bothriopsis* constitute a well-supported clade, the phylogenetic position of *Lachesis* is much less clear. If, as we hypothesize, *Lachesis* is sister to the other genera of the South American group, then knowledge of the geographic history of this genus is critical for understanding the origin of the group. Unfortunately, as Zamudio and Greene (1997) noted, "we cannot at this point exclude the hypothesis that Central American *Lachesis* are remnants of initial colonization of the tropics (from the north) rather than more recent immigrants from South America." Thus, the South American group may have originated in southern Central America with subsequent dispersal to South America prior to the differentiation of *Bothrocophias*, *Bothrops*, and *Bothriopsis*. Alternatively, this group may have originated in South America with later colonization of Central America by the common ancestor of *L. stenophrys* and *L. melanocephala*. Evolution of these two species was likely precipitated by the uplift of the Talamancan highlands.

One species of the South American group (*Bothrops punctatus*) barely extends into Panama, whereas another species (*B. asper*) has expanded its range well into Mexico (a relatively recent event). The ancestors of the two species of lanceheads in the Lesser Antilles (*B. lanceolatus* and *B. caribbaeus*) reached those islands relatively recently as well (Hedges, 1996). As ongoing phylogenetic studies continue to improve our estimation of American pitviper relationships, the historical biogeography of these snakes will be further clarified.

Geological history, ancient climates, and even random processes like waif dispersal have all influenced the evolution of New World venomous snakes. Although many important questions have been answered—thanks in large part to sophisticated phylogenetic analyses—much remains to be learned and tested. For example, general differences in foraging mode between coralsnakes (active foragers) and pitvipers (many are primarily ambush foragers) are likely to have had a strong influence on the evolution of these snakes, and we may be able to gain deeper understanding of variation in such features as coloration (aposematic versus cryptic), reproductive mode (egg laying versus live-bearing), and head scalation (large platelike scales versus many tiny scales) through investigation of this possibility. This is but one of the mysteries awaiting future students of venomous snake biology. Clearly there is still much to occupy the curious naturalist.

Acknowledgments

We thank Jonathan Campbell and William Lamar for inviting us to contribute this chapter; we are honored to have been included. We thank Jonathan Campbell for all he has taught us, for his guidance, and for his kind support. Financial support for our work on venomous snake systematics has come from the University of Texas at Tyler (Department of Biology, College of Arts and Sciences, and President's Faculty-Student Summer Research Award), California Academy of Sciences (Charles Stearns Grant-in-Aid of Herpetological Research), Carnegie Museum of Natural History (Collection Study Grant in Herpetology), East Tennessee State University (College of Arts and Sciences Grants, Presidential Grants-in-Aid), the University of Texas at Arlington chapter of the Phi Sigma Biological Society, and the North Texas Herpetological Society. The great progress in venomous snake systematics has resulted from the tireless efforts of many people—especially collection managers, curators, and field collectors—who may not be listed as authors of particular papers. We are fortunate to know some of these biologists and thank them and their respective institutions for helpful collaboration in our studies: R. W. McDiarmid, G. R. Zug, R. P. Reynolds, S. W. Gotte, and J. A. Poindexter III (USNM); W. E. Duellman, L. Trueb, and J. Simmons (KU); R. C. Drewes and J. V. Vindum (CAS); J. J. Wiens and S. P. Rogers (CM); D. R. Frost, C. W. Myers, and L. S. Ford (AMNH); H. K. Voris and A. R. Resetar (FMNH); J. A. Campbell and P. C. Ustach (UTA); J. Aparicio E. (CBF); G. Scrocchi (FUL); and L. Gonzales A. (NK). We thank our generous colleagues who shared their work prior to publication: Jonathan A. Campbell, Todd Castoe, Paul T. Chippindale, Marlis R. Douglas, Michael E. Douglas, Joshua V. Feltham, Jinzhong Fu, Andrew T. Holycross, Viera Kovac, Amy Lathrop, Robert Murphy, Chris Parkinson, Louis W. Porras, J. Adrián Quijada-Mascareñas, Maria da Graça Salomão, Gordon W. Schuett, Roger S. Thorpe, and Wolfgang Wüster. Thoughtful criticism of parts of the manuscript was provided by Toby Breland, Todd Castoe, Brian E. Fontenot, Matthew E. Gifford, Don Killebrew, Chris Parkinson, Eric Smith, and Rod Wittenberg. We thank Jonathan Campbell, William Lamar, and Kelly Zamudio for reading the manuscript in its entirety and for providing many helpful suggestions. During completion of this project, students and colleagues at our respective institutions patiently endured our prolonged periods of self-enforced exile. When we did emerge from our offices, these great people were very supportive of our efforts and we thank them heartily for that. Our families have always been supportive of our unusual interests, and we are certainly grateful. Carol Gutberlet has continued in her fine tradition of patience and encouragement; thank you, Carol.

Venom Poisoning by North American Reptiles

Robert Norris

No comprehensive treatise on venomous reptiles would be complete without a discussion of the medical impact these creatures have on humans. This chapter discusses the medically important venomous reptiles of North America—both snakes and lizards. The discussion includes an overview of known information regarding the composition of venoms, an analysis of the clinical effects that can be expected in cases of human venom poisoning, and a review of management principles in the field and in the hospital. To the extent possible I include species-specific information that may be useful to the physician or researcher interested in the effects of an individual snake's venom.

A number of North American venomous snake species have been reclassified in recent years, and the medical literature has not kept pace with these changes. Therefore, in the sections below I include former names as they were used in medical manuscripts.

VENOMOUS LIZARDS, FAMILY HELODERMATIDAE

Epidemiology

It is impossible to know the precise incidence of bites by venomous lizards because many of them go unreported. The medical importance of helodermatid bites as far as the general population is concerned is small. The Good Samaritan Regional Poison Center in Phoenix, Arizona, manages an average of only one case per year (Brown and Carmony, 1991). Almost all victims are intentionally interacting with the animal at the time of the bite, and such bites are termed illegitimate. Truly legitimate (or accidental) bites are notably rare (Russell and Bogert, 1981). With the current rise in interest in these animals in herpetoculture, however, it is likely that the overall number of bites that occur each year will increase.

Venoms

The venoms of the two species of Helodermatidae are complex and very toxic (Albritton et al., 1970; Mebs, 1995). The electrophoretic patterns of *Heldoderma suspectum* and *H. horridum* venoms are remarkably similar, meaning that they have similar compositions (Stahnke et al., 1970). Russell and Bogert (1981) reported a venom yield of 17 mg (dry weight) from *H. suspectum*, and Stahnke et al. (1970) de-

scribed its venom as being as toxic to lab animals as that of *Crotalus atrox*.

Proteins make up approximately 62% of *H. suspectum* venom, and enzymes including L-amino acid oxidase, phospholipases, hyaluronidase, and kallikreins constitute the major physiologically active components (Mebs, 1995; Stahnke et al., 1970; Sullivan and Wingert, 1989). Serotonin is also present (Sullivan and Wingert, 1989). There does not appear to be any significant acetylcholine esterase, nucleotidase, ATPase, DNAase, RNAase, or fibrinogen coagulase activity (Russell, 1983). Although proteases are present, the overall proteolytic activity of the venoms appears to be low (Russell, 1983). There are no neurotoxins or enzymes that significantly affect systemic blood coagulation (Cooke and Loeb, 1913; Mebs, 1995). Although there have been anecdotal cases of coagulation disturbances following helodermatid bites (Bou-Abboud and Kardassakis, 1988; Preston, 1989), any systemic disturbances in blood clotting are indirect and due to local damage to the endothelial lining of blood vessels at the bite site (Strimple et al., 1997). Hyaluronidase stimulates swelling (Russell, 1983) and spread of the venom within tissues. L-amino acid oxidase can act like thrombin, splitting fibrinogen and causing blood clots in the microvasculature of the bite site (Gold and Willis, 1994). Phospholipases split lecithin into isolecithin, which damages cell membranes (Gold and Wingert, 1994). Kallikreins (serine proteases such as gilatoxin, horridum toxin, and helodermatine) cause the release of potent vasoactive kinins (probably bradykinin) from plasma precursors (kininogen) (Datta and Tu, 1997; Mebs, 1995; Strimple et al., 1997). These circulating kinins can cause a precipitous fall in blood pressure due to vasodilatation and leakage of fluid from the intravascular space.

Clinical Features

Given the toxicity of *Heloderma* venoms, it is fortunate that their delivery apparatus is much less efficient than that of the solenoglyph snakes. If the lizard is able to clamp on and chew, however, a significant envenoming can occur within seconds (Hooker and Caravati, 1994). Significant poisoning occurs in approximately 70% of bites (Bou-Abboud and Kardassakis, 1988), but bites are rarely severe (Ernst, 1992). In Russell's experience (Russell and Bogert, 1981), only 9 of 15 bites resulted in envenomation. Severity is based on a number of variables including the size and health of the lizard, the duration of attachment, which teeth made contact, whether clothing was interposed between the teeth and the skin, and the degree of agitation on the part of the lizard prior to the bite (Hooker and Caravati, 1994).

Helodermatid bites can cause severe local pain and significant soft tissue swelling (Bou-Abboud and Kardassakis, 1988; Hooker and Caravati, 1994; Stahnke et al., 1970; Strimple et al., 1997). Patients who have experienced the pain of both pitviper bites and helodermatid bites describe those of the venomous lizards as being much more intense (Albritton et al., 1970). The pain can persist for 12 hours or more, and sometimes the entire limb is swollen (Mebs, 1995). Generally, however, the degree of swelling is less than that seen with rattlesnake poisoning (Russell, 1983) (see Pls. 1366 and 1367). Significant bleeding is usually not a problem (Albritton et al., 1970; Mebs, 1995). The local tissues may appear cyanotic, but tissue necrosis is uncommon (Mebs, 1995; Russell and Bogert, 1981). Local and regional lymph nodes can become swollen and tender as a result of the intense inflammatory response that follows envenoming. Given the relatively weak attachment of the lizard's dentition to the supporting connective tissues, teeth are often avulsed during a bite and may be left embedded in the wounds (Sullivan et al., 1995).

Systemically, the victim may feel weak, dizzy, chilled, and nauseated, and may sweat profusely (Albritton et al., 1970; Bou-Abboud and Kardassakis, 1988; Datta and Tu, 1997; Hooker and Caravati, 1994; Russell, 1983; Stahnke et al., 1970). The majority of these systemic signs and symptoms are secondary to shock, which can occur quickly due to venom-induced release of circulating plasma kinins (see above; Bou-Abboud and Kardassakis, 1988; Mebs, 1995; Russell, 1983). In rare cases the victim may experience muscle fasciculations or complain of "numbness" of the affected body part. Such numbness is likely secondary to local tissue swelling (Russell and Bogert, 1981). Primary neurotoxicity is not seen, and respiratory weakness, while reported in animal models (Stahnke et al., 1970), is not a component of venom poisoning in humans (Russell and Bogert, 1981).

Prevention

If potential victims would refrain from handling these animals, the vast majority of bites could be prevented.

Field Management of Helodermatid Bites

The first priority in treating a victim of helodermatid bite may indeed be removal of the lizard from the person's body (Engelhardt, 1912). It may take as long as 15 minutes to get *H. suspectum* to release its grip (Hooker and Caravati, 1994). Removal can best be achieved by using a strong object to pry the lizard's jaws apart. Some have reported success in applying a noxious stimulus (such as a lighted flame) to the underside of the animal's jaw or immersing it in cold or hot water in an effort to encourage it to release its grip (Miller, 1995; Streiffer, 1986; Strimple et al., 1997).

Once freed from the lizard, the victim should be transported as quickly as feasible to a medical facility. While preparing the victim for transport, the wounds can be quickly washed, dressed, and splinted at heart level. These interventions make intuitive sense, but no specific field management principles for helodermatid bites have been scientifically evaluated. There is no evidence to suggest any benefit from measures such as incision, suction, constriction bands, tourniquets, or pressure-immobilization. Applying ice to the bite site could risk inducing additional vasospasm and tissue injury (Russell and Bogert, 1981). Friar Nentvig's recommendation in the eighteenth century to "cut away the affected parts immediately" should be considered extreme (Brown and Carmony, 1991).

A victim who develops signs of shock (dizziness, sweating, weak and rapid pulse, etc.) should be placed in a supine position with legs elevated, and the local emergency medical services system should be activated. Paramedics may treat the victim with intravenous fluids in an attempt to reverse circulatory shock.

Hospital Management of Helodermatid Bites

While a rapid history is obtained and a focused physical examination takes place, the victim should be placed on cardiac and oxygen monitors, and intravenous lines established. Evidence of venom poisoning such as a drop in blood pressure and/or a significant rise in the heart rate (beyond that expected with the stress and pain of the situation) should be sought.

Shock should be managed by the rapid administration of intravenous saline solutions. If there is no response to 2 liters of fluid in an adult or 20–40 ml/kg in a child, adding a colloidal fluid such as albumin should be considered. If hypotension persists after adequate volume resuscitation, the use of vasopressor drugs such as dopamine may be considered in order to support tissue perfusion.

When the patient is stable, attention can be directed at evaluating and treating the wounds and managing the victim's pain. The bite site should be cleansed with soap and water. The puncture wounds should then be precisely anesthetized with local anesthetic and the wounds explored and probed with a small needle to look for retained teeth (Sullivan and Wingert, 1989). Soft tissue radiographs can be used to augment the search for teeth (Hooker and Caravati, 1994), although their sensitivity is limited. The wounds should then be dressed with a sterile, dry dressing, and the extremity splinted and elevated to reduce swelling. Prophylactic antibiotics are probably unnecessary (Strimple et al., 1997; Sullivan and Wingert, 1989) although there are no case series available on which to base this recommendation. The victim's tetanus immunization status should be updated as needed.

Pain control can usually be obtained with narcotic analgesics, but large doses may be required (Albritton et al., 1970). Some physicians have recommended the use of the rapid-acting narcotic fentanyl, which does not stimulate release of histamine (Strimple et al., 1997). Drugs such as morphine, which do cause histamine release, can precipitate iatrogenic hypotension in a potentially unstable victim (Strimple et al., 1997). In addition, intraarterial and intravenous injections of anesthetic agents such as lidocaine and regional nerve blocks have been used to reduce pain and ameliorate vasospasm (Russell, 1983; Stahnke et al., 1970). Infiltrating large volumes of local anesthetic agents into the bite site is not recommended as this may worsen soft tissue distension and increase pressure (Russell and Bogert, 1981). Steroids have no role in the management of helodermatid envenoming unless the victim experiences a rare allergic reaction to the venom (Russell, 1983).

Diagnostic Studies

Blood work is minimally helpful in guiding therapy. There is frequently an elevation of white blood cells on the complete

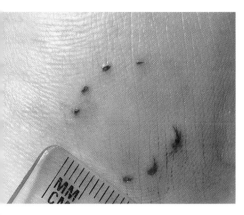

Plate 1366. *Heloderma horridum* bite to the hand demonstrating multiple puncture wounds. Photo by Michael Cardwell.

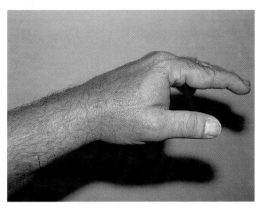

Plate 1367. Soft tissue swelling related to mild venom poisoning from *Heloderma horridum*. Photo by Michael Cardwell.

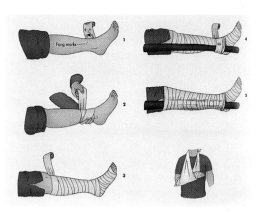

Plate 1368. The Australian pressure-immobilization technique. Reproduced with permission from Norris and Minton, 2001.

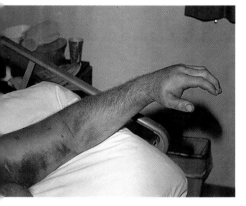

Plate 1369. Severe swelling and bruising 20 hours following a bite to the hand by a newborn *Crotalus atrox*. Photo by David Hardy.

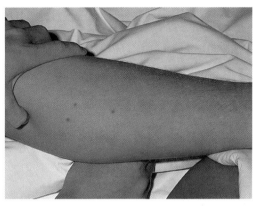

Plate 1370. This bite by a 1-m *Crotalus atrox* to the mid-calf region was a dry bite. Photo by David Hardy.

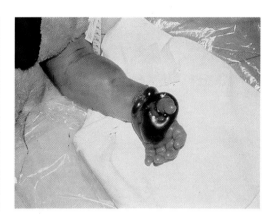

Plate 1371. Large hemorrhagic bleb after an unidentified rattlesnake bite in southern California. Photo by Sean Bush.

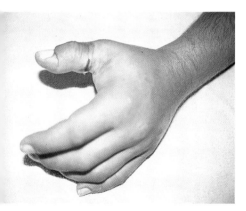

Plate 1372. Hemorrhagic bleb that formed at the bite on a young man who presented several hours after being bitten by a *Crotalus atrox*. Photo by Robert Norris.

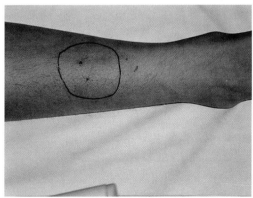

Plate 1373. Minimal local findings following a bite by a venom A–producing *Crotalus scutulatus*. The child experienced a drop in blood pressure, drooping eyelids, and was lethargic. Photo by Sean Bush.

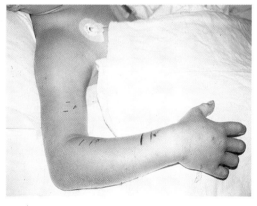

Plate 1374. Young boy bitten 24 hours previously on the right hand by an *Agkistrodon contortrix*. Note the degree of swelling into the shoulder. Photo by Robert Norris.

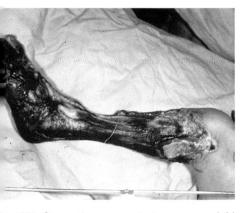

Plate 1375. Severe tissue necrosis in a young child necessitating a below-the-knee amputation following a bite by a 1.5-m *Crotalus adamanteus*. Photo by Joe Gararo.

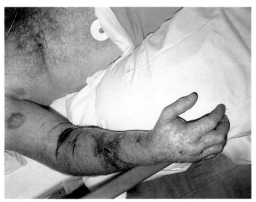

Plate 1376. Severe *Crotalus atrox* bite to the upper extremity 10 hours afterward. Note the extensive swelling and bruising. Photo by David Hardy.

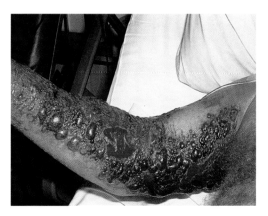

Plate 1377. The same patient as in Plate 1376 photographed four days after the bite. Multiple hemorrhagic and serum-filled vesicles are present. Photo by David Hardy.

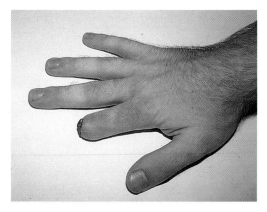

Plate 1378. Amputation of index finger at the proximal interphalangeal joint following a bite by a 1-m *Crotalus atrox*. Photo by Tanith Tyrr.

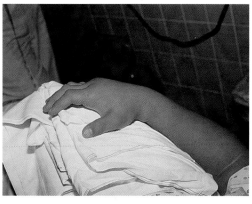

Plate 1379. *Crotalus cerastes* bite manifesting moderate swelling. Photo by David Hardy.

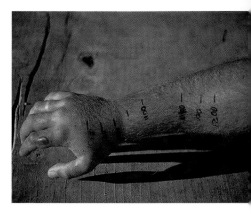

Plate 1380. Hemorrhagic bleb and soft tissue swelli following a *Crotalus cerastes* bite. Photo by Steph Secor.

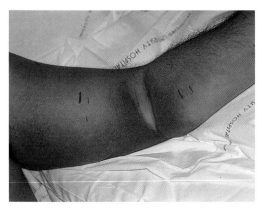

Plate 1381. *Crotalus lepidus lepidus* bite at 24 hours. Note the degree of subcutaneous bruising in the tissues remote from the bite site (left hand). Photo by Robert Norris.

Plate 1382. *Crotalus lepidus klauberi* bite to the index finger. Photo by David Hardy.

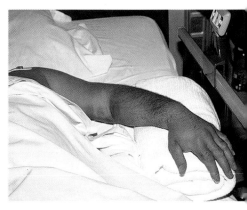

Plate 1383. *Crotalus molossus* bite with significa swelling. Photo by David Hardy.

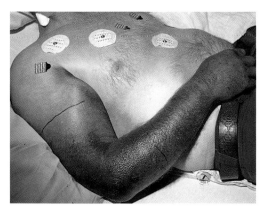

Plate 1384. Extensive ecchymosis following severe venom poisoning by *Crotalus oreganus* (northern Pacific rattlesnake) in an elderly man (two days after the bite). This patient developed a prolonged, recurrent coagulopathy despite aggressive antivenom treatment. Photo by Robert Norris.

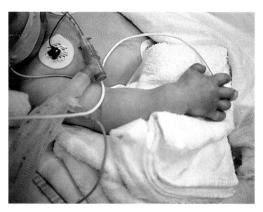

Plate 1385. Severe swelling and bruising in a child severely poisoned by *Crotalus oreganus* (southern Pacific rattlesnake). Photo by Sean Bush.

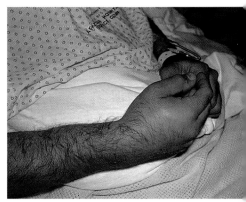

Plate 1386. Swelling of the hand and wrist 12 ho after a *Crotalus polystictus* bite to the thumb. Photo David Hardy.

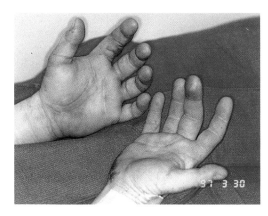

Plate 1387. Hemorrhagic blisters occurring a few hours after bites to both hands by a *Crotalus ruber*. Photo by Sean Bush.

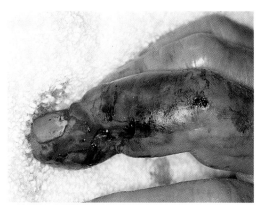

Plate 1388. Hemorrhagic blebs and swelling six hours after a *Crotalus ruber* bite to the long finger. The patient experienced a severe decrease in his platelet count. Photo by Sean Bush.

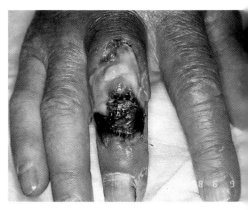

Plate 1389. Tissue necrosis seven weeks after a *Crot ruber* bite, same patient as Plate 1388. Photo by S Bush.

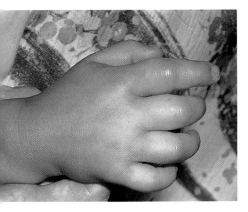

Plate 1390. Soft tissue swelling following the bite of a venom B–producing *Crotalus scutulatus*. Photo by David Hardy.

Plate 1391. Hemorrhagic blebs and soft tissue swelling shortly after a bite to the finger by a venom B–producing *Crotalus scutulatus*. Photo by David Hardy.

Plate 1392. Tissue necrosis 10 days after the bite in the same patient as shown in Plate 1391. Photo by David Hardy.

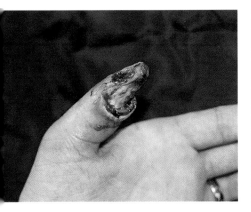

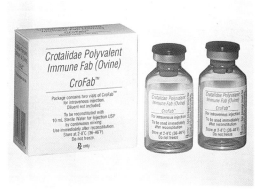

Plate 1393. Severe necrosis leading to amputation of the limb following a *Crotalus viridis* bite. Photo by Jarrod Northman.

Plate 1394. Circular area of tissue damage on the foot of a pig injected with *Crotalus atrox* venom and treated with Extractor suction for 30 minutes (left) compared with a pig injected with venom and receiving no treatment (right) (Bush et al., 2000a). Photo by Sean Bush.

Plate 1395. CroFab antivenom packaging. Photo courtesy of Savage Laboratories.

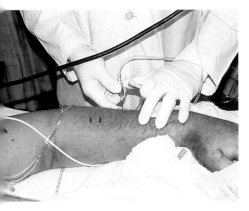

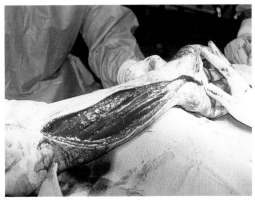

Plate 1396. Checking the pressure inside the forearm muscle compartment in a patient bitten on the left hand by a *Crotalus oreganus* (southern Pacific rattlesnake). Photo by Robert Norris.

Plate 1397. Fasciotomy performed on the patient in Plate 1396. Intracompartmental pressures were severely elevated despite high-dose antivenom therapy and elevation. Photo by Robert Norris.

Plate 1398. *Crotalus atrox* bite to the ring finger at three days. Photo by David Hardy.

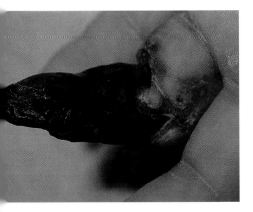

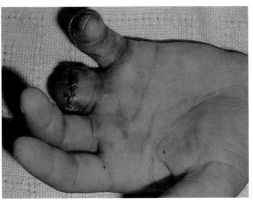

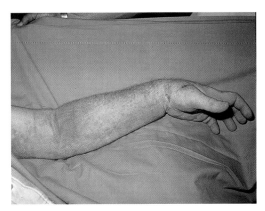

Plate 1399. Same patient as shown in Plate 1398, photographed at six days. Note the severe necrosis of the digit. Photo by David Hardy.

Plate 1400. Completed amputation of the distal ring finger in the patient from Plates 1398 and 1399. Photo by David Hardy.

Plate 1401. At day 13 the patient from Plates 1376–1377 manifests permanent functional disability to the extremity. Photo by David Hardy.

Plate 1402. Instituto Butantan, São Paulo, Brazil. Photo courtesy of João Luiz Costa Cardoso.

Plate 1403. Ashaninka Indian family, Rio Bren, Acre, Brazil. Copyright Stephen Pierini.

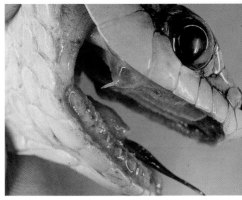

Plate 1404. *Philodryas olfersii* showing fang. Copyrig David A. Warrell.

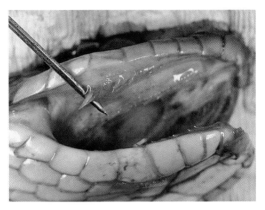

Plate 1405. *Hydrodynastes gigas* showing maxillary tooth. Copyright David A. Warrell.

Plate 1406. Venom being milked from *Bothrops jararacussu*. Copyright David A. Warrell.

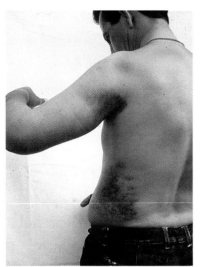

Plate 1407. Extensive and distant bruising two days after a bite b *Philodryas olfersii* on th left hand, posterior aspect. Copyright Joã Luiz Costa Cardoso, Brazil.

Plate 1408. Same patient as in Plate 1407, frontal aspect.

Plate 1409. Bite on the right hand by *Philodryas viridissimus*, 1 m TL. Huampami, Río Cenepa, Amazonas, Peru. Photo by John E. Cadle.

Plate 1410. On the left is a patient bitten on the rig hand by a *Micrurus corallinus* in São Paulo State, Brazil; n absence of local swelling, bilateral ptosis, facial paralys and inability to open the mouth. On the right is the sna involved. Copyright João Luiz Costa Cardoso, Brazil.

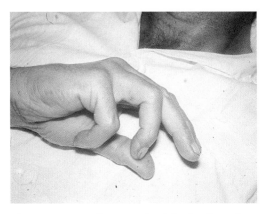

Plate 1411. Patient bitten on the right ring finger by a *Micrurus corallinus* in São Paulo State, Brazil; note absence of local envenoming. Photo courtesy of João Luiz Costa Cardoso, Brazil.

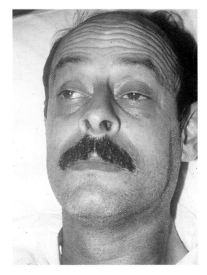

Plate 1412. Same patient as in Plate 1411 showing bilateral ptosis and external ophthalmoplegia (divergent squint). The patient is contracting the frontalis muscle, causing puckering of the brow, in order to try to keep his eyes open.

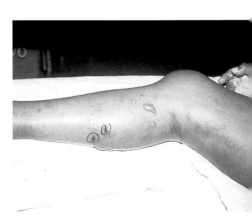

Plate 1413. Local effects of envenoming by *Agkistroc bilineatus*. Photo courtesy of Victor Rolando Alvarac Hospital Instituto Guatemalteco de Seguridad Social

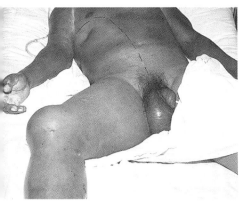

te 1414. Same patient as in Plate 1413 showing ensive swelling including the scrotum.

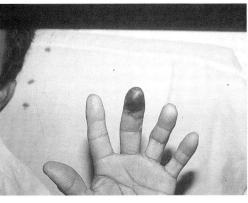

Plate 1415. Bite by a *Bothriechis bicolor*. Photo courtesy of Victor Rolando Alvarado, Hospital Instituto Guatemalteco de Seguridad Social.

Plate 1416. A 30-year-old man bitten on the left wrist by a *Bothriopsis bilineata* six days earlier near Lago Agrio, Napo, Ecuador, showing bruising on the bitten hand extending up the arm to the back of the shoulder. Copyright David A. Warrell.

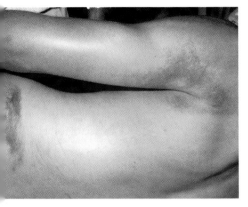

te 1417. Same patient as in Plate 1416, posterior ect, showing the site of intramuscular antivenom ction on the left hip.

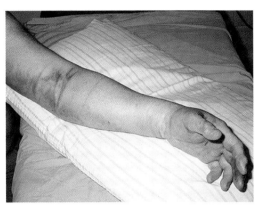

Plate 1418. A 57-year-old man bitten by a *Bothriopsis bilineata* from Pastaza, Ecuador, showing local hemorrhagic blisters and ecchymoses with swelling and bruising of the arm. Copyright David A. Warrell.

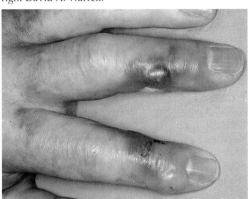

Plate 1419. Same patient as in Plate 1418, showing hand.

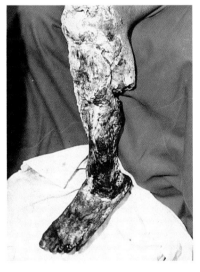

te 1420. An 11-year-old boy bitten two weeks earlier by *hrops asper* near Pedro Vicente Maldonado, Ecuador, treated only with antibiotic. Above-knee amputation s performed. Photo courtesy of David Gaus.

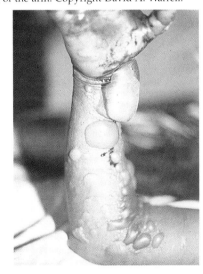

Plate 1421. Bite by *Bothrops asper* (*barba amarilla*) in Guatemala. Photo courtesy of Victor Rolando Alvarado, Hospital Instituto Guatemalteco de Seguridad Social.

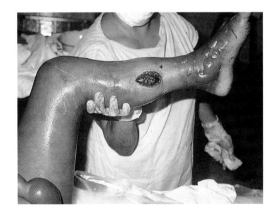

Plate 1422. A 14-year-old Waorani boy bitten by a *Bothrops atrox* on the left foot near Cononaco, Pastaza, Ecuador, showing local blistering, extensive swelling (involving the scrotum), and bulging hemorrhagic muscles following attempted fasciotomy. Copyright David A. Warrell.

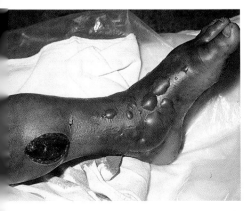

te 1423. Same patient as in Plate 1422, showing early mpt at fasciotomy.

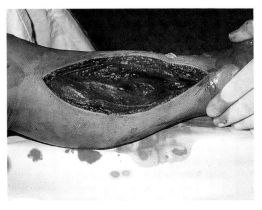

Plate 1424. Same patient as in Plate 1423, showing fasciotomy.

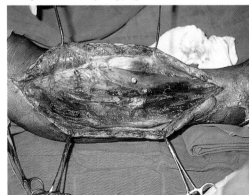

Plate 1425. Second surgical debridement of necrotic tissue in the anterior tibial compartment in an Amerindian woman bitten by a *Bothrops atrox* in Pará, Brazil. Copyright David A. Warrell.

Plate 1426. Necrotic and infected contents of the anterior tibial compartment in a patient bitten by a *Bothrops marajoensis* 1m in TL on Marajó Island, Brazil, 27 days earlier. Copyright David A. Warrell.

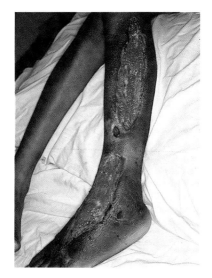

Plate 1427. Results of anterior tibial compartment syndrome in a 10-year-old Shuar girl bitten by a *Bothrops atrox* four weeks earlier in Pastaza, Ecuador. Copyright David A. Warrell.

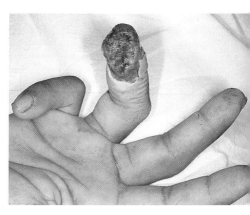

Plate 1428. Healing necrotic lesion of the right ri finger of a woman bitten three weeks earlier by *Bothro atrox* while pulling up mandioca roots near Belé Brazil. Copyright David A. Warrell.

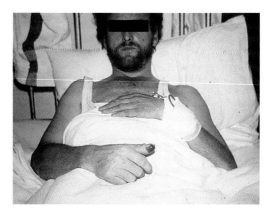

Plate 1429. Necrotic thumb of a 35-year-old British nature photographer bitten by a *Bothrops atrox* on the Coppename River, Suriname, two weeks earlier. Note the arteriovenous shunt on his left wrist used for hemodialysis for renal failure caused by the envenoming. Copyright D. P. Healey.

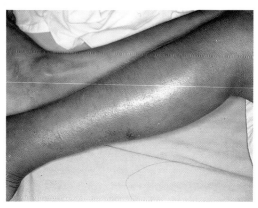

Plate 1430. A nine-year-old Quechua girl bitten on the left calf by a *Bothrops atrox* five days earlier near Puyo, Pastaza, Ecuador, showing tense, hot, red, fluctuant swelling denoting an abscess. Copyright David A. Warrell.

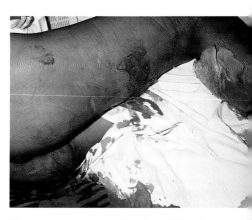

Plate 1431. Extensive bleeding following surgic drainage of an abscess in a 19-year-old man bitten by *Bothrops atrox* behind the right knee in La Merced, Jun Peru. Copyright David A. Warrell.

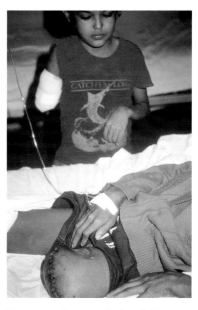

Plate 1432. Boys aged 18 and 10 years, sons of seringueiros (rubber gatherers), bitten by a *Bothrops atrox* in Acre, Brazil, while fishing and brought to the hospital in Rio Branco, where their necrotic limbs were amputated. Copyright David A. Warrell.

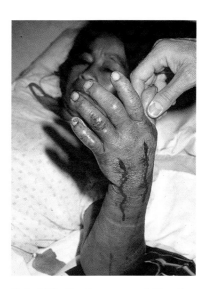

Plate 1433. Quechua woman bitten five days earlier by a *Bothrops atrox* in Pastaza, Ecuador, and still bleeding two days after surgical incisions were made. Copyright David A. Warrell.

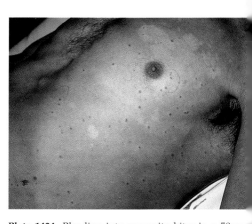

Plate 1434. Bleeding into mosquito bites in a 50-ye old man bitten by a *Bothrops atrox* near Pôrto Vell Rondônia, Brazil. Copyright David A. Warrell.

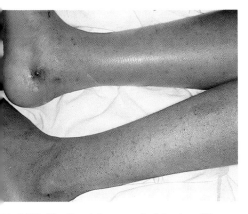

Plate 1435. Bleeding into mosquito bites in a 15-year-boy bitten by a *Bothrops atrox* at La Merced, Junín, u. Copyright David A. Warrell.

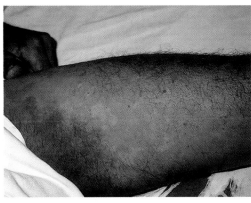

Plate 1436. Bruising over the inguinal lymph nodes in a 50-year-old man bitten on the left leg by a *Bothrops atrox* near Pôrto Velho, Rondônia, Brazil. Copyright David A. Warrell.

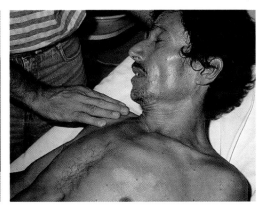

Plate 1437. Neck stiffness caused by subarachnoid hemorrhage in a 50-year-old seringueiro bitten 48 hours earlier by a *Bothrops atrox* near Pôrto Velho, Rondônia, Brazil. Copyright David A. Warrell.

Plate 1438. A 29-year-old man bitten on the left hand a *Bothrops jararaca* 122.5 cm in TL two hours earlier anto Amaro, Marrecas, São Paulo, Brazil. Note fang cture marks and swelling extending to the wrist. yright David A. Warrell.

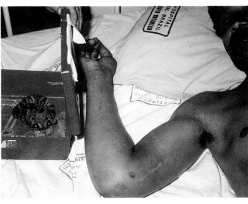

Plate 1439. Swelling, redness, inflammation, and bruising of the right arm several hours after a bite on the elbow by a *Bothrops jararaca*. The living snake was brought to the hospital. Copyright David A. Warrell.

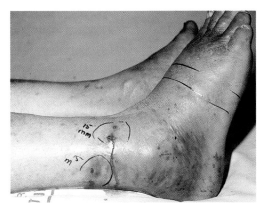

Plate 1440. A 54-year-old man bitten twice on the right ankle by a *Bothrops jararaca* eight hours earlier in São Paulo, Brazil. Note fang marks and swelling and bruising of the foot and ankle. Copyright David A. Warrell.

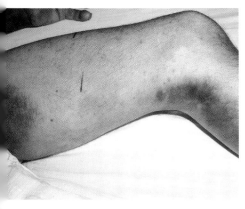

te 1441. Same patient as in Plate 1440 showing bruis-extending up the bitten limb after four days.

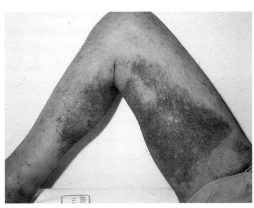

Plate 1442. Same patient as in Plate 1441 12 days after the bite. Copyright David A. Warrell.

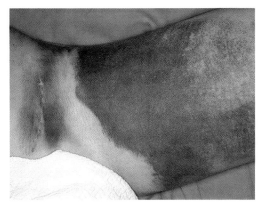

Plate 1443. Extensive bruising of the thigh and over the inguinal lymph nodes of a 13-year-old boy bitten by a *Bothrops jararaca*, 60 cm in TL, 48 hours earlier near Guarulhos, São Paulo, Brazil. Copyright David A. Warrell.

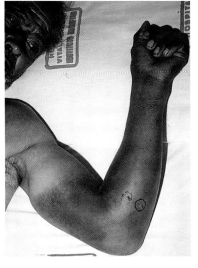

e 1444. Swelling, bruising, and erythema on the left of a man bitten below the left elbow by a *Bothrops raca* 24 hours earlier near São Paulo, Brazil. Copy-t David A. Warrell.

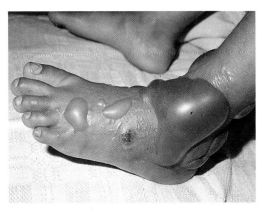

Plate 1445. Blistering on the foot of a boy bitten on the left ankle at Lapa, São Paulo, Brazil, by a *Bothrops jararaca* two hours earlier. A tight tourniquet had been applied above the ankle. Copyright David A. Warrell.

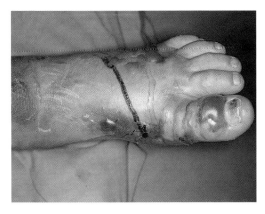

Plate 1446. Same patient as in Plate 1443 showing local hemorrhagic blisters and swelling 36 hours after the bite. Copyright David A. Warrell.

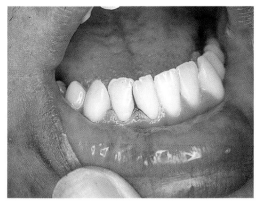

Plate 1447. Bleeding from the gingival sulci in patients bitten by *Bothrops jararaca* two hours earlier near São Paulo, Brazil. Copyright David A. Warrell.

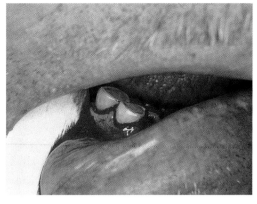

Plate 1448. Bleeding from the gingival sulci in patients bitten by *Bothrops jararaca* three hours earlier near São Paulo, Brazil. Copyright David A. Warrell.

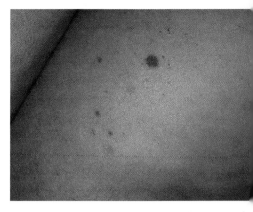

Plate 1449. Purpura and discoid ecchymoses, cut neous manifestations of hemorrhagin activity. Cop right David A. Warrell.

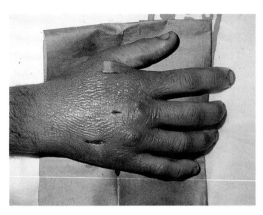

Plate 1450. Drainage of a local abscess that formed at the site of a *Bothrops jararaca* bite on the dorsum of the right hand. Copyright David A. Warrell.

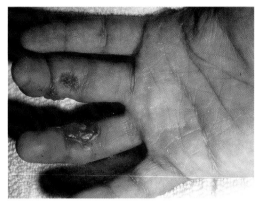

Plate 1451. Deformities resulting from bites by a *Bothrops jararaca* on adjacent fingers. Copyright David A. Warrell.

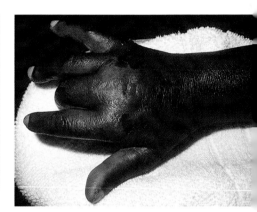

Plate 1452. Deformities resulting from bite by a *Bothrops jararaca* on the back of the right hand. Copyright Dav A. Warrell.

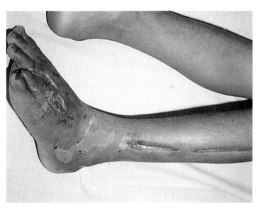

Plate 1453. Long-term results of fasciotomy for anterior tibial compartment syndrome and amputation of the fourth toe in a patient bitten by a *Bothrops jararaca* on the dorsum of the left foot. Copyright David A. Warrell.

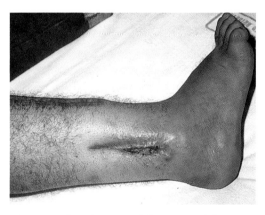

Plate 1454. Complications of fasciotomy following a bite by a *Bothrops jararaca*, 113 cm in TL, five months earlier. Copyright David A. Warrell.

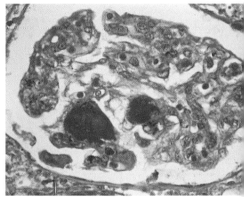

Plate 1455. Histological section of a glomerulus fr the kidney of a patient bitten by a *Bothrops jarar* near Belo Horizonte, Brazil. There are two large fib thrombi (staining red) inside the glomerular capilla loops. Copyright Carlos Amaral, Belo Horizonte, Bra

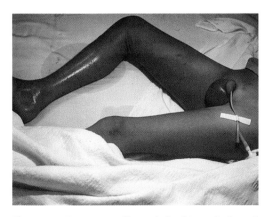

Plate 1456. Intense swelling of the bitten limb and scrotum of an 11-year-old boy bitten on the right foot by a *Bothrops jararacussu* at Cachoeira Paulista, São Paulo State, Brazil, 60 hours earlier. Photo courtesy of M. T. Jorge.

Plate 1457. Extensive swelling and bruising on a three-year-old girl bitten on the left thigh by a *Bothrops jararacussu* 1.59 m in TL. Photo courtesy R. Milani Jr.

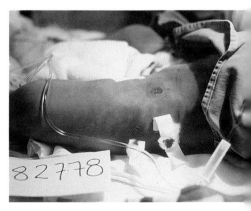

Plate 1458. Same patient as in Plate 1457. The fa punctures are 5 cm apart.

Plate 1459. *Bothrops jararacussu*, female, 1.59 m in TL, [res]ponsible for fatal envenoming of the patient shown [in] Plates 1457 and 1458 at Miracatu, near Juquitiba, São [Pau]lo State, Brazil.

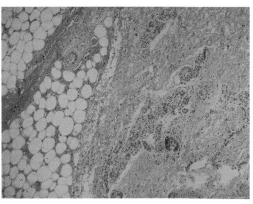

Plate 1460. Histological section of skin near the site of a bite by *Bothrops jararacussu* on a three-year-old girl (Plates 1457 and 1458), showing hemorrhage and necrosis in the dermis and hemorrhage in subcutaneous fat.

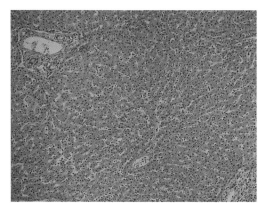

Plate 1461. Histological section of the liver of a three-year-old girl fatally envenomed by *Bothrops jararacussu* (Plates 1457–1460) showing polymorphonuclear cell infiltrate of the liver sinusoids, consisting mainly of eosinophils.

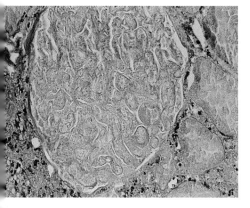

Plate 1462. Histological appearance of a renal biopsy [tak]en from a 35-year-old man 30 days after he was bitten by [*Bo*]*throps jararacussu*. There is renal cortical necrosis. The [glo]merulus is acellular with necrotic tubular epithelial cells [and] some nuclear debris remaining in the interstitium.

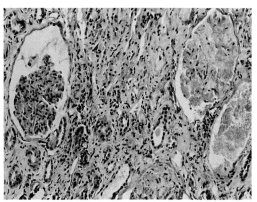

Plate 1463. Same patient as in Plate 1462. Renal biopsy showing necrotic glomeruli on the right with viable glomerulus and tubules on the left.

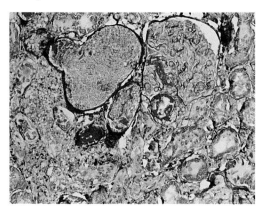

Plate 1464. Same patient as in Plate 1462. Renal biopsy (Masson's stain). In the glomerulus on the right, a capillary appears to be occluded with red-staining proteinaceous material, also seen in the wall of arterioles. This is probably fibrin, and the appearances suggest disseminated intravascular coagulation.

Plate 1465. Conjunctival inflammation in a woman [in]to whose right eye venom was squirted by a *Bothrops* [jara]*racussu*.

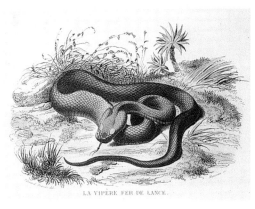

LA VIPÈRE FER DE LANCE.

Plate 1466. "La vipère fer de lance." Illustration of the yellow phase of *Bothrops lanceolatus* from Martinique in Lacépède's *Histoire naturelle des serpents* (1789).

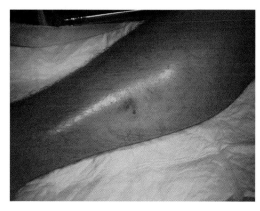

Plate 1467. Intense local swelling with blistering two hours after a bite on the calf by a *Bothrops lanceolatus*. Copyright Laurent Thomas, Fort-de-France, Martinique.

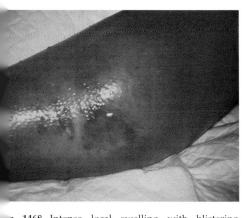

Plate 1468. Intense local swelling with blistering [two] days after a bite on the calf by a *Bothrops lanceolatus*. [Cop]yright Laurent Thomas, Fort-de-France, Martinique.

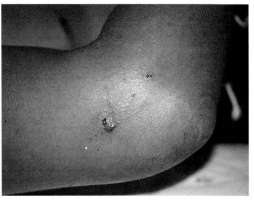

Plate 1469. A 35-year-old man bitten on the right elbow by a *Bothrops lanceolatus* in Martinique four days earlier. Swelling had spread to the trunk. Copyright Laurent Thomas, Fort-de-France, Martinique.

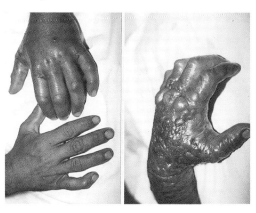

Plate 1470. A 31-year-old man whose left hand was bitten by a *Bothrops moojeni* while he was moving a pile of wood near São José do Rio Preto, São Paulo State, Brazil. Left, 12 hours after the bite; right, three days after the bite and immediately before fasciotomy. Copyright João Aris Kouyoumdjian.

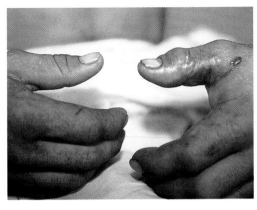

Plate 1471. A 23-year-old man bitten on the left thumb by a *Bothrops moojeni* two days earlier when he put his hand into an armadillo burrow. Copyright João Aris Kouyoumdjian.

Plate 1472. Colony of *Bothrops moojeni* maintained for commercial venom production near Uberlândia, Minas Gerais, Brazil. Copyright David A. Warrell.

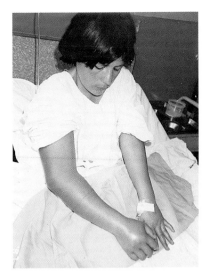

Plate 1473. Woman bitten on the right hand by a *Bothrops pictus* in Lima, Peru, showing extensive local swelling. Copyright Ciro Maguiña.

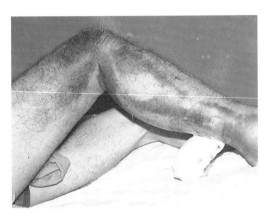

Plate 1474. Extensive swelling and bruising of the bitten limb of a man bitten by a *Bothrops pictus* in Lima, Peru. Copyright Ciro Maguiña.

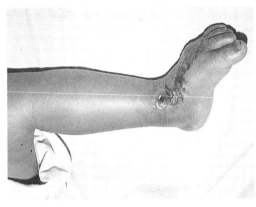

Plate 1475. Local envenoming caused by the bite of a *Cerrophidion godmani* in Guatemala. Photo courtesy of Victor Rolando Alvarado, Hospital Instituto Guatemalteco de Seguridad Social.

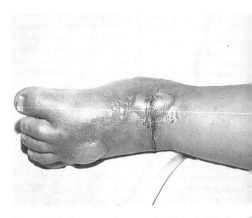

Plate 1476. Same patient as in Plate 1475 showing dorsal aspect of foot.

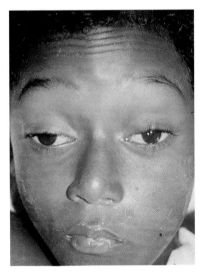

Plate 1477. Boy showing early neurotoxicity after a bite by a *Crotalus durissus marajoensis* on Marajó Island, Brazil. Copyright Pedro Pardal, Belém, Brazil.

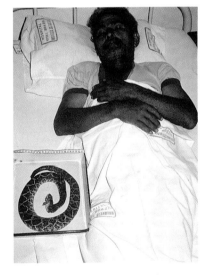

Plate 1478. A 54-year-old man bitten on the right hand at Santa Isabel, São Paulo State, Brazil, by a *Crotalus durissus terrificus* 100.3 cm in TL, showing absence of local envenoming but myasthenic facies. Copyright David A. Warrell.

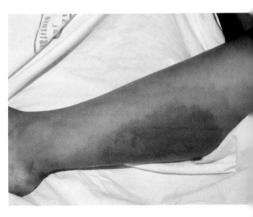

Plate 1479. A 15-year-old girl bitten by a *Crotalus durissus terrificus* at Guarulhos, São Paulo, Brazil, two hours earlier. There is mild swelling but marked erythema at the site of the bite on the left calf. Copyright David A. Warrell.

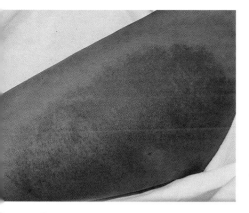

1480. Same patient as in Plate 1479.

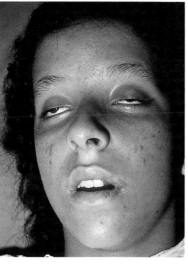

Plate 1481. Same patient as in Plate 1479 showing the development of ptosis, external ophthalmoplegia, facial paralysis, and inability to open the mouth two hours after the bite. Copyright David A. Warrell.

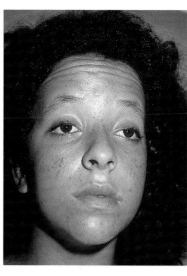

Plate 1482. Same patient as in Plate 1479 showing the development of ptosis, external ophthalmoplegia, facial paralysis, and inability to open the mouth 21 hours after the bite. Copyright David A. Warrell.

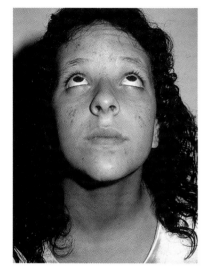

Plate 1483. Same patient as in Plate 1479 showing almost complete recovery five days after the bite. Copyright David A. Warrell.

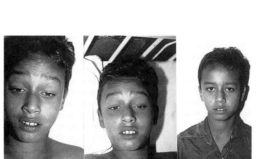

Plate 1484. A 12-year-old boy bitten by a *Crotalus durissus terrificus* at São José do Rio Preto, São Paulo, Brazil, showing (left and middle) myasthenic facies on admission and (right) almost complete recovery three days later. Copyright João Aris Kouyoumdjian.

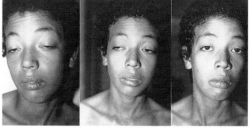

Plate 1485. A 13-year-old boy bitten by a *Crotalus durissus terrificus* at São José do Rio Preto, São Paulo, Brazil, showing (left) mental confusion on admission to hospital, (middle) myasthenic facies 36 hours after the bite, and (right) almost complete recovery 60 hours after the bite. Copyright João Aris Kouyoumdjian.

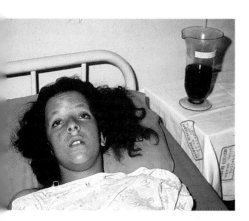

1486. Same patient as in Plate 1479 showing ~~my~~asthenic facies and intense myoglobinuria nine ~~hou~~rs after the bite. Copyright David A. Warrell.

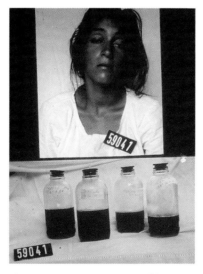

Plate 1487. Woman envenomed by a *Crotalus durissus terrificus* in São Paulo State, Brazil, showing myasthenic/neurotoxic facies and intense myoglobinuria persisting for 48 hours. Copyright João Luiz Costa Cardoso, São Paulo, Brazil.

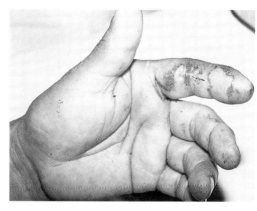

Plate 1488. Left index finger bitten by a *Crotalus durissus terrificus* in the Sandia Valley, Peru. The wound has been incised and sutured and there is mild local swelling. Copyright Ciro Maguiña.

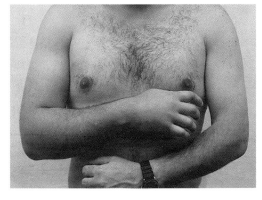

Plate 1489. A 28-year-old man bitten on the right index finger 30 hours earlier by a *Lachesis muta muta* from Mato Grosso, Brazil, showing swelling of the entire arm and local blistering.

Plate 1492. Residual deformity after a bite by a *Lachesis muta* near Leticia, Colombia. Copyright Dr. Juan Silva-Haad, courtesy of João Luiz Costa Cardoso, São Paulo, Brazil.

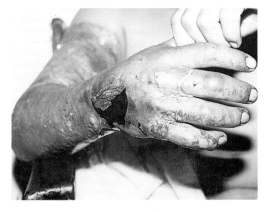

Plate 1495. Same patient as in Plate 1494.

Plate 1498. Persistent bleeding from fang marks three hours after the bite, indicating that the blood is incoagulable as a result of consumption coagulopathy. Copyright David A. Warrell.

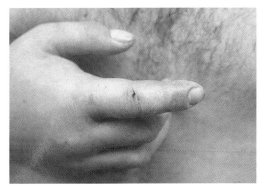

Plate 1490. Same patient as in Plate 1489.

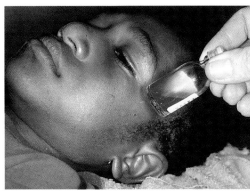

Plate 1493. The 20-minute whole-blood clotting test. Blood from a snakebite victim was placed in a glass vessel and left undisturbed for 20 minutes. It remains liquid, indicating consumption coagulopathy caused by venom procoagulant enzymes. Copyright David A. Warrell.

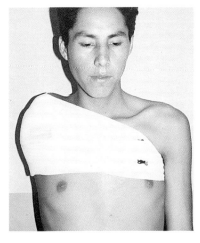

Plate 1496. Same patient as in Plate 1494, following amputation of his gangrenous right arm.

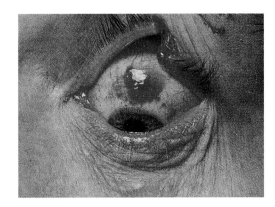

Plate 1499. Bite injury inflicted on the upper eyelid and conjunctiva of a pet shop owner by a *Boa constrictor*. From the *British Medical Journal* 305 (1992):1304, reproduced with permission.

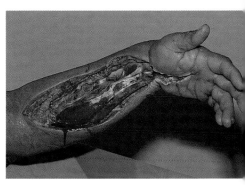

Plate 1491. Fasciotomy of the forearm of a patie bitten by a *Lachesis stenophrys* in Costa Rica. Photo Alejandro Solórzano.

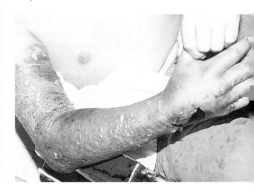

Plate 1494. Disastrous consequences of the applicat of a tight tourniquet around the upper arm of a pati bitten by a *Bothrops atrox* in Peru. Copyright Ciro Magui

Plate 1497. Shuar shamans from Tutinenza Pumbuenza, Amazonas, Ecuador, treating a child bit by a snake. One holds in his hand a foreign body— "illness" extracted from the girl's stomach by suction the bowl is the hallucinogenic liquid *natem* (*Banister sis*), an extract of liana rich in LSD-like alkaloids. Co right Erwin Patzelt. Reproduced from *Ecuador in Shadow of the Volcanoes* by Acosta-Solis et al. with mission of Ediciones Libri Mundi, Quito, Ecuador.

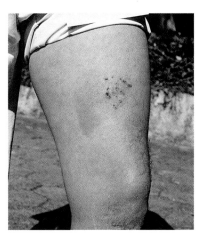

Plate 1500. Effects of the bite of a *Eunectes murinus* three days earlier in Brazil. Copyright João Luiz Costa Cardoso.

blood count (CBC; Bou-Abboud and Kardassakis, 1988). Serum chemistries are generally normal, although there may be an elevation of creatinine phosphokinase (CPK) as a marker of muscle damage (Bou-Abboud and Kardassakis, 1988; Preston, 1989). Measuring cardiac markers (troponin I or T, harbingers of myocardial injury) is prudent if the victim has chest pain, an abnormal electrocardiogram (ECG; see below), or an elevation of total CPK. In very rare cases of severe bites there may be an elevation in coagulation times (e.g., prothrombin time and partial thromboplastin time), a decrease in plasma fibrinogen, an increase of fibrin degradation products (FDPs), and a decrease in platelet count, all of which are consistent with mild coagulopathy (Bou-Abboud and Kardassakis, 1988; Russell, 1983; Russell and Bogert, 1981).

An ECG should be obtained on any victim with hypotension or chest pain. There is one report (Bou-Abboud and Kardassakis, 1988) of an apparent myocardial infarction following a *H. s. cinctum* bite in a young man who suffered profound hypotension (but who also had a prior history of cocaine use).

Antivenom

Although two experimental antivenoms have been produced for helodermatid bites (one by the Poisonous Animal Research Lab, Arizona State University, and one by the Venom Poisoning Center, Los Angeles County–University of Southern California Medical Center; Ernst, 1992), there is no commercially available antivenom for bites by venomous lizards. Given the excellent outcome in almost all cases, the clinical need for an antivenom (and the impetus to develop a commercial product) is prohibitively small. Conservative, supportive care achieves an excellent outcome in almost all such bites.

Disposition

When a "dry bite" is suspected (i.e., no venom is injected), the victim should be kept in the emergency department for a minimum of 6 hours. If after this period the patient remains asymptomatic (with the exception of some slight soreness at the site of the bites, proportional to any nonvenomous bite wound of similar severity), discharge to a reliable home setting is appropriate. Any victim of a helodermatid bite with signs or symptoms of envenoming should be admitted to the hospital for at least 24 hours of observation and treatment. If there is hypotension, chest pain, or the rare case of coagulation dysfunction, the patient should be admitted initially to an intensive care unit.

Morbidity and Mortality

Tenderness at the bite site may persist for three to four weeks, but necrosis is notably rare (Russell and Bogert, 1981).

There is considerable controversy over whether or not any otherwise healthy person has ever died from the bite of a venomous lizard. There are many case reports in the literature of deaths (Brennan, 1924; Woodson, 1943, 1947), but most of these can be explained by other complicating factors such as cardiac disease or chronic alcoholism (Lowe and Limbacher, 1961; Woodson, 1943). The fact that there has not been a fatality reported due to Helodermatidae in more than 50 years (Mebs, 1995) illustrates that the risk of death is extremely low.

If—and this is doubtful—the lethal dose for humans is as low as the predicted 5–8 mg (Phisalix, 1911), and given an average venom yield of 17 mg (Russell and Bogert, 1981), then a lethal bite could occur. This would be most likely if a small child or an infirm, elderly adult was the victim; if the lizard was a large specimen (particularly one of the larger *H. horridum*; Datta and Tu, 1997); and if the bite exposure was prolonged.

CORALSNAKES, FAMILY ELAPIDAE

Epidemiology

Throughout the range of the American coralsnakes, the incidence of coralsnake bites is probably no more than 2% of all venomous snakebites (and probably significantly less than that in the United States). Parrish and Khan (1967b) estimated approximately 20 bites by coralsnakes in the United States each year. The 2001 report of the American Association of Poison Control Centers (AAPCC), however, listed 68 such cases for that year (Litovitz et al., 2002). But that report includes insufficient detail to analyze the circumstances surrounding the bites or even the reliability of identification of the involved serpents. Most coralsnake bites involve *Micrurus* species; very few bites by the smaller *Micruroides euryxanthus* are reported.

Most bites occur in the victim's own yard or garden (Parrish, 1980). In the largest published series on coralsnake bites (including 20 cases they treated locally and 19 cases on which they consulted), Kitchens and Van Mierop (1987a) reported only 6 bites that were truly legitimate or accidental, meaning that the victim was completely unaware of the animal until after the bite occurred. In 14 cases the victim was handling the animal and sustained an illegitimate bite. In 9 of these the victim misidentified the animal as a harmless scarlet kingsnake. In 85% of the cases the snake had to be shaken off or pulled free from the skin. In Neill's (1957a) case series from the 1950s, at least half of the victims were deliberately handling the snake when bitten.

Venoms

Up until the late 1880s the venomous potential of U.S. coralsnakes was still being debated. It was not until True (1883) reported four cases of documented venom poisoning that the issue was finally settled. Although the venoms of American coralsnakes are indeed very potent, they have been given almost mythical qualities. Hence some of the names attached to the coralsnake, such as "ten pace snake," "minute snake," and "knock 'em dead snake" (Russell, 1983).

Micrurus venoms are complex protein mixtures, and as is the case with many genera of snakes that span large geographical regions, there are significant interspecific differences in venom composition (Davidson and Eisner, 1996). The primary toxic components (alpha neurotoxins) of coralsnake venoms are low-molecular-weight, basic polypetides that block the nicotinic acetylcholine receptors of neuromuscular junctions (Chang, 1979). This has been likened to the effect of curare, the paralytic poison used by some South American tribes to tip their arrows. Coral snake neurotoxins, however, have a more delayed onset and a longer duration of action than curare (Russell, 1983). While many elapid venoms demonstrate neurotoxicity related to acetylcholine esterase activity, this component is not a major constituent of North American coralsnake venoms (Davidson and Eisner, 1996).

Micrurus venoms exhibit much less proteinase activity than do crotaline venoms (Russell et al., 1997). They do have significant amounts of phospholipase activity and hyaluronidase, with variable amounts of L-amino acid oxidase (Minton, 1974; Russell et al., 1997). A component phospholipase A_2 (PLA_2) may cause myonecrosis and CPK release (Nishioka et al., 1993). PLA_2 may also have some cardiotoxic properties (Davidson and Eisner, 1996). Hypotension related to a precipitous fall in aortic pressure and cardiac output (with concomitant rises in hepatosplanchnic and pulmonary artery pressures) has been demonstrated in dog studies (Ramsey et al., 1972). These cardiotoxic effects are uncommon in human venom poisoning and were not noted in Kitchens and Van Mierop's (1987a) cases. Coralsnake venoms have little phosphodiesterase, 5'-nucleotidase and no phosphomonoesterase activity (Russell et al., 1997). They lack procoagulant, defibrinogenating, hemorrhagic, necrotizing, and proteolytic properties (Sanchez et al., 1992).

The venom of *Micruroides euryxanthus* is clearly distinct from that of *M. fulvius* and *M. tener*, although the three may contain some common antigens (Cohen and Seligmann, 1967). It is quite neurotoxic, but the animal's small size and short fangs greatly limit the risk of serious poisoning in humans (Ernst, 1992).

Clinical Features

Most published accounts of New World coralsnake bites have come from the United States and involved *M. fulvius* or *M. tener*.

Micrurus fulvius and *M. tener*

Due to their small mouths and relatively inefficient venom delivery apparatus, coralsnake bites in humans generally occur to the hands and fingers because the snake is usually being handled when the bite occurs (Russell, 1967a). In one study, 39% of coralsnake bite victims thought the snake was a harmless kingsnake when they picked it up (Kitchens and Van Mierop, 1987a). Envenoming is estimated to occur in approximately 40% of *Micrurus* bites (Parrish et al., 1966; Parrish and Khan, 1967b; Russell, 1983).

While crotaline venoms are capable of inducing a wide variety of systemic derangements in human victims (see below), bites by coralsnakes produce neurological dysfunction as their major consequence. Local findings are usually minimal (Kitchens and Van Mierop, 1987a; Parrish and Khan, 1967b). Bite marks may, in fact, be difficult to find (Norris and Dart, 1989; Russell, 1983). There is little in the way of redness or soft tissue swelling (Campbell, 1979). Local pain is relatively common and may be described as "burning" and radiating up the extremity (Gloyd, 1938a; Werler and Darling, 1950). Hypesthesias or paresthesias may also occur (Banner, 1988; Van Mierop, 1976b), but tissue necrosis is not seen.

The first findings of significance are usually abnormalities in cranial nerve function (including ptosis, diplopia, dysarthria, and dysphonia) (Campbell, 1979; Kitchens and Van Mierop, 1987a; McCollough and Gennaro, 1963a, 1970; Ramsey and Klickstein, 1962; Russell, 1983; Weis and McIsaac, 1971; Werler and Darling, 1950). A classic finding is that of myasthenic or neurotoxic facies (an odd expression due to lax facial muscles; Nishioka et al., 1993). Pupils may be pinpoint (Russell, 1983), and the victim may exhibit excessive salivation (McCollough and Gennaro, 1963a, 1970; Van Mierop, 1976b). As cranial nerve dysfunction progresses, systemic muscle weakness begins and may progress to complete paralysis (including paralysis of res-

piratory muscles) (McCollough and Gennaro, 1963a, 1970; Neill, 1957a; Ramsey and Klickstein, 1962). Deep tendon reflexes may be abnormal (McCollough and Gennaro, 1963a; Weis and McIsaac, 1971). There may occasionally be alterations in mental status (e.g., drowsiness or "euphoria," which may be compounded by any alcohol the victim has imbibed; Neill, 1957a; Parrish and Khan, 1967b; Weis and McIsaac, 1971). The precise mechanism behind such altered mental status is unclear. In some cases it may be related to hypoxia secondary to respiratory failure (Banner, 1988). Usually, however, the victim's mental state is clear (McCollough and Gennaro, 1963a). Occasionally hypotension may occur and may be associated with cardiovascular or respiratory failure (Banner, 1988). Cardiovascular collapse and seizures may occur in severe cases (McCollough and Gennaro, 1963a; Russell, 1983). Additional findings may include nausea and vomiting, abdominal discomfort, headache, and diaphoresis (Campbell, 1979; Gaar, 1996; Kitchens and Van Mierop, 1987a; McCollough and Gennaro, 1963a; Van Mierop, 1976b).

Coralsnake venoms contain little if any anticoagulant properties (Davidson and Eisner, 1996), and laboratory or clinical coagulopathies are thus not expected.

While the onset of symptoms may immediately follow coralsnake bites, it is important to realize that there may be a significant delay (up to 13 hours) before any significant systemic findings appear (Kitchens and Van Mierop, 1987a). Once symptoms begin, however, their progression can be alarmingly rapid and difficult to halt (McCollough and Gennaro, 1963a; Ramsey and Klickstein, 1962).

Micruroides euryxanthus

The clinical findings following venom poisoning by *Micruroides euryxanthus* may include some pain (that may persist for several hours) and paresthesias, lacrimation, headache, difficulty focusing, photophobia, nausea, abdominal pain, weakness, and drowsiness (Russell 1967, 1983; Russell and Picchioni, 1983). Symptoms usually resolve within 24 hours but may persist up to four days (Russell, 1967a).

Micrurus distans distans and *M. laticollaris*

The signs and symptoms of venom poisoning by *M. distans distans* and *M. laticollaris* appear to be quite similar to those following *M. fulvius* bites (Dart et al., 1992; Pettigrew and Glass, 1985). At least one death due to *M. d. distans* has been reported in the medical literature (Dart et al., 1992), that of an elderly man who misidentified the snake as a harmless milksnake.

Prevention

Not handling these reptiles would eliminate the vast majority of bites. Children and the uninitiated should be particularly careful about attempting to handle any snake that has not been positively identified. Young children, unaware of the danger, may be particularly attracted to these brightly colored serpents.

Field Management of Elapid Bites

Given the number of harmless snakes that may be confused for coralsnakes by the lay public and the substantial delay in symptomatology that may occur following bites by *Micrurus* species, it is prudent to make a positive identification of the snake. This can be done by getting a close look at the offending specimen, noting especially the color pattern of the head and body, or by bringing the snake in for identification if this can be done safely. As mentioned below under the discussion of antivenom, precise identification has significant implications in terms of antivenom administration in coralsnake bites.

In Kitchens and Van Mierop's review (1987a) of 20 patients bitten by *M. fulvius* in Florida, the average time to presentation to medical care was two and a half hours. The delay in seeking care was variously attributed to delay in onset of signs and symptoms, alcohol intoxication, and misidentification of the snake as a harmless specimen. It is important that any prehospital actions not delay transportation of the victim to appropriate medical care even if there are no early signs or symptoms of envenoming.

There is nothing to suggest that a constriction band (impeding lymphatic and superficial venous return), suction, or local ice therapy would be of any benefit. Incisions and electric shock, which carry significant risks of doing additional harm, should be strictly avoided (Dart and Gustafson, 1991).

While there is no literature evaluating its efficacy, the Australian pressure-immobilization technique (Pl. 1368) should be used. It has been demonstrated to impede the systemic distribution of Australian elapid venoms (Sutherland et al., 1979; Sutherland and Coulter, 1981) and, anecdotally, to delay the onset of signs and symptoms of venom poisoning in human cases (Balmain and McCelland, 1982; Murrell, 1981; Pearn et al., 1981; Sutherland, 1995). Because there is no significant risk of local tissue complications following *Micrurus* or *Micruroides* venom poisoning, and because the major threat is systemic neuromuscular paralysis, this technique may be a reasonable temporizing measure while the victim is transported to medical care (Hardy and Bush, 1998; Norris, 1999). The technique must be applied accurately (i.e., within a relatively narrow range of pressures—approximately 55–70 mm Hg) for it to be effective (Howarth et al., 1994). In Australia, people are instructed to apply the wrap as tightly as they would for a sprained ankle (Edmondson, 1979; White, 1991). If the wrap is too loose or too tight, venom uptake will not be slowed (and may in fact be enhanced). Success of the technique also depends on splint immobilization and avoidance of exertion. Walking, even for a few minutes, will likely increase flow from the site, even in upper extremity bites (Howarth et al., 1994). Studies are needed to definitively evaluate the efficacy of pressure-immobilization in coralsnake bites.

Hospital Management of Elapid Bites

Although there is a reasonably well validated grading scale for judging the severity of pitviper bites (see below), it is highly dependent on the presence of local signs and symptoms and on a steady progression of findings. Such findings are often absent in coralsnake bites, and therefore the scale cannot be used in this scenario. Although Parrish and Khan (1967b) proposed a grading scale specifically for coralsnake bites, its clinical utility is very limited. The physician treating a victim of *Micrurus* or *Micruroides* venom poisoning must remain highly vigilant for evidence of envenoming and must be ready to intervene quickly should the victim's clinical status deteriorate.

Concurrent with conducting a rapid history and physical examination, intravenous lines should be established and monitoring of cardiac and respiratory status initiated. A careful evaluation searching for any evidence of neurologic dysfunc-

tion or cardiovascular derangement is paramount. It is especially important for the medical team to watch carefully for any evidence of weakening respiratory drive or diminished ability to protect the airway. If this occurs, the patient requires prompt endotracheal intubation in order to prevent aspiration and its significant complications (hypoxia, pneumonia, death). If signs of cranial nerve dysfunction appear, prophylactic intubation is prudent (Kitchens and Van Mierop, 1987a). Frequent reassessment of respiratory function using simple measuring devices such as a bedside peak flow meter may be of benefit. It is unwise to administer sedative agents to a coralsnake bite victim unless the patient is going to be intubated (Gold and Wingert, 1994).

Diagnostic Studies

Micrurus and *Micruroides* venoms do not cause major hemostatic or blood cell abnormalities (Gaar, 1996); therefore, no routine laboratory studies will be required for most victims bitten by these snakes. Occasionally there will be an increase in the serum CPK and some spilling of the muscle protein myoglobin into the urine, both reflecting a degree of myotoxicity (C. H. Campbell, 1979; Kitchens and Van Mierop, 1987a).

In the setting of severe venom poisoning with respiratory or cardiovascular instability, sampling arterial blood to evaluate the pH and partial pressures of oxygen and carbon dioxide (arterial blood gases) is prudent. Likewise, a chest radiograph and electrocardiogram should be obtained in serious cases, especially if endotracheal intubation is required.

Antivenom

Current recommendations are to begin antivenom therapy, when possible, in any person bitten by a snake positively identified as *Micrurus* regardless of whether or not signs or symptoms of venom poisoning are present. This is especially true if the period of fang contact was such that a significant quantity of venom may have been introduced (Gaar, 1996; Heard et al., 1999; Kitchens and Van Mierop, 1987a; Van Mierop, 1976b). This reasoning is based on observations that systemic findings may be significantly delayed following coralsnake bites, and once they begin may progress rapidly and unabatedly even in the presence of delayed antivenom infusion (Dart and Sullivan, 1996; Heard et al., 1999; Kitchens and Van Mierop, 1987a). It has been estimated that approximately 25% of patients will receive antivenom unnecessarily (i.e., they would not have developed neurological signs or symptoms in the absence of antivenom) if this approach is used (Kitchens and Van Mierop, 1987a).

While the future of the product is unclear, there is currently a single antivenom for coralsnake bites available in the United States: Antivenin (*Micrurus fulvius*) (Wyeth-Ayerst Laboratories, Philadelphia, Pa.). The starting dose for this product is 3–7 vials given intravenously (Russell, 1983). The higher end of the range should be used if significant signs or symptoms are already present (McCollough and Gennaro, 1970). If after the initial infusion neurologic or cardiovascular findings progress, additional antivenom should be given, although it is extremely rare for more than 10 vials to be required (Otten, 1983). At the time of this writing, it is unclear whether Wyeth-Ayerst Laboratories will continue producing this antivenom given its infrequent use and thus low profitability.

Additional antivenoms produced for *Micrurus* species are listed in Table 63 in the next chapter, "Snakebites in Central and South America." Although there may be significant antigenic dissimilarity between venoms of different *Micrurus* species, cross protection by several of the various antivenoms is likely (Cohen and Seligmann, 1967; McCollough and Gennaro, 1968; Ramsey and Klickstein, 1962; Rawat et al., 1994). As an example, Wyeth antivenom produced using *M. fulvius* venom appears to be effective for *M. distans* venom as well (Dart et al., 1992). Nevertheless, it is always best to use an antivenom produced specifically for the offending species when possible (Otten, 1983).

Coralsnake antivenom should be administered in a fashion similar to pitviper antivenom (see below). The risks of allergic reactions (both acute reactions and delayed serum sickness) are similar to those associated with pitviper antivenom, and the same admonitions regarding skin testing are true. Kitchens and Van Mierop (1987a) reported 39 cases of *M. fulvius* bites in which 17 patients received antivenom (median dose, 6.5 vials). Most of the patients received antivenom within eight hours of the bite. Of those who received the equine-derived antivenom, 6 developed acute hives and 1 experienced an apparent anaphylactic reaction. The latter patient was a horse keeper. Four of the patients receiving antivenom developed delayed serum sickness severe enough to be treated with steroids.

If there is a serious risk of antivenom allergy or if antivenom is not available, it is possible to manage a victim of severe coralsnake bite with respiratory and peripheral paralysis using only conservative measures. These patients can be endotracheally intubated and ventilated mechanically until their neurological symptoms are resolved (Kitchens and Van Mierop, 1987a). Mechanical ventilation can, however, be required for many days to weeks in severe cases (Gaar, 1996).

Management of *Micruroides euryxanthus* venom poisoning is purely supportive in the vast majority of cases. If the situation is one of respiratory instability but an intact cardiovascular status, conservative management of the patient's airway and breathing (with intubation and mechanical ventilation) is likely to achieve an optimal outcome. In the unlikely event of a life-threatening situation with severe cardiovascular instability unresponsive to supportive measures, a trial of any available *Micrurus* antivenom might be considered. While many believe that there would be little cross protection from these agents (Russell, 1983; Van Mierop, 1976b), there is some immunodiffusion evidence for cross reactivity (Russell, 1967a).

Disposition

Any person possibly bitten by a coralsnake should be admitted for a minimum of 24 hours of close observation, even if antivenom is withheld. The delayed onset of signs and symptoms followed by precipitous deterioration make this a judicious course of action.

Morbidity and Mortality

Cranial nerve dysfunction can lead to difficulty swallowing and handling secretions, and can lead to aspiration pneumonia (Kitchens and Van Mierop, 1987a) and possibly death.

Muscle weakness can persist for days to months, and uncomfortable radiating paresthesias may persist for weeks (Kitchens and Van Mierop, 1987a). Permanent sequelae in victims who survive the bite are exceedingly rare (Gaar, 1996; Gómez and Dart, 1995; Kitchens and Van Mierop, 1987a).

The estimated LD_{100} for a human adult has been put at 4–5 mg of dried venom (Fix, 1980; Minton and Minton, 1969). Since the venom yield for an average adult coralsnake is 2–6 mg (Fix

and Minton, 1976), it is clearly possible for *Micrurus* bites to lead to death, particularly in small children or in the elderly and infirm (Dart et al., 1992). In 8 of 12 adult *Micrurus* specimens, venom extraction yielded more than 6 mg of dried venom, and more than 12 mg was obtained from 4 individuals (Fix and Minton, 1976).

Deaths due to coralsnake bites are exceedingly rare. Parrish (1963) reviewed 460 deaths caused by venomous animals in the 48 contiguous United States from 1950 to 1959, and only 2 of these deaths were attributable to coralsnakes—less than the number caused by exotic venomous snakes that had been imported into the United States during that same period. The primary cause of death in coralsnake bites is respiratory failure (Banner, 1988; Gaar, 1996; McCollough and Gennaro, 1963a; Parrish and Khan, 1967b). Cardiovascular instability can also contribute to a lethal outcome (C. H. Campbell, 1979). Historically, the mortality rate for untreated *Micrurus* bites was estimated to be 10–20% (McCollough and Gennaro, 1963a; Neill, 1957a; Parrish and Khan, 1967b). Death from respiratory failure has occurred in as little as 1–2 hours and as long afterward as 26 hours (McCollough and Gennaro, 1963a). There has not, however, been a documented death due to *Micrurus* in the United States since the Wyeth antivenom became available in the 1960s (Russell, 1983).

There have been no deaths reported from bites of *Micruroides euryxanthus*, despite the fact that its venom is quite toxic (Boyden, 1980; Davidson and Eisner, 1996; Russell, 1967a).

PITVIPERS, FAMILY VIPERIDAE

Epidemiology

The only systematic attempt to define the epidemiology of venomous snakebites in the United States was done by Parrish (1966) using data obtained in the late 1950s. Parrish surveyed selected hospitals and general practitioners, surgeons, internists, pediatricians, and orthopedists to estimate the number of patients treated for venomous snakebite, and also reviewed death certificates of patients with fatal bites. He estimated that there were approximately 6,680 treated bites in the United States in 1959, with 15 deaths. Between 1962 and 1966 in Florida, there were an estimated 200 bites by venomous snakes and 3 deaths each year (McCollough and Gennaro, 1968). All these numbers have likely changed given the changes in population demographics (of both humans and snakes) and changes in lifestyles that have occurred since the 1950s and 1960s. The AAPCC collected records of 6,440 snakebites reported to 64 centers covering 48 states and the District of Columbia in 2001 (Litovitz et al., 2002). Of these, 2,127 were by native venomous species, 96 were by exotic venomous species, 1,922 were by unknown species, 2,129 were by nonvenomous native species, and 166 were by nonvenomous exotic species. Clearly these numbers underestimate the magnitude of the problem in the United States as there is no requirement to report snakebites to any health agency. A large percentage of snakebites are likely treated without input from poison control centers, especially in areas of the country where physicians see a number of bites and are comfortable with treatment decisions. A more up-to-date, systematic survey is needed, but funding has been a problem. For the time being, Russell's (1988) estimates of the scope of this problem in the United States are the best available. He estimated approximately 8,000 venomous bites each year, with 70% inflicted by rattlesnakes, 20% by copperheads, 9% by cottonmouths, and less than 1% by coralsnakes. Clearly, the relative importance of each of these groups of snakes will vary by location. For example, in both the Houston and Temple, Texas, areas, *Agkistrodon contortrix* accounts for more than half of all treated venomous snakebites (Burch et al., 1988; White and Weber, 1991).

The snakes of greatest medical importance in the United States include *Crotalus adamanteus*, *C. atrox*, *C. horridus*, *C. oreganus*, *C. scutulatus*, *C. viridis*, and *Sistrurus miliarius*. Pygmy rattlesnakes are responsible for approximately 44% of the venomous snakebites in Florida (Tu, 1977).

In Mexico, as many as 28,000 bites by venomous snakes occur each year (Gómez and Dart, 1995), with the most important snakes being *C. atrox*, *C. simus*, and *Bothrops asper* (see "Central and South American Snakebites" for discussions of *C. simus* and *B. asper*). *Crotalus atrox* is probably responsible for most of the serious bites and deaths in northern Mexico (Minton and Weinstein, 1986).

Venom Yields

Venom yields for North American venomous snakes are listed in Table 57. Without doubt, the largest yields are those obtained from large *C. adamanteus* and *C. atrox* specimens, which can produce in excess of 1 g (dry weight; Glenn and Straight, 1982). The sheer volume of venom such a snake can possess is impressive—as much as 4.5 ml (Glenn and Straight, 1982). It appears likely that of these two snakes, *C. atrox* consistently delivers higher venom loads in its bites (Gennaro et al., 1961). Venom yield appears to be directly related to total length (Jones, 1971).

Venoms

Crotaline venoms are arguably the most complex naturally occurring toxins. They are mixtures of enzymes, low-molecular-weight polypeptides, metal ions, and other, as yet poorly studied, components.

Studies of reptile venoms are notoriously fraught with difficulty. Of major importance is the degree of variability. Venoms vary not only between species but also between different populations and individuals within a single species, and even in the same individual based on its age, health, geographic origin, and the time of year (Glenn et al., 1983; Glenn and Straight, 1985b; Hayes, 1991; Mebs and Kornalik, 1984; Ownby et al., 1976). Juvenile crotalines tend to produce venom that, on a weight-for-weight basis, is more toxic than that of adult animals of the same species. This largely accommodates for young snakes' significantly reduced venom yield and may also be related to differences in preferred prey in juveniles (Hayes, 1991; Ownby et al., 1976). Juvenile pitvipers can clearly inflict a serious, even life-threatening bite (see Pl. 1369).

The numerous variables involved in venom production make it very difficult to fully describe the venom composition for any particular snake species, although generalizations can be made. Much of the local tissue destruction for which the pitvipers are so well known is due to proteolytic enzymes. Various metalloproteinases have been determined to stimulate necrosis by yielding activated tumor necrosis factor alpha (TNF α), which is a major mediator of inflammation (Holstege et al., 1997). The sequence of events initiated by these metalloproteinases and activated TNF α results in the production of endogenous human metalloproteinases that further amplify

inflammation and necrosis (Holstege et al., 1997; Moura-da-Silva et al., 1996).

Some of the most toxic crotaline venoms contain phospholipase A_2 neurotoxins. These include the venoms of *Crotalus durissus terrificus* (crotoxin), *C. scutulatus* (Mojave toxin), *C. viridis concolor* (concolor toxin), and *C. horridus* (canebrake toxin). The LD_{50} values for these species can be 10–80 times lower than for rattlesnakes that lack these neurotoxins (Glenn and Straight, 1989). Such neurotoxins have been discovered in 6 of 27 North American rattlesnake venoms tested to date (Lee, 1972; Weinstein et al., 1985). They appear to block neuromuscular transmissions in a noncompetitive fashion by blocking calcium channels on the presynaptic side of the neuromuscular junction (Holstege et al., 1997), thus preventing acetylcholine release, which is required for muscle activation.

Many crotaline venoms contain thrombinlike enzymes (TLEs) that may cause abnormalities in the blood coagulation function of the snakebite victim. TLEs are glycoproteins (procoagulant amino acid esterases) that cleave off a portion of the clotting precursor, fibrinogen, yielding an abnormal, unstable fibrin clot that is rapidly broken down (Kitchens, 1992; Russell, 1983; Van Mierop and Kitchens, 1980). This results in the formation of widespread tiny intravascular clots that are rapidly dissolved and result in secondary consumption of serum clotting factors. TLEs, unlike true thrombin, do not directly activate coagulation factors VIII, XIII, or plasminogen; do not complex with antithrombin III (and therefore are unaffected by heparin therapy); and have no direct effect on the cellular components of the blood, including platelets (Kitchens, 1992; Kitchens and Van Mierop, 1983; Russell, 1983). TLEs also do not appear to have a significant direct effect on levels of circulating clotting factors (Weiss et al., 1969). While these components do not significantly affect platelets directly, an associated slight reduction in platelet count can occur, possibly due to mechanical destruction by fibrin strands or to action of plasmin on platelet membranes (Kitchens and Van Mierop, 1983).

Some crotaline bites are followed by significant drops in platelet counts. There are probably multiple mechanisms by which this can occur, including effects of venom phospholipases on platelet cell membranes, direct stimulation of platelet clumping, and destruction of platelets at sites of vascular damage and inflammation (Holstege et al., 1997).

Many venoms contain hemorrhagins, all of which, to date, have been metalloproteinases (Chugh and Sakhuja, 1991; Weissenberg et al., 1991). These substances cause the vasculature to become leaky (by working on the basement membranes) and allow red blood cells to seep out of the vessels (Chugh and Sakhuja, 1991; Weissenberg et al., 1992). These agents are largely responsible for the impressive degree of soft tissue bruising seen following many significant pitviper bites (Bjarnason and Fox, 1994).

A number of crotaline venoms (such as those of *C. adamanteus* and *C. atrox*) can stimulate release of bradykinin in bite victims. This powerful peptide can induce a drop in blood pressure and can stimulate nausea, vomiting, and diarrhea, as well as compounding local pain (Minton, 1974).

Agkistrodon bilineatus

Significant individual variability has been found in this snake's venom (Tan and Ponnudurai, 1990). It tends to have moderate hyaluronidase and alkaline phosphomonoesterase activities, high L-amino acid oxidase and 5'-nucleotidase

Table 57. Venom yields of some North American venomous reptiles.

Species	Yield (per individual)	Comments	Reference
Heloderma suspectum	17 mg (mean)		Russell and Bogert, 1981
		Lethal human dose probably about one-half of the possible venom yield (very unlikely that this volume could be expressed in a single bite)	Minton and Minton, 1969
Heloderma horridum	—	Due to its typically larger size, the venom yield for this lizard is likely to exceed that for *H. suspectum*	
Micrurus fulvius	2–12 mg		Fix and Minton, 1976
Micrurus tener		Estimated human lethal dose: 4–5 mg	Fix, 1980; Minton and Minton, 1969
Agkistrodon contortrix	40–70 mg	Probably 100 mg or more necessary to kill a human	Minton and Minton, 1969
Agkistrodon c. phaeogaster	43.4 mg (0.146 ml) (mean)		DeWit, 1982
Agkistrodon c. contortrix	57.5 mg (mean)		Russell, 1982
Agkistrodon c. mokasen	57.8 mg (0.20 ml) (mean)		Minton, 1953
Agkistrodon c. laticinctus	50 mg (mean)		Russell, 1967b
Agkistrodon piscivorus	100–150 mg	Estimated human lethal dose: 100–150 mg	Minton and Minton, 1969
	158 mg (mean)		Wolff and Githens, 1939b
	1,090 mg	One extraction of a 152 cm TL specimen	Wolff and Githens, 1939a
Crotalus adamanteus	450 gm (mean)		Klauber, 1956
	848 mg (maximum)		
	400 mg (mean)		Glenn and Straight, 1982
	1,000 mg (maximum)	Estimated human lethal dose: 90–100 mg	Dowling, 1975; Weiss et al., 1969
Crotalus atrox	277 mg (mean)		Klauber, 1956
	1,145 mg (maximum)		
	400 mg (mean)		Glenn and Straight, 1982
	1,150 mg (maximum)	Estimated human lethal dose: 100 mg	Minton and Minton, 1969
Crotalus cerastes	33 mg (mean)		Klauber, 1956
	63 mg (maximum)		
	30 mg (mean)		Glenn and Straight, 1982
	80 mg (maximum)		
Crotalus horridus	140 mg (mean)		Glenn and Straight, 1982
	300 mg (maximum)		
	139 mg (mean)		Klauber, 1956
		Estimated human lethal dose: 70–100 mg	Minton and Minton, 1969
Crotalus h. atricaudatus	229 mg (maximum)		Klauber, 1956
Crotalus intermedius	2.2 mg	A single milking of a single snake	Minton, 1977
Crotalus lepidus	30 mg (0.1 ml)	Yield may be as much as 129 mg dry weight	Glenn and Straight, 1982
Crotalus l. klauberi	24, 25, 33 mg	3 milkings of one snake	Minton, 1977; Minton and Weinstein, 1984
Crotalus mitchellii mitchellii	32 mg (mean)		Klauber, 1956
	90 mg (maximum)		
	33 mg (mean)		Glenn and Straight, 1982
	90 mg (maximum)		
Crotalus m. pyrrhus	227 mg (mean)		Klauber, 1956
	308 mg (maximum)		
	200 mg (mean)		Glenn and Straight, 1982
	350 mg (maximum)		
Crotalus m. stephensi	73 mg (mean)		Klauber, 1956
	129 mg (maximum)		
Crotalus molossus molossus	286 mg (mean)		Klauber, 1956
	540 mg (maximum)		
Crotalus m. estebanensis	32 mg	A single milking	Klauber, 1956
Crotalus oreganus oreganus	112 mg (mean)		Klauber, 1956
	289 mg (maximum)		
	90 mg (mean)		Glenn and Straight, 1982
	190 mg (maximum)		
Crotalus o. abyssus[1]	97 mg (mean)		Klauber, 1956
	137 mg (maximum)		
Crotalus o. cerberus[1]	112 mg (mean)		Klauber, 1956
	150 mg (maximum)		
Crotalus o. concolor[1]	6–34 mg	Males produce approximately twice as much venom as females	Glenn and Straight, 1977
	13 mg (mean)		Glenn and Straight, 1982
	34 mg (maximum)		
	22 mg (mean)		Klauber, 1956
Crotalus o. helleri[1]	112 mg (mean)		Klauber, 1956
	390 mg (maximum)		
	112 mg (mean)		Glenn and Straight, 1982
	390 mg (maximum)		

Table 57—cont.

Species	Yield (per individual)	Comments	Reference
Crotalus o. lutosus[1]	110 mg (mean)		Klauber, 1956
	234 mg (maximum)		
	110 mg (mean)		Glenn and Straight, 1982
	240 mg (maximum)		
Crotalus polystictus	101.3 mg		Minton, 1977; Minton and Weinstein, 1984
Crotalus pricei	8 mg (mean)		Klauber, 1956
Crotalus ravus	7.0 mg	A single milking	Minton, 1977
Crotalus ruber	300–350 mg	Adults 110 cm TL	Mackessy, 1985
	28–35 mg	Juveniles 53–58 cm TL	
	150–350 mg	Estimated human lethal dose: 100 mg	Dowling, 1975
		Estimated typical bite by an adult: 240 mg (0.72 ml) and, exceptionally, 550 mg (1.65 ml)	Amaral, 1928b
Crotalus r. exsul	54 mg	A single milking	Klauber, 1956
Crotalus r. lucasensis	234 mg (mean)		Klauber, 1956
	707 mg (maximum)		
	230 mg (mean)		Glenn and Straight, 1982
	710 mg (maximum)		
Crotalus r. ruber	363 mg (mean)		Klauber, 1956
	668 mg (maximum)		
	350 mg (mean)		Glenn and Straight, 1982
	670 mg (maximum)		
Crotalus scutulatus scutulatus	77 mg (mean)		Klauber, 1956
	141 mg (maximum)		
	70 mg (mean)		Glenn and Straight, 1982
	150 mg (maximum)		
	50–90 mg (typical adult)	Estimated human lethal dose: 10–15 mg	Minton and Minton, 1969
Crotalus tigris	6.4–11 mg (adult) (0.18 ml)		Klauber, 1972; Minton and Weinstein, 1984; Weinstein and Smith, 1990
	10 mg (mean)		
Crotalus viridis viridis	44 mg (mean)		Klauber, 1956
	162 mg (maximum)		
	44 mg (mean)		Glenn and Straight, 1982
	165 mg (maximum)		
Crotalus v. nuntius	51 mg (mean)		Klauber, 1956
	72 mg (maximum)		
Crotalus willardi willardi	37 mg	A single milking	Klauber, 1956
Sistrurus catenatus	25–35 mg	Probably can yield 5–6 mg per bite	Minton and Minton, 1969
	31 mg (mean)	Estimated lethal human dose: 30–40 mg	
Sistrurus c. catenatus	31 mg (mean)		Klauber, 1956
Sistrurus c. tergeminus	37 mg	A single milking	Klauber, 1956
Sistrurus miliarius	20–30 mg (typical adult)		Minton and Minton, 1969
	35 mg (maximum)		Klauber, 1972
		Typical bite, approximately 20 mg	Ernst, 1992
Sistrurus m. barbouri	18 mg (mean)		Klauber, 1956
	30 mg (mean)		Glenn and Straight, 1982
	50 mg (estimated maximum)		
	34 mg (mean)		Allen and Maier, 1941

[1] Taxa formerly allied with *Crotalus viridis*.

activity, and low arginine ester hydrolase and protease activity (Tan and Ponnudurai, 1990). A myotoxic phospholipase A_2 enzyme has been isolated (Mebs and Samejima, 1986).

Agkistrodon contortrix

There are no major biological differences in the ways the venoms of the various copperhead subspecies act (Tan and Ponnudurai, 1990). It does appear that ontogenic variation occurs, however, with juvenile venoms being antigenically distinguishable from those found in adults (Minton, 1967).

Copperhead venoms are moderately proteolytic (Van Mierop, 1976a, 1976b), and while they contain a TLE, they rarely cause significant hemostatic abnormalities or hemorrhage (Burch et al., 1988; Van Mierop, 1976a). Unlike *A. piscivorus* (see below), the venom of this species cleaves both fibrinopeptides A and B from fibrinogen, but it cleaves B at a much faster rate (Dyr et al., 1990; Herzig et al., 1970; Van Mierop and Kitchens, 1980). As fibrinopeptide A must be cleaved in appreciable amounts before visible clot formation occurs (Herzig et al., 1970), *A. contortrix* venom is not particularly procoagulant (Van Mierop and Kitchens, 1980). *Agkistrodon contortrix* venom may stimulate bradykinin release (Minton, 1974). A myotoxic phospholipase A_2 enzyme has been isolated from *A. c. contortrix* and *A. c. mokasen* (Mebs and Samejima, 1986).

Agkistrodon piscivorus

As in the copperheads, the venoms of the various cottonmouth subspecies do not show major biological differences (Tan and Ponnudurai, 1990). Cottonmouth venom has relatively high hyaluronidase and proteolytic activity, but little coagulant effect (Tan and Ponnudurai, 1990; Van Mierop, 1976a, 1976b). It does have an amino acid esterase with thrombinlike activity, but it cleaves only fibrinopeptide B from fibrinogen, and thus lacks significant procoagulant function (Van Mierop, 1976a, 1976b). Cottonmouth venom has been known to induce hemolysis, and in severe cases to render the blood nearly incoagulable (McCollough and Gennaro, 1968). Like the venom of *A. contortrix*, it can stimulate the release of bradykinin and has high PLA$_2$ activity (Mebs and Samejima, 1986; Van Mierop, 1976b).

Crotalus adamanteus

The venom of this, the largest of the North American pitvipers, has a TLE (crotalase) that is capable of clotting fibrinogen (Bajwa et al., 1980; Corrigan and Jeter, 1990; Damus et al., 1972; Kitchens, 1992; Markland and Damus, 1971; Weiss, 1970). This results in secondary activation of plasminogen from endothelial cells (Kitchens and Van Mierop, 1983; Ouyang et al., 1992). It does not activate platelets, although production of fibrin strands can lead to a reduction in platelet count and red blood cell hemolysis due to microangiopathic cell lysis (Damus et al., 1972). The fibrin clot produced is highly unstable because only fibrinopeptide A is cleaved from fibrinogen, and cross-linking is therefore incomplete (Kitchens and Van Mierop, 1983; Van Mierop and Kitchens, 1980). A benign defibrination syndrome has been reported following bites by this snake (Kitchens, 1992). Clinically significant bleeding is uncommon even with defibrination (Hasiba et al., 1975).

Crotalus adamanteus venom has high hemorrhagic activity (Minton, 1974). It also possesses a low-molecular-weight basic peptide that can interfere with neuromuscular transmission (Lee, 1972) and could potentially, as in animal models (Bonilla et al., 1971), cause death by producing cardiac muscle ischemia and myocardial failure. This small peptide is similar in structure to crotamine from *C. durissus terrificus* (Aird et al., 1991; Bonilla et al., 1971) and constitutes 2–8% of the venom's protein composition (Minton, 1974).

Crotalus adamanteus venom is highly necrotizing, mildly proteolytic, and contains high concentrations of phosphodiesterase (Minton, 1974; Van Mierop, 1976b). It can stimulate bradykinin release in victims, which can produce severe pain and profound, transient hypotension (Van Mierop, 1976b).

Crotalus atrox

Research with this snake has shed light on the amount of variation that can occur in the venom of a single species with age and geographic origin (Minton and Weinstein, 1986). Reid and Theakston (1978) studied the venom composition of three specimens and found a number of quantitative and qualitative differences as the individuals aged. Venom toxicity was highest in snakes less than 13 months of age, with large amounts of hemorrhagic activity. Venoms obtained up to 8 months caused a significant defibrination due to the action of a TLE. From 9 to 10 months the venoms clotted plasma, but not fibrinogen, via thromboplastin activity. The venom of snakes older than 10 months no longer had procoagulant activity. Although venom

toxicity decreases with age in this snake, this is more than made up for by the significant increases in venom yield in older, larger snakes (Glenn and Straight, 1982). Venoms of this widely distributed snake also vary geographically, with western populations having greater lethality and lower protease activity than eastern populations (Minton and Weinstein, 1986).

Crotalus atrox venoms in general are highly proteolytic and hemorrhagic (Anaya et al., 1992; De Mesquita et al., 1991; Glenn and Straight, 1982; Perez et al., 1984). They may contain as many as seven hemorrhagins (Bjarnason and Fox, 1989), have a strong platelet-aggregating action (causing a drop in platelet count [thrombocytopenia]), and are strongly fibrinogenolytic (Bajwa et al., 1980; Budzynski et al., 1984; Corrigan and Jeter, 1990; Markland and Damus, 1971; Russell, 1983). The quantities of TLEs found in *C. atrox* venom are variable (Budzynski et al., 1984; Russell, 1983). Like *C. adamanteus* venom, western diamondback venom also has a dose-dependent ability to stimulate release of plasminogen activator from damaged endothelial cells (Budzynski et al., 1984; Ouyang et al., 1992; Warrell, 1986). It can stimulate bradykinin release as well, thus worsening pain and shock (Minton, 1974).

Crotalus atrox venom has been found to possess a myocardial depressant factor that has a negative effect on cardiac muscle contractility (De Mesquita et al., 1991). The clinical significance of this component is unclear. Some *C. atrox* populations have also been found to have neurotoxins similar to Mojave toxin (see below; Farstad et al., 1997; Weinstein et al., 1985). This component was found in animals with ranges that overlapped with *C. scutulatus*, and Minton and Weinstein (1986) suggested a possible genetic exchange between these two species in these areas.

Crotalus basiliscus

This venom may, in some populations, contain a component structurally related to Mojave toxin (Glenn and Straight, 1989; Rael et al., 1986). It also contains proteases (Martínez et al., 1990; Minton, 1974).

Crotalus horridus

The toxicity of this snake's venom combined with its impressive size, long fangs, and high venom yield make it potentially one of North America's most dangerous snakes (Glenn et al., 1994). Fortunately, its relatively mild temperament offsets, to some degree, its lethal potential (Van Mierop, 1976b).

As is the case with many species of rattlesnakes, there is significant geographic and ontogenic variation in the venom's toxicity (Glenn and Straight, 1982, 1985b; Glenn et al., 1983; Reid and Theakston, 1978; Straight et al., 1991). A study of pooled juvenile *C. horridus* (3–18 months of age) venoms demonstrated lower protease activity and greater lethality than adult venom (Bonilla et al., 1973). The venom of newborns (5 days old), however, was 10 times less toxic than venom collected at 182 days of age, and there was a steady rise in potency throughout the first year of life.

Four venom patterns have been described for this snake (Glenn et al., 1994). Type A venoms are largely neurotoxic and are found variably in the southern portions of the range. This venom type is found primarily in Oklahoma, southern Arkansas, and Louisiana, and in southeastern South Carolina south through eastern Georgia to northern Florida. Type B venom is hemorrhagic and proteolytic, and is found consistently in the northern portion of the range and variably in the southeast. Type A + B venom contains all of these activities and is found in areas of apparent intergradation in southwestern Arkansas and northern Louisiana. Type C venom, found variably in the southeastern portion of the range, especially Florida, has none of these components and is a relatively weak venom.

The neurotoxic component, canebrake toxin, is a PLA_2, that comes in multiple isomeric forms with two components, acidic and basic (Glenn et al., 1994). Canebrake toxin is analogous to the neurotoxins found in several other rattlesnake venoms and contributes significantly to the toxicity of specimens in which it is found (Aird et al., 1991; Glenn et al., 1983).

Other components isolated from *C. horridus* venom include a small basic peptide distinct from canebrake toxin that functions as a myotoxin (Carroll et al., 1997; Straight et al., 1991) and a fibrinogen-clotting enzyme (Anderson, 1998). This enzyme, a procoagulant esterase, cleaves fibrinopeptide A from fibrinogen and can produce defibrination syndrome (Van Mierop and Kitchens, 1980). A platelet-activating protein (crotalocytin) has also been isolated from the venom of some specimens (Anderson, 1998; Ouyang et al., 1992; Schmaier and Colman, 1980; Schmaier et al., 1980). Crotalocytin has no fibrinogen clotting activity and is therefore not a TLE (Schmaier and Colman, 1980; Schmaier et al., 1980), although there does appear to be a separate TLE (Bonilla, 1975). A bradykinin-releasing enzyme may also be present (Deutsch and Diniz, 1955).

Crotalus intermedius

This snake has a moderately toxic crotaline venom with strong hemorrhagic activity in laboratory experiments (Minton, 1977).

Crotalus lepidus

The venom of this small pitviper is very potent in its hemorrhagic activity (Soto et al., 1989). Its toxicity appears to be quite variable, however, depending on the individual's geographic origin (Glenn et al., 1983; Minton and Weinstein, 1984).

Crotalus molossus molossus

The venom of the black-tailed rattlesnake may have a strong platelet-aggregating action (causing thrombocytopenia) and appears to be strongly fibrinolytic (Corrigan and Jeter, 1990; Hardy et al., 1982).

Crotalus oreganus

Western rattlesnake (*C. o. oreganus*, formerly *C. viridis oreganus*) venom contains a component that activates factor X (Ouyang et al., 1992) and a hemorrhagic toxin (Martínez et al., 1990). There is no evidence of Mojave toxin (Rael et al., 1986). It does have metalloprotease activity (Mackessy, 1996), and this function is approximately fivefold greater in adults than in juveniles (Mackessy, 1988). This factor is likely responsible for local tissue necrosis that can occur after bites by adults (Mackessy, 1996).

More southerly populations of western rattlesnakes, *C. o. helleri* (formerly *C. viridis helleri*), also appear to lack Mojave toxin (Glenn and Straight, 1985b; Rael et al., 1986). These venoms can, however, contain a low-molecular-weight myotoxin, peptide C, that is homologous to crotamine (Aird et al., 1991; Maeda et al., 1978; Rael et al., 1986; Straight et al., 1991). A com-

ponent capable of activating factor X in the coagulation cascade may also be present (Ouyang et al., 1992; Russell, 1983).

The venom of the Grand Canyon rattlesnake, *C. o. abyssus* (formerly *C. viridis abyssus*), has at least 18 fractions and appears to be very similar to that of the Great Basin rattlesnake, *C. o. lutosus* (formerly *C. v. lutosus*; Young et al., 1980). The venom is high in hemorrhagic and hemolytic properties but does not appear to contain any PLA_2 neurotoxic activity (Adame et al., 1990).

Crotalus o. concolor (formerly *C. viridis concolor*) has the most toxic venom of any *C. oreganus* or *C. viridis* group tested, although there appears to be wide variability among individuals in populations (Glenn and Straight, 1977, 1978). It is, in fact, one of the most potent venoms found in North America (Glenn and Straight, 1977). It is noted for a PLA_2, presynaptic neurotoxin, concolor toxin, which is present in variable amounts in individual snakes (Glenn and Straight, 1977, 1990; Weinstein et al., 1985). Concolor toxin is antigenically related to crotoxin, Mojave toxin, canebrake toxin, and vegrandis toxin (from *C. durissus vegrandis*; Kaiser et al., 1986).

Crotalus polystictus

Due to its relatively long fangs compared with its body size (Glenn and Straight, 1982) and its relatively large venom yield, this snake should be considered dangerous (Hardy, 1982; Minton, 1977; Minton and Weinstein, 1984). Beyond these factors, however, as Sherman Minton (1977) noted, the venom is "in no way exceptional."

Crotalus pricei pricei

With its relatively short fangs, relatively low venom yield, and mild disposition, this snake is not particularly dangerous, although its venom is toxic and bites should be taken seriously (Ernst, 1992; Ownby et al., 1976). The venom does not appear to have any significant protease activity (Minton and Weinstein, 1984).

Crotalus ravus

The toxicity of *C. ravus* venom appears to be intermediate between that of *Sistrurus catenatus* and *S. miliarius* (Minton, 1977), with which it was formerly classified.

Crotalus ruber

The red diamond rattlesnake has a relatively large venom yield (Glenn and Straight, 1982) that contains high levels of proteolytic enzymes, especially in adults (6–15 times that found in juvenile snakes; Glenn and Straight, 1985b; Mackessy, 1985; Straight et al., 1992). The venom of neonate snakes, however, has a lower LD_{50} than that of adults (Glenn and Straight, 1985b). The venoms of specimens from Baja and southern California are similar, although PLA enzymes are more consistently present in Baja specimens (Glenn and Straight, 1985b; Straight et al., 1992). *Crotalus ruber* venom contains at least three proteolytic hemorrhagins (which degrade fibrinogen and cause myonecrosis; Straight et al., 1992), but no Mojave toxin (Rael et al., 1986). The venom of *C. r. exsul* is nearly identical with that of *C. r. ruber* from farther north (see below) and contains trace amounts of a phospholipase enzyme (Straight et al., 1992).

Crotalus scutulatus salvini

A study of a single specimen (Glenn and Straight, 1978) found an intraperitoneal LD_{50} in mice of 0.18 mg/kg (versus 0.09–3.5 for *C. scutulatus scutulatus*; see below). The venom of three specimens from Mexico had Mojave toxin and lacked hemorrhagic activity (Glenn et al., 1983).

Crotalus scutulatus scutulatus

Studies of this snake's venom have yielded insight into the remarkable degree of variability that can occur within a widely distributed species. Specimens from some regions (venom A populations) have Mojave toxin in their venom (Weinstein et al., 1985). Mojave toxin has at least two major subunits: an acidic peptide and a basic protein with PLA_2 activity (Farstad et al., 1997; Glenn et al., 1983; Meier and Stocker, 1995). Mojave toxin is a presynaptic neurotoxin that has been isolated in specimens from California, Texas, southwestern Utah, and western Arizona (Farstad et al., 1997; Glenn et al., 1983; Glenn and Straight, 1989; Rael et al., 1984). Specimens from central Arizona (venom B populations) lack this toxin, and a zone of intergradation occurs between Phoenix and Tucson (Glenn and Straight, 1989; Glenn et al., 1983; Wilkinson et al., 1991). The lethal potential of *C. s. scutulatus* goes up with increasing quantities of Mojave toxin in its venom (Glenn and Straight, 1978, 1989). Mojave toxin has been demonstrated by immunodiffusion and ELISA studies to be antigenically similar to crotoxin (*C. durissus terrificus*) and concolor toxin (*C. o. concolor*; Aird et al., 1990; Kaiser et al., 1986), and various isoforms of Mojave toxin exist (Rael et al., 1984; Weinstein and Smith, 1990).

Venom B has significant proteolytic and hemorrhagic effects while venom A lacks these effects (Glenn et al., 1983; Hardy, 1983; Wilkinson et al., 1991). The hemorrhagic toxin is a fibrinogenolytic metalloproteinase (Martínez et al., 1990). Venom from specimens around Tucson has weak fibrinolytic properties, no clotting activity, insignificant platelet aggregation, and generally does not cause systemic hemostatic defects (Corrigan and Jeter, 1990).

Crotalus tigris

Although this snake has a relatively low venom yield, its venom is considered by some to be "the most lethal of rattlesnake venoms" (Weinstein and Smith, 1990). The venom has a high concentration of a neurotoxin (Weinstein and Smith, 1990; Weinstein et al., 1985) antigenically related to Mojave toxin. It also has a component that is immunologically identical with myotoxic crotamine (Weinstein and Smith, 1990). It contains low but significant protease activity, but has no known hemolytic activity (Weinstein and Smith, 1990).

Crotalus viridis

Ontogenic differences also occur in this snake's venom (Fiero et al., 1972). The venom of juveniles from two weeks to three months of age is approximately twice as lethal as that of adults (Glenn and Straight, 1982). A common misconception is that juvenile rattlesnakes are unable to control the quantity of venom they inject, making bites by these snakes potentially more dangerous. Studies with *C. viridis* have shown, however, that young snakes can indeed meter their venom delivery (Hayes, 1992, 1995). It is the increased toxicity of juvenile

venoms that likely explains the serious potential of bites by these small serpents.

Crotalus viridis venom has at least 21 different protein components (Anaya et al., 1992). The venom is best known for myotoxin *a* (Aird et al., 1991; Ownby et al., 1976), a nonenzymatic, low-molecular-weight polypeptide that produces pronounced vacuolization of muscle fibers and weak lysing of red blood cells (Cameron and Tu, 1977). Myotoxin *a* constitutes approximately 18% of the crude venom (Cameron and Tu, 1977) but is only one of several myotoxins present (another being viritoxin; Ownby et al., 1984). Myotoxin *a* is found in large amounts in specimens from Montana, Wyoming, North Dakota, South Dakota, and Nebraska; and in small amounts or not at all in those from New Mexico and Texas (Straight et al., 1991). Myotoxin *a* is chemically and functionally similar to crotamine from *C. durissus terrificus* (Ownby et al., 1983).

Crotalus viridis venom also has a neurotoxic component (Lee, 1972). Glenn and Straight (1990) surveyed 46 populations of *C. viridis* for the presence of Mojave toxin and found 3 (of 14) specimens from southwest New Mexico and 1 (of 1) from northern Arizona that possessed this component. They theorized that the presence of this neurotoxin was due to prior hybridization with *C. scutulatus* in New Mexico and with *C. o. concolor* in Arizona.

The venom also contains direct hemorrhagic metalloproteinases (Ownby et al., 1984) that appear to digest the alpha chain of fibrinogen (Li et al., 1993) and a kallikrein-like enzyme (Anaya et al., 1992) that stimulates bradykinin release in victims, resulting in increased pain and possibly hypotension.

Sistrurus catenatus

While extremely adverse outcomes following bites by this snake are uncommon, its venom potency should not be underestimated. Some researchers have found its venom to be nearly as toxic as that of *C. scutulatus* (Glenn et al., 1983; Weinstein and Smith, 1990). It contains significant proteinase and phospholipase activity that can destroy fibrinogen/fibrin and platelets, respectively (Hankin et al., 1987).

Sistrurus miliarius

Pygmy rattlesnake venom is strongly hemorrhagic and tissue toxic, but it contains no neurotoxins (Ernst, 1992; Van Mierop, 1976b). It is somewhat unusual in that it contains appreciable quantities of serotonin and related tryptamine compounds (Welsh, 1967).

Clinical Features

While the venom components of different pitvipers can be extremely variable, there is a fairly typical clinical presentation of "classic" crotaline venom poisoning that consists of pain, soft tissue swelling (edema), bruising of the tissues (ecchymosis) with or without coagulation disturbances, and possible tissue death (necrosis). Even so, every bite involves a unique snake, a unique person, and a unique set of circumstances. This makes accurately predicting what to expect following snake envenoming a challenging task. While generalizations can be made, the treating physician must be alert for unusual effects.

The signs and symptoms of crotaline venom poisoning can be broken down into local and systemic effects, the presence and severity of which have important implications in terms of management decisions and outcome (see below).

Approximately 25% of bites from pitvipers are "dry," that is, they result in no venom injection (Parrish et al., 1966; see Pl. 1370). The precise operant factors in such cases are a source of controversy. There may be some "short-circuiting" of the feedback loop between the foveal organs and the venom delivery mechanism so that no venom is injected. Alternatively, the snake may "choose" to withhold venom it will need for its next meal in dealing with an antagonist that is clearly too large to eat. Whatever the reason, a victim fortunate enough to have sustained a dry bite will have no more symptoms or findings than would be expected from simple puncture wounds.

Local Signs and Symptoms

Most pitviper bites are marked by severe pain at the site of the wound (often described as "burning" or "searing" and as starting within seconds or minutes of the bite) and local soft tissue swelling that progresses outward from the bite site, proximally and distally. Swelling can encompass the entire extremity and can even spread to the trunk and unbitten extremities. There is often bruising of the skin (both locally and more distally) due to blood leaking from damaged blood vessels (hemorrhagin effects). Because much venom absorption takes place through the victim's lymphatic system, the regional lymph nodes are often swollen and tender very soon after the bite (Russell et al., 1975).

Over a period of several hours to days, blisters and blebs can form on the bitten extremity; these may be filled with clear tissue fluid or with blood (see Pl. 1371). They are particularly common if there has been a delay in reaching medical care (see Pl. 1372).

Local findings tend to be most severe following bites by *C. adamanteus*, *C. atrox*, *C. horridus*, *C. oreganus*, and *C. viridis* (Russell, 1983). With some species, pain is minimal, even in the face of a significant envenoming. An important example is the bite of venom A–producing *C. scutulatus*. Bites by these snakes can produce minimal local findings resulting in an underestimation of severity (see Pl. 1373). Local findings following envenoming by venom B–producing *C. scutulatus* tend to approximate those of "typical" rattlesnakes.

The most common serious outcome following pitviper bites in North America is local tissue necrosis. This can include skin, muscles, tendons, and neurovascular bundles. In particularly severe cases, skin grafts, muscle and tendon transfers, or even amputation may be required to treat this complication (see Morbidity and Mortality, below).

Systemic Signs and Symptoms

Systemic findings can involve essentially any organ system of the body and reflect the severity of venom poisoning. Findings can range from a total absence of systemic complaints to profound shock, respiratory failure, renal failure, and death. Common early findings in significant bites include nausea, vomiting, a sense of weakness and anxiety, and profuse sweating (diaphoresis; Minton, 1974).

Victims will often complain of a change in taste (such as a minty or metallic taste or a "numb" mouth). In addition, tiny muscle fasciculations termed myokymia may be present either at the bite site or on other parts of the body. These fasciculations

are particularly common following bites by *Crotalus oreganus*, *C. adamanteus*, and *C. horridus* (Russell, 1983; Van Mierop, 1976b; Watt, 1978). They are likely due to the interaction of venom components with ionized calcium at nerve membranes, causing enhanced excitability (Brick and Gutmann, 1982; Holstege et al., 1997). A similar mechanism may be responsible for paresthesias (tingling) of the face and digits, another common complaint (Brick and Gutmann, 1982). Major neurological findings following pitviper bites are, however, relatively uncommon. Primary neurotoxicity can be seen following bites by snakes known to possess PLA_2 neurotoxins (see Venoms, above) such as venom A–producing *C. scutulatus*, *C. horridus*, and *C. oreganus concolor*, as well as *C. durissus* of South America. Cranial nerve dysfunction and muscle weakness (including the muscles of respiration) have been reported following *C. scutulatus* poisoning (Banner, 1988; Clark et al., 1997; Jansen et al., 1992; Wingert and Chan, 1988).

Poisoning by a number of species of pitvipers, particularly rattlesnakes, can disrupt blood coagulation. Interestingly, and in sharp contrast to some of the Asian and African vipers, these coagulation disturbances are usually manifested only by laboratory abnormalities (see below) with no clinical evidence of serious bleeding. Occasionally, however, severe bleeding may occur in the gastrointestinal tract, the genitourinary system, the central nervous system, the respiratory system, etc. In addition, snake venom–induced vessel wall damage can stimulate intravascular clotting and defibrination syndrome (consumptive coagulopathy; Van Mierop, 1976b). In general, the coagulation defects that follow crotaline venom poisoning can be broken down into four categories (Holstege et al., 1997). Most common is a combined defibrination syndrome and venom-induced thrombocytopenia. Less common are isolated defibrination and isolated venom-induced thrombocytopenia. The final, and fortunately the rarest, form is true, disseminated intravascular coagulation (DIC), which can result in systemic infarction of tissues, hemolysis, and widespread bleeding.

The following descriptions of clinical findings for some North American pitviper bites are a compilation of signs and symptoms that could be expected in a typical significant bite by that animal. It must be emphasized that unusual or unexpected findings can occur, and the medical care provider must remain vigilant.

Agkistrodon contortrix

The majority of bites tend to be mild (Lawrence et al., 1996), although severe bites and fatalities can occur (Parrish and Carr, 1967; White and Weber, 1991). Poisoning is characterized by soft tissue swelling and pain, along with lymphadenopathy (Chotkowski, 1949; Krochmal and Anderson, 1976; Scharman and Noffsinger, 2001; see Pl. 1374). There may be some bruising of the tissues and blisters, although these are less common and much less severe than with many other pitviper bites (Glass, 1987; Russell and Picchioni, 1983; Whitley, 1996).

Agkistrodon piscivorus

Cottonmouth bites commonly cause ecchymosis (bruising of the skin) and swelling (Roberts et al., 1985). Pain tends to be more severe than with copperhead bites but less than with most rattlesnake bites (Russell, 1983). Vesicles and bullae are also less common than with rattlesnake bites (Russell, 1983), but tissue necrosis can occur (Banner, 1988). Occasionally, myokymia is seen (Russell, 1983).

Crotalus adamanteus

Significant envenoming can produce remarkable bruising of the tissues, swelling, and pain, sometimes involving the entire bitten extremity (Parrish and Thompson, 1958; Russell, 1980a, 1980b, 1983; Van Mierop and Kitchens, 1980; Watt et al., 1956). Pain is usually pronounced (more than with most other pitviper bites), and over the first 8–36 hours petechiae, vesicles, and hemorrhagic bullae may develop (Russell, 1983). Ultimately, wounds inflicted by this snake may become severely necrotic and can involve extensive portions of the involved extremity (Migliore, 1963; Minton, 1974; Russell et al., 1975; Van Mierop, 1976b; see Pl. 1375).

Victims may experience a change in taste (a minty, rubbery, or metallic quality) and numbness/tingling of the tongue, mouth, scalp, hands, and feet (which can begin within minutes of the bite; Russell, 1983). Muscle fasciculations, especially of the face and extremities, are common and portend significant poisoning (Buntain, 1983; Hardy, 1982; McCreary, 1959; Russell and Picchioni, 1983; Van Mierop, 1976b; Van Mierop and Kitchens, 1980; Watt and Pollard, 1954). Pupils may be constricted (Van Mierop, 1976b; Watt and Gennaro, 1965) and vision altered (Watt and Pollard, 1954). Neurologic dysfunction can become so pronounced that paralysis and respiratory failure occur, though this is rare (Russell, 1983; Watt and Pollard, 1954; Watt et al., 1956). Sweating and chills are common (Russell, 1983), and shock can occur in severe bites (Kitchens and Van Mierop, 1983; Parrish and Thompson, 1958; Tenery and Koefoot, 1955). Early hypotension can be due to venom-induced bradykinin release (Van Mierop, 1976b).

A severe bite can cause incoagulable blood due to venom TLEs, but often in the absence of any clinically significant bleeding (as other coagulation components besides fibrinogen are unaffected; Hasiba et al., 1975; Kitchens, 1992; Kitchens and Van Mierop, 1983; Van Mierop and Kitchens, 1980; Weiss et al., 1969). In one series (Kitchens and Van Mierop, 1983) of 10 patients bitten by this snake, all developed incoagulable blood, but none developed more severe bleeding than slight oozing from needle-stick sites. On rare occasions, however, victims may present with significant and life-threatening hemorrhage (McCollough and Gennaro, 1968). Any victim with nonclotting blood must be considered to have a severe envenomation and be treated accordingly.

Crotalus atrox

Western diamondback bites are characterized by significant soft tissue swelling that may spread to involve the entire extremity and even the trunk (Burgess and Dart, 1991; Clark et al., 1997; Guisto, 1995; Reid, 1978; Rivers, 1976; Russell, 1983; Seifert et al., 1997; Sivaprasad and Cantini, 1982; see Pl. 1376). Severe pain and ecchymoses are prominent (Burgess and Dart, 1991; Guisto, 1995; Russell, 1983). Perioral paresthesias and muscle fasciculations may occur (Clark et al., 1997; Gold and Wingert, 1994; Sivaprasad and Cantini, 1982). Over a period of hours to days, petechiae, serum-filled vesicles, and hemorrhagic bullae may appear (Budzynski et al., 1984; see Pl. 1377). These are more common if medical care is delayed (Russell, 1983). Crotalus atrox bites can result in sufficient

local tissue damage to require local amputation (Rivers, 1976; see Pl. 1378).

Abnormal taste sensations (Clark et al., 1997; Wingert and Chan, 1988) and changes in vision (Crane and Irwin, 1985) similar to those seen in some victims of C. adamanteus bites can occur. Patients presenting with nonclotting blood are likely to have been bitten by juvenile specimens and should be considered to have severe venom poisoning (Reid and Theakston, 1978). Victims may go into profound shock (Burgess and Dart, 1991; Hardy, 1997; Sivaprasad and Cantini, 1982).

Crotalus cerastes

Sidewinder bites can cause pain, swelling, ecchymosis, and hemorrhagic bleb formation (Hardy, 1992; Lowell, 1957; Tanen et al., 2001; see Pls. 1379 and 1380). The swelling tends not to be particularly severe (Holstege et al., 1997), but it can involve the entire extremity and trunk (Tanen et al., 2001). Systemic effects may include dizziness, nausea, chills, coagulopathy, and shock (Hardy, 1992; Lowell, 1957; Tanen et al., 2001).

Crotalus horridus

Significant timber rattlesnake bites are characterized by severe pain, massive soft tissue swelling, ecchymosis, and, at times, severe tissue damage (Bond and Burkart, 1997; Brick and Gutmann, 1982; Brick et al., 1978; Ruggiero, 1958; Schmaier et al., 1980; Tallon et al., 1981; Wingert and Chan, 1988). Patients may present with paresthesias (particularly of the face, scalp, and extremities), diffuse muscle fasciculations (Bond and Burkart, 1997; Bond and Clancy, 1992; Brick and Gutmann, 1982; Brick et al., 1978; Gold and Wingert, 1994; Ruggiero, 1958; Wingert and Chan, 1988), and occasionally altered taste sensations (Wingert and Chan, 1988). Other systemic findings may include headache, nausea, vomiting, diarrhea, and shock (Carroll et al., 1997; Kitchens et al., 1987; Lewis, 1994; Ruggiero, 1958). Depending on the geographic provenance of the snake, victims may present with neurologic dysfunction such as difficulty speaking or swallowing (Carroll et al., 1997; see above, under Venoms). Coagulopathy may also be present, with occasional clinical bleeding manifested by petechiae, gingival bleeding, hematemesis, blood in the stool, and hematuria (Bond and Burkart, 1997, 1998; Furlow and Brennan, 1985; Tallon et al., 1981). Myonecrosis following C. horridus bites may be extensive (Carroll et al., 1997).

Crotalus lepidus

Bites by these snakes can produce significant soft tissue swelling, subcutaneous ecchymosis, and hemorrhagic blebs (Hardy, 1992; see Pls. 1381 and 1382). Local tissue damage is seen in animal models of venom poisoning and is probably a possiblity in humans as well (Minton, 1977).

Crotalus molossus

Black-tailed rattlesnake bites appear to be characterized by significant soft tissue swelling, bruising, and the formation of blisters (Hardy et al., 1982; see Pl. 1383). Tissue loss appears to be less common than with bites of some of the more virulent pitvipers (Hardy et al., 1982; Russell, 1969).

Crotalus oreganus

Bites by snakes from northwestern ranges (referred to in the medical literature as *C. viridis oreganus*) are characterized by pain, soft tissue swelling, and ecchymosis (Butner, 1983; Russell, 1983; Russell and Picchioni, 1983; see Pl. 1384). Vesicles or hemorrhagic bullae may be seen (Russell, 1983). Lymph nodes may be swollen and tender (Butner, 1983). Tissue damage can be significant, especially after bites by adult specimens (Mackessy, 1996). Systemic findings may include anxiety; numbness of the mouth, tongue, or digits; altered taste sensations; and myokymia (Butner, 1983; Gold and Wingert, 1994; Russell, 1980a, 1980b, 1983). Of 73 bites by this snake treated at a referral hospital in northern California between 1988 and 1998, approximately 10% were dry bites, 32% were mild, 44% were moderate, and 15% were severe (Offerman et al., 2001).

Bites by more southern Pacific rattlesnakes (formerly *C. viridis helleri*) can produce impressive pain, soft tissue swelling, and ecchymosis (Bush and Siedenburg, 1999; Davidson, 1988; Reid, 1978; Russell, 1980a, 1980b, 1983; Russell and Picchioni, 1983; Russell et al., 1975; see Pl. 1385). Also prominent are altered taste sensations, paresthesias (particularly of the mouth, tongue, and digits) and myokymia (Bush and Siedenburg, 1999; Russell, 1980a, 1980b, 1983; Russell et al., 1975). Serum-filled vesicles or hemorrhagic bullae may occur, and tissue necrosis can complicate these bites (Russell, 1983; Russell and Picchioni, 1983). Although no evidence of Mojave toxin has been found in this snake's venom (see above), there has been some speculation that a neurotoxic component may be present in certain populations, particularly in areas where the range overlaps with that of *C. scutulatus* (Bush and Siedenburg, 1999). Systemic findings may include weakness, diaphoresis, fever, systemic bleeding (including oozing from venipuncture sites and hematemesis), shock, and altered mental status (possibly even coma; Davidson, 1988; Reid, 1978).

Bites by snakes formerly listed as *C. viridis concolor* (=*C. oreganus concolor*) can result in systemic myokymia and potentially in rhabdomyolysis (Holstege et al., 1997). Those by snakes formerly classified as *C. v. lutosus* result in pain, soft tissue swelling, ecchymosis, and possible tissue necrosis (Adame et al., 1990). Coagulopathy and shock have also been reported (Adame et al., 1990; Dart and Gustafson, 1991).

Crotalus polystictus

Bites by this snake are not well represented in the literature. It appears that significant bites can cause soft tissue swelling, local ecchymosis, and slight pain (Hardy, 1982; see Pl. 1386). Muscle fasciculations; odd, metallic taste sensation; and numbness of the face and extremities have occurred (Hardy, 1982). Blebs can form at the bite site, and necrosis can occur (Hardy, 1982).

Crotalus pricei

The few bites that have been reported have been relatively typical for pitvipers. Soft tissue swelling, ecchymosis, bleb formation, and lymphadenopathy have been seen (Bernstein et al., 1992). Minor necrosis can occur, but signs of clinical bleeding have not been described (Bernstein et al., 1992). Local findings and systemic symptoms may be more impressive than expected from such a small rattlesnake (Minton and Weinstein, 1984).

Crotalus ruber

Bites by this snake can produce massive soft tissue swelling, pain, ecchymosis, hemorrhagic blebs (Clarke, 1961; Klauber, 1972; Lyons, 1971; Russell, 1983), and necrosis (Mackessy, 1985; see Pls. 1387–1389). Systemic effects may include nausea and vomiting, coagulopathy (decreased platelets and fibrinogen), clinical bleeding, and hemolysis (with resulting anemia; Kitchens, 1992; Lyons, 1971; Minton, 1974).

Crotalus scutulatus

Of particular importance is the fact that some patients bitten by this snake exhibit a delay in the onset of signs and symptoms (Sullivan et al., 1995) that could lead to a dangerous underestimation of severity in early stages.

Bites by venom A–producing specimens can present with prominent neurotoxic findings and little in the way of local findings (Russell, 1969; Russell and Puffer, 1970; Russell et al., 1975). Paresthesias and muscle fasciculations can be prominent (Clark et al., 1997). Those bitten by venom B animals present with more typical pitviper signs and symptoms, including local swelling and pain, and hematological abnormalities with potential for local tissue loss (Bush and Jansen, 1995; Sullivan and Wingert, 1989; see Pls. 1390–1392). Muscle necrosis (rhabdomyolysis) with complicating renal failure has also been reported (Farstad et al., 1997).

Of 15 cases of *C. scutulatus* bites reported from southern Arizona, all were moderate or severe envenomings (Hardy, 1983). All had soft tissue swelling, 10 had soft tissue ecchymoses, and 6 developed blebs. Three patients developed some degree of necrosis, and hypotension on arrival was noted in 3. Neurologic findings were noted in only 1 case (ptosis). This victim also had soft tissue swelling, but no ecchymosis or blebs. Half of the cases had abnormal laboratory findings (slight decreases in fibrinogen, increased FDP, and/or a drop in platelet counts). No victim demonstrated any evidence of systemic bleeding.

In cases of *C. scutulatus* bites manifesting neurotoxicity, double vision and difficulty swallowing and speaking have been noted (Farstad et al., 1997; Hardy, 1983; Rhoten and Gennaro, 1968). With progression, skeletal muscle weakness can occur (Clark et al., 1997; Farstad et al., 1997). This can ultimately lead to respiratory and cardiovascular collapse, and potentially to death (Banner, 1988; Farstad et al., 1997; Hardy, 1983; Jansen et al., 1992). Fortunately, however, respiratory failure is uncommon (Gold and Wingert, 1994).

Crotalus tigris

There is essentially no literature available on bites by this snake. Despite its potency, the venom apparently has caused little in the way of local reactions or systemic signs and symptoms in humans (Ernst, 1992).

Crotalus viridis

Prairie rattlesnake bites cause significant pain, swelling, and ecchymosis (Russell, 1980a, 1980b, 1983; Russell and Picchioni, 1983; Ryan and Caravati, 1994). Tissue loss can occur (see Pl. 1393). Cole (1996) reported a case of nonhemorrhagic cerebral infarct attributed to this snake.

Sistrurus catenatus

Bites by massasaugas can produce soft tissue swelling, pain, redness, and ecchymosis (Burgess and Dart, 1991; Hankin et al., 1987), but less so than is seen with most other pitviper bites (Russell, 1983; Russell and Picchioni, 1983; Russell et al., 1975; Wingert and Wainschel, 1975). Blebs can also occur (Russell, 1983). In addition, the victim can experience weakness or malaise, faintness, nausea, diaphoresis, fever, and even shock (Hankin et al., 1987; LaPointe, 1953; Parrish and Khan, 1966). Muscle fasciculations do not appear to be a major component of this syndrome (Russell, 1983).

Sistrurus miliarius

Pygmy rattlesnake bites tend to produce less edema than those of other rattlesnakes, but may cause ecchymosis and, rarely, blebs (Ahlstrom et al., 1991; Russell, 1983; Russell and Picchioni, 1983; Wingert and Wainschel, 1975). The pain can be impressive, and necrosis can occur (Migliore, 1965; Russell, 1983; Van Mierop, 1976b). There generally are no paresthesias or fasciculations (Russell, 1983). Nausea may occur, but it is generally slight (Russell, 1983). Hematuria and renal failure have been reported (Ahlstrom et al., 1991; Hutchison, 1929).

Field Management of Crotaline Bites

The same variables that complicate characterization of any particular species' venom or its effects compound the difficulty and uncertainty of research into treatment modalities for snakebite. Add to this the infinite number of variables involved in any particular snakebite event (such as the age, health, and size of the victim; the motivating factors of the snake; the circumstances surrounding rescue attempts), and it becomes clear why it is hard to make broad recommendations on how to treat a snakebite.

The most important principle in field management of any snakebite is rapid transportation to a medical facility properly equipped to deal with the problem. It would be foolish to wait for the onset of clinical signs of venom poisoning before beginning movement to definitive care. If the identity of the biting snake is unclear, it is reasonable to make a brief attempt to identify it as long as this does not put the victim or the rescuer at risk for additional bites. There is no need to kill or capture the snake. With some exceptions, most North American pitvipers produce a characteristic syndrome of poisoning that is relatively well covered by appropriate polyvalent antivenoms.

Even if someone has attempted to kill the snake, it must still be handled with extreme caution. Russell (1983) mentioned a patient who pricked himself on a fang of a *C. adamanteus* that had reportedly been dead for several days and received a mild envenoming. Griffen and Donovan (1986) described a young man who received a moderately severe envenomation from a preserved *C. atrox* rattlesnake head and required antivenom therapy. There has even been a reported fatality in an elderly man bitten on the hand by the fresh decapitated head of a *C. horridus* (Carroll et al., 1997; Kitchens et al., 1987). Despite massive doses of antivenom, the victim succumbed to shock, rhabdomyolysis, and renal failure.

Beyond rapid transportation to medical care, no other specific, scientifically based recommendations for first aid interventions can be made. It is of utmost importance that no further harm be inflicted on the victim and that nothing delays movement to the hospital.

Incisions into the wound (or more proximally along the extremity) should be strictly avoided as they only increase local tissue damage, enhance the risk of infection, and add additional risk of trauma to vital structures below the skin (nerves, arteries, etc.). In an animal survival study, incisions actually hastened the time to death (Leopold et al., 1957).

Application of ice should also be avoided due to the risk of inducing vasoconstriction and possibly tissue ischemia at the site. In the 1950s, cryotherapy was touted for management of snakebite. The bitten extremity was packed in ice for hours to weeks in the mistaken belief that the cold temperatures would inhibit action of the venom components while the body's natural defenses detoxified the substances. Often this therapy was combined with application of a tight ligature to the extremity. When the subsequent incidence of amputations in victims rose dramatically (Van Mierop, 1976b), it became clear that severe cold and anoxic injuries were being superimposed on venom effects (McCollough and Gennaro, 1968). Cryotherapy subsequently fell completely out of favor.

In the late 1980s interest developed in the use of electric shock therapy for snakebite (Guderian et al., 1986) with the idea that electric current might alter the activity or kinetics of venom components. Various devices were recommended, including outboard motors and modified stun guns (Guderian et al., 1986; McPartland and Foster, 1988). All research to date has failed to demonstrate any beneficial effects from such therapy in terms of morbidity or mortality (Dart and Lindsey, 1988; Hardy, 1992; Howe and Meisenheimer, 1988; Johnson et al., 1987; Stoud et al., 1989), and there have been some serious complications following the use of electricity in snakebite victims (Dart and Gustafson, 1991; Hardy, 1997). Its use for this purpose should be completely abandoned.

Many authors have recommended the use of tourniquets or constriction bands for pitviper bites. Tourniquets that completely obstruct blood flow into and out of the extremity should definitely be avoided as they worsen tissue ischemia and bite site necrosis. More loosely fitting constriction bands, applied to limit only superficial venous and lymphatic flow, are slightly more controversial. Although the bands have been demonstrated to reduce systemic spread of pitviper venom in animal models (Burgess et al., 1992), restricting tissue-toxic venoms to the bite site may do more harm than good. Constriction bands may actually worsen local tissue effects and should be avoided.

Even a technique as intuitively safe as mechanical suction is not without controversy. While mouth suction has long been recognized as a bad idea (as it may inoculate the wound with oral bacteria and could, theoretically, lead to problems for a rescuer with open lesions of the mouth or throat), mechanical suction has often been regarded as safe and possibly effective. Two abstracts (Bronstein et al., 1985, 1986) published regarding the most commonly recommended device in North America, the Extractor (Sawyer Products, Safety Harbor, Fla.), suggested that it might be capable of retrieving some quantity of deposited venom. Why neither of these abstracts went on to formal, peer-reviewed publication is unclear. In a critical review of the Extractor, Hardy (1992) pointed out that the maximum amount of venom that could be retrieved with the device was inconsequential compared with the amount injected in a typical pitviper defensive bite. Alberts et al. (2000) used radio-labeled albumin and saline to demonstrate that the Extractor removed essentially none of the mixture. Recent animal data have also cast doubt on the safety of the device. In a small-animal study, Bush et al. (2000a) noted an increased incidence of wound necrosis in pigs injected with *C. atrox* venom and treated with the Extractor for 30 minutes compared with control envenomed pigs that received no treatment (see Pl. 1394). This may have been related to enhanced tissue ischemia or a local sequestering of venom caused by the vacuum effect of the device. In addition, there was no difference in soft tissue swelling between the two groups, suggesting no benefit in the device. If a suction device has been applied by the victim in the field, it should be removed as soon as possible (Bush and Hardy, 2001).

Some researchers have suggested that pressure-immobilization, which appears to be quite effective in limiting the spread of many elapid venoms (Balmain and McCelland, 1982; Sutherland et al., 1979), could be applied to pitviper bites (Grenard, 2000; Sutherland and Coulter, 1981). There may, however, be significant risk in using this technique when a necrotizing venom is involved, as it might worsen local necrosis (Greenland and Hoffman, 1982; Hardy and Bush, 1998; Russell, 1982). Some evidence of this is already present in the literature (Hardy, 1992). It is conceivable that there might be benefit to the technique in cases of bites by pitvipers whose venoms have PLA_2 neurotoxins as their primary lethal components (and often causing less in the way of local tissue destruction; Hardy and Bush, 1998). A great deal of research will be necessary, however, before this technique can be routinely recommended for pitviper bites.

Thus, we are left with rapid transportation of the snakebite victim to medical care as the only currently justifiable, scientifically sound means of field management. It may be reasonable to apply a splint to the extremity to reduce movement of the bitten area and possibly limit edema formation to some degree, but this technique has not been adequately studied either. In one animal survival study, immobilization did prolong survival (Leopold et al., 1957).

Given the increasing safety of newer antivenoms, it is possible that we may someday be able to administer antivenom outside the hospital setting. Even the newer antibody fragment antisera, however, are too slowly absorbed by anything other than the intravenous route to be effective (Theakston, 1997). In regions of the United States where paramedics with intravenous skills are available, where rattlesnake bites are more common, and where transport times to hospitals are prolonged, it is conceivable that the new antivenom CroFab (see below) could one day be given in the field, saving considerable time.

Hospital Management of Crotaline Bites

Hospital management of a pitviper bite victim requires significant clinical judgment and a high degree of vigilance because the patient's clinical condition can change suddenly. The treating physician must either have significant experience in dealing with these emergencies or be willing to get help from available resources such as regional poison control centers.

When the victim arrives, several questions must be answered. Was the victim in fact bitten by a snake? Was the snake venomous? Did venom poisoning occur? How severe is the poisoning? Are there concomitant factors (such as co-morbid medical problems of the victim) that will complicate treatment? The answers to the first two questions may be obvious, especially if a herpetologist or herpetoculturist is the victim. The remaining answers may be more obscure.

The patient should be quickly placed in a critical care setting (such as an emergency department), and appropriate cardiac and respiratory monitoring started. Two intravenous lines should be established in order to give the victim any necessary fluids and medications, including antivenom if indicated. While these lines are being started, blood for laboratory testing should be drawn. The treating physician should obtain a rapid history to determine the pertinent facts regarding the bite, and should perform a brief physical examination looking for local findings and any evidence of systemic toxicity. Vital signs should be closely monitored, again seeking evidence of systemic poisoning. If the victim has any shortness of breath, signs of shock, or a history of heart or lung disease, oxygen should be started. If there is evidence of respiratory failure, the patient may need to have an artificial airway placed (endotracheal intubation) and mechanical ventilation started. Bites to the head and neck present particular risk to the airway due to soft tissue swelling, and must be managed aggressively with airway control (Danzl and Carter, 1988; Dart and Gustafson, 1991; Lewis, 1994).

If the victim is in shock, rapid infusion of saline solution through the intravenous lines is critical. If after the administration of approximately 2 liters of fluid in an adult (20–40 ml/kg in a child) the victim is not stabilized, a change to albumin-containing fluid is indicated. Evidence suggests that this colloidal fluid will stay in the leaky vasculature for longer periods than saline solutions (Schaeffer et al., 1978).

When evaluating the bitten extremity, it is useful to mark several locations—at the bite site and more proximally—and to measure circumferences at these sites every 15 minutes so that progressive swelling can be assessed. The advancing edge of edema can also be marked. These measurements should continue until it is clear that the situation has stabilized. If the extremity continues to swell between measurements, it is clear that there is progressive toxicity and antivenom will be needed.

Determination of the severity of pitviper venom poisoning is achieved by evaluating the presence and extent of local and systemic findings and laboratory abnormalities (Table 58; Parrish, 1955; Wood et al., 1955). Care must be exercised, however, in relying on grading schemes. Snake venom poisoning is a dynamic process, and an apparently minor envenomation can quickly progress to a more serious situation. It is particularly important not to underestimate the degree of venom poisoning when a venom A–producing *C. scutulatus* is the offending animal (Otten and McKimm, 1983) given the paucity of local findings following some of these bites.

Diagnostic Evaluation

Laboratory studies are useful to assess the severity of venom poisoning and to monitor for potential complications. Appropriate tests include a complete blood count (CBC), serum electrolytes, creatine phosphokinase (CPK), blood urea nitrogen (BUN), creatinine (Cr), blood glucose, and liver function tests. An analysis of coagulation function should include a check of the protime (PT) or international normalized ratio (INR), the partial thromboplastin time (PTT), fibrinogen, and fibrin degradation products (FDPs). The urine should be checked each time the patient voids to assess for blood and protein, and the stool should be checked for blood.

In the common scenario of combined defibrination syndrome and venom-induced thrombocytopenia, the lab results will reveal a drop in fibrinogen, a rise in FDPs, an increase in coagulation times (PT, INR, and PTT), and a drop in platelets (Holstege et al., 1997). In cases with isolated defibrination, the platelet count will be normal (Holstege et al., 1997). In isolated venom-induced thrombocytopenia, however, the platelets will

Table 58. Clinical grading scale for pitviper bites.

Severity	Local findings	Systemic findings	Laboratory test results
Nonenvenomation (dry bite)	None or simple puncture wounds	None	Normal
Mild bite	Puncture wounds Pain (may be significant) Local soft tissue swelling	None	Normal
Moderate bite	As for mild Swelling and pain may be more severe	Mild (nausea, vomiting, muscle fasciculations, paresthesias, etc.)	Mildly abnormal (e.g., mildly abnormal coagulation studies or blood counts)
Severe bite	Generally severe pain and swelling If deep intramuscular or intravenous envenoming, local findings may be misleadingly mild	More severe (respiratory difficulty, hypotension/shock, clinical hemorrhage, etc.)	Very abnormal

be low, but other coagulation parameters should be normal (Holstege et al., 1997). Fortunately, in most of these cases actual bleeding is uncommon, unless the abnormalities are severe or there is additional trauma or surgical insult (Holstege et al., 1997). In the rare case of true DIC syndrome, all these results are abnormal and there is evidence of hemolysis, diffuse bleeding, and possibly tissue ischemia (Holstege et al., 1997).

In addition to a drop in platelet count, the CBC may reveal a decrease in hemoglobin/hematocrit due to bleeding or hemolysis and an elevated white blood cell count (without any concomitant infection). Serum CPK levels may be increased, indicating skeletal muscle damage (rhabdomyolysis; Reid, 1978). Rhabdomyolysis can be due to either direct venom-induced muscle damage or diffuse myokymia (see below under *C. horridus*). If the CPK is elevated significantly, the urine should be checked for myoglobin. In rare cases where there is kidney or liver involvement, the studies specific for these organs will be abnormal as well.

It is prudent to draw a blood sample for typing and cross matching (Van Mierop and Kitchens, 1980). Even though the need for blood products is uncommon (see below), both venom and antivenom can interfere with this process later (Krochmal and Anderson, 1976; McCreary, 1959; Van Mierop and Kitchens, 1980; Watt and Gennaro, 1965).

In cases of severe bites or in patients with significant underlying medical problems, markers of cardiac damage (isoenzymes and troponins) and an electrocardiogram should be obtained. If the victim is severely poisoned or has other major underlying medical problems, a chest radiograph and arterial blood gases can be obtained to further evaluate the cardiorespiratory status.

After assessment of the initial diagnostic studies, any tests that returned abnormal results should be repeated at regular intervals (e.g., every two to four hours) until stable. If the initial results are normal, they should be rechecked in several hours if clinical evidence of venom poisoning is present (signs or symptoms). Below I summarize published results of laboratory tests for individual species.

Agkistrodon piscivorus* and *A. contortrix Significant coagulopathies or evidence of muscle damage (e.g., elevated CPK) are uncommon in bites by these species (Banner, 1988; Kitchens, 1992).

Crotalus adamanteus Platelet counts are usually normal or minimally reduced due to platelet destruction secondary to fibrin clot production or plasmin activation (Damus et al., 1972;

Kitchens and Van Mierop, 1983; Van Mierop, 1976a; Weiss et al., 1969). Fibrinogen is often reduced due to the effects of the TLE in this snake's venom (Corrigan and Jeter, 1990; Kitchens and Van Mierop, 1983). Other coagulation factors are usually unaffected (Kitchens and Van Mierop, 1983; Van Mierop, 1976a; Weiss, 1970). Interestingly, one may see markedly abnormal coagulation and incoagulable blood in an otherwise minor envenoming (Kitchens and Van Mierop, 1983; Van Mierop and Kitchens, 1980).

Crotalus atrox Commonly seen are drops in fibrinogen, the appearance of FDPs, and a decrease in platelets (Anderson, 1998; Budzynski et al., 1984; Burgess and Dart, 1991; Clark et al., 1997; Corrigan and Jeter, 1990; Griffen and Donovan, 1986; Hardy, 1992; Reid, 1978). PT and PTT may be elevated (Budzynski et al., 1984) and clotting defects can be persistent (Minton, 1974).

Crotalus horridus Laboratory analysis may demonstrate severe thrombocytopenia (Anderson, 1998; Bond and Burkart, 1997; Brick et al., 1978; Furlow and Brennan, 1985; Schmaier et al., 1980; Tallon et al., 1981). Other coagulation abnormalities may include an increase in the PT and PTT, a drop in fibrinogen, and increased FDPs (Anderson, 1998; Bismuth et al., 1983; Bond and Clancy, 1992; Bond and Burkart, 1997, 1998; Brick et al., 1978; Schmaier et al., 1980; Tallon et al., 1981). The precise mechanisms causing profound thrombocytopenia are unclear (Bond and Burkart, 1997). Crotalocytin undoubtably plays a role but does not appear to be responsible for this venom's resistance to antivenom therapy (see below; Bond and Burkart, 1997). An as yet unidentified venom component that is poorly covered by antivenom may be responsible (Bond and Burkart, 1997).

Myokymia in these patients can be severe enough to induce rhabdomyolysis, and markers of such damage should be checked (Bond and Clancy, 1992; Carroll et al., 1997; Kitchens et al., 1987).

Crotalus molossus The venom of black-tailed rattlesnakes can cause a drop in platelets and fibrinogen, and an elevation in coagulation times (Hardy et al., 1982).

Crotalus oreganus Laboratory findings following significant envenoming may include coagulopathy (low platelet counts, elevated coagulation times, diminished fibrinogen, and the presence of FDPs (Davidson, 1988; Kitchens, 1992; LaGrange and Russell, 1970; Silvani et al., 1980). Serum CPK values may be elevated (Butner, 1983).

Crotalus polystictus Bites can result in a decrease in platelets and fibrinogen and an increase in FDPs (Hardy, 1982).

Crotalus pricei A transient drop in platelet count without other evidence of coagulopathy has been reported (Bernstein et al., 1992).

Crotalus ruber Laboratory tests may reveal coagulopathy with thrombocytopenia, decreased fibrinogen, and the presence of FDPs (Kitchens, 1992; Minton, 1974). Hemolysis may occur as well, with a drop in hematocrit (Lyons, 1971).

Crotalus scutulatus The treating physician must be vigilant for evidence of rhabomyolysis (by assessing serial CPK levels) (Bush and Jansen, 1995; Carroll et al., 1997; Jansen et al., 1992).

Crotalus viridis Bites by this snake can cause coagulopathy (increased coagulation times and FDPs and thrombocytopenia) and elevations in CPK due to myotoxicity (Cole, 1996; Ryan and Caravati, 1994).

Sistrurus catenatus Diminished fibrinogen and elevated FDPs, PT, and PTT have been reported following bites by this snake (Burgess and Dart, 1991; Hankin et al., 1987). Russell (1983), however, found no significant blood changes in patients bitten by this species.

Sistrurus miliarius Russell (1983) found no significant blood changes in patients bitten by this species. Kitchens (1992), however, found evidence of defibrination in 2 of 36 patients. Migliore (1965) also noted a case with laboratory evidence of coagulation dysfunction. Ahlstrom et al. (1991) reported a case with decreased fibrinogen, positive D-dimers, thrombocytopenia, and decreased hematocrit. This patient subsequently developed myoglobinuria and acute renal failure, which was thought to be due to intravascular thrombosis.

Antivenom

The mainstay of modern treatment of venomous snakebite worldwide is antivenom therapy. Antivenoms are antibody molecules, or fragments of these molecules, given to the victim of a bite in order to block the deleterious effects of venom components circulating in the blood. Essentially, the victim is given passive immunization against further venom effects. The greatest benefit from antivenom is in reversing systemic toxicity—cardiovascular, neurotoxic, gastrointestinal, and coagulation abnormalities (Dart et al., 2001). It is important to realize, however, that once venom components are bound to their target tissues, it may be impossible to completely prevent their effects, especially in terms of local tissue damage, regardless of the amount of antivenom administered. Antivenom should therefore be started as soon as possible after its need is identified (see below). In an envenomed victim with an indication for antivenom, it can be said that "time is tissue." In most clinical scenarios it is highly unlikely that antivenom can be started within an hour of the bite. Effectiveness in reducing local tissue damage is thus limited given the rapidity with which tissue necrosis proceeds (Dart and McNally, 2001; Lindsey, 1985; Smith and Ownby, 1985; Theakston, 1997).

There are, at the time of this writing, two antivenoms approved in the United States for management of pitviper venom poisoning. The first, Antivenin (Crotalidae) Polyvalent

(ACP), produced by Wyeth-Ayerst Laboratories of Philadelphia, Pennsylvania, has been available since 1954. It is an equine product containing whole immunoglobulin antibodies (IgG) to venom proteins from *Crotalus adamanteus*, *C. atrox*, *C. durissus terrificus*, and *Bothrops atrox*. Being an equine product that is minimally purified, it contains significant amounts of contaminating proteins such as equine albumin (Sjostrom et al., 1994) and carries significant risks of allergic complications (see below). It is indicated for treatment of significant poisoning by any North American pitviper. At the time of this writing it is uncertain that Wyeth-Ayerst will continue to manufacture this product.

In October 2000 the U.S. Food and Drug Administration approved a second antivenom for use in this country, CroFab, distributed by Savage Laboratories of Melville, New York (see Pl. 1395). This is an ovine product produced by injecting sheep with one of four venoms (*C. adamanteus*, *C. atrox*, *C. scutulatus* [venom A producing], or *Agkistrodon piscivorus*). The sheep antibodies are then collected, and the IgG molecules are cleaved with papain into Fab and Fc fragments. The Fab fragments are the protective components of the immunoglobulin molecules, while the Fc fragments are responsible for the majority of acute immunologic reactions (Dart et al., 1997). The Fc fragments are therefore discarded and the Fab fragments are concentrated by passing the serum over an affinity column to which venom proteins have been adsorbed. The desirable antibody fragments bind to the column as extraneous substances are washed away. The Fab fragments are then eluted off the column. Equal amounts of Fab produced from the four different snake venoms are combined to produce the final monoclonal, polyvalent CroFab. Experience to date suggests that CroFab is safer and more effective than ACP in neutralizing North American pitviper venoms (Consroe et al., 1995). One disadvantage of the smaller molecular size of the Fab fragments is their more rapid clearance from the body and the resulting need to redose the product during treatment (Dart et al., 1997, 2001; see below).

The decisions as to when to administer antivenom and in what dose (Table 59) are aided by categorizing the severity of poisoning according to parameters that have been used for a number of years. Antivenom is currently administered only intravenously because studies have demonstrated better tissue distribution and clinical protection when it is given by this route rather than injected into the bite site or intramuscularly (McCollough and Gennaro, 1963b).

Administration of Wyeth's ACP begins with reconstituting the lyophylized product. Ten milliliters of warm sterile water or saline are placed into each vial, and the vial is gently agitated under warm running water to get the proteins back into solution. This can be an arduous process and can take about 20 minutes. Once the antivenom has been reconstituted, each vial is then placed in a larger volume of fluid (250–1,000 ml) for intravenous administration. The manufacturer recommends applying a skin test to predict possible allergy to the product. While this is currently standard when using Wyeth's antivenoms in the United States, skin testing is largely a medical-legal procedure. The test, which takes 20–30 minutes to administer and read, is notoriously inaccurate, with as many as 10–36% of patients with a negative test still manifesting an acute reaction to the antiserum once it is begun (Jurkovich et al., 1988; Spaite et al., 1988; Weber and White, 1993). Even in the presence of a positive skin test, antivenom can still usually be administered to patients with significant venom poisoning, often

Table 59. Starting doses of antivenoms commercially available in the United States.

Manufacturer/Product	Starting dose (vials, given intravenously)		Notes
Coralsnakes (*Micrurus fulvius*, *M. tener*)			
Wyeth[a]/Antivenin (*Micrurus fulvius*)	3–6		Give more vials if signs or symptoms progress (rarely are more than 10 vials required).
Pitvipers (all North American species)			
Protherics, Inc./CroFab	Dry bite:	0	After initial dose, watch for 1 hour. If patient fails to stabilize, repeat the starting dose (and continue this pattern until stable). After stable, give 2 more vials every 6 hours for 3 more doses.
	Mild:	4–6	
	Moderate:	4–6	
	Severe:	6[b]	
Wyeth[a]/Antivenin (Crotalidae) Polyvalent	Dry bite:	0	If signs, symptoms, or laboratory abnormalities progress, give 5 further doses of vials as needed.
	Mild:	0 or 5[c]	
	Moderate:	10	
	Severe:	15	

[a] It is unclear at the time of this writing whether or not this company will continue manufacturing antivenoms.
[b] No studies of dosing in severe bites have been published.
[c] Many victims with mild bites and no progression can be managed without use of ACP.

without any acute reaction (LoVecchio and DeBus, 2001; Offerman et al., 2001; Wingert and Chan, 1988). Finally, the skin test alone can stimulate an acute reaction in a susceptible patient and has caused serum sickness (Spaite et al., 1988; Weber and White, 1993). Thus, applying a skin test may be a poor use of time in the face of a serious poisoning when antivenom is clearly indicated. In this scenario, it is reasonable to briefly discuss the issue with the patient if possible and to omit the skin test, choosing instead to use the time to get the antivenom infusion started.

Before initiating the ACP infusion, it may be helpful to expand the victim's intravascular volume by giving a bolus of intravenous saline, and to premedicate with intravenous antihistamines (such as diphenhydramine and cimetidine). As the infusion is begun, the physician should be in immediate attendance to intervene if an acute reaction occurs. If the patient reacts negatively, the infusion is stopped and medications are given to halt the reaction (epinephrine, more antihistamines, and steroids as needed). If the poisoning is severe, the antivenom may be restarted at a slower rate and after further diluting the mixture, if possible.

Precise recommendations regarding the starting doses for CroFab are still being refined. The current recommended starting dose for progressive mild or moderate rattlesnake poisoning is four to six vials, reconstituted and diluted in 250 ml of saline and given intravenously over one hour. If it is a severe bite, six vials should be given. The patient is then observed over the next hour to determine whether the signs and symptoms are reversed (as evidenced by stabilization of local findings and normalization of systemic effects and laboratory values). If findings continue to progress, an additional four to six vials are administered, and this is repeated until improvement occurs. After stabilization, two vials are given every six hours for three additional doses. This repeat dosing appears to be necessary due to the relatively short half-life of CroFab in the circulation compared with the half-life of venom proteins in the depot site or due to dissociation over time of the Fab-venom complexes, allowing release of free venom back into the circulation (Dart et al., 1997, 2001).

Because CroFab is less likely to cause allergic reactions (see below), the manufacturer does not recommend any skin test or premedication. Nevertheless, all drugs that might be necessary

to treat an acute allergic reaction must be immediately available whenever any antivenom is being infused.

Coagulation dysfunction during the acute phase of crotaline venom poisoning is usually quite responsive to antivenom therapy, but it can recur in a delayed fashion for at least two weeks following the bite (Bogdan et al., 2000; Boyer et al., 2001; Clark et al., 1997; Dart et al., 1997; Seifert et al., 1997). The clinical significance of this fact is unclear. Certainly any patient exhibiting such dysfunction should be warned about this possibility and told to seek medical care if bleeding symptoms recur, and also to avoid elective surgery for several weeks.

Special Notes regarding Antivenom Therapy

Agkistrodon contortrix Bites by this relatively nontoxic species rarely require therapy with Wyeth's ACP (Russell, 1988) because the risk of complications from the use of this product tends to outweigh the potential benefits in most poisonings. There is evidence, however, of its efficacy in the rare event of a life-threatening bite (Brubacher et al., 1999). The efficacy of CroFab in treating copperhead bites remains to be seen. It is not currently listed as being indicated for such bites, but this is due to regulatory restrictions placed on the company by the U.S. Food and Drug Administration. As no *Agkistrodon* bites were included in the premarket clinical studies, these animals cannot be listed as covered species in the package information. It is very likely, however, that CroFab will provide excellent coverage for all New World *Agkistrodon* species.

Agkistrodon piscivorus Although the package insert for CroFab (available on-line at http://www.fda.gov/cber/label/cropro100200LB.pdf) lists only rattlesnake bites as indications for its use (for reasons noted above), it is almost certainly very effective for cottonmouth bites, as *A. piscivorus* venom is used in its production (Consroe et al., 1995).

Crotalus adamanteus Despite the fact that this venom is one of the four used in the manufacture of Wyeth's ACP, massive doses have been needed to manage severe bites (Buntain, 1983). ACP is usually very effective at reversing the defibrination syndrome seen in many cases of *C. adamanteus* bites (Van Mierop and Kitchens, 1980), although low platelet counts may be refractory to ACP therapy (Kitchens and Van Mierop, 1983). As expected, CroFab is quite effective against this venom (Consroe et al., 1995).

Crotalus horridus ACP is noted for its poor reversal of thrombocytopenia in bites by this species (Anderson, 1998; Bond and Burkhart, 1998). The precise mechanism for this refractory thrombocytopenia is unclear (Bond and Burkart, 1997; Furlow and Brennan, 1985), as crotalocytin (see above) has been shown in animal models to be deactivated by ACP (Schmaier et al., 1980; Schmaier and Colman, 1980). Possibly there is some other, as yet unidentified, venom component operant in thrombocytopenia that is poorly covered by ACP (Bond and Burkart, 1997). Other coagulation abnormalities (such as elevation of the PT and PTT, and drop in fibrinogen) are more responsive to antivenom therapy (Bond and Burkhart, 1998; Bond and Clancy, 1992).

Crotalus molossus ACP appears to be effective in managing the systemic effects (coagulation dysfunction) of this snake's venom (Hardy et al., 1982). In preliminary animal studies, it took moderately higher doses of CroFab to protect against this venom compared with that of most other pitvipers tested (Consroe et al., 1995).

Crotalus oreganus Larger doses of CroFab were required in animal studies to protect against the venom of southern specimens of this species (formerly classified as *C. viridis helleri*), and ACP demonstrated lack of protection against these same snakes (Consroe et al., 1995). Human clinical data on the efficacy of CroFab are currently being gathered.

There has been concern that ACP may be less effective against the venom of snakes formerly classified as *C. viridis concolor* (Glenn and Straight, 1977). CroFab will probably provide adequate coverage of this venom given the close relationship between concolor toxin and Mojave toxin.

Crotalus polystictus ACP appears to give good coverage for this snake's venom (Hardy, 1982).

Crotalus ruber Wyeth's ACP had relatively poor neutralizing activity of one phospholipase component found in this venom (Straight et al., 1992).

Crotalus scutulatus Given that ACP does not contain significant amounts of antibodies protective against Mojave toxin, bites by venom A–producing specimens may require higher doses of this antivenom (Farstad et al., 1997; Glenn and Straight, 1977, 1978; Jansen et al., 1992; Russell and Lauritzen, 1966; Wingert and Chan, 1988). CroFab does contain antibodies against Mojave toxin and thus should provide excellent coverage at standard doses.

Venom B toxicity is likely to be effectively treated with either ACP (Glenn et al., 1983) or CroFab.

Crotalus viridis Wyeth's ACP has a reputation for inability to prevent myonecrosis following significant bites by this species (Cameron and Tu, 1977). This may be related to low titers of antibodies against myotoxins found in the venom (Cameron and Tu, 1977; Ownby and Colberg, 1986; Ownby et al., 1983, 1984, 1985; Smith and Ownby, 1985). In animal models ACP does protect against the venom's lethal effects (Ownby et al., 1983).

Sistrurus catenatus Both ACP and CroFab appear to be effective against *Sistrurus* venoms despite the fact that no member of this genus is used in their production (Consroe et al., 1995; Hankin et al., 1987).

Sistrurus miliarius Antivenom does appear to be effective in treating these bites, and CroFab appears to offer better coverage (at least in animal models) than ACP (Consroe et al., 1995).

Antivenom Use in Pregnancy Snake venom poisoning can have dire consequences in pregnancy, even leading to fetal death and miscarriage (Dunnihoo et al., 1992; Pantanowitz and Guidozzi, 1996; Parrish and Khan, 1966). Antivenom appears to be safe for pregnant women and can prevent some of these complications (Gold and Wingert, 1994; Van Mierop, 1976b). If an acute reaction occurs to the antivenom, however, epinephrine should be avoided if possible due to the sensitivity of the uterine arteries to its effects (with resulting severe reduction of blood flow to the fetus); ephedrine is preferred (Pantanowitz and Guidozzi, 1996; Sullivan and Wingert, 1989).

Antivenom Allergy Two categories of allergic reactions can occur following antivenom use: early (or acute) reactions and late (delayed) reactions. Early reactions can be either anaphylactic or anaphylactoid. In anaphylactic reactions, foreign antivenom proteins cause cross-linking of IgE antibodies on mast cells and basophils in the victim's blood and tissues, generating the release of physiologically active mediators (e.g., histamine) that can result in hives, bronchospasm, swelling of the upper airway, and shock. In the more common anaphylactoid reaction, antivenom proteins cause direct release of mediators from mast cells and basophils, without involvement of antibodies but with precisely the same clinical results. Management of either form of acute reaction may require use of epinephrine, antihistamines, intravenous fluids, steroids, bronchodilating aerosols, and medications to support the blood pressure (vasopressors).

Twenty to 25% of patients who receive ACP experience an acute reaction (Burgess and Dart, 1991; Dart and Gustafson, 1991; Jurkovich et al., 1988; Spaite et al., 1988; Weber and White, 1993), which can be mild (hives and wheezing) or severe (airway swelling and shock). Deaths due to acute reactions to ACP have occurred on rare occasions (Dart and Gustafson, 1991; Jurkovich et al., 1988). In early studies using CroFab (Dart et al., 2001), 19% of patients experienced some degree of early reaction to the product. All reactions reported to date have been mild or moderate in severity, and easily treated with standard medications (Clark et al., 2002; Dart et al., 2001; Gold et al., 2002).

Late serum reactions, also known as serum sickness, involve deposition of immune complexes into the victim's vascular tissues. IgG- and IgM-class antibodies are produced over time by the patient against antivenom proteins in the circulation. These antibodies bind to the proteins, and the antigen-antibody complexes become deposited in the vascular system stimulating an intense inflammatory response. Manifestations may include hives, fever, muscle and joint aches, kidney problems, and peripheral nerve problems that appear several days to two weeks following antivenom therapy. Management of serum sickness involves use of steroids (such as oral prednisone) to reduce the inflammatory response and antihistamines for symptomatic relief. Treatment with steroids is generally continued until all symptoms have subsided, and then the agent is tapered off with a gradually reducing dose over one to two weeks.

As many as 60–80% of victims treated with ACP develop serum sickness (Burgess and Dart, 1991; Corrigan et al., 1978; Wingert and Wainschel, 1975). In premarket studies with CroFab, 23% of patients developed signs and symptoms consistent with serum sickness (Dart et al., 2001). The majority of these patients had received an early batch of the product that was ultimately determined to contain an unexpectedly high concentration of Fc antibody fragment contaminants. Changes in the production process resolved this problem, and the ensuing rate for serum sickness was closer to 6%.

Blood Products

Although venom poisoning by a number of pitviper species can cause hematologic and hemostatic abnormalities, in most cases these changes are identifiable only through laboratory tests; actual clinically significant bleeding is unusual. Nevertheless, victims occasionally exhibit major bleeding or severe hemolysis and require transfusion of blood products. In all such cases, antivenom must be administered prior to beginning infusion of blood products in order to keep the transfused components from being destroyed by circulating venom and adding to the problem. Giving blood products in the absence of antivenom therapy is unlikely to be of any benefit (Burgess and Dart, 1991). Antivenom alone, however, is often effective in reversing coagulopathy (Bogdan et al., 2000; Reid and Theakston, 1978). If venom poisoning results in severe anemia, red blood cells can be transfused. If severe coagulopathy is present, coagulation factors may be needed (in the form of fresh frozen plasma or factor concentrates). If significant bleeding is present in the face of an abnormal platelet count or if the count is low enough to make spontaneous hemorrhage a likely possibility (e.g., less than 20,000/mm^3), then platelet transfusion is needed (Burgess and Dart, 1991). Low platelet counts will respond to antivenom alone in many cases, but to a variable degree (Bush et al., 2000b; Rawat et al., 1994; Riffer et al. 1987). Platelet counts may rebound following antivenom infusion only to fall again later (Anderson, 1998). In some cases (e.g., *C. horridus* bites), thrombocytopenia may be relatively refractory to antivenom therapy alone (Bond and Burkart, 1997; Bond and Clancy, 1992). Even if platelet transfusions are used, the effect on platelet count may be transient, with a recurrent, rapid drop (Anderson, 1998; Bond and Burkhart, 1997, 1998; Furlow and Brennan, 1985). In most cases there are no ill effects from such recurrent or delayed reductions in platelet counts (Brown and Carmony, 1991; Rao et al., 1998), although patients should be warned of this possibility and the need to avoid elective surgery for some weeks after the bite.

Wound Care

Management of the bitten extremity should include ruling out any retained fangs in the wound and cleansing the area to the extent possible. This is followed by application of a padded splint, with cotton placed between the digits. The extremity should then be elevated above the level of the heart (after antivenom, if indicated, has been started).

The victim's tetanus status should be updated if appropriate. The decision to begin prophylactic antibiotics is usually at the discretion of the attending physician. Research indicates that the incidence of secondary bacterial infections following pitviper bites is actually quite low (Clark et al., 1993; Lawrence et al., 1996). Many treating physicians still opt to administer prophylactic antibiotics for a few days in all but the most inconsequential bites, although there is no evidence that it actually reduces the risk of infection (Lawrence et al., 1996). The mouths and fangs of these snakes do harbor an array of bacteria (mostly Gram-negative organisms) that could secondarily infect a necrotic wound and compound tissue loss (Fischer et al., 1961; Goldstein et al., 1979; Parrish, 1980). Antibiotics are more likely to be of benefit if ill-advised incisions were made into the bite site in the field. In such cases, a broad-spectrum agent such as a cephalosporin can be given.

Over the first several days following the bite, any hemorrhagic or clear blisters that develop on the extremity should be sharply debrided (Russell, 1983). Any coagulation disturbances that may have been present should be resolved or treated before such debridement is carried out in order to avoid stimulating bleeding and potentially increasing tissue loss. Similar debridement of necrotic tissue should be carried out as wound margins become demarcated.

Physical therapy should be started as soon as possible, to hasten the victim's return to maximal recovery, especially following bites to the hand.

Surgical Interventions

Although there was a time when some physicians considered pitviper bite to be a surgical disease, it has become clear that the role for surgery in managing these cases is small. Hemorrhagic blebs should be debrided in order to relieve pain and assess the degree of underlying necrosis (Holstege et al., 1997; see above). Likewise, necrotic tissue should be debrided as needed. Much less commonly, surgery may be indicated when venom has been deposited inside muscle compartments, resulting in swelling of the muscles within their nondistensible sheaths. When this occurs, the rising pressure within the sheaths can cut off blood flow to the muscles (termed a compartment syndrome). The likelihood of this occurring is greatest for bites by large snakes with particularly long fangs, such as *C. adamanteus*, whose fangs may reach 2.5 cm in length (Glass, 1982). The actual incidence of compartment syndrome, however, is quite low following venomous snakebite (Clark et al., 1993; Curry et al., 1985; Garfin, 1982; Kunkel et al., 1983–1984; Watt, 1985; White and Weber, 1991). The difficulty lies in differentiating the rare compartment syndrome from the typical scenario in which the victim has a painful, swollen, discolored limb due to superficial swelling outside the muscle compartment. Making this distinction may require measurement of the actual pressures inside the compartments. This is done simply by placing a small needle into the suspect muscle belly so that a pressure reading can be obtained (see Pl. 1396). If the pressure reading exceeds the intravascular pressure necessary to achieve blood flow to the muscles (above approximately 30–40 mm Hg), then a surgical procedure (fasciotomy) is required to open up the compartment and allow room for swelling (see Pl. 1397). A fasciotomy should always be preceded by objective recorded measurements of the intracompartmental pressures.

It has been suggested that elevated intracompartmental pressures might be reduced by giving intravenous mannitol in addition to antivenom (Sullivan et al., 1995). This hyperosmolar agent causes a shift of fluid from tissues and interstitial spaces into the vascular space, from which it can be excreted via the urine (diuresis). While this therapy has been used in other causes of compartment syndrome (Better, 1999), it has never been objectively studied as an adjunct to management of snake venom poisoning. Mannitol infusion can result in complications, particularly in victims with unstable vital signs (Walter et al., 1998), and should be undertaken only with caution and while monitoring the victim's cardiovascular status and intra-compartmental pressures.

In addition, a pitviper bite to a digit can cause enough swelling to impair vascular flow to the appendage. In the setting of a compromised (pale, pulseless) finger, the surgeon may need to make an incision through the skin on one side of the digit (digital dermotomy) to allow room for swelling and to preserve circulation (Holstege et al., 1997; Wasserman, 1988; Watt, 1985; White and Weber, 1991).

There is no benefit to routine surgical exploration of snakebite wounds, or to routine fasciotomy in the absence of objective evidence of compartment syndrome (Garfin et al., 1984). These procedures only add surgical trauma to the venom-induced tissue injury and prolong the victim's hospital stay and recovery period.

Steroids

There is no role for routine use of steroids in pitviper venom poisoning. They have never been shown to be beneficial in terms of treating primary venom effects, and there is some evidence that they may be harmful—accentuating venom effects or interfering with the body's normal wound repair systems (Russell and Emery, 1961). The only role for steroids is in mitigating the effects of acute or delayed serum reactions to antivenom (see above) or in the unusual case of an allergic reaction to the venom itself (see below).

Disposition

Victims of apparent pitviper bites should be observed closely. In apparent dry bites (i.e., local findings limited to simple puncture wounds and no systemic symptoms or laboratory abnormalities), victims can be discharged home with a reliable adult after 6–8 hours of observation. Anyone clearly envenomed should be admitted to the hospital for at least 24 hours regardless of whether or not antivenom is needed. This is done to monitor for any deterioration in clinical status. If the offending reptile may have been C. scutulatus (particularly venom A producing), then it may be reasonable to admit the patient for observation even if the bite appears to be dry—again, to watch for unexpected deterioration (Bush and Cardwell, 1999).

Management of Renal Insufficiency

Fortunately, significant renal damage following snake venom poisoning in North America is uncommon (Danzig and Abels, 1961), unlike the situation in other areas of the world (Myint-Lwin et al., 1985). When it does occur, it is usually multifactorial in origin—related to shock, deposition of muscle and blood proteins in the kidney filtering system, and direct venom nephrotoxicity (Ahlstrom et al., 1991; Jansen et al., 1992). Most cases are transient with eventual resumption of normal renal function. In rare patients, hemodialysis is necessary to carry

them over the period of severe renal shutdown. It is extremely uncommon, however, for renal failure to be permanent, mandating lifelong dialysis or renal transplant.

Venom Allergy

People who have had previous bites or who work closely with snake venoms can become sensitized to venom proteins (Parrish and Thompson, 1958; Reimers et al., 2000; Ryan and Caravati, 1994; Tanen et al., 2001). It is possible that even more casual contact with venom can sensitize some susceptible individuals (Brooks et al., 2001). Once sensitization occurs, a subsequent bite can result in an acute anaphylactic reaction in the victim that can be more immediately life-threatening than the direct venom effects. These cases can present with rapid onset of shock, airway swelling, and respiratory distress, with or without hives. In addition, venom can cause endogenous release of bradykinin and histamine in nonsensitized victims, causing a similar anaphylactoid presentation (Reimers et al., 2000). The precise etiology of systemic collapse can be unclear in such cases. Is this a case of direct intravascular venom poisoning or is it an anaphylactic/-oid reaction? When in doubt, the treating physician must treat for both, giving epinephrine, antihistamines, and steroids to ameliorate anaphylaxis, and antivenom to treat venom poisoning. In many of these cases the administration of epinephrine subcutaneously, intramuscularly, or intravenously in the field may be necessary to keep the patient alive during transport to the hospital. Paramedical personnel in the United States are fully trained in using epinephrine and antihistamines to treat anaphylaxis in the prehospital setting but must think of this possibility when treating a snakebite victim who is unconscious, in shock, or both.

People at unavoidable increased risk of snake venom poisoning who are known to be sensitive to snake venoms (as manifested by allergic symptoms when working with venoms or prior allergic reaction following a bite) should be prescribed some form of epinephrine self-administration kit (e.g., EpiPen, Dey, Napa, Calif.). Epinephrine must always be immediately available to such individuals whenever they are involved in tasks that could potentially expose them to venom.

Morbidity and Mortality

The number of deaths in North America due to venomous snakebite is quite low compared with many other areas of the world. Estimates of deaths due to snakebite in the United States are often quoted as approximately 9–14 per year (Parrish and Carr, 1967; Russell, 1983). This is almost certainly an overestimate today. Between 1983 and 1998 there were only 10 such deaths reported to the AAPCC, and while that is certainly an underestimate (many deaths are not reported to poison control centers), it probably better describes the magnitude of the problem today. In Mexico, however, as many as 150 people die each year as a result of venomous snakebite (Gómez and Dart, 1995).

The most lethal species of pitvipers in North America include Crotalus adamanteus, C. atrox, C. simus, and Bothrops asper (see "Snakebites in Central and South America" for discussions of C. simus and B. asper); C. scutulatus, C. horridus, C. oreganus, and C. viridis are all capable of delivering fatal bites as well. Even species that are commonly considered relatively benign, such as

A. contortrix (Amaral, 1927i) and *C. cerastes*, have caused fatalities on rare occasions (Russell, 1960).

Hardy (1986, 1997) reviewed 10 deaths that occurred in Arizona between 1969 and 1996. He found that almost all could be attributed to one of a few factors: a delay in presentation (or failure to seek care at all), inadequate treatment of shock (insufficient fluid resuscitation or use of vasopressor drugs to try to raise blood pressure instead of giving fluids), or inadequate or delayed use of antivenom. The final case involved either a massive envenoming or an allergic reaction to venom in a victim with known frequent exposure to snake venoms. Hardy concluded that at least 7 of the 10 deaths were preventable.

The factors that predispose a victim to a bad outcome following a serious envenoming include age (the very young and the very old may be at increased risk), the presence of serious underlying disorders that complicate management (e.g., heart or lung disease), delays in reaching medical care, inadequate intravenous fluid administration in patients with shock, and, most important, inadequate or delayed antivenom administration (Hardy, 1986; Russell, 1983).

Before antivenom was available, the mortality rate for pitviper envenoming in the United States varied between 5% and 25% (Russell, 1983). The current rate is certainly less than 1% (Parrish, 1980), and may decline further as CroFab comes into wider use.

A much more likely outcome of pitviper bite in North America is long-term local complications. Tissue loss, with permanent disability and possible need for amputation, occurs with some regularity (Minton, 1974; Tenery and Koefoot, 1955; Watt et al., 1956; see Pls. 1398–1400). Approximately 10–15% of victims will experience significant tissue necrosis (Hardy, 1992; Lawrence et al., 1996). The precise incidence of permanent functional disability is unknown, as this has never been carefully evaluated. It may be as high as 30% in upper extremity bites (Cowin et al., 1998; Grace and Omer, 1980; see Pl. 1401). Multiple surgical procedures may be needed to debride dead tissue and to place tendon or skin grafts. Some underlying medical conditions may increase the victim's risk of tissue loss, such as a history of smoking tobacco or abuse of methamphetamines (Holstege et al., 1997). Patients may experience persistent swelling and stiffness and loss of strength in the bitten extremity for months following pitviper bites (Hardy et al., 1982). Specific prognoses are discussed below.

Agkistrodon contortrix

Almost all patients bitten by copperheads do uniformly well with appropriate conservative therapy (Whitley, 1996).

Agkistrodon piscivorus

Deaths from cottonmouth bites have been recorded (McCollough and Gennaro, 1968; Parrish, 1963; Parrish and Donnell, 1967).

Crotalus adamanteus

This snake has been considered to cause the greatest number of snakebite deaths in the United States (Russell, 1983). The lethal venom dose for humans has been estimated to be approximately 90–100 mg (Dowling, 1975; Weiss et al., 1969), or roughly one-tenth of the total venom yield of an exceptionally large specimen. Complaints of numbness and tingling as well as abnormal co-agulation can persist for weeks following a bite by this species (Van Mierop and Kitchens, 1980; Watt and Pollard, 1954).

Crotalus atrox

The western diamondback probably ranks number two in terms of deaths in the United States and number one in northern Mexico (Minton and Weinstein, 1986; Watt, 1985).

Crotalus horridus

Given the large size of this snake and its highly virulent venom, its lethal potential should not be underestimated.

Crotalus lepidus

Despite its small size and fangs (Ownby et al., 1976) this snake should be considered capable of inflicting a serious bite in an adult.

Crotalus oreganus

Tissue necrosis, possibly severe enough to require amputation or tissue grafting, may occur (Butner, 1983; Mackessy, 1996; Silvani et al., 1980). Fatalities by snakes in this species formerly classified as *C. viridis concolor* appear to be very uncommon, despite their extremely potent venom. No fatalities had ever been recorded according to a 1977 report, perhaps because these snakes occur in low densities in areas sparsely inhabited by people (Glenn and Straight, 1977). Further limiting its medical importance is this snake's small size, low venom yield, and mild disposition (Glenn and Straight, 1977). Similarly rare are deaths due to Great Basin rattlesnakes (formerly *C. v. lutosus*), but tissue necrosis can occur (Adame et al., 1990).

Crotalus polystictus

Local wound necrosis has been reported following its bite (Hardy, 1982).

Crotalus pricei

Secondary bite site infection complicated one reported bite by this snake (Bernstein et al., 1992).

Crotalus ruber

The estimated lethal dose for humans is approximately 100 mg of venom (Dowling, 1975).

Crotalus scutulatus

Despite the facts that the venom of this snake is the most toxic pitviper venom in the United States, and that a single typical bite carries enough venom to be potentially lethal to a healthy adult (Ernst, 1992), the number of deaths attributed to it are few (Watt, 1985). Venom A–producing specimens can perhaps cause death by respiratory or circulatory failure (Banner, 1988; Hardy, 1983). Morbidity may include significant tissue loss and renal failure (Farstad et al., 1997; Hardy, 1983).

Crotalus tigris

Despite its low venom yield, any bites by this snake must be taken seriously due to the venom's high degree of toxicity (Weinstein and Smith, 1990).

Sistrurus catenatus

The estimated lethal dose for humans is approximately 30–40 mg, more than a typical adult can yield on milking, and much less than anticipated in a single bite (Minton and Minton, 1969). Deaths, however, have been reported (Menne, 1959; Stebbins, 1954). Tissue damage can occur but does not tend to be severe (Hankin et al., 1987).

Sistrurus miliarius

The lethal dose for humans is unknown, and given their low venom yields, it is unlikely that pygmy rattlesnakes can deliver a fatal bite to an adult human (Ernst, 1992; Minton and Minton, 1969; Van Mierop, 1976b). Severe bites requiring prolonged hospitalization have occurred in children (Guidry, 1953; Van Mierop, 1976b), and necrosis has been reported (Snyder et al., 1968; Van Mierop, 1976b).

Prevention

Prevention of most cases of venomous snakebite in North America would be easily achieved if potential victims would refrain from handling or intentionally disturbing these animals. Exceptions might be in professions where periodic snake handling is required (zoos, museums, and especially laboratories dedicated to extracting venoms for research and antivenom production). "Accidental bites" (bites in which the victim had no intention of interacting with the snake and may not have even seen the snake prior to being bitten) can be reduced when extra vigilance is used in "snake country." Wearing appropriate footwear (especially at night), visually inspecting areas where hands or feet will land when hiking or climbing, and staying on open paths away from ground cover that can conceal a resting snake can reduce the chances of being bitten.

Prior Planning

While preventive strategies can reduce the risk of snakebite, they cannot completely eliminate the problem. All too often sojourners in the field (campers, hikers, researchers, etc.) and those who work around venomous snakes on a daily basis (both professionally and as an avocation) give little forethought to the steps they would take if a bite should occur. What management would they apply in the prehospital setting? Where would they go for medical care, and how would they get there? Where is the nearest source of appropriate antivenom for likely involved species?

It is strongly recommended that those at risk have a preconceived plan of action (Hardy 1994b, 1994c). Research and zoological institutions should have a formal snakebite emergency plan. It would be very helpful for such organizations to have a prearranged relationship with a physician who is either knowledgeable in venomous snakebite management or willing to become so.

Future Directions for Research

There continues to be great need for research into snakebite management. Areas of interest include antivenoms, snake venom detection kits, and immunization.

Antivenoms

Much success has been achieved in developing safer and more effective antivenoms (e.g., CroFab), but work needs to continue in this area. The current extremely high cost of antivenoms available in the United States makes the economic impact of venomous snakebite in this country a real problem. Perhaps in the foreseeable future there will exist cheap, effective antivenoms produced entirely without the use of horses, sheep, or other vertebrates—perhaps using biogenetic techniques.

Also of concern is a possible future absence of a commercially available antivenom in the United States for use in significant coralsnake bites. If Wyeth-Ayerst discontinues manufacturing Antivenin (*Micrurus fulvius*), clinicians may find themselves without this tool in their armamentarium when faced with these uncommon bites. While sound conservative care (especially respiratory support) alone will likely lead to a favorable outcome, the availability of a safe, effective antivenom for *M. fulvius* and *M. tener* could reduce the costs and potential complications of treating such bites. Costs might be reduced by decreasing the need for respiratory support in an intensive care unit, and complications such as aspiration pneumonia and possible death could be minimized. Possible alternatives if Wyeth-Ayerst discontinues manufacturing its coralsnake antivenom would include a new manufacturer assuming production of a suitable product (unlikely due to the high costs involved in obtaining FDA approval for new drugs) or importing another country's antivenom for compassionate use in the United States.

Snake Venom Detection Kits

In some areas of the world, significant work has been done to develop snake venom detection kits that can be used clinically in the management of patients. Such kits may be especially helpful in rapidly identifying the offending species (through samples done on wound aspirate, blood, or urine) and in determining the levels of circulating venom in the victim's bloodstream (as an assessment of severity; Amuy et al., 1997). In the latter instance, the test might provide guidance for antivenom administration—as long as circulating venom proteins were still detectable, antivenom administration would continue (Amuy et al., 1997). Unfortunately, very little work has been done in this area regarding North American venomous snakes (Amuy et al., 1997; Theakston et al., 1977).

Immunization

There has been intermittent interest in the possibility of immunizing humans against the effects of snake venoms. In North America, the risk of snake venom poisoning to the general public is much too low to even consider such an approach. Those who interact with venomous snakes on a daily basis, however, would benefit if immunization were possible. Unfortunately, it does not appear that such an approach will be feasible. Evidence from cases of victims with histories of repeated snakebites fail to indicate any apparent protective effects from previous bites (Parrish, 1959). It is much more likely that repeated low-dose exposure to snake venom in an attempt to stimulate immunity would actually sensitize the person to the venom so that a subsequent bite might be *more* likely to be fatal due to anaphylaxis.

CONCLUSIONS

Reptile venom poisoning is clearly much less of a medical concern in North America than it is in many other regions of the world. Despite the low incidence of bites and the rarity of deaths in this region, there is need for continued research to develop simple, efficacious field management techniques; to further enhance our antivenom armamentaria; and to develop bedside testing technologies that will help guide treating physicians in making decisions regarding antivenom choices and dosing. Also needed is further research into snake venoms themselves and their potential application to human disease states such as cardiovascular disease, stroke, and cancer. Unfortunately, funding for such research has been difficult to obtain. Individuals with interests (either amateur or professional) in the herpetological sciences should do all within their power to encourage the allocation of research money by government and private industry to these important areas.

Snakebites in Central and South America: Epidemiology, Clinical Features, and Clinical Management

David A. Warrell

Snakes featured prominently in pre-Columbian religion in Mesoamerica, notably as the "feathered serpent" at the Temple of Quetzalcoatl at Teotihuacan and Chichén Itzá and as the Olmec earth serpents at La Venta's Altar 4. The mosaic faces at La Venta have been convincingly identified as those of rattlesnakes (*Crotalus simus*; Luckert, 2001). The importance of the rattlesnake to pre-Columbian Americans is illustrated by its threatening position in relation to the Aztec zodiac man (Kingsborough et al., 1831–1848; Fig. 253) and its inclusion in the ancient Mayan codices (J. C. Lee, 1996). The snake god (of wisdom) was one of the seven Inca deities. Klauber (1972) reviewed the role of rattlesnakes in the medicine, myth, and legend of pre-Columbian Indians.

Early accounts of the European invaders' encounters with venomous snakes were published from the sixteenth century onward. Pedro de Cieça de Leon (1554) (see Klauber, 1972), who traveled in Venezuela, Colombia, and Peru, described the fatal bite of the rattlesnake, or cascabel. Padre Luís Rodrigues, a Jesuit missionary, was bitten by a *cascavel* (*Crotalus durissus cascavella*) at Christmas 1560 near Bahia, Brazil (Leite, 1954, 3:93; see below). In 1566, Diego de Landa described two very venomous snakes in Yucatán, a rattlesnake and the taxinchan (*Bothrops asper*) (J. C. Lee, 1996). Pedro de Magalhães Gandavo described the dangerous cascavel in Brazil (Gandavo, 1576). Francisco Hernández (1615) was the first to illustrate a rattlesnake (*C. s. simus*) from Mexico. His account was plagiarized by Johann Nieremberg (Nierembergii, 1635), who added a new picture of a rattlesnake, described as teuhtlacocauhqui, king of the serpents (Fig. 254). Death ensued within 24 hours of the strike of this snake unless appropriate treatment was applied. A bite by the ahucyactli, which lacked a rattle, caused bleeding at the site of the bite, from scars, and through all the bodily orifices; and the bite of the "chiappa" caused bleeding and necrosis.

Willem Piso and George Marcgrave, based in Recife (Pernambuco), Brazil, described many species of snakes, including the boiçininga (*C. d. cascavella*), ibiboboca (cobra de coral [genus *Micrurus*]), and çurucucu (*Lachesis muta*), and the effects of their bites (Piso and Marcgraf, 1658; Fig. 255). In Venezuela, Padre Josef Gumilla (1741) described the venomous cascabel, the coralsnakes, and the deadly rica (rieca) or verrugosa (*Lachesis muta*). José Gonçalves da Fonseca (1749), traveling in the Rio Negro in Brazil, described the case of an Amerindian soldier who was bitten on the finger by a surucucu while hunting. He experienced agonizing pain and lost the power of speech but made a dramatic recovery in only a few hours after taking a tra-

ditional remedy made of birds' beaks. Edward Bancroft provided some early descriptions of the snakes of Guyana (Bancroft, 1769). He mentioned the ibonuna (coralsnake) but emphasized that it was the labarra (now known as labaria, *Bothrops atrox*) "whose poison is, of all others, the most fatal." At the Conception Plantation in Demarary (Demarara), an Afro slave carpenter was bitten on the right forefinger while trying to turn a piece of timber. He was just able to kill the labaria before falling to the ground and dying "in less than 5 minutes." The victim's blood "had suffered a fatal dissolution by the poison" resulting in purple spots on every part of the external surface of the body and bleeding from eyes, ears, lungs, etc. (Bancroft, 1769).

Sonnini de Manoncourt (1776) was contemptuous of the herbal remedies for snakebite used by the inhabitants of French Guiana but convinced himself of the efficacy of eau de luce (alkali volatil, or sal volatile—ammonium carbonate—in amber oil). During a journey into the interior he found a young Amerindian who had been bitten on his big toe a few hours earlier by a serpent à grage, whose venom was considered far more dangerous than that of the rattlesnake. (The description of this species, whose local name alluded to the scales on its back being like a grater used for making manioc flour, indicates that it was *Lachesis muta*.) The bitten limb was grossly swollen and tense up to the thigh, and the victim was delirious with a high fever. He had already received a variety of indigenous treatments including binding of the snake's head to the scarified wound, ingestion of its liver, and plant remedies. Repeated topical application of a compress soaked in eau de luce brought a dramatic improvement in symptoms, and the patient recovered in three days. Eau de luce proved equally effective for a second patient, an African bitten twice on the ankle by the same species. In Suriname, Stedman (1796) gave a dramatic account of a man bitten by a small snake, known locally as oroocookoo (owroekoekoe; *Bothrops atrox*), which in less than a minute caused swelling, excruciating pain, and convulsions. The victim drank a locally approved remedy, the snake's gall, but soon developed fits of increasing violence and promptly died. In the nineteenth century, several European travelers and naturalists in Brazil made observations about venomous snakes, the effects of their bites, and traditional treatments in this region. Koster (1816), while traveling in the northeast of Brazil, heard about the mandingueiros, who were able to handle venomous snakes and cure their bites. One man whom they had cured of a rattlesnake bite continued to suffer: the bitten leg remained

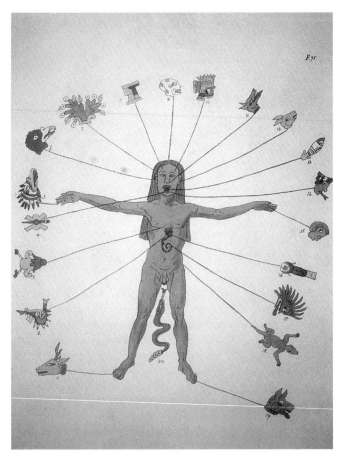

Fig. 253. Aztec version of the European zodiac man from *Antiquities of Mexico*. From Kingsborough, 1831.

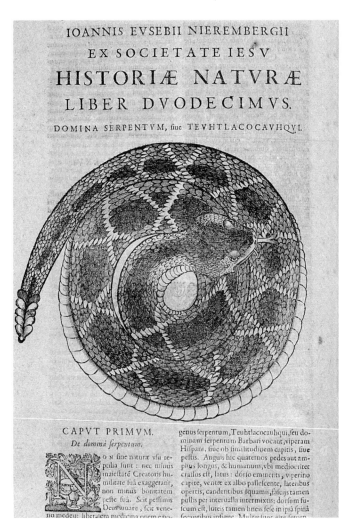

Fig. 254. The second published representation of a rattlesnake (from Mexico) in *Historia Naturae*, published in Antwerp by Nierembergii in 1635. Photograph by David A. Warrell.

swollen, there was discharge from the wound, and the man had violent pains in all his limbs at the time of the full moon. Saint-Hilaire (1833, 2:226) found that venomous reptiles were formidable enemies of the farmers in Espirito Santo. On one fazenda, 14 of the workers had been bitten by venomous snakes, but only 1 had died.

In the modern era, Vital Brazil Mineiro da Campanha (1865–1950; Fig. 256) was a great pioneer in the study of Latin American venomous snakes, their venoms, and the production of specific therapeutic antivenoms. Stimulated by an epidemic of bubonic plague in the port of Santos in 1899, the authorities set up an antiserum production laboratory in São Paulo State in 1899. The Instituto Butantan was officially opened in 1901 under the direction of Vital Brazil and began antivenom production in 1905. More than 100 years later this institute (Pl. 1402) remains the center of excellence for research on venomous animals in South America. It has been celebrated in poetry (Rudyard Kipling: "Poison of asps—a Brazilian snake-farm") and classical music (Ottorino Respighi: "Impressões Brasileiras—Butantã"). During its first 50 years the Instituto Butantan treated 7,562 patients with antivenom with only 181 deaths (Swaroop and Grab, 1954).

EPIDEMIOLOGY

The incidence of snakebite is determined by the frequency of contact between snakes and humans, which depends on their population densities, diurnal and seasonal variations in activity, and particular human activities such as agriculture. Some species seem far more irritable, or willing to strike, than others. The severity of the resulting envenoming depends on the dose of venom injected, which is determined by the mechanical efficiency of the bite and the species, size, and age of the snake. Some believe in the concept of a defensive bite. The composition and potency of the snake's venom depends on the species and, within a species, on the geographical location, season, and age of the snake. The health, age, body weight, and specific immunity of the human victim may also affect the outcome, as, most crucially, will the nature and timing of first aid and medical treatment. Most bites are inflicted on the lower limbs of farmers, plantation workers, herdsmen, and hunters in rural areas. Snakebite truly deserves to be considered an occupational disease, with the high political profile that classification confers. In northwest Colombia, for example, 46% of bite victims are farmers and 71% are bitten on the lower limbs (Otero et al., 1992b), and in Chanchamayo, Peru, the peak incidence of snakebites occurs during the coffee-harvesting season (March–June). The snakes are often trodden on inadvertently at night and in undergrowth. Exceptions are the bites on the upper body, face, and arms inflicted by arboreal species such as *Bothriopsis bilineata*. Severe flooding, by concentrating the human and snake populations in shrinking areas of dry land, has given rise to epidemics of snakebite in Colombia and other countries. Invasions of virgin jungle during construction of the

Fig. 255. Frontispiece of *De Indiae utriusque re naturali et medica*, published in Amsterdam by Piso and Marcgraf in 1658. Photograph by David A. Warrell.

Trans-Amazonian Highway in Brazil and irrigation and hydroelectric schemes have also led to an increased incidence of snakebite.

SNAKEBITES IN CENTRAL AND SOUTH AMERICA

In 1954 Swaroop and Grab estimated that 3,000–4,000 people died as a result of snakebites in Central and South America (including Mexico) each year. In 1998, some 5,000 out of 300,000 bites were estimated to have resulted in death (Chippaux, 1998). Such estimates, based on hospital and Ministry of Health returns, are notoriously inaccurate. Gutiérrez et al. (1999) suggested that there might be 4,500–5,000 bites per year in Central America alone. In most rural areas of tropical countries, only a minority of those bitten by snakes seek the help of Western-style hospitals. Most prefer traditional herbal treatments from shamans (*curanderos/curadores*; Pl. 1497) or witch doctors (*brujos*). For example, in northwest Colombia, 54% of patients admitted to hospital with snakebites had already been treated by shamans or traditional healers (Otero et al., 2002).

Generally, numbers of bites, deaths, and permanently crippled patients are not accurately recorded in official national

Fig. 256. Vital Brazil as a young man. Photograph courtesy of João Luiz Costa Cardoso, Brazil.

statistics. In the few areas of the world where population surveys have been carried out, surprisingly high rates of snakebite-related mortality have been discovered. Thus, in southeastern Senegal, West Africa, there were 14 deaths per 100,000 population per year (Trape et al., 2001). No study of this type has yet been attempted in a Latin American country. Although the risk of snakebite in indigenous communities may be high, visitors, even those involved in high-risk activities, are rarely bitten. Hardy (1994b) calculated that the risk to field biologists in Central America was one bite per 500,000 person-hours working in the habitat of *Bothrops asper*.

SNAKEBITES AMONG INDIGENOUS AMERICANS

Snakebite data from Amerindian groups are the least likely to be recorded, except in anthropological studies. Chagnon (1968), working among the Yanomamö of Roraima, Brazil, and southern Venezuela, found that 2% of adult deaths were caused by snakebites. Among the Waorani (Waodani) Indians of eastern Ecuador, 45% had had at least one snakebite; 95% of the adult male population had been bitten at least once, and almost half had been bitten more than once. Throughout five generation genealogies, 4% of deaths were attributable to snakebite (Larrick et al., 1978, 1979; Fig. 257). In Acre, western Brazil, preliminary inquiries in 1992 suggested that during the past 40 years snakebite had accounted for 3.3% of all deaths and 24% of deaths in the 15–44-year-old age group among 100 families of Kaxinawa Indians of the Rio Tejo, Upper Juruá rubber extraction area (Paulo Brígido de Alencar, pers. comm.; Fig. 258). A survey of forest-dwelling Amazonian Indians and rubber

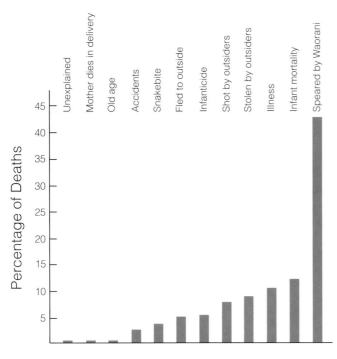

Fig. 257. Causes of mortality among the Waorani of eastern Ecuador. From *Ecuador in the Shadow of the Volcanoes* by Acosta-Solis et al. Published by permission of Ediciones Libri Mundi, Quito, Ecuador.

Fig. 258. Kaxinawa man, Acre, Brazil. Copyright Stephen Pierini.

Fig. 259. A seringueiro, or collector of natural rubber, in the jungles of Amazonian Brazil. Photograph by David A. Warrell.

Fig. 260. Seringueiro boy and collected latex, Rio Juruá, Acre, Brazil. Copyright Stephen Pierini.

tappers (*seringueiros, caucheros*; Figs. 259 and 260) of the Juruá Valley showed that 30% of the population had been bitten during their lifetime. Seventeen percent of the Katukina people interviewed but only 8% of Ashaninkas (Pl. 1403) had been bitten. Mortality was estimated at about 400 deaths per 100,000 population per lifetime, the majority of bites being attributed to *Bothrops atrox*, *Lachesis muta*, and *Bothriopsis bilineata* (Pierini et al., 1996). Among Siona-Secoya Indians at San Pablo de Kantesyia, Río Aguarico, Napo Province, Ecuador, bites were caused by undefined *Bothrops* species (6 cases), *Bothriopsis bilin-*

eata (5 cases), *Bothrocophias hyoprora* (2 cases), *Lachesis muta*, and *B. atrox* (1 case each) (Touzet, 1986).

SNAKEBITES IN INDIVIDUAL COUNTRIES

Argentina

Esteso (1985) estimated an average of 1,150–1,250 cases of snakebite each year, 80% caused by *Bothrops diporus*, 18% by *B. alternatus*, 2% by *Crotalus durissus terrificus*, and only 0.01% by *Micrurus pyrrhocryptus*.

Aruba

Twelve cases of bites by the only indigenous front-fanged snake present, *Crotalus durissus unicolor*, were reported during a seven-year period (Hardy, 1992b). The adjacent islands of Curaçao and Bonaire (Netherlands Antilles) have no venomous front-fanged snakes.

Belize

Between 1980 and 1985, eight deaths were reported among 57 cases of snakebite (Martin, 1988–1989).

Bolivia

From 1948 to 1950, 63–115 deaths per year were attributed to deaths caused by venomous animals (Swaroop and Grab, 1954). Little recent information is available about the frequency of snakebites, but the majority of bites seen at the Clínica Bethesda in El Chapare (the tropics) are caused by *Bothrops* species. In the absence of treatment, most victims die of hemorrhage or extensive local necrosis complicated by infection. Two subspecies of *Crotalus durissus* known as cascabel (*C. d. terrificus* and *C. d. collilineatus*) occur in Bolivia, while *Lachesis muta* is known, misleadingly, as *cascabel pua* (Kempff-Mercado, 1977). Hospitals near Cochabamba (at Ibuelo, Villa Tunari, and Ivirgazama) admit 25–30 cases of snakebite each year. Amputations are commonly required. Antivenom is scarce, but deaths are rare. *Crotalus* accounts for 70% of bites and *Bothrops* for 30% (Stuart Fisher, pers. comm., 1998).

Brazil

In the nineteenth century, Sigaud (1844) described snakebite as common among the indigenous Amerindians of Brazil and a frequent cause of death in hunters. During their travels in Brazil (1817–1820), Spix and Martius (1824) met many people who had survived snakebites but were left weak and troubled with swollen and ulcerated legs. At the beginning of the twentieth century, Vital Brazil estimated 4,800 deaths from 19,200 probable bites in Brazil, most of the victims being previously healthy and productive people (Brazil, 1911). In 1949, an estimated 2,000 deaths occurred (Swaroop and Grab, 1954). During 1990–1993 the number of snakebite cases averaged 27,200 per year with 120 deaths per year, the overall case fatality being 0.5% (1.87% for *Crotalus* bites). *Bothrops atrox* is responsible for most bites in the Amazon region, *B. jararaca* dominates in the most populated areas of southeastern Brazil (where *B. jararacussu* has a notoriously high case fatality), *B. moojeni* in the central savanna region, and *B. erythromelas* in the dry northeastern part of the

country (Cardoso, 2000). In Belo Horizonte, Minas Gerais, 310 cases of snakebite were admitted to Hospital João XXIII over seven years. Fifty-six percent were caused by *Bothrops*, 32% by *Crotalus*, and 1% by *Lachesis* (Caiaffa et al., 1997).

At Cuiabá, Mato Grosso, 307 cases of snakebite were documented from 1993 to 1998 (Carvalho and Nogueira, 1998). Ninety-nine percent of clinically important bites were caused by *Bothrops moojeni* and *B. neuwiedi* (sensu lato). Of 108 severe cases of snakebite reported in 15 years in Goiás, Brazil, 65% were attributable to *Crotalus durissus collilineatus* (Vêncio and de Oliveira, 1980). In São José do Rio Preto, São Paulo State, 32% of snakebite victims were coffee plantation workers, and 88% of all bites were attributed to *Bothrops moojeni* (Kouyoumdjian and Polizelli, 1988). A survey carried out in 24 municipal districts in Amazonas State revealed an incidence of snakebite at least six times greater than the official returns suggested, with a case fatality of 1.3% and an annual mortality of 1.1 per 100,000 population (Cruz-Rocha et al., 1997). Over a period of eight years, an average of 197 bites per year were reported by the 34 municipalities of Amazonas, with a case fatality of 1% (Borges et al., 1999). About 200 cases of snakebites are admitted each year to a specialist hospital in Manaus, Brazil; 80% are caused by *Bothrops* species (Alcideia R. R. de Souza, pers. comm.). In Roraima State between 1992 and 1998, 309 cases of snakebite were reported; 82% were attributed to *Bothrops* species, 13.4% to *Crotalus*, 4.3% to *Lachesis*, and 0.5% to *Micrurus*. The case fatality was 3.9% (Nascimento, 2000). See Cardoso et al., 2003, for a valuable new review of Brazilian venomous snakes and the effects and management of envenomation by them.

Chile

The only venomous snakes in mainland Chile are opisthoglyphous colubrids, of which *Tachymenis peruvianus* and *Philodryas chamissonis* are the most important. Few reports of bites by these species have been published in the national medical literature (the first was in 1938; Schenone and Reyes, 1965), and no fatalities have occurred in Chile (Donoso-Barros, 1966; Schenone and Reyes, 1965). *Pelamis platurus* has been found on rare occasions in the waters off Easter Island (Isla de Pascua; Donoso-Barros, 1966), but no bites have been reported.

Colombia

Marinkelle (1966) estimated 821 deaths between 1945 and 1949 in Colombia, an incidence of 1.56 per 100,000 population per year. In the 1990s an average of 2,675 (±333 1 S.D.) cases of snakebite were reported each year. Twenty-five percent of these occurred in Antioquia and Chocó, where there is an incidence of 28–38 bites per 100,000 population per year. In this area of northwestern Colombia, *Bothrops* species are responsible for 95% of bites, with a case fatality of 5% and an incidence of permanent sequelae of 6% (Otero, 2000). In Bucaramanga, Santander, in eastern Colombia, 91% of 55 victims admitted over five years had been bitten by *Bothrops* species (Badillo et al., 1989). At Leticia (Amazonas) and Yopal (Casanare) in eastern Colombia, 56 cases of snakebite were admitted during a nine-month period (1996/7) with 1 fatality (Pineda et al., 2002).

Costa Rica

In 1943, 24 deaths were attributed to bites from venomous animals (Swaroop and Grab, 1954). Annual mortality (per

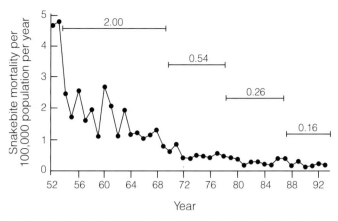

Fig. 261. The declining mortality from snakebite in Costa Rica. From Gutiérrez and Rojas, 1999.

100,000 population) has since declined, from about 5 in 1952 to 0.15 in 1996 (Gutiérrez and Rojas, 1999; Fig. 261). In 1979, 477 bites were reported (22.4/100,000 population) with a mortality of 0.75 per 100,000 (Bolaños, 1982). Between 1990 and 2000, the total number of snakebites varied from 423 (1999) to 590 (1992), averaging 504 per year. During this period the country's population increased from 2.8 to 3.8 million. The number of deaths ranged from 7 (1992) to 0 (2000). Incidence was maximal during the rainy season (May–November), and 46% of the victims were agricultural workers (Sasa and Vázquez, 2003). At San Isidro de El General, on the south Pacific versant of Costa Rica, 166 children (aged 1–13 years) were admitted with snakebite between 1972 and 1981; 49% of the bites were caused by *Bothrops asper* (Montalvan et al., 1983). In Limón on the Atlantic coast, 80 children bitten by snakes were admitted to the Tony Facio Hospital between 1985 and 1995 with a case fatality of 2.5%. *Bothrops asper* was responsible for the majority of identified cases. The incidence of snakebites in the region as a whole was 20 per 100,000 population per year (Saborio et al., 1998).

Ecuador

Between 1900 and 1946, 2,182 cases of snakebite were treated at Luis Vernaza Hospital in Guayaquil, with 87 deaths (Swaroop and Grab, 1954). In the year 1983–1984, 2,980 doses of antivenom were distributed throughout the country, which, at an average dose of two to three ampules per patient, suggests that more than 1,000 snakebite patients must have been treated. However, the Ministerio de Salud Pública estimates an annual requirement of 7,000–10,000 doses to treat the 1,200–1,400 cases of bites reported each year from 19 of the 21 provinces (Gonzalo Rivadeneira Naranjo, pers. comm.). Records from individual hospitals augment the information available. In the Santo Domingo de los Colorados Hospital, 62 snakebite patients were admitted during the year 1987–1988 (Mancheno and Vera, unpublished data), and in Hospital Vozandes del Oriente, Shell-Mera, Pastaza, an average of about 34 patients were admitted each year from 1980 to 1989 (Kerrigan, 1991). Chippaux (1998), quoting various sources, estimated more than 1,000 bites, 16–28 envenomings, and 0.2–1.2 deaths per 100,000 population per year, with a case fatality of 2.3–3.3%.

El Salvador

There are relatively few bites; a high proportion are caused by *Crotalus simus*.

French Guiana

Chippaux et al. (1984) and Chippaux (2002) reported an incidence of 45–590 bites, a morbidity of 75, and a mortality of 1.5 per 100,000 population per year. The case fatality was 2.2%. Among soldiers stationed in the country, the incidence of snakebite is 32 per 100,000 per year (Chippaux, 2002). During a period of 10 years, three fatalities were recorded (in Cayenne), attributed to *Crotalus d. durissus* (Hulin et al., 1982), *Bothrops*, and *Micrurus* (Chippaux, 1987). The intensive care unit in Cayenne reported 11 cases of snakebite during a 2-year period (Hulin et al., 1982). Four were attributed to *Lachesis muta*, 2 to *Bothrops atrox*, and the 1 fatal case to *C. d. durissus*. According to V. Debons (Starace, 1998), *Bothrops atrox* is the most frequent cause of envenoming cases seen in the hospital in Cayenne, but the rattlesnake is the most dangerous venomous snake.

Guatemala and Honduras

Guatemala and Honduras together record between 600 and 1,000 cases of snakebite each year (Gutiérrez et al., 1999).

Guyana

The literature on snakebite in Guyana is sparse and dates from the eighteenth and nineteenth centuries. Bites by *Bothrops atrox* (Bancroft, 1769), *Erythrolamprus aesculapii*, and *Xenodon severus* (Quelch, 1893) have been reported. David Attenborough (1956) saw an Amerindian bitten by a labaria (*B. atrox*). From 2000 to 2002, the Ministry of Health in Georgetown reported an average of 209 bites per year (male:female, 3.1:1), but fatalities were not recorded (Paul O'Reilly and Stan Brock, pers. comm.). It was clear from my discussions with staff at the country's only tertiary referral hospital in that city in 2002 that snakebite was a common cause of admission, especially in the rainy season. *Bothrops atrox* (labaria, but this name is also used nonspecifically) is the commonest snake in many areas and is responsible for most bites both in the coastal region and upcountry. Amerindians such as the Macushi of the Iwokrama Rain Forest Conservation Development Area are frequent victims of snakebites but usually rely on traditional treatments (Graham Watkins, pers. comm.). Other species responsible for bites include *Bothriopsis bilineata* (parrotsnake; see below), *Crotalus durissus* ssp. (rattlesnake), and *Lachesis muta* (bushmaster).

Martinique

Between 1991 and 1998 between 12 and 27 (average 20) *Bothrops lanceolatus* bites were recorded each year on the island (Laurent Thomas, pers. comm.).

Nicaragua

About 800 cases occur each year (Gutiérrez et al., 1999).

Panama

Between 1925 and 1951 the Gorgas Hospital in Panama City recorded 55 cases of snakebite, with seven deaths (Jutzy et al., 1953). Ten of the 19 identified snakes were *Bothrops asper*. Currently, more than 2,000 cases are thought to occur each year (Gutiérrez et al., 1999).

Paraguay

Most snakebites in the Paraguayan Chaco are attributable to *Bothrops diporus* and *B. mattogrossensis*. Among 323 snakebite cases admitted to a hospital in Asunción from 1945–1971, 53.5% were attributed to *B. neuwiedi* sensu lato, 37% to *B. jararaca*, and 4% to *Crotalus durissus terrificus* (Grassi and Ramírez, 1973).

Peru

The highest incidence of snakebites is at altitudes below 3,000 m on the Pacific coast and in the eastern Amazon region during the rainy season, December–April. High-risk occupations include agriculture, oil prospecting, mining, fishing, and hunting. There is even thought to be a small risk to tourists; for example, in the ruins of Machu Picchu (*Bothrops andianus*; see below). The most important among about 60 venomous species are *Bothrops atrox* and *Bothriopsis bilineata* in the Amazon region, and on the Pacific coast, *Bothrops barnetti* in the north and *B. pictus* and *B. roedingeri* in the central region. In 1999, 1,170 bites were recorded for the whole country. Between 1975 and 1992, 20–30 patients a year were admitted to the hospital in La Merced, Chanchamayo, but in the three years from 1998 to 2000, 170 cases were admitted (Villanueva Forero, 2000). In Pucallpa, in the department of Ucayali, 262 bites were recorded in 2000 (241 by *Bothrops*, 2 by *Lachesis*), with one death and 13 sequelae (Armando Yarleque and Luis Muñante, pers. comm.). At the regional hospital of Loreto, 65 cases of snakebite were admitted in the year 1998–1999 (Mosquera Leiva, 2000). The annual incidence of snakebites in Peru has been estimated at 4,500, with a 3% case fatality (Julio Demarini Caro, pers. comm., 2002).

Saint Lucia

An average of 12 bites by *Bothrops caribbaeus* occur each year, mainly near Anse la Raye and in the Roseau Valley. The last death was in the early 1990s.

Suriname

Bites by venomous snakes are said to be relatively rare (Oostburg, 1973), although potentially dangerous species such as *Bothrops atrox*, *Bothriopsis bilineata*, rattlesnakes, and *Lachesis muta* are common in the interior, and two cases of severe envenoming by *B. atrox* are described below.

Trinidad

Trinidad has four species of venomous snakes, Tobago none (Murphy, 1997). In the nineteenth century De Verteuil (1858) noted that although venomous snakes were common, bites were rare. He described two cases of fatal envenoming by *Micrurus lemniscatus diutius* (De Verteuil, 1858), and Mole (1924) recorded a fatal bite by an unidentified species of coralsnake and severe envenoming by a specimen of *Lachesis muta* from which the patient recovered. At Port-of-Spain General Hospital, 12 children were admitted with snakebites during the five-year period 1985–1989 but only 2 had actually been envenomed, probably by *Bothrops asper* (Bratt and Boos, 1992a, 1992b).

Uruguay

Only 15 deaths were attributed to bites by venomous animals during the period 1935–1946 (Swaroop and Grab, 1954). In the capital, Montevideo, only 41 cases were reported in a five-year period. *Bothrops alternatus* (crucera) and *B. pubescens* (yarará) were responsible (Revista Médica del Uruguay, 1983).

Venezuela

During the period 1947–1949, 271–635 snakebites per year with 122–149 resulting deaths were reported, an annual death rate of 3.1 per 100,000 population (Swaroop and Grab, 1954). In more recent years, between 2,500 and 3,000 bites are estimated to occur each year, with an average of 250 deaths (Roze, 1966a). Data from the Anuarios de Epidemiología y Estadística Vital indicate 13,618 bites and 1,448 deaths from 1955 to 1968, a case fatality of 9.4% (Dao-L., 1971). Between 1978 and 1982 there were 7.7 bites per 100,000 population per year with a 4.97% case fatality. Most patients were bitten by *Bothrops asper*. Fewer than 10% of patients were bitten by *Crotalus* or *Micrurus* species. At Leopoldo Manrique Hospital in Caracas, 60 cases of snakebite were admitted from 1996 to 1997. Among the 32 cases in which the snake could be identified, 26 were attributed to *Bothrops asper* (referred to as *B. lanceolatus*), 4 to *B. venezuelensis*, and 2 to *B. atrox*. There were no deaths (Rodriguez-Acosta et al., 2000).

Some of Venezuela's offshore islands are inhabited by crotalines. *Crotalus durissus cumanensis* is found on Morro de la Iguana and Tamarindo (Islas los Testigos), and this subspecies and *Porthidium lansbergii* occur on Isla de Margarita, but there are no reports of bites.

VENOM APPARATUS

The oral glands of snakes include sublingual, supralabial, and infralabial glands with mucous and serous secretions; Duvernoy's glands of Colubridae; and the venom glands of Elapidae and Viperidae, which produce toxic secretions.

Eighty percent of colubrid snakes have some kind of Duvernoy's gland behind and below the eye, surrounded by muscles that may help to express its secretions (*adductores superficialis*, *medialis*, and *profundus* and *retractor quadrati*). Elapid and viperid venom glands consist of a main gland behind and below the eye and an anterior accessory gland. In elapids, the gland is compressed by the *adductor externus superficialis* (=*levator anguli oris*) and *pterygoideus* muscles, while in viperids this is accomplished by a *compressor glandulae* together with *adductor externus profundus* and *pterygoideus* muscles (Kochva, 1978).

Some coralsnakes have infralabial glands in the lower jaw that also secrete venom, which is conducted by shallow grooves in the mandibular teeth (Dix, 1978).

Colubrid snakes capable of envenoming humans are either opisthoglyphous (Pls. 1237, 1404, 1405) or aglyphous (Pl. 1339), with the fangs or enlarged grooveless teeth being at the posterior end of the maxilla. Elapids, including seasnakes, are proteroglyphous, their front fangs being mounted on a relatively immovable maxillary. Vipers are solenoglyphous; that is, their fangs are mounted on a rotatable maxillary so that they can be erected during the strike (Figs. 262–264) and folded flat against the upper jaw when not in use (Fig. 265).

Colubrids tend to hold on and chew after striking in order to engage their posterior maxillary fangs or teeth, but in some cases a rapid strike and disengagement has proved sufficient to result in envenoming. Coralsnakes also sustain their grip and chew after the strike. Crotaline snakes strike with a stabbing

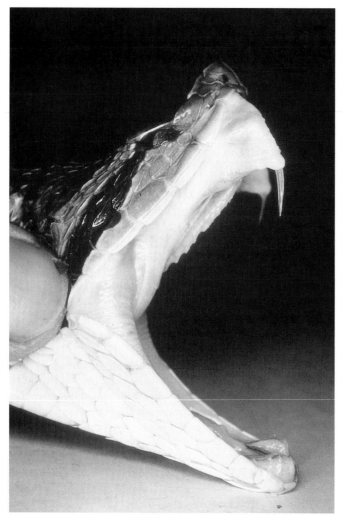

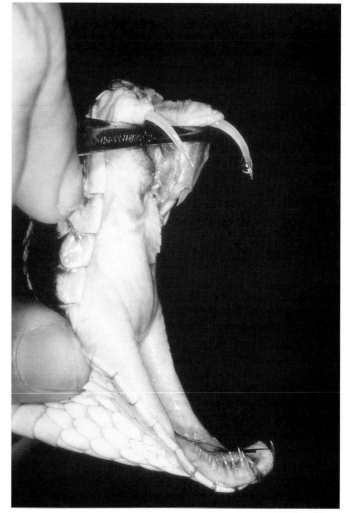

Fig. 262. Erect fangs of *Bothrops jararaca*. Copyright David A. Warrell.

Fig. 263. Erect fangs of *Bothrops jararacussu*. Copyright David A. Warrell.

motion of their long, erect front fangs and disengage immediately, although *Atropoides*, *Bothriechis*, some *Bothriopsis*, and juveniles of many species are exceptions.

"Dry" Bites

Whether or not snakes can control the release of venom during the strike, or even regulate the dose of venom injected according to the size of the prey (Hayes, 1995), remains controversial. Nevertheless, bites by venomous species that do not result in envenoming are well documented, even when puncture marks in the skin of the victim confirm penetration by the fangs. Russell et al. (1997) quoted figures for "dry" bites of 58% for Panama, 40% for Central American countries (1925–1931), and 45% for Guatemala (1980–1990). Among 40 cases of snakebite seen in Uberlândia, Brazil, 30% of *Bothrops* bites and 43% of *Crotalus* bites resulted in no clinical or laboratory evidence of local or systemic envenoming (Silveira and Nishioka, 1995); only 34 of 37 bites by *B. moojeni* in São José do Rio Preto, São Paulo State, Brazil, resulted in signs of envenoming (Kouyoumdjian and Polizelli, 1988). It is not clear whether these dry bites represent a mechanically ineffective bite or an intentionally defensive bite in which the snake withholds its venom.

VENOM COMPOSITION AND PROPERTIES

Venom is easily milked from viperid and elapid snakes by encouraging the snake to strike through a membrane (Pl. 1406) or by gentle massage over the venom glands. Increasingly, short-term general anesthesia using agents such as sevoflurane, halothane, or even carbon dioxide is being used to assist this process.

Snake venoms are complex mixtures of enzymes, toxins, and smaller peptides. More than 90% of the dry weight of venom consists of polypeptides. These venoms are a rich source of enzymes (molecular weight [Mw] 13–150 kDa), which form 80–95% of viperid and 25–70% of elapid venoms. Digestive hydrolases include proteinases, exo- and endopeptidases, phosphodiesterases, and phospholipases. Hyaluronidase, present in all snake venoms, promotes the spread of other venom components through tissues.

Procoagulant enzymes are found in the venoms of Central and South American vipers (Hutton and Warrell, 1993). Thrombinlike enzymes (serine proteases) such as batroxobin (*B. asper*, *B. marajoensis*, *B. moojeni*), reptilase (*B. atrox*), and mutase (*Lachesis muta*) split fibrinopeptides from the fibrinogen molecule, resulting in nonpolymerized fibrin. Unlike physiological thrombin, the action of snake venom thrombinlike enzymes is not inhibited by heparin (Nahas et al., 1975). Thrombinlike

Fig. 264. Erect fangs of *Crotalus durissus terrificus*. Copyright David A. Warrell.

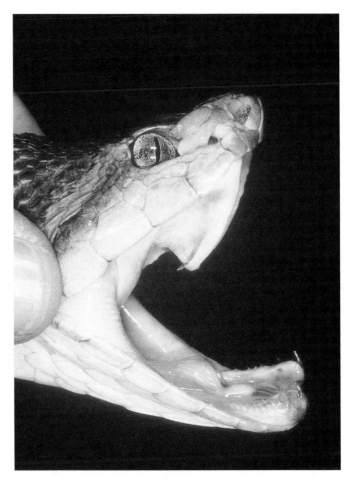

Fig. 265. Partially collapsed fangs of *Bothrops atrox*, Icoaraci, Distrito de Belém, Pará, Brazil. Copyright David A. Warrell.

enzymes are also found in the venoms of *Bothrops alternatus, B. brazili, B. jararaca, B. neuwiedi* (sensu lato), *B. jararacussu,* and *Bothriopsis bilineata.*

Prothrombin-activating enzymes are found in many *Bothrops* venoms, including those of *B. erythromelas* and *B. asper,* and also in the venoms of *Bothriopsis taeniata* and *B. bilineata.*

Factor X–activating enzymes are found in most *Bothrops* venoms, including *B. jararacussu* and *B. erythromelas,* and in *Bothriopsis taeniata* venom. Venoms of some vipers, such as *Atropoides mexicanus,* possess little or no procoagulant activity and do not result in defibrination.

Phospholipases attack the phospholipid constituents of cell membranes, leading to cell lysis. Some phospholipases A_2 damage muscle. These consist of enzymatically active (aspartate 49) and enzymatically inactive (lysine 49) components known as the *Bothrops* myotoxins. Crotamine and myotoxin *a* from *Crotalus* venoms cause monocytes to swell by opening their voltage-dependent sodium channels.

Some phospholipases A_2, like the prototype β-bungarotoxins (from the venom of the Chinese krait, *Bungarus multicinctus*), bind to the presynaptic membrane at peripheral neuromuscular junctions and cause paralysis by preventing the release of acetylcholine from nerve endings. The first snake neurotoxin ever isolated was crotoxin from the venom of *Crotalus durissus terrificus.* Crotoxin consists of a basic B component (phospholipase), Mw 12 kDa, and an acidic A component (crotapotin),

Mw 10 kDa. These toxins have a triphasic action, initially inhibiting, then facilitating, and finally blocking release of acetylcholine (Marlas and Bon, 1982).

Metalloproteinases are the hemorrhagic factors responsible for life-threatening spontaneous systemic hemorrhage following envenoming by Viperidae. They may contain disintegrin and cysteine-rich domains (e.g., jararhagin from *B. jararaca* venom). Studies of the mechanism of local tissue damage caused by *B. asper* venom have demonstrated that metalloproteinases cause hemorrhage, myonecrosis, blistering, and edema (Lomonte et al., 1994), and that synthetic matrix metalloproteinase inhibitors such as Batimastat can prevent such local tissue damage (Escalante et al., 2000). The myotoxin II (PLA_2 isoform) from this venom also releases interleucin-6 (IL-6), a cytokine, from macrophages, which stimulates a local inflammatory response and contributes to the destructive effects of envenoming (Lomonte et al., 1993; Rucavado et al., 2002).

Kininogenases (arginine ester hydrolases) release bradykinin from bradykininogen, as first demonstrated in *B. jararaca* venom (Rocha e Silva et al., 1949).

Polypeptide neurotoxins (Mw 5–10 kDa) are found in elapid (including seasnake) venoms. The alpha neurotoxins (also known as curarimimetic or postsynaptic toxins) found in some coralsnake (*Micrurus*) venoms compete with acetylcholine for binding sites at peripheral neuromuscular junctions. Elapid cytotoxins (cardiotoxins), present in some *Micrurus* venoms, cause cardiovascular changes in some animals but probably not in humans.

Low-molecular-weight (Mw < 1.5 kDa) compounds in venoms include metal constituents of enzymes, lipids, nucleosides, carbohydrates, and amines (such as 5-hydroxytryptamine and acetylcholine). Venoms of *Bothrops jararaca*, *B. alternatus*, *B. atrox*, *B. cotiara*, *B. insularis*, *B. neuwiedi* (sensu lato), *Crotalus durissus terrificus*, *Lachesis*, *Atropoides mexicanus*, *A. picadoi*, and possibly others contain oligopeptide enzyme inhibitors that block the action of bradykinin-deactivating enzymes and angiotensin-converting enzyme (ACE), so lowering the blood pressure of the prey or human victim. These structures were the prototypes of the widely used synthetic drugs known as ACE inhibitors, which are dipeptidyl-carboxypeptidase inhibitors. C-type natriuretic peptide is another blood pressure–lowering component of *B. jararaca* venom (Murayama et al., 1997).

Lethal Potency of Venoms

The median lethal dose (LD_{50}) of many Central and South American snake venoms has been measured in laboratory mice (Mebs, 1978; Sanchez et al., 1992). Some examples of figures for intravenous LD_{50}, in decreasing order of lethal potency, are listed below:

Crotalus durissus collilineatus	1.86 μg/20 g mouse
C. d. terrificus	1.93
Bothrops jararacussu	2.8
B. moojeni	7.8
B. neuwiedi (sensu lato)	12.1
Micrurus frontalis (sensu lato)	15.0
B. alternatus	15.0
B. jararaca	16.7
B. atrox	28.7
Lachesis muta	113.8

Intraspecies Variation in Venom Composition

The best-known example of geographical variation in the venom composition of a single species or subspecies is *Crotalus durissus* in Brazil. Crotamine, a phospholipase myotoxin that causes contraction of the leg extensors in mice, is found in specimens of in *C. d. terrificus* from northwestern São Paulo and Argentina, and in *C. d. cascavella* from Paraná and Ceará, but not in specimens of *C. d. collilineatus* from northeastern Brazil and Goiás. Crotamine may or may not be present in the venom of snakes from southeastern São Paulo and Minas Gerais (Schenberg, 1959). In several species of Central and South American vipers, venom composition changes as the snake grows older (ontogenic variation). The venom of *B. asper* shows decreasing lethal potency and proteolytic, hemorrhagic, and edema-forming effects with age, but increasing hemolytic and myonecrotic effects. The venom of *B. atrox* shows decreasing lethal potency and number of protein constituents but increasing protein concentration, and the venoms of other *Bothrops* species show decreasing lethal potency and procoagulant activity. Venoms of *C. d. terrificus* and *C. simus* (previously *C. d. durissus*) show a decrease in crotoxin and other myotoxic hemorrhagic edema-producing and proteolytic activities with age, and the venom of *Lachesis stenophrys* shows increasing lethal potency and proteolytic activity (Saravia et al., 2002; Warrell, 1987).

CLINICAL FEATURES OF ENVENOMING

The extensive multilingual literature on snakebite in South America is characterized by a tendency to rationalize the clinical features into four discrete syndromes—bothropic, crotalic, elapidic, and lachetic envenoming—following the influential writings of Gastão Rosenfeld of the Instituto Butantan, São Paulo, Brazil (see Rosenfeld, 1971). Although this approach may be justified on pragmatic grounds to "permit diagnosis of the accident and the consequent therapeutic handling and prognosis without identification of the snake . . . because most physicians are unable to classify venomous snakes and it is rare for the patient or family to bring the snake that caused the accident" (Rosenfeld, 1971), it has tended to conceal important differences in the features of envenoming caused by different genera and species. It is clear, for example, that envenoming by *Bothrops lanceolatus* and *B. caribbaeus* has some distinctive pathophysiological features, such as the occlusion of major arteries (see below). Many accounts of series of cases observed at a particular hospital mention that some of the victims brought the snake responsible for the bite, but the clinical and laboratory findings are usually grouped together, making it impossible to discern whether envenoming by a particular species had any distinctive features. Another problem is the arbitrary grading of clinical severity (mild, moderate, and severe), which is rarely validated on prognostic grounds; often represents a casual grouping of symptoms, signs, and results of investigations; and ignores the sometimes rapid evolution of envenoming after the patient has been admitted to the hospital.

Symptoms and signs in victims of snakebite are the result of anxiety; the direct effect of different venom components on the tissues; indirect effects such as complement activation, autopharmacological release of endogenous vasoactive mediators, and the release of inflammatory mediators such as cytokines; acquired hypersensitivity to venom components (anaphylaxis); effects of treatment; and complications such as secondary bacterial infections.

ENVENOMING BY COLUBRIDAE

At least 45 New World genera in the family Colubridae include rear-fanged, or opisthoglyphous, species that have several enlarged, grooved teeth at the rear of the mouth on the posterior ends of the maxillae (McKinstry, 1983). The enlarged teeth aid in conduction of serous secretions produced in the Duvernoy's gland (Rosenberg et al., 1985; Sakai et al., 1984). These secretions have multiple roles (Kardong, 1980b, 1982, 1996, 2002; Weinstein and Kardong, 1994), including that of envenoming potential prey (Rodríguez-Robles, 1994). Even secretions not normally employed in prey acquisition may be incidentally toxic (Kardong, 1996). Most colubrids have Duvernoy's glands, sometimes also referred to as parotid glands (Kapus, 1964; Phisalix, 1922), although the latter term is erroneous (Tyler et al., 2001). Duvernoy's glands are branched, tubular structures situated behind each eye (Kochva, 1978; Rodríguez-Robles, 1994; Taub, 1967).

About three dozen New World colubrid genera include aglyphous species that have enlarged, nongrooved teeth at the rear of the mouth and salivary glands that are histologically similar to the Duvernoy's gland (Taub, 1967). At least 10 types of oral glands are collectively represented in the Colubridae, and several may be present in a single species (Kochva, 1978; Kochva and Gans, 1970; Taub, 1966). Whether or not enlarged teeth (grooved or not) are present, a bite from a colubrid snake can introduce toxic substances.

Many opisthoglyphs are capable of delivering a fatal bite to small vertebrate prey such as lizards and frogs (Duellman, 1958b; Goodman, 1953). The low-pressure venom delivery system that colubrids use to inject venom is often inefficient as a defense mechanism, however, and members of this group are rarely dangerous to humans (Kardong and Lavin-Murcio, 1993; Kardong and Young, 1991). We know little about the toxic effects of colubrid saliva and other secretions, and we know nothing about geographical variation in these products. Secondary envenoming may be just as dangerous to humans as colubrid venom. For example, a snake that has recently consumed a toad may have residue of that toad's defensive parotid secretions in its mouth. Alternatively, toxic secretions from the snake's oral glands may be present before, during, or just after feeding. New World genera such as *Erythrolamprus*, *Helicops*, *Hydrodynastes*, *Leptodeira*, *Oxybelis*, and *Xenodon* are known to bite with or without evidence of envenoming.

Studies of the Duvernoy's secretions of *Hydrodynastes gigas* (Glenn et al., 1992) and *Philodryas* (Assakura et al., 1992) have demonstrated toxicities in mice higher than those of some viperids in the genera *Bothrops* and *Crotalus*. Investigations of other species' glandular secretions have revealed myotoxins (Prado-Franceschi et al., 1998), neurotoxins (Heleno et al., 1997; Levinson et al., 1976), and proteolytic components (Finley et al., 1994; Laporta-Ferreira and Salomão, 1991; Mackessy, 2002). Many species of colubrids have not been investigated owing to their small size or secretive nature, and the effect of their venom on humans is unknown. While the risk from these species should not be exaggerated, it is prudent to recognize the potential danger.

At least 37 colubrid genera worldwide include species that have been implicated in venomous bites to humans (Minton, 1996; Valls-Moraes and Lema, 1997; Gutiérrez and Sasa, 2002; Prado-Franceschi and Hyslop, 2002). The first documented cases of envenoming by snakes previously thought to be nonvenomous involved a mock viper, *Xenodon severus*, and a false coral, *Erythrolamprus aesculapii*, in Guyana (Minton and Minton, 1980; Quelch, 1893). Because venomous colubrids are

found throughout most of the family's geographical range, and because their toxins are many, varied, and distinct from those of elapids and viperids (Minton and Weinstein, 1987), it is likely that colubrid oral secretions have evolved independently several times within these groups (Minton, 1996). Although it is questionable whether any colubrid snake can be regarded as definitely nonvenomous, it seems likely that continued investigation will establish other primary roles for many of their toxic secretions.

Envenoming by several species of opisthoglyphous colubrid snakes in Africa and Asia have resulted in human deaths, and three or four Latin American species have also been implicated in these very rare fatal accidents (Minton, 1990b). No colubrid species native to North America has been implicated in bites causing more than localized symptoms of envenoming (Minton, 1986), and opisthoglyphs are uncommon in the United States and Canada. Nevertheless, familiar species that have traditionally been regarded as inoffensive, such as gartersnakes, have produced symptoms of envenoming in humans (Hayes and Hayes, 1985; Minton, 1979a, 1979b; Vest, 1981a). Tables 60–62 list the 4 genera reputed to have caused human fatalities, 24 genera that have been implicated in human envenoming (Minton, 1996; Valls-Moraes and Lema, 1997), and 13 genera that have envenomed the authors and their colleagues or are suspected of being

Table 61. Distribution of rear-fanged or mildly venomous colubrid snakes by genus in the Caribbean region.

Genus	Caribbean region	Saint Lucia	Martinique
Alsophis	X		
Clelia	X	X	
Diadophis	X		
Leptodeira	X		
Liophis	X	X	X
Mastigodryas	X		

Note: Genera listed are those implicated in human envenomings according to the literature or to field experiences known to us, as well as those likely to cause envenoming. The list is not exhaustive.

Table 60. Distribution of rear-fanged or mildly venomous colubrid snakes by genus in North and Central America, including islands.

Genus	Canada	United States	Mexico	Belize	Guatemala	Honduras	El Salvador	Nicaragua	Costa Rica	Panama
Clelia			X	X	X	X	X	X	X	X
Coluber	X	X	X	X	X					
Coniophanes		X	X	X	X	X	X	X	X	X
Conophis			X	X	X	X	X	X	X	?
Crisantophis					X	X	X	X	X	
Diadophis	X	X	X							
Erythrolamprus						X		X	X	X
Heterodon	X	X	X							
Hypsiglena	X	X	X							
Leptodeira		X	X	X	X	X	X	X	X	X
Leptophis		X		X	X	X	X	X	X	X
Liophis									X	X
Mastigodryas										X
Oxybelis		X	X	X	X	X	X	X	X	X
Pliocercus			X	X	X	X	X	X	X	X
Rhinobothryum						X		X	X	X
Symphimus			X	X						
Thamnophis	X	X	X	X	X	X	X	X	X	X
Trimorphodon		X	X		X	X	X	X	X	
Xenodon[a]			X	X	X	X	X	X	X	X

Note: Genera listed include those implicated in human envenomings according to the literature or to field experiences known to us, as well as those likely to cause envenoming. The list is not exhaustive.

[a] Capable of causing systemic and allegedly fatal envenoming.

Table 62. Distribution of rear-fanged or mildly venomous colubrid snakes by genus in South America, including islands.

Genus	Colombia	Venezuela	Trinidad/ Tobago	Guyana	Suriname	French Guiana	Brazil	Ecuador	Peru	Bolivia	Paraguay	Uruguay	Argentina	Chile
Alsophis								X	X					X
Apostolepis	X			X		X	X		X	X	X		X	
Boiruna							X						X	
Clelia	X	X	X	X	X	X	X	X	X	X	X	X	X	
Coniophanes	X						X	X	X					
Conophis	X													
Elapomorphus						X	X			X	X	X	X	
Erythrolamprus	X	X	X	X	X	X	X	X	X	X			X	
Helicops	X	X	X	X	X	X	X	X	X	X		X	X	
Hydrodynastes	X	X		X	X	X	X			X	X		X	
Hydrops	X	X	X	X	X	X	X	X	X	X	X		X	
Leptodeira	X	X	X	X	X	X	X	X	X	X	X		X	
Leptophis	X	X	X	X	X	X	X	X	X	X	X	X	X	
Liophis	X	X	X	X	X	X	X	X	X	X	X	X	X	
Lystrophis							X			X	X	X	X	
Mastigodryas	X	X	X	X	X	X	X	X	X	X	X	X	X	
Oxybelis	X	X	X	X	X	X	X	X	X	X				
Phalotris[a]							X			X	X	X	X	
Philodryas[a]	X	X		X	X	X	X	X	X	X	X	X	X	X
Pliocercus	X	?					?	X						
Ptychophis							X							
Rhinobothryum	X	X		?	X	X	X	X	X	?	X			
Tachymenis[a]						?			X	X				X
Thamnodynastes	X	X	X	X	X	X	X	X	X	X	X	X	X	
Tomodon							X				X	X	X	
Tropidodryas							X							
Waglerophis	X			X	X	X	X	X	X		X		X	
Xenodon[a]	X	X		X	X	X	X	X	X	X	X		X	
Xenoxybelis	X	X		X	X	X	X	X	X	X	X		X	

Note: Genera listed include those implicated in human envenomings according to the literature or to field experiences known to us, as well as those likely to cause envenoming. The list is not exhaustive.
 a Known to be capable of causing systemic and allegedly fatal envenoming.

capable of envenoming. Twenty genera occur from Canada and the United States through Central America; 29 are found in South America, including on offshore islands; and 6 occur in the Caribbean region. Some of these species resemble venomous elapids or viperids and are discussed further in the species accounts under Similar Species.

Severe envenoming is usually thought to be possible only if the snake is able to engage its rear fangs and chew on the wound. All severe colubrid envenomings exhibit somewhat similar features. The interval between the bite and the appearance of signs of systemic envenoming may be many hours. Early systemic symptoms include nausea, vomiting, colicky abdominal pain, and headache. More severe symptoms include bleeding from old and recent wounds, spontaneous gingival bleeding, epistaxis, hematemesis, melena, subarachnoid or intracerebral hemorrhage, hematuria, and extensive ecchymoses. Intravascular hemolysis and microangiopathic hemolysis have been described. Most fatalities resulted from renal failure many days after the bite. Local effects of envenoming by dangerous African and Asian colubrid snakes are usually trivial (with the possible exception of *Dispholidus typus*, the boomslang) but in Latin America envenoming often entails considerable local swelling and bruising (Pls. 1407 and 1408, Fig. 266). Laboratory investigations reveal incoagulable blood, defibrin(ogen)ation, elevated fibrin(ogen) degradation products, thrombocytopenia, and anemia, sometimes with evidence of hemolysis and, rarely, renal failure. These abnormalities are explained by disseminated intravascular coagulation triggered by venom prothrombin activators.

Local or systemic envenoming has been reported following bites by some 40 species from 26 genera of New World colubrid snakes. Most of these are disussed individually below. Some of the reports are difficult to evaluate because they were written by nonmedically qualified herpetologists who were unable to distinguish between direct effects of the venom and allergic effects in those who may have been previously sensitized. Systemic envenoming may be wrongly inferred when the victim develops symptoms resulting from anxiety and hyperventilation (e.g., lightheadedness, acroparesthesiae, and carpopedal spasm). Auto-observations and self-reported cases of envenoming are rarely supported by results of laboratory investigations. Particularly tantalizing are reports of fatal envenoming by colubrids in which little or no clinical informa-

tion is provided. It may be impossible to decide whether the fatality was caused by the venom itself, by treatment, or by some intercurrent chronic condition. In most cases of envenoming reported by herpetologists, the identification of the snake responsible can be assumed reliable; however, this may not always be the case (D. G. Cook, 1984; Johnson, 1988). For these reasons, the literature on toxic colubrids should be read critically and future cases should if possible be examined and investigated by physicians.

COLUBRID SNAKES CAUSING SYSTEMIC AND ALLEGEDLY FATAL ENVENOMING

Genus *Phalotris* (Pls. 1230–1232)

Phalotris lemniscatus trilineatus (formerly *Elapomorphus bilineatus*), Argentine black-headed snake, cabeça-preta

In Rio Grande do Sul, Lema (1978b) was bitten between his index and middle fingers by a specimen 20 cm in TL that did not release immediately. Soon after, an unbearable burning sensation spread through the bitten hand. Two hours later, the bitten area was mildly red and swollen and he had developed a severe headache. There was bleeding and severe pain at the site of the fang punctures. He became oliguric, his urine appearing cloudy and brownish and eventually "Coca-Cola" colored, suggesting hemoglobinuria, hematuria, or both. Pain and "phlebitis" involved the entire bitten arm. He continued to bleed from his mouth and required blood transfusion. He developed renal failure and on the fourth day passed melena stool, indicating gastrointestinal hemorrhage. The "phlebitis" persisted for 20 days, the gingival bleeding for 8 days, and the renal failure for 6 days. Eventually, he made a complete recovery.

Remarks This species is clearly capable of causing fatal envenoming, but nothing is known of the nature of its venom. The features described by Lema are reminiscent of severe envenoming by African and Asian colubrids: coagulopathy, spontaneous systemic hemorrhage, possible intravascular hemolysis, and acute renal failure.

Genus *Philodryas* (Pls. 1233–1240)

Philodryas olfersii (Pls. 1237–1238, 1404, 1407, 1408), Amazonian green racer, cobra cipó, cobra verde

Bites by *P. olfersii* are common in parts of Brazil. In Cuiabá, Mato Grosso, two-thirds of "medically unimportant" bites are inflicted by this species (Carvalho and Nogueira, 1998). Martins (1916) described and illustrated envenoming in a 21-year-old man bitten on the finger by this species. The bitten finger felt hot, very painful, and stiff. Within two hours swelling had extended to the elbow, and it persisted for six days. There were no generalized symptoms. Silva-Júnior (1956) also quoted this case (2a observação) together with a second case in which there was pain and swelling (5a observação). Kraus and Werner (1931) illustrated swelling and bruising of the arm following a bite by this species. Other descriptions of local symptoms caused by bites of *P. olfersii* refer to immediate swelling and intense pain with enlargement of local lymph glands (Lema, 1978a). In Misiones, Argentina, pain, swelling, bruising, and mild coagulopathy developed in a 26-year-old man, and similar

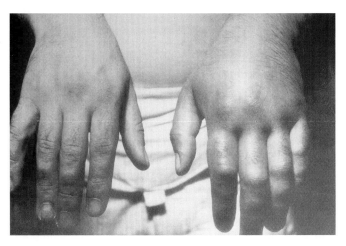

Fig. 266. Persistent swelling following a bite by *Hydrodynastes gigas* in a zookeeper. Copyright Dave Ball.

symptoms but without coagulopathy developed in a 21-year-old woman (Orduna et al., 1994 [The snake illustrated is *Liophis miliaris semiaureus*, not *P. olfersii*!]; Martino et al., 2001). Nickerson and Henderson (1976) described a case in which one fang punctured the skin for about four seconds. There was swelling of the whole hand within seven hours followed by painful enlargement of the regional lymph nodes. The swelling persisted for four days. On Ilha Solteira, Brazil, a male herpetologist was bitten on the first finger and thumb. He noticed a transient (20 seconds) accentuation of his red-green vision, severe pain locally and in the axillary lymph nodes, and bruising. He had to keep the arm in a sling for 20 days (Pedro Federsoni, pers. comm.). Kuch (1999) reported envenoming by *P. o. latirostris*. Ribeiro et al. (1999) reviewed case records of 43 patients admitted to Hospital Vital Brazil, Instituto Butantan, from 1982 to 1990 with *P. olfersii* bites. Seventy-two percent of the bites were inflicted on hands. In all 11 cases in which blood coagulability was tested, it proved to be normal. The only recorded systemic symptoms were in a 2-year-old child who vomited three times and developed abdominal pain. Ribeiro et al. (1999) pointed out that the clinical symptoms might be confused with symptoms of mild envenoming by a viper, leading to inappropriate treatment with antivenom.

Brief details have been published of two children bitten by *P. olfersii* in Cachoeira do Sul, Brazil, where this species is known as cobra cipó or cobra verde. One of them is said to have died after developing massive local swelling and hypovolemic shock ("third spacing") attributable to vascular damage (Secretaria da Saúde, 1996; see also Salomão and Di-Bernardo, 1995).

In French Guiana, bites by *Philodryas* species were reported to have caused inflammation graded 2 out of a maximum of 3 (2/3+), necrosis (1/3+), and hemorrhage (1/3+), but no further details were given (Chippaux, 1987).

In Brazil, a patient bitten on the arm by *P. olfersii* experienced inexplicable persistent muscle weakness in the legs for 14 days, long after the other symptoms and signs of envenoming had disappeared (Silva and Buononato, 1984).

Venom Gland and Venom Properties of *Philodryas* The anatomy and histology of the salivary glands of a related species, *P. patagoniensis*, have been studied in detail (Lopes et al., 1982). The venom of *P. olfersii* possesses fibrin(ogen)olytic, hemorrhagic, and edema-forming proteins, but has no thrombinlike, procoagulant, phospholipase A_2, or platelet-aggregating activity (Assakura et al., 1992, 1994). Postsynaptic neurotoxic activity, more potent in avian than murine nerve muscle preparations, was demonstrated by Prado-Franceschi et al. (1996), and a myotoxin with some potassium channel–blocking activity by Prado-Franceschi et al. (1998).

Remarks More is known about the structure of the venom apparatus, composition of venom, and effects of envenoming for *P. olfersii* than for any other Latin American colubrid. It is clear that the vast majority of those bitten are not envenomed, but that on the rare occasions when the snake is enabled to inject its venom, local pain, swelling, and bruising may result. Systemic envenoming is extremely rare but must be regarded as potentially life-threatening through the same pathophysiological processes that have resulted in fatal envenoming by colubrid snakes in Africa and Asia.

Genus *Tachymenis*

Tachymenis peruvianus, culebra de cola corta, culebra listada (Pl. 1312)

According to Schenone and Reyes (1965), bites by this species in Chile cause local pain that spreads rapidly to affect the whole limb. The progressively swollen limb is pale or violaceous in color. Ecchymoses or blisters containing serosanguinous fluid develop at the site of the bite, and there is also bruising along the path of lymphatics. These symptoms resolve in four to seven days. The majority of patients experience generalized symptoms including fever, restlessness, and distress. No deaths have been reported in Chile, but Vellard (1955) and Lema (1978b) mentioned a fatal case from Peru without giving any clinical details.

Remarks Nothing is known about the venom of this potentially dangerous species.

Genus *Xenodon* (Pls. 1340–1358)

This genus is widespread from Mexico throughout Central and South America, with one species, *X. severus*, attaining a large size. These snakes frequently feed on *Bufo marinus*, which produces copious quantities of toxic secretions when stressed.

Xenodon severus, Amazonian false viper (Pls. 1356 and 1357)

Bites in Guyana were reported to cause local pain and swelling (Quelch, 1893), but in Ecuador, Orcés (1948) cited a report by Jorge Olállo of the death of a child from the bite of this species (local name yana yuta). In Chanchamayo, Peru, a patient developed local pain, swelling, a small bruise, and mildly prolonged clotting times (Julio Demarini Caro, pers. comm.).

COLUBRID SNAKES CAUSING LOCAL ENVENOMING

Genus *Alsophis* (Pl. 1024)

Snakes of this genus are found throughout the Greater and Lesser Antilles, in Chile, and in the Galápagos Archipelago.

Alsophis cantherigerus (formerly *Dromicus angulifer* and *A. angulifer*), jubo

Bites of this species are reported to cause local bruising and swelling (Neill, 1954). The first report of envenoming was by Don Felipe Poey (1873) in Cuba, who described the case of a 60-year-old man bitten on the hand. The pain was so severe that he could not sleep, and swelling spread rapidly up to the axilla and onto his side over the next six hours. The signs persisted for six days, but he was disabled for months (Poey, 1873). Another patient, bitten on the thumb by this species in a suburb of Havana, developed marked inflammation of the hand, arm, and the adjacent area of the chest (Jaume, 1983; Jaume and Garrido, 1980).

Alsophis portoricensis, Puerto Rican racer

The patient reported by Heatwole and Banuchi (1966) was bitten on the index finger. There was immediate swelling, itching, pain, and hematoma formation at the site of the bite. Over the next few hours swelling and pain spread to involve the entire arm, axilla, and adjacent part of the chest, with enlargement of epitrochlear and axillary lymph nodes and later development of discoid ecchymoses, lymphangitis, and inflammation of the arm. There was residual atrophy of the tip of the bitten finger.

Genus *Apostolepis* (Pls. 1026–1033)

This genus comprises small, semifossorial snakes similar to *Leptomicrurus* in body shape. I know of no published cases of envenoming involving *Apostolepis*, but rumors persist in South America that it is capable of doing so.

Genus *Boiruna*

Boiruna maculata (Pls. 1045 and 1046)

This species is said to have caused envenoming in Brazil (Santos-Costa and Di-Bernardo, 2001; Santos-Costa et al., 2000).

Genus *Clelia* (Pls. 1056–1061)

Clelia plumbea, muçurana (Pl. 1059)

In Goiânia, Goiás, Brazil, a 1.4-m specimen bit a four-year-old girl on the thigh. Ten hours later there was swelling and bruising up to the groin with visible enlargement of inguinal glands. Blood coagulation was normal. The symptoms subsided over the next three days (Pinto-Leite et al., 1991). Chippaux (1987), writing about envenoming in French Guiana, recorded inflammatory (2/3+), necrotic (1/3+), and hemorrhagic (2/3+) effects of *C. clelia* bites without giving further details.

Genus *Coluber*

This genus is Holarctic in distribution, and although no North American species of *Coluber* has been implicated, several Old World species have been responsible for severe bites (Mamonov, 1977). There is evidence that at least one Old World species produces a salivary neurotoxin (Bedry et al., 1998).

Genus *Coniophanes* (Pls. 1062–1064)

Coniophanes imperialis (Pls. 1062 and 1063)

Two bites, one self-induced, caused local pain, itching, and burning, with redness, numbness, and swelling involving half the bitten limb and persisting for three or more days (Brown, 1939). Other species in this genus, including *C. piceivittis* (Pl. 1064) in Costa Rica, are capable of causing local pain and swelling (Minton and Mebs, 1978). *Coniophanes fissidens*, while less willing to bite, can also produce a painful wound.

Genus *Conophis*

Conophis lineatus (Pl. 1065) and *C. vittatus*, guarda camino

Bites by these species in southern Mexico and Central America have caused local pain and bleeding with bruising and swelling, sometimes involving the entire bitten limb (Campbell, 1998; Johanboeke, 1974; Taylor and Smith,1939; Wellman, 1963). Ditmars (1931) described a bite inflicted on Douglas March in Honduras by a specimen of *C. lineatus* 45 cm in TL. There was immediate burning pain and local swelling.

Johnson (1988) described and illustrated a bite inflicted by *C. vittatus* in Jalisco, Mexico. There was transient burning pain at the site of the bite on a finger, followed by swelling that spread to involve the dorsum of the hand. A bite originally thought to have been caused by *Stenorrhina freminvillei* (Pl. 1039) in Yucatán, Mexico (D. G. Cook, 1984), was reattributed by Johnson (1988) to *C. lineatus concolor* on the basis of the published photograph of the snake involved. A chewing bite on the thumb caused immediate pain and bleeding followed by swelling and numbness, which spread to the wrist.

Genus *Crisantophis*

Crisantophis nevermanni, guarda camino (Pl. 1072)

Bites are said to be capable of causing local envenoming (Villa, 1969).

Genus *Diadophis*, Ringnecked Snakes (Pls. 1074 and 1075)

These snakes are usually small and inoffensive, but some populations reach considerable size, and their use of enlarged rear teeth and copious salivary secretions during prey handling justifies caution (Anton, 1994). Shaw and Campbell (1974) reported a *Diadophis* bite that produced a burning sensation.

Genus *Elapomorphus* (Pls. 1095 and 1096)

This genus includes small, slender, semifossorial snakes similar in habits to *Leptomicrurus*. Historic citations of envenomings credited to *Elapomorphus* may, in fact, be allocatable to the recently partitioned genus *Phalotris*, but these genera are closely related, and species of *Elapomorphus* should be handled with caution (Lema, 1978a; Minton, 1996).

Genus *Erythrolamprus* (Pls. 1100–1116)

Erythrolamprus aesculapii (some populations formerly known as *E. venustissimus*), false coralsnake

Quelch (1893, 1898) was bitten on the finger by a large specimen in Georgetown, Guyana. Within 30 minutes severe pain and swelling developed. In São Paulo, Brazil, a 24-year-old man employed by the Instituto Butantan was bitten on the index finger. Within 15 minutes he developed pain and swelling, which had spread up to the elbow by the next day. His symptoms disappeared during the next four days. There were no systemic symptoms (Martins, 1916; also mentioned by Silva-Júnior, 1956). Martins carried out some simple experiments with the venom but was unable to demonstrate any effect on blood coagulation.

Greene and McDiarmid (1981) reported substantial pain and swelling from the bite of an *Erythrolamprus*. Campbell and Lamar (pers. comm.) are aware of at least two unreported cases of severe envenoming from *E. bizona*, but have sustained several bites from this species with no ill effects.

Genus *Helicops*

Helicops angulatus, South American watersnake (Pl. 1127)

Local soreness, swelling, stiffness, and bruising have been reported to follow bites (Campbell and Lamar, pers. comm.; Quelch, 1898).

Genus *Heterodon*, Hognosed Snakes (Pls. 1128–1131)

Snakes of this North American genus feed primarily on anurans, especially toads, and have enlarged teeth on the posterior of the maxillary. These teeth do not bear grooves (Kapus, 1964) despite reports to the contrary (Ditmars, 1912), and may function primarily in deflating anurans by piercing their body wall and lungs (Edgren, 1955; Pope, 1947). McAlister (1963) tested the saliva of *H. platirhinos* and found that it was toxic to small anurans. Kapus (1964) discovered considerable variation in size of the Duvernoy's gland among the species of *Heterodon*. He found the gland to be relatively small in *H. simus*, larger in *H. nasicus*, and absent from *H. platirhinos*. However, Young (1992) found a Duvernoy's gland in *H. platirhinos* and studied the effects of this gland's secretions on smooth muscle and the neuromuscular junction.

Heterodon nasicus (Pl. 1128)

This North American species is a popular pet in the United Kingdom and other European countries. Species of *Heterodon* can rarely be induced to bite humans, but Bragg (1960) described the effects of a bite he received from a specimen of *H. nasicus* after he had been handling frogs and the captive snake apparently grabbed his thumb in a feeding response. This was an unusual bite in that he allowed the snake to chew on his thumb with jaw movements typical of swallowing for 10–15 minutes. After this time he noted a "pricking" sensation, and within about 2 hours there was some swelling near the bite, but the area was not sore. Within about 3.5 hours most of the dorsal surface of the hand was swollen and there was a slight burning. The wrist and proximal section of the digits became swollen within 4.5 hours, and the hand was so edematous that it could not be closed. Occasional twinges of pain were experienced 6.5 hours following the bite, and these increased in intensity and frequency for several hours. The swelling on the bitten extremity did not begin to subside until about 24 hours after the bite, and did not completely disappear for several days.

Morris (1985) was bitten on his right fourth finger by a specimen of *H. nasicus* that retained its grip for about 2 minutes. Within about 10 minutes some pain was felt around the site of the bite, and within about 15 minutes the area had become swollen and purplish. Twenty-five minutes after the bite the swelling included all of the second interphalangeal joint of the bitten finger. For about 8 hours following the bite a throbbing pain was intermittently felt in the finger and ulnar side of the wrist, and about 11 hours afterward edema included the base of the finger and much of the hand. Blisters formed on the lateral and dorsal surfaces of the finger at the nail base. The puncture wound continued to ooze blood and fluid until the following day, and about 26–27 hours postbite the finger and hand remained badly swollen and the dorsum and palm of the hand were numb. By 48 hours the swelling had subsided but the area remained discolored and sensitive to the touch.

Bites can cause painful swelling and discoloration with persistent oozing from the fang punctures. In one reported case, pain and swelling began within a few minutes. Bruising involved the bitten foot and ankle, swelling persisted for 3 weeks, and full recovery took almost 3 months (Walley, 2002).

Incorrect use of the English name "western hognosed viper" has caused confusion for poison centers and clinical toxicologists as this may suggest *Porthidium hespere* from Colima, Mexico, and raises inappropriate questions about antivenom treatment. A more distinctive English name for *Porthidium hespere*, Colima hognosed pitviper, is now recommended.

Heterodon platirhinos (Pls. 1129 and 1130)

A specimen of *H. platirhinos* accidentally snagged its teeth on someone's forearm near the wrist while it was writhing and feigning death (Grogan, 1974). A burning sensation similar to a bee sting was experienced at the site of the bite within about 10 minutes, and it intensified over the next several hours. Within 15 minutes the area around the bite began to swell and to become discolored. Forty-five minutes following the bite the discolored area increased to about 2.5 cm in diameter and the victim became nauseated, a feeling that intensified over the next few hours. Other symptoms included anxiety and nervousness that persisted for about four hours. The following day the area around the bite was still swollen, reddish, and painful to touch. Two days after the bite all pain was gone, although some discoloration around the bite persisted for several more days. Minton (1979a) mentioned pain and swelling suffered by a youth who was bitten by *H. platirhinos*.

Genus *Hydrodynastes*, False Water Cobras (Pls. 1132, 1133, 1405)

Hydrodynastes gigas (formerly *Cyclagras gigas*), cobra de Paraguay, false cobra, Boipevussu snake, South American false water cobra

This species, which may exceed 3 m in TL, has enlarged posterior maxillary teeth (Pl. 1405) and a Duvernoy's gland secretion with high proteolytic activity (Hill and Mackessy, 2000). Apart from mechanical trauma caused by the teeth of this powerful snake, there have been many cases of local envenoming and perhaps hypersensitivity reactions, mostly unreported. Painful swelling, which may be extensive, persistent, and associated with bruising, has resulted from prolonged chewing bites inflicted on zookeepers and other snake handlers (see Fig. 266; Warrell, 1996). Manning et al. (1999) described the case of an 18-year-old male pet store employee who was bitten on the wrist. The snake retained its grip for 1.5 minutes. Mild swelling developed, and after nine hours the victim experienced three episodes during which his muscles became paralyzed, causing him to fall, and he was unable to move or speak. The swelling and numbness eventually extended up to the elbow. Some premature atrial extrasystoles were recorded on the electrocardiogram. Laboratory tests showed a total white cell count at the upper limit of normal. There was no objective evidence of muscle paralysis. One wonders whether these bizarre symptoms were occasioned by anxiety.

Genus *Hydrops*, South American Mudsnakes (Pls. 1134–1136)

Snakes of this genus have not been implicated in human envenomings, but their enlarged rear maxillary teeth and overall size dictate caution in handling them.

Genus *Hypsiglena*, Nightsnakes (Pl. 1137)

Hypsiglena torquata, spotted nightsnake

A large adult spotted nightsnake (44.9 cm in TL) was observed by Jameson and Jameson (1956) while it rasped a Texas earless lizard (*Holbrookia texana*), which succumbed within three minutes. Campbell and Lamar (pers. comm.) observed a small *H. torquata* bite and kill two adult *Arizona elegans* when all three freshly collected specimens were placed in the same container. The rapidity with which the snake's saliva acted on its prey suggests that bites to humans may produce at least mild symptoms of envenoming (Vest, 1988).

Genus *Leptodeira*, Cat-Eyed Snakes (Pls. 1163–1170)

Local pain, redness, swelling, stiffness, and profuse bleeding from fang marks have been reported after bites by *L. annulata ashmeadii* (Pl. 1165) in Colombia (Campbell and Lamar, pers. comm.), by *L. a. ashmeadii* in Venezuela (Gorzula, 1982), and by *L. septentrionalis* (Pl. 1170; Minton, 1986). Multiple bites by an individual of *L. a. annulata* (Pls. 1163 and 1164) in Brazil caused no effects (Mark O'Shea, pers. comm.). A person bitten by a specimen of *L. a. annulata* near Shell-Mera, Pastaza, Ecuador, developed no signs of envenoming (Warrell et al., unpublished data).

Genus *Leptophis*, Parrotsnakes (Pls. 1171–1175)

Leptophis ahaetulla

Multiple bites by a specimen of *L. a. praestans* (Pl. 1173) 1.5 m in TL in Belize caused persistent bleeding from the wounds, pain, and then numbness in the bitten hand and forearm that lasted for several hours (Mark O'Shea, pers. comm.). Swelling and severe pain have been described after bites by *L. ahaetulla* (Minton and Mebs, 1978; Zwinenberg, 1977).

Leptophis diplotropis

Persistent stinging pain has been reported after bites (Hardy and McDiarmid, 1969; Zweifel and Norris, 1955).

Genus *Liophis* (Pls. 1179–1189)

Oral secretions of swampsnakes of this genus (which now includes *Leimadophis*) have been reported to have toxic properties (Alcock and Rogers, 1902).

Liophis miliaris, swampsnake (Pl. 1183)

Intense pain, itching, paresthesia, local bleeding, and edema have been described following bites (Santos-Costa and Di-Bernardo, 2001).

Genus *Lystrophis*, South American Hognosed Snakes (Pls. 1190–1195)

Snakes of this genus have not been reported to cause human envenoming, but there are anecdotal accounts of captive specimens alleging that their bites caused a stinging sensation (Campbell and Lamar, pers. comm.). *Lystrophis* species are notable for their resemblance to North American *Heterodon* and have color patterns similar to sympatric species of viperids and elapids.

Genus *Mastigodryas*, Whipsnakes (Pls. 1196 and 1197)

These species range from Panama throughout South America. Traditionally confused and combined with the genus *Dryadophis*, they are medium to large snakes. Several species defend themselves with vigor when threatened. All possess enlarged, nongrooved rear teeth, and *M. bifossatus* (Pl. 1196) is known to secrete a neurotoxin (Fontana et al., 1996; Heleno et al., 1997).

Genus *Oxybelis*, Vinesnakes

Oxybelis aeneus, brown vinesnake (Pl. 1204),
O. fulgidus (Pl. 1205)

In Colombia, where *O. aeneus* is known as bejuca, bejuquilla or bejuquilla mojosa, it was thought by Dunn (1944a) to be the commonest cause of snakebites. Villa (1962) suggested that a bite could result in wasting of the bitten limb similar to that caused by poliomyelitis. A bite by *O. fulgidus* (Pl. 1205) (which, given the location, must have been *O. aeneus*) in Coahuila, Mexico, resulted in itching, reddening, and swelling, and later in numbness and blister formation. The symptoms were transient (Crimmins, 1937). Chippaux (1987) recorded inflammation (2/3+) as a symptom of *O. fulgidus* bite. A. Hyatt Verrill described a fatal bite in a horse in Central America (Orcés, 1948).

The defensive ability of large *O. fulgidus*, which deliver slashing strikes with great accuracy, is impressive. Nonetheless, Jonathan Campbell and William Lamar (pers. comm.) have experienced numerous defensive bites from snakes of the genus *Oxybelis* with no ill effects. Swelling of the hand and forearm followed a bite by *O. fulgidus* in French Guiana (Starace, 1998).

Genus *Oxyrhopus*, Calico Snakes (Pls. 1206–1229)

Oxyrhopus rhombifer (Pls. 1221–1224)

An eight-year-old child developed minor symptoms six hours after being bitten by this species in Brazil (Lema, 1978a; Thales de Lema, pers. comm.).

Genus *Philodryas* (Pls. 1233–1240)

Philodryas aestivus (Pl. 1233)

Human envenoming has been reported by Fowler and Salomão (1994).

Philodryas baroni (Pl. 1234)

In Argentina, a specimen 90 cm in TL bit a 22-year-old male herpetologist on the thumb but withdrew immediately. There was immediate slight burning pain with minimal local bleeding. Swelling was evident after five minutes; after one hour the whole hand was swollen and there were petechial hemorrhages in the skin. Swelling progressed to mid-forearm level, and there were ecchymoses along the line of lymphatics up to the axilla. Recovery was complete within 48 hours (Kuch and Jesberger, 1993).

Philodryas chamissonis (formerly *Dromicus chamissonis*), culebra de cola larga (in Chile)

In Chile, bites by this species are said to produce symptoms very similar to those described for *Tachymenis peruvianus*: local pain of variable intensity spreading rapidly to involve the entire limb, associated with swelling, bruising, and serohemorrhagic blisters (Schenone and Reyes, 1965). Arzola and Schenone (1994) described and illustrated two cases of bites by *P. chamissonis* (referred to as *Dromicus chamissonis*) in Chile, both inflicted by a specimen 110 cm in TL. A 17-year-old youth bitten on the index finger within 10 hours had developed severe pain, swelling, and bruising, which extended up the arm. There was evidence of mild coagulopathy (the prothrombin time was prolonged with thrombocytopenia) and muscle damage (serum creatine kinase concentration was elevated). An 11-year-old boy bitten in the antecubital fossa experienced severe local pain and swelling up to the elbow, and after 48 hours had developed a large hematoma on the back of his forearm. Kuch (1999) also reported envenoming by this species.

Philodryas olfersii (see pp. 721–22; Pls. 1237, 1238)

Philodryas patagoniensis (formerly *P. schotti*) (Pl. 1239)

In Brazil, Martins (1916) was bitten on the thumb by a specimen 1.36 m in TL. Puncture marks were visible from two posterior maxillary teeth, two from the pterygoic-palatine series, and two mandibular teeth. There was an intense burning sensation lasting about 90 minutes and then a feeling of deadness and stiffness in the bitten digit. Argentine *P. patagoniensis* venom exhibited hemorrhagic, proteolytic, and fibrinogen-degrading activity (Acosta et al., 2003).

Nishioka and Silveira (1994) described a five-year-old boy who developed mild swelling and warmth of the bitten leg and mildly abnormal blood coagulation after being bitten by this species. The snake was misidentified and the patient treated inappropriately with *Bothrops* antivenom.

Philodryas viridissimus (Pls. 1240, 1409)

A bite by this species causing considerable edema, pain, and discoloration was illustrated by Campbell and Lamar (1989) (Pl. 1409). Another case developed swelling sufficient to prompt fasciotomy. A case of envenoming was described in Venezuela (Rodríguez-Acosta et al., 1997).

Genus *Pliocercus*, False Coralsnakes (Pls. 1245–1265)

Species of this genus resemble coralsnakes in color, pattern, and defensive behavior. Evidence has been offered that *Pliocercus* should be transferred to the genus *Urotheca*, and some herpetologists place them in that genus.

Pliocercus elapoides, Central American false coralsnake (Pls. 1245–1263)

A 23-year-old man suffered a rapid strike by a specimen 20 cm in TL in Chiapas, Mexico. There was searing pain and tender swelling of the axillary lymph nodes (Seib, 1980).

Genus *Ptychophis*

Ptychophis flavovirgatus, watersnake

This species is not known to have caused envenoming in humans, but it has large serous glands, enlarged rear maxillary teeth, and is prone to bite repeatedly when threatened. Lema (1978a) considered it to be potentially dangerous.

Genus *Rhinobothryum*, Ringed Treesnake (Pls. 1273 and 1274)

This genus includes two species of large, nocturnal snakes that are brightly patterned like coralsnakes. I am unaware of any medically important bites involving *Rhinobothryum*, but in view of their large heads, grooved teeth at the rear of the maxillae, and willingness to bite when molested, they should be treated with caution.

Genus *Symphimus* (Pl. 1311)

Snakes of this genus have a limited distribution in Mexico and adjacent Belize. Although *Symphimus* species are generally regarded as inoffensive insectivores, the bite of *S. mayae* has caused extensive swelling and intense local pain in at least one instance. The victim was attempting to smuggle the snake and had placed it in his underwear. The bite was sustained in a particularly delicate location.

Genus *Thamnodynastes*, Mock Vipers (Pls. 1314–1320)

Thamnodynastes strigatus (Pl. 1317), *T. strigilis* (formerly *T. nattereri*) (Pl. 1318), and *Thamnodynastes* sp.

Duvernoy's gland secretions from Venezuelan *Thamnodynastes* (probably *T. strigilis*) were proteolytic, hemorrhagic in mice and chick embryos, and neurotoxic in mice (Lemoine, Salgueiro, and Rodriguez-Acosta, unpublished data). Bites by these species are reported to cause local pain and swelling (Fig. 267; Lema, 1978a; Martins, 1916; Santos-Costa and Di-Bernardo, 2001). In Brazil, a patient bitten on the dorsum of the foot by *Thamnodynastes* sp. (probably *T. strigatus*) developed painful swelling which spread rapidly and caused difficulty walking (Thales de Lema, pers. comm.).

Genus *Thamnophis*, Gartersnakes and Ribbonsnakes (Pls. 1321–1323)

These snakes are among the most familiar reptiles in North America. Many thousands have been kept as pets by youngsters without incident. A bite from the coast gartersnake, *T. elegans*

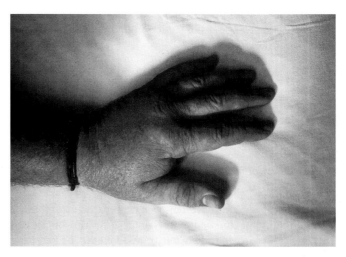

Fig. 267. Effects of a bite by a *Thamnodynastes* from Goiás, Brazil, on the middle finger of the left hand of a 49-year-old male. The snake was about 50 cm in TL and the bite produced instant stinging pain. Copyright Ed George.

terrestris, caused swelling and discoloration of the hand and arm of an 11-year-old boy who allowed the snake to chew on him for about 10 minutes. He was hospitalized for several days (DeLisle, 1982; Gans, 1978; Minton, 1976). Accounts ascribing this case to *Thamnophis couchi* are incorrect (Minton, 1990b). The eastern gartersnake, *T. sirtalis*, has also been reported to envenom humans (Hayes and Hayes, 1985; Nichols, 1986). Perhaps the most implicated and studied species is the wandering gartersnake, *T. elegans vagrans* (Pl. 1321; Finley et al., 1994; Jansen, 1987; Kardong and Luchtel, 1986; Vest, 1981b), whose bite produces marked edema and ecchymosis (Minton, 1986; Vest, 1981a). A woman bitten on the foot by a specimen of *T. proximus* (Pl. 1323) in Guanacaste, Costa Rica, suffered a swollen ankle that remained mildly uncomfortable for two days (A. Solórzano, pers. comm.). A bite by *T. marcianus* (Pl. 1322) in Texas produced marked pain and local swelling (Samuelson, 2001).

Genus *Tomodon*, Mock Vipers (Pl. 1324)

These snakes, which resemble *Thamnodynastes* species, occur in south-central South America and possess grooved, enlarged teeth at the rear of the maxillae.

Tomodon dorsatus, mock viper (Fig. 268)

A bite causing mild pain and swelling was reported from Brazil (Lema, 1978a; Thales de Lema, pers. comm.).

Genus *Trimorphodon*, Lyresnakes (Pls. 1327–1329)

These snakes attain impressive dimensions, especially *T. biscutatus* (Pl. 1327), which may exceed 1.5 m.

Trimorphodon biscutatus (Pl. 1327)

Bites can cause localized pain and swelling (Lowe et al., 1986; W. W. Lamar, pers. comm.). The potent oral secretions of *T. biscutatus* have been studied (see Cowles and Bogert, 1935; Dugès, 1882–1883, 1901b). This species produced the largest venom yield of seven North American colubrids tested by Hill and Mackessy (1997). An induced bite by a specimen 55 cm in TL from Arizona, which was allowed to chew on a finger for 30–45

Fig. 268. *Tomodon dorsatus* threatening. Copyright Ivan Sazima.

seconds, produced stinging pain, a feeling of heat, and itching and swelling of the finger lasting about 24 hours (Foley, 2002).

Genus *Waglerophis*, Mock Vipers (Pls. 1334–1339)

These snakes reach large proportions and have wide mouths. Like their close relatives in the genus *Xenodon*, they feed on large anurans and have enlarged, nongrooved teeth on the posterior maxillae. Although apparently there are no published reports implicating *Waglerophis* in human envenoming, this is another species best regarded with suspicion. One of the primary authors of this volume sustained a glancing bite on the right index finger from a small *Waglerophis* in central Brazil (Campbell and Lamar, pers. comm.). A sharp pain not caused by the teeth was felt immediately and the wound bled copiously. There were no further symptoms.

Genus *Xenoxybelis*, Sharpnose Snakes (Pl. 1360)

These snakes were long placed in the genus *Oxybelis*. Because of their overall close relationship to *Oxybelis* they merit caution, but I am unaware of any reported envenomings.

ENVENOMING BY ELAPIDAE

Seasnakes

Seasnakes mainly bite people who handle them incautiously, either fishermen removing them from their nets or beachcombers who pick up stranded snakes. The head may easily be mistaken for the tail. Bites by seasnakes are usually painless and may not be noticed by waders or swimmers who tread on or collide with them. Teeth may be left in the wound. There is minimal or no local swelling, and local lymph nodes are rarely involved. The most important effects of envenoming are generalized muscle breakdown (rhabdomyolysis) attributable to venom phospholipases A_2 and paralysis caused by presynaptic phospholipase A_2 neurotoxins and polypeptide postsynaptic neurotoxins. Headache, a thick-feeling tongue, thirst, sweating, and vomiting are early symptoms. Generalized aching, stiffness, and tenderness of muscles all over the body become noticeable between 30 minutes and several hours after the bite. Trismus, reminiscent of tetanus, is common. Passive stretching of muscles is painful. Later there is progressive flaccid paralysis, starting with ptosis and paralysis of muscles innervated by the cranial nerves, as with other elapid envenomings. Paralysis of the muscles of deglutition and respiration is life-threatening. Muscle pigment (myoglobin) appears in plasma and in the urine 3–8 hours after the bite. Myoglobinemia and myoglobinuria are suspected when the serum/plasma appears brownish and the urine dark reddish brown, black, or Coca-Cola-colored. Myoglobin and potassium released from damaged muscles may cause acute renal failure, while hyperkalemia, also the result of muscle breakdown, may become sufficiently severe within 6–12 hours of the bite to cause cardiac arrest (Warrell, 1994).

Pelamis platurus, pelagic seasnake or yellow-bellied seasnake (Pls. 283–290)

Edward Taylor (1953a) quoted an early sixteenth-century sighting of this species by the conquistador Gonzalo Fernández de Oviedo y Valdes off the coast of Costa Rica in the Bahía de Culebras. A seventeenth-century traveler, Ravenau de Lussan, averred that "their bite is venomous and mortal, and there is no human remedy that is able to prevent a sudden death to a person once bitten" (Taylor, 1953a). Later travelers were impressed by "considerable numbers [of yellow-bellied seasnakes] in the Bay of Panama" (Tennent, 1861). This species is found along the Pacific coast of the Americas, from California in the north to northern Chile and Isla de Pascua (Easter Island) in the south. Despite its wide distribution there have been few reported fatalities attributable with certainty to this species. In South Africa, FitzSimons (1912) claimed that many fatalities had occurred from people mistaking this snake for an eel and catching hold of it. He reported that a naval officer had died in 4 hours and a sailor in 2.5 hours after the bite, while a third patient had recovered. Other deaths were recorded off the Torres Strait Islands near the coast of Papua New Guinea; in the River Ganges, India; and in Vietnam (Warrell, 1994). In Latin America, human fatalities have been claimed in Panama (Curran and Kauffeld, 1937) and Colombia. Medem (1969) described a case in the Río Guapí, Cauca, Colombia, where the local fishermen do not regard this species as dangerous. A snake that had climbed a submerged cable bit a man on the hand. The victim vomited, was unable to eat, and was treated with coralsnake antivenom, but he died less than 10 hours after the bite. Solórzano (1995b) reviewed the scanty literature on bites by this species and described a bite inflicted by a single fang on the back of the hand of William W. Lamar. There was instant pain, slight swelling, and discoloration, and later deep pain and slight stiffness involving the wrist and thumb lasting from 1 to 28 hours after the bite. No systemic symptoms developed. Six cases of bites without envenoming were mentioned briefly by Kropach (1972).

Coralsnakes (*Leptomicrurus* and *Micrurus*)

Two of the first reported fatalities from *Micrurus* bites were described by Dr. Otto Wucherer (after whom one of the causative organisms of lymphatic filariasis, *Wuchereria bancroftii*, was named) in 1867 (Wucherer, 1867); one was a young German at Filadélfia, Minas Gerais, the other a young woman at Vila da Barra do Rio Grande (Silva-Júnior, 1956).

Although coralsnake bites never constitute more than a few percent of snakebite cases in any particular area, the case fatality remains high (e.g., 25% in Brazil *fide* Rosenfeld, 1971).

Coralsnake venoms are best known for their neurotoxic effects. Local signs are usually reported as being minimal, consisting of mild swelling and some erythema, or entirely absent (Pls. 1410–1412). However, local symptoms may be severe and persistent, including pain of variable intensity, paresthesiae such as numbness radiating up the bitten limb, and in some cases extensive swelling. The earliest symptom of systemic envenoming may be nausea, retching, and repeated vomiting, sometimes with abdominal pain, but the use of emetic herbal medicines may confuse the interpretation of these symptoms. Other early preparalytic symptoms include contraction of the frontalis muscle causing puckering of the brow before ptosis is demonstrable (Pl. 1412); blurred vision, perhaps attributable to paralysis of visual accommodation; paresthesiae, especially around the mouth; hyperacusis; loss of the sense of smell and taste; headache; dizziness; vertigo; and signs of autonomic nervous system stimulation such as hypersalivation producing unusually sticky secretions, congestion of the conjunctivae, and piloerection (gooseflesh). Kitchens and Van Mierop (1987) described "euphoria" in 15% of victims of *M. fulvius* in Florida.

Paralysis is usually first detectable as ptosis and external ophthalmoplegia (Pls. 1410–1412) because ocular muscles are most sensitive to neuromuscular blockade. These signs may appear from as early as 15 minutes to as late as many hours after bites by coralsnakes. Later, the facial muscles, palate, jaws, tongue, vocal cords, neck muscles, and muscles of deglutition may become paralyzed. The pupils are dilated. Many patients are unable to open the mouth, but this can be overcome by force. Respiratory arrest may be precipitated by obstruction of the upper airway by the paralyzed tongue or inhaled vomitus. Intercostal muscles are affected before the limbs, diaphragm, and superfical muscles, and even in patient with almost total flaccid paralysis, slight movements of the digits may be possible, allowing the patient to signal. Loss of consciousness, generalized convulsions, and shock in patients who have respiratory paralysis is explained by cerebral hypoxia. However, the drowsiness or sleepiness before the development of evident paralysis that has been described in some victims of coralsnake bites suggests the possibility of some direct effect of venom toxins on the central nervous system. Drooping eyelids from physiological tiredness may be misconstrued as ptosis unless the extent of lid retraction is assessed formally by asking the patient to look upward. Symptoms of systemic envenoming include headache, malaise, and generalized myalgia. High serum concentrations of skeletal muscle enzymes (creatine kinase, lactic dehydrogenase, aminotransferases) in some reported cases suggest generalized rhabdomyolysis caused by venom myotoxins such as the acidic myotoxic phospholipase A_2 in the venom of *M. n. nigrocinctus* described by Arroyo et al. (1987). Like many snake venoms, coralsnake venoms show variable hemolytic activity against erythrocytes of different mammalian species *in vitro*. A number of human envenomings, however, showed evidence of clinically significant intravascular hemolysis such as hemoglobinuria (sometimes wrongly recorded as hematuria if the urine was tested with reagent sticks rather than by microscopy), a fall in hemoglobin concentration, and, in at least one autopsied case, hemoglobin pigment in the renal tubules (Machado and Rosenfeld, 1971). Although coralsnake venoms have cardiovascular effects in some experimental animals, this phenomenon has not been satisfactorily demonstrated in human victims. Neurotoxic effects are completely reversible, either acutely in response to antivenom or (e.g., in the case of *Micrurus frontalis* [sensu lato] envenoming) by anticholinesterases such as neostigmine and edrophonium (Fig. 269). Paralysis may also, in time, resolve spontaneously.

Genus *Leptomicrurus*

One case of a bite by a *Leptomicrurus* species (probably *L. narduccii*) was recorded from the Selva Central of Peru (Demarini Caro, 1992). The victim, an oil company manager, was given the snake as a present. It bit him on the finger causing some pain, slight swelling, and much anxiety. There was dyspnea of uncertain significance, without other convincing signs of neurotoxicity, but the patient recovered within six to eight hours (J. Demarini Caro, pers. comm.).

Genus *Micrurus* (Pls. 26–282)

Micrurus alleni (Pls. 28–32)

Transient symptoms lasting only 30 minutes were described in a patient bitten in Costa Rica (Bolaños, 1984). A bite inflicted

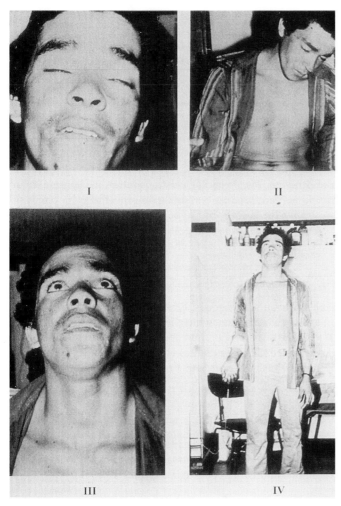

Fig. 269. Effects of neostigmine in a patient envenomed by *Micrurus frontalis* in São Paulo State, Brazil: (I) and (II) before, and (III) and (IV) after treatment with anticholinesterase, showing a marked improvement in neuromuscular transmission. From Vital Brazil and Vieira, 1990, reproduced with permission.

by a juvenile Costa Rican specimen resulted in immediate pain but no lasting symptoms (W. W. Lamar, pers. comm.).

Micrurus altirostris (formerly *M. frontalis altirostris*) (Pls. 213–215)

An account of a fatal bite in Uruguay by a coralsnake that must have been of this species is featured in a short story by Rudyard Kipling (Roze, 1996).

Micrurus annellatus (Pls. 33–37)

Roze (1996) recorded symptoms of a bite by *M. annellatus* in Oxapampa, Pasco, Peru. There was immediate pain radiating up the bitten limb that lasted for a few hours and residual reddening and local stinging pain with persistent numbness of the bitten finger.

Micrurus bocourti (Formerly *M. ecuadorianus*) (Pls. 44–46)

In Los Ríos, Ecuador, a man was bitten on the finger by a specimen 40 cm in TL. The snake tried to hold on, chewing, but was immediately removed. The man soon felt severe pain in the digit and what was described as "severe vertigo" (Kuch and

Freire-Lascano, 1998). The pain spread along the bitten arm to his chest. Five hours after the bite he developed ptosis and disturbances of visual accommodation causing blurred vision. He vomited three times. There was local paralysis confined to the bitten index and adjacent middle fingers. These symptoms resolved after about six hours, but the two fingers remained paralyzed for a month. A second serious case of envenoming by this species in Guayaquil was also reported (Kuch and Freire-Lascano, 1998).

Micrurus clarki (Pls. 54 and 55)

Bolaños (1984) reported a case of fatal envenoming in Colombia in which the patient did not receive specific antivenom.

Micrurus corallinus (Pls. 56–58, 1410–1412)

At Santa Catarina, Florianópolis, Brazil, Coelho et al. (1992) observed two cases of envenoming by this species. A 66-year-old man was bitten on the foot by a specimen 84 cm in TL. He presented to a hospital three hours later with malaise, dysphagia, cramping abdominal pain, and paralysis of all four limbs. He had myasthenic facies with ptosis, external ophthalmoplegia, fixed pupils, conjunctival congestion, paralysis of the tongue, and palate, and inability to speak. Apparently his first neurological symptom was dysphagia, one hour after the bite. Laboratory tests returned normal results. After receiving specific antivenom, his neurological symptoms gradually resolved; first the external ophthalmoplegia and pupillary paralysis, and last the ptosis. A 60-year-old man who had been bitten on the foot by a *M. corallinus* presented to a hospital two hours later with intense myalgia, muscle weakness, and blurred vision. Dysphagia had been his first symptom. He had myasthenic facies, ptosis, external ophthalmoplegia, conjunctival congestion, and muscle fasciculations. There was no local swelling at the site of the bite. After treatment with specific antivenom, his symptoms resolved without any signs of respiratory paralysis, but ptosis persisted for three days. Also in Brazil, Machado and Rosenfeld (1971) described the autopsy of a 50-year-old man who had died 6.5 hours after a bite by *M. corallinus*. At the site of the bite there was local edema, necrosis, and hemorrhage with infiltration by polymorpho- and basophil-leukocytes. An interesting finding was cylinders of hemoglobin in the renal tubules suggesting intravascular hemolysis.

A driver at the Instituto Butantan bitten on the finger by a specimen of *M. corallinus* almost immediately developed numbness and weakness of the bitten and adjacent fingers, headache, cramps of the lower limbs, vomiting, and diarrhea. He was found to have ptosis, photophobia, decreased muscle tone but retention of superficial (cremasteric) and tendon reflexes, hyperesthesia, and hematuria. Treatment with specific antivenom was complicated by an anaphylactic reaction, but he eventually recovered (Yered, 1942, in Silva-Júnior, 1956). Vital Brazil reported a bite by this species in Santa Rita, São Paulo State. After several days of symptoms the victim made a full recovery (Brazil, 1938, in Silva-Júnior, 1956).

In Brazil, a 19-year-old man complained of numbness of the entire bitten arm, pain in the chest, blurred vision, and muscular fatigue after being bitten by *M. corallinus*. There was mild ptosis, hypersalivation, and impaired vision; his walking was unsteady. Despite treatment with specific antivenom, he developed respiratory paralysis and aphonia and died six hours after the bite (Vital Brazil, 1980).

Remarks This Brazilian species is one of the commoner causes of bites by coralsnakes, which are admittedly rare. Local pain and swelling are negligible, but paresthesiae and weakness of the bitten limb may precede the usual progression of paralysis starting with ptosis and progressing to potentially fatal bulbar and respiratory paralysis. Vomiting, diarrhea, generalized myalgias, muscle cramps, and fasciculations are other signs of systemic envenoming, and some reports suggest the possibility of intravascular hemolysis.

Micrurus diastema (Pls. 59–78)

Roze (1996) mentioned a symptomless bite by *M. d. sapperi* (Pls. 75–78) in Los Tuxtlas, Mexico.

Micrurus dumerilii (Pls. 84–93)

A coffee plantation worker in Pueblo Rico, Antioquia, Colombia, suffered local pain, vomiting, headache, and bilateral VIth cranial nerve paralysis after being bitten (Otero et al., 1992b).

Micrurus filiformis (Pls. 228 and 229)

This species can strike and bite violently if restrained. William Lamar was bitten twice on the palm of the hand when he caught a specimen less than 20 cm in TL that was swimming in a river. No symptoms developed (Roze, 1996).

Micrurus frontalis (Pls. 230–234)

According to Vital Brazil and Vieira (1990) this species is responsible for about 1% of all snakebites in São Paulo State, Brazil. A 20-year-old man seen 2 hours after being bitten was experiencing local pain and paresthesia. He also complained of blurred vision and was found to have ptosis, external ophthalmoplegia, and respiratory distress and was unable to stand. His symptoms responded to neostigmine, an anticholinesterase drug, and he made a complete recovery. A 38-year-old man also presented with local pain, itching along the arm, and faintness. He had muscle weakness, blurred vision, diplopia, drowsiness, and muscle fasciculation, and he also responded to neostigmine. A case of probable *M. frontalis* envenoming was seen in Santa Catarina, Florianópolis, Brazil. This 35-year-old man presented 3 hours after being bitten on the foot with agitation, vomiting, myalgia, ptosis, and mydriasis. Eighteen hours after the bite he was found to have generalized muscle fasciculations, intense myalgia, paralysis of the lower limbs, epigastric pain, dysphonia, blurred vision, stupor, mydriasis, ptosis, and respiratory difficulty. Laboratory test results were normal. Since no specific antivenom was available, he was treated with neostigmine, and after 12 hours his symptoms were greatly improved (Coelho et al., 1992). At Agudo, Rio Grande do Sul, Brazil, a 35-year-old man was bitten on the hand. There were no local changes, and laboratory results were normal; however, 2 hours and 45 minutes after the bite he developed nausea, blurred vision, ptosis, and dyspnea. Three hours after the bite he was treated with specific antivenom and neostigmine, and 4 hours later his symptoms had resolved. When the neostigmine was stopped, his symptoms recurred with muscular fasciculations in the lower limbs and bradycardia. These symptoms resolved after neostigmine treatment was restored (Secretaria da Saúde, 1996).

Thirty minutes after the little finger of a 5-year-old boy was penetrated by one fang he felt numbness spreading up to the axilla, pain in the chest, distress, and difficulty breathing. His symptoms slowly receded after he had been given specific antivenom half an hour after the bite (Vital Brazil, *in* Silva-Júnior, 1956).

Remarks Clinical features of envenoming resemble those following bites by *M. corallinus*, the other medically important coralsnake in Brazil. The striking difference is in the victims' response to anticholinesterase. Prolonging the biological life of acetylcholine, the physiological transmitter at neuromuscular junctions, can produce dramatic improvement in paralysis caused by *M. frontalis* but appears ineffective when used for victims of *M. corallinus*, suggesting that the predominant neurotoxic effect of *M. frontalis* venom is postsynaptic.

Micrurus hemprichii (Pls. 235–239)

Near Manaus, Amazonas, Brazil, a patient was bitten by this interesting coralsnake, which feeds at least in part on onychophorans. There was mild local swelling, abdominal pain, and repeated vomiting (Santos et al., 1995). A symptomless bite occurred when a herpetologist in Peru was handling an adult specimen (Campbell and Lamar, pers. comm.).

Micrurus langsdorffi (Pls. 116–120)

Two people bitten by this species in Amazonian Peru (one suffered multiple bites) developed only local swelling and pain (Campbell and Lamar, pers. comm.).

Micrurus laticollaris (Pls. 195–197)

A 27-year-old man was bitten on the finger by this species, which he had mistaken for *Lampropeltis*, near Acapulco, Mexico. Fifteen minutes later he felt nauseated and the bitten finger had become numb. Two hours after the bite he arrived at a hospital with local swelling and distention of local lymphatics. Twelve hours after the bite he had lost his sense of taste and developed ptosis, blurred vision, and slurred speech. He found it difficult to chew. Over the next 48 hours he developed weakness of the limbs and respiratory distress. There was evidence of gastrointestinal bleeding and hematuria. Elevated serum levels of lactate dehydrogenase and creatine kinase suggested hemolysis and muscle damage, but no myoglobin was detected in urine or serum. Edrophonium did not improve his muscle weakness (Pettigrew and Glass, 1985). Eventually, this patient made a complete recovery, reporting that his sense of taste was normal 25 days after the bite.

Remarks Loss of the senses of smell and taste is a fascinating effect of envenoming by some elapid snakes (e.g., Australasian elapids such as *Pseudechis* species and Asian cobras) and by some neurotoxic vipers (such as *Bitis atropos*). It implies a specific effect on the olfactory nerves, which in some snakebite victims may be permanently damaged.

Micrurus lemniscatus (Pls. 244–258)

A patient reported by Vital Brazil died 17 hours after a bite by this species, after developing impaired vision, paralysis, and internal hemorrhage (Silva-Júnior, 1956). A 21-year-old man bitten on the thumb by an adult *M. lemniscatus* in Amazonian Peru developed ptosis and difficulty walking 48 hours after the bite. Although he recovered, his symptoms persisted for several weeks. In Corumbaiba, Goiás, Brazil, a 61-year-old man bitten on the finger by a specimen of *M. l. carvalhoi* (Pls. 245–247) developed bursts of intense pain along the bitten arm that persisted for many hours despite the use of conventional analgesics. No neurotoxic symptoms developed (Nishioka et al., 1993). In St. Joseph, Trinidad, two laborers who were playing with a coralsnake (*M. lemniscatus diutius*) 137 cm in TL were bitten on the lip and tongue and died seven and eight hours later, respectively, after developing convulsions (De Verteuil, 1858).

Micrurus mipartitus, rabo de ají, cabeza de chocho, coral rabo de candela (Pls. 198–206)

Angel-Mejía (1987b) described three cases of bites by this species in Medellín, Antioquia, Colombia. A 5-year-old girl was bitten on her foot by a snake 47 cm in TL. After 4 hours she became distressed and was unable to sleep. Twelve hours after the bite she developed ptosis, paralysis of all four limbs, and respiratory difficulties, but she eventually recovered. A 27-year-old woman was bitten by a snake 30 cm in TL. Thirty minutes later she became nauseated, and after 6 hours exhibited hypersalivation, ptosis, and impaired visual accommodation. A striking symptom was generalized pain in the teeth. After being mechanically ventilated she recovered. A 50-year-old man bitten on his hand by a snake 41 cm in TL developed local pain and itching. After 4.5 hours there was paresthesia, ptosis, dysarthria, inability to protrude the tongue, and respiratory distress. He developed complete flaccid paralysis but eventually recovered.

A 2-year-old child bitten in Las Cruces, Urrao, Antioquia, Colombia, developed hypersalivation, dysphagia, ptosis, intercostal muscle paralysis resulting in respiratory failure, and bilateral paralysis of the VIth cranial nerves (Otero et al., 1992b: fig. 14). Bolaños (1984) recorded four cases of *M. mipartitus* envenoming from Colombia. One developed no symptoms, one with moderately severe symptoms recovered without antivenom, one severely envenomed patient recovered after receiving antivenom three days after the bite, and the fourth patient died without receiving antivenom. In Bucaramanga, eastern Colombia, one case of mild envenoming by this species was reported (Badillo et al., 1989). At Darién, Panama, Charles Myers suffered a chewing bite lasting several seconds on the finger from a *M. mipartitus* 38.5 cm in TL (Roze, 1996). There was transient pain and progressive swelling that spread to the wrist. Four bites by *M. m. decussatus* in Popayán, Colombia, two of them fatal, were reported by Ayerbe (1981) and Ayerbe et al. (1977, 1979, 1990). A man bitten by a snake 40.4 cm in TL developed ptosis, hypersalivation, dysphagia, an unsteady gait, difficulty talking, and eventually respiratory failure with cyanosis. There was no local envenoming. He died 6 hours after the bite. A 52-year-old woman bitten by the same subspecies developed hemolysis, hemoglobinuria, and renal failure with bilateral renal cortical necrosis but with no neurotoxic symptoms (Roze, 1996).

Micrurus multifasciatus

This species is said to be nervous and to bite readily (Campbell and Lamar, 1989), but no human envenomings have been reported.

Micrurus nigrocinctus (Pls. 144–157)

In Costa Rica only about 2% of all snakebites, about 8 cases a year, are caused by coralsnakes, even though *M. nigrocinctus* is very common there (Bolaños, 1984). Only 1 of 166 snakebites reported in children in southwestern Costa Rica was caused by this species (Montalvan et al., 1983). A severely envenomed patient in Costa Rica recovered after receiving specific antivenom eight hours after the bite (Bolaños, 1984). A man bitten on the index finger by a specimen 60 cm in TL in Costa Rica developed immediate intense pain radiating from the bite up the arm, and, after 45 minutes, to the chest. Swelling of the hand appeared in 15 minutes and extended up the forearm. He became nauseated after 45 minutes, and after two hours vomited, became dizzy, and then lost consciousness. He was treated at Puntarenas Hospital (with analgesia only) and in San José (with suero anticoral) but spent six days in the hospital. During the first three months of convalescence the bitten hand was numb, but it then became hypersensitive to heat. He eventually made a full recovery (Roze, 1996).

Micrurus nigrocinctus bites seem to cause more severe and persistent local pain and swelling than those of other coralsnakes, but two biologists bitten while handling this species at La Selva Biological Station, Costa Rica, developed no signs of envenoming (Hardy, 1994c).

Micrurus pyrrhocryptus (formerly *M. frontalis pyrrhocryptus*) (Pls. 261 and 262)

Esteso (1985) estimated that 27 coralsnake bites in Argentina over a period of 20 years were attributable to this species. In Córdoba, Argentina, Esteso et al. (1989) observed 7 cases. There was immediate pricking pain, and 5–10 minutes later paresthesiae spread up the bitten limb. Diplopia and blurred vision developed 30 minutes after the bite, followed by sleepiness, chest tightness, profuse salivation, and tachyardia. After about 60 minutes there was ptosis and coma, and two to six hours after the bite patients died from respiratory failure unless appropriate treatment had been given. Esteso (1985) described fatal envenoming by this species in three children and one adult. Bolaños (1984) reported a mild case of envenoming by this species (as *M. frontalis*) in Argentina in which specific antivenom was given 15 minutes after the bite. These accounts contrast with the impression of Abalos (quoted in Roze, 1996) that no bites by coralsnakes had been reported in Argentina.

Micrurus ruatanus

The inhabitants of Roatán Island, Islas de Bahia, Honduras, do not regard this species as venomous (Campbell and Lamar, 1989).

Micrurus spixii (Pls. 266–274)

This species, one of the largest coralsnakes, is capable of biting through clothing, and some individuals are highly irritable (Campbell and Lamar, 1989). In Manaus, Amazonas, Brazil, a herpetologist was bitten and experienced persistent, severe generalized pains in the joints, the bones, and in all the tooth sockets (the late Paulo Buhrnheim, pers. comm.). A similar case occurred when a herpetologist in Cali, Colombia, was bitten by a captive specimen (Campbell and Lamar, pers. comm.).

Remarks Generalized pain in the teeth (odontalgia) was also mentioned by a victim of *M. mipartitus* envenoming (see above).

Micrurus steindachneri (Pls. 176 and 177)

At Veracruz, Pastaza, Ecuador, a 46-year-old mestiza was bitten on the index finger by a specimen of *M. s. orcesi* 30 cm in TL. She developed persistent pain and swelling of the finger and hand but was discharged from the hospital the next day. Results of laboratory tests were normal (Case LA, no. 17; Warrell et al., unpublished data).

Micrurus surinamensis (Pls. 275–278, Fig. 11)

This aquatic species, the stoutest of the coralsnakes, was responsible for a case of fatal envenoming at Leticia, Amazonas, Colombia (Silva-Haad, *in* Roze, 1996). The victim was bitten on the foot while standing in a river.

ENVENOMING BY VIPERIDAE (CROTALINAE)

Pitvipers are responsible for the vast majority of snakebites, envenomings, and related deaths and cases of permanent disability in Latin America. Destructive effects of envenoming may be purely local, in the region of the bite wound, or may be local and systemic, the most obviously life-threatening effects being shock (fall in blood pressure), bleeding, defective blood coagulation, kidney failure, and, in the case of South American rattlesnakes, neuromyotoxicity.

Local Envenoming

Envenoming by vipers, notably by the pitvipers (Crotalinae), usually produces more severe local effects than envenoming by other snakes. Local swelling at the site of the bite may appear within 15 minutes but, rarely, may be delayed for several hours. Swelling spreads rapidly, sometimes to involve the entire bitten limb and adjacent areas of the trunk. There is associated pain, tenderness, inflammation, and enlargement of regional lymph nodes; for example, at the elbow (epitrochlear) and in the axilla in the case of bites on the arm, and in the inguinal and femoral regions in the case of bites on the leg. Bruising may extend from the site of the bite up the bitten limb, especially in lines along the path of superficial lymphatics and over regional lymph nodes (Pls. 1436, 1439–1444, 1474). There may be persistent bleeding from the fang marks if the blood has been rendered incoagulable by the venom. Massively swollen limbs can accommodate many liters of leaked (extravasated) blood leading to hypovolemic shock when the circulating blood volume is seriously depleted. Blistering may appear at the site of the bite within the first 12 hours (Pls. 1413, 1414, 1422–1424, 1445, 1446, 1471). Blisters (small vesicles or large bullae) contain clear or bloodstained (serosanguinous) fluid. Necrosis (gangrene) of skin, subcutaneous tissue, and muscle (Pls. 1420, 1421, 1425–1429) develops in up to 10% of hospitalized cases, especially following bites by Central American rattlesnakes (*C. simus*), South American lanceheads (*Bothrops*) and bushmasters (*Lachesis*). Bites on the digits (fingers and toes) (Pls. 1428, 1429, 1453) and in areas draining into the tight fascial compartments, such as the anterior tibial compartment, are particularly likely to cause necrosis (Pls. 1425–1427, 1453, 1454). Increased tissue pressure within these relatively indistensible fascial compartments may reduce blood flow so that ischemia contributes, together with direct effects of the venom, to muscle necrosis. The absence of detectable local swelling 2 hours after a viper bite usually means that no venom has been injected, but there are important exceptions to this rule. Fatal systemic envenoming by the tropical rattlesnake (*C. d. terrificus*) may occur in the absence of local signs. The most serious complication of local envenoming is necrosis (gangrene), requiring surgical debridement or even amputation and resulting in permanent disability. Secondary bacterial infections may present as discrete local fluctuant swellings (subcutaneous abscesses) or more diffuse cellulitis attributable to a variety of bacteria derived from the snake's venom, fangs, and mouth; from the patient's skin; or introduced by unsterile incisions. Secondary infestation with fly larvae (myiasis) has also been described (Dao-L., 1971).

Systemic Envenoming

Disturbances of blood clotting and abnormal bleeding are characteristic of envenoming by Viperidae. Bleeding for more than about 10 minutes from the fang puncture wounds (Pl. 1498) and from new injuries such as venepuncture sites and old partially healed wounds is the first clinical evidence that the blood's clotting factors have been consumed as a result of venom activity. Spontaneous systemic hemorrhage, a sign of circulating metalloproteinase hemorrhagins, is most often detected in the gums (gingival sulci; Pls. 1447 and 1448). Blood-staining of saliva and sputum usually reflects bleeding from the gums or from the nose (epistaxis). Bleeding into the lungs (hemoptysis) is rarely detected clinically. The urine may become cloudy or frankly bloodstained (hematuria) a few hours after the bite. Other types of spontaneous bleeding are ecchymoses, intracranial and subconjunctival hemorrhages, and bleeding into the floor of the mouth and into the gastrointestinal and genitourinary tracts. Women may develop menorrhagia, and pregnant women may suffer antepartum or postpartum hemorrhages with abortion of the fetus. Severe headache and neck stiffness (meningism; Pl. 1437) suggest subarachnoid hemorrhage, while lateralizing neurological signs (e.g., hemiplegia), irritability, loss of consciousness, and convulsions suggest intracranial hemorrhage (Pls. 1409, 1416–1419) or cerebral thrombosis (Pl. 1410). Abdominal distention, tenderness, and peritonism with signs of hemorrhagic shock but no external blood loss suggest retroperitoneal or intraperitoneal hemorrhage.

Blockage (thrombosis) of major arteries (cerebral, pulmonary, coronary) is unique to envenoming by the two Caribbean species of *Bothrops*, *B. lanceolatus* and *B. caribbaeus* (see below; Pls. 1410, 1413, 1414).

Circulatory Shock and Hypotension

Some patients bitten by South American pitvipers may suddenly feel faint, lose their vision, and collapse unconscious a short time after being bitten. This early, profound, but usually transient fall in blood pressure is almost certainly due to autopharmacological effects of the venom. Venom kininogenases activate human bradykininogen to release bradykinin, which lowers blood pressure. Venom oligopeptides inhibit both the breakdown of bradykinin and the activation of angiotensin I to angiotensin II, thus increasing the degree of shock. Pitviper venoms may also have a direct effect on the heart.

Inflammatory Response

Local and systemic inflammatory responses, triggered by venom components such as phospholipases A_2 and mediated by cytokines such as interleukin (IL)-1β and IL-6, and their possible role in the pathogenesis of local necrosis, fever, shock, and other phenomena, has been little studied in human snakebite patients. However, the potential importance of these mechanisms has been suggested by experimental studies in animals (Lomonte et al., 1993; Rucavado et al., 2002).

Acute Renal Failure

This is a well-known complication of severe envenoming by Central and South American pitvipers. Mechanisms include a direct effect of venom toxins on the renal tubule; renal ischemia attributable to profound systemic hypotension; and narrowing or obstruction by fibrin thrombi of renal arterioles, spontaneous bleeding into the kidneys, and the damaging effect on the nephron of the filtration of muscle and blood pigments (myoglobin and hemoglobin).

Neurotoxic Envenoming

Envenoming by some subspecies of tropical rattlesnake (*C. d. terrificus*, *C. d. collilineatus*) can cause typical neurotoxicity reminiscent of elapid envenoming that occasionally results in life-threatening respiratory paralysis. Venom phospholipases A_2 are responsible for this presynaptic neuromuscular blockade and also for the generalized rhabdomyolysis and myoglobinuria reminiscent of seasnake envenoming.

Genus *Agkistrodon* (Pls. 291–318)

Agkistrodon bilineatus, cantil (Pls. 291–299, see also 300 and 301)

This species is "greatly feared throughout its range" (Gloyd and Conant, 1990) and in some parts of Central America is regarded as more dangerous than even *Bothrops asper*. Although the consequences of a bite may be merely local pain, swelling, and discoloration, bites by adult snakes can cause massive swelling, blistering, and necrosis (Pls. 1413 and 1414). Campbell and Lamar (1989) suggested that in one out of every six cases, necrosis may require amputation. Some bites have caused death in a matter of hours. At Motul, Yucatán, Mexico, a woman died a few hours after being bitten by a specimen 30 cm in TL (Gaige, 1936). Alvarez del Toro (1983) referred to "spontaneous amputation" of the necrotic wound, when the gangrenous tissues fell off in fragments, exposing the underlying bones. In Sonora, Mexico, where it is known as pichicuate, the cantil is feared more than any other reptile. Two doctors interviewed by Bogert and Oliver (1945) had treated and lost patients bitten by this species.

In Honduras, Cruz (1987) described the effects of envenoming as being similar to a *Bothrops* bite but more severe considering that the snake is less than 1 m long. There is immediate severe pain, oozing of blood from the fang puncture marks, considerable edema, epistaxis, bleeding from the gums, frank hematuria, generalized petechiae, shock, renal failure, and local necrosis. He reported two fatal cases.

In Nicaragua, *A. bilineatus* is responsible for numerous bites and is regarded as the country's most dangerous snake. Villa (1962) described and illustrated two men bitten—one on the ankle and the other on the finger—by this species, known locally as castellana, one of whom developed swelling up to the knee and the other of the whole arm, but who recovered in two and five days, respectively, after receiving Wyeth antivenom.

Genus *Atropoides*, Jumping Pitvipers (Pls. 319–368)

Unlike most vipers, *Atropoides* species strike and then hold on and chew. In one case the jaws had to be prized off with a machete. Writing of *A. mexicanus* in Honduras, Douglas March noted, "When he bites he hangs on and will make a half dozen punctures unless he is quickly and forcibly disengaged" (March, 1929a). In Costa Rica in 1979, 3 of 477 bites (0.63%) were by *A. mexicanus* (referred to as *A. nummifer*; Bolaños, 1984). The effects of envenoming seem to be mild—transient pain and mild swelling. In one part of Honduras the local people insist that this snake (*A. mexicanus*) is nonvenomous. A man bitten on the finger developed nothing more than pain. Laboratory studies of *Atropoides* venoms suggest that human victims are unlikely to develop consumption coagulopathy and incoagulable blood, but among 10 species of Costa Rican pitviper venoms tested on mice, that of *A. picadoi* proved the most hemorrhagic (Gutiérrez and Chaves, 1980).

Genus *Bothriechis*, Palm-Pitvipers (Pls. 369–426)

Bothriechis aurifer, yellow-blotched palm-pitviper (Pls. 369–372)

In Baja Verapaz, Guatemala, a seven-year-old girl bitten on the hand died the next day (Campbell and Lamar, 1989).

Bothriechis bicolor, Guatemalan palm-pitviper (Pls. 373–377)

Bites by this species are capable of causing marked local envenoming (Pl. 1415).

Bothriechis lateralis, side-striped palm-pitviper (Pls. 378–383)

In Costa Rica, where this species is known as lora, Picado T. (1930) described and illustrated two cases of severe envenoming in men who were bitten on the finger while picking coffee or pruning trees. There was tense swelling, in one man extending above the wrist and in the other involving the whole arm and shoulder, with extensive hematomas and large blisters from which drained serosanguinous fluid. A study of 477 cases of snakebite in Costa Rica in 1979 revealed that 41 (8.6%) were attributable to *B. lateralis* (Bolaños, 1984). In southwestern Costa Rica, there were 3 cases of bites by this species among 166 child victims of snakebite (Montalvan et al., 1983). Bolaños (1984) regarded bites by this pitviper (and by *B. schlegelii* and *Porthidium nasutum*) as being of only moderate medical importance unless they affected the fingers, in which case permanent disability frequently resulted.

Bothriechis marchi (formerly *B. nigroviridis marchi*), Honduran palm-pitviper (Pls. 384–387)

March (1929b) heard that three men had been killed in Honduras by a snake known locally as tamagá verde, which was named as a new subspecies later in the same year. At La

Cumbre, a 50-year-old man was struck on the shoulder as he brushed past a large rock on which the snake was resting. Nineteen hours later he presented in a state of collapse with swelling of the right shoulder and trunk down to and including the hip. He complained of severe head pains, difficulty breathing, dizziness, and exhaustion after a sleepless night. He had photophobia with inflammation and congestion of the conjunctivae. He recovered after antivenom treatment. A herpetologist who was bitten on the finger by a specimen of *B. marchi* applied a tight band around the base of the digit and later developed some necrosis of the fingertip (Thomas Häfner, pers. comm.).

Bothriechis nigroviridis, black-speckled palm-pitviper (Pls. 388–390)

According to Campbell and Lamar (1989), bites by this species can cause severe pain, nausea, and asphyxia and have been implicated in human fatalities.

Bothriechis schlegelii, eyelash palm-pitviper (Pls. 395–414, see also 415–420)

Several members of a trail gang cutting through the jungle in Honduras died after being bitten on the hands and face by this species (Ditmars, 1931). In Costa Rica in 1979, *B. schlegelii* was responsible for 90 of 477 snakebite cases (18.9%) analyzed by Bolaños (1984). At one time this species caused three to six deaths per year in Costa Rica. Four of a series of 27 autopsied snakebite cases in San José, Costa Rica, were attributed to *B. schlegelii* (Mekbel and Céspedes, 1963). In southwestern Costa Rica, 7 of 166 cases of snakebites in children were attributed to this species (Montalvan et al., 1983). Lieske (1963) illustrated a 38-year-old man bitten on the big toe by *B. schlegelii* who presented 30 hours after the bite with marked edema of the lower leg, local hematoma, bleeding gums, and a temperature of 38 °C. For 72 hours after the bite there was bleeding from the gums, nosebleed, and hematuria, but after 14 days the man was discharged from the hospital. This species is regarded as the most important cause of snakebite in Popayán, Cauca, Colombia. A coffee plantation worker died after being bitten on the tongue (Ayerbe et al., 1977, 1979). Among 218 cases of pitviper bites in Antioquia and Chocó (1989–1990), 12 (5.5%) were caused by this species, known locally as víbora de tierra fría, granadilla, or cabeza de candado. Eleven showed only mild local envenoming, and 1 had systemic dysfunction (Otero et al., 1992b). In a later series of 39 cases from this area, there was only 1 case of mild envenoming caused by *B. schlegelii* (Otero et al., 2002).

In Chiapas, Mexico, *B. schlegelii* is regarded as one of the most dangerous snakes present. Its arboreal habit results in bites on the face, neck, and other parts of the upper body, which make the effects all the more severe (Alvarez del Toro, 1983).

Of 10 Costa Rican pitviper venoms studied by Gutiérrez and Cháves (1980), those of *Bothriechis schlegelii* and *Bothrops asper* were the most myotoxic, and those of *B. lateralis* and *Cerrophidion godmani* were the most proteolytic.

Genus *Bothriopsis* (Pls. 427–453)

Bothriopsis bilineata, parrotsnake (Pls. 427–430, 1416–1419)

Silva-Júnior (1956) cited an early reference to a fatal bite by this species in "Uruguai" by the famous Mineiro poet, Vasílio da Gama (1740–1795). More recently, this species is increasingly recognized as an important cause of snakebite throughout the entire Amazon region. In Leticia, Amazonas, Colombia, 14 of 93 cases of snakebite seen between 1973 and 1978 were attributed to *B. b. smaragdina* (Silva-Haad, 1982a) and during the period 1982–1987, 9 of 279 cases (3.4%) seen at the same hospital were attributed to this species (Silva, 1989). Eight of 262 cases of identified snakebites from the Selva Central of Peru were attributed to *B. bilineata* (Julio Demarini Caro, pers. comm., 2002), and among 65 cases seen at the regional hospital of Loreto, Iquitos, Peru, 7.7% were caused by this snake (known locally as loro machaco; Mosquera Leiva, 2000). The Siona-Secoya Indians of Napo, Ecuador, identified *B. b. smaragdina* as the species most often responsible for bites (Touzet, 1986); 5 of 16 cases in which the snake was identified were attributed to this species. Bites were on the wrists, hands, and arms. All of the victims developed bleeding gums; one lost consciousness, vomited blood, and developed fever; and three bled from the fang puncture wounds. A little girl bitten on the forearm by this species, known as orito machácuy at Hacienda Primavera, Río Napo, Ecuador, developed "nervous shock," local swelling, and bleeding from the mouth, nose, and eyes. She was treated by a local brujo, and two days later all signs of envenoming had resolved (Touzet, 1983). At Santa Cecilia on the Río Aguarico, Ecuador, two trail cutters were bitten by this species (known locally as loro, meaning "parrot"; Duellman, 1978).

In a group of 55 snakebite cases admitted to Hospital Vozandes del Oriente in Shell-Mera, Pastaza, Ecuador, in which the snake responsible was brought for identification, 21 (38%) were caused by *B. b. smaragdina*, known locally as oro palito or palo verde (Warrell et al., unpublished data). A high proportion of bites by this species are inflicted on the hands, upper body, and face, reflecting its arboreal nature. Among a series of 230 snakebite cases recruited to a comparative study of three different antivenoms at the same hospital (1997–2002), *B. b. smaragdina* was responsible for seven bites inflicted on the head, two on the shoulders, one on the back, and many on the hands and upper limbs (Warrell et al., unpublished data).

Common clinical features include local swelling and bruising, profound coagulopathy, and spontaneous bleeding (Pls. 1413–1417). A 14-year-old Shuar girl (Case EA, no. 7, Warrell et al., unpublished data) was bitten on the dorsum of her foot at Makuma, Morona-Santiago, Ecuador, by a specimen of *B. b. smaragdina* 65 cm in TL. She developed local pain, swelling, and bruising up to the knee, and when seen in the hospital was feverish (40 °C) and was bleeding from her nose and gums. There was hematuria, her blood was incoagulable, and she had a low platelet count (145×10^9/l). She made an uneventful recovery after treatment with specific antivenom. A pregnant 37-year-old mestiza (Case FA, no. 6, Warrell et al., unpublished data) was bitten on the finger in Puyo, Pastaza, Ecuador, while reaching into a cupboard in her garden. She developed pain and swelling in the finger and hand and was found to have incoagulable blood but a normal platelet count. She recovered uneventfully after being treated with specific antivenom; her pregnancy proceeded normally. A seven-months'-pregnant, 25-year-old Quechua woman was bitten on the dorsum of her foot at Pitacocha, Pastaza, Ecuador. When seen in the hospital six hours after the bite she had painful swelling of the foot and leg and was bleeding from the gums. Her blood was incoagulable. She made a good recovery after treatment with specific antivenom, and her pregnancy proceeded normally (Warrell et al., unpublished data). A 7-year-old Shuar boy (Case LAH, no. 21, Warrell et al., unpublished data) was bitten on the forehead at Nueva Vida, Pastaza, Ecuador. When admitted to the hospital three hours later he exhibited painful swelling, bruising, and erythema of the forehead and both eyelids. He had vomited on the way to the hospital. His blood was incoagulable. The peripheral leukocyte count was $14.3 \times 10^9/l$ (55% neutrophils). He made an uneventful recovery after being treated with specific antivenom.

Near Lago Agrio, Napo, Ecuador, a 30-year-old farmer was bitten on the left wrist while cutting with a machete (Warrell et al., unpublished data). He was admitted to the hospital with local pain and swelling and bleeding gums. When antivenom was injected intramuscularly into his left buttock, he developed an extensive hematoma indicating that his blood was incoagulable at the time. Six days after the bite there was still bruising of the arm, adjacent areas of the trunk, and at the site of the antivenom injection (Pls. 1416 and 1417). A 57-year-old English toxinologist was bitten on the index and middle fingers of his left hand while milking a specimen of *B. b. smaragdina* from Pastaza in Quito, Ecuador (Warrell et al., unpublished data). There was immediate pain, followed 10 minutes later by local swelling, nausea, and symptoms of venom hypersensitivity causing anaphylaxis. His blood became incoagulable and he developed bruising and swelling of the bitten limb with enlarged, tender epitrochlear and axillary glands. A blood-filled blister developed at the site of the bite (Pls. 1418 and 1419). Unusual complications of *B. bilineata* bites are local abscess formation (from one, *Escherichia coli* was cultured) and necrosis (Warrell et al., unpublished data).

At Phillipai, Mazaruni, Guyana, a 32-year-old diamond miner was bitten twice on the trunk by *B. b. bilineata* (parrotsnake) while sleeping in bed. After some preliminary treatment in Mazaruni District, he was flown to Georgetown and admitted to the intensive care unit of the country's only tertiary referral hospital, where he died (Starbroek News, 1999).

Bothriopsis chloromelas (formerly *B. oligolepis* and so designated in Campbell and Lamar, 1989), lamón (Pls. 431–433)

This species is still recognized in Peru as *B. oligolepis* and is common around Oxapampa, Pasco, and Huatziroki (near La Merced), Junín, Peru. Oxapampa Hospital admits about 20 cases of bites by this species, known locally as "lamón," each year, but there have been no recent fatalities. Bites occur in the area of Villa Rica, Palcazu, Porte Bermudez, Iscozacin, and Pozuzo (elevation 1,000–2,000 m).

Bothriopsis medusa, viejita (Pls. 434 and 435)

According to Campbell and Lamar (1989), the venom of this species has only a mild effect on humans.

Bothriopsis oligolepis (formerly *B. peruviana* and so designated in Campbell and Lamar, 1989), loro machaco (Pls. 436 and 437)

This species is recognized in Peru as *B. peruviana*. Demarini Caro (1992) described and illustrated a 22-year-old man who was bitten at the base of his middle and ring fingers by a specimen of *B. oligolepis* (also illustrated and referred to as *B. peruviana*) in the Selva Central of Peru. On admission to hospital three hours after the bite, there was painful swelling of the affected hand. He was treated with antivenom (Anti-Botrópico

INS) and made an uneventful recovery over the next four days. Three other cases of bites by this species were recorded in the same area, constituting 2.8% of all identified bites (Demarini Caro, 1992). In a larger series of 230 cases of identified bites surveyed by the same author in the same region, 20 were attributed to this species, and 23 cases of proven bites have been observed in La Merced, Chanchamayo, Peru at the time of this writing (Julio Demarini Caro, pers. comm.). Clinical features include pain, swelling, blistering, but no necrosis, with incoagulable blood and more frequent spontaneous systemic bleeding than with *Bothrops atrox* envenoming. A 10-year-old girl was bitten by a specimen 86 cm in TL near La Merced and presented with local swelling and bleeding that persisted for three days despite treatment with two vials of antivenom. She was transferred to a specialist hospital in Lima, where she died six days after the bite. A coffee plantation worker bitten on the leg by a snake that fell from a tree developed massive local swelling, epistaxis, and hematuria, and finally came to the hospital 36 hours after the event. Two hours after receiving antivenom he started to have generalized seizures and died of suspected cerebral hemorrhage (Julio Demarini Caro, pers. comm.).

Bothriopsis pulchra (formerly *Bothriopsis albocarinata*, *Bothriechis albocarinata*, and *Bothrops albocarinatus*; possibly the same species as *B. alticola*) (Pls. 438–443)

An 18-year-old mestiza (Case MQ, no. 15, Warrell et al., unpublished data) was bitten on the heel, near Puyo, Pastaza, Ecuador, by a specimen 25 cm in TL that she referred to as oro palito. There was local pain, persistent bleeding from the site of the bite, and swelling that extended up to the knee within the first 24 hours after the bite. Her blood remained coagulable, there was no fever, and she was not treated with antivenom.

Bothriopsis taeniata (formerly *Bothrops castelnaudi* and *Bothrops taeniatus*) (Pls. 444–453)

Among 985 cases of snakebite surveyed in the Selva Central of Peru, 2 were caused by this species with no fatalities or necrotic sequelae (Julio Demarini Caro, pers. comm., 2002). At Mera, Pastaza, Ecuador, an 11-year-old girl (Case LC, no. 9, Warrell et al., unpublished data) was bitten on the lower leg. When she was first seen in the hospital 30 minutes after the bite, there was no swelling but she was complaining of pain. There was local redness and bleeding from the fang punctures, and she was vomiting. Her blood was incoagulable, peripheral leukocyte count $9.5 \times 10^9/l$ (70% neutrophils). She was treated with antivenom, and after repeated doses over 24 hours, blood coagulability was eventually restored. She developed extensive bruising and massive swelling of the foot, leg, and thigh. She became feverish (39 °C) 12 hours after the bite, and after 48 hours a local blister formed that was drained of serosanguinous fluid. She eventually made a complete recovery.

At Vera Cruz, Pastaza, Ecuador, a 56-year-old mestizo (Case JC, no. 16, Warrell et al., unpublished data) was bitten on the left leg by a very large *B. taeniata* (approximately 1.5 m in TL). On admission to the hospital 5.5 hours after the bite there was pain and swelling of the bitten limb with persistent bleeding from the fang punctures although his blood was coagulable. He complained of dizziness, sleepiness, and repeated vomiting. The peripheral leukocyte count was

21.3 × 10⁹/l. He had persistent hematuria. Swelling quickly spread to involve the entire limb. He was treated with antivenom. The next day, at fasciotomy, the anterior tibial compartment was found to be under high pressure and its contained muscles dark and necrotic looking. Anterior, lateral, and posterior fasciotomies were performed, but pus was later found in the posterior compartment; 13 days after the bite, an above-knee amputation was performed. He had required a nine-unit blood transfusion.

Remarks   These two cases of proven *B. taeniata* bites indicate that the venom of this species can cause severe local swelling, in both cases involving the entire bitten limb, and also tissue damage, which led to amputation in the second case.

Genus *Bothrocophias* (Pls. 454–485)

Bothrocophias hyoprora (formerly *Porthidium hyoprora*) (Pls. 466–472)

In Leticia, Amazonas, Colombia, this species was responsible for 0.35% of identified bites (Silva, 1989). On the Río Aguarico, Napo, Ecuador, 2 of 16 identified bites in Siona-Secoya Indians were attributed to this species. The bites, on the feet, were painful and caused swelling that spread to the ankle; in one case there was bleeding from the gums. No local necrosis developed in either case (Touzet, 1986). At Moretecocha, Pastaza, Ecuador, a 38-year-old Quechua woman (Case BS, no. 27, Warrell et al., unpublished data) was bitten on the middle and third fingers of the right hand by an identified specimen of *B. hyoprora*. There was bleeding from the site of the bite and slight swelling of the hand. When she was admitted to the hospital five hours later, there was no bleeding but she was crying with intense pain that required strong analgesia. Her blood was coagulable and the hemoglobin concentration and peripheral leukocyte count were normal. On the day after her admission, whole blood clotting time increased from 7 to 15 minutes and she was treated with antivenom. Her pain persisted for the next two days and there was persistent oozing of blood from the fang punctures.

In northeastern Peru, *B. hyoprora* (known locally as jergón pudridora) is said to cause extensive necrosis (Campbell and Lamar, pers. comm.).

Bothrocophias microphthalmus (formerly *Bothrops microphthalmus*) (Pls. 473–484)

At Topo, Tungurahua, Ecuador, a 28-year-old man (Case TR, no. 5, Warrell et al., unpublished data) was bitten on the left forearm by an identified specimen of *B. microphthalmus*. The distance between the fang punctures was 25 mm, suggesting a very large snake. There was immediate swelling, redness, and bruising. On admission to the hospital one hour later there was no spontaneous systemic bleeding but his blood was incoagulable and he had hematuria. The peripheral leukocyte count was 17.2 × 10⁹/l. He was treated with polyspecific antivenom, which eventually restored blood coagulability permanently. Swelling extended up to the elbow, but he was discharged after two days. Among 262 identified cases of snakebite from the Selva Central of Peru, 4 were attributed to this species (Julio Demarini Caro, pers. comm., 2002). Clinical signs included local swelling (involving the whole arm in a patient bitten by a specimen 85 cm in TL) bruising, and blistering, but without development of local necrosis or systemic bleeding.

Genus *Bothrops* (Pls. 486–662)

Bothrops alternatus, urutu in Brazil, yarará grande in Argentina, crucera in Uruguay (Pls. 488–491)

North of Arraial do Rio Verde, Brazil, Spix and Martius (1824) found that the urutú had the reputation of being one of the most poisonous serpents of the country. "Its bite is said to occasion almost certain death."

In his survey of 6,601 snakebite cases from Central and South America, Fonseca (1949) attributed 384 (5.82%) to this species, with eight deaths—a case fatality of 2.0%. At the Instituto Butantan, before 1945, this species was the fourth most common cause of bites; there were 507 cases, with a case fatality of 4.3% (Silva-Júnior, 1956). During the years 1954–1965 only 3 bites by this species were recorded at the Instituto Butantan (0.1% of all cases), and there were no deaths (Rosenfeld, 1971). In Catanduva, São Paulo State, Brazil, 32 cases of bites by this species were admitted to the hospital between 1985 and 1992 (Bauab et al., 1994). All of these patients developed local pain and swelling. Blood clotting time was prolonged (more than 12 minutes) in 97%, and there was bleeding (usually from the gums) in 41%. Local blistering developed in 32%, with necrosis in 9%. Specific antivenom was used and there were no fatalities. These findings contrast with the urutu's reputation in rural Brazil for either killing or crippling its victims. Silva-Júnior described one Brazilian patient with gangrene of the hand and forearm, requiring amputation, resulting from the bite of this species (1956: fig. 73), and another patient with scarring over the anterior tibial compartment following a bite four years previously (1956: fig. 75). Abalos and Pirosky (1963) regarded this species as being responsible for a large proportion of the snakebites in Argentina. They illustrated a young boy with gangrene below the knee, exposing the bare tibia and fibula, following a bite by *B. alternatus*. Esteso (1985) attributed 18% of bites in Argentina to this species.

Bothrops ammodytoides, yarará ñata (Pls. 492 and 493)

Although Campbell and Lamar (1989) commented on this species' irritable temperament and speculated that it might be capable of causing human fatalities, Esteso (1985) and Abalos and Pirosky (1963) reported that bites were either unknown or infrequent and doubted that this species poses a medical problem to humans.

Bothrops andianus, jergona (Pls. 494–498)

Carrillo de Espinoza (1983) reported that this species was very common in the ruins of Machu Picchu, Peru, and she considered that it posed a risk of fatal accidents to the many tourists visiting this area. Although snakes are frequently observed, especially on Huayna Picchu, only two bites to tourists have been noted in five recent years. Among 230 identified cases of snakebite in the Selva Central of Peru, only 1 was attributable to this species. The patient was bitten at Vilkanota, near Machu Picchu, by a specimen 45 cm in TL and developed pain, swelling, local bruising, prolonged clotting times, and moderate leukocytosis, but no systemic bleeding. No necrosis ensued (Julio Demarini Caro, pers. comm.).

Bothrops asper (includes *B. xanthogrammus*), terciopelo, barba amarilla, nauyaca, etc. (Pls. 499–517, 1363, 1420, 1421)

This species is an important cause of snakebite throughout its range in Mexico, Guatemala, Honduras, Nicaragua, Costa Rica, Panama, western Colombia (including Isla de Gorgona), Ecuador (La Costa), Peru, Venezuela, and Trinidad. This irritable, fast-moving, and agile snake can grow to about 2.5 m in TL. The average venom yield is 458 mg (dry weight), and the maximum known is 1,530 mg (Bolaños, 1984). In Yucatán, Mexico, it is, with *Crotalus simus*, the leading cause of snakebites. In Costa Rica it is regarded as the most dangerous snake present, causing 46% of bites and 30% of all hospitalized snakebite cases, with a case fatality that was 7.0% in 1947 but has now declined to almost 0% (Bolaños, 1984). In southwestern Costa Rica, 49% of bites in children were attributed to this species (Montalvan et al., 1983). In Antioquia and Chocó in Colombia, this species causes 50–70% of bites with a case fatality of 5% and an incidence of sequelae of 6% (Otero et al., 1992b). In the state of Lara, northwestern Venezuela, this species (referred to as *B. atrox*) was responsible for 78% of envenomings and all of the snakebite deaths (Dao-L., 1971). In La Costa, Ecuador, it is implicated in more than 80% of all cases of snakebite envenoming, "of which many result in permanent sequelae, and not a few in the death of the patients" (Freire-Lascano and Kuch, 1994). *Bothrops xanthogrammus* is no longer distinguished as a separate species (Campbell and Lamar, 1992; Theakston et al., 1995). In Cauca, southwestern Colombia, *B. asper* is the primary cause of snakebites as well (Ayerbe et al., 1977), and in Panama this species is thought to pose the greatest risk of envenoming. One out of three of Eichelbaum's cases died (Eichelbaum, 1927). *Bothrops asper* was responsible for all of 10 bites inflicted on biology field workers in Middle America (Hardy, 1994c; see below) and claimed the life of Douglas March, a well-known herpetologist who worked mainly in Honduras. This species' habit of living close to human dwellings increases the risk of bites, many of which occur indoors (Sasa and Vázquez, 2003).

Bothrops asper is regarded as being more excitable and unpredictable than *B. atrox* and has a reputation for being aggressive. In Trinidad, Mole (1924) observed it eject its venom for a distance of at least 6 feet (1.8 m), in fine jets, from the tips of its fangs.

According to Russell et al. (1997), *B. asper* bites cause pain, oozing from the fang punctures, local swelling that may continue to increase for 36 hours, bruising that spreads from the site of the bite, numbness, mild fever, bleeding from the gums and nose, hemoptysis, gastrointestinal bleeding, hematuria, hypotension, nausea and vomiting, impaired consciousness, and splenic tenderness. In untreated cases, local necrosis is frequent and may require amputation (Pl. 1420). Hardy (1994c) reviewed 10 cases of bites by specimens of *B. asper* ranging in TL from 1.0 to 2.0 m in people involved in field biology projects in Middle America. Three of the bites were at or above knee level, 3 were on the hand, and 1 was on the upper arm. One patient was not envenomed. Local swelling was sometimes massive, and in 3 cases local necrosis required surgical reconstruction (Pl. 1421). Four patients showed spontaneous systemic bleeding from the gums or from the gastrointestinal, respiratory, or urinary tracts. A 26-year-old man bitten on the lower leg by a snake 1.8 m in TL in Petén, Guatemala, developed local necro-

sis, and 14 days after the bite required laparotomy for closure of multiple intestinal perforations. He was mechanically ventilated following a respiratory arrest, had a below-knee amputation, and required peritoneal dialysis for acute renal failure (Hardy, 1994c). Other complications in this series of bites were anemia (2 cases), disseminated intravascular coagulation (1 case), and acute renal failure (2 cases). Seven of the victims received antivenom in the field, and all but the unenvenomed patient eventually received antivenom. In a series of 244 cases of snakebite treated in Antioquia and Chocó (1989–1990), 44.5% were attributed to *Bothrops asper* (referred to as *B. atrox*), known in this area as mapaná, equis, cuatro narices, or boquidorá (Otero et al., 1992b). Of these patients, 97.2% developed local swelling, 12.4% had multiple local blisters containing serosanguinous fluid, and 9.2% developed necrosis. Nonspecific symptoms such as nausea, vomiting, headache, tachycardia, and sweating were experienced by 23%. Gingival bleeding occurred in 23%; fever in 20.3%; hypotension in 14.3%; macroscopic hematuria in 12.9%; hematemesis, melena, hemoptysis, and epistaxis in less than 10%; incoagulable blood in 62%; thrombocytopenia in 31%; and elevated serum creatinine in 10.6%. Local soft tissue infections attributed to *Proteus mirabilis*, *Staphylococcus aureus*, *Acinetobacter calcoaceticum*, *E. coli*, *Pseudomonas aeruginosa*, and *Klebsiella pneumoniae* developed in 10.6% of the *Bothrops* victims. All of the patients who developed soft tissue infection had severe local envenoming with areas of necrosis; 5% had DIC, prolonged thrombin and partial thromboplastin times, and thrombocytopenia; 3.2% developed compartmental syndromes. Six patients suffered intracranial hemorrhages, and 1 developed a subcapsular hematoma of the liver. A woman in the third month of pregnancy developed hemothorax and spontaneous abortion. Six percent of the patients bitten by *Bothrops* developed acute renal failure. Use of traditional medicine, delay in reaching hospital for 6 or more hours, and being bitten by a snake more than 1 m in TL were associated with a bad prognosis, as was being bitten by *B. asper* rather than any other pitviper. Causes of death in 12 patients were septicemia (5), intracranial hemorrhage (3), acute renal failure with hyperkalemia and metabolic acidosis (2), and hemorrhagic shock (1). Sequelae in 13 patients were the result of extensive necrosis, atrophy, and contractures from muscle necrosis and peripheral nerve palsies. The risk of sequelae was increased in patients who had undergone traditional treatment and whose hospital admission had been delayed for 12 or more hours.

A later study from the same area of Colombia surveyed 39 patients who were transferred to a university hospital in Medellín, Antioquia (Otero et al., 2002). In this series, 29 (74.4%) patients had been bitten by *B. asper*. This species was responsible for envenoming 11 of the 15 patients who developed acute renal failure; 3 of 5 with intracranial hemorrhage; 11 of 12 who developed soft tissue infections (abscesses, necrotizing fasciitis, or cellulitis); 3 children who developed compartmental syndromes; and a 26-year-old woman, 30 weeks pregnant, who presented with antepartum hemorrhage, abruptio placentae, and fetal death. The four deaths (10.3%) were associated with acute renal failure and intracranial hemorrhage. Fourteen patients (36%) had sequelae from muscle necrosis and amputations and from the effects of strokes.

In Trinidad, where *B. asper* is known as mapepire balsain, valsain, or mapepire barcin (Murphy, 1997), a six-year-old boy was admitted to Port-of-Spain General Hospital two hours after being bitten by a large specimen. He had vomited blood on three occasions. The bitten leg was swollen, tender, and bruised; he had proteinuria, hematuria, and nasogastric fluid aspirate strongly positive for blood (indicating gastrointestinal hemorrhage). His blood was incoagulable, prothrombin and partial thromboplastin times were grossly prolonged, and the leukocyte count was elevated at $15.2 \times 10^9/l$, but his platelet count was normal at $328 \times 10^9/l$. He was treated with antivenom (presumably Wyeth polyspecific Crotalidae) and given fresh frozen plasma. Normal blood coagulation was restored and local symptoms improved by the third day of admission, but hematuria persisted until the fifth day (Bratt and Boos, 1992b).

Barrantes et al. (1985) studied the coagulopathy caused by *B. asper* envenoming in 18 patients in Costa Rica. Platelet counts were normal, but prothrombin and partial thromboplastin times were prolonged and fibrinogen and factors II, V, VIII, IX, X, and XI, antithrombin III, and plasminogen were all reduced. Factors VII and XII were normal. These results indicated venom-induced defibrination. Kornalík and Vorlová (1990) studied a 60-year-old patient whose finger had been punctured by a single fang of a juvenile *B. asper*. Four hours after the bite there was spontaneous bleeding from the gums, hemoptysis, and hematuria. Antivenom treatment was withheld because of allergy. Over the next eight days there was hypofibrinogenemia, elevated fibrin(ogen) degradation products, and prolonged prothrombin and activating partial prothrombin times, suggesting disseminated intravascular coagulation leading to consumption coagulopathy. The patient was treated with fibrinogen, cryoprecipitate, and vitamin K. Coagulation tests had returned to normal 12 days after the bite. The venom of the juvenile snake had strong prothrombin-converting activity, whereas adult *B. asper* venom has mainly thrombinlike activity. Autopsies of 26 snakebite victims in Costa Rica showed that 68% had renal lesions, hemoglobinuric nephrosis (7 patients), thrombotic microangiopathy (DIC) (4 patients), acute tubular necrosis (3 patients), and renal cortical necrosis (3 patients) (Vargas-Baldares, 1978). Mekbel and Céspedes (1963) reviewed the autopsies of 27 snakebite victims in San José, Costa Rica, 13 of which were caused by *B. asper*. There was bilateral renal cortical necrosis in 7 cases, thrombi in the glomerular capillaries in 6 cases, focal tubular degeneration in 4, and acute tubular necrosis in 1 case. A typical history was of a 37-year-old man bitten on the foot by *B. asper*, known locally as terciopelo or tiznada. Two hours after the bite he was given one ampule of antivenom intramuscularly. On admission to the hospital 30 hours after the bite, there was pain in the bitten limb and a history of blood-stained saliva. The bitten limb was swollen and hot, the prothrombin time was prolonged, and the urine contained albumin, red cells, and a few white cells. Despite further antivenom treatment he died 13 days after the bite. In this series of 27 fatal cases, which included four bites attributed to *Bothriechis schlegelii* and two by unidentified snakes, the cause of death was intracranial hemorrhage in 10 cases, diffuse hemorrhage in 2, bilateral renal cortical necrosis in 6, toxemia in 4, shock in 4, and acute renal tubular necrosis in 1.

Remarks *Bothrops asper* is responsible for many cases of severe envenoming resulting in death or permanent disability. The range of clinical manifestations of envenoming is similar to that of *B. atrox* (see below), but *B. asper* seems even more inclined to strike if cornered, molested, or inadvertently trodden on or touched. Its size and its habit of raising its head high off the ground can result in bites above the knee level. Like *B. atrox*, its willingness to colonize plantations and gardens in

areas of cleared jungle and even to enter human dwellings brings it into contact with people.

Bothrops atrox, South American lancehead; common lancehead; fer-de-lance; yoperojobobo in Bolivia; caissaca or jararaca in Brazil; mapaná, equis, or cuatronarices in Colombia; equis in Ecuador; jergón in Peru; and, inappropriately, fer-de-lance outside Latin America (Pls. 518–534, 1365; see also 535, 1364)

Throughout its range, the Amazon region, this species is the most important cause of snakebite mortality and morbidity. Thus, in Manaus, Amazonas, Brazil, *B. atrox* was responsible for 76% of bites with an overall case fatality of 1% (Borges et al., 1999); in Roraima, Brazil, it was blamed for 82% of bites (case fatality 3.9%; Nascimento, 2000); and in Leticia, Amazonas, Colombia, 94% of bites were caused by pitvipers, 95.5% of which were *B. atrox* (Silva-Haad, 1989). In northeastern Peru, 60% of bites were attributed to this species (Arévale, *in* Soini, 1974b), and in Pebas, Loreto, Peru, all of a group of 100 snakebite cases were attributed to *B. atrox* (Scott Humfeld, pers. comm.). At the Hospital Regional de Loreto in Iquitos, 63% of snakebite cases were caused by *B. atrox* (Mosquera Leiva, 2000); and at the Hospital de Apoyo, La Merced, Chanchamayo, Peru, 36.5% of snakebites were caused by this species (Villanueva Forero, unpublished data). Among 74 snakebite patients admitted to Barros Barreto Hospital in Belém, Pará, Brazil, all but 1 were proved to be due to *B. atrox* (Pardal et al., 2004); however, the immunodiagnostic method did not distinguish between *B. atrox* and *B. marajoensis*. On geographical grounds, 5 of these patients must have been bitten by *B. marajoensis* (see below). In Pastaza, Ecuador, 45% of a group of 55 patients admitted to the Hospital Vozandes del Oriente who brought the snake responsible had been bitten by *B. atrox* (Warrell et al., unpublished data). Among the 73 patients with proven bites by *B. atrox* (and *B. marajoensis*) in Belém, Pará, Brazil, all had pain, local swelling, and inflammation; 33 had regional lymphadenopathy; 29 exhibited local bleeding; 19 had local erythema; and 13 showed ecchymoses (Pardal et al., 2004). Three developed local blistering. Fifty-four patients experienced headache and nausea. Spontaneous systemic bleeding was observed from the gingival sulci in 11, as hemoptysis in 6, as macroscopic hematuria in 4, as purpura in 4, as subconjunctival hemorrhage in 1, and as hematemesis in 1. Thirty-one had incoagulable blood on admission. Swelling reached a maximum in about 24 hours. Seven patients developed local abscesses and 2 developed local necrosis requiring surgical debridement, but no amputations were required. Laboratory screening detected no elevation of serum creatine kinase, but 29 patients had elevated serum creatinine concentrations. Fibrinogen and α_2 antiplasmin concentrations were reduced, while fibrin(ogen) degradation production and D-dimer were elevated. Many patients showed a transient leukocytosis, but only 9 had thrombocytopenia (platelets less than $150 \times 10^9/l$).

Among 230 patients with systemic envenoming by *Bothrops* species recruited to a trial of three antivenoms at Hospital Vozandes, Shell, Pastaza, Ecuador, the majority had bites attributable to *B. atrox*, known locally as equis (Warrell et al., unpublished data). Five patients had been bitten by *B. atrox* while washing, bathing, or wading in rivers. The series included five pregnant women (from six weeks to full term), but in no case did envenoming cause any complications. One woman bitten postpartum, however, had persistent vaginal bleeding. Among 12 patients who developed local abscesses at the site of the bite, one had gas gangrene. Pus aspirated from the abscesses in the other cases cultured the following organisms: *Morganella morganii* (2), *Escherichia coli* (4), *Proteus mirabilis* (3), *P. vulgaris* (2), *Acinetobacter baumannii* (2), *Staphylococcus aureus* (1), and *Pseudomonas* (1).

A seven-year-old Shuar girl was bitten on the ankle after treading on a small *B. atrox* in her garden at Ischpingo, Pastaza, Ecuador (Warrell et al., unpublished data). Her parents took no action because the snake was so small, but 9 hours later she began to bleed from the gums, and 26 hours after the bite she suddenly complained of headache and almost immediately lost consciousness. She was flown to the Hospital Vozandes del Oriente, Shell, Pastaza, arriving 36 hours after the bite. On admission she was found to be unconscious (Glasgow Coma Score 4). She was bleeding from the nose, mouth, vagina, and rectum. She had bled into one eye, and the pupil of the other eye was fixed and dilated. The bitten leg was swollen up to the groin and was ecchymotic with a hemarthrosis in the knee. Her blood pressure was 50/40 mm Hg, pulse rate 164 per minute, respiratory rate 26–32 per minute. During endotracheal intubation, blood was aspirated from the lungs. She was mechanically ventilated. The hematocrit was 28%, platelet count $150 \times 10^9/l$. Eight ampules of Instituto Butantan polyspecific antivenom were administered over 26 hours. The spontaneous bleeding ceased, but she became hypothermic and remained hypotensive (blood pressure 70/50 mm Hg, pulse 78 per minute). She was flown to Quito, where a cerebral CT scan showed massive intracerebral hemorrhage with a fluid level indicating that the blood was incoagulable (Fig. 270); she died shortly afterward.

On his way back from hunting wild boar with his father, a 14-year-old Waorani boy at Cononaco, Ecuador, took one step off the path and was bitten on the calf by a ñenenenca (*B. atrox*) 1.5 m in TL (Warrell et al., unpublished data). He fainted almost immediately and was taken to Coca and then flown to the Hospital Vozandes del Oriente at Shell, Pastaza. On admission he was bleeding from the gums and vomiting blood. There was progressive swelling of the entire bitten limb and adjacent area of trunk and genitalia (Pls. 1422–1424). He was treated with Mexican Myn antivenom (later proved to be ineffective *fide*

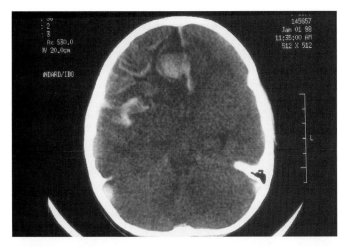

Fig. 270. Cerebral CT scan of a seven-year-old Shuar girl bitten by a small *Bothrops atrox* at Ischpingo, Pastaza, Ecuador, 48 hours earlier, showing massive intracerebral hemorrhage. The fluid level indicates that the blood was incoagulable. Copyright David A. Warrell.

Theakston et al., 1995), which failed to restore blood coagulability, and despite repeated blood transfusions over the next 48 hours his hemoglobin concentration fell from 12 to 5 g/dl. He bled from exploratory fasciotomies (Pls. 1422–1424), developed abdominal distention with other signs of massive intra- or retroperitoneal hemorrhage, lapsed into coma, and died 68 hours after the bite.

While reaching down to pull an armadillo out of its hole near Macas, Ecuador, at 0600, a 54-year-old mestizo was bitten on the left shoulder by a female *B. atrox* 1.6 m in TL. He took a traditional remedy, "Pepa de Aguacate," and alcohol to relieve the severe pain. One hour later he arrived at the Hospital Vozandes del Oriente at Shell, Pastaza, complaining of agonizing pain in the bitten shoulder extending into the neck. Examination revealed swelling of his arm and shoulder, blood pressure 80/60 mm Hg, pulse 52 per minute. His blood was incoagulable; hemoglobin 14.2 g/dl, hematocrit 43%, leukocytes $15.5 \times 10^9/l$, platelets $300 \times 10^9/l$. The urine contained erythrocytes. Plasma electrolytes, creatinine, and urea were normal. He was treated with two vials of Instituto Butantan anti-bothropic antivenom at 0840 hours, together with 5 l of intravenous fluid over the first 24 hours. Six hours later the dose of antivenom was repeated as his blood was still incoagulable, and 6 hours later, blood coagulability was restored. After passing only 100 ml of urine he became anuric. Hypotension with an inappropriately low pulse rate of less than 60 per minute was treated with intravenous fluids, but 24 hours after admission, dopamine was started because his systolic blood pressure had dropped to 70 mm Hg. For a while, dopamine 20 μg/kg/minute maintained his blood pressure at about 110 mm Hg. He became breathless, and a chest radiograph demonstrated diffuse pulmonary edema, for which he was treated with increasing doses of furosamide. However, he passed no urine. There was biochemical evidence of renal failure, creatinine increasing to 3.7 mg/dl, urea to 87 mg/dl, and potassium to 5.2 mmol/l. About 30 hours after the bite he suffered a respiratory arrest from which he could not be resuscitated (Jeffrey Maudlin, pers. comm.).

A 37-year-old British wildlife photographer was bitten by a specimen of *B. atrox* while removing it from a net near the Coppename River in upcountry Suriname. One fang entered his right thumb, and less than a minute later he suffered a complete loss of vision lasting three or four minutes. This symptom, indicating a sudden fall in blood pressure, is described by many victims of *Bothrops* envenoming. There was severe pain in the bitten thumb, hand, and arm. By the next morning, after a sleepless night, there was bruising of the whole arm with tender, swollen lymph glands at the elbow and in the axilla. During the next 24 hours his gums swelled and bled, he vomited blood and bile, passed black diarrhea stools suggesting melena, felt hot and thirsty, suffered severe pain in the bitten limb, and could not sleep. After 48 hours he was able to sleep for the first time but woke with his mouth filled with congealed blood. At last he managed to board a passing truck and travel to the capital, Paramaribo, where he was admitted to the hospital pale, jaundiced, and dehydrated, having passed a small amount of urine only once since the bite. Investigations revealed a hemoglobin of 5.4 g/dl, normal serum electrolytes, but a blood urea of 62 mmol/l and serum creatinine of 1,540 μmol/l, indicating renal failure. The local doctors held out very little hope for his survival but treated him with antibiotics, tetanus toxoid, and corticosteroids. The next day, five days after the bite, he was flown to London, still with anorexia, insomnia, anuria, and persistent hiccups indicative of his renal failure. On examination at

Guy's Hospital, London, he was found to be exhausted, distressed, and pale, with retinal hemorrhages, a necrotic lesion on the thumb, but no residual swelling of the bitten limb. His pulse and blood pressure were normal. His hemoglobin was 7 g/dl, with marked thrombocytopenia ($20,000 \times 10^9/l$); prolonged prothrombin, kaolin cephalin, and reptilase clotting times; hypofibrinogenemia (1.32 g/l); and elevated fibrin(ogen) degradation products. The blood film showed abnormalities of red cell morphology indicative of microangiopathic hemolysis. The blood urea was 62 mmol/l, serum creatinine 1,590 μmol/l with normal serum electrolytes. Initially, he was treated with peritoneal dialysis and transfusion of blood and platelet concentrates. An arteriovenous shunt was inserted and he was treated with hemodialysis and heparinized (Pl. 1429). Eight days after the bite, a [^{99}Tc^m] diethylenetriaminepentaacetic acid (DTPA) renal scan showed evidence of acute tubular necrosis. Thrombocytopenia and coagulopathy persisted until finally, nine days after the bite (and after consultation with the author), he was treated with Wyeth antivenom, after which there was sustained and eventually complete recovery. He started to pass urine 16 days after the bite. Surgical debridement of the necrotic area on his thumb was carried out 23 days after the bite (D. P. Healey and J. S. Cameron, pers. comm.).

A second case of *B. atrox* envenoming was reported from Suriname, where this species is known as oroekoekoe in the marshy coastal region and as boesie-oroekoekoe (bush oroekoekoe) in the savanna region and hilly interior of the country. A Dutch scientist was bitten on the thumb by a specimen of *B. atrox* approximately 47 cm in TL. Smarting pain spread up the arm, and there was persistent oozing of blood from the bite wound. He applied a tourniquet around the upper arm and incised and sucked at the wound. Polyspecific antivenom was injected locally. Swelling involved the whole hand, and he developed a severe headache. Later he developed an abscess at the site of the bite and an urticarial rash, presumably a reaction to the antivenom treatment. He recovered after 10 days (Oostburg, 1973).

In French Guiana, 2 of 11 cases of snakebite admitted to an intensive care unit in Cayenne were attributed to *B. atrox*, one of which was 70 cm in TL (Hulin et al., 1982). These two men, one Creole and one Palikour Amerindian, were bitten on the calf and foot while clearing undergrowth or gardening in the forest. There was severe pain and swelling. Both had incoagulable blood but with normal platelet counts. They were treated with antivenom (Syntex do Brasil, São Paulo) one and nine hours after the bite, respectively, and both recovered without developing local necrosis.

In Bucaramanga, eastern Colombia, 91% of 55 snakebite cases were caused by *Bothrops* (principally *B. atrox*); the case fatality was 2%. There were 3 cases of cerebrovascular accidents (6% of all cases). Other complications included local infections (16%), necrosis (14%), amputations (8%), and compartmental syndromes (8%) (Badillo et al., 1989).

Remarks Bites and envenoming by *B. atrox* are frequent and familiar environmental hazards of the Amazon region. The snake is usually trodden on in jungle areas, on riverbanks, in cleared areas of plantations, in people's gardens, and even in their dwellings. A number of patients claim to have encountered and been bitten by *B. atrox* in rivers. Envenoming differs from that caused by other *Bothrops* species—other than *B. asper*—only in its frequency and severity. Local envenoming involves pain, swelling that often involves the entire limb (Pls. 1422–1424),

inflammation, local lymphadenopathy, bruising (Pl. 1426), blistering, local abscess formation (Pls. 1430 and 1431), and necrosis that may require amputation and result in permanent physical disability (Pls. 1425–1429, 1432). Systemic effects include early transient hypotensive collapse and spontaneous systemic bleeding from many different sites. Bleeding may be from gums, as hemoptysis, hematemesis, melena, bleeding from the urinary tract and genital tract, bleeding into the skin (Pls. 1434–1436), and subarachnoid (Pl. 1437) and intracranial hemorrhage (Fig. 270), as well as persistent bleeding from the fang marks, from other sites of recent trauma, or from partially healed wounds. Acute renal failure is an important complication.

Bothrops barnetti, Barnett's lancehead, sancarranca or macanche in Peru (Pls. 536 and 537)

This species, the main cause of snakebites in the northern coastal region of Peru, is much feared by locals and is known to defend itself vigorously when confronted (O. Pesantes and P. Venegas, pers. comm.).

Bothrops brazili, Brazil's lancehead (Pls. 536 and 537)

Three cases of proven bites by *B. brazili* were treated at a specialist unit in Manaus, Brazil (Alcideia R. R. de Souza, pers. comm.). Two were from Apuí on the Trans-Amazonian Highway south of Manaus. One developed an intracranial hemorrhage. According to Campbell and Lamar (1989), this snake is greatly feared by the Amerindians of southeastern Colombia. Chippaux (1987) listed the clinical effects of envenoming by this species in French Guiana as inflammatory (graded 3 out of a maximum of 3, or 3/3+), necrotic (2/3+), and hemorrhagic (3/3+).

Bothrops caribbaeus, Saint Lucia lancehead (Pls. 545 and 546; Figs. 271 and 272)

Although bites by this species are uncommon on Saint Lucia, local and systemic complications with rare fatalities have been observed. A 32-year-old man was bitten on the lower leg by a snake 60 cm in TL. Despite treatment with Wyeth polyvalent crotalid antivenin, the bitten limb developed extensive swelling

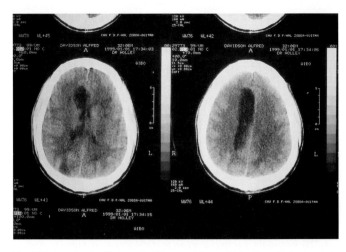

Fig. 271. Cerebral CT scan of a 32-year-old man bitten by a *Bothrops caribbaeus* 60 cm in TL in Saint Lucia, six days after the bite, showing multiple cerebral infarcts.

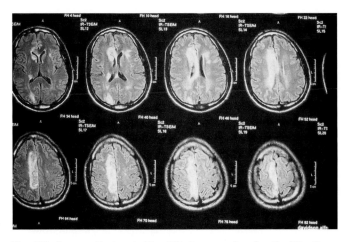

Fig. 272. Same patient as in Fig. 271, three weeks after the bite. From Numeric et al., 2002, reproduced with permission.

with "cellulitis." Six days after the bite the man developed aphasia and weakness of the left arm and leg. Results of laboratory tests were normal apart from a raised creatine kinase (1,212 units/l) and C reactive protein and peripheral leukocyte count (30.4 × 10^9/l). Partial thromboplastin time was normal, fibrinogen was slightly raised, D-dimer was detectable, and the platelet count was normal. His hematocrit and hemoglobin were slightly reduced. He had left hemiplegia with left facial paralysis and aphasia. Cerebral imaging revealed multiple areas of cerebral ischemia, especially in the territory of the right anterior cerebral artery (Fig. 271). Swelling had extended to the entire bitten limb, the abdominal wall, and the upper chest, and there was an area of necrosis at the site of the bite. By August 2003, he had made a complete recovery (Fig. 272; Numeric et al., 2002). "BothroFav" should be considered for treatment of severe envenoming by this species, but at present it is available only in Martinique.

Bothrops cotiara, cotiara (Pls. 547–549)

There were 96 cases of bites by this species among the 6,601 surveyed by Fonseca (1949), with one fatality. From 1954 to 1965 one case was reported at Hospital Vital Brazil, São Paulo (Rosenfeld, 1971).

Bothrops erythromelas, Caatinga lancehead (Pls. 550–557)

This species is an important cause of snakebites in the dry northeastern region of Brazil, especially Natal. Spontaneous systemic hemorrhage is said to be more frequent than is the case with bites by other Bothrops species, and local effects of envenoming less pronounced (Hui Wen Fan, pers. comm.). However, Vellard (1938a) found that in animals the venom was less hemorrhagic and necrotizing but more neurotropic and coagulant than other Bothrops venoms, making this species potentially dangerous to humans despite its small venom yield.

Bothrops insularis, golden lancehead (Pls. 562–564)

This species has an exceptionally toxic venom judged by LD$_{50}$ measurements in birds. When tested in rodents, however, the lethal toxicity is not much different from that of B. jararaca (M. Buononato, pers. comm.). No cases of human envenoming have been formally reported, but it is said that lighthouse keepers, early colonists, and several fishermen who landed on Ilha

Queimada Grande died after being bitten, probably because of the remote location. Two bites from captive specimens in São Paulo were managed without problems.

Bothrops jararaca, jararaca in Brazil, yararaca in Argentina, yarará in Paraguay (Pls. 567–572, 1438–1455)

This species, the best known venomous snake in the wealthy and heavily populated southeast of Brazil, was responsible for 3,446 of the 6,601 snakebite cases surveyed by Fonseca (1949) between 1902 and 1945 (52%), with 25 deaths (0.7%). Of 1,718 admissions to the Hospital Vital Brazil in São Paulo during the period 1954–1965, 625 were identified as being caused by this species (36%) (a large proportion of the bites were unidentified, so B. jararaca may have been responsible for quite a few more). In two large randomized comparative trials of antivenom treatment conducted at the Hospital Vital Brazil involving 121 and 170 patients bitten by Bothrops species, 43 of 44 and 86 of 87 were victims of B. jararaca bites (Cardoso et al., 1993; Jorge et al., 1995). The average TL of the snakes responsible for bites was 65 (range 30–128) cm (Cardoso et al., 1993). Typical clinical features included local swelling, petechiae (purpura), bruising and blistering of the bitten limb (Pls. 1438–1446), spontaneous systemic bleeding from the gums (Pls. 1447 and 1448) and into the skin (purpura; Pl. 1449), subconjunctival hemorrhage, and incoagulable blood.

Bothrops jararaca is responsible for 97% of the snakebite cases admitted to the Hospital Vital Brazil (Jorge and Ribeiro, 1990). Systemic envenoming is potentially lethal through hemostatic disorders (Kamiguti et al., 1986; Maruyama et al., 1990), intracranial hemorrhage (Kouyoumdjian, 1990), shock, and renal failure (Amaral et al., 1986). The incidence of local necrosis is 6–10%, and of local abscesses also about 5–10%. The bacterial flora of local collections of pus near the site of the bite (Pl. 1450) and in the snake's mouth was studied by Jorge et al. (1990; see above). A randomized placebo-controlled trial of chloramphenicol prophylaxis showed no advantage in giving this treatment (Miguel Tanús Jorge, pers. comm.). Local necrosis may result in life-threatening complications such as tetanus and septicemia, while the resulting chronic ulceration may eventually undergo malignant transformation to a squamous cell carcinoma. In a series of 779 cases of snakebite in which the snake was identified as B. jararaca 20–140 cm long, the incidence of symptoms was pain (92%), local swelling (92%), bruising (51%), local blisters (13%), local necrosis (14%), local abscesses (8%), and incoagulable blood (55%). There were no fatalities. The incidence of necrosis was 6% in patients bitten by snakes 20–39 cm long and 43% in those bitten by snakes 100–140 cm long (Ribeiro et al., 2001).

In a group of patients with proven bites by B. jararaca who were admitted to the Hospital Vital Brazil in 1989 and 1990, initial serum venom antigen levels correlated with clinical severity and plasma fibrinogen concentrations. A multiple logistical regression model showed three independent risk factors for severity: (1) bites at sites other than leg or forearm, (2) serum venom antigen level equal to or more than 400 ng/ml, and (3) the use of a tourniquet (França et al., in press).

The venom of B. jararaca, which has been studied more than any other Latin American snake venom, exhibits thrombinlike, factor X–activiating, prothrombin-activating, and platelet-aggregating activity. In a study of 34 patients in São Paulo, there was evidence of factors released by endothelial cells including von Willebrand factor, tissue plasminogen activator, and plasminogen activator inhibitor type I (Kamiguti et al., 1991). Twenty-two of 38 patients envenomed by *B. jararaca*, also studied in São Paulo, had incoagulable blood with very high levels of thrombin-anti-thrombin III complex and D-dimer (Kamiguti et al., 1992). Serum venom hemorrhagin levels were higher in patients with spontaneous systemic hemorrhage than in controls, and patients with bleeding and thrombocytopenia had high hemorrhagin and thrombomodulin levels. Hemorrhagin levels were inversely correlated with platelet counts (Kamiguti et al., 1992). Jararhagin, the principal hemorrhagin of *B. jararaca* venom, is a 52 kDa soluble zinc-dependent metalloproteinase with disintegrin and cysteine-rich domains (Paine et al., 1992). It was through the action of *B. jararaca* venom in animals that bradykinin (Rocha e Silva et al., 1949) and, eventually, the angiotensin-converting enzyme inhibitors and bradykinin-potentiating peptides were discovered. Although the widespread use of antivenom in Brazil has reduced the case fatality of *B. jararaca* envenoming to less than 1%, morbidity from the necrotic local effects of envenoming is not uncommon, especially when bites involve digits or fascial compartments (Pls. 1451–1454).

A 13-year-old boy bitten at Santa Isabel, São Paulo, Brazil, by a *B. jararaca* 60 cm in TL developed blood-filled blisters at the site of the bite (Pl. 1446), bleeding gums, and nonclotting blood (Warrell et al., unpublished data). Bruising extended up to the groin. He was treated with 60 ml of Instituto Butantan *Bothrops* polyspecific antivenom 2 hours and 25 minutes after the bite. Blood coagulability was restored within 24 hours.

In a retrospective study of 3,139 cases of largely *B. jararaca* bites in São Paulo, prognostic factors for amputation (Pl. 1453), which was carried out in 21 cases (0.67%), were analyzed by Jorge et al. (1999). Risk of amputation was associated with bites by large snakes (more than 60 cm in TL) and with the formation of local blistering and abscesses.

Bothrops jararacussu, jararacuçu (Pls. 573–580, 1456–1465)

The local and specific name of this species comes from the Tupi word *yararakusú*, indicating a large jararaca (*B. jararaca*). Other local names are urutu dourado, urutu amarela, and surucucu tapete. The average venom yield (dry weight) is 247 (range 149–385) mg and, exceptionally, up to 1,000 mg at one milking. Its lethal potency exceeds that of other *Bothrops* species and approaches that of the neotropical rattlesnake *Crotalus durissus terrificus* (Sánchez et al., 1992) (see p. 718). Fortunately, this species is a relatively rare cause of human snakebites. In Latin America from 1902 to 1945, 657 (9.95%) of 6,601 cases of snakebites were attributed to *B. jararacussu*, with 11 deaths (Fonseca, 1949). During the 12-year period 1954–1965, 14 of 1,718 snakebite cases recorded at the Hospital Vital Brazil, Instituto Butantan, São Paulo, were caused by this species, with 1 death (Rosenfeld, 1971). In a later series of 730 cases at the same hospital, 1.2% were caused by *B. jararacussu*. In Santa Catarina, Brazil, 7 of 29 *Bothrops* bites were attributed to this species (Queiroz and Moritz, 1989). A detailed review of 29 proven cases of bites treated and studied in São Paulo over a 20-year period included 3 fatal cases (Milani et al., 1997). Severe signs of local (Pl. 1456) and systemic envenoming, including local necrosis, shock, spontaneous systemic bleeding, and renal failure, were seen only in patients bitten by snakes longer than 50 cm in TL. Bites by shorter specimens were more likely to cause incoagulable blood. Fourteen patients developed incoagulable blood, six developed local necrosis (which required

amputation in one), and five developed local abscesses. Two became shocked, and four developed renal failure. The three fatal cases, aged 3, 11, and 65 years, died 18 hours 45 minutes, 27 hours 45 minutes, and 83 hours, respectively, after being bitten. Causes of death were respiratory and circulatory failure despite large doses of specific antivenom and intensive care unit management. Autopsies of two patients revealed acute renal tubular necrosis, cerebral edema, hemorrhagic rhabdomyolysis at the site of the bite, and disseminated intravascular coagulation. In one survivor with chronic renal failure, renal biopsy showed bilateral cortical necrosis; this patient remained dependent on hemodialysis for his chronic renal failure. The efficacy of available polyspecific *Bothrops* antivenom was not impressive, and it has since been suggested that anti-*Bothrops* and anti-*Crotalus* antivenoms should be given in combination. In Argentina, however, four locally produced antivenoms showed good cross neutralization of *B. jararacussu* venom from Misiones (De Roodti et al., 1999).

While playing near her house in Miracatu, São Paulo State, Brazil, a three-year-old girl was bitten three times in the thigh (Pls. 1457–1459) by a *B. jararacussu* 1.59 m in TL (Pl. 1459). After initial specific antivenom treatment at a local hospital she was transferred to São Paulo. She had been vomiting and was found to be shocked, tachycardic, and anuric since the bite. There was persistent bleeding from the bite site and local ecchymoses. On admission to an intensive care unit three hours after the bite she was comatose, pale, peripherally cyanosed, and hypothermic with a weak pulse, very poor peripheral circulation, and irregular gasping respirations. She deteriorated rapidly, becoming bradycardic and apneic. She was resuscitated and given more polyspecific antivenom but again deteriorated. There were three puncture wounds, approximately 5 cm apart, on the left thigh (Pls. 1457 and 1458) and swelling of the entire limb and adjacent area of her trunk. There was evidence of hypovolemic shock and disseminated intravascular coagulation. Despite further antivenom (including *Crotalus* antivenom), plasma expanders, blood transfusion, vasoactive drugs, and ventilatory support, she became profoundly acidotic with electrolyte disturbances, acute renal failure, profound anemia, leukocytosis ($52 \times 10^9/l$), and thrombocytopenia ($89 \times 10^9/l$) with profound coagulopathy. She died 18 hours and 45 minutes after the bite (Milani et al., 1997). At autopsy, extensive rhabdomyolysis with hemorrhagic foci but no inflammatory infiltration of leukocytes was found at the site of the bite (Pl. 1460). There was a polymorphonuclear cell infiltrate of the liver sinusoids consisting mainly of eosinophils (Pl. 1461).

A 35-year-old farmer who was bitten on the forearm by a 1.1-m-long *B. jararacussu* developed acute renal failure. An open renal biopsy carried out 30 days after the bite because of persistent oliguria showed diffuse cortical and medullary necrosis (Pl. 1462); a few glomeruli appeared viable (Pl. 1463), fibrin was detected in the walls of arterioles, and there were fibrin thrombi in some glomerular capillaries (Pl. 1464; Milani et al., 1997).

The severity of envenoming in these cases explains why the jararacussu is feared more than any other *Bothrops* species in Brazil and adjacent countries. Its great size, enormous triangular head, bulky body, and striking markings add to its reputation. The risk of death and severe sequelae is well known. In one notorious incident near Belo Horizonte, a large jararacussu bit several members of a family and their dog in quick succession, killing three of them. A tendency for unusually large individuals of various species of *Bothrops* to be called jararacussu in

Brazil may invalidate some published accounts. The first reported case of anterior pituitary insufficiency following snakebite (and still the only report outside Asia), occurred at Bento Gonçalves, Brazil (Wolff, 1958); however, this location is more than 250 km southeast of the southernmost limit of this species' distribution (Lema and Leitão de Araujo, 1980). Other identified cases reported in the literature (for review, see Milani et al., 1997) confirm the clinical picture of rapidly developing massive local swelling and necrosis, profound coagulopathy with life-threatening spontaneous systemic hemorrhage, suspicion of neurotoxic symptoms, hypotension and shock (to which the venom's bradykinin-potentiating and angiotensin-converting enzyme-inhibiting effects must contribute), and acute renal failure. At São Sebastão, Brazil, a 36-year-old woman died 40 minutes after a bite by a *B. jararacussu* more than 1 m in TL. Autopsy revealed fibrin clots in the heart, lungs, and skin (Benvenuti et al., 2003). A worker at Instituto Butantan, São Paulo, who received a squirt of venom in her eye suffered intense pain and inflammation but no permanent effects (Pl. 1465).

Bothrops lanceolatus, vipère jaune, Martinique lancehead (Pls. 584–587, 1466–1469; Figs. 273–275)

"La vipère jaune de la Martinique" was described in Rochefort's *Histoire Naturelle des Antilles*, published in Lyon in 1667, but this author—and later Lacépède (1788–89), who illustrated the yellow form of this species (Pl. 1466)—emphasized its very variable coloration. Lacépède reported that its venom was so deadly that no one had survived a bite, the victims usually dying within six hours (Lacépède, 1788–89, 1:355–358). Specimens of *B. lanceolatus* from Martinique were preserved in the Cabinet du Roi in Paris, which formed the basis for the Musée National d'Histoire Naturelle. This snake was the scourge of black slaves working in the sugarcane plantations of Martinique (in the same way that the black scorpion, *Tityus trinitatis*, caused many deaths in the workforce in the Trinidad plantations [Lalung, 1934]). In his famous treatise "Enquête sur le serpent de la Martinique" (Figs. 273 and 274), Rufz mentioned the high mortality from bites and described some of the distinctive clinical features (Rufz, 1859). His case histories included examples of massive local swelling (case II), pus formation (case III), absence of bleeding despite fatal envenoming (case IV), necrosis requiring amputation (cases V–VII), two cases of tetanus

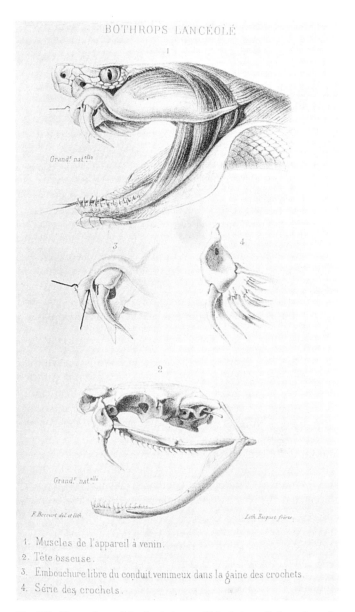

Fig. 274. Illustrations of the fer-de-lance of Martinique, *Bothrops lanceolatus*. From Rufz, 1859.

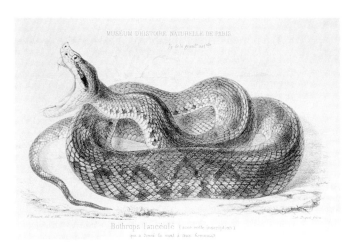

Fig. 273. Illustration of the fer-de-lance of Martinique, *Bothrops lanceolatus*. From Rufz, 1859.

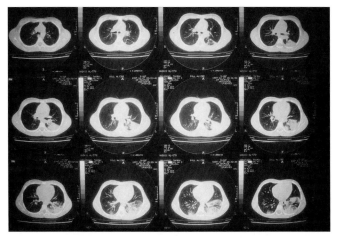

Fig. 275. An eight-year-old girl bitten by a *Bothrops lanceolatus* three days before this photograph was taken. Spiral CT scan of the chest showing pulmonary infarctions, from which she recovered. Copyright Laurent Thomas.

complicating envenoming and amputation (cases VI and VII), two cases of strokes (cases VIII and IX), and one of blindness (case X). The two cases of hemiplegia described by Rufz are of particular interest because thrombosis of cerebral and other major arteries is a distinctive feature of envenoming by *B. lanceolatus* and *B. caribbaeus*.

Rufz described the case of a 35-year-old black woman bitten on the hand by a snake 80 cm in TL while handling bagasse (dry refuse of sugarcane). The hand began to swell, but she did not seem to be in much distress. Later the wound was "cupped," and traditional herbal remedies were applied about 9 hours after the bite. She became unable to move her right arm and leg and lost her power of speech although sensation was intact. She recovered from the bite, but after two years the neurological deficit persisted. Rufz had seen four cases in which the victims permanently lost their ability to speak. In all, local signs of envenoming were mild. In another case, a 26-year-old black woman bitten on the knuckle of her little finger by a snake 35 cm in TL became paralyzed in the arm and leg on the opposite side 15 hours later and lost her speech. A 17-year-old boy was left permanently blind after a bite by a small snake (Rufz, 1859, 257–274).

More recently, Estrade et al. (1989) in Fort-de-France, Martinique, described a 22-year-old woman who was admitted to the hospital two hours after a bite by *B. lanceolatus* with two fang marks 15 mm apart and local, very painful, inflammatory edema of the ankle and calf. There were no other abnormal signs apart from fever (38 °C). On the next day, however, she became breathless, with a respiratory rate of 40 breaths per minute, and developed a fever of 38.5 °C. Arterial blood gases revealed hypoxia and hypocapnia. A perfusion scan of the lungs and pulmonary angiogram confirmed bilateral pulmonary emboli and she was treated with heparin. Three days after the bite she had thrombocytopenia ($31 \times 10^9/1$), reduced factors II and V, and detectable circulating soluble complexes but normal fibrinogen, fibrin(ogen) degradation products, and euglobulin lysis time. Swelling involved the entire bitten limb and extended up to the costal margin; at the site of the bite there was an area of necrosis. She made a complete recovery, and 21 days later the pulmonary perfusion scan was normal. These authors cite an unpublished thesis by Dra. M.-N. Ca in which 13 of 53 cases of envenoming by *B. lanceolatus* were found to have disseminated intravascular coagulation. However, Thomas et al. (1995), who studied 50 cases in Fort-de-France from 1991 to 1994, found that blood coagulation was normal in 80% of the patients. Clinically, hemorrhage was rare except in the form of small ecchymoses around the bite wound. Disseminated intravascular coagulation, defined by thrombocytopenia, decreased fibrinogen and prothrombin concentrations, prolonged activated prothrombin time, and detection of fibrin(ogen) degradation productions, was found in only 4 cases. The striking finding in this study was 11 cases of thrombosis of major arteries, occurring an average of 36 (range 12–96) hours after the bite. There were two cases of pulmonary embolism (Fig. 275), six cerebral infarctions, one myocardial infarction, and two combined cerebral and myocardial infarctions. Among the 11 patients who developed thromboses, 5 showed normal blood coagulation, 3 showed evidence of disseminated intravascular coagulation, and 3 had isolated thrombocytopenia. The degree of thrombocytopenia was more marked in thrombotic cases. Thomas et al. (1996) reported an incidence of about 20 cases of snakebite per year in Martinique, and studied 65 cases in the period 1991–1995. Thirty percent of these patients developed major arterial thromboses within the

first 48 hours after the bite. Twelve cases developed thrombosis an average of 33 (range 8–96) hours after the bite. There were six cerebral infarctions, two myocardial infarctions, two combined cerebral and myocardial infarctions, and two cases of pulmonary embolism. Three patients died with massive strokes, and three were left with permanent neurological deficits. All those developing thrombosis had been bitten by snakes 70 cm or more in TL. A new specific antivenom, now manufactured by Aventis-Pasteur as "BothroFav," was introduced in 1993. Its early use prevented arterial thromboses but had no effect on the incidence of local necrosis or abscess formation. Among 63 patients treated with this antivenom over a 45-month period, there were no cases of arterial thrombosis (Bucher et al., 1997). Clinical severity grading on admission to hospital, beloved of physicians who treat snakebites in the Americas, did not predict mortality; neither did laboratory measurements made at this time (Bucher et al., 1997; Thomas et al., 1998). However, quantitation of serum venom antigenemia by enzyme immunoassay on admission did distinguish patients with severe envenoming from others (Bucher et al., 1997). More than one-third of patients with swelling involving more than half the bitten limb (Pls. 1467–1469) presented with primary bacterial infections. Bacteria grown from the oral cavity of *B. lanceolatus* included *Aeromonas hydrophila*, *Morganella morganii*, *Proteus vulgaris*, and *Clostridium* species (Thomas et al., 1998). Bogarín et al. (1999) demonstrated no coagulant or defibrinating effect of *B. lanceolatus* venom in mice. In concentrations up to 100 µg/ml, the venom did not clot human citrated plasma.

Remarks The world literature on snakebite contains only a few isolated reports of confirmed thrombosis of major arteries following snakebites. Against this background, the clinical observations of major vascular occlusions in victims of *B. caribbaeus* (Figs. 271 and 272; see above) and *B. lanceolatus* constitute a unique syndrome (Wüster et al., 2002b). The discovery that the venom of *B. lanceolatus* has no procoagulant activity on human plasma *in vitro* and that many of the human patients who develop thromboses have a normal blood coagulation profile apart from thrombocytopenia strongly suggests that the mechanism of thrombosis involves activation of vascular endothelium, platelets, or both. The introduction of an effective specific antivenom has resulted in a striking improvement in the prognosis of victims of snakebite in Martinique, but the local effects of envenoming remain challenging.

Bothrops leucurus, white-tailed lancehead

Spix (1824) reported that inhabitants of Bahía had died within a few hours of being bitten by this snake.

Bothrops lojanus, Lojan lancehead (Pl. 596)

According to Orcés (1948), bites by this species are less dangerous than those by many other *Bothrops* species.

Bothrops marajoensis (Pls. 597, 1426)

Three patients among 74 admitted to Barros Barreto Hospital, Belém, Pará, Brazil, had been bitten in the seasonally flooded, relatively open eastern half of Marajó Island occupied by this species: 1 each at Cachoeira Arari, Pontadepedras, and Soure (Pardal et al., 2004). Their clinical features were indistinguishable from those of the remaining cases of *B. atrox* envenoming. Another man, bitten in eastern Marajó Island on the side of his calf by a snake 1 m in TL, arrived at the hospital 27 days later. Surgical exploration revealed an anterior tibial compartment containing necrotic muscle and pus (Pl. 1426; Warrell et al., unpublished data).

Bothrops moojeni, caissaca, Brazilian lancehead
(Pls. 598–604, 1470–1472; Figs. 276–278)

This species is an important cause of snakebite in the central savanna area of Brazil. At São José do Rio Preto, São Paulo State, near the border with Minas Gerais, 88% of snakebite cases were attributable to this species (Kouyoumdjian and Polizelli, 1988). Among 37 cases of proven bites by B. moojeni, 34 had been envenomed. All of the victims had local pain and swelling (pls. 1470, 1471; Fig. 276), which started immediately in 35 cases. Abnormal blood coagulation appeared in 27, but only two showed spontaneous systemic hemorrhage such as hematuria and gastrointestinal hemorrhage. In 11 of the victims there were complications: 4 developed necrosis, 5 developed local infection, one patient required a fasciotomy two days after the bite, one patient died three days after the bite, and one patient was left with chronic disability due to muscle contractures. There

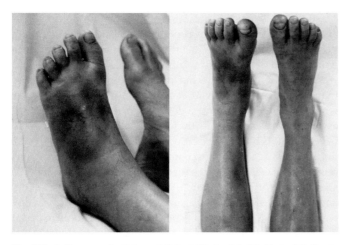

Fig. 276. *Bothrops moojeni* bite on left foot, São José do Rio Preto, São Paulo State, Brazil. Copyright João Aris Kouyoumdjian.

was an impression of higher incidences of coagulopathy and local necrosis than with bites by *B. jararaca*. The same authors compared patients bitten by snakes 30–53 cm in TL with those bitten by snakes 80–147 cm in TL in a series of 22 cases of proven *B. moojeni* envenoming collected over a 19-month period (Kouyoumdjian and Polizelli, 1989). There was one death (7.6%). Bites by larger snakes were associated with more local complications but a lower incidence of coagulopathy. In the same district, a 13-year-old boy bitten by a *B. moojeni* 71 cm in TL developed local pain and swelling and applied a tourniquet. Two hours after the bite he was treated with five vials of Instituto Butantan *Bothrops* polyspecific antivenom. Five hours after the bite he became confused and developed decerebrate rigidity. He was transferred to the university hospital nine hours after the bite, by which time he was comatose with irregular pupils but with no spontaneous systemic bleeding and normal blood coagulation. A cranial CT scan revealed an extensive right frontal extradural hematoma (Fig. 277; Kouyoumdjian, 1990; Kouyoumdjian et al., 1991). Near Uberlândia, Minas Gerais, a 30-year-old man was apparently bitten by a *B. moojeni* while he was drunk. The next day he was treated with antivenom and referred to a local hospital, where his severe neurological impairment was recognized as being separate from his drunken state. A cerebral CT scan confirmed a large intracranial hemorrhage with a fluid level indicating that the blood was incoagulable (Fig. 278). Near Uberlândia, Pentapharm do Brasil maintains a large captive colony of *B. moojeni* (Pl. 1472) for commercial venom production. Between 1981 and 1999, 25 technicians performed 370,768 venom extractions, incurring 12 snakebites and one case of venom being splashed into the eye. Four cases showed local swelling, one victim had a grossly prolonged clotting time, and two developed anaphylaxis from acquired hypersensitivity to the venom. The patient who had venom splashed into the eye felt local pain, complained of transient loss of vision, and developed a conjunctival hemorrhage. Two of the bites were dry (Nishioka et al., 2000b). One proven and two probable cases of bites by *B. moojeni* near Uberlândia developed local abscesses requiring incision and drainage (Jorge et al., 1998). *Aeromonas hydrophila*, an organism particularly associated with bites by reptiles and fish, was cultured from the pus in all cases. Chloramphenicol is the recommended treatment.

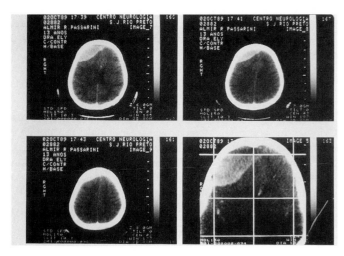

Fig. 277. Cerebral CT scan of a 13-year-old boy bitten nine hours earlier by a *Bothrops moojeni* 71 cm in TL near São José do Rio Preto, São Paulo, Brazil. There is an extensive right frontal extradural hematoma. Copyright João Aris Kouyoumdjian.

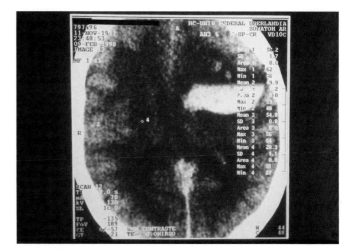

Fig. 278. Cerebral CT scan of a 30-year-old man bitten by a *Bothrops moojeni* near Uberlândia, Minas Gerais, Brazil, 24 hours earlier. There is a large intracranial hemorrhage with a fluid level indicating that the blood was incoagulable. Courtesy of M. Jorge, Uberlândia.

Bothrops neuwiedi, Neuwied's lancehead (Pls. 636–662)

This once familiar species has now become a complex of seven species; all occur in Brazil, and three are also found in adjacent countries. Spix (1824) was informed by local people that bites by *Bothrops neuwiedi* (sensu lato) were very dangerous. It was responsible for 236 of the 6,601 snakebite records collected by Fonseca (1949) during the period 1902–1945, with one death (0.4%). Only 3 cases were admitted to the Hospital Vital Brazil in São Paulo during the period 1954–1965 (Rosenfeld, 1971). Jorge and Ribeiro (2000) reviewed 18 cases of *B. neuwiedi* (sensu lato) bites admitted to the hospital in São Paulo between 1975 and 1992. All had pain, 83% had swelling, 50% had bruising, 17% developed necrosis, and 5% developed abscesses. Coagulopathy was detected in 12%. Sixteen of the patients were treated with antivenom. Compared with *B. jararaca* envenoming, fewer of the *B. neuwiedi* victims showed coagulopathy.

In Germany, a 36-year-old man who kept about 100 snakes in his home was bitten on the finger by a specimen of *B. neuwiedi* (sensu lato). Within one hour there was hemorrhagic "necrosis" and swelling of the finger extending onto the hand. Five hours after the bite his blood was incoagulable with reduced fibrinogen concentration, elevated fibrin(ogen) degradation products and D-dimer, but a normal platelet count. *In vitro* studies showed that the venom activated prothrombin and factor X but not factor XIII (Dempfle et al., 1990).

In a fatal case of *B. diporus* (Pls. 640 and 641) envenoming in Argentina, gastroduodenal hemorrhage 12 days after the bite was attributed to stress ulceration and excessive doses of corticosteroids (Esteso, 1985). Among 500 cases of snakebite per year reported from 1960 to 1975 in Argentina, 80% were attributed to *B. diporus* (Esteso, 1985). Bites by *B. neuwiedi* (sensu lato) have been reported from other countries, including Uruguay, where *B. pubescens* (Pls. 658 and 659) occurs (Revista Médica del Uruguay, 1983).

Bothrops pictus, desert lancehead, víbora, jergón de la costa (Pls. 613, 614, 1473, 1474)

This is the most abundant species of pitviper in the semi-desert coastal areas of central and northern Peru and in the departments of Huancavelica and Ayacucho, where it is responsible for most cases of snakebite. It is one of only two species of *Bothrops* (the other being *B. roedingeri*) in the department of Lima. During the period 1990–1998, 23 patients bitten by this species were admitted to the Hospital Nacional Cayetano Heredia in Lima (Maguiña et al., 1998). The most common symptoms were local pain and swelling (Pl. 1473) followed by general malaise, weakness, and fever in 2 cases. One patient developed oliguria, and 5 had microscopic hematuria. Eighty-seven percent had local erythema, 48% had bruising (Pl. 1474), 22% had serosanguinous blisters, and 13% developed necrosis. Sixty-three percent had peripheral leukocytosis, 31% had microscopic hematuria, 20% had pyuria, and 30% showed increased blood urea and creatinine levels. Among 8 patients tested, 6 had prolonged prothrombin times and 5 had prolonged partial thromboplastin times. One patient required transfer to a specialist unit for treatment of acute renal failure, but there were no deaths in this series. Seventy percent were treated with Instituto Nacional de Salud polyspecific antivenom. All but 3 of the patients were treated with prophylactic antibiotics, and perhaps as a result, none developed bacterial cellulitis (Maguiña et al., 1998). Maguiña et al. (1998)

reviewed three other studies of *B. pictus* envenoming in Lima and speculated that the El Niño phenomenon might have led to an increase in numbers of snakebite cases in the area.

Bothrops punctatus (formerly *Bothriopsis punctata*) (Pls. 620–624)

In the Antioquia region of Colombia this species is responsible for about 6% of snakebites (Otero, 2000). Fourteen (6.4%) of 218 pitviper bite cases surveyed in Antioquia and Chocó were caused by this species, known locally as rabo de chucha (Otero et al., 1992b). Acute renal failure has been reported as a complication of envenoming (Otero et al., 2002).

Bothrops roedingeri (Pls. 625 and 626)

This species is said to be responsible for snakebites in the coastal area of central Peru.

Genus *Cerrophidion* (Pls. 663–680)

Cerrophidion godmani, toboba de altura, Godman's montane pitviper (Pls. 667–672, 1475, 1476)

Only 2 (0.42%) of 477 snakebites in Costa Rica in 1979 were caused by this species (Bolaños, 1984). Bites are not frequent, and their effect is usually confined to local pain and swelling, although the venom is moderately hemorrhagic in mice (Gutiérrez et al., 1980). In southwestern Costa Rica, one child was bitten by this species but no symptoms developed other than local pain (Montalvan et al., 1983). In Chiapas, Mexico, where it is known as nauyaca del frío, this snake is not regarded as aggressive. It is not greatly feared by the local people, who believe that its bites can be cured with home remedies (Alvarez del Toro, 1982). The venom contains phosopholipase myotoxins (Lizano et al., 2000). Three patients in Guatemala bitten by this species, two of them children, developed fever and swelling, and three cases in Guatemala City were mild. A 14-year-old boy was bitten on the hand and experienced intense localized pain and dizziness. Within an hour there was extensive swelling of the bitten arm, but he was discharged from the hospital after 3 days. Two adults bitten by snakes from Baja Verapaz developed persistent severe pain throughout the bitten limb; swelling and bruising; a red, itching rash over the body (suggestive of urticaria); nausea; headache; faintness; and near collapse. Massive swelling continued for 5 days and recovery took 7–10 days (Campbell and Lamar, 1989).

Cerrophidion petlalcalensis (Pls. 673–675)

This species, from the extreme south of the Sierra Madre Oriental in Veracruz, Mexico, was responsible for biting a photographer on the finger. A suction extractor was applied, but within 15 minutes the finger began to swell and pain increased. A polyvalent antivenom was injected locally and intramuscularly, but swelling extended to the lower half of the forearm after three hours and lasted for three days (López-Luna et al., 1999).

Genus *Crotalus*, Rattlesnakes (Pls. 752–1010)

The two species of Latin American (tropical) rattlesnakes, *Crotalus simus* (Pls. 956–966) in Central America and *C. durissus*

(Pls. 795–824) in South America, pose a serious medical problem in many parts of their ranges. Envenoming by *C. durissus* subspecies results in distinctive clinical features attributable to venom neurotoxins (crotoxin and crotamine) present in populations in certain geographical areas (see Venom Composition and Properties, above). *Crotalus durissus* neurotoxins disable neuromuscular transmission, resulting in progressive paralysis reminiscent of elapid envenoming. Victims exhibit ptosis, external ophthalmoplegia, paralysis of muscles of the face and tongue, and eventually, in some cases, life-threatening respiratory paralysis (Pls. 1478–1485). Phospholipase A$_2$ neurotoxins also damage skeletal and perhaps cardiac muscle, causing generalized tenderness, aching, inflammation, and pain on movement or passive stretching of muscles throughout the body reminiscent of seasnake envenoming (see above). Release of muscle pigment (myoglobin) into the bloodstream results in passage of dark red/brown or black urine (myoglobinuria; Pls. 1486 and 1487) and may have a secondary damaging effect on renal tubules, causing acute tubular necrosis. Other life-threatening clinical effects encountered throughout the range of *C. durissus* in South America are hemostatic disturbances (incoagulable blood and spontaneous systemic hemorrhage), hypotension, and shock. Local envenoming, however, is usually trivial and restricted to pain, mild swelling, and erythema (Pls. 1478–1480, 1488).

In contrast, envenoming by *C. simus* in Central America produces clinical effects more reminiscent of rattlesnake bites in North America. Local envenoming may be severe, with massive swelling, blistering, and necrosis, provoking surgeons to carry out fasciotomies, and in some cases leading to amputation and permanent physical handicap. Systemic envenoming involves some hemostatic disorders such as hypofibrinogenemia, but spontaneous systemic bleeding is most unusual, renal failure has rarely been reported, and neurotoxicity is uncertain. This clinical difference is consistent with the results of a recent comparison of venom composition in *C. d. terrificus*, *C. d. cumanensis*, and *C. simus* ("*C. d. durissus*"). Only the venom of newborn *C. simus* contains the crotoxin responsible for neurotoxic envenoming by *C. d. terrificus* and *C. d. cumanensis* (Saravia et al., 2002). Douglas March's description of paralysis of cervical muscles producing the "broken neck" sign in Honduras (March, 1928b) has not been confirmed elsewhere in the distribution of *C. simus*.

Crotalus durissus, South American rattlesnakes (Pls. 795–824)

***Crotalus durissus cascavella* (Pls. 797 and 798)**   At Christmas 1560, Padre Luís Rodrigues, a Jesuit missionary, was visiting a plantation near Bahia, Brazil, when he was bitten by a cascavel (*C. d. cascavella*) as thick as his arm that he had not seen. This snake was considered the most venomous in Brazil, and since no one had escaped death after its bite, he resigned himself to his fate. He collapsed with generalized pain and for 20 days could sleep no more than 6 hours altogether. So severe were the permanent effects of his ordeal that when he returned to Portugal in 1565, he was considered unfit to continue his vocation and so was dismissed by the Jesuits (Leite, 1954, 3:93, 536). Spix (1824) mentioned that those bitten by this snake usually died within 24 hours.

***Crotalus durissus collilineatus* (Pls. 799–802)**   In Goiás, Brazil, 65% of a series of 108 cases of snakebite were attributed

to *C. d. collilineatus* (Vêncio and de Oliveira, 1980). In a continuing study of patients bitten by rattlesnakes in Uberlândia, Minas Gerais, Brazil, all the dead snakes brought to the hospital by their victims proved to be *C. d. collilineatus*, which is responsible for 24% of all snakebites in this area (Miguel Jorge, pers. comm.). Local signs and symptoms included moderate pain, paresthesiae (such as itching), mild swelling, and warmth and redness of the skin. Systemic symptoms included severe generalized myalgia, diplopia, visual impairment probably attributable to paralysis of visual accommodation, and ptosis. Many patients were drowsy. Two complained of a bitter taste in the mouth. Some reported passing dark or red urine. One woman complained of abnormal menstrual bleeding, and there were some cases of respiratory paralysis (Jorge M. et al., unpublished data). Among 249 patients bitten by rattlesnakes admitted to the Hospital Vital Brazil in São Paulo, between 1974 and 1990, one had been bitten by a captive specimen of *C. d. collilineatus* but developed no signs of envenoming (Jorge and Ribeiro, 1992).

Near Uberlândia, Brazil, a 38-year-old man bitten on the foot by a specimen of *C. d. collilineatus* 86 cm in TL developed typical features of South American rattlesnake envenoming, including severe generalized myalgia, dark urine, ptosis, and ophthalmoplegia. After treatment with specific antivenom he made a complete recovery; however, at a follow-up visit a week after his discharge from hospital, he showed signs of a local infection at the site of the bite. *Escherichia coli* and *Staphylococcus aureus* were cultured from blister aspirate. Local infection is common after bites by *Bothrops* but is most unusual after *Crotalus* bites (Nishioka et al., 2000a).

***Crotalus durissus cumanensis*, cascabel (Pls. 803–809)**   This subspecies, which occurs in Colombia and Venezuela, is capable of causing fatal envenoming (Lancini, 1979). In the state of Lara, western Venezuela, 24 of 325 cases of snakebite admitted between 1953 and 1959 were attributed to this rattlesnake. At the site of the bite victims exhibited congestion and redness. The swelling spread to involve the whole of the bitten limb, the edema was tense, sometimes with small nonhemorrhagic blisters, but necrosis was never observed. Local pain was immediate and extensive. Bruises were seen in 6 cases. Systemic symptoms included nausea; headache; blurred vision; generalized cramps, especially in the affected limb; trembling; distress; and inability to move the affected limb in all cases. The famous "broken neck" sign ("la nuca quebrada"; see also March, 1928b) was seen in only half the cases. Neck stiffness became marked 24 hours after the bite in 80% of cases. Strabismus was marked in 30% and was mild in 70%. Sweating, nausea, and vomiting occurred occasionally (Dao-L., 1971). Swelling of a foot and leg after a bite by this subspecies is illustrated in Dao-L., 1971. Marinkelle (1966) speculated that *C. durissus* was second only to *Bothrops atrox* (and *B. asper*) as a cause of fatal snakebite in Colombia, but there is no evidence to support this statement.

***Crotalus durissus durissus* (Pls. 795 and 796)**   A 40-year-old Creole man bitten on the calf by a cascabel in French Guiana suffered pain, mild local swelling, shock, distress, and paralysis of extraocular muscles and muscles of deglutition (Hulin et al., 1982). Twenty-four hours after the bite, the results of blood coagulation tests were within normal limits (fibrinogen 1.8 g/l, platelets 160×10^9/l). He was treated with 50 ml of antivenom (Syntex do Brasil, São Paulo) at that time and was mechanically ventilated, but he developed circulatory failure secondary to refractory ventricular tachycardia and died 36 hours after admission.

***Crotalus durissus marajoensis* (Pls. 810 and 811)** A boy bitten by this subspecies on Marajó Island was admitted to Barros Baretto Hospital in Belém with typical myopathic or neuropathic facies (Pl. 1477; Pedro Pardal, pers. comm.).

***Crotalus durissus ruruima* (Pls. 812 and 813)** In Roraima Province, Brazil, 13.4% of 309 snakebite cases between 1992 and 1998 were attributed to this subspecies (Nascimento, 2000). A British herpetologist in his twenties was bitten on the thumb by a small specimen on Ilha Maracá, Roraima, Brazil. There was local swelling and pain, which had spread to the elbow 12 hours after the bite. He was transferred to the hospital in Boa Vista for treatment with Instituto Butantan antivenom (anticrotálico). At no stage did he develop any systemic symptoms (Mark O'Shea, pers. comm.); however, the victim of a bite by this subspecies had died in this hospital within the previous year.

A 31-year-old Amerindian community health-care worker was bitten on the toes by a rattlesnake while bathing in Tiger Pond near Karasabai in the Pakaraima Mountains of western Guyana, which is in the area of distribution of *C. d. ruruima*. While being loaded into an air ambulance 21 hours after the bite, the patient began to vomit dark blood and died a few minutes later (Stan Brock, pers. comm.).

***Crotalus durissus terrificus,* cascavel, cascabel (Pls. 814–816, 1478–1488)** Of the 6,601 snakebite cases surveyed in Latin America, Fonseca (1949) attributed 738 (11.2%) to this subspecies, with 90 deaths (12.2%). During the years 1954–1965, 143 *C. d. terrificus* bite cases (out of 1,718 total cases of snakebite; 8.3%) were admitted to the Hospital Vital Brazil in São Paulo, with 17 deaths (11.9%) (Rosenfeld, 1971). During the period 1990–1993, bites by *C. durissus* ssp. accounted for 7.7% of the 65,911 identified snakebites reported in Brazil, with a case fatality of 1.9%, the highest for any genus (Brasil, 1998). In Marília, São Paulo State, and southern Minas Gerais, rattlesnake bites are at least as common as bites by lanceheads.

Far more has been published on the clinical effects of envenoming and the properties of the venom of this subspecies than those of any of the other Latin American rattlesnakes. The principal clinical effects of the venom are neurotoxic, myotoxic, and thrombinlike. Its principal toxins are the neuro/myotoxins crotoxin, crotamine, and gyroxin; the platelet aggregator convulxin; and a thrombinlike enzyme. The venom's lethal toxicity, higher than that of any other Latin American snake venom, is attributable to crotoxin, a phospholipase A_2 complex. In experimental conditions crotoxin with crotamine damages peripheral nerve endings and causes myonecrosis. The geographical variation of crotamine content of rattlesnake venoms in Brazil and Argentina has already been discussed (see above; Schenberg, 1959). Minton and Minton (1971) suggested that the crotamine content of the venom might be responsible for the "broken neck" sign in human victims of envenoming, resulting from paralysis of the cervical flexor muscles, first reported after a rattlesnake bite in Honduras (March, 1928b) but not elsewhere in Middle America. These comments are controversial as far as bites by Central American rattlesnakes (*C. simus*) are concerned (see below).

Comparative studies of the biological activities of the venoms of the three Brazilian subspecies (*C. d. terrificus, C. d. collilineatus,* and *C. d. cascavella*) indicate that most activities are common to all three subspecies (Santoro et al., 1999). The earliest detailed description of symptoms of envenoming by *C. d. terrificus* is in Sigaud's "Du climat et des maladies du Brésil" (1844). A 50-year-old leprosy patient in Rio de Janeiro, against all medical advice, induced a cascavel to bite him on the hand in the hope that it might cure his disease. Swelling eventually involved the entire bitten limb, and pain spread from the hand to become generalized. Paralytic symptoms started within 2 hours of the bite, first affecting his lips and, in succession, causing difficulty with speaking, swallowing, and eventually with breathing. There was sweating, hypersalivation, persistent nosebleed, and bleeding into some of his lepromatous skin lesions. Initially he was agitated and passed excessive volumes of urine, but later he became progressively somnolent and tachycardic. He died about 24 hours after the bite. Rosenfeld's clinical descriptions of envenoming by *C. d. terrificus* in Brazil (Rosenfeld, 1971) have not been bettered, although his concepts of pathophysiology have had to be revised. Local symptoms at the site of the bite include pain, paresthesiae such as formication or anesthesia, but little or no swelling (Pl. 68) and no local necrosis. Rosenfeld denied the occurrence of erythema, but this has been reported in several parts of Brazil (Sano-Martins et al., 2001; Pls. 1479 and 1480). Systemic envenoming usually starts with symmetrical ptosis, external ophthalmoplegia, and facial weakness resulting in the characteristic myopathic/neurotoxic facies (Pls. 1481–1483). Paresis of the pupils may impair visual accommodation (responsible for the frequent complaint of blurred vision) and result in loss of pupillary reflexes and dilated pupils (mydriasis), which Rosenfeld (1971) regarded as a fatal prognostic sign. Uncommonly, respiratory muscle involvement may lead to respiratory failure (Amaral et al., 1991). Among 249 patients bitten by rattlesnakes who were admitted to hospital in São Paulo, 3 developed respiratory distress requiring endotracheal intubation (Jorge and Ribeiro, 1992). A striking symptom described by some Brazilian patients was "corpo estranho na garganta," a sensation of having a foreign body in the throat. Some developed hiccups. Notably, the venom of South American rattlesnakes induces generalized breakdown of skeletal muscle (rhabdomyolysis) causing myalgias, stiffness, and tenderness of the muscles; a massive increase in serum concentrations of myoglobin and muscle enzymes such as creatine kinase; and the passage of dark brown, black, or Coca-Cola–colored urine (Pls. 1484 and 1485). This pigment was originally misidentified as hemoglobin and attributed to intravascular hemolysis (Rosenfeld, 1971), but the work of Dr. Marisa Azevedo-Marques and her colleagues in Riberão Preto, São Paulo State, Brazil, proved conclusively that there was no hemolysis, only rhabdomyolysis (Azevedo-Marques et al., 1985, 1987; Cupo et al., 1988, 1990; Rossi et al., 1989). There is no obvious reason why venom phospholipase A_2 myotoxins should not attack myocardial as well as skeletal muscle. In a well-documented case treated in Londrina, São Paulo State, there were clinical, electrocardiographic, biochemical, and histological features strongly suggesting venom-induced myocardial damage (Siqueira et al., 1990; Fig. 279).

In Campinas, São Paulo State, Brazil, *C. d. terrificus* is responsible for 30% of venomous snakebites in children (Bucaretchi et al., 2002). During a 16-year period (1984–1999), 31 children bitten by rattlesnakes were admitted; only 1 showed no envenoming. Local swelling and erythema were present in two-thirds of the children. Ptosis developed in 27, myalgia in 23, dark urine in 17, dilated pupils in 17, unequal pupils in 2, constricted pupils in 1, and spontaneous bleeding in 1. Plasma concentra-

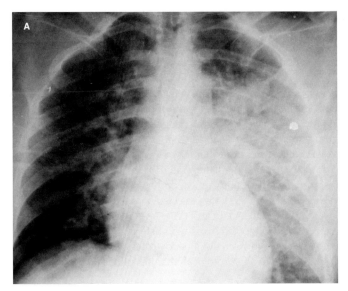

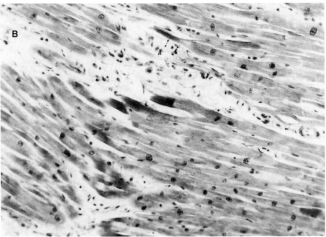

Fig. 279. Evidence of myocardial damage in a 32-year-old woman bitten by a *Crotalus durissus terrificus* near Londrina, São Paulo, Brazil: (A) chest x-ray showing acute pulmonary edema that developed 24 hours after the bite; (B) histological appearance of heart muscle at autopsy (the patient died six days after the bite) showing foci of necrosis with an inflammatory infiltrate consisting predominantly of lymphocytes. There was no evidence of preexisting heart disease.

tions of creatine kinase and lactate dehydrogenase had increased within six hours of the bite in most patients, indicating rhabdomyolysis. This was complicated by hypocalcemia in 8 of 20 patients, 1 of whom developed tetany. There were no deaths, and no patients developed local wound infections (Bucaretchi et al., 2002). In the 3 children with acute renal failure, antivenom treatment had been delayed more than nine hours after the bite.

Blood coagulation disturbances have been observed in about half the patients bitten by this subspecies (Jorge and Ribeiro, 1992), and hypofibrinogenemia without thrombocytopenia has been reported (Amaral et al., 1988), but spontaneous systemic bleeding has only rarely been observed in human patients. Twenty-four patients admitted to the hospital in Belo Horizonte, Minas Gerais, Brazil, showed coagulopathy whose pattern was consistent with the action of a venom component very similar to physiological thrombin (Sano-Martins et al., 2001). Although convulxin and crotoxin can cause platelet aggregation, thrombocytopenia is uncommon in envenomed patients. Spontaneous systemic bleeding occurs in less than

5% of cases (Jorge and Ribeiro, 1992). Fatal envenoming has been attributed to coagulopathy (Ribeiro et al., 1998), myocardial damage (Sano-Martins et al., 2001; Siqueira et al., 1990), hypotension and shock, rhabdomyolysis, renal failure, spontaneous hemorrhage, spontaneous rupture of the spleen (Lopez et al., 1972), and respiratory paralysis. In Belo Horizonte, Minas Gerais, Magalhães et al. (1986) treated two severe cases of envenoming with rhabdomyolysis. Clinical features included blurred vision, headache, generalized myalgia that prevented sleep, incoagulable blood, ptosis, dilated pupils, and diplopia. Changes in blood biochemistry included reduction in calcium concentration and increases in uric acid, phosphate, creatine kinase, aminotransferases, lactic dehydrogenase, and myoglobin (Magalhães et al., 1986). A 14-year-old boy bitten on the leg by a specimen of *C. d. terrificus* developed blurred vision, headache, and generalized myalgia three hours after the bite. Twenty-four hours after the bite he was given specific antivenom. His urine contained "hemoglobin" (4+) (in fact, myoglobin), and his blood was incoagulable. He was drowsy but rousable with ptosis, bilateral mydriasis, and diplopia, and his muscles were generally painful on palpation. At the site of the bite puncture marks and a circumscribed hyperemic area were present. He had a normal hemoglobin concentration, a neutrophil leukocytosis (15.2 × 10^9/l), normal platelet count, and a creatine kinase concentration of 12,390 mU/ml. Within eight days he made a complete recovery. The phospholipase A_2 myotoxins in the venom of *C. d. terrificus* damaged skeletal muscle type I and IIa fibers, releasing cardiac muscle as well as skeletal muscle isoenzymes of creatine kinase.

Acute renal failure is a well-recognized complication of *C. d. durissus* envenoming and a potential cause of death. In Belo Horizonte, Minas Gerais, Brazil, Amaral et al. (1986) reported on 63 snakebite victims suffering from acute renal failure, among whom 31 (49%) had been bitten by *C. d. terrificus*. Pigment nephropathy, caused by passage of myoglobin through the renal tubules, has been blamed for renal damage, but it seems likely that other effects of envenoming—including hypotension, shock, acidosis, potassium and other products of skeletal muscle breakdown, and perhaps a venom factor acting directly on the renal tubules—may be involved in its evolution.

Among the 249 cases of rattlesnake bites treated in São Paulo (all but 1 attributed to *C. d. terrificus*), 13% developed oliguria or anuria and required dialysis for renal failure; 4.8% developed spontaneous systemic bleeding—into the tissues, from the gums (8 cases), nose (1), vagina (2), and intracranial (1). At the Hospital Vital Brazil in São Paulo, Jorge et al. (1997a) reviewed 97 cases of bites by *C. d. terrificus* in which the victim brought the snake. Eight of the patients (8.2%) showed no envenoming. Most of the clinical features were similar in patients bitten by larger (more than 40 cm in TL) and smaller (less than 40 cm in TL) snakes, but myalgia and dark urine were significantly more frequent in the 79 victims of the larger snakes compared with the 18 bitten by smaller snakes. Oliguria (6 cases), bleeding gums (4), respiratory muscle paralysis leading to respiratory failure (2), shock (2), and need for renal dialysis (2) occurred only in patients bitten by larger snakes. There were no real differences in epidemiological features between victims of smaller and larger rattlesnakes. In Botucatu, São Paulo State, *C. d. terrificus* is responsible for 20% of snakebites. Among 40 cases examined by Barraviera et al., (1989), there were two deaths, both occurring five days after the bite. One was attributed to acute tubular necrosis and the other to renal failure and extensive hepatic necrosis perhaps related to his chronic alcoholism.

In Argentina *C. d. terrificus* is responsible for 2% of snakebites (Esteso, 1985). In Peru this species occurs only in the Sandia Valley, Puno, near the border with Bolivia and is responsible for few bites (Pl. 1488). In many parts of the Amazon region of Peru (e.g., Pucallpa) the name cascabel is used, misleadingly, for young *Bothrops atrox* because of their tendency to vibrate the tail when disturbed.

Crotalus durissus unicolor, Aruba Island rattlesnake (Pls. 819–821)

In Aruba Island, Dutch Antilles, 12 bites were inflicted on four individuals during a seven-year period by this normally docile snake, known locally as cascabel (Hardy, 1992). A 26-year-old man who was bitten on the finger developed a burning sensation that spread up the arm. Within an hour he developed blurred vision, which persisted for 24 hours. There was weakness of the muscles in the bitten arm, paresthesia, and hyperesthesia, which lasted for one month. He was subsequently bitten on eight further occasions without any serious effects. Two of the other three victims were bitten and suffered no ill effects, but the third experienced residual weakness and spasticity in the affected limb. In another case, the drunken victim picked up the snake and was bitten but recovered after antivenom treatment (Howard Reinert, pers. comm.). Venezuelan antivenom suero antiofidico polyvalente, raised against *C. d. cumanensis* venom, is recommended to treat envenoming by this subspecies (Hardy, 1992).

Crotalus durissus vegrandis (Pls. 822–824)

This subspecies is confined to the states of Monagas and Anzoátegui, Venezuela. Lancini (1979) illustrated swelling of the whole hand following a bite on the finger.

Crotalus simus, Central American rattlesnake (Pls. 956–966)

Costa Rica Rattlesnakes are abundant in the dry Pacific area of Guanacaste. Fourteen snakebite victims whose cases were reviewed by Bolaños et al. (1981) developed local pain, swelling, inflammation, nausea, headache, spontaneous systemic bleeding (epistaxis, hematemesis, microscopic and frank hematuria), coagulopathy (prolonged prothrombin, partial thromboplastin, and thrombin times with reduced fibrinogen concentration), local bruising, redness, and in some cases abscesses; however, there was no evidence of the neurological signs, shock, or acute renal failure described following South American rattlesnake bites.

Honduras March (1928b) described two extraordinary cases treated in San Pedro Sula, Honduras. A man was bitten on the finger by a rattlesnake 165 cm in TL. Although he was treated with anticrotalic antivenom from Brazil, swelling spread up his forearm. Thirty minutes after the bite he became blind and developed paralysis of the neck muscles so that his head dropped down and his chin rested on his chest. He was sweaty, collapsed, and pale but was roused with stimulants and apparently left the hospital, after only 18 hours, in good condition. A second man was bitten on the hand by a rattlesnake 60 cm in TL. Five hours after the bite he was said to be delirious, very nervous, almost blind, and suffering severe pain in the head and spine. Treatment with anticrotalic serum produced immediate

improvement. It is difficult to know the extent to which psychological factors contributed to the symptoms of these two patients, who may well have been terrified of dying of rattlesnake bite.

Cruz (1987) described a different clinical picture. Rattlesnake bites produced immediate severe pain and progressive swelling with bruising, erythema, local lymphadenopathy, and moderate local necrosis, but spontaneous systemic bleeding from the gums, neurotoxicity, and renal complications were never observed. On the other hand, a victim from the Atlantic coast (La Ceiba) developed fatigue, dilated pupils, restlessness, insomnia, confusion, dyspnea, and coma before he died.

Russell et al. (1997) also averred that Central American rattlesnake bites cause pain and acute swelling that can involve the entire limb along with bruising, blistering, nausea, and vomiting. Local tissue necrosis is said to be common in untreated cases. However, neurological manifestations are rare, as are fatalities.

Genus *Lachesis*, Bushmaster (Pls. 681–701, 1489–1492)

In Brazil the bushmaster is known as surucucú, pico-de-jaca and serpiente verrugoso, in Colombia as verrugosa, in Venezuela as cuaima concha de piña, in Trinidad as mapepire ananas or mapepire z'ananna, and in French Guiana as grage à grand carreaux or serpent à grage. These names refer to the protruberances on its skin, which resemble the skin of the jackfruit (jaca, *Artocarpus heterophyllus*), breadfruit (*A. altilis*), pineapple (*Ananas comosus*), warts, or a flour grater. The genus now comprises four species: *L. stenophrys* from the Caribbean coast of Central America; *L. melanocephala* from southwestern Costa Rica; *L. acrochorda* from Panama, western Colombia, and northwestern Ecuador; and *L. muta* from elsewhere in South America.

The great fear engendered by bushmasters is well illustrated by an episode described by the famous German film director Werner Herzog: "While filming *Aguirre, the Wrath of God* in the Peruvian Amazon jungle, one of my lumber men, who always worked barefooted, was cutting down a tree when he suddenly felt a snake strike him twice. It was a chu chupe [also shushupe/shuchupe, local names for *Lachesis muta* in Peru], the most dangerous snake of all. It normally takes a few minutes before cardiac arrest occurs and breathing stops. He took the saw, the power was cut off and he thought about it for five seconds. He then grabbed the saw again, started it up and cut off his foot. That saved his life because our camp with the doctor and the serum was 20 minutes away." According to Ditmars (1933), "a man bitten in the thigh by an eight foot Bushmaster died in less than ten minutes—the long fangs apparently wounding an important blood vessel." Such a rapid death is exceptionally unusual, however, and it seems highly likely that had Werner Herzog's lumberman waited for 20 minutes to receive antivenom and other medical treatment, he would have survived complete with his foot! Piso and Marcgraf (1658) featured this species under the name çurucucu, reporting that bites caused pain, dizziness, colic, delirium, fever, and death within 24 hours: "the blood corrodes, then flows through the nostrils, ears, hands and feet."

Lachesis acrochorda, Chocoan bushmaster (Pls. 681–683)

In Ecuador *L. acrochorda* is reported to cause some bites in the Montañas de Muisne and Rio Cayapas regions (Theakston et al.,

1995). In Antioquia and Chocó, Colombia, *L. acrochorda* was implicated in only 2% of bites. Five patients developed nausea, sweating, and hypotension, but no neurotoxic symptoms, diarrhea, or bradycardia were observed (Otero Patiño et al., 1993).

Lachesis melanocephala (Pls. 684 and 685)

This species has a reputation for being unusually aggressive (Campbell and Lamar, 1989). Ripa (2001) was bitten on the hand by a specimen 1.2 m in TL. Agonizing local pain and severe systemic symptoms evolved almost immediately, and within 40 minutes he had developed dizziness, loss of coordination, temporary losses of consciousness, nausea, sweating, tachycardia, swollen tongue, hypersalivation, projectile vomiting, explosive diarrhea, intense stabbing pains in the trunk and lower back, muscle cramps, fall in blood pressure, respiratory distress, inability to stand up, and a generalized feeling of numbness. Prothrombin time was prolonged. Despite treatment with 14 ampules of antivenom soon after the bite, the swelling progressed to involve the entire arm and adjacent area of trunk, reaching its maximum in 60 hours and resolving after one month without any necrosis. Painful enlargement of axillary lymph nodes persisted for four months. Ripa was also bitten on the hand by a specimen of *L. melanocephala*, 1.5 m in TL, but on that occasion there were no systemic symptoms but only intense local pain, swelling up to the elbow, and stiffness and soreness of the fingers that lasted for a month (Ripa, 2001).

Lachesis muta (Pls. 686–698)

Unlike *L. melanocephala*, this species is not particularly aggressive even after dark, and humans, even the indigenous Amerindians who hunt in its habitat, are rarely bitten. In Leticia, Colombia, only two *Lachesis muta* bites were identified in 12 years (Silva-Haad, 1982a), with a third fatal case reported more recently (Hardy and Silva-Haad, 1998). In Cayenne, French Guiana, however, 4 of 11 snakebite admissions during a 2-year period were attributed to *L. muta* (Hulin et al., 1982). There is a tendency for people who have been bitten by a large snake to apply the name of a large and notorious species such as bushmaster or jararacussu to the perpetrator. This may explain reports of unbelievably large numbers of *Lachesis* bites in some places. For example, in Manaus, Amazonas, Brazil, 17% of snakebite cases were attributed to this species (Bard et al., 1994), and Hardy (1995) quoted government data suggesting that over 4.5 years in Brazil, *L. muta* was responsible for 15,000 of 200,000 reported snakebites (7.5%) with a case fatality of 1.4%, compared with less than 0.5% in *Bothrops* bites.

The incidence of bushmaster bites has also been exaggerated by studies in which the prevalence of enzyme immunoassay antibodies (EIA) was measured (18% in Ecuador, Theakston et al., 1981; and 35% in French Guiana, Chippaux and Theakston, 1987). At a specialist center in Manaus, Amazonas, Brazil, where 200 snakebite cases are admitted each year, only 10 proven cases of *Lachesis* bites have been observed over a number of years (Alcideia de Souza, pers. comm.).

The symptoms and signs of envenoming (local swelling, blistering, bruising, and necrosis with coagulopathy, spontaneous systemic bleeding, shock, and renal failure) may be confused with those caused by other pitvipers. However, a distinctive syndrome has been described in a proportion of cases. There is early nausea, abdominal colic, repeated vomiting, and watery diarrhea with profuse sweating. In Leticia, on the Colombia-Brazil border, Silva-Haad (1982a) described two patients bitten by specimens of *L. muta* 2.65 and 1.85 m in TL. Vomiting, severe abdominal colic, profuse diarrhea, hypotension, bradycardia, impaired consciousness, and other manifestations of shock may develop as soon as 15 minutes after the bite, while local effects of envenoming may leave permanent impairment (Pl. 1492). In Amazonas State, Brazil, 6.2% of patients had vomiting, 0.9% had faintness, 4.6% felt dizziness, 4.1% felt nausea, 2.4% felt abdominal pain, and 1.9% had visual disturbances, symptoms suggesting the possibility of envenoming by *L. muta* (Borges et al., 1999). Near Manaus, Amazonas, Brazil, a patient became hypotensive, shocked, and stuporose 90 minutes after being bitten by a bushmaster (Bard et al., 1994). In Venezuela a patient developed intense sweating, vomiting, watery diarrhea, hypersalivation, conjunctival suffusion, hypotension, bradycardia, and respiratory distress 45 minutes after being bitten by a juvenile bushmaster (Torres et al., 1995). This patient also showed neurotoxic signs: divergent strabismus, dysarthria, and dysphagia.

Mole (1924) reproduced an account by A. B. Carr, who was bitten on the thumb while reaching into a lappe (*Agouti paca*) burrow in Trinidad. He incised the bite wound, applied and ingested a proprietary herbal remedy called Melidor's Antidote to Snakebite, and used a ligature, but there was severe pain and a feeling of cold with shivering and giddiness. There was intense swelling of the bitten hand and pain spreading to the armpit and chest with cramping abdominal pain followed by vomiting of black material that he thought was congealed blood from the lungs. The swelling began to subside within 18 hours of the bite, but Carr was unfit for work for five weeks and suffered necrosis and persistent numbness of the bitten thumb.

Hulin et al. (1982) described four men (Caucasian, Palikour and Oyampi Amerindian, and Creole) in French Guiana, aged between 15 and 64 years, bitten by snakes between 1.5 and 2.5 m in TL on foot, ankle, and calf while hunting or gardening. One showed no signs of envenoming, but the other three had severe pain and local swelling, two had incoagulable blood, and the fourth had hypofibrinogenemia (0.1 g/l) and elevated fibrin(ogen) degradation products in the serum. All four were treated with 50 ml of Soro Anti-ofidico-purificado (Syntex do Brasil, São Paulo) 1–50 hours after the bite. Two of the patients developed extensive local necrosis, associated in one with necrosis of tendons at the ankle joint. Both required skin grafts but were left with extensive scarring, and in one, permanent arthrodesis of the ankle. The other two patients escaped without local necrosis. Systemic complications in the three envenomed patients included pulmonary edema (1) patient, oliguric renal failure (2), paralytic ileus (1), and staphylococcal septicemia (1). The three envenomed patients were in the hospital for 45, 26, and 60 days.

In Chanchamayo, Junín, Peru, 12 proven cases of bites by *L. muta* up to 2.17 m in TL have been recorded over 20 years with no deaths or amputations. The autonomic symptoms described by Silva-Haad (1982a) were not observed. Two patients bitten on their hands were left with permanent contractures, and hypotension and hemorrhage were commonly recorded on admission. One patient was severely confused. A 45-year-old Peruvian tourist was bitten on the upper arm when he put his hand on a rope by a walkway to a waterfall at Mazamari, Chanchamayo, Peru. The snake was 1.7 m in TL. He developed pain, swelling, and bruising; was mildly hypotensive; and evinced great anxiety. He was treated with three vials of Anti-

Lachesis antivenom and transferred to Lima, where he made a full recovery (Julio Demarini Caro, pers. comm.).

A 28-year-old man was bitten on the finger, with one fang only, by a specimen of *L. m. muta* 1.82 m in TL from Mato Grosso, Brazil (Jorge et al., 1997b). Pain and local swelling developed almost immediately, and within an hour he had become nauseated, had vomited, and had experienced two episodes of profuse watery diarrhea. There was pain at the site of the bite, dryness of the mouth, and abdominal colic. He was found to be pale, drowsy but fully rousable, with cold skin, profuse sweating, conjunctival congestion, and exaggerated bowel sounds. His pulse rate and blood pressure were normal. He had a peripheral leukocyte count of $24.7 \times 10^9/l$, moderate depletion of fibrinogen and factor V, but normal levels of factors II, VIII, IX, and X with a normal platelet count. He developed swelling of the whole arm with local blisters containing serous fluid (Pls. 1489 and 1490). After treatment with monospecific antivenom he made a complete recovery (Jorge et al., 1997b).

Hemostatic abnormalities are commonly described in patients bitten by bushmasters: incoagulable blood, hypofibrinogenemia, increased fibrin(ogen) degradation products with normal or increased platelet counts (Bard et al., 1994; Hulin et al., 1982; Silva-Haad, 1982a; Torres et al., 1995). Persistent bleeding from the fang marks and venepuncture sites, local ecchymoses, epistaxis, and hematuria and bleeding from the bowel have been reported. Complications include bacterial infection of necrotic local lesions, permanent crippling deformity, acute renal failure, pulmonary edema, paralytic ileus, and staphylococcal septicemia. Jorge et al. (1997b) reviewed the venom properties. An acidic kininogenase (serine protease) may contribute to hypotension and shock in human victims and to the manifestations of autonomic nervous system stimulation such as vomiting, diarrhea, sweating, hypersalivation, and bradycardia (Diniz and Oliveira, 1992).

Lachesis stenophrys (Pls. 699–701, 1491)

In Switzerland a 64-year-old man was bitten in the calf by a specimen of *L. stenophrys* 2.7 m in TL from Costa Rica that had been kept in captivity for nearly 30 years. He was admitted to the hospital 45 minutes later and treated in an intensive care unit for shock and coagulopathy. His platelet count fell from $257 \times 10^9/l$ on admission to $98 \times 10^9/l$ on the third day after the bite. The INR (normally less than 1.3) was 2.6 on admission, the prothrombin time was prolonged, the fibrinogen concentration fell to 0.9 g/l the day after the bite, fibrin(ogen) degradation products exceeded 2,000 µg/l, factor II levels were mildly reduced, but factor V and factor VII levels were normal (Rosenthal et al., 2002). He was treated with norepinephrine, which stabilized his blood pressure; Wyeth polyvalent Crotalidae antivenin; and wound debridement and was discharged in good health after four days. He was readmitted one week later complaining of abdominal pain, diarrhea, and vomiting, with peripheral leukocytosis ($13.4 \times 10^9/l$) but normal blood coagulation. He developed intestinal obstruction, and at emergency laparotomy was found to have a necrotic ileum and caecum. Histology confirmed hemorrhagic necrosis of the bowel. He was found to have obstruction of the superior mesenteric artery attributable to venom-induced thrombosis. The patient made a complete recovery after extensive resection of the ischemic bowel. Ripa (2001) was bitten on the thumb by a juvenile specimen 45 cm in TL. There was intense burning pain and swelling, which

reached the elbow in 6 hours and persisted for more than one week, but no systemic symptoms. He was bitten again by a juvenile specimen of *L. stenophrys*, 57 cm in TL, on the finger (Ripa, 2001). Within 20 minutes, there was abdominal pain, vomiting and diarrhea, and pain in the lower back. He felt faint and became hypotensive (63/50 mm Hg), drowsy, feverish with chills, and experienced sweating with a sensation of a swollen tongue. There was swelling of the entire arm, which subsided after 25 days, but the bitten finger remained swollen for more than four months and took a year to recover normal function. A man bitten by a captive specimen 1.3 m in TL developed severe hypotension with impalpable pulse and periods of unconsciousness within 15–20 minutes of the bite (Ripa, 2001). None of these three bites was complicated by local necrosis. In Limón Province, Costa Rica, *L. stenophrys* was responsible for 3 of 164 snakebite cases during a 10-year period (Cerdas et al., 1986). Bolaños et al. (1982) described 4 cases from Costa Rica. Three of the victims died within 3–5 days despite antivenom treatment. They had developed shock associated with massive local swelling and secondary infection, but spontaneous bleeding appeared less common than with envenoming by *Bothrops* species. Bolaños et al. observed bleeding from the fang marks, epistaxis, hematemesis, hemoptysis, and hematuria in the 4 cases. The only survivor was left with severe contractions of the bitten arm. Eichelbaum (1927) reported two deaths from Panama.

Treatment of *Lachesis* Envenoming

Although the lethal potency of *Lachesis* venom is relatively low (Sanchez et al., 1992), the injected dose may be very large. Specific activity against the venom of *Lachesis* species is claimed for more than 10 commercially produced monospecific and polyspecific antivenoms (Theakston and Warrell, 1991; Theakston et al., 1995). Two Colombian antivenoms showed very little efficacy in neutralizing the effects of Ecuadorian *L. muta* venom, while Instituto Butantan monospecific Soro antilaquetico showed only moderate activity (Theakston et al., 1995). No proper clinical trials of antivenom treatment have been carried out, but anecdotal reports suggest disappointing activity for the currently available antivenoms. In Costa Rica, three out of four patients treated with polyspecific antivenom one or two hours after the bite died three to five days later (Bolaños et al., 1982). Anti-Botropico, Crotalico, Laquesico antivenom (Instituto Clodomiro Picado, Costa Rica) and Wyeth polyvalent antivenom in doses of 5–20 ampoules were used in four of the five cases reported by Ripa (2001). The efficacy is hard to assess, but hypotension and systemic symptoms seemed to decrease after the start of antivenom treatment, although local swelling continued to advance. There is likely to be geographical variation in venom composition within the genus, perhaps explaining the absence of autonomic nervous system excitation in Colombia, the relative mildness of hemorrhagic manifestations in Costa Rica, the surprising absence of local necrosis in the two cases of *L. melanocephala* and three cases of *L. stenophrys* envenoming described by Ripa (2001), and the differences between biological activities of venom samples from Brazil and Peru (Sanchez et al., 1992). Recommended ancillary treatments include vasoactive drugs such as dopamine, epinephrine (adrenaline), or norepinephrine (noradrenaline) for hypotension; correction of hypovolemia; dialysis for renal failure; surgical debridement of necrotic tissue; and antimicrobial treatment for secondary bacterial infections.

Genus *Porthidium*, Hognosed Pitvipers (Pls. 715–751)

Porthidium arcosae, Manabí hognosed pitviper (Pls. 715–719)

This species, together with *P. nasutum*, is thought to be responsible for numerous cases of mild envenoming in the coastal region of Ecuador.

Porthidium dunni (formerly *P. brachystoma* and *P. lansbergii*—in part) (Pls. 720–722)

This species is greatly feared around Tehuantepec, southern Mexico, where it is thought to be a frequent cause of serious accidents (Campbell and Lamar, 1989).

Porthidium hespere, Colima hognosed pitviper (Pl. 723)

This Mexican species is capable of causing severe pain, swelling, and permanent stiffness (Campbell, 1976).

Porthidium lansbergii, mapaná, tamagá (Pls. 724–730)

In Panama, four bites without fatalities were attributed to this species (referred to as *Bothrops brachystoma*; Eichelbaum, 1927). In Bucaramanga, eastern Colombia, a bite by this species caused "moderately severe envenoming: moderate local pain and swelling, local bleeding with blistering and bruising, mild systemic symptoms and moderate abnormalities of blood coagulation" (Badillo et al., 1989).

Porthidium nasutum, rainforest hognosed pitviper, tamagá

Porthidium nasutum, known locally as patoco, patoquilla, or veinticuatro, was responsible for 34 (15.6%) of 218 pitviper bites in Antioquia and Chocó, Colombia (Otero et al., 1992b). Only 1 of a second series of 39 snakebites from the same area was attributed to *Porthidium* (Otero et al., 2002). Rafael Otero (pers. comm.) believes that *P. nasutum* and *P. lansbergii* between them account for 15–30% of snakebites in this region. Bites to a finger may result in necrosis, and there is at least one case of intracranial hemorrhage (Rafael Otero, pers. comm.). In northwestern Ecuador, bites by this species and *P. arcosae* are said to be common but not severe. At La Selva Biological Station in Costa Rica, three people bitten on their feet, despite wearing sandals, were not envenomed (Hardy, 1994a). In southwestern Costa Rica, this species was responsible for three bites in children, 1.9% of all snakebites. One of these patients was mildly and two were moderately envenomed (Montalvan et al., 1983). In Central America, opinions vary about the danger of bites by *P. nasutum*. Although this snake is a frequent cause of bites, Bolaños (1984) did not consider the consequences to be severe because of its small size. Daniel (1949), however, reported some fatalities, and Amaral (1927d) thought *P. nasutum* had been responsible for "a great many bites and quite a few deaths . . . being very vicious and secreting a very active venom." In Panama, *P. nasutum* and *P. lansbergii* were implicated in 5% of all snakebite deaths (Russell et al., 1997). Alvarez del Toro (1983) also considered the venom of *P. nasutum* to be potent, and Picado T. (1936) found it much more toxic than that of *P. ophryomegas*. Someone in Guatemala who had been bitten by most of the local species reported that its bite was more painful than any other and resulted in considerable necrosis. Bites by *P. nasutum* may be misattributed to *Bothrops asper*.

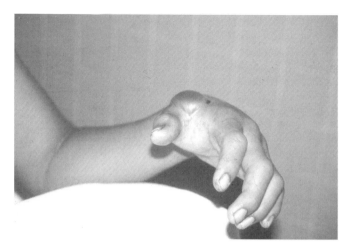

Fig. 280. Bite from a Guatemalan *Porthidium ophryomegas*, showing blister formation on hand. Photograph courtesy of Victor Rolando Alvarado, Hospital Instituto Guatemalteco de Seguridad Social.

Porthidium ophryomegas, slender hognosed pitviper, toboba (also used for *Atropoides mexicanus*) (Pls. 738–742, Fig. 280)

There are said to be no reported deaths from bites by this species, but it is quick to strike and some serious cases of envenoming have required hospitalization (Fig. 280; Campbell and Lamar, 1989). In Costa Rica, this species was responsible for 3 (0.63%) of 477 cases of snakebite reported in 1979 (Bolaños, 1984).

LABORATORY INVESTIGATION OF SNAKEBITE VICTIMS

Hematological Tests

Systemic envenoming is usually associated with a neutrophil leukocytosis: counts above $20 \times 10^9/l$ indicate severe envenoming. Initially, the hematocrit may be high from hemoconcentration when there is generalized increase in capillary permeability (e.g., following bites by Central American *Crotalus simus*). Later, the hematocrit falls because of bleeding into the bitten limb and elsewhere, and from intravascular hemolysis (possible in some cases of *Micrurus* envenoming) or microangiopathic hemolysis in patients with disseminated intravascular coagulation (viper bites). Thrombocytopenia is common in patients severely envenomed by vipers.

Twenty-Minute Whole Blood Clotting Test and Other Tests of Blood Coagulation

Incoagulable blood is a cardinal sign of systemic envenoming by most Viperidae and some of the medically important Colubridae. For clinical purposes, a simple, bedside, all-or-nothing test of blood coagulability is usually adequate. Incoagulable blood suggests a fibrinogen concentration less than about 0.5 g/l (Sano-Martins et al., 1994). A few milliliters of blood taken by venepuncture is placed in a new, clean, dry glass vessel; left undisturbed at room temperature for 20 minutes; then tipped once to see if there is clotting or not (Pl. 1493; Warrell et al., 1977).

More sensitive tests that are rapid and relatively simple to perform are whole blood or plasma prothrombin times and detection of elevated concentrations of fibrin(ogen) degradation products by agglutination of sensitized latex particles or of D-dimer.

Biochemical Tests

Serum concentrations of creatine kinase, aspartate transferase, and blood urea are commonly raised in patients with severe envenoming because of local muscle damage at the site of the bite. Generalized rhabdomyolysis, caused by seasnake, some coralsnake, and tropical rattlesnake bites, produces a steep rise in serum creatine kinase and other muscle-derived enzymes, myoglobin, and potassium concentrations. Plasma is stained brownish by myoglobin and pink by hemoglobin. Patients with intravascular hemolysis or rhabdomyolysis have black urine. Blood urea or serum creatinine and potassium concentrations should be measured in patients who become oliguric, especially in cases with a high risk of renal failure (*C. d. terrificus*, *Bothrops* spp., seasnakes, and Colubridae).

All snakebite patients should be encouraged to empty the bladder on admission. The urine should be examined for blood/hemoglobin and protein (by "stix" test) and for microscopic hematuria and red cell casts.

Electrocardiographic abnormalities include sinus bradycardia, ST-T changes, various degrees of atrioventricular block, and evidence of hyperkalemia. Shock may induce myocardial ischemia or infarction in patients with diseased coronary arteries.

Immunodiagnosis

Detection of venom antigens in body fluids of snakebite victims has improved diagnosis, understanding of pathophysiological mechanisms, assessment of first aid methods, and control of antivenom treatment (Ho et al., 1986a, 1986b; Theakston et al., 1979). Enzyme immunoassays (EIA) have been the most widely used for research. Venom detection kits are not available commercially in Latin America.

TREATMENT OF SNAKEBITE VICTIMS

For an overview of treatment of snakebites, see Meier and White, 1995.

Herbal and Other Traditional Treatments of Snakebite in Latin America

In rural areas of Central and South America, most snakebite victims, whether they be Amerindians or more recent settlers, first seek treatment from traditional therapists such as shamans (curador/curanderos de cobra, curandeiros; Quechua, sukanka), sorcerers, or witch doctors, known in Ecuador as brujos (Pl. 1497) and in Brazil as mandingueiros or mandinguentos (Koster, 1816). In Chanchamayo, Junín, Peru, Ashaninka curanderos known as shiripriaris use a plant remedy that they misleadingly describe as antivenom. In northeastern Peru, shamans often employ special songs believed to cure snakebite (W. W. Lamar, pers. comm.). A decoction made from "jergón sacha" (*Dracontium* sp.) is also favored (W. W. Lamar, pers. comm.). In Antioquia and Chocó, Colombia, 60% of a group of 244 snakebite victims surveyed used these traditional therapists as their first resort (Otero et al., 1992b). Remedies included plasters made of vegetable matter, tobacco, gunpowder, brandy, and hot water; drinks made from concoctions of herbs believed to have medicinal properties (Otero et al., 2000); and even the drinking of petroleum (gasoline;

Otero et al., 1992b). Other folk treatments include inhalations; moxibustion; and application of the black snake stone (piedra negra, for example, in Chocó, Colombia, and Loja, Ecuador), a chicken's cloaca, the snake's head, or petroleum (Otero et al., 1992b; Touzet, 1983). European travelers in Brazil in the nineteenth century were impressed by the diversity and apparent efficacy of herbal remedies for snakebite. Spix and Martius (1824) discovered the use of leaves and roots of *Chiococco anguifuga* and *C. foliis*, "raiz preta" or "raiz de cobra," known in Europe as "cainca." Other ingredients included "loco" (*Plumbago scandens*), "picaõ" (*Bidens graveolens*), "St. Anne's herb" (*Kuhnia arguta*), and *Spilanthes brasiliensis* (Sigaud, 1844; Spix and Martius, 1824). Saint-Hilaire (1833, 2:226) was persuaded of the efficacy of immediate local application of gunpowder thinned in lemon juice followed by ingestion of a decoction "milhomens" (*Aristolochia grandiflora*) and a tisane made with "jarro" or "jarrinha" (*A. macroura*) in snakebite victims in Espirito Santo. In Goiás Province, "herva d'urubú" was the accepted cure for snakebite (Saint-Hilaire, 1847, 1:98). Especifico Pessoa, a proprietary treatment for snakebite of plant origin, is used extensively throughout South America. Its exact composition is a closely guarded secret, but it may be based on the leguminous plant *Apoleia leiocarpa* or the root of the "cabeça de negro" (*Annona coriacea*), which contains cabenegrins that have some activity against venom components *in vitro*. In northeastern Brazil, where it has been used for more than 70 years, it was registered with the Department of Health in the state of Ceará in 1926 by A. Pexedes Pessoa. Its clinical efficacy and safety have not been established.

First Aid

The patient should be reassured and moved to the nearest hospital or dispensary as quickly, comfortably, and passively as possible, preferably on a stretcher. The bitten limb should be immobilized with a splint or sling and all unnecessary movement discouraged.

Most traditional first aid methods are potentially harmful and should not be used. Local incisions and suction do not remove venom effectively and may introduce infection, damage tissues, and cause persistent bleeding. Vacuum extractors (Bush et al., 2000a), potassium permanganate, and ice packs may potentiate local necrosis. Electric shocks may act as counterirritants but are dangerous and have not been proved beneficial. Tourniquets and compression bands can cause gangrene (Pls. 1494–1496), increased fibrinolysis and bleeding in the occluded limb, peripheral nerve palsies, compartmental ischemia, and intensification of local signs of envenoming.

The pressure-immobilization method developed by the late Struan Sutherland and his colleagues in Australia involves using a long crepe bandage to wrap the entire bitten limb as tightly as for a sprained ankle, starting at the toes or fingers and incorporating a splint (Sutherland and Tibballs, 2001; Fig. 281). In animals, a pressure of about 55 mm Hg was effective in preventing systemic uptake of Australian elapid and some other venoms. Anecdotal experience supports the use of the method. In several reported cases, however, patients rapidly deteriorated after release of the pressure bandage. Prospective clinical studies are needed to assess the risks and benefits of this interesting technique. In the meantime, it is recommended in Latin America as first aid *only* for bites by seasnakes and coralsnakes. The method is not recommended for bites by vipers, because their venoms cause massive local swelling and necrosis and these effects may be accentuated by the bandage, which by

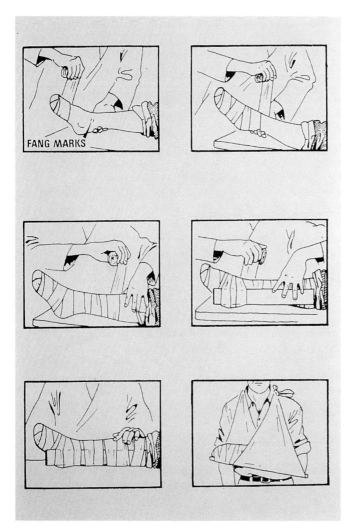

Fig. 281. Pressure-immobilization technique.

raising pressure in fascial compartments will increase the risk of ischemic necrosis.

Pursuing and killing the snake is not recommended, but if the snake has been killed it should be taken with the patient to the hospital. It must not be handled, however, as even a severed head can inject venom.

Patients being transported to the hospital should lie on the left side to prevent aspiration of vomit. Persistent vomiting can be treated with chlorpromazine by intravenous injection (25–50 mg for adults, 1 mg/kg for children). Syncope, shock, angioedema, and other autonomic symptoms can be treated with 0.1% epinephrine (adrenaline) by intramuscular injection (0.5 ml for adults, 0.01 ml/kg for children) and an antihistamine such as chlorpheniramine maleate by intravenous injection (10 mg for adults, 0.2 mg/kg for children). Respiratory distress and cyanosis should be treated by clearing the airway and giving oxygen, and, if necessary, with assisted ventilation. If the patient is unconscious and no femoral or carotid pulses can be detected, cardiopulmonary resuscitation must be started immediately.

MEDICAL TREATMENT IN THE HOSPITAL

Clinical Assessment

In most cases of snakebite there are uncertainties about the species and the quantity and composition of the venom injected that can be resolved only by admitting the patient for at least 24 hours' observation. Local swelling is usually detectable within 15 minutes of pitviper envenoming, but may not develop in patients bitten by South American rattlesnakes, coralsnakes, and seasnakes. Fang marks are sometimes invisible. Tender enlargement of regional lymph nodes draining the bitten area is an early sign of envenoming by Viperidae and some Colubridae and coralsnakes. All the patient's gingival sulci should be examined meticulously because this is usually the first site of spontaneous bleeding (Pls. 1447 and 1448); other common sites of bleeding are nose, conjunctivae, skin, and gastrointestinal tract. Persistent bleeding from fang punctures, venepuncture sites, and other wounds implies incoagulable blood (Pl. 1498). Hypotension and shock are important signs of hypovolemia or cardiotoxicity after viper bites. Ptosis is the earliest sign of neurotoxic envenoming (Pls. 1410–1412, 1481–1485). Respiratory muscle power should be assessed objectively and repeatedly, for example, by measuring vital capacity. Trismus and generalized muscle tenderness suggest rhabdomyolysis (seasnake and, rarely, coralsnake bites). If a procoagulant venom is suspected, coagulability of whole blood should be checked at the bedside using the 20-minute whole blood clotting test described above.

Antivenom Treatment

The most important decision is whether or not to give antivenom, the only specific treatment for envenoming. There is now abundant evidence that in patients with severe envenoming the benefits of this treatment far outweigh the risks of antivenom reactions. Antivenom has reduced the mortality of systemic envenoming by *C. d. terrificus* in Brazil from 72 to 12% (Rosenfeld, 1971). Antivenoms are effective in reversing hypotension and coagulopathies. Antivenom, also known as antivenin, antivenene, and antisnakebite serum, is the partially purified immunoglobulin (whole IgG, F(ab')2, or Fab fragments) of horses or sheep that have been immunized with venom. Table 63 lists the antivenoms currently available to treat envenoming by snakes in the Western Hemisphere.

General Indications for Antivenom

Antivenom is indicated if there are signs of systemic envenoming such as the following: (1) hemostatic abnormalities such as spontaneous systemic bleeding, incoagulable blood, or thrombocytopenia; (2) neurotoxicity; (3) hypotension and shock, abnormal ECG, or other evidence of cardiovascular dysfunction; and (4) generalized rhabdomyolysis. Supporting evidence of severe envenoming is a neutrophil leukocytosis (greater than 10×10^9/l), elevated serum enzymes such as creatine kinase and aminotransferases, hemoconcentration, severe anemia, myoglobinuria, hemoglobinuria, methemoglobinuria, hypoxemia, and acidosis.

In the absence of systemic envenoming, local swelling involving more than half the bitten limb, extensive blistering or bruising, bites on digits, and rapid progression of swelling are indications for antivenom, especially in patients bitten by vipers.

Special Indications for Antivenom

In the United States, "some immediate pain" or "any symptoms or signs" after bites by coralsnakes (*Micruroides*

Table 63. Antivenoms available for treatment of envenoming by American snakes (in alphabetical order by manufacturer).

Warning! Availability of antivenoms, manufacturers' contact information, and other details change frequently. Some of this information may already be obsolete.

1. Aventis-Pasteur SA, France
   Avenue Général Leclerc, 69007 Lyon, France
   Phone: 33-7273-7707 or 33-7280-4000; fax: 33-7273-7997
   Web: www.aventispasteur.com
   Monospecific ("BothroFav"): *Bothrops lanceolatus, ?B. caribbaeus*

2. Centro de Biotecnologia, Venezuela
   Facultad de Farmacia–Universidad Central, Av. de Los Llustres, Los Chaguaramos, Caracas, Venezuela
   Phone: 582-693-6615102; fax: 582-693-1026
   Polyspecific: *Crotalus durissus cumanensis*, "*Bothrops venezuelae*" (=*B. venezuelensis*), "*B. colombiensis*" (=?*B. asper* or *B. atrox*)

3. Fundaçao Ezequiel Dias, Brazil
   Rua Conde Pereira Carneiro 80, 30500 Belo Horizonte, MG Brazil
   Phone: 5531-332-2077/7222; fax: 5531-332-2534
   Antibotropico: *Bothrops alternatus, B. jararaca, B. jararacussu, B. moojeni, B. neuwiedi* (sensu lato)
   Antibotropico crotalico: *Bothrops alternatus, B. jararaca, B. jararacussu, B. atrox, B. moojeni, B. neuwiedi* (sensu lato), *Crotalus d. terrificus*
   Anticrotalico: *Crotalus d. terrificus*
   Antibotropico laquetico: *Bothrops alternatus, B. jararaca, B. jararacussu, B. atrox, B. moojeni, B. neuwiedi* (sensu lato), *Lachesis muta*

4. Gerencia General de Biológicos y Reactivos, Ministerio de Salud, Mexico M Escobado 20 CP, 11400 México, DF Mexico
   Phone: 52-527-6127/7368; fax: 52-527-6693
   Anti-*Crotalus*: *Crotalus basiliscus, C. atrox*, "*C. durissus*" (=*C. simus*), *C. molossus*
   Anti-*Bothrops*: *Agkistrodon bilineatus, Bothrops asper*
   Suero antiofidico export lyophilized: "*Bothrops atrox*" (?*B. asper*), "*Crotalus d. terrificus*" (?*C. simus*), Mexican and South American *Bothrops* and *Crotalus* spp.

5. Instituto Butantan, Brazil
   Av. Vital Brazil, 1500 Caixa Postal 65, 05504 São Paulo, SP Brasil
   Phone: 5511-3726-7222; fax: 5511-3726-1505
   Polyspecific ("Antibotropico") *Bothrops*: *B. alternatus, B. atrox, B. cotiara, B. erythromelas, B. insularis, B. jararaca, B. jararacussu, B. moojeni, B. neuwiedi* (sensu lato), "*B. pradoi*" (=*B. leucurus*)
   Monospecific ("Anticrotalico"): *Crotalus durissus terrificus*
   Polyspecific ("Antiophidico polyvalente"): *Bothrops, Crotalus durissus terrificus*, and *Lachesis muta*
   Polyspecific ("Antielapidico"): *Micrurus corallinus, M. frontalis*

6. Instituto Clodomiro Picado, Costa Rica
   Facultad de Microbiologia, Universidad de Costa Rica, San José, Costa Rica
   Fax: 506-292-0485
   Polyspecific: *Bothrops asper*, "*Crotalus durissus*" (=*C. simus*), *Lachesis* spp.
   Monospecific: *Micrurus nigrocinctus, M. mipartitus* (?and *M. multifasciatus*)

7. Instituto de Higiene, Uruguay
   Calle Alfredo Navarro 3051, Montevideo, Uruguay
   Phone: 598-2471288; fax: 598-4873074
   Bispecific ("Suero antiofidico bivalente anti-bothropico"): *Bothrops alternatus* and "*B. neuwiedi*" (=*B. pubescens*)

8. Instituto Nacional de Higiene y Medicina Tropical "Leopoldo Izquieta Perez," Ecuador
   Casilla, Postal 3961, Guayaquil, Ecuador
   Fax: 5934-394189
   Anti-Bothrops polyvalent: *B. atrox, B. asper*, "*B. xanthogrammus*" (=*B. asper*)

9. Instituto Nacional de Microbiologia "Dr. Carlos G. Malbran," Argentina
   Av. Velez Sarsfield 563, Buenos Aires, Argentina
   Antibothrops bivalente: *Bothrops alternatus*, "*B. neuwiedi*" (=*B. diporus*), *B. ammodytoides*
   Antibothrops tetravalente: *Bothrops alternatus, B. diporus, B. jararaca, B. jararacussu*
   Anticrotalus: *Crotalus durissus terrificus*
   Antimicrurus: "*Micrurus frontalis*" (=*M. pyrrhocryptus*), *M. corallinus*
   Tropical trivalente: *Bothrops alternatus*, "*B. neuwiedi*" (=*B. diporus*), *Crotalus durissus terrificus*

10. Instituto Nacional de Salud, Colombia
    Av. Eldorado con Carrera 50, ZonaG, Santa Fe de Bogotá DE, Colombia
    Tel/Fax: 57-1-222-0577
    Polyspecific: *Bothrops* spp., *Crotalus durissus cumanensis, Lachesis muta* (?and/or *L. acrochorda*)
    Monospecific: *Bothrops* spp.

11. Instituto Nacional de Salud, Peru
    Calle Cápac Yupanqui Nr. 1400, Jesús Maria, Lima 11, Peru
    Phone: 57-471-9920; fax: 57-471-0179
    E-mail: postmaster@ins.sld.pe
    Web: www.ins.sld.pe
    Antibotrópico polivalente: *B. atrox, B. brazili, B. pictus, B. barnetti*, "*B. hypoprora*" (=*Bothrocophias hyoprora*)
    Antilachésico monovalente: *Lachesis* spp.
    Anticrotálico monovalente: *Crotalus durissus terrificus*

Table 63—cont.

12. Instituto Vital Brazil, Brazil
    Rua Vital Brazil Filho 64, Santa Rosa, 24230-340 Niteroi, RJ Brazil
    Phone: 5521-711-0012; fax: 5521-714-3198
    Sôro Antibotrópico: *Bothrops alternatus, B. cotiara, B. jararaca, B. jararacussu, B. moojeni, "B. pradoi"* (=*B. leucurus*)
    Sôro Anticrotálico: *Crotalus d. terrificus*
    Sôro Antiofidico polyvalente: *Bothrops alternatus, B. cotiara, B. jararaca, B. jararacussu, B. moojeni, "B. pradoi"* (=*B. leucurus*), *Crotalus durissus terrificus*

13. Laboratorios Bioclon/Silanes, Mexico
    Calzada de Tlalpan, No 4687, CP 14050, México DF, Mexico
    Phone: 525-488-3735; fax: 525-604-2368
    Antivipmyn Suero Antiviperino: *Crotalus basiliscus, Bothrops asper* (also claimed to cover other *Crotalus, Sistrurus,* and *Agkistrodon* spp.)
    Antivipmyn Suero Antiviperino, Polivalente equino: *"Bothrops atrox"* (?*B. asper*), *Crotalus* (covers against same spp. as above)

14. Laboratorios de Biológicos y Reactivos de Mexico SA de CV (Birmex), Mexico
    Amores 1240, Col del Valle CO 03100, México DF, Mexico
    Phone: 5559-2697; fax: 5559-0722
    Polyspecific: North and Central American *Crotalus* spp. and *Bothrops* spp.

15. Protherics, Ltd., USA
    1207 17th Avenue South (Suite 103), Nashville, TN 37212 USA
    Phone: 615-327-1027; fax: 615-320-1212
    Distributed by Altana, Inc., Melville, NY 11747, 800-231-0206, ext. 3058, Jackie Beltrani
    Protherics Ltd., UK
    Blaenwaun Farm, Ffostrasol, Llandysul, Ceredigian SA44 5JT, UK
    Phone: 44-1239-851122; fax: 44-1239-858800
    Polyspecific ("CroFab"): *Agkistrodon contortrix contortrix, A. piscivorus, Crotalus adamanteus, C. atrox, C. horridus atricaudatus, C. h. horridus, C. scutulatus, C. m. molossus, Sistrurus miliarius barbouri, "C. viridis helleri"* (=*C. oreganus helleri*)

16. Wyeth-Ayerst Laboratories, USA
    P.O. Box 8299, Philadelphia, PA 19101-1245, USA
    Phone: 215-688-4400; fax: 215-964-9743
    Polyspecific ("Wyeth Antivenin [Crotalidae] polyvalent"): *Crotalus* spp., *C. durissus* (=*C. simus* and *C. durissus*), *Agkistrodon* spp. (*A. piscivorus*), *A. contortrix, A. bilineatus, Gloydius* spp., *Bothrops* spp., *Sistrurus* spp., and *Lachesis muta* (production discontinued, but some stocks still in use)
    Monospecific ("Antivenin [*Micrurus fulvius*]"): *Micrurus fulvius* and *M. tener* (production likely to be discontinued soon)

euryxanthus, Micrurus fulvius, and *M. tener*) are regarded by some as indications for immediate antivenom treatment (Russell, 1980b).

Prediction of Antivenom Reactions

Skin and conjunctival tests do not predict early (anaphylactic) or late (serum sickness type) antivenom reactions and should not be used (Malasit et al., 1986).

Contraindications to Antivenom

Patients with severe asthma, hay fever, or eczema (atopy) and those who have reacted previously to antiserum are at increased risk of developing severe antivenom reactions. Antivenom should be given to such patients only if there is evidence of severe envenoming. Reactions may be prevented or ameliorated by pretreatment with subcutaneous epinephrine (adrenaline), intravenous antihistamine, and hydrocortisone or continuous intravenous infusion of highly dilute (1 : 100,000) epinephrine (adrenaline) while antivenom is being given. Rapid desensitization is not recommended.

Selection and Administration of Antivenom

Antivenom should be given only if its stated range of specificity includes the species responsible for the bite. In view of the geographical variation in venom composition and antigenicity within a single species (Warrell, 1987), the ideal antivenom for treating a particular patient would be one raised against the venom of the local population of the species of snake involved. For example, the effectiveness of Instituto Butantan polyspecific anti-*Bothrops* (Sôro Antibotrópico) was tested in mice against 11 regional venom pools of the *Bothrops atrox* complex. Although venoms from populations used in raising the antivenom were effectively neutralized, there was a wide range of efficacy against venom of other regional populations (Wüster et al., unpublished data). Opaque solutions should be discarded because precipitation of protein indicates loss of activity and increased risk of reactions. Expiration dates quoted on ampules are often very conservative for commercial reasons. Liquid and lyophilized antivenoms stored below 8 °C usually retain most of their activity for five years or more. Monospecific (monovalent) antivenom is ideal if the biting species is known. Polyspecific (polyvalent) antivenoms are used in many countries because of the difficulty in identifying the species responsible for bites. Polyspecific antivenoms may be just as effective as monospecific ones provided that a larger dose is used to compensate for the lower concentration of specific neutralizing antibody per unit of immunoglobulin. Apart from the specific activity against the venoms used for immunization in the production of antivenoms, there may be some paraspecific activity, extending to the venoms of related species.

It is almost never too late to give antivenom while signs of systemic envenoming persist, but ideally, antivenom should be given as soon as it is indicated. Antivenom has proved effective up to two days after seasnake bites and in patients still defibrinated weeks after bites by Viperidae. In contrast, local envenoming is probably not reversible unless antivenom is given within a few hours of the bite. The intravenous route is the most effective and should always be employed where technical skills and equipment allow (but see below). Infusion of antivenom diluted in approximately 5 ml of isotonic fluid/kg body weight is easier to control than intravenous "push" or bolus injection of undiluted antivenom given at the rate of about 4 ml/min, but there is no difference in the incidence or severity of antivenom reactions in patients treated by these two methods (Malasit et al., 1986).

Treatment of Snakebites during Expeditions to Remote Locations

Snakebites may occur during expeditions or collecting trips to areas remote from medical facilities. If a medically qualified person is present and antivenom and other drugs (especially epinephrine/adrenaline for treating early antivenom reactions) are available, treatment can proceed as described above, following the usual criteria for antivenom administration. However, in the absence of someone capable of administering antivenom intravenously and of recognizing and dealing with potentially life-threatening antivenom reactions, it is much more difficult to decide what treatment is appropriate. Hardy (1994c) reviewed 10 cases of field researchers bitten by *B. asper* in Mexico and Central America and discussed the role of first aid and early antivenom treatment in these circumstances. If it is decided to give antivenom, the dose can be divided between a number of sites and the antivenom given by deep intramuscular injection into the anterolateral part of the thigh followed by massage to promote its absorption. Antivenom should not be injected into the gluteal region (buttock) as absorption from this fatty area is particularly slow and unreliable. Unfortunately, intramuscular antivenom, even if administered correctly, is absorbed slowly and the resulting circulating levels of therapeutic antivenom take hours to match those achieved within 20 or 30 minutes by intravenous injection. Using intramuscular injection, smaller IgG fragments, such as Fab, are not absorbed more rapidly and do not prove more effective therapeutically than conventional F(ab')$_2$ or even whole IgG (Chaves et al., 2003; Rivière et al., 1998; R. D. G. Theakston and D. A. Warrell, unpublished data). Decision making may be helped by the algorithm shown in Figure 282. It is important to realize that intramuscular injections may cause massive superficial bruising and deep muscle hematomas in patients with incoagulable blood. To reduce this risk, pressure pads should be firmly bandaged over all injection sites.

Dose of Antivenom

Manufacturers' recommendations are based on mouse protection tests and may be very misleading. Few clinical trials have been performed to establish appropriate starting doses, and in most countries antivenom is used empirically. Many hospitals in the rural tropics give a standard dose of one to two ampules to every patient who claims to have been bitten, irrespective of clinical severity. This practice squanders scarce,

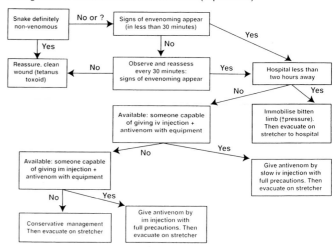

Fig. 282. Algorithm to guide the use of antivenom in victims of snakebite at remote locations. "Antivenom with equipment" means appropriate specific antivenom for the species of snake involved together with epinephrine (adrenaline) (for intramuscular injection), antihistamine, and hydrocortisone (for intravenous intramuscular injection) for treating an antivenom reaction if one occurs. "Immobilize bitten limb (±pressure)" means immobilization with a splint or sling (bites by pitvipers and colubrids) and pressure-immobilization (Fig. 281) in the case of coralsnake or seasnake bites.

expensive antivenom and exposes nonenvenomed patients to the risk of reactions.

CHILDREN MUST BE GIVEN THE SAME DOSE OF ANTIVENOM AS ADULTS. However, the total volume of fluid administered (volume of liquid or reconstituted freeze-dried antivenom plus intravenous fluid) should be calculated according to body weight (total volume not exceeding 5 ml/kg body weight) to avoid volume overload in a child.

Response to Antivenom

Often there is marked symptomatic improvement soon after antivenom has been injected. In shocked patients, the blood pressure may rise and consciousness may return. Neurotoxic signs usually take several hours to improve. Spontaneous systemic bleeding usually stops within 15–30 minutes, and blood coagulability is restored within six hours of antivenom provided a neutralizing dose has been given. More antivenom should be given if severe signs of envenoming persist after one to two hours, or if blood coagulability is not restored within about six hours.

Recurrent Envenoming

Systemic envenoming may recur hours or days after an initially good response to antivenom (Ho et al., 1986a, 1986b, 1990; Warrell et al., 1986), especially if rapidly cleared Fab antivenom (e.g., Protherics CroFab) is used (Ariaratnam et al., 1999, 2001; Meyer et al., 1997). This is explained by continuing absorption of venom from the injection site after clearance of antivenom from the bloodstream. The phenomenon has been rediscovered by those using CroFab to treat pitviper bites in North America. The apparent serum half-lives of antivenoms in envenomed patients range from 26 to 95 hours. Patients should therefore be assessed daily for at least three or four days to ensure that the effects of envenoming have been permanently controlled.

Antivenom Reactions

Early (anaphylactic) reactions develop within 10–180 minutes of starting antivenom in 3–84% of patients. The incidence increases with dose. Symptoms include itching, urticaria, cough, nausea, vomiting, other autonomic manifestations, fever, and tachycardia. Up to 40% of patients with early reactions develop systemic anaphylaxis: hypotension, bronchospasm, and angio-edema. Deaths are rare. Early antivenom reactions are rarely the result of type I IgE-mediated hypersensitivity reactions to equine or ovine serum proteins. They are usually the result of complement activation by immune complexes or aggregates in the antivenom (Malasit et al., 1986).

Pyrogenic reactions result from contamination of the antivenom with endotoxinlike compounds during manufacture. Fever, rigors, vasodilatation, and a fall in blood pressure develop one to two hours after treatment. In children, febrile convulsions may be precipitated.

Late reactions of serum sickness type may develop 5–24 (mean 7) days after antivenom. The incidence of those reactions and the speed of their development increases with the dose of antivenom. Clinical features include fever, itching, urticaria, arthralgia (including the temperomandibular joint), lymphadenopathy, periarticular swellings, mononeuritis multiplex, albuminuria, and, rarely, encephalopathy. This is a classical immune complex disease.

Prevention of Antivenom Reactions

Routine prophylaxis with epinephrine (adrenaline), H_1-antihistamines, and hydrocortisone is widely used, but for reasons of efficacy and safety *it is not recommended for routine use* except in patients with a high risk of severe reactions (see above). In Brazil, the Ministério da Saúde recommends routine prophylaxis with histamine H_1 and H_2 antagonists and hydrocortisone (Brasil, 1998). However, there is no evidence of efficacy (Bucaretchi et al., 2002).

Treatment of Antivenom Reactions

Epinephrine (adrenaline) is the effective treatment for early anaphylactic reactions; 0.5–1.0 ml of 0.1% (1 in 1,000, 1 mg/ml) is given by intramuscular injection to adults (to children, 0.01 ml/kg) at the first signs of a reaction. The dose may be repeated within 5–10 minutes if the reaction is not controlled. Patients with profound hypotension, severe bronchospasm, or laryngeal edema may be given epinephrine (adrenaline) by slow intravenous injection (0.5 mg diluted in 20 ml of isotonic saline over 10–15 minutes). A histamine anti-H_1 blocker such as chlorpheniramine maleate (10 mg for adults, 0.2 mg/kg for children) should be given by intravenous injection to combat the effects of histamine released during the reaction. Histamine anti-H_2 blockers, such as cimetidine, may have a role. Pyrogenic reactions are treated by cooling the patient and giving antipyretics. Late reactions respond to an oral H_1-antihistamine such as chlorpheniramine (2 mg six-hourly for adults, 0.25 mg/kg/day in divided doses for children) or to oral prednisolone (5 mg six-hourly for 5–7 days for adults, 0.7 mg/kg/day in divided doses for children).

Supportive Treatment

Neurotoxic Envenoming

Bulbar and respiratory paralysis may lead to death from aspiration, airway obstruction, or respiratory failure. A clear airway must be maintained. If respiratory distress develops, a cuffed endotracheal tube should be inserted or tracheostomy performed. Provided they are adequately ventilated, patients with neurotoxic envenoming remain fully conscious with intact sensation. Patients have been effectively ventilated manually (by Ambu bag/anesthetic bag) for 30 days and have recovered after 10 weeks of mechanical ventilation. Although artificial ventilation was first suggested for neurotoxic envenoming more than 100 years ago, patients continue to die because they are denied this simple procedure. Anticholinesterases have a variable but potentially useful effect in patients with neurotoxic envenoming from coralsnake bites, especially when postsynaptic neurotoxins are involved. The Tensilon test (used in patients with suspected myasthenia gravis) should be carried out in all cases of severe neurotoxic envenoming after antivenom has been given. Atropine sulphate (0.6 mg for adults, 50 µg/kg for children) or glycopyrronium bromide (200–400 µg for adults, 4–8 µg/kg max, 200 µg for children) is given by intravenous injection followed by an intravenous injection of edrophonium chloride (10 mg for adults, 0.25 mg/kg for children). Patients who respond convincingly can be maintained on neostigmine methyl sulphate (50–100 µg/kg) and atropine, four-hourly or by continuous infusion.

Rhabdomyolysis Caused by South American Rattlesnake Bites

Myoglobin and other muscle constituents released into the circulation as a result of generalized skeletal muscle breakdown in patients envenomed by South American rattlesnakes may cause a number of serious complications, notably acute renal failure. By analogy with the treatment of crush syndrome, renal damage should be actively prevented by correcting hypovolemia and acidosis and by the use of intravenous mannitol. Hyperkalaemia and hypocalcemia (Bucaretchi et al., 2002) are potentially life-threatening complications of severe rhabdomyolysis.

Hypotension and Shock

Intravenous fluids should be infused in patients with swelling of more than half the bitten limb if the central venous pressure is low or there is other clinical evidence of hypovolemia. A plasma expander such as fresh whole blood or fresh frozen plasma may be indicated. If this fails to improve the blood pressure, a selective vasoconstrictor such as dopamine (starting dose 2.5–5 µg/kg/min by intravenous infusion) can be used.

Decreasing Urine Output (Oliguria) and Renal Failure

Urine output, serum creatinine, urea, and electrolytes should be measured each day in patients with severe envenoming and in those bitten by species known to cause renal failure (e.g., *Crotalus durissus, Bothrops* spp. seasnakes). If urine output drops below 400 ml in 24 hours, urethral and central venous catheters should be inserted. If urine flow fails to increase after cautious rehydration, diuretics should be tried (e.g., frusemide) by slow intravenous injection, 100 mg followed by 200 mg; and if that is unsuccessful, mannitol. Dopamine (2.5 µg/kg/min by intravenous infusion) is sometimes effective. If these measures are ineffective, the patient should be placed on strict fluid balance. Peritoneal- or hemodialysis or hemofiltration will usually be required.

Local Infection at the Site of the Bite

Bites by *Bothrops* spp. are likely to be complicated by local infections caused by bacteria in the snake's venom or on its fangs. Among 312 pitviper bite victims in eastern Ecuador, 38 developed local abscesses at the site of the bite, while 1 showed features of gas gangrene (Kerrigan, 1992). In Goiânia, Goiás, Brazil, 16% of *Bothrops* victims developed local abscesses, as did 9% of snakebite cases at the Hospital Vital Brazil in São Paulo. A discrete abscess often forms at the site of the bite, from which pus can be aspirated for bacterial culture. Organisms commonly implicated are *Morganella morganii*, *Escherichia coli*, *Providencia rettgeri*, *Aeromonas hydrophila*, *Pseudomonas paucimobilis*, *Proteus mirabilis*, *Streptococcus* Group D, *Enterobacter* spp., *Klebsiella* spp., *Bacteroides* spp., and *Clostridium* spp. (Andrade et al., 1989; Arroyo et al., 1980; Garcia-Lima and Laure, 1987; Jorge et al., 1990, 1994, 1998; Kerrigan, 1992). At Hospital Vozandes Oriente, Shell, Pastaza, Ecuador, 114 patients bitten by pitvipers were randomized to prophylactic gentamicin and chloramphenicol or no antibiotic treatment. The incidence of local wound abscesses was 1 out of 59 patients in the antibiotic-treated group and 3 out of 55 patients in the patients who did not receive antibiotics, an insignificant difference (Kerrigan et al., 1997). An unpublished randomized study of parenteral chloramphenicol prophylaxis in patients with *Bothrops* bites in Brazil has also shown that routine antibiotics prophylaxis is not effective (M. T. Jorge et al., unpublished data).

Treatment with penicillin, chloramphenicol, or erythromycin is justified only if the wound has been incised or tampered with in any way or if there is already evidence of local infection. A booster dose of tetanus toxoid should be given in all cases. An aminoglycoside such as gentamicin should be added for 48 hours if there is evidence of local necrosis.

Management of Local Envenoming

Bullae are best left intact. The bitten limb should not be elevated as this increases the risk of intracompartmental ischemia. Once definite signs of necrosis have appeared (blackened anesthetic area with putrid odor or signs of sloughing), surgical debridement, immediate split skin grafting, and broad-spectrum antibiotic cover are indicated.

Intracompartmental Syndrome and Fasciotomy

Increased pressure within tight fascial compartments such as the digital pulp spaces and anterior tibial compartment may cause ischemia. This complication is most likely after bites by *Crotalus simus*, *Agkistrodon bilineatus*, and *Bothrops* spp. The signs are excessive pain, weakness of the compartmental muscles and pain when they are passively stretched, hypoesthesia of skin supplied by nerves running through the compartment, and obvious tenseness of the compartment. Detection of arterial pulses by palpation or Doppler does not exclude intracompartmental ischemia. Intracompartmental pressures

exceeding 45 mm Hg carry a high risk of ischemic necrosis. Fasciotomy may be justified in these circumstances, but it did not prove effective in saving envenomed muscle in experimental animals. Fasciotomy is contraindicated until blood coagulability has been restored and blood loss compensated by transfusion. Intravenous infusion of mannitol proved effective in reducing intracompartmental pressure in two out of three patients with compartment syndrome caused by *B. asper* bites (Otero et al., 2002). Early and adequate antivenom treatment will prevent the development of intracompartmental syndromes in most cases. Necrosis of digits is especially common.

Hemostatic Disturbances

Once specific antivenom has been given to neutralize venom procoagulants, restoration of coagulability and platelet function may be accelerated by giving fresh whole blood, fresh frozen plasma, cryoprecipitates (containing fibrinogen, factor VIII, fibronectin, and some factors V and XIII), or prothrombin complex concentrates, and platelet concentrates. Heparin has been used for a variety of snakebites, usually with disastrous results. *In vitro*, it does not inhibit the thrombin generated by *Bothrops* venoms (Nahas et al., 1975).

Other Drugs

Corticosteroids, antifibrinolytic agents (aprotinin-Trasylol and ε-aminocaproic acid), antihistamines, and a variety of traditional herbal remedies have been used, but none has proved effective and most are potentially harmful.

THE SPECIAL DANGERS OF SNAKEBITE FOR HABITUAL SNAKE HANDLERS AND HERPETOLOGISTS

Many herpetologists and people whose business or pleasure is to handle snakes have been bitten, been envenomed, and even succumbed to envenoming. Two of my friends died following snakebites, and several more have had a close brush with death. "Snake people" expose themselves to special risks, but they also have a few potential advantages over those unaccustomed to dealing with snakes. The risks include being bitten on the dominant hand while alone and in a remote location, sensitization to snake venom through previous exposure to venom (not always to the venom of the snake that has just bitten them), and ill-placed self-confidence that may lead them to underestimate the risks and ignore normal first aid and medical guidelines. Herpetologists have an advantage in being in a better position to identify the snake that has bitten them, but even experienced people may be misled by juvenile coloration or a too-hasty assumption that the snake is a nonvenomous mimic. In Latin America, it must be assumed that all viperid and elapid snakes and most colubrids are capable of envenoming. Response to a bite should follow the guidelines given above, even if the venomous snake is a small specimen and the expert victim makes the unwarranted presumption that it was a dry bite. In the case of bites in remote geographical locations, attempting to delay the development of systemic envenoming by the use of appropriate first aid methods (for example, pressure-immoblization in the case of bites by neurotoxic species) is particularly important in order to buy time before the victim reaches proper medical care.

All those who habitually search for and handle snakes and all field workers in snake-infested areas should anticipate and prepare for a snakebite emergency. First aid and evacuation procedures must be rehearsed in advance; some special equipment and training will be necessary.

Snake Venom Anaphylaxis

In the same way that some beekeepers become hypersensitive to bee venom through frequent stings, herpetologists and other snake handlers may be sensitized to snake venom components. Large-molecular-weight constituents such as phospholipases and hyaluronidase are especially allergenic. Exposure is by bites, through venom entering cracks on the fingers, and, in the case of those who work with venoms, through contact of aerosolized venom with mucous membranes of the respiratory tract and conjunctivae. Snake-venom-specific IgE has been detected in people who have been bitten repeatedly by snakes and have shown anaphylactic features after bites (Reimers et al., 2000). This confirms type I hypersensitivity.

Symptoms suggestive of venom sensitization are rhinitis and conjunctivitis (sneezing, itching of the nose and eyes, swelling of the eyelids, and congestion of the conjunctivae); breathlessness related either to asthma (narrowing of the smaller airways causing wheezing) or angio-edema (swelling and obstruction of the upper airway); an urticarial rash (nettlerash, itchy, red, raised hives); shock from a fall in blood pressure manifested by impaired vision, fainting, and sometimes a feeling of impending death; and gastrointestinal symptoms (nausea, vomiting, abdominal cramps, and violent diarrhea). Milder symptoms of this type should be an early warning that sensitization is developing. These symptoms will come on very soon after exposure to snake venom.

The treatment of anaphylaxis is epinephrine (adrenaline) as described above for the treatment of early antivenom reactions. People who know or suspect that they are hypersensitive to venom should equip themselves with self-injectable epinephrine (in the form of EpiPen or Anapen) and ensure that they and their companions know how to use the apparatus. Symptoms of anaphylaxis developing within minutes and up to 30 minutes after a snakebite should always raise the possibility of venom hypersensitivity. However, the differential diagnosis is complicated by the fact that early hypotensive collapse (without the other features of anaphylaxis described above) is not uncommon as a direct result of envenoming by *Bothrops* and *Lachesis*. If in doubt, administer epinephrine and implement urgent resuscitation and other medical care.

PREVENTION OF SNAKEBITE

To reduce the risk of bites, never disturb, attack, corner, or handle snakes, even if they are thought to be harmless species or appear to be dead. Never keep venomous species as pets or as performing animals. In snake-infested areas wear boots, socks, and long trousers for walks in undergrowth or deep sand, and always use a flashlight at night. Collecting firewood; dislodging logs and boulders with bare hands; pushing sticks or fingers into burrows, holes, and crevices; climbing rocks and trees covered with dense foliage; and swimming in overgrown lakes and rivers are particularly hazardous activities. Unlighted paths and gutters are especially dangerous after heavy rains. Fishermen should not touch seasnakes caught in nets or on lines, and swimmers and divers should not aggravate them and should avoid wading in the sea, especially in muddy estuaries, in sand, or near coral reefs, in areas where seasnakes are present. It is futile and undesirable from all points of view to attempt to exterminate venomous snakes. Various substances toxic to snakes, such as insecticides and methylbromide, have been used to keep human dwellings free of these animals. However, no effective repellent that is harmless to snakes has yet been discovered.

OTHER DANGEROUS REPTILES OF LATIN AMERICA

Venomous reptiles in the families Helodermatidae, Elapidae, and Viperidae are not the only dangerous reptiles in the Western Hemisphere. Among the giant constricting snakes, members of the genus *Eunectes* are large, powerful, and have been implicated in attacks (Matthews, 1995; Murphy and Henderson, 1997; Pl. 1500). Boids in the genera *Boa* (Pl. 1499), *Corallus*, *Epicrates*, and *Eunectes* (Pl. 1500) as well as some large colubrids such as *Drymarchon* and *Lampropeltis* have long teeth and are capable of producing severe mechanical damage when they bite. Large crocodilians are well-known sources of danger to humans, and even sea turtles (*Dermochelys*) can be hazardous to small boats and their occupants (F. Medem, pers. comm.).

Acknowledgments

I am very grateful to many friends and colleagues who have assisted my studies of venomous snakes and snakebite in Latin America and the Caribbean over the last 15 years. Special thanks are due to R. David G. Theakston and Aura Kamiguti Shisuko in Liverpool, U.K.; João Luiz Costa Cardoso, Hui Wen Fan, Francisco França, and their colleagues at the Hospital Vital Brazil, Instituto Butantan, São Paulo, Brazil; Miguel Jorge, Lindioneza Ribeiro, and Sergio Nishioka at the Federal University of Uberlândia, Minas Gerais; Pedro Pardal at the Hospital Universitario João de Barros Barreto, Belém, Pará, Brazil; Roger Smalligan, Steve Nelson, Judy Cole, and their colleagues at the Hospital Vozandes El Oriente, Shell, Ecuador; the staff of the Fundación Herpetólogica Gustavo Orcés, Quito, Ecuador, especially Jean-Marc Touzet and Maria Elena Barragan; Ronald Guderian, Manuel Calvopiña, and Angel Guevara, Laboratory of Clinical Investigations, Hospital Vozandes, Quito, Ecuador; Antonio Freire-Lascano in Guayaquil; Armando Yarlequé, Julio Demarini Caro and their colleagues and the staff of the Museo Nacional Javier Prado, Universidad de San Marcos, Lima, Peru; Juan Manuel Renjifo at the Instituto Nacional de Salud, Bogotá, Colombia; Wolfgang Wüster, Giuseppe Puorto, Maria da Graça Salomão, and their colleagues at the University of Bangor, U.K., and Instituto Butantan, São Paulo, Brazil; José-Maria Gutiérrez, Mahmood Sasa, and colleagues at Instituto Clodomiro Picado, San José, Costa Rica; Laurent Thomas and colleagues in Fort-de-France, Martinique; and David L. Hardy Sr. for his constructive review and Eunice Berry for her extraordinary efforts in preparing the manuscript.

GLOSSARY

Some of the scientific and medical terms used in this book are defined here. We have made no effort to provide a comprehensive list of terms; instead, we have defined those that we think readers will most need to know in order to understand the text and keys. These definitions apply only to our usage of particular words within this work.

12S and 16S rRNA Mitochondrial genes that code for RNA that is incorporated into the structure of ribosomes (tiny cellular structures that participate in the production of proteins). Nucleotide sequences from these genes have been used in several important studies of pitviper phylogeny (e.g., Parkinson et al., 2002).

AAPCC American Association of Poison Control Centers.

Abruptio placentae Premature separation of the placenta during pregnancy.

Abscess A localized collection of pus in a cavity.

Acetycholine A compound released at neuromuscular junctions and at many autonomic nerve endings that functions in the transmission of the nerve impulse.

Acidosis Accumulation of acid (hydrogen ions) in the body.

Acroparesthesia Tingling, numbness, and stiffness of the hands and feet often caused by overbreathing.

Acuminate Pointed.

Acute tubular necrosis Damage to the renal tubules (nephrons) associated with kidney failure.

Afibrinogenemia Absence of plasma fibrinogen. This abnormality of the blood-clotting mechanism may result in prolonged bleeding from sites of injury. Snake venoms induce afibrinogenemia by stimulating conversion of fibrinogen to fibrin, which is broken down by the body's fibrinolytic system.

Aglyphous Referring to a snake whose maxillary teeth have no grooves or canals; by inference, a snake that has no fangs. See also **Opisthoglyphous, Proteroglyphous, Solenoglyphous**.

Albuminuria Leakage of albumin into the urine.

Alignment See **Sequence alignment**.

Allopatric Living apart. Two species whose ranges do not overlap are said to be allopatric.

Allozyme Any one of a group of functionally identical or similar enzymes produced by alleles of the same gene. In phylogenetic analysis, the gene (represented by an enzyme product such as lactate dehydrogenase) is considered to be the character, and the different alleles (represented in this case by molecules of lactate dehydrogenase with slightly different molecular structures) are the character states.

Amelanistic Lacking black pigment.

Anal See **Cloacal**.

Anaphylaxis A sudden, overwhelming reaction to exposure to a molecule (allergen) to which the body has been sensitized, consist-ing of shock, bronchospasm, urticaria, angio-edema, and gastrointestinal symptoms.

Anesthetic Without feeling.

Angio-edema Intense swelling—usually of the lips, gums, tongue, and upper airway—as part of an anaphylactic reaction.

Angle of the jaw The angle formed by the articulation of the quadrate bone of the skull and the compound bone of the lower jaw.

Annulus See **Ring**.

Anorexia Lack of appetite.

Antepartum hemorrhage Bleeding from the uterus before the end of pregnancy.

Anterior tibial compartment The tight, relatively indistensible connective tissue chamber on the outside of the shin containing the muscles that flex the ankle and evert the foot.

Anticholinesterase A compound that inhibits acetylcholinesterase, the enzyme normally responsible for curtailing the action of acetylcholine, a physiological transmitter at neuromuscular junctions.

Antigenic Possessing the ability to stimulate an immune antibody response.

Antipyretic A drug to reduce fever.

Antisnakebite serum See **Antivenom**.

Antivenene See **Antivenom**.

Antivenin See **Antivenom**.

Antivenom Serum or purified immunoglobulin (IgG) or fractions of immunoglobulin (F(ab')$_2$, Fab) from an animal (usually a horse or sheep) that has been intensively immunized with one or more snake venoms.

Anuria Failure to pass urine.

Aphonia Inability to speak.

Apical pit A tiny pore or pores near the apex of individual scales in snakes. These structures are usually most easily seen in preserved specimens if the outer layer of epidermis is removed from an individual scale, dried, and examined under magnification.

Apneic Not breathing.

Apomorphy A derived character. The designation of a character state as apomorphic is relative to the level of the comparison being made. For example, in a phylogenetic analysis of all snakes, the rattle of rattlesnakes would be considered an apomorphy; but in a phylogenetic analysis of the *Crotalus atrox* group, presence of a rattle would be considered ancestral, or plesiomorphic. See also **Ingroup, Outgroup, Plesiomorphy, Synapomorphy,** and **Symplesiomorphy**.

Arenicolous Inhabiting sandy areas.

Arid tropical scrub See **Tropical arid forest**.

Arroyo Spanish for ravine.

Asphyxia Suffocation.

Asulcate The side of the hemipenis opposite the side bearing the sulcus spermaticus.

Atopy Hereditary allergies such as asthma, hay fever, and eczema.

Atresic Involuted, as of a part such as an ovarian follicle not destined to produce a functional ovum.

Atrial extrasystoles Abnormal premature contractions of the atria (heart chambers) resulting in an irregular pulse.

Atrioventricular block Defective conduction of the heartbeat from the atria to the ventricles.

Atrophy Wasting.

Autapomorphy A derived characteristic that is unique to a particular species or other taxonomic group.

Autonomic nervous system The part of the nervous system responsible for self-regulating secretion by glands, control of the heartbeat and caliber of blood vessels, etc.

Autopharmacological Causing activation of the body's own systems (especially for altering blood pressure), as by some venom components.

Axillary Concerning the axilla or armpit.

Band An element of skin pattern that is darker or paler than the ground color and that runs perpendicularly across the vertebral line; it may extend onto the ventral scales, but it does not completely encircle the body (see **Ring**). Synonymous with crossband.

Bifid Divided into two lobes or branches.

Bifurcate To branch or divide into two parts.

Bleb A blister or large, flaccid vesicle containing serum or blood.

Blotch A discrete area that differs from the ground color, either darker or paler, and that is generally as long as or longer than wide and not transversely widened to form a band or ring. Many snakes have a primary series of blotches along the middorsum and one to several smaller series of blotches laterally. Counts of body blotches in pitvipers do not include paired nape blotches (if present) or those on the tail.

Bootstrap support See **Nonparametric bootstrap**.

Boreal forest A type of temperate vegetation occurring across northern North America and on the tops of a few high peaks in central and northern Mexico. Some of the dominant trees of this forest are firs (*Abies* and *Pseudotsuga*), pines (*Pinus*), junipers (*Juniperus*), and alders (*Alnus*). Various coarse bunchgrasses (*Agrostis*, *Festuca*, *Muhlenbergia*) often form a dense understory.

Bradycardia An abnormally slow heart rate.

Bradykinin A polypeptide hormone that causes vasodilatation, fall in blood pressure, pain, and gastrointestinal muscle cramping.

Branch-and-bound search An algorithm in the computer program PAUP* that is guaranteed to find all shortest (i.e., most parsimonious) trees based on a particular set of data.

Bronchospasm Constriction of the airways in the lungs (bronchi and bronchioles).

Bulbar (paralysis) Concerning the medulla oblongata (between the spinal cord and the brain) or paralysis of muscles innervated by nerves arising there.

Bulla (pl. **bullae**) A large (usually greater than 2 cm in diameter) blister, typically containing serum or blood. See also **Bleb**.

Button The first permanent rattle acquired by a young rattlesnake. As a rattlesnake matures, the button usually breaks off. At birth, rattlesnakes have a "prebutton," that is lost in the first molt, exposing the button.

Calyces Small pockets surrounded by ridges on the distal portion of the hemipenes of many snakes.

Calyculate Having small, superficial pockets or sunken interspaces between the retiform ridges, as on the apices of the hemipenial lobes of many snakes.

Canaliculate Grooved or channeled longitudinally.

Canthal The scale or scales situated along the upper surface of the canthus rostralis. These scales lie behind the level of the prenasal and postnasal suture and in front of the supraocular. If these scales are large and in contact along the midline, they are more properly called prefrontals.

Canthorostral A small scale between the rostral and internasals-canthals. These scales are characteristic of some species of *Bothrocophias*.

Canthus rostralis The area between the supraocular and the rostral where the dorsum of the snout turns downward on the side. It is

delimited as a sharp ridge in many vipers but is rounded in most rattlesnakes and in coralsnakes.

Capillary permeability The degree of leakiness (porosity) of the smallest blood vessels (capillaries) in the tissues.

Capitate Pertaining to a snake hemipenis that has an apical region clearly separated from the basal part of the organ by a groove.

Cardiotoxicity The action of some venom components in disturbing the function of the heart.

Cardiovascular Concerning the heart, blood vessels, and circulation.

Carpopedal spasm Spasms of the hands and feet, often associated with overbreathing (see **Acroparesthesia**).

Case fatality The proportion (percentage) of fatal cases among those suffering from a particular condition or disease.

Caudal Pertaining to the tail or posterior end of the body or part of the body.

Ceja de la montaña Spanish for "brow of the mountain." A vegetation type that covers the upper parts (1,000–3,350 m) of the eastern slopes of the Andes in Peru and Bolivia. It occurs in areas of high rainfall and is composed of cloud forest vegetation.

Cellulitis Superficial inflammation of the skin and subcutaneous tissues caused by infection.

Cerebral edema Swelling of the brain.

Cerro Spanish for "mountain."

Chaparral A vegetation type found along the western coast of the southwestern United States and the Baja California Peninsula. The dominant shrubs of the dry habitat are chamise (*Adenostoma*), mananita (*Arctostaphylos*), sage (*Artemisia*), coyote bush (*Baccharis*), wild lilac (*Ceanothus*), and scrub oaks (*Quercus*).

Character A feature of an organism. Characters range from single nucleotide positions in DNA sequences to large anatomical features.

Character state One of two or more conditions that a character can exhibit; for example, for the character eye color, two character states could be brown and green.

Character weighting In a parsimony analysis, characters assigned a greater weight add more steps to (i.e., exert more influence over) the phylogenetic hypothesis. When analyzing nucleotide data, transversions may be assigned more weight because they occur less frequently than transitions.

Chinshield A large, elongated scale lying directly behind the first pair of infralabials along either side of the midline on the ventral surface of the head. Chinshields are always arranged in pairs, with a single pair most frequently present in snakes.

Chromosome A long, threadlike association of genes in the nucleus of all eukaryotic cells that is most visible during mitosis and meiosis. Chromosomes consist of DNA and protein.

Cladistics A method and philosophy of phylogenetic analysis based on the work of Willi Hennig (1966) in which only synapomorphies are considered to be informative about phylogenetic relationships.

Cline A geographic character gradient. A character that continuously varies geographically is said to be clinal.

Cloacal The ventrally located plate immediately preceding the vent, sometimes improperly referred to as the anal scale. In snakes this scale is larger than other scales of the ventral series and may be single or divided by a diagonal suture. This scale should not be included in the ventral series. The body of a snake is measured from the rostral to the posterior edge of the cloacal plate.

Cloud forest A montane forest type characterized by cool temperatures, frequent fogs and high humidity, and lush, dense vegetation that includes numerous hardwood tree species. Cloud forest usually occurs above 1,000 m on the windward escarpments of tropical mountains. The lower belt of cloud forest is sometimes referred to as subtropical wet forest and the higher belt as lower montane wet forest or montane rainforest. The biological diversity of cloud forests is greater than that of any other habitat with the possible exception of the great lowland rainforests.

Coagulopathy Disturbance of blood coagulation.

Codon A unit of three nucleotides that codes for a single amino acid. The 64 combinations of the four nucleotides code for 20 amino acids. Redundancy occurs in the third position, so many substitutions in this position do not affect the protein product.

Colicky Descriptive of a kind of spasmodic abdominal pain that builds up to a peak and then subsides in regular cycles.

Colloidal Pertaining to a colloid—a suspension of particles (e.g., proteins) in fluid.

Colubrid A snake of the family Colubridae. Most members of this family are considered harmless, although many species have enlarged teeth on the rear of the maxillae (opisthoglyphic dentition), and a few species are known to produce venom dangerous to humans.

Comatose Unconscious.

Compartmental syndrome A group of clinical symptoms and signs suggesting raised pressure in a tight connective tissue (fascial) compartment, such as the anterior tibial compartment, which may cause ischemic damage to the contents of that compartment.

Condyle An articular prominence on a bone.

Congener A member of the same genus.

Conjunctiva The mucous membrane covering the outer surface of the eye.

Conjunctivitis Inflammation of the conjunctiva.

Consistency index A measure of homoplasy (or "goodness of fit") in a data set, calculated by dividing the minimum number of steps possible (equal to the number of characters when all characters are binary) by the actual number of steps of the tree. The consistency index is inflated by addition of autapomorphies, and characters showing total homoplasy have the same consistency index as characters showing partial homoplasy. The retention and rescaled consistency indices avoid both problems.

Constriction band A ligature applied proximal to a venomous bite site just tightly enough to block return of superficial flow in the veins and lymph vessels (i.e., arterial flow beyond the band is intact) in an effort to limit circulation of toxins.

Contracture Sustained contraction of a muscle.

Convergence The occurrence of the same (or at least very similar) trait in separate lineages that does not meet the criterion of homology; this is a type of homoplasy, and it introduces "noise" that may obscure phylogentic signal in the data.

Convulsions Generalized seizures or epileptic fits.

Cordillera Spanish for "mountain range."

Corpora lutea Secretory tissue in the ovary that forms from the collapsed follicle after ovulation and produces progesterone.

Cranial nerves Those nerves arising directly from the base of the brain.

Creatine kinase (also **Creatine phosphokinase**) An enzyme detectable in serum that originates from muscle.

Creatinine A breakdown product of muscle normally present in serum whose level reflects kidney function.

Cremasteric (reflex) A superficial reflex (part of the neurological examination) in which stimulation of the skin of the thigh causes retraction of the testicle.

Crepuscular Active in the twilight.

Crescentric Resembling a crescent.

Crotch The V- or U-shaped area where the two lobes bifurcate from one another on the hemipenes of some snakes.

Crown The anterior part of the top of the head, usually corresponding to the anterior portion of the frontal area forward to the tip of the snout.

Curarimimetic Acting like the drug curare, which blocks neuromuscular transmission by competitive inhibition of acetylcholine.

Cyanosis Blueness of the skin and mucous membranes (lips, tongue) indicating decreased oxygen content of blood hemoglobin (desaturation).

Cyanotic Characterized by cyanosis.

Cytochrome *b* A mitochondrial gene that codes for the protein of that name.

Cytokines Macrophage products that mediate inflammation (e.g., tumor necrosis factor, leukotrienes, interleukins, interferons).

Cytolytic Capable of dissolving or disintegrating cells.

D-dimer Fibrin(ogen) breakdown products whose molecules are cross-linked, indicating that cross-linked (polymerized) fibrin had been deposited in the circulation and then degraded by fibrinolysis.

Debride To cut away localized dead tissue.

Decerebrate rigidity A sign of severe (mid)brain dysfunction in which the limbs are held straight and rigid, the wrists are flexed, the ankles are extended, the neck is extended, and the eyes deviate upward.

Deciduous forest A widespread type of temperate forest consisting of a variety of hardwood trees. See also **Tropical deciduous forest**.

Defibrination Removal of fibrin(ogen) from the blood.

Defibrinogenation Removal of fibrinogen from the blood.

Deglutition Swallowing.

Deletion The loss of one or more consecutive nucleotides from a gene. See also **Gap, Insertion**, and **Sequence alignment**.

Dentary One of the major bones of the lower jaw in reptiles. In snakes and lizards this bone bears the teeth of the lower jaw.

Dentition The arrangement of teeth.

Dialysis Artificial removal of metabolic products such as urea and creatinine, normally excreted by the kidney, by using selective diffusion through the peritoneal membrane (peritoneal dialysis) or filtration of the blood (hemodialysis).

Diaphoresis Marked by profuse sweating.

DIC See **Disseminated intravascular coagulation**.

Dichromatism The state of having two independent color varieties.

Digital pulp space The cushionlike connective tissue compartment on the palmar or plantar surface of the ends of the distal phalanges of the fingers and toes.

Digits Fingers and toes.

Dimorphism Difference (as of form, color, size) between two individuals.

Diploid Containing two sets of chromosomes ($2n$), one set inherited from each parent.

Diplopia Double vision resulting from paralysis of eye muscles causing a squint.

Discordant Dissimilar with respect to one or more characters.

Disseminated intravascular coagulation (DIC) Activation of the blood-clotting system combined with breakdown of the resulting fibrin. This leads to depletion of blood-clotting factors (e.g., afibrinogenemia), incoagulable blood, and damage to blood vessel walls, causing spontaneous systemic bleeding and, sometimes, blockage of small arteries by fibrin thrombi (clots) causing damage to various organs and tissues.

Distal Pertaining to the part of a structure, such as the tail or hemipenis, that is relatively farther removed from the center of the body than some other part of that structure.

Diurnal Active by day.

Dorsal scale row number The number of longitudinal scale rows encircling the body of a snake at a certain point, exclusive of the ventrals. Often counts are made at three points along a snake's body: a head's length behind the head, at midbody, and a head's length in front of the vent. A dorsal scale formula of 23-21-19 specifies these three counts. If only one figure is given, it is the midbody count. The dorsal scale rows are most easily counted in oblique or diagonal series, starting with a paraventral.

Dorsum The upper surface of an animal or part thereof; for example, the dorsum of the head extends from the internasal through the parietal regions.

Dry bite A bite by a venomous snake in which a fang or fangs punctures the skin but no envenoming results.

Dysarthria Difficulty articulating words, usually caused by paralysis or loss of control of the muscles involved.

Dysphagia Difficulty swallowing.

Dysphonia Defective speaking.

Dyspnea Difficult or labored breathing.

Ecchymosis Superficial bruising of the skin that is larger and more extensive than petechiae or purpura.

Ectothermic Property of an animal, such as a reptile, that must use environmental energy and behavioral adaptations to regulate its body temperature; these animals are often referred to as "cold-blooded."

Eczema Atopic disease of the skin (dermatitis).

Edema Swelling resulting from accumulation of fluid in the tissues.

Egg tooth A structure on the tip of the snout that is used to cut or break through the egg membranes or leathery shell at the time of hatching.

Elapid A snake of the family Elapidae. In the New World this family includes the coralsnakes (*Leptomicrurus, Micrurus, Micruroides*) and the pelagic seasnake (*Pelamis*). All members of this family are proteroglyphous, and all New World species should be considered dangerous. Some authorities place the seasnakes in a separate family.

Electrocardiogram (ECG) A diagnostic study in which electrodes attached to the skin record the electrical impulses of the heart, giving information regarding the heart's rate, rhythm, and function.

Electrophoretic pattern The pattern of separation of component parts of a venom in an electrical field.

Emarginate Pertaining to a margin that is notched or scalloped.

Embolus (or **embolism**) Blockage of an artery by a clot that has traveled in the bloodstream from a distant site. For example, a clot formed in the deep veins of the calf may break off and be carried in the bloodstream to obstruct in a branch of the pulmonary artery.

Emetic Causing vomiting.

Encephalopathy Disease or dysfunction of the brain, usually associated with unconsciousness.

Endothelial Concerning the endothelium—flattened cells (epithelium) lining blood and other vessels, serosal cavities such as the peritoneal and pleural cavities, and hollow organs.

Endotracheal intubation Passing a tube (via the nose or mouth) into the trachea to ensure a patent airway and allow artificial ventilation.

Envenoming (or **envenomation**) The effects (clinical, pathophysiological, etc.) of injection of venom into the body. *Envenomation* and *envenomization* are corruptions of the English word *envenoming*, used in North America and Australia.

Eosinophil A kind of leukocyte (white blood corpuscle) found in the blood and tissues whose granules stain bright red with eosin. These cells are particularly associated with allergic/hypersensitivity reactions.

Eosinophilia Excessive numbers of eosinophils in the bloodstream.

Epididymis The band of tissue on the amniote testis that is homologous to the cranial part of the opisthonephros and to part of the archinephric duct of anamniotes.

Epigastric Concerning the upper central part of the abdomen below the sternum and upper rib (costal) margin.

Epistaxis Nosebleed.

Epitrochlear At the inner side of the elbow next to the prominent inner condyle of the humerus; the site of lymph glands that may become painfully enlarged following snakebite on the hand or forearm.

Erythema Redness.

Erythremia A greater than normal number of erythrocytes in the blood.

Erythrocyte Red blood corpuscle.

Esterase Any of a class of enzymes that accelerate the hydrolysis or synthesis of esters.

Evergreen forest Sometimes refers to forests containing primarily coniferous trees. Coniferous forests are found primarily in temperate forests of northern and southern latitudes but also in the Gulf Coastal Plain of the United States and the mountainous region of the western United States, Mexico, and northern Central America. Sometimes refers to tropical forests in relatively equitable climates that tend to have few deciduous species. See **Tropical evergreen forest**.

Extensors The muscles that straighten the back, neck, or limbs (opposite of flexors).

External ophthalmoplegia Paralysis of the extraocular muscles responsible for moving the eyeball and hence directing the gaze. The results of this paralysis are strabismus (squint) and diplopia (double vision).

Extradural (hematoma) An accumulation of blood within the skull (or vertebral canal) but outside the dura mater, the outermost and thickest of the three membranes (meninges) covering the brain and spinal cord.

F84 model One of the models of nucleotide sequence evolution used in maximum likelihood analyses.

Fang Any hollow or grooved tooth borne on the maxillary bone of the upper jaw in snakes that is longer than other teeth and serves in the conduction of venom.

Fascial compartment A tissue space containing muscles, nerves, blood vessels, etc., contained within walls of fibrous connective tissue that are relatively indistensible.

Fasciculation Repeated involuntary local contractions of groups of muscle fibers innervated by single motor nerve filaments. It is visible through the skin and can be difficult to differentiate from shivering.

Fasciotomy Surgical opening and decompression of a fascial compartment.

FDPs See **Fibrin(ogen) degradation products**.

Femoral Concerning the femur or thigh.

Fibrin A component of a blood clot, formed by an enzyme (e.g., thrombin) acting on fibrinogen.

Fibrinogen A precursor protein circulating in the blood that is partially cleaved by thrombin to yield one of the components (fibrin) of a blood clot.

Fibrin(ogen) degradation products Fragments of fibrin or fibrinogen detectable in the blood and urine when there has been abnormal breakdown of fibrinogen (e.g., by thrombinlike enzymes in crotaline snake venoms) or the formation and deposition of fibrin and its breakdown by endogenous (and/or snake venom) defibrinating enzymes.

Fibrinogenolytic Able to destroy fibrinogen, usually by means of an enzyme.

Fibrinolytic Able to destroy fibrin, usually by means of an enzyme.

Flaccid paralysis Paralysis resulting from damage to peripheral nerves or defective neuromuscular transmission caused by pre- or postsynaptic snake venom toxins. Affected muscles are flaccid (floppy), in contrast to the spasticity resulting from central nervous system damage (as in stroke).

Flounces With reference to snake hemipenes, simple linear ridges or folds of tissue that parallel one another and encircle the organ.

Follicle A small structure in the ovary that contains the developing ovum and secretes estrogens.

Foramen Any small opening or perforation, such as that found in a bone.

Formication A sensation of ants crawling over the skin.

Fossa A groove or depression in an organ.

Foveal Any of the small scales surrounding the loreal pit of viperid snakes that have no other regular designations. These scales usually lie exterior to the lacunals, above the supralabials, below the loreal, and anterior to the level of the eye. More specifically, the prefoveals usually lie within the area bordered by the nasals, loreal, prelacunal, and supralabials, and may extend forward between the nasals and supralabials to make contact with the rostral. The subfoveals lie below the pit between the lacunals and supralabials; the postfoveals lie along the lower posterior border of the pit, between the sublacunal and supralabials but in front of the interoculabials.

Frontal The scale or scales lying on top of the head between the supraoculars; or pertaining to this region. Many snakes—including coralsnakes, *Agkistrodon*, and *Sistrurus*—have a single large, flat, symmetrical scale in this region; however, most pitvipers have a number of irregularly disposed scales, keeled or not, occupying this space (see **Intersupraoculars**).

Frontalis The muscle responsible for raising the eyebrows and puckering the forehead.

Gallery forest A forest growing along a watercourse in a region otherwise mostly devoid of trees.

Gangrene Necrosis (death) of tissue usually associated with the foul odor of putrefaction (rotting flesh) caused by bacterial infection.

Gap A space inserted into a nucleotide sequence in order to achieve alignment of homologous nucleotide sites; it may represent an actual deletion in that sequence or an insertion in other comparative sequences. Gaps may be treated as characters in phylogenetic analyses.

Gas gangrene Necrotic tissue in which anaerobic bacteria (*Clostridia*) are multiplying and creating bubbles of gas.

Gingival (sulci) The margins of the gums and teeth where the effect of snake venom hemorrhagins causing spontaneous bleeding may be evident.

Glomerular capillaries Tiny blood vessels through whose walls excretory products are filtered into the nephrons to form the urine in globular tufts (glomeruli) in the kidney.

Grasslands See **Savanna**.

Ground color The basic color between the various elements of pattern; the background color. Snakes with spots, blotches, or bands have a ground color; ringed snakes, such as some coralsnakes, have no identifiable ground color.

Gular Pertaining to the throat region or ventral surface of the neck; or a scale in this region not having another designation.

Head cap In coralsnakes, the black pigment that extends posteriorly from the top of the snout often to cover most or all of the parietal scales.

Hemarthrosis Accumulation of blood in the joint (synovial) cavity.

Hematemesis The vomiting of blood.

Hematocrit The relative volume (percentage) of red blood corpuscles in the blood assessed after centrifugation; an indirect measure of the hemoglobin concentration and an indicator of hemoconcentration or hemodilution.

Hematoma A collection of blood in the tissues.

Hematuria Passage of red blood corpuscles in the urine. This may be detectable by the naked eye (macroscopic hematuria) or only by examination under a microscope (microscopic hematuria).

Hemipenis One of the paired copulatory organs of snakes or lizards. When inverted, the hemipenes (pl.) lie ventrolaterally in the base of the tail. Hemipenes tend to be ornate, with spines and calyces that provide useful taxonomic characters.

Hemiplegia Paralysis of one side of the body after a stroke.

Hemoconcentration Relative decrease in the volume of plasma and increase in the volume of red blood corpuscles in the blood. In snakebite victims it indicates leakage of plasma into the tissues of the bitten limb and elsewhere resulting from increased permeability of blood vessel walls under the influence of venom toxins.

Hemodialysis In patients with kidney failure, the removal of substances normally excreted by the kidney using an artificial kidney machine.

Hemofiltration A method of removing waste products from the blood of patients with kidney failure by convection under pressure through a permeable membrane.

Hemoglobinemia Presence of free hemoglobin in the plasma, staining it pink, as a result of intravascular hemolysis, which releases hemoglobin from red blood corpuscles.

Hemoglobinuria Passage of the blood pigment hemoglobin in the urine.

Hemolysis (intravascular) The breakdown of red blood corpuscles in the circulation; for example, as a result of the action of venom phospholipases A_2.

Hemolysis (microangiopathic) The breakdown of red blood corpuscles in the circulation as a result of fibrin deposition onto the endothelial lining of blood vessels or other causes of small blood vessel damage.

Hemolytic The property of breaking down red blood corpuscles.

Hemoptysis Coughing up blood.

Hemorrhagic Characterized by bleeding.

Hemorrhagin A snake venom toxin (metalloproteinase) that disrupts the cells lining the inside of blood vessels, allowing red blood cells to leak into surrounding tissues.

Hemostatic disorder A disturbance of the normal blood-clotting mechanisms that stop bleeding after injury.

Hemothorax Accumulation of blood in the virtual (pleural) cavity surrounding the lungs.

Hemotoxic A substance that causes the dissolution of red blood cells.

Heteromorphic Having different forms.

Heuristic search A tree-searching algorithm used to conduct maximum parsimony analyses in PAUP*; although faster than a branch-and-bound search, it is not guaranteed to find the shortest tree.

Homologue (Homology) Two characters in two taxa are homologues if (1) they are the same as the character that is found in the ancestor of the taxa or (2) they are different but descended from the ancestral character with modification.

Homoplasy A character state that changes more than once.

Homoplasy indices Three measures for assessing the amount of homoplasy in a phylogenetic data set have been proposed: consistency index, rescaled consistency index, and retention index.

Hypapophysis A ventral bony projection from the centra of cervical or anterior trunk vertebrae.

Hyperacusis Heightened hearing.

Hyperesthesia Heightened sense of touch and pain.

Hyperkalemia Increased concentration of potassium in the blood; for example, as a result of kidney failure or breakdown of muscle.

Hypersensitivity A type of allergic reaction in which the immune system (inappropriately) manufactures (IgE) antibodies against a foreign substance (allergen). If the hypersensitive person is again exposed to the same allergen, the specific IgE to that substance in the blood and tissues may bring about a violent and potentially fatal anaphylactic reaction.

Hypocapnia Depletion of carbon dioxide in the blood resulting from overbreathing.

Hypoesthesia Diminished sense of touch.

Hypofibrinogenemia A deficiency of plasma fibrinogen (see **Afibrinogenemia**).

Hypotension Low blood pressure, as in shock.

Hypothermic Decreased body temperature.

Hypovolemia A depletion of circulating blood volume causing hypotension and shock. In snakebite victims it is usually the result of leakage of plasma or blood into the tissues of the bitten limb and elsewhere.

Hypoxia Deficiency of oxygen in the tissues.

Imbricate Overlapping, as the shingles on a roof. Used in reference to the scales of reptiles that have their posterior margins overlapping adjacent scales.

Immune complex (disease) Damage to organs and tissues such as the kidney by antigen-antibody complexes.

Incidence The number of new events (e.g., snakebites) during a given period in a population of a given size; hence, the frequency of occurrence of a particular event or phenomenon. The incidence of snakebite might be 50 per 100,000 population per year.

Indel An insertion or a deletion in a nucleotide sequence (indicated by a gap in an aligned sequence).

Infarction Severe damage to or death of part of an organ or tissue resulting from sudden cessation of its blood supply, as in myocardial or pulmonary infarction.

Infracephalic Pertaining to the venter of the head.

Infralabials The series of scales along the lip of the lower jaw exclusive of the anterior median mental scale. The notation 9/10 would indicate 9 infralabials on the right side and 10 on the left.

Ingroup A group of organisms for which phylogenetic relationships are being determined in a particular study.

Inguinal In the region of the groin or inguinal ligament at the top of the inside of the thigh.

Insertion The gain of one or more consecutive nucleotides within a nucleotide sequence. See also **Deletion, Gap Sequence alignment**.

Intercanthals The scales on top of the snout between the canthals.

Interchinshields The scales lying between the paired, elongate chinshields. These scales are present in a few species of rattlesnakes.

Intercostals The muscles connecting adjacent ribs.

Intergenial A pair of small scales sutured off the ends of the first infralabials, lying with the mental suture on the midline of the chin immediately behind the mental.

Intergrade The offspring of individuals of two different subspecies of populations of the same species, or an individual that comes from a locality that is geographically intermediate between two subspecies. Many of the characteristics that distinguish the parental populations are often intermediate in intergrades.

Internasals The scales or plates in snakes and lizards that run across the top of the front of the snout between the prenasals and make contact with the prenasals and/or the rostral. Most snakes have two internasals.

Interoculabials The scales between, but not including, the suboculars and supralabials. The fewest of these usually occur below the anteriormost subocular. In some species the interoculabial series is incomplete or absent, with the suboculars and supralabials in contact or the supralabials reaching the eye.

Interphalangeal Between adjacent phalanges (bones of the fingers or toes).

Intersupraoculars The scales lying on top of the head between the supraoculars. The scales in this area often are disposed in an irregular fashion. The number of intersupraoculars lying between the supraoculars is generally taken as the lowest number of contiguous scales. If only one large scale is present, it is called the frontal.

Intraperitoneal Within the cavity lining the abdomen.

Intubation See **Endotracheal intubation**.

In vitro Performed (as an experiment) in an artificial environment— for example, in a test tube—rather than in a living body (*in vivo*).

Ischemia Deficient blood supply.

Isoenzyme Multiple forms of an enzyme whose synthesis is controlled by more than one gene. See also **Allozyme**.

Jacobson's organ A sensory structure located in the roof of the mouth of some reptiles such as snakes and lizards. Sensory particles are picked up from the surrounding environment by the tongue, which is subsequently protruded into the blind sac that is the Jacobson's organ.

Juxtaposed Disposed in a side-by-side fashion.

Karyotype A method of organizing the chromosomes of a cell in relation to number, size, and type.

Keeled Used in reference to scales that possess a median ridge; the keel may or may not extend to the tip of the scale.

Kinesis Physical movement including quantitative, qualitative, and positional change.

Kinins A group of peptides that cause inflammation and dilatation of blood vessels (e.g., bradykinin).

Labials See **Infralabials** and **Supralabials**.

Lacrimation Tearing.

Lacunal Any one of the scales that form the inner border of the loreal pit in crotaline snakes. These scales are usually large and curve outward to form part of the outer border of the pit as well. Small scales lying near but entirely outside the pit and having no other designation (e.g., supralabials, loreals, preoculars, etc.) are called foveals. The external aperture of the pit is generally triangular with one apex pointing posteriorly toward the eye; the pit is bounded in front by the prelacunal, below by the sublacunal, and above by the supralacunal.

Lacunolabial The single large scale that is formed in some crotaline snakes from the fusion of the prelacunal and the second (rarely the third) supralabial. It is often said of snakes having this condition that "the second labial enters the pit."

Laryngeal Concerning the larynx and vocal cords.

Lateral Refering to a position away from the midline of the body.

LD₅₀ The venom dose predicted to kill 50% of the organisms that receive it (see also **Median lethal dose**).

LD₁₀₀ The venom dose predicted to kill 100% of the organisms that receive it.

Lepidosis The arrangement and pattern of the scales (syn. **Scutellation**).

Leukocyte White blood corpuscles found in the blood and tissues.

Leukocytosis Increased number of white blood corpuscles in the blood.

Llanos Extensive grassy plains, usually with few trees except along watercourses. This habitat is widespread in eastern Colombia and Venezuela.

Loreals The scales lying on the side of the head between the postnasal and preoculars. There is much variation in the location and number of these scales: in most coralsnakes loreal scales are absent, most crotalines have at least one per side, and many have two or more. In some snakes the postnasal and upper preocular may contact each other, displacing the loreal(s) to above or below the point of contact.

Loreal pit A deep depression on the side of the head of crotaline snakes; thus the name pitviper. The pit is located behind the nostril and in front of the eye, but most of the pit lies below a line drawn from the nostril to the center of the eye. The loreal pit is the external opening to an extremely sensitive infrared-detecting organ.

Lorilabials In lizards, one or more scales arranged in a longitudinal row between the supralabials and loreals.

Lymphadenopathy Swollen, tender lymph glands (nodes).

Lymphangitis Inflammation of lymphatics such that they can be seen as fine red lines extending up the limb of a snakebite victim.

Lymphatics Vessels or channels forming a vascular system separate from veins for conveying larger molecules from the tissues to the bloodstream. Larger-molecular-weight venom components spread from the site of the snakebite through lymphatics, causing inflammation (lymphangitis) and bruising along these channels and around the lymph nodes into which they drain.

Lymph gland Small, nodular structure found in locations such as the armpits, neck, and groin and from which further lymphatics proceed eventually to drain into the venous system. These structures are part of the reticuloendothelial system, which has important immunological functions. In snakebite victims lymph glands may become enlarged, tender, painful, and bruised when large-molecular-weight venom toxins drain into them. This can be a valuable early sign that venom is spreading from the site of the bite.

Lymph node See **Lymph gland**.

Lyophilized Freeze-dried, as in the case of some sera (antivenoms), to promote a longer shelf life.

Lysis Breakdown.

Macroscopic As seen or visible to the naked eye.

Malaise A generalized but vague and nonspecific feeling of being unwell.

Malignant transformation Change from normal tissue into a malignant cancerous growth, as in the case of squamous cell carcinoma arising at the site of a chronic snakebite-induced ulcer.

Matrix The fleshy tip of the tail in rattlesnakes on which each successive rattle is formed. In a few populations, the matrix is shriveled or withered, precluding development of a string of rattles.

Maxillae The bones in the upper jaw of reptiles; there is one maxilla on either side of the head. In venomous snakes these bones are modified to support the fangs, and they may form a rotatable joint with the prefrontal.

Medial Pertaining to a position toward the midline of the body.

Median lethal dose (LD₅₀) Experimentally, the dose of any noxious substance (venom, toxin, poison) capable of killing half of a group of experimental animals (usually mice) within a defined time frame.

Mediator A chemical messenger in the body produced by a particular cell or organelle and capable of specifically stimulating another, usually after binding to a specific receptor.

Melanic See **Melanistic**.

Melanistic Characterized by the development of black or nearly black skin. This condition occurs either as a characteristic of a species or as an individual variation. As used in this text, *melanistic* refers to a condition affecting overall pattern, whereas *melanic* or *melanized* refers to an element of pattern, such as a melanic ring.

Melena Passage of black, tarry stools composed of altered blood: a sign of gastrointestinal hemorrhage.

Meningism Pain, rigidity, and spasm on attempting to flex the neck indicative of inflammation and irritation of the meninges (membranes covering the brain and spinal cord) as a result of hemorrhage into the cerebrospinal fluid compartment surrounding the central nervous system (subarachnoid hemorrhage) or infection (meningitis).

Menorrhagia Excessive menstrual bleeding.

Mental The median triangular scale at the anterior edge of the lower jaw of snakes and lizards. This scale is bordered on both sides by the first infralabials.

Meristic Divided into discrete entities; features that are countable (such as scales) are said to be meristic.

Mesial spines The spines located just above the crotch of the hemipenis of certain snakes.

Mesic Having a moderate to large amount of moisture.

Mesquite-grassland A seasonally dry vegetation type occurring on the high tableland of Mexico at elevations of 1,500–2,100 m. This habitat is also found on the Gulf coast of northeastern Mexico and along the foothills of eastern and southern Sonora. Characteristic plants include grasses (*Andropogon*, *Bouteloua*, *Spartina*), mesquite (*Prosopis*), legumes (*Acacia*, *Mimosa*), cacti (*Opuntia*), and agaves.

Metabolic acidosis Excessive accumulation of acidic products of metabolism (such as lactic acid) or acidic poisons as the result of increased production of these compounds or the inability of a failing kidney to excrete acidic products of the body's metabolism.

Methemoglobinuria Passage of chocolate-colored oxidized (ferric) hemoglobin in the urine as a result of the oxidizing effect of venoms, poisons, or drugs.

Microangiopathic Caused by abnormalities of small blood vessels.

Mitochondrion An organelle in eukaryotic cells that serves as the site of cellular respiration.

Monad Referring to a pattern in coralsnakes in which the black rings occur as single elements. The sequence of rings in monadal snakes is red-yellow-black-yellow-red. See also **Triad**.

Mononeuritis multiplex Simultaneous inflammation and damage of two or more peripheral nerves remote from one another, as occurs in some victims of serum sickness after antivenom treatment.

Monophyletic group A group that includes all of the descendants of a most recent common ancestor. Since monophyletic groups are not artificial constructs (they were actually produced by nature), they are also called natural groups.

Monospecific Referring to an antivenom raised by immunizing an animal with only one venom.

Monovalent Pertaining to an antivenom effective against the venom of only one species; same as monospecific.

Montane dry forest A type of vegetation usually found between elevations of 600 and 1,500 m and characterized by thorny shrubs and low deciduous trees, agaves, and cacti, and many kinds of grasses. Many of the rainshadow valleys of Middle America contain this type of forest. Portions of montane dry forest are sometimes referred to as subtropical dry forest or lower montane dry forest.

Montane moist forest A type of forest found mostly at elevations above 1,000 m that experiences a well-defined dry season and receives an amount of rainfall intermediate between that received by montane dry and montane wet forests. In Mexico and northern Central America, lower montane moist forest lies just below montane moist forest and is generally equivalent to pine-oak forest.

Montane wet forest A type of very humid forest usually found at elevations well above 1,500 m and corresponding to the upper portion of the cloud forest; the lower portion of cloud forest is often referred to as subtropical or lower montane wet forest. See also **Cloud forest**.

Moxibustion A kind of folk medicine treatment in which materials are burnt in or on the wound.

Mucous membrane A thin, moist layer of mucus-secreting cells covering or lining such structures as the eye, nasopharynx, and mouth.

Multiple hits Two or more base substitutions at the same nucleotide site. Nucleotide sites with a relatively rapid substitution rate become "saturated" over time as a result of multiple hits.

Mutation A change in the composition or arrangement of nucleotides within a molecule of DNA. Point mutations, which affect single nucleotide positions, introduce genetic variation that is particularly useful for reconstructing phylogenetic history. See also **Substitution, Transition,** and **Transversion**.

Myalgia Pain or aching of the muscles.

Myasthenic (facies) The characteristic drooping eyelids and slack cheeks seen in patients suffering from myasthenia gravis, a disease in which there is defective neuromuscular transmission. Similar symptoms appear in victims of seasnake, coralsnake, and South American tropical rattlesnake bites.

Mydriasis Dilatation of the pupils.

Myocardial infarction Severe damage or death of an area of heart muscle supplied by an artery that has been blocked by ruptured atheromatous plaque or thrombus, as in a heart attack.

Myoglobin Brown muscle pigment.

Myoglobinemia The presence in the blood of myoglobin that has leaked from muscles damaged by, for example, phosopholipase A_2 toxins in the venom of the South American tropical rattlesnake. In this case, the plasma/serum may be stained a brownish color.

Myoglobinuria The passage of myoglobin in the urine. The urine is dark brown, black, or Coca-Cola colored.

Myokymia See **Fasciculation**.

Myonecrosis Death of muscle cells as a result, for example, of the action of venom phospholipases A_2 and other myotoxins.

Myopathic (facies) The appearance caused by slack facial muscles in people suffering from muscle diseases or the effects of snake venom neurotoxins or myotoxins.

Myotoxin A toxin that damages muscle.

Naked With reference to snake hemipenes, devoid of ornamentation such as spines on the basal area and proximal portion of the lobes.

Nape The dorsal part of the neck. In snakes, the nape generally refers to the part of the neck just behind the head.

Nasals See **Prenasal** and **Postnasal**.

Nausea A feeling of sickness or the need to vomit.

ND4 A mitochondrial gene that codes for the fourth subunit of the protein NADH dehydrogenase.

Necrosis Death of tissues (gangrene).

Nephron The tiny renal tubule in which urine is formed in the kidney by filtration of constituents of the plasma through the glomerular capillary membrane.

Nephrosis Disease of the kidney.

Neurasthenia A condition characterized by general lassitude, irritability, lack of concentration, worry, and hypochondria.

Neuromuscular junction The anatomical site for transmission of the excitatory impulse from a motor nerve ending to the muscle fiber it innervates. This is the site of action of pre- and postsynaptic venom toxins.

Neurotoxicity Effects of some snake venom toxins (neurotoxins) on nerve endings and on the neuromuscular junction.

Neurotoxin A toxin that acts specifically on the nervous system in a harmful way, either causing excessive stimulation or interrupting neuromuscular transmission with resulting paralysis.

Nocturnal Active at night.

Nonparametric bootstrap A method for assessing confidence in clades recovered through phylogenetic analysis (Felsenstein, 1985). Hillis and Bull (1993) suggested that clades with bootstrap proportions of 70 or higher are likely to be accurate.

Norther A cold front from the mid-latitude frontal storms of the westerly wind belt. Mexico, Central America, and even northern South America are subject to these cold fronts from October to May.

Nuchal Pertaining to the region immediately behind the head.

Ocellus (pl. **Ocelli**) An element of pattern that resembles an eye.

Odontalgia Pain in a tooth or teeth.

Olfactory (nerve) The sensory cranial nerve (I) responsible for the sense of smell and hence fine taste.

Oliguric Passing reduced volumes of urine.

Ontogenic Related to the development of the individual.

Operational taxonomic unit (OTU) A general name for any terminal group used in a phylogenetic analysis; often these are species, but in some studies they are populations, genera, or higher taxa.

Opisthoglyphous Referring to a snake in which the posterior maxillary teeth are enlarged, usually with grooves or channels; such snakes are sometimes called rear-fanged. See also **Aglyphous**, **Proteroglyphous**, **Solenoglyphous**.

Oropel The local name in parts of Nicaragua, Costa Rica, and Panama for the yellow color phase of *Bothriechis schlegelii*.

Osteoderm A small dermal bone that is located under an epidermal scale of *Heloderma*. Osteoderms are found in many other lizards and crocodilians.

Outgroup One or more organisms or groups of organisms that are closely related to the ingroup and that are used to root the optimal ingroup tree(s).

Oviductal Pertaining to the oviducts, such as eggs.

Ovine Pertaining to sheep.

Palatine One of a pair of dermal bones in the roof of the mouth.

Palsy Paralysis.

Papillate Bearing small, nipplelike projections; sometimes used in reference to the microornamentation of hemipenes.

Paralytic ileus Intestinal obstruction caused by paralysis of the smooth muscle whose (peristaltic) contractions are normally responsible for propelling the contents of the gastrointestinal tract.

Páramo Isolated cold, humid meadows occurring above the treeline (2,600–3,800 m) in the northern Andes and Mérida Andes (in Colombia, Ecuador, Peru, and Venezuela). The vegetation is characterized by grasses (*Calamagrostis*, *Festuca*), *Baccharis*, *Diplostephium*, and, perhaps the most distinctive páramo plant genus, *Espeletia*.

Paraphyletic group A group that includes some but not all of the descendants of the most recent common ancestor of that group. Examples: the old use of Reptilia is paraphyletic with respect to Aves. Such unnatural groups should not be given taxonomic recognition.

Paraspecific In the case of antivenoms, paraspecific neutralizing activity is the ability of some monospecific and polyspecific antivenoms to neutralize venoms other than those used in the immunizing procedure to raise these antivenoms. Paraspecific activity is usually confined to venoms of closely related species (e.g., within the genus *Bothrops*).

Paratenic Referring to a host that permits the maintenance but not the development of a larval parasite. It differs from the intermediate host in that it is not necessary for the life cycle of the parasite.

Paraventrals The scales composing the longitudinal series that are situated on either side of the ventrals. The paraventral scales are usually slightly larger than more dorsally located scales. In snakes having most of the dorsal scales keeled, the paraventrals are usually smooth or weakly keeled. *Paraventral* also refers to the area on either side of the ventrals.

Paravertebral Lying on either side of the vertebral line; often used in reference to the rows of dorsals lying to either side of the vertebral row.

Paresthesiae/Paresthesias Altered, disturbed, or abnormal sensations such as "pins and needles," tingling, burning, and formication implying disordered function of sensory nerves, as may be the case in a limb bitten by a coralsnake.

Parietal eye A sensory structure that opens by means of the parietal foramen, a hole in the top of the skull that lies along the middorsal line in the parietal or frontoparietal region. The parietal eye is thought to detect temperature, and in some species of lizards it is capable of light reception.

Parietals Typically, a pair of large scales on the back of the dorsum of a snake's head. In most vipers, the parietals are fragmented into many small scales. The parietal region is located on top of the head posterior to the frontal region and supraoculars.

Parsimony The principle that states that the simplest explanation for a given phenomenon should be the correct explanation; in maximum parsimony analysis as applied to phylogenetic reconstruction, the phylogeny requiring the fewest character state changes (or steps) is viewed as the simplest explanation of the data and is thus taken to be the best estimate of relationships.

Parturition The process of giving birth.

Pathophysiology Disturbance of physiological function attributable to disease, such as envenoming.

Peak flow meter A hand-held device that allows measurement of expiratory airflow (representative of airway patency and respiratory muscle function).

Periarticular In the region of a joint.

Peripheral Outer parts of the body, such as the extremities.

Peritoneal dialysis Irrigation of the peritoneal cavity with specially designed electrolyte solutions so that excretory products in the blood such as urea, creatinine, and potassium diffuse through the peritoneal (semipermeable) membrane and can be drained off together with water extracted by osmosis. Used to treat patients with kidney failure.

Peritonism/peritonitis Extreme pain, sensitivity, and rigidity of the abdomen resulting from irritation and inflammation of the peritoneal lining by blood or intestinal contents that have leaked into it, or from infection.

Petechia (pl. **Petechiae**) A tiny (pinhead-sized) circular bleed in the skin from a single dermal capillary loop, which in victims of viper bite reflects thrombocytopenia or venom hemorrhagin activity (effectively the same as Purpura).

Phenetics A school of taxonomy in which taxa are classified according to an objective measure of their similarity to other taxa; this approach does not produce a natural classification.

Phlebitis Inflammation of veins often associated with thrombosis. Phlebitis involving superficial veins may be visible and palpable.

Phospholipase An enzyme that acts on phospholipids, which are important components of cell membranes. Certain of these enzymes have been found in the venom of many snakes, including vipers and elapids.

Photophobia Abnormal intolerance of light.

Phylogenetic systematics A method described by Hennig (1966) for discovering natural groups through the study of shared, derived characters (synapomorphies).

Phylogeny The historical relationships of different lineages to one another; often summarized in a branching diagram known as a phylogenetic tree.

Physiography The description of the relief features of the earth's surface.

Piloerection Contraction of smooth muscle attached to hairs in the skin, causing erection of the hairs and the appearance of "gooseflesh" (horripilation).

Pine-oak forest A widespread forest type occurring mostly at elevations above 1,000 m in the seasonally dry highlands of Mexico and northern Central America. This vegetation type comprises many communities, including oak scrub, pine forest, pine-oak woodland, and piñon-juniper woodland. See also **Montane moist forest**.

Platelet aggregation The sticking together of platelets in the circulation producing clumps, an important method of controlling bleeding at sites of injury. Many snake venom toxins cause platelet aggregation.

Plates Large, usually flat scales; typically used in reference to the enlarged scales on top of a snake's head or on its belly.

Plesiomorphy An ancestral (or primitive) character state.

Polyphyletic group A group that includes multiple independently derived lineages; cf. **Monophyletic group**.

Polyspecific In the case of antivenoms, referring to a hyperimmune serum raised in animals against the venoms of two or more snake species.

Polyvalent Said of an antivenom effective against multiple species of venomous animals; same as polyspecific.

Postnasal The scale bordering the posterior margin of the nostril; it may be conjoined above and/or below with the prenasal.

Postocular The scale or scales bordering the posterior periphery of the eye.

Postsynaptic In the case of snake venom neurotoxins, polypeptides shaped like two fingers and a thumb that bind to the alpha component of the acetylcholine receptor on the muscle side of the neuromuscular junction, competitively inhibiting the action of acetylcholine and resulting in paralysis of the muscle.

Prefoveal See **Foveal**.

Prefrontals The scales on top of the snout behind the internasals and in front of the frontal(s). The scales in this region may be paired and meet at the midline or may be fragmented into numerous smaller scales including the canthals and intercanthals.

Prehensile Adapted for seizing by wrapping around; the arboreal vipers have a prehensile tail.

Premontane Pertaining to the lower piedmont region or foothills of a mountain or mountain range; used to describe several types of forest that occur in these areas.

Prenasal The scale bordering the anterior margin of the nostril. This scale may be conjoined above and/or below with the postnasal.

Preocular The scale or scales bordering the anterior periphery of the eye.

Presynaptic In the case of snake venom neurotoxins, phospholipase A_2 and other compounds that bind at specific sites on the nerve terminal at the neuromuscular junction, initially discharging and later inactivating and irreversibly damaging the structure and causing paralysis of the muscles innervated by the nerve terminal.

Preventrals Scales lying anteriorly in the ventral series, wider than long, but not in contact on both sides with the paraventral row of dorsal scales.

Procoagulant (enzyme) Toxic snake venom enzymes that activate particular steps in the blood coagulation cascade. For example, some activate factor X, some prothrombin, some factor XIII, etc.

Prognosis The outlook or chances of recovery in patients suffering from a disease or envenoming.

Protease An enzyme that breaks down proteins.

Proteolytic Causing breakdown of proteins, for example by enzymes, venoms, or toxins.

Proteroglyphous Referring to a snake with fangs attached to a relatively akinetic maxillary bone that is located in the front of the mouth. At rest, the fangs are not folded against the roof of the mouth. See also **Aglyphous**, **Opisthoglyphous**, **Solenoglyphous**.

Proximal Pertaining to the part of a particular structure, such as the tail or hemipenis, that is closer to the center of the body than some other part of that structure.

Psammophilous Having an affinity for sandy ground.

Pterygoid One of a pair of dermal bones lying behind the palatines in the roof of the mouth.

Ptosis Drooping of and inability to retract the upper eyelids because of paralysis of the *levator palpebrae superioris* muscles innervated by the IIId cranial nerves. This is the earliest and most sensitive sign of venom neurotoxicity.

Puna An essentially treeless, windswept vegetation type occurring at elevations of about 3,400–4,400 m and even higher on the dry tablelands of the high Andes (from southern Ecuador to northern Argentina). The dominant plants are bunchgrasses (*Festuca, Poa, Stipa*), low shrubs (*Adesmia, Parastephia*), and sometimes small, scattered trees (*Polylepis*). In some areas along the eastern side of the altiplano, the puna is more humid and bromeliads (*Puya, Tillandsia*) may be abundant.

Purpura See **Petechiae**.

Putrid Concerning rotting flesh (necrotic/gangrenous infected tissue).

Rainforest A humid, tropical, relatively aseasonal vegetation type characterized by gigantic trees, lianas, palms, and epiphytes. Rainforest occurs throughout much of the Middle American Caribbean lowlands from Veracruz, Mexico, to Panama; it is also found locally on the Pacific coast in Guatemala, Costa Rica, and Panama. In South America, rainforest occurs along the Pacific lowlands from Colombia through Ecuador to extreme northern Peru, in the lower Río Orinoco Basin and Trinidad, throughout most of the Amazon Basin, and along an Atlantic corridor in Brazil from the state of Rio Grande do Norte to Santa Catarina.

Rainshadow Refers to the dry conditions on the leeward side of some mountain ranges. Warm, moisture-laden air coming off a large body of water (e.g., an ocean) rises as it is swept up the windward slopes of mountains. As it rises, the air cools, condensing the water vapor, and most of the moisture is lost on the windward side of the mountain range, often creating luxuriant cloud forest vegetation. By the time the air reaches the leeward side of the mountain, it is relatively dry and promotes xeric or rainshadow vegetation.

Rattle The sound-producing appendage on the tail of rattlesnakes.

Rattle matrix The fleshy tip of the tail of rattlesnakes on which each new rattle is formed.

Recrudescence The state of becoming renewed or active.

Rectilinear In reference to a mode of movement in which a snake moves forward in a straight line with no lateral movement.

Regional nerve block A technique in which an anesthetic is injected in the vicinity of a major nerve in an effort to alleviate pain occurring more distally along that nerve's area of distribution.

Renal Concerning the kidney.

Renal cortical necrosis Irreparable damage to the outer portion of both kidneys, usually the result of a sustained period of profound shock (hypotension).

Renal failure Kidney failure.

Renal tubules See **Nephron**.

Rescaled consistency index The product of the retention index and the consistency index.

Respiratory distress See **Dyspnea**.

Retention index Proposed by Farris (1989) to overcome problems with the consistency index, the retention index measures the fraction of apparent synapomorphy to actual synapomorphy.

Retroperitoneal hematoma Collection of blood beneath the membrane covering the organs and blood vessels at the back of the abdomen.

Reversal The change of a character state back into a previously occurring state; for example, an ancestral condition (lack of a rattle) being evolved from a derived condition (presence of a rattle) as in *Crotalus catalinensis*.

Rhabdomyolysis Generalized breakdown of skeletal muscle resulting from generalized action of venom myotoxins (phospholipases A_2) spread through the bloodstream.

Rhinitis Inflammation (usually allergic and atopic) of the mucous membranes lining the nose causing sneezing and nasal discharge.

Rictus The point, somewhat anterior to the angle of the jaw, where the lips of the upper and lower jaws come together.

Rigors Bouts of violent shaking, shivering, and teeth-chattering associated with alternate feelings of fever and chills. These result from circulating pyrogens (cytokines) released as a result of infection, intoxication, or immunological reactions.

Ring An element of pattern that consists of a solid color that completely encircles the body of a snake. Rings have been variously described as broad, wide, or long; because of their orientation around the long axis of the body, we prefer the last-named term. Counts of black body rings in coral snakes include the nape ring. Synonymous with annulus (pl. annuli).

Rostral The median scale covering the anterior tip of the snout in snakes and lizards. This scale is usually bordered by the first infralabials, the prenasals, and the internasals.

Rugose Rough, wrinkled. The dorsal aspect of some pitvipers is rugose owing to the presence of heavy keels and high neural spines.

Saddle A dorsal blotch that extends down the sides but is longer along the midline than it is laterally.

Saturation The occurrence of consecutive substitutions at one nucleotide site within the historical period during which ingroup species were diversifying. Its effect is to obscure phylogenetic relationships. See **Multiple hits**.

Savanna A large, grassy plain often containing scattered groves of trees, palms, or palmettos. Savannas may occur on flat coastal plains or in interior drainages. They are sometimes the result of clearing by humans, but many savannas are thought to be relatively old and to be created by edaphic conditions.

Saxicolous Inhabiting rocky areas.

Scutellation See **Lepidosis.**

Sensu lato In the broad or unrestricted sense; often used with names of taxa to indicate that the name is being used more inclusively than is sanctioned by current practice.

Sensu stricto In the narrow or restricted sense; often used with names of taxa to indicate that the name is being used more exclusively than is sanctioned by current practice.

Septicemia Generalized spread of bacteria or other pathogenic organisms throughout the bloodstream, associated with severe systemic inflammatory manifestations and often with prostration and shock ("blood poisoning").

Sequelae Aftereffects of a disease or envenoming that may be persistent.

Sequence alignment The process of identifying homologous nucleotide positions in nucleic acid (DNA or RNA) sequences from two or more individuals.

Sequence divergence The percentage difference between two nucleotide sequences.

Serohemorrhagic, Serosanguineous Containing serum and blood (e.g., pathological discharges or contents of blisters/bullae).

Serotonin A peptide that causes smooth muscle constriction in blood vessels (vasoconstriction).

Shoulders The proximal outer basal margins of a divided hemipenis, such as that found in pitvipers.

Sierra Spanish for "mountain range."

Solenoglyphous Referring to a snake with fangs attached to a relatively kinetic maxillary bone that is located in the front of the mouth. At rest, the fangs are folded against the roof of the mouth. See also **Aglyphous, Opisthoglyphous, Proteroglyphous.**

Spermiogenesis Transformation of a spermatid into a spermatozoan.

Spinulate With reference to microornamentation of snake hemipenes, the areas of the organ covered by small spinules.

Splenic Concerning the spleen.

Spontaneous bleeding Bleeding that arises without obvious injury at a site distant from the snakebite, for example, nosebleed, bleeding gums, vomiting, or passing blood in the stools or urine.

State See **Character state.**

Strabismus Paralysis of extraocular muscle(s) (squint) causing double vision (diplopia).

Strict consensus tree A phylogenetic tree used to summarize only those relationships in common among multiple trees.

Stupor Reduced level of consciousness without being completely unconscious (comatose).

Subarachnoid Beneath the innermost layer of the meninges (membranes covering the brain and spinal cord) in the (subarachnoid) space containing the cerebrospinal fluid. This may be a site of spontaneous bleeding (subarachnoid hemorrhage).

Subcaudals The scales lying on the ventral side of the tail in snakes, extending from immediately behind the cloacal plate to (but not including) the tail spine. In some snakes these scales are entire (undivided), whereas in other species they are paired (divided).

Submetacentric Chromosomes whose centromeres are approximately midway between each end, thereby forming two chromosome arms of similar length.

Subocular A scale bordering the lower periphery of the eye, but not the margin of the upper lip (in which case it would be considered a supralabial). Many species of pitvipers have several suboculars, but some have a single elongate scale.

Substitution A change from one nucleotide to another. The two types of substitution are transitions and transversions.

Subtelocentric Referring to chromosomes with a more terminally placed centromere, forming very unequal chromosome arms.

Subtropical dry forest See **Montane dry forest.**

Subtropical moist forest See **Montane moist forest.**

Subtropical wet forest See **Montane wet forest.**

Successive approximations A method developed by Farris (1969) in which characters are reweighted according to their consistency indices computed from a previous analysis. The procedure is repeated until relationships remain the same. Its purpose is to decrease false phylogenetic signal caused by homoplasy in certain parts of the tree.

Successive weighting See **Successive approximations.**

Sulcate Pertaining to the side of the hemipenis bearing the sulcus spermaticus.

Sulcus spermaticus A well-defined longitudinal groove on the outer surface of the everted hemipenis that transports spermatozoa. In species with divided hemipenes, this groove is also divided, with a branch extending to the apex of each hemipenial lobe.

Superciliary Any one of a small series of scales lying above the eye and along the outer edge of the supraocular. Some of these scales are raised into spinelike projections on *Bothriechis schlegelii* and *B. supraciliaris*. A term often used as a synonym is *supraciliary*.

Supracephalic On top of the head, such as scales.

Supracloacal keels Well-developed keels on the scales covering the lateral portion of the body above the vent. These keels occur in certain species of coralsnakes, typically only in males; however, large females of some species also develop keels in this region. Sometimes called supra-anal keels or tubercles.

Supralabials The series of scales along the lip of the upper jaw, exclusive of the anterior median rostral. The notation 9/10 indicates 9 supralabials on the right side and 10 on the left.

Supraocular In snakes, usually a large plate that lies on top of the head over either eye. In some species (e.g., *Atropoides nummifer*, *A. picadoi*) this scale may be either fragmented into many small scales or reduced to a small elongate scale. In other species (e.g., *Ophryacus undulatus*, *O. melanurum*) the supraocular is divided into many small scales, one or several of which may form a spine or hornlike process above the eye.

Surgical debridement Surgical excision of dead, infected, or nonviable tissue, for example, at the site of a viper bite.

SVL Standard abbreviation for snout-to-vent length.

Sympatric Coexistent; two species living in the same general region are said to be sympatric.

Symplesiomorphy A shared, ancestral character state; not indicative of phylogenetic relationship.

Synapomorphy A shared, derived character state; indicative of phylogenetic relationship.

Syncope Fainting.

Syndrome A group of clinical symptoms, signs, or results of investigations that occur together more commonly than by chance, suggesting a common cause.

Tachycardia Rapid heart (pulse) rate.

Tail length In snakes, the distance from the posterior edge of the cloacal plate to the tip of the tail.

Tail spine The terminal scale on the tip of the tail in snakes. In most species it is elongate and spinelike, but in some (e.g., *Bothriechis*) it is short and blunt. It is replaced by a rattle in rattlesnakes. The tail spine varies in size and shape among individuals of a species, and it usually becomes longer and more pointed with age.

Temporal The scale or scales lying behind the postoculars, above the supralabials, and below the parietals. The temporals are often arranged in two vertical rows, the anterior and posterior temporals, named according to their location. The notation 1 + 2 indicates that a snake has 1 anterior and 2 posterior temporals on each side of the head.

Tendon reflex The reflex contraction that occurs when a tendon is suddenly stretched (e.g., when a tendon hammer is used to tap the patella tendon below the kneecap during a neurological examination). The presence and nature of the resulting muscle contraction (in this case the knee jerk) indicates whether the neuromuscular reflex arc is intact.

Tepui Any one of a series of tabletop mountains of the Guiana Shield. These mountains are erosional remnants of the Cretaceous and Tertiary uplifts.

Tetanus Wound infection with the bacterium *Clostridium tetani*, which produces a neurotoxin causing muscular rigidity and spasms.

Thornforest A relatively short, scrubby forest occurring along portions of the western coast of Mexico, at the northern end of the Yucatán Peninsula, in a few interior valleys in Central America, and in the Caribbean coastal plain of northern South America. Leguminous trees (*Acacia, Caesalpinia, Cassia, Mimosa*) are characteristic vegetation.

Thrombin A proteolytic enzyme that facilitates the clotting of blood by promoting the conversion of fibrinogen to fibrin.

Thrombinlike enzyme A component of some snake venoms that acts on fibrinogen, converting it to an abnormal, unstable fibrin clot that is rapidly broken down.

Thrombocytopenia Reduction in the number of circulating blood platelets, which may result in abnormal bleeding (petechiae, purpura, and bruising).

Thrombotic microangiopathy Blockage of small arterioles by a clot (thrombus) sometimes causing gangrene of the areas of skin, muscle, and other tissue supplied by the arterioles.

TL Total length.

Total length The distance from the front face of the rostral to the tip of the tail; in other words, the combined head-body length and tail length.

Tourniquet A band applied around the upper part of the limb tightly enough to obliterate the arteries supplying that limb with blood.

Transition A nucleotide substitution from a purine to another purine or from a pyrimidine to another pyrimidine.

Transversely divided Referring to a scale that is partitioned across its long axis into two smaller scales. Examples are the upper preocular in most *C. lepidus* and the first infralabial in *C. ruber* and some populations of *C. simus*.

Transversion A nucleotide substitution from a purine to a pyrimidine or from a pyrimidine to a purine.

Trauma Injury.

Tree length The number of character state changes required to explain the character state distribution observed among OTUs given that particular tree topology.

Triad A grouping of three similar items. This term frequently is applied to the groups of black rings found in the pattern of some coralsnakes and their mimics in which *black*-yellow-*black*-yellow-*black* ring sequences are separated from one another by red rings.

Trismus Spasm or rigidity of the muscles responsible for clenching the jaws shut (masseter muscles) seen in tetanus and in patients envenomed by seasnakes.

Tropical arid forest A type of xeric vegetation, sometimes called arid tropical scrub in Mexico, characteristic of the lower elevations (100–600 m) of the driest rainshadow valleys in Mexico and northern Central America. This forest usually experiences less than 500 mm of precipitation each year. The vegetation is sparse and comprises various grasses, cacti, and thorny leguminous shrubs.

Tropical deciduous forest A vegetation type occurring at low elevations in the semiarid tropics characterized by species of trees (belonging to the genera *Bursera, Ipomoea, Lysiloma, Tabebuia*) that lose their leaves during the dry season. This type of forest is widespread, occurring principally along the western coast of Mexico and parts of Central America and at scattered locales in South America.

Tropical evergreen forest A vegetation type occurring at low elevations in the semihumid tropics characterized by species of trees (belonging to the genera *Bursera, Cedrela, Ceiba*) that are not deciduous. This type of forest is not as wet or tall as rainforest, and it usually experiences at least a short but well-defined dry season.

Tropical moist forest See **Rainforest**.

Troponin A muscle protein specific to heart muscle.

Tumefaction The process of swelling.

Type-locality The geographic locality at which a holotype (a specimen designated by an author as the type in the original description), lectotype (a specimen chosen as the type if the author failed to designate a type in the original description), or neotype (a specimen chosen as the type to replace a type that has been lost or destroyed) was collected.

Urticaria A rapidly evolving allergic rash consisting of numerous raised circular areas of skin that may be red against a white background or white against a red background and are usually intensely itchy. Also known as wheals, hives, or nettlerash. The areas may coalesce, causing extensive sheets of intracutaneous edema. When severe and generalized, they give the sufferer the appearance of a "Michelin man."

Vacuolization Creation of holes or spaces within cells.

Vasodilatation Opening up of blood vessels.

Vasopressor A drug that increases the tension in blood vessel walls and is given to patients suffering from shock to support blood pressure and organ perfusion.

Venepuncture Sampling of blood from a vein using needle and syringe.

Venter The undersurface of an animal.

Ventrals In snakes, the large, transversely elongated plates covering the belly from the neck to the cloacal plate. When the ventral series are counted, the first ventral is the anteriormost scale bordered on either side by the continuous, longitudinal row of dorsal scales that is adjacent to the ventrals (paraventrals); the cloacal plate is not counted in the ventral series.

Vertigo A kind of severe dizziness in which the surroundings seem to be spinning, caused by disturbance to the balancing mechanism in the middle ear, the VIIIth cranial nerve, or its connections in the brain.

Vesicle A tiny, fluid-filled spot on the skin (as in chickenpox) that may be the beginning of a blister or bulla near the site of a snakebite.

Vicariant event, Vicariance Event such as mountain building or habitat fragmentation that interrupts gene flow among parts of a population and may lead to speciation.

Viperid A snake in the family Viperidae. Members of this family are solenoglyphous and should be considered potentially dangerous. The family is divided into the true vipers (Viperinae, viperines), which lack a heat-sensitive pit and are restricted to Eurasia and Africa, and the pitvipers (Crotalinae, crotalines), which have a heat-sensitive pit in the loreal region and are widespread in parts of both the Old and New Worlds. New World viperids include the cantil, copperhead, and cottonmouth (*Agkistrodon*); jumping pitvipers (*Atropoides*); palm-pitvipers (*Bothriechis*); forest-pitvipers (*Bothriopsis*); toadheaded pitvipers (*Bothrocophias*); lanceheads (*Bothrops*); montane pitvipers (*Cerrophidion*); bushmasters (*Lachesis*); Mexican horned pitvipers (*Ophryacus*); hognosed pitvipers (*Porthidium*); and rattlesnakes (*Crotalus* and *Sistrurus*).

Visual accommodation Adjustment of the size of the pupil to allow focused vision on distant and near objects. Paralysis of the pupil, usually in the dilated condition (mydriasis), can result from exposure to neurotoxic venom. This will prevent visual accommodation and contribute to the symptom of blurred vision.

Vital capacity The maximum volume of air that can be forcibly breathed out of the lungs after a full inspiration. This volume is reduced in patients developing paralysis of their respiratory (breathing) muscles, such as the diaphragm, as a result of neurotoxic envenoming.

Vitellogenesis Yolk formation.

Vomeronasal organ See **Jacobson's organ**.

Weighting See **Character weighting**.

Xanthic Having yellow pigment or tending toward a yellow color.

Xeric Having relatively little moisture.

LITERATURE CITED

Journal Abbreviations

Am. Midl. Nat.	American Midland Naturalist
Am. Mus. Novitat.	American Museum Novitates
Ann. Emerg. Med.	Annals of Emergency Medicine
Ann. Mag. Nat. Hist.	Annals of the Magazine of Natural History
Bull. Am. Mus. Nat. Hist.	Bulletin of the American Museum of Natural History
Bull. Antivenin Inst. Am.	Bulletin of the Antivenin Institute of America
Bull. Chicago Herpetol. Soc.	Bulletin of the Chicago Herpetological Society
Bull. Maryland Herpetol. Soc.	Bulletin of the Maryland Herpetological Society
Comp. Biochem. Physiol.	Comparative Biochemistry and Physiology
Field Mus. Nat. Hist. Publ., Zool. Ser.	Field Museum of Natural History, Zoological Series
Herpetol. Rev.	Herpetological Review
JAMA	Journal of the American Medical Association
J. Herpetol.	Journal of Herpetology
Mem. Inst. Butantan	Memórias do Instituto Butantan
Occas. Pap. Mus. Zool. Univ. Michigan	Occasional Papers of the Museum of Zoology, University of Michigan
Proc. Acad. Nat. Sci. Philadelphia	Proceedings of the Academy of Natural Sciences of Philadelphia
Proc. California Acad. Sci.	Proceedings of the California Academy of Sciences
Proc. Zool. Soc. London	Proceedings of the Zoological Society of London
Rev. Biol. Trop.	Revista de Biología Tropical
Southwest. Nat.	Southwestern Naturalist
Syst. Biol.	Systematic Biology
Syst. Zool.	Systematic Zoology
Trans. Kansas Acad. Sci.	Transactions of the Kansas Academy of Science
Trans. Roy. Soc. Trop. Med. Hyg.	Transactions of the Royal Society of Tropical Medicine and Hygiene
Trans. San Diego Soc. Nat. Hist.	Transactions of the San Diego Society of Natural History

For abbreviations not listed here, see http://research.amnh.org/herpetology/amphibia/serial_and_book_titles.html

Abalos, J. W. 1949. Cuáles son los animales venenosos de la Argentina? Tucumán, Argentina. 23 pp.

——. 1961. Distribución y densidad de las serpientes venenosas de Santiago del Estero. Acta Krausi Cuaderno del Instituto Nacional de Microbiología (Buenos Aires) 3: 69–70.

——. 1972. Serpentario Córdoba. Universidad Nacional de Córdoba, Argentina. 22 pp.

——. 1977. ¿Qué sabe usted de víboras? Edit. Losada, Buenos Aires. 175 pp.

Abalos, J. W., and E. C. Baez. 1963 [dated 1961]. Variaciones del diseño en *Bothrops neuwiedii meridionalis* de Santiago del Estero. Acta Zoológica Lilloana 19: 479–486.

Abalos, J. W., E. C. Baez, and R. Nader. 1964. Serpientes de Santiago del Estero. Acta Zoológica Lilloana 20: 211–283.

Abalos, J. W., and E. Bucher. 1970. Zoo-epidemiología del ofidismo en Santiago del Estero. Boletín de la Academia Nacional de Ciéncias du Córdoba 47(2–4): 259–272.

Abalos, J. W., and C. C. Mischis. 1975. Elenco sistemático de los ofidios Argentinos. Boletín de la Academia Nacional de Ciéncias du Córdoba 51(1–2): 55–76.

Abalos, J. W., and R. Nader. 1962. La coral *Micrurus lemniscatus frontalis* de Santiago del Estero. Anales del Instituto Nacional de Microbiología (Buenos Aires) 1: 83–94.

Abalos, J. W., and I. Pirosky. 1963. Venomous Argentine serpents, ophidism and snake antivenin. Pp. 363–371 in H. L. Keegan and W. V. Macfarlane (eds.), Venomous and poisonous animals and noxious plants of the Pacific region. Pergamon, Oxford.

Ab'Saber, A. N. 1977. Os domínios morfoclimáticos da América do Sul. Boletim do Instituto de Geografia da Universidade de São Paulo 52: 1–21.

Abuys, A. 1982. Enige korrekties en aanvullende gegevens t.a.v. het boekje "Surinaamse slangen in kleur" van Joep Moonen e. a., 1979. Litteratura Serpentium 2(1): 34–42.

——. 1987a. De slangen van Suriname, deel XVII: familie Elapidae, subfamilie Micrurinae (genera *Leptomicrurus* en *Micrurus*). Litteratura Serpentium 7(4): 198–208.

——. 1987b. The snakes of Surinam, part XVIII: family Elapidae, subfamily Micrurinae. Litteratura Serpentium 7(4): 185–194, 221–242.

——. 1987c. A new coral snake (genus *Micrurus*) from Surinam. Litteratura Serpentium 7(5): 215–220.

——. 1987d. De slangen van Suriname, deel XIX: familie Viperidae, subfamilie Crotalinae. Litteratura Serpentium 7(6): 303–317.

——. 1988a. De slangen van Suriname, deel XX: familie Viperidae, subfamilie Crotalinae (het geslacht *Lachesis*). Litteratura Serpentium 8(1): 44–52.

——. 1988b. De slangen van Suriname, deel XXI: familie Viperidae, subfamilie Crotalinae (het genus *Bothrops*). Litteratura Serpentium 8(2): 78–94.

——. 1988c. An addition to the article "A new coral snake (genus *Micrurus*) from Surinam." Litteratura Serpentium 8(3): 106.

Achával, F. 1976. Reptiles. Pp. 26–29 in A. Langguth (ed.), Lista de las especies de vertebrados del Uruguay (reptiles). Museo Nacional de Historia Natural, Montevideo.

——. 1979 [dated 1977]. Lista comentada de los reptiles que habitan en la zona de influencia de la represa de Salto Grande. Seminario sobre Medio Ambiente y Represas (Montevideo) 1: 173–181.

——. 2001. Actualización sistemática y mapas de distribución de los reptiles del Uruguay. Smithsonian Herpetological Information Service 129: 1–21.

Achával, F., A. Melgarejo, and M. Meneghel. 1976. Víboras venenosas del Uruguay. Instituto de Investigación de Ciéncias Biológicas, Montevideo. 6 pp.

——. 1978. Ofidios del área de influencia de Salto Grande (aspectos biológicos y referencias sobre ofidismo). V Reunión sobre Aspectos de Desarrollo Ambiental. Salto, Argentina, 6–10 November 1978. 31 pp.

Acosta, J. C., and R. A. Martori. 1999. Relevamiento de un ensamble herpetológico en el monte de la Provincia de San Juan, Argentina. P. 23 in Abstracts of the V Congreso Latinoamericano de Herpetología, Montevideo, 12 al 17 de diciembre de 1999.

Acosta, O., L. C. Leiva, M. E. Peichoto, S. Maruñak, P. Teibler, and L. Rey. 2003. Hemorrhagic activity of the Duvernoy's gland secretion of the xenodontine colubrid *Philodryas patagoniensis* from the northeast region of Argentina. Toxicon 41: 1007–1012.

Acosta, S., A. Giraudo, and S. Montanelli. 1994. Composición de la ofiofauna (Reptilia: Serpentes) del Parque Nacional Iguazu, Provincia de Misiones, Argentina. Boletín de la Asociación Herpetológica Argentina 10(1): 6–8.

Acosta de Pérez, O., S. Maruñak, R. Ruiz, P. Koscinczuk, and P. Teibler. 1997. Hemorrhage induced by venoms of serpents from Argentina. Acta Physiologica, Pharmacologica et Therapeutica Latinoamericana 47(4): 221–224.

Acosta-Solís, M. 1944. Nuevas contribuciones al conocimiento de la provincia de Esmeraldas. Editorial Ecuador, Quito. 606 pp.

Adame, B. L., J. G. Soto, D. J. Secraw, J. C. Perez, J. L. Glenn, and R. C. Straight. 1990. Regional variation of biochemical characteristics and antigeneity in Great Basin rattlesnake (*Crotalus viridis lutosus*) venom. Comp. Biochem. Physiol. B 97: 95–101.

Adams, C. E., J. K. Thomas, K. J. Strnadel, and S. L. Jester. 1994. Texas rattlesnake roundups: implications of unregulated commercial use of wildlife. Wildlife Society Bulletin 22(2): 324–330.

Adler, K. 1960. On a brood of *Sistrurus* from northern Indiana. Herpetologica 16(1): 38.

——. 1976. New genera and species described in Holbrook's "North American herpetology." Pp. xxix–xlix in Holbrook's North American herpetology. Facsimile Reprints in Herpetology. Society for the Study of Amphibians and Reptiles, Ithaca, New York.

Aguilar, A. S., E. C. N. Rubião, O. M. P. Bastos, and A. R. Melgarejo. 1999. Parasitismo por *Porocephalus stilesi* (Sambon, 1910) (Pentastomida) em *Lachesis muta rhombeata* Wied, 1824 (Serpentes: Viperidae). P. 24 in Abstracts of the V Congreso Latinoamericano de Herpetología, Montevideo, 12 al 17 de diciembre de 1999.

Ahl, E. 1927. Zwei neue Korallenottern der Gattung *Elaps*. Zoologischer Anzeiger (Leipzig) 70: 251–252.

Ahlbrandt, L., K. Jones, and M. Fordyner. 2002. Geographic distribution; *Crotalus horridus* (Timber rattlesnake). Herpetol. Rev. 33(3): 227.

Ahlstrom, N. G., W. Luginbuhl, and C. C. Tisher. 1991. Acute anuric renal failure after pigmy rattlesnake bite. Southern Medical Journal 84: 783–785.

Aird, S. D. 1984. Natural history notes: *Crotalus viridis viridis* (prairie rattlesnake). Coloration. Herpetol. Rev. 15(1): 18–19.

Aird, S. D., and N. Jorge da Silva. 1991. Comparative enzymatic composition of Brazilian coral snake (*Micrurus*) venoms. Comp. Biochem. Physiol. B 99: 287–294.

Aird, S. D., W. G. Kruggel, and I. I. Kaiser. 1990. Amino acid sequence of the basic subunit of the Mojave rattlesnake (*Crotalus s. scutulatus*). Toxicon 28: 669–673.

——. 1991. Multiple myotoxin sequences from the venom of a single prairie rattlesnake (*Crotalus viridis viridis*). Toxicon 29: 265–268.

Aird, S. D., C. S. Seebart, and I. I. Kaiser. 1988. Preliminary fractionation and characterization of the venom of the Great Basin rattlesnake (*Crotalus viridis lutosus*). Herpetologica 44(1): 71–85.

Alberts, M. B., M. Shalit, and F. L. Galbo. 2000. Suction as initial treatment of venomous snakebite (abstract). Academic Emergency Medicine 7: 496.

Albritton, D. C., H. M. Parrish, and E. R. Allen. 1970. Venenation by the Mexican beaded lizard (*Heloderma horridum*): report of a case. South Dakota Journal of Medicine 23: 9–11.

Alcock, A., and L. Rogers. 1902. On the toxic properties of the saliva of certain "non-poisonous" colubrines. Proceedings of the Royal Society of London 70: 445–454.

Aldridge, R. D. 1975. Environmental control of spermatogenesis in the rattlesnake *Crotalus viridis*. Copeia 1975(3): 493–496.

——. 1979a. Seasonal spermatogenesis in sympatric *Crotalus viridis* and *Arizona elegans* in New Mexico. J. Herpetol. 13: 187–192.

——. 1979b. Female reproductive cycles of the snakes *Arizona elegans* and *Crotalus viridis*. Herpetologica 35: 256–261.

——. 1993. Male reproductive anatomy and seasonal occurrence of mating and combat behavior of the rattlesnake *Crotalus v. viridus*. J. Herpetol. 27: 481–484.

——. 2002. The link between mating season and male reproductive anatomy in the rattlesnakes *Crotalus viridis oreganus* and *Crotalus viridis helleri*. J. Herpetol. 36(2): 295–300.

Aldridge, R. D., and W. S. Brown. 1995. Male reproductive cycle, age at maturity, and cost of reproduction in the timber rattlesnake (*Crotalus horridus*). J. Herpetol. 29: 399–407.

Aldridge, R. D., and D. Duvall. 2002. Evolution of the mating season in the pitvipers of North America. Herpetological Monographs 16: 1–25.

Alemán G. C. 1952. Apuntes sobre reptiles y anfibios de la región Baruta–El Hatillo. Memoria de la Sociedad de Ciencias Naturales La Salle 12(31): 11–30.

——. 1953. Contribución al estudio de los reptiles y batracios de la Sierra de Perijá. Memoria de la Sociedad de Ciencias Naturales La Salle 13(35): 205–225.

Alexander, C. C., and E. P. Alexander. 1957. *Oochoristica crotalicola*, a new anoplocephalid cestode from California rattlesnakes. Journal of Parasitology 43: 365.

Alfaro, A. 1907. Notas herpetológicas. Páginas Ilustradas Revista Semanal 4(129): 2060–2062.

——. 1912. Notas herpetológicas. Boletin de Fomento (Costa Rica) 2: 734–741.

Allen, C. E. 1940. Behavior of *Micrurus frontalis frontalis*. Copeia 1940(1): 51–52.

Allen, E. R. 1938. The copperhead in northern Florida. Copeia 1938(1): 50.

——. 1940. Poisonous snakes of Florida. Florida Fish and Game Magazine 1(10): 6–9.

——. 1949a. Observations on the feeding habits of the juvenile cantil. Copeia 1949(3): 225–226.

——. 1949b. Range of cane-brake rattlesnake in Florida. Copeia 1949(1): 73–74.

Allen, E. R., and E. Maier. 1941. The extraction and processing of snake venom. Copeia 1941(4): 248–252.

Allen, E. R., and W. T. Neill. 1950. The pigmy rattlesnakes. Florida Wildlife 5: 10–11.

——. 1957. Some interesting rattlesnakes from southern British Guiana. Herpetologica 13(1): 67–74.

——. 1959a. Studies on the amphibians and reptiles of British Honduras. Publication of the Research Division of the Ross Allen Reptile Institute 2: 1–76.

——. 1959b. Doubtful records in British Honduras. Herpetologica 15(4): 227–233.

Allen, E. R., and R. Slatten. 1945. A herpetological collection from the vicinity of Key West, Florida. Herpetologica 3(1): 25–26.

Allen, E. R., and D. Swindell. 1948. Cottonmouth moccasin of Florida. Herpetologica 4(suppl. 1): 1–16.

Allen, J. A. 1869. Catalogue of the reptiles and batrachians found in the vicinity of Springfield, Massachusetts, with notice of all other species known to inhabit the state. Proceedings of the Boston Society of Natural History 12: 171–206.

Allen, M. J. 1933. Report on a collection of amphibians and reptiles from Sonora, Mexico, with a description of a new lizard. Occas. Pap. Mus. Zool. Univ. Michigan 259: 1–15.

Allen, P. H. 1956. The rain forests of Golfo Dulce. University of Florida Press, Gainesville. 417 pp.

Allen, W. B. 1956. The effects of a massasauga bite. Herpetologica 12(2): 151.

Allen, W. B., Jr. 1992. The snakes of Pennsylvania. Reptile and Amphibian Magazine, Pottsville, Pa. 33 pp.

Almeida, M. T., and M. Martins. 1999. Historia natural de *Bothrops neuwiedi pubescens* (Serpentes, Viperidae). P. 26 in Abstracts of the V Congreso Latinoamericano de Herpetología, Montevideo, 12 al 17 de diciembre de 1999.

Almeida-Santos, S. M., and M. G. Salomão. 1997. Long-term sperm storage in the female Neotropical rattlesnake, *Crotalus durissus terrificus* (Viperidae: Crotalinae). Japanese Journal of Herpetology 17(2): 46–52.

———. 2002. Reproduction in Neotropical pitvipers, with emphasis on species of the genus *Bothrops*. Pp. 445–462 in G. W. Schuett, M. Höggren, M. E. Douglas, and H. W. Greene (eds.), Biology of the vipers. Eagle Mountain Publishing, Eagle Mountain, Utah.

Almeida-Santos, S. M., L. F. Schmidt de Aguiar, and R. Lucchesi Balestrin. 1998. Natural history notes: *Micrurus frontalis* (coral snake). Male combat. Herpetol. Rev. 29(4): 242.

Almendáriz, A. 1991. Lista de vertebrados del Ecuador. Anfibios y reptiles. Politécnica 16(3): 86–165.

Alsberg, C. L. 1913. Biochemical studies upon the venom of *Heloderma suspectum*. Pp. 229–244 in L. Loeb (ed.), The venom of *Heloderma*. Carnegie Institution, Washington, D.C.

Altini, G. 1942. I rettili dei Laghi Chapala, Patzcuaro e Peten raccolti nel 1932 dal Prof. Allesandro Ghigi e dal Prof. Alula Taibel. Atti della Società Italiana di Scienze Naturali e del Museo Civico di Storia Naturale di Milano 81(3–4): 153–195.

Alvarado-Diaz, J., D. del C. Huacuz-Elias, and I. Suazo-Ortuño. 1997. Geographic distribution: *Porthidium hespere*. Herpetol. Rev. 28: 98.

Alvarez, B. B., J. A. Cespedez, M. L. Lions, A. Hernando, and R. Aguirre. 1996. Herpetofauna de las provincias de Corrientes, Chaco y Formosa (Argentina). Facena 12: 119–134.

Alvarez, B. B., M. L. Lions, R. Aguirre, J. A. Cespedez, and A. Hernando. 1995. Herpetofauna del área de influencia del embalse de la represa de Yacyretá (Argentina-Paraguay). Facena 11: 57–73.

Alvarez, T., and P. Huerta. 1974. Nuevo registro de *Crotalus atrox* para la Península de Baja California. Revista de la Sociedad Mexicana de Historia Natural 35: 113–115.

Alvarez del Toro, M. 1952. Los animales silvestres de Chiapas. Departamento de Prensa y Turismo, Tuxtla Gutiérrez, Chiapas, México. 247 pp.

———. 1960. Los reptiles de Chiapas. Instituto Zoológico del Estado, Tuxtla Gutiérrez, Chiapas, México. 204 pp.

———. 1972. Los reptiles de Chiapas, 2d ed. Gobierno del Estado, Publicación del Instituto de Historia Natural del Estado, Departamento de Zoología, Tuxtla Gutiérrez, Chiapas, México. 178 pp.

———. 1983 [dated 1982]. Los reptiles de Chiapas, 3d ed. Gobierno del Estado, Publicación del Instituto de Historia Natural del Estado, Departamento de Zoología, Tuxtla Gutiérrez, Chiapas, México. 248 pp.

Alvarez del Toro, M., and H. M. Smith. 1956. Notulae herpetologicae Chiapasiae I. Herpetologica 12(1): 3–17.

Alves, A. L., A. R. Melgarejo G., D. de V. R. Ventura, F. L. B. De Moraes, H. E. Belluomini, H. M. Canter, I. Staciarini, P. A. Federsoni Jr., R. Q. Dos Santos, and S. G. F. Leite. 1991. Cartilha de ofidismo (cobral). 3d ed. Centro Nacional de Epidemiologia, Brasilia. 32 pp.

Amaral, A. do. 1922a [dated 1921]. Contribuição para o conhecimento dos ophidios do Brasil. Parte I. Quatro novas espécies de serpentes brasileiras. Anexos das Mem. Inst. Butantan 1(1): 1–38.

———. 1922b [dated 1921]. Contribuição para o conhecimento dos ophidios do Brasil. Parte II. Biologia da nova espécie, *Lachesis insularis*. Anexos das Mem. Inst. Butantan 1(1): 39–44.

———. 1922c [dated 1921]. Contribution towards the knowledge of snakes in Brazil. Part I. Four new species of Brazilian snakes. Anexos das Mem. Inst. Butantan 1(1): 49–81.

———. 1923. New genera and species of snakes. Proceedings of the New England Zoölogical Club 8: 85–105.

———. 1924. On the biological differentiation of the Neotropical species of snakes, *Bothrops atrox* (Linné, 1758), *B. jararaca* (Wied, 1824), and *B. jararacussu* Lacerda, 1884. American Journal of Tropical Medicine 4: 447–452.

———. 1925a. South American snakes in the collection of the United States National Museum. Proceedings of the U.S. National Museum 67(24): 1–70.

———. 1925b. A general consideration of snake poisoning and observations on Neotropical pit-vipers. Contributions of the Harvard Institute of Tropical Biology and Medicine 2: 1–64.

———. 1925c. On the oviparity of *Lachesis muta* Daudin, 1803. Copeia 1925(149): 93–94.

———. 1926a. Notas de ophiologia. I. Nota de nomenclatura ophiologica sôbre o amprego do nome generico *Micrurus* em vez de *Elaps*. Revista do Museu Paulista 14: 3–6.

———. 1926b. Notas de ophiologia. 1.ª nota de ophiologia. Sôbre a invalidez de um genero e algunas espécies de ophidios sul-Americanos. Revista do Museu Paulista 14: 17–33.

———. 1926c. Nota de nomenclatura ophiologica. 4. Sôbre a differenciacao dos genericos *Lachesis*, *Trimeresurus*, e *Bothrops*. Revista do Museu Paulista 14: 34–40.

———. 1926d. Tres sub-espécies novas de *Micrurus corallinus*: *Micrurus corallinus riesei*, *M. corallinus corallinus*, e *M. corallinus dumerilii*. Revista do Museu Paulista 15: 12–25.

———. 1926e. Da invalidez de espécie de Colubrideo Elapineo *Micrurus ibiboboca* (Merrem) e redescripção de *M. lemniscatus* (L.). Revista do Museu Paulista 15: 28–40.

———. 1926f. Sôbre a *Lachesis muta* Daudin, 1803, especie ovipara. Revista do Museu Paulista 15: 42–46.

———. 1926g. Ophidios sul-americanos do Museu Carnegie e especies novas de Griffin. Revista do Museu Paulista 15: 64–73.

———. 1926h. Variaçãoes das marcas dorsaes de *Crotalus terrificus* Laurenti, 1768. Revista do Museu Paulista 15: 88–94.

———. 1926i. Ophidia from South America in the Carnegie Museum: a critique of Dr. L. E. Griffin's Catalog of the Ophidia from South America at present (June, 1916) contained in the Carnegie Museum. Annals of Carnegie Museum 16(8): 319–323.

———. 1926j. Novos generos e especies de ophidios brasileiros. Archivos do Museu Nacional, Rio de Janeiro 26: 96–121.

———. 1926k. Studies of Neotropical Ophidia. II. On *Micrurus mipartitus* and allied forms. Proceedings of the New England Zoölogical Club 9: 61–66.

———. 1926l. Nomes vulgares de ophidios do Brasil. Boletim do Museu Nacional, Rio de Janeiro, 2(2): 19–29.

———. 1926m [dated 1925]. Ophidios de Matto Grosso. Commissão de Linhas Telegráficas Estratégicas de Matto Grosso ao Amazonas 84(5): 1–29.

———. 1927a. Studies of Neotropical Ophidia. IV. A new form of Crotalidae from Bolivia. Bull. Antivenin Inst. Am. 1(1): 5–6.

———. 1927b. Studies of Neotropical Ophidia. V. Notes on *Bothrops lansbergii* and *B. brachystoma*. Bull. Antivenin Inst. Am. 1(1): 22.

———. 1927c. The snake-bite problem in the United States and in Central America. Bull. Antivenin Inst. Am. 1(2): 31–35.

———. 1927d. Studies of Neotropical Ophidia. VII. An interesting collection of snakes from west Colombia. Bull. Antivenin Inst. Am. 1(2): 44–47.

———. 1927e. Studies on Nearctic Ophidia. I. *Crotalus godmani* Schmidt, 1922, a synonym of *C. mitchelli* Cope, 1961. Bull. Antivenin Inst. Am. 1(2): 47–48.

———. 1927f. Studies of Nearctic Ophidia. II. *Crotalus pricei* Van Denburgh, 1896, a synonym of *C. triseriatus* (Wagler, 1830). Bull. Antivenin Inst. Am. 1(2): 48–54.

———. 1927g. Notes on Nearctic poisonous snakes and treatment of their bites. Bull. Antivenin Inst. Am. 1(3): 61–76.

———. 1927h. Excursão á Ilha Quiemada Grande: noteas sôbre a biologia de uma *Lachesis* ali existente. Coletânea de Trabalhos do Instituto Butantan 1918–1924 2: 49–57.

———. 1927i. Contribuição á biologia dos ophideos brasileiros (habitat, habitos, e alimentação). 1.a Nota prévia. Col. Trab. Inst. Butantan 1918–1924 2: 177–187.

———. 1927j. The anti-snake-bite campaign in Texas and in the subtropical United States. Bull. Antivenin Inst. Am. 1(3): 77–85.

——. 1928a. Studies of Neotropical Ophidia. XI. Snakes from the Santa Marta region, Colombia. Bull. Antivenin Inst. Am. 2(1): 7–8.

——. 1928b. Studies on snake venoms. I. Amounts of venom secreted by Nearctic pit vipers. Bull. Antivenin Inst. Am. 1(4): 103–104.

——. 1929a. Studies on Nearctic Ophidia. III. Notes on *Crotalus tigris* Kennicott, 1859. Bull. Antivenin Inst. Am. 2(4): 82–85.

——. 1929b. Studies of Nearctic Ophidia. IV. On *Crotalus tortugensis* Vandenburgh and Slevin, 1921, *Crotalus atrox elegans* Schmidt 1922, and *Crotalus atrox lucasensis* (Vandenburgh, 1920). Bull. Antivenin Inst. Am. 2(4): 85–86.

——. 1929c. Studies of Nearctic Ophidia. V. On *Crotalus confluentus* Say, 1823, and its allied forms. Bull. Antivenin Inst. Am. 2(4): 86–97.

——. 1929d. Studies of Nearctic Ophidia. VI. Phylogeny of the rattlesnakes. Bull. Antivenin Inst. Am. 3(1): 6–8.

——. 1929e. Studies of Neotropical Ophidia. XII. On the *Bothrops lansbergi* group. Bull. Antivenin Inst. Am. 3(1): 19–27.

——. 1929f. Key to the rattlesnakes of the genus *Crotalus* Linné, 1758. Bull. Antivenin Inst. Am. 3(1): 4–6.

——. 1930a [dated 1929]. Estudos sôbre ophidios neotropicos. XVII. Valor sistemático de varias formas de ophidios neotropicos. Mem. Inst. Butantan 4: 3–68.

——. 1930b [dated 1929]. Contribuição ao conhecimento dos ophidios do Brasil. IV. Lista remissiva dos ophidios do Brasil. Mem. Inst. Butantan 4: 71–125.

——. 1930c [dated 1929]. Estudos sôbre ophidios neotropicos. XVIII. Lista remissiva dos ophidios da região neotrópica. Mem. Inst. Butantan 4: 129–271.

——. 1930d. Studies of Neotropical Ophidia. XV. A rare Brazilian snake. Bull. Antivenin Inst. Am. 4(1): 13–16.

——. 1930e. Studies of Neotropical Ophidia. 25. A new race of *Bothrops neuwiedii*. Bull. Antivenin Inst. Am. 4(3): 65–67.

——. 1930f. Campanhas antiophídicas. Mem. Inst. Butantan 5: 193–232.

——. 1931a. Studies of Neotropical Ophidia. XXIII. Additional notes on Colombian snakes. Bull. Antivenin Inst. Am. 4(4): 85–89.

——. 1931b. Studies of Neotropical Ophidia. XXVI. Ophidia of Colombia. Bull. Antivenin Inst. Am. 4(4): 89–94.

——. 1931c [dated 1930]. Animaes venenosos do Brasil. Instituto Butantan. Typografia Levi, São Paulo. 65 pp.

——. 1932. Estudos sôbre ophidios neotropicos. XXIX. Novas notas sôbre especies da Colombia. Mem. Inst. Butantan 7: 103–123.

——. 1933a [dated 1932]. Contribuição ao conhecimento dos ophidios do Brasil. 5. Uma nova raça de *Bothrops neuwiedii*. Mem. Inst. Butantan 7: 97–98.

——. 1933b. Mecanismo e gênero de alimentação das serpentes do Brasil. Boletim do Museu de Biologia, São Paulo, 1: 2–4.

——. 1934a [dated 1933–1934]. Notas sôbre chromatismo de ophidios. III. Um caso de xanthismo e um novo de albinismo observados no Brasil. Mem. Inst. Butantan 8: 151–153.

——. 1934b [dated 1933–1934]. Estudos sôbre ophidios neotropicos. 31. Sôbre a especie *Bothrops alternata* D. & B., 1854 (Crotalidae). Variações. Redescripção. Mem. Inst. Butantan 8: 161–182.

——. 1935. Estudios sôbre ophidios neotropicos. XXXIII. Novas especies de ophídios da Colombia. Mem. Inst. Butantan 9: 219–223.

——. 1937a. New species of ophidians from Colombia. C. R. XII Congr. Inst. Zool. (Lisbon 1935) 3: 1762–1767.

——. 1937b. Remarks on the ophiological fauna of Colombia. C. R. XII Congr. Inst. Zool. (Lisbon 1935) 3: 1768–1776.

——. 1937c [dated 1935–36]. Contribuição ao conhecimento dos ophidios do Brasil. VIII. Lista remissiva dos ophidios do Brasil. 2d ed. Mem. Inst. Butantan 10: 87–162.

——. 1938 [dated 1937]. Contribuição ao conhecimento dos ofidios do Brasil. Synopse das crotalideas do Brasil. Mem. Inst. Butantan 11: 217–229.

——. 1944a. Notas sôbre a ofiologia neotrópica e brasilica. II. Sôbre *Bothrops lansbergii lansbergii* (Schlegel, 1841); *Trimeresurus dunni* Hartweg and Oliver, 1938; *T. lansbergii annectens* Schmidt, 1936.

Papéis Avulsos do Departamento de Zoologia, São Paulo, 5(2): 7–12.

——. 1944b. Notas sôbre a ofiologia neotrópica e brasílica. IV. Da invalidez da espécie *Bothrops pessoai* A. Prado, 1939. Papéis Avulsos do Departamento de Zoologia, São Paulo, 5: 19–28.

——. 1944c. Notas sôbre a ofiologia neotrópica e brasílica. XI. Subespecies de *Micrurus lemniscatus* (L.) e suas afinidades com *M. frontalis* (Dm. e. Bibr.). Papéis Avulsos do Departamento de Zoologia, São Paulo, 5(11); 83–94.

——. 1944d. Notas sôbre a ofiologia neotrópica e brasílica. V. Sôbre a invalidez específica de *Crotalus unicolor*. Papéis Avulsos do Departamento de Zoologia, São Paulo, 5: 29–40.

——. 1944e. Notas sôbre a ofiologia neotropica e brasílica: sôbre a aplicacão do nome genérico *Trimeresusurus*, em vez de *Bothrops*, a serpentes neotrópicas. Papéis Avulsos do Departamento de Zoologia, São Paulo, 5: 13–18.

——. 1945. Animais veneniferos, venenos, e antivenenos. Caça e Pesca, n.p. 60 pp.

——. 1948a. Ofídios de Mato Grosso (Contribuição II para o conhecimento dos ofidios do Brasil). Commissão de Linhas Telegráficas Estratégicas de Mato Grosso ao Amazonas 84(5): 1–43.

——. 1948b. Ofidios do Pará. Boletim do Museu Paraense Emílio Goeldi 10: 149–159.

——. 1955a [dated 1954]. Contribuição ao conhecimento dos ofidios neotrópicos. 35. A propósito da revalidação de *Coluber lanceolatus* Lacepéde, 1789. Mem. Inst. Butantan 26: 207–214.

——. 1955b [dated 1954]. Contribuição ao conhecimento dos ofidios do Brasil 15. Situação taxonómica de algumas formas de Crotalidae, Lachesinae, recentemente descritas. Mem. Inst. Butantan 26: 215–220.

——. 1955c [dated 1954]. Contribuição ao conhecimento dos ofidios neotrópicos. 36. Redescrição da espécie *Bothrops hyoprora* Amaral, 1935. Mem. Inst. Butantan 26: 221–225.

——. 1974 [dated 1973]. Ofionimia ameríndia na ofiologia Brasiliense. Mem. Inst. Butantan 37: 1–15.

——. 1978. Serpentes do Brasil: iconografia Colorida, 2d ed. Edições Melhoramentos. Editora Universidade de São Paulo. 247 pp.

Amaral, C. F. S., O. A. Da Silva, M. López, and E. R. P. Pedroso. 1980. Afibrinogenemia following snake bite (*Crotalus durissus terrificus*). American Journal of Tropical Medicine and Hygiene 29(6): 1453–1455.

Amaral, C. F. S., R. A. Malgalhães, and N. A. D. Rezende. 1991. Respiratory abnormalities following *Crotalus durissus* snakebite. Revista do Instituto de Medicina Tropical de São Paulo 33(4): 251–255.

Amaral, C. F. S., N. A. Rezende, T. M. G. Pedrosa, et al. 1988. Afibrinogenemia secundária a acidente ofídico crotálico (*Crotalus durissus terrificus*). Revista do Instituto de Medicina Tropical de São Paulo 30: 288–292.

Amaral, C. F. S., N. A. D. Rezende, O. A. D. Silva, M. M. F. Ribeiro, R. A. Malgalhães, R. J. D. Reis, J. G. Carneiro, and J. R. S. Castro. 1986. Acute renal insufficiency secondary to ophidian bothropic and crotalic accidents. Revista do Instituto de Medicina Tropical de São Paulo 28(4): 220–227.

Ambrose, M. S. 1956. Snakebite in Central America. Pp. 323–329 in E. E. Buckley and N. Porges (eds.), Venoms. American Association for the Advancement of Science, Washington, D.C.

Amuy, E., A. Alap-Giron, B. Lomont, M. Thelestam, and J. M. Gutierrez. 1997. Development of immunoassays for determination of circulating venom antigen during envenomations by coral snakes (*Micrurus* species). Toxicon 35: 1605–1616.

Anaya, M., E. D. Rael, D. S. Lieb, J. C. Perez, and R. J. Salo. 1992. Antibody detection of venom protein variation within a population of rattlesnake *Crotalus v. viridis*. J. Herpetol. 26: 473–482.

Anderson, J. D. 1962. A new subspecies of the ridged-nosed rattlesnake, *Crotalus willardi*, from Chihuahua, Mexico. Copeia 1962(1): 160–163.

Anderson, J. D., and W. Z. Lidicker Jr. 1963. A contribution to our knowledge of the herpetofauna of the Mexican state of Aguascalientes. Herpetologica 19(1): 40–51.

Anderson, O. I., and J. R. Slater. 1941. Life zone distribution of the Oregon reptiles. Occasional Papers, Department of Biology, College of Puget Sound 12–15: 109–119.

Anderson, P. 1941. The cottonmouth in northern Missouri. Copeia 1941(3): 178.

——. 1942. Amphibians and reptiles of Jackson County, Missouri. Bulletin of the Chicago Academy of Science 6: 203–220.

——. 1947. Observations on the denning habits of the prairie rattlesnake, *Crotalus viridis viridis* (Rafinesque). Natural History Miscellanea, Chicago Academy of Sciences 9: 1–2.

——. 1965. The reptiles of Missouri. University of Missouri Press, Columbia. 330 pp.

Anderson, P. C. 1998. Bites by copperhead snakes in mid-Missouri. Missouri Medicine 95: 629–632.

Anderson, R. C. 2000. Nematode parasites of vertebrates: their development and transmission, 2d ed. CAB International, Wallingford, United Kingdom. 672 pp.

Anderson, S. G., and C. L. Ownby. 1997. Systematic hemorrhage induced by proteinase H from *Crotalus admanteus* (eastern diamondback rattlesnake) venom. Toxicon 35(8): 1301–1313,

Andersson, L. G. 1899. Catalogue of Linnean type-specimens of snakes in the Royal Museum in Stockholm. Bihang till Kongliga Svenska Vetenskaps-Akademiens Handlingar 24(4): 1–35.

——. 1900. Catalogue of Linnean type-specimens of Linnaeus's Reptilia in the Royal Museum of Stockholm. Bihang till Kongliga Svenska Vetenskaps-Akademiens Handlingar 26: 1–29.

Andrade, D. V., and A. S. Abe. 1999. Relationship of venom ontogeny and diet in *Bothrops*. Herpetologica 55(2): 200–204.

——. 2000. Water collection by the body in a viperid snake, *Bothrops moojeni*. Amphibia-Reptilia 21(4): 485–492.

Andrade, D. V., A. S. Abe, and M. C. dos Santos. 1996. Is the venom related to diet and tail color during *Bothrops moojeni* ontogeny? J. Herpetol. 30: 285–288.

Andrade, J. G., R. N. L. Pinto, A. L. S. S. de Andrade, C. M. Martelli, and F. Zicker. 1989. Estudo bacteriológico de abscessos causados por picada de serpentes do genero *Bothrops*. Revista do Instituto de Medicina Tropical de São Paulo 31(6): 363–367.

Andrews, C. E., and C. B. Pollard. 1953. Report of snake bites in Florida and treatment: venoms and antivenoms. Journal of the Florida Medical Association 40: 388–437.

Andrews, E. W. 1937. Notes on snakes from the Yucatan Peninsula. Field Mus. Nat. Hist. Publ., Zool. Ser., 20(25): 355–359.

Andrews, J. S. 1995. A preliminary atlas of the reptiles and amphibians of Vermont. Vermont Reptile and Amphibian Scientific Advisory Group, Middlebury. 64 pp.

Andrle, R. F. 1964. A biogeographical investigation of the Sierra de Tuxtla in Veracruz, Mexico. Ph.D. dissertation, Louisiana State University. 236 pp.

Angel-Mejía., R. 1982. Serpientes de Colombia. Guía práctica para su clasificación y tratamiento del envenenamiento causado por sus mordeduras. Revista Facultad Nacional de Agronomía Medellín 36(1): 1–171.

——. 1987a. Serpientes de Colombia. Su relación con el hombre. Academia de Medicina de Medillín, Colombia. 231 pp.

——. 1987b. Serpientes de Colombia. Su relación con el hombre. Ediciones Especiales del Fondo Rotatorio de Publicaciones, Secretaría de Educación y Cultura de Antioquia. Academia de Medicina de Medellín, Homenaje, Medellín, Colombia. 229 pp.

Anonymous. 1870. *Heloderma horridum* from Guaymas. Proc. California Acad. Sci. 4: 55.

Anthony, J. 1955. Essai sur l'évolution anatomique de l'appareil venimeux des ophidians. Annales des Sciences Naturelles 17: 7–53.

Anton, T. G. 1993. Massasaugas in Lake County, Illinois: the Ryerson population. Pp. 71–77 in B. Johnson and V. Menzies (eds.), International symposium and workshop on the conservation of the eastern massasauga rattlesnake *Sistrurus catenatus catenatus*. Toronto Zoo, Toronto.

——. 1994. Observations of predatory behavior in the regal ringneck snake (*Diadophis punctatus regalis*) under captive conditions. Bull. Chicago Herpetol. Soc. 29(5): 95.

——. 2000. Natural history notes: *Sistrurus catenatus* (massasauga). Litter size. Herpetol. Rev. 31(4): 248.

Antonio, F. B. 1980. Mating behavior and reproduction of the eyelash viper (*Bothrops schlegeli*) in captivity. Herpetologica 36(3): 231–233.

Antonio, F. B., and J. B. Barker. 1983. An inventory of phenotypic aberrancies in the eastern diamondback rattlesnake (*Crotalus adamanteus*). Herpetol. Rev. 14(4): 108–110.

Applegate, R. D. 1995. Natural history notes: *Sistrurus catenatus catenatus* (eastern massasauga): food habits. Herpetol. Rev. 26(4): 206.

Appun, K. F. 1961. En los trópicos. Imprenta Universitaria Central de Venezuela, Caracas. 519 pp.

Aquino, A. L., N. J. Scott, and M. Motte. 1996. Lista de anfibios y reptiles del Museo Nacional de Historia Natural del Paraguay (Marzo de 1980–Septiembre de 1995). Pp. 331–400 in O. R. Martínez (ed.), Colecciones de flora y fauna del Museo Nacional de Historia Natural del Paraguay. Ministerio de Agricultura y Ganadería, Asunción, Paraguay.

Aragón, F., and F. Gubensek. 1981. *Bothrops asper* venom from the Atlantic and Pacific zones of Costa Rica. Toxicon 19: 797–805.

Araujo, P. 1969. Nouvelle espèce d'*Ophidascaris* Baylis 1921, parasite du serpent crotale (*Crotalus durissus terrificus*). Annales de Parasitologie Humaine et Comparé 44(4): 441–450.

——. 1971. Observations sur le développement de l'ébauche génitale chez des larves du 3° stade de *Polydelphis quadrangularis* (Schneider, 1866) (Nematoda, Ascaridoidea). Annales de Parasitologie Humaine et Comparé 46(6): 699–707.

Arbingast, S. A. 1975. Atlas of Mexico, 2d ed. Bureau of Business Research, University of Texas at Austin, Austin, Texas. 164 pp.

Ariaratnam, C. A., W. P. Meyer, G. Perera, M. Eddleston, S. A. Kuleratne, W. Attapattu, R. Sheriff, A. M. Richards, R. D. G. Theakston, and D. A. Warrell. 1999. A new monospecific ovine Fab fragment antivenom for treatment of envenoming by the Sri Lankan Russell's viper (*Daboia russelii russelii*): a preliminary dose-finding and pharmacokinetic study. American Journal of Tropical Medicine and Hygiene 61(2): 259–265.

Ariaratnam, C. A., L. Sjöström, Z. Raziek, S. A. Kularatne, R. W. Arachchi, M. H. Sheriff, R. D. Theakston, and D. A. Warrell. 2001. An open, randomized comparative trial of two antivenoms for the treatment of envenoming by Sri Lankan Russell's viper (*Daboia russelii russelii*). Trans. Roy. Soc. Trop. Med. Hyg. 95: 74–80.

Armstrong, B. L., and J. B. Murphy. 1979. The natural history of Mexican rattlesnakes. Special Publication of the Museum of Natural History, University of Kansas, No. 5. 88 pp.

Arnberger, L. P. 1948. Gila monster swallows quail eggs whole. Herpetologica 4(6): 209–210.

Arny, S. A. 1948. A survey of the reptiles and amphibians of the Delta National Wildlife Refuge. Master's thesis, Tulane University.

Arrington, O. N. 1930. Notes on the two poisonous lizards with special reference to *Heloderma suspectum*. Bull. Antivenin Inst. Am. 4(2): 29–35.

Arroyo, O., R. Bolaños, and G. Muñoz. 1980. The bacterial flora of venoms and mouth cavities of Costa Rican snakes. Bulletin of the Pan American Health Organization 14: 280–285.

Arroyo, O., J. P. Rosso, O. Vargas, J. M. Gutiérrez, and L. Cerdas. 1987. Skeletal muscle necrosis induced by phospholipase A_2 isolated from the venom of the coralsnake (*Micrurus nigrocinctus nigrocinctus*). Comp. Biochem. Physiol. B 87: 949–952.

Arzola, J., and H. Schenone. 1994. Dos nuevos casos de ofidismo en Chile. Boletin Chileno de Parasitologia 49: 69–70.

Ashton, K. G. 1999. Shedding aggregations of *Crotalus virdis concolor*. Herpetol. Rev. 30(4): 211–213.

——. 2000. Notes on the island populations of the western rattlesnake, *Crotalus viridis*. Herpetol. Rev. 31(4): 214–217.

——. 2001. Body size variation among mainland populations of the western rattlesnake (*Crotalus viridis*). Evolution 55(12): 2523–2533.

Ashton, K. G., and A. de Queiroz. 2001. Molecular systematics of the western rattlesnake, *Crotalus viridis* (Viperidae), with comments on the utility of the D-loop in phylogenetic studies of snakes. Molecular Phylogenetics and Evolution 21(2): 176–189.

Ashton, K. G., and J. Johnson. 1998. Natural history notes: *Crotalus viridis concolor* (midget faded rattlesnake). Drinking from skin. Herpetol. Rev. 29(3): 170.

Ashton, K. G., and T. M. Patton. 2001. Movement and reproductive biology of female midget faded rattlesnakes, *Crotalus viridis concolor*, in Wyoming. Copeia 2001(1): 229–234.

Ashton, K. G., H. M. Smith, and D. Chiszar. 1997. Geographic distribution: *Crotalus viridis viridis* (prairie rattlesnake). Herpetol. Rev. 28(3): 159.

Ashton, R. E. 1976. Endangered and threatened amphibians and reptiles in the United States. Society for the Study of Amphibians and Reptiles, Herpetological Circular No. 5. 65 pp.

——. 1978. Identification manual to the amphibians and reptiles of Florida. University of Florida Interpretation Series No. 1. Florida State Museum Associates, Gainesville. 25 pp.

Ashton, R. E., Jr., and P. S. Ashton. 1981. Handbook of reptiles and amphibians of Florida. Part one. The snakes. Windward Publishing, Miami. 176 pp.

Assakura, M. T., M. da Graça Salomão, G. Puorto, and F. R. Mandelbaum. 1992. Hemorrhagic, fibrinolytic and edema-forming activities of the venom of the colubrid snake *Philodryas olfersi* (green snake). Toxicon 30: 427–438.

Assakura, M. T., A. P. Reichl, and F. R. Mandelbaum. 1994. Isolation and characterisation of five fibrin(ogen)olytic enzymes from the Duvernoy's secretion of *Philodryas olfersii* (green snake). Toxicon 32: 819–831.

Ast, J. C. 2001. Mitochondrial DNA evidence and evolution in Varanoidea (Squamata). Cladistics 17: 211–226.

Astort, E. 1988. La cascabel. Pp. 1–3 in Anfíbios y reptiles. Fauna Argentina 2. Centro Editor de América Latina, Tucumán, Argentina.

Atkinson, D. A. 1901. The reptiles of Allegheny County, Pa. Annals of Carnegie Museum 1: 145–157.

——. 1907. Notes on a collection of batrachians and reptiles from Central America. Ohio Naturalist 7(7): 151–157.

Atkinson, D. A., and M. G. Netting. 1927. The distribution and habits of the massasauga. Bull. Antivenin Inst. Am. 1(2): 40–44.

Attenborough, D. 1956. Zooquest to Guiana. Lutterworth Press, Cambridge, U.K. 146 pp.

Audubon, J. W. 1906. Audubon's western journal, 1849–1850. Arthur H. Clark, Cleveland. 249 pp.

Auth, D. L. 1994. Checklist and bibliography of the amphibians and reptiles of Panama. Smithsonian Herpetological Information Service 98: 1–59.

Auth, D. L., H. M. Smith, B. C. Brown, and D. Lintz. 2000. A description of the Mexican amphibian and reptile collection of the Strecker Museum. Bull. Chicago Herpetol. Soc. 35(4): 65–85.

Avila, L. J., and M. Morando. 1998. Natural history notes: *Bothrops ammodytoides* (yarará ñata, Patagonian lancehead). Prey. Herpetol. Rev. 29(3): 169.

Avila, L. J., and J. C. Moreta. 1995. *Bothrops neuwiedi bolivianus* Amaral. Cuadernos de Herpetología 9(1): 57.

Avise, J. C., J. Arnold, R. M. Ball, E. Bermingham, T. Lamb, J. E. Neigel, C. A. Reeb, and N. C. Saunders. 1987. Intraspecific phylogeography—the mitochondrial-DNA bridge between population genetics and systematics. Annual Review of Ecology and Systematics 18: 489–522.

Axtell, R. W. 1956. [Size maxima in the western diamond-backed rattlesnake.] Texas Journal of Science 8(3): frontispiece.

——. 1959. Amphibians and reptiles of the Black Gap Wildlife Management Area, Brewster County, Texas. Southwest. Nat. 4(2): 88–109.

Axtell, R. W., and M. D. Sabath. 1963. *Crotalus pricei miquihuanus* from the Sierra Madre of Coahuila, Mexico. Copeia 1964(1): 161–164.

Axtell, R. W., and A. O. Wasserman. 1953. Interesting herpetological records from southern Texas and northern Mexico. Herpetologica 9: 1–6.

Ayerbe, S. 1979. Pautas para el manejo de las mordeduras de serpiente. Cuadernos de Medicina, Facultad de Medicina, Universidad del Cauca, Popayán (Colombia) 4(1–2): 46–55.

——. 1981. Ofidiotoxicosis micrúrica en el Cauca. Reporte de un caso fatal. Popayán (mimeo), 7 pp.

——. 1990. Bothropic envenomation in Colombia: changes in hematological tests (abstract). Journal of Toxicology—Toxin Reviews 9(1): 130–131.

——. 1995. Pautas para el manejo de las mordeduras de serpientes. Temas de Pediatría 133: 1–10.

——. 2000. Ofidismo en el Departamento del Cauca, Colombia. Epidemiología, etiología, clínica y complicaciones. Revista de la Facultad de Ciencias de la Salud, Universidad del Cauca, Popayán, Colombia, 2(4): 21–27.

——. 2001. Tratamiento del ofidismo en el Departamento del Cauca, Colombia. Revista de la Facultad de Ciencias de la Salud, Universidad del Cauca, Popayán, Colombia, 3(1): 20–26.

Ayerbe, S., and F. J. López. 2002. Descripción de una nueva especie de serpiente coral (Elapidae: *Micrurus*). Memorias II Simposio de Investigación en Ciencias Biológicas, Departamento de Biología, Universidad del Cauca, Asociación Colombiana de Ciencias Biológicas, Capítulo Popayán. Ponencia 12, February 12–13, 2002. 2 pp.

Ayerbe, S., L. M. Otero, D. Galvez, and A. Paredes. 1977. Estudio retrospectivo sobre ofidiotoxicosis en el Departmento del Cauca. 1ª Parte. Cuadernos de Medicina, Facultad de Medicina, Universidad del Cauca, Popayán (Colombia) 2: 1–7.

Ayerbe, S., A. Paredes, and D. A. Gálvez. 1979. Estudio retrospectivo sobre ofidiotoxicosis en el Departamento del Cauca. 2ª Parte. Aspectos clinicos, epidemiológicos y complicaciones. Cuadernos de Medicina, Facultad de Medicina, Universidad del Cauca, Popayán (Colombia) 4(1–2): 33–45.

Ayerbe, S., M. A. Tidwell, and M. Tidwell. 1990. Observaciones sobre la biología y comportamiento de la serpiente coral "rabo de aji" (*Micrurus mipartitus*). Descripción de una subespecie nueva. Novedades Colombianas, Museo de Historia Natural, Universidad del Cauca, Popayán, 2: 30–41.

Azevedo, A. C. P. 1960. Notes on coral snakes (Serpentes, Elapidae). I. About the eggs of coral snakes. II. A new observation of the behavior of *Micrurus frontalis multicinctus* and its relationship with folklore. Iheringia, Zoologia 14: 1–13.

——. 1961. Notas sôbre cobras corais (Serpentes-Elapidae) III a VII. Iheringia, Zoologia 18: 1–23.

——. 1962a. Anomalias observadas em serpentes do genero *Micrurus* Wagler, 1824 (Serpentes, Elapidae). Iheringia, Zoologia 26: 1–6.

——. 1962b. Sôbre uma população de *Micrurus frontalis frontalis* (D. & B., 1854) de Lagoa Santa, Minas Gerais, Brasil (Serpentes, Elapidae). Iheringia, Zoologia 27: 1–3.

——. 1964. Variaçães cromáticas em *Micrurus corallinus* (Wied, 1820) (Serpentes: Elapidae). Iheringia, Zoologia 34: 1–15.

Azevedo-Marques, M. M., P. Cupo, T. M. Coimbra, S. E. Hering, M. A. Rossi, and C. J. Laure. 1985. Myonecrosis, myoglobinuria, and acute renal failure induced by South American rattlesnake (*Crotalus durissus terrificus*) envenomation in Brazil. Toxicon 23: 621–636.

Azevedo-Marques, M. M., S. E. Hering, and P. Cupo. 1987. Evidence that *Crotalus durissus terrificus* South American rattlesnake envenomation in humans causes myolysis rather than hemolysis. Toxicon 25(11): 1163–1168.

Baarslag, A. F. 1950. The pilot blacksnake and timber rattlesnake in Vermont. Copeia 1950(4): 322–323.

Babb, R. D., J. K. Aitken, and D. Delisle. 1989. Life history notes: *Micruroides euryxanthus* (Arizona coral snake). Size. Herpetol. Rev. 20(2): 53.

Babbitt, L. H. 1932. Some remarks on Connecticut herpetology. Bulletin of the Boston Society of Natural History 63: 23–28.

Babbitt, L. H., and T. E. Graham. 1972. Snakes of Massachusetts. Massachusetts Wildlife 23(6): 7–9, 14–19.

Babcock, H. L. 1925. Rattlesnakes in Massachusetts. Bulletin of the Boston Society of Natural History 35: 5–10.

——. 1929. The snakes of New England. Boston Society of Natural History, Natural History Guides, No. 1, 30 pp.

Babero, B. B., and F. H. Emmerson. 1974. *Thubunaea cnemidophorus* in Nevada rattlesnakes. Journal of Parasitolgy 60: 595.

Babis, W. A. 1949. Notes on the food of the indigo snake. Copeia 1949(2): 147.

Badillo, R., M. Casas, and G. Gamarra. 1989. Ofidiotoxicosis en el Hospital Universitario Ramón González Valencia de Bucaramanga. Acta Médica Colombiana 14(6): 352–368.

Badman, J. A. 2001. Geographic distribution: *Crotalus tigris*. Herpetol. Rev. 32(3): 194.

Bahena-Basave, H. 1995. Geographic distribution: *Micrurus browni*. Herpetol. Rev. 26(1): 46.

Bailey, R. M. 1942. An intergeneric hybrid rattlesnake. American Naturalist 76: 376–385.

Bailey, V. 1905. Report on the biological survey collection of lizards and snakes from Texas. North American Fauna 25: 38–51.

Baird, S. F. 1854. On the serpents of New-York; with a notice of a species not hitherto included in the fauna of the state. C. Van Benthuysen, Albany, N.Y. 28 pp.

———. 1859a. Reptiles of the boundary, with notes by the naturalists on the survey. Pp. 1–35 in W. H. Emory (ed.), Report on the United States and Mexican Boundary Survey, vol. 2. Zoology of the Boundary. GPO, Washington, D.C.

———. 1859b. Report on reptiles collected on the survey. Reports of explorations and surveys, to ascertain the most practicable and economical route for a railroad from the Mississippi River to the Pacific Ocean, vol. 10(4): 13–16. Washington, D.C.

———. 1875. Affinities of *Heloderma horridum*. Annual Record of Science and Industry 1874: 308.

Baird, S. F., and C. Girard. 1852. Descriptions of new species of reptiles collected by the U.S. Exploring Expedition, Captain Wilkes. Proc. Acad. Nat. Sci. Philadelphia 6: 174–177.

———. 1853. Catalogue of North American reptiles in the Museum of the Smithsonian Institution. Part I—Serpents. GPO, Washington, D.C. 172 pp.

Bajwa, S. S., F. S. Markland, and F. E. Russell. 1980. Fibrinolytic enzyme(s) in western diamondback rattlesnake (*Crotalus atrox*) venom. Toxicon 18: 285–290.

Baker, R. E. 1983. The western cottonmouth in Osage County, Oklahoma. Mountain Boomer, Bulletin of the Oklahoma Herpetological Society 8: 56–57.

———. 1985. Late season capture of the western cottonmouth, *Agkistrodon piscivorus leucostoma*, in northern Osage County, Oklahoma. Mountain Boomer, Bulletin of the Oklahoma Herpetological Society 10: 23.

Baker, R. H., and R. G. Webb. 1967 [dated 1966]. Notas acerca de los anfibios, reptiles y mamíferos de la Pesca, Tamaulipas. Revista de la Sociedad Mexicana de Historia Natural 27: 179–190.

Baker, R. H., R. G. Webb, and E. Stern. 1971. Amphibians, reptiles, and mammals from north-central Chiapas. Anales del Instituto de Biología, Universidad Nacional Autónoma de México 42: 77–86.

Baker, R. J., G. A. Mengden, and J. J. Bull. 1972. Karyotypic studies of thirty-eight species of North American snakes. Copeia 1972(2): 257–265.

Baldauf, R. J. 1957. Records of *Ancistrodon piscivorus leucostoma* (Troost). Copeia 1957(3): 229.

Baldwin, A. S. 1999. Case report on an untreated human envenomation by the western massasauga rattlesnake *Sistrurus catenatus tergeminus*. Bull. Maryland Herpetol. Soc. 35(1): 14–20.

Ball, R. L. 1975. Geographic distribution: *Sistrurus miliarius streckeri* (western pigmy rattlesnake). Herpetol. Rev. 6(2): 45.

Balmain, R., and K. L. McClelland. 1982. Pantyhose compression bandage: first-aid measure for snake bite. Medical Journal of Australia 2: 240–241.

Bancroft, E. 1769. An essay on the natural history of Guiana, in South America. T. Becket and P. A. DeHondt, London. 402 pp.

Banks, R. C. 1962. A history of explorations for vertebrates on Cerralvo Island, Baja California. Proc. California Acad. Sci., 4th ser., 30(6): 117–125.

Banner, W. 1988. Bites and stings in the pediatric patient. Current Problems in Pediatrics 18: 9–69.

Banta, B. H. 1962. The amphibians and reptiles from the state of Aguascalientes, Mexico, in the collections of the California Academy of Sciences. Wasmann Journal of Biology 20(1): 99–105.

———. 1965a. An annotated chronological bibliography of the herpetology of the state of Nevada. Wasmann Journal of Biology 23: 1–224.

———. 1965b. A distributional check list of the recent reptiles inhabiting the state of Nevada. Biological Society of Nevada Occasional Papers 5: 1–8.

Banton, H. J. 1930. A snake doctor of the Mosquito Coast. Military Surgery 67: 474–478.

Barbour, R. W. 1950. The reptiles of Big Black Mountain, Harlan County, Kentucky. Copeia 1950(2): 100–107.

———. 1956. A study of the cottonmouth, *Ancistrodon piscivorus* Troost, in Kentucky. Transactions of the Kentucky Academy of Science 17: 33–41.

———. 1962. An aggregation of copperheads, *Agkistrodon contortrix*. Copeia 1962(3): 640.

———. 1971. Amphibians and reptiles of Kentucky. University Press of Kentucky, Lexington. 334 pp.

Barbour, T. 1905. The vertebrata of Gorgona Island, Colombia. V. Reptilia and Amphibia. Bulletin of the Museum of Comparative Zoology 46: 98–102.

———. 1906. Vertebrata from the savanna of Panama. IV. Reptilia and amphibia. Bulletin of the Museum of Comparative Zoology 46(12): 224–229.

———. 1912. A contribution to the zoögeography of the East Indian islands. Memoirs of the Museum of Comparative Zoology 44(1): 1–203.

———. 1913. Reptiles collected by the Yale Peruvian expedition of 1912. Proc. Acad. Nat. Sci. Philadelphia 65: 505–507.

———. 1914. A contribution to the zoogeography of the West Indies, with special reference to amphibians and reptiles. Memoirs of the Museum of Comparative Zoology 64(2): 209–347.

———. 1916. Amphibians and reptiles from Tobago. Proceedings of the Biological Society of Washington 29: 221–224.

———. 1921. Some reptiles from Old Providence Island. Proceedings of the New England Zoölogical Club 7: 81–85.

———. 1922. Rattlesnakes and spitting cobras. Copeia 1922: 36–38.

———. 1923. Notes on reptiles and amphibians from Panama. Occas. Pap. Mus. Zool. Univ. Michigan 129: 1–16.

———. 1926. Reptiles and amphibians: their habits and adaptations. Houghton Mifflin, Boston. 125 pp.

———. 1928. Reptiles from the Bay Islands. Proceedings of the New England Zoölogical Club 10: 55–61.

———. 1930. The bushmaster in the Canal Zone. Bull. Antivenin Inst. Am. 4(1): 11.

Barbour, T., and A. do Amaral. 1924. Notes on some Central American snakes. Occasional Papers of the Boston Society of Natural History 5: 129–132.

———. 1928. A new elapid from western Panama. Bull. Antivenin Inst. Am. 1(4): 100.

Barbour, T., and W. S. Brooks. 1923. The Sapo Mountains and the Sambú Valley. A biological reconnaissance in southeastern Panama. Geographical Review 13: 211–222.

Barbour, T., and A. Loveridge. 1929a. On *Bothrops atrox* (Linné). Bull. Antivenin Inst. Am. 2(4): 108.

———. 1929b. On some Honduranian and Guatemalan snakes with the description of a new arboreal pit viper of the genus *Bothrops*. Bull. Antivenin Inst. Am. 3(1): 1–3.

———. 1929c. Reptiles and amphibians [of the Corn Islands]. Bulletin of the Museum of Comparative Zoology 69: 138–146.

———. 1929d. Typical amphibians and reptiles in the Museum of Comparative Zoology. Bulletin of the Museum of Comparative Zoology 69(10): 203–360.

Barbour, T., and G. K. Noble. 1920. Amphibians and reptiles from southern Peru collected by the Peruvian expedition of 1914–1915 under the auspices of Yale University and the National Geographic Society. Proceedings of the U.S. National Museum 58: 609–620.

Bard, R., J. C. de Lima, R. P. de Sa Neto, S. G. de Oliveira, and M. C. dos Santos. 1994. Ineficacia do antiveneno botrópico na neutralização da atividade coagulante do veneno de *Lachesis muta*. Relato de caso comprovação experimental. Revista do Instituto de Medicina Tropical de São Paulo 36: 77–81.

Barker, D. G. 1991. An investigation of the natural history of the New Mexico ridgenose rattlesnake, *Crotalus willardi obscurus*. Unpublished report to the New Mexico Department of Game and Fish. 99 pp.

——. 1992. Variation, infraspecific relationships, and biogeography of the ridgenose rattlesnake, *Crotalus willardi*. Pp. 89–106 in J. A. Campbell and E. D. Brodie Jr. (eds.), Biology of the pitvipers. Selva, Tyler, Texas.

Barrantes, A., V. Solís, and R. Bolaños. 1985. Alteración de los mecanismos de la coagulación en el envenenamiento por *Bothrops asper* (Terciopelo). Toxicon 23: 399–407.

Barraviera, B., J. C. Bonjorno Jr., D. Arkaki, M. A. Domingues, P. C. Pereira, R. P. Mendes, J. M. Machado, D. A. Meira. 1989. A retrospective study of 40 victims of *Crotalus* snake bites. Analysis of the hepatic necrosis observed in one patient. Revista da Sociedade Brasileira Medicina Tropical 22(1): 5–12.

Barrera, A. 1963 [dated 1962]. La península de Yucatán como provincia biótica. Revista de la Sociedad Mexicana de Historia Natural 23: 71–105.

Barrio, A. 1961a [dated 1960]. Consideraciones en torno a *Crotalus terrificus crotaminicus* Moura Goncalves. Physis 22(63): 141–147.

——. 1961b [dated 1960]. Distribución del género *Bothrops* Wagler (Ophidia, Crotalidae) en la provincia de Buenos Aires. Physis 22(63): 211–215.

Barrio, A., and O. V. Brazil. 1954. Acción neuromuscular de los venenos de *Crotalus terrificus terrificus* (Laur.). Revista del Instituto Malbran (Buenos Aires) 16(1): 22–40.

Barrio, A., and M. E. Miranda. 1967a [dated 1966]. Estudio comparativo morfológico e inmunológico entre diferentes entidades del género *Micrurus* Wagler (Ophidia, Elapidae) de la Argentina. Mem. Inst. Butantan 33(3): 869–880.

——. 1967b [dated 1966]. Las diferentes poblaciones de *Bothrops alternata* Duméril y Bibron (Ophidia, Crotalidae) de la Argentina, consideradas desde el punto de vista morfológico y antigénico. Mem. Inst. Butantan 33(3): 887–892.

Barrio, C. L. 2001. Geographic distribution: *Micrurus dumerilii carinicauda*. Herpetol. Rev. 32(4): 279.

Barrio-Amorós, C. L., and D. Calcaño. 2003. First record of *Micrurus lemniscatus* (Linnaeus, 1758) from western Venezuela with comments on coral snakes from the eastern Andean piedmont. Herpetozoa 16(1–2): 73–78.

Bartholomew, B., and R. D. Nohavec. 1995. Saltation in snakes with a note on escape saltation in a *Crotalus scutulatus*. Great Basin Naturalist 55(3): 282–283.

Bartlett, R. D., and P. Bartlett. 1999. A field guide to Florida reptiles and amphibians. Gulf Publishing, Houston, Texas. 280 pp.

Basey, H. E. 1988. Discovering Sierra reptiles and amphibians. 2d ed. Yosemite Association, U.S. Department of Interior. 50 pp.

Bates, H. W. 1862. Contributions to an insect fauna of the Amazon Valley, Lepidoptera: Heliconiidae. Transactions of the Linnean Society of London 23: 495–566.

Bates, L. B. 1928. Snakes and snake-bite accidents of the Panama Canal Zone. Bull. Antivenin Inst. Am. 2(2): 31–33.

Batistic, R. F., P. A. Federsoni Jr., S. C. R. Calixto, and N. Vitello. 1999. Partenogênese facultiva em *Bothrops moojeni*: um caso. P. 36, Abstracts of the V Congreso Latinoamericano de Herpetología, Montevideo, 12 al 17 de diciembre de 1999.

Bauab, F. A., G. R. Junqueira, M. C. Morato-Corradini, P. V. Silveira, and S. de A. Nishioka. 1994. Clinical and epidemiological aspects of the "urutu" lance-headed viper (*Bothrops alternatus*) bite in a Brazilian hospital. Tropical Medicine and Parasitology 45: 243–245.

Bauer, A. M., R. Günther, and M. Klipfel. 1995. The herpetological contributions of Wilhelm C. H. Peters (1813–1883). Facsimile

Reprints in Herpetology, Society for the Study of Amphibians and Reptiles. 714 pp.

Baxter. 1930. [Article on coralsnake.] Augusta Chronicle, August 17.

Baxter, G. T., and M. D. Stone. 1985. Amphibians and reptiles of Wyoming, 2d ed. Wyoming Game and Fish Department, Cheyenne. 137 pp.

Bayless, L. E. 1979. New herpetological records from southern West Virginia, USA. Proceedings of the West Virginia Academy of Science 51(2): 65–67.

Beaman, K. R., and L. L. Grismer. 1994. *Crotalus enyo* (Cope): Baja California rattlesnake. Catalogue of American Amphibians and Reptiles 589.1–589.6.

Beaman, K. R., and N. Wong. 2001. *Crotalus catalinensis* Cliff, Santa Catalina Island rattleless rattlesnake. Catalogue of American Amphibians and Reptiles 733.1–733.4.

Bean, B. A. 1924. A curious fish trap. Copeia 1924(131): 57–58.

Beane, J. C. 1998. New distributional records for reptiles from North Carolina. Herpetol. Rev. 29(1): 56–58.

Beaupre, S. J. 1993. An ecological study of oxygen consumption in the mottled rock rattlesnake, *Crotalus lepidus lepidus*, and the black-tailed rattlesnake, *Crotalus molossus molossus*, from two populations. Physiological Zoology 66(3): 437–454.

——. 1995a. Effects of geographically variable thermal environments on bioenergetics of mottled rock rattlesnakes. Ecology 76(5): 1655–1665.

——. 1995b. Comparative ecology of the mottled rock rattlesnake, *Crotalus lepidus*, in Big Bend National Park. Herpetologica 51(1): 45–56.

——. 1996. Field metabolic rate, water flux, and energy budgets of mottled rock rattlesnakes, *Crotalus lepidus*, from two populations. Copeia 1996(2): 319–329.

Beaupre, S. J., and D. Duvall. 1998a. Integrative biology of rattlesnakes. BioScience 48(7): 531–538.

——. 1998b. Variation in oxygen consumption of the western diamondback rattlesnake (*Crotalus atrox*): implications for sexual size dimorphism. Journal of Comparative Physiology B 168: 497–506.

Beaupre, S. J., D. Duvall, and J. O'Leile. 1998. Ontogenetic variation in growth and sexual size dimorphism in a central Arizona population of the western diamondback rattlesnake (*Crotalus atrox*). Copeia 1998(1): 40–47.

Beaupre, J. J., and K. G. Roberts. 2001. Natural history notes: *Agkistrodon contortrix contortrix* (southern copperhead), chemotaxis, arboreality, and diet. Herpetol. Rev. 32(1): 44–45.

Beavers, R. A. 1976. Food habits of the western diamondback rattlesnake, *Crotalus atrox*, in Texas (Viperidae). Southwest. Nat. 20(4): 503–515.

Beçak, W. 1965. Constituição cromossômica e mecanismo de determinação do sexo em ofídios sul-americanos. I. Aspectos cariotípicos. Mem. Inst. Butantan 32: 37–78.

——. 1971. Karyotypes, sex chromosomes, and chromosomal evolution in snakes. Pp. 53–96 in W. Bücherl, E. Buckley, and V. Deulofeu (eds.), Venomous animals and their venoms, vol. 1. Academic Press, New York.

Beçak, W., and M. L. Beçak. 1969. Cytotaxonomy and chromosomal evolution in serpents. Cytogenetics 8(4): 247–362.

Bechtel, H. B. 1978. Color and pattern in snakes (Reptilia, Serpentes). J. Herpetol. 12: 521–532.

——. 1995. Reptile and amphibian color pattern variants. Kreiger, Malabar, Fla.

Beck, D. D. 1985a. Life history notes: *Heloderma suspectum cinctum* (banded Gila monster). Pattern/coloration. Herpetol. Rev. 16(2): 53.

——. 1985b. The natural history, distribution, and present status of the Gila monster in Utah. Unpublished report submitted to the Utah Division of Wildlife Resources. 78 pp.

——. 1990. Ecology and behavior of the Gila monster in southwestern Utah. J. Herpetol. 24(1): 54–68.

——. 1993. A retrospective of "The Gila monster and its allies." Pp. xvii–xx in C. M. Bogert and R. Martín del Campo, The Gila monster and its allies. Reprinted by the Society for the Study of Amphibians and Reptiles, Oxford, Ohio. 242 pp.

——. 1995. Ecology and energetics of three sympatric rattlesnake species in the Sonoran Desert. J. Herpetol. 29(2): 211–223.

——. 2004. Biology of Gila monsters and beaded lizards. University of California Press.

Beck, D. D., M. R. Dhohm, T. Garland, A. Ramírez-Bautista, and C. H. Lowe. 1995. Locomotor performance and activity energetics of helodermatid lizards. Copeia 1995: 577–585.

Beck, D. D., and C. H. Lowe. 1991. Ecology of the beaded lizard, *Heloderma horridum*, in a tropical dry forest in Jalisco, Mexico. J. Herpetol. 25: 395–406.

——. 1994. Resting metabolism of helodermatid lizards: allometric and ecological relationships. Journal of Comparative Physiology B, 164(2): 124–129.

Beck, D. D., and A. Ramírez-Bautista. 1991. Combat behavior of the beaded lizard, *Heloderma h. horridum*, in Jalisco, Mexico. J. Herpetol. 25(4): 481–484.

Beckers, G., and T. Leenders. 1994. Color patterns of Costa Rican coral snakes. Report 320, Department of Ecology, Research Group Animal Ecology, University of Nijmegen, the Netherlands. 27 pp.

Beckers, G. J., T. Leenders, and H. Strijbosch. 1996. Coral snake mimicry: live snakes not avoided by a mammalian predator. Oecologia 106: 461–463.

Beddard, F. E. 1907. Contributions to the knowledge of the systematic arrangement and anatomy of certain genera and species of Squamata. Proc. Zool. Soc. London 1907: 36–68.

Bedry, R., et al. 1998. Is the saliva of the European whip snake (*Coluber viridiflavus*) neurotoxic? Toxicon 36(12): 1729–1730.

Beebe, [C.] W. 1905. Two bird-lovers in Mexico. Houghton Mifflin, Boston. 407 pp.

—— 1919. The higher vertebrates of British Guiana with special reference to the fauna of Bartica District No. 7. List of amphibia, reptilia and mammalia. Zoologica (New York) 2(7): 205–227.

——. 1946. Field notes on the snakes of Kartabo, British Guiana, and Caripito, Venezuela. Zoologica (New York) 31(1–4): 11–52.

——. 1947. Snake skins and color. Copeia 1947(3): 205–206.

——. 1952. High jungle. Readers Union, London. 234 pp.

Behler, J. L., B. Winn, and R. H. Hayes Jr. 1997. Snake fauna of St. Catherines Island, Georgia. Herpetol. Rev. 28(3): 162.

Belding, L. 1887. Reptiles of the cape region of lower California. West American Scientist 3(24): 97–99.

Bellairs, A. 1969. The life of reptiles, 2 vols. Weidenfeld and Nicolson, London. 590 pp.

Belluomini, H. E. 1971. Extraction and quantities of venom obtained from some Brazilian snakes. Pp. 97–118 in W. Bücherl, E. Buckley, and V. Deulofeu (eds.), Venomous animals and their venoms, vol. 1. Academic Press, New York.

Belluomini, H. E., P. De Biasi, G. Puorto, W. Fernandes, and A. L. Domingues. 1991. Amostras de poulação de *Bothrops atrox* (Linnaeus 1758) apreciadas nas quantidades de veneno obtidas e dados ecológicos (Serpentes: Viperidae: Crotalinae). Boletim do Museu Paraense Emílio Goeldi, Zoologia 7(1): 53–69.

Benítez-Gálvez, J. E. 1997. Los ofidios de Puebla. Gobierno del Estado de Puebla, Puebla, México. 123 pp.

Benson, S. B. 1932. Three new rodents from lava beds of southern New Mexico. University of California Publications in Zoology 38: 335–344.

Benvenuti, L. A., F. O. de S. França, K. C. Barbaro, J. R. Nunes, and J. L. C. Cardoso. 2003. Pulmonary haemorrhage causing rapid death after *Bothrops jararacussu* snakebite—a case report. Toxicon 42(3): 331–334.

Berg, C. 1884. Reptiles in C. L. Holmberg, Viajes al Tandil y a La Tina. Acta Académica, Córdova 5: 93–96.

——. 1898. Contribuciones al conocimiento de la fauna herpetológica Argentina y de los paises limítrofes. Anales del Museo Nacional de Historia Natural de Buenos Aires 6: 1–35.

Berger, T. J. 1974. Geographic distribution: *Sistrurus miliarius streckeri* (western pigmy rattlesnake). Herpetol. Rev. 5(1): 21.

Berish, J. E. D. 1998. Characterization of rattlesnake harvest in Florida. J. Herpetol. 32(4): 551–557.

Berlandier, J. L. 1980. Journey to Mexico during the years 1826 to 1834, 2 vols. Trans. S. M. Ohlendorf, J. M. Bigelow, and M. M. Standifer. Texas State Historical Association and the Center for Studies in Texas History at the University of Texas at Austin. 672 pp.

Berna, H. J., and J. W. Gibbons. 1991. Life history notes: *Agkistrodon piscivorus piscivorus* (eastern cottonmouth). Diet. Herpetol. Rev. 22(4): 130–131.

Bernstein, J. N., R. C. Dart, and D. Hardy. 1992. Natural history of envenomation by the twin spotted rattlesnake (*Crotalus p. pricei*). Veterinary and Human Toxicology 34: 341.

Berthold, A. A. 1846 [dated 1845]. Ueber verschiedene neue oder seltene Reptilien aus New Granada und Crustacien aus China. Abhandlungen der Gesellschaft der Wissenschaften zu Göttingen 3: 3–32.

Berthold, G. 1959. Algunas consideraciones sobre la tigre mariposa (*Bothrops medusa*), su veneno y mordedura. Memoria de la Sociedad de Ciencias Naturales La Salle 19(52): 17–22.

Bertoni, A. W. 1914. Fauna Paraguayana. Catálogos sistemáticos de los vertebrados del Paraguay. Peces, batracios, reptiles, aves, y mamíferos conocidos hasta 1913. Pp. 1–83 in M. S. Bertoni (ed.), Descripción física y económica del Paraguay. Asunción.

——. 1939. Catálogos sistemáticos de los vertebrados del Paraguay. Revista de la Sociedad Científica del Paraguay 4(4): 47–49.

Best, I. B. 1978. Field sparrow reproductive success and nesting ecology. Auk 95: 9–22.

Best, T. L., and H. C. James. 1984. Rattlesnakes (genus *Crotalus*) of the Pedro Armendariz lava field, New Mexico. Copeia 1984(1): 213–215.

Best, T. L., H. C. James, and F. H. Best. 1983. Herpetofauna of the Pedro Armendariz lava field, New Mexico. Texas Journal of Science 35(3): 245–256.

Better, O. S. 1999. Rescue and salvage of casualties suffering from the crush syndrome after mass disasters. Military Medicine 164: 366–369.

Betz, T. W. 1963. The gross ovarian morphology of the diamond-backed water snake, *Natrix rhombifera*, during the reproductive cycle. Copeia 1963(4): 692–697.

Beyer, G. E. 1898. Contributions on the life histories of certain snakes. American Naturalist 32: 17–24.

——. 1900. Louisiana herpetology with a check-list of the batrachians and reptiles of the state. Proceedings of the Louisiana Society of Naturalists for 1897–99: 25–46.

Bhatt, B. D., M. J. Zuckerman, J. A. Foland, and L. G. Guerra. 1988. Rattlesnake meat ingestion—a common Hispanic folk remedy. Western Journal of Medicine 149: 605.

Biardi, J. E., R. G. Coss, and D. G. Smith. 2000. California ground squirrel (*Spermophilus beecheyi*) blood sera inhibits crotalid venom proteolytic activity. Toxicon 38(5): 713–721.

Biasi, P. de, H. E. Belluomini and W. Fernandes. 1977a [dated 1976–1977]. Quantidades de veneno obtidas na extração de serpentes *Bothrops pradoi* (Hoge, 1948) (Serpentes, Viperidae, Crotalinae). Mem. Inst. Butantan 40–41: 155–166.

Biasi, P. de, S. Hyakutake, H. E. Belluomini, and C. A. Santa Rosa. 1977b [dated 1976–1977]. Contribuição ao estudo epidemiológico das Leptospiroses em serpentes do Brasil: 1—Levantamento sorológico em *Bothrops pradoi* Hoge, 1948 (Viperidae: Crotalinae). Mem. Inst. Butantan 40–41: 173–180.

Bielema, B. J. 1973. The eastern massasauga (*Sistrurus catenatus*) in west-central Illinois. Master's thesis, Western Illinois University.

Bigney, A. J. 1892. Notes on *Elaps fulvius*. Proceedings of the Indiana Academy of Science 1: 151–152.

Bingham, A. M. 1989. Portrait of an explorer: Hiram Bingham, discoverer of Machu Picchu. University of Iowa Press, Ames. 381 pp.

Bini, L. M., J. A. Diniz Filho, F. Bonfim, and R. P. Bastos. 2000. Local and regional species richness relationships in viperid snake assemblages from South America: unsaturated patterns at three different spatial scales. Copeia 2000(3): 799–805.

Bisbal, F. J. 1990. Inventario preliminar de la fauna del Cerro Santa Ana, de tado Venezuela. Acta Científica Venezolana 41: 177–185.

Bishop, L. A., T. M. Farrell, and P. G. May. 1996. Sexual dimorphism in a Florida population of the rattlesnake *Sistrurus miliarius*. Herpetologica 52(3): 360–364.

Bishop, S. C. 1927. The amphibians and reptiles of Allegany State Park. New York State Museum Handbook 3. University of the State of New York, Albany, New York. 141 pp.

Bishopp, F. C., and H. L. Trembley. 1945. Distribution and hosts of certain North American ticks. Journal of Parasitology 31: 1–54.

Bismuth, C., N. Chouvalidze, F. Baud, C. Soria, L. Drouet, and G. Tobelem. 1983. Defibrination pure après morsure de crotale horridus. Presse Medicale 12: 91–93.

Bjarnason, J. B., and J. W. Fox. 1989. Hemorrhagic toxins from snake venoms. Journal of Toxicology—Toxin Reviews 7: 121–209.

——. 1994. Hemorrhagic toxins from snake venoms: structure, function, target substrates, and relationship to mammalian reproductive proteins. Presented at Eleventh Meeting of the European Section of the International Society of Toxinology. Toxicon 32: 382.

Black, E. R., and C. T. McAllister. 2001. Geographic distribution: *Micrurus fulvius tener* (Texas coral snake). Herpetol. Rev. 32(2): 123–124.

Blair, K. B., F. C. Killebrew, H. M. Smith, and D. Chiszar. 1997. Mexican amphibians and reptiles in the West Texas A&M University Natural History Museum. Bulletin of the Chicago Herpetological Museum 32(8): 174–177.

Blair, W. F. 1958. Distributional patterns of vertebrates in the southwestern United States in relation to past and present environments. Pp. 433–468 in C. L. Hubbs (ed.), Zoogeography. American Association for the Advancement of Science Publication 51. AAAS, Washington, D.C.

Blanchard, F. N. 1922. The amphibians and reptiles of western Tennessee. Occasional Papers of the Museum of Zoology at University of Michigan 177: 1–18.

Blanchard, R. 1889. Remarques critiques sur les serpents du genre *Thanatophis* Posada-Arango. Bulletin de la Société Zoologique de France 14: 346–349.

Blaney, R. M. 1971. An annotated check list and biogeographic analysis of the insular herpetofauna of the Apalachicola Region, Florida. Herpetologica 27(4): 406–430.

Blaney, R. M., and P. K. Blaney. 1978. Notes on three species of *Micrurus* (Serpentes: Elapidae) from Mexico. Herpetol. Rev. 9(3): 92.

——. 1979. Variation in the coral snake, *Micrurus diastema*, in Quintana Roo, Mexico. Herpetologica 35(3): 276–278.

Blem, C. R. 1981. Reproduction of the eastern cottonmouth *Agkistrodon piscivorus piscivorus* (Serpentes: Viperidae) at the northern edge of its range. Brimleyana 5: 117–128.

——. 1982. Biennial reproduction in snakes: an alternate hypothesis. Copeia 1982(4): 961–963.

——. 1987a. Range portrayal and reality: "bias" or scaling problem. Herpetol. Rev. 18(1): 9.

——. 1987b. More accurate range portrayal: conclusions. Herpetol. Rev. 18(1): 10.

——. 1997. Lipid reserves of the eastern cottonmouth (*Agkistrodon piscivorus*) at the northern edge of its range. Copeia 1997(1): 53–59.

Blem, C. R., and L. B. Blem. 1995. The eastern cottonmouth (*Agkistrodon piscivorus*) at the northern edge of its range. J. Herpetol. 29: 391–398.

Blihovde, W. B., and K. J. Irwin. 2001. Geographic distribution: *Sistrurus miliarius* (pigmy rattlesnake). Herpetol. Rev. 32(1): 61.

Blody, D. A. 1983. Notes on the reproductive biology of the eyelash viper *Bothrops schlegeli* in captivity. Herpetol. Rev. 14(2): 45–46.

Blum, H. F., and C. R. Spealman. 1933. Note on the killing of rattlesnakes by "sunlight." Copeia 1933(3): 150–151.

Bober, M. A., J. L. Glenn, R. C. Straight, and C. L. Ownby. 1988. Detection of myotoxin a–like proteins in various snake venoms. Toxicon 26: 665–673.

Böckeler, W. 1988. A small guide to snakes of the Paraguayan Chaco. Zoologische Institut di Universität D, Kiel, Germany. 101 pp.

Bocourt, M. F. 1868. Descriptions de quelques crotaliens nouveaux appartenant au genre *Bothrops*, recueillis dans le Guatemala.

Annales des Sciences Naturelles—Zoologie et Biologie Animale, 5th ser., 10: 201–202.

——. 1875. Observations sur les moeurs de l'*Heloderma horridum* Wiegmann par M. F. Sumichrast. Comptes Rendus Hebdomadaires des Séances de l'Académie des Sciences, Paris, 80: 676–679.

——. 1876. Note sur quelques reptiles de l'isthme de Tehuantepec (Mexique) donnés par M. Sumichrast au Muséum. Journal de Zoologie (Paris) 5(5–6): 386–411.

——. 1878. Etudes sur les reptiles. Mission scientifique au Mexique et dans l'Amérique centrale—recherches zoologiques, livraison 5: 281–360. Imprimerie Impériale, Paris.

Boettger, O. 1886. Aufzählung der von den Philippinen bekannten Reptilien und Batrachier. Bericht der Senckenbergischen Naturforschenden Gesellschaft in Frankfurt am Main 1885/1886: 91–134.

——. 1891. Reptilien und Batrachier aus Bolivia. Zoologischer Anzeiger (Leipzig) 14: 343–347.

——. 1898. Katalog der Reptiliensammlung im Museum der Senckenbergischen Naturforschenden Gesellschaft in Frankfurt am Main. II. Teil (Schlangen). Geb. Knauer, Frankfurt am Main. 160 pp.

Bogarín, G., M. Romero, G. Rojas, C. Lutsch, M. Casadamont, J. Lang, R. Otero, and J. M. Gutiérrez. 1999. Neutralization, by a monospecific *Bothrops lanceolatus* antivenom, of toxic activities induced by homologous and heterologous *Bothrops* snake venoms. Toxicon 37: 551–557.

Bogdan, G. M., R. C. Dart, S. C. Falbo, J. McNally, and D. Spaite. 2000. Recurrent coagulopathy after antivenom treatment of crotalid snakebite. Southern Medical Journal 93: 562–566.

Bogert, C. M. 1942. Field note on the copulation of *Crotalus atrox* in California. Copeia 1942(4): 262.

——. 1943. Dentitional phenomena in cobras and other elapids with notes on adaptive modifications of fangs. Bull. Am. Mus. Nat. Hist. 81: 285–360.

——. 1954. Amphibians and reptiles of the world. Pp. 1189–1390 in F. Drimmer (ed.), The animal kingdom, vol. 2, book 3. Greystone Press, New York.

——. 1956. The world's only venomous lizard. Animal Kingdom 59(4): 105–109.

——. 1959. The Gila monster. Audubon Magazine 61: 160–163.

——. 1960. The influence of sounds on the behavior of amphibians and reptiles. Pp. 137–320 in W. E. Lanyon and W. Tavolga (eds.), Animal sounds and communication. American Institute for Biological Sciences, Washington, D.C.

——. 1968. A new arboreal pit viper of the genus *Bothrops* from the Isthmus of Tehuantepec, Mexico. Am. Mus. Novitat. 2341: 1–14.

Bogert, C. M., and W. G. Degenhardt. 1961. An addition to the fauna of the United States, the Chihuahua ridge-nosed rattlesnake in New Mexico. Am. Mus. Novitat. 2064: 1–15.

Bogert, C. M., and R. Martín del Campo. 1956. The Gila monster and its allies. The relationships, habits, and behavior of the lizards of the family Helodermatidae. Bull. Am. Mus. Nat. Hist. 109(1): 1–238.

Bogert, C. M., and J. A. Oliver. 1945. A preliminary analysis of the herpetofauna of Sonora. Bull. Am. Mus. Nat. Hist. 83(6): 297–426.

Boie, F. 1827. Bemerkungen über Merrem's versuch eines Systems der Amphibien. Isis von Oken 20(6): 508–566.

Bolaños, R. 1971. Nuevos recursos contra el ofidismo en Centroamérica, 2d ed. Ministerio de Salubridad Pública, Universidad de Costa Rica, San José. 29 pp.

——. 1972. Toxicity of Costa Rican snake venoms for the white mouse. American Journal of Tropical Medicine and Hygiene 21: 360–363.

——. 1982. Las serpientes venenosas de Centro América y el problema del ofidismo. Primera parte. Aspectos zoológicos, epidemiológicos, y biomédicos. Revista Costarricense de Ciencias Médicas 3: 165–184.

——. 1983 [dated 1982]. Serpientes venenosas de Centro América: distribución, características, y patrones cardiológicos. Mem. Inst. Butantan 46: 275–291.

——. 1984. Serpientes, venenos, y ofidismo en Centroamérica. Editorial Universidad de Costa Rica, San José. 136 pp.

Bolaños, R., L. Cerdas, and J. W. Abalos. 1978a. Venoms of coral snakes (*Micrurus* spp.): report on a multivalent antivenin for the Americas. Bulletin of the Pan American Health Organization 12: 23–27.

Bolaños, R., L. Cerdas, and R. T. Taylor. 1975. The production and characteristics of a coral snake (*Micrurus mipartitus hertwigi*) antivenin. Toxicon 13: 139.

Bolaños, R., A. Flores, R. T. Taylor, and L. Cerdas. 1974. Color patterns and venom characteristics in *Pelamis platurus*. Copeia 1974(4): 909–912.

Bolaños, R., O. Marín, E. Mora Medina, and E. A. Alfaro. 1981. El accidente ofídico por cascabela (*Crotalus durissus durissus*) en Costa Rica. Acta Médica Costarricense 24: 211–214.

Bolaños, R., and J. R. Montero. 1970. *Agkistrodon bilineatus* Günther from Costa Rica. Rev. Biol. Trop. 16: 277–279.

Bolaños, R., G. Muñoz, and L. Cerdas. 1978b. Toxicidad, neutralización, inmunoelectroforesis de los venenos de *Lachesis muta* de Costa Rica y Colombia. Toxicon 16: 295–300.

Bolaños, R., O. Rojas, and C. E. Ulloa Flores. 1982. Aspectos biomédicos de cuatro casos de mordedura de serpiente por *Lachesis muta* (Ophidia: Viperidae) en Costa Rica. Rev. Biol. Trop. 30: 53–58.

Bolette, D. P. 1997a. First record of *Pachysentis canicola* (Acanthocephala: Oligacanthorhynchida) and the occurrence of *Mesocestoides* sp. tetrathyridia (Cestoidea: Cyclophyllidae) in the western diamondback rattlesnake, *Crotalus atrox* (Serpentes: Viperidae). Journal of Parasitology 83(4): 751–752.

——. 1997b. Oligacanthorhynchid cystacanths (Acanthocephala) in a long-nosed snake, *Rhinocheilus lecontei* (Colubridae), and a Mojave rattlesnake (*Crotalus scutulatus*) from Maricopa County, Arizona. Southwest. Nat. 42: 232–236.

——. 1998. Helminths of the prairie rattlesnake, *Crotalus viridis viridis* (Serpentes: Viperidae), from western South Dakota. Journal of the Helminthological Society of Washington 65(1): 105–107.

Bond, G. R., and K. Burkart. 1997. Thrombocytopenia following timber rattlesnake envenomation. Ann. Emerg. Med. 30: 40–44.

——. 1998. Thrombocytopenia after rattlesnake envenomation. Ann. Emerg. Med. 31: 140–141.

Bond, G. R., and C. Clancy. 1992. Relative antivenin unresponsiveness of thrombocytopenia and myokymia following timber rattlesnake bite. Veterinary and Human Toxicology 34: 341.

Bonilla, C. A. 1975. Defibrinating enzyme from timber rattlesnake (*Crotalus h. horridus*) venom. Thrombosis Research 6: 151–169.

Bonilla, C. A., M. R. Faith, and S. A. Minton. 1973. L-amino acid oxidase, phosphodiesterase, total protein and other properties of juvenile timber rattlesnake (*C. h. horridus*) venom at different stages of growth. Toxicon 11: 301–303.

Bonilla, C. A., K. Fiero, and L. P. Frank. 1971. Isolation of a basic protein neurotoxin from *Crotalus adamanteus* venom. Pp. 343–357 in A. deVries and E. Kochva, eds. Toxins of animal and plant origin, vol. 1. Gordon and Breach Science Publishers, New York.

Bonnaterre, P.-J. 1790. Ophiologie. Pp. 1–76 in Tableau encyclopédique et méthodique des trois règnes de la nature (Encyclopédie méthodique). Panckoucke, Paris.

Boos, H. 1975. Checklist of Trinidad snakes. Journal of the Trinidad and Tobago Field Naturalists' Club 1975: 22–28.

——. 1984a [dated 1983–1984]. A consideration of the terrestrial reptile fauna on some offshore islands north west of Trinidad. Living World: Journal of the Trinidad and Tobago Field Naturalists' Club 1983–1984: 19–26.

——. 1984b. The status and distribution of important reptiles and amphibians in Trinidad and Tobago. Food and Agricultural Organization, United Nations. 19 pages.

——. 2001. The snakes of Trinidad and Tobago. Texas A&M Press, College Station. 270 pp.

Boos, H., and V. Quesnel. 1968. Reptiles of Trinidad and Tobago. Public Branch, Ministry of Education and Culture, Trinidad and Tobago. 39 pp.

Booth, E. S. 1959. Amphibians and reptiles collected in Mexico and Central America from 1952 to 1958. Department of Biological Science, Walla Walla College Publications 24: 1–9.

Borges, C. C., M. Sadahiro, and M. C. dos Santos. 1999. Aspectos epidemiológicos e clínicos dos acidentes ofídicos ocorridos nos municípios do Estado do Amazonas. Revista da Sociedade Brasileira de Medicina Tropical 32: 637–646.

Borges, R. C. 1999. Serpentes peçonhentas brasileiras. Atheneu, São Paulo. 148 pp.

Borges-Nojosa, D. M., and J. S. Lima-Verde. 1999. Geographic distribution: *Lachesis muta rhombeata* (South American bushmaster). Herpetol. Rev. 30(4): 235.

Bostic, D. L. 1971. Herpetofauna of the Pacific coast of north central Baja California, Mexico, with a description of a new subspecies of *Phyllodactylus xanti*. Trans. San Diego Soc. Nat. Hist. 16(10): 237–263.

——. 1975. A natural history guide to the Pacific coast of north central Baja California and adjacent islands. Biological Educational Expeditions, Vista, Calif. 184 pp.

Bothner, R. C. 1974. Some observations on the feeding habits of the cottonmouth in southeastern Georgia. J. Herpetol. 8: 257–258.

Bou-Abboud, C. F., and D. G. Kardassakis. 1988. Acute myocardial infarction following a Gila monster (*Heloderma suspectum cinctum*) bite. Western Journal of Medicine 148: 577–579.

Boulenger, G. A. 1882. Account of the reptiles and batrachians collected by Mr. Edward Whymper in Ecuador in 1879–80. Ann. Mag. Nat. Hist., 5th ser., 9(54): 457–467.

——. 1883. Observations on *Heloderma*. Proc. Zool. Soc. London 1882(4): 631–632.

——. 1885a. Catalogue of lizards in the British Museum (Natural History), 2d ed., 2 vols. Taylor and Francis, London.

——. 1885b. A list of reptiles and batrachians from the province of Rio Grande do Sul, Brazil, sent to the Natural-History Museum by Dr. H. von Ihering. Ann. Mag. Nat. Hist., 5th ser., 15(87): 191–196.

——. 1885c. Second list of reptiles and batrachians from the province of Rio Grande do Sul, Brazil, sent to the Natural-History Museum by Dr. H. von Ihering. Ann. Mag. Nat. Hist., 5th ser., 16(92): 85–88.

——. 1886. A synopsis of the reptiles and batrachians of the province of Rio Grande do Sul, Brazil. Ann. Mag. Nat. Hist., 5th ser., 18(108): 423–445.

——. 1891a. The anatomy of *Heloderma*. Nature 44: 444.

——. 1891b. Reptilia and batrachia. Pp. 128–136 in E. Whymper (ed.), Supplementary appendix to Travels amongst the Great Andes of the Equator. John Murray, London.

——. 1893. Catalogue of the snakes in the British Museum (Natural History), vol. 1., Taylor and Francis, London. 448 pp.

——. 1894a. List of reptiles and batrachians collected by Dr. J. Bohls near Asunción, Paraguay. Ann. Mag. Nat. Hist., 6th ser., 13(76): 342–348.

——. 1894b. Catalogue of the snakes in the British Museum (Natural History), vol. 2. Taylor and Francis, London. 382 pp.

——. 1896a. Remarks on the dentition of snakes and on the evolution of the poison-fangs. Proc. Zool. Soc. London 1896: 614–616.

——. 1896b. Catalogue of the snakes in the British Museum (Natural History), vol. 3. Taylor and Francis, London. 727 pp.

——. 1898a. A list of the reptiles and batrachians collected by the late Prof. L. Balzan in Bolivia. Annali del Museo Civico Storia Naturale Giacomo Doria (Genova), 2d ser., 19: 128–133.

——. 1898b. An account of the reptiles and batrachians collected by Mr. W. F. H. Rosenberg in western Ecuador. Proc. Zool. Soc. London 1898: 107–126.

——. 1898c. A list of reptiles, batrachians and fishes collected by Cav. Guido Baggiani in the northern Chaco. Annali del Museo Civico Storia Naturale Giacomo Doria (Genova), 2d ser., 19(39): 125–128.

——. 1900. Report on a collection made by Messrs. F. V. McConnell and J. J. Quelch at Mount Roraima in British Guiana. In E. R. Lankester (ed.), Transactions of the Linnaean Society of London, Zoology, 2d ser., 8(2): 51–76.

——. 1902a. Descriptions of new batrachians and reptiles from northwestern Ecuador. Ann. Mag. Nat. Hist., 7th ser., 9: 51–57.

——. 1902b. List of fishes, batrachians, and reptiles collected by the late Mr. P. O. Simons in the provinces of Mendoza and Cordova, Argentina. Ann. Mag. Nat. Hist., 7th ser., 9: 336–339.

——. 1902c. Descriptions of new batrachians and reptiles from the Andes of Peru and Bolivia. Ann. Mag. Nat. Hist., 7th ser., 10: 394–402.

——. 1903. Descriptions of new snakes in the collection of the British Museum. Ann. Mag. Nat. Hist., 7th ser., 12: 350–354.

——. 1905. Descriptions of new snakes in the collection of the British Museum. Ann. Mag. Nat. Hist., 7th ser., 15: 453–456.

——. 1907. Description of a new pit-viper from Brazil. Ann. Mag. Nat. Hist., 7th ser., 20: 338.

——. 1912. Descriptions of new reptiles from the Andes of South America preserved in the British Museum. Ann. Mag. Nat. Hist., 8th ser., 10: 420–424.

——. 1913. On a collection of batrachians and reptiles made by Dr. H. G. F. Spurrell, F.Z.S., in the Choco, Colombia. Proc. Zool. Soc. London 1913: 1019–1038.

——. 1914. On a second collection of batrachians and reptiles made by Dr. H. G. F. Spurrell, F.Z.S., in the Choco, Colombia. Proc. Zool. Soc. London 1914: 813–817.

——. 1920a. Descriptions of four new snakes in the collection of the British Museum. Ann. Mag. Nat. Hist., 9th ser., 6: 108–111.

——. 1920b. A monograph of the South Asian, Papuan, Melanesian and Australian frogs of the genus *Rana*. Rec. Indian Mus. 20: 1–226.

Boundy, J. 1992. Geographic distribution: *Crotalus viridis viridis* (prairie rattlesnake). Herpetol. Rev. 23(4): 124.

——. 1994a. County records for Florida amphibians and reptiles. Herpetol. Rev. 25(2): 78–79.

——. 1994b. Range extensions for Louisiana amphibians and reptiles. Herpetol. Rev. 25(3): 128–129.

——. 1994c. County records for Texas amphibians and reptiles. Herpetol. Rev. 25(3): 129.

——. 1995. Maximum lengths of North American snakes. Bull. Chicago Herpetol. Soc. 30(6): 109–122.

Boundy, J., and T. G. Balgooyen. 1988. Record lengths for some amphibians and reptiles from the western United States. Herpetol. Rev. 19(2): 26–27.

Bouskila, A. 1995. Interactions between predation risk and competition: a field study of kangaroo rats and snakes. Ecology 76(1): 165–178.

Bovee, E. C. 1962. An isosporan coccidian *Isospora dirumpens*, from the Florida diamondback rattlesnake, *Crotalus adamanteus* (abstract). Journal of Protozoology 9(suppl. 19): 459–466.

Bowler, J. K. 1974. Venomous snakes of Pennsylvania. Pennsylvania Game News 45(7): 28–31.

——. 1977. Longevity of reptiles and amphibians in North American collections as of 1 November, 1975. Society for the Study of Amphibians and Reptiles, Miscellaneous Publications, Herpetological Circular 6. 32 pp.

Bowman, D. D. 1984. *Hexametra leidyi*, new species (Nematoda: Ascarididae) from North America pit vipers (Reptilia: Viperidae). Proceedings of the Helminthological Society of Washington 51(1): 54–61.

Boyden, T. W. 1980. Snake venom poisoning: diagnosis and treatment. Arizona Medicine 37: 639–641.

Boyer, D. A. 1933. A case report on the potency of the bite of a young copperhead. Copeia 1933(2): 97.

Boyer, D. M., L. A. Mitchell, and J. B. Murphy. 1989. Reproduction and husbandry of the bushmaster (*Lachesis m. muta*), at the Dallas Zoo. International Zoo Yearbook 28: 190–194.

Boyer, D. R. 1957. Sexual dimorphism in a population of the western diamond-backed rattlesnake. Herpetologica 13(3): 213–217.

Boyer, L. V., S. A. Seifert, and J. S. Cain. 2001. Recurrence phenomena after immunoglobulin therapy for snake envenomations, part 2: guidelines for clinical management with crotaline Fab antivenom. Ann. Emerg. Med. 37: 196–201.

Bradley, W. G., and J. E. Deacon. 1966. Distribution of the Gila monster in the northern Mojave Desert. Copeia 1966(2): 365–366.

Bradt, G. W. 1932. The mammals of the Malpais, an area of black lava rock in the Tularosa Basin, New Mexico. Journal of Mammalogy 13: 321–328.

Bragg, A. N. 1960. Is *Heterodon* venomous? Herpetologica 16(2): 121–123.

Brandt, L. A., K. L. Montgomery, A. W. Saunders, and F. J. Mazzotti. 1993. Natural history notes: *Gopherus poyphemus* (gopher tortoise). Herpetol. Rev. 24(4): 149.

Branson, E. B. 1904. Snakes of Kansas. Kansas University Science Bulletin 2(13): 353–430.

Brasil. 1998. Manual de diagnóstico e tratamento de acidentes por animais peçonhentos. Fundação Nacional da Saúde, Ministério da Saúde, Brasília.

Bratt, D. E., and H. E. A. Boos. 1992a. *Bothrops atrox* snakebite. West Indian Medical Journal 41: 53–55.

——. 1992b. *Bothrops atrox* snakebite in a 6-year-old child. West Indian Medical Journal 41(3): 130.

Brattstrom, B. H. 1952. Diurnal activities of a nocturnal animal. Herpetologica 8(3): 61–63.

——. 1955. The coral snake "mimic" problem and protective coloration. Evolution 9(2): 217–219.

——. 1964. Evolution of the pit vipers. Trans. San Diego Soc. Nat. Hist. 13(11): 185–267.

——. 1965. Body temperatures of reptiles. Am. Midl. Nat. 73: 367–422.

Brattstrom, B. H., and T. R. Howell. 1954. Notes on some collections of reptiles and amphibians from Nicaragua. Herpetologica 10(2): 114–123.

Bravo, H. 1927. Flagelados encontrados en batracios y reptiles del Valle de México. Memorias y Revista de la Sociedad Científica Antonio Alzate 48: 385–390.

Brazil, O. V. 1996. Vital Brazil e o Instituto Butantan. Editora da Unicamp, Campinas.

Brazil, V. 1911. A defesa contra o ophidismo. Pocai & Weiss, São Paulo. 152 pp.

——. 1914. La défense contre l'ophidisme. Translated by J. Maibon. Pocai & Weiss, São Paulo. 319 pp.

Breckenridge, W. J. 1944. Reptiles and amphibians of Minnesota. University of Minnesota Press, Minneapolis. 202 pp.

Breder, C. M., Jr. 1946. Amphibians and reptiles of the Río Chucunaque drainage, Darien, Panama, with notes on their life histories and habits. Bull. Am. Mus. Nat. Hist. 86(8): 377–453.

Bremer, K. 1988. The limits of amino acid sequence data in angiosperm phylogenetic reconstruction. Evolution 42: 795–803.

Brennan, G. A. 1924. A case of death from *Heloderma* bite. Copeia 1924(129): 45.

Briceño-Rossi, A. L. 1934a. El problema del ofidismo en Venezuela. Litografía y Tipografía Casa de Especialidades, Caracas. 187 pp.

——. 1934b. El problema del ofidismo en Venezuela. Boletín del Ministerio de Salubridad y Agricultura y Cría 2(14): 1079–1177.

Brick, J. R., and L. Gutmann. 1982. Rattlesnake venom induced myokymia. Muscle and Nerve 5(suppl.): 98–100.

Brick, J. R., L. Gutmann, J. Brick, K. N. Apelgren, and J. E. Riggs. 1978. Timber rattlesnake venom-induced myokymia: evidence for peripheral nerve origin. Neurology 37: 1545–1546.

Brickell, J. 1805. [On two species of *Crotalus*.] Philadelphia Medical and Physical Journal, vol. 2, part 1, sec. 3, p. 164.

Bridegam, A. S., B. E. Smith, C. M. Garrett, and D. T. Roberts. 1990. Cannibalism in two species of arboreal pitviper, *Trimeresurus wagleri* and *Bothriechis schlegelii*. Herpetol. Rev. 21(3): 54–55.

Briggler, J. T., and J. W. Prather. 2002. Natural history notes: *Crotalus horridus* (timber rattlesnake). Cave use. Herpetol. Rev. 33(2): 139.

Brimley, C. S. 1915. List of the reptiles and amphibians of North Carolina. Journal of the Elisha Mitchell Scientific Society 30: 195–206.

——. 1923. The copperhead moccasin at Raleigh, N.C. Copeia 1923(124): 113–116.

——. 1944. Amphibians and reptiles of North Carolina. Carolina Biological Supply Company, Elon College, Burlington, N.C. 63 pp.

Broadley, D. G. 1957. Fatalities from the bites of *Dispholidus* and *Thelotornis* and personal case history. Journal of the Herpetological Association of Rhodesia 1: 5.

——. 1990. FitzSimons' Snakes of Southern Africa. Delta Books, Johannesburg. 387 pp.

Brodie, E. D., III. 1992. Correlational selection for color pattern and antipredator behavior in the garter snake *Thamnophis ordinoides*. Evolution 46: 1284–1298.

———. 1993. Differential avoidance of coral snake banded patterns by free-ranging avian predators in Costa Rica. Evolution 47: 227–235.

Brodie, E. D., III, and A. F. Agrawal. 2001. Maternal effects and the evolution of aposematic signals. Proceedings of the National Academy of Sciences 98: 7884–7887.

Brodie, E. D., III, and E. D. Brodie Jr. 1999. Predator-prey arms races. Bioscience 49: 557–568.

Brodie, E. D., III, and F. J. Janzen. 1995. Experimental studies of coral snake mimicry: generalized avoidance of ringed patterns by free-ranging avian predators. Functional Ecology 9: 186–190.

Brodie, E. D., III, and A. J. Moore. 1995. Experimental studies of coral snake mimicry: do snakes mimic millipedes? Animal Behaviour 49: 534–536.

Brodie, E. D., III, A. J. Moore, and F. J. Janzen. 1995. Visualizing and quantifying natural selection. Trends in Ecology and Evolution 10: 313–318.

Brodie, E. D., Jr. 1981. Phenological relationships of model and mimic salamanders. Evolution 35: 988–994.

Brodie, E. D., Jr., and R. R. Howard. 1973. Experimental study of Batesian mimicry in the salamanders *Plethodon jordani* and *Desmognathus ochrophaeus*. Am. Midl. Nat. 90: 38–46.

Brongersma, L. D. 1940. Snakes from the Leeward Group, Venezuela, and eastern Colombia. Pp. 115–137 in P. Wagenaar Hummelinck (ed.), Studies on the fauna of Curaçao, Aruba, Bonaire, and the Venezuelan islands, vol. 2. P. den Boer, Utrecht.

———. 1967a [dated 1966]. Note on *Leptomicrurus collaris* (Schlegel) (Reptilia, Serpentes). Zoologische Mededelingen 41(17): 243–254.

———. 1967b [dated 1966]. Poisonous snakes of Surinam. Mem. Inst. Butantan 33(1): 73–79.

Bronstein, A. C., F. E. Russell, and J. B. Sullivan. 1986. Negative pressure suction in the field treatment of rattlesnake bite victims (abstract). Veterinary and Human Toxicology 28: 485.

Bronstein, A. C., F. E. Russell, J. B. Sullivan, N. B. Egen, and B. R. Rumack. 1985. Negative pressure suction in field treatment of rattlesnake bite (abstract). Veterinary and Human Toxicology 28: 297.

Brooks, D. E., K. A. Graeme, and K. Katz. 2001. Life threatening anaphylaxis after first time Crotalidae envenomation (abstract). Journal of Toxicology—Clinical Toxicology 39: 558.

Brooks, D. R. 1978. Systematic status of proteocephalid cestodes from reptiles and amphibians in North America with descriptions of three new species. Proceedings of the Helminthological Society of Washington 45(1): 1–28.

Brothers, D. R. 1992. An introduction to snakes of the Dismal Swamp region of North Carolina and Virginia. Edgewood Probes, Inc., Boise, Idaho. 139 pp.

Brower, A. V. Z. 1994. Phylogeny of *Heliconius* butterflies inferred from mitochodrial DNA sequences (Lepidoptera: Nymphaline). Molecular Phylogeny and Evolution 3: 159–174.

———. 1996. Parallel race formation and the evolution of mimicry in *Heliconius* butterflies: a phylogenetic hypothesis from mitochondrial DNA sequences. Evolution 50: 195–221.

Brower, J. V. Z. 1958a. Experimental studies of mimicry in some North American butterflies. Part I. Evolution 12: 32–47.

———. 1958b. Experimental studies of mimicry in some North American butterflies. Part III. Evolution 12: 273–285.

Brower, L. P., P. B. McEvoy, K. L. Williamson, and M. A. Flannery. 1972. Variation in cardiac glycoside content of monarch butterflies from natural populations in eastern North America. Science 177: 426–429.

Brower, L. P., and C. M. Moffitt. 1974. Palatability dynamics of cardenolides in the monarch butterfly. Nature 249: 280–283.

Brower, L. P., F. H. Pough, and H. R. Meck. 1970. Theoretical investigations of automimicry. I. Single trial learning. Proceedings of the National Academy of Sciences 66: 1059–1066.

Brown, A. E. 1893. Notes on some snakes from tropical America lately living in the collection of the Zoological Society of Philadelphia. Proc. Acad. Nat. Sci. Philadelphia 45: 429–435.

———. 1901. A review of the genera and species of American snakes, north of Mexico. Proc. Acad. Nat. Sci. Philadelphia 53: 10–110.

———. 1903a. Texas reptiles and their faunal relations. Proc. Acad. Nat. Sci. Philadelphia 55: 543–558.

———. 1903b. Note on *Crotalus scutulatus* Kenn. Proc. Acad. Nat. Sci. Philadelphia 55: 625.

———. 1908. Generic types of Neartic Reptilia and Amphibia. Proc. Acad. Nat. Sci. Philadelphia 60: 112–127.

Brown, B. C. 1939. The effect of *Coniophanes* poisoning in man. Copeia 1939(2): 109.

———. 1950. An annotated check list of the reptiles and amphibians of Texas. Baylor University Press, Waco, Texas. 257 pp.

Brown, B. C., and L. M. Brown. 1967. Notable records of Tamaulipan snakes. Texas Journal of Science 19(3): 323–326.

Brown, B. C., and M. B. Mittleman. 1947. A range extension for *Crotalus m. molossus* Baird and Girard in Texas. Herpetologica 4(1): 23–24.

Brown, B. C., and H. M. Smith. 1942. A new subspecies of Mexican coral snake. Proceedings of the Biological Society of Washington 55: 63–66.

Brown, C. W., and C. H. Ernst. 1986. A study of variation in eastern timber rattlesnakes, *Crotalus horridus* Linnae [*sic*] (Serpentes, Viperidae). Brimleyana 12: 57–74.

Brown, D. E. (ed.). 1994. Biotic communities: southwestern United States and northwestern Mexico. University of Utah Press, Salt Lake City. 342 pp.

Brown, D. E., and N. B. Carmony. 1991. Gila monster: facts and folklore of America's Aztec lizard. High-Lonesome Books, Silver City, N.M. 131 pp.

Brown, D. G., and D. Duvall. 1993. Habitat associations of prairie rattlesnakes (*Crotalus viridis*) in Wyoming. Herpetological Natural History 1(1): 5–12.

Brown, E. E. 1979. Some snake food records from the Carolinas. Brimleyana 1: 113–124.

Brown, E. R., J. W. Haberman, and J. K. Kappell. 1970. Productive collecting sites for *Sistrurus catenatus edwardsi/tergeminus* in southeast Colorado. Journal of the Colorado-Wyoming Academy of Science 7(1): 44.

Brown, H. A., R. B. Bury, D. M. Darda, L. V. Diller, C. R. Peterson, and R. M. Storm. 1995. Reptiles of Washington and Oregon. Seattle Audubon Society, Seattle. 176 pp.

Brown, J. F. W., W. M. Marden, and D. L. Hardy, Sr. 2000. Natural history notes: *Crotalus scutulatus scutulatus* (Mojave rattlesnake). Defensive behavior. Herpetol. Rev. 31(1): 45.

Brown, N. L. 2000a. Geographic distribution: *Crotalus atrox* (western diamondback rattlesnake). Herpetol. Rev. 31(1): 54–55.

———. 2000b. Geographic distribution: *Crotalus molossus* (blacktail rattlesnake). Herpetol. Rev. 31(1): 55.

Brown, P. R. 1997. A field guide to snakes of California. Gulf Publishing, Houston, Texas. 215 pp.

Brown, T. W. 1970. Autecology of the sidewinder (*Crotalus cerastes*) at Kelso Dunes, Mojave Desert, California. Diss. Abstr. B31(10): 6336–6337.

Brown, T. W., and H. B. Lillywhite. 1992. Autecology of the Mojave desert sidewinder (*Crotalus cerastes cerastes*) at Kelso Dunes, Mojave Desert, California. Pp. 279–308 in J. A. Campbell and E. D. Brodie Jr. (eds.), Biology of the pitvipers. Selva, Tyler, Texas.

Brown, W. H., and C. H. Lowe Jr. 1955. Technique for obtaining maximum yields of fresh labial gland secretions from the lizard *Heloderma suspectum*. Copeia 1955(1): 63.

Brown, W. M., E. M. Prager, A. Wang, and A. C. Wilson. 1982. Mitochondrial DNA sequences of primates: tempo and mode of evolution. Journal of Molecular Evolution 18: 225–239.

Brown, W. S. 1982. Overwintering body temperatures of timber rattlesnakes (*Crotalus horridus*) in northeastern New York. J. Herpetol. 16(2): 145–150.

———. 1991. Female reproductive ecology in a northern population of the timber rattlesnake, *Crotalus horridus*. Herpetologica 47(1): 101–115.

———. 1992. Emergence, ingress, and seasonal captures at dens of northern timber rattlesnakes, *Crotalus horridus*. Pp. 251–258 in J. A.

Campbell and E. D. Brodie Jr. (eds.), Biology of the pitvipers. Selva, Tyler, Texas.

———. 1993. Biology, status, and management of the timber rattlesnake (*Crotalus horridus*): a guide for conservation. Herpetology Circular No. 22. Society for the Study of Amphibians and Reptiles, Lawrence, Kans.

———. 1995. Heterosexual groups and the mating season in a northern population of timber rattlesnakes, *Crotalus horridus*. Herpetological Natural History 3: 127–133.

Brown, W. S., and D. B. Greenberg. 1992. Vertical-tree ambush posture in *Crotalus horridus*. Herpetol. Rev. 23(3): 67.

Brown, W. S., and F. M. MacLean. 1983. Conspecific scent-trailing by newborn timber rattlesnakes, *Crotalus horridus*. Herpetologica 39(4): 430–436.

Brown, W. S., D. W. Pyle, K. R. Greene, and J. B. Friedlaender. 1982. Movements and temperature relationships of timber rattlesnakes (*Crotalus horridus*) in northeastern New York. J. Herpetol. 16: 151–161.

Brubacher, J. R., D. Lachmanen, and R. S. Hoffman. 1999. Efficacy of Wyeth polyvalent antivenin used in the pretreatment of copperhead envenomation in mice. Wilderness and Environmental Medicine 10: 142–145.

Brugger, K. E. 1989. Red-tailed hawk dies with coral snake in talons. Copeia 1989(2): 508–510.

Brukoff, B. 2001. Machu Picchu. Bulfinch Press of Little, Brown, Boston. 127 pp.

Brush, S. W., and G. W. Ferguson. 1986. Predation of lark sparrow eggs by a massasauga rattlesnake. Southwest. Nat. 31: 260–261.

Bryant, H. N. 1991. The polarization of character transformations in phylogenetic systematics: role of axiomatic and auxiliary assumptions. Syst. Zool. 40: 433–445.

Bryson, R. W., Jr., J. Banda, and D. Lazcano. 2002a. Natural history notes: *Crotalus lepidus maculosus* (Durangan rock rattlesnake). Diet. Herpetol. Rev. 33(2): 139–140.

———. 2002b. Natural history notes: *Crotalus pricei pricei* (Price's twinspotted rattlesnake). Habitat selection. Herpetol. Rev. 33(2): 140.

Bryson, R. W., Jr., and A. T. Holycross. 2001. Natural history notes: *Crotalus willardi amabilis* (Del Nido ridgenose rattlesnake). Diet. Herpetol. Rev. 32(4): 262.

Bryson, R. W., Jr., and D. Lazcano. 2002. Reproduction and mating behavior in the Del Nido ridgenose rattlesnake, *Crotalus willardi amabilis*. Southwest. Nat. 47(2): 310–312.

Bryson, R. W., Jr., and J. M. Mueller. 2001. Geographical distribution: *Crotalus lepidus lepidus* (mottled rock rattlesnake). Herpetol. Rev. 32(2): 122.

Bucaretchi, F., S. R. F. Herrera, S. Hyslop, E. C. Baracat, and R. J. Veira. 2002. Snakebites by *Crotalus durissus* ssp. in children in Campinas, São Paulo, Brazil. Revista do Instituto Medicina Tropical de São Paulo 44: 133–138.

Bucher, B., D. Canonge, L. Thomas, B. Tyburn, A. Robbe-Vincent, V. Choumet, C. Bon, J. Ketterle, and J. Lang. 1997. Clinical indicators of envenoming and serum levels of venom antigens in patients bitten by *Bothrops lanceolatus* in Martinique. Trans. Roy. Soc. Trop. Med. Hyg. 91(2): 186–190.

Buckle, A. C., J. Riley, and G. F. Hill. 1997. The *in vitro* development of the pentastomid *Porocephalus crotali* from the infective instar to the adult stage. Parasitology 115: 503–512.

Budzynski, A. Z., B. V. Pandya, R. N. Rubin, B. S. Brizuela, T. Soszka, and G. J. Stewart. 1984. Fibrinogenolytic afibrinogenemia after envenomation by western diamondback rattlesnake (*Crotalus atrox*). Blood 63: 1–14.

Bullock, T. H., and R. B. Cowles. 1952. Physiology of an infra-red receptor: The facial pit of pit vipers. Science 115: 541–543.

Bullock, T. H., and R. P. J. Diecke. 1956. Properties of an infra-red receptor. Journal of Physiology 134: 47–87.

Buntain, W. L. 1983. Successful venomous snakebite neutralization with massive antivenin infusion in a child. Journal of Trauma—Injury, Infection, and Critical Care 23: 1012–1014.

Buongermini P. E., and T. Waller. 1999. Geographic distribution: *Bothrops moojeni* (Brazilian lancehead). Herpetol. Rev. 30(1): 53.

Burbrink, F. T. 2001. Systematics of the eastern ratsnake complex (*Elaphe obsoleta*). Herpetological Monographs 15: 1–53.

Burbrink, F. T., R. Lawson, and J. B. Slowinski. 2000. Mitochondrial DNA phylogeography of the polytypic North American rat snake (*Elaphe obsoleta*): a critique of the subspecies concept. Evolution 54: 2107–2118.

Burch, J. M., R. Agarwal, K. L. Mattox, D. V. Feliciano, and G. L. Jordan. 1988. The treatment of crotalid envenomation without antivenin. Journal of Trauma—Injury, Infection, and Critical Care 28: 35–43.

Burchfield, P. M. 1975. Raising the fer-de-lance *Bothrops atrox* in captivity. International Zoo Yearbook 15: 173–174.

———. 1982. Additions to the natural history of the crotaline snake *Agkistrodon bilineatus taylori*. J. Herpetol. 16: 376–382.

Burchfield, P. M., T. F. Beimler, and C. D. Hairston. 1982. A range extension for *Crotalus molossus nigrescens* in Tamaulipas, Mexico. Herpetol. Rev. 13(4): 131–132.

Burger, J. W. 1934. The hibernation habits of the rattlesnake of the New Jersey pine barrens. Copeia 1934(3): 142.

Burger, R. M. 1997. Predation by two species of coral snakes in Limón Province, Costa Rica. Bull. Chicago Herpetol. Soc. 32(7): 145.

———. 2001. The herpetofauna of Caño Palma Biological Station, Tortugero, Costa Rica. Bull. Chicago Herpetol. Soc. 36(12): 243–253.

Burger, W. L. 1950. A preliminary study of the subspecies of the jumping viper *Bothrops nummifer*. Bulletin of the Chicago Academy of Sciences 9(3): 59–67.

———. 1955. A new subspecies of the coral snake, *Micrurus lemniscatus*, from Venezuela, British Guiana, and Trinidad; and a key for the identification of associated species of coral snakes. Boletín del Museo de Ciencias Naturales, Caracas, 1(2): 1–19.

———. 1971. Genera of pitvipers (Serpentes: Crotalidae) Ph.D. dissertation, University of Kansas. 186 pp.

Burger, W. L., and M. M. Hensley. 1949. Notes on a collection of reptiles and amphibians from northwestern Sonora. Chicago Academy of Sciences, Natural History Miscellanea 35: 1–6.

Burger, W. L., and W. B. Robertson. 1951. A new subspecies of the Mexican moccasin, *Agkistrodon bilineatus*. University of Kansas Science Bulletin 24(5): 213–218.

Burger, W. L., and P. W. Smith. 1950. The coloration of the tail tip of young fer-de-lances: sexual dimorphism rather than adaptive coloration. Science 112(2911): 431–433.

Burgess, J. L., and R. C. Dart. 1991. Snake venom coagulopathy: use and abuse of blood products in the treatment of pit viper envenomation. Ann. Emerg. Med. 20: 795–801.

Burgess, J. L., R. C. Dart, N. B. Egen, and M. Mayersohn. 1992. Effects of constriction bands on rattlesnake venom absorption: a pharmacokinetic study. Ann. Emerg. Med. 21: 1086–1093.

Burkett, R. D. 1966. Natural history of the cottonmouth moccasin, *Agkistrodon piscivorus* (Reptilia). Publications of the Museum of Natural History, University of Kansas, 17: 435–491.

Burmeister, G. H. C. 1861. Reise durch die La Plata Staaten, 1857–1860. Halle. 538 pp.

Burns, B. 1969. Oral sensory papillae in sea snakes. Copeia 1969(3): 617–619.

Bursey, C. R., S. R. Goldberg, and S. M. Secor. 1995. *Hexametra boddaertii* (Nematoda: Ascaridae) in the sidewinder, *Crotalus cerastes* (Crotalidae), from California. Journal of the Helminthological Society of Washington 62(1): 78–80.

Busby, W. H., and J. R. Parmelee. 1996. Historical changes in a herpetofaunal assemblage in the Flint Hills of Kansas. Am. Midl. Nat. 135(1): 81–91.

Bush, F. M. 1959. Foods of some Kentucky herptiles. Herpetologica 15(2): 73–77.

Bush, S. P., and M. D. Cardwell. 1999. Mojave rattlesnake (*Crotalus scutulatus scutulatus*) identification. Wilderness and Environmental Medicine 10: 6–9.

Bush, S. P., and D. L. Hardy. 2001. Immediate removal of Extractor is recommended. Ann. Emerg. Med. 38: 607–608.

Bush, S. P., K. G. Hegewald, S. M. Green, M. D. Cardwell, and W. K. Hayes. 2000a. Effects of a negative pressure venom extraction device (Extractor) on local tissue injury after artificial rattlesnake envenomation in a porcine model. Wilderness and Environmental Medicine 11: 180–188.

Bush, S. P., and P. W. Jansen. 1995. Severe rattlesnake envenomation with anaphylaxis and rhabdomyolysis. Ann. Emerg. Med. 25: 845–848.

Bush, S. P., and E. Siedenburg. 1999. Neurotoxicity associated with suspected southern Pacific rattlesnake (*Crotalus viridis helleri*) envenomation. Wilderness and Environmental Medicine 10: 247–249.

Bush, S. P., V. H. Wu, and S. W. Corbett. 2000b. Rattlesnake venom-induced thrombocytopenia response to antivenin (Crotalidae) polyvalent: a case series. Academic Emergency Medicine 7: 181–185.

Bushar, L. M., M. Maliga, and H. K. Reinert. 2001. Cross-species amplification of *Crotalus horridus* microsatellites and their application in phylogenetic analysis. J. Herpetol. 35(3): 532–537.

Bushar, L. M., H. K. Reinert, and L. Gelbert. 1998. Genetic variation and gene flow within and between local populations of the timber rattlesnake, *Crotalus horridus*. Copeia 1998(2): 411–422.

Bushey, C. L. 1978. Man's effect upon a colony of *Sistrurus catenatus catenatus* in northwestern Illinois (1834–1975). Pp. 96–103 in Proceedings of the Fifth Midwestern Prairie Conference, Iowa State University, Ames.

Butler, J. A., T. W. Hull, and R. Franz. 1995. Neonatal aggregations and maternal attendance of young in the eastern diamondback rattlesnake, *Crotalus adamanteus*. Copeia 1995(1): 196–198.

Butner, A. N. 1983. Rattlesnake bites in northern California. Western Journal of Medicine 139: 179–183.

Buttenhoff, P. A., and R. C. Vogt. 1995. Natural history notes: *Bothrops asper* (Nauyaca). Cannibalism. Herpetol. Rev. 26(3): 146–147.

Byrd, E. E., and J. F. Denton. 1938. New trematodes of the subfamily Reniferinae, with a discussion of the systematics of the genera and species assigned to the subfamily group. Journal of Parasitology 24: 379–401.

Caballero y Caballero, E. 1954. Estudios helmintológicos de la región oncocercosa de México y de la República de Guatemala. Nemátod. 8ª Parte. Anales del Instituto de Biología, Universidad Nacional Autónoma de México, 25: 259–274.

Cadle, J. E. 1983 [dated 1982]. Problems and approaches in the interpretation of the evolutionary history of venomous snakes. Mem. Inst. Butantan 46: 255–274.

———. 1985. The Neotropical colubrid snake fauna (Serpentes: Colubridae): lineage components and biogeography. Syst. Zool. 34: 1–20.

———. 1988. Phylogenetic relationships among advanced snakes: a molecular perspective. University of California Publications in Zoology 119: 1–77.

———. 1992. Phylogenetic relationships among vipers: immunological evidence. Pp. 41–48 in J. A. Campbell and E. D. Brodie Jr. (eds.), Biology of the pitvipers. Selva, Tyler, Texas.

Cadle, J. E., and G. C. Gorman. 1981. Albumin immunological evidence and the relationships of sea snakes. J. Herpetol. 15: 329–334.

Cadle, J. E., and H. W. Greene. 1993. Phylogenetic patterns, biogeography, and the ecological structure of Neotropical snake assemblages. Pp. 281–293 in D. Schluter and R. E. Ricklefs (eds.), Species diversity in ecological communities: historical and geographical perspectives. University of Chicago Press, Chicago.

Cadle, J. E., and V. M. Sarich. 1981. An immunological assessment of the phylogenetic position of New World coral snakes. Journal of Zoology 195: 157–167.

Caiaffa, W. T., C. M. Antunes, H. R. de Oliveira, and C. R. Diniz. 1997. Epidemiological and clinical aspects of snakebite in Belo Horizonte, southeast Brazil. Revista do Instituto de Medicina Tropical de São Paulo 39(2): 113–118.

Calleffo, M. E. V. 1999. Dados preliminares do levantamento herpetologico na U.H.E. Sergio Motta, Porto Primavera–MS/SP, Brasil. P. 42 in Abstracts of the V Congreso Latinoamericano de Herpetología, Montevideo, 12 al 17 de diciembre de 1999.

Camarillo R., J. L. 1995. Distribution records for some amphibians and reptiles from Mexico. Bull. Maryland Herpetol. Soc. 31(4): 195–197.

Camarillo R., J. L., and J. A. Campbell. 1993. A second confirmed population of the rare Mexican rattlesnake, *Crotalus transversus* (Serpentes: Viperidae). Texas Journal of Science 45(2): 178–179.

———. 2002. Observaciones sobre la historia natural de *Crotalus transversus* (Squamata: Viperidae). Boletín de la Sociedad Herpetológica Mexicana 10(1): 7–9.

Camarillo [R.], J. L., and G. Casas-Andreu. 1998. Notas sobre la herpetofauna del área comprendida entre Zacualtipán, Hidalgo, y Huayacocotlaa, Veracruz. Anales Instituto de Biología Universidad Autónoma de México, Serie Zoología, 69(2): 231–237.

Cameron, D. L., and A. T. Tu. 1977. Characterization of myotoxin a from the venom of the prairie rattlesnake (*Crotalus viridis viridis*). Biochemistry 16: 2546–2552.

Cameron, H. A. 1898. *Heloderma horridum* (*suspectum*). Journal of Homeopathy 1: 295–306.

Camin, J. H. 1953. Observations on the life history and sensory behavior of the snake mite, *Ophionyssus natricis* (Gervais) (Acarina: Macronyssidae). Chicago Academy of Science Special Publications 10: 1–75.

Camp, C. L. 1916. Notes on the local distribution and habits of the amphibians and reptiles of southeastern California in the vicinity of the Turtle Mountains. Univ. California Publs. Zool. 12: 503–544.

———. 1923. Classification of the lizards. Bull. Am. Mus. Nat. Hist. 48(11): 289–481.

Campbell, B. 1934. Report on a collection of reptiles and amphibians made in Arizona during the summer of 1933. Occas. Pap. Mus. Zool. Univ. Michigan 289: 1–10.

Campbell, C. H. 1979. Symptomatology, pathology and treatment of the bites of elapid snakes. Pp. 898–921 in C. Y. Lee (ed.), Snake venoms. Springer-Verlag, New York.

Campbell, J. A. 1973a. A captive hatching of *Micrurus fulvius tenere* (Serpentes, Elapidae). J. Herpetol. 7(3): 312–315.

———. 1973b. Life history: *Bothrops bilineatus*. HISS News Journal 1(3): 191.

———. 1976. A new terrestrial pit viper of the genus *Bothrops* (Reptilia, Serpentes, Crotalidae) from western Mexico. J. Herpetol. 10(3): 151–160.

———. 1977. The distribution, variation, and natural history of the Middle American highland pitvipers, *Bothrops barbouri* and *Bothrops godmani*. Master's thesis, University of Texas at Arlington. 152 pp.

———. 1979a. *Crotalus scutulatus* (Viperidae) in Jalisco, Mexico. Southwest. Nat. 24(4): 693–694.

———. 1979b. A new rattlesnake (Reptilia, Serpentes, Viperidae) from Jalisco, Mexico. Trans. Kansas Acad. Sci. 81(4): 365–369.

———. 1982a. A confusing specimen of rattlesnake from Cerro Tancítaro, Michoacán, Mexico. Southwest. Nat. 27(3): 353.

———. 1982b. The biogeography of the cloud forest herpetofauna of Middle America with special reference to the Sierra de las Minas of Guatemala. Ph.D. dissertation, University of Kansas. 322 pp.

———. 1985. A new species of highland pitviper of the genus *Bothrops* from southern Mexico. J. Herpetol. 19(1): 48–54.

———. 1988a. The distribution, variation, natural history, and relationships of *Porthidium barbouri* (Viperidae). Acta Zoologica Mexicana, new ser., 26: 1–32.

———. 1988b. *Crotalus transversus*. Catalogue of American Amphibians and Reptiles 450.1–450.3

———. 1998. The amphibians and reptiles of northern Guatemala, Yucatán, and Belize. University of Oklahoma Press, Norman. 367 pp.

———. 1999. Distribution patterns of amphibians in Middle America. Pp. 111–210 in W. E. Duellman (ed.), Patterns of distribution of amphibians. Johns Hopkins University Press, Baltimore.

———. 2000. A new species of venomous coral snake (Serpentes: Elapidae) from high desert in Puebla, Mexico. Proceedings of the Biological Society of Washington 113(1): 291–297.

———. 2001 [dated 2000]. The herpetofauna of the mesic upland forests of the Sierra de Las Minas and Montañas del Mico of Guatemala. Pp. 80–92 in J. D. Johnson, R. G. Webb, and O. A. Flores-Villela (eds.), Mesoamerican herpetology: systematics, zoogeography, and conservation. Centennial Museum, special publ. University of Texas at El Paso.

Campbell, J. A., and B. L. Armstrong. 1979. Geographic variation in the Mexican Pygmy Rattlesnake, *Sistrurus ravus*, with the description of a new subspecies. Herpetologica 35(4): 304–317.

Campbell, J. A., and E. D. Brodie Jr. (eds.). 1992. Biology of the pitvipers. Selva, Tyler, Texas. 467 pp.

Campbell, J. A., E. D. Brodie Jr., D. G. Barker, and A. H. Price. 1989a. An apparent natural hybrid rattlesnake and *Crotalus willardi* (Viperidae) from the Peloncillo Mountains of New Mexico. Herpetologica 45(3): 344–349.

Campbell, J. A., D. R. Formanowicz Jr., and E. D. Brodie Jr. 1989b. Potential impact of rattlesnake roundups on natural populations. Texas Journal of Science 41(3): 301–318.

Campbell, J. A. and D. R. Frost. 1993. Anguid lizards of the genus *Abronia*: revisionary notes, descriptions of four new species, a phylogenetic analysis, and key. Bull. Am. Mus. Nat. Hist. 216: 1–121.

Campbell, J. A., and W. W. Lamar. 1989. The venomous reptiles of Latin America. Cornell University Press, Ithaca, N.Y. 425 pp.

———. 1992. The taxonomic status of miscellaneous Neotropical viperids, with the description of a new genus. Occasional Papers of the Museum, Texas Tech University 153: 1–31.

Campbell, J. A., and E. N. Smith. 2000. A new species of arboreal pitviper from the Atlantic versant of northern Central America. Rev. Biol. Trop. 48(4): 1001–1013.

Campbell, J. A., and A. Solórzano. 1992. The distribution, variation, and natural history of the Middle American montane pitviper, *Porthidium godmani*. Pp. 223–250 in J. A. Campbell and E. D. Brodie Jr. (eds.), Biology of the pitvipers. Selva, Tyler, Texas.

Campbell, J. A., and J. P. Vannini. 1988a. A new subspecies of beaded lizard, *Heloderma horridum*, from the Motagua Valley of Guatemala. J. Herpetol. 22: 457–468.

———. 1988b. Preliminary checklist of the herpetofauna of Finca El Faro, El Palmar, Quezaltenango, Guatemala. Publicación Ocasional Fundación Interamericana de Investigación Tropical 1: 1–10.

———. 1989. Distribution of amphibians and reptiles in Guatemala and Belize. Western Foundation of Vertebrate Zoology 4(1): 1–21.

Campbell, J. A., and D. H. Whitmore Jr. 1989. A comparison of the skin keratin biochemistry in vipers with comments on its systematic value. Herpetologica 45(2): 242–249.

Camper, J. D. 2001. County records of amphibians and reptiles from northeastern South Carolina. Herpetol. Rev. 32(3): 200–201.

Campos, S., E. Escobar, F. Lazo, A. Yarleque, N. A. Marsh, P. M. Peyser, B. C. Whaler, J. L. Creighton, and P. J. Gaffney. 1988. Partial separation and characterization of a thrombin-like enzyme from the venom of the Peruvian bushmaster snake, *Lachesis muta muta*. P. 107 in H. Pirkle and F. S. Markland (eds.), Hemostasis and animal venoms. Marcel Dekker, New York.

Canese, A. 1966. Animales venenosos del Paraguay. Revista Paraguaya de Microbiología 1(1): 56–72.

Canseco-Márquez, L., and J. A. Campbell. 2003. Variation in the Zapotitlán coralsnake, *Micrurus pachecogili* (Serpentes: Elapidae). Southwest. Nat. 48(4): 705–707.

Canseco-Márquez, L., G. Gutiérrez-Mayen, and J. Salazar-Arenas. 2000. New records and range extensions for some amphibians and reptiles from Puebla, Mexico. Herpetol. Rev. 31(4): 259–263.

Cantino, P. D., H. N. Bryant, K. de Queiroz, M. J. Donoghue, T. Eriksson, D. M. Hillis, and M. S. Y. Lee. 1999. Species names in phylogenetic nomenclature. Syst. Biol. 48: 790–807.

Cantino, P. D., and K. de Queiroz. 2000. PhyloCode: a phylogenetic code of biological nomenclature. www.ohio.edu/phylocode/.

Capocaccia, L. 1961. Catalogo dei tipi di rettili del Museo Civico di Storia Naturale di Genova. Annali del Museo Civico Storia Naturale Giacomo Doria (Genova) 72: 86–111.

Cardinale, L., and L. J. Avila. 1997. Natural history notes: *Bothrops alternatus* (vibora de la cruz). Reproduction. Herpetol. Rev. 28(4): 205.

Cardoso, J. L. C. 2000. Snakebites in Brazil: epidemiological and clinical aspects (abstract). Pp. 12–13 in Simposio Internacional—El Envenenamiento Ofídico: Un Problema de Salud Pública en Latino América. 30 Aniversario del Instituto Clodomiro Picado de la Universidad de Costa Rica, 5–6 April 2000, San José, Costa Rica.

Cardoso, J. L. C., and R. B. Brando. 1982. Acidentes por animais peçonhentos clínica e tratamento. Biblioteca Brasileira de Livro Médico. Santos, São Paulo. 25 pp. + 60 slides.

Cardoso, J. L. C., H. W. Fan, F. O. S. França, M. T. Jorge, R. P. Leite, S. A. Nishioka, A. Avila, I. S. Sano-Martins, S. C. Tomy, M. L. Santoro, et al. 1993. Randomized comparative trial of three antivenoms in the treatment of envenoming by lance-headed vipers (*Bothrops jararaca*) in São Paulo, Brazil. Quarterly Journal of Medicine 86(5): 315–325.

Carl, G. 1980. Distributional records of Johnson County, Texas. Herpetol. Rev. 11(4): 116–117.

Carl, G., K. H. Peterson, and R. M. Hubbard. 1982a. Reproduction in captive Uracoan rattlesnakes, *Crotalus vegrandis*. Herpetol. Rev. 13(2): 42–43.

———. 1982b. Reproduction in captive Aruba Island rattlesnakes, *Crotalus unicolor*. Herpetol. Rev. 13(3): 89–90.

Carl, G. C. 1968. The reptiles of British Columbia, 3d ed., rev. British Columbia Provincial Museum, Department of Education, Handbook No. 3. 65 pp.

Carpenter, C. C. 1958. Reproduction, young, eggs, and food of Oklahoma snakes. Herpetologica 14(2): 113–115.

———. 1960. A large brood of western pigmy rattlesnakes. Herpetologica 16(2): 142–143.

———. 1979. A combat ritual between two male pygmy rattlesnakes (*Sistrurus miliarius*). Copeia 1979(4): 638–642.

Carpenter, C. C., and J. C. Gillingham. 1990. Ritualized behavior in *Agkistrodon* and allied genera. Pp. 523–531 in H. K. Gloyd and R. Conant (eds.), Snakes of the *Agkistrodon* complex: a monographic review. Society for the Study of Amphibians and Reptiles, Ithaca, N.Y. 614 pp.

Carpenter, C. C., J. C. Gillingham, and J. B. Murphy. 1976. The combat ritual of the rock rattlesnake (*Crotalus lepidus*). Copeia 1976(4): 764–780.

Carpenter, C. C., J. B. Murphy, and G. C. Carpenter. 1978. Tail luring in the death adder, *Acanthophis antarcticus* (Reptilia, Serpentes, Elapidae). J. Herpetol. 12: 574–577.

Carr, A. F., Jr. 1937 [dated 1936]. The Gulf-island cottonmouths. Proceedings of the Florida Academy of Science 1: 86–90.

———. 1940. A contribution to the herpetology of Florida. University of Florida Publication, Biological Science Series 3(1): 1–118.

———. 1950. Outline for a classification of animal habitats in Honduras. Bull. Am. Mus. Nat. Hist. 94: 565–594.

———. 1963. Life Nature Library: the reptiles. Time-Life Books, New York. 192 pp.

———. 1973. The American wilderness: the Everglades. Time-Life Books, Alexandria, Va. 184 pp.

———. 1994. A naturalist in Florida: a celebration of Eden. Yale University Press, New Haven, Conn. 264 pp.

Carr, A. F., Jr., and M. H. Carr. 1942. Notes on the courtship of the cottonmouth moccasin. Proceedings of the New England Zoölogical Club 20: 1–6.

Carr, A. F., Jr., and C. J. Goin. 1955. Guide to the reptiles, amphibians, and fresh-water fishes of Florida. University of Florida Press, Gainesville, Florida. 341 pp.

Carrillo de Espinoza, N. 1970. Contribución al conocimiento de los reptiles del Perú (Squamata, Crocodylia, Testudinata: Reptilia). Publicaciones del Museo de Historia Natural "Javier Prado," Serie A, Zoología, 22: 1–64.

———. 1977. Arañas y serpientes muy venenosas en el departamento de Lima. Publicaciones del Museo de Historia Natural "Javier Prado," Serie de Divulgación 8: 1–8.

——. 1983. Contribución al conocimiento de las serpientes venenosas del Perú de las familias Viperidae, Elapidae e Hydrophiidae (Ophidia: Reptilia). Publicaciones del Museo de Historia Natural "Javier Prado," Universidad Nacional Mayor de San Marcos, Serie A, Zoología, 30: 1–55.

Carrillo de Espinoza, N., and J. Icochea. 1995. Lista taxonómica preliminar de los reptiles vivientes del Perú. Publicaciones del Museo de Historia Natural "Javier Prado," Universidad Nacional Mayor de San Marcos, Serie A, Zoología, 49: 1–27.

Carroll, R. B., E. L. Hall, and C. S. Kitchens. 1997. Canebrake rattlesnake envenomation. Ann. Emerg. Med. 30(1): 45–48.

Carvalho, M. A. de, and F. Nogueira. 1998. Snakes from the urban area of Cuiabá, Mato Grosso: ecological aspects and associated snakebites. Cadernos de Saúde Pública (Rio de Janeiro) 14: 753–763.

Casais e Silva, L. L. 1996. Geographic distribution: *Micrurus lemniscatus*. Herpetol. Rev. 27(2): 88–89.

Casais e Silva, L. L., and T. Brazil Nunes. 1996. Geographic distribution: *Micrurus corallinus* (coral snake). Herpetol. Rev. 27(1): 34.

Casas-Andreu, G. 1979. Ejemplares tipo de la colección herpetológica del Instituto de Biología, UNAM. Anales del Instituto de Biología, Universidad Nacional Autónoma de México 50, Serie Zoología, 1: 657–650.

——. 1981. Lista preliminar de los anfibios y reptiles de la costa de Jalisco. Instituto de Biología, Universidad Nacional Autónoma de México. 5 pp.

——. 1990. Geographic distribution: *Pelamis platurus* (yellowbelly sea snake). Herpetol. Rev. 21(2): 41.

——. 1992. Anfibios y reptiles de las Islas Marías y otras islas adyacentes a la costa de Nayarit, México. Aspectos sobre su biogeografía y conservación. Anales del Instituto de Biología, Universidad Nacional Autónoma de México, Serie Zoológía, 63: 95–112.

——. 1997. Distribución de la culebra de mar *Pelamis platurus* en el Pacífico Mexicano. Revista de la Sociedad Mexicana de Historia Natural 47: 157–166.

Casas-Andreu, G., and W. López-Forment C. 1978. Notas sobre *Micrurus browni taylori* Schmidt and Smith, en Guerrero, México. Anales del Instituto de Biología, Universidad Nacional Autónoma de México 49(1): 291–294.

Casas-Andreu, G., F. R. Méndez-de la Cruz, and J. L. Camarillo. 1996. Anfibios y reptiles de Oaxaca. Lista, distribución, y conservación. Acta Zoológica Mexicana 69: 1–35.

Case, T. J. 1978. A general explanation for insular size trends in terrestrial vertebrates. Ecology 59: 1–18.

Casper, G. S. 1996. Geographic distributions of the amphibians and reptiles of Wisconsin. Milwaukee Public Museum, Milwaukee. 87 pp.

Castoe, T. A. 2002. Microhabitat selection in *Porthidium nasutum* (Serpentes: Viperidae) in Costa Rica, with comments on ontogenetic variation. Herpetol. Rev. 33(3): 174–175.

Castoe, T. A., P. T. Chippindale, J. A. Campbell, L. K. Ammerman, and C. L. Parkinson. 2003. Molecular systematics of the Middle American jumping pitvipers (genus *Atropoides*) and phylogeography of the *Atropoides nummifer* complex. Herpetologica 59(3): 420–431.

Castro, F. 1998. Ecología e historia natural de las serpientes en el Chocó biogeográfico. Pp. 41–46 in R. Otero Patiño, R. Angel Mejía, and M. E. García (eds.), Primer simposio colombiano de toxinología. Memorias Colciencias, Medellín, el 12–14 de marzo de 1998.

Castro, F., G. Kattan K., and C. Murcia D. 1982. Serpientes corales verdaderas y falsas del Valle del Cauca. COAGRO (Cooperativa Agroindustrial do Estado do Rio de Janeiro) 4: 15–21.

Catesby, M. 1731–1743. The natural history of Carolina, Florida, and the Bahama Islands, 2 vols. W. Innys, London.

Catlin, W. P. 1950. A new Florida record for *Sistrurus miliarius barbouri*. Copeia 1950(1): 59–60.

Cavalli-Sforza, L. L., and A. W. F. Edwards. 1967. Phylogenetic analysis: models and estimation procedures. Evolution 32: 550–570.

Cavanaugh, C. J. 1994. Natural history notes: *Crotalus horridus* (timber rattlesnake). Longevity. Herpetol. Rev. 25(2): 70.

Cei, J. M. 1975. *Liolaemus melanops* Burmeister and the subspecific status of the *Liolaemus fitzingeri* group (Sauria-Iguanidae). J. Herpetol. 9(1): 217–222.

——. 1979a. The Patagonian herpetofauna. Pp. 309–339 in W. E. Duellman (ed.), The South American herpetofauna: its origin, evolution, and dispersal. Monograph No. 7 of the Museum of Natural History, University of Kansas, Lawrence.

——. 1979b. Remarks on the South American iguanid lizard *Liolaemus anomalus* Koslowsky, and the synonymy of *Phrynosaura werneri* Müller (Reptilia, Lacertilia, Iguanidae). J. Herpetol. 13(2): 183–186.

——. 1987 [dated 1986]. Reptiles del centro, centro-oeste y sur de la Argentina. Herpetofauna de las zonas áridas y semiáridas. Museo Regionale di Scienze Naturali, Torino, Monografie 4. 527 pp.

——. 1993. Reptiles del noroeste, nordeste y este de la Argentina. Museo Regionale di Scienze Naturali, Torino, Monografie 14. 929 pp.

Cendrero, L., F. de Buen, M. A. Freiberg, C. C. Olrog, and J. Yepes. 1972. Zoología hispanoamericana. Vertebrados. Editorial Porrúa, México, D.F. 1160 pp.

Cerdas, L. G., A. Cornavaca, and R. López. 1986. Ofidismo en la región Atlántica de Costa Rica: análisis de 164 casos. Acta Médica Costarricense 29: 113–117.

Chace, G. E., and H. M. Smith. 1968. Two additional examples of Gloyd's linked albinism in the prairie rattlesnake, *Crotalus viridis*. J. Herpetol. 2(3–4): 165–166.

Chadwick, L. E., and H. E. Rahn. 1954. Temperature dependence of rattling frequency in the rattlesnake, *Crotalus v. viridis*. Science 119: 442–443.

Chagnon, N. A. 1968. Yanomamö: the fierce people. Holt, Rinehart, Winston, New York. 142 pp.

Chamberlain, E. B. 1935. Notes on the pygmy rattlesnake, *Sistrurus miliarius* Linnaeus, in South Carolina. Copeia 1935(3): 146–147.

Chambrier, A. du, C. Vaucher, and F. Renaud. 1992. Etude des caractères morpho-anatomiques et des flux géniques chez quatre *Proteocephalus* (Cestoda: Proteocephalidae) parasites de *Bothrops jararaca* du Brésil et description de trois espèces nouvelles. Systematic Parasitology 23: 141–156.

Chance, B. 1970. A note on the feeding habits of *Micrurus fulvius fulvius* (cannibalism). Bull. Maryland Herpetol. Soc. 6: 56.

Chaney, A. H., and E. A. Liner. 1986. Natural history notes: *Crotalus pricei miquihuanus* (Miquihuanan twin spotted rattlesnake). Herpetol. Rev. 17(4): 89.

Chang, C. C. 1979. The action of snake venoms on nerve and muscle. Pp. 309–376 in C. Y. Lee (ed.), Snake venoms. Springer-Verlag, New York.

Chapman, B. R., and S. D. Castro. 1972. Additional vertebrate prey of the loggerhead shrike. Wilson Bulletin 84(4): 496–497.

Charland, M. B. 1989. Size and winter survivorship in neonatal western rattlesnakes (*Crotalus viridis*). Canadian Journal of Zoology 67: 1620–1625.

Charland, M. B., and P. T. Gregory. 1989. Feeding rate and weight gain in postpartum rattlesnakes: do animals that eat more always grow more? Copeia 1989(1): 211–214.

——. 1990. The influence of female reproductive status on thermoregulation in a viviparous snake, *Crotalus viridis*. Copeia 1990(4): 1089–1098.

Charlesworth, B. 1994. The genetics of adaptation: lessons from mimicry. American Naturalist 144: 839–847.

Charlesworth, D., and B. Charlesworth. 1975. Theoretical genetics of Batesian mimicry. I. Single-locus models. Journal of Theoretical Biology 55: 283–303.

——. 1976a. Theoretical genetics of Batesian mimicry II. Evolution of supergenes. Journal of Theoretical Biology 55: 305–324.

——. 1976b. Theoretical genetics of Batesian mimicry III. Evolution of dominance. Journal of Theoretical Biology 55: 325–337.

Chaves, F., G. D. Loría, A. Salazar, and J. M. Gutiérrez. 2003. Intramuscular administration of antivenoms in experimental envenomation by *Bothrops asper*: comparison between Fab and IgG. Toxicon 40: 237–244.

Cheatham, M. 1988. Geographic distribution: *Agkistrodon piscivorus leucostoma* (western cottonmouth). Herpetol. Rev. 19(1): 19.

Chenoweth, W. L. 1948. Birth and behavior of young copperheads. Herpetologica 4(5): 162.

———. 1950. Records of amphibians and reptiles from New Mexico. New Mexico Quarterly 26: 257–288.

Chernov, S. A. 1957. Systematic position of the poisonous snake *Ancistrodon rhodostoma* (Boie) (Serpentes, Crotalidae) in connection with its craniology. Zool. Zhur., Moskva 36: 790–792.

Chiasson, R. B., D. L. Bentley, and C. H. Lowe. 1989. Scale morphology in *Agkistrodon* and closely related crotaline genera. Herpetologica 45(4): 430–438.

Chippaux, J.-P. 1987 [dated 1986]. Les serpents de la Guyane française. Coll. Faune Tropicale 27. ORSTOM [Organisation de Recherche Scientifique et Technique pour l'Outre-mer], Paris. 165 pp.

———. 1998. Snake-bites: appraisal of the global situation. Bulletin of the World Health Organization 76: 515–524.

———. 2002. Les envenimations ophidiennes en Guyane française. Med Trop. Marseille 62: 177–184.

Chippaux, J.-P., J. Galtier, and J. F. Lefait. 1984. Epidemiologie des envenimations en Guyane française. Bulletin de la Société de Pathologie Exotique 77: 206–215.

Chippaux, J.-P., L. Sanite, and D. Heuclin. 1988. Serpents de Guyane. SEPANGUY, Cayenne, French Guiana. 55 pp.

Chippaux, J.-P., and R. D. G. Theakston. 1987. Epidemiological studies of snakebite in French Guiana. Annals of Tropical Medicine and Parasitology 81(3): 301–304.

Chippindale, P. T., A. H. Price, J. J. Wiens, and D. M. Hillis. 2000. Phylogenetic relationships and systematic revision of central Texas hemidactyliine plethodontid salamanders. Herpetological Monographs 14: 1–80.

Chiszar, D., L. J. Livo, R. R. J. Smith, and H. M. Smith. 1995. Geographic distribution: *Crotalus viridis* (western rattlesnake). Herpetol. Rev. 26(3): 156.

Chiszar, D., and C. W. Radcliffe. 1989. The predatory strike of the jumping viper (*Porthidium nummifer*). Copeia 1989(4): 1037–1039.

Chiszar, D., K. Scudder, H. M. Smith, and C. W. Radcliffe. 1976. Observation of courtship in the western massasauga (*Sistrurus catenatus tergeminus*). Herpetologica 32(3): 337–338.

Chiszar, D., and H. M. Smith. 1993. Geographic distribution: *Crotalus viridis viridis* (prairie rattlesnake). Herpetol. Rev. 24(4): 156.

———. 1994. Natural history notes: *Crotalus viridis* (prairie rattlesnake). Record rattle-string. Herpetol. Rev. 25(3): 123.

———. 2002. Colubrid envenomations in the United States. Journal of Toxicology—Toxin Reviews 21(1–2): 85–104.

Chiszar, D., H. M. Smith, and R. Defusco. 1993. Life history notes: *Crotalus viridis viridis* (prairie rattlesnake). Diet. Herpetol. Rev. 24(3): 106.

Chiszar, D., A. Walters, J. Urbaniak, H. M. Smith, and S. P. Mackessy. 1999. Discrimination between envenomated and nonenvenomated prey by western diamondback rattlesnakes (*Crotalus atrox*): chemosensory consequences of venom. Copeia 1999(3): 640–648.

Chotkowski, L. A. 1949. The treatment of snake-bite poisoning: a report of two cases involving the copperhead. New England Journal of Medicine 241: 600–603.

Chrapliwy, P. S., and C. M. Fugler. 1955. Amphibians and reptiles collected in Mexico in the summer of 1953. Herpetologica 11(2): 121–128.

Christiansen, J. L., and R. M. Bailey. 1988. The snakes of Iowa. Iowa Conservation Commission, Des Moines. 15 pp.

———. 1990. The snakes of Iowa. Iowa Department of Natural Resources, Nongame Technical Series No. 1: 1–16.

Christman, B. L., and C. W. Painter. 1998. Geographic distribution: *Crotalus molossus* (blacktail rattlesnake). Herpetol. Rev. 29(4): 249.

Christman, B. L., C. W. Painter, R. D. Jennings, and A. W. Lamb. 2000. Geographic distribution: *Crotalus viridis cerberus* (Arizona black rattlesnake). Herpetol. Rev. 31(4): 255.

Christman, S. P. 1980. Patterns of geographic variation in Florida snakes. Bulletin of the Florida State Museum, Biological Sciences, 25: 157–256.

Christman, S. P., C. A. Young, S. Gonzalez, K. Hill, G. Navratil, and P. Delis. 2000. New records of amphibians and reptiles from Hardee County, Florida. Herpetol. Rev. 31(2): 116–117.

Chugh, K. S., and V. Sakhuja. 1991. Renal disease caused by snake venom. Pp. 471–493 in A. T. Tu (ed.), Handbook of natural toxins: reptile venoms and toxins, vol. 5. Marcel Dekker, New York.

Cifelli, R. L., J. I. Kirkland, A. Weil, A. L. Deino, and B. J. Kowallis. 1997. High-precision ^{40}Ar/^{39}Ar geochronology and the advent of North America's late Cretaceous terrestrial fauna. Proceedings of the National Academy of Sciences 94: 11163–11167.

Cifelli, R. L., and R. L. Nydam. 1995. Primitive helodermatid-like platynotan from the early Cretaceous of Utah. Herpetologica 51(3): 286–291.

Clark, A. W., and E. Schultz. 1980. Rattlesnake shaker muscle, 2: fine structure. Tissue and Cell 12(2): 335–352.

Clark, D. R. 1963. Variation and sexual dimorphism in a brood of the western pygmy rattlesnake (*Sistrurus*). Copeia 1963(1): 157–159.

Clark, H. C. 1925. Snakes of the Ulua River Valley. Annual Report United Fruit Company Medical Department 14: 286–297.

———. 1942. Venomous snakes. Some Central American records: incidence of snake-bite accidents. American Journal of Tropical Medicine 22: 37–49.

———. 1951. Annual report of the Gorgas Memorial Laboratory, 1951. GPO, Washington, D.C. 36 pp.

Clark, L. 1953. The rivers ran east. Funk and Wagnalls, New York. 366 pp.

Clark, P. J., and R. F. Inger. 1942. Scale reduction studies in certain non-colubrid snakes. Copeia 1942(4): 230–232.

Clark, R. F. 1949. Snakes of the hill parishes of Louisiana. Journal of the Tennessee Academy of Science 24(4): 244–261.

———. 1959. Poisonous snakes of Kansas. Kansas School Naturalist 5(3): 1–16.

Clark, R. F., P. E. McKinney, P. B. Chase, and F. G. Walter. 2002. Immediate and delayed allergic reactions to Crotalidae polyvalent immune Fab (ovine) antivenom. Annals of Emergency Medicine 39:671–676.

Clark, R. F., B. S. Selden, and B. Furbee. 1993. The incidence of wound infection following crotalid envenomation. Journal of Emergency Medicine 11: 583–586.

Clark, R. F., S. R. Williams, S. P. Nordt, and L. V. Boyer-Hassen. 1997. Successful treatment of crotalid-induced neurotoxicity with a new polyspecific crotalid Fab antivenom. Ann. Emerg. Med. 30: 54–57.

Clark, R. W. 2002. Diet of the timber rattlesnake, *Crotalus horridus*. J. Herpetol. 36(3): 494–499.

Clark, W. C., and H. K. Voris. 1969. Venom neutralization by rattlesnake serum albumin. Science 164: 1402–1404.

Clarke, C. A., and P. M. Sheppard. 1971. Further studies on the genetics of the mimetic butterfly *Papilio memnon*. Philosophical Transactions of the Royal Society of London B 263: 35–70.

Clarke, C. A., P. M. Sheppard, and I. W. B. Thornton. 1968. The genetics of the mimetic butterfly *Papilio memnon*. Philosophical Transactions of the Royal Society of London B 254: 37–89.

Clarke, G. K. 1961. Report on a bite by a red diamond rattlesnake, *Crotalus ruber ruber*. Copeia 1961(4): 418–422.

Clarke, J. A., J. T. Chopko, and S. P. Mackessy. 1996. The effect of moonlight on activity patterns of adult and juvenile prairie rattlesnakes (*Crotalus viridis viridis*). J. Herpetol. 30(2): 192–197.

Clarkson, R. W., and J. C. DeVos Jr. 1986. The bullfrog, *Rana catesbiana* Shaw, in the lower Colorado River, Arizona–California. J. Herpetol. 20(1): 42–49.

Clench, W. J. 1925. A possible manner of snake distribution. Copeia 1925(142): 40.

Cliff, F. S. 1954. Snakes of the islands in the Gulf of California, Mexico. Trans. San Diego Soc. Nat. Hist. 12(5): 67–98.

Cobb, V. A., and C. R. Peterson. 1999. Natural history notes: *Crotalus viridis lutosus* (Great Basin rattlesnake). Mortality. Herpetol. Rev. 30(1): 45–46.

Cochran, D. M. 1943. Poisonous reptiles of the world: a wartime handbook. Smithsonian Institution, War Background Studies 10: 1–37.

——. 1946. Notes on the herpetology of the Pearl Islands, Panama. Smithsonian Miscellaneous Collections 106(4): 1–8.

——. 1961. Type specimens of reptiles and amphibians in the United States National Museum. Bulletin of the U.S. National Museum 220: 1–291.

Cochran, P. A., and J. R. Hodgson. 1997. A note on reproduction by the rainforest hognosed pitviper (*Porthidium nasutum*) in Panama. Bull. Maryland Herpetol. Soc. 33(2): 63–64.

Cochran, P. A., and J. D. Lyons. 1986. New distributional records for Wisconsin: amphibians and reptiles. Transactions of the Wisconsin Academy of Sciences, Arts, and Letters 74: 138–141.

Cochrane, T. T., and P. G. Jones. 1981. Savannas, forests, and wet season potential evapotranspiration in tropical South America. Tropical Agriculture (Trinidad) 58(3): 185–190.

Cockerell, T. D. A. 1896. Reptiles and batrachians of Mesilla Valley, N. Mex. American Naturalist 30: 325–327.

Coe, C. H. 1891. The poisonous snakes of Florida. Scientific American 64: 401.

Coelho, L. K., E. Silva, C. Espositto, and M. Zanin. 1992. Clinical features and treatment of Elapidae bites: report of three cases. Human and Experimental Toxicology 11: 135–137.

Cogger, H. G. 1992. Reptiles and amphibians of Australia, 3d ed. Cornell University Press, Ithaca, N.Y. 775 pp.

—— (ed.). 1999. Reptiles and amphibians. Little Guides. Federal Street Press, Springfield, Mass. 320 pp.

Cogo, J. C., J. P. Prado-Franceschi, M. A. Cruz-Hofling, A. P. Corrado, and M. A. Rodrigues-Simioni. 1993. Effect of *Bothrops insularis* venom on the mouse and chick nerve-muscle preparation. Toxicon 31: 1237–1247.

Cohen, A. C., and B. C. Myers. 1970. A function of the horns (supraocular scales) in the sidewinder rattlesnake, *Crotalus cerastes*, with comments on other horned snakes. Copeia 1970(3): 574–575.

Cohen, P. and E. B. Seligmann Jr. 1967 [dated 1966]. Immunological studies of coral snake venom. Mem. Inst. Butantan 33(1): 339–347.

Cole, C. J. 1990. Chromosomes of *Agkistrodon* and other viperid snakes. Pp. 533–538 in H. K. Gloyd and R. Conant (eds.), Snakes of the *Agkistrodon* complex: a monographic review. Society for the Study of Amphibians and Reptiles, Ithaca, N.Y. 614 pp.

Cole, M. 1996. Cerebral infarct after rattlesnake bite. Archives of Neurology 53: 957–958.

Collins, J. T. 1982. *Crotalus stejnegeri*. Catalogue of American Amphibians and Reptiles 303.1–303.2.

——. 1985. Amphibians. Pp. 145–158 in J. T. Collins (ed.), Natural Kansas. University Press of Kansas, Lawrence.

——. 1991. Viewpoint: a new taxonomic arrangement for some North American amphibians and reptiles. Herpetol. Rev. 22(2): 42–43.

——. 1993. Amphibians and reptiles in Kansas. Public Education Series No. 13. Museum of Natural History, University of Kansas, Lawrence. 397 pp.

Collins, J. T., and J. L. Knight. 1980. *Crotalus horridus* Linnaeus. Timber rattlesnake. Catalogue of American Amphibians and Reptiles 253.1–253.2.

Collins, R. F. 1980. Stomach contents of some snakes from eastern and central North Carolina. Brimleyana 4: 157–159.

Collins, R. F., and C. C. Carpenter. 1970. Organ position–ventral scute relationship in the water moccasin (*Agkistrodon piscivorus leucostoma*), with notes on food habits and distribution. Proceedings of the Oklahoma Academy of Science 49: 15–18.

Coloma, L. A., and S. R. Ron. 2001. Ecuador Megadiverso: anfibios, reptiles, aves, mamíferos. Serie de Divulgación 1. Museo de Zoología, Pontificia Universidad Católica del Ecuador, Quito. 138 pp.

Coloma, L. A., A. Quiguano, and S. Ron. 2000. Reptiles de Ecuador: lista de especies y distribución. Crocodylia, serpentes, y testudines. Version 1.1. 25 Mayo 2000. Museo de Zoología, Pontificia Universidad Católica del Ecuador, Quito, http://www.puce.edu.ec/Zoologia/repecua.htm (accessed 10 August 2001).

Comroe, D. B. 1948. *Kalicephalus conoidus*, n. sp. (Strongylata), a nematode from the rattlesnake *Crotalus triseriatus*. Transactions of the American Microscopical Society 67: 280–284.

Conant, R. 1938. The reptiles of Ohio. Am. Midl. Nat. 20: 1–200.

——. 1951. The reptiles of Ohio. University of Notre Dame Press, Notre Dame, Ind. 284 pp.

——. 1955. Notes on three Texas reptiles, including an addition to the fauna of the state. Am. Mus. Novitat. 1726: 1–6.

——. 1958. A field guide to reptiles and amphibians of the United States and Canada east of the 100th meridian. Houghton Mifflin, Boston. 366 pp.

——. 1969. Some rambling notes on rattlesnakes. Archives of Environmental Health 19: 768–769.

——. 1975. A field guide to reptiles and amphibians of eastern and central North America, 2d ed. Houghton Mifflin, Boston. 429 pp.

——. 1977. The Florida water snake (Reptilia, Serpentes, Colubridae) established at Brownsville, Texas, with comments on other herpetological introductions in the area. J. Herpetol. 11: 217–220.

——. 1982. The origin of the name "cantil" for *Agkistrodon bilineatus*. Herpetol. Rev. 13: 118.

——. 1984. A new subspecies of the pit viper *Agkistrodon bilineatus* (Reptilia; Viperidae) from Central America. Proceedings of the Biological Society of Washington 97: 135–141.

——. 1986. Phylogeny and zoogeography of the genus *Agkistrodon* in North America. Pp. 89–92 in Z. Rocek (ed.), Studies in herpetology: proceedings of the European Herpetological Meeting (3d Ordinary General Meeting of the Societas Europaea Herpetologica), Prague, 1985. Charles University, Prague.

——. 1990. The fossil history of the genus *Agkistrodon* in North America. Pp. 539–543 in H. K. Gloyd and R. Conant (eds.), Snakes of the *Agkistrodon* complex: a monographic review. Ithaca, N.Y., Society for the Study of Amphibians and Reptiles. 614 pp.

——. 1992. Comments on the survival status of members of the *Agkistrodon* complex. Greater Cincinnati Herpetological Society Contributions in Herpetology 1992: 29–33.

——. 1997. The great barrancas. Bull. Chicago Herpetol. Soc. 32(9): 189–196.

Conant, R., and W. Bridges. 1939. What snake is that? D. Appleton-Century, New York. 163 pp.

Conant, R., and J. T. Collins. 1998. A field guide to reptiles and amphibians of eastern and central North America. Houghton Mifflin, Boston. 616 pp.

Conley, K. E., and S. L. Lindstedt. 1996. Minimal cost per twitch in rattlesnake muscle. Nature 383(6595): 71–72.

Consroe, P., N. B. Egen, F. E. Russell, K. Gerrish, D. C. Smith, A. Sidki, and J. T. Landon. 1995. Comparison of a new ovine antigen binding fragment (Fab) antivenin for United States Crotalidae with the commercial antivenin for protection against venom-induced lethality in mice. American Journal of Tropical Medicine and Hygiene 53: 507–510.

Cook, D. G. 1984. A case of envenomation by the Neotropical colubrid snake *Stenorrhina feminvillei*. Toxicon 22: 823–827.

Cook, F. A. 1943. Snakes in Mississippi. Survey Bulletin, Mississippi Game and Fish Commission, Jackson, Mississippi, Pittman-Robertson Project. 73 pp.

——. 1954. Snakes of Mississippi. State Game and Fish Commission, Public Relations Department, Jackson, Miss. 73 pp.

Cook, F. R. 1984. Introduction to Canadian amphibians and reptiles. National Museum of Canada, Ottawa. 200 pp.

Cook, P. M., M. P. Rowe, and R. W. Van Devener. 1994. Allometric scaling and interspecific differences in the rattling sounds of rattlesnakes. Herpetologica 50(3): 358–368.

Cook, S. F., Jr. 1955. Rattlesnake hybrids: *Crotalus viridis* × *Crotalus scutulatus*. Copeia 1955(2): 139–141.

Cooke, E., and L. Loeb. 1913. General properties and actions of the venom of *Heloderma*, and experiments in immunization. Pp. 51–95 in L. Loeb (ed.), The venom of *Heloderma*. Carnegie Institution Publication No. 177, Washington, D.C.

Cooper, J. E. 1972. Review of Studies on the cavernicole fauna of Mexico, by Reddell and Mitchell. Herpetol. Rev. 4(3): 75.

Cooper, J. E., and F. Groves. 1959. The rattlesnake, *Crotalus horridus*, in the Maryland piedmont. Herpetologica 15(1): 33–34.

Cooper, J. G. 1859. Report upon the reptiles collected on the survey. Reports of explorations and surveys, to ascertain the most practicable and economical route for a railroad from the Mississippi River to the Pacific Ocean. United States and Pacific Railroad Exploration and Survey, 47th Parallel, 2d ser., 12(4): 292–306.

Cooper, W. E., Jr. 1989. Prey odor discrimination in the varanoid lizards *Heloderma suspectum* and *Varanus exanthematicus*. Ethology 81: 250–258.

——. 1994. Chemical discrimination by tongue-flicking in lizards: a review with hypotheses on its origin and its ecological and phylogenetic relationships. Journal of Chemical Ecology 20: 439–488.

Cooper, W. E., Jr., and J. Arnett. 1995. Strike-induced chemosensory searching in the Gila monster. Copeia 1995(1): 89–96.

Cooper, W. E., Jr., C. S. Deperno, and J. Arnett. 1994. Prolonged post-strike elevation in tongue-flicking rate with rapid onset in the Gila monster, *Heloderma suspectum*: relation to diet and foraging and implications for evolution of chemosensory searching. Journal of Chemical Ecology 20: 2867–2881.

Cope, E. D. 1860a [dated 1859]. Catalogue of the venomous serpents in the museum of the Academy of Natural Sciences of Philadelphia, with notes on the families, genera, and species. Proc. Acad. Nat. Sci. Philadelphia 11: 332–347.

——. 1860b. An enumeration of the genera and species of rattlesnakes, with synonymy and references. Smithsonian Contributions to Knowledge 12: 119–126.

——. 1860c. Supplement to "A catalogue of the venomous serpents in the museum of the Academy of Natural Sciences of Philadelphia, with notes on the families, genera, and species." Proc. Acad. Nat. Sci. Philadelphia 12: 72–74.

——. 1860d. Catalogue of the Colubridae in the Museum of the Academy of Natural Sciences of Philadelphia, with notes and descriptions of new species. Proc. Acad. Nat. Sci. Philadelphia 12: 241–266.

——. 1861. Contributions to the ophiology of lower California, Mexico, and Central America. Proc. Acad. Nat. Sci. Philadelphia 13: 292–306.

——. 1862. Catalogues of the reptiles obtained during the explorations of the Parana, Paraguay, Vermejo, and Uraguay [sic] rivers by Capt. Thos. J. Page, U.S.N., and those procured by Lieut. N. Michler, U.S. Top. Eng., commander of the expedition conducting the survey of the Atrato River. Proc. Acad. Nat. Sci. Philadelphia 14: 346–359.

——. 1864. Contributions to the herpetology of tropical America. Proc. Acad. Nat. Sci. Philadelphia 16: 166–181.

——. 1865. Third contribution to the herpetology of tropical America. Proc. Acad. Nat. Sci. Philadelphia 17: 185–189.

——. 1867 [dated 1866]. On the Reptilia and Batrachia of the Sonoran Province of the Nearctic region. Proc. Acad. Nat. Sci. Philadephia 18: 300–314.

——. 1868. An examination of the Reptilia and Batrachia obtained by the Orton expedition to Equador and the upper Amazon, with notes on other species. Proc. Acad. Nat. Sci. Philadelphia 20: 96–119.

——. 1869. Remarks on *Heloderma suspectum*. Proc. Acad. Nat. Sci. Philadelphia 21: 5.

——. 1870 [dated 1869]. Seventh contribution to the herpetology of tropical America. Proceedings of the American Philosophical Society 11: 147–169.

——. 1871. Ninth contribution to the herpetology of tropical America. Proc. Acad. Nat. Sci. Philadelphia 23: 200–224.

——. 1872. Report on the recent reptiles and fishes of the survey, collected by Campbell Carrington and C. M. Dawes. Pp. 467–476 in F. V. Hayden (ed.), Preliminary report of the United States Geological Survey of Montana.

——. 1874. Description of some species of reptiles obtained by Dr. John F. Bransford, assistant surgeon, United States Navy, while attached to the Nicaraguan surveying expedition in 1873. Proc. Acad. Nat. Sci. Philadelphia 26: 64–72.

——. 1875. Check-list of North American Batrachia and Reptilia with a systematic list of the higher groups, and an essay on geographical distribution based on specimens contained in the United States National Museum. GPO, Washington, D.C. 104 pp.

——. 1876a [dated 1875]. On the Batrachia and Reptilia of Costa Rica. Journal of the Academy of Natural Sciences of Philadelphia, 2d ser., 8(4): 93–154.

——. 1876b [dated 1875]. Report on the reptiles brought by Professor James Orton from the middle and upper Amazon and Western Peru. Journal of the Academy of Natural Sciences of Philadelphia, 2d ser.,8: 159–188.

——. 1877. Synopsis of the cold-blooded vertebrata procured by Prof. James Orton during his exploration of Peru in 1876–77. Proceedings of the American Philosophical Society 17: 33–49.

——. 1879. Eleventh contribution to the herpetology of tropical America. Proceedings of the American Philosophical Society 18: 261–277.

——. 1884a. Review of Garman's North American reptiles and batrachians. American Naturalist 18: 513–515.

——. 1884b [dated 1883]. Notes on the geographical distribution of Batrachia and Reptilia in western North America. Proceedings of the Academy of Natural Sciences 35: 10–35.

——. 1885a [dated 1884]. Twelfth contribution to the herpetology of tropical America. Proceedings of the American Philosophical Society 22: 167–194.

——. 1885b. A contribution to the herpetology of Mexico. Proceedings of the American Philosophical Society 22: 379–404.

——. 1886 [dated 1885]. Thirteenth contribution to the herpetology of tropical America. Proceedings of the American Philosophical Society 23: 271–287.

——. 1887. Catalogue of batrachians and reptiles of Central America and Mexico. Bulletin of the U.S. National Museum 32: 1–98.

——. 1892 [dated 1891]. A critical review of the characters and variations of the snakes of North America. Proceedings of the U.S. National Museum 14(882): 589–694.

——. 1893. Prodromus of a new system of the nonvenomous snakes. American Naturalist 27: 477–483.

——. 1894. On the lungs of the Ophidia. Proceedings of the American Philosophical Society 33: 217–224.

——. 1895 [dated 1894]. The classification of the Ophidia. Transactions of the American Philosophical Society 18(2): 186–219.

——. 1896. The geographical distribution of Batrachia and Reptilia in North America. American Naturalist 30: 886–902, 1003–1026.

——. 1900. The crocodilians, lizards, and snakes of North America. Annual Report of the U.S. National Museum 1898: 153–1270.

Cordeiro, C. L., and A. R. Hoge. 1974 [dated 1973]. Contribuição ao conhecimento das serpentes do estado de Pernambuco. Mem. Inst. Butantan 37: 261–290.

Cornett, J. W. 1979. Geographic distribution: *Crotalus ruber* (red diamond rattlesnake). Herpetol. Rev. 19(4): 119.

Correa-Sánchez, F., M. A. Casariego-Madorell, and F. Luna-Castellanos. 2001. Natural History notes: *Porthidium dunni* (Dunn's hognosed pitviper). Diet. Herpetol. Rev. 32(4): 264.

Correa-Sánchez, F., A. González-Ruiz, E. Godínez-Cano, J. Alfonso, and J. A. Delgadillo-Espinosa. 1999. Natural history notes: *Crotalus lepidus morulus* (rock rattlesnake). Reproduction. Herpetol. Rev. 30(3): 168.

Corrigan, J. J., and M. A. Jeter. 1990. Mojave rattlesnake (*Crotalus scutulatus scutulatus*) venom: in vitro effects on platelets, fibrinolysis, and fibrinogen clotting. Veterinary and Human Toxicology 32: 439–441.

Corrigan, P., F. E. Russell, and J. Wainschel. 1978. Clinical reactions to antivenin. Toxicon 16: 457–465.

Coss, R. G., K. L. Guse, N. S. Poran, and D. G. Smith. 1993. Development of antisnake defenses in California ground squirrels (*Spermophilus beechey*): II. Microevolutionary effects of relaxed selection from rattlesnakes. Behaviour 124(1–2): 137–164.

Costa-Prudente, A. L. da, S. A. A. Morato, and J. C. de Moura-Leite. 1995. Registro de um híbrido natural entre *Bothrops alternatus* Duméril, Bibron et Duméril, 1854, e *Bothrops neuwiedi* Wagler, 1824 (Serpentes: Viperidae). Biociências (Porto Alegre) 3: 231–238.

Cott, H. B. 1940. Adaptive coloration in animals. Methuen, London. 508 pp.

Coues, E. 1875. Synopsis of the reptiles and batrachians of Arizona; with critical and field notes, and an extensive synonymy. Report upon geographical and geological explorations and surveys west of the one hundreth meridian, in charge of First Lieut. Geo. M. Wheeler, Engineer Department, United States Army, Washington, D.C. 5(5): 585–633.

Coues, E., and H. C. Yarrow. 1878a. Notes on the herpetology of Dakota and Montana. Bulletin of the United States Geological and Geographic Survey 4(1): 259–291.

——. 1878b. Notes on the natural history of Fort Macon, North Carolina, and vicinity, no. 4. Proc. Acad. Nat. Sci. Philadelphia 30: 21–28.

Coupe, B. 2001. Arboreal behavior in timber rattlesnakes (*Crotalus horridus*). Herpetol. Rev. 32(2): 83–85.

Cover, J. F. 1983. Captive maintenance and propagation of the eyelash viper (*Bothrops schlegeli*). Pp. 304–322 in D. Marcellini (ed.), Proceedings of the Sixth Reptile Symposium on Captive Propagation, Thurmont, Md.

Cowan, I. T. 1937. A review of the reptiles and amphibians of British Columbia. Report of the Provincial Museum of Natural History for the Year 1936: 16–25

Cowell, Adrian. 1990. The decade of destruction. Henry Holt, New York. 215 pp.

Cowin, D. J., T. Wright, and J. A. Cowin. 1998. Long-term complications of snake bites to the upper extremity. Journal of the Southern Orthopedic Association 7: 205–211.

Cowles, R. B. 1938. Unusual defense postures assumed by rattlesnakes. Copeia 1938(1): 13–16.

——. 1941. Observations on the winter activities of desert reptiles. Ecology 22(2): 125–140.

——. 1945. Some of the activities of the sidewinder. Copeia 1945(4): 220–222.

——. 1953. The sidewinder: master of desert travel. Pacific Discovery 6(2): 12–15.

——. 1957 [dated 1956]. Sidewinding locomotion in snakes. Copeia 1956(4): 211–214.

——. 1962. Semantics in biothermal studies. Science 135: 670.

Cowles, R. B., and C. M. Bogert. 1935. Observations on the California lyre snake, *Trimorphodon vandenburghi* Klauber, with notes on the effectiveness of its venom. Copeia 1935: 80–85.

——. 1936. The herpetology of the Boulder Dam region (Nevada, Arizona, Utah). Herpetologica 1(2): 33–42.

——. 1944. A preliminary study of the thermal requirements of desert reptiles. Bull. Am. Mus. Nat. Hist. 83(5): 261–296.

Cowles, R. B., and R. L. Phelan. 1958. Olfaction in rattlesnakes. Copeia 1958(2): 77–83.

Cox, D. C., and W. W. Tanner. 1995. Snakes of Utah. Brigham Young University, Provo, Utah. 92 pp.

Cox, M. K., and W. L. Franklin. 1989. Terrestrial vertebrates of Scotts Bluff National Monument, Nebraska. Great Basin Naturalist 49(4): 597–613.

Crabtree, C. B., and R. W. Murphy. 1984. Analysis of maternal-offspring allozymes in *Crotalus viridis*. J. Herpetol. 18(1): 75–80.

Crane, D. B., and J. S. Irwin. 1985. Rattlesnake bite of glans penis. Urology 26: 50–52.

Cranwell, J. A. 1943. Para la herpetofauna de Misiones. Revista Argentina de Zoogeografía 3(1–2): 65–66.

Crawford, R. 1936. A study of the massasauga as found in Trumbull County, Ohio. Master's thesis, University of Southern California, Los Angeles.

Creaser, C. W. 1927. The northward distribution of venomous snakes in Michigan. Papers of the Michigan Academy of Science, Arts and Letters 8: 369–370.

Crimmins, M. L. 1927a. Notes on the Texas rattlesnakes. Bull. Antivenin Inst. Am. 1(1): 23–24.

——. 1927b. Facts about Texas snakes and their poison. Texas State Journal of Medicine 23(3): 198–203.

——. 1937. A case of *Oxybelis* poisoning in man. Copeia 1937(4): 233.

——. 1946. The treatment of poisonous snake bites in Texas. Texas Academy of Science 24: 54–61.

Crosman, A. M. 1956. A longevity record for Gila monster. Copeia 1956(1): 54.

Cross, C. L. 2002. Natural history notes: *Agkistrodon piscivorus piscivorus* (eastern cottonmouth). Diet. Herpetol. Rev. 33(1): 55–56.

Cross, C. L., and C. Marshall. 1998. Natural history notes: *Agkistrodon piscivorus piscivorus* (eastern cottonmouth). Herpetol. Rev. 29(1): 43.

Cross, J. K., and M. S. Rand. 1979. Climbing activity in wild-ranging Gila monsters, *Heloderma suspectum* (Helodermatidae). Southwest. Nat. 24(4): 703–705.

Crother, B. I. 1990. Review of The venomous reptiles of Latin America. Quarterly Review of Biology 65: 516–517.

——. 1999. Evolutionary relationships. Pp. 269–334 in B. I. Crother (ed.), Caribbean amphibians and reptiles. Academic Press, San Diego, California.

—— (ed.). 2001. Scientific and standard English names of amphibians and reptiles of North America north of Mexico, with comments regarding confidence in our understanding. Society for the Study of Amphibians and Reptiles, Herpetological Circular No. 29. 82 pp.

Crother, B. I., J. A. Campbell, and D. M. Hillis. 1992. Phylogeny and historical biogeography of the palm-pitvipers, genus *Bothriechis*: Biochemical and morphological evidence. Pp. 1–20 in J. A. Campbell and E. D. Brodie Jr. (eds.), Biology of the pitvipers. Selva, Tyler, Texas.

Croulet, C. 1963. A taste of the tropics. Bulletin of the Philadelphia Herpetological Society 1963 (January–June): 1–5.

Cruz, G. A. 1987. Serpientes venenosas de Honduras. Editorial Universitaria, Tegucigalpa. 160 pp.

Cruz, G. A., L. D. Wilson, and J. Espinosa. 1979. Two additions to the reptile fauna of Honduras, *Eumeces managuae* Dunn and *Agkistrodon bilineatus* (Gunther), with comments on *Pelamis platurus* (Linnaeus). Herpetol. Rev. 10: 26–27.

Cruz-Rocha, M. A., C. C. Borges, A. Verçosa-Dias, A. L. Boechat, J. A. Loureiro, G. A. Borja, C. S. Paiva, C. S. Mello, F. S. Maciel, L. W. Bindá, et al. 1997. Incidence of accidents caused by poisonous snakes in twenty-four municipal districts of Amazonas State. Journal of Venomous Animals and Toxins 3(1): 253.

Cuesta-Terrón, C. 1920 [dated 1919]. Datos para una monografía sobre la fauna erpetológica de la península de la Baja California. Boletin de la Dirección de Estudios Biológicos, Mexico 2(4): 398–402.

——. 1921a. Datos para una monografía de la fauna erpetológica de la península de la Baja California. Memorias y Revista de la Sociedad Científica Antonio Alzate 39: 161–171.

——. 1921b. Los crotalianos mexicanos. Memorias y Revista de la Sociedad Científica Antonio Alzate 39: 173–194.

——. 1930a. Los reptiles ponzoñosos mexicanos. 1. El escorpión (*Heloderma horridum* Wiegmann). Folletos Divulgativos Científicos del Instituto di Biología, Mexico, 2: 1–11.

——. 1930b. Los crotalianos mexicanos: su clasificación, ecología y distribución geográfica. Anales del Instituto de Biología, Universidad Nacional Autónoma de México 1(3): 187–199.

——. 1931. Los crotalianos mexicanos. Anales del Instituto de Biología, Universidad Nacional Autónoma de México 2(1): 47–72.

——. 1932. Los coralillos mexicanos. Anales del Instituto de Biología, Universidad Nacional Autónoma de México 3(1): 5–14.

Cuffey, R. J. 1971. Pacific sea snakes—a highly mobile newly recognized substrate for bryozoans (abstract). Proceedings of the Second International Bryozoan Association. Durham, U.K., 6–16 September 1971.

Cullings, K. W., D. J. Morafkka, J. Hernandez, and J. W. Roberts. 1997. Reassessment of phylogenetic relationships among pitviper genera based on mitochondrial cytochrome *b* gene sequences. Copeia 1997(2): 429–432.

Cundall, D. 1983. Activity of head muscles during feeding by snakes: a comparative study. American Zoologist 23: 383–396.

Cundall, D., V. Wallach, and D. A. Rossman. 1993. The systematic relationships of the snake genus *Anomochilus*. Zoological Journal of the Linnean Society 109: 275–299.

Cunha, A. C. M., and A. R. Melgarejo. 1991. Um exemplar de "cobra coral" *Micrurus corallinus* (Merrem, 1820) compadrão anomalo de coloração (Serpentes: Elapidae). Resumos XVIII Congr. Bras. Zool., Univ. Fed. BA Salvador I–II: 339.

Cunha, O. R. da. 1967. Ofídios da Amazônia. Primeira ocorrência de *Bothrops bilineatus bilineatus* (Wied) nas matas dos arredores de Belém, Pará (Ophidia, Crotalidae). Boletim do Museu Paraense Emílio Goeldi, Zoologia 66: 1–12.

Cunha, O. R. da, and F. P. Nascimento. 1972. Ofídios da Amazônia. 3. Sôbre a ocorrência de *Bothrops lichenosus* Roze, 1958 no Brasil (Ophidia, Crotalidae). Revista Brasileira de Biologia 32(1): 27–32.

———. 1973. Ofídios da Amazônia. 4. As cobras corais (genero *Micrurus*) da região leste do Pará (Ophidia, Elapidae)—nota preliminar. Papéis Avulsos Museu Paraense Emílio Goeldi 20: 273–286.

———. 1975a. Ofídios da Amazônia. 5. *Bothrops lichenosus* Roze, 1958, sinonimo de *Bothrops castelnaudi* Duméril, Bibron e Duméril, 1854, com nova descrição e comentários. Boletim do Museu Paraense Emílio Goeldi, Zoologia 80: 1–15.

———. 1975b. Ofídios da Amazônia. VII. As serpentes peçonhentas do genero *Bothrops* (Jararacas) e *Lachesis* (Surucucu) da região leste do Pará (Ophidia, Viperidae). Boletim do Museu Paraense Emílio Goeldi, Zoologia 83: 1–42.

———. 1978. Ofídios da Amazônia. X. As cobras da região leste do Pará. Papéis Avulsos Museu Paraense Emílio Goeldi 31: 218.

———. 1982a. Ofídios da Amazônia. XIV. As especies de *Micrurus*, *Bothrops*, *Lachesis* e *Crotalus* do sul do Pará e oeste do Maranhão, incluindo áreas de cerrado deste estado (Ophidia: Elapidae e Viperidae). Boletim do Museu Paraense Emílio Goeldi, Zoologia 112: 1–58.

———. 1982b. Ofídios da Amazônia. XVII. Revalidação de *Micrurus ornatissimus* (Jan, 1858) diferenciada de *M. langsdorffi* (Wagler, 1824) e distribuição geográfica das duas espécies (Ophidia: Elapidae). Boletim do Museu Paraense Emílio Goeldi, Zoologia 116: 1–17.

———. 1991. Ofídios da Amazônia. XXII. Revalidação e redescrição de *Micrurus albicinctus* Amaral, de Rondônia, e sôbre a validade de *Micrurus waehnerorum* Meise, do Amazonas (Ophidia: Elapidae). Boletim do Museu Paraense Emílio Goeldi, Zoologia 7(1): 43–52.

———. 1993. Ofídios da Amazônia. As cobras da região leste do Pará. Papéis Avulsos Museu Paraense Emílio Goeldi, n. ser., Zool., Belém 9(1): 1–191.

Cunha, O. R. da, F. P. do Nascimento, and T. C. S. Avila-Pires. 1985. Contribuções do Museu Paraense Emílio Goeldi au Projeto Carajás. Os répteis da área de Carajás, Pará, Brasil (Testudines e Squamata). Papéis Avulsos Museu Paraense Emílio Goeldi 40: 9–87.

Cunningham, G. R., S. M. Hickey, and C. M. Gowen. 1996. Natural history notes: *Crotalus viridis viridis* (prairie rattlesnake). Behavior. Herpetol. Rev. 27(1): 24.

Cunningham, J. D. 1955. Arboreal habits of certain reptiles and amphibians in southern California. Herpetologica 11(3): 217–220.

———. 1959. Reproduction and food of some California snakes. Herpetologica 15(1): 17–19.

Cupo, P., M. M. Azevedo-Marques, and S. E. Hering. 1988. Clinical and laboratory features of South American rattlesnake (*Crotalus durissus terrificus*) envenomation in children. Trans. Roy. Soc. Trop. Med. Hyg. 82: 924–929.

———. 1990. Acute myocardial infarction–like enzyme profile in human victims of *Crotalus durissus terrificus* envenoming. Trans. Roy. Soc. Trop. Med. Hyg. 84: 447–451.

Curran, C. H. 1935. Rattlesnakes. Natural History (New York) 36(4): 331–340.

Curran, C. H., and C. Kauffeld. 1937. Snakes and their ways. Harper and Brothers, New York. 285 pp.

Curry, S. C., J. C. Kraner, D. B. Kunkel, P. J. Ryan, M. V. Vance, R. K. Requa, and S. B. Ruggeri. 1985. Noninvasive vascular studies in management of rattlesnake envenomations to extremities. Ann. Emerg. Med. 14: 1081–1084.

Curtis, L. 1949a. Notes on the eggs of *Heloderma horridum*. Herpetologica 5(6): 148.

———. 1949b. The snakes of Dallas County, Texas. Field and Laboratory 17: 5–13.

———. 1952. Cannibalism in the Texas coral snake. Herpetologica 8(2): 27.

Curtiss, C. F. 1926. The snakes of Iowa. Agricultural Experimental Station, Iowa State College of Agriculture and Mechanic Arts Bulletin 239: 147–192.

Cushing, P. E. 1997. Myrmecomorphy and myrmecophily in spiders: a review. Florida Entomologist 80: 165–193.

Cuvier, G. 1817. Le règne animal distribué d'après son organisation, pour servir de base à l'histoire naturelle des animaux et d'introduction à l'anatomie comparée, vol. 2. Deterville, Paris. 532 pp.

Cypert, E. 1961. The effects of fires in the Okefenokee Swamp in 1954 and 1955. Am. Midl. Nat. 66: 485–503.

Czaplicki, J. A., and R. H. Porter. 1974. Visual cues mediating the selection of goldfish (*Carassius auratus*) by two species of *Natrix*. J. Herpetol. 8: 129–134.

D'Alessandro, A. 1972. Tratamiento de las mordeduras de viboras. Acta Médica Valle 3: 74–76.

D'Alessandro, S. E., and C. H. Ernst. 1995. Additional geographical records for reptiles in Virginia. Herpetol. Rev. 26(4): 212–214.

Dalrymple, G. H. 1988. The herpetofauna of Long Pine Key, Everglades National Park, in relation to vegetation and hydrology. Pp. 72–86 in R. C. Szaro, K. E. Severson, and D. R. Patton (technical coordinators), Management of amphibians, reptiles, and small mammals in North America. General Technical Report RM-166. USDA Forest Service, Fort Collins, Colo.

Dalrymple, G. H., F. S. Bernardino Jr., T. M. Steiner, and R. J. Nodell. 1991a. Patterns of species diversity of snake community assemblages, with data on two Everglades snake assemblages. Copeia 1991(2): 517–521.

Dalrymple, G. H., T. M. Steiner, R. J. Nodell, and F. S. Bernardino Jr. 1991b. Seasonal activity of the snakes of Long Pine Key, Everglades National Park. Copeia 1991(2): 294–302.

Dammann, A. E. 1961. Some factors affecting the distribution of sympatric species of rattlesnakes (genus *Crotalus*) in Arizona. Ph.D. dissertation, University of Michigan.

Damus, P. S., F. S. Markland Jr., T. M. Davidson, and J. D. Shanley. 1972. A purified procoagulant enzyme found in the venom of Eastern diamondback rattlesnake (*Crotalus adamanteus*): in vitro and in vivo studies. Journal of Laboratory and Clinical Medicine 79: 906–923.

Daniel, Hno. 1949. Las serpientes en Colombia. Revista Facultad Nacional de Agronomía (Medellín) 9(36): 301–333.

———. 1959. La colgadora y sus actividades. Progreso, Medellín 27: 38–42.

Danzig, L. E., and G. H. Abels. 1961. Hemodialysis of acute renal failure following rattlesnake bite, with recovery. JAMA 175: 136–137.

Danzl, D. F., and G. L. Carter. 1988. "Kiss and yell," a rattlesnake bite to the tongue. Ann. Emerg. Med. 17: 549.

Dao-L., L. 1971. Emponzoñamiento ofídico en el Estado Lara. Gaceta Medica de Caracas 79: 383–410.

Dart, R. C., and R. A. Gustafson. 1991. Failure of electric shock treatment for rattlesnake envenomation. Ann. Emerg. Med. 20: 659–661.

Dart, R. C., and D. Lindsey. 1988. Snakebites and shocks. Ann. Emerg. Med. 17: 1262.

Dart, R. C., and J. McNally. 2001. Efficacy, safety, and use of snake antivenoms in the United States. Ann. Emerg. Med. 37: 181–188.

Dart, R. C., P. C. O'Brien, B. S. Garcia, J. C. Jarchow, and J. McNally. 1992. Neutralization of *Micrurus distans distans* venom by antivenom (*Micrurus fulvius*). Journal of Wilderness Medicine 3: 377–381.

Dart, R. C., S. A. Seifert, L. V. Boycr, R. F. Clark, E. Hall, P. McKinney, J. McNally, C. S. Kitchens, S. C. Curry, G. M. Bogdan, S. B. Ward, and S. Porter. 2001. A randomized multicenter trial of Crotalinae polyvalent immune Fab (ovine) antivenom for the treatment for crotaline snakebite in the United States. Archives of Internal Medicine 161: 2030–2036.

Dart, R. C., S. A. Seifert, L. Carroll, R. F. Clark, E. Hall, L. V. Boyer-Hassen, S. C. Curry, C. S. Kitchens, and R. A. Garcia. 1997. Affinity-purified, mixed monoclonal specific crotalid antivenom ovine Fab for the treatment of crotalid venom poisoning. Ann. Emerg. Med. 30: 33–39.

Dart, R. C., and J. B. Sullivan. 1996. Elapid snake envenomations. Pp. 1453–1454 in A. L. Harwood-Nuss (ed.), The clinical practice of emergency medicine. Philadelphia, Lippincott-Raven.

Darwin, C. 1839. Journal of researches into the geology and natural history of the various countries visited by H.M.S. Beagle, under the command of Captain Fitzroy, R.N. from 1832 to 1836. Henry Colburn, London. 614 pp.

Darwin, C. [1859] 1952. The origin of species by means of natural selection: or the preservation of favoured races in the struggle for life. John Murray, London. 502 pp. Reprint, Encyclopaedia Britannica, Chicago. 251 pp.

Datta, G., A. Dong, J. Witt, and A. T. Tu. 1995. Biochemical characterization of basilase, a fibrinolytic enzyme from Crotalus basiliscus basiliscus. Archives of Biochemistry and Biophysics 317(2): 365–373.

Datta, G., and A. T. Tu. 1997. Structure and other chemical characterizations of gila toxin, a lethal toxin from lizard venom. Journal of Peptide Research 50: 443–450.

Daudin, F. M. 1801–1803. Histoire naturelle générale et particulière des reptiles; ouvrage faisant suite à l'histoire naturelle générale et particulière, composée par Leclerc de Buffon, et rédigée par C. S. Sonnini, membre de plusiers sociétés savantes. 8 vols. F. Dufort, Paris.

——. 1803. Division des ophidiens en vingt-trois genres. Bulletin Société Scientifique Philomatique Paris 3(72): 187–188.

David, P., and I. Ineich. 1999. Les serpents venimeux du monde: systématique et repartition. Dumerilia 3: 3–499.

Davidson, F. F., and E. A. Dennis. 1990. Evolutionary relationships and implications for the regulation of phospholipase A$_2$ from snake venom to human secreted forms. Journal of Molecular Evolution 31: 228–238.

Davidson, T. M. 1988. Intravenous rattlesnake envenomation. Western Journal of Medicine 148: 45–47.

Davidson, T. M., and J. Eisner. 1996. United States coral snakes. Wilderness and Environmental Medicine 7: 38–45.

Davidson, T. M., S. F. Schafer, and J. Moseman. 1993. Central and South American pit vipers. Journal of Wilderness Medicine 4: 416–440.

Davis, D. D. 1936. Courtship and mating behavior in snakes. Field Mus. Nat. Hist. Publ., Zool. Ser., 20(22): 257–290.

Davis, H. T., and C. S. Brimley. 1944. Poisonous snakes of the eastern United States with first aid guide. North Carolina Museum, Raleigh. 16 pp.

Davis, J. B. 2002. Natural history notes: Agkistrodon piscivorus (cottonmouth). Predation. Herpetol. Rev. 33(2): 136–137.

Davis, W. B. 1938. White-throated sparrow killed by a copperhead. Condor 40: 183.

Davis, W. B., and J. R. Dixon. 1957. Notes on Mexican snakes (Ophidia). Southwest. Nat. 2(1): 19–27.

——. 1959. Snakes of the Chilpancingo region, Mexico. Proceedings of the Biological Society of Washington 72: 79–92.

——. 1961. Reptiles (exclusive of snakes) from the Chilpancingo region, Mexico. Proceedings of the Biological Society of Washington 74: 37–56.

Davis, W. B., and H. M. Smith. 1953. Snakes of the Mexican state of Morelos. Herpetologica 8(4): 133–143.

Deacon, J. E., and W. G. Bradley. 1965. Distribution of the Gila monster in the northern Mohave Desert. Desert Research Institute, University of Nevada, Preprint No. 7: 1–4.

Dean, B. 1938. Note on the sea-snake, Pelamis platurus (Linnaeus). Science 88(2276): 145.

De Franco Montalvan, D., I. Alvarez Trejos, and L. A. Mora Walter. 1983a. Mordedura de ofidios venenosos en niños en la región Pacífico sur. Análisis de ciento sesenta casos. Acta Médica Costarricense 26: 61–70.

——. 1983b. Terápia de la mordedura de ofidios venenosos en niños en la región Pacífico sur. Análisis de ciento sesenta casos. Acta Médica Costarricense 26: 76–80.

Degenhardt, W. G., C. W. Painter, and A. H. Price. 1996. Amphibians and reptiles of New Mexico. University of New Mexico Press, Albuquerque. 431 pp.

DeGraff, R. M., and D. D. Rudis. 1983. Amphibians and reptiles of New England: habitats and natural history. University of Massachusetts Press, Amherst, Mass. 85 pp.

DeKay, J. 1842. Zoology of New York, part III: reptiles and amphibians. State of New York, Albany. 2 vols. 415 pp.

de la Peña, M. 1986. Guia de flora y fauna del Paraná medio, vol. 1. Martín R. de la Peña, Santa Fe, Argentina. 110 pp.

Delavan, W. 1939. Corvus and a copperhead. Field Ornithology 1: 6–7.

Delgadillo-Espinosa, J., E. Godínez-Cano, F. Correa-Sánchez, and A. González-Ruiz. 1999. Natural history notes: Crotalus willardi silus (ridge-nosed rattlesnake). Reproduction. Herpetol. Rev. 30(3): 168–169.

DeLisle, H. F. 1982. Venomous colubrid snakes. Bull. Chicago Herpetol. Soc. 17(1): 1–17.

DeLisle, H., G. Cantu, J. Feldner, P. O'Connor, M. Peterson, and P. Brown. 1986. The distribution and present status of the herpetofauna of the Santa Monica Mountains of Los Angeles and Ventura Counties, California. Southwestern Herpetologists Society Special Publication No. 2. 94 pp.

Dellinger, S. C., and J. D. Black. 1938. Herpetology of Arkansas, part I: the reptiles. Occasional Papers of the University of Arkansas Museum 1: 1–47.

Demarini Caro, J. C. 1992. Ofidismo: aspectos etiologicos, clinicos y terapeuticos. Tesis doctoral, Universidad Peruana Cayetano Heredia, Lima-Peru.

De Mesquita, L. C. M., H. S. Selistre, and J. R. Giglio. 1991. The hypotensive activity of Crotalus atrox (western diamondback rattlesnake) venom: identification of its origin. American Journal of Tropical Medicine and Hygiene 44: 90–105.

Demeter, B. J. 1986. Combat behavior in the Gila monster (Heloderma suspectum cinctum). Herpetol. Rev. 17(1): 9–11.

D'Empaire, A., J. E. Serrano, G. Cook, R. Govea, M. A. Leal, J. M. Rios, and H. Cuenca. 1921. Geografía médica del Zulia. Trabajo de contribución al Tecer Congreso Venszolano de Medicina. Chap. 4, Fauna, pp. 76–83. Empresa Panorama, Maracaibo.

Dempfle, C. E., R. Kohl, J. Harenberg, W. Kirschstein, D. Schlauch, and D. L. Heene. 1990. Coagulopathy after snake bite by Bothrops neuwiedi: case report and results of in vitro experiments. Blut 61: 369–374.

de Queiroz, K. 1985. The ontogenetic method for determining character polarity and its relevance to phylogenetic systematics. Syst. Zool. 34: 280–299.

——. 1998. The general lineage concept of species, species criteria, and the process of speciation: a conceptual unification and terminological recommendation. Pp. 57–75 in D. Howard and S. H. Berlocher (eds.), Endless forms: species and speciation. Oxford University Press, New York.

de Queiroz, K., and J. Gauthier. 1990. Phylogeny as a central principle in taxonomy: phylogenetic definitions of taxon names. Syst. Zool. 39: 307–322.

——. 1992. Phylogenetic taxonomy. Annual Review of Ecology and Systematics 23: 449–480.

——. 1994. Toward a phylogenetic system of biological nomenclature. Trends in Ecology and Evolution 9: 27–31.

de Queiroz, L. P., and R. D. Moritz. 1989. Acidente botrópico em Florianópolis. Arquivos Catarinensis de Medicina 18: 163–166.

Deraniyagala, A. W. C. T. 1955. A colored atlas of some some vertebrates from Ceylon, vol. 3. Government Press, Colombo.

De Roodti, A. R., J. C. Vidal, S. Litwin, J. C. Dokmetjian, J. A. Dolab, S. E. Hajos, and L. Segre. 1999. Neutralización cruzada de veneno de *Bothrops jararacussu* por sueros antiofidicos heterologos. Medicina (Buenos Aires) 59: 238–242.

Desiderio, M. H. G., N. M. Serra Freire, R. S. Critalli, P. O. Scherer, and L. SaFreire. 1996. *Travassosascaris araujoi* (Sprent, 1978); um novo hospedeiro. Parasitología al Dia 20(1–2): 66–67.

Despax, R. 1910. Mission géodésique de l'Equateur. Collections recueillies par M. le Dr. Rivet. Liste des ophidiens et description des espèces nouvelles (note préliminaire). Bulletin du Muséum National d'Histoire Naturelle, Paris, 16: 368–376.

———. 1911. Reptiles et batraciens de l'Equateur recueillis par M. le Dr. Rivet. Ministère de l'Instruction Publique, Mission du Service Géographique de l'Armée pour la mesure d'un arc de méridien équatorial en Amérique du Sud (1899–1906) 9: 17–44.

Desportes, C. 1941. Sur un *Hastospiculum* parasite du crotali. Annales de Parasitologie Humaine et Comparé 18(4–6): 198–208.

Deutsch, H. F., and C. R. Diniz. 1955. Some proteolytic activities of snake venoms. Journal of Biological Chemistry 216: 17–26.

DeVault, T. L., and A. R. Krochmal. 2002. Scavenging by snakes: an examination of the literature. Herpetologica 58(4): 429–436.

De Verteuil, L. A. A. G. 1858. Trinidad: its geography, natural resources, administration, present condition, and prospects. Ward and Lock, London.

———. 1884. Trinidad: its geography, natural resources, administration, present condition, and prospects, 2d ed. Cassell, London.

Devincenzi, G. J. 1925. Fauna herpetológica del Uruguay. Anales del Museo Nacional de Historia Natural, Montevideo, 2d ser., 2(1): 1–65.

DeWit, C. A. 1982. Yield of venom from the Osage copperhead, *Agkistrodon contortrix phaeogaster*. Toxicon 20: 525–527.

Dexter, R. W. 1944. New records of reptiles from Portage County, Ohio. Copeia 1944(4): 252.

Dial, B. E., and R. E. Smith. 1964. The reptiles and amphibians of Dallas and Tarrant Counties, Texas. John K. Strecker Herpetological Society, Fort Worth, Texas. 42 pp.

Díaz-Gómez, O. 1971. Accidentes por animales ponzoñosos. La Tribuna Médica (Bogotá) 1971: 6–12.

Di-Bernardo, M., M. Borges-Martins, and L. H. Cappellari. 2001. Geographic distribution: *Micrurus lemniscatus* (South American coral snake). Herpetol. Rev. 32(1): 60–61.

Dice, L. R. 1939. The Sonoran biotic province. Ecology 20(2): 118–129.

Dickerman, R. W., and C. W. Painter. 2001. Natural history notes: *Crotalus lepidus lepidus* (mottled rock rattlesnake), diet. Herpetol. Rev. 32(1): 46.

Dickinson, W. E. 1949. Field guide to the lizards and snakes of Wisconsin. Milwaukee Public Museum Popular Science Handbook Series No. 2: 1–70.

Diener, R. A. 1961. Notes on a bite of the broad-banded copperhead, *Ancistrodon contortrix laticinctus* Gloyd and Conant. Herpetologica 17(2): 143–144.

Diesing, C. M. 1851. Systema Helminthum. Vindobonae, 2 vols. 588 pp.

Diller, L. V. 1990. Field observations on the feeding behavior of *Crotalus viridis lutosus*. J. Herpetol. 24: 95–97.

Diller, L. V., and D. R. Johnson. 1988. Food habits, consumption rates, and predation rates of western rattlesnakes and gopher snakes in southwestern Idaho. Herpetologica 44(2): 228–233.

Diller, L. V., and R. L. Wallace. 1984. Reproductive biology of the northern Pacific rattlesnake (*Crotalus viridis oreganus*). Herpetologica 40(2): 182–193.

———. 1996. Comparative ecology of two snake species (*Crotalus viridis* and *Pituophis melanoleucus*) in southwestern Idaho. Herpetologica 52(3): 343–360.

———. 2002. Growth, reproduction, and survival in a population of *Crotalus viridis oreganus* in north central Idaho. Herpetological Monographs 16: 26–45.

Diniz, M. R. V., and E. B. Oliveira. 1992. Purification and properties of a kininogen from the venom of *Lachesis muta* (bushmaster). Toxicon 30: 247–258.

Dirksen, L., P. L. Ibisch, J. Köhler, and W. Böhme. 1995. Zur Herpetofauna der semihumiden Samaipata-Region, Bolivien. II. Reptilien. Herpetofauna 17: 15–28.

Ditmars, R. L. 1901. Collecting reptiles in South Carolina. Fifth Annual Report of the New York Zoological Society: 73–76.

———. 1904. Observations on lacertilians. Eighth Annual Report of the New York Zoological Society 1904: 146–160.

———. 1905a. The reptiles in the vicinity of New York. American Museum Journal 5: 93–140.

———. 1905b. A new species of rattlesnake. Ninth Annual Report of the New York Zoological Society 1904: 197–200.

———. 1907. The reptile book; a comprehensive popularized work on the structure and habits of the turtles, tortoises, crocodilians, lizards, and snakes which inhabit the United States and northern Mexico. Doubleday Page, New York. 472 pp.

———. 1910. Reptiles of the world: tortoises and turtles, crocodilians, lizards, and snakes of the Eastern and Western Hemispheres. Sturgis and Walton, New York. 373 pp.

———. 1912. The feeding habits of serpents. Zoology 1(11): 197–238.

———. 1913. Two litters of the fer-de-lance. Bulletin of the New York Zoological Society 16: 957.

———. 1928a. The lizards. Bulletin of the New York Zoological Society 33(3): 79–132.

———. 1928b. A reptile reconnaissance in Honduras. Bull. Antivenin Inst. Am. 2(2): 25–29.

———. 1930. The poisonous serpents of the New World. Bulletin of the New York Zoological Society 33: 78–132.

———. 1931. Snakes of the world. Macmillan, New York. 207 pp.

———. 1932. Thrills of a naturalist's quest. Macmillan, New York. 268 pp.

———. 1933. Reptiles of the world, rev. ed. Macmillan, New York.

———. 1936. The reptiles of North America: a review of the crocodilians, lizards, snakes, turtles, and tortoises inhabiting the United States and northern Mexico. Doubleday, Doran, New York. 476 pp.

———. 1937. Snakes of the world. Macmillan, New York. 270 pp.

———. 1949. A field book of North American snakes. Doubleday, Garden City, New York. 305 pp.

Ditmars, R. L., and W. Bridges. 1935. Snake-hunters' holiday. Appleton-Century, New York. 309 pp.

Dix, M. W. 1978. The venom gland in the lower jaw of the coral snake (*Micrurus nigrocinctus mosquitensis* Schmidt). Pp. 16–28 in P. Rosenberg (ed.), Toxins: animal, plant, and microbial. Pergamon, Oxford [also publ. as Toxicon suppl. 1].

Dixon, J. R. 1956. The mottled rock rattlesnake *Crotalus lepidus lepidus*, in Edwards County, Texas. Copeia 1956(2): 126–127.

———. 1979. Origin and distribution of reptiles in lowland tropical rainforests of South America. Pp. 217–249 in W. E. Duellman (ed.), The South American herpetofauna: its origin, evolution, and dispersal. Monograph No. 7 of the Museum of Natural History, University of Kansas, Lawrence.

———. 1987. Amphibians and reptiles of Texas. Texas A&M University Press, College Station. 434 pp.

———. 2000. Amphibians and reptiles of Texas, 2d ed. Texas A&M University Press, College Station. 421 pp.

Dixon, J. R., C. A. Ketchersid, and C. S. Lieb. 1972. The herpetofauna of Queretaro, Mexico, with remarks on taxonomic problems. Southwest. Nat. 16(3–4): 225–237.

Dixon, J. R., and P. A. Medica. 1965. Noteworthy records of reptiles from New Mexico. Herpetologica 21(1): 72–75.

Dixon, J. R., M. Sabbath, and R. Worthington. 1962. Comments on snakes from central and western Mexico. Herpetologica 18(2): 91–100.

Dixon, J. R., and P. Soini. 1977. The reptiles of the upper Amazon Basin, Iquitos region, Peru. II. Crocodilians, turtles, and snakes. Contributions to Biology and Geology of the Milwaukee Public Museum 12: 1–91.

———. 1986. The reptiles of the upper Amazon basin, Iquitos region, Peru, 2d ed. Milwaukee, Milwaukee Public Museum. 154 pp.

Dixon, J. R., and O. W. Thornton Jr. 1996. Geographic distribution: *Agkistrodon contortrix laticinctus* (broad-banded copperhead). Herpetol. Rev. 27(1): 33.

Dixon, J. R., and R. G. Webb. 1965. *Micrurus laticollaris* Peters, from Jalisco, Mexico. Southwest. Nat. 10: 77.

Doan, T. M., and W. Arrizábal-Arriaga. 2002. Microgeographic variation in species composition of the herpetofaunal communities of Tampopata region, Peru. Biotropica 34(1): 101–117.

Dobie, J. F. 1965. Rattlesnakes. Little, Brown, Boston. 201 pp.

Dodd, C. K., Jr., and B. G. Charest. 1988. The herpetofaunal community of temporary ponds in north Florida sandhills: species composition, temporal use, and management implications. Pp. 87–97 in R. C. Szaro, K. E. Severson, and D. R. Patton (technical coordinators), Management of amphibians, reptiles, and small mammals in North America. General Technical Report RM-166. USDA Forest Service, Fort Collins, Colo.

Doello-Jurado, M. 1916. Cuál es la serpiente mencionada por Darwin con el nombre de "*Trigonocephalus crepitans*"? Physis 2(11): 287–290.

Domínguez, P., T. Alvarez, and P. Huerta. 1974. Colección de anfibios y reptiles del noroeste de Chihuahua, Mexico. Revista de la Sociedad Mexicana de Historia Natural 35: 117–141.

Donoso-Barros, R. 1966. Reptiles de Chile. Ediciones de la Universidad de Chile, Santiago. 458 pp.

——. 1967. Notas sobre ofidios colectados por el Dr. Emilio Ureta en la Amazonía boliviana. Publicación Ocasional del Museo Nacional de Historia Natural, Santiago 12: 1–8.

Dorcas, M. E. 1992. Relationships among montane populations of *Crotalus lepidus* and *Crotalus triseriatus*. Pp. 71–88 in J. A. Campbell and E. D. Brodie Jr. (eds.), Biology of the pitvipers. Selva, Tyler, Texas.

Douglas, M. E., M. R. Douglas, G. W. Schuett, L. W. Porras, and A. T. Holycross. 2002. Phylogeography of the western rattlesnake (*Crotalus viridis*) complex, with emphasis on the Colorado Plateau. Pp. 11–50 in G. W. Schuett, M. Höggren, M. E. Douglas, and H. W. Greene (eds.), Biology of the vipers. Eagle Mountain Publishing, Eagle Mountain, Utah.

Dowling, H. G. 1957. A review of the amphibians and reptiles of Arkansas. Occasional Papers of the University of Arkansas Museum 3: 1–51.

——. 1959. Classification of the serpents: a critical review. Copeia 1959(1): 38–52.

——. 1965. The puzzle of the *Bothrops*; or a tangle of serpents. Animal Kingdom 68(1): 18–21.

——. 1975. Yearbook of herpetology. Herpetological Information Search Systems, New York. 256 pp.

Dowling, H. G., and W. E. Duellman. 1978. Systematic herpetology: a synopsis of families and higher categories. Herpetological Information Search Service Publication 7. 240 pp.

Dowling, H. G., and J. M. Savage. 1960. A guide to the snake hemipenis: a survey of basic structure and systematic characteristics. Zoologica 45: 17–31.

Drake, J. J. 1958. The brush mouse *Peromyscus boylii* in southern Durango. Publications of the Museum, Michigan State University, Biological Series 1: 99–132.

Drda, W. J., and D. A. Kluepfel. 1979. Geographic distribution: *Agkistrodon piscivorus leucostoma* (western cottonmouth). Herpetol. Rev. 19(4): 118.

Duarte, M. R., G. Puorto, and F. L. Franco. 1995. A biological survey of the pitviper *Bothrops insularis* Amaral (Serpentes, Viperidae): an endemic and threatened offshore island snake of southeastern Brazil. Studies on Neotropical Fauna and Environment 30: 1–13.

Duellman, W. E. 1950. A case of *Heloderma* poisoning. Copeia 1950(2): 151.

——. 1954. The amphibians and reptiles of Jorullo Volcano, Michoacán, Mexico. Occas. Pap. Mus. Zool. Univ. Michigan 560: 1–24.

——. 1957. Notes on snakes from the Mexican state of Sinaloa. Herpetologica 13(3): 237–240.

——. 1958a. A preliminary analysis of the herpetofauna of Colima, Mexico. Occas. Pap. Mus. Zool. Univ. Michigan 589: 1–22.

——. 1958b. A monographic study of the colubrid snake genus *Leptodeira*. Bull. Am. Mus. Nat. Hist. 114(1): 1–152.

——. 1960. A distributional study of the amphibians of the Isthmus of Tehuantepec. Publications of the Museum of Natural History, University of Kansas, 13: 19–72.

——. 1961. The amphibians and reptiles of Michoacán, Mexico. Publications of the Museum of Natural History, University of Kansas, 15(1): 1–148.

——. 1963. Amphibians and reptiles of the rainforests of southern El Petén, Guatemala. Publications of the Museum of Natural History, University of Kansas, 15(5): 205–249.

——. 1965a. Amphibians and reptiles from the Yucatan Peninsula, Mexico. Publications of the Museum of Natural History, University of Kansas, 15(12): 577–614.

——. 1965b. A biogeographic account of the herpetofauna of Michoacán, Mexico. Publications of the Museum of Natural History, University of Kansas, 15(14): 627–709.

——. 1966. The Central American herpetofauna: an ecological perspective. Copeia 1966(4): 700–719.

——. 1978. The biology of an equatorial herpetofauna in Amazonian Ecuador. Miscellaneous Publications of the Museum of Natural History, University of Kansas, 65: 1–352.

——. 1979a. The South American herpetofauna: a panoramic view. Pp. 1–28 in W. E. Duellman (ed.), The South American herpetofauna: its origin, evolution, and dispersal. Monograph No. 7 of the Museum of Natural History, University of Kansas, Lawrence.

——. 1979b. The herpetofauna of the Andes: patterns of distribution, origin, differentiation, and present communities. Pp. 371–459 in W. E. Duellman (ed.), The South American herpetofauna: its origin, evolution, and dispersal. Monograph No. 7 of the Museum of Natural History, University of Kansas, Lawrence.

—— (ed.). 1979c. The South American herpetofauna: its origin, evolution, and dispersal. Monograph No. 7 of the Museum of Natural History, University of Kansas, Lawrence. 485 pp.

Duellman, W. E., and B. Berg. 1962. Type specimens of amphibians and reptiles in the Museum of Natural History, University of Kansas. Publications of the Museum of Natural History, University of Kansas, 15: 185–204.

Duellman, W. E., and J. R. Mendelson. 1995. Amphibians and reptiles from northern Departamento Loreto, Peru: taxonomy and biogeography. University of Kansas Science Bulletin 55(10): 329–376.

Duellman, W. E., and A. W. Salas. 1991. Annotated checklist of the amphibians and reptiles of Cuzco amazonico, Peru. Occasional Papers, Museum of Natural History, University of Kansas, 143: 1–13.

Duellman, W. E., and A. Schwartz. 1958. Amphibians and reptiles of southern Florida. Bulletin of the Florida State Museum 3: 181–324.

Dueñas, C., L. D. Wilson, and J. R. McCranie. 2001 [dated 2000]. A list of the amphibians and reptiles of El Salvador, with notes on additions and deletions. Pp. 93–99 in J. D. Johnson, R. G. Webb, and O. A. Flores-Villela (eds.), Mesoamerican herpetology: systematics, zoogeography, and conservation. Centennial Museum, special publ. University of Texas at El Paso.

Dufton, M. J., and R. C. Hider. 1983. Classification of phospholipases A according to sequence: evolutionary and pharmacological considerations. Journal of Biochemistry 137: 545–551.

Dugand, A. 1975. Serpentifauna de la llanura costera del Caribe. Caldasia 11(53): 61–82.

Dugès, A. A. D. 1869. Catálogo de animales vertebrados observados en la República Mexicana. Naturaleza 1: 137–145.

——. 1876–1877. Apuntes para la monografía de los crótalos de México. Naturaleza 4: 1–29. (Pp. 1–16 published in 1876.)

——. 1882–1883. Nota sobre el colcoatl ó *Trimorphodon (Dipsas) biscutata*, D.B. Naturaleza 6: 145–148.

——. 1885. Nota sobre las coralillas (*Elaps*, Schneider). Naturaleza 7: 200–203.

——. 1888. Erpetología del Valle de México. Naturaleza, 2d ser., 1: 97–146.

——. 1889. Un punto curioso de geografía zoológica. Naturaleza, 2d ser., 1: 209–211.

——. 1890. Fauna del estado de Guanajuato. Pp. 287–295 in A. L. Velasco (ed.), Geografía y estadística del estado de Guanajuato. Geografía y estadística de la República Mexicana, vol. 5. Secretaria de Fomento, México, D.F.

——. 1891. *Elaps diastema*, var. *Michoacanensis*, A. Dug. Naturaleza, 2d ser., 1: 487.

——. 1894. Lista de algunas reptiles y batracios de Tabasco y Chiapas. Naturaleza, 2d ser., 2: 375–377.

——. 1896a. Reptiles y batracios de los E. U. Mexicanos. Naturaleza, 2d ser., 2: 479–485.

——. 1896b. Note sur l'*Elaps michoacanensis*. Bulletin du Muséum National d'Histoire Naturelle, Paris 44(2): 60–61.

——. 1897. Sur l'*Heloderma horridum*, Wiegm. Actes de la Société Scientifique du Chili 7: 113–117.

——. 1899. Venin de l'*Heloderma horridum* (Wiegm.). Pp. 134–137 in Cinquantenaire de la Société de Biologie. Masson, Paris. 740 pp.

——. 1901a. Contribución al estudio del escorpión. Anuario de la Academía Mexicana de Ciencias Exactas, Físicas, y Naturales 5: 85–91.

——. 1901b. Glándulas salivares de los ofidianos. Rev. Cient. Ind. 1(6): 100–104.

Duke, J. A. 1967. Herpetological dietary: bioenvironmental and radiological–safety feasibility studies, Atlantic–Pacific interoceanic canal. Battelle Memorial Institute, Columbus, Ohio. 35 pp.

Dullemeijer, P. 1958. A comparative functional-anatomical study of the heads of some Viperidae. Gegenbaurs Morphologisches Jahrbuch (Leipzig) 99: 881–985.

——. 1959. The mutual structure influence of the elements in a pattern. Archives Neérlandaises de Zoologie 13(suppl.): 74–88.

Duméril, A. C. 1853. Prodrome de la classification des reptiles ophidiens. Mémoires de l'Académie des Sciences, Paris 23: 399–536.

Duméril, A. M. C., G. Bibron, and A. Duméril. 1854. Erpétologie générale ou histoire naturelle complète des reptiles, vol. 7: 781–1536. Librairie Encyclopédique de Roret, Paris.

Duncan, C. J., and P. M. Sheppard. 1965. Sensory discrimination and its role in the evolution of Batesian mimicry. Behaviour 24: 269–282.

Dundee, H. A. 1994a. Natural history notes: *Crotalus horridus* (timber rattlesnake). Coloration. Herpetol. Rev. 25(1): 28.

——. 1994b. Geographic distribution: *Crotalus horridus* (timber rattlesnake). Herpetol. Rev. 25(1): 33–34.

——. 1996. Some reallocations of type localities of reptiles and amphibians described from the Major Stephen H. Long Expedition to the Rocky Mountains, with comments on some of the statements made in the account written by Edwin James. Tulane Studies in Zoology and Botany 30: 75–89.

Dundee, H. A., and W. L. Burger. 1948. A denning aggregation of the western cottonmouth. Chicago Academy of Sciences, Natural History Miscellanea 21: 1–2.

Dundee, H. A., and D. A. Rossman. 1989. The amphibians and reptiles of Louisiana. Louisiana State University Press, Baton Rouge. 300 pp.

Dundee, H. A., D. A. White, and V. Rico-Gray. 1986. Observations on the distribution and biology of some Yucatan Peninsula amphibians and reptiles. Bull. Maryland Herpetol. Soc. 22(2): 37–50.

Dunkle, D. H., and H. M. Smith. 1937. Notes on some Mexican ophidians. Occas. Pap. Mus. Zool. Univ. Michigan 363: 1–15.

Dunn, E. R. 1915a. Number of young produced by certain snakes. Copeia 1915(22): 37.

——. 1915b. List of reptiles and amphibians from Clark County, Va. Copeia 1915(25): 62–63.

——. 1919. Two new crotaline snakes from western Mexico. Proceedings of the Biological Society of Washington 32: 213–216.

——. 1923. Some snakes from northwestern Peru. Proceedings of the Biological Society of Washington 36: 185–188.

——. 1928. Notes on *Bothrops lansbergi* and *Bothrops ophryomegas*. Bull. Antivenin Inst. Am. 2(2): 29–30.

——. 1933. Amphibians and reptiles from El Valle de Anton, Panama. Occasional Papers of the Boston Society of Natural History 8: 65–79.

——. 1936. The amphibians and reptiles of the Mexican expedition of 1934. Proc. Acad. Nat. Sci. Philadelphia 88: 471–477.

——. 1937. Notes on some Colombian reptiles. Proceedings of the Biological Society of Washington 50: 11–14.

——. 1939. A new pit viper from Costa Rica. Proceedings of the Biological Society of Washington 52: 165–166.

——. 1940a. New and noteworthy herpetological material from Panama. Proc. Acad. Nat. Sci. Philadelphia 92: 105–123.

——. 1940b. Some aspects of herpetology in lower Central America. Transactions of the New York Academy of Sciences, ser. 2, 2(6): 156–158.

——. 1942. New or noteworthy snakes from Panama. Notulae Naturae (Philadelphia) 108: 1–8.

——. 1944a. Los géneros de anfibios y reptiles de Colombia. Tercera parte: reptiles, orden de las Serpientes. Caldasia 3(12): 155–224.

——. 1944b. Herpetology of the Bogotá area. Revista de la Academia Colombiana de Ciencias Exactas, Físicas, Naturales 6: 68–81.

——. 1945. The amphibians and reptiles of the Colombian islands San Andrés and Providencia. Caldasia 4: 363–365.

——. 1946. A small herpetological collection from eastern Peru. Proceedings of the Biological Society of Washington 59: 17–20.

——. 1947. Snakes of the Lérida Farm (Chiriqui Volcano, western Panama). Copeia 1947(2): 153–157.

——. 1949. Relative abundance of some Panamanian snakes. Ecology 30(1): 39–57.

——. 1951. Venomous reptiles of the tropics. Pp. 741–754 in G. C. Shattuck (ed.), Diseases of the tropics. Appleton-Century-Crofts, New York. 803 pp.

——. 1954. The coral snake "mimic" problem in Panama. Evolution 8: 97–102.

Dunn, E. R., and J. R. Bailey, 1939. Snakes from the uplands of the Canal Zone and of Darien. Bulletin of the Museum of Comparative Zoology 86: 1–22.

Dunn, E. R., and M. T. Dunn. 1940. Generic names in herpetology proposed by E. D. Cope. Copeia 1940(2): 69–76.

Dunn, E. R., and J. T. Emlen Jr. 1932. Reptiles and amphibians from Honduras. Proc. Acad. Nat. Sci. Philadelphia 84: 21–32.

Dunn, E. R., and L. C. Stuart. 1951a. On the legality of restriction of type locality. Science 113: 677–678.

——. 1951b. Comments on some recent restrictions of type localities of certain South and Central American amphibians and reptiles. Copeia 1951(1): 55–61.

Dunnihoo, D. R., B. M. Rush, R. B. Wise, G. G. Brooks, and W. N. Otterson. 1992. Snake bite poisoning in pregnancy: a review of the literature. Journal of Reproductive Medicine 37: 653–658.

Dunson, W. A. (ed.). 1975. The biology of sea snakes. University Park Press, Baltimore, Md. 530 pp.

Dunson, W. A., and G. W. Ehlert. 1971. Effects of temperature, salinity, and surface water flow on the distribution of the sea snake. Limnology and Oceanography 16: 845–853.

Dunson, W. A., and J. Freda. 1985. Water permeability of the skin of the amphibious snake, *Agkistrodon piscivorus*. J. Herpetol. 19(1): 93–98.

Durant, W. 1939. The story of civilization. Simon and Schuster, New York. 754 pp.

Durham, F. E. 1956. Amphibians and reptiles of the North Rim, Grand Canyon, Arizona. Herpetologica 12(3): 220–224.

Dury, R., and W. Gessing Jr. 1940. Additions to the herpetofauna of Kentucky. Herpetologica 2(2): 31–32.

Duvall, D., S. J. Arnold, and G. W. Schuett. 1992. Pitviper mating systems: ecological potential, sexual selection, and microevolution. Pp. 321–336 in J. A. Campbell and E. D. Brodie Jr. (eds.), Biology of the pitvipers. Selva, Tyler, Texas.

Duvall, D., M. J. Goode, W. K. Hayes, J. K. Leonhardt, and D. G. Brown. 1990. Prairie rattlesnake vernal migration: field experimental analyses and survival value. National Geographic Research 6: 457–469.

Duvall, D., M. B. King, and K. J. Gutzwiller. 1985. Behavioral ecology and ethology of the prairie rattlesnake. National Geographic Research 1: 80–111.

Dyr, J. E., J. Suttnar, J. Simak, H. Fortova, and F. Kornalik. 1990. The action of fibrin-promoting enzyme from the venom of *Agkistrodon contortrix contortrix* on rat fibrinogen and plasma. Toxicon 28: 1364–1367.

Eaton, T. H., Jr. 1935. Amphibians and reptiles of the Navaho country. Copeia 1935(3): 150–151.

Echternacht, A. A. 1973. The color pattern of *Sonora michoacanensis* (Dugès) (Serpentes, Colubridae) and its bearing on the origin of the species. Breviora 410: 1–18.

Edgren, R. A., Jr. 1948. Notes on a litter of young timber rattlesnakes. Copeia 1948(2): 132.

———. 1955. The natural history of the hognosed snakes, genus *Heterodon*: a review. Herpetologica 11: 105–117.

Edmondson, K. W. 1979. Treatment of snakebite. Medical Journal of Australia 2: 257.

Edmunds, M. 1972. Defensive behaviour in Ghanaian praying mantids. Zoological Journal of the Linnean Society 51: 1–32.

———. 1974. Defence in animals: a survey of antipredator defenses. Longman, London. 357 pp.

———. 1978. On the association between *Myrmarachne* spp. (Salticidae) and ants. Bulletin of the British Arachnological Society 4: 149–160.

———. 1990. The evolution of cryptic coloration. Pp. 3–23 in D. L. Evans and J. O. Schmidt (eds.), Insect defenses: adaptive mechanisms and strategies of prey and predators. State University New York Press, Albany.

———. 1993. Does mimicry of ants reduce predation by wasps on salticid spiders? Memoirs of the Queensland Museum 11: 507–512.

———. 2000. Why are there good and poor mimics? Biological Journal of the Linnean Society 70: 459–466.

Egler, S. G., M. E. Oliveira, and M. Martins. 1996. Natural history notes: *Bothrops atrox*. Foraging behavior. Herpetol. Rev. 27(1): 22–23.

Eichelbaum, H. R. 1927. Cases of snake-bite treated in Almirante Hospital, Panama, the years 1922–26, inclusive. Bull. Antivenin Inst. Am. 1(2): 35–36.

Eisner, T. 1970. Chemical defense against predation in arthropods. Pp. 157–217 in E. Sondheimer and J. B. Simeone (eds.), Chemical ecology. Academic Press, New York.

Ellis, M. M., and J. Henderson. 1913. The Amphibia and Reptilia of Colorado, Part I. University of Colorado Studies 10(2): 39–129.

———. 1915. Amphibia and Reptilia of Colorado, Part II. University of Colorado Studies 11(4): 253–263.

Elton, N. W. 1948. The venomous snakes of Panama. Safety Zone (Panama Canal Zone). 7 pp.

Emery, J. A., and F. E. Russell. 1961. Studies with cooling measures following injection of *Crotalus* venom. Copeia 1961(3): 322–326.

Emsley, M. 1977. Snakes, and Trinidad and Tobago. Bull. Maryland Herpetol. Soc. 13(4): 201–304.

Endler, J. A. 1992. Signals, signal conditions, and the direction of evolution. American Naturalist 139(suppl.): s125–s153.

———. 1993. The color of light in forests and its implications. Ecological Monographs 63: 1–27.

Engelhardt, G. P. 1912. Notes on the Gila monster. Copeia 1912(7): 1–2.

———. 1932. Notes on poisonous snakes in Texas. Copeia 1932(1): 37–38.

Engels, W. L. 1952. Vertebrate fauna of North Carolina coastal islands, II: Shackleford Banks. Am. Midl. Nat. 47(3): 702–742.

Enzeroth, R., B. Chobotar, and E. Scholtseck. 1985. *Sarcocystis crotali*—new species with the Mojave rattlesnake (*Crotalus scutulatus scutulatus*) and mouse (*Mus musculus*) cycle. Archiv für Protistenkunde 129(1–4): 19–23.

Ernst, C. H. 1964. A study of sexual dimorphism in American *Agkistrodon* fang lengths. Herpetologica 20(3): 214.

———. 1965. Fang length comparisons of American *Agkistrodon*. Transactions of the Kentucky Academy of Science 26: 12–18.

———. 1992. Venomous reptiles of North America. Smithsonian Institution Press, Washington, D.C. 236 pp.

Ernst, C. H., S. C. Belfit, S. W. Sekscienski, and A. F. Laemmerzahl. 1997. The amphibians and reptiles of Ft. Belvoir and northern Virginia. Bull. Maryland Herpetol. Soc. 33(1): 1–62.

Escalante, T., A. Franceschi, A. Rucavado, and J. M. Gutiérrez. 2000. Effectiveness of Batimastat, a synthetic inhibitor of matrix metalloproteinases, in neutralizing local tissue damage induced by BaP1, a hemorrhagic metalloproteinase from the venom of the snake *Bothrops asper*. Biochemical Pharmacology 60: 269–274.

Espinal, M. R. 1994. Especies de anfibios y reptiles conocidos en el Parque Nacional El Cusuco. En evaluación ecológica rápida 1993 (EER) Parque Nacional El Cusuco y Cordillera del Merendón. Fundación Ecológica Hector Rodrigo Pastor Fasquelle, Documento Técnico. Nature Conservancy and PACA, San Pedro Sula. 129 pp.

Espinal, M. R., and J. R. McCranie, and L. D. Wilson. 2001 [dated 2000]. The herpetofauna of Parque Nacional La Muralla, Honduras. Pp. 100–108 in J. D. Johnson, R. G. Webb, and O. A. Flores-Villela (eds.), Mesoamerican herpetology: systematics, zoogeography, and conservation. Centennial Museum, special publ. University of Texas at El Paso.

Esqueda, L. F., and E. La Marca. 1999. New reptilian species records from the Cordillera de Mérida, Andes of Venezuela. Herpetol. Rev. 30(4): 238–240.

Esqueda, L. F., E. La Marca, M. Natera, and P. Battiston. 2001. Noteworthy reptilian state records and a lizard species new to the herpetofauna of Venezuela. Herpetol. Rev. 32(3): 198–200.

Esslinger, J. H. 1962. Morphology of the egg and larva of *Porocephalus crotali* (Pentastomida). Journal of Parasitology 48(3): 457–462

Estes, E. T. 1958. Timber rattlesnake in Jefferson County, Illinois. Herpetologica 14(2): 68.

Estes, R., K. de Queiroz, and J. Gauthier. 1988. Phylogenetic relationships within Squamata. Pp. 119–281 in R. Estes and G. Pregill (eds.), Phylogenetic relationships of the lizard families: essays commemorating Charles L. Camp. Stanford University Press, Stanford, Calif.

Esteso, S. C. 1985. Ofidismo en la República Argentina. Arpon, Córdoba, Argentina.

Esteso, S. C., T. Vazquez, A. Olmos, and R. Palacios. 1989. Ofidismo por *Micrurus frontalis pyrrhocryptus*. Siete casos ocurridos en la provincia de Córdoba, Argentina, en los ultimos 25 años. Prensa Médica Argentina 76: 376–378.

Estol, C. O. 1981. Scale microdermatoglyphics of the viperid snake genera *Bothrops* and *Trimeresurus*: taxonomic relationships. Ph.D. dissertation, New York University. 214 pp.

Estrade, G., D. Garnier, F. Bernasconi, and Y. Donatien. 1989. Embolie pulmonaire et coagulation intravasculaire disséminée après une morsure de serpent *Bothrops lanceolatus*. Archives des Maladies du Coeur et des Vaisseaux 82: 1903–1905.

Etheridge, R. 1961. Additions to the herpetological fauna of Isla Cerralvo in the Gulf of California, Mexico. Herpetologica 17(1): 57–60.

Ettling, J. 1988. Geographic distribution: *Agkistrodon piscivorus leucostoma* (western cottonmouth). Herpetol. Rev. 19(3): 60.

Evans, H. E. 1947a. Notes on Panamanian reptiles and amphibians. Copeia 1947(3): 166–170.

———. 1947b. Herpetology of Crystal Lake, Sullivan County, N.Y. Herpetologica 4(1): 19–21.

Evans, P. D. 1940. Notes on Missouri snakes. Copeia 1940(1): 53–54.

Evans, P. D., and H. K. Gloyd. 1948. The subspecies of the massasauga, *Sistrurus catenatus*, in Missouri. Bulletin of the Chicago Academy of Sciences 8(9): 225–232.

Eveleigh, R. 2000. Paradise for pit vipers. Minnesota Herpetological Society Newsletter 20(10): 1–4.

Evenden, F. G., Jr. 1946. Notes on the herpetology of Elmore County, Idaho. Copeia 1946(4): 256–257.

Evermann, B. W., and H. W. Clark. 1914. The snakes of the Lake Maxinkuckee Region. Proceedings of the Indiana Academy of Science 24: 337–348.

Ewan, J. 1932. Pacific rattlesnake at high altitude on San Jacinto Peak, California. Copeia 1932(1): 36.

Ewing, H. E. 1924. A new mite from the lung sac of a rattlesnake. Proceedings of the Entomological Society of Washington 26(6): 179.

Fain, A. 1967 [dated 1966]. Pentastomida of snakes. Mem. Inst. Butantan 33(1): 167–174.

Falcetti, C. A., and F. L. Franco. 1999. Serpentes da região de Tapiraí, Estado de São Paulo (Reptilia: Serpentes). P. 57 in Abstracts of the V Congreso Latinoamericano de Herpetología, Montevideo, 12 al 17 de diciembre de 1999.

Falck, E. G. J. 1940. Food of an eastern rock rattlesnake in captivity. Copeia (1940): 135.

Fantham, H. B., and A. Porter. 1954. The endoparasites of some North American snakes and their effects on the Ophidia. Proc. Zool. Soc. London 123: 867–898.

Faria, R. G., and V. L. C. Brites. 1999a. Estudos taxonómicos de Bothrops moojeni Hoge, 1966 (Serpentes, Crotalinae) da zona geográfica do triângulo e Alto Paranaíba–MG. P. 58 in Abstracts of the V Congreso Latinoamericano de Herpetología, Montevideo, 12 al 17 de diciembre de 1999.

———. 1999b. Estudos ecológicos de Bothrops moojeni Hoge, 1966 (Serpentes, Crotalinae) da zona geográfica do triângulo e Alto Paranaíba–MG. P. 58 in Abstracts of the V Congreso Latinoamericano de Herpetología, Montevideo, 12 al 17 de diciembre de 1999.

Farrell, T. M., P. G. May, and M. A. Pilgrim. 1995. Reproduction in the rattlesnake, Sistrurus miliarius barbouri, in central Florida. J. Herpetol. 29(1): 21–27.

Farris, J. S. 1969. A successive approximation approach to character weighting. Syst. Zool. 18: 374–385.

———. 1983. The logical basis of phylogenetic analysis. Pp. 7–36 in N. I. Platnick and V. A. Funk (eds.), Advances in cladistics, vol. 2. Columbia University Press, New York.

———. 1989. The retention index and the rescaled consistency index. Cladistics 5: 417–419.

Farstad, D., T. Thomas, T. Chow, S. Bush, and P. Stiegler. 1997. Mojave rattlesnake envenomation in southern California: a review of suspected cases. Wilderness and Environmental Medicine 8: 89–93.

Feldner, J. J. 1990. Review of The venomous reptiles of Latin America. Herpetology 21: 27–30.

Felsenstein, J. 1978. Cases in which parsimony and compatibility methods will be positively misleading. Syst. Zool. 27: 401–410.

———. 1981. Evolutionary trees from DNA sequences: a maximum likelihood approach. Journal of Molecular Evolution 17: 368–376.

———. 1982. Numerical methods for inferring evolutionary trees. Quarterly Review of Biology 57: 379–404.

———. 1985. Confidence limits on phylogenies: an approach using the bootstrap. Evolution 39: 783–791.

———. 1988. Phylogenies from molecular sequences: inference and reliability. Annual Review of Genetetics 22: 521–565.

———. 1993. PHYLIP (Phylogeny Inference Package), Version 3.5c. Department of Genetics, University of Washington, Seattle.

———. 2004. Inferring phylogenies. Sinauer, Sunderland, Mass. 664 pp.

Fenton, M. B., and L. E. Licht. 1990. Why rattle snake? J. Herpetol. 24(3): 274–279.

Ferguson, D. E. 1952. The distribution of amphibians and reptiles of Wallowa County, Oregon. Herpetologica 8(3): 66–68.

———. 1954. An annotated list of the amphibians and reptiles of Union County, Oregon. Herpetologica 10(3): 149–152.

———. 1961. The herpetofauna of Tishomingo County, Mississippi, with comments on its zoogeographic affinities. Copeia 1961(4): 391–396.

Fernandes, R., and M. B. Gandolfi. 2000. Répteis. Pp. 48–50 in Espécies ameaçadas de extinção do Municipio do Rio de Janeiro—flora e fauna. Secretaria Municipal do Meio Ambiente, Prefeitura da Cidade do Rio de Janeiro, Rio de Janeiro. 68 pp.

Fernandes, W., and O. Pesantes-Segura. 1989. Relacionamento entre as especies do grupo Bothrops atrox (Serpentes: Viperidae) pela eletroforese do plasma. P. 75 in XVI Congresso Brasileiro de Zoologia, Universidade Federal da Paraíba, 22 a 27 de Janeiro de 1989, João Pessoa, PB.

Fernández-Barrán, E., and M. A. Freiberg. 1951. Nombres vulgares de reptiles y batracios de la Argentina. Physis 20(58): 303–319.

Ferner, J. W., M. Bramilage, and W. S. Bryant 1999. Geographic distribution: Agkistrodon contortrix mokasen (northern copperhead). Herpetol. Rev. 30(2): 112.

Ferrarezzi, H., and E. M. X. Freire. 2001. New species of Bothrops Wagler, 1824, from the Atlantic forest of northeastern Brazil (Serpentes, Viperidae, Crotalinae). Boletim do Museu Nacional, Rio de Janeiro, new ser., 440: 1–10.

Ferrari-Perez, F. 1886. Catalogue of animals collected by the geographical and exploring commission of the Republic of Mexico, part III: reptiles and amphibians. Proceedings of the U.S. National Museum 9: 182–199.

Fiero, M. K., M. W. Seifert, T. J. Weaver, and C. A. Bonilla. 1972. Comparative study of juvenile and adult prairie rattlesnake (Crotalus viridis viridis) venoms. Toxicon 10: 81–82.

Finley, R. B., D. Chiszar, and H. M. Smith. 1994. Field observations of salivary digestion of rodent tissue by the wandering garter snake, Thamnophis elegans vagrans. Bull. Chicago Herpetol. Soc. 29: 5–6.

Finneran, L. C. 1948. Reptiles at Branford, Connecticut. Herpetologica 4(4): 123–126.

———. 1953. Aggregation behavior of the female copperhead, Agkistrodon contortrix, during gestation. Copeia 1953(1): 61–62.

Fischer, F. J., H. W. Ramsey, J. Simon, and J. F. Gennaro. 1961. Antivenin and antitoxin in the treatment of experimental rattlesnake venom intoxication (Crotalus adamanteus). American Journal of Tropical Medicine and Hygiene 10: 75–79.

Fischer, J. G. 1813. Zoognosia tabulis synopticus illustrata, in usum praelectionum Academiae Imperialis medico-chirurgicae Mosquensis edita. 3d ed. vol. 1, pt. 3 (Reptiles, Poissons): 57–117. Nicolai Sergeidis Vsevolozsky, Moscow.

———. 1856. Die Familie der Seeschlangen systematisch beschrieben. Abhandlungen aus dem Gebiet der Naturwissenschaften, Hamburg 3: 1–78.

———. 1880. Neue Amphibien und Reptilien. Archiv für Naturgeschichte 46(1): 215–227.

———. 1881. Herpetologische Bemerkungen vorzugsweise über Stucke der Sammlung des Naturhistorischen Museums in Bremen. Abhandlungen des Naturwissenschaftlichen vereins zu Bremen 7: 225–238.

Fitch, H. S. 1949a. Road counts of snakes in western Louisiana. Herpetologica 5(4): 87–90.

———. 1949b. Study of snake populations in central California. Am. Midl. Nat. 41: 513–579.

———. 1959. A patternless phase of the copperhead. Herpetologica 15(1): 21–24.

———. 1960. Autecology of the copperhead. Publications of the Museum of Natural History, University of Kansas, 13(4): 85–288.

———. 1970. Reproductive cycles in lizards and snakes. Miscellaneous Publications of the Museum of Natural History, University of Kansas 52: 1–247.

———. 1985a. Variation in clutch and litter size in New World reptiles. Miscellaneous Publications of the Museum of Natural History, University of Kansas, 76: 1–76.

———. 1985b. Observations on rattle size and demography of prairie rattlesnakes (Crotalus viridis) and timber rattlesnakes (Crotalus horridus) in Kansas. Occasional Papers, Museum of Natural History, University of Kansas, 118: 1–11.

———. 1998. The Sharon Springs roundup and prairie rattlesnake demography. Trans. Kansas Acad. Sci. 101(3–4): 101–113.

———. 1999. A Kansas snake community: composition and changes over 50 years. Krieger Publishing, Malabar, Florida. 165 pp.

Fitch, H. S., and A. L. Clarke. 2002. An exceptionally large natural assemblage of female copperheads (Agkistrodon contortrix). Herpetol. Rev. 33(2): 94–95.

Fitch, H. S., and B. Glading. 1947. A field study of a rattlesnake population. California Fish and Game 33(2): 103–123.

Fitch, H. S., and G. R. Pisani. 1993. Life history traits of the western diamondback rattlesnakes (Crotalus atrox) studied from roundup samples in Oklahoma. Occasional Papers, Museum of Natural History, University of Kansas, 156: 1–24.

Fitch, H. S., and H. W. Shirer. 1971. A radiotelemetric study of spatial relationships in some common snakes. Copeia 1971(1): 118–128.

Fitch, H. S., and H. Twining. 1946. Feeding habits of the Pacific rattlesnake. Copeia 1946(2): 64–71.

Fitzgerald, L. A., and C. W. Painter. 2000. Rattlesnake commercialization: long-term trends, issues, and implications for conservation. Wildlife Society Bulletin 28(1): 235–253.

Fitzinger, L. J. 1826a. Kritischke Bemerkungen über J. Wagler's Schlangenwerk. Isis von Oken 9: 882–902.

——. 1826b. Neue Classification der Reptilien nach ihren natürlichen Verwandtschaften: nebst einer Verwandtschafts-Tafel und einem Verzeichnisse der Reptilien-Sammlung des K. K. Zoologischen Museums zu Wien. J. G. Heubner, Vienna. 66 pp.

——. 1843. Systema reptilium, fasciculus primus. Amblyglossae. Vindobonae, Braumüller und Seidel, Vienna. 106 pp.

FitzSimons, D. C., and H. M. Smith, 1958. Another rear-fanged South African snake lethal to humans. Herpetologica 14: 198–202.

FitzSimons, F. W. 1912. The snakes of South Africa, their venom and the treatment of snakebite. T. M. Miller, Cape Town. 547 pp.

Fix, J. D. 1980. Venom yield of the North American coral snake and its clinical significance. Southern Medical Journal 73: 737–738.

Fix, J. D., and S. A. Minton. 1976. Venom extraction and yields from the North American coral snake, Micrurus fulvius. Toxicon 14: 143–145.

Fleay, D. 1937. Black snakes in combat. Proceedings of the Royal Zoological Society, New South Wales 1937(August): 40–42.

Fleet, R. R., and J. C. Kroll. 1978. Litter size and parturition behavior in Sistrurus miliarius streckeri. Herpetol. Rev. 9(1): 11.

Fleischman, L. J. 1985. Cryptic movement in the vine snake Oxybelis aeneus. Copeia 1985(1): 242–245.

Fleming, J. 1822. The philosophy of zoology; or a general view of the structure, functions, and classification of animals. Hurst, Robinson, London. Vol. 1, 432 pp., vol. 2, 618 pp.

Flores-Villela, O. 1990. Review of The venomous reptiles of Latin America. Copeia 1990(3): 900–901.

Flores-Villela, O., and P. Gerez. 1988. Conservación en México: síntesis sobre vertebrados terrestres, vegetación y uso del suelo. Instituto Nacional de Investigaciones sobre Recursos Bióticos. Xalapa, Veracruz.

Flores-Villela, O., and E. Hernández-García. 1989. New state records from northern Guerrero, Mexico. Herpetol. Rev. 20(1): 15–16.

Flores-Villela, O., E. Hernández-García, and A. Nieto Montes de Oca. 1991. Catálogo de anfibios y reptiles. Serie Catálogos del Museo de Zoología "Alfonso L. Herrera" 3: 1–222.

Flores-Villela, O., F. Mendoza, E. Hernández, M. Mancilla, E. Godínez, and I. Goyenechea-Mayer. 1992. Ophryacus undulatus in the Mexican state of Hidalgo. Texas Journal of Science 44: 249–250.

Flores-Villela, O., G. Pérez-Higadera [sic], R. C. Vogt, and M. Palma Muñoz. 1987. Claves para los géneros y las especies de anfibios y reptiles de la región de los Tuxtlas. Universidad Nacional Autónoma de México, Mexico City. 27 pp.

Flury, A. G. 1949. Range extensions for two west Texas snakes. Copeia 1949(4): 293.

Fogell, D. D., T. J. Leonard, and J. D. Fawcett. 2002a. Natural history notes: Agkistrodon contortrix phaeogaster (Osage copperhead). Breeding. Herpetol. Rev. 33(3): 209–210.

——. 2002b. Natural history notes: Crotalus horridus horridus (timber rattlesnake). Habitat. Herpetol. Rev. 33(3): 211–212.

——. 2002c. Natural history notes: Crotalus horridus horridus (timber rattlesnake). Climbing. Herpetol. Rev. 33(3): 212.

Fogelman, B., W. Byrd, and E. Hanebrink. 1986. Observations on the male combat dance in the cottonmouth (Agkistrodon piscivorus). Bull. Chicago Herpetol. Soc. 21: 26–28.

Foley, D. H., III. 2002. Notes on the effects of Trimorphodon biscutatus venom on a human. Herpetol. Rev. 33(3): 176–177.

Fonseca, F. da. 1949. Animais peçonhentos. Instituto Butantan, São Paulo. 376 pp.

Fontana, M. D., M. G. Heleno, and O. Vital Brazil. 1996. Mode of action of Duvernoy's gland extracts from the colubrid Dryadophis bifossatus in the chick biventer cervicis nerve-muscle preparation. Toxicon 34(10): 1187–1190.

Fontenot, L. W., and W. F. Font. 1996. Helminth parasites of four species of aquatic snakes from two habitats in southeastern Louisiana. Journal of the Helminthological Society of Washington 63(1): 66–75.

Foote, R., and J. A. MacMahon. 1977. Electrophoretic studies of rattlesnake (Crotalus and Sistrurus) venom: taxonomic implications. Comp. Biochem. Physiol. B 57: 235–241.

Force, E. R. 1930. The amphibians and reptiles of Tulsa County, Oklahoma, and vicinity. Copeia 1930(2): 25–39.

Ford, N. B., and G. M. Burghardt. 1993. Perceptual mechanisms and the behavioral ecology of snakes. Pp. 117–164 in R. A. Seigel and J. T. Collins (eds.), Snakes: ecology and behavior. McGraw-Hill, New York.

Ford, N. B., V. A. Cobb, and W. W. Lamar. 1990. Reproductive data on snakes from northeastern Texas. Texas Journal of Science 42(4): 355–368.

Ford, R. S. 1981. Geographic distribution: Heloderma suspectum cinctum (banded Gila monster). Herpetol. Rev. 12(2): 64.

Forrester, D. J., R. M. Shealy, and S. H. Best. 1970. Porocephalus crotali (Pentastomida) in South Carolina. Journal of Parasitology 56: 977.

Fountain, P. 1902. The great mountains and forests of South America. Longmans, Green, London. 306 pp.

Fouquette, M. J., Jr., and D. A. Rossman. 1963. Noteworthy records of Mexican amphibians and reptiles in the Florida State Museum and the Texas Natural History collection. Herpetologica 19(3): 185–201.

Fowler, H. W. 1907. Amphibians and reptiles of New Jersey. Annual Report of the New Jersey State Museum 1906: 23–250, 402–408.

Fowler, I. R., and M. G. Salomão. 1994. Activity patterns in the colubrid snake genus Philodryas and their relationship to reproduction and snakebite. Bull. Chicago Herpetol. Soc. 29(10):229–232.

Fowlie, J. A. 1965. The snakes of Arizona. Azul Quinta Press, Fallbrook, Calif. 164 pp.

França, F. O. S., K. C. Barbaro, H. W. Fan, J. L. C. Cardoso, I. S. Martins, S. C. Tomy, M. H. Lopes, D. A. Warrell, and R. D. G. Theakston. (In press.) Relationship between venom antigenaemia and severity of Bothrops jararaca envenoming in Brazil. Trans. Roy. Soc. Trop. Med. Hyg.

Franco, F. L., and M. T. O. Malmann-Franco. 1999. Presencia de hemiclitoris em Bothrops jararacussu (Serpentes: Viperidae: Crotalinae). P. 62 in Abstracts of the V Congreso Latinoamericano de Herpetología, Montevideo, 12 al 17 de diciembre de 1999.

Franke, A. 1881. Die Reptilien und Amphibien Deutschlands. Nach einigen Beobachtungen geschildert von Ad. Francke. Veit, Leipzig.

Franklin, C. J., and J. Franklin. 1999. Geographic distribution: Bothriechis schlegelii (eyelash palm-pitviper). Herpetol. Rev. 30(2): 112.

Fraser, D. F. 1964. Micrurus limbatus, a new coral snake from Veracruz, Mexico. Copeia 1964(3): 570–573.

——. 1973. Variation in the coral snake, Micrurus diastema. Copeia 1973(1): 1–17.

Freddy, D. J., and J. L. Kogutt. 1978. Geographic distribution: Crotalus viridis ssp. (western rattlesnake). Herpetol. Rev. 9(3): 108.

Freed, P. 1993. Herpetofauna. Pp. 31–32 in T. A. Parker III, R. B. Foster, L. H. Emmons, P. Freed, A. B. Forsyth, B. Hoffman, and B. D. Gill, A biological assessment of the Kanuku Mountain region of southwestern Guyana. RAP Working Papers 5. Conservation International, Washington, D.C.

——. 1997. Record small size for the western pigmy rattlesnake. Bull. Chicago Herpetol. Soc. 32(2): 27.

Freeman, S. and J. C. Herron. 2001. Evolutionary analysis, 2d ed. Prentice Hall, Upper Saddle River, N.J.

Freiberg, M. A. 1939. Enumeración sistematica de los reptiles de Entre Rios y lista de los ejemplares que los representam en el Museo de Entre Rios. Memorias del Museo Entre Rios (Paraná) Zool. 11: 1–28.

——. 1968. Ofidios ponzoñosos de la Argentina. Ciencia e Investigación (Buenos Aires) 24(8): 338–353.

——. 1972. Clase VII. Los reptiles (Reptilia). Pp. 447–634 in L. Cendrero (ed.), Zoología hispanoamericana. Editorial Porrúa, Mexico, D.F.

——. 1982. Snakes of South America. T. F. H. Publications, Neptune, N.J. 189 pp.

——. 1984. El mundo de los ofidios. Albatross, Buenos Aires. 152 pp.

Freire, E. M. X. 2001. Geographic distribution: *Micrurus corallinus* (painted coral snake). Herpetol. Rev. 32(1): 60.

Freire-Lascano, A. 1991. Dos nuevas especies de *Bothrops* en el Ecuador. Universidad Técnica de Machala, Publicaciones de Trabajos Científicos del Ecuador. 11 pp.

Freire-Lascano, A., F. García, W. Wüster, and U. Kuch. 2003. *Bothriopsis taeniata* or *Bothrops taeniatus* (speckled forest-pitviper). Juvenile size. Herpetol. Rev. 34(3).

Freire-Lascano, A., and U. Kuch. 1992. Bermerkungen zur Systematik einiger Grubenottern Ecuadors. Zusammenfassungen Jahrestagung der Deutschen Gesellschaft für Herpetologie und Terrarienkunde 16(20): 14–15.

——. 1994. A note on the geographical distribution of *Bothrops asper* (Garman, 1883) in Ecuador. Snake 26: 135–139.

——. 2000. Natural history: *Bothrops campbelli*. Diet and reproduction. Herpetol. Rev. 31(1): 45.

Freitas, M. A. de. 1999. Serpentes da Bahia e do Brasil. Editora Dall, Bahia, Brazil. 79 pp.

Frey, J. K. 1996. Natural history notes: *Crotalus lepidus* (rock rattlesnake). Aquatic behavior. Herpetol. Rev. 27(3): 145.

Froom, B. 1964. The massasauga rattlesnake. Canadian Audubon 26: 78–80.

——. 1967. Ontario snakes. Department of Lands and Forests, Toronto. 36 pp.

Frost, D. [R.], and S. Aird. 1978. Geographic distribution: *Micrurus laticollaris*. Herpetol. Rev. 9(2): 62.

Frost, D. R., and J. T. Collins. 1988. Nomenclatural notes on reptiles of the United States. Herpetol. Rev. 19(4): 73–74.

Frost, D. R., and D. M. Hillis. 1990. Species in concept and practice: herpetological applications. Herpetologica 46(1): 87–104.

Fu, J., and R. W. Murphy. 1997. Phylogeny of Chinese *Oreolalax* and the use of functional outgroups to select among multiple equally parsimonious trees. Asiatic Herpetological Research 7: 38–43.

——. 1999. Discriminating and locating character covariation: an application of permutation tail probability analyses. Syst. Biol. 48: 380–395.

Fuentes, O., and A. Rodríguez-Acosta. 1997. A new record of *Bothrops brazili* Hoge, 1953 (Serpentes: Crotalidae) in Venezuela. Acta Biologica Venezuelica 17(3): 71–77.

Fugler, C. M. 1960. New herpetological records for British Honduras. Texas Journal of Science 12(1–2): 8–13.

——. 1983. Lista preliminar de los anfibios y reptiles de Tumi Chucua. Museo Nacional de Historia Natural de Bolivia Comunicación 2: 4–11.

——. 1984. Tercera contribución a la fauna herpetológica del oriente boliviano. Revista Ecología en Bolivia 5: 63–72.

Fugler, C. M., and J. Cabot. 1995. Herpetologica boliviana: una lista comentada de las serpientes de Bolivia con datos sobre su distribución. Ecología en Bolivia 24: 41–90.

Fugler, C. M., and J. R. Dixon. 1961. Notes on the herpetofauna of the El Dorado area of Sinaloa, Mexico. Publications of the Museum, Michigan State University, Biological Series 2(1): 1–21.

Fugler, C. M., and A. B. Walls. 1978. Snakes of the Upano Valley of Amazonian Ecuador. Journal of the Tennessee Academy of Science 53(3): 81–87.

Fugler, C. M., and R. G. Webb. 1956. Distributional notes on some reptiles and amphibians from southern and central Coahuila. Herpetologica 12(3): 167–171.

Fuhrmann, O. 1927. Brasilianische Cestoden aus Reptilien und Vögeln. Abhandlungen der Senckenbergischen Naturforschenden Gesellschaft (Frankfurt am Main) 410: 389–401.

Fukada, H. 1964. A small collection of snakes of the Kyoto University expedition to the upper Amazon. Bulletin of the Kyoto Gakugei University, ser. B, 23: 19–26.

Funderburg, J. B. 1968. Eastern diamondback rattlesnake feeding on carrion. J. Herpetol. 2: 161–162.

Funk, R. S. 1963. On the reproduction of *Micruroides euryxanthus* (Kennicott). Copeia 1963(1): 219.

——. 1964. On the food of *Crotalus m. molossus*. Herpetologica 20(2): 134.

——. 1965. Food of *Crotalus cerastes laterorepens* in Yuma County, Arizona. Herpetologica 21(1): 15–17.

——. 1966. Notes about *Heloderma suspectum* along the western extremity of its range. Herpetologica 22(4): 254–258.

Furlow, T. G., and L. V. Brennan. 1985. Purpura following timber rattlesnake (*Crotalus horridus horridus*) envenomation. Cutis 35: 234–236.

Furtado, M. F. D., M. Maruyama, A. S. Kamiguti, and L. C. Antonio. 1991. Comparative study of nine *Bothrops* snake venoms from adult female snakes and their offspring. Toxicon 29(2): 219–226.

Gaar, G. G. 1996. Assessment and management of coral and other exotic snake envenomations. Journal of the Florida Medical Association 83: 178–182.

Gaddy, L. L. (ed.). 1982. Man's impact on the vegetation, avifauna, and herpetofauna of South Carolina's Barrier Islands: a habitat approach to carrying capacity. South Carolina Wildlife and Marine Resources Department, Columbia.

Gadow, H. 1905. The distribution of Mexican amphibians and reptiles. Proc. Zool. Soc. London 1905(2): 191–244.

——. 1908. Through southern Mexico. Witherly, London. 527 pp.

——. 1910. The effect of altitude upon the distribution of Mexican amphibians and reptiles. Zoologische Jahrbücher. Abteilung für Systematik, Ökologie, und Geographie der Tiere 6: 689–714.

——. 1911. Isotely and coral snakes. Zoologische Jahrbücher. Abteilung für Systematik, Ökologie, und Geographie der Tiere 31: 1–24.

Gaige, H. T. 1936. Some reptiles and amphibians from Yucatan and Campeche, Mexico. Publication of the Carnegie Institution of Washington 457: 289–304.

Gaige, H. T., N. Hartweg, and L. C. Stuart. 1937. Notes on a collection of amphibians and reptiles from eastern Nicaragua. Occas. Pap. Mus. Zool. Univ. Michigan (357): 1–8.

Gallardo, J. M. 1972. Observaciones biológicas sobre una falsa yarara, *Tomodon ocellatus* Duméril, Bibron, and Duméril (Reptilia, Ophidia). Neotropica 18(56): 57–63.

——. 1977. Reptiles de los alrededores de Buenos Aires. Editorial Universitaria de Buenos Aires, Buenos Aires. 213 pp.

——. 1979. Composición, distribución y origen de la herpetofauna Chaqueña. Pp. 299–307 in W. E. Duellman (ed.), The South American herpetofauna: its origin, evolution, and dispersal. Monograph No. 7 of the Museum of Natural History, University of Kansas, Lawrence.

——. 1982. Anfibios y reptiles del Parque Nacional El Palmar de Colón, Provincia de Entre Ríos. Anales de Parques Nacionales (Buenes Aires) 15: 65–75.

Galligan, J. H., and W. A. Dunson. 1979. Biology and status of timber rattlesnake (*Crotalus horridus*) populations in Pennsylvania. Biological Conservation 15: 13–58.

Gandavo, P. de M. 1576. Historia da província Santa Cruz. Antonio Gonsalvez, Lisboa.

Gann, T., and M. Gann. 1939. Archeological investigations in the Corozal District of British Honduras. Smithsonian Institution, Bulletin of the Bureau of American Ethnology 123: 1–66.

Gannon, V. P. J., and D. M. Secoy. 1984. Growth and reproductive rates of a northern population of the prairie rattlesnake, *Crotalus v. viridis*. J. Herpetol. 81: 13–19.

——. 1985. Seasonal and daily activity patterns in a Canadian population of the prairie rattlesnake, *Crotalus viridis*. Canadian Journal of Zoology 63: 86–91.

Gans, C. 1961. Mimicry in procryptically colored snakes of the genus *Dasypeltis*. Evolution 15: 72–91.

——. 1964. Empathic learning and the mimicry of African snakes. Evolution 18: 705.

——. 1973. Another case of presumptive mimicry in snakes. Copeia 1973(4): 801–802.

——. 1978. Reptilian venoms: some evolutionary considerations. Pp. 1–39 in C. Gans and K. A. Gans (eds.), Biology of the Reptilia, vol. 8. Physiology B. Academic Press, London.

——. 1987. Automimicry and Batesian mimicry in uropeltid snakes: pigment, proportions, pattern, and behavior. Journal of the Bombay Natural History Society 83(suppl.): 153–158.

Gans, C., and D. Baic. 1974. Convergent surface structures in the sound producing scales of some snakes (Reptilia: Serpentes). Pp. 265–272 in L. Arvie (ed.), Recherches biologiques contemporaines, dédiés à la mémoire de Dr. Manfred Gabe, 1916–1973. Imprimerie Vagner, Nancy, France.

——. 1977. Regional specialization of reptilian scale surfaces: relation of texture and biologic role. Science 195: 1348–1350.

Gans, C., and A. S. Gaunt. 1998. Biology of the Reptilia, vol. 19. Morphology G. Visceral organs. Society for the Study of Amphibians and Reptiles, Ithaca, N.Y. 660 pp.

Gans, C., and P. F. A. Maderson. 1973. Sound producing mechanisms in recent reptiles: review and comment. American Zoologist 13: 1195–1203.

Gans, C., and N. D. Richmond. 1957. Warning behavior in snakes of the genus *Dasypeltis*. Copeia 1957: 269–274.

García, A., and G. Ceballos. 1994. Guía de campo de los reptiles y anfibios de la costa de Jalisco, México. Fundación Ecológica de Cuixmala, A. C., Instituto de Biología, Universidad Nacional Autónoma de México. 184 pp.

García, E. 1896. Los ofidios venenosos del Cauca. Métodos empíricos y racionales empleados contra los accidentes producidos por la mordedura de esos reptiles. Librería Colombiana, Cali, Colombia. 102 pp.

García, V. E., and J. C. Perez. 1984. The purification and characterization of an antihemorrhagic factor in woodrat (*Neotoma micropus*) serum. Toxicon 22(1): 129–138.

Garcia-Lima, E. and C. J. Laure. 1987. A study of bacterial contaminations of rattlesnake venom. Revista da Sociedade Brasileira de Medicina Tropical 20: 19–21.

García-López, R. and F. Sandner-Montilla. 1962. Estudio bioquímico y electroforético de las ponzoñas de las principales serpientes de la fam. Crotalidae venezolanas y su actividad biológica en el hombre. Memoria de la Sociedad de Ciencias Naturales La Salle 22(6): 5–33.

García-Pérez, J. E. 1995. Una nueva especie de cascabel (Serpentes: Crotalidae) para el bolsón árido de Lagunillas, Cordillera de Mérida, Venezuela. Revista de Ecología Latinoamericana 3(2): 7–12.

Garel, T., and S. Matola. 1996. A field guide to the snakes of Belize. Belize Zoo and Tropical Education Center, Belize City. 147 pp.

Garfin, S. R. 1982. Rattlesnake bites: current hospital therapy. Western Journal of Medicine 137: 411–412.

Garfin, S. R., R. R. Castilonia, S. J. Mubarak, A. R. Hargens, F. E. Russell, and W. H. Akeson. 1984. Rattlesnake bites and surgical decompression: results using a laboratory model. Toxicon 22: 177–182.

Garman, S. 1877 [dated 1876]. Reptiles and batrachians collected by Allen Lesley, Esq., on the Isthmus of Panama. Proceedings of the Boston Society of Natural History 18: 402–413.

——. 1881. New and little-known reptiles and fishes in the museum collections. Bulletin of the Museum of Comparative Zoology 8: 85–93.

——. 1882. The scream of the young burrowing owl sounds like the warning of the rattlesnake. Nature 27: 174.

——. 1884a [dated 1883]. The reptiles and batrachians of North America. Memoirs of the Museum of Comparative Zoology 8(3): 1–185.

——. 1884b. The North American reptiles and batrachians. A list of the species occurring north of the Isthmus of Tehuantepec, with references. Bulletin of the Essex Institute 16: 1–46.

——. 1887a. Reptiles and batrachians from Texas and Mexico. Bulletin of the Essex Institute 19: 119–138.

——. 1887b. On West Indian reptiles in the Museum of Comparative Zoology, at Cambridge, Mass. Proceedings of the American Philosophical Society 24: 278–286.

——. 1888. The rattle of the rattlesnake. Bulletin of the Museum of Comparative Zoology 13(10): 259–268.

——. 1889. On the evolution of the rattlesnake. Proceedings of the Boston Society of Natural History 24: 170–182.

——. 1890a. The "Gila monster." Bulletin of the Essex Institute 22: 60–69.

——. 1890b. Notes on Illinois reptiles and amphibians, including several species not before recorded from the northern states. Bulletin of the Illinois Natural History Survey 3: 185–190.

——. 1892a. The reptiles of the Galapagos islands from the collections of Dr. Geo. Baur. Bulletin of the Essex Institute 24: 73–87.

——. 1892b. On reptiles collected by Dr. Geo. Baur near Guayaquil, Ecuador. Bulletin of the Essex Institute 24: 88–95.

——. 1892c. On Texan reptiles. Bulletin of the Essex Institute 24: 98–109.

——. 1908. The reptiles of Easter Island. Bulletin of the Museum of Comparative Zoology 52(1): 1–13.

Garrido, O. H. 1980. Notas sobre mordidas de jubo, *Alsophis* (Serpentes: Colubridae). Miscelanea Zoologica, La Habana, 11: 2–3.

Garton, J. S., and R. W. Dimmick. 1969. Food habits of the copperhead in middle Tennessee. Journal of the Tennessee Academy of Science 44: 113–117.

Gasc, J.-P. and M. T. Rodrigues. 1980. Liste préliminaire des serpents de la Guyane française. Bulletin du Muséum National d'Histoire Naturelle, Paris, 4th ser., 2, A(2): 559–598.

Gasparini, J. L., C. Zamprogno, and I. Saxima. 1993. Dieta de "jararaca-de-rabo-branco" ou "jararacuçu," *Bothrops pradoi*. P. 189 in Resumos do III Congreso Latinoamericano de Herpetología, Unicamp, Campinas, São Paulo.

Gates, G. O. 1956a. Mating habits of the Gila monster. Herpetologica 12(3): 184.

——. 1956b. A record length for the Arizona coral snake. Herpetologica 12(2): 155.

——. 1957. A study of the herpetofauna in the vicinity of Wickenburg, Maricopa County, Arizona. Trans. Kansas Acad. Sci. 60(4): 403–418.

Gatti, C. 1955. Las culebras venenosas del Paraguay. Revista Médica del Paraguay 1: 81–100.

Gavrilets, S., and A. Hastings. 1998. Coevolutionary chase in two-species systems with applications to mimicry. Journal of Theoretical Biology 191: 415–427.

Gebhard, J. 1853. In the Sixth Report of the State Cabinet of Natural History, New York, p. 22.

Gehlbach, F. R. 1957 [dated 1956]. Annotated records of southwestern amphibians and reptiles. Trans. Kansas Acad. Sci. 59(3): 364–372.

——. 1965. Herpetology of the Zuni Mountains region, northwestern New Mexico. Proceedings of the U.S. National Museum 116(3505): 243–332.

——. 1970. Death-feigning and erratic behavior in leptotyphlopid, colubrid, and elapid snakes. Herpetologica 26(1): 24–34.

——. 1972. Coral snake mimicry reconsidered: the strategy of self-mimicry. Forma et Functio 5: 311–320.

Gehlbach, F. R., and B. B. Collette. 1957. A contribution to the herpetofauna of the highlands of Oaxaca and Puebla, Mexico. Herpetologica 13(3): 227–231.

Gennaro, J. F., R. S. Leopold, and W. M. Merriam. 1961. Observations on the actual quantity of venom introduced by several species of crotalid snakes in their bite. Anatomical Record 139: 303.

Genter, D. L. 1984. Natural history notes: *Crotalus viridis* (prairie rattlesnake). Food. Herpetol. Rev. 15(2): 49–50.

Gentry, G. 1941. Herpetological collections from counties in the vicinity of the Obey River drainage of Tennessee. Journal of the Tennessee Academy of Science 16(3): 329–332.

——. 1955. An annotated checklist of the amphibians and reptiles of Tennessee. Journal of the Tennessee Academy of Science 30(2): 168–251.

——. 1956. An annotated checklist of the amphibians and reptiles of Tennessee. Journal of the Tennessee Academy of Science 31(3): 242–251.

Gentry, J., and M. H. Smith. 1968. Food habits and burrow associates of *Peromyscus polionotus*. Journal of Mammalogy 49: 562–565.

George, I. D. 1930a. Notes on the extraction of venom at the serpentarium of the Antivenin Institute at Tela, Honduras. Bull. Antivenin Inst. Am. 4(3): 57–59.

——. 1930b. Short report of work on the snake farm at Lancetilla, Tela, Honduras. Report of the Medical Department of the United Fruit Company, Boston, Massachusetts, 18: 326–332.

Gerhardt, R. P., P. M. Harris, and M. A. Vásquez-Marroquin. 1993. Food habits of nesting great black hawks in Tikal National Park, Guatemala. Biotropica 25: 349–352.

Gerstäcker, F. 1968. Wild sports in the Far West: the narrative of a German wanderer beyond the Mississippi, 1837–1843. Duke University Press, Durham, N.C. 409 pp. [Reprint of 1854 translation; original published in 1844 as *Streif- und Jagdzüge durch die Vereinigten Staaten Nordamerikas*.]

Geyer, C. A. 1847. Beobachtungen über gemeine Klapperschlange Nordamerikas, mit dem Beinamen der "Schrecklichen" (*Crotalus horridus*). Allgemeine Deutsche Naturhistorische Zeitung 2: 373–386.

Gibbons, J. W. 1972. Reproduction, growth, and sexual dimorphism in the canebrake rattlesnake (*Crotalus horridus atricaudatus*). Copeia 1972(2): 222–226.

——. 1993. Keeping all the pieces: perspectives on natural history and the environment. Smithsonian Institution Press, Washington, D.C. 182 pp.

Gibbons, J. W., and M. E. Dorcas. 2002. Defensive behavior of cottonmouths (*Agkistrodon piscivorus*) toward humans. Copeia 2002(1): 195–198.

Gibbons, J. W., R. R. Haynes, and J. L. Thomas. 1990. Poisonous plants and venomous animals of Alabama and adjoining states. University of Alabama Press, Tuscaloosa. 345 pp.

Gibbons, J. W., and P. J. West. 2000. Snakes of Georgia and South Carolina. Savannah River Ecology Laboratory Herp Outreach Publication No. 1. University of Georgia, Athens. 28 pp.

Gibbs, H. L., A. Prior, P. J. Weatherhead, and G. Johnson. 1997. Genetic structure of populations of the threatened eastern massasauga rattlesnake, *Sistrurus c. catenatus*: evidence from microsatellite DNA markers. Molecular Ecology 6: 1123–1132.

Gifford, M. E. 2002. Cryptic diversity in the *Ameiva chrysolaema* species complex (Squamata: Teiidae) as revealed by analysis of morphology and mitochondrial DNA. Master's thesis, University of Texas at Tyler. 138 pp.

Gillingham, J. C., and R. E. Baker. 1981. Evidence for scavenging behavior in the western diamondback rattlesnake (*Crotalus atrox*). Zeitschrift Tierpsychologie 55: 217–227.

Gillingham, J. C., C. C. Carpenter, and J. B. Murphy. 1983. Courtship, male combat, and dominance in the western diamondback rattlesnake, *Crotalus atrox*. J. Herpetol. 17: 265–270.

Gilmore, C. W. 1928. Fossil lizards of North America. Memoirs of the National Academy of Sciences 12: 1–201.

Girard, C. F. 1855 [dated 1854]. Abstract of a report to Lieut. James M. Gillis, U.S.N., upon reptiles collected during the U.S.N. astronomical expedition to Chile. Proc. Acad. Nat. Sci. Philadelphia 7: 226–227.

——. 1858. Herpetology. United States Exploring Expedition during the years 1838, 1839, 1840, 1841, 1842, under the command of Charles Wilkes, U.S.N., vol. 20. C. Sherman, Philadelphia. 496 pp.

Girard, R. 1958. Indios selváticos de la Amazonía Peruana. Libro Mex, México, D.F. 356 pp.

Giraudo, A., and R. Abranson. 1994. Comentarios sobre los ophidios registrados en una localidad del centro de la Providencia de Misiones, Argentina. Boletín de la Asociación Herpetológica Argentina 10(1): 8–10.

Giraudo, A., and A. O. Contreras. 1994. Lista preliminar de los reptiles registrados en el Departamento Neembucu, Paraguay. Boletín de la Asociación Herpetológica Argentina 10(1): 1–4.

Gistel, J. N. F. X. 1848. Naturgeschichte de Thierreichs. Für höhere Shulen bearbeitet. Hoffman'sche, Stuttgart. 216 pp.

Githens, T. S. 1935. Snake bite in the United States. Scientific Monthly 1935 (August): 163–167.

Githens, T. S., and L. W. Butz. 1929. Venoms of North American snakes and their relationship. Bull. Antivenin Inst. Am. 2: 100–104.

Githens, T. S., and I. D. George. 1931. Comparative studies of the venoms of certain rattlesnakes. Bull. Antivenin Inst. Am. 5(2): 31–35.

Glaser, H. S. R. 1948. Bactericidal activity of *Crotalus* venom *in vitro*. Copeia 1948(4): 245–247.

——. 1970. The distribution of amphibians and reptiles in Riverside County, California. Natural History Series No. 1. Riverside Museum Press, Riverside, Calif. 40 pp.

Glass, T. G. 1982. Treatment of rattlesnake bites. JAMA 247: 461.

——. 1987. Poisonous snakebite. Pp. 973–976 in R. E. Rakel (ed.), Conn's current therapy. Saunders, Philadelphia.

Glenn, J. L., and H. E. Lawler. 1987. Life history notes: *Crotalus scutulatus salvini* (Huamantlan rattlesnake). Behavior. Herpetol. Rev. 18(1): 15–16.

Glenn, J. L., L. Porras, R. Nohavec, and R. Straight. 1992. Analysis of the Duvernoy's gland and oral secretions of *Hydrodynastes gigas*. Pp. 19–26 in P. D. Strimple and J. L. Strimple (eds.), Contributions in herpetology. Greater Cincinnati Herpetological Society, Cincinnati.

Glenn, J. L., and R. Straight. 1977. The midget faded rattlesnake (*Crotalus viridis concolor*) venom: lethal toxicity and individual variability. Toxicon 15: 129–133.

——. 1978. Mojave rattlesnake (*Crotalus scutulatus scutulatus*) venom: variation in toxicity with geographical origin. Toxicon 16: 81–84.

——. 1982. The rattlesnakes and their venom yield and lethal toxicity. Pp. 3–119 in A. T. Tu (ed.), Rattlesnake venoms. Marcel Dekker, New York.

——. 1985a. Distribution of proteins immunologically similar to Mojave toxin among species of *Crotalus* and *Sistrurus*. Toxicon 23: 28.

——. 1985b. Venom properties of the rattlesnakes (*Crotalus*) inhabiting the Baja California region of Mexico. Toxicon 23(5): 769–776.

——. 1987. Variations in the venom of *Crotalus lepidus klauberi*. Toxicon 25: 142.

——. 1989. Intergradation of two different venom populations of the Mojave rattlesnake (*Crotalus scutulatus scutulatus*) in Arizona. Toxicon 27: 411–418.

——. 1990. Venom characteristics as an indicator of hybridization between *Crotalus viridis viridis* and *Crotalus scutulatus scutulatus* in New Mexico. Toxicon 28(7): 857–862.

Glenn, J. L., R. Straight, M. C. Wolfe, and D. L. Hardy. 1983. Geographical variation in *Crotalus scutulatus scutulatus* (Mojave rattlesnake) venom properties. Toxicon 21: 119–130.

Glenn, J. L., R. C. Straight, and T. B. Wolt. 1994. Regional variation in the presence of canebrake toxin in *Crotalus horridus* venom. Comp. Biochem. Physiol. C 107: 337–346.

Gliesch, R. 1925. As cobras do Estado do Rio Grande do Sul. Almanak Agricola Brazileiro 1925: 97–118.

——. 1931. A Urutu (*Lachesis=Bothrops=alternata* D. e B.). Egatea—Revista da Escola de engenharia de Porto Alegre 16(3–4): 96–102.

Glissmeyer, H. R. 1951. Egg production of the Great Basin rattlesnake. Herpetologica 7: 24–27.

Gloyd, H. K. 1928. The amphibians and reptiles of Franklin County, Kansas. Trans. Kansas Acad. Sci. 31: 115–141.

——. 1932 [dated 1931]. The herpetological fauna of the Pigeon Lake region, Miami County, Kansas. Papers of the Michigan Academy of Science, Arts, and Letters 15: 389–409

——. 1933a. On the effect of moccasin venom upon a rattlesnake. Science 78: 13–14.

——. 1933b. An unusual feeding of the prairie rattlesnake. Copeia 1933(2): 98.

——. 1934a [dated 1933]. Studies on the breeding habits and young of the copperhead, *Agkistrodon mokasen* Beauvois. Papers of the Michigan Academy of Sciences, Arts and Letters 19: 587–604.

——. 1934b. The broad-banded copperhead: a new subspecies of *Agkistrodon mokasen*. Occasional Papers of the Museum of Zoology of the University of Michigan 283: 1–6.

——. 1935a [dated 1934]. Studies on the breeding habits and young of the copperhead, *Agkistrodon mokasen* Beauvois. Papers of the Michigan Academy of Sciences, Arts, and Letters 20: 661–668.

——. 1935b [dated 1934]. Some aberrant color patterns in snakes. Papers of the Michigan Academy of Sciences, Arts, and Letters 20: 661–668.

——. 1935c. The subspecies of *Sistrurus miliarius*. Occasional Papers of the Museum of Zoology of the University of Michigan 322: 1–7.

——. 1936a [dated 1935]. The cane-brake rattlesnake. Copeia 1935(4): 175–178.

——. 1936b. The subspecies of *Crotalus lepidus*. Occasional Papers of the Museum of Zoology of the University of Michigan 337: 1–5.

——. 1936c. A Mexican subspecies of *Crotalus molossus* Baird and Girard. Occas. Pap. Mus. Zool. Univ. Michigan 325: 1–5.

——. 1936d. The status of *Crotalus unicolor* Van Lidth de Jeude and *Crotalus pulvis* Ditmars. Herpetologica 1(2): 65–68.

——. 1937. A herpetological consideration of faunal areas in southern Arizona. Bulletin of the Chicago Academy of Sciences 5(5): 79–136.

——. 1938a. A case of poisoning from the bite of a black coral snake. Herpetologica 1(5): 121–124.

——. 1938b. The snakes of Goose Pond Hill. Chicago Naturalist 1(4): 121–123.

——. 1940. The rattlesnakes, genera *Sistrurus* and *Crotalus*. A study in zoogeography and evolution. Special Publications of the Chicago Academy of Sciences 4: 1–270.

——. 1944. Texas snakes. Texas Geographic Magazine 8(2): 1–18.

——. 1946. Some rattlesnake dens of South Dakota. Chicago Naturalist 9: 87–97.

——. 1947a [dated 1946]. Some rattlesnake dens of South Dakota. Chicago Naturalist 9(4): 87–97.

——. 1947b. Notes on the courtship and mating behavior of certain snakes. Chicago Academy of Sciences, Natural History Miscellanea 12: 1–4.

——. 1948a. Another account of the "dance" of the western diamond rattlesnake. Chicago Academy of Sciences, Natural History Miscellanea 34: 1–3.

——. 1948b. Description of a neglected subspecies of rattlesnake from Mexico. Chicago Academy of Sciences, Natural History Miscellanea 17: 1–4.

——. 1955. A review of the massasaugas, *Sistrurus catenatus*, of the southwestern United States. Bulletin of the Chicago Academy of Sciences 10(6): 83–98.

——. 1957 [dated 1956]. Distribution of the Mexican moccasin: a correction. Copeia 1956(4): 259.

——. 1958. Aberrations in the color pattern of some crotalid snakes. Bulletin of the Chicago Academy of Science 10(12): 185–195.

——. 1969. Two additional subspecies of North American crotalid snakes, genus *Agkistrodon*. Proceedings of the Biological Society of Washington 83: 219–232.

——. 1972. A subspecies of *Agkistrodon bilineatus* (Serpentes: Crotalidae) on the Yucatan Peninsula, Mexico. Proceedings of the Biological Society of Washington 84: 327–334.

——. 1977. Descriptions of new taxa of crotalid snakes from China and Ceylon (Sri Lanka). Proceedings of the Biological Society of Washington 90: 1002–1015.

——. 1979. A new generic name for the hundred-pace viper. Proceedings of the Biological Society of Washington 91: 963–964.

Gloyd, H. K., and W. A. Bevan. 1946. A case of intraspecific poisoning in the Great Basin rattlesnake. Chicago Academy of Sciences, Natural History Miscellanea 3: 1–3.

Gloyd, H. K., and R. Conant. 1938. The subspecies of the copperhead, *Agkistrodon mokasen* Beauvois. Bulletin of the Chicago Academy of Sciences 5: 163–166.

——. 1943. A synopsis of the American forms of *Agkistrodon* (copperheads and moccasins). Bulletin of the Chicago Academy of Sciences 7(2): 147–170.

——. 1990. Snakes of the *Agkistrodon* complex: a monographic review. Society for the Study of Amphibians and Reptiles, Oxford, Ohio. 614 pp.

Gloyd, H. K., and C. F. Kauffeld. 1940. A new rattlesnake from Mexico. Bulletin of the Chicago Academy of Sciences 6(2): 11–14.

Gloyd, H. K., and H. M. Smith. 1942. Amphibians and reptiles from the Carmen Mountains, Coahuila. Bulletin of the Chicago Academy of Sciences 6(13): 231–235.

Gmelin, J. F. 1788. Caroli a Linné Systema naturae per regna tria naturae, 13th ed., vol. 1, part 2, pp. 501–1032. G. E. Beer, Leipzig.

——. 1789. Caroli a Linné Systema naturae per regna tria naturae, 13th ed., vol. 1, part 3, pp. 1033–1516. G. E. Beer, Leipzig.

Godínez-Cano, E., F. Mendoza-Quijano, M. Mancilla Moreno, and E. Hernández-García. 1995. Natural history notes: *Ophryacus undulatus* (Mexican pit viper). Herpetol. Rev. 26(3): 149.

Godman, F. D. 1915. Biologia Centrali-Americana. Zoology, botany, and archaeology. Taylor and Francis, London. 149 pp.

Golay, P. 1985. Checklist and keys to the terrestrial proteroglyphs of the world. Elapsoidea. Gilbert Rey, Geneva. 90 pp.

Golay, P., D. Chiszar, H. M. Smith, and F. van Breukelen. 1999. The proper name for the Venezuelan red-tailed coral snake. Acta Biológica Venezuelica 19(4): 73–75.

Golay, P., H. M. Smith, D. G. Broadley, J. R. Dixon, C. McCarthy, J. C. Rage, B. Schätti, and M. Toriba. 1993. Endoglyphs and other major venomous snakes of the world. *Azemiops*, Herpetological Data Center, Geneva, Switzerland. 478 pp.

Gold, B. S., R. C. Dart, and R. A. Barish. 2002. Bites of venomous snakes. New England Journal of Medicine 347:347–356.

Gold, B. S., and W. A. Wingert. 1994. Snake venom poisoning in the United States: a review of therapeutic practice. Southern Medical Journal 87: 579–589.

Goldberg, S. R. 1997. Reproduction in the western coral snake, *Micruroides euryxanthus* (Elapidae), from Arizona and Sonora Mexico. Great Basin Naturalist 57(4): 363–365.

——. 1999a. Reproduction in the blacktail rattlesnake, *Crotalus molossus* (Serpentes: Viperidae). Texas Journal of Science 51(4): 323–328.

——. 1999b. Reproduction in the tiger rattlesnake, *Crotalus tigris* (Serpentes: Viperidae). Texas Journal of Science 51: 31–36.

——. 2000a. Reproduction in the speckled rattlesnake, *Crotalus mitchelli* (Serpentes: Viperidae). Bulletin of the Southern California Academy of Sciences 99(2): 101–104.

——. 2000b. Reproduction in the twin-spotted rattlesnake, *Crotalus pricei* (Serpentes: Viperidae). Western North American Naturalist 60(1): 98–100.

Goldberg, S. R., and D. D. Beck. 2001. Natural history notes: *Heloderma horridum* (beaded lizard). Reproduction. Herpetol. Rev. 32(4): 255–256.

Goldberg, S. R., and C. R. Bursey. 1990. Redescription of the microfilaria, *Piratuba mitchelli* (Smith) (Onchocercidae) from the Gila monster, *Heloderma suspectum* Cope (Helodermatidae). Southwest. Nat. 35(4): 458–460.

——. 1991. Gastrointestinal helminths of the reticulate Gila monster, *Heloderma suspectum suspectum* (Sauria: Helodermatidae). Journal of the Helminthological Society of Washington 58(1): 146–149.

——. 1999. Natural history notes: *Crotalus lepidus* (rock rattlesnake), *Crotalus molossus* (blacktail rattlesnake), *Crotalus pricei* (twin-spotted rattlesnake), *Crotalus tigris* (tiger rattlesnake). Endoparasites. Herpetol. Rev. 30(1): 44–45.

——. 2000a. Natural history notes: *Crotalus mitchelli* (speckled rattlesnake) and *Crotalus willardi* (ridgenose rattlesnake). Endoparasites. Herpetol. Rev. 31(2): 104.

——. 2000b. Natural history notes: *Micruroides euryxanthus* (western coral snake). Endoparasites. Herpetol. Rev. 31(2): 105–106.

Goldberg, S. R., C. R. Bursey, and A. T. Holycross. 2001. Natural history notes: *Sistrurus catenatus* (desert massasauga). Endoparasites. Herpetol. Rev. 32(4): 265.

——. (In press.) *Abbreviata terrapenis* (Nematoda: Physalopteridae): an accidental parasite of the banded rock rattlesnake, *Crotalus lepidus klauberi* (Serpentes: Viperidae). Journal of Wildlife Diseases.

Goldberg, S. R., C. R. Bursey, and C. W. Painter. 2002. Helminths of the western diamondback rattlesnake, *Crotalus atrox*, from southeast New Mexico rattlesnake roundups. Southwest. Nat. 47(2): 307–310.

Goldberg, S. R., and A. T. Holycross. 1999. Reproduction in the desert massasauga, *Sistrurus catenatus edwardsi*, in Arizona and Colorado. Southwest. Nat. 44(4): 531–535.

Goldberg, S. R., and C. H. Lowe. 1997. Reproductive cycle of the Gila monster, *Heloderma suspectum*. J. Herpetol. 31: 161–166.

Goldberg, S. R., and P. C. Rosen. 2000. Reproduction in the Mojave rattlesnake, *Crotalus scutulatus* (Serpentes: Viperidae). Texas Journal of Science 52(2): 101–109.

Goldman, E. A. 1951. Biological investigations in Mexico. Smithsonian Miscellaneous Collections 115: 1–476.

Goldstein, E. J. C., D. M. Citron, H. Gonzalez, F. E. Russell, and S. M. Finegold. 1979. Bacteriology of rattlesnake venom and implications for therapy. Journal of Infectious Diseases 140: 818–821.

Gomes, J. F. 1913. Uma nova cobra venenosa do Brasil. Annaes Paulistas de Medicina e Cirurgia (São Paulo) 1(3): 65–66.

——. 1918a. Contribuição para o conhecimento dos ophidios do Brazil. II. Ophidios do Museu Rocha (Ceará). Revista do Museu Paulista 10: 503–527.

——. 1918b. Contribuição para o conhecimento dos ophidios do Brazil—III. 1.—Ophidios do Museu Paraense. Mem. Inst. Butantan 1(1): 57–77.

Gómez, H. F., and R. C. Dart. 1995. Clinical toxicology of snakebite in North America. Pp. 619–644 in J. Meier and J. White (eds.), Handbook of clinical toxicology of animal venoms and poisons. CRC Press, Boca Raton, Fla.

Gomulkiewicz, R., J. N. Thompson, R. D. Holt, S. L. Nuismer, and M. E. Hochberg. 2000. Hot spots, cold spots, and the geographic mosaic theory of coevolution. American Naturalist 156: 156–174.

Gonçalves, J. M. 1956. Purification and properties of crotamine. Pp. 261–274 in E. E. Buckley and N. Porges (eds.), Venoms: papers presented at the First International Conference on Venoms, December 27–30, 1954, Berkeley, California. American Association for the Advancement of Science, Washington, D.C.

González-A., L. 1998. La herpetofauna del Izozog. Ecología en Bolivia 1998: 45–52.

González, A., J. L. Camarillo, F. Mendoza, and M. Mancilla. 1986. Impact of expanding human populations on the herpetofauna of the Valley of Mexico. Herpetol. Rev. 17(1): 30–31.

González-Romero, A., and S. Alvarez-Cárdenas. 1989. Herpetofauna de la región del Pinacate, Sonora, Mexico: un inventario. Southwest. Nat. 34(4): 519–526.

González-Ruiz, A., E. Godinez-Cano, and I. Rojas-Gonzalez. 1996. Captive reproduction of the Mexican Acaltetepon, *Heloderma horridum*. Herpetol. Rev. 27(4): 192.

Goode, M. J., and D. Duvall. 1989. Body temperature and defensive behavior of free-ranging prairie rattlesnakes, *Crotalus viridis*. Animal Behaviour 38: 360–362.

Goodman, J. D. 1951. Some aspects of the role of parasitology in herpetology. Herpetologica 7: 65–67.

——. 1953. Further evidence of the venomous nature of the saliva of *Hypsiglena ochrorhyncha*. Herpetologica 9(4): 174–176.

——. 1958. Material ingested by the cottonmouth, *Agkistrodon piscivorus*, at Reelfot Lake, Tennessee. Copeia 1958(2): 149.

Goodman, R. H., Jr., G. R. Stewart, and T. J. Moisi. 1997. Natural history notes: *Crotalus cerastes cerastes* (Mojave Desert sidewinder). Longevity. Herpetol. Rev. 28(2): 89.

Goodrich, R. L., R. W. Murphy, J. Nyhan, and M. J. Wong. 1978. Geographic distribution: *Crotalus ruber lucasensis* Van Denburgh (San Lucan diamond rattlesnake). Herpetol. Rev. 9(3): 108.

Gordon, B. L. 1982. A Panama forest and shore: natural history and Amerindian culture in Bocas del Toro. Boxwood Press, Pacific Grove, Calif. 178 pp.

Gorzula, S. 1982. Life history: *Leptodeira annulata ashmeadi*. Envenomation. Herp. Rev. 13(2): 47.

Gorzula, S., and J. Celsa Señaris. 1998. Contribution to the herpetofauna of the Venezuelan Guayana I. A database. Scientia Guaianae, No. 8. Caracas. 269 pp.

Gosner, K. L. 1987. Observations on Lesser Antillean pit vipers. J. Herpetol. 21(1): 78–80.

Gowanloch, J. N. 1934. Poisonous snakes of Louisiana. Louisiana Conservation Review 4(3): 1–16.

Gowanloch, J. N., and C. A. Brown. 1943. Poisonous snakes, plants, and black widow spider of Louisiana. Louisiana Department of Conservation, New Orleans. 133 pp.

Grace, T. G., and G. E. Omer. 1980. The management of upper extremity pit viper wounds. Journal of Hand Surgery 5: 168–177.

Graf, W., S. G. Jewett, Jr., and K. L. Gordon. 1939. Records of amphibians and reptiles from Oregon. Copeia 1939(2): 101–104.

Graham, G. L. 1977. The karyotype of the Texas coral snake, *Micrurus fulvius tenere*. Herpetologica 33(3): 345–348.

Graham, J. B. 1974. Body temperatures of the sea snake *Pelamis platurus*. Copeia 1974(2): 531–533.

Graham, J. B., I. Rubinoff, and M. K. Hecht. 1971. Temperature physiology of the sea snake *Pelamis platurus*: an index of its colonization potential in the Atlantic Ocean. Proceedings of the National Academy of Sciences 68: 1360–1363.

Grant, C. 1952. Probably the first legislation to protect a poisonous animal. Herpetologica 8: 64.

Grant, C., and H. M. Smith. 1959. Herptiles from San Luis Potosi. Herpetologica 15(1): 54–56.

Grant, G. S. 1970. Rattlesnake predation on the clapper rail. Chat 34: 20–21.

Grantsau, R. 1991. As cobras venenosas do Brasil. Bandeirantes, São Bernardo de Campo, São Paulo. 101 pp.

Grassi, J., and C. M. Ramírez. 1973. Nuestra experiencia en 323 enfermos picados por serpientes venenosas del Paraguay. Revista de la Asociación Médica Paraguaya 5(1): 21–43.

Graves, B. M. 1989a. Defensive behavior of female prairie rattlesnakes (*Crotalus viridis*): changes after parturition. Copeia 1989(3): 791–794.

——. 1989b. Life history notes: *Crotalus viridis viridis* (prairie rattlesnake). Predation. Herpetol. Rev. 20(3): 71–72.

Graves, B. M., and D. Duvall. 1987. An experimental study of aggregation and thermoregulation in prairie rattlesnakes (*Crotalus viridis viridis*). Herpetologica 43: 259–264.

——. 1993. Reproduction, rookery use, and thermoregulation in free-ranging, pregnant *Crotalus v. viridis*. J. Herpetol. 27: 33–41.

Graves, B. M., D. Duvall, M. B. King, S. L. Lindstedt, and W. A. Gern. 1986. Initial den location by neonatal prairie rattlesnakes: functions, causes, and natural history in chemical ecology. Pp. 285–304 in D. Duvall, D. Müller-Schwarze, and R. M. Silverstein (eds.), Chemical signals in vertebrates, vol. 4. Ecology, evolution, and comparative biology. Plenum, New York.

Gray, J. E. 1825. A synopsis of the genera of reptiles and Amphibia, with a description of some new species. Annals of Philosophy, new ser., 10: 193–217.

——. 1829. Synopsis generum reptilium et amphibiorum. Isis von Oken 22(2): 187–206.

——. 1831. A synopsis of the species of the class Reptilia. 110 pp. Appendix to E. Griffith and E. Pidgeon, The class Reptilia arranged by the Baron Cuvier with specific descriptions. Whittaker, Treacher, and Co., London.

——. 1842. Synopsis of the species of rattle-snakes, or family of Crotalidae. Zoological Miscellany, London, 2: 47–51.

——. 1845. Catalogue of the specimens of lizards in the collection of the British Museum. Taylor and Francis, London. 289 pp.

——. 1849. Catalogue of the specimens of lizards in the collection of the British Museum. British Museum (Natural History) Department of Zoology, London. 125 pp.

Gray, J. E., and J. Neill. 1845. Journals of expeditions of discovery into central Australia, and overland from Adelaide to King George's Sound, in the years 1840–1. T. and W. Boone, London.

Graybeal, A. 1995. Naming species. Syst. Biol. 44(2): 237–250.

Greding, E. J., Jr. 1964. Food of *Ancistrodon c. concortrix* [*sic*] in Houston and Trinity Counties, Texas. Southwest. Nat. 9: 105.

———. 1972. Mordedura y alimentación de la culebra centroamericana *Conophis lineatus dunni* Smith. Rev. Biol. Trop. 20: 29–30.

Green, N. B. 1937. The amphibians and reptiles of Randolph County, West Virginia. Herpetologica 1(4): 113–116.

———. 1943. The snakes of West Virginia. West Virginia Conservation 6: 7–18.

Green, N. B., and T. K. Pauley. 1987. Amphibians and reptiles in West Virginia. University of Pittsburgh Press, Pittsburgh, Pa. 241 pp.

Greene, H. W. 1972. Mexican reptiles in the Senckenberg Museum. Carnegie Museum. Privately printed. 15 pp.

———. 1973a. Defensive tail display by snakes and amphisbaenians. J. Herpetol. 7(3): 143–161.

———. 1973b. The food habits and feeding behavior of New World coral snakes. Master's thesis, University of Texas at Arlington. 66 pp.

———. 1984. Feeding behavior and diet of the eastern coral snake, *Micrurus fulvius*. Pp. 147–162 in R. A. Seigel et al. (eds.), Vertebrate ecology and systematics. Special Publications of the Museum of Natural History, University of Kansas, No. 10.

———. 1986. Natural history and evolutionary biology. Pp. 99–108 in M. E. Feder and G. V. Lauder (eds.), Predator-prey relationships: perspectives and approaches from the study of lower vertebrates. University of Chicago Press, Chicago.

———. 1988. Antipredator mechanisms in reptiles. Pp. 1–152 in C. Gans and R. B. Huey (eds.), Biology of the Reptilia, vol. 16. Ecology B. Defense and life history. A. R. Liss, New York.

———. 1992. The ecological and behavioral context for pitviper evolution. Pp. 107–118 in J. A. Campbell and E. D. Brodie Jr. (eds.), Biology of the pitvipers. Selva, Tyler, Texas.

———. 1994. Systematics and natural history, foundations for understanding and conserving biodiversity. American Zoologist 34: 48–56.

———. 1997. Snakes: the evolution of mystery in nature. University of California Press, Berkeley. 351 pp.

Greene, H. W., and J. A. Campbell. 1972. Notes on the use of caudal lures by arboreal green pit vipers. Herpetologica 28(1): 32–34.

———. 1992. The future of pitvipers. Pp. 421–427 in J. A. Campbell and E. D. Brodie Jr. (eds.), Biology of the pitvipers. Selva, Tyler, Texas.

Greene, H. W., and D. L. Hardy. 1989. Natural death associated with skeletal injury in the terciopelo, *Bothrops asper* (Viperidae). Copeia 1989(4): 1036–1037.

Greene, H. W., and R. W. McDiarmid. 1981. Coral snake mimicry: does it occur? Science 213: 1207–1212.

———. 2004. Wallace and Savage: heroes, theories, and venomous snake mimicry. In M. A. Donnelly, B. I. Crother, C. Guyer, M. H. Wake, and M. E. White (eds.), Ecology and evolution in the tropics. University of Chicago Press, Chicago.

Greene, H. W., and G. V. Oliver. 1965. Notes on the natural history of the western massasauga. Herpetologica 21(3): 225–228.

Greene, H. W., and W. F. Pyburn. 1973. Comments on aposematism and mimicry among coral snakes. Biologist 55: 144–148.

Greene, H. W., and M. A. Santana. 1983. Field studies of hunting behavior by bushmasters. American Zoologist 23: 897.

Greene, H. W., and R. L. Seib. 1983. *Micrurus nigrocinctus* (Corál, Coral Snake, Coralillo). Pp. 406–408 in D. H. Janzen (ed.), Costa Rican Natural History. University of Chicago Press, Chicago.

Greenhall, A. M. 1936. The care of the bushmaster and of certain lizards in the New York Zoological Park. Copeia 1936(1): 66–67.

Greenland, S., and J. R. Hoffman. 1982. Australian work in first-aid of poisonous snakebite. Ann. Emerg. Med. 11: 228.

Gregory, P. T. 1982. Reptilian hibernation. Pp. 53–154 in C. Gans and F. H. Pough (eds.), Biology of the Reptilia, vol. 13. Physiology D. Academic Press, New York.

———. 1984. Communal denning in snakes. Pp. 57–75 in R. A. Seigel, L. E. Hunt, J. L. Knight, L. Malaret, and N. L. Zuschlag (eds.), Vertebrate ecology and systematics: a tribute to Henry S. Fitch. Special Publications of the Museum of Natural History, University of Kansas, No. 10.

Gregory, P. T., and R. W. Campbell. 1984. The reptiles of British Columbia. British Columbia Provincial Museum Handbook No. 44. British Columbia Provincial Museum, Victoria, British Colombia. 102 pp.

Gregory, P. T., J. M. Macartney, and K. W. Larsen. 1987. Spatial patterns and movements. Pp. 366–395 in R. A. Seigel, J. T. Collins, and S. S. Novak (eds.), Snakes: ecology and evolutionary biology. McGraw-Hill, New York.

Grenard, S. 2000. Veno- and arterio-occlusive tourniquets are not only harmful, they are unnecessary. Toxicon 30: 1305–1306.

Griffen, D., and J. W. Donovan. 1986. Significant envenomation from a preserved rattlesnake head (in a patient with a history of immediate hypersensitivity to antivenin). Ann. Emerg. Med. 15: 955–958.

Griffin, L. E. 1916. A catalog of the Ophidia from South America at present (June, 1916) contained in the Carnegie Museum with descriptions of some new species. Memoirs of Carnegie Museum 7(3): 163–228.

Griffith, E., and E. Pidgeon. 1831. The class Reptilia, arranged by the Baron C. Cuvier, with specific descriptions. The animal kingdom arranged in conformity with its organization by the Baron Cuvier, with additional descriptions of all the species hitherto named, and of many others, vol. 9. Whittaker, London. 481 pp.

Grinnell, J., and C. L. Camp. 1917. A distributional list of the amphibians and reptiles of California. University of California Publications in Zoology 17: 127–208.

Griscom, L. 1924. Bird hunting among the wild Indians of western Panama. Nat. Hist. 24: 509–519.

Grismer, L. L. 1990. The reptiles and amphibians of Baja California. Tucson Herpetological Society Newsletter 3: 2–6.

———. 1993. The insular herpetofauna of the Pacific Coast of Baja California, Mexico. Herpetological Natural History 1(2): 1–10.

———. 1994a. Geographic origins for the reptiles on islands in the Gulf of California, Mexico. Herpetological Natural History 2(2): 17–40.

———. 1994b. Ecogeography of the peninsular herpetofauna of Baja California, Mexico, and its utility in historical biogeography. Herpetology of the North American Deserts: proceedings of a symposium. Southwestern Herpetologists' Society, Special Publication No. 5: 89–125.

———. 1994c. The origin and evolution of the peninsular herpetofauna of Baja California, Mexico. Herpetological Natural History 2(1): 51–106.

———. 1999a. An evolutionary classification of reptiles on islands in the Gulf of California, Mexico. Herpetologica 55(4): 446–469.

———. 1999b. Checklist of amphibians and reptiles on islands in the Gulf of California, Mexico. Bulletin of the Southern California Academy of Science 98: 45–56.

———. 2002. The amphibians and reptiles of Baja California, its Pacific islands, and the islands in the Sea of Cortés: natural history, distribution and identification. University of California Press, Berkeley. 409 pp.

Grismer, L. L., B. D. Hollingsworth, M. R. Cryder, and H. Wong. 1997. Geographic distribution: *Crotalus enyo enyo* (Baja California rattlesnake). Herpetol. Rev. 28(1): 51.

Grismer, L. L., J. A. McGuire, and B. D. Hollingsworth. 1994. Report on the herpetofauna of the Vizcaino Peninsula, Baja California, Mexico, with a discussion of its biogeographic and taxonomic implications. Bulletin of the Southern California Academy of Sciences 93: 45–80.

Grismer, L. L., and E. Mellink. 1994. The addition of *Sceloporus occidentalis* to the herpetofauna of Isla de Cedros, Baja California, Mexico, and its historical and taxonomic implications. J. Herpetol. 28(1): 120–126.

Grismer, L. L., and J. J. Sigala-Rodríguez. 2000. Preliminary report of the natural history of the rattleless rattlesnake, *Crotalus catalinensis* (abstract). Joint Meeting of the American Society of Ichtyologists and Herpetologists, Herpetologists' League, Society for the Study of Amphibians and Reptiles, 14–20 June 2000, La Paz, Baja California Sur, Mexico.

Grobman, A. 1978. An alternative solution to the coral snake mimic problem (Reptilia, Serpentes, Elapidae). J. Herpetol. 12: 1–11.

Grocott, R. G., and G. G. Sadler. 1958. The poisonous snakes of Panama. Panama Canal Printing Plant, Mt. Hope, Canal Zone. 38 pp.

Grogan, W. L., Jr. 1974. Effects of accidental envenomation from the saliva of the eastern hognose snake, *Heterodon platyrhinos*. Herpetologica 30(3): 248–249.

Groombridge, G. 1986a. Phyletic relationships among viperine snakes. Pp. 219–222 in Z. Rocek (ed.), Studies in herpetology: proceedings of the European herpetological meeting (3d ordinary general meeting of the Societas Europaea Herpetologica), Prague, 1985. Charles University, Prague.

——. 1986b. Comments on the *M. pterygoideus glandulae* of crotaline snakes (Reptilia: Viperidae). Herpetologica 42(4): 449–457.

Groves, F. 1961. A feeding record of the palm viper, *Bothrops schlegelli*. Herpetologica 17(4): 277.

Groves, J. D. 1977. Aquatic behavior in the northern copperhead, *Agkistron* [sic] *contortrix mokasen*. Bull. Maryland Herpetol. Soc. 13: 114–115.

Groves, J. D., and W. Altimari. 1979. First breeding of the St. Lucia serpent in captivity. International Zoo Yearbook 19: 101–102.

Grzimek, B. (ed.). 1975. Grzimek's animal life encyclopedia, vol. 6. Reptiles. Van Nostrand Reinhold, New York. 589 pp.

Guderian, R. H., C. D. Mackenzie, and J. F. Williams. 1986. High voltage shock treatment for snakebite. Lancet 2: 229.

Guenther, K. 1931. A naturalist in Brazil: the record of a year's observation of her flora, her fauna, and her people. Houghton Mifflin, Boston. 400 pp.

Guichenot, A. 1855. Animaux nouveaux ou rares recueillis pendant l'expédition dans les parties centrales de l'Amérique du Sud, de Rio de Janeiro à Lima, et de Lima au Pará; exécutée par ordre du gouvernement français pendant les années 1843 à 1847, sous la direction du Comte Francis de Castelnau, tome 2. Reptiles. P. Bertrand, Paris. 95 pp.

Guidry, E. V. 1953. Herpetological notes from southeastern Texas. Herpetologica 9(1): 49–56.

Guilford, T. 1990. The secrets of aposematism: unlearned responses to specific colours and patterns. Trends in Ecology and Evolution 5: 323.

Guimarães Guedes, A. 2000. Geographic distribution: *Micrurus frontifasciatus* (Bolivian coral snake). Herpetol. Rev. 31(4): 255.

Guisto, J. A. 1995. Severe toxicity from crotalid envenomation after early resolution of symptoms. Ann. Emerg. Med. 26: 387–389.

Gumbart, T. C., and K. A. Sullivan. 1990. Predation on yellow-eyed junco nestlings by twin-spotted rattlesnakes. Southwest. Nat. 353: 367–368.

Gumilla, S. J. 1741. El Orinoco ilustrado, historia natural, civil, y geográfica de este gran Río y de sus caudalosas vertientes, 2 vols. Manuel Fernández, Madrid. 580 pp.

Günther, A. C. L. G. 1858. Catalogue of the colubrine snakes in the collection of the British Museum. Taylor and Francis, London. 281 pp.

——. 1859a. On the genus *Elaps* of Wagler. Proc. Zool. Soc. London 27: 79–89.

——. 1859b. Second list of cold-blooded vertebrates collected by Mr. Fraser in the Andes of Western Ecuador. Proc. Zool. Soc. London 1859: 402–420.

——. 1861. Account of the reptiles sent by Dr. Wucherer from Bahía. Proc. Zool. Soc. London 1861: 12–18.

——. 1863a. The reptiles of British India. The Ray Society. Taylor and Francis, London. 452 pp.

——. 1863b. Third account of the snakes in the collection of the British Museum. Ann. Mag. Nat. Hist., 3d ser., 12: 348–365.

——. 1868. Sixth account of new species of snakes in the collection of the British Museum. Ann. Mag. Nat. Hist., 4th ser., 1: 413–429.

——. 1895–1902. Biologia Centrali-Americana. Reptilia and Batrachia. Porter, London. 326 pp.

Guo, Y. M., S. H. Mao, and F. Y. Yin. 1987. Comparison of cobra plasma albumins with those of banded krait and sea snake. Comp. Biochem. Physiol. B 87: 559–566.

Gutberlet, R. L., Jr. 1993. Descriptive morphology and phylogenetic postion of the Mexican black-tailed pitviper. Master's thesis, University of Texas at Arlington. 94 pp.

——. 1995. A new locality for Rowley's palm pitviper, *Bothriechis rowleyi* (Serpentes: Viperidae), a Mexican relict. Southwest. Nat. 40: 124–125.

——. 1998a. The phylogenetic position of the Mexican black-tailed pitviper (Squamata: Viperidae: Crotalinae). Herpetologica 54(2): 184–206.

——. 1998b. Phylogenetic relationships of New World pitvipers (Squamata: Crotalinae) as inferred from gross anatomy, epidermal microstructure, and mitochondrial DNA. Ph.D. dissertation, University of Texas at Arlington. 175 pp.

Gutberlet, R. L., Jr., and J. A. Campbell. 2001. Generic recognition for a neglected lineage of South American pivipers (Squamata: Viperidae: Crotalidae), with the description of a new species from the Colombian Chocó. Am. Mus. Novitat. 3316: 1–15.

Gutberlet, R. L., Jr., and M. B. Harvey, 1998. Comments on the proposed conservation of the specific names of *Trigonocephalus pulcher* Peters, 1862, *Bothrops albocarinatus* Shreve, 1934 (Reptilia: Serpentes) by the designation of a neotype for *T. pulcher*. Bulletin of Zoological Nomenclature 55: 29–32.

Gutberlet, R. L., and M. B. Harvey. 2002. Phylogenetic relationships of New World pitvipers as inferred from anatomical evidence. Pp. 51–68 in G. W. Schuett, M. Höggren, M. E. Douglas, and H. W. Greene (eds.), Biology of the vipers. Eagle Mountain Publishing, Eagle Mountain, Utah.

Guthrie, J. E. 1926. The snakes of Iowa. Iowa State Agricultural Experiment Station Bulletin 239: 147–192.

——. 1927. Rattlesnake eggs in Iowa. Copeia 1927(162): 12–14.

Gutiérrez, J. M., C. Avila, Z. Camacho, and B. Lomonte. 1990. Ontogenetic changes in the venom of the snake *Lachesis muta stenophrys* (bushmaster) from Costa Rica. Toxicon 28: 419–426.

Gutiérrez, J. M., and R. Bolaños. 1979. Cariotipos de las principales serpientes coral (Elapidae: *Micrurus*) de Costa Rica. Rev. Biol. Trop. 27: 57–73.

——. 1980. Karyotype of the yellow-bellied sea snake, *Pelamis platurus* (Linnaeus) and its position in the chromosomal evolution of the subfamily Hydrophiinae. J. Herpetol. 14: 161–165.

——. 1981. Polimorfismo cromosómico intraespecífico en la serpiente de coral *Micrurus nigrocinctus* (Ophidia: Elapidae). Rev. Biol. Trop. 29: 115–122.

Gutiérrez, J. M., and F. Chaves. 1980. Effectos proteolítico, hemorrágico, y mionecrótico de los venenos de serpientes costarricenses de los géneros *Bothrops*, *Crotalus*, y *Lachesis*. Toxicon 18: 315–321.

Gutiérrez, J. M., F. Chaves, and R. Bolaños. 1980. Estudio comparativo de venenos de ejemplares recién nacidos y adultos de *Bothrops asper*. Rev. Biol. Trop. 28: 341–351.

Gutiérrez, J. M., and B. Lomonte. 1995. Phospholipase A_2 myotoxins from *Bothrops* snake venoms. Toxicon 33(11): 1405–1424.

Gutiérrez, J. M., and G. Rojas. 1999. Instituto Clodomiro Picado: ciencia y tecnología endógenas en la solución de un problema de salud pública en Centroamérica. Interciencia (San José, Costa Rica) 24: 182–186.

Gutiérrez, J. M., G. Rojas, and R. Aymerich. 1999. El envenamiento ofídico en Centroamerica: fisiopatología y tratamiento. Universidad de Costa Rica, Instituto Clodomiro Picado, San José. 23 pp.

Gutiérrez, J. M., G. Rojas, and L. Cerdas. 1987. *Lachesis muta melanocephala*, a new Costa Rican subspecies of the bushmaster. Toxicon 25: 713.

Gutiérrez, J. M., and M. Sasa. 2002. Bites and envenomations by colubrid snakes in Mexico and Central America. Journal of Toxicology—Toxin Reviews 21 (1–2): 105–115.

Gutiérrez, J. M., A. Solórzano, L. Cerdas, and J. P. Vannini. 1988. Karyotypes of five species of coral snakes (*Micrurus*). J. Herpetol. 22(1): 109–112.

Gutiérrez, J. M., R. T. Taylor, and R. Bolaños. 1979. Cariotipos de diez especies de serpientes costarricenses de la familia Viperidae. Rev. Biol. Trop. 27: 309–319.

Guyer, C. 1994. The reptile fauna: diversity and ecology. Pp. 210–216 and 382–383 in L. McDade, K. S. Bawa, H. A. Hespenheide, and G. S. Hartshorn (eds.), La Selva: ecology and natural history of a Neotropical rain forest. University of Chicago Press, Chicago.

Haas, G. 1938. A note on the origin of solenoglyph snakes. Copeia 1938(1): 73–78.

——. 1952. The head muscles of the genus *Causus* (Ophidia, Solenoglypha) and some remarks on the origin of the Solenoglypha. Proc. Zool. Soc. London 122: 573–592.

——. 1962. Remarques concernant les relations phylogéniques des diverses familles d'ophidiens fondées sur la différenciation de la musculature mandibulaire. Colloque Internationale du Centre National de la Recherche Scientifique 104: 215–239.

Hadley, W. F., and C. Gans. 1972. Convergent ontogenetic change of color pattern in *Elaphe climacophora* (Colubridae: Reptilia). J. Herpetol. 6(1): 75–78.

Haeckel, E. 1866. Generelle Morphologie der Organismen: Allgemeine Grundzuge der organischen Formen-Wissenschaft, mechanisch begrundet durch die von Charles Darwin reformirte Descendenz-Theorie. Georg Riemer, Berlin. 462 pp.

Haefner, U., and W. Frank. 1984. Host specificity and host range of the genus *Sarcocystis* in three snake–rodent life cycles. Zentralblatt für Bakteriologie, Mikrobiologie, und Hygiene, ser. A, 256(3): 296–299.

Hafernik, J., and L. Saul-Gershenz. 2000. Beetle larvae cooperate to mimic bees. Nature 405: 35.

Hagmann, G. 1909. Die Reptilien der Insel Mexiana, Amazonestrom. Zoologische Jahrbücher 28: 473–504.

Hahn, D. E. 1971. Noteworthy herpetological records from Honduras. Herpetol. Rev. 3: 111–112.

Hahn, D. E., and C. J. May. 1972. Noteworthy Arizona herpetofaunal records. Herpetol. Rev. 4(3): 91–92.

Hall, C. D. 1997. Minnesota county biological survey: amphibian and reptile results, 1988–1994. Pp. 58–62 in J. J. Moriarty and D. Jones (eds.), Minnesota's amphibians and reptiles, their conservation and status: proceedings of a symposium. Serpent's Tale Natural History Book Distributors, Lanesboro, Minn.

Hall, E. R. 1929. A den of rattlesnakes in eastern Nevada. Bull. Antivenin Inst. Am. 3(3): 79–80.

Hall, E. R., and W. W. Dalquest. 1963. The mammals of Veracruz. Publications of the Museum of Natural History, University of Kansas, 14(14): 165–362.

Hall, H. H., and H. M. Smith. 1947. Selected records of reptiles and amphibians from southeastern Kansas. Trans. Kansas Acad. Sci. 49: 447–454.

Hall, R. J. 1994. Herpetological diversity of the Four Holes Swamp, South Carolina. U.S. Department of Interior Resource Publication 198: 1–43.

Haller, E. C. P., and M. Martins. 1999. Historia natural da urutu, *Bothrops alternatus* (Serpentes: Viperidae: Crotalinae). P. 69 in Abstracts of the V Congreso Latinoamericano de Herpetología, Montevideo, 12 al 17 de diciembre de 1999.

Haller, R. 1971. The diamondback rattlesnakes. Herpetology 5(3): 1–34.

Hallock, L. A. 1991. Habitat utilization, diet and behavior of the eastern massasauga (*Sistrurus catenatus*) in southern Michigan. Master's thesis, Michigan State University.

Hallowell, E. 1845. Description of reptiles from South America, supposed to be new. Proc. Acad. Nat. Sci. Philadelphia 2: 241–247.

——. 1852. Descriptions of new species of reptiles inhabiting North America. Proc. Acad. Nat. Sci. Philadelphia 6: 177–182.

——. 1853. Report of an expedition down the Zuni and Colorado Rivers by L. Sitgreaves. U.S. Senate, Executive Document No. 59, 32d Congress, 2d Session, Washington, D.C., pp. 106–147.

——. 1854. Descriptions of new reptiles from California. Proc. Acad. Nat. Sci. Philadelphia 7: 91–97.

——. 1855. Contributions to South American herpetology. Journal of the Academy of Natural Sciences of Philadelphia 2(3): 33–36.

——. 1861 [dated 1860]. Report upon the Reptilia of the north Pacific exploring expedition, under command of Capt. John Rogers, U.S.N. Proc. Acad. Nat. Sci. Philadelphia 12: 480–510.

Halloy, M., R. Etheridge, and G. M. Burghardt. 1998. To bury in the sand: phylogenetic relationships among lizard species of the *boulengeri* group, *Liolaemus* (Reptilia: Squamata: Tropiduridae), based on behavioral characters. Herpetological Monographs 12: 1–37.

Halstead, B. W. (ed.). 1970. Poisonous and venomous marine animals of the world, vol. 3. GPO, Washington, D.C. 1006 pp.

Halter, C. R. 1923. The venomous coral snake. Copeia 1923 (123): 105–107.

Haltom, W. L. 1931. Alabama reptiles. Alabama Museum of Natural History Museum Paper No. 11. 145 pp.

Hambrick, P. S. 1975. New county records and range extensions for Texas amphibians and reptiles. Herpetol. Rev. 6(3): 79–80.

Hamel, P. B. 1996. Natural history notes: *Agkistrodon piscivorus leucostoma* (western cottonmouth). Carrion feeding. Herpetol. Rev. 27(3): 143.

Hamilton, W. J., Jr. 1950. Food of the prairie rattlesnake. Herpetologica 6(2): 34.

Hamilton, W. J., Jr., and J. A. Pollack. 1955. The food of some crotalid snakes from Fort Benning, Georgia. Natural History Miscellanea 140: 1–4.

Hammack, S. H., and F. Antonio. 1991. Life history notes: *Bothriechis nigroviridis* (speckled palm viper). Maximum size. Herpetol. Rev. 22(4): 131.

Hammerson, G. A. 1982. Amphibians and reptiles in Colorado. Colorado Division of Wildlife, Denver.

——. 1999. Amphibians and reptiles in Colorado, 2d ed. University Press of Colorado and Colorado Division of Wildlife, Niwot. 484 pp.

Hammerson, G. A., L. Valentine, and L. J. Livo. 1991a. Geographic distribution: *Crotalus viridis* (western rattlesnake). Herpetol. Rev. 22(2): 67.

——. 1991b. Geographic distribution: *Sisturus catenatus* (massasauga). Herpetol. Rev. 22(2): 68.

Hammond, D. M., and P. L. Long. 1973. The Coccidia. University Park Press, Baltimore, Md.

Hanken, J., and D. B. Wake. 1982. Genetic differentiation among plethodontid salamanders (genus *Bolitoglossa*) in Central and South America: implications for the South American invasion. Herpetologica 38: 272–287.

Hankin, F. M., M. D. Smith, J. A. Penner, and D. S. Louis. 1987. Eastern massasauga rattlesnake bites. Journal of Pediatric Orthopedics 7: 201–205.

Harding, J. H. 1997. Amphibians and reptiles of the Great Lakes region. University of Michigan Press, Ann Arbor. 378 pp.

Hardy, D. L. 1982. Envenomation by the Mexican lance-headed rattlesnake *Crotalus polystictus*: a case report. Toxicon 20: 1089–1091.

——. 1983. Envenomation by the Mojave rattlesnake (*Crotalus scutulatus scutulatus*) in southern Arizona. Toxicon 21(1): 111–118.

——. 1986. Fatal rattlesnake envenomation in Arizona, 1969–1984. Journal of Toxicology—Clinical Toxicology 24(1): 1–10.

——. 1992a. A review of first aid measures for pitviper bite in North America with an appraisal of Extractor suction and stun gun electroshock. Pp. 405–414 in J. A. Campbell and E. D. Brodie (eds.), Biology of the pitvipers. Selva, Tyler, Texas.

——. 1992b. The Aruba Island rattlesnake or cascabel (*Crotalus durissus unicolor*): epidemiology and treatment aspects of envenomation. International Symposium and Workshop on the Conservation and Research of the Aruba Island Rattlesnake, 5–7 February, Palm Beach, Aruba Island.

——. 1994a. Venomous snakes of Costa Rica: comments on feeding behavior, venom, and human envenoming. Part I. Sonoran Herpetologist 7(12): 108–113.

——. 1994b. *Bothrops asper* (Viperidae) snakebite and field researchers in Middle America. Biotropica 26: 198–207.

——. 1994c. Snakebite and field biologists in Mexico and Central America: report on ten cases with recommendations for field management. Herpetological Natural History 2(2): 67–82.

———. 1995. Venomous snakes of Costa Rica: comments on feeding behavior, venom, and human envenoming. Part II. Sonoran Herpetologist 8(1): 2–5.

———. 1997. Fatal bite by a captive rattlesnake in Tucson, Arizona. Sonoran Herpetologist 10: 38–39.

Hardy, D. L., and S. P. Bush. 1998. Pressure/immobilization as first aid for venomous snakebite in the United States. Herpetol. Rev. 29: 204–208.

Hardy, D. L., Sr., and H. W. Greene. 1995. Natural history notes: *Crotalus molossus molossus* (blacktail rattlesnake). Maximum size. Herpetol. Rev. 26(2): 101.

Hardy, D. L., M. Jeter, and J. J. Corrigan. 1982. Envenomation by the northern blacktail rattlesnake (*Crotalus molossus molossus*): report of two cases and the in vitro effects of the venom on fibrinolysis and platelet aggregation. Toxicon 20: 487–493.

Hardy, D. L., Sr., and J. J. Silva-Haad. 1998. A review of venom toxinology and epidemiology of envenoming of the bushmaster (*Lachesis*) with report of a fatal bite. Bull. Chicago Herpetol. Soc. 33: 113–123.

Hardy, L. M., and R. W. McDiarmid. 1969. The amphibians and reptiles of Sinaloa, Mexico. Publications of the Museum of Natural History, University of Kansas, 18(3): 39–252.

Harlan, R. 1826. Genera of North American reptiles, and a synopsis of the species. Journal of the Academy of Natural Sciences of Philadelphia 5: 317–372.

Harris, H. S., Jr. 1974. The New Mexican ridge-nosed rattlesnake. National Parks Conservation Magazine 48(3): 22–24.

———. 1975. Distributional survey (Amphibia/Reptilia). Maryland and District of Columbia. Bull. Maryland Herpetol. Soc. 11: 73–167.

Harris, H. S., Jr., and R. S. Simmons. 1972a. A checklist of the rattlesnakes (*Crotalus durissus* group) of South America. Bull. Maryland Herpetol. Soc. 8(1): 27–32.

———. 1972b. Keys to the Neotropical species and subspecies of the *Crotalus durissus* group. Bull. Maryland Herpetol. Soc. 8(2): 33–40.

———. 1975. An endangered species, the New Mexican ridge-nosed rattlesnake. Bull. Maryland Herpetol. Soc. 11: 1–7.

———. 1976. The paleogeography and evolution of *Crotalus willardi*, with a formal description of a new subspecies from New Mexico, United States. Bull. Maryland Herpetol. Soc. 12(1): 1–22.

———. 1977a. A preliminary account of insular rattlesnake populations, with special reference to those occurring in the Gulf of California and off the Pacific Coast. Bull. Maryland Herpetol. Soc. 13: 92–110.

———. 1977b. Additional notes concerning cannibalism in pit vipers. Bull. Maryland Herpetol. Soc. 13(2): 121–122.

———. 1978a [dated 1976–1977]. A new subspecies of *Crotalus durissus* (Serpentes: Crotalidae) from the Rupununi Savanna of southwestern Guyana. Mem. Inst. Butantan 40–41: 305–311.

———. 1978b. A preliminary account of the rattlesnakes with the descriptions of four new subspecies. Bull. Maryland Herpetol. Soc. 14(3): 105–211.

Harris, J. B. 1991. Phospholipases in snake venom and their effects on nerve and muscle. Pp. 91–129 in A. L. Harvey (ed.), Snake toxins. Pergamon Press, New York.

———. 1997. Toxic phospholipases in snake venom: an introductory review. Pp. 235–250 in R. S. Thorpe, W. Wüster, and A. Malhotra (eds.), Venomous snakes: ecology, evolution and snakebite. Clarendon Press, Oxford.

———. 1998. Phospholipases A_2 that show neurotoxic activity. Pp. 425–449 in G. S. Bailey (ed.), Enzymes from snake venoms. Alaken, Inc., Fort Collins, Colo.

Hartdegen, R. W., and B. Aucone. 2001. Natural history notes: *Micrurus surinamensis surinamensis* (NCN). Arboreality. Herpetol. Rev. 32(4): 264.

Hartdegen, R. W., M. J. Russell, and R. Buice. 1999. An enteric parasite study of Neotropical herpetofauna. Herpetol. Rev. 30(1): 26–28.

Hartline, P. H., L. Kass, and M. S. Loop. 1978. Merging of modalities in the optic tectum: infrared and visual integration in rattlesnakes. Science 199: 1225–1229.

Hartman, F. A. 1911. Description of a little-known rattlesnake, *Crotalus willardi*, from Arizona. Proceedings of the U.S. National Museum 39(1800): 569–570.

Hartmann, P. A., and M. T. de Almeida. 2001. Natural history notes: *Bothrops jararaca* (jararaca pitviper), caudal luring. Herpetol. Rev. 32(1): 45.

Hartsell, S., C. Caravati, and E. Martin. 1994. Gila monster envenomation. Ann. Emerg. Med. 24: 731–735. [Erratum of authors' names published 1995, Ann. Emerg. Med. 25: 47.]

Hartweg, N., and J. A. Oliver. 1938. A contribution to the herpetology of the Isthmus of Tehuantepec. III. Three new snakes from the Pacific slope. Occas. Pap. Mus. Zool. Univ. Michigan 390: 1–9.

———. 1940. A contribution to the herpetology of the Isthmus of Tehuantepec. IV. Miscellaneous Publications of the Museum of Zoology, University of Michigan 47: 1–31.

Harvey, A. L. (ed.). 1991. Snake toxins. International encyclopedia of pharmacology and therapeutics. Pergamon, New York.

Harvey, M. B. 1994. A new species of montane pitviper (Serpentes: Viperidae: *Bothrops*) from Cochabamba, Bolivia. Proceedings of the Biological Society of Washington 107: 60–66.

———. 1998. Reptiles and amphibians of Parque Nacional Noel Kempff Mercado. Pp. 144–166, 348–355 in T. J. Killeen and T. S. Schulenberg (eds.), A biological assessment of Parque Noel Kempff Mercado, Bolivia. Conservation International, Washington, D.C.

Harvey, M. B., J. Aparicio-E., and L. González-A. 2003. Revision of the venomous snakes of Bolivia. Part 1. The coralsnakes (Elapidae: *Micrurus*). Annals of Carnegie Museum, 72: 1–52.

Harvey, M. B., and R. L. Gutberlet Jr. 1995. Microstructure, evolution, and ontogeny of scale surfaces in cordylid and gerrhosaurid lizards. Journal of Morphology 226: 121–139.

———. 2000. A phylogenetic analysis of the tropidurine lizards (Squamata: Tropiduridae), including new characters of squamation and epidermal microstructure. Zoological Journal of the Linnean Society 128: 189–233.

Harvey, P. H., and M. D. Pagel. 1991. The comparative method in evolutionary biology. Oxford: Oxford University Press. 239 pp.

Harwood, P. D. 1930. A new species of *Oxysomatium* (Nematoda) with some remarks on the genera *Oxysomatium* and *Aplectana*, and observations on life history. Journal of Parasitology 17(2): 61–73.

———. 1932. The helminths parasitic in the Amphibia and Reptilia of Houston, Texas, and vicinity. Proceedings of the U.S. National Museum 81: 1–71.

Hasegawa, M., H. Kishino, and T. Yano. 1985. Dating of the human–ape splitting by a molecular clock of mitochondrial DNA. Journal of Molecular Evolution 21: 160–174.

Hasiba, U., L. M. Rosenbach, D. Rockwell, and J. H. Lewis. 1975. DIC-like syndrome after envenomation by the snake *Crotalus horridus horridus*. New England Journal of Medicine 292: 505–507.

Hatt, R. T. 1930. Collectors' days and nights in Yucatán. Natural History (New York) 30(6): 617–626.

Hauser, D. L., and W. Presch. 1991. The effect of ordered characters on phylogenetic reconstruction. Cladistics 7: 243–265.

Haverly, J. E., and K. V. Kardong. 1996. Sensory deprivation effects on the predatory behavior of the rattlesnake, *Crotalus viridis oreganus*. Copeia 1996(2): 419–428.

Hay, O. P. 1887a. The massasauga and its habits. American Naturalist 21(3): 211–218.

———. 1887b. The amphibians and reptiles of Indiana. Annual Report of the Indiana Board of Agriculture 28: 201–233.

———. 1892. The batrachians and reptiles of the state of Indiana. Pp. 409–602 in Indiana Department of Geological Natural Resources, 17th Annual Report, 1891.

Hayes, M., and F. Cliff. 1982. A checklist of the herpetofauna of Butte County, the Butte Sink, and Sutter Buttes, California. Herpetol. Rev. 13(3): 85–86.

Hayes, M. P., J. A. Pounds, and W. W. Timmerman. [1989.] An annotated list and guide to the amphibians and reptiles of Monteverde, Costa Rica. Society for the Study of Amphibians and Reptiles, Herpetological Circular No. 17. 67 pp.

Hayes, W. K. 1986. Observations of courtship in the rattlesnake, *Crotalus viridis oreganus*. J. Herpetol. 20: 246–249.

——. 1991. Ontogeny of striking, prey-handling, and envenomation behavior of prairie rattlesnakes (*Crotalus v. viridis*). Toxicon 29: 867–875.

——. 1992. Factors associated with the mass of venom expended by prairie rattlesnakes (*Crotalus v. viridis*) feeding on mice. Toxicon 30: 449–460.

——. 1995. Venom metering by juvenile prairie rattlesnakes, *Crotalus v. viridis*: effects of prey size and experience. Animal Behaviour 50(1): 33–40.

Hayes, W. K., and R. Hayes. 1985. Human envenomation from the bite of the eastern garter snake, *Thamnophis s. sirtalis* (Serpentes: Colubridae). Toxicon 23: 719–721.

Hayes, W. K., I. I. Kaiser, and D. Duvall. 1992. The mass of venom expended by prairie rattlesnakes when feeding on rodent prey. Pp. 383–388 in J. A. Campbell and E. D. Brodie Jr. (eds.), Biology of the pitvipers. Selva, Tyler, Texas.

Hayes, W. K., P. Lavín-Murcio, and K. V. Kardong. 1995. Northern Pacific rattlesnakes (*Crotalus viridus oreganus*) meter venom when feeding on prey of different sizes. Copeia 1995(2): 337–343.

Haynes, K. F., K. V. Yeargan, and C. Gemano. 2001. Detection of prey by a spider that aggressively mimics pheromone blends. Journal of Insect Behavior 14: 535–544.

Haynes, K. F., K. V. Yeargan, J. G. Millar, and B. B. Chastain. 1996. Identification of sex pheromone of *Tetanolia mynesalis* (Lepidoptera: Noctuidae), a prey species of the bolas spider, *Mastophora hutchinisoni*. Journal of Chemical Ecology 22: 75–89.

Heard, K., G. F. O'Malley, and R. C. Dart. 1999. Antivenom therapy in the Americas. Drugs 58: 5–15.

Heatwole, H. 1974. Shark predation on sea snakes. Copeia 1974(3): 780–781.

——. 1987. Sea snakes, 2d ed. Kreiger, Malabar, Fla. 148 pp.

Heatwole, H., and I. B. Banuchi. 1966. Envenomation by the colubrid snake, *Alsophis portoricensis*. Herpetologica 22(2): 132–134.

Heatwole, H., and H. Cogger. 1993. Family Hydrophiidae. Pp. 310–318 in C. J. Glasby, G. J. B. Ross, and P. L. Beesley (eds.), Fauna of Australia, vol. 2. Amphibia and Reptilia. Australian Government Publication Service, Canberra.

Heatwole, H., and E. Davison. 1976. A review of caudal luring in snakes with notes on its occurrence in the Saharan sand viper, *Cerastes vipera*. Herpetologica 32(3): 332–336.

Heatwole, H., and E. P. Finnie. 1980. Seal predation on a sea snake. Herpetofauna 11: 24.

Heatwole, H., and R. Seymour. 1978. Cutaneous oxygen uptake in three groups of aquatic snakes. Australian Journal of Zoology 26: 481–486.

Hecht, M. K., C. Kropach, and B. M. Hecht. 1974. Distribution of the yellow-bellied sea snake, *Pelamis platurus*, and its significance in relation to the fossil record. Herpetologica 30(4): 387–396.

Hecht, M. K., and D. Marien. 1956. The coral snake mimic problem: a reinterpretation. Journal of Morphology 98: 335–365.

Heckel, J.-O., D. C. Sisson, and C. F. Quist. 1994. Apparent fatal snakebite in three hawks. Journal of Wildlife Diseases 30(4): 616–619.

Hedges, S. B. 1996. The origin of West Indian amphibians and reptiles. Pp. 95–128, in R. Powell and R. W. Henderson (eds.), Contributions to West Indian herpetology: a tribute to Albert Schwartz. Society for the Study of Amphibians and Reptiles, Ithaca, N.Y.

——. 1999. Distribution patterns of amphibians in the West Indies. Pp. 211–254 in W. E. Duellman (ed.), Patterns of distribution of amphibians. Johns Hopkins University Press, Baltimore.

Heinrich, G. 1996. Natural history notes: *Micrurus fulvius fulvius* (eastern coral snake). Diet. Herpetol. Rev. 27(1): 25.

Heinrich, G., and K. R. Studenroth Jr. 1996. Natural history notes: *Agkistrodon piscivorus conanti* (Florida cottonmouth). Diet. Herpetol. Rev. 27(1): 22.

Heise, P. J., L. R. Maxson, H. G. Dowling, and S. B. Hedges. 1995. Higher-level snake phylogeny inferred from mitochondrial DNA sequences of 12S rRNA and 16S rRNA genes. Molecular Biology and Evolution 12: 256–265.

Heleno, M. G., A. M. T. Gregio, S. Hyslop, M. D. Fontana, and O. Vital-Brasil. 1997. Partial purification of a neurotoxic component from a Duvernoy's gland extract of the aglyphous colubrid *Mastigodryas bifossatus*. Journal of Venomous Animals and Toxins 3 (1): 209.

Hemprich, W. 1820. Grundriss der Naturgeschichte für höhere Lehranstalten. A. Rucker, Berlin. 432 pp.

Henderson, R. W. 1978. Notes on *Agkistrodon bilineatus* (Reptilia, Serpentes, Viperidae) in Belize. J. Herpetol. 12: 412–413.

Henderson, R. W., J. R. Dixon, and P. Soini. 1978. On the seasonal incidence of tropical snakes. Milwaukee Public Museum Contributions in Biology and Geology 17: 1–15.

——. 1979. Resource partitioning in Amazonian snake communities. Milwaukee Public Museum Contributions in Biology and Geology 22: 1–11.

Henderson, R. W., and L. G. Hoevers. 1975. A checklist and key to the amphibians and reptiles of Belize, Central America. Milwaukee Public Museum Contributions in Biology and Geology 5: 1–63.

——. 1977. The seasonal incidence of snakes at a locality in northern Belize. Copeia 1977(2): 349–355.

Henderson, R. W., M. N. Nickerson, and S. Ketcham. 1976. Short-term movements of the snakes *Chironius carinatus*, *Helicops angulatus*, and *Bothrops atrox* in Amazonian Peru. Herpetologica 32(3): 304–310.

Hendy, M. D., and D. Penny. 1982. Branch and bound algorithms to determine minimal evolutionary trees. Mathematical Bioscience 59: 277–290.

——. 1989. A framework for the quantitative study of evolutionary trees. Syst. Zool. 38: 297–309.

Henle, K., and A. Erhl. 1991. Zur Reptilienfauna Perus nebst Beschreibung eines neuen *Anolis* (Iguanidae) und zweier neuer Schlangen (Colubridae). Bonner Zoologische Beiträge 42(2): 143–180.

Hennig, W. 1966. Phylogenetic systematics. University of Illinois Press, Urbana. 263 pp.

Henning, W. L. 1938. Amphibians and reptiles of a 2,220-acre tract in central Missouri. Copeia 1938(2): 91–92.

Henry, G. M. 1925. Notes on *Ancistrodon hypnale*, the hump-nosed viper. Ceylon Journal of Science, Spolia Zeylanica 13: 257–258.

Hensley, M. M. 1949. Mammal diet of *Heloderma*. Herpetologica 5(6): 152.

——. 1950a. Notes on the natural history of *Heloderma suspectum*. Trans. Kansas Acad. Sci. 53(2): 268–269.

——. 1950b. Results of a herpetological reconnaissance in extreme southwestern Arizona and adjacent Sonora, with a description of a new subspecies of the Sonoran whipsnake, *Masticophis bilineatus*. Trans. Kansas Acad. Sci. 53(2): 270–288.

——. 1959. Albinism in North American amphibians and reptiles. Publications of the Museum of Michigan State University 1(4): 133–159.

Hensley, M. M., and P. W. Smith. 1962. Noteworthy herpetological records from the Mexican states of Hidalgo and Tabasco. Herpetologica 18(1): 70–71.

Herman, D. W. 1982. Geographic distribution: *Sistrurus miliarius miliarius* (Carolina pigmy rattlesnake). Herpetol. Rev. 13(2): 53

Herman, D. W., and B. Baker. 1982. Geographic distribution: *Sistrurus miliarius miliarius* (Carolina pigmy rattlesnake). Herpetol. Rev. 13(2): 53.

Hermann, R. 1921. Kanibalismus und Ophiophagie bei brasilischen Schlangen. Zeitschr. Deutsch. Ver. Wiss. Kunst S. Paulo 2: 270–277.

Hernández, F. 1615. Cuatro libros de la naturaleza y animales que están recividos en el uso de medicina en la Nueva España. Mexico City.

——. 1648. Rerum medicarum novae hispaniae thesaurus seu plantarum animalium mineralium mexicanorum historia, 2d ed. Mascardi, Rome. 1040 pp.

Hernández-Camacho, J. I., R. Alvarez-León, and J. M. Renjifo-Rey. (In press.) Pelagic sea snake *Pelamis platurus* (Linnaeus, 1766) (Reptilia:

Serpentes: Hydrophiidae) is found in the Caribbean coast of Colombia. Memória de la Fundación La Salle de Ciencias Naturales.

Hernández-García, E., F. Mendoza-Quijano, I. Goyenechea-Mayer, and E. Godínez-Cano. 1992. Life history notes: *Ophryacus undulatus* (horned pit viper). Digestive disturbance. Herpetol. Rev. 23(3): 81–82.

Herreid, C. F., II. 1961. Snakes as predators of bats. Herpetologica 17: 271–272.

Herrera, A. L. 1890. Notas acerca de los vertebrados del Valle de México. Naturaleza, 2d ser., 1: 299–342.

——. 1891. El clima del Valle de México y la biología de los vertebrados. Part 1. Naturaleza, 2d ser., 2(1–2): 38–86.

——. 1899. Sinonimia vulgar y científica de los principales vertebrados mexicanos. Secretaria de Fomento, México, D.F. 31 pp.

——. 1904. Catálogo de la colección de reptiles y batracios del Museo Nacional, 2d ed. Museo Nacional, México, D.F. 65 pp.

Herzig, R. H., O. D. Ratnoff, and J. R. Shainoff. 1970. Studies on the procoagulant fraction of southern copperhead snake venom: the preferential release of fibrinopeptide B. Journal of Laboratory and Clinical Medicine 76: 451–465.

Heyer, W. R. 1967. A herpetofaunal study of an ecological transect through the Cordillera de Tilaran, Costa Rica. Copeia 1967(2): 259–271.

Heyrend, F. L., and A. Call. 1951. Growth and age in western striped racer and Great Basin rattlesnake. Herpetologica 7: 28–40.

Hibbits, T. D. 1991. Geographic distribution: *Sisturus catenatus* (massasauga). Herpetol. Rev. 22(2): 68.

Hibbits, T. D., M. P. Hibbits, and T. J. Hibbits. 1996. New distributional records of reptiles from western and Trans-Pecos Texas, USA. Herpetol. Rev. 27(4): 217–218.

Hidalgo, H. 1980. Occurrence of *Pelamis platurus* (Linnaeus) in El Salvador. Herpetol. Rev. 11(4): 117.

Higgins, S. B. 1870. Culebras y reptiles venenosos. Gaitán, Bogotá. 167 pp.

——. 1873. Ophidians. Boericke and Tafel, New York.

Higley, W. K. 1889. Reptilia and Batrachia of Wisconsin. Transactions of the Wisconsin Academy of Science 7: 155–176.

Hill, H. R. 1935. New host records of the linguatulid, *Kiricephalus coarctatus* (Diesing) in the United States. Bulletin of the Southern California Academy of Science 34: 226–267.

Hill, R. E., and S. P. Mackessy. 1997. Venom yields from several species of colubrid snakes and differential effects of ketamine. Toxicon 35: 671–678.

——. 2000. Characterisation of venom (Duvernoy's secretion) from 12 species of colubrid snakes and partial sequence of four venom proteins. Toxicon 38: 1663–1687.

Hillis, D. M. 1987. Molecular versus morphological approaches to systematics. Annual Review of Ecology and Systematics 18: 23–42.

Hillis, D. M., M. W. Allard, and M. M. Miyamoto. 1993. Analysis of DNA sequence data: phylogenetic inference. Methods in Enzymology 242: 456–487.

Hillis, D. M., and J. J. Bull. 1993. An empirical test of boot strapping as a method for assessing confidence in phylogenetic analysis. Syst. Biol. 42: 182–192.

Hillis, D. M., and J. P. Huelsenbeck. 1992. Signal, noise, and reliability in molecular phylogenetic analyses. Journal of Heredity 83: 189–195.

——. 1994. Support for dental HIV transmission. Nature 369: 24–25.

Hillis, D. M., B. K. Mable, and C. Moritz. 1996. Applications of molecular systematics: the state of the field and a look to the future. Pp. 515–543 in D. M. Hillis, C. Moritz, and B. K. Mable (eds.), Molecular systematics, 2d ed. Sinauer, Sunderland, Mass.

Himes, J. G. 1999. New parish records of amphibians and reptiles from Louisiana. Herpetol. Rev. 30(3): 175–176.

Hirth, H. F. 1964. Observations of the fer-de-lance, *Bothrops atrox*, in coastal Costa Rica. Copeia 1964(2): 453–454.

——. 1966a. The ability of two species of snakes to return to a hibernaculum after displacement. Southwest. Nat. 11: 49–53.

——. 1966b. Weight changes and mortality of three species of snakes during hibernation. Herpetologica 22(1): 8–12.

Hirth, H. F., R. C. Pendleton, A. C. King, and T. R. Downard. 1969. Dispersal of snakes from a hibernaculum in northwestern Utah. Ecology 50: 332–339.

Hitchiner, J. A. 1987. Reproduction in captive eyelash vipers, *Bothrops schlegelii*. Herpetol. Rev. 18(3): 55.

Ho, M., K. Silamut, N. J. White, J. Karbwang, S. Looareesuwan, R. E. Phillips, and D. A. Warrell. 1990. Pharmacokinetics of three commercial antivenoms in patients envenomed by the Malayan pit viper, *Calloselasma rhodostoma*, in Thailand. American Journal of Tropical Medicine and Hygiene 42(3): 260–266.

Ho, M., D. A. Warrell, S. Looareesuwan, R. E. Phillips, P. Chanthavanich, J. Karbwang, W. Supanaranond, C. Viravan, R. A. Hutton, and S. Vejcho. 1986a. Clinical significance of venom antigen levels in patients envenomed by the Malayan pit viper (*Calloselasma rhodostoma*). American Journal of Tropical Medicine and Hygiene 35(3): 579–587.

Ho, M., M. J. Warrell, D. A. Warrell, D. Bidwell, and A. Voller. 1986b. Review of A critical reappraisal of the use of enzyme-linked immunosorbent assays in the study of snakebite. Toxicon 24: 211–221.

Hoard, R. S. 1939. New lower California reptile records. Journal of Entomology and Zoology 31(1): 4–5.

Hobert, J. P. 1997. The massasauga rattlesnake (*Sistrurus catenatus*) in Colorado. Master's thesis, University of Northern Colorado.

Hobert, J. P., S. Boback, C. Montgomery, E. Bergman, B. Hill, and S. P. Mackessy. 1997. Geographic distribution: *Sistrurus catenatus edwardsii* (desert massasauga). Herpetol. Rev. 28(1): 52–53.

Hoessle, C. 1963. A breeding pair of western diamondback rattlesnakes, *Crotalus atrox*. Bulletin of the Philadelphia Herpetological Society 11: 65–66.

Hoevers, L. 1967. Herpetological collections from the Atkinson-Maduni-Laluni area, east Demerara, Guyana. Timehri 43: 34–50.

Hoevers, L. G., and R. W. Henderson. 1974. Additions to the herpetofauna of Belize (British Honduras). Milwaukee Public Museum Contributions in Biology and Geology 2: 1–6.

Hoffman, R. L. 1945. Notes on the herpetological fauna of Alleghany County, Virginia. Herpetologica 2(7–8): 199–204.

——. 1953. Interesting herpesian records from Camp Pickett, Virginia. Herpetologica 8(4): 171–174.

Hoffstetter, R. 1962. Revue des récentes acquisitions concernant l'histoire et la systématique des squamates. Colloque Internationale du Centre National de la Recherche Scientifique 104: 243–279.

Hoge, A. R. 1948 [dated 1947]. Notas erpetológicas. 3. Uma nova espécie de *Trimeresurus*. Mem. Inst. Butantan 20: 193–202.

——. 1949. Notas erpetológicas 7. Sôbre a ocorrência de *Trimeresurus hyoprora* (Amaral) no Brasil. Boletim do Museu Paraense Emílio Goeldi 10: 325–329.

——. 1950. Notas erpetológicas. 7. Fauna erpetológica da Ilha da Queimada Grande. Mem. Inst. Butantan 22: 151–172.

——. 1953a [dated 1952]. Notas erpetológicas. 1. Contribuição ao conhecimento dos ofídios do Brasil central. Mem. Inst. Butantan 24(2): 179–214.

——. 1953b [dated 1952]. Notas erpetológicas. 2a. Contribuição ao conhecimento dos ofídios do Brasil central. Mem. Inst. Butantan 24(2): 215–223.

——. 1953c [dated 1952]. Snakes from the Uaupés Region. Mem. Inst. Butantan 24(2): 225–230.

——. 1953d [dated 1952]. Notas erpetológicas. Revalidação de *Bothrops lanceolata* (Lacépede). Mem. Inst. Butantan 24(2): 231–236.

——. 1953e [dated 1952]. Notas erpetológicas. Anomalia na lepidose e pigmentação das escamas dorsales em *B. jararaca* e *B. alternata*. Mem. Inst. Butantan 24(2): 237–240.

——. 1954 [dated 1953]. A new *Bothrops* from Brazil—*Bothrops brazili*, sp. nov. Mem. Inst. Butantan 25(1): 15–21.

——. 1956 [dated 1955]. Uma nova espécie de *Micrurus* (Serpentes-Elapidae) do Brasil. Mem. Inst. Butantan 27: 67–72.

——. 1958. Três notas sôbre serpentes brasileiras. I. Sôbre a posição genérica de *Coluber bicinctus* Hermann, 1804 e *Xenodon gigas*

Duméril, 1853 (Colubridae). II. Sôbre a posição sistematica de *Enicognathus joberti* Sauvage, 1884 (Colubridae). III. Dimorfismo sexual em *Micrurus s. surinamensis* (Cuvier, 1817) (Elapidae). Papéis Avulsos do Departamento de Zoologia, São Paulo 13: 217–224.

———. 1959 [dated 1957–1958]. Note sur la position systématique de *Trigonocephalus* (*Bothrops*) *pubescens* Cope 1869. Mem. Inst. Butantan 28: 83–84.

———. 1964 [dated 1960–1962]. Serpentes da Fundação Surinaam Museum. Mem. Inst. Butantan 30: 51–64.

———. 1966 [dated 1965]. Preliminary account on Neotropical Crotalinae (Serpentes, Viperidae). Mem. Inst. Butantan 32: 109–184.

———. 1967. Serpentes do Território Federal do Amapá. Atlas de Symposia sôbre a Biota Amazonica 5: 217–223.

———. 1979. Distribuição e dispersão de *Crotalus durissus*. Anais da Academia Brasileira de Ciências 51(3): 570–571.

Hoge, A. R., and H. E. Belluomini. 1959a [dated 1957–1958]. Aberrações cromáticas em serpentes brasileiras. Mem. Inst. Butantan 28: 95–98.

———. 1959b [dated 1957–1958]. Uma nova espécie de *Bothrops* do Brasil (Serpentes). Mem. Inst. Butantan 28: 195–206.

———. 1964 [dated 1960–1962]. Notas sôbre *Bothrops fonsecai* Hoge e Belluomini, *Bothrops alternatus* Duméril, Bibron et Duméril e *Bothrops cotiara* Gomes. Mem. Inst. Butantan 30: 97–102.

Hoge, A. R., H. E. Belluomini, and W. Fernandes. 1977a [dated 1976/77]. Variação do número de placas ventrais de *Bothrops jararaca* em função dos climas (Viperidae, Crotalinae). Mem. Inst. Butantan 40–41: 11–17.

Hoge, A. R., H. Belluomini, and G. Schreiber. 1953. Intersexuality in a highly isolated population of snakes. Caryologia 6(suppl.): 964–965.

———. 1961. Anomalis sexuais em *Bothrops insularis* (Amaral) 1921 (Serp. Crot.). Anállise estatística da terceira amostra, desdobramento e comparções com duas amostras anteriores. Anais da Academia Brasileira de Ciências 33(2): 259–264.

Hoge, A. R., H. Belluomini, G. Schreiber and A. M. Penha. 1960 [dated 1959]. Sexual abnormalities in *Bothrops insularis* (Amaral 1921). Mem. Inst. Butantan 29: 17–88.

Hoge, A. R., C. L. Cordeiro, and S. A. R. W. D. L. Romano. 1976. A new species of *Micrurus* from Brazil (Serpentes: Elapidae). Sociedade Brasileira para o Progresso da Ciência 28(7): 417–418.

———. 1977b [dated 1976–1977]. Redescription of *Micrurus donosoi* Hoge, Cordeiro et Romano (Serpentes: Elapinae). Mem. Inst. Butantan 40–41: 71–73.

Hoge, A. R., and P. A. Federsoni Jr. 1978 [dated 1976–1977]. Observações sôbre uma ninhada de *Bothrops atrox* (Linnaeus, 1758), Serpentes: Viperidae: Crotalinae. Mem. Inst. Butantan 40–41: 19–36.

———. 1981. Matunenção e criação de serpentes em cativeiro. Revista Bioterios 1: 63–73.

Hoge, A. R., and A. R. Lancini. 1960 [dated 1959]. Nota sôbre *Micrurus surinamensis nattereri* Schmidt e *Micrurus pyrrhocryptus* Cope. Mem. Inst. Butantan 29: 9–13.

———. 1962. Sinopsis de las serpientes venenosas de Venezuela. Publicaciones Ocasionales del Museo de Ciencias Naturales, Caracas (Zool.) 1: 1–24.

Hoge, A. R., and S. A. R. W. D. L. Romano. 1966 [dated 1965]. *Leptomicrurus* in Brasil (Serpentes: Elapidae). Mem. Inst. Butantan 32: 1–8.

———. 1969. Espécies registradas para o Brasil (Serpentes). Ciência e Cultura, Suppl. (São Paulo) 21: 454.

———. 1971a. Neotropical pit vipers, sea snakes, and coral snakes. Pp. 211–293 in W. Bucherl and E. Buckley (eds.), Venomous animals and their venoms, vol. 2. Venomous vertebrates. Academic Press, New York.

———. 1971b. *Micrurus hemprichii hemprichii* recorded for Brazil. Mem. Inst. Butantan 35: 107–109.

———. 1973 [dated 1972]. Sinopse das serpentes peçonhentas do Brasil. Serpentes, Elapidae e Viperidae. Mem. Inst. Butantan 36: 109–207.

Hoge, A. R., and S. A. R. W. L. Romano-Hoge. 1981a [dated 1978–1979]. Poisonous snakes of the world. Part 1. Check list of the pit vipers, Viperoidea, Viperidae, Crotalinae. Mem. Inst. Butantan 42–43: 179–309.

———. 1981b [dated 1978–1979]. Sinopse das serpentes peçonhentas do Brasil. Mem. Inst. Butantan 42–43: 373–496.

———. 1983 [dated 1980–1981]. Notes on micro and ultrastructure of "oberhauschen" in Viperoidea. Mem. Inst. Butantan 44–45: 81–118.

Hoge, A. R., S. A. R. W. D. L. Romano, and C. L. Cordeiro. 1977c [dated 1976–77]. Contribuição ao conhecimento das serpentes do Maranhão, Brazil [Serpentes: Boidae, Colubridae e Viperidae]. Mem. Inst. Butantan 40–41: 37–52.

Hoge, A. R., S. A. R. W. L. Romano, P. A. Federsoni Jr., and C. L. S. Cordeiro. 1975 [dated 1974]. Nota prévia. Lista das espécies de serpentes coletadas na região da usina hidroelectrica de Ilha Solteira—Brasil. Mem. Inst. Butantan 38: 167–178.

Hoge, A. R., C. R. Russo, M. C. Santos, M. F. D. Furtado. 1981 [dated 1978–1979]. Snakes collected by Projeto Rondon XXII to Piauí, Brazil. Mem. Inst. Butantan 42–43: 87–94.

Hoge, A. R., N. P. Santos, C. Heitor, L. A. Lopes, and I. M. de Souza. 1973 [dated 1972]. Serpentes coletadas pelo projeto Rondon VII em Iauareté, Brasil. Mem. Inst. Butantan 36: 221–232.

Hoge, A. R., and P. Souza Santos. 1953. Submicroscopic structure of "stratum corneum" of snakes. Science 118: 410–411.

Holbrook, J. E. 1838. North American herpetology, vol. 2. J. Dobson, Philadelphia. 125 pp.

———. 1840. North American herpetology, vol. 4. J. Dobson, Philadelphia. 126 pp.

———. 1842. North American herpetology, 2d ed., vol. 3. J. Dobson, Philadelphia. 128 pp.

Holdridge, L. R. 1967. Life zone ecology. Tropical Science Center, San José, Costa Rica. 187 pp.

Holland, R. L., H. M. Smith, and D. Chiszar. 1995. Geographic distribution: *Crotalus viridis viridis* (prairie rattlesnake). Herpetol. Rev. 26(4): 210.

Hollerman, W. H., and L. J. Weiss. 1976. The thrombin-like enzyme from *Bothrops atrox* snake venom. Properties of the enzyme purified by affinity chromatography on p-aminobenzamidine-substituted agarose. Journal of Biological Chemistry 251: 1663.

Hollingsworth, B. D., and E. Mellink. 1996. Natural history notes: *Crotalus exsul lorensoensis* (San Lorenzo Island rattlesnake). Arboreal behavior. Herpetol. Rev. 27(3): 143–144.

Holm, T. C. 1702. A short description of the province of New Sweden, now called by the English, Pennsylvania, in America. Stockholm. Reprinted in the Memoirs of the Historical Society of Pennsylvania, vol. 3, Philadelphia, 1834.

Holman, J. A. 1960. Physiographic provinces and distribution of some reptiles and amphibians in Johnson County, Indiana. Copeia 1960(1): 56–58.

———. 1976. Snakes of the Split Rock Formation (Middle Miocene), central Wyoming. Herpetologica 32: 419–426.

———. 1977. Upper Miocene snakes (Reptilia, Serpentes) from southeastern Nebraska. J. Herpetol. 11: 323–335.

———. 1981. A herpetofauna from an eastern extension of the Harrison Formation, Early Miocene: Arikareean, Cherry County, Nebraska. Journal of Vertebrate Paleontology 1: 49–56.

———. 1995. Pleistocene amphibians and reptiles in North America. Oxford University Press, New York. 243 pp.

Holman, J. A., and J. H. Harding. 1999. Michigan snakes: a field guide and pocket reference. 2d ed. Michigan State University, East Lansing. 72 pp.

Holmback, E. 1981. Life history notes: *Crotalus atrox*. Herpetol. Rev. 12(2): 70.

———. 1985. Natural history notes: *Crotalus atrox* (western diamondback rattlesnake). Coloration. Herpetol. Rev. 16(3): 78.

Holstege, C. P., M. B. Miller, M. Wermuth, B. Furbee, and S. C. Curry. 1997. Crotalid snake envenomation. Critical Care Clinics 13: 889–921.

Holt, E. G. 1924. Additional records for the Alabama herpetological catalogue. Copeia 1924(136): 100–101.

Holycross, A. T. 1995. Natural history notes: *Crotalus viridis* (western rattlesnake). Phenology. Herpetol. Rev. 26(1): 37–38.

——. 1998. Geographic distribution: *Crotalus tigris* (tiger rattlesnake). Herpetol. Rev. 29(2): 111.

——. 2000a. Natural history notes: *Crotalus atrox* (western diamondback rattlesnake). Morphology. Herpetol. Rev. 31(3): 177–178.

——. 2000b. Natural history notes: *Crotalus viridis viridis* (prairie rattlesnake). Morphology. Herpetol. Rev. 31(3): 178.

——. 2000c. Natural history notes: *Crotalus willardi obscurus* (New Mexico ridgenose rattlesnake). Caudal dichromatism. Herpetol. Rev. 31(4): 246.

——. 2001. Geographic distribution: *Crotalus molossus*. Herpetol. Rev. 32(3): 194.

——. 2002. Natural history notes: *Sistrurus catenatus edwardsii* (desert massasauga). Maximum length. Herpetol. Rev. 33(1): 59.

Holycross, A. T., and J. D. Fawcett. 2002. Observations on neonatal aggregations and associated behaviors in the prairie rattlesnake, *Crotalus viridis viridis*. Am. Midl. Nat. 148: 183–186.

Holycross, A. T., and S. R. Goldberg. 2001. Reproduction in northern populations of the ridgenose rattlesnake, *Crotalus willardi* (Serpentes: Viperidae). Copeia 2001: 473–481.

Holycross, A. T., L. K. Kamees, and C. W. Painter. 2001. Observations of predation on *Crotalus willardi obscurus* in the Animas Mountains, Hidalgo County, New Mexico. Southwest. Nat. 46(3): 363–364.

Holycross, A. T., and S. P. Mackessy. 2002. Variation in the diet of *Sistrurus catenatus edwardsii* (massasauga) with emphasis on *S. catenatus edwardsii* (desert massasauga). J. Herpetol. 36(3): 454–464.

Holycross, A. T., C. W. Painter, D. G. Barker, and M. E. Douglas. 2002a. Foraging ecology of the threatened New Mexico rattlesnake, *Crotalus willardi obscurus*. Pp. 243–252 in G. W. Schuett, M. Höggren, M. E. Douglas, and H. W. Greene (eds.), Biology of the vipers. Eagle Mountain Publishing, Eagle Mountain, Utah.

Holycross, A. T., C. W. Painter, D. B. Prival, D. E. Swann, M. J. Schroff, T. Edwards, and C. R. Schwalbe. 2002b. Diet of *Crotalus lepidus klauberi* (banded rock rattlesnake). J. Herpetol. 36(4): 589–597.

Holycross, A. T., and M. Rubio. 2000. Geographic distribution: *Sistrurus catenatus edwardsii* (desert massasauga). Herpetol. Rev. 31(1): 57.

Holycross, A. T., and S. W. Smith. 1997. Geographic distribution: *Crotalus willardi obscurus* (New Mexico ridgenose rattlesnake). Herpetol. Rev. 28(2): 97.

Holycross, D. A. T., and L. J. Smith. 2001. Geographic distribution: *Crotalus molossus*. Herpetol. Rev. 32(3): 194.

Hoogmoed, M. S. 1979. The herpetofauna of the Guianan Region. Pp. 241–280 in W. E. Duellman (ed.), The South American herpetofauna: its origin, evolution, and dispersal. Monograph No. 7 of the Museum of Natural History, University of Kansas, Lawrence.

——. 1983 [dated 1982]. Snakes of the Guianan region. Mem. Inst. Butantan 46: 219–254.

——. 1993. The herpetofauna of floating meadows. Pp. 199–213 in P. E. Ouboter (ed.), Freshwater ecosystems of Suriname. Kluwer, the Netherlands.

Hoogmoed, M. S., and U. Gruber. 1983. Spix and Wagler type specimens of reptiles and amphibians in the Natural History Museums in Munich (Germany) and Leiden (the Netherlands). Spixiana 9: 319–415.

Hooker, K. R., and E. M. Caravati. 1994. Gila monster envenomation. Ann. Emerg. Med. 24: 731–735.

Hopkins, H. H. 1890. Observations on the copperhead snake, *Ancistrodon contortrix*. Transactions of the Maryland Academy of Science 1890: 89–96.

Houttuyn, M. 1764. Natuurlyke historie van uitvoerige beschryving der dieren, planten en mineraalen, volgens het samenstel van den Heer Linnaeus, vol. 6, part 1. 558 pp.

Howarth, D. M., A. E. Southee, and M. Whyte. 1994. Lymphatic flow rates and first-aid in simulated peripheral snake or spider envenomation. Medical Journal of Australia 161: 695–700.

Howe, N. R., and J. L. Meisenheimer. 1988. Electric shock does not save snakebitten rats. Ann. Emerg. Med. 17: 245–256.

Howell, T. R. 1957. Birds of a second-growth rain forest area of Nicaragua. Condor 59: 74–111.

Howland, J. M., E. F. Enderson, R. L. Bezy, B. H. Sigafus, and A. Titcomb. 2002. Geographic distribution: *Crotalus tigris* (tiger rattlesnake). Herpetol. Rev. 33(2): 149.

Hoy, P. R. 1883. Catalogue of the cold-blooded vertebrates of Wisconsin. Geology of Wisconsin 1: 422–426.

Hoy, W. E., J. T. Penney, H. W. Freeman, W. R. Kelley, and N. H. Seebeck Jr. 1953. New distributional records for reptiles and amphibians in South Carolina. Copeia 1953(1): 59–60.

Hrdlicka, A. 1908. Physiological and medical observations among the Indians of Southwestern United States and northern Mexico. Bulletin of the Bureau of American Ethnology 34:1–460.

Huang, S. Y., and J. C. Pérez. 1980. Comparative studies on hemorrhagic and of proteolytic activities of snake venoms. Toxicon 18: 421–426.

Hubbard, R. M. 1980. Captive propagation in the lancehead rattlesnake, *Crotalus polystictus*. Herpetol. Rev. 11(2): 33–34.

Hubbard, W. E. 1939. *Entonyssus ewingi* n. sp., an ophidian lung mite. Am. Midl. Nat. 21: 657–662.

Hudnall, J. A. 1979. Surface activity and horizontal movements in a marked population of *Sistrurus miliarius barbouri*. Bull. Maryland Herpetol. Soc. 15: 134–138.

Hudson, G. E. 1942. The amphibians and reptiles of Nebraska. Nebraska Conservation Bulletin 24: 1–146.

Hudson, R., and G. Carl. 1985. Natural history notes: *Crotalus horridus*. Coloration. Herpetol. Rev. 16(1): 28–29.

Hudson, R. G. 1954. An annotated list of the reptiles and amphibians of the Unami Valley, Pennsylvania. Herpetologica 10(1): 67–72.

Huelsenbeck, J. P. 1995. Performance of phylogenetic methods in simulation. Syst. Biol. 44: 17–48.

Huelsenbeck, J. P., and K. A. Crandall. 1997. Phylogeny estimation and hypothesis testing using maximum-likelihood. Annual Review of Ecology and Systematics 28: 437–466.

Hughes, R. C., J. R. Baker, and C. B. Dawson. 1941. The trematodes of reptiles. Part II. Host catalogue. Proceedings of the Oklahoma Academy of Science 21: 37–43.

Hughes, R. C., J. W. Higginbotham, and J. W. Clary. 1942. The trematodes of reptiles. Part I. Systematic section. Am. Midl. Nat. 27: 109–134.

Huheey, J. E. 1988. Mathematical models of mimicry. American Naturalist 131 (suppl.): S22–S41.

Huheey, J. E., and A. Stupka. 1967. Amphibians and reptiles of Great Smoky Mountains National Park. University of Tennessee Press, Knoxville. 98 pp.

Hulin, A., O. A. Och, and J.-M. Desbordes. 1982. Envenimations par des crotalidés en Guyane Française. Médicine d'Afrique Noire 29: 249–255.

Hulme, J. H. 1952. Observation of a snake bite by a cottonmouth moccasin. Herpetologica 8(2): 51.

Hulse, A. C. 1973. Herpetofauna of the Fort Apache Indian Reservation, east central Arizona. J. Herpetol. 7(3): 275–282.

Hulse, A. C., C. J. McCoy, and E. J. Censky. 2001. Amphibians and reptiles of Pennsylvania and the Northeast. Cornell University Press, Ithaca, N.Y. 419 pp.

Humboldt, A., and A. Bonpland. 1813. Recueil d'observations de zoologie et anatomie comparée faites dans l'Océan Atlantique, dans l'intérieur du Nouveau Continent et dans la Mer du Sud pendant les années 1799, 1800, 1801, 1802 et 1803, vol. 2: 1–8. F. Schoell, G. Dufour, Paris.

Hummelinck, D. W. 1940. A survey of the mammals, lizards, and mollusks. Studies on the fauna of Curaçao, Aruba, Bonaire, and the Venezuelan islands 1–3: 1–129.

Humphrey, R. R. 1936. Notes on altitudinal distribution of rattlesnakes. Ecology 17(2): 328–329.

Hunter, J., and C. T. Mitchell. 1967. Association of fishes with flotsam in the offshore waters of Central America. Fishery Bulletin 66: 13–29.

Hunter, M. L. 1985. Are there rattlesnakes in Maine? Habitat 2(6): 40–41.

Hunter, M. L., J. Albright, and J. Arbuckle (eds.). 1992. The amphibians and reptiles of Maine. Maine Agricultural Experiment Station Bulletin 838. 188 pp.

Hunter, M. L., Jr., A. J. K. Calhoun, and M. McCollough. 1999. Maine amphibians and reptiles. University of Maine Press, Orono. 254 pp.

Hurter, J. 1898. A contribution to the herpetology of Missouri. Transactions of the Academy of Science of St. Louis 7: 499–503.

——. 1911. Herpetology of Missouri. Transactions of the Academy of Science of St. Louis 20(5): 59–274.

Hurter, J., and J. K. Strecker Jr. 1909. The amphibians and reptiles of Arkansas. Transactions of the Academy of Science of St. Louis 18(2): 1–27.

Hutchison, R. H. 1929. On the incidence of snake-bite poisoning in the United States and the results of the newer methods of treatment. Bull. Antivenin Inst. Am. 3(2): 43–57.

Hutton, R. A., and D. A. Warrell. 1993. Action of snake venom components on the haemostatic system. Blood Reviews 7: 176–189.

Ibáñez, D. R., F. A. Arosemena, F. A. Solís, and C. A. Jaramillo. 1995a [dated 1994]. Anfibios y reptiles de la Serranía Piedras—Pacora, Parque Nacional Chagres. Scientia (Panamá) 9(1): 17–31.

Ibáñez, D. R., C. A. Jaramillo, M. Arrunátegui, Q. Fuenmayor, and F. A. Solís. 1995b. Inventario biológico del Canal de Panamá. Estudio herpetológicio. Scientia (Panamá), número especial 2: 11–159.

Ibáñez, D. R., and F. A. Solís. 1993 [dated 1991]. Las serpientes de Panamá: Lista de especies, comentarios taxonómicos y bibliografía. Scientia (Panamá) 6(2): 27–52.

Ibáñez, D. R., F. A. Solís, C. A. Jaramillo, and A. S. Rand. 2001. An overview of the herpetology of Panama. Pp. 159–170 in J. D. Johnson, R. G. Webb, and O. A. Flores-Villela (eds.), Mesoamerican herpetology: systematics, zoogeography, and conservation. Centennial Museum, special publ. University of Texas at El Paso.

ICZN. See International Commission on Zoological Nomenclature

Iglésias, F. A. 1958. Caatingas e chapadões (notas, impressões e reminiscências do Meio-Norte Brasileiro)—1912–1919, 2d ed., 2 vols. Companhia Editorial Nacional, São Paulo. 1044 pp.

Ihering, R. von. 1881. Über den Giftapparat de Korallenschlange. Zoologischer Anzeiger (Leipzig) 4: 409–412.

——. 1911 [dated 1910]. As cobras do Brazil. Primeira parte. Revista do Museu Paulista, São Paulo 8: 273–379.

Ingersoll, E. 1883. The rattlesnake. Manhattan 2: 35–45.

Instituto Geográfico "Augustín Codazzi." 1977a. Atlas de Colombia. Instituto Geográfico Augustín Codazzi, Bogotá.

——. 1977b. Carta ecológica de Colombia, 1:500,000. Instituto Geográfico Augustín Codazzi, Bogotá. 20 sheets.

——. 1977c. Zonas de vida o formaciones vegetales de Colombia: memoria explicativa sobre el mapa ecológico. Instituto Geográfico Augustín Codazzi, Bogotá.

International Commission of Zoological Nomenclature. 1999. Opinion 1939. *Trigonocephalus pulcher* Peters, 1862 (currently *Bothrops pulcher*, *Bothriechis pulcher* or *Bothrops pulchra*; Reptilia, Serpentes): defined by the holotype, and not a neotype; *Bothrops campbelli* Freire Lascano, 1991: specific name placed on the Official List. Bulletin of Zoological Nomenclature 56: 218–220.

——. 2000a. Opinion 1939. *Crotalus ruber* Cope, 1892 (Reptilia, Serpentes): specific name given precedence over that of *Crotalus exsul* Garman, 1884. Bulletin of Zoological Nomenclature 57(3): 189–190.

——. 2000b. International Code of Zoological Nomenclature, 4th ed. International Trust for Zoological Nomenclature, Natural History Museum, London.

Irish, F. J., E. E. Williams, and E. Seling. 1988. Scanning electron microscopy of changes in epidermal structure occurring during the shedding cycle in squamate reptiles. Journal of Morphology 197: 105–126.

Irwin, K. J. 1979. Two aberrant crotalid snakes from Kansas. Herpetol. Rev. 10(3): 85.

Irwin, K. J., and L. K. Irwin. 2002. Geographic distribution: *Agkistrodon contortrix* (copperhead). Herpetol. Rev. 33(2): 149.

Itoh, N., N. Tanaka, S. Mihashi, and I. Yamashima. 1987. Molecular cloning and sequence analysis of cDNA for batroxobin, a thrombin-like snake venom enzyme. Journal of Biological Chemistry 262: 3132–3135.

Ivanov, M. 1999. The first European pitviper from the Miocene of Ukraine. Acta Palaeontol. Polonica 44: 327–334.

Iverson, J. B. 1978. Reproductive notes on Florida snakes. Florida Scientist 41: 201–207.

Jackson, D. R., and R. Franz. 1981. Ecology of the eastern coral snake (*Micrurus fulvius*) in northern peninsular Florida. Herpetologica 37(4): 213–228.

Jackson, E. 1970. The natural history story of Chiricahua National Monument. Southwest Parks and Monuments Association, Globe, Arizona. 76 pp.

Jackson, J. F. 1979. Effects of some ophidian tail displays on the predatory behavior of grison (*Galictis* sp.). Copeia 1979(1): 169–172.

Jackson, J. F., and D. L. Martin. 1980. Caudal luring in the dusky pigmy rattlesnake, *Sistrurus miliarius barbouri*. Copeia 1980(4): 926–927.

Jackson, J. J. 1983. Snakes of the southeastern United States. Georgia Extension Service, Athens. 112 pp.

Jacob, J. S. 1977. An evaluation of the possibility of hybridization between the rattlesnakes *Crotalus atrox* and *C. scutulatus* in the southwestern United States. Southwest. Nat. 22: 469–485.

——. 1981. Population density and ecological requirements of the western pigmy rattlesnake in Tennessee. Report for the Tennessee Wildlife Resources Agency, project #E-1-2.

Jacob, J. S., and J. S. Altenbach. 1977. Sexual color dimorphism in *Crotalus lepidus klauberi* Gloyd (Reptilia, Serpentes, Viperidae). J. Herpetol. 11(1): 81–84.

Jacob, J. S., and C. W. Painter. 1980. Overwinter thermal ecology of *Crotalus viridis* in the north central plains of New Mexico. Copeia 1980: 799–805.

Jacob, J. S., S. R. Williams, and R. P. Reynolds. 1987. Reproductive activity of male *Crotalus atrox* and *C. scutulatus* (Reptilia: Viperidae) in northeastern Chihuahua, Mexico. Southwest. Nat. 32: 273–276.

Jaeger, E. C. 1957. North American deserts. Stanford University Press, Stanford, California. 308 pp.

James, E. 1823. Account of an expedition from Pittsburgh to the Rocky Mountains, performed in the years 1819, 1820 . . . , vol. 1. Longman, Hurst, Rees, Orme, and Brown, London.

Jameson, D. L., and A. G. Flury. 1949. The reptiles and amphibians of the Sierra Vieja range of southwestern Texas. Texas Journal of Science 1(2): 54–77.

Jameson, D. L., and A. M. Jameson. 1956. Food habits and toxicity of the venom of the night snake. Herpetologica 12(3): 240.

Jan, G. 1857. Cenni sul Museo Civico di Milano ed indice sistematico dei rettili ed anfibi esposti nel medesimo. Milan. 61 pp.

——. 1858. Plan d'une iconographie descriptive des ophidiens et description sommaire de nouvelles espèces de serpents. Revue et Magasin de Zoologie (Paris), 2d ser., 9: 438–449, 514–527.

——. 1859a. Plan d'une iconographie descriptive des ophidiens, et description sommaire de nouvelles espèces de serpents. Revue et Magasin de Zoologie (Paris), 2d ser., 10: 122–130, 148–157.

——. 1859b. Additions et rectifications aux Plan et prodrome de l'iconographie descriptive des ophidiens. Revue et Magasin de Zoologie (Paris), 2d ser., 10: 505–512.

——. 1859c. Spix: Serpentes brasilienses beurtheilt nach Autopsie der original Exemplare und auf die Nomenclatur von Dumeril und Bibron zurückgeführt. Archiv für Naturgeschichte 25(1): 272–275.

——. 1863a. Elenco sistematico degli ofidi descritti e disegnati per l'iconografia generale. A. Lombardi, Milano. 143 pp.

——. 1863b. Enumerazione sistematica degli ofidi appartenenti al gruppo Coronellidae. Archivio per la Zoologia, l'Anatomia, e la Fisiologia 21(2): 213–330.

Jan, G., and F. Sordelli. 1860–1881. Iconographie générale des ophidiens, 3 vols. J. B. Bailliere, Milan.

Janeiro-Cinquini, T. R. F., F. F. Leinz, and E. C. Farias. 1993. Ovarian cycle of the *Bothrops jararaca*. Mem. Inst. Butantan 55: 33–36.

Jansen, D. W. 1987. The myonecrotic effect of Duvernoy's gland secretion of the snake *Thamnophis elegans vagrans*. J. Herpetol. 21(1): 81–83.

Jansen, E., I. Kristensen, J. Maduro, V. Rooze, and R. Stanley (eds.). 1982. Discover Aruba's wildlife. STINAPA [Stichting Nationale Parken Nederlandse Antillean] 26. 61 pp.

Jansen, P. W., R. M. Perkin, and D. Van Stralen. 1992. Mojave rattlesnake envenomation: prolonged neurotoxicity and rhabdomyolysis. Ann. Emerg. Med. 21: 322–325.

Janzen, D. H. 1980. Two potential coral snake mimics in a tropical deciduous forest. Biotropica 12: 77–78.

Jaramillo, C., and A. S. Rand. 1996. Serpientes venenosas de la Isla Barro Colorado y areas aledañas. Instituto Smithsonian de Investigaciones Tropicales, Panamá. 6 pp.

Jaume, M. L. 1983. Notas sobre mordeduras tóxicas de serpientes (Reptilia-Serpentes-Colubridae). Revista Cubana de Medicina Tropical 35: 224–230.

Jaume, M. L., and O. H. Garrido. 1980. Notas sobre mordeduras de jubo Alsophis cantherigerus Bibron (Reptilia, Serpentes, Colubridae) en Cuba. Revista Cubana de Medicina Tropical 32: 145–148.

Jellen, B. C., C. A. Phillips, M. J. Dreslik, and D. B. Shepard. 2001. Reproductive ecology of the eastern massasauga rattlesnake, Sistrurus catenatus catenatus. Pp. 87–88 in Abstracts for 2001 Joint Annual Meetings of the Herpetologists' League and the Society for the Study of Amphibians and Reptiles, Bloomington, Indiana, 27–31 July.

Jensen, A. S. 1900. Lagoa Santa Egnens Slanger. Et Bidrag til det indre Brasiliens Herpetologi. Saertryk af Vidensk. Meddelengen fra den naturh. Foren. i Kbhvn. Copenhagen (1900): 99–111.

Jensen, J. B. 2001. Distribution records of Georgia herpetofauna. Herpetol. Rev. 32(1): 64.

Jensen, J. B., B. W. Mansell, and P. E. Moler. 1994. Geographic distribution: Crotalus horridus (timber rattlesnake). Herpetol. Rev. 25(4): 166.

Jensen, J. B., and R. A. Moulis. 1997. Early rewards from the Georgia Herp Atlas. Herpetol. Rev. 29(4): 212–214.

———. 1999. The Georgia Herp Atlas: Year II county records. Herpetol. Rev. 30(4): 240–247.

Jermiin, L. S., G. J. Olsen, K. L. Mengersen, S. Easteal. 1997. Majority-rule consensus of phylogenetic trees obtained by maximum-likelihood analysis. Molecular Biology and Evolution 14: 1296–1302.

Jiggins, C. D., and W. O. McMillan. 1997. The genetic basis of an adaptive radiation: warning colour in two Heliconius species. Proceedings of the Royal Society of London B 264: 1167–1175.

Jiménez-Lang, N., R. Vidal-López, and R. Luna-Reyes. 2002. Registro adicional de Bothriechis rowleyi (Serpentes: Viperidae) en Chiapas, México. Boletín de la Sociedad Herpetológica Mexicana 10(2): 43–45.

Jiménez-Porras, J. M. 1964a. Intraspecific variations in composition of venom of the jumping viper, Bothrops nummifera. Toxicon 2: 187–195.

———. 1964b. Venom proteins of the fer-de-lance, Bothrops atrox from Costa Rica. Toxicon 2: 155–166.

———. 1967. Differentiation between Bothrops nummifer and Bothrops picadoi by means of the biochemical properties of their venoms. Pp. 307–321 in F. E. Russell and P. R. Saunders (eds.), Animal toxins. Pergamon, Oxford.

Johanboeke, M. M. 1974. Effects of a bite from Conophis lineatus (Squamata: Colubridae). Bulletin of the Philadelphia Herpetological Society 22: 39.

John-Adler, H., C. H. Lowe, and A. F. Bennett. 1983. Thermal dependence of locomotor energetics and aerobic capacity of the Gila monster (Heloderma suspectum). Journal of Comparative Physiology 151: 119–126.

Johnson, A. S., H. O. Hillstead, S. F. Shanholtzer, and G. F. Shanholtzer. 1974. An ecological survey of the coastal region of Georgia. National Park Service Scientific Monograph Series 3: 1–233.

Johnson, E. K., K. V. Kardong, and S. P. Mackessy. 1987. Electric shocks are ineffective in treatment of lethal effects of rattlesnake envenomation in mice. Toxicon 25: 1347–1349.

Johnson, E. K., K. V. Kardong, and C. L. Owenby. 1987. Observations on white and yellow venoms from an individual southern Pacific rattlesnake, Crotalus viridis helleri. Toxicon 25 (11): 1169–1180.

Johnson, G. 1995. Spatial ecology, habitat preference, and habitat management of the eastern massasauga, Sistrurus c. catenatus, in a New York weakly-minerotrophic peatland. Ph.D. dissertation, State University of New York, Syracuse.

Johnson, J. D. 1974 [dated 1973]. New records of reptiles and amphibians from Chiapas, Mexico. Trans. Kansas Acad. Sci. 76(3): 223–224.

———. 1988. Comments on the report of envenomation by the colubrid snake Stenorrhina freminvillei. Toxicon 26(6): 519–521.

———. 1989. A biogeographic analysis of the herpetofauna of northwestern Nuclear Central America. Milwaukee Public Museum Contributions to Biology and Geology 76: 1–66.

Johnson, J. D., and J. R. Dixon. 1984. Taxonomic status of the Venezuelan macagua, Bothrops colombiensis. J. Herpetol. 18(3): 329–332.

Johnson, L. F., J. S. Jacob, and P. Torrance. 1982. Annual testicular and androgenic cycles of the cottonmouth (Agkistrodon piscivorus) in Alabama. Herpetologica 38(1): 16–25.

Johnson, M. L. 1942. A distributional check-list of the reptiles of Washington. Copeia 1942(1): 15–18.

———. 1952. Herpetological notes from north-eastern Brazil. Copeia 1952(4): 283–284.

———. 1995 [dated 1954]. Reptiles of the State of Washington. Northwest Fauna 3: 5–80.

Johnson, R. G. 1955. The adaptive and phylogenetic significance of vertebral form in snakes. Evolution 9: 367–388.

———. 1956. The origin and evolution of the venomous snakes. Evolution 10: 56–65.

Johnson, T. B., and G. S. Mills. 1982. A preliminary report on the status of Crotalus lepidus, C. pricei, and C. willardi in southeastern Arizona. Unpublished report, U.S. Fish and Wildlife Service, Phoenix, Ariz.

Johnson, T. R. 1979. Missouri's venomous snakes. Missouri Conservationist 40(6): 4–7.

———. 1987. The amphibians and reptiles of Missouri. Missouri Department of Conservation, Jefferson City. 368 pp.

———. 2000. The amphibians and reptiles of Missouri, 2d ed. Missouri Department of Conservation, Jefferson City. 400 pp.

Jones, A. 1997. Big reptiles, big lies. Reptile and Amphibian Magazine 51: 22–27.

Jones, J. M. 1971. Relationship of specimen size to venom extracted from the copperhead, Agkistrodon contortrix. Copeia 1971(1): 162–163.

———. 1976. Variations of venom proteins in Agkistrodon snakes from North America. Copeia 1976(3): 558–562.

Jones, J. M., and P. M. Burchfield. 1971. Relationship of specimen size to venom extracted from the copperhead, Agkistrodon contortrix. Copeia 1971: 162–163.

Jones, K. B. 1983. Movement patterns and foraging ecology of Gila monsters (Heloderma suspectum Cope) in northwestern Arizona. Herpetologica 39(3): 247–253.

———. 1988. Distribution and habitat associations of herpetofauna in Arizona: comparison by habitat type. Pp. 109–128 in R. C. Szaro, K. E. Severson, and D. R. Patton (technical coordinators), Management of amphibians, reptiles, and small mammals in North America. General Technical Report RM-166. USDA Forest Service, Fort Collins, Colo.

Jones, K. B., D. R. Abbas, and T. Bergstedt. 1981. Herpetological records from central and northeastern Arizona. Herpetol. Rev. 12(1): 16.

Jones, L. L. C. 1981. Geographic distribution: Crotalus viridis helleri (southern Pacific rattlesnake). Herpetol. Rev. 12(2): 65.

Jopson, H. G. M. 1940. Reptiles and amphibians from Georgetown County, South Carolina. Herpetologica 2(2): 39–43.

Jorge, M. T., J. L. Cardoso, S. C. Castro, L. Ribeiro, F. O. S. França, M. E. Sbrogio de Almeida, A. S. Kamiguti, I. S. Sano-Martins, M. L. Santoro, J. E. C. Mancau, et al. 1995. A randomised "blinded" comparison of two doses of antivenom in the treatment of Bothrops envenoming in São Paulo, Brazil. Trans. Roy. Soc. Trop. Med. Hyg. 89(1): 111–114.

Jorge, M. T., S. de A. Nishioka, R. B. de Oliveira, L. A. Ribeiro, and P. V. Silveira. 1998. Aeromonas hydrophila soft-tissue infection as a complication of snake bite: report of three cases. Annals of Tropical Medicine and Parasitology 92(2): 213–217.

Jorge, M. T., J. S. de Mendonça, L. A. Ribeiro, M. L. da Silva, E. J. Kusano, and C. L. Cordeiro. 1990. Flora bacteriana dacavidade oral, presas y veneno de *Bothrops jararaca*: possível fonte de infecção no local da picada. Revista do Instituto de Medicina Tropical de São Paulo 32: 6–10.

Jorge, M. T., and L. A. Ribeiro. 1990. Acidentes por serpentes peçonhentas do Brasil. Revista da Associação Medica Brasileira 36: 66–77.

——. 1992. Epidemiology and clinical features of South American rattlesnakes (*Crotalus durissus*) envenomation. Revista do Instituto de Medicina Tropical de São Paulo 34(4): 347–354.

——. 2000. Envenoming by the South American pitviper *Bothrops neuwiedi* Wagler. Annals of Tropical Medicine and Parasitology 94(7): 731–734.

Jorge, M. T., L. A. Ribeiro, M. L. R. da Silva, E. J. Uro Kusano, and J. S. De Mendonça. 1994. Microbiological studies of abscesses complicating *Bothrops* snakebite in humans: a prospective study. Toxicon 32: 743–748.

Jorge, M. T., L. A. Ribeiro, and S. de A. Nishioka. 1997a. A comparison of clinical and epidemiological aspects of bites by small and large South American rattlesnakes. Tropical Doctor 27: 106–107.

Jorge, M. T., L. A. Ribeiro, and J. L. O'Connell. 1999. Prognostic factors for amputation in the case of envenoming by snakes of the *Bothrops* genus (Viperidae). Annals of Tropical Medicine and Parasitology 94: 401–408.

Jorge, M. T., I. S. Sano-Martins, S. C. Tomy, S. C. Castro, R. A. Ferrari, L. A. Ribeiro, and D. A. Warrell. 1997b. Snakebite by the bushmaster (*Lachesis muta*) in Brazil: case report and review of the literature. Toxicon 35(4): 545–554.

Jorge da Silva, N. 1993. The snakes of Samuel hydroelectric power plant and vicinity, Rondônia, Brazil. Herpetological Natural History 1: 37–86.

——. 1996. Geographic distribution: *Micrurus lemniscatus* (coral snake). Herpetol. Rev. 27(1): 34.

Jorge da Silva, N., Jr., S. D. Aird, C. Seebart, and I. I. Kaiser. 1989. A gyroxin analog from the venom of the bushmaster (*Lachesis muta muta*). Toxicon 27(7): 763–771.

Jorge da Silva, N., Jr., P. R. Griffin, and S. D. Aird. 1991. Comparative chromatography of Brazilian coral snakes (*Micrurus*) venom. Comp. Biochem. Physiol. B 100(1): 117–126.

Jorge da Silva, N., and J. W. Sites Jr. 1999. A revision of the *Micrurus frontalis* complex (Serpentes, Elapidae). Herpetological Monographs 13: 142–194.

——. 2001. Phylogeny of South American triad coral snakes (Elapidae: *Micrurus*) based on molecular characters. Herpetologica 57(1): 1–22.

Joron, M., and J. Mallet. 1998. Diversity in mimicry: paradox or paradigm. Trends in Ecology and Evolution 13: 461–466.

Joron, M., I. R. Wynne, G. Lamas, and J. Mallet. 1999. Variable selection and the coexistence of multiple mimetic forms of the butterfly *Heliconius numata*. Evolutionary Ecology 13: 721–754.

Joseph, E. L. 1838. History of Trinidad. Henry James Mills, London. 269 pp.

Jouventin, P., G. Pasteur, and J. P. Cambefort. 1977. Observational learning of baboons and avoidance of mimics: exploratory tests. Evolution 31: 214–218.

Jukes, T. H. and C. R. Cantor. 1969. Evolution of protein molecules. Pp. 21–132 in H. M. Munro (ed.), Mammalian protein metabolism. Academic Press, New York.

Juliá-Zertuche, J. 1982. Una nueva subespecie de "vibora de cascabel pigmea" de la Sierra de Sinaloa. Resumenes del Sexto Congreso Nacional de Zoología, Ciencias del Mar, Universidad Autónoma de Sinaloa, Mazatlán, Sinaloa, Diciembre.

Juliá-Zertuche, J., and C. H. Treviño. 1978. Una nueva subespecie de *Crotalus lepidus* encontrada en Nuevo León. Resumenes del Segundo Congreso Nacional de Zoologia, Monterrey, Nuevo León, México.

Juliá-Zertuche, J., and M. Varela-J. 1978. Una *Bothrops* de México, nueva para la ciencia. Mem. Primer Congreso Nacional Zool.,

Escuela Nac. Agric. (Universidad Autónoma de Chiapas) 1977: 209–210.

Jurkovich, G. J., A. Luterman, K. McCullar, M. L. Ramenofsky, and P. W. Curreri. 1988. Complications of Crotalidae antivenin therapy. Journal of Trauma—Injury, Infection, and Critical Care 28: 1032–1037.

Jutzy, D. A., S. H. Biber, N. W. Elton, and E. C. Lowry. 1953. A clinical and pathological analysis of snake bites in the Panama Canal zone. American Journal of Tropical Medicine and Hygiene 2(1): 129–141.

Kaiser, E., and H. Michl. 1971. Chemistry, biochemistry, pharmacology, and toxicology of *Bothrops* and *Lachesis*. Pp. 307–318 in W. Bucherl and E. Buckley (eds.), Venomous animals and their venoms, vol. 2. Venomous vertebrates. Academic Press, New York.

Kaiser, I. I., J. L. Middlebrook, M. H. Crumrine, and W. W. Stevenson. 1986. Cross-reactivity and neutralization by rabbit antisera raised against crotoxin, its subunits, and two related toxins. Toxicon 24: 669–678.

Kamiguti, A. S., J. L. C. Cardoso, R. D. G. Theakston, I. S. Sano-Martins, R. A. Hutton, F. P. Rugman, D. A. Warrell, and C. R. Hay. 1991. Coagulopathy and haemorrhage in human victims of *Bothrops jararaca* envenoming in Brazil. Toxicon 29: 961–972.

Kamiguti, A. S., S. Matsunaga, M. Spir, I. S. Sano-Martins, and L. Nahas. 1986. Alterations of the blood coagulation system after accidental human inoculation by *Bothrops jararaca* venom. Brazilian Journal of Medical and Biological Research 19: 199–204.

Kamiguti, A. S., F. P. Rugman, R. D. G. Theakston, F. O. França, H. Ishii, and C. R. Hay. 1992. The role of venom haemorrhaging in spontaneous bleeding in *Bothrops jararaca* envenoming. Thrombosis Haemostasis 67: 484–488.

——. 2002. Colubrid snakes and Duvernoy's "venom" glands. Journal of Toxicology—Toxin Reviews 21 (1–2): 1–19.

Kane, Joe. 1996. Savages. Knopf, New York. 273 pp.

Kapan, D. D. 2001. Three-butterfly system provides a field test of müllerian mimicry. Nature 409: 338–340.

Kappler, A. 1881. Holländische-Guiana. Erlebnisse und Erfahrungen während eines 43 jährigen Aufenthalts in der Kolonie Surinam. W. Kohlhammer, Stuttgart. 495 pp.

Kapus, E. J. 1964. Anatomical evidence for *Heterodon* being poisonous. Herpetologica 20(2): 137–138.

Kardong, K. V. 1973. Lateral jaw and throat musculature of the cottonmouth snake *Agkistrodon piscivorus*. Morph. Jahrb. 119: 316–335.

——. 1977. Kinesis of the jaw apparatus during swallowing in the cottonmouth snake, *Agkistrodon piscivorus*. Copeia 1977(2): 338–348.

——. 1980a. Gopher snakes and rattlesnakes: presumptive Batesian mimicry. Northwest Science 54: 1–4.

——. 1980b. Evolutionary patterns in advanced snakes. American Zoologist 20: 269–282.

——. 1982. The evolution of the venom apparatus in snakes from colubrids to viperids to elapids. Mem. Inst. Butantan 46: 105–118.

——. 1986. Biogeography of New World pit vipers. Exploration of Nature 5(18): 35–40.

——. 1990. General skull, bone, and muscle variation in *Agkistrodon* and related genera. Pp. 573–581 in H. K. Gloyd and R. Conant (eds.), Snakes of the *Agkistrodon* complex: a monographic review. Society for the Study of Amphibians and Reptiles, Oxford, Ohio.

——. 1996. Snake toxins and venoms: an evolutionary perspective. Herpetologica 52(1): 36–46.

——. 2002. Colubrid snakes and Duvernoy's "venom" glands. Journal of Toxicology—Toxin Reviews 21(1–2): 1–19.

Kardong, K. V., and P. A. Lavin-Murcio. 1993. Venom delivery of snakes as high-pressure and low-pressure systems. Copeia 1993: 644–650.

Kardong, K. V., and D. L. Luchtel. 1986. Ultrastructure of Duvernoy's gland from the wandering garter snake, *Thamnophis elegans vagrans* (Serpentes: Colubridae). Journal of Morphology 188: 1–13.

Kardong, K. V., and B. A. Young. 1991. Fangs and snakes: how do open grooves inject venom into enclosed spaces? American Zoologist 31: 51A.

Karges, J. P. 1978. Texas amphibians and reptiles: some new distributional records, part I. Herpetol. Rev. 9(4): 143–145.

——. 1979a. Texas amphibians and reptiles: some new distributional records, part II. Herpetol. Rev. 10(4): 119–121.

——. 1979b. An aberrant pattern morph in a western diamondback rattlesnake, *Crotalus atrox*, from southern Texas. Trans. Kansas Acad. Sci. 82(4): 205–208.

Kathariner, L. 1900. Die Nase der im Wasser lebenden Schlangen als Luftweg und Geruchsorgan. Zoologische Jahrbücher, Abt. Syst. 13: 415–442.

Kauffeld, C. F. 1943a. Field notes on some Arizona reptiles and amphibians. Am. Midl. Nat. 29(2): 342–359.

——. 1943b. Growth and feeding of new-born Price's and green rock rattlesnakes. Am. Midl. Nat. 29(3): 607–614.

——. 1957. Snakes and snake hunting. Hanover House, Garden City, N.Y.

——. 1964. Coronado Island rattlesnake. Animaland 17(3): 2–4.

Kauffeld, C. F., and H. K. Gloyd. 1939. Notes on the Aruba rattlesnake, *Crotalus unicolor*. Herpetologica 1(6): 156–160.

Kauffeld, I. 1940. A glimpse into Mexico. News Bulletin of the Staten Island Zoological Society 7(3): 3–4.

Kauffman, F. E. 1928. The pygmy or ground rattler. Bull. Antivenin Inst. Am. 1(4): 118.

Keasey, M. S., III. 1969. Some records of reptiles at the Arizona–Sonoran Desert Museum. International Zoo Yearbook 9: 16–17.

Keegan, H. L. 1944. Indigo snakes feeding upon poisonous snakes. Copeia 1944(1): 59.

Keegan, H. L., and T. F. Andrews. 1942. Effects of crotalid venom on North American snakes. Copeia 1942(4): 251–254.

Keegan, K. A., R. N. Reed, A. T. Holycross, and Charles W. Painter. 1999. Natural history notes: *Crotalus willardi* (ridgenose rattlesnake). Maximum length. Herpetol. Rev. 30(2): 100.

Keenlyne, K. D. 1972. Sexual differences in feeding habits of *Crotalus horridus horridus*. J. Herpetol. 6(3–4): 234–237.

Keenlyne, K. D. 1978. Reproductive cycles in two species of rattlesnakes. Am. Midl. Nat. 100: 368–375.

Keenlyne, K. D., and J. R. Beer. 1973a. Food habits of *Sistrurus catenatus catenatus*. J. Herpetol. 7: 382–384.

——. 1973b. Note on the size of *Sistrurus catenatus catenatus* at birth. J. Herpetol. 7: 381–382.

Keiser, E. D., Jr. 1971. The poisonous snakes of Louisiana and the emergency treatment of their bites. Louisiana Conservationist 23(7–8): 1–16.

——. 1982. The poisonous snakes of Mississippi with suggestions for the emergency treatment of their bite. Mississippi Outdoors 1982(4): 1a–16a.

——. 1993. Life history notes: *Agkistrodon piscivorus leucostoma* (western cottonmouth). Behavior. Herpetol. Rev. 24(1): 34.

Kelly, H. A. 1936. Snakes of Maryland. Natural History Society of Maryland, Baltimore. 103 pp.

Kemper, W. F., S. L. Lindstedt, L. K. Hartzler, J. W. Hicks, and K. E. Conley. 2001. Shaking up glycolysis: sustained, high lactate flux during aerobic rattling. Proceedings of the National Academy of Sciences 98(2): 723–728.

Kempff-Mercado, N. 1975. Ofidios de Bolivia. Acad. Nac. Cienc. Bolivia, La Paz. 46 pp.

——. 1977. El genero *Bothrops* en Bolivia. Boletín científico del Centro Nacional de Doenças Tropicais 3: 8–14.

Kennedy, J. P. 1964. Natural history notes on some snakes of eastern Texas. Texas Journal of Science 16(2): 210–215.

Kennicott, R. 1855. Catalogue of animals observed in Cook County, Illinois. Transactions of the Illinois State Agriculture Society 1: 577–595.

——. 1861a [dated 1860]. Descriptions of new species of North American serpents in the Museum of the Smithsonian Institution, Washington. Proc. Acad. Nat. Sci. Philadelphia 12: 328–338.

——. 1861b. On three new forms of rattlesnakes. Proc. Acad. Nat. Sci. Philadelphia 13: 204–208.

Keogh, J. S. 1998. Molecular phylogeny of elapid snakes and a consideration of their biogeographic history. Biological Journal of the Linnean Society 63: 177–203.

Keogh, J. S., R. Shine, and S. Donnellan. 1998. Phylogenetic relationships of terrestrial Australo-Papuan elapid snakes (subfamily Hydrophiinae) based on cytochrome b and 16S rRNA sequences. Molecular Phylogenetics and Evolution 10: 67–81.

Kerrigan, K. R. 1991. Venomous snakebite in eastern Ecuador. American Journal of Tropical Medicine and Hygiene 44: 93–99.

——. 1992. Bacteriology of snakebite abscess. Tropical Doctor 22: 158–160.

Kerrigan, K. R., B. L. Mertz, S. J. Nelson, and J. D. Dye. 1997. Antibiotic prophylaxis for pit viper envenomation: prospective, controlled trial. World Journal of Surgery 21: 369–373.

Keyler, D., and B. Oldfield. 1992. Velvet tails in the Blufflands. Minnesota Volunteer, May–June: 32–43.

Kiel, J. L. 1975. A review of parasites in snakes. Southwestern Veterinarian 28(3): 1–12.

Killebrew, F. C., K. B. Blair, D. Chiszar, and H. M. Smith. 1996. New records for amphibians and reptiles from Texas. Herpetol. Rev. 27(2): 90–91.

Killebrew, F. C., and T. L. James. 1983. Natural history notes: *Crotalus viridis viridis* (prairie rattlesnake). Coloration. Herpetol. Rev. 14(3): 74.

Kimball, D. W. (ed.). 1978. The timber rattlesnake in New England—a symposium. Western Massachusetts Herpetological Society, Springfield. 14 pp.

King, F. W. 1932. Herpetological records and notes from the vicinity of Tucson, Arizona, July and August, 1930. Copeia 1932(4): 175–177.

King, M. B., and D. Duvall. 1990. Prairie rattlesnake seasonal migrations: episodes of movement, vernal foraging, and sex differences. Animal Behaviour 39(5): 924–935.

King, M. B., D. McCarron, D. Duvall, G. Baxter, and W. Gern. 1983. Group avoidance of conspecific but not interspecific chemical cues by prairie rattlesnakes (*Crotalus viridis*). J. Herpetol. 17: 196–198.

Kingsborough, E. K. 1831–1848. Antiquities of Mexico. Robert Havell, London.

Kinney, C., G. Abishahin, and B. A. Young 1998. Hissing in rattlesnakes: redundant signaling or inflationary epiphenomenon? Journal of Experimental Zoology 280(2): 107–113.

Kirtland, J. P. 1838. Report on the zoology of Ohio. Second Annual Report of the Geological Survey of Ohio, pp. 157–200.

Kishino, H., T. Miyata, and M. Hasegawa. 1990. Maximum likelihood inference of protein phylogeny and the origin of chloroplasts. Journal of Molecular Evolution 31: 151–160.

Kissner, K. J., M. R. Forbes, and D. M. Secoy. 1997. Rattling behavior of prairie rattlesnakes (*Crotalus viridis viridis*, Viperidae) in relation to sex, reproductive status, body size, and body temperature. Ethology 103(12): 1042–1050.

Kitchens, C. S. 1992. Hemostatic aspects of envenomation by North American snakes. Hematology/Oncology Clinics of North America 6: 1198–1195.

Kitchens, C. S., S. Hunter, and L. H. S. Van Mierop. 1987. Severe myonecrosis in a fatal case of envenomation by the canebrake rattlesnake (*Crotalus horridus atricaudatus*). Toxicon 25: 455–458.

Kitchens, C. S., and H. S. Van Mierop. 1983. Mechanism of defibrination in humans after envenomation by the eastern diamondback rattlesnake (*Crotalus ademanteus*). American Journal of Hematology 14(4): 345–354.

——. 1987a. Envenomation by the eastern coral snake (*Micrurus fulvius fulvius*). A study of 39 victims. JAMA 258(12): 1615–1618.

——. 1987b. Severe myonecrosis in a fatal case of envenomation by the canebrake rattlesnake, *Crotalus horridus atricaudatus*. Toxicon 25(4): 455–458.

Klappenbach, M. A., and B. Orejas-Miranda. 1969. Anfibios y reptiles. Nuestra Tierra 11: 1-68.

Klauber, L. M. 1927. Some observations on the rattlesnakes of the extreme southwest. Bull. Antivenin Inst. Am. 1(1): 7–21.

——. 1929. Range extensions in California. Copeia 1929(170): 15–22.

——. 1930a. Differential characteristics of the southwestern rattlesnakes allied to *Crotalus atrox*. Bulletins of the Zoological Society of San Diego 6: 1–72.

——. 1930b. New and renamed subspecies of *Crotalus confluentus* Say, with remarks on related species. Trans. San Diego Soc. Nat. Hist. 6(5): 95–144.

——. 1930c. A list of amphibians and reptiles of San Diego County, California. Bulletins of the Zoological Society of San Diego 5: 2–7.

——. 1931a. A statistical survey of the snakes of the southern border of California. Bulletins of the Zoological Society of San Diego 8: 1–93.

——. 1931b. *Crotalus tigris* and *Crotalus enyo*, two little known rattlesnakes of the southwest. Trans. San Diego Soc. Nat. Hist. 6(24): 353–370.

——. 1932a. A herpetological review of the Hopi Snake Dance. Bulletins of the Zoological Society of San Diego 9: 1–82.

——. 1932b. Amphibians and reptiles observed en route to Hoover Dam. Copeia 1932(3): 118–128.

——. 1934. An addition to the fauna of New Mexico and a deletion. Copeia 1934(1): 52.

——. 1935a. The feeding habits of a sea snake. Copeia 1935(4): 182.

——. 1935b. A new subspecies of *Crotalus confluentus*, the prairie rattlesnake. Trans. San Diego Soc. Nat. Hist. 8: 75–90.

——. 1936a. *Crotalus mitchelli*, the speckled rattlesnake. Trans. San Diego Soc. Nat. Hist. 8: 149–184.

——. 1936b. Key to the rattlesnakes with summary of characteristics. Trans. San Diego Soc. Nat. Hist. 8(2): 185–276.

——. 1936c. A statistical study of the rattlesnakes. I. Introduction. Occasional Papers of the San Diego Society of Natural History 1: 1–24.

——. 1937. A statistical study of the rattlesnakes. IV. The growth of the rattlesnakes. Occasional Papers of the San Diego Society of Natural History 3: 1–56.

——. 1938a. A statistical study of the rattlesnakes. V. Head dimensions. Occasional Papers of the San Diego Society of Natural History 4: 1–53.

——. 1938b. Notes from a herpetological diary, I. Copeia 1938(4): 191–197.

——. 1939a. Studies of reptile life in the arid Southwest. Bulletins of the Zoological Society of San Diego 14: 1–100.

——. 1939b. A statistical study of the rattlesnakes. VI. Fangs. Occasional Papers of the San Diego Society of Natural History 5: 1–61.

——. 1940a. Notes from a herpetological diary, II. Copeia 1940(1): 15–18.

——. 1940b. The rattlesnakes, genera *Sistrurus* and *Crotalus*: a study in zoogeography and evolution (Review). Copeia 1940(3): 206–207.

——. 1940c. A statistical study of the rattlesnakes. VII. The rattle, part 1. Occasional Papers of the San Diego Society of Natural History 6: 1–62.

——. 1941a. Four papers on the application of statistical methods to herpetological problems. Bulletins of the Zoological Society of San Diego 17: 1–95.

——. 1941b. A new species of rattlesnake from Venezuela. Trans. San Diego Soc. Nat. Hist. 9(30): 333–336.

——. 1943. 1. Tail-length differences in snakes with notes on sexual dimorphism and the coefficient of divergence. 2. A graphic method of showing relationships. Bulletins of the Zoological Society of San Diego 18: 1–76.

——. 1944. The sidewinder, *Crotalus cerastes*, with a description of a new subspecies. Trans. San Diego Soc. Nat. Hist. 10(8): 91–126.

——. 1948. Answer 2 to query no. 106. Earliest printed illustration of rattlesnakes. Isis 39(4): 334–335.

——. 1949a. The relationship of *Crotalus ruber* and *Crotalus lucasensis*. Trans. San Diego Soc. Nat. Hist. 11(5): 57–60.

——. 1949b. Some new and revived subspecies of rattlesnakes. Trans. San Diego Soc. Nat. Hist. 11(6): 61–116.

——. 1949c. The subspecies of the ridge-nosed rattlesnake, *Crotalus willardi*. Trans. San Diego Soc. Nat. Hist. 11(8): 121–140.

——. 1952. Taxonomic studies of the rattlesnakes of mainland Mexico. Bulletins of the Zoological Society of San Diego 26: 1–143.

——. 1956. Rattlesnakes: their habits, life histories, and influence on mankind, 2 vols. University of California Press, Berkeley. 1476 pp.

——. 1957 [dated 1956]. *Agkistrodon* or *Ancistrodon*? Copeia 1956(4): 258–259.

——. 1963. A new insular subspecies of the speckled rattlesnake. Trans. San Diego Soc. Nat. Hist. 13(5): 73–80.

——. 1971. Classification, distribution, and biology of the venomous snakes of northern Mexico, the United States, and Canada: *Crotalus* and *Sistrurus*. Pp. 115–156 in W. Bucherl and E. Buckley (eds.), Venomous animals and their venoms, vol. 2. Venomous vertebrates. Academic Press, New York.

——. 1972. Rattlesnakes: their habits, life histories, and influence on mankind, 2d ed., 2 vols. University of California Press, Berkeley. 1533 pp.

——. 1997. Rattlesnakes: their habits, life histories, and influence on mankind, 2d ed., 2 vols. Reprint, University of California Press, Berkeley. 1580 pp.

Klawe, W. L. 1963. Observations on the spawning of four species of tuna (*Neothunnus macropterus, Katsuwonus pelamis, Auxis thazard,* and *Euthynnus lineatus*) in the eastern Pacific Ocean, based on the distribution of their larvae and juveniles. Inter-American Tropical Tuna Commission Bulletin 6: 447–540.

——. 1964. Food of the black and yellow sea snake, *Pelamis platurus*, from Ecuadorian coastal waters. Copeia 1964(4): 712–713.

Klemens, M. W. 1993. Amphibians and reptiles of Connecticut and adjacent regions. Connecticut Geological and Natural History Survey Bulletin 112: 1–318.

Klemmer, K. 1963. Liste der rezenten Giftschlangen: Elapidae, Hydropheidae, Viperidae, und Crotalidae. Pp. 255–264 in Die Giftschlangen der Erde. N. G. Elwert Universitäts- und Verlags-Buchhandlung, Marburg.

Klimstra, W. D. 1959. Food habits of the cottonmouth in southern Illinois. Chicago Academy of Science, Natural History Micellanea 168: 1–8.

Klopfer, P. H. 1957. An experiment on empathic learning in ducks. American Naturalist 91: 61–63.

Kluge, A. G. 1991. Boine snake phylogeny and research cycles. Miscellaneous Publications of the Museum of Zoology, University of Michigan 178: 1–58.

——. 1993. *Calabaria* and the phylogeny of erycine snakes. Zoological Journal of the Linnean Society 107: 293–351.

Kluge, A. G., and J. S. Farris. 1969. Quantitative phyletics and the evolution of anurans. Syst. Zool. 18: 1–32.

Knapp, R. A., and R. C. Sargent. 1989. Egg-mimicry as a mating strategy in the fantail darter, *Etheosoma flabellare*: females prefer males with eggs. Behavioral Ecology and Sociobiology 25: 321–326.

Knight, A., L. D. Densmore III, and E. D. Real. 1992. Molecular systematics of the *Agkistrodon* complex. Pp. 49–70 in J. A. Campbell and E. D. Brodie Jr. (eds.), Biology of the pitvipers. Selva, Tyler, Texas. 467 pp.

Knight, A., and D. P. Mindell. 1993. Substitution bias, weighting of DNA sequence evolution, and the phylogenetic position of Fea's viper. Syst. Biol. 42: 18–31.

——. 1994. On the phylogenetic relationship of Colubrinae, Elapidae, and Viperidae and the evolution of front-fanged venom systems in snakes. Copeia 1994(1): 1–9.

Knight, A., D. Styler, S. Pelikan, J. A. Campbell, L. D. Densmore III, and D. P. Mindell. 1993. Choosing among hypotheses of rattlesnake phylogeny: a best-fit rate test for DNA sequence data. Syst. Biol. 42(3): 356–367.

Knight, R. L., and A. W. Ericson. 1976. High incidence of snakes in the diet of nesting red-tailed hawks. Raptor Research 10(4): 108–111.

Knopf, G. N., and D. W. Tinkle. 1961. The distribution and habits of *Sistrurus catenatus* in northwest Texas. Herpetologica 17(2): 126–131.

Koch, E. D., and C. R. Peterson. 1995. Amphibians and reptiles of Yellowstone and Grand Teton National Parks. University of Utah Press, Salt Lake City. 188 pp.

Kocholaty, W. F., E. Boyles-Ledford, J. Daly, and T. A. Billings. 1971. Oxicity and some enzymatic properties and activities in the venoms of Crotalidae, Elapidae, and Viperidae. Toxicon 9: 131–138.

Kochva, E. 1958. The head muscles of Vipera palaestinae and their relation to the venom gland. Journal of Morphology 102: 23–53.

——. 1962. On the lateral jaw musculature of the Solenoglypha with remarks on some other snakes. Journal of Morphology 110: 227–284.

——. 1978. Oral glands of the Reptilia. Pp. 43–162 in C. Gans and K. A. Gans (eds.), Biology of the Reptilia, vol. 8. Physiology B. Academic Press, London.

Kochva, E., and C. Gans. 1970. Salivary glands of snakes. Clinical Toxicology 3: 363–387.

Koenig, H. F., and J. L. La Grone. 2000. Geographic distribution: Crotalus molossus (blacktail rattlesnake). Herpetol. Rev. 31(4): 254–255.

Kofron, C. P. 1978. Foods and habitats of aquatic snakes (Reptilia, Serpentes) in a Louisiana swamp. J. Herpetol. 12: 543–554.

——. 1979. Reproduction of aquatic snakes in south-central Louisiana. Herpetologica 35(1): 44–50.

Köhler, G. 2001. Reptilien und Amphibien Mittelamerikas, vol. 2: Schlangen. Herpeton, Offenbach, Germany. 174 pp.

Kornacker, P. M. 1999. Checklist and key to the snakes of Venezuela. Pako-Verlag, Rheinbach, Germany. 270 pp.

Kornalík, F., and Z. Vorlová. 1990. Non-specific therapy of a hemorrhagic diathesis after a bite by a young Bothrops asper (barba amarilla): a case report. Toxicon 28(12): 1497–1501.

Koslowsky, J. 1895. Batracios y reptiles de Rioja y Catamarca (Republica Argentina) recogidos durante los meses de Febrero a Mayo de 1895 (expedición del Director del Museo). Revista del Museo de La Plata 6: 357–370.

——. 1898a. Enumeración sistemática y distribución geográfica de los reptiles argentinos. Revista del Museo de La Plata 8: 161–200.

——. 1898b. Ofidios de Mato-Grosso (Brasil). Revista del Museo de La Plata 8: 3–32.

Koster, H. 1816. Travels in Brazil. London, Longman. 501 pp.

Koster, W. J. 1951. The distribution of the Gila monster in New Mexico. Herpetologica 7(3): 97–101.

Kouyoumdjian, J. A. 1990. Intracranial haemorrhage after snakebite. Mem. Inst. Butantan 52(suppl.): 45–46.

Kouyoumdjian, J. A., and C. Polizelli. 1988. Acidentes ofídicos causados por Bothrops moojeni: relato de 37 casos. Revista do Instituto de Medicina Tropical de São Paulo 30: 424–432.

——. 1989. Acidentes ofídicos causados por Bothrops moojeni: correlato do quadro clínico com o tamanho da serpente. Revista do Instituto de Medicina Tropical de São Paulo 31(2): 84–90.

Kouyoumdjian, J. A., C. Polizelli, S. M. A. Lobo, and S. M. Guimares. 1991. Fatal extradural haematoma after snake bite (Bothrops moojeni). Trans. Roy. Soc. Trop. Med. Hyg. 85: 552.

Kozloff, E. N. 1976. Plants and animals of the Pacific Northwest. University of Washington Press, Seattle. 264 pp.

Kramer, E. 1978. Typenkatalog der Schlangen des NMB, Stand 1977. Revue Suisse de Zoologie 85(3): 657–665.

Kraus, F., D. G. Mink, and W. M. Brown. 1996. Crotaline intergeneric relationships based on mitochondrial DNA sequence data. Copeia 1996(4): 763–773.

Kraus, F., and G. W. Schuett. 1980. Geographic distribution: Crotalus scutulatus scutulatus (Mojave rattlesnake). Herpetol. Rev. 11(3): 81.

Kraus, R., and F. Werner. 1931. Giftschlangen und die Serumbehandlung der Schlangenbisse. Gustav Fischer, Jena.

Kreis, H. A. 1940. Beitrage zur Kenntnis parasitische Nematoden. IX. Parasitische Nematoden aus dem Naturhistorischen Museum Basel. Zentralblatt für Bakteriologie, Parasitenkunde, Infektionskrankheiten, und Hygiene. 1. Abteilung. Originale 145(3): 163–208.

Krochmal, L., and P. C. Anderson. 1976. Copperhead bites: update on therapy. Missouri Medicine 73(4): 169–172, 178.

Kropach, C. 1971a. Sea snake (Pelamis platurus) aggregations on slicks in Panama. Herpetologica 27(2): 131–135.

——. 1971b. Another color variety of the sea snake Pelamis platurus from Panama Bay. Herpetologica 27(3): 326–327.

——. 1972. Pelamis platurus as a potential colonizer of the Caribbean Sea. Bulletin of the Biological Society of Washington 2: 267–269.

——. 1975. The yellow bellied sea snake, Pelamis platurus, in the eastern Pacific. Pp. 185–213 in W. A. Dunson (ed.), The biology of sea-snakes. University Park Press, Baltimore, Md.

Kropach, C., and J. D. Soule. 1973. An unusual association between an ectoproct and a sea snake. Herpetologica 29(1): 17–19.

Krysko, K. L., and K. R. Abdelfattah. 2002. Natural history notes: Micrurus fulvius (eastern coral snake). Prey. Herpetol. Rev. 33(1): 57–58.

Kuch, U. 1997a. Comment on the proposed conservation of the specific and subspecific names of Trigonocephalus pulcher Peters, 1863 [recte 1862] and Bothrops albocarinatus Shreve, 1934 (Reptilia, Serpentes) by the designation of a neotype for T. pulcher (Case 2921; see BZN 54: 35–38). Bulletin of Zoological Nomenclature 54: 245–249.

——. 1997b. Mimikry bei Schlangen. Reptilia 2: 25–32.

——. 1999. Notes on two cases of human envenomation by the South American colubrid snakes Philodryas olfersii latirostris Cope, 1862, and Philodryas chamissonis (Wiegmann, 1834) (Squamata: Serpentes: Colubridae). Herpetozoa 12: 11–16.

——. 2001. Geographic distribution: Bothriechis schlegelii (eyelash palm pit viper). Herpetol. Rev. 32(1): 58.

Kuch, U., F. Ayala-V., and A. Freire L. 2002. First record of Micrurus peruvianus Schmidt, 1936, from Ecuador. Herpetozoa 15(3–4): 182–183.

Kuch, U., C. Boada, F. García, J. Torres, and A. Freire. (In press.) Bothrops asper (terciopelo or equis). Diet. Herpetol. Rev.

Kuch, U., and A. Freire-Lascano. 1993a. Geographical distribution and variation of the eyelash palm-pitviper, Bothriechis schlegelii (Berthold, 1846), in Ecuador (abstract). Second World Congress of Herpetology, Adelaide, Australia, 26 Dec. 1993–6 Jan. 1994.

——. 1993b. A contribution to the knowledge of the Chocoan forest pitviper, Bothriopsis punctata (García, 1896) (abstract). Second World Congress of Herpetology, Australia, 26 Dec. 1993–6 Jan. 1994.

——. 1995a. Bemerkungen zur geographischen Verbreitung und Variabilität von Schlegels Palmen-Lansenotter, Bothriechis schlegelii (Berthold, 1846), in Ecuador. Herpetozoa 8: 49–58.

——. 1995b. Notes on morphology, reproduction and medical importance of the poorly known small-eyed lancehead, Bothrops microphthalmus Cope, 1876, in Ecuador (Squamata: Serpentes: Viperidae). Herpetozoa 8: 81–83.

——. 1998. Human envenomation from the bite of the Ecuadorian coral snake, Micrurus bocourti (Jan, 1872). Snake 28: 41–43.

Kuch, U., and A. Hohmeister. 1998. Bothriechis schlegelii (Berthold). Sauria (Berlin) 20(suppl.): 441–448.

Kuch, U., and U. Jesberger. 1993. Human envenomation from the bites of the South American colubrid snake species Philodryas baroni Berg, 1895. Snake 25: 63–65.

Kuch, U., D. Mebs, J. M. Gutiérrez, and A. Freire. 1996. Biochemical and biological characterization of Ecuadorian pitviper venoms (genera Bothriechis, Bothriopsis, Bothrops, and Lachesis). Toxicon 34: 714–717.

Kumar, V., T. A. Rejent, and W. B. Elliott. 1973. Anticholinesterase activity of elapid venoms. Toxicon 11: 131–138.

Kunkel, D. B., S. C. Curry, M. V. Vance, and P. J. Ryan. 1983–1984. Reptile envenomations. Journal of Toxicology—Clinical Toxicology 21: 503–526.

Lacépède, B. G. E. 1788–1789. Histoire naturelle des quadrupèdes ovipares et des serpents, 2 vols. Hôtel de Thou, Paris. 1178 pp.

——. 1802. The natural history of oviparous quadrupeds and serpents. Arranged and published from the papers and collections of the Count de Buffon by the Count de Lacépède, translated by Robert Kerr. T. Cadel and W. Davis, London.

——. 1804. Mémoire sur plusieurs animaux de la Nouvelle-Hollande dont la description n'a pas encore été publiée. Annales du Muséum National d'Histoire Naturelle, Paris 4(21): 184–211.

Lacerda, J. B. 1884. Leçons sur le venin des serpents du Brésil et sur la méthode de traitement des morsures venimeuses par le permanganate de potasse. Librairie Lombaerts, Rio de Janeiro. 194 pp.

Ladd, C. G., and G. G. Galbraith. 1989. Geographic distribution: *Agkistrodon c. contortrix* (southern copperhead). Herpetol. Rev. 20(1): 13.

LaGrange, R. G., and F. E. Russell. 1970. Blood platelet studies in man and rabbits following *Crotalus* envenomation. Proceedings of the Western Pharmacology Society 13: 99–105.

Lainson, R., F. P. Nascimento, and J. J. Shaw. 1991. Some new species of *Caryospora* (Apicomplexa: Eimeridae) from Brazilian snakes, and redescription of *C. jaracae* Carini, 1939. Memórias do Instituto Oswaldo Cruz (Rio de Janeiro) 86(3): 349–364.

Lainson, R., and J. J. Shaw. 1973. Coccidia of Brazilian snakes: *Isispora decipiens*, *Eimeria micruri*, *E. liophi*, and *E. leimadophi* spp. n., with redescriptions of *Caryospora brasiliensis* Carini, 1932, and *Eimeria poecilogyri* Carini, 1933. Journal of Parasitology 20(3): 358–362.

Lalung, H. de. 1934. Le serpent de la Martinique. Sa légende, ses moeurs, ses ennemis. Comment les caraïbes et les nègres soignaient ses piqûres. Laboratoires Corbière, Paris. 77 pp.

Lamar, W. W. 1997. Checklist and common names of the reptiles of the Peruvian lower Amazon. Herpetological Natural History 5(1): 73–76.

——. 1998. *Lachesis muta*: cantante y bailarin? (abstract). Primer Simpôsio. *Lachesis muta*: um desafio biológica e toxinólogico. Instituto Vital Brazil, Niteroi, Rio de Janeiro, September 1998.

——. 2003. A new species of slender coralsnake, genus *Leptomicrurus* (Serpentes: Elapidae), from Colombia. Rev. Biol. Trop. 51(1–2): 17–20.

Lamar, W. W., and M. Sasa. 2003. A new species of hognosed pitviper, genus *Porthidium* (Serpentes: Viperidae), from Costa Rica. Rev. Biol. Trop. 51(1–2): 21–24.

Lamson, G. H. 1935. The reptiles of Connecticut. Connecticut Geological and Natural History Survey Bulletin 54: 1–35.

Lanave, C., G. Preparata, C. Saccone, and G. Serio. 1984. A new method for calculating evolutionary substitution rates. Journal of Molecular Evolution 20: 86–93.

Lancini, A. R. 1962a. Una nueva especie de serpiente coral (Serpentes: Elapidae) del Perú. Publicaciones Ocasionales del Museo de Ciencias Naturales, Caracas, 2: 1–3.

——. 1962b. Un cambio de nombre para una serpiente coral (Elapidae: *Micrurus*) del Peru. Publicaciones Ocasionales del Museo de Ciencias Naturales, Caracas, 3: 1.

——. 1962c. Contribución al conocimiento de los ofidios del cordon litoral. Los ofidios de Curupao, Estado Miranda (Venezuela). Acta Biológica Venezuelica 3(11): 161–172.

——. 1962d. Notas taxonomicas sobre una pequeña colección de serpientes del Río Palmar, Estado Zulia (Venezuela). Acta Biológica Venezuelica 3(13): 195–200.

——. 1967 [dated 1966]. *Crotalus vegrandis* Klauber. Redescripción y distribución. Mem. Inst. Butantan 33(3): 725–734.

——. 1968. Las serpientes del Valle de Caracas. Estudio de Caracas, I. Ecología Vegetal, Fauna, Universidad Central de Venezuela, Caracas 1968: 297–325.

——. 1970. Los ofidios. Oficina Central de Información, Caracas. 23 pp.

——. 1978. Un nuevo record de serpiente "Mapanare" para Venezuela. Natura 65: 16–17.

——. 1979. Serpientes de Venezuela. E. Armitano, Caracas. 262 pp.

——. 1983 [dated 1982]. Serpientes de Venezuela: distribución geográfica y altitudinal de generos de serpientes en Venezuela. Mem. Inst. Butantan 46: 95–103.

Lancini, A. R., and P. M Kornacker. 1989. Die Schlangen von Venezuela. Verlag Armitano, Caracas. 381 pp.

Lande, R., and S. J. Arnold. 1983. The measurement of selection on correlated characters. Evolution 37: 1210–1226.

Landreth, H. F. 1973. Orientation and behavior of the rattlesnake, *Crotalus atrox*. Copeia 1973(1): 26–31.

Landy, M. J., D. A. Langebartel, E. O. Moll, and H. M. Smith. 1966. A collection of snakes from Volcán Tacaná, Chiapas, Mexico. Journal of the Ohio Herpetological Society 5(3): 93–101.

Langebartel, D. A., and H. M. Smith. 1954. Summary of the Norris collection of reptiles and amphibians from Sonora, Mexico. Herpetologica 10(2): 125–136.

Lanyon, L. M. 1985. Detecting internal inconsistencies in distance data. Syst. Zool. 34: 397–403.

LaPointe, J. 1953. Case report of a bite from the massasauga, *Sistrurus catenatus catenatus*. Copeia 1953(2): 128–129.

Laporta-Ferreira, I. L., and M. G. Salomão. 1991. Morphology, physiology, and toxicology of the oral gland of a tropical cochleophagous snake, *Sibynomorphus neuweidi* (Colubridae-Dipsadinae). Zoologischer Anzeiger 227: 198–208.

Lardie, R. L. 1976. Large centipede eaten by a western massasauga. Bulletin of the Oklahoma Herpetological Society 1: 40.

——. 1979. Herpetological records from northwestern Oklahoma. Herpetol. Rev. 10(1): 24–25.

——. 1999. Geographic distribution: *Agkistrodon contortrix laticinctus* (broad-banded copperhead). Herpetol. Rev. 30(2): 112.

Lardner, P. J. 1969. Diurnal and seasonal locomotory activity in the Gila monster, *Heloderma suspectum* Cope. Ph.D. dissertation, University of Arizona. 99 pp.

Larget, B., and D. L. Simon. 1999. Markov chain Monte Carlo algorithms for the Bayesian analysis of phylogenetic trees. Molecular Biology and Evolution 16: 750–759.

Larrick, J. W., J. A. Yost, and J. Kaplan. 1978. Snakebite among the Waorani Indians of eastern Ecuador. Trans. Roy. Soc. Trop. Med. Hyg. 72: 542–543.

Larrick, J. W., J. A. Yost, J. Kaplan, G. King, and J. Mayhall. 1979. Patterns of health and disease among the Waorani Indians of eastern Ecuador. Medical Anthropology 3: 147–189.

Laughlin, H. E. 1959. Stomach contents of some aquatic snakes from Lake McAlester, Pittsburg County, Oklahoma. Texas Journal of Science 11: 83–85.

Laurent, R. F., and E. M. Terán. 1981. Lista de anfibios y reptiles de la Provincia de Tucumán. Fundación Miguel Lillo, Micelanea 71: 1–15.

Laurenti, J. N. 1768. Specimen medicum exhibens Synopsin Reptilium emendatatum cum experimentis circa venena et antidota reptilium austriacorum. Joan. Thom. Trattnern, Vienna. 214 pp.

Laveran, A. 1902. Sur quelques hemogregarines des Ophidiens. Comptes Rendus de l'Académie des Sciences, Paris, 135: 1036–1040.

Lavilla, E. O., and G. J. Scrocchi. 1991. Aportes a la herpetología del Chaco argentino. I. Lista comentada de los taxa colectados por la expedición PRHERP 1985. Acta Zoológica Lilloana 40(1): 21–32.

——. 1999. Anfibios y reptiles de Tariquía. Pp. 83–92 in J. A. González, G. J. Scrocchi, and E. O. Lavilla (eds.), Relevamiento de la biodiversidad de la Reserva Nacional de Flora y Fauna Tariquía (Tarija, Bolivia). Fundación Miguel Lillo, San Miguel de Tecumán, Argentina.

Lavín-Murcio, P., and K. V. Kardong. 1995. Scents related to venom and prey as cues in the poststrike trailing behavior of rattlesnakes, *Crotalus viridis oreganus*. Herpetologica 51(1): 39–44.

Lavín-Murcio, P., B. G. Robinson, and K. V. Kardong. 1993. Cues involved in relocation of struck prey by rattlesnakes, *Crotalus viridis oreganus*. Herpetologica 49(4): 463–469.

Lawrence, W. T., A. Giannopoulos, and A. Hansen. 1996. Pitviper bites: rational management in locales in which copperheads and cottonmouths predominate. Annals of Plastic Surgery 36: 276–285.

Lawson, D. 1997 [dated 1996–1997]. Sexual dimorphism and reproduction of the pitviper *Porthidium ophryomegas* (Serpentes: Viperidae) in Guatemala. Rev. Biol. Trop. 44–45: 671–674.

Lazcano-Barrero, M. A., and A. Muñoz-Alonzo. 1989. Life history notes: *Bothrops godmani* (Godman's viper). Size. Herpetol. Rev. 20(2): 53.

Lazell, J. D., Jr. 1964. The lesser Antillean representatives of *Bothrops* and *Constrictor*. Bulletin of the Museum of Comparative Zoology 132(3): 245–273.

——. 1976. This broken archipelago. Quadrangular, New York. 260 pp.

——. 1989. Wildlife of the Florida Keys: a natural history. Island Press, Washington, D.C. 253 pp.

Leavitt, B. B. 1957. Water moccasin preys on pied-billed grebe. Wilson Bulletin 69: 112–113.

Lee, C. Y. 1972. Chemistry and pharmacology of polypeptide toxins in *Snake venoms*. Annual Review of Pharmacology 12: 265–286.

Lee, D. S. 1968. Herpetofauna associated with central Florida mammals. Herpetologica 24(1): 83–84.

Lee, J. C. 1980. An ecogeographic analysis of the herpetofauna of the Yucatan Peninsula. Miscellaneous Publications of the Museum of Natural History, University of Kansas, 67: 1–75.

——. 1996. The amphibians and reptiles of the Yucatán Peninsula. Cornell University Press, Ithaca. 500 pp.

Lee, J. R. 1996. Natural history notes: *Agkistrodon piscivorus piscivorus* (eastern cottonmouth). Coloration. Herpetol. Rev. 27(1): 22.

Lee, M. S. Y. 2000. Tree robustness and clade significance. Syst. Biol. 49: 829–836.

Leenders, T., 1995. The snakes of Rara Avis, Costa Rica, II. Pit vipers (Crotalinae). Litteratura Serpentium 15(1): 4–12.

——. 2001. A guide to amphibians and reptiles of Costa Rica. Zona Tropical, Miami. 305 pp.

Leenders, T., G. Beckers, and H. Strijbosch. 1996. Natural history notes: *Micrurus mipartitus* (NCN). Polymorphism. Herpetol. Rev. 27(1): 25.

Lehr, E. 2001. New records for amphibians and reptiles from Departamentos Pasco and Ucayali, Peru. Herpetol. Rev. 32(2): 130–132.

Leitão de Araujo, M. 1978. Notas sôbre ovos de serpentes (Boidae, Colubridae, Elapidae e Viperidae). Iheringia, Zoologia 51: 9–37.

Leitão de Araujo, M., and L. A. M. Ely. 1980. Notas sôbre a biologia de tanatofídios criados em cativeiro—segunda parte. (Ophidia—Elapidae e Viperidae). Iheringia, Zoologia 55: 9–26.

Leite, S. 1954. Cartas dos primeiros Jesuítas do Brasil, 3 vols . São Paulo, Comissão do IV Centenário da Cidade de São Paulo. 1715 pp.

Leloup, P. 1975. Observations sur la reproduction de *Bothrops moojeni* Hoge en captivité. Acta Zoologica et Pathologica Antverpiensia 62: 173–201.

Lema, T. de. 1960a. Sôbre a espécie *Bothrops cotiara* (Gomes, 1913) e sua ocorrência no estado do Rio Grande do Sul (Serpentes: Crotalidae). Iheringia, Zoologia 13: 6–10.

——. 1960b. Ampliação da descrição original de *Bothrops cotiara* (Gomes, 1913)—Serpentes: Crotalidae. Iheringia, Zoologia 13: 11–19.

——. 1960c. Tendência ao estriamento dad marcas dorsais no crotalídeos—Descrição de dois casos novos. Iheringia, Zoologia 13: 28–33.

——. 1962. Sôbre a espécie *Bothrops itapetiningae* (Boulenger, 1907) e sua ocorrência no Estado do Rio Grande do Sul, Brasil (Serpentes, Crotalidae). Iheringia, Zoologia 21: 1–12.

——. 1971a. Análise geográfica dos répteis do Río Grande do Sul. Arquivos do Museu Nacional, Rio de Janeiro, 54: 61–62.

——. 1971b. Serpentes peçonhentas do Rio Grande do Sul. Iheringia, série divulgação, 1: 25–32.

——. 1972. Sôbre *Micrurus putumayensis* Lancini, 1962 e sua ocorrência no Brasil (Serpentes, Elapidae). Iheringia, Zoologia 41: 35–58.

——. 1978a. Cobras não venenosas que matam. Natureza em revista 4: 38–46.

——. 1978b. Relato de um envenenamento por uma cobra não venenosa. Natureza em revista 1978: 62–63.

——. 1983 [dated 1982]. Fauna de serpentes da província pampeana e inter-relações com as provincias limitrofes. Mem. Inst. Butantan 46: 173–182.

——. 1987. Estriamento em *Bothrops alternatus* (Duméril, Bibron, et Duméril, 1854) (Serpentes, Viperidae, Crotalinae). Acta Biologica Leopoldensia 9(2): 241–244.

——. 1989. A nomenclatura vulgar das espécies de serpentes ocorrentes no Estado Rio Grande do Sul, Brasil sul, e a proposição de sua unificação (Reptilia, Serpentes). Acta Biologica Leopoldensia 11(1): 25–46.

Lema, T. de, M. L. Araujo, and A. C. P. Azevedo. 1983. Contribução para o conhecimento da alimentação e do modo alimentar de serpentes do Brasil. Comunicaciones Museo Ciências Pontifícia Universidade Católica do Rio Grande do Sul 26: 41–121.

Lema, T. de, and A. C. P. Azevedo. 1969. Ocorrência de *Micrurus decoratus* (Jan) no Rio Grande do Sul, Brasil (Serpentes, Elapidae). Iheringia, Zoologia 37: 113–117.

Lema, T. de, and M. E. Fabián-Beurmann. 1977. Levantamento preliminar dos répteis da região da fronteira Brasil–Uruguai. Iheringia, Zoologia 50: 61–92.

Lema, T. de, M. E. Fabián-Beurmann, M. Leitão de Araujo, M. L. M. Alves, and M. I. Vieira. 1980. Lista de répteis encontrados na região da Grande Pôrto Alegre, Estado do Río Grande do Sul, Brasil. Iheringia, Zoologia 55: 27–36.

Lema, T. de, and M. Leitão de Araujo. 1980. Sôbre *Bothrops jararacussu* Lacerda, 1884, do extremo sul do Brasil e sua ocorrência no Estado do Rio Grande do Sul (Ophidia, Viperidae). Iheringia, Zoologia 56: 63–70.

Lemos-Espinal, J. A., D. Auth, D. Chiszar, and H. M. Smith. 2002a. Year 2000 snakes from Chihuahua, Mexico. Bull. Chicago Herpetol. Soc. 37(3): 51–55.

——. 2002b. Year 2001 snakes from Chihuahua, Mexico. Bull. Chicago Herpetol. Soc. 37(10): 180–182.

Lemos-Espinal, J. A., D. Chiszar, and H. M. Smith. 1994. The distribution of the prairie rattlesnake (*Crotalus v. viridis*) in Mexico. Bull. Maryland Herpetol. Soc. 30(4): 143–148.

——. 2000a. Geographic distribution: *Crotalus lepidus lepidus* (mottled rock rattlesnake). Herpetol. Rev. 31(2): 113.

Lemos-Espinal, J., H. M. Smith, R. E. Ballinger, G. R. Smith, and D. Chiszar. 1997. A herpetological collection from northern Chihuahua, Mexico. Bull. Chicago Herpetol. Soc. 32(9): 198–201.

Lemos-Espinal, J., H. M. Smith, and D. Chiszar. 2000b. New distributional and variational data on some species of snakes from Chihuahua, Mexico. Bull. Chicago Herpetol. Soc. 35(2): 19–24.

León, N. 1889. Nombres de animales en Tarasco y Castellano, con su correspondiente clasificación cientifica. Anales del Museo Michoacano 2: 186–192.

Leopold, A. S. 1950. Vegetation zones of Mexico. Ecology 31(4): 507–518.

——. 1959. Wildlife of Mexico, the game birds and mammals. University of California Press, Berkeley. 568 pp.

——. 1967. Grizzlies of the Sierra del Nido. Pacific Discovery 20(5): 30–32.

Leopold, R. S., G. S. Huber, and R. H. Kathan. 1957. An evaluation of the mechanical treatment of snake bite. *Military Medicine* 120: 414–416.

LeRay, W. J. 1930. The rattlesnake *Sistrurus catenatus* in Ontario. Canadian Field Naturalist 44(9): 201–203.

Lescure, J., and J. P. Gasc. 1986. Partage de l'espace forestier par les amphibiens et les reptiles en amazonie du nord-ouest. Caldasia 15(71–75): 705–723.

Levine, N. D. 1980. Some corrections of coccidian (Apicomplexa: Protozoa) nomenclature. Journal of Parasitology 66(5): 830–834.

Levinson, S. R., M. H. Evans, and F. Groves. 1976. A neurotoxic component of the venom from Blanding's tree snake (*Boiga blandingi*). Toxicon 14: 307–312.

Leviton, A. E. 1953. Catalogue of the amphibian and reptile types in the Natural History Museum of Stanford University. Herpetologica 8: 121–132.

Leviton, A. E., and B. H. Banta. 1964. Midwinter reconnaissance of the herpetofauna of the cape region of Baja California, Mexico. Proc. California Acad. Sci., 4th ser., 30(7): 127–156.

Leviton, A. E., R. H. Gibbs Jr., E. Heal, and C. E. Dawson. 1985. Standards in herpetology and ichthyology. Part I. Standard symbolic codes for institutional resource collections in herpetology and ichthyology. Copeia 1985(3): 802–832.

Lewis, J. V. 1994. Rattlesnake bite of the face: case report and review of the literature. American Surgeon 60: 681–682.

Lewis, P. O. 2001. Phylogenetic systematics turns over a new leaf. Trends in Ecology and Evolution 16: 30–37.

Lewis, T. H. 1949. Dark coloration in the reptiles of the Tularosa Malpais, New Mexico. Copeia 1949(3): 181–184.

———. 1950. The herpetofauna of the Tularosa Basin and Organ Mountains of New Mexico with some ecological features of the Chihuahuan desert. Herpetologica 6(1): 1–10.

———. 1951. Dark coloration in the reptiles of the Malpais of the Mexican border. Copeia 1951(4): 311–312.

Leybold, F. 1873. Excursión a las pampas argentinas. Hojas de mi diario. Imprenta Nacional, Santiago de Chile. 107 pp.

Leydig, F. 1872. Die in Deutschland lebenden Arten der Saurier. Laupp, Tübingen.

Leynaud, G. C., and E. H. Bucher. 1999. La fauna de serpientes del Chaco Sudamericano: diversidad, distribución geográfica y estado de conservación. Academia Nacional de Ciencias (Córdoba, Argentina) Miscelanea 98: 1–46.

Li, Q., T. R. Colberg, and C. L. Ownby. 1993. Purification and characterization of two high molecular weight hemorrhagic toxins from Crotalus viridis viridis venom using monoclonal antibodies. Toxicon 31: 711–722.

Liais, E. 1872. Climats, géologie, faune, et géographie botanique de Brésil. Paris. 640 pp.

Lidikay, C. E. 1997. Biochemistry of helodermatid venom. Stanislaus Journal of Biochemical Reviews 1997 (May), 4 pp. [On-line publication.]

Lidth de Jeude, T. W. van. 1887. On a collection of reptiles and fishes from the West Indies. Notes Leyden Mus. 9: 129–139.

Liem, K. F., H. Marx, and G. B. Rabb. 1971. The viperid snake Azemiops: its comparative cephalic anatomy and phylogenetic position in relation to Viperinae and Crotalinae. Fieldiana: Zoology 59: 65–126.

Lieske, H. 1963. Symptomatik und Therapie von Giftschlangenbissen. Pp. 121–160 in Die Giftschlangen der Erde. N. G. Elwert Universitäts un Verlags-Buchhandlung, Marburg.

Lillegraven, J. A., M. J. Kraus, and T. M. Brown. 1979. Paleogeography of the world of the Mesozoic. Pp. 277–308 in J. A. Lillegraven, Z. Kielan-Jaworowska, and W. A. Clemens (eds.), Mesozoic mammals: the first two-thirds of mammalian history. University of California Press, Berkeley.

Lillywhite, H. B. 1982. Cannibalistic carrion ingestion by the rattlesnake, Crotalus viridis. J. Herpetol. 16(1): 95.

Lind, A. J., and H. H. Welsh. 1994. Ontogenetic changes in foraging behaviour and habitat use by the Oregon garter snake, Thamnophis atratus hydrophilus. Animal Behaviour 48: 1261–1273.

Linder, A. D., and E. Fichter. 1977. The amphibians and reptiles of Idaho. Idaho State University Press, Pocatello. 78 pp.

Lindner, D. 1962. Feeding observations of Micruroides. Bulletin of the Philadelphia Herpetological Society 10(2–3): 31.

Lindsay, G. E. 1962. The Belvedere expedition to the Gulf of California. Trans. San Diego Soc. Nat. Hist. 13(1): 1–44.

———. 1964. Sea of Cortez expedition of the California Academy of Sciences. Proc. California Acad. Sci., 4th ser., 30(11): 211–242.

———. 1966. The Gulf Islands expedition of 1966. Proc. California Acad. Sci., 4th ser., 30(16): 309–355.

Lindsey, D. 1985. Controversy in snake bite—time for a controlled appraisal. Journal of Trauma—Injury, Infection, and Critical Care 25: 462–463.

Lindsey, P. 1979. Combat behavior in the dusky pygmy rattlesnake, Sistrurus miliarius barbouri, in captivity. Herpetol. Rev. 19(3): 93.

Lindström, L., R. V. Alatalo, J. Mappes, M. Riipi, and L. Vertainen. 1999. Can aposematic signals evolve by gradual change? Nature 397: 249–251.

Liner, E. A. 1964. Notes on four small herpetological collections from Mexico. I. Introduction, turtles and snakes. Southwest. Nat. 8(4): 221–227.

———. 1997. The herpetofauna of Terrebonne Parish, Louisiana. Bull. Chicago Herpetol. Soc. 32(8): 169–172.

Liner, E. A., and A. H. Chaney. 1973. Life history: Micrurus fulvius tenere. HISS News Journal 1(6): 186.

———. 1986. Natural history notes: Crotalus lepidus lepidus (mottled rock rattlesnake). Reproduction. Herpetol. Rev. 17(4): 89.

Liner, E. A., R. M. Johnson, and A. H. Chaney. 1976. Amphibian and reptile records and range extensions for Mexico. Herpetol. Rev. 7(4): 177.

Liner, E. A., and R. E. Olson. 1973. Adults of the lizard Sceloporus torquatus binocularis Dunn. Herpetologica 29(1): 53–55.

Link, G. 1951. Records of the coral snake Micrurus fulvius in Indiana and Ohio. Natural History Miscellanea 92: 1–5.

Linnaeus, C. 1746. Mus. Adolpho-Fridericianum, quod . . . Subpraesidio . . . C. Linnaei . . . submittit L. Balk . . . . Homiae, 48 pp.

———. 1754. Hans Maj:ts Adolf Frideriks vår allernådigste konungs naturalie samling innehållande sällsynte och främmande djur, som bevaras på kongl. lust-slottet Ulriksdahl beskrefne och afritade samt på nådig befallning utgifne af Carl Linnaeus. Stockholm.

———. 1758. Systema naturae per regna tria naturae, secundum classes, ordines, genera, species cum characteribus, differentiis, synonymis, locis. 10th ed. Stockholm, Laurentii Salvii. 826 pp. [Reprinted 1956 by Unwin Brothers, London.]

———. 1766. Systema naturae per regna tria naturae, secundum classes, ordines, genera, species cum characteribus, differentiis, synonymis, locis. 12th ed. Stockholm, Laurentii Salvii. 532 pp.

Linsdale, J. M. 1927. Amphibians and reptiles of Doniphan County, Kansas. Copeia 1927(164): 75–81.

———. 1932. Amphibians and reptiles from lower California. University of California Publications in Zoology 38(6): 345–386.

———. 1940. Amphibians and reptiles in Nevada. Proceedings of the American Academy of Arts and Sciences 73(8): 197–257.

Linzey, D. W. 1972. Snakes of Alabama. Strode Publishers, Huntsville, Ala. 136 pp.

Linzey, D. W., and M. J. Clifford. 1981. Snakes of Virginia. University Press of Virginia, Charlottesville. 173 pp.

Linzey, D. W., and A. V. Linzey. 1968. Mammals of the Great Smoky Mountains National Park. Journal of the Elisha Mitchell Scientific Society 84(3): 384–414.

Lira-da-Silva, R. M., L. L. Casais-e-Silva, I. Biondi de Queiroz, and T. Brazil Nunes. 1994. Contribuição a biologia de serpentes da Bahia, Brasil. I. Vivíparas. Revista Brasileira de Zoologia 11(2): 187–193.

Litovitz, T. L., W. Klein-Schwartz, G. C. Rodgers, D. J. Cobaugh, J. Youniss, J. C. Omslaer, M. E. May, A. D. Woolf, and B. E. Benson. 2002. 2001 annual report of the American Association of Poison Control Centers Toxic Exposure Surveillance System. American Journal of Emergency Medicine 20: 391–452.

Little, E. L., Jr. 1940. Amphibians and reptiles of the Roosevelt Reservoir Area, Arizona. Copeia 1940(4): 260–265.

Little, E. L., Jr., and J. G. Keller. 1937. Amphibians and reptiles of the Jornada Experimental Range, New Mexico. Copeia 1937(4): 216–222.

Liu, C.-Z., H.-C. Peng, and T.-F. Huang. 1995. Crotavirin, a potent platelet aggregation inhibitor purified from the venom of the snake Crotalus viridis. Toxicon 33(10): 1289–1298.

Livezey, R. L. 1949. An aberrant pattern of Agkistrodon mokeson austrinus. Herpetologica 5(4): 93.

Livezey, R. L., and R. S. Peckham. 1953. Some snakes from San Marcos, Guatemala. Herpetologica 8(4): 175–177.

Lizano, S., Y. Angulo, B. Lomonte, J. W. Fox, G. Lambeau, M. Lazdunski, and J. M. Gutiérrez. 2000. Two phospholipase A_2 inhibitors from the plasma of Cerrophidion (Bothrops) godmani which selectively inhibit two different group-II phospholipase A_2 myotoxins from its own venom: isolation, molecular cloning and biological properties. Biochemical Journal 346(3): 631–639.

Lobeck, A. K. 1948. The physiographic provinces of North America [map]. Geographical Press, Columbia University, New York.

Lockington, W. N. 1880. List of California reptiles and batrachia collected by Mr. Dunn and Mr. W. J. Fisher in 1876. American Naturalist 14: 295–296.

Loeb, L., C. L. Alsberg, E. Cooke, E. P. Corson-White, M. S. Fleisher, H. Fox, T. S. Githens, S. Leopold, M. K. Meyers, M. E. Rehfuss, D. Rivas, and L. Tuttle. 1913. The venom of *Heloderma*. Publications of Carnegie Institution (Washington, D.C.) 177: 1–244.

Loennberg, E. 1894. Notes on reptiles and batrachians collected in Florida in 1892 and 1893. Proceedings of the U.S. National Museum 17(1003): 317–339.

———. 1896. Linnean type-specimens of birds, reptiles, batrachians, and fishes in the Zoological Museum of the Royal University in Upsala. Bihang till Kongliga Svenska Vetenskaps-Akademiens Handlingar 22, 4(1): 1–45.

———. 1902. On a collection of snakes from northwestern Argentina and Bolivia containing new species. Annals and Magazine of Natural History 7: 457–462.

Loewen, S. L. 1947a. Notes on a rattlesnake in captivity. Turtox News 25: 53–54.

———. 1947b. On some reptilian cestodes of the genus *Oochoristica* (Anoplocephalidae). Transactions of the American Microscopical Society 59: 511—518.

Logier, E. B. S. 1958. The snakes of Ontario. University of Toronto Press, Toronto. 94 pp.

Logier, E. B. S., and G. C. Toner. 1955. Check-list of the amphibians and reptiles of Canada and Alaska. Contributions of the Royal Ontario Museum of Zoology and Palaeontology 41: 1–88.

Lohoefener, R., and R. Altig. 1983. Mississippi herpetology. Mississippi State University Research Center National Space Technology Laboratories Bulletin 1: 1–66.

Lokke, J. 1985. A question of parental care in the timber rattlesnake, *Crotalus horridus*. Nebraska Herpetological Newsletter 6: 4–5.

Lomonte, B., L. Cerdas, A. Solórzano, and S. Martínez. 1989. El suero de neonatos de *Clelia clelia* (Serpentes: Colubridae) neutraliza la acción hemorrágica del veneno de *Bothrops asper* (Serpentes: Viperidae). Rev. Biol. Trop. 38: 325–326.

Lomonte, B., J. A. Gene, J. M. Gutiérrez, and L. Cerdas. 1983. Estudio comparativo de los venenos de serpeinte cascabel (*Crotalus durissus durissus*) de ejemplares adultos y recien nacidos. Toxicon 21: 379–384.

Lomonte, B., J. Lundgren, B. Johansson, and U. Bagge. 1994. The dynamics of local tissue damage induced by *Bothrops asper* snake venom and myotoxin II on the mouse cremaster muscle: an intravital and electron microscopic study. Toxicon 32: 41–55.

Lomonte, B., A. Tarkowski, and L. A. Hanson. 1993. Host response to *Bothrops asper* snake venom. Analysis of edema formation, inflammatory cells and cytokine release in a mouse model. Inflammation 17(2): 93–105.

Long, E. G. 1974. The serpent's tale. Reptiles and amphibians of St. Lucia. Iouanaloa, ser. 2, University of West Indies Extra-Mural Dept., St. Lucia. 46 pp.

Loomis, R. B. 1948. Notes on the herpetology of Adams County, Iowa. Herpetologica 4(4): 121–122,

———. 1951. Increased rate of ecdysis in *Crotalus* caused by chiggers damaging a facial pit. Herpetologica 7: 83–84.

Lopes, R. A., M. G. Contrera, J. R. da Costa, S. O. Petenusci, and J. S. Lima-Verde. 1982. Les glands salivaires de *Philodryas patagoniensis* Girard, 1857 (Serpentes: Colubridae). Etude morphologique, morphometrique, et histochimique. Archives d'Anatomie Microscopique et de Morphologie Experimentale 71: 175–182.

Lopez, M., L. G. Foscarini, J. M. Alvares, I. Diniz Filho, U. D. Marra, and N. P. M. M. Procópio. 1972. Traitemento intensivo das complicações do acidente ofídico. Revista Medica de Minas Gerais 23: 107–112.

López-Luna, M. A., R. C. Vogt, and M. A. de la Torre-Loranca. 1999. A new species of montane pitviper from Veracruz, Mexico. Herpetologica 55(3): 382–389.

———. 2002. Biochemistry and pharmacology of Colubrid snake venoms. Journal of Toxicology—Toxin Reviews 21 (1–2): 43–83.

LoVecchio, F., and D. M. DeBus. 2001. Snakebite envenomation in children: a 10-year retrospective review. Wilderness and Environmental Medicine 12: 184–189.

Loveridge, A. 1928a. Note on *Agkistrodon bilineatus* Günther. Bull. Antivenin Inst. Am. 2(2): 52.

———. 1928b. On *Bothrops lansbergii* (Schlegel). Bull. Antivenin Inst. Am. 2(3): 64–65.

———. 1938. Food of *Micrurus fulvius fulvius*. Copeia 1938(4): 201–202.

———. 1944. Cannibalism in the common coral snake. Copeia 1944(4): 254.

Lowe, C. H., Jr. 1942. Notes on the mating of desert rattlesnakes. Copeia 1942(4): 261–262.

———. 1948a. Effects of venom of *Micruroides* upon *Xantusia vigilis*. Herpetologica 4(4): 136.

———. 1948b. Territorial behavior in snakes and the so-called courtship dance. Herpetologica 4(4): 129–135.

———. 1955. The eastern limit of the Sonoran Desert in the United States with additions to the known herpetofauna of New Mexico. Ecology 36: 343–345.

——— (ed.). 1964. The vertebrates of Arizona. University of Arizona Press, Tucson. 259 pp.

Lowe, C. H., Jr., and H. P. Limbacher. 1961. The treatment of poisonous bites and stings. II: Arizona coral snake and Gila monster bite. Arizona Medicine 18: 128–131.

Lowe, C. H., Jr., and K. S. Norris. 1950. Aggressive behavior in male sidewinders, *Crotalus cerastes*, with a discussion of aggressive behavior and territoriality in snakes. Chicago Academy of Sciences, Natural History Miscellanea 66: 1–13.

———. 1954. Analysis of the herpetofauna of Baja California, Mexico. Trans. San Diego Soc. Nat. Hist. 12(4): 47–64.

———. 1955. Analysis of the herpetofauna of Baja California, Mexico. III. New and revived reptilian subspecies of Isla de San Estéban, Gulf of California, Sonora, Mexico, with notes on other satellite islands of Isla Tiburón. Herpetologica 11(2): 89–96.

Lowe, C. H., Jr., C. R. Schwalbe, and T. B. Johnson. 1986. The venomous reptiles of Arizona. Arizona Game and Fish Department, Phoenix. 115 pp.

Lowell, J. A. 1957. A bite by a sidewinder rattlesnake. Herpetologica 13(2): 135–136.

Lucas, R. S., and J. V. Vindum. 2000. New county records from Colusa, Glenn, Pumas, and Yuba Counties, Mendocino and Plumas National Forests, California. Herpetol. Rev. 31(3): 194.

Luckert, K. W. 2001. Serpents and snakes. Pp. 138–139 in D. Carrasco (ed.), The Oxford encyclopaedia of Meso-American cultures, vol. 3. Oxford University Press, Oxford.

Ludlow, M. E. 1981. Observations on *Crotalus v. viridis* (Rafinesque) and the herpetofauna of the Ken-Caryl Ranch, Jefferson County, Colorado. Herpetol. Rev. 12(2): 50–52.

Ludwig, M., and H. Rahn. 1943. Sperm storage and copulatory adjustments in the prairie rattlesnake. Copeia 1943(1): 15–18.

Luederwalt, H., and J. P. Fonseca. 1923. A Ilha de Alcatrazes. Revista do Museu Paulista 13: 441–512.

Luján-Medina, F. 1973. Nota sobre *Bothrops pictus* Tschudi. Rebiol 2(2): 191–201.

Lumholtz, C. [1902] 1987. Unknown Mexico, 2 vols. Scribner's, New York. 1120 pp. Reprint, Dover, New York.

Luna-Medina, L. E. 1992. Icaros: magic melodies among the mestizo shamans of the Peruvian Amazon. Pp. 231–253 in E. J. Matteson Langdon and G. Baer (eds.), Portals of power: shamanism in South America. University of New Mexico Press, Albuquerque.

Luna-Reyes, R. 1997. Distribución de la herpetofauna por tipos de vegetación en el polígono I de la Reserva de la Biosfera "El Triunfo," Chiapas, Mexico. Tésis, Universidad Nacional Autónoma de México. 144 pp.

Lutterschmidt, W. I. 1992. Geographic distribution: *Crotalus horridus* (timber rattlesnake). Herpetol. Rev. 23(1): 26.

Lutz, A., and O. de Mello. 1922. *Elaps ezequieli* e *Rhinostoma bimaculatum*, cobras novas do estado de Minas Geraes. Memórias do Instituto Oswaldo Cruz (Rio de Janeiro) 15: 235–239.

——. 1923. Duas novas espécies de colubrideos brasileiros. Folletos Medicos (Rio de Janeiro) 4: 2–3.

Luykx, P., J. B. Slowinski, and J. R. McCranie. 1992. The karyotype of the coral snake *Micrurus ruatanus*. Amphibia-Reptilia 13(3): 289–292.

Lyman, V. A. 1949. Incidence of rattlesnakes in Panama. Herpetologica 5(2): 44.

Lynch, J. D., and H. M. Smith. 1965. New or unusual amphibians and reptiles from Oaxaca, Mexico. I. Herpetologica 21(3): 168–177.

——. 1966. New or unusual amphibians and reptiles from Oaxaca, Mexico. II. Trans. Kansas Acad. Sci. 69(1): 58>–75.

Lynn, W. G. 1936. Reptile records from Stafford County, Virginia. Copeia 1936(3): 169–171.

Lyon, M. W., Jr., and C. A. Bishop. 1936. Bite of the prairie rattlesnake *Sistrurus catenatus* Raf. Proceedings of the Indiana Academy of Science 45: 253–256.

Lyons, W. J. 1971. Profound thrombocytopenia associated with *Crotalus ruber ruber* envenomation: a clinical case. Toxicon 9: 237–240.

Mabee, P. M. 2000. The usefulness of ontogeny in interpreting morphological characters. Pp. 84–114 in J. J. Wiens (ed.), Phylogenetic analysis of morphological data. Smithsonian Institution Press, Washington, D.C.

Macartney, J. M. 1985. The ecology of the northern Pacific rattlesnake, *Crotalus viridis oreganus*, in British Columbia. Master's thesis, University of Victoria.

——. 1989. Diet of the northern Pacific rattlesnake, *Crotalus viridis oreganus*, in British Columbia. Herpetologica 45(3): 299–304.

Macartney, J. M., and P. T. Gregory. 1988. Reproductive biology of female rattlesnakes (*Crotalus viridis*) in British Columbia. Copeia 1988(1): 47–57.

Macartney, J. M., P. T. Gregory, and M. B. Charland. 1990. Growth and sexual maturity of the western rattlesnake, *Crotalus viridis*, in British Columbia. Copeia 1990(2): 528–542.

Macartney, J. M., P. T. Gregory, and K. W. Larsen. 1988. A tabular survey of data on movements and home ranges of snakes. J. Herpetol. 22(1): 61–73.

Macartney, J. M., K. W. Larsen, and P. T. Gregory. 1989. Body temperatures and movements of hibernating snakes, *Crotalus* and *Thamnophis*, and thermal gradients of natural hibernacula. Canadian Journal of Zoology 67(1): 108–114.

MacDougall, T. 1971. The Chima wilderness. Explorers Journal 49(2): 86–103.

Machado, J. C., and G. Rosenfeld. 1971. Achados anátomo-patológicos en necropsia de paciente falecido por enbenenamento elapídico. Mem. Inst. Butantan 35: 41–43.

Machado, O. 1945a. Estudo comparativo das Elapideas do Brasil. Boletim Instituto Vital Brazil 5(2): 37–46.

——. 1945b. Estudo comparativo das Crotalideas do Brasil. Boletim Instituto Vital Brazil 5(2): 47–66.

——. 1945c. Variacões do desenho da *Bothrops jararaca*. Boletim Instituto Vital Brazil 5(2): 75–76.

Mackessy, S. P. 1985. Fractionation of red diamond rattlesnake (*Crotalus ruber ruber*) venom: protease, phosphodiesterase, L-amino acid oxidase activities and effects of metal ions and inhibitors on protease activity. Toxicon 23: 337–340.

——. 1988. Venom ontogeny in the Pacific rattlesnakes *Crotalus viridis helleri* and *C. v. oreganus*. Copeia 1988(1): 92–101.

——. 1993. Fibrinogenolytic proteases from the venoms of juvenile and adult northern Pacific rattlesnakes (*Crotalus viridis oreganus*). Comp. Biochem. Physiol. B 106(1): 181–189.

——. 1996. Characterization of the major metalloprotease isolated from the venom of the northern Pacific rattlesnake, *Crotalus viridis oreganus*. Toxicon 34(11–12): 1277–1285.

——. 1998. A survey of the herpetofauna of southeastern Colorado with a focus on the current status of two candidates for protected species status: the massasauga rattlesnake and the Texas horned lizard. Final report to the Colorado Division of Wildlife. Unpublished report.

——. 2002. Biochemistry and pharmacology of colubrid snake venoms. Journal of Toxicology—Toxin Reviews 21(1–2): 43–83.

Mackessy, S. P., J. Hobert, R. Donoho, C. Montgomery, and K. Waldron. 1996. Geographic distribution: *Sistrurus catenatus* (massasauga). Herpetol. Rev. 27(1): 36.

Maclean, W. P. 1968. A case of intersexuality in *Bothrops moojeni* Hoge. Copeia 1968(1): 170.

Maclean, W. P., R. Kellner, and H. Dennis. 1977. Island lists of West Indian amphibians and reptiles. Smithsonian Herpetological Information Service 40: 1–47.

Macphail, N. P. 1929. A case report. Bull. Antivenin Inst. Am. 2(4): 81–82.

Maeda, N., N. Tamiya, T. R. Pattabhiraman, and F. E. Russell. 1978. Some chemical properties of the venom of the rattlesnake, *Crotalus viridis helleri*. Toxicon 16: 431–441.

Magalhães, M. R., F. E. Costa Paulino, and N. Jorge da Silva Jr. 1991. Geographic distribution: *Bothrops alternatus* (urutu). Herpetol. Rev. 22(2): 66–67.

Magalhães, O. 1922. Contribuição para o estudo dos ophidios brasileiros. Folletos Medicos (Rio de Janeiro) 3(11): 81–82.

——. 1925. Contribuição para o estudo dos ophidios brasileiros (1). Memórias do Instituto Oswaldo Cruz (Rio de Janeiro) 18: 151–155.

——. 1958. Campanha antiofídica em Minas Gerais. Memórias do Instituto Oswaldo Cruz (Rio de Janeiro) 56(2): 291–371.

Magalhães, R. A., M. M. F. Ribeiro, N. A. de Rezende, and C. F. S. Amaral. 1986. Rabdomióilise secundária a acidente ofídico crotálico (*Crotalus durissus terrificus*). Revista do Instituto de Medicina Tropical de São Paulo 28: 228–233.

Maguiña, C., C. Henríquez, L. Ilquimiche, R. Mostorino, E. Gotuzzo, P. Legua, J. Echevarría, and C. Seas. 1998. Ofidismo por *Bothrops pictus* en el Hospital Nacional Cayetano Heredia: estudio prospectivo de 23 casos. Folia Dermatológica Peruana 9(1–2): 41–48.

Mahaney, P. A. 1997a. Natural history notes: *Crotalus pricei* (twin-spotted rattlesnake). Reproduction. Herpetol. Rev. 28(4): 205.

——. 1997b. Taxon management account: twin-spotted rattlesnake *Crotalus pricei* ssp. American Zoo and Aquarium Association Snake Advisory Group. 9 pp.

Mahendra, B. 1938. Some remarks on the phylogeny of the Ophidia. Anatomischer Anzeiger 86: 321–368.

Malasit, P., D. A. Warrell, P. Chanthavanich, C. Viravan, J. Mongkolsapaya, B. Singhthong, and C. Supich. 1986. Prediction, prevention, and mechanism of early (anaphylactic) antivenom reactions in victims of snakebites. British Medical Journal 292: 17–20.

Malcolm, S. B. 1990. Mimicry: status of a classical evolutionary paradigm. Trends in Ecology and Evolution 5: 57–61.

Malhotra, A., and R. S. Thorpe. 1997. New perspectives on the evolution of South-East Asian pit-vipers (genus *Trimeresurus*) from molecular studies. Pp. 115–118 in R. S. Thorpe, W. Wüster, and A. Malhotra (eds.), Venomous snakes: ecology, evolution, and snakebite. Clarendon Press, Oxford.

——. 2000. A phylogeny of the *Trimeresurus* group of pitvipers: new evidence from a mitochondrial gene tree. Molecular Phylogenetics and Evolution 16: 199–211.

Malkin, B. 1956. Seri ethnozoology: A preliminary report. Davidson Journal of Anthropology 2(1): 73–83.

——. 1958. Cora ethnozoology, herpetological knowledge; a bioecological and cross cultural approach. Anthropological Quarterly 31: 73–90.

——. 1962. Seri ethnology. Occasional Papers of the Idaho State College Museum 7: 1–59.

Mallet, J. 1989. The genetics of warning colour in Peruvian hybrid zones of *Heliconius erato* and *H. melpomene*. Proceedings of the Royal Society of London B 236: 163–185.

——. 1993. Speciation, raciation, and color pattern evolution in *Heliconious* butterflies: evidence from hybrid zones. Pp. 226–260 in R. G. Harrison (ed.), Hybrid zones and the evolutionary process. Oxford University Press, New York.

——. 1999. Causes and consequences of a lack of coevolution in Müllerian mimicry. Evolutionary Ecology 13: 777–806.

——. 2001. Mimicry: an interface between psychology and evolution. Proceedings of the National Academy of Sciences 98: 8928–8930.

Mallet, J., and N. H. Barton. 1989. Strong natural selection in a warning color hybrid zone. Evolution 43: 421–431.

Mallet, J., N. Barton, G. Lamas M., J. Santisteban C., M. Muedas M., and H. Eeley. 1990. Estimates of selection and gene flow from measures of cline width and linkage disequilibrium in *Heliconius* hybrid zones. Genetics 124: 921–936.

Mallet, J., and L. E. Gilbert. 1995. Why are there so many mimicry rings? correlations between habitat, behaviour and mimicry in *Heliconius* butterflies. Biological Journal of the Linnean Society 55: 159–180.

Mallet, J., and M. Joron. 1999. Evolution of diversity in warning color and mimicry: polymorphisms, shifting balance, and speciation. Annual Review of Ecology and Systematics 30: 201–233.

Mallet, J., W. O. McMillan, and C. D. Jiggins. 1998. Mimicry and warning color at the boundary between species and races. Pp. 390–403 in S. Berlocher and D. Howard (eds.), Endless forms: species and speciation. Oxford University Press, New York.

Mallet, J., and M. C. Singer. 1987. Individual selection, kin selection, and the shifting balance in the evolution of warning colours: the evidence from butterflies. Biological Journal of the Linnean Society 32: 337–350.

Malnate, E. V. 1944. Notes on South Carolinian reptiles. Am. Midl. Nat. 32: 728–731.

——. 1971. A catalog of primary types in the herpetological collections of the Academy of Natural Sciences, Philadelphia (ANSP). Proc. Acad. Nat. Sci. Philadelphia 123: 345–375.

——. 1990. A review and comparison of hemipenial structure in the genus *Agkistrodon* (sensu lato). Pp. 583–588 in H. K. Gloyd and R. Conant (eds.), Snakes of the *Agkistrodon* complex: a monographic review. Society for the Study of Amphibians and Reptiles, Ithaca, N.Y. 614 pp.

Mamonov, G. 1977. Case report of envenomation by the mountain racer *Coluber ravergieri* in USSR. Snake 9(1): 27–28.

Mancheno-V., F., and L. Vera-M. Mordeduras de serpientes. Incidencia de 62 casos en el Hospital Santo Domingo de los Colorados, Período Octubre 1987–Octubre 1988. Mimeograph.

Manion, S. 1968. *Crotalus willardi*—the Arizona ridge-nosed rattlesnake. Herpetology 2(3): 27–30.

Mankau, S. K., and E. A. Widmer. 1977. Prevalence of Mesocestoides (Eucestoda: Mesocestoididea) Tetrathyridia in Southern California reptiles with notes on the pathology in the Crotalidae. Japanese Journal of Parasitology 26(4): 256–259.

Manning, B., M. Galbo, and G. Klapman. 1999. First report of a symptomatic South American false water cobra envenomation (abstract 72). Journal of Toxicology—Clinical Toxicology 37: 613.

Manning, F. B. 1923. Hearing in rattlesnakes. Journal of Comparative Psychology 3(4): 241–247.

Manzani, P. R., and C. Arzabe. 1995. Geographic distribution: *Bothrops atrox* (common lancehead). Herpetol. Rev. 26(4): 209.

Manzani, P. R., R. A. Moreno, and M. N. Mattar. 1997. Geographic distribution: *Bothrops fonsecai* (Fonseca's lancehead). Herpetol. Rev. 28(4): 210.

Manzanilla Puppo, J., A. Fernández-Badillo, and R. Visbal García. 1996. Fauna del Parque Nacional Henri Pittier, Venezuela: composición y distribución de los reptiles. Acta Científica Venezolana 47: 191–204.

Mao, S. H., and B. Y. Chen. 1980. Sea snakes of Taiwan. National Science Council Spec. Pub. No. 4., Taipei. 64 pp.

Mao, S. H., B. Y. Chen, and H. M. Chang. 1977. The evolutionary relationships of sea snakes suggested by immunological cross-reactivity of transferrins. Comp. Biochem. Physiol. A 57: 403–406.

Mao, S. H., B. Y. Chen, F. Y. Yin, and Y. W. Guo. 1983. Immunotaxonomic relationships of sea snakes to terrestrial elapids. Comp. Biochem. Physiol. A 74: 869–872.

Mao, S. H., H. C. Dessauer, and B. Y. Chen. 1978. Fingerprint correspondence of hemoglobins and the relationships of sea snakes. Comp. Biochem. Physiol. B 59: 353–361.

Maple, W. T. 1968. The overwintering adaptations of *Sistrurus catenatus catenatus* in northeastern Ohio. Master's thesis, Kent State University. 64 pp.

Maple, W. T., and L. P. Orr. 1968. Overwintering adaptations of *Sistrurus c. catenatus* in northeastern Ohio. J. Herpetol. 2: 179–180.

March, D. D. H. 1928a. Field notes on barba amarilla (*Bothrops atrox*). Bull. Antivenin Inst. Am. 1(4): 92–97.

——. 1928b. Field notes on the Neotropical rattlesnake (*Crotalus terrificus*). Bull. Antivenin Inst. Am. 2(3): 55–61.

——. 1929a. Notes on *Bothrops nummifera*, mano de piedra or timbo. Bull. Antivenin Inst. Am. 3(1): 27–29.

——. 1929b. Notes on *Bothrops nigroviridis*. Bull. Antivenin Inst. Am. 3(2): 58.

Marchisin, A. 1978. Observations on an audio-visual "warning" signal in the pigmy rattlesnake, *Sistrurus miliarius* (Reptilia, Serpentes, Crotalidae). Herpetol. Rev. 9(3): 92–93.

Marcuzzi, G. 1950. Ofidios existentes en las colecciones de los museos de Caracas (Venezuela). Novedades Científicos del Museo de Historia Natural La Salle (Zoología) (Caracas) 3: 1–20.

Marcy, D. 1945. Birth of a brood of *Crotalus basiliscus*. Copeia 1945(3): 169–170.

Marineros, L. 2000. Guía de las serpientes de Honduras. Dirección General de Biodiversidad. Secretaría de Recursos Naturales y Ambiente, Tegucigalpa. 252 pp.

Marinkelle, C. J. 1966. Accidents by venomous animals in Colombia. Industrial Medicine and Surgery 35(11): 988–992.

Markezich, A. L. 2002. New distribution records of reptiles from western Venezuela. Herpetol. Rev. 33(1): 69–74.

Markezich, A. L., and D. C. Taphorn. 1993. A variational analysis of populations of *Bothrops* (Serpentes: Viperidae) from western Venezuela. J. Herpetol. 27(3): 248–254.

Markland, F. S., and P. S. Damus. 1971. Purification and properties of a thrombin-like enzyme from the venom of *Crotalus adamanteus* (Eastern diamondback rattlesnake). Journal of Biological Chemistry 246: 6460–6473.

Marlas, G., and C. Bon. 1982. Relationship between the pharmacological action of crotoxin and its phospholipase activity. European Journal of Biochemistry 125: 157–165.

Marmie, W., S. Kuhn, and D. Chiszar. 1990. Behavior of captive-raised rattlesnakes (*Crotalus enyo*) as a function of rearing conditions. Zoo Biology 9(3): 241–246.

Marques, O. A. V. 1992. História natural de *Micrurus corallinus* (Serpentes, Elapidae). Dissertação de Mestrado, Universidade de São Paulo. 80 pp.

——. 2000. Tail displays of the false coral snake *Simophis rhinostoma* (Colubridae). Amphibia-Reptilia 22: 127–129.

——. 2002. Natural history of the coral snake *Micrurus decoratus* (Elapidae) from the Atlantic forest in southeast Brazil, with comments on possible mimicry. Amphibia-Reptilia 23(2): 228–232.

Marques, O. A. V., A. Eterovic, and I. Sazima. 2001. Serpentes da Mata Atlântica. Guia ilustrado para a Serra do Mar. Holos Editora, Ribeirão Preto, São Paulo, Brazil. 184 pp.

Marques, O. A. V., M. Martins, and I. Sazima. 2002. A new insular species of pitviper from Brazil, with comments on evolutionary biology and conservation of the *Bothrops jararaca* group (Serpentes, Viperidae). Herpetologica 58(3): 303–312.

Marques, O. A. V., and A. A. Oliveira. 1991. Atividade e habitos alimentares em *Micrurus corallinus* (Serpentes: Elapidae). Resumos XVIII Congr. Bras. Zool., Univ. Fed. BA Salvador, p. 310.

Marques, O. A. V., and I. Sazima. 1997. Diet and feeding behavior of the coral snake, *Micrurus corallinus*, from the Atlantic forest in Brazil. Herpetological Natural History 5: 88–91.

Marr, J. C. 1944. Notes on amphibians and reptiles from the central United States. Am. Midl. Nat. 32(2): 478–490.

Marshall, J. T. 1957. Birds of pine-oak woodland in southern Arizona and adjacent Mexico. Pacific Coast Avifauna 32: 1–125.

Marshall, L. G., R. F. Butler, R. E. Drake, G. H. Curtis, and R. H. Tedford. 1979. Calibration of the Great American Interchange. Science 204: 272–279.

Martin, B. E. 1974. Distribution and habitat adaptations in rattlesnakes of Arizona. Bulletin of the New York Herpetological Society 10(3–4): 3–12.

——1975a. An occurrence of the Arizona ridge-nosed rattlesnake, *Crotalus willardi willardi*, observed feeding in nature. Bull. Maryland Herpetol. Soc. 11: 66–67.

——. 1975b. Notes on a brood of the Arizona ridge-nosed rattlesnake (*Crotalus willardi willardi*). Bull. Maryland Herpetol. Soc. 11: 64–65.

——. 1975c. A brood of the Arizona ridge-nosed rattlesnake (*Crotalus willardi willardi*) bred and born in captivity. Bull. Maryland Herpetol. Soc. 11: 187–189.

——. 1976. A reproductive record for the New Mexican ridge-nosed rattlesnake (*Crotalus willardi obscurus*). Bull. Maryland Herpetol. Soc. 12: 126–128.

Martin, D. J. 1973. A spectrographic analysis of burrowing owl vocalizations. Auk 90: 564–678.

Martin, D. L. 1984. An instance of sexual defense in the cottonmouth, *Agkistrodon piscivorus*. Copeia 1984: 772–774.

Martin, J. H., and R. M. Bagby. 1972. Temperature-frequency relationship of the rattlesnake rattle. Copeia 1972(3): 482–485.

Martin, J. R., and J. T. Wood. 1955. Notes on the poisonous snakes of the Dismal Swamp area. Herpetologica 11(3): 237–238.

Martin, P. S. 1955a. Zonal distribution of vertebrates in a Mexican cloud forest. American Naturalist 89(849): 347–361.

——. 1955b. Herpetological records from the Gómez Farías region of southwestern Tamaulipas, Mexico. Copeia 1955(3): 173–180.

——. 1958. A biogeography of reptiles and amphibians in the Gómez Farías region, Tamaulipas, Mexico. Miscellaneous Publications of the Museum of Zoology, University of Michigan 101: 1–102.

Martin, T. E. 1988–1989. Snakebite injury in Belize (its incidence and how best to manage it). Medical Corps International 6: 11–16; 7: 60–70.

Martin, W. H. 1982. The timber rattlesnake in the Northeast: its range, past and present. Bulletin of the New York Herpetological Society 17: 15–20.

——. 1992. Phenology of the timber rattlesnake (*Crotalus horridus*) in an unglaciated section of the Appalachian Mountains. Pp. 259–277 in J. A. Campbell and E. D. Brodie Jr. (eds.), Biology of the pitvipers. Selva, Tyler, Texas.

——. 1993. Reproduction of the timber rattlesnake (*Crotalus horridus*) in the Appalachian Mountains. J. Herpetol. 27: 133–143.

——. 1996. Natural history notes: *Crotalus horridus* (timber rattlesnake). Reproductive phenology. Herpetol. Rev. 27(3): 144–145.

Martin, W. H., J. C. Mitchell, and R. Hoggard. 1992. Geographic distribution: *Crotalus horridus* (timber rattlesnake). Herpetol. Rev. 23(3): 91.

Martín del Campo, R. 1935. Nota acerca de la distribución geográfica de los reptiles ponzoñosos en México. Anales del Instituto de Biología, Universidad Nacional Autónoma de México, 6(3–4): 291–300.

——. 1936. Contribuciónes al conocimiento de la fauna de Actopán, Hgo. IV. Vertebrados observados en la época de las secas. Anales del Instituto de Biología, Universidad Nacional Autónoma de México 7(2–3): 271–286.

——. 1937a. Reptiles ponzoñosos de México: las víboras de cascabel. Folletos de Divulgación Científica, Publicados por el Instituto de Biología, México, 27: 1–18.

——. 1937b. Contribución al conocimiento de los batracios y reptiles del Valle del Mezquital, Hgo. Anales del Instituto de Biología, Universidad Nacional Autónoma de México, 7: 489–512.

——. 1938a. Tres *Bothrops* de Chiapas, dos de ellas nuevas para la fauna de México. Anales del Instituto de Biología, Universidad Nacional Autónoma de México, 9: 227–229.

——. 1938b. Ensayo de interpretación del libro undécimo de la Historia de Sahagún. Anales del Instituto de Biología, Universidad Nacional Autónoma de México, 9(3–4): 379–391.

——. 1940a. Los vertebrados de Pátzcuaro. Anales del Instituto de Biología, Universidad Nacional Autónoma de México, 11(2): 481–492.

——. 1940b. Nota acerca de algunos vertebrados de las lagunas de Cempoala y sus alrededores. Anales del Instituto de Biología, Universidad Nacional Autónoma de México, 11(2): 741–743.

——. 1942 [dated 1941]. Nota sobre el segundo hallazo de *Sistrurus ravus* en el Distrito Federal. Anales del Instituto de Biología, Universidad Nacional Autónoma de México, 12(2): 762.

——. 1950. Serpientes ponzoñosas de México. Revista Mexicana de Ciencias Médicas y Biológicas 8: 103–115.

——. 1953. Contribución al conocimiento de la herpetología de Nuevo León. Universidad 11: 115–152.

——. 1955. Productos biológicas del Valle de México. Revista Mexicana de Estudios Antropológicos 14(1): 53–77.

——. 1979. Un manuscrito inédito de Alfredo Dugès. Anales del Instituto de Biología, Universidad Nacional Autónoma de México, 50(1): 665–672.

——. 1984 [dated 1983]. Herpetología mexicana antigua. II. Nomenclatura y taxonomicá de las serpientes. Anales del Instituto de Biología, Universidad Nacional Autónoma de México, 54, Ser. Zool. 1: 177–198.

Martínez, A. M., R. A. Martínez, and S. B. Montanelli. 1992. Actualización de la distribución de los ofidios venenosos (Crotalidae y Elapidae) de la Provincia de Misiones, Argentina, y su relación con una distribución de suero antiofídico. Acta Zoológica Lilloana 41: 307–310.

Martínez, M., E. D. Rael, and N. L. Maddux. 1990. Isolation of a hemorrhagic toxin from Mojave rattlesnake (*Crotalus scutulatus scutulatus*) venom. Toxicon 28: 685–694.

Martinez, R. R., J. C. Perez, E. E. Sanchez, and R. Campos. 1999. The antihemorrhagic factor of the Mexican ground squirrel (*Spermophilus mexicanus*). Toxicon 37(6): 949–954.

Martínez, V. 1983. Panamá: nuevo ámbito de distribución para la serpiente venenosa *Bothrops picadoi* (Dunn). ConCiencia (Universidad de Panamá) 10(1): 26–27.

Martínez, V., and R. Bolaños. 1982. The bushmaster, *Lachesis muta muta* (Linnaeus) [Ophidia: Viperidae], in Panama. Rev. Biol. Trop. 30(1): 100–101.

Martínez-Cadillo, E., C. B. Ferreyra, and A. Zavaleta. 1991. Haemolytic activity of venoms from snakes of the genera *Bothrops*, *Lachesis*, *Crotalus*, and *Micrurus* (Serpentes: Viperidae and Elapidae). Rev. Biol. Trop. 39(2): 311–314.

Martino, O. A., T. A. Orduna, M. O. Espinosa. 2001. Atlas de patalogia humana provocada por la agresion de animales. Fundación "Dra María Cristina Peña," Buenos Aires.

Martins, M., and M. Gordo. 1993. Life history notes: *Bothrops atrox* (common lancehead). Diet. Herpetol. Rev. 24(4): 151–152.

Martins, M., O. A. V. Marques, and I. Sazima. 2002. Ecological and phylogenetic correlates of feeding habits in Neotropical pitvipers of the genus *Bothrops*. Pp. 307–328 in G. W. Schuett, M. Höggren, M. E. Douglas, and H. W. Greene (eds.), Biology of the vipers. Eagle Mountain Publishing, Eagle Mountain, Utah.

Martins, M., and M. E. Oliveira. 1998. Natural history of snakes in forests of the Manaus region, Central Amazonia, Brazil. Herpetological Natural History 6(2): 78–150.

Martins, N. 1916. Das Opisthoglyphas brasileiras e o seu veneno. Dissertação (Cadeira de Historia Natural), Faculdade de Medicina de Rio de Janeiro. Typografia America, Rio de Janeiro.

Martof, B. S. 1956. Amphibians and reptiles of Georgia. University of Georgia Press, Athens. 94 pp.

——. 1963. Some observations on the herpetofauna of Sapelo Island, Georgia. Herpetologica 19(1): 70–72.

Martof, B. S., W. M. Palmer, J. R. Bailey, and J. R. Harrison. 1980. Amphibians and reptiles of the Carolinas and Virginia. University of North Carolina Press, Chapel Hill. 264 pp.

Maruyama, M., A. S. Kamiguti, J. L. C. Cardoso, I. S. Sano-Martins, A. M. Chudzinski, M. L. Santoro, P. Morena, S. C. Tomy, L. C. Antonio, H. Mihara, et al. 1990. Studies on blood coagulation and fibrinolysis in patients bitten by *Bothrops jararaca* (jararaca). Thrombosis Haemostasis 63: 449–453.

Marx, H. 1958. Catalogue of type specimens of reptiles and amphibians in the Chicago Natural History Museum. Fieldiana: Zoology 36(4): 407–496.

Maslin, T. P. 1942. Evidence for the separation of the crotalid genera *Trimeresurus* and *Bothrops*, with a key to the genus *Trimeresurus*. Copeia 1942(1): 18–24.

——. 1950. Herpetological notes and records from Colorado. Herpetologica 6(3): 89–95.

——. 1959. An annotated check list of amphibians and reptiles of Colorado. University of Colorado Studies, Series in Biology 6: 1–98.

——. 1965. The status of *Sistrurus catenatus* in Colorado. Southwest. Nat. 10(1): 31–34.

Mason, R. T., and D. Crews. 1985. Female mimicry in garter snakes. Nature 316: 59–61.

——. 1986. Pheromone mimicry in garter snakes. Pp. 279–283 in D. Duvall, D. Müller-Schwarze, and R. M. Silverstein (eds.), Chemical signals in vertebrates, vol. 4. Plenum, New York.

Masterson, J. R. 1938. Colonial rattlesnake lore, 1714. Zoologica, New York Zoological Society, 23(9): 213–216.

Mather, C. M., and J. R. Dixon. 1976. Geographic records of some South Texas amphibians and reptiles. Herpetol. Rev. 7(3): 127.

Mather, H. M., S. Mayne, and T. M. McMonagle. 1978. Severe envenomation from "harmless" pet snake. British Medical Journal 20: 1324–1325.

Matlack, R. S., and R. L. Rehmeier. 2002. Status of the western diamondback rattlesnake (*Crotalus atrox*) in Kansas. Southwest. Nat. 47(2): 312–316.

Matthews, R. 1995. Nightmares of nature. HarperCollins, London. 256 pp.

Matthey, R. 1931a. Chromosomes de sauriens: Helodermatidae, Varanidae, Xantusiidae, Anniellidae, Anguidae. Bulletin de la Société Vaudoise des Sciences Naturelles 57: 269.

——. 1931b. Chromosomes de reptiles: Sauriens, ophidiens, cheloniens. L'évolution de la formule chromosomiale chez les sauriens. Revue Suisse de Zoologie 38: 117–186.

Mattison, C. 1996. Rattler! A natural history of rattlesnakes. Blandford, London. 144 pp.

Maudslay, A. C., and A. P. Maudslay. 1899. A glimpse at Guatemala. John Murray, London. 272 pp.

Mauger, D., and T. P. Wilson. 1999. Population characteristics and seasonal activity of *Sistrurus catenatus catenatus* in Will County, Illinois: implications for management and monitoring. Pp. 110–124 in B. Johnson and M. Wright (eds.), Second International Symposium and Workshop on the Conservation of the Eastern Massassauga Rattlesnake, *Sistrurus catenatus catenatus*: Population and Habitat Management Issues in Urban, Bog, Prairie, and Forested Ecosystems. Toronto Zoo, Toronto.

Maxell, B. A., J. K. Werner, P. Hendricks, and D. L. Flath. 2003. Herpetology in Montana. Northwest Fauna No. 5. Society for Northwestern Vertebrate Biology, Seattle. 135 pp.

May, P. G., T. M. Farrell, S. T. Heulett, M. A. Pilgrim, L. A. Bishop, D. J. Spence, A. M. Rabatsky, M. G. Campbell, A. D. Aycrigg, and W. E. Richardson II. 1996. Seasonal abundance and activity of a rattlesnake (*Sistrurus miliarius barbouri*) in Central Florida. Copeia 1996(2): 389–401.

Mayr, E. 1954. Notes on nomenclature and classification. Syst. Zool. 3: 86–89.

——. 1982. The growth of biological thought. Belknap Press of Harvard University Press, Cambridge, Mass. 974 pp.

McAlister, W. H. 1963. Evidence of mild toxicity in the saliva of the hognose snake (*Heterodon*). Herpetologica 19(2): 132–137.

McAllister, C. T. 1990. Geographic distribution: *Crotalus atrox* (western diamondback rattlesnake). Herpetol. Rev. 21(4): 97.

McAllister, C. T., and J. E. Kessler. 2001. Geographical distribution: *Agkistrodon piscivorus leucostoma* (western cottonmouth). Herpetol. Rev. 32(2): 121.

McAllister, C. T., S. J. Upton, D. G. Barker, and C. W. Painter. 1996. *Sarcocystis* sp. (Apicomplexa) from the New Mexico ridgenose rattlesnake, *Crotalus willardi obscurus* Harris, 1974, from Sonora, Mexico. Journal of the Helminthological Society of Washington 63(1): 128–130.

McAllister, C. T., S. J. Upton, S. E. Trauth, and J. R. Dixon. 1995. Coccidian parasites (Apicomplexa) from snakes in the southcentral and southwestern United States: new host and geographic records. Journal of Parasitology 81(1): 63–68.

McAllister, C. T., and R. Ward. 1986. More distributional records of amphibians and reptiles from Texas. Herpetol. Rev. 17(1): 28–30.

McAllister, K. R. 1995. Distribution of amphibians and reptiles in Washington State. Northwest Fauna 3: 81–112.

McCann, C. 1935. Male ratsnakes (*Zamenis mucosus*) fighting. Journal of the Bombay Natural History Society 38: 409.

McCarthy, C. J. 1985. Monophyly of elapid snakes (Serpentes: Elapidae). An assessment of the evidence. Zoological Journal of the Linnean Society 83: 79–93.

——. 1986. Relationships of the laticaudine sea snakes (Serpentes: Elapidae: Laticaudinae). Bulletin of the British Museum of Natural History (Zoology) 50: 127–161.

McCauley, R. H., Jr. 1945. The reptiles of Maryland and the District of Columbia. Privately printed, Hagerstown, Md. 194 pp.

McCauley, R. H., Jr., and C. S. East. 1940. Amphibians and reptiles from Garrett County, Maryland. Copeia 1940(2): 120–123.

McCollough, N. C., and J. F. Gennaro. 1963a. Coral snake bites in the United States. Journal of the Florida Medical Association 49: 968–972.

——. 1963b. Evaluation of the venomous snakebite in the southern United States from parallel clinical and laboratory investigations. Journal of the Florida Medical Association 49: 959–967.

——. 1968. Diagnosis, symptoms, treatment and sequelae of envenomation by *Crotalus adamanteus* and genus *Ancistrodon*. Journal of the Florida Medical Association 55: 327–329.

——. 1970. Treatment of venomous snakebite in the United States. Clinical Toxicology 3: 483–500.

McCord, J. S., and M. E. Dorcas. 1989. Geographic distribution: new Texas herpetological distributional records from the University of Texas at Arlington Collection of Vertebrates. Herpetol. Rev. 20(4): 94–96.

McCoy, C. J., Jr. 1961. Birth season and young of *Crotalus scutulatus* and *Agkistrodon contortrix laticinctus*. Herpetologica 17(2): 140.

——. 1962. Noteworthy amphibians and reptiles from Colorado. Herpetologica 18(1): 60–62.

——. 1971 [dated 1970]. The snake fauna of Middlesex, British Honduras. J. Herpetol. 4(3–4): 135–140.

——. 1982. Amphibians and reptiles in Pennsylvania. Carnegie Museum of Natural History Special Publications 6: 1–91.

——. 1984. Ecological and zoogeographic relationships of amphibians and reptiles of the Cuatro Ciénagas Basin. Journal of the Arizona–Nevada Academy of Science 19: 49–59.

——. 1990. Review of The venomous reptiles of Latin America. Herpetologica 46: 245–247.

McCoy, C. J., Jr., and E. J. Censky. 1992. Biology of the Yucatan hognosed pitviper, *Porthidium yucatanicum*. Pp. 217–222 in J. A. Campbell and E. D. Brodie Jr. (eds.), Biology of the pitvipers. Selva, Tyler, Texas.

McCoy, C. J., Jr., and W. L. Minckley. 1969. *Sistrurus catenatus* (Reptilia: Crotalidae) from the Cuatro Ciénagas Basin, Coahuila, México. Herpetologica 25(2): 152–153.

McCoy, C. J., Jr., and N. D. Richmond. 1966. Herpetological type-specimens in Carnegie Museum. Annals of Carnegie Museum 38(10): 233–264.

McCoy, C. J., Jr., and D. H. Van Horn. 1962. Herpetozoa from Oaxaca and Chiapas. Herpetologica 18(3): 180–186.

McCranie, J. R. 1976. *Crotalus polystictus*. Catalogue of American Amphibians and Reptiles 180.1–180.2.

——. 1980a. *Crotalus adamanteus* Beauvois, Eastern diamondback rattlesnake. Catalogue of American Amphibians and Reptiles 252.1–252.2.

——. 1980b. *Crotalus pricei*. Catalogue of American Amphibians and Reptiles 266.1–266.2.

——. 1981. *Crotalus basiliscus*. Catalogue of American Amphibians and Reptiles 283.1–283.2.

——. 1983. *Crotalus pusillus* Klauber, southwestern Mexican dusky rattlesnake. Catalogue of American Amphibians and Reptiles 313.1–313.2.

——. 1984. *Crotalus vegrandis*. Catalogue of American Amphibians and Reptiles 350.1–350.2.

——. 1986. *Crotalus unicolor*. Catalogue of American Amphibians and Reptiles 389.1–389.2.

——. 1988. Description of the hemipenis of *Sistrurus ravus* (Serpentes: Viperidae). Herpetologica 44(1): 123–126.

——. 1991. *Crotalus intermedius*. Catalogue of American Amphibians and Reptiles 519.1–519.4.

——. 1993. Additions to the herpetofauna of Honduras. Caribbean Journal of Science 29(3–4): 254–255.

——. 2001. Benque Viejo and *Porthidium yucatanicum* (Squamata: Viperidae) in Belize. Caribbean Journal of Science 37(3–4): 284–285.

McCranie, J. R., and L. Porras. 1978. Geographic distribution: *Bothrops yucatanicus* (Yucatan hognose viper). Herpetol. Rev. 9(3): 108.

McCranie, J. R., and L. D. Wilson. 1978. A second Mexican specimen of *Crotalus willardi obscurus* from the Sierra San Luis, Chihuahua, with comments on other members of the herpetofauna. Herpetol. Rev. 9(3): 108–109.

——. 1979. Commentary on taxonomic practice in regional herpetological publications: review of A preliminary account of the rattlesnakes with the description of four new subspecies by Herbert S. Harris Jr. and Robert S. Simmons (1978, Bull. Maryland Herpetol. Soc., 14[3]: 105–211), with comments on other Harris and Simmons rattlesnake papers. Herpetol. Rev. 10: 18–21.

——. 1987. The biogeography of the herpetofauna of the pine-oak woodlands of the Sierra Madre Occidental of Mexico. Milwaukee Public Museum Contributions to Biology and Geology 72: 1–30.

——. 1991. *Geophis fulvoguttatus* Mertens and *Micrurus browni* Schmidt and Smith: additions to the snake fauna of Honduras. Amphibia-Reptilia 12(1): 112–114.

McCreary, T. 1959. Poisonous snake bites: report of a case. JAMA 170: 268–272.

McCrystal, H. K., and R. J. Green. 1986. Natural history notes: *Agkistrodon contortrix pictigaster* (Trans-Pecos copperhead). Feeding. Herpetol. Rev. 17(3): 61.

McCrystal, H. K., and M. J. McCoid. 1986. *Crotalus mitchellii*. Catalogue of American Amphibians and Reptiles 388.1–388.4.

McCrystal, H. K., C. R. Schwalbe, and D. F. Retes. 1996. Selected aspects of the ecology of the Arizona ridge-nosed rattlesnake (*Crotalus willardi willardi*) and the banded rock rattlesnake (*Crotalus lepidus klauberi*). Final Report to Arizona Game and Fish Department, Phoenix.

McDiarmid, R. W. 1963. A collection of reptiles and amphibians from the highland faunal assemblage of western Mexico. Natural History Museum of Los Angeles County Contributions in Science 68: 1–15.

McDiarmid, R. W., J. A. Campbell, and T. A. Touré. 1999. Snake species of the world: a taxonomic and geographic reference, vol. 1. Herpetologists' League, Washington, D.C. 511 pp.

McDiarmid, R. W., J. F. Copp, and D. E. Breedlove. 1976. Notes on the herpetofauna of western Mexico: new records from Sinaloa and the Tres Marías Islands. Natural History Musem of Los Angeles County Contributions in Science 275: 1–17.

McDiarmid, R. W., and M. F. Foster. 1987. Additions to the reptile fauna of Paraguay, with notes on a small herpetological collection from Amambay. Studies on Neotropical Fauna and Environment 22(1): 1–9.

McDowell, S. B. 1967. *Aspidomorphus*, a genus of New Guinea snakes of the family Elapidae, with notes on related genera. Journal of Zoology (London) 151: 497–543.

——. 1968. Affinities of the snakes usually called *Elaps lacteus* and *E. dorsalis*. Journal of the Linnean Society (Zoology) 47: 561–578.

——. 1969. *Toxicocalamus*, a New Guinea genus of snakes of the family Elapidae. Journal of Zoology (London) 159: 443–511.

——. 1970. On the status and relationships of the Solomon Island elapid snakes. Journal of Zoology (London) 161: 145–190.

——. 1972. The genera of sea-snakes of the *Hydrophis* group (Serpentes: Elapidae). Transactions of the Zoological Society of London 32: 195–247.

——. 1986. The architecture of the corner of the mouth of colubroid snakes. J. Herpetol. 20: 353–407.

——. 1987. Systematics. Pp. 3–50 in R. A. Seigel, J. T. Collins, and S. Novak (eds.), Snakes: ecology and evolutionary biology. Macmillan, New York.

McDowell, S. B., and C. M. Bogert. 1954. The systematic position of *Lanthanotus* and the affinities of the anguinomorphan lizards. Bull. Am. Mus. Nat. Hist. 105: 1–142.

McDuffie, G. T. 1961. Notes on the ecology of the copperhead in Ohio (abstract). Journal of the Ohio Herpetological Society 3: 26–27.

McGuire, J. A. 1991. Life history notes: *Crotalus enyo cerralvensis* (Cerralvo Island rattlesnake). Behavior. Herpetol. Rev. 22(3): 100.

McGuire, J. A., and K. B. Heang. 2001. Phylogenetic systematics of southeast Asian flying lizards (Iguania: Agamidae: *Draco*) as inferred from mitochondrial DNA sequence data. Biological Journal of the Linnean Society 72: 203–229.

McGurty, B. M. 2002. Natural history notes: *Heloderma suspectum* (Gila monster). Egg predation by juveniles. Herpetol. Rev. 33(3): 205.

McKee, E. D., and C. M. Bogert. 1934. The amphibians and reptiles of Grand Canyon National Park. Copeia 1934(4): 178–180.

McKinney, C. O., and R. E. Ballinger. 1966. Snake predators of lizards in western Texas. Southwest. Nat. 11(3): 410–412.

McKinstry, D. M. 1983. Morphologic evidence of toxic saliva in colubrid snakes: a checklist of world genera. Herpetol. Rev. 14(1): 12–15.

McMillan, W. O., C. D. Jiggins, and J. Mallet. 1997. What initiates speciation in passion-vine butterflies? Proceedings of the National Academy of Sciences 94: 8626–8633.

McPartland, J. M., and R. Foster. 1988. Stun-guns and snakebites. Lancet 2: 1141.

McPeak, R. H. 2000. Amphibians and reptiles in Baja California. Sea Challengers, Monterey, Calif. 104 pp.

Meacham, A., and C. Myers. 1961. An exceptional pattern variant of the coral snake, *Micrurus fulvius* (L.). Quarterly Journal of the Florida Academy of Science 21(1): 56–58.

Mealer, B. 2001. Snake, rattle, and roll: this spring, no viper is safe. Esquire, March, p. 60.

Means, D. B. 1978. Reproductive ecology of the female eastern diamondback rattlesnake. Abstract in Proc. of the Joint Meeting of the 58th Ann. Meeting of the Assoc. of Ichthyologists and Herpetologists, 26th Ann. Meeting of the Herpetologists' League, and 26th Ann. Meeting of the Society for the Study of Amphibians and Reptiles, 31 May–2 June 1978, Arizona State University, Tempe, Ariz.

——. 1985. Radio-tracking the eastern diamondback rattlesnake. National Geographic Research 18: 529–536.

——. 1992. Southern copperhead. Pp. 242–246 in P. E. Moler (ed.), Rare and endangered biota of Florida. University Press of Florida, Gainesville.

——. 1994. Diamonds in the rough. North Florida Journal 2: 1–28.

——. 1998. Geographic distribution: *Agkistrodon contortrix contortrix* (southern copperhead). Herpetol. Rev. 29(3): 175.

——. 1999. Venomous snakes of Florida. Florida Wildlife 53(5): 13–20.

Mebs, D. 1968. Some studies on the biochemistry of the venom gland of *Heloderma horridum*. Toxicon 5(3): 225–226.

——. 1978. Pharmacology of reptilian venoms. Pp. 437–560 in C. Gans and K. A. Gans (ed.), Biology of the Reptilia, vol. 8. Physiology B. Academic Press, London.

——. 1995. Clinical toxicology of Helodermatidae lizard bites. Pp. 361–366 in J. Meier and J. White (eds.), Handbook of clinical toxicology of animal venoms and poisons. CRC Press, Boca Raton.

Mebs, D., and F. Kornalik. 1984. Intraspecific variation in content of a basic toxin in eastern diamondback rattlesnake (*Crotalus adamanteus*) venom. Toxicon 22: 831–833.

Mebs, D., and H. W. Raudonat. 1967 [dated 1966]. Biochemical investigations on *Heloderma* venom. Memoria do Instituto Butantan, Simposio Internacional 33(3): 907–911.

Mebs, D., and Y. Samejima. 1986. Isolation and characterization of myotoxic phospholipases A_2 from crotalid venoms. Toxicon 24: 161–168.

Medem, F. 1965. Bibliografía comentada de reptiles colombianos. Revista de la Academia Colombiana de Ciencias Exactas, Físicas y Naturales 12(47): 299–346.

——. 1969 [dated 1968]. El desarrollo de la herpetología en Colombia. Revista de la Academia Colombiana de Ciencias Exactas, Físicas y Naturales 13(50): 149–199.

——. 1979. Los anfibios y reptiles de las Islas Gorgona y Gorgonilla. Pp. 189–218 in H. Prahl, F. Guhl, and M. Grogl (eds.), Gorgona. Universidad de los Andes, Bogotá.

Meek, G. 1946. Creatures of mystery. J. W. Burke, Macon, Ga.

Meek, S. E. 1906 [dated 1905]. An annotated list of a collection of reptiles from southern California and northern Lower California. Field Mus. Nat. Hist. Publ., Zool. Ser., 7(1): 1–19.

——. 1910. Notes on batrachians and reptiles from the islands north of Venezuela. Field Mus. Nat. Hist. Publ., Zool. Ser., 7(12): 415–418.

Megonigal, J. P. 1985. Field notes: *Agkistrodon contortrix mokasen* and *Lampropeltis getulus getulus*. Catesbeiana 5: 16.

Mehrtens, J. M. 1987. Living snakes of the world in color. Sterling, New York. 480 pp.

Meier, J. 1986. Individual and age-dependent variations in the venom of the fer-de-lance (*Bothrops atrox*). Toxicon 24: 41–46.

Meier, J., and K. F. Stocker. 1995. Biology and distribution of venomous snakes of medical importance and the composition of snake venoms. Pp. 367–412 in J. Meier and J. White (eds.), Handbook of clinical toxicology of animal venoms and poisons. CRC Press, Boca Raton.

Meier, J., and J. White (eds.). 1995. Handbook of clinical toxicology of animal venoms and poisons. CRC Press, Boca Raton. 752 pp.

Meise, W. 1938. Eine neue korallenschlange aus dem Amazonasgebiet. Zoologischer Anzeiger (Leipzig) 123(1–2): 20–22.

Mekbel, S. T., and R. Céspedes. 1963. Las lesiones renales en el ofidismo. Acta Médica Costarricense 6: 111–118.

Melgarejo, A. R. 1978 [dated 1977]. Observaciones sobre nacimiento en el laboratorio de *Bothrops neuwiedi pubescens* (Cope, 1870) (Ophidia, Crotalinae). Revista de Biología del Uruguay 5(1): 35–41.

Melgarejo, A. R., A. C. Cunha, and A. S. Aguilar. 1999a. Reprodução de *Lachesis muta rhombeata* Wied, 1824 (Serpentes: Viperidae). P. 82 in Abstracts of the V Congreso Latinoamericano de Herpetología, Montevideo, 12 al 17 de diciembre de 1999.

Melgarejo, A. R., M. D. Meneghel, and F. Achával. 1980. Sobre un ejemplar de *Bothrops alternatus* (Serpentes: Viperidae) con aberraciones cromáticas y morfológicas; estudio revisivo de la especie para Uruguay (abstract). Pp. 142–143 in VIII Cong. Latinoamer. Zool., Mérida.

Melgarejo, A. R., M. S. Stavola, and T. A. Gomes. 1999b. Ofidismo no Estado do Rio de Janeiro–Brasil. P. 82 in Abstracts of the V Congreso Latinoamericano de Herpetología, Montevideo, 12 al 17 de diciembre de 1999.

Mellink, E. 1990. Life history notes: *Crotalus scutulatus* (Mohave rattlesnake). Reproduction. Herpetol. Rev. 21(4): 93.

Mello, K. 1978. Geographic distribution: *Crotalus viridis cerberus* (Arizona black rattlesnake). Herpetol. Rev. 9(1): 22.

Mello-leitão, C. 1947. Zoogeografia do Brasil, 2d ed. Editora Nacional, São Paulo. 648 pp.

Mendelson, J. R., III, and W. B. Jennings. 1992. Shifts in the relative abundance of snakes in a desert grassland. J. Herpetol. 26(1): 38–45.

Meneses, O. 1974a. Ofidios y ofidismo en el Peru. I. Las serpientes venenosas del Perú. Revista del Instituto Zoonosis e Investigación Pecuaria 2(3–4): 69–77.

——. 1974b. Ofidios y ofidismo en el Peru. II. Aspectos ecológicos de la fauna ofídica ponzoñosa. Revista del Instituto Zoonosis e Investigación Pecuaria 2(3–4): 79–84.

Menne, H. A. L. 1959. Lets over het voorkomen van ratelslangen in Canada. Lacerta 18: 4–6.

Merkord, G. W. 1975. Range extensions and new county records of some Texas amphibians and reptiles. Herpetol. Rev. 6(3): 79.

Merrem, B. 1820. Versuch eines Systems der Amphibien. Johann Christian Krieger, Marburg. 191 pp.

Mertens, R. 1929. Herpetologische Mitteilungen. XII. Über einige Amphibien und Reptilien aus Süd-Bolivien. Zoologischer Anzeiger (Leipzig) 86: 57–62.

——. 1930. Bemerkungen über die von Herrn Dr. K. Lafrentz in Mexiko gesammelten Amphibien und Reptilien. Abhandlungen und Berichte aus dem Museum für Natur- und Heimatkunde zu Magdeburg 6(2): 153–161.

——. 1941. Eine neue Korallennatter aus Mexico. Senckenbergiana Biologica 23(46): 216–217.

——. 1942. Amphibien und Reptilien I. (Ausbeute der Hamburger Sudperu-Expedition.) In E. Titschack (ed.), Beitrage zur Fauna Perus 2(1): 277–287.

——. 1952a. Neues über die Reptilienfauna von El Salvador. Zoologischer Anzeiger (Leipzig) 148: 87–94.

——. 1952b. Die Amphibien und Reptilien von El Salvador auf Grund der Reisen von R. Mertens und A. Zilch. Abhandlungen der Senckenbergischen Naturforschenden Gesellschaft (Frankfurt am Main) 487: 1–83.

——. 1956. Das Problem der Mimikry bei Korallenschlangen. Zoologische Jahrbücher. Abteilung für Systematik, Ökologie, und Geographie der Tiere 84(6): 541–576.

——. 1957a. Zooligische Beobachtungen im Nebel von Rancho Grande, Venezuela. Natur und Volk 87(10): 337–334.

——. 1957b. Gibt es eine Mimikry bei Korallenschlangen? Natur und Volk 87: 56–66.

——. 1963. Liste der rezenten Amphibien und Reptilien. Helodermatidae, Varanidae, Lanthanotidae. Tierreich (Berlin) 79: 1–26.

——. 1965. Wenig bekannte "Seitenwinder" unter den Wüstenottern Asiens. Natur und Museum 95: 346–352.

——. 1966. Ueber die Inselotter, *Bothrops insularis*. Salamandra 2(3): 72–74.

——. 1967. Die herpetologische Sektion des Natur-Museums und Forschungs-Institutes Senckenberg in Frankfort a. M. nebst einem Verzeichnis ihrer Typen. Senckenbergiana Biologica 48: 1–106.

Messeling, E. 1953. Rattlesnakes in southwestern Wisconsin. Wisconsin Conservation Bulletin 18: 21–23.

Meszler, R. M., and D. B. Webster. 1968. Histochemistry of the rattlesnake facial pit. Copeia 1968(4): 722–728.

Metter, D. E. 1963. A rattlesnake that encountered a porcupine. Copeia 1963(1): 161.

Meyer, J. R. 1969. A biogeographic study of the amphibians and reptiles of Honduras. Ph.D. dissertation, University of Southern California. 589 pp.

Meyer, J. R., and L. D. Wilson. 1971. Taxonomic studies and notes on some Honduran amphibians and reptiles. Bulletin of the Southern California Academy of Sciences 70(3): 106–114.

Meyer, W. P., A. G. Habib, A. A. Onayade, A. Yakubu, D. C. Smith, A. Nasidi, I. J. Daudu, D. A. Warrell, and R. D. Theakston. 1997. First clinical experience with a new bovine Fab *Echis ocellatus* snakebite antivenom in Nigeria: randomized comparative trial with Institute Pasteur serum (IPSER) Africa antivenom. American Journal of Tropical Medicine and Hygiene 56(3): 291–300.

Meylan, P. A. 1982. The squamate reptiles of the Inglis IA fauna (Irvingtonian: Citrus County, Florida). Bulletin of the Florida State Museum, Biological Sciences, 27(3): 1–85.

Middendorf, G. A., and W. C. Sherbrooke. 1992. Canid elicitation of blood-squirting in a horned lizard (*Phyrnosoma cornutum*). Copeia 1992: 519–527.

Migliore, A. D. 1963. Rattlesnake envenomation: report of two cases. Medical Times 91: 1076–1085.

——. 1965. Envenomation by *Sistrurus miliarius*: report of two cases of pygmy rattlesnake poisoning. Arizona Medicine 22: 367–374.

Migone, L. E. 1929. Apuntes de climatología y nosografía médica del Paraguay. Rev. Soc. Cienc. Paraguay 2(5): 203–222.

Mijares-Urrutia, A., and A. Arends R. 2000. Herpetofauna of Estado Falcón, northwestern Venezuela: a checklist with geographical and ecological data. Smithsonian Herpetological Information Service 123: 1–30.

Milá de la Roca, F. 1932. Introducción al estudio de los ofidios de Venezuela. Boletin de la Sociedad Venezolana de Ciencias Naturales 1(10): 381–392.

———. 1935. Notas sobre ofidios venenosos venezolanos. Descripción provisional de la "tigra mariposa." Caracas Médico 2(6): 319–333.

Milani Junior, R., M. T. Jorge, F. P. Ferraz de Campos, F. P. Martins, A. Bousso, J. L. Cardoso, L. A. Ribeiro, H. W. Fan, F. O. França, I. S. Sano-Martins. 1997. Snakebites by the jararacuçu (*Bothrops jararacussu*): clinicopathological studies of 29 proven cases in São Paulo State, Brazil. Quarterly Journal of Medicine 90: 323–334.

Miller, A. H., and R. C. Stebbins. 1964. The lives of desert animals in Joshua Tree National Monument. University of California Press, Berkeley.

Miller, D. M., R. A. Young, T. W. Gatlin, and J. A. Richardson. 1982. Amphibians and reptiles of the Grand Canyon. Grand Canyon Natural History Association Monograph 4. Prescott, Arizona. 144 pp.

Miller, L. 1920. The hidden people: the story of a search for Incan treasure. Scribner's, New York.

Miller, M. F. 1995. Gila monster envenomation (letter). Ann. Emerg. Med. 25: 720.

Mills, R. C. 1948. A check list of the reptiles and amphibians of Canada. Herpetologica 4(suppl. 2): 1–15.

Milstead, W. W. 1960a. Relict species of the Chihuahuan Desert. Southwest. Nat. 5(2): 75–88.

———. 1960b. Supplementary notes on the herpetofauna of the Stockton Plateau. Texas Journal of Science 12(3–4): 228–231.

Milstead, W. W., J. S. Mecham, and H. McClintock. 1950. The amphibians and reptiles of the Stockton Plateau in northern Terrell County, Texas. Texas Journal of Science 2: 543–562.

Minckley, C. O., and W. E. Rinne. 1972. Another massasauga from Mexico. Texas Journal of Science 23(3): 432–433.

Minton, J. A. 1949. Coral snake preyed upon by the bullfrog. Copeia 1949(4): 288.

Minton, S. A., Jr. 1944. Introduction to the study of the reptiles of Indiana. Am. Midl. Nat. 32: 438–477.

———. 1951 [dated 1950]. Injuries by venomous animals in Indiana. Proceedings of the Indiana Academy of Science 60: 315–323.

———. 1953. Variation in venom samples from copperheads (*Agkistrodon contortrix mokeson*) and timber rattlesnakes (*Crotalus horridus horridus*). Copeia 1953(4): 212–215.

———. 1956. Some properties of North American pitviper venoms and their correlation with phylogeny. American Association for the Advancement of Science Publ. 44: 145–151.

———. 1957a. Snakebite. Scientific American 196(1): 114–122.

———. 1957b. Variation in yield and toxicity of venom from a rattlesnake (*Crotalus atrox*). Copeia 1957(4): 265–268.

———. 1959 [dated 1958]. Observations of amphibians and reptiles of the Big Bend region of Texas. Southwest. Nat. 3(1–4): 28–54.

———. 1967. Observations on toxicity and antigenic makeup of venoms from juvenile snakes. Pp. 211–222 in F. E. Russell and P. R. Saunders (eds.), Animal toxins. Pergamon, Oxford.

———. 1969. The feeding strike of the timber rattlesnake. J. Herpetol. 3(3–4): 121–124.

———. 1972. Amphibians and reptiles of Indiana. Indiana Academy of Science Monograph No. 3. 346 pp.

———. 1974. Venom diseases. Charles C. Thomas, Springfield, Ill. 235 pp.

———. 1975. A note on the venom of an aged rattlesnake. Toxicon 13: 73–74.

———. 1976. A list of colubrid envenomations. Kentucky Herpetologist 1976 (7): 4–5.

———. 1977. Toxicity of venoms from some little known Mexican rattlesnakes. Toxicon 15: 580–581.

———. 1979a. Beware: nonpoisonous snakes. Natural History (New York) 87: 56–61.

———. 1979b. Beware: nonpoisonous snakes. Clinical Toxicology 15: 259–265.

———. 1983a. Scientists make rare find in southern Indiana: cottonmouth. Outdoor Indiana, September, pp. 14–18.

———. 1983b. *Sisturus catenatus* (Rafinesque) massasauga. Catalogue of American Amphibians and Reptiles 332.1–332.2.

———. 1985. Observations on toxicity and antigenic makeup of venoms from juvenile snakes. Pp. 211–222 in F. E. Russell and P. R. Saunders (eds.), Animal toxins. Pergamon, Oxford.

———. 1986. Venomous bites by "nonvenomous" snakes. Wilderness Medicine 3: 6–7.

———. 1990a. Immunological relationships in *Agkistrodon* and related genera. Pp. 589–600 in H. K. Gloyd and R. Conant (eds.), Snakes of the *Agkistrodon* complex: a monographic review. Society for the Study of Amphibians and Reptiles, Ithaca. 614 pp.

———. 1990b. Venomous bites by nonvenomous snakes: an annotated bibliography of colubrid envenomation. Journal of Wilderness Medicine 1: 119–127.

———. 1992. Serologic relationships among pitvipers: evidence from plasma albumins and immunodiffusion. Pp. 155–161 in J. A. Campbell and E. D. Brodie Jr. (eds.), Biology of the pitvipers. Selva, Tyler, Texas.

———. 1996. Are there any nonvenomous snakes? An update on colubrid envenoming. Advances in Herpetoculture 1: 127–134.

———. 2001. Amphibians and reptiles of Indiana, 2d ed., revised. Indiana Academy of Science, Indianapolis. 404 pp.

Minton, S. A., and M. S. da Costa. 1975. Serological relationships of sea snakes and their evolutionary implications. Pp. 33–55 in W. Dunson (ed.), The biology of sea snakes. University Park Press, Baltimore.

Minton, S. A., Jr., H. G. Dowling, and F. E. Russell. 1968. Poisonous snakes of the world. A manual for use by the U.S. amphibious forces. GPO, Washington, D.C. 212 pp.

Minton, S. A., Jr., and D. Mebs. 1978. Vier bissfälle durch Colubriden. Salamandra 14: 41–43.

Minton, S. A., Jr., and M. R. Minton. 1969. Venomous reptiles. Scribner, New York. 274 pp.

———. 1971. Venomous reptiles. London, George Allen and Unwin. 274 pp.

———. 1980. Venomous reptiles, rev. ed. Scribner, New York. 308 pp.

———. 1991. Rattlesnakes and Mexican folk medicine. Herpetol. Rev. 22(4): 116.

Minton, S. A., Jr., and B. Minton de Cervantes. 1977. Observations on the snakes of Querétaro, Mexico. Bull. Chicago Herpetol. Soc. 12(3): 69–74.

Minton, S. A., Jr., R. E. Olson, W. W. Tanner, R. W. Murphy, and B. H. Brattstrom. 1999. Comments on the proposed precedence of the specific name of *Crotalus ruber* Cope, 1892, over that of *Crotalus exsul* Garman, 1884 (Reptilia, Serpentes). Bulletin of Zoological Nomenclature 56(2): 148–149.

Minton, S. A., Jr., and S. A. Weinstein. 1984. Protease activity and lethal toxicity of venoms from some little known rattlesnakes. Toxicon 22(5): 828–830.

———. 1986. Geographic and antogenetic variation in venom of the western diamondback rattlesnake (*Crotalus atrox*). Toxicon 24(1): 71–80.

———. 1987. Colubrid snake venoms: immunologic relationships, electrophoretic patterns. Copeia 1987 (4): 993–1000.

Minton de Cervantes, B., and S. A. Minton. 1975. Geographic distribution: *Micrurus fulvius microgalbineus* (Tamaulipan coral snake). Herpetol. Rev. 6(4): 116.

Miranda, L. C., M. O. Ribera A., J. Sarmiento T., E. Salinas, and C. Navia R. (eds.). 1991. Plan de manejo de la reserva de la biósfera Estación Biológica del Bení 1991. Academia Nacional de Ciencias de Bolivia, La Paz.

Miranda, M. E., G. A. Couturier, and J. D. Williams. 1983. Guía de los ofidios bonaerenses, 2d ed. Asociación Cooperativa del Jardin Zoologica de La Plata, Buenos Aires. 72 pp.

Miranda Ribeiro, A. 1915. *Lachesis lutzi*, uma variedade de *L. pictus* Tschudi. Archivos do Museu Nacional, Rio de Janeiro, 17: 3–4.

Mitchell, J. C. 1986. Cannibalism in reptiles: a worldwide review. Society for the Study of Amphibians and Reptiles, Herpetological Circular No. 15. 37 pp.

——. 1994. The reptiles of Virginia. Smithsonian Institution Press, Washington, D.C. 352 pp.

Mitchell, J. C., and K. K. Reay. 1999. Atlas of amphibians and reptiles in Virginia. Virginia Department of Game and Inland Fisheries, Wildlife Diversity Division, Special Publication No. 1. 122 pp.

Mitchell, J. D. 1903. The poisonous snakes of Texas with notes on their habits. Transactions of the Texas Academy of Science 5: 19–48.

Mitchell, S. W., and E. T. Reichert. 1883. A partial study of the poison of Heloderma suspectum (Cope). Medical News, Philadelphia 42: 209–212.

Mittleman, M. B. 1935. A Gila monster bit me! Field and Stream 60(3 July): 72–73.

——. 1947. Miscellaneous notes on Indiana amphibians and reptiles. Am. Midl. Nat. 38(2): 466–484.

Mittleman, M. B., and R. C. Goris. 1974. Envenomation from the bite of the Japanese colubrid snake Rhabdophis tigrinus (Boie). Herpetologica 30: 113–119.

——. 1978. Death caused by the bite of the Japanese colubrid snake Rhabdophis tigrinus (Boie) (Reptilia, Serpentes, Colubridae). J. Herpetol. 12(1): 109–111.

Mittleman, M. B., and H. M. Smith. 1949. Remarks on the Mexican subspecies of the coral snake Micrurus nigrocinctus. Trans. Kansas Acad. Sci. 52(1): 86–88.

Miyata, K. 1982. A check list of the amphibians and reptiles of Ecuador with a bibliography of Ecuadorian herpetology. Smithsonian Herpetological Information Service 54: 1–70.

Mocquard, M. F. 1877. Sur une nouvelle espèce d'Elaps, E. heterochilus. Bulletin de la Société Philomathique de Paris 7(11): 39–41.

——. 1899a. Reptiles et batraciens recueillis au Mexique par M. León Diguet en 1896 et 1897. Bulletin de la Société Philomathique de Paris 9(1): 154–169.

——. 1899b. Contribution à la faune herpétologique de la Basse Californie. Nouvelles Archives du Muséum National d'Histoire Naturelle, 4th ser., 1: 297–344.

——. 1905. Diagnoses de quelques espèces nouvelles de reptiles. Bulletin du Muséum National d'Histoire Naturelle, Paris, 1st ser., 11(2): 76–79.

——. 1908–1909. Etudes sur les reptiles. Mission scientifique au Mexique et dans l'Amérique centrale . . . Recherches zoologiques. Part 3. Imprimerie Impériale, Paris.

Moesel, J. 1918. The prairie rattler in western and central New York. Copeia 1918(58): 67–68.

Mole, R. R. 1914. Trinidad snakes. Proceedings of the Agricultural Society of Trinidad and Tobago 14(603): 363–369.

——. 1924. The Trinidad snakes. Proc. Zool. Soc. London 1: 235–278.

——. 1926. The snakes of Trinidad. Port of Spain Gazette, January 10–July 15.

Mole, R. R., and F. W. Urich. 1894a. A preliminary list of the reptiles and batrachians of the island of Trinidad. Journal of the Trinidad Field Naturalists' Club 2(3): 77–90.

——. 1894b. Biological notes upon some of the Ophidia of Trinidad, B.W.I., with a preliminary list of the species recorded from the island. Proc. Zool. Soc. London 1894: 499–518.

Molenaar, G. J. 1992. Anatomy and physiology of infrared sensitivity of snakes. Pp. 367–453 in C. Gans and P. S. Ulinski (eds.), Biology of the Reptilia, vol. 17. Neurology C. Sensorimotor integration. University of Chicago Press, Chicago.

Monroe, J. E. 1962. Chromosomes of rattlesnakes. Herpetologica 17(4): 217–220.

Montalvan, D. de F., I. A. Trejos, and L. A. M. Watler. 1983. Mordedura de Ofidios venenosos en niños en la región pacífico sur. Análisis de ciento sesenta casos. Acta Médica Costarricensis 26(2): 61–70.

Montgomery, C., T. Childers, E. Bergman, J. D. Manzer, J. Sifert, B. Hill, and S. P. Mackessy. 1998. Geographic distribution: Sistrurus catenatus (massasauga). Herpetol. Rev. 29(2): 116.

Moon, B. R. 2001. Muscle physiology and the evolution of the rattling system in rattlesnakes. J. Herpetol. 35(3): 497–500.

Moonen, J. 1982. De Boomowroekoekoe Bothrops castelnaudi Dumeril, Bibron and Dumeril 1854, een weinig bekende gifslang uit zuidelijk Suriname. Paramaribo Zoo Medelingen 1. 4 pp.

Moonen, J., W. Eriks, and K. van Deursen. 1978. Surinaamse Slangeninkleur. C. Kersten, Paramaribo. 119 pp.

Moore, R. G. 1976. Seasonal and daily activity patterns and thermoregulation in the southwestern speckled rattlesnake (Crotalus mitchelli pyrrhus) and the Colorado desert sidewinder (Crotalus cerastes lateroreprens). Ph.D. diss., University of California, Davis.

——. 1978. Seasonal and daily activity patterns and thermoregulation in the southwestern speckled rattlesnake (Crotalus mitchelli pyrrhus) and the Colorado desert sidewinder (Crotalus cerastes laterorepens). Copeia 1978(3): 439–442.

Morafka, D. J. 1977. A biogeographical analysis of the Chihuahuan Desert through its herpetofauna. Dr. W. Junk, The Hague. 313 pp.

Morales, V. R., and R. W. McDiarmid. 1996. Annotated checklist of the amphibians and reptiles of Pakitza, Manu National Park Reserve Zone, with comments on the herpetofauna of Madre de Dios, Peru. Pp. 503–522 in D. E. Wilson and A. Sandoval (eds.), Manu: the biodiversity of southeastern Peru. National Museum of Natural History, Washington, D.C.

Morato de Carvalho, C. 2002. Descrição de uma nova espécie de Micrurus do estado de Roraima, Brasil (Serpentes, Elapidae). Papéis Avulsos da Universidade de São Paulo 42(8): 183–192.

Moravec, J., I. A. Tuanama, and A. M. Burgos. 2001. Reptiles recently recorded from the surroundings of Iquitos (Departamento Loreto, Peru). Casopis Náodního Muzea Rada Prírodovedná 170(1–4): 47–68.

Morelet, A. 1871. Travels in Central America, including accounts of some regions unexplored since the Conquest. Leypoldt, Holt, and Williams, New York. 430 pp.

Moreno, A. 1873. El Tepotzo. Nota sobre este reptil. Naturaleza 2: 336–338.

Moreno, E., and R. Bolaños. 1977. Hemogregarinas en serpentes de Costa Rica. Rev. Biol. Trop. 25(1): 47–57.

Morgan, B. B. 1943. The Physaloptera (Nematoda) of reptiles. Nat. Canada (Quebec) 70: 179–185.

Mori, N., and H. Sugihara. 1988. Kallikrein-like enzyme from Crotalus ruber ruber, red rattlesnake, venom. International Journal of Biochemistry 20(12): 1425–1434.

——. 1989. Characterization of kallikrein-like enzyme from Crotalus ruber ruber, red rattlesnake, venom. International Journal of Biochemistry 21(1): 83–90.

Moro, S. 1996. Osteología craneal y musculatura mandibular de tres especies de Bothrops (Serpentes: Crotalidae). Acta Zoológica Lilloana 43(2): 293–316.

Morris, M. A. 1985. Envenomation from the bite of Heterodon nasicus (Serpentes: Colubridae). Herpetologica 41(3): 361–363.

Morrissette, J., J. Kratezschmar, B. Haendler, R. El-Hayek, J. Mochca-Morales, B. M. Martin, J. R. Patel, R. L. Moss, W-D. Schleuning, R. Coronado, and L. D. Possani. 1995. Primary structure and properties of helothermine, a peptide toxin that blocks ryanodine receptors. Biophysical Journal 68: 2280–2288.

Mosauer, W. 1932a. Adaptive convergence in the sand reptiles of the Sahara and of California: a study in structure and behavior. Copeia 1932(2): 72–78.

——. 1932b. The amphibians and reptiles of the Guadalupe Mountains of New Mexico and Texas. Occas. Pap. Mus. Zool. Univ. Michigan 246: 1–18.

——. 1932c. On the locomotion of snakes. Science 76: 583–585.

——. 1933. Locomotion and diurnal range of Sonora occipitalis, Crotalus cerastes, and Crotalus atrox as seen from their tracks. Copeia 1933(1): 14–16.

——. 1935. The myology of the trunk region of snakes and its significance for ophidian taxonomy and phylogeny. Publications University of California at Los Angeles, Biol. Sci. 1: 81–120.

——. 1936. The reptilian fauna of sand dune areas of the Vizcaino Desert and of northwestern Lower California. Occas. Pap. Mus. Zool. Univ. Michigan 329: 1–22.

Mosauer, W., and E. L. Lazier. 1933. Death from insolation in desert snakes. Copeia 1933(3): 149.

Moseley, T. 1966. Coral snake bite: recovery following respiratory paralysis. Annals of Surgery 163: 943–948.

Mosimann, J. E., and G. B. Rabb. 1952. The herpetology of Tiber Reservoir Area, Montana. Copeia 1952(1): 23–27.

Moski, H. 1954. A large litter of copperheads (*Agkistrodon contortrix mokeson*). Copeia 1954(1): 67.

Mosquera Leiva, C. E. 2000. Ofidismo en la Amazon. Estudio clinico-epidemiologico de los accidentes ofidicos en el Hospital Regional de Loreto. Estudio retrospectico de 65 casos ocurridos en los años de 1998 y 1999. Unpublished ms.

Mount, R. H. 1975. The reptiles and amphibians of Alabama. Auburn Printing Company, Auburn, Ala. 347 pp.

Mount, R. H., and J. Cecil. 1982. Natural history notes: *Agkistrodon piscivorus* (cottonmouth). Hybridization. Herpetol. Rev. 13(3): 95–96.

Mount, R. H., and G. W. Folkerts. 1968. Distribution of some Alabama reptiles and amphibians. Herpetologica 24(3): 259–262.

Moura-da-Silva, A., G. Laing, and M. Paine. 1996. Processing of pro-tumor necrosis factor-alpha by venom metalloproteinases: A hypothesis explaining local tissue damage following snake bite. European Journal of Immunology 26: 2000–2005.

Moura Gonçalves. 1956. Estudos sôbre venenos de serpientes brasileiras. II. *Crotalus terrificus crotaminicus*, subespécie biológica. Anais da Academia Brasileira de Ciências 28(3): 365–367.

Mudde, P., and T. Van Dijk. 1985. Herpetologische waarnemingen in Costa Rica (13). Slangen (Serpentes). Lacerta 43: 76–180.

Mulcahy, D. G., J. R. Mendelson III, K. W. Setser, and E. Hollenbeck. 2003. *Crotalus cerastes* (sidewinder). Prey/predator weight-ratio. Herpetol. Rev. 34(1): 64.

Müller, F. 1877. Mittheilungen aus der herpetologischen Sammlung des Basler Museums. 39 pp.

——. 1878a. Mitteilungen aus der herpetologischen Sammlung des Basler Museums. Verhandlungen der Naturforschenden Gesellschaft in Basel 6: 389–427.

——. 1878b. Katalog der im Museum und Universitätskabinet zu Baselaufgestellen Amphibien und Reptilien nebst Anmerkungen. Verhandlungen der Naturforschenden Gesellschaft in Basel 6: 559–709.

——. 1879. *Ituna* and *Thyridia*; a remarkable case of mimicry in butterflies. Transactions of the Entomological Society of London 1879: xx–xxix.

——. 1880. Katalog der herpetologischen Sammlung des Basler Museums (Erster Nach.). 49 pp.

——. 1882. Erster Nachtrag zum Katalog der herpetologischen Sammlung des Basler Museums. Verhandlung der Naturforschenden Gesellschaft in Basel 7: 120–165.

——. 1885. Vierter Nachtrag zum Katalog der herpetologischen Sammlung des Basler Museums. Verhandlung der Naturforschenden Gesellschaft in Basel 7(3): 668–717.

Müller, J. W. 1865. Reisen in den Vereinigten Staaten, Canada und Mexiko. III. Beiträge zur Geschichte, Statistik, und Zoologie von Mexiko. Dritte Abtheilung. Die Wirbelthiere Mexikos. III. Amphibia. Brockhaus, Leipzig. 643 pp.

Müller, L. 1923. Ueber neue oder seltene mittel- und sudamerikanische Amphibien und Reptilien. Mitteilungen aus dem Zoologischen Museum in Berlin 11(1): 77–93.

——. 1926. Neue Reptilien und Batrachier der zoologischen Sammlung der bayerischen Staates. Zoologischer Anzeiger (Leipzig) 65: 193–200.

——. 1927. Amphibien und reptilien der Ausbeute Prof. Breslau's in Brasilien 1913–14. Abhandlungen der Senckenbergischen Naturforschenden Gesellschaft (Frankfurt am Main) 40(3): 259–304.

Müller, P. 1968. Die herpetofauna der Insel von São Sebastião (Brasilien). Saarbrucher Zeitung Verl. und Druckerei, Saarbrucken. 68 pp.

——. 1969a. Vertebratenfaunen brasilianischer Inseln als Indikatoren für glaziale und postglaziale Vegetationsfluktuationen. Zoologischer Anzeiger (Leipzig) 33(suppl.): 97–107.

——. 1969b. Herpetologische Beobachtungen auf der Insel Marajo. Deutschlands führender Aquarien- und Terrarien- Zeitschrift 22(4): 117–121.

——. 1971. Herpetologische Reiseeindrucke aus Brasilien. Salamandra 7(1): 9–30.

——. 1973. The dispersal centres of terrestrial vertebrates in the Neotropical realm. Dr. W. Junk, The Hague. 244 pp.

Muñoz-Alonzo, L. A. 1988. Estudio herpetofaunísctico del Parque Ecológico Estatal de Omiltemi, Mpio. de Chilapancingo, Guerrero. Tésis Biol. Fac. Ciencias, UNAM. 102 pp.

Munro, D. F. 1947. Effect of a bite by *Sistrurus* on *Crotalus*. Herpetologica 4(2): 57.

Murayama, N., M. A. F. Hayashi, H. Ohi, L. A. Ferreira, V. V. Hermann, H. Saito, Y. Fujita, S. Higuchi, B. L. Fernandes, T. Yamane, A. C. de Camargo, et al. 1997. Cloning and sequence analysis of a *Bothrops jararaca* cDNA encoding a precursor of 7 bradykinin-potentiating peptides and a C-type natriuretic peptide. Proceedings of the National Academy of Sciences 94: 1189–1193.

Murphy, J. B., C. C. Carpenter, and J. C. Gillingham. 1978. Caudal luring in the green tree python, *Chondropython viridis* (Reptilia, Serpentes, Boidae). J. Herpetol. 12: 117–119.

Murphy, J. B., and L. A. Mitchell. 1984. Miscellaneous notes on the reproductive biology of reptiles. 6. Thirteen varieties of the genus *Bothrops* (Serpentes, Crotalidae). Acta Zoologica et Pathologica Antverpiensia 78: 199–214.

Murphy, J. B., L. A. Mitchell, and J. A. Campbell. 1979. Miscellaneous notes on the reproductive biology of reptiles. III. The Uracoan rattlesnake, *Crotalus vegrandis* Klauber (Serpentes, Viperidae). J. Herpetol. 13(3): 373–374.

Murphy, J. C. 1997. Amphibians and reptiles of Trinidad and Tobago. Krieger, Malabar, Fla. 245 pp.

Murphy, J. C., and R. W. Henderson. 1997. Tales of giant snakes. Kreiger, Malabar, Fla. 221 pp.

Murphy, R. C. 1917 [dated 1916]. Natural history observations from the Mexican portion of the Colorado desert, with a note on the Lower California pronghorn and a list of birds. Proceedings of the Linnean Society of New York (28–29): 43–101.

Murphy, R. W. 1975. Two new blind snakes (Serpentes: Leptotyphlopidae) from Baja California, Mexico, with a contribution to the biogeography of peninsular and insular herpetofauna. Proceedings of the California Academy of Science, 4th ser., 40: 93–107.

——. 1983a. Paleobiogeography and genetic differentiation of the Baja California herpetofauna. Occasional Papers of the California Academy of Sciences (137): 1–48.

——. 1983b. The reptiles: origin and evolution. Pp. 130–158 in T. J. Case and M. L. Cody (eds.), Island biogeography in the Sea of Cortez. University of California Press, Berkeley.

——. 1983c. A distributional checklist of the reptiles and amphibians on the islands in the Sea of Cortez. Pp. 429–437 in T. J. Case and M. L. Cody (eds.), Island biogeography in the Sea of Cortez. University of California Press, Berkeley.

——. 1988. The problematic phylogenetic analysis of interlocus heteropolymer isozyme characters: a case study from sea snakes and cobras. Canadian Journal of Zoology 66: 2628–2633.

Murphy, R. W., W. E. Cooper Jr., and W. S. Richardson. 1983. Phylogenetic relationships of the North American five-lined skinks, genus *Eumeces* (Sauria: Scincidae). Herpetologica 39: 200–211.

Murphy, R. W., and B. Crabtree. 1985a. Evolutionary aspects of isozyme patterns, number of loci, and tissue-specific gene expression in the prairie rattlesnake, *Crotalus viridis viridis*. Herpetologica 41: 451–470.

——. 1985b. Genetic relationships of the Santa Catalina Island Rattleless Rattlesnake, *Crotalus catalinensis* (Serpentes: Viperidae). Acta Zoologica Mexicana, new ser., 9: 1–16.

——. 1988. Genetic identification of a natural hybrid rattlesnake: *Crotalus scutulatus scutulatus × C. viridis viridis*. Herpetologica 44(1): 119–123.

Murphy, R. W., and K. D. Doyle. 1998. Phylophenetics: frequencies and polymorphic characters in genealogical estimation. Syst. Biol. 47: 737–761.

Murphy, R. W., J. Fu, A. Lathrop, J. V. Feltham, and V. Kovac. 2002. Phylogeny of the rattlesnakes (*Crotalus* and *Sistrurus*) inferred from sequences of five mitochondrial DNA genes. Pp. 69–92 in G. W. Schuett, M. Höggren, M. E. Douglas, and H. W. Greene (eds.), Biology of the vipers. Eagle Mountain Publishing, Eagle Mountain, Utah.

Murphy, R. W., V. Kovac, O. Haddrath, G. S. Oliver, A. Fishbein, and N. E. Mandrak. 1995. MtDNA gene sequence, allozyme, and morphological uniformity among red diamond rattlesnakes, *Crotalus ruber* and *Crotalus exsul*. Canadian Journal of Zoology 73(2): 270–281.

Murphy, R. W., D. J. Morafka, and R. D. MacCulloch. 1989. Phylogenetic relationships of rattlesnakes as revealed by protein electrophoresis (abstract). Symposium of the Texas Herpetological Society, p. 10.

Murphy, R. W., and J. R. Ottley. 1984. Distribution of amphibians and reptiles on islands in the Gulf of California. Annals of Carnegie Museum 53(8): 207–230.

Murphy, T. D. 1964. Box turtle, *Terrapene carolina*, in stomach of copperhead, *Agkistrodon contortrix*. Copeia 1964(1): 221.

Murray, K. F. 1955. Herpetological collections from Baja California. Herpetologica 11(1): 33–48.

Murrell, G. 1981. The effectiveness of the pressure/immobilization first aid technique in the case of a tiger snake bite. Medical Journal of Australia 2: 295.

Myers, C. W. 1954. Subspecific identity of *Crotalus horridus* in Washington County, Missouri. Copeia 1954(4): 300–301.

——. 1965. Biology of the ringneck snake, *Diadophis punctatus*, in Florida. Bulletin of the Florida State Museum 10(2): 43–90.

——. 1969a. The ecological geography of cloud forest in Panama. Am. Mus. Novitat. 2396: 1–52.

——. 1969b. Snakes of the genus *Coniophanes* in Panama. Am. Mus. Novitat. 2372: 1–28.

——. 1972. The status of herpetology in Panamá. Pp. 199–209 in M. L. Jones (ed.), The Panamanian biota: some observations prior to a sea-level canal. Bulletin of the Biological Society of Washington 2: 1–270.

——. 1984. Subcircular pupil shape in the snake *Tantalophis* (Colubridae). Copeia 1984(1): 215–216.

Myers, C. W., and J. A. Campbell. 1981. A new genus and species of colubrid snake from the Sierra Madre del Sur of Guerrero, Mexico. Am. Mus. Novitat. 2708: 1–20.

Myers, C. W., J. W. Daly, and B. Malkin. 1978. A dangerously toxic new frog (*Phyllobates*) used by Emberá Indians of western Colombia, with discussion of blowgun fabrication and dart poisoning. Bull. Am. Mus. Nat. Hist. 161(2): 307–366.

Myers, C. W., and A. S. Rand. 1969. Checklist of amphibians and reptiles of Barro Colorado Island, Panama, with comments on faunal change and sampling. Smithsonian Contributions to Zoology 19: 1–11.

Myers, G. S. 1945. Nocturnal observations on sea-snakes in Bahia Honda, Panama. Herpetologica 3(1): 22–23.

Myers, N. 1984. The primary source. Norton, New York. 399 pp.

Myint-Lwin, D. A. Warrell, R. E. Phillips, Tin-Nu-Swe, Tun-Pe, and Maung-Maung-Lay. 1985. Bites by Russell's viper (*Vipera russelli siamensis*) in Burma: haemostatic, vascular, and renal disturbances and response to treatment. Lancet 2: 1259–1264.

Nadeau, M. R. 1978. Geographic distribution: *Crotalus scutulatus scutulatus* (Mojave rattlesnake). Herpetol. Rev. 9(4): 142.

Nahas, L., A. S. Kamiguti, and M. A. R. Barros. 1979. Thrombin-like and factor X-activator components of *Bothrops* snake venoms. Thrombos. Haemostas. (Stuttgart) 41(2): 314–328.

Nahas, L., A. S. Kamiguti, H. W. Rzeppa, I. S. Sano, and S. Matsunaga. 1975. Effect of heparin on the coagulant action of snake venoms. Toxicon 13: 457–463.

Nahas, L., A. S. Kamiguti, M. C. C. Sousa, E. Silva, M. A. A. Ribiero de Barros, and P. Morena. 1983. The inactivating effect of *Bothrops jararaca* and *Waglerophis merremii* snake plasma on the coagulant activity of various snake venoms. Toxicon 19: 749–755.

Nascimento, F. P., T. C. S. Avila-Pires, and O. R. Rodrigues da Cunha. 1987. Os répteis da área de Carajás, Pará, Brasil (Squamata). II. Boletim do Museu Paraense Emílio Goeldi, Zoologia 3(1): 33–65.

——. 1988. Répteis squamata de Rondônia e Mato Grosso colectados atraves do programa polonoroeste. Boletim do Museu Paraense Emílio Goeldi, Zoologia 4(1): 21–66.

Nascimento, F. P., T. C. S. Avila-Pires, I. N. F. F. dos Santos, and A. C. Marinho Lima. 1991. Répteis de Marajó, Pará, Brasil. I. Revisão bibliográfica e novos registros. Boletim do Museu Paraense Emílio Goelldi, Zoologia 7(1): 25–41.

Nascimento, S. P. 2000. Epidemiological characteristics of snakebites in the State of Roraima, Brazil, 1992–1998. Cadernos de Saúde Pública (Rio de Janeiro) 16: 271–276.

National *Crotalus* News. 1993a. Quarterly Publication of the National *Crotalus* Society 1(3): 4–5.

——. 1993b. Quarterly Publication of the National *Crotalus* Society 1(4): 4–5.

——. 1994. Quarterly Publication of the National *Crotalus* Society 2(3): 4–6.

——. 1995. Quarterly Publication of the National *Crotalus* Society 3(4): 3–7.

Necker, W. L. 1939. Poisonous snakes of Illinois. Chicago Naturalist 2: 35–47.

Neill, W. T. 1947a. Hibernation of amphibians and reptiles in Richmond County, Georgia. Herpetologica 4(3): 107–114.

——. 1947b. Size and habits of the cottonmouth moccasin. Herpetologica 3(6): 203–205.

——. 1948. The yellow tail of juvenile copperheads. Herpetologica 4(5): 161.

——. 1949. A checklist of the amphibians and reptiles of Georgia. Ross Allen's Reptile Institute, Silver Springs, Fla. 4 pp.

——. 1951. Notes on the natural history of certain North American snakes. Publications of the Research Division of Ross Allen's Reptile Institute 1: 47–60.

——. 1952. The pygmy rattlesnake, *Sistrurus miliarius barbouri*, in southwestern Florida. Copeia 1952(1): 48.

——. 1954. Evidence of venom in snakes of the genera *Alsophis* and *Rhadinaea*. Copeia 1954(1): 59–60.

——. 1957a. Some misconceptions regarding the eastern coral snake, *Micrurus fulvius*. Herpetologica 13(2): 111–118.

——. 1957b. The vipers of Queimada Grande. Nature Magazine, April, pp. 188–191.

——. 1958. The occurrence of amphibians and reptiles in saltwater areas, and a bibliography. Bulletin of Marine Science of the Gulf and Caribbean 8(1): 1–97.

——. 1959. Additions to the British Honduras herpetofaunal list. Herpetologica 15(4): 235–240.

——. 1960a. Nature and man in British Honduras. Maryland Naturalist 30(1–4): 2–14.

——. 1960b. The caudal lure of various juvenile snakes. Quarterly Journal of the Florida Academy of Science 23: 173–200.

——. 1961. Giant rattlesnakes—past and present. Florida Wildlife 15: 10–13.

——. 1962. The reproductive cycle of snakes in a tropical region, British Honduras. Quarterly Journal of the Florida Academy of Sciences 25(3): 234–253.

——. 1963. Polychromatism in snakes. Quarterly Journal of the Florida Academy of Sciences 26: 194–216.

——. 1964. Viviparity in snakes: Some ecological and zoogeographical considerations. American Naturalist 48: 35–55.

——. 1965. New and noteworthy amphibians and reptiles from British Honduras. Bulletin of the Florida State Museum, Biological Sciences, 9(3): 77–130.

——. 1966. Notes on *Bothrops hyoprora* (Serpentes, Crotalidae). Herpetologica 22(3): 235–239.

——. 1968. Snake eats snake. Florida Wildlife 21: 22–25.

Neill, W. T., and R. Allen. 1955. Metachrosis in snakes. Quarterly Journal of the Florida Academy of Sciences 18(3): 207–215.

——. 1959a. Studies on the amphibians and reptiles of British Honduras. Publications of the Research Division, Ross Allen's Reptile Institute 2(1): 1–76.

——. 1959b. Additions to the British Honduras herpetofaunal list. Herpetologica 15(4): 235–240.

——. 1960. Noteworthy snakes from British Honduras. Herpetologica 16(3): 145–162.

——. 1962. Reptiles of the Cambridge Expedition to British Honduras, 1959–1960. Herpetologica 18(2): 79–91.

Nelson, D. J. 1950. A treatment for helminthiasis in Ophidia. Herpetologica 6: 57–59.

Nelson, E. W. 1922. Lower California and its natural resources. Memoirs of the National Academy of Sciences (Washington, D.C.) 16(1): 1–194.

Nelson, M. A. 1988. Geographic distribution: *Sistrurus miliarius streckeri* (western pigmy rattlesnake). Herpetol. Rev. 19(1): 20–21.

Nemuras, K. 1967. Notes on the herpetology of Panama: part 4. Dry season in the tropics. Bull. Maryland Herpetol. Soc. 3(3): 63–71.

Netting, M. G. 1930. The poisonous snakes of Pennsylvania and the treatment of snake-bite. Annals of Carnegie Museum 19: 175–184.

——. 1932. The poisonous snakes of Pennsylvania. Carnegie Museum of Vertebrate Zoology, Pamphlet 1.

Nevares, M., and A. Quijada-Mascareñas. 1989. Life history notes: *Crotalus scutulatus scutulatus* (Mojave rattlesnake). Mating behavior. Herpetol. Rev. 20(3): 71.

Nicéforo-María, H. 1929a. Rabo de Chucha del Chocó. Revista de la Sociedad Colombiana de Ciencias Naturales 4(103): 185–188.

——. 1929b. Observaciones acerca de algunos nombres científicos que emplea el Dr. Evaristo García en su obra titulada Los ofidios venenosos del Cauca. Revista de la Sociedad Colombiana de Ciencias Naturales 18(103): 189–191.

——. 1930a. La colgadora o víbora: *Bothrops schlegelii*. Boletín del Instituto de La Salle (Bogotá) 17(125): 129–132.

——. 1930b. Los reptiles de Villavicencio en el museo de La Salle. Revista de la Sociedad Colombiana de Ciencias Naturales 19: 40–54.

——. 1930c. Los reptiles y batracios de Honda (Tolima) en el Museo de La Salle. Revista de la Sociedad Colombiana de Ciencias Naturales 19(106): 96–104.

——. 1933. Las serpientes de Villavicencio. Pp. 199–237 in Libro conmemorativo del segundo centenario de Don José Celestino Bruno Mutis y Bosio, 1732–1932. Imprenta Nacional, Bogotá.

——. 1938. Las serpientes colombianas de hocico proboscidiforme, grupo *Bothrops lansbergii-nasuta-hyoprora*. Revista de la Academia Colombiana de Ciencias Exactas, Físicas, y Naturales 2(7): 417–421.

——. 1939. Contribución al estudio de la ofiología colombiana. Revista de la Academia Colombiana de Ciencias Exactas, Físicas, y Naturales 3(9–10): 91–94.

——. 1942. Los ofidios de Colombia. Revista de la Academia Colombiana de Ciencias Exactas, Físicas, y Naturales 5(17): 84–101.

——. 1964. Herpetología. Boletín del Instituto de La Salle (Bogotá) 204: 129–135.

——. 1975. Contribución al estudio de las serpientes de Colombia II. Boletín del Instituto de La Salle (Bogotá) 215: 1–4.

Nichols, A. 1986. Envenomation by a bluestripe garter snake, *Thamnophis sirtalis sirtalis*. Herp. Rev. 17(1): 6.

Nickerson, M. A., and R. W. Henderson. 1976. A case of envenomation by the South American colubrid, *Philodryas olfersi*. Herpetologica 32(2): 197–198.

Nickerson, M. A., and C. E. Mays. 1968. More aberrations in the color patterns of rattlesnakes (genus *Crotalus*). Wasmann Journal of Biology 26(1): 125–131.

——. 1970 [dated 1969]. A preliminary herpetofaunal analysis of the Graham (Pinaleno) mountain region, Graham Co., Arizona, with ecological comments. Trans. Kansas Acad. Sci. 72(4): 492–505.

Nickerson, M. A., and A. E. McDaniels. 1967. Amphibious behavior in northern copperheads, *Agkistrodon contortrix mokeson* (Daudin). Herpetologica 31(1): 60–61.

Nickerson, M. A., R. A. Sajdak, R. W. Henderson, and S. Ketcham. 1978. Notes on the movements of some Neotropical snakes (Reptilia, Serpentes). J. Herpetol. 12(3): 419–422.

Nierembergii, I. E. 1635. Historia naturae, maxime peregrinae, libris XVI. Distincta Antverpiae, Belthasaris Moreti.

Nikol'skii, A. M. 1916. Fauna of Russia and adjacent countries. Translated by the Israel Program for Scientific Translations. 1964.

Nishioka, S. A., M. T. Jorge, P. V. P. Silveira, and L. A. Ribeiro. 2000a. South American rattlesnakebite and soft-tissue infection: report of a case. Revista da Sociedade Brasileira de Medicina Tropical 33: 401–402.

Nishioka, S. A., and P. V. Silveira. 1994. *Philodryas patagoniensis* bite and local envenoming. Revista do Instituto de Medicina Tropical de São Paulo 36(3): 279–281.

Nishioka, S. A., P. V. P. Silveira, and L. B. Menzes. 1993. Coral snake bite and severe local pain. Annals of Tropical Medicine and Parasitology 87: 429–431.

Nishioka, S. A., P. V. P. Silveira, F. M. Peixoto-Filho, et al. 2000b. Occupational injuries with captive lance-headed vipers (*Bothrops moojeni*): experience from a snake farm in Brazil. Tropical Medicine and International Health 5: 507–510.

Nixon, K. C., and J. M. Carpenter. 1993. On outgroups. Cladistics 9: 413–426.

Nobile, M., V. Magnelli, L. Lagostena, J. Mochca-Morales, L. D. Possani, and G. Prestipino. 1994. The toxin helothermine affects potassium currents in newborn rat cerebellar granule cells. Journal of Membrane Biology 139: 49–55.

Nobile, M., F. Noceti, and G. Prestipino. 1996. Helothermine, a lizard venom toxin, inhibits calcium current in cerebellar granules. Experimental Brain Research 110: 15–20.

Noble, G. K., and A. Schmidt. 1937. The structure and function of the facial and labial pits of snakes. Proceedings of the American Philosophical Society 7(3): 262–288.

Noguchi, H. 1909. Snake venoms. An investigation of venomous snakes with special reference to the phenomena of their venoms. Carnegie Institution, Washington D.C. 315 pp.

Nogueira, C., and P. H. Valdujo. 2001. Geographic distribution: *Bothrops alternatus* (urutu). Herpetol. Rev. 32(1): 58.

Norell, M. A., and K. Gao. 1997. Braincase and phylogenetic relationships of *Estesia mongoliensis* from the Late Cretaceous of the Gobi Desert and the recognition of a new clade of lizards. Am. Mus. Novitat. 3211: 1–25.

Norell, M. A., M. C. McKenna, and M. J. Novacek. 1992. *Estesia mongoliensis*, a new fossil varanoid from the Late Cretaceous Barun Goyot formation of Mongolia. Am. Mus. Novitat. 3045: 1–24.

Norman, D. R. 1994. Amphibians and reptiles of the Paraguayan Chaco, vol. 1. D. Norman, San José, Costa Rica. 281 pp.

Norris, K. S. 1967. Color adaptations in desert reptiles and its thermal relationships. Pp. 162–229 in Milstead (ed.), Lizard ecology: a symposium. University of Missouri Press, Columbia. 300 pp.

Norris, K. S., and C. H. Lowe. 1964. An analysis of background color matching in amphibians and reptiles. Ecology 45: 565–580.

Norris, R. L. 1999. Envenomations. Pp. 1625–1637, in R. S. Irwin, F. B. Cerr, and J. M. Rippe (eds.), Intensive care medicine, 4th ed., 2 vols. Lippincott-Raven, Philadelphia.

Norris, R. L., and R. C. Dart. 1989. Apparent coral snake envenomation in a patient without fang marks. American Journal of Emergency Medicine 7: 402–405.

Norris, R. L., and S. A. Minton. 2001. Non–North American venomous reptile bites. Pp. 927–951 in P. S. Auerbach (ed.), Wilderness medicine. Mosby, St. Louis.

Norton, A. H. 1929. The rattlesnake in Maine. Maine Naturalist 9: 25–28.

Nuismer, S. L., J. N. Thompson, and R. Gomulkiewicz. 2000. Coevolutionary clines across selection mosaics. Evolution 54: 1102–1115.

Numeric, P., V. Moravie, M. Didier, D. Chatot-Henry, S. Cirille, B. Bucher, and L. Thomas. 2002. Multiple cerebral infarctions following a snakebite by *Bothrops caribbaeus*. American Journal of Tropical Medicine and Hygiene 67(3): 287–288.

Nussbaum, R. A., E. D. Brodie Jr., and R. M. Storm. 1983. Amphibians and reptiles of the Pacific Northwest. University of Idaho Press, Moscow. 332 pp.

Nussbaum, R. A., and R. F. Hoyer. 1974. Geographic variation and the validity of subspecies in the rubber boa, *Charina bottae* (Blainville). Northwest Science 48: 219–229.

Nutter, R. B. 1927. Report of snake-bite cases. Bull. Antivenin Inst. Am. 1(2): 38–39.

Nydam, R. L. 2000. A new taxon of helodermatid-like lizard from the Albian-Cenomanian of Utah. Journal of Vertebrate Paleontology 20(2): 285–294.

Obrecht, C. B. 1946. Notes on South Carolina reptiles and amphibians. Copeia 1946(2): 71–74.

Obst, F. J. 1977. Die herpetologische Sammlung des Staatlichen Museums für Tierkunde Dresden und ihre Typusexamplare. Zoologische Abhandlungen Staatliches Museum für Tierkunde in Dresden 34(13): 171–186.

Ocaranza, F. 1930. Sistemática de los animales ponzoñosos de la América Latina y acción biológica de sus venenos. Medicina 10(121): 357–374.

Ochoterena, I. 1934. Distribución geográfica de los animales de México. Reseñas Científicas 9: 23–41.

Odermatt, C. 1940. Beitrage zur Kenntniss des Gebisses von *Heloderma*. Vierteljahresschrift der Naturforschenden Gesellschaft in Zürich 85(3–4): 98–141.

Offerman, S. R., T. S. Smith, and R. W. Derlet. 2001. Does the aggressive use of polyvalent antivenin for rattlesnake bites result in serious acute side effects? Western Journal of Medicine 175: 88–91.

Ogawa, H., and Y. Sawai. 1986. Fatal bite of the yamakagashi (*Rhabdophis tigrinus*). Snake 18: 53–54.

Ohmart, R. D., B. W. Anderson, and W. C. Hunter. 1988. The ecology of the lower Colorado River from Davis Dam to the Mexico–United States international boundary: a community profile. USFWS Biological Report 85 (7.19). 296 pp.

Oken, L. 1816. Lehrbuch der Naturgeschichte, Dritter Theil. Zoologie. Zweite Abteilung. Fleischtiere. August Schmid, Jena. 1270 pp.

Oldfield, B., and D. Keyler. 1989. Survey of timber rattlesnake (*Crotalus horridus*) distribution along the Mississippi River in western Wisconsin. Transactions of the Wisconsin Academy of Sciences, Arts, and Letters 77: 27–34.

———. 1997. Timber rattlesnakes: velvet tails of Minnesota's blufflands. Pp. 22–26 in J. J. Moriarty and D. Jones (eds.), Minnesota's amphibians and reptiles, their conservation and status: proceedings of a symposium. Serpent's Tale Natural History Book Distributors, Lanesboro, Minn.

Oldfield, B., and J. J. Moriarty. 1994. Amphibians and reptiles native to Minnesota. University of Minnesota Press, Minneapolis. 240 pp.

Oldham, M. J. 1985. Natural history notes: *Sistrurus catenatus catenatus* (eastern massasauga). Pattern. Herpetol. Rev. 16(2): 57.

Olin, N. 1930. Reminiscences of Milwaukee in 1835–1836. Wisconsin Magazine of History 13: 201–223.

Oliver, J. A. 1937. Notes on a collection of amphibians and reptiles from the state of Colima, Mexico. Occas. Pap. Mus. Zool. Univ. Michigan 360: 1–30.

———. 1958. Snakes in fact and fiction. Macmillan, New York. 199 pp.

Olson, R. E. 1967. Peripheral range extensions and some new records of Texas amphibians and reptiles. Texas Journal of Science 19(1): 99–106.

Oostburg, B. F. J. 1973. Case report. A snakebite in Surinam. Tropical and Geographical Medicine 25: 187–189.

Oppel, M. 1811a. Mémoire sur la classification des reptiles. Ordre II. Reptiles à écailles. Section II. Ophidiens. Annales du Musée National d'Histoire Naturelle, Paris 16: 254–295, 376–393.

———. 1811b. Die Ordnungen, Familien, und Gattungen der Reptilien als Prodrom einer Naturgeschichte derselben. Joseph Lindauer, Munich. 86 pp.

Orcés, G. 1942. Los ofidios venenosos del Ecuador. Flora (Quito) 2: 147–155.

———. 1943. Ofidios venenosos del Ecuador. Flora (Quito) 3: 165–170.

———. 1948. Notas sobre los ofidios venenosos del Ecuador. Revista Filosofia Letras (Quito) 3: 231–250.

Orduna, T. A., O. A. L. Martino, P. Bernachea, and S. Maulen. 1994. Ofidismo provocado por mordedura de culebra del genero *Philodryas*. Prensa Médica Argentina 81: 636–638.

Orr, R. T. 1965. An expedition to the Sea of Cortez. Animals 6: 86–91.

———. 1982. Vertebrate biology, 5th ed. Saunders, Philadelphia. 568 pp.

Orrengo-Aravena. 1971. Rept. La Pampa. Biblioteca Pam. Serie Folleto 14.

Ortenburger, A. I. 1925. Preliminary list of the snakes of Oklahoma. Proceedings of the Oklahoma Academy of Science 5: 83–87.

———. 1929. Reptiles and amphibians from southeastern Oklahoma and southwestern Arkansas. Copeia 1929(170): 8–12.

Ortenburger, A. I., and R. D. Ortenburger. 1927 [dated 1926]. XVII. Field observations on some amphibians and reptiles of Pima County, Arizona. Proceedings of the Oklahoma Academy of Science 6: 101–121.

Ortenburger, R. D. 1924. Notes on the Gila monster. Proceedings of the Oklahoma Academy of Science 4: 22.

Orth, J. C. 1939. Moth larvae in a copperhead's stomach. Copeia 1939(1): 54–55.

Orton, J. 1876. The Andes and the Amazon; or, across the continent of South America, 3d ed. Harper and Brothers, New York. 645 pp.

O'Shea, M. T. 1989. New departmental records for northeastern Honduran herpetofauna. Herpetol. Rev. 20(1): 16.

Oshima, M. 1920. Notes on the venomous snakes from the islands of Formosa and Riu Kiu. Annual Report of the Institute of Science, Government of Formosa, Taihoku 8(2): 1–99.

Osorio Tafall, B. F. 1948. La Isla de Cedros, Baja California. Ensayo monográfico. Boletin Sociedad Mexicana de Geografía y Estadística 66(3): 318–402.

Otero, R. 1994. Manual de diagnóstico y tratamiento del accidente ofídico. Editorial Universidad de Antioquia, Medellín, Colombia. 87 pp.

———. 2000. Epidemiología y aspectos clínicos del accidente ofídico en Colombia: envenenamiento bothrópico grave (abstract). Pp. 14–16 in Simposio internacional—el envenenamiento ofídico: un problema de salud pública en Latino América, 5–6 April 2000, San José, Costa Rica.

Otero-P., R., R. Fonnegra-G., and S. Luz Jiménez-R. 2000. Plantas utilizadas contra mordeduras de serpientes en Antioquia y Chocó, Colombia. Grandacolor, Medellín.

Otero, R., J. Gutiérrez, M. B. Mesa, E. Duque, O. Rodriguez, J. Luis Arango, F. Gomez, A. Toro, F. Cano, L. Maria Rodriguez L., et al. 2002. Complications of *Bothrops*, *Porthidium*, and *Bothriechis* snakebites in Colombia: a clinical and epidemiological study of 39 cases attended in a university hospital. Toxicon 40(8):1107–1114.

Otero, R., R. G. Osorio, R. Valderrama, and C. A. Giraldo. 1992a. Efectos farmacológicos y enzimáticos de los venenos de serpientes de Antioquia y Chocó (Colombia). Toxicon 30(5–6): 611–620.

Otero, R., G. S. Tobón, L. Fernando Gómez, R. Osorio, R. Valderrama, D. Hoyos, J. E. Urreta, S. Molina, and J. J. Arboleda. 1992b. Accidente ofídico en Antioquia y Chocó. Aspectos clínicos y epidemiológicos (marzo de 1989–febrero de 1990). Acta Médica Colombiana 17: 229–249.

Otero Patiño, R., G. S. Tobón Jaramillo, L. F. Gómez, et al. 1993. Bites from the bushmaster (*Lachesis muta*) in Antioquia and Chocó, report of five accidents (abstract). Toxicon 31: 97–179.

Otten, E. J. 1983. Antivenin therapy in the emergency department. American Journal of Emergency Medicine 1: 83–93.

Otten, E. J., and D. McKimm. 1983. Venomous snakebite in a patient allergic to horse serum. Ann. Emerg. Med. 12: 624–627.

Ottley, J. R. 1981a. Geographic distribution: *Heloderma horridum exasperatum* (Rio Fuerte beaded lizard). Herpetol. Rev. 12(2): 64.

———. 1981b. Geographic distribution: *Heloderma suspectum suspectum* (reticulate Gila monster). Herpetol. Rev. 12(2): 65.

———. 1981c. Geographic distribution: *Crotalus viridis helleri* (southern Pacific rattlesnake). Herpetol. Rev. 12(2): 65.

Ottley, J. R., and L. E. Hunt. 1981. *Crotalus viridis helleri*: geographic distribution. Herpetol. Rev. 12: 65.

Ouyang, C., C. M. Teng, and T. F. Huang. 1992. Characterization of snake venom components acting on blood coagulation and platelet function. Toxicon 30: 945–966.

Over, W. H. 1923. Amphibians and reptiles of South Dakota. South Dakota Geological and Natural History Survey Bulletin 12: 1–34.

Oviedo y Valdes, G. F. 1535. Historia general y natural de las Indias. Seville, Spain.

Owings, D. H., R. G. Coss, D. McKernon, M. P. Rowe, and P. C. Arrowood. 2001. Snake directed behavior of rock squirrels (*Spermophilus variegatus*): population differences and snake species discrimination. Behaviour 138: 575–595.

Ownby, C. L., D. Cameron, and A. T. Tu. 1976. Isolation of myotoxic component from rattlesnake (*Crotalus viridis viridis*) venom. American Journal of Pathology 85: 149–166.

Ownby, C. L., and T. R. Colberg. 1986. Ability of polyvalent (Crotalidae) antivenom to neutralize local myonecrosis induced by *Crotalus atrox* venom. Toxicon 24: 201–203.

Ownby, C. L., T. R. Colberg, P. L. Claypool, and G. V. Odell. 1984. In vivo test of the ability of antiserum to myotoxin a from prairie rattlesnake (*Crotalus viridis viridis*) venom to neutralize local myonecrosis induced by myotoxin a and homologous crude venom. Toxicon 22: 99–105.

Ownby, C. L., T. R. Colberg, and G. V. Odell. 1985. Ability of a mixture of antimyotoxin a serum and polyvalent (Crotalidae) antivenin to neutralize myonecrosis, hemorrhage, and lethality induced by prairie rattlesnake (*Crotalus viridis viridis*) venom. Toxicon 23: 317–324.

Ownby, C. L., G. V. Odell, W. M. Woods, and T. R. Colberg. 1983. Ability of antiserum to myotoxin a from prairie rattlesnake (*Crotalus viridis viridis*) venom to neutralize local myotoxicity and lethal effects of myotoxin a and homologous crude venom. Toxicon 21: 35–45.

Owen, R. P. 1940. A list of the reptiles of Washington. Copeia 1940(3): 169–172.

Owens, V. 1949. New snake records and notes, Morgan County, Missouri. Herpetologica 5(2): 49–50.

Pacheco-Cruz, S. 1958. Diccionario de la fauna yucateca. Secretaria de Educación Pública, Mérida, México. 381 pp.

Page, J. L. 1930. Climate of Mexico. Monthly Weather Review Supplement 33: 1–30.

Page, L. A. 1966. Diseases and infections in snakes: a review. Bulletin of the Wildlife Disease Association 2: 111–126.

Pagel, M. 1999. The maximum likelihood approach to reconstructing ancestral character states of discrete characters on phylogenies. Syst. Biol. 48: 612–622.

Paine, M. J., H. P. Desmond, R. D. G. Theakston, and J. M. Crampton. 1992. Purification and molecular characterisation of a high molecular weight haemorrhagic metalloproteinase, jararhagin, from *Bothrops jararaca* venom. Journal of Biological Chemistry 267: 22869–22876.

Painter, C. W. 1998. Geographic distribution: *Crotalus atrox*. Herpetol. Rev. 29(4): 249.

Painter, C. W., L. A. Fitzgerald, and M. L. Heinrich. 1999. Natural history notes: *Crotalus atrox* (western diamondback rattlesnake). Herpetol. Rev. 30(1): 44.

Painter, C. W., and C. M. Milensky. 1993. Geographic distribution: *Crotalus tigris* (tiger rattlesnake). Herpetol. Rev. 24(4): 155–156.

Palis, J. G. 1993. Life history notes: *Agkistrodon piscivorus conanti* (Florida cottonmouth). Prey. Herpetol. Rev. 24(2): 59, 62.

Palisot de Beauvois, A. M. F. J. 1799. Memoir on Amphibia. Serpentes. Transactions of the American Philosophical Society 4: 362–381.

Pallas, P. S. 1776. Reise durch verschiedene Provinzen des Rusischen Reichs. St. Petersburg. Gedruckt bey der Kayserlichen Acad. der Wissenschaften 1771–1776, 3 vols.

Palmer, B. K., and J. C. Devos Jr. 1986. Geographic distribution: *Micruroides euryxanthus euryxanthus* (Arizona coral snake). Herpetol. Rev. 17(1): 27.

Palmer, T. 1992. Landscape with reptile: rattlesnakes in an urban world. Ticknor and Fields, New York. 340 pp.

Palmer, W. M. 1965. Intergradation among the copperheads (*Agkistrodon contortrix* Linnaeus) in the North Carolina coastal plain. Copeia 1965(2): 146–247.

———. 1971. Distribution and variation of the Carolina pigmy rattlesnake, *Sistrurus miliarius miliarius* Linnaeus, in North Carolina. J. Herpetol. 5(1–2): 39–44.

———. 1974. Poisonous snakes of North Carolina. State Museum of Natural History, North Carolina Department of Agriculture, Raleigh. 22 pp.

———. 1978. *Sistrurus miliarius* (Linnaeus), pygmy rattlesnakes. Catalogue of American Amphibians and Reptiles 220.1–220.2.

Palmer, W. M., and A. L. Braswell. 1995. Reptiles of North Carolina. University of North Carolina Press, Chapel Hill. 412 pp.

Palmer, W. M., A. L. Braswell, and D. L. Stephen. 1974. Noteworthy herpetological records from North Carolina. Bull. Maryland Herpetological Society 10(3): 81–87.

Palmer, W. M., and D. E. Whitehead. 1961. Herpetological collections and observations in Hyde and Tyrrell Counties, North Carolina. Journal of the Elisha Mitchell Scientific Society 77: 280–289.

Palmer, W. M., and G. M. Williamson. 1971. Observations on the natural history of the Carolina pigmy rattlesnake, *Sistrurus miliarius miliarius* Linnaeus. Journal of the Elisha Mitchell Scientific Society 87: 20–25.

Pandya, B. V., R. N. Buin, S. A. Olexa, and A. Z. Budzynski. 1983. Unique degradation of human fibrinogen by proteases from western diamondback rattlesnake (*Crotalus atrox*) venom. Toxicon 21(4): 515–526.

Panger, M. A., and H. W. Greene. 1998. Natural history notes: *Micrurus nigrocinctus* (coral snake). Reproduction. Herpetol. Rev. 29(1): 46.

Pantanowitz, L., and F. Guidozzi. 1996. Management of snake and spider bite in pregnancy. Obstetrical and Gynecological Surgery 51: 615–620.

Pardal, P. P. de O., S. M. Souza, M. R. de C. da C. Monteiro, H. W. Fan, J. L. C. Cardoso, F. O. S. França, S. C. Tomy, I. S. Sano-Martins, M. C. C. Cirillo de Sousa-e-Silva, M. Colombini, et al. 2004. Clinical trial of two antivenoms for the treatment of *Bothrops* and *Lachesis* bites in the northeastern Amazon region of Brazil. Trans. Roy. Soc. Trop. Med. Hyg.

Parham, H. J. 1937. A nature lover in British Columbia. H. F. and G. Witherby, London. 292 pp.

Parker, H. W. 1926. The reptiles and batrachians of Gorgona Island, Colombia. Ann. Mag. Nat. Hist., 9th ser., 17: 549–554.

———. 1930. Two new reptiles from southern Ecuador. Ann. Mag. Nat. Hist., 10th ser., 5: 568–571.

———. 1932. Some new or rare reptiles and amphibians from southern Ecuador. Ann. Mag. Nat. Hist., 10th ser., 9: 21–26.

———. 1934. Reptiles and amphibians from southern Ecuador. Ann. Mag. Nat. Hist., 10th ser., 14: 264–273.

———. 1935. The frogs, lizards, and snakes of British Guiana. Proc. Zool. Soc. London 1935: 505–530.

———. 1938. The vertical distribution of some reptiles and amphibians in southern Ecuador. Ann. Mag. Nat. Hist., 11th ser., 2: 438–450.

———. 1966. *Ancistrodon* not *Agkistrodon* (Reptilia-Serpentes) Z.N.(S.) 671. Bulletin of Zoological Nomenclature 22: 300–302.

———. 1977. Snakes: a natural history, 2d ed. Rev. and enl. by A. G. C. Grandison. British Museum, London; Cornell University Press, Ithaca, N.Y. 108 pp.

Parker, J. M., and S. H. Anderson. 2002. Natural history notes: *Crotalus viridis concolor* (midget faded rattlesnake). Maximum length. Herpetol. Rev. 33(2): 140.

Parker, M. V. 1937. Some amphibians and reptiles from Reelfoot Lake. Journal of the Tennessee Academy of Science 12: 60–86.

Parker, S. A., and D. Stotz. 1977. An observation on the foraging behavior of the Arizona ridge-nosed rattlesnake, *Crotalus willardi willardi* (Serpentes: Crotalidae). Bull. Maryland Herpetol. Soc. 13: 123.

Parker, W. S., and W. S. Brown. 1973. Species composition and population changes in two complexes of snake hibernacula in northern Utah. Herpetologica 29(4): 319–326.

———. 1974. Mortality and weight changes of Great Basin rattlesnakes (*Crotalus viridis*) at a hibernaculum in northern Utah. Herpetologica 30: 234–239.

Parker, W. S., and M. V. Plummer. 1987. Population ecology. Pp. 253–301 in R. A. Seigel, J. T. Collins, and S. Novak (eds.), Snakes: ecology and evolutionary biology. McGraw-Hill, New York.

Parkinson, C. L. 1999. Molecular systematics and biogeographical history of pitvipers as determined by mitochondrial ribosomal DNA sequences. Copeia 1999(3): 576–586.

Parkinson, C. L., J. A. Campbell, and P. Chippindale. 2002. Multigene phylogenetic analysis of pitvipers, with comments on their biogeography. Pp. 93–110 in G. W. Schuett, M. Höggren, M. E. Douglas, and H. W. Greene (eds.), Biology of the vipers. Eagle Mountain Publishing, Utah.

Parkinson, C. L., S. M. Moody, and J. E. Ahlquist. 1997. Phylogenetic relationships of the "*Agkistrodon* complex" based on mitochondrial DNA sequence data. Pp. 63–78 in R. S. Thorpe, W. Wüster, and A. Malhotra (eds.), Venomous snakes: ecology, evolution and snakebite. Clarendon Press, Oxford.

Parkinson, C. L., K. R. Zamudio, and H. W. Greene. 2000. Phylogeography of the pitviper clade *Agkistrodon*: historical ecology, species status, and conservation of cantiles. Molecular Ecology 9: 411–420.

Parks, H. B., and V. L. Cory. 1936. Biological survey of the east Texas Big Thicket area. Sam Houston State Teachers College, Huntsville, Texas. 51 pp.

Parmalee, P. W. 1955. Reptiles of Illinois. Illinois State Museum Popular Science Series 5: 1–88.

Parrish, H. M. 1955. Poisonous snakebites resulting in lack of venom poisoning. Virginia Medical Monthly 82: 130–135.

———. 1957. Mortality from snake bites, United States, 1950–54. Public Health Report 72: 1027–1030.

———. 1959. Effects of repeated poisonous snakebites in man. American Journal of the Medical Sciences 237: 277–286.

———. 1963. Analysis of 460 fatalities from venomous animals in the United States. American Journal of the Medical Sciences 245(February): 129–141.

———. 1964a. Snakebite injuries in Louisiana. Journal of the Louisiana State Medical Society 116(7): 249–257.

———. 1964b. Texas snakebite statistics. Texas State Journal of Medicine 60: 592–598.

———. 1966. Incidence of treated snakebites in the United States. Public Health Reports 81: 269–276.

———. 1980. Poisonous snakebites in the United States. Vantage, New York. 469 pp.

Parrish, H. M., and C. A. Carr. 1967. Bites by copperheads (*Ancistrodon contortrix*) in the United States. JAMA 201: 927–932.

Parrish, H. M., and H. D. Donnell. 1967. Bites by cottonmouths (*Ancistrodon piscivorus*) in the United States. Southern Medical Journal 60: 429–434.

Parrish, H. M., and L. P. Donovan. 1964. Facts about snakebites in Alabama. Journal of the Medical Association of the State of Alabama 33(10): 297–305.

Parrish, H. M., J. C. Goldner, and S. L. Silberg. 1966. Poisonous snakebites causing no venenation. Postgraduate Medicine 39: 265–269.

Parrish, H. M., and M. S. Khan. 1966. Snakebite during pregnancy. Obstetrics and Gynecology 27: 468–471.

———. 1967a. Bites by coral snakes: report of a case and suggested therapy. JAMA 182: 949.

———. 1967b. Bites by coral snakes: report of 11 representative cases. American Journal of Medical Science 253: 561–568.

Parrish, H. M., A. W. MacLaurin, and R. L. Tuttle. 1956. North American pitvipers: bacterial flora of the mouths and venom glands. Virginia Medical Monthly 83: 383–385.

Parrish, H. M., and R. E. Thompson. 1958. Human envenomation from bites of recently milked rattlesnakes: a report of three cases. Copeia 1958(2): 83–86.

Pasteur, G. 1982. A classificatory review of mimicry systems. Annual Review of Ecology and Systematics 13: 169–199.

Patterson, R. A. 1967. Some physiological effects caused by venom from the Gila monster, *Heloderma suspectum*. Toxicon 5:5–10.

Patzelt, E. 1979. Fauna del Ecuador, 2d ed. Editorial Las Casas, Quito. 198 pp.

Paukstis, G. L. 1977. Geographic distribution: *Sistrurus miliarius streckeri* (western pygmy rattlesnake). Herpetol. Rev. 8(1): 14.

Pauly, G. B., and M. F. Benard. 2002. Natural history notes: *Crotalus viridis oreganus* (northern Pacific rattlesnake). Costs of feeding. Herpetol. Rev. 33(1): 56–57.

Pawley, R. 1969. Observations on a prolonged food refusal period of an adult fer-de-lance. International Zoo Yearbook 9: 58–59.

Pearn, J., J. Morrison, N. Charles, and V. Muir. 1981. First-aid for snake-bite: efficacy of a constrictive bandage with limb immobilization in the management of human envenomation. Medical Journal of Australia 2: 293–295.

Péfaur, J. E. 1992. Checklist and bibliography (1960–85) of the Venezuelan herpetofauna. Smithsonian Herpetological Information Service No. 89. 54 pp.

Péfaur, J. E., J. Davila, E. Lopez, and A. Nuñez. 1978. Distribución y clasificación de los reptiles del Departamento de Arequipa. Bulletin de l'Institut Français d'Etudes Andines 7(1–2): 129–139.

Péfaur, J. E., and J. A. Rivero. 2000. Distribution, species-richness, endemism, and conservation of Venezuelan amphibians and reptiles. Amphibian and Reptile Conservation 2(2): 42–70.

Pegler, S. T., D. Chiszar, H. M. Smith. 1995. Geographic distribution: *Sistrurus catenatus tergeminus* X *edwardsii* (massasauga). Herpetol. Rev. 26(1): 47.

Peñaranda B., E. 1995. Natural history notes: *Bothrops neuwiedi* (yoperojobobo, Neuwied's lancehead). Herpetol. Rev. 26(4): 205–206.

Peñaranda-B., E., A. Calvo-C., and J. Peñaranda. 1994. Biología reproductiva de *Bothrops neuwiedi* (Serpentes, Viperidae) en cautiverio: resultados preliminares. Ecología en Bolivia 23: 57–70.

Penn, G. A., Jr. 1940. Notes on the summer herpetology of De Kalb County, Alabama. Journal of the Tennessee Academy of Science 15: 352–355.

Penn, G. H. 1942. The life history of *Porocephalus crotali*, a parasite of the Louisiana muskrat. Journal of Parasitology 28: 277–283.

———. 1943. Herpetological notes from Cameron Parish, Louisiana. Copeia 1943(1): 58–59.

Peracca, M. G. 1897a. Intorno ad una piccola raccolta di rettili di Cononacco (Perú Orientale). Bollettino Musei Zoologia Anatomia Comparata Università Torino 12(284): 1–7.

———. 1897b. Viaggio del Dott. Alfredo Borelli nel Chaco boliviano e nella Republica Argentina. Bollettino Musei Zoologia Anatomia Comparata Università Torino 12(274): 1–19.

———. 1910. Descrizione di alcune nuove specie di ofidii del Museo Zoologico della Reale Università di Napoli. Annali del Museo Zoologico della Reale Università di Napoli 3(12): 1–3.

Perales, J., H. Moussatche, S. Marangoni, B. Oliveira, and G. B. Domont. 1994. Isolation and partial characterization of an antibothropic complex from the serum of South American didelphidae. Toxicon 32(10): 1237–1249.

Perales, J., R. Munoz, and H. Moussatche. 1986. Isolation and partial characterization of a protein fraction from the opossum (*Didelphis marsupialis*) serum, with protecting property against the *Bothrops jararaca* snake venom. Anais da Academia Brasileira de Ciências 58: 155–162.

Peres-Neto, P. R., and F. Marques. 2000. When are random data not random, or is the PTP test useful? Cladistics 16: 420–424.

Pérez, D. R., and L. J. Avila. 2000. Geographic distribution: *Bothrops neuwiedi diporus* (lancehead). Herpetol. Rev. 31(4): 254.

Perez, J. C., V. E. Garcia, and S. Y. Huang. 1984. Production of a monoclonal antibody against hemorrhagic activity of *Crotalus atrox* (western diamondback rattlesnake) venom. Toxicon 22: 967–973.

Pérez, J. C., S. Pichyangkul, and V. E. García. 1979. The resistance of 3 species of warm-blooded animals to Western diamondback rattlesnake (*Crotalus atrox*) venom. Toxicon 17(6): 601–608.

Pérez-Higadera [*sic*], G., R. C. Vogt, and O. A. Flores-Villela. 1987. Lista anotada de los anfibios y reptiles de la región de Los Tuxtlas, Veracruz. Estación de Biología Tropical Los Tuxtlas, Instituto de Biología, Universidad Nacional Autónoma de México. 23 pp.

Pérez-Higareda, G. 1978. Reptiles and amphibians from the Estación de Biología Tropical Los Tuxtlas (U.N.A.M.), Veracruz, Mexico. Bull. Maryland Herpetol. Soc. 14(2): 67–74.

——. 1980. Additions to and notes on the known snake fauna of the Estación de Biología Tropical Los Tuxtlas, Veracruz, México. Bull. Maryland Herpetol. Soc. 16(1): 23–26.

Pérez-Higareda, G., and H. M. Smith. 1990. The endemic coral snakes of the Los Tuxlas region, southern Veracruz, Mexico. Bull. Maryland Herpetol. Soc. 26(1): 5–13.

——. 1991. Ofidiofauna de Veracruz. Análisis taxonómico y zoogeográfico. Universidad Nacional Autónoma de México, Publicación Especial 7. 122 pp.

Pérez-Higareda, G., H. M. Smith, and J. Juliá-Zertuche. 1985. A new jumping viper, *Porthidium olmec*, from southern Veracruz, Mexico (Serpentes: Viperidae). Bull. Maryland Herpetol. Soc. 21(3): 97–106.

Pérez-Ramos, E., L. Saldaña de la Riva, and Z. Uribe-Peña. 2000. A checklist of the reptiles and amphibians of Guerrero, Mexico. Anales del Instituto de Biología, Universidad Nacional Autónoma de México, Serie Zoología, 71(1): 21–40.

Pérez-Santos, C. 1986a. Las serpeintes del Atlántico. Museo de Ciencias Naturales de Madrid. 83 pp.

——. 1986b. Las serpeintes del Tolima. T. Torreblanca, Madrid. 96 pp.

Pérez-Santos, C., and A. G. Moreno. 1986. Distribución altitudinal de las serpientes del Colombia. Revista Española de Herpetología 1: 11–27.

——. 1988. Ofidios de Colombia. Museo Regionale di Scienze Naturali Torino, Monografía 6. 517 pp.

——. 1989. Addenda y corrigenda al libro "Ofidios de Colombia." Bollettino Museo Regionale di Scienze Naturali di Torino 7: 1–17,

——. 1991a. Serpientes de Ecuador. Museo Regionale di Scienze Naturali di Torino, Monografía 11. 538 pp.

——. 1991b. Distribución y amplitud altitudinal de las serpientes en Ecuador. Revista Española de Herpetología 5: 125–140.

Pérez-Santos, C., A. G. Moreno, and A. Garhart. 1993. Checklist of the snakes of Panama. Revista Española de Herpetología 7: 113–122.

Perkins, C. B. 1951 Hybrid rattlesnakes. Herpetologica 7(3): 146.

Perkins, R. M., and M. J. R. Lentz. 1934. Contribution to the herpetology of Arkansas. Copeia 1934(3): 139–140.

Perry, J. 1978. An observation of "dance" behavior in the western cottonmouth, *Agkistrodon piscivorus leucostoma* (Reptilia, Serpentes, Viperidae). J. Herpetol. 12: 429–431.

Perry, J. J. 1997. Taxon management account: twin-spotted rattlesnake *Crotalus willardi* ssp. American Zoo and Aquarium Association Snake Advisory Group. 13 pp.

Pesantes-Segura, O. 1989. Relações entre algumas espécies do gênero *Bothrops* pela eletroforese do plasma e morfologia do hemipênis (Serpentes: Viperidae). M. Sc. dissertation, Universidade Estadual Paulista Júlio de Mesquita Filho, Rio Claro, São Paulo, Brasil.

——. 2000. Prevención y tratamiento de accidentes por serpientes venenosas. Centro Ecológico Recreacional Huachipa, Sedapal, Lima, Perú. 38 pp.

Pesantes-Segura, O., and J. Cárdenas. 1996. Status taxonómico de *Bothrops pictus* and *B. roedingeri* (Serpentes: Viperidae). P. 179 in IV Congreso Latinoamerica de Herpetología, Santiago, Chile.

Pesantes-Segura, O., and F. O. Cutti. (In press.) *Bothrops menesis*, a new species from Peru (Serpentes: Viperidae).

Pesantes-Segura, O., and W. Fernandes. 1989. Afinidade de *Bothrops erythromelas* aferida atraves da eletroforese do plasma e da morfologia do hemipenis (Serpentes: Viperidae). P. 74 in XVI Congresso Brasileiro de Zoologia, Universidade Federal da Paraíba, 22 a 27 de Janeiro de 1989, João Pessoa, Paraíba.

Pesce, H., and H. Lumbreras. 1965. Ofidismo de Lima por *Bothrops pictus*. Anales de la Facultad de Medicina de Lima, 39th ser., 7(3): 1153–1188.

Pessôa, S. B. 1967. Notas sôbre hemogregarinas de serpentes brasileiras: V. Hemogregarinas da cascavel. Revista Brasil Biol. 27(4): 381–384.

Pessôa, S. B., and P. De Biasi. 1972. *Trypanosoma cascavelli* sp. n. parasita de cascavel: *Crotalus durissus terrificus* (Laurent). Atas Sociedade de Biologia do Rio de Janeiro 15(2): 67–70.

Pessôa, S. B., P. De Biasi, and G. Puorto. 1974. Nota sôbre a freqüência de hemoparasitas em serpentes do Brasil. Mem. Inst. Butantan 38: 69–118.

Peters, J. A. 1942. Reptiles and amphibians of Cumberland County, Illinois. Copeia 1942(3): 182–183.

——. 1953. Snakes and lizards from Quintana Roo, Mexico. Lloydia 16(3): 227–232.

——. 1954. The amphibians and reptiles of the coast and coastal sierra of Michoacán, Mexico. Occas. Pap. Mus. Zool. Univ. Michigan 554: 1–37.

——. 1955. Herpetological type localities in Ecuador. Revista Ecuatoriana de Entomología y Parasitología 2(3–4): 335–352.

——. 1960a. The snakes of Ecuador. A check list and key. Bulletin of the Museum of Comparative Zoology 122: 491–541.

——. 1960b. Notes on the faunistics of southwestern and coastal Michoacan, with lists of reptilia and amphibia collected in 1950 and 1951. Pp. 319–334 in P. D. Brand (ed.), Coalcoman and Motines del Oro, an ex-distrito of Michoacan Mexico. Institute for Latin American Studies, University of Texas at Austin.

——. 1967. On Venezuelan snakes. Copeia 1967(2): 496–498.

——. 1968. A replacement name for *Bothrops lansbergii venezuelensis* Roze, 1959 (Viperidae, Serpentes). Proceedings of the Biological Society of Washington 81: 319–322.

Peters, J. A., and B. Orejas-Miranda. 1970. Catalogue of the Neotropical Squamata: part I. Snakes. Bulletin of the U.S. National Museum 297: 1–347.

Peters, W. C. H. 1859. Über die von Hrn. Hofmann in Costa Rica gesammelten und an das Konigl. Zoologische Museum gesandten Schlangen. Monatsberichte der Preussischen Akademie der Wissenschaften zu Berlin 1859: 275–278.

——. 1861a. Die Beschreibung von zwei neuen Schlangen, *Mizodon variegatus* aus Westafrika und *Bothriopsis quadriscutata*. Monatsberichte der Preussischen Akademie der Wissenschaften zu Berlin 1861: 358–360.

——. 1861b. Über eine Sammlung von Schlangen aus Huanusco in Mexico welche das Konigl zoologisch Museum Kurzlich von Dr. Hille erworben hat. Monatsberichte der Preussischen Akademie der Wissenschaften zu Berlin 1861: 460–462.

——. 1862 [dated 1861]. Über neue Schlangen des konigl. zoologischen Museums: *Typhlops striolatus*, *Geophidium dubium*, *Streptophorus (Ninia) maculatus*, *Elaps hippocrepis*. Monatsberichte der Preussischen Akademie der Wissenschaften zu Berlin 1861: 922–925.

——. 1863a [dated 1862]. Präparate . . . zur kraniologischen Unterscheidung der Schlangengattung *Elaps* und . . . Mittheilung über eine neue Art der Gattung Simotes. Monatsberichte der Preussischen Akademie der Wissenschaften zu Berlin 1862: 635–638.

——. 1863b [dated 1862]. Über die kraniologischen Verschiedenheiten der Grubenottern (Trigonocephali) und über eine neue Art der Gattung *Bothriechis*. Monatsberichte der Preussischen Akademie der Wissenschaften zu Berlin 1862: 670–674.

——. 1869. Eine Mittheilung über mexicanisch Amphibien, welche Hr. Berkenbusch in Puebla auf Veranlassung des Hrn. Legationsraths von Schlozer dem Zoologischen Museum zugesandt hat. Monatsberichte der Preussischen Akademie der Wissenschaften zu Berlin 1869: 874–881.

——. 1871. Über eine von hrn. Dr. Robert Abendroth in dem Hochlande von Peru gemachte Sammlung von Amphibien, welche derselbe dem Königl. zoologischen Museum geschenkt hat. Monatsberichte der Preussischen Akademie der Wissenschaften zu Berlin 1871: 397–404.

——. 1881. Über das Vorkommen schildförmiger Verbreiterungen der Dornfortsatze bei Schlangen und über neue oder weniger bekannte Arten dieser Abtheilen der Reptilien. Sitzungsberichte der Gesellschaft Naturforschender Freunde zu Berlin 1881: 49–52.

Petersen, R. C. 1970. Connecticut's venomous snakes. Timber rattlesnake and northern copperhead. State Geological and Natural History Survey of Connecticut, Bulletin 103. 40 pp.

Peterson, H. W., R. Garrett, and J. P. Lantz. 1952. The mating period of the giant tree frog, *Hyla dominicensis*. Herpetologica 8: 63.

Peterson, H. W., and H. M. Smith. 1974. Observations on sea snakes in the vicinity of Acapulco, Guerrero, Mexico. Bull. Chicago Herpetol. Soc. 8(3–4): 29.

Peterson, K. H. 1982. Reproduction in captive *Heloderma suspectum*. Herpetol. Rev. 13(4): 122–124.

Peterson, K. H., and R. A. Odum. 1985. Reproduction and notes on the maintenance of arboreal and terrestrial montane *Bothrops* at Houston Zoological Gardens. Pp. 187–197 in F. Caporaso, S. McKeown, and K. H. Peterson (eds.), Ninth International Herpetological Symposium on Captive Propagation and Husbandry, 26–30 June 1985, San Diego, California.

Peterson, R. C., and R. W. Fritsch. 1986. Connecticut's venomous snakes: Timber rattlesnake and northern copperhead, 2d ed. Connecticut Geological and Natural History Survey, Bulletin 111. 48 pp.

Pettigrew, L. C., and J. P. Glass. 1985. Neurologic complications of a coral snake bite. Neurology 35(4): 589–592.

Petzing, J. E., M. J. Dreslik, C. A. Phillips, C. D. Smith, A. R. Kuhns, D. B. Shepard, J. G. Palis, E. O. Moll, D. J. Olson, T. G. Anton, et al. 2000. New amphibian and reptile county records in Illinois. Herpetol. Rev. 31(3): 189–194.

Petzing, J. E., and C. A. Phillips. 1998. Geographic distribution: *Agkistrodon contortrix* (copperhead). Herpetol. Rev. 29(2): 111.

Petzold, H. G. 1963. Notizen zur Fortpflanzungs-biologie und Jugendentwicklung zweier Grubenottern (Serpentes: Crotalidae: *Crotalus atrox* und *Agkistrodon p. piscivorus*). Bijdragen tot de Dierkunde, Universiteit van Amsterdam, 33: 61–69.

Pfaffenberger, G. S., N. M. Jorgensen, and D. D. Woody. 1989. Parasites of prairie rattlesnakes, *Crotalus viridis viridis*, and gopher snakes, *Pituophis melanoleucus sayi*, from the eastern high plains of New Mexico, USA. Journal of Wildlife Diseases 25(2): 305–306.

Pfennig, D. W., W. R. Harcombe, and K. S. Pfennig. 2001. Frequency-dependent Batesian mimicry. Nature 410: 323.

Phillips, C. A., R. A. Brandon, and E. O. Moll. 1999. Field guide to amphibians and reptiles of Illinois. Illinois Natural History Survey Manual No. 8. 282 pp.

Phillipson, W. R. 1952. The immaculate forest. Hutchinson, London. 223 pp.

Philpot, V. B., Jr., E. Ezekiel, Y. Laseter, R. G. Yeager, and R. L. Sternholm. 1978. Neutralization of crotalid venoms by fractions from snake sera. Toxicon 16: 603–610.

Philpot, V. B., and R. G. Smith. 1950. Neutralization of pit viper venom by kingsnake serum. Proceedings of the Society for Experimental Biology and Medicine 74: 521–524.

Phisalix, M. 1911. Note sur les effets mortels réciproques des morsures de l'*Heloderma suspectum* Cope et de la *Vipera aspis* Laur. et sur les caractères differentiels de leurs venins. Bulletin du Museum d'Histoire Naturelle, Paris, 17: 485–491.

———. 1914. Anatomie comparée de la tête et de l'appareil venimeux chez les serpents. Annales des Sciences Naturelles, Zoologie, 9th ser. 19 pp.

———. 1922. Animaux venimeux et venins, 2 vols. Masson, Paris. 1,520 pp.

Piacentine, J., S. C. Curry, and P. J. Ryan. 1986. Life-threatening anaphylaxis following Gila monster bite. Ann. Emerg. Med. 15: 959–961.

Pianka, E. R., and H. M. Smith. 1959. Distributional records for certain Mexican and Guatemalan reptiles. Herpetologica 15: 119–120.

Picado T., C. 1930. Venom of Costa Rican arboreal vipers. Bull. Antivenin Inst. Am. 4(1): 1–3.

———. 1931a. Serpientes venenosas de Costa Rica. Secretaría de Salubridad y Protección Social, San José. 219 pp.

———. 1931b. Epidermal microoornaments of the Crotalinae. Bull. Antivenin Inst. Amer. 4: 104–105.

———. 1936 [dated 1933–1934]. Serpentes venenosas occorrentes em Costa Rica. Mem. Inst. Butantan 8: 389–397.

Pickwell, G. B. 1972. Amphibians and reptiles of the Pacific States. Dover, New York. 234 pp.

Pickwell, G. V. 1971. Knotting and coiling behavior in the pelagic sea snake *Pelamis platurus* (L.). Copeia 1971(2): 348–350.

———. 1972. The venomous sea snakes. Fauna 4: 17–32.

Pickwell, G. V., R. L. Bezy, and J. E. Fitch. 1983. Northern occurrences of the sea snake, *Pelamis platurus*, in the eastern Pacific, with a record of predation on the species. California Fish and Game 69(3): 172–177.

Pickwell, G. V., and W. A. Culotta. 1980. *Pelamis* and *P. platurus*. Catalogue of American Amphibians and Reptiles 255.1–255.4.

Pickwell, G. V., J. A. Vick, W. H. Shipman, and M. M. Grenan. 1973. Production, toxicity, and preliminary pharmacology of the venom from the sea snake *Pelamis platurus* with observations on its probable threat to man along Middle America. Pp. 247–265 in L. R. Worthen (ed.), Food-drugs from the sea, proceedings of the Third Conference, Marine Technology Society, Washington, D.C.

Pierini, S. V., D. A. Warrell, A. de Paulo, and R. D. G. Theakston. 1996. High incidence of bites and stings by snakes and other animals among rubber tappers and Amazonian Indians of the Juruá Valley, Acre State, Brazil. Toxicon 34: 225–236.

Pifano, F. 1935. Contribución al estudio de las serpientes ponzoñosas de Estado Yaracuy. Privately printed, Caracas. 16 pp.

———. 1938. Corales ponzoñosas de los valles de Yaracuy. Pesquisas experimentales con la ponzoño del *Micrurus lemniscatus* (Linneo, 1758). Publicaciones de Asociación Médica del Estado Yaracuy 1: 10–15.

Pifano-C., F., and A. Rodríguez-Acosta. 1996. Ecological niche and redescription of *Crotalus vegrandis* (Serpentes: Crotalidae) in Venezuela. Brenesia 45–46: 159–175.

Pifano-C., F., and M. Römer. 1949a. Ofidios ponzoñosos de Venezuela I. Nueva comprobación en Venezuela del *Bothrops medusa* (Sternfeld, 1920) Amaral, 1929, y redescripción de la especie. Archivos Venezolanos de Patología Tropical y Parasitología Médica 1(2): 277–300.

———. 1949b. Ofidios ponzoñosas de Venezuela II. Sobre las serpientes ponzoñosas venezolanas del grupo *Bothrops lansbergii*. Archivos Venezolanos de Patología Tropical y Parasitología Médica 1(2): 301–326.

Pifano-C., F., Romer, M. and F. Sandner-Montilla. 1950. Serpientes ponzoñosas de Venezuela III. *Bothrops schlegelii* (Berthold, 1846) Jan, 1875: su existencia en Venezuela. Archivos Venezolanos de Patología Tropical y Parasitología Médica 2(1): 261–264.

Pilsbry, H. A., and J. H. Ferriss. 1919 [dated 1918]. Mollusca of the southwestern states. IX. The Santa Catalina, Rincon, Tortillita, and Galiuro Mountains. X. The mountains of the Gila headwaters. Proc. Acad. Nat. Sci. Philadelphia 70: 282–333.

Pineda, D., K. Ghotme, M. E. Aldeco, and P. Montoya. 2002. Accidentes ofidicos en Yopal y Leticia, Colombia, 1996–1997. Biomedica (Bogotá) 22(1): 14–21.

Pinto-Leite, N. R., N. Jorge da Silva, and S. D. Aird. 1991. Human envenomation by the South American opisthoglyph *Clelia clelia plumbea* (Wied). Toxicon 29: 1512–1516.

Pisani, G. R., J. T. Collins, and S. R. Edwards. 1972. A re-evaluation of the subspecies of *Crotalus horridus*. Trans. Kansas Acad. Sci. 75: 255–263.

Pisani, G. R., and B. R. Stephenson. 1991. Food habits in Oklahoma: *Crotalus atrox* in fall and early spring. Trans. Kansas Acad. Sci. 94(3–4): 137–141.

Piso, W., and G. Marcgraf. 1658. De Indiae utriusque re naturali et medica libri quatuordecim. Danielem Elzevirios, Amsterdam.

Pizzatto, L., and R. R. Madi. 2002. Natural history notes: *Micrurus corallinus* (coral snake). Endoparasites. Herpetol. Rev. 33(3): 215.

Platt, S. G., A. W. Hawkes, and T. R. Rainwater. 2001. Diet of the canebrake rattlesnake (*Crotalus horridus atricaudatus*): an additional record and review. Texas Journal of Science 53(2): 115–120.

Platt, S. G., and T. R. Rainwater. 1998. Distribution records and life history notes for amphibians and reptiles in Belize. Herpetol. Rev. 29(4): 250–251.

——. 2000. Natural history notes: *Agkistrodon piscivorus* (cotton-mouth). Diet. Herpetol. Rev. 31(4): 244.

Platt, S. G., K. R. Russell, W. E. Snyder, L. W. Fontenot, and S. Miller. 1999. Distribution and conservation status of selected amphibians and reptiles in the Piedmont of South Carolina. Journal of the Elisha Mitchell Scientific Society 115(1): 8–19.

Plummer, M. V. 2000. Natural history notes: *Crotalus scutulatus* (Mojave rattlesnake). Thermal stress. Herpetol. Rev. 31(2): 104–105.

Poey, F. 1873. Mordedura de un jubo. Genio Científico de la Habana 1: 94–98.

Polis, G. A., and C. A. Myers. 1985. A survey of intraspecific preda-tion among reptiles and amphibians. J. Herpetol. 19(1): 99–107.

Ponce-Campos, P., R. Romero-Contreras, and S. M. Huerta-Ortega. 2000. Geographic distribution: *Crotalus lepidus maculosus* (Duran-gan rock rattlesnake). Herpetol. Rev. 31(2): 113.

Ponce-Campos, P., and E. N. Smith. (In press.) Geographic distribu-tion: *Micrurus proximans* (Nayarit coralsnake). Herpetol. Rev.

Pook, C. E., W. Wüster, and R. S. Thorpe. 2000. Historical biogeogra-phy of the western rattlesnake (Serpentes: Viperidae: *Crotalus viridis*), inferred from mitochondrial DNA sequence information. Molecular Phylogenetics and Evolution 15(2): 269–282.

Pope, C. H. 1944–1945. The poisonous snakes of the New World. Bul-letin of the New York Zoological Society 47(1944): 83–90, 111–120, 143–152; 48(1945): 17–23, 44–47.

——. 1946. Snakes of the northeastern United States. New York Zoo-logical Society, New York. 52 pp.

——. 1947. Amphibians and reptiles of the Chicago area. Chicago Museum of Natural History, Chicago. 275 pp.

——. 1955. The reptile world. Knopf, New York. 325 pp.

Pope, T. E. B. 1926. The massasauga in Wisconsin. Yearbook of the Public Museum, Milwaukee, 1: 171–180.

Pope, T. E. B., and W. E. Dickinson. 1928. The amphibians and rep-tiles of Wisconsin. Bulletin of the Public Museum of the City of Mil-waukee 8(1): 1–138.

Poran, N. S., and R. G. Cross. 1990. Development of antisnake defenses in California ground squirrels, *Spermophilus beecheyii*. Behavioral and immunological relationships. Behaviour 112(3–4): 222–245.

Poran, N. S., R. G. Cross, and E. Benjamini. 1987. Resistance of California ground squirrels, *Spermophilus beecheyi*, to the venom of the northern Pacific rattlesnake, *Crotalus viridis oreganus*: a study of adaptive variation. Toxicon 25(7): 767–778.

Porras, L., J. R. McCranie, and L. D. Wilson. 1981. The systematics and distribution of the hognose viper *Bothrops nasuta* Bocourt (Ser-pentes: Viperidae). Tulane Studies in Zoology and Botany 22(2): 85–107.

Porter, C. A., M. W. Haiduk, and K. de Queiroz. 1994. Evolution and phylogenetic significance of ribosomal gene location in chromo-somes of squamate reptiles. Copeia 1994: 302–313.

Porto, M., and D. M. Teixeira. 1995. Geographic distribution: *Bothrops leucurus* (white-tailed lancehead). Herpetol. Rev. 26(3): 156.

Posada-Arango, A. 1889a. Apuntamientos para la ofiología colom-biana. Anales de la Academia de Medicina de Medellín 2(2): 45–49.

——. 1889b. Note sur quelques solénoglyphes de Colombie. Bulletin de la Société Zoologique de France 14: 343–345.

——. 1909. Las serpientes. Pp. 252–284 in Carlos A. Molina (ed.), Estu-dios científicos del Doctor Andrés Posada con algunos otros escritos suyos sobre diversos temas y con ilustraciones o grabados. Imprenta Oficial, Medellín, Colombia.

Pough, F. H. 1964. A coral snake "mimic" eaten by a bird. Copeia 1964(1): 223.

——. 1966. Ecological relationships of rattlesnakes in southeastern Arizona with notes on other species. Copeia 1966(4): 676–683.

——. 1976. Multiple cryptic effects of crossbanded and ringed pat-terns of snakes. Copeia 1976(4): 834–836.

——. 1988a. Mimicry and related phenomena. Pp. 154–229 in C. Gans and R. B. Huey (eds.), Biology of the Reptilia, vol. 16. Ecology B. A. R. Liss, New York.

——. 1988b. Mimicry of vertebrates: are the rules different? American Naturalist 131(suppl.): 67–102.

Pough, F. H., R. M. Andrews, J. E. Cadle, M. L. Crump, A. H. Savitzky, and K. D. Wells. 2001. Herpetology, 2d ed. Prentice Hall, Upper Saddle Creek, N.J.

Pough, F. H., C. M. Janis, and J. B. Heiser. 1999. Vertebrate life, 5th ed. Prentice Hall, Upper Saddle River, N.J. 733 pp.

Poulton, E. B. 1908. Essays on evolution. Oxford University Press, Oxford.

Pounds, J. A., and M. P. Fogden. 2000. Amphibians and reptiles of Monteverde. Pp. 537–540 in N. M. Nadkarni and N. T. Wheelwright (eds.), Monteverde: ecology and conservation of a tropical cloud forest. Oxford University Press, New York.

Powell, J. W. 1895. The exploration of the Colorado River and its canyons. Meadville, Pa., Flood and Vincent. 400 pp.

Powell, R., and J. Parmerlee. 1980. Geographic distribution: *Crotalus durissus* (tropical rattlesnake). Herpetol. Rev. 11(4): 116.

Powers, A. 1974. Description of a female *Micrurus diastema mac-dougalli* Rooze from Progreso, Oaxaca, Mexico. Bull. Maryland Her-petol. Soc. 10(4): 103–104.

Prado, A. 1939 [dated 1938–1939]. Notas ofiológicas. I. Sôbre as ser-pentes do grupo *Bothrops lansbergii*, com a descrição de uma nova espécie. Mem. Inst. Butantan 12: 1–4.

——. 1945. Serpentes do Brasil. Edição de Sitios e Fazendas, São Paulo. 134 pp.

Prado, A., and A. R. Hoge. 1948 [dated 1947]. Notas ofiológicas. 21. Observações sôbre serpentes do Perú. Mem. Inst. Butantan 20: 283–296.

Prado-Franceschi, J., and S. Hyslop. 2002. South American colubrid envenomations. Journal of Toxicology—Toxin Reviews 21(1–2): 117–158.

Prado-Franceschi, J., S. Hyslop, J. C. Cogo, A. L. Andrade, M. Assakura, M. A. Cruz-Hofling, and L. Rodrigues-Simioni. 1996. The effects of Duvernoy's gland secretion from the xenodontine colubrid *Philodryas olfersii* on striated muscle and the neuromus-cular junction: partial characterization of a neuromuscular fraction. Toxicon 34(4): 459–466.

Prado-Franceschi, J., S. Hyslop, J. C. Cogo, A. L. Andrade, M. T. Assakura, A. P. Reichl, M. A. Cruz-Hofling, and L. Rodrigues-Simioni. 1998. Characterization of a myotoxin from the Duvernoy's gland secretion of the xenodontine colubrid *Philodryas olfersii* (green snake): effects on striated muscle and the neuromuscular junction. Toxicon 36(10): 1407–1421.

Prado-Franceschi, J., and O. Vital Brazil. 1981. Convulxin, a new toxin from the venom of the South American rattlesnake, *Crotalus duris-sus terrificus*. Toxicon 19(6): 875–888.

Pregill, G. K., J. A. Gauthier, and H. W. Greene. 1986. The evolution of helodermatid squamates, with the description of a new taxon and an overview of Varanoidea. Trans. San Diego Soc. Nat. Hist. 21(11): 167–202.

Pregill, G. K., and S. L. Olson. 1981. Zoogeography of West Indian vertebrates in relation to Pleistocene climatic cycles. Annual Review of Ecology and Systematics 12: 75–98.

Prentiss, D. J. 1994. Natural history notes: *Coluber constrictor priapus* (southern black racer): Prey. Herpetol. Rev. 25(2): 70.

Preston, C. A. 1989. Hypotension, myocardial infarction, and coagu-lopathy following Gila monster bite. Journal of Emergency Medi-cine 7: 37–40.

Preston, W. B. 1982. The amphibians and reptiles of Manitoba. Man-itoba Museum of Man and Nature, Winnipeg. 128 pp.

Price, A. H. 1980. *Crotalus molossus* Baird and Girard, black-tailed rat-tlesnake. Catalogue of American Amphibians and Reptiles 242.1–242.2.

——. 1982. *Crotalus scutulatus* (Kennicott), Mojave rattlesnake. Cata-logue of American Amphibians and Reptiles 291.1–291.2.

——. 1988. Observation on maternal behavior and neonate aggrega-tion in the western diamondback rattlesnake, *Crotalus atrox*. South-west. Nat. 33: 370–373.

——. 1998. Poisonous snakes of Texas. Texas Parks and Wildlife Press, Austin. 112 pp.

Price, R. M. 1982. Dorsal snake scale microdermatoglyphics: ecolog-ical indicator or taxonomic tool? J. Herpetol. 16: 294–306.

Prieto, A. A., and E. R. Jacobson. 1968. A new locality for melanistic *Crotalus molossus molossus* in southern New Mexico. Herpetologica 24(4): 339–340.

Prior, K. A., and P. J. Weatherhead. 1994. Response of free-ranging eastern massasauga rattlesnakes to human disturbance. J. Herpetol. 28(2): 255–257.

Prival, D. B. 2000. Ecology and conservation of the twin-spotted rattlesnake, *Crotalus pricei*. Master's thesis, University of Arizona. 137 pp.

Prival, D. B., M. J. Goode, D. E. Swann, C. R. Schwalbe, and M. J. Schroff. 2002. Natural history of a northern population of twin-spotted rattlesnakes, *Crotalus pricei*. J. Herpetol. 36(4): 598–607.

Prival, D. B., and C. R. Schwalbe. 2000. Conservation management of commercially valuable snake species at Chiricahua National Monument. Unpublished report. Southwest Parks and Monuments Association, Tucson, Ariz.

Procter, J. B. 1918. On the variation of the pit viper, *Lachesis atrox*. Proc. Zool. London 1918(8): 163–182.

Puorto, G. 1992. Serpentes brasileiras de importância médica. Pp. 143–149 in S. Schvartsman (ed.), Plantas venenosas e animais peçonhentos. Sarvier, São Paulo.

Puorto, G., M. da Graça Salomão, R. D. G. Theakston, R. S. Thorpe, D. A. Warrell, and W. Wüster. 2001. Combining mitochondrial DNA sequences and morphological data to infer species boundaries: phylogeography and lanceheaded pitvipers in the Brazilian Atlantic forest, and the status of *Bothrops pradoi* (Squamata: Serpentes: Viperidae). Journal of Evolutionary Biology 14: 527–538.

Pylka, J. M, J. A. Simmons, and E. G. Wever. 1971. Sound production and hearing in the rattlesnake. Herpetol. Rev. 3(6): 107.

Quaintance, C. W. 1935. Reptiles and amphibians from Eagle Creek, Greenlee County, Arizona. Copeia 1935(4): 183–185.

Queiroz, L. P. de, and R. D. Moritz. 1989. Acidente botrópico em Florianópolis. Arquivos Catarinenses de Medicina 18: 163–166.

Quelch, J. J. 1893. Venom in harmless snakes. Journal of the Linnean Society (Zoology) 17: 30–31.

——. 1898. The poisonous snakes of British Guiana. Timehri 2(12): 26–36.

Quesnel, V. C. 1986. An unusual prey for the marine toad, *Bufo marinus*. Living World: Journal of the Trinidad and Tobago Field Naturalists' Club 1985–1986: 25.

Quinn, H. R. 1977. Further notes on reproduction in *Crotalus willardi* (Reptilia, Serpentes, Crotalidae). Bull. Maryland Herpetol. Soc. 13: 111.

——. 1979. Reproduction and growth of the Texas coral snake (*Micrurus fulvius tenere*). Copeia 1979(3): 453–463.

——. 1981. Natural history notes: *Crotalus lepidus lepidus* (mottled rock rattlesnake). Coloration. Herpetol. Rev. 12(3): 79–80.

——. 1983. Two new subspecies of *Lampropeltis triangulum* from Mexico. Trans. Kansas Acad. Sci. 86(4): 113–135.

——. 1987. Morphology, isozymes, and mitochondrial DNA as systematic indicators in *Crotalus viridis*. Ph.D. dissertation, University of Houston, University Park.

Quintero, M. T., A. Acevedo-Hernández, and S. R. Gaitán. 1990. Presence of the mite *Ophionyssus natricis* (Macroyssidae) in snakes from Mexico. Veterinaria (Mexico) 21(2): 163–166.

Quintini N., J. 1927. Contribución a la geografía médica del ferrocarril de Santa Bárbara al vigía en los Estados Zulia y Mérida. Capítulo: Los animales ponzoñosos. Memorias del V Congreso Venezolano Medicina (Caracas) 1: 305–311.

——. 1936. Contribución al estudio del género *Bothrops* en el Estado Trujillo. Sobre un ejemplar del grupo *B. lansbergii*. Caracas Médico 3(9): 493–498.

Rabatsky, A. M., and T. M. Farrell. 1996. The effects of age and light level on foraging posture and frequency of caudal luring in the rattlesnake, *Sistrurus miliarius barbouri*. J. Herpetol. 30(4): 558–561.

Rabinowitz, A. 2000. Jaguar: one man's struggle to establish the world's first jaguar preserve. Island Press, Washington, D.C. 378 pp.

Radcliffe, W. C., and T. P. Maslin. 1975. A new subspecies of the red rattlesnake, *Crotalus ruber*, from San Lorenzo Sur Island, Baja California Norte, Mexico. Copeia 1975(3): 490–493.

Rado, T. A., and P. G. Rowlands. 1981. A range extension and low elevational record for the Arizona ridge-nosed rattlesnake (*Crotalus w. willardi*). Herpetol. Rev. 12(1): 15.

Radovanovic, M. 1935. Anatomische Studien am Schlangenkopf. Jena. Z. Naturw. 69: 321–421.

Rael, E. D., R. A. Knight, and H. Zepeda. 1984. Electrophoretic variants of Mojave rattlesnake (*Crotalus scutulatus scutulatus*) venoms and migration differences of Mojave toxin. Toxicon 22: 980–985.

Rael, E. D., R. J. Salo, and H. Zepeda. 1986. Monoclonal antibodies to Mojave toxin and use for isolation of cross-reacting proteins in *Crotalus* venoms. Toxicon 24: 661–668.

Rafinesque, C. S. 1815. Analyse de la nature ou tableau de l'univers et des corps organisés. Jean Barravecchia, Palermo. 224 pp.

——. 1817. Dissertation on water snakes, sea snakes, and sea serpents. American Monthly Magazine and Critical Review 1(6): 431–442.

——. 1818. Natural history of the *Scytalus Cupreus*, or copper-head snake. American Journal of Science 1(1): 84–88.

Rage, J.-C. 1984. Serpents. Handbuch der Paläoherpetologie / Encyclopedia of paleoherpetology, part 11. Gustav Fischer, Stuttgart.

——. 1987. Fossil history. Pp. 51–76 in R. A. Seigel, J. T. Collins, and S. S. Novak (eds.), Snakes: ecology and evolutionary biology. Macmillan, New York.

Rage, J.-C., and J. A. Holman. 1984. Des serpents (Reptilia, Squamata) de type nord-américain dans le Miocène français: évolution parallèle ou dispersion? Geobios 17: 89–104.

Rahn, H. 1942a. Effect of temperature on color change in the rattlesnake. Copeia 1942(3): 178.

——. 1942b. The reproductive cycle of the prairie rattler. Copeia 1942(4): 233–240.

Rakowitz, V. A., R. R. Fleet, and F. L. Rainwater. 1983. New distributional records of Texas amphibians and reptiles. Herpetol. Rev. 14(3): 85–89.

Ramírez-Bautista, A. 1994. Manual y claves ilustradas de los anfibios y reptiles de la región de Chamela, Jalisco, México. Universidad Nacional Autónoma de México, Cuadernos del Instituto de Biología 23: 1–127.

Ramírez-Bautista, A., G. Gutiérrez-Mayen, and A. González-Romero. 1995. Clutch sizes in a community of snakes from the mountains of the Valley of Mexico. Herpetol. Rev. 26(1): 12–13.

Ramírez-Bautista, A., G. Pérez-Higareda, and G. Casas-Andreu. 1981. Lista preliminar de los anfibios y reptiles de la region de Los Tuxtlas, Veracruz. Instituto de Biología, Universidad Nacional Autónoma de México. 6 pp.

Ramírez-Velásquez, A. 2001. Temacuil o *Heloderma negro*. Unidad de Divulgación y Fondo Editorial Instituto de Historia Natural y Ecología, Tuxtla Gutiérrez. 6 pp.

——. 2002. Contribución al conocimiento de la historia natural de la víbora chatilla (*Porthidium dunni*), en Chiapas (Reptilia, Serpentes, Viperidae). Unpublished ms.

Ramírez-Velásquez, A., and C. A. Guichard-Romero. 1989. El escorpión negro: combates ritualizados. Cuadernillos de Divulgación sobre Flora y Fauna de Chiapas, Instituto de Historia Natural, Tuxtla Gutiérrez. 20 pp.

Ramsey, G. F., and G. D. Klickstein. 1962. Coral snake bite: report of a case and suggested therapy. JAMA 182: 949–951.

Ramsey, H. W., W. J. Taylor, I. B. Boruchow, and G. K. Snyder. 1972. Mechanism of shock produced by an elapid snake (*Micrurus f. fulvius*) venom in dogs. American Journal of Physiology 222: 782–786

Ramsey, L. W. 1948. Combat dance and range extension of *Agkistrodon piscivorus leucostoma*. Herpetologica 4(6): 228.

——. 1951. New localities for several Texas snakes. Herpetologica 7(4): 176.

Rand, A. S., and C. W. Myers. 1990. The herpetofauna of Barro Colorado Island, Panama: an ecological summary. Pp. 386–409 in A. H. Gentry (ed.), Four Neotropical rainforests. Yale University Press, New Haven, Conn.

Rand McNally. 1984. The new international atlas. Rand McNally, Chicago. 1376 pp.

Rao, R. B., M. Palmer, and M. Touger. 1998. Thrombocytopenia after rattlesnake envenomation. Ann. Emerg. Med. 31: 139–140.

Raufman, J. P. 1996. Bioactive peptides from lizard venoms. Regulatory Peptides 61: 1–18.

Raun, G. G. 1965. A guide to Texas snakes. Texas Memorial Museum Notes 9: 1–85.

Raun, G. G., and F. R. Gehlbach. 1972. Amphibians and reptiles in Texas. Bulletin of the Dallas Museum of Natural Hisoty 2(1): 1–61.

Raven, P. H., and D. I. Axelrod. 1974. Angiosperm biogeography and past continental movements. Annals of the Missouri Botanical Garden 61: 539–673.

Ravenau de Lussan. 1693. Journal du voyage fait à Mer du Sud. Jacques Lefebvre, Paris.

Raw, Y., R. Guidolin, H. Higashi, and E. M. Kelen. 1991. Antivenins in Brazil: preparation. Pp. 557–581 in A. T. Tu (ed.), Handbook of natural toxins, vol. 5. Reptile venoms and toxins. Marcel Dekker, New York.

Rawat, S., G. Laing, D. C. Smith, D. Theakston, and J. Landon. 1994. A new antivenom to treat eastern coral snake (*Micrurus fulvius fulvius*) envenoming. Toxicon 32: 185–190.

Read, V. M. St. J. 1986. An onychophoran from the summit of Mt. Aripo, Trinidad, with notes on other animals from that locality. Living World: Journal of the Trinidad and Tobago Field Naturalists' Club 1985–1986: 28–30.

Reams, R. D., C. J. Franklin, and J. M. Davis. 1999. Natural history notes: *Micrurus fulvius tener* (Texas coral snake). Diet. Herpetol. Rev. 30(4): 228–229.

Recinos, A. 1913. Monografía del Departamento de Huehuetenango. Editorial del Ministerio de Educación Pública, Guatemala. 269 pp.

——. 1954. Monografía del Departamento de Huehuetenango. Colección Monografías 2. Editorial del Ministerio de Educación Pública, Guatemala. 403 pp.

Reddell, J. R., and R. W. Mitchell (eds.). 1971. Studies on the cavernicole fauna of Mexico. Bull. Assoc. Mexican Cave Stud. 4: 1–239.

Redmer, M., and S. R. Ballard. 1995. Recent distributional records for amphibians and reptiles in Illinois. Herpetol. Rev. 26(1): 49–53.

Redmond, W. H., A. C. Echternacht, and A. F. Scott. 1990. Annotated checklist and bibliography of amphibians and reptiles of Tennessee (1835 through 1989). Miscellaneous Publication No. 4, Center for Field Biology, Austin Peay State University, Clarksville, Tennessee. 173 pp.

Reese, R. W. 1971. Notes on a small herpetological collection from northeastern Mexico. J. Herpetol. 5(1–2): 67–69.

Rego, A. A. 1982a [dated 1980–1981]. Sôbre a identificacão das espécies de *Porocephalus* (Pentastomida) que ocorrem em ofídios da América tropical. Mem. Inst. Butantan 44–45: 219–232.

——. 1982b [dated 1980–1981]. Notas sôbre alguns pentastomídeos de répteis. Mem. Inst. Butantan 44–45: 233–238.

Reichel-Dolmatoff, G. 1968. Simbolismo de los Indios Tukanos del Vaupes. Universidad de los Andes, Bogota. 269 pp.

Reid, H. A. 1956. Sea-snake bite research. Trans. Roy. Soc. Trop. Med. Hyg. 50(6): 517–542.

——. 1978. Bites by foreign venomous snakes in Britain. British Medical Journal 1: 1598–1600.

Reid, H. A., and R. D. G. Theakston. 1978. Changes in coagulation effects by venoms of *Crotalus atrox* as snakes age. American Journal of Tropical Medicine and Hygiene 27: 1053–1057.

Reid, M. and A. Nichols. 1970. Predation by reptiles on the periodic cicada. Bull. Maryland Herpetol. Soc. 6: 57.

Reimers, A. R., M. Weber, and U. R. Muller. 2000. Are anaphylactic reactions to snake bites immunoglobulin E–mediated? Clinical and Experimental Allergy 30: 276–282.

Reinert, H. K. 1978. The ecology and morphological variation of the massasauga rattlesnake (*Sistrurus catenatus*). Master's thesis, Clarion State College.

——. 1981. Reproduction by the massasauga (*Sistrurus catenatus catenatus*). Am. Midl. Nat. 105: 393–395.

——. 1984a. Habitat separation between sympatric snake populations. Ecology 65: 478–486.

——. 1984b. Habitat variation within sympatric snake populations. Ecology 65: 1673–1682.

——. 1990. A profile and impact assessment of organized rattlesnake hunts in Pennsylvania. Journal of the Pennsylvania Academy of Science 64(3): 136–144.

——. 1992. Radiotelemetric field studies of pitvipers: data acquisition and analysis. Pp. 185–197 in J. A. Campbell and E. D. Brodie Jr. (eds.), Biology of the pitvipers. Selva, Tyler, Texas.

Reinert, H. K., L. M. Bushar, G. L. Rocco, M. Goode, and R. A. Odum. 2002. Distribution of the Aruba Island rattlesnake, *Crotalus unicolor*, on Aruba, Dutch West Indies. Caribbean Journal of Science 38(1–2): 126–128.

Reinert, H. K., D. Cundall, and L. M. Bushar. 1984. Foraging behavior of the timber rattlesnake, *Crotalus horridus*. Copeia 1984(4): 976–981.

Reinert, H. K., and W. R. Kodrich. 1982. Movements and habitat utilization by the massasauga, *Sistrurus catenatu catenatus*. J. Herpetol. 16(2): 162–171.

Reinert, H. K., and R. R. Rupert Jr. 1999. Impacts of translocation on behavior and survival of timber rattlesnakes, *Crotalus horridus*. J. Herpetol. 33(1): 45–61.

Reinert, H. K., and R. T. Zappalorti. 1988a. Timber rattlesnakes (*Crotalus horridus*) of the Pine Barrens: their movement patterns and habitat preference. Copeia 1988(4): 964–978.

——. 1988b. Field observation of the association of adult and neonatal timber rattlesnakes, *Crotalus horridus*, with possible evidence for conspecific trailing. Copeia 1988(4): 1057–1059.

Reiskind, J. 1977. Ant-mimicry in Panamanian clubionid and salticid spiders (Araneae: Clubionidae, Salticidae). Biotropica 9: 1–8.

Rendahl, H. 1937. Einige reptilien aus Ecuador und Bolivia. Arkiv för Zoologi 29A(13): 1–19.

Rendahl, H., and G. Vestergren. 1940. Notes on Colombian snakes. Arkiv för Zoologi 33A(1): 1–16.

——. 1941. On a small collection of snakes from Ecuador. Arkiv för Zoologi 33A(5): 1–16.

Rendón-R., A., T. Alvarez, and O. Flores-Villela. 1998. Herpetofauna de Santiago Jalahui, Oaxaca, Mexico. Acta Zoologica Mexicana 75: 17–45.

Renjifo, J. M. 1979. Systematics and distribution of crotalid snakes in Colombia. Master's thesis, University of Kansas, Lawrence. 64 pp.

Renjifo, J. M., and M. Lundberg. 1999. Anfibios y reptiles de Urrá. Editorial Clina, Medellín, Colombia. 96 pp.

——. 2003. Una nueva especie de serpiente coral (*Micrurus*, Elapidae) de la región de Urrá, Tierra Alta, Córdoba, noroccidente de Colombia. Revista de la Academia Colombiana de Ciencias Exactas, Físicas, Naturales 27(102): 141–144.

Resetar, A. 1992. The eastern massasauga (*Sistrurus catenatus*) in Indiana: a preliminary historical survey. Pp. 138–141 in B. Johnson and V. Menzies (eds.), International workshop and symposium on the conservation of the eastern massasauga rattlesnake. Toronto Zoo, Toronto.

Retzios, A. D., and F. S. Markland Jr. 1992. Purification characterization and fibrinogen cleavage sites of three fibrinolytic enzymes from the venom of *Crotalus basiliscus basiliscus*. Biochemistry 31(19): 4547–4557.

Reuss, T. 1930. Über eine neurotoxische Otterngruppe Europas, Mesocoronis, 1927, und über ihre Stellung unter den Solenoglyphen der Welt. Glasnik Zemaljskog Muzeja, Serajevo 42: 57–114.

Revista Médica del Uruguay. 1983. Ofidismo y arachnidismo en el Uruguay. Revista Médica del Uruguay 7: 1–37.

Reyes, D. S. 1889. El lagarto de costra. Naturaleza, ser. 2, 1: 277–278.

Reynolds, R. P. 1978. Resource use, habitat selection, and seasonal activity of a Chihuahuan snake community. Ph.D. diss., University of New Mexico, Albuquerque. 100 pp.

——. 1982. Seasonal incidence of snakes in northeastern Chihuahua, Mexico. Southwest. Nat. 27(2): 161–166.

Reynolds, R., T. Fritts, S. Gotte, J. Icochea, and G. Tello. 1997. Amphibians and reptiles I: assessment of the lower Urubamba region. Biodiversity Assessment and Monitoring, Smithsonian Institution's Monitoring and Assessment of Biodiversity Program Series 1: 213–221.

Reynolds, R. P., and J. Icochea M. 1997. Amphibians and reptiles of the upper Rio Comainas, Cordillera del Condor. Pp. 82–86, 202–206 in T. S. Schulenberg and K. Awbrey (eds.), The Cordillera del

Condor region of Ecuador and Peru: a biological assessment. Rapid Assessment Program Working Papers No. 7. Conservation International, Washington, D.C.

Reynolds, R. P., and G. V. Pickwell, 1984. Records of the yellow-bellied sea snake, *Pelamis platurus*, from the Galápagos Islands. Copeia 1984(3): 786–789.

Reynolds, R. P., and N. J. Scott Jr. 1982. Use of mammalian resource by a Chihuahuan snake community. Pp. 99–118 in N. J. Scott Jr. (ed.), Herpetological communities: a symposium of the Society for the Study of Amphibians and Reptiles and the Herpetologists' League, August 1977. U.S. Fish and Wildlife Service, Wildlife Research Report No. 13.

Reynoso, F. 1990. Geographic distribution: *Crotalus enyo enyo* (Lower California rattlesnake). Herpetol. Rev. 21(1): 23.

Rhoten, W. B., and J. F. Gennaro. 1968. Treatment of the bite of the Mojave rattlesnake. Journal of the Florida Medical Association 55: 324–326.

Ribeiro, L. A., M. J. Albuquerque, V. A. de Campos, G. Katz, N. Y. Takaoka, M. L. Lebrao, and M. T. Jorge. 1998. Obitos por serpentes peçonhentas no Estado de São Paulo: avaliacão de 43 casos, 1988–1993. Revista da Associação Medica Brasileira 44(4): 312–318.

Ribeiro, L. A., and M. T. Jorge. 1989. Changes in blood coagulation in patients bitten by young and adult *Bothrops jararaca* snakes. Revista do Hospital Clinica Fac. Medico, São Paulo 44(4): 143–145.

———. 1990. Clinical and epidemiological features of bites by adult and young *Bothrops jararaca*. Revista do Instituto de Medicina Tropical de São Paulo 32(6): 436–442.

Ribeiro, L. A., M. T. Jorge, and M. L. Lebrão. 2001. Prognostic factors for local necrosis in *Bothrops jararaca* (Brazilian pitviper) bites. Trans. Roy. Soc. Trop. Med. Hyg. 95(6): 630–634.

Ribeiro, L. A., G. Puorto, and M. T. Jorge. 1999. Bites by the colubrid snake *Philodryas olfersii*: a clinical and epidemiologial study of 43 cases. Toxicon 37: 943–948.

Richards, R. L. 1990. Quaternary distribution of the timber rattlesnake (*Crotalus horridus*) in southern Indiana. Proceedings of the Indiana Academy of Science 99: 113–122.

Ride, W. D. L., C. W. Sabrosky, G. Bernardi, and R. V. Melville (eds.). 1985. International Code of Zoological Nomenclature, 3d ed. University of California Press, Berkeley. 388 pp.

Riedle, D. 1996. Some occurrences of the western diamondback rattlesnake (*Crotalus atrox*) in Kansas. Kansas Herpetological Society Newsletter 105: 18–19.

Rieppel, O. 1980. The phylogeny of anguinomorph lizards. Birkhäuser, Basel. 86 pp.

Riffer, E., S. C. Curry, and R. Gerkin. 1987. Successful treatment with antivenin of marked thrombocytopenia without significant coagulopathy following rattlesnake bite. Ann. Emerg. Med. 16: 1297–1299.

Riley, J. 1981. Some observations on the development of *Porocephalus crotali* (Pentastomida: Porocephalidae) in the western diamondback rattlesnake (*Crotalus atrox*). International Journal for Parasitology 11(2): 127–132.

Riley, J., and J. T. Self. 1979. On the systematics of the pentastomid genus *Porocephalus* (Humbolt, 1811) with descriptions of two new species. Systematic Parasitology 1(1): 25–42.

Ringler, S. B. 1977. The herpetofauna of Ossabaw Island, Chatham County, Georgia. Herpetol. Rev. 8(2): 39.

Ripa, D. 1994a. Reproduction of the Central American bushmaster (*Lachesis muta stenophrys*) and the black-headed bushmaster (*Lachesis muta melanocephala*) for the first time in captivity. Bull. Chicago Herpetol. Soc. 29(8): 165–183.

———. 1994b. The reproduction of the Central American bushmasters (*Lachesis melanocephala* and *Lachesis muta stenophrys*) for the first time in captivity. Vivarium 5(5): 36–37.

———. 1996. The bushmaster: a natural history. League of Florida Herpetological Societies Newsletter, June. 4 pp.

———. 1997. Range extension for *Bothrops leucurus*. Bull. Chicago Herpetol. Soc. 32(2): 25–26.

———. 1999. Keys to understanding the bushmasters (genus *Lachesis* Daudin, 1803). Bull. Chicago Herpetol. Soc. 34(3): 45–92.

———. 2001. The bushmasters (genus *Lachesis* Daudin 1803): morphology in evolution and behavior. CD-ROM. Ripa Ecologica, Wilmington, N.C.

Ritland, D. B. 1991. Revising a classic butterfly mimicry scenario—demonstration of Müllerian mimicry between Florida viceroys (*Limenitis archippus floridensis*) and queens (*Danaus gilippus berenice*). Evolution 45: 918–934.

Ritland, D. B., and L. P. Brower. 1991. The viceroy butterfly is not a Batesian mimic. Nature 350: 497–498.

Rivero-Blanco, C., and J. R. Dixon. 1979. Origin and distribution of the herpetofauna of the dry lowland regions of northern South America. Pp. 281–298 in W. E. Duellman (ed.), The South American herpetofauna: its origin, evolution, and dispersal. Monograph No. 7 of the Museum of Natural History, University of Kansas, Lawrence.

Rivers, I. L. 1976. I—Some comments on snakebite treatment in the United States and II—an account of a human envenomation by an adult western diamondback rattlesnake (*Crotalus atrox* Baird and Girard). Biological Society of Nevada 42: 1–6.

Rivière, G., V. Choumet, B. Saliou, M. Debray, and C. Bon. 1998. Absorption and elimination of viper venom after antivenom administration. Journal of Pharmacology and Experimental Therapeutics 285: 490–495.

Roberts, A. R., and J. Quarters. 1947. *Sistrurus* in Michigan. Herpetologica 4(1): 6.

Roberts, D. T., and S. H. Hammack. 1995. Captive reproduction and husbandry of the speckled forest-pitviper *Bothriopsis taeniata* (Wagler) at the Dallas Zoo. Snake 27(1): 53–55.

Roberts, J. B., and H. B. Lillywhite. 1983. Lipids and the permeability of epidermis from snakes. Journal of Experimental Zoology 228(1): 1–10.

Roberts, R. S., T. A. Csencsitz, and C. W. Heard. 1985. Upper extremity compartment syndromes following pit viper envenomation. Clinical Orthopaedics and Related Research 193: 184–188.

Robison, H. W. 1972. Geographic distribution: *Micrurus fulvius tenere*. Herpetol. Rev. 4(5): 170–171.

Rocha, C. F. D., H. G. Bergallo, and D. Vrcibradic. 1997. Natural history notes: *Bothrops pradoi* (Prado's lancehead). Unusual mortality. Herpetol. Rev. 28(3): 153–154.

Rocha, C. F. D., M. van Sluys, G. Puorto, R. Fernandes, J. D. Barros Filho, R. R. Silva, F. A. Néo, and A. Melgarejo. 2000. Répteis. Pp. 79–87 in H. G. Bergallo, C. F. D. da Rocha, M. A. S. Alves, and M. van Sluys (eds.), Fauna ameaçada de extinção do Estado do Rio de Janeiro. Editora da Universidade do Estado do Rio de Janeiro, Rio de Janeiro. 168 pp.

Rocha e Silva, M., W. T. Beraldo, and G. Rosenfeld. 1949. Bradykinin, a hypotensive and smooth muscle stimulating factor released from plasma globulin by snake venoms and by trypsin. American Journal of Physiology. 156: 261–273.

Rodas J., T. 1938. Contribución al estudio de las serpientes venenosas de Guatemala. Tipografía Nacional, Guatemala City. 152 pp.

Rodgers, T. L., and W. L. Jellison. 1942. A collection of amphibians and reptiles from western Montana. Copeia 1941(1): 10–13.

Rodrigues, M. T. 2000. A fauna de répteis e anfíbios das Caatingas. Avaliação identificação de ações prioritárias para a conservação, utilização sustentável e repartição de benefícios da biodiversidade do bioma Caatinga. Documento para discussão no GT répteis e anfíbios. 12 pp.

Rodrigues-García, J., G. Pérez-Higareda, H. M. Smith, and D. Chiszar. 1998. Natural history notes: *Micrurus diastema* and *M. limbatus* (diastema coral snake and Tuxtlan coral snake, respectively). Diet. Herpetol. Rev. 29(1): 45.

Rodríguez, J. P., and F. Rojas-Suárez. 1995. Libro rojo de la fauna venezolana. Provita, Fundación Polar, Wildlife Conservation Society, Profauna—Ministerio del Ambiente y los Recursos Naturales Renovables, Unión Internacional para la Conservación de la Naturaleza, Caracas. 444 pp.

Rodríguez, L. B., and J. E. Cadle. 1990. A preliminary overview of the herpetofauna of Cocha Cashu, Manu National Park, Peru. Pp.

410–425 in A. H. Gentry (ed.), Four Neotropical rainforests. Yale University Press, New Haven, Conn.

Rodríguez-Acosta, A., I. Aguilar, M. Girón, and V. Rodríguez-Pulido. 1998. Haemorrhagic activity of Neotropical rattlesnake (*Crotalus vegrandis* Klauber, 1941) venom. Natural Toxins 6(1): 15–18.

Rodríguez-Acosta, A., M. E. Girón, I. Aguilar, and O. Fuentes. 1997. A case of envenomation by a "non-venomous" snake (*Philodryas viridissimus*) and comparison between this snake's Duvernoy's gland secretion and northern South America rattlesnake's venoms. Archivos Venezolanos de Medicina Tropical 1: 29–32.

Rodríguez-Acosta, A., W. Uzcategui, R. Azuaje, I. Aguilar, and M. E. Giron. 2000. Analisis clínico y epidemiológico de los accidentes por mordeduras de serpientes del genero *Bothrops* en Venezuela. Revista Cubana de Medicina Tropical 52(2): 90–94.

Rodríguez-Robles, J. A. 1994. Are the Duvernoy's gland secretions of colubrid snakes venoms? J. Herpetol. 28(3): 388–390.

Roge [*sic*], A. R., and S. A. R. W. L. Romano. 1977 [dated 1976–1977]. *Lachesis muta rhombeata* [Serpentes: Viperidae: Crotalinae]. Mem. Inst. Butantan 40–41: 53–54.

Rohl, E. 1949. Fauna descriptiva de Venezuela (vertebrados), 2d ed. Tipografía Americana, Caracas.

Rojas, G., J. M. Gutiérrez, J. A. Gene, M. Gómez, and L. Cerdas. 1987. Neutralization of toxic and enzymatic activities of 4 venoms from snakes of Guatemala and Honduras by polyvalent antivenom produced in Costa Rica. Rev. Biol. Trop. 35(1): 59–68.

Rokosky, E. J. 1941. Notes on new-born jumping vipers, *Bothrops nummifera*. Copeia 1941(4): 267.

———. 1942. Notes on *Trimeresurus nigroviridis marchi*. Copeia 1943(4): 260.

Romano, S. A. R. W. L. 1972 [dated 1971]. Notes on *Leptomicrurus* Schmidt (Serpentes, Elapidae). Mem. Inst. Butantan 35: 111–115.

Roodt, A. R., J. C. Vidal, S. Litwin, J. C. Dokmetjian, J. A. Dolab, S. E. Hajos, and L. Segre. 1999. Neutralización cruzada de veneno de *Bothrops jararacussu* por sueros antiofidicos heterologos. Medicina (Buenos Aires) 59: 238–242.

Rooij, N. de. 1922. Reptiles and amphibians of Curacao. Bijdragen tot de Dierkunde, Universiteit van Amsterdam, 1922: 249–253.

Rosado-López, L., and F. A. Laviada-Arrigunada. 1977. Accidente ofídico. Communicación de 38 casos. Prensa Médica Méxicana 42: 409–412.

Rosen, D. E. 1976. A vicariance model of Caribbean biogeography. Syst. Zool. 24: 431–464.

Rosen, P. C., and S. R. Goldberg. 2003. Female reproduction in the western diamond-backed rattlesnake, *Crotalus atrox* (Serpentes: Viperidae), from Arizona. Texas Journal of Science 54(4): 347–356.

Rosenberg, H. I., A. Bdolah, and E. Kochva. 1985. Lethal factors and enzymes in the secretion from Duvernoy's gland of three colubrid snakes. Journal of Experimental Zoology 233: 5–14.

Rosenfeld, G. 1971. Symptomatology, pathology, and treatment of snake bite in South America. Pp. 345–384 in W. Bucherl and E. E. Buckley (eds.), Venomous animals and their venoms, vol. 2. Academic Press, New York.

Rosenfeld, G. E., M. A. Kelen, and L. Nahas. 1959 [dated 1958]. Regeneration of fibrinogen after defibrination by bothropic venom in man and dogs. Relationship with clotting and bleeding times. Revista Clinica, São Paulo, 34: 36–44.

Rosenthal, R., J. Meier, A. Koelz, et al. 2002. Intestinal ischemia after bushmaster (*Lachesis muta*) snakebite—a case report. Toxicon 40: 217–220.

Rossi, J. V., and J. J. Feldner. 1993. Life history notes: *Crotalus willardi willardi* (Arizona ridgenose rattlesnake). Arboreal behavior. Herpetol. Rev. 24(1): 35.

Rossi, M. A., L. C. Peres, F. Paola, P. Cupo, S. E. Hering, and M. M. Azevedo-Marques. 1989. Electron-microscopic study of systemic myonecrosis due to poisoning by tropical rattlesnake (*Crotalus durissus terrificus*) in humans. Archives of Pathology and Laboratory Medicine 113: 169–173.

Rossman, D. A. 1960. Herpetofaunal survey of the Pine Hills area of southern Illinois. Quarterly Journal of the Florida Academy of Science 22: 207–225.

Rossman, D. A., and K. L. Williams. 1966. Defensive behavior of the South American colubrid snakes *Pseustes sulphureus* (Wagler) and *Spilotes pullatus* (Linnaeus). Proceedings of the Louisiana Academy of Sciences 29: 152–156.

Roth, E. D., P. G. May, and T. M. Farrell. 1999. Pigmy rattlesnakes use frog-derived chemical cues to select foraging sites. Copeia 1999(3): 772–774.

Roudabush, R. L., and G. R. Coatney. 1937. On some blood protozoa of reptiles and amphibians. Transactions of the American Microscopical Society 56: 291–297.

Roux-Esteve, R. 1983 [dated 1982]. Les spécimens-types du genre *Micrurus* (Elapidae) conservés au Museum National d'Histoire Naturelle de Paris. Mem. Inst. Butantan 46: 79–94.

Rowe, M. P., R. G. Coss, and D. H. Owings. 1986. Rattlesnake rattles and burrowing owl hisses: a case of acoustic Batesian mimicry. Ethology 72: 53–71.

Rowe, M. P., and D. H. Owings. 1978. The meaning of the signal of rattling by rattlesnakes to California ground squirrels. Behaviour 66(2): 252–267.

Roze, J. A. 1952. Colección de reptiles del Profesor Scorza, de Venezuela. Acta Biológica Venezuelica 1(5): 93–114.

———. 1953. Ofidios de Camurí Chico, Macuto, D.F., Venezuela, colectados por el Rvdo. Padre Cornelius Vogl. Boletin de la Sociedad Venezolana de Ciencias Naturales 19(79): 200–211.

———. 1954. Nota preliminar sobre los ofidios de la expedición franco–venezolana al alto Orinoco. Archivos Venezolanos de Patología Tropical y Parasitología Médica 2(2): 227–234.

———. 1955. Revisión de las corales (Serpentes: Elapidae) de Venezuela. Acta Biologica Venezuelica 1(17): 453–500.

———. 1957 [dated 1955]. Ofidios coleccionados por la expedición franco–venezolana al Alto Orinoco, 1951 a 1952. Boletín del Museo de Ciencias Naturales, Caracas, 1 (3–4): 179–195.

———. 1958a. On Hallowell's type specimens of reptiles from Venezuela in the collection of the Academy of Natural Science of Philadelphia. Notulae Naturae (Philadelphia) 309: 1–4.

———. 1958b. Resultados zoológicos de la expedición de la Universidad Central de Venezuela a la región del Auyantepui en la Guayana venezolana, Abril 1956. 5. Los reptiles del Auyantepui, Venezuela, basándose en las collecciones de las expediciones de Phelps–Tate, del American Museum of Natural History, 1937–1938, y de la Universidad Central de Venezuela, 1956. Acta Biologica Venezuelica 2(22): 243–270.

———. 1958c. Los reptiles del Chimantá Tepui (Estado Bolívar, Venezuela) colectados por la expedición botánica del Chicago Natural History Museum. Acta Biologica Venezuelica 2(25): 299–314.

———. 1959. Taxonomic notes on a collection of Venezuelan reptiles in the American Museum of Natural History. Am. Mus. Novitat. 1934: 1–14.

———. 1964. La herpetología de la Isla de Margarita, Venezuela. Memoria de la Sociedad de Ciencias Naturales La Salle 24(69): 209–241.

———. 1966a. La taxonomía y zoogeografía de los ofidios en Venezuela. Ediciones de la Biblioteca, Universidad Central de Venezuela, Caracas. 362 pp.

———. 1966b. On the synonymy and type specimens of the coral snakes *Micrurus corallinus* and *M. ibiboboca* (Marcgravii). Copeia 1966(2): 369–371.

———. 1967. A checklist of the New World venomous coral snakes (Elapidae), with descriptions of new forms. Am. Mus. Novitat. 2287: 1–60.

———. 1970a. Ciencia y fantasía sobre las serpientes de Venezuela. Editorial Fondo de Cultura Científica, Caracas. 162 pp.

———. 1970b. *Micrurus*. Pp. 196–220 in J. A. Peters and B. Orejas-Miranda (eds.), Catalogue of Neotropical Squamata. Part I. Snakes. Bulletin of the U.S. National Museum 297.

———. 1974. *Micruroides*, *M. euryxanthus*. Catalogue of American Amphibians and Reptiles 163.1–163.4.

———. 1983 [dated 1982]. New World coral snakes (Elapidae): a taxonomic and biological summary. Mem. Inst. Butantan 46: 305–338.

——. 1987. Summary of coral snakes (Elapidae) from Cerro de la Neblina, Venezuela, with description of a new subspecies. Revue Française d'Aquariologie, Herpétologie 14(3): 109–112.

——. 1989. New species and subspecies of coral snakes, genus *Micrurus* (Elapidae), with notes on type specimens of several species. Am. Mus. Novitat. 2932: 1–15.

——. 1994. Notes on the taxonomy of venomous coral snakes (Elapidae) of South America. Bull. Maryland Herpetol. Soc. 30: 177–185.

——. 1996. Coral snakes of the Americas—bibliography, identification, and venoms. Kreiger, Malabar, Fla. 328 pp.

Roze, J. A., and A. Bernal-Carlo. 1988 [dated 1987]. Las serpientes venenosas del género *Leptomicrurus* (Serpentes, Elapidae) de Suramérica con descripción de una nueva subspécie. Bolletin del Museo Regionale de Sciènze Naturale di Torino 5: 573–608.

Roze, J. A., and N. Jorge da Silva. 1990. Coral snakes (Serpentes, Elapidae) from hydroelectric power plant of Samuel, Rondonia, Brazil, with description of a new species. Bull. Maryland Herpetol. Soc. 26(4): 169–176.

Roze, J. A., and G. M. Tilger. 1983. *Micrurus fulvius*. Catalogue of American Amphibians and Reptiles 316.1–316.4.

Roze, J. A., and C. P. Trebbau M. 1958. Un nuevo genero de corales venenosas (*Leptomicrurus*) para Venezuela. Acta Científica Venezolana 9(6–7): 128–130.

Rubinoff, I., and C. Kropach. 1970. Differential reactions of Atlantic and Pacific predators to sea snakes. Nature 228: 1288–1290.

Rubio, M. V. 1972. In search of the rare cascabel. Bulletin of the New York Herpetological Society 8(3–4): 6–15.

——. 1998. Rattlesnake: portrait of a predator. Smithsonian Institution Press, Washington, D.C. 240 pp.

Rucavado, A., T. Escalante, C. F. P. Teixeira, C. M. Fernandes, C. Diaz, and J. M. Gutiérrez. 2002. Increments in cytokines and matrix metalloproteinases in skeletal muscle after injection of tissue-damaging toxins from the venom of the snake *Bothrops asper*. Mediators of Inflammation 11: 121–128.

Rudolph, D. C., and S. J. Burgdorf. 1997. Timber rattlesnakes and Louisiana pine snakes of the West Gulf Coast Plain: hypotheses of decline. Texas Journal of Science 49(suppl. 3): 111–122.

Rufino, N. 1998. Geographic distribution: *Micrurus collaris* (coral snake). Herpetol. Rev. 29(3): 178.

Rufz, E. 1859. Enquête sur le serpent de la Martinique (vipère fer-de-lance, Bothrops lancéolé etc.), 2d ed. Germer Baillière, Paris.

Ruggiero, A. 1958. Rattlesnake poisoning. New York State Journal of Medicine 58: 3114–3116.

Ruick, J. D., Jr. 1948. Collecting coral snakes, *Micrurus fulvius tenere*, in Texas. Herpetologica 4(6): 215–216.

Ruiz, J. M. 1951. Sôbre a distinção genérica dos Crotalidae baseada em alguns caracteres osteológicos. Mem. Inst. Butantan 23: 109–114.

Ruiz, R. I., L. I. Ruiz, A. Z. Martínez-Vargas, M. S. Arruz, and J. M. Gutiérrez. 1993. Toxicity and neutralization of venoms from Peruvian snakes of the genera *Bothrops* and *Lachesis* (Serpentes: Viperidae). Rev. Biol. Trop. 41(3): 351–357.

Ruiz de Alarcón, H. 1629. Treatise on the heathen superstitions and customs that today live among the Indians native to New Spain. Translated and edited by J. Richard Andrews and Ross Hassig. University of Oklahoma Press, Norman, 1984. 406 pp.

Rundquist, E. M. 2000. Results of the eleventh and twelfth annual KHS herpetofaunal counts for 1999–2000, held 1 April–31 May. Kansas Herpetological Society Newsletter 122: 11–16.

Rundquist, E. M., E. Stegall, D. Grow, and P. Gray. 1978. New herpetological records from Kansas. Trans. Kansas Acad. Sci. 81: 73–77.

Rüppell, E. 1845. Verzeichniss der in dem Museum der Senckenbergischen Gesselshaft aufgestellten Sammlung. Verhandelingen Museum Senckenberg 3: 293–316.

Russell, A. P., and Aaron M. Bauer. 1993. The amphibians and reptiles of Alberta. University of Calgary Press and University of Alberta Press. 264 pp.

Russell, F. E. 1960. Rattlesnake bites in Southern California. American Journal of Medical Science 239: 1.

——. 1967a. Bites by the Sonoran coral snake, *Micruroides euryxanthus*. Toxicon 5: 39–42.

——. 1967b. Pharmacology of animal venoms. Clinical Pharmacology and Therapeutics 8: 849–873.

——. 1969. Clinical aspects of snake venom poisoning in North America. Toxicon 7: 33–37.

——. 1980a. Snake venom poisoning in the United States. Annual Review of Medicine 31: 247–259.

——. 1980b. Snake venom poisoning. Lippincott, Philadelphia.

——. 1982. Pressure and immobilization for snakebite remains speculative. Ann. Emerg. Med. 11: 701.

——. 1983. Snake venom poisoning, 2d ed. Scholium International, Great Neck, N.Y. 562 pp.

——. 1988. AIDS, cancer, and snakebite—what do these three have in common? Western Journal of Medicine 148: 84–85.

Russell, F. E., and C. M. Bogert. 1981. Gila monster: its biology, venom, and bite—a review. Toxicon 19(3): 341–359.

Russell, F. E., R. W. Carlson, W. Wainschel, and J. Osborne. 1975. Snake venom poisoning in the United States: experiences with 550 cases. JAMA 233: 341–344.

Russell, F. E., and J. A. Emery. 1961. Effects of corticosteroids on the lethality of *Ancistrodon contortrix* venom. American Journal of the Medical Sciences 241: 507–511.

Russell, F. E., and L. Lauritzen. 1966. Antivenins. Trans. Roy. Soc. Trop. Med. Hyg. 60: 797–810.

Russell, F. E., and A. L. Picchioni. 1983. Snake venom poisoning. Clinical Toxicology Consultant 5: 73–87.

Russell, F. E., and H. W. Puffer. 1970. Pharmacology of snake venoms. Clinical Toxicology 3: 433–444.

Russell, F. E., F. G. Walter, T. A. Bey, and M. C. Fernandez. 1997. Snakes and snakebite in Central America. Toxicon 35: 1469–1522.

Ruthven, A. G. 1907. A collection of reptiles and amphibians from southern New Mexico and Arizona. Bull. Am. Mus. Nat. Hist. 23: 483–603.

——. 1911. A biological survey of the sand dune region of the south shore of Saginaw Bay: amphibians and reptiles. Michigan Geological and Biological Survey Publication No. 4, Biological Series 2: 257–272.

——. 1912. The amphibians and reptiles collected by the University of Michigan–Walker Expedition in southern Vera Cruz, Mexico. Zoologische Jahrbücher. Abteilung für Systematik, Ökologie, und Geographie der Tiere 32: 295–332.

——. 1922. The amphibians and reptiles of the Sierra Nevada de Santa Marta, Colombia. Miscellaneous Publications of the Museum of Zoology, University of Michigan 8: 1–69.

——. 1923. The reptiles of the Dutch Leeward Islands. Occas. Pap. Mus. Zool. Univ. Michigan 143: 1–10.

Ruthven, A. G., C. Thompson, and H. T. Gaige. 1928. The herpetology of Michigan. University Museums, University of Michigan, Michigan Handbook Series No. 3. 229 pp.

Ryan, K. C., and E. M. Caravati. 1994. Life-threatening anaphylaxis following envenomation by two different species of Crotalidae. Journal of Wilderness Medicine 5: 263–268.

Saavedra R., D., A. Restrepo M., and N. Caro M. 1975. Ofidiotoxicosis botrópica en Colombia. Parte 1: aspectos clínicos y hematológicos. Antioquia Médica 25(1): 13–26.

Sabath, M., and R. Worthington. 1959. Eggs and young of certain Texas reptiles. Herpetologica 15(1): 31–32.

Saborio, P., M. Gonzalez, and M. Cambronero. 1998. Accidente ofídico en niños en Costa Rica: epidemiología y detección de factores de riesgo en el desarrollo de absceso y necrosis. Toxicon 36(2): 359–66.

Saenz, D., S. J. Burgdorf, D. C. Rudolph, and C. M. Duran. 1996. Natural history notes: *Crotalus horridus* (timber rattlesnake). Climbing. Herpetol. Rev. 27(3): 145.

Saenz, D., D. C. Rudolph, and J. H. Williamson. 1999. Geographic distribution: *Crotalus horridus* (timber rattlesnake). Herpetol. Rev. 30(3): 174.

Sage, R. D., and E. E. Capredoni. 1971. La distribución de la cascabel (*Crotalus durissus terrificus* Laurentius) en Argentina y su significado zoogeográfico (Reptilia, Serpentes). Neotropica 17(54): 133–136.

Sahagun, Fray B. de. 1829. Historia general de las cosas de Nueva Espana. 3 vols. Impr. del Ciudadano Alejandro Valdes, Mexico, 1829–1830. Bound with Sahagun, Historia de la conquista de Mexico. Imprenta de Gavan a cargo de Mariano Arevalo, Mexico.

Saint Girons, H. 1989. Systématique des serpents venimeux. Pp. 25–37 in Société herpétologique de France (ed.), Serpents, venins, envenimations. Fondation Marcel-Mérieux, Lyon.

Saint-Hilaire, A. de. 1833. Voyage dans le district des diamans et sur le littoral du Brésil, vol. 2. Paris, Librairie-Gide, Paris.

——. 1847. Voyage aux sources du Rio de S. Francisco et dans le province de Goyaz, vol. 1. Arthur Bertrand, Paris.

——. 1975. Viagem às nascentes do Rio São Francisco. Itatiaia Editora, Belo Horizonte, Brazil. 190 pp.

Sajdak, R. A. 2000. Natural history notes: Micrurus circinalis (Trinidad northern coral snake). Arboreality. Herpetol. Rev. 31(2): 105.

——. 2001. Patriarchs of the bluffs. Fauna, May–June: 8–21.

Sajdak, R. A., and A. W. Bartz. (In press.) Natural history notes: Crotalus horridus (timber rattlesnake). Arboreality, diet. Herpetol. Rev.

Sakai, A., M. Honma, and Y. Sawai. 1984. Study on the toxicity of venoms expressed from Duvernoy's gland of certain Asian colubrid snakes. Snake 16: 16–20.

Saldarriaga-Córdoba, M. M. 1998. Ecología y biología de los ofidios venenosos de Antioquia y Chocó. Pp. 47–56 in R. Otero Patiño, R. Angel Mejía, and M. E. García (eds.), Primer Simposio Colombiano de Toxinología, marzo 12, 13, y 14 de 1998. Memorias Colciencias, Medillín.

Salomão, E. L., and M. Di-Bernardo. 1995. Philodryas olfersi: uma cobra comum que mata. Caso registrado na área da 8° Delegacia Regional de Saúde. Arquivos da Sociedade Brasileira de Zootecnia 14–16: 21.

Salomão, M. G., S. M. A. Santos, and G. Puorto. 1995. Activity pattern of Crotalus durissus (Viperidae, Crotalidae): feeding, reproduction, and snakebite. Studies on Neotropical Fauna and Environment 30(2): 101–106.

Salomão, M. G., W. Wüster, R. S. Thorpe, J.-M. Touzet, and BBBSP. 1997. DNA evolution of South American pitvipers of the genus Bothrops (Reptilia: Serpentes: Viperidae). Pp. 89–98 in R. S. Thorpe, W. Wüster, and A. Malhotra (eds.), Venomous snakes: ecology, evolution, and snakebite. Clarendon Press, Oxford.

——. 1999. MtDNA phylogeny of neotropcial pitvipers of the genus Bothrops (Squamata: Serpentes: Viperidae). Kaupia 8: 127–134.

Salvin, O. 1860. On the reptiles of Guatemala. Proc. Zool. Soc. London 1860: 451–461.

——. 1861. On a collection of reptiles from Guatemala. Proc. Zool. Soc. London 1861: 227–229.

Samuelson, P. 2001. Louie Porras: reflections of a herpetologist. Part 2. Reptiles 9(1): 24–29.

Sanchez, E. F., T. V. Freitas, D. L. Ferreira-Alves, D. T. Velarde, M. R. Diniz, M. N. Codeiro, G. Agostini-Cotta, and C. R. Diniz. 1992. Biological activities of venoms from South American snakes. Toxicon 30(1): 95–104.

Sanchez, E. F., A. Magalhães, and C. R. Diniz. 1987. Purification of a hemorrhagic factor LHF-1 from the venom of the bushmaster snake Lachesis muta muta. Toxicon 25: 611.

Sánchez, F. C., A. González Ruiz, E. Godínez Cano, and J. A. Delgadillo Espinoza. 1999. Natural history notes: Crotalus lepidus morulus. Reproduction. Herpetol. Rev. 30(3): 168.

Sánchez-Herrera, O. 1980. Herpetofauna of the Pedregal de San Angel. Bull. Maryland Herpetol. Soc. 16(1): 9–18.

Sánchez-Herrera, O., and M. Alvarez del Toro. 1980. A range extension for Thecadactylus rapicauda (Gekkonidae) in Mexico, and note on two snakes from Chiapas. Bull. Maryland Herpetol. Soc. 13(2): 49–51.

Sánchez-Herrera, O., and W. López-Forment C. 1987. Anfibios y reptiles de la región de Acapulco, Guerrero, México. Anales del Instituto de Biología, Universidad Nacional Autónoma de México, Serie Zoología, 58(2): 735–750.

Sánchez-Herrera, O., and G. López-Ortega. 1987. Noteworthy records of amphibians and reptiles from Tlaxcala, Mexico. Herpetol. Rev. 18(2): 41.

Sánchez-Herrera, O., H. M. Smith, and D. Chiszar. 1981. Another suggested case of ophidian deceptive mimicry. Trans. Kansas Acad. Sci. 84(3): 121–127.

Sanders, J. S., and J. S. Jacob. 1981. Thermal ecology of the copperhead (Agkistrodon contortrix). Herpetologica 37(4): 264–270.

Sandner-Montilla, F. 1952. Serpientes Bothrops de Venezuela. Monografias Científicos del Instituto de Terapeutica Experimental de los Laboratorios "Veros" Limitada, Bogotá, No. 9. 4 pp.

——. 1961. Ofidios ponzoñosas de Venezuela. Bothrops venezuelae Sp. nov. Novedades Científicos del Museo de Historia Natural La Salle (Zoología) (Caracas) 30: 1–36.

——. 1965. Manual de las serpientes ponzoñosas de Venezuela. Talleres Tipografía Miguel Angel García y Hijo, Caracas. 112 pp.

——. 1966. El caso de anomalía en Bothrops venezuelae. Instituto de Investigación de Ofidiología Venezolana (Caracas) 1: 1–17.

——. 1976. Una nueva especie del genero Bothrops (Serpientes: Crotalidae, Lachesinae) de la Gran Sabana, Edo. Bolívar, Venezuela. Memorias Científicas de Ofidiología, Contribuciones Periódicas del Instituto Venezolano de Oficiología 1: 1–4.

——. 1978. Bothrops castelnaudi Duméril, Bribron [sic] et Duméril, 1854. Su existencia en Venezuela y el paso a sinonimía de Bothrops lichenosus Roze, 1958. Memorias Científicas de Ofidiología, Contribuciones Periódicas del Instituto Venezolano de Ofidiología 2: 1–8.

——, F. 1979a. La necesaria revalidación de Bothrops lanceolatus (Lacépède, 1789) y el paso a sinonimía de B. colombiensis (Hallowell, 1845). Memorias Científicas de Ofidiología, Contribuciones Periódicas del Instituto Venezolano de Ofidiología 3: 1–7.

——. 1979b. Una nueva especie del género Bothrops (Serpentes, Crotalidae, Bothropinae) de la region de Guanare, Estado Portuguesa, Venezuela. Memorias Científicas de Ofidiología, Contribuciones Periódicas del Instituto Venezolano de Ofidiología 4: 1–19.

——. 1980. Una nueva especie del género Crotalus (Serpentes, Crotalidae, Crotalinae) del sur del estado Guarico, Venezuela. Memorias Científicas de Ofidiología, Contribuciones Periódicas del Instituto Venezolano de Ofidiología 5: 1–12.

——. 1981. Una nueva subespecie de Bothrops lanceolatus (Lacépède, 1789) Fam. Crotalidae. Memorias Científicas de Ofidiología, Contribuciones Periódicas del Instituto Venezolano de Ofidiología 6: 1–15.

——. 1983 [dated 1982]. Serpientes Crotalinae de Venezuela. Mem. Inst. Butantan 46: 193–194.

——. 1985a. Edición dedicada al más insigne herpetólogo de todos los tiempos: el profesor doctor Afranio do Amaral. Memorias Científicas de Ofidiología, Contribuciones Periódicas del Instituto Venezolano de Ofidiología 7: 1–77.

——. 1985b. La creación de la familia Micruridae Fam. Nov. para las corales de America de la superfamilia Elapoidea y la proposición para la creación de la familia Oxyuranidae de la misma superfamilia, para proteroglifas australianas. Memorias Científicas de Ofidiología, Contribuciones Periódicas del Instituto Venezolano de Ofidiología 8: 1–22.

——. 1989. Una nueva subespecie de Bothrops lansbergi (Schlegel, 1841) de la familia Crotalidae: Bothrops lansbergi hutmanni n. Ssp. Memorias Científicas de Ofidiología, Contribuciones Periódicas del Instituto Venezolano de Ofidiología 9: 1–16.

——. 1990. Una nueva subespecie de Bothrops lanceolatus (Lacépède, 1789), género Bothrops Wagler, familia Crotalidae Gray, del Estado Carabobo y regiones adyacentes: Bothrops lanceolatus nacaritae, ssp. nov. Memorias Científicas de Ofidiología, Contribuciones Periódicas del Instituto Venezolano de Ofidiología 10: 33–37.

——. 1994. Mini-información sobre serpientes venezolanas. Instituto Venezolano de Ofidiología, Caracas. 40 pp.

Sandner-Montilla, F., and M. Römer. 1961. Ofidios ponzoñosos de Venezuela, Bothrops pifanoi Sp. nov. Novedades Científicos del Museo de Historia Natural La Salle (Zoología) (Caracas) 29: 1–15.

Sano-Martins, I. S., H. W. Fan, S. C. B. Castro, S. C. Tomy, F. O. França, M. T. Jorge, A. S. Kamiguti, D. A. Warrell, and R. G. G. Theakston. 1994. Reliability of the simple 20-minute whole blood clotting test (WBCT20) as an indicator of low plasma fibrinogen concentration in patients envenomed by Bothrops snakes. Toxicon 32: 1045–1050.

Sano-Martins, I. S., S. C. Tomy, D. Campolina, M. B. Dias, S. C. de Castro, M. C. de Sousa-e-Silva, C. F. Amaral, N. A. Rezende, A. S. Kamiguti, D. A. Warrell, et al. 2001. Coagulopathy following lethal and non-lethal envenoming of humans by the South American rattlesnake (*Crotalus durissus*) in Brazil. Quarterly Journal of Medicine 94: 551–559.

Sant'anna, S., K. F. Grego, and W. Fernandes. 2001. Natural history notes: *Bothrops leucurus* (white-tailed lancehead), reproduction. Herpetol. Rev. 32(1): 45–46.

Santesson, C. G. 1897. Über das Gift von *Heloderma suspectum* Cope, einer giftigen Eidesche. Nordiskt Medicinskt Arkiv 30: 1–48.

Santiago, Q. S. 1979. Diagnostic and therapeutic measure for copperhead snake bite. West Virginia Medical Journal 75: 62–64.

Santoro, M. L., M. C. C. Sousa-e-Silva, L. R. C. Gonçalves, S. M. Almeida-Santos, D. F. Cardoso, I. L. Laporta-Ferreira, M. Saiki, C. A. Peres, and I. S. Sano-Martins. 1999. Comparison of the biological activities in venoms from three subspecies of the South American rattlesnake (*Crotalus durissus terrificus, C. durissus cascavella* and *C. durissus collilineatus*). Comp. Biochem. Physiol. C 122(1): 61–73.

Santos, E. 1943. As cobras venenosas: como conhece-las e evita-las. Biblioteca Agricola Popular Brazileira. 107 pp.

———. 1981. Anfíbios e répteis do Brasil (vida e costumbres), 3d ed. Itatiaia Editora, Belo Horizonte, Brazil. 263 pp.

Santos, M. C. dos, L. C. L. Ferreira, W. D. da Silva, and M. de F. D. Furtado. 1993. Characterization of the biological activities of the "yellow" and "white" venoms of *Crotalus durissus ruruima* compared with the venom of *Crotalus durissus terrificus*: neutralizing power of antivenoms against the venoms of *Crotalus durissus ruruima*. Toxicon 31(11): 1459–1469.

Santos, M. C. dos, M. Martins, A. L. Boechat, et al. 1995. Serpentes de interesse médico da Amazônia biologia venenos e tratamento de acidentes. Universidade do Amazonas, Manaus, Brazil.

Santos, S. M. A., and V. J. Germano. 1996. Natural history notes: *Crotalus durissus* (Neotropical rattlesnake). Prey. Herpetol. Rev. 27(3): 143.

Santos-Costa, M. C. dos, and M. Di-Bernardo. 2001 [dated 2000]. Human envenomation by an aglyphous colubrid snake *Liophis miliaris* (Linnaeus, 1758). Cuadernos de Herpetologica 14(2): 153–154.

Santos-Costa, M. C., Outeral, A. B., D'Agostini, F. M., and L. H. Cappellari. 2000. Envenomation by the Neotropical colubrid *Boiruna maculata* (Boulenger, 1896): a case report. Revista do Instituto de Medicina Tropical de São Paulo 42(5): 283–286.

Saravia, P., E. Rojas, V. Arce, C. Guevara, J. C. Lopez, E. Chaves, R. Velasquez, G. Rojas, and J. M. Gutiérrez. 2002. Geographic and ontogenic variability in the venom of the Neotropical rattlesnake *Crotalus durissus*: pathophysiological and therapeutic implications. Rev. Biol. Trop. 50: 337–346.

Sasa, M. 1996. Morphological variation in the lancehead snake *Bothrops asper* (Garman) from Middle America. Master's thesis, University of Texas at Arlington.

———. 1997. *Cerrophidion godmani* in Costa Rica: a case of extremely low allozyme variation? J. Herpetol. 31(4): 569–572.

———. 2002. Morphological variation in the lancehead pitviper *Bothrops asper* (Garman) (Serpentes: Viperidae) from Middle America. Rev. Biol. Trop. 50(1): 259–271.

Sasa, M., and R. Barrantes. 1998. Allozyme variation in populations of *Bothrops asper* (Serpentes: Viperidae) in Costa Rica. Herpetologica 54(4): 462–469.

Sasa, M., and E. N. Smith. 2001. Phylogenetic analysis of monadal coral snake genus *Micrurus* from Middle America. Pp. 131–132 in Abstracts for 2001 Joint Annual Meetings of the Herpetologists' League and the Society for the Study of Amphibians and Reptiles, Indianapolis, 27–31 July.

Sasa, M., and A. Solórzano. 1995. The reptiles and amphibians of Santa Rosa National Park, with comments about the herpetofauna of xerophytic areas. Herpetological Natural History 3: 113–126.

Sasa, M., and S. Vázquez. 2003. Snakebite envenomation in Costa Rica: a revision of incidence in the decade 1990–2000. Toxicon 41(1): 19–22.

Sasaki, A., I. Kawaguchi, and A. Yoshimori. 2001. Spatial mosaic and interfacial dynamics in a Müllerian mimicry system. Theoretical Population Biology 61: 49–71.

Sauer, C. O. 1950. Geography of South America. Pp. 319–344 in J. H. Steward (ed.), Handbook of South American Indians, vol. 6. Physical anthropology, linguistics, and cultural geography of South American Indians. Smithsonian Institution Bureau of American Ethnology, Bulletin 143. GPO, Washington, D.C. 715 pp.

Savage, J. M. 1959. An illustrated key to the turtles, lizards, and snakes of the western United States and Canada, vol. 2. Naturegraph Pocket Keys. Naturegraph Co., Healdsburg, Calif. 36 pp.

———. 1960. Evolution of a peninsular herpetofauna. Syst. Zool. 9(3–4): 184–211.

———. 1966. The origins and history of the Central American herpetofauna. Copeia 1966: 719–766.

———. 1967. Evolution of the insular herpetofauna. Pp. 219–227 in R. N. Philbrick (ed.), Proceedings of the Symposium on the Biology of the California Islands, Santa Barbara Botanical Gardens, Santa Barbara, Calif.

———. 1973. A preliminary handlist of the herpetofauna of Costa Rica. University of Southern California, Los Angeles. 17 pp.

———. 1974a. Type localities for species of amphibians and reptiles described from Costa Rica. Rev. Biol. Trop. 22(1): 71–122.

———. 1974b. The Isthmian link and the evolution of Neotropical mammals. Los Angeles County Museum Contributions in Science 260: 1–51.

———. 1980. A handlist with preliminary keys to the herpetofauna of Costa Rica. Allan Hancock Foundation, University of Southern California, Los Angeles. 111 pp.

———. 1982. The enigma of the Central American herpetofauna: dispersals or vicariance? Annals of the Missouri Botanical Garden 69: 464–547.

———. 1990. Review of The venomous reptiles of Latin America. Recent Publications in Natural History 8: 5–6.

———. 2002. The amphibians and reptiles of Costa Rica. University of Chicago Press, Chicago. 934 pp.

Savage, J. M., and F. S. Cliff. 1953. A new subspecies of sidewinder, *Crotalus cerastes,* from Arizona. Chicago Academy of Sciences, Natural History Miscellanea 119: 1–7.

Savage, J. M., and B. I. Crother. 1989. The status of *Pliocercus* and *Urotheca* (Serpentes: Colubridae), with a review of included species of coral snake mimics. Zoological Journal of the Linnean Society 95: 335–362.

Savage, J. M., and J. B. Slowinski. 1990. Short note: a simple consistent terminology for the basic color patterns of the venomous coral snakes and their mimics. Herpetological Journal 1: 530–532.

———. 1992. The colouration of the venomous coral snakes (family Elapidae) and their mimics (families Aniliidae and Colubridae). Biological Journal of the Linnaean Society 45: 235–254.

———. 1996. Evolution of colouration, urotomy, and coral snake mimicry in the snake genus *Scaphiodontophis* (Serpentes: Colubridae). Biological Journal of the Linnean Society 57: 129–194.

Savage, J. M., and J. L. Vial. 1974. The venomous coral snakes (genus *Micrurus*) of Costa Rica. Rev. Biol. Trop. 21(2): 295–349.

Savage, J. M., and J. Villa. 1986. Introduction to the herpetofauna of Costa Rica. Contributions to Herpetology 3. Society for the Study of Amphibians and Reptiles. 207 pp.

Savage, T. 1967. The diet of rattlesnakes and copperheads in the Great Smoky Mountains National Park. Copeia 1967(1): 226–227.

Savary, W. 1999. Natural history notes: *Crotalus molossus* (northern blacktail rattlesnake). Brood defense. Herpetol. Rev. 30(1): 45.

Savitzky, A. H. 1978. The origin of the New World proteroglyphous snakes and its bearing on the study of venom delivery systems in snakes. Ph.D. dissertation, University of Kansas, Lawrence.

———. 1992. Embryonic development of the maxillary and prefrontal bones of crotaline snakes. Pp. 119–142 in J. A. Campbell and E. D. Brodie Jr. (eds.), Biology of the pitvipers. Selva, Tyler, Texas.

Savitzky, B. A. C. 1992. Laboratory studies on piscivory in an opportunistic pitviper, the cottonmouth, *Agkistrodon piscivorus.* Pp.

347–368 in J. A. Campbell and E. D. Brodie Jr. (eds.), Biology of the pitvipers. Selva, Tyler, Texas.

Say, T. 1819. Notes on herpetology. American Journal of Science [Silliman's Journal] 1(3): 256–265.

Sazima, I. 1989a [dated 1988]. Um estudo de biologia comportamental de jararaca, *Bothrops jararaca*, com uso de marcas naturais. Mem. Inst. Butantan 50: 83–99.

———. 1989b. Comportamento alimentar de jararaca, *Bothrops jararaca*: encontros provocados na natureza. Ciência e Cultura 41: 500–505.

———. 1991. Caudal luring in two Neotropical pitvipers, *Bothrops jararaca* and *B. jararacussu*. Copeia 1991(1): 245–248.

———. 1992. Natural history of the jararaca pitviper, *Bothrops jararaca*, in southeastern Brazil. Pp. 199–216 in J. A. Campbell and E. D. Brodie Jr. (eds.), Biology of the pitvipers. Selva, Tyler, Texas.

Sazima, I., and A. S. Abe. 1991. Habits of five Brazilian snakes with coral-snake pattern, including a summary of defensive tactics. Studies on Neotropical Fauna and Environment 26(3): 159–164.

Sazima, I., and P. R. Manzani. 1998. Natural history notes: *Bothrops fonsecai* (Fonseca's lancehead). Herpetol. Rev. 29(2): 102–103.

Schad, G. A. 1962. Studies on the genus *Kalicephalus*. Canadian Journal of Zoology 40: 1035–1165.

Schaefer, G. C. 1969. Sex independent ground color in the timber rattlesnake, *Crotalus horridus horridus*. Herpetologica 25(1): 65–66.

Schaefer, N. 1976. The mechanism of venom transfer from the venom duct to the fang in snakes. Herpetologica 32(1): 71–76.

Schaeffer, P. J., K. E. Conley, and S. L. Lindstedt. 1996. Structural correlates of speed and endurance in skeletal muscle: the rattlesnake tailshaker muscle. Journal of Experimental Biology 199(2): 351–358.

Schaeffer, R. C., R. W. Carlson, V. K. Puri, G. Callahan, F. E. Russell, and M. H. Weil. 1978. The effects of colloidal and crystalloidal fluids on rattlesnake venom shock in the rat. Journal of Pharmacology and Experimental Therapeutics 206: 687–695.

Schargel, W. E., and J. E. García-Pérez. [1999]. Lista de anfibios y reptiles del Edo. Portuguesa. Museo de Zoología, Universidad Nacional Experimental de Los Llanos Occidentales Ezequiel Zamora, Guanare, Venezuela. Unpublished ms.

Scharman, E. J., and V. D. Noffsinger. 2001. Copperhead snakebites: clinical severity of local effects. Ann. Emerg. Med. 38: 55–61.

Schätti, B. 1986 [dated 1985]. Catalogue des types et des exemplaires figures du Musée d'Histoire Naturelle de Neuchatel. II. Ophidiens. Biblio. Mus. Ville de Neuchatel 1985: 98–108.

Schätti, B., and E. Kramer. 1991. A new pitviper from Ecuador, *Bothrops mahnerti* n. sp. Revue Suisse de Zoologie 98: 9–14.

———. 1993. Ecuadorianische Grubenottern der Gattungen *Bothriechis*, *Bothrops*, und *Porthidium* (Serpentes: Viperidae). Revue Suisse de Zoologie 100: 235–278.

Schätti, B., E. Kramer, and J. M. Touzet. 1990. Systematic remarks on a rare crotalid snake from Ecuador, *Bothriechis albocarinatus* (Shreve), with some comments on the generic arrangements of arboreal Neotropical pitvipers. Revue Suisse de Zoologie 97: 877–885.

Schätti, B., and H. M. Smith. 1997. *Trigonocephalus pulcher* Peters, 1863 (currently *Bothrops pulcher*) and *Bothrops albocarinatus* Shreve, 1934 (currently *Bothriechis oligolepis albocarinatus*) (Reptilia, Serpentes): proposed conservation of the specific and subspecific names by the designation of a neotype for *T. pulcher*. Bulletin of Zoological Nomenclature 54: 35–38.

Schenberg, S. 1959. Geographical pattern of crotamine distribution in the same rattlesnake subspecies. Science 129(3359): 1361–1363.

———. 1960 [dated 1959]. Analize da crotamina no veneno individual de cascaveis recebidas pelo Instituto Butantan. Mem. Inst. Butantan 29: 213–226.

Schenone, H., and H. Reyes. 1965. Animales ponzoñosos de Chile. Boletin Chileno de Parasitologia 20: 104–108.

Schiestl, F. P., M. Ayasse, H. F. Paulus, C. Löfstedt, B. S. Hansson, F. Ibarra, and W. Francke. 2000. Sex pheromone mimicry in the early spider orchid (*Ophrys sphegodes*): patterns of hydrocarbons as the key mechanisms for pollination by sexual deception. Journal of Comparative Physiology A 186: 567–574.

Schinz, H. R. 1822. Das Thierreich eingetheilt nach dem Bau der Thiere als Grundlage ihrer Naturgeschichte und der vergleichenden Anatomie von dem Herrn Ritter von Cuvier, vol. 2. J. G. Cotta, Stuttgart and Tübingen. 189 pp.

Schlegel, H. 1826. Notice sur l'erpétologie de l'ile de Java; par M. Boié (ouvrage manuscrit). Bulletin des Sciences Naturelles et de Géologie 9(2): 233–240.

———. 1837. Essai sur la physionomie des serpens, 2 vols. Arnz, Leiden. 857 pp.

———. 1841. Description d'une nouvelle espèce du genre *Trigonocéphale* (*Trigonocephalus Lansbergii*). Magasin de Zoologie 1841: 1–3.

Schmaier, A. H., W. Claypool, and R. W. Colman. 1980. Crotalocytin: recognition and purification of a timber rattlesnake platelet aggregating protein. Blood 56: 1013–1019.

Schmaier, A. H., and R. W. Colman. 1980. Crotalocytin: characterization of the timber rattlesnake platelet activating protein. Blood 56: 1020–1028.

Schmidt, H. 1945. Argentinische Kreichtiere, Lurche, Fische, und Insekten. Verlag Hans Schmidt, San Andres, Argentina. 270 pp.

Schmidt, K. P. 1922. The amphibians and reptiles of Lower California and the neighboring islands. Bull. Am. Mus. Nat. Hist. 46(11): 607–707.

———. 1928a. Notes on American coral snakes. Bull. Antivenin Inst. Am. 2(3): 63–64.

———. 1928b. Reptiles collected in Salvador for the California Institute of Technology. Field Mus. Nat. Hist. Publ., Zool. Ser., 12(16): 193–201.

———. 1932a. Stomach contents of some American coral snakes with the descriptions of a new species of *Geophis*. Copeia 1932(1): 6–9.

———. 1932b. A new subspecies of coral snake from Guatemala. Proc. California Acad. Sci., 4th ser., 20(7): 265–267.

———. 1933a. Preliminary account of the coral snakes of Central America and Mexico. Field Mus. Nat. Hist. Publ., Zool. Ser., 20: 29–40.

———. 1933b. Amphibians and reptiles collected by the Smithsonian biological survey of the Panama Canal Zone. Smithsonian Miscellaneous Collections 89: 1–20.

———. 1936a. A preliminary account of coral snakes of South America. Field Mus. Nat. Hist. Publ., Zool. Ser., 20(19): 189–203.

———. 1936b. Notes on Central American and Mexican coral snakes. Field Mus. Nat. Hist. Publ., Zool. Ser., 20(20): 205–216.

———. 1936c. New amphibians and reptiles from Honduras in the Museum of Comparative Zoology. Proceedings of the Biological Society of Washington 49: 43–50.

———. 1937. The history of *Elaps collaris* Schlegel, 1837–1937. Field Mus. Nat. Hist. Publ., Zool. Ser., 20(26): 361–364.

———. 1939. A new coral snake from British Guiana. Field Mus. Nat. Hist. Publ., Zool. Ser., 24(6): 45–47.

———. 1941. The amphibians and reptiles of British Honduras. Field Mus. Nat. Hist. Publ., Zool. Ser., 22(8): 475–510.

———. 1952. The Surinam coral snake *Micrurus surinamensis*. Fieldiana: Zoology 34(4): 25–34.

———. 1953a. Hemprich's coral snake, *Micrurus hemprichi*. Fieldiana: Zoology 34(13): 165–170.

———. 1953b. The Amazonian coral snake, *Micrurus spixi*. Fieldiana: Zoology 34(14): 171–180.

———. 1953c. A check list of North American amphibians and reptiles, 6th ed. American Society of Ichthyologists and Herpetologists, Chicago. 280 pp.

———. 1954. The annellated coral snake, *Micrurus annellatus* Peters. Fieldiana: Zoology 34(30): 319–325.

———. 1955. Coral snakes of the genus *Micrurus* in Colombia. Fieldiana: Zoology 34(34): 337–359.

———. 1957a. The venomous coral snakes of Trinidad. Fieldiana: Zoology 39(8): 55–63.

———. 1957b. Anent the "dangerous" bushmaster. Copeia 1957(3): 233.

——. 1958. Some rare or little-known Mexican coral snakes. Fieldiana: Zoology 39(19): 201–212.

Schmidt, K. P., and E. W. Andrews. 1936. Notes on snakes from Yucatan. Field Mus. Nat. Hist. Publ., Zool. Ser., 20(18): 167–187.

Schmidt, K. P., and D. D. Davis. 1941. Field book of snakes of the U.S. and Canada. Putnam, New York. 354 pp.

Schmidt, K. P., and R. F. Inger. 1951. Amphibians and reptiles of the Hopkins–Branner expedition to Brazil. Fieldiana: Zoology 31(42): 439–465.

——. 1957. Living reptiles of the world. Hanover House, Garden City, N.Y. 287 pp.

Schmidt, K. P., and D. W. Owens. 1944. Amphibians and reptiles of northern Coahuila, Mexico. Field Mus. Nat. Hist. Publ., Zool. Ser., 29(6): 97–115.

Schmidt, K. P., and F. J. W. Schmidt. 1925. New coral snakes from Peru. Report on results of the Captain Marshall Field expeditions. Field Mus. Nat. Hist. Publ., Zool. Ser., 12(10): 129–134.

Schmidt, K. P., and F. A. Shannon. 1947. Notes on the amphibians and reptiles of Michoacan, Mexico. Fieldiana: Zoology 31(9): 63–85.

Schmidt, K. P., and H. M. Smith. 1943. Notes on coral snakes from Mexico. Field Mus. Nat. Hist. Publ., Zool. Ser., 29(2): 25–31.

Schmidt, K. P., and T. F. Smith. 1944. Amphibians and reptiles of the Big Bend region of Texas. Field Mus. Nat. Hist. Publ., Zool. Ser., 29(5): 75–96.

Schmidt, K. P., and W. F. Walker. 1943a. Peruvian snakes from the University of Arequipa. Field Mus. Nat. Hist. Publ., Zool. Ser., 24(26): 279–296.

——. 1943b. Snakes of the Peruvian coastal region. Field Mus. Nat. Hist. Publ., Zool. Ser., 24(27): 297–324.

Schneider, A. F. 1866. Monographie der Nematoden. Reimer, Berlin. 357 pp.

Schneider, J. G. 1799–1801. Historiae amphibiorum naturalis et literariae, 2 vols. Friederici Frommann, Jena. 640 pp.

Schoefer, N. 1976. The mechanism of venom transfer from the venom duct to the fang in snakes. Herpetologica 32(1): 71–76.

Schöttler, W. H. A. 1951. Toxicity of the principal snake venoms of Brazil. American Journal of Tropical Medicine and Hygiene 31: 489–500.

Schouten, G. B. 1931. Contribuciones al conocimiento de la fauna herpetológica del Paraguay y de los paises limítrofes. Revista de la Sociedad Científica del Paraguay 3(1): 5–32.

——. 1937. Fauna herpetológica del Paraguay. Novena Reunión de la Sociedad Argentina de Patologia Regional 2: 1218–1232.

Schreiber, G., A. R. Hoge, H. E. Belluomini, and A. M. Penha. 1958. Further researches on intersexuality in a highly isolated population of snakes. Proceedings of the X International Congress of Genetics (Montreal 1958), vol. 2: 254–255.

Schroeder, W. W. 1979. Geographic distribution: Crotalus adamanteus (eastern diamondback rattlesnake). Herpetol. Rev. 10(2): 60.

Schuett, G. W. 1982. A copperhead (Agkistrodon contortrix) brood produced from autumn copulations. Copeia 1982(3): 700–702.

——. 1984. Calloselasma rhodostoma (Malayan pit viper): feeding mimicry. Herpetol. Rev. 15: 112.

——. 1992. Is long-term sperm storage an important component of the reproductive biology of temperate pitvipers? Pp. 169–184 in J. A. Campbell and E. D. Brodie Jr. (eds.), Biology of the pitvipers. Selva, Tyler, Texas.

——. 1997. Body size and agonistic experience affect dominance and mating success in male copperheads. Animal Behavior 54: 213–224.

Schuett, G. W., D. L. Clark, and F. Kraus. 1984. Feeding mimicry in the rattlesnake Sistrurus catenatus, with comments on the evolution of the rattle. Animal Behaviour 32: 625–626.

Schuett, G. W., E. W. A. Gergus, and F. Kraus. 2001. Phylogenetic correlation between male–male fighting and mode of prey subjugation in snakes. Acta Ethologica 4: 31–49.

Schuett, G. W., and J. C. Gillingham. 1986. Sperm storage and multiple paternity in the copperhead, Agkistrodon contortrix. Copeia 1986(3): 807–811.

——. 1988. Courtship and mating of the copperhead, Agkistrodon contortrix. Copeia 1988(2): 374–381.

Schuett, G. W., and F. Kraus. 1980a. Geographic distribution: Crotalus viridis viridis (prairie rattlesnake). Herpetol. Rev. 11(3): 81

——. 1980b. Geographical distribution: Sistrurus catenatus edwardsi (desert massasauga). Herpetol. Rev. 11(3): 81.

——. 1982a. Natural history notes: Agkistrodon contortrix pictigaster (Trans-Pecos copperhead). Neonates. Herpetol. Rev. 13(1): 17.

——. 1982b. Natural history notes: Crotalus viridis concolor (midget faded rattlesnake). Coloration. Herpetol. Rev. 13(1): 17–18.

Schuett, G. W., E. M. Nowak, and R. A. Repp. 2002. Natural history notes: Crotalus cerberus (Arizona black rattlesnake). Diet and prey size. Herpetol. Rev. 33(3): 210–211.

Schuler, W. 1982. Zur Funktion von Warnfarben: die Reaktion jünger Stare aus wespenähnlich Schwarzgelbe attrapen. Zeitschrift Tierpsychologie 58: 66–78.

Schuler, W., and E. Hesse. 1985. On the function of warning coloration: a black and yellow pattern inhibits prey-attack by naïve domestic chicks. Behavioral Ecology and Sociobiology 16: 249–255.

Schultz, E., A. W. Clark, A. Suzuki, and R. G. Cassens. 1980. Rattlesnake shaker muscle: 1. A light microscopic and histological study. Tissue and Cell 12(2): 323–334.

Schwab, S. 1988. Faunal checklist of the Aripo Savannas (Scientific Reserve). Living World: Journal of the Trinidad and Tobago Field Naturalists' Club 1987–1988: 6–13.

Schwammer, H. 1983. Herpetologische Beobachtungen aus Colorado/USA. Aasfressen bei Sistrurus catenatus edwardsi/tergeminus und Verhaltensmimikry bei Pituophis melanoleucus. Aquaria 30: 90–93.

Schwaner, T. D., P. R. Baverstock, H. C. Dessauer, and G. A. Mengden. 1985. Immunological evidence for the phylogenetic relationships of Australian elapid snakes. Pp. 177–184, in G. Grigg, R. Shine, and H. Ehmann (eds.), Biology of Australasian frogs and reptiles. Royal Zoological Society of New South Wales, Sydney.

Schwardt, H. H. 1938. Reptiles of Arkansas. University of Arkansas Agricultural Experiment Station Bulletin 357: 1–47.

Schwartwelder, J. 1950. Snake-bite accidents in Louisiana: with data on 306 cases. Journal of Tropical Medicine 30: 575–587.

Schwartz, A. 1952. Three new mammals from southern Florida. Journal of Mammalogy 33: 381–385.

Schwartz, A., and W. A. Babis. 1949. Extension of range of Crotalus lepidus klauberi. Copeia 1949(1): 74.

Schwartz, A., and R. W. Henderson. 1985. A guide to the identification of the amphibians and reptiles of the West Indies exclusive of Hispaniola. Milwaukee Public Museum, Milwaukee. 165 pp.

——. 1988. West Indian amphibians and reptiles: a check-list. Milwaukee Public Museum, Contributions in Biology and Geology 74: 1–264.

——. 1991. Amphibians and reptiles of the West Indies: descriptions, distributions, and natural history. University of Florida Press, Gainesville. 720 pp.

Schwartz, A., and R. Thomas. 1975. A check-list of West Indian amphibians and reptiles. Carnegie Museum of Natural History Special Publication 1: 1–216.

Schwartz, V., and D. M. Golden. 2002. A field guide to reptiles and amphibians of New Jersey. New Jersey Division of Fish and Wildlife, Vineland. 90 pp.

Scott, D. E., R. U. Fischer, J. D. Congdon, and S. A. Busa. 1995. Whole body lipid dynamics and reproduction in the eastern cottonmouth, Agkistrodon piscivorus. Herpetologica 51(4): 472–487.

Scott, N. J. 1969. A zoogeographic analysis of the snakes of Costa Rica. Ph.D. dissertation, University of Southern California. 390 pp.

Scott, N. J. 1983a. Bothrops asper (terciopelo, fer-de-lance). Pp. 383–384 in D. H. Janzen (ed.), Costa Rican natural history. University of Chicago Press, Chicago.

——. 1983b. Crotalus durissus (cascabel, tropical rattlesnake). Pp. 393–394 in D. H. Janzen (ed.), Costa Rican natural history. University of Chicago Press, Chicago.

Scott, N. J., and J. W. Lovett. 1975. A collection of reptiles and amphibians from the Chaco of Paraguay. University of Connecticut Occasional Papers (Biological Sciences Series) 2(16): 257–266.

Scott, N. J., J. M. Savage, and D. C. Robinson. 1983. Checklist of the reptiles. Pp. 367–374 in D. H. Janzen (ed.), Costa Rican natural history, University of Chicago Press, Chicago.

Scrocchi, G. J. 1990. El género Micrurus (Serpentes: Elapidae) en la República Argentina. Bolletin del Museo Regionale di Sciènze Naturale di Torino 8: 343–368.

———. 1991. Análisis preliminar de la osteología cranial del género Micrurus Wagler (Ophidia: Elapidae). Acta Zoológica Lilloana 41: 311–327.

Sealy, J. B. 1996. Natural history notes: Crotalus horridus (timber rattlesnake). Mating. Herpetol. Rev. 27(1): 23–24.

Seaton, F. H. 1949. A large Micrurus. Herpetologica 5(5): 149.

Seba, A. 1734–1765. Locupletissimi rerum naturalium thesauri accurata descriptio, et iconibus artificiosissimis expressio, per universam physices historiam, 4 vols. J. Westenium, G. Smith, and Janssonio-Waesbergios, Amsterdam.

Secor, S. M. 1992. A preliminary analysis of the movement and home range of the sidewinder, Crotalus cerastes. Pp. 389–394 in J. A. Campbell and E. D. Brodie Jr. (eds.), Biology of the pitvipers. Selva, Tyler, Texas.

———. 1994a. Ecological significance of movements and activity range for the sidewinder, Crotalus cerastes. Copeia 1994(3): 631–645.

———. 1994b. Natural history of the sidewinder, Crotalus cerastes. In Herpetology of the North American deserts: proceedings of a symposium. Southwestern Herpetologists' Society, Special Publication No. 5: 281–301.

———. 1995. Ecological aspects of foraging mode for the snakes Crotalus cerastes and Masticophis flagellum. Herpetological Monographs 9: 169–186.

Secor, S. M., B. C. Jayne, and A. F. Bennett. 1992. Locomotor performance and energetic cost of sidewinding by the snake Crotalus cerastes. Journal of Experimental Biology 163: 1–14.

Secor, S. M., and K. A. Nagy. 1994. Bioenergetic correlates of foraging mode for the snakes Crotalus cerastes and Masticophis flagellum. Ecology 75: 1600–1614.

Secretaria da Saúde. 1996. Importância medico-sanitária dos acidentes com cobra verde ou cobra cipó. Curare. Boletim de Divulgação Centro Informação Toxicologica, do Rio Grande do Sul, Pôrto Alegre, 1(2): 7–8.

Seib, R. L. 1978. Geographic distribution: Crotalus mitchelli pyrrhus (southwestern speckled rattlesnake). Herpetol. Rev. 9(1): 22.

———. 1980. Human evenomation from the bite of an aglyphous false coral snake, Pliocercus elapoides (Serpentes: Colubridae). Toxicon 18: 399–401.

———. 1985. Feeding ecology and organization of Neotropical snake faunas. Ph.D. dissertation, University of California at Berkeley. 229 pp.

Seifert, R. P. 1983. Bothrops schlegelii (oropel [gold morph], bocaracá, eyelash viper, palm viper). Pp. 384–385 in D. H. Janzen (ed.), Costa Rican natural history. University of Chicago Press, Chicago.

Seifert, S. A., L. V. Boyer, R. C. Dart, R. S. Porter, and L. Sjostrom. 1997. Relationship of venom effects to venom antigen and antivenom serum concentrations in a patient with Crotalus atrox envenomation treated with Fab antivenom. Ann. Emerg. Med. 30: 49–53.

Seifert, W. 1972. Habitat, variations, and intergradation of the Trans-Pecos copperhead Agkistrodon contortrix pictigaster in Texas. Bulletin of the Dallas Museum of Natural History 2(2): 1–10.

Seigel, R. A. 1983. Final report on the ecology and management of the massasauga, Sistrurus catenatus, at the Squaw Creek National Wildlife Refuge, Holt County, Missouri. Report to the Missouri Department of Conservation. 14 pp.

———. 1986. Ecology and conservation of an endangered rattlesnake, Sistrurus catenatus, in Missouri. Biological Conservation 35: 333–346.

Seigel, R. A., and C. A. Sheil. 1999. Populations viability analysis: applications for the conservation of massasaugas. Pp. 17–22 in B. Johnson and M. Wright (eds.), Second International Symposium and Workshop on the Conservation of the eastern massasauga rattlesnake, Sistrurus catenatus catenatus: population and habitat management issues in urban, bog, prairie, and forested ecosystems. Toronto Zoo, Toronto.

Seigel, R. A., C. A. Sheil, and J. S. Doody. 1998. Changes in a population of an endangered rattlesnake, Sistrurus catenatus, following a severe flood. Biological Conservation 83(2): 127–131.

Self, J. T., and R. E. Kuntz. 1967. Host–parasite relations in some Pentastomida. Journal of Parasitology 53: 202–206.

Selous, P. S. 1900. Notes and observation regarding the habits and characteristics of the massasauga or ground rattlesnakes, Sistrurus catenatus, during captivity. Michigan Academy of Science First Report: 89–92.

Selye, C. W., Jr., and G. K. Williamson. 1982. Life history notes: Gopherus polyphemus (Gopher tortoise). Burrow associates. Herpetol. Rev. 13(2): 48.

Serié, P. 1915. Suplemento a la fauna erpetológica argentina. Anales del Museo Nacional de Buenos Aires 27: 93–109.

———. 1921. Catálogo de los ofidios argentinos. Anales de la Sociedad Científica Argentina 92: 145–175.

———. 1936. Nueva enumeración sistemática de los ofidios argentinos. Inst. Mus. Univ. Nac. La Plata. Obra Cincuentenario: 33–68.

Servedio, M. R. 2000. The effects of predator learning, forgetting, and recognition errors on the evolution of warning coloration. Evolution 54: 751–763.

Sexton, O. J. 1958 [dated 1956–1957]. The distribution of Bothrops atrox in relation to food supply. Bol. Mus. Cienc. Nat. (Caracas) 2–3: 47–54.

———. 1960. Experimental studies of artificial Batesian mimics. Behaviour 15: 244–251.

Sexton, O. J., and H. Heatwole. 1965. Life history notes on some Panamanian snakes. Caribbean Journal of Science 5(1–2): 39–43.

Sexton, O. J., P. Jacobson, and J. E. Bramble. 1992. Geographic variation in some activities associated with hibernation in Nearctic pitvipers. Pp. 337–346 in J. A. Campbell and E. D. Brodie Jr. (eds.), Biology of the pitvipers. Selva, Tyler, Texas.

Shaffer, L. L. 1991. Pennsylvania amphibians and reptiles. Pennsylvania Fish Commission, Harrisburg. 161 pp.

Shannon, F. A. 1951. Notes on a herpetological collection from Oaxaca and other localities in Mexico. Proceedings of the U.S. National Museum 101(3284): 465–484.

———. 1953. Case reports of two Gila monster bites. Herpetologica 9(3): 125–127.

Shannon, F. A., and H. M. Smith. 1950 [dated 1949]. Herpetological results of the University of Illinois field expedition, spring 1949. I. Introduction, Testudines, Serpentes. Trans. Kansas Acad. Sci. 52(4): 499–514.

Shaw, C. E. 1948a. A note on the food habits of Heloderma suspectum. Herpetologica 4(4): 145.

———. 1948b. The male combat "dance" of some crotalid snakes. Herpetologica 4(4): 137–145.

———. 1950. The Gila monster in New Mexico. Herpetologica 6(2): 37–39.

———. 1951. Male combat in American colubrid snakes with remarks on combat in other colubrid and elapid snakes. Herpetologica 7(4): 149–168.

———. 1962. Sea snakes at the San Diego Zoo. International Zoo Yearbook 4: 49–52.

———. 1964a. Beaded lizards—dreaded but seldom deadly. Zoonooz 37: 10–15.

———. 1964b. A snake easily ruffled but unrattled. Zoonooz 37: 1–7.

———. 1964c. Note on Crotalus catalinensis birthing. Zoonooz 37: 8

———. 1971. The coral snakes, genera Micrurus and Micruroides, of the United States and northern Mexico. Pp. 156–172 in W. Bucherl and E. E. Buckley (eds.), Venomous animals and their venoms, vol. 2. Venomous vertebrates. Academic Press, New York.

Shaw, C. E., and S. Campbell. 1974. Snakes of the American West. Knopf, New York. 332. pp.

Shaw, G. 1802. General zoology, or systematic natural history, vol. 3. Amphibia. G. Kearsley, London. 615 pp.

Sheppard, P. M. 1959. The evolution of mimicry; a problem in ecology and genetics. Cold Spring Harbor Symposium on Quantitative Biology 24: 131–140.

Sheppard, P. M., J. R. G. Turner, K. S. Brown, W. W. Benson, and M. C. Singer. 1985. Genetics and the evolution of Muellerian mimicry in *Heliconius* butterflies. Philosophical Transactions of the Royal Society of London B 308: 433–613.

Sheppegrell, W. 1928. A coral snake record. Bull. Antivenin Inst. Am. 2(3): 78–79.

Sherbrooke, W. C. 1996. Reactions of Costa Rican hummingbirds to models of two color-morphs of the eyelash palm-pitviper (*Bothriechis schlegelii*). Sonoran Herpetologist 9(1): 2–3.

Sherbrooke, W. C., and G. A. Middendorf. 2001. Blood-squirting variability in horned lizards (Phrynosoma). Copeia 2001: 1114–1122.

Sherbrooke, W. C., and R. R. Montanucci. 1988. Stone mimicry in the round-tailed horned lizard, *Phrynosoma modestum* (Sauria, Iguanidae). Journal of Arid Environments 14: 275–284.

Shine, R. 1977. Reproduction in Australian elapid snakes II. Female reproductive cycles. Australian Journal of Zoology 25: 655–666.

Shine, R. 1978. Sexual size dimorphism and male combat in snakes. Oecologia (Berlin) 33: 269–277.

Shine, R., P. Harlow, M. P. Lemaster, I. T. Moore, and R. T. Mason. 2000a. The transvestite serpent: why do male garter snakes court (some) other males? Animal Behaviour 59: 349–359.

Shine, R., D. O'Connor, and R. T. Mason. 2000b. Female mimicry in garter snakes: behavioural tactics of "she-males" and the males that court them. Canadian Journal of Zoology 78: 1391–1396.

———. 2000c. Sexual conflict in the snake den. Behavioral Ecology and Sociobiology 48: 392–401.

Shine, R., B. Phillips, H. Waye, M. LeMaster, and R. T. Mason. 2001. Benefits of female mimicry in snakes. Nature 414: 267.

Shoop, W. L., and K. C. Corkum. 1982. *Proteocephalus micruricola* sp. n. (Cestoda: Proteocephalidae) from *Micrurus diastema affinis* in Oaxaca, Mexico. Proceedings of the Helminthological Society of Washington 49(1): 62–64.

Shreve, B. 1934. Notes on Ecuadorian snakes. Occasional Papers of the Boston Society of Natural History 8: 125–132.

———. 1938. A new *Agkistrodon* from Mexico. Copeia 1938(1): 9.

———. 1947a. On Venezuelan reptiles and amphibians collected by Dr. H. G. Kugler. Bulletin of the Museum of Comparative Zoology 99(5): 519–537.

———. 1947b. On Colombian reptiles and amphibians collected by Dr. R. E. Schultes. Caldasia 4(19): 311–316.

———. 1953. Notes on the races of *Micrurus frontalis* (Duméril, Duméril and Bibron). Breviora 16: 1–6.

Shufeldt, R. W. 1882. The bite of the Gila monster (*Heloderma suspectum*). American Naturalist 16: 907–908.

———. 1890. Contributions to the study of *Heloderma suspectum*. Proc. Zool. Soc. London 1890: 148–244.

Shuntov, V. P. 1963. Morskie zmei. Priroda (Moskow) 3: 103–104.

———. 1971. [Sea snakes of the north Australian shelf.] Ekologiya 1971(4): 65–72. (Consultants Bureau English Translation, 1972.)

Siddall, M. E. 1995. Another monophyly index: revisiting the jackknife. Cladistics 11: 33–56.

Sievert, G., and L. Sievert. 1988. A field guide to reptiles of Oklahoma. Department of Wildlife Conservation, Oklahoma City. 96 pp.

Sigala-Rodríguez, J. J. 1996. Contribuciones sobre fauna herpetofauna del estado de Aguascalientes: *Crotalus polystictus*, Serpiente de cascabel de rombos. Boletín Informativo Biocalli, II Epoca. Departamento de Biología, Universidad Autónoma de Aguascalientes 7: 28–31.

———. 1998. Reflexiones sobre el estudio de la serpiente de cascabel *Crotalus willardi obscurus*. Boletín Informativo Biocalli, II Epoca. Departamento de Biología, Universidad Autónoma de Aguascalientes 9: 31–36.

———. 1999. Mapeo del hábitat de la serpiente de cascabel *Crotalus willardi obscurus* en las montañas Peloncillo, Arizona, y Nuevo México. Boletín Informativo Biocalli, II Epoca. Departamento de Biología, Universidad Autónoma de Aguascalientes 11: 37–41.

Sigala-Rodríguez, J. J., and J. Vázquez-Díaz. 1996. Serpientes venenosas de Aguascalientes. Cuadernos de Trabajo, Agricultura y Recursos Naturales 56: 1–36.

Sigaud, J.-F.-X. 1844. Du climat et des maladies du Brésil, ou statistique médical de cet empire. Fortin, Masson, Paris.

Silva, D. F. 2001. Revisão sistemática do gênero *Lachesis* Daudin, 1803 (Serpentes: Viperidae: Crotalinae). Ph.D. dissertation, Universidade Federal do Rio de Janeiro. 59 pp.

Silva, M. V., and M. A. Buononato. 1984. Relato clínico de envenenamento humano por *Philodryas olfersi*. Mem. Inst. Butantan 47–48: 121–126.

Silva, M. V., Jr. 1956. O ofidismo no Brasil. Serv. Nac. Educ. Sanit., Min. Saúde, Rio de Janeiro. 346 pp.

Silva, O. A., M. López, and P. Godoy. 1979. Intensive care unit treatment of acute renal failure following snake bite. American Journal of Tropical Medicine and Hygiene 28: 401–407.

Silva, V. X. 2000. Revisão sistemática do complexo *Bothrops neuwiedi* (Serpentes, Viperidae, Crotalinae), 2 vols. Ph.D. dissertation, Universidade de São Paulo. 375 pp.

Silva-Haad, J. 1982a [dated 1980–1981]. Accidentes humanos por los serpientes de los géneros *Bothrops* y *Lachesis*. Mem. Inst. Butantan 44–45: 403–423.

———. 1982b. Las serpientes del género *Bothrops* en la Amazonia colombiana. Comando Unificado del Sur, Amazonia 82: 45–50.

———. [Silva, J. J.] 1989. Las serpientes del género *Bothrops* en la Amazonia colombiana. Acta Médica Colombiana 14(3): 148–165.

———. 1994. Los *Micrurus* de la Amazonia colombiana. Biología y toxicología experimental de sus venenos. Colombia Amazónica 7(1–2): 41–138.

Silva-Haad, J., and R. A. Rodríguez R. 1985. Las serpientes *Micrurus* de la Amazonia colombiana. Amazonia 85: 26–28.

Silva-Júnior, M. 1956. O ofidismo no Brasil. Ministério da Saúde, Serviço Nacional de Educação Sanitária, Rio de Janeiro. 136 pp.

Silvani, S. H., S. De Valentine, B. L. Scurran, and J. M. Karlin. 1980. Poisonous snakebites of the extremities. Journal of the American Podiatry Association 70: 172–176.

Silveira, P. V. P., and S. Nishioka de A. 1995. Venomous snakebite without clinical envenoming ("dry-bite"). A neglected problem in Brazil. Tropical and Geographical Medicine 47: 82–85.

Silveira-Bérnils, R. 1994. Medidas conservacionistas concernentes a herpetofauna, adotadas no estado do Paraná. Herpetologia no Brazil 1: 125–127.

Simons, L. H. 1986. Natural history notes: *Crotalus atrox* (western diamondback rattlesnake). Pattern. Herpetol. Rev. 17(1): 20–22.

Simpson, G. G. 1961. Principles of animal taxonomy. Columbia University Press, New York. 247 pp.

Sinclair, R. 1965. Tennessee snakes. Pp. 24–26 in Amphibians and reptiles of Tennessee. Tennessee State Game and Fish Commission, Nashville.

Siqueira, J. E. de, M. de L. Higuchi, N. Nabut, A. Lose, J. K. Souza, and M. Nakashima. 1990. Lesão miocárdica em acidente ofídico pela espécie *Crotalus durissus terrificus* (Cascavel), relato de caso. Arquivos Brasileiros de Cardiologia 54: 323–325.

Sisk, N. R., and J. F. Jackson. 1997. Tests of two hypotheses for the origin of the crotaline rattle. Copeia 1997(3): 485–495.

Sivaprasad, R., and E. M. Cantini. 1982. Western diamondback rattlesnake (*Crotalus atrox*) poisoning. Postgraduate Medicine 71: 223–230.

Sjostrom, L., I. H. Al-Abdulla, S. Rawat, D. C. Smith, and J. Landon. 1994. A comparison of ovine and equine antivenoms. Toxicon 32: 427–433.

Skutch, A. F. 1960. The laughing reptile hunter of tropical America. Animal Kingdom 63: 115–119.

———. 1971. A naturalist in Costa Rica. University of Florida Press, Gainesville.

Slater, J. R. 1939. The amphibians and reptiles of the state of Washington. Occasional Papers, Department of Biology, College of Puget Sound 3: 6–31.

———. 1941. The distribution of amphibians and reptiles in Idaho. Occasional Papers, Department of Biology, College of Puget Sound 14: 78–109.

Slavens, F. L., and K. Slavens. 2000. Reptiles and amphibians in captivity: breeding, longevity, and inventory. Slaveware, Seattle. 400 pp.

Slevin, J. R. 1926. Expedition to the Revillagigedo Islands, Mexico in 1925, III. Notes on a collection of reptiles and amphibians from Tres Marías and Revillagigedo Islands, and west coast of Mexico, with description of a new species of *Tantilla*. Proc. California Acad. Sci. 15(3): 195–207.

——. 1939. Notes on a collection of reptiles and amphibians from Guatemala. 1. Snakes. Proc. California Acad. Sci., 4th ser., 23(26): 393–414.

——. 1942. Notes on a collection of reptiles from Boquete, Panama, with the description of a new species of *Hydromorphus*. Proc. California Acad. Sci., 4th ser., 23(32): 463–480.

Slowinski, J. B. 1991. The phylogenetic relationships of the New World coral snakes (Elapidae: *Leptomicrurus*, *Micruroides*, and *Micrurus*) based on biochemical and morphological data. Ph.D. dissertation, University of Miami.

——. 1993. "Unordered" versus "ordered" characters. Syst. Biol. 42: 155–165.

——. 1995. A phylogenetic analysis of the New World coral snakes (Elapidae: *Leptomicrurus*, *Micruroides*, and *Micrurus*) based on allozymic and morphological characters. J. Herpetol. 29: 325–338.

Slowinski, J. B., J. Boundy, and R. Lawson. 2001. The phylogenetic relationships of Asian coral snakes (Elapidae: *Calliophis* and *Maticora*) based on morphological and molecular characters. Herpetologica 57: 233–245.

Slowinski, J. B., and C. Guyer. 1993. Testing whether certain traits have caused amplified diversification: an improved method based on a model of random speciation and extinction. American Naturalist 142: 1019–1024.

Slowinski, J. B., and J. S. Keogh. 2000. Phylogenetic relationships of elapid snakes based on cytochrome b mtDNA sequences. Molecular Phylogenetics and Evolution 15: 157–164.

Slowinski, J. B., A. Knight, and A. Rooney. 1997. Inferring species trees from gene trees: a phylogenetic analysis of the Elapidae (Serpentes) based on the amino acid sequences of venom protein. Molecular Phylogenetics and Evolution 8: 349–362.

Slowinski, J. B., and S. L. Rasmussen. 1985. Natural history notes: *Crotalus viridis viridis*. Coloration. Herpetol. Rev. 16(1): 29.

Smith, C. 1992. Life history notes: *Crotalus adamanteus* (eastern diamondback rattlesnake). Behavior. Herpetol. Rev. 23(4): 118.

——. 1994. Geographic distribution: *Crotalus adamanteus* (eastern diamondback rattlesnake). Herpetol. Rev. 25(4): 166.

——. 1997. Natural history notes: *Agkistrodon contortrix contortrix* (southern copperhead). Diet. Herpetol. Rev. 28(3): 153.

Smith, C. F., and L. Radford. 1989. Cannibalism in the Colombian rattlesnake *Crotalus durissus cumanensis*. Journal of the Northern Ohio Association of Herpetologists 15(1): 34.

Smith, D. D., N. A. Laposha, R. Powell, and J. S. Parmerless Jr. 1985. Natural history notes: *Crotalus molossus* (blacktail rattlesnake). Anomaly. Herpetol. Rev. 16(3): 78–79.

Smith, E. N., and R. L. Gutberlet Jr. 2001. Generalized frequency coding: a method of preparing polymorphic multistate characters for phylogenetic analysis. Syst. Biol. 50: 156–169.

Smith, H. M. 1931. Additions to the herpetological fauna of Riley County, Kansas. Copeia 1931(3): 143.

——. 1935. Miscellaneous notes on Mexican lizards. Kansas University Science Bulletin 22(6): 119–155.

——. 1938. Notes on reptiles and amphibians from Yucatan and Campeche, Mexico. Occas. Pap. Mus. Zool. Univ. Michigan 388: 1–22.

——. 1939. An annotated list of the Mexican amphibians and reptiles in the Carnegie Museum. Annals of Carnegie Museum 27(21): 311–320.

——. 1940. Descriptions of new lizards and snakes from Mexico and Guatemala. Proceedings of the Biological Society of Washington 53: 55–64.

——. 1941a. Notes on Mexican snakes of the genus *Trimeresurus*. Zoologica (New York) 26: 61–64.

——. 1941b. On the Mexican snakes of the genus *Pliocercus*. Proceedings of the Biological Society of Washington 54: 119–124.

——. 1942. Additional notes on Mexican snakes of the genus *Pliocercus*. Proceedings of the Biological Society of Washington 55: 159–164.

——. 1943a. Summary of the collections of snakes and crocodilians made in Mexico under the Walter Rathbone Traveling Scholarship. Proceedings of the U.S. National Museum 93(3169): 393–504.

——. 1943b. The validity of *Crotalus viridis decolor* Klauber. Copeia 1943(4): 251.

——. 1944a. Snakes of the Hoogstraal expeditions to northern Mexico. Field Mus. Nat. Hist. Publ., Zool. Ser., 29(8): 135–152.

——. 1944b. Notes on a small collection of reptiles and amphibians from Tabasco, Mexico. Journal of the Washington Academy of Sciences 34(5): 154–156.

——. 1944c. Additions to the list of Mexican amphibians and reptiles in the Carnegie Museum. Annals of Carnegie Museum 30(9): 89–92.

——. 1946a. Handbook of lizards: lizards of the United States and of Canada. Comstock Publishing, Ithaca, N.Y. 557 pp.

——. 1946b. Preliminary notes and speculations on the *Triseriatus* group of rattlesnakes in Mexico. Kansas University Science Bulletin 31(3): 75–101.

——. 1947a [dated 1946]. Notas sobre una colleción de reptiles y anfibios de Chiapas, Mex. Revista de la Sociedad Mexicana de Historia Natural 7(1–4): 63–74.

——. 1947b. Notes on Mexican amphibians and reptiles. Journal of the Washington Academy of Sciences 37(11): 408–412.

——. 1947c. The influence of the Balcones Escarpment on the distribution of amphibians and reptiles in Texas. Bulletin of the Chicago Academy of Sciences 8(1): 1–16.

——. 1956. Handbook of amphibians and reptiles of Kansas, 2d ed. Miscellaneous Publications of the Museum of Natural History, University of Kansas, No. 9. 356 pp.

——. 1958. Handlist of the snakes of Panama. Herpetologica 14(4): 222–224.

——. 1959. Herpetozoa from Guatemala, I. Herpetologica 15(4): 210–216.

——. 1960a [dated 1959]. New and noteworthy reptiles from Oaxaca, Mexico. Trans. Kansas Acad. Sci. 62(4): 265–271.

——. 1960b. Herpetozoa from Tabasco. Herpetologica 16(3): 222–223.

——. 1963. New distributional records of amphibians and reptiles from South Dakota and Wyoming. Herpetologica 19(2): 147–148.

——. 1970 [dated 1969]. The first herpetology of Mexico. Herpetology 3(1): 1–16.

——. 2001. Searching for herps in Mexico in the 1930s, II. Bull. Chicago Herpetol. Soc. 36(2): 31–42.

Smith, H. M., E. R. Allen, and R. L. Holland. 1970. A new atavistic hyperxanthic chromotype in the coralsnake *Micrurus fulvius* (Linnaeus). J. Herpetol. 4(1–2): 80–83.

Smith, H. M., and E. D. Brodie Jr. 1982. A guide to field identification: reptiles of North America. Western Publishing, N.Y. 240 pp.

Smith, H. M., L. E. Brown, et al. 1998. *Crotalus ruber* Cope, 1892 (Reptilia, Serpentes): proposed precedence of the specific name over that of *Crotalus exsul* Garman, 1884. Bulletin of Zoological Nomenclature 55(4): 229–232.

Smith, H. M., and H. K. Buechner. 1947. The influence of the Balcones Escarpment on the distribution of amphibians and reptiles in Texas. Bulletin of the Chicago Academy of Sciences 8(1): 1–16.

Smith, H. M., and D. Chiszar. 1996. Species-group taxa of the false coral snake genus *Pliocercus*. Pamus Publishing, Pottsville, Pa. 112 pp.

——. 1997. New records for amphibians and reptiles from Texas. Herpetol. Rev. 28(2): 99–100.

——. 2001. A new subspecies of cantil (*Agkistrodon bilineatus*) from central Veracruz, Mexico (Reptilia: Serpentes). Bull. Maryland Herpetol. Soc. 37: 130–136.

Smith, H. M., and P. S. Chrapliwy. 1958. New and noteworthy Mexican herptiles from the Lidicker collection. Herpetologica 13(4): 267–271.

Smith, H. M., and O. Flores-Villela. 1994. Deletion of the coral snake *Micrurus fulvius* from the herpetofaunal concept of Michoacán, Mexico. Bull. Maryland Herpetol. Soc. 30(2): 76–77.

Smith, H. M., and H. K. Gloyd. 1964. Nomenclatorial notes on the snake names *Scytale, Boa scytale,* and *Agkistrodon mokasen.* Herpetologica 19(4): 280–283.

Smith, H. M., and C. Grant. 1958a. Noteworthy herptiles from Jalisco, Mexico. Herpetologica 14(1): 18–23.

———. 1958b. New and noteworthy snakes from Panama. Herpetologica 14(4): 207–215.

Smith, H. M., G. A. Hammerson, D. Chiszar, and C. Ramotnik. 1993. Geographic distribution: *Crotalus viridis viridis* (prairie rattlesnake). Herpetol. Rev. 24(4): 156.

Smith, H. M., and R. L. Holland. 1971. Noteworthy snakes and lizards from Baja California. J. Herpetol. 5(1–2): 56–59.

Smith, H. M., R. L. Holland, and R. L. Brown. 1971. The prairie rattlesnake in Baja California del Sur. J. Herpetol. 5(3–4): 200.

Smith, H. M., and M. J. Landy. 1965. New and unusual snakes of the genus *Pliocercus* from Oaxaca, Mexico. Chicago Academy of Sciences, Natural History Miscellanea 183: 1–4.

Smith, H. M., and D. A. Langebartel. 1949. Notes on a collection of reptiles and amphibians from the Isthmus of Tehuantepec, Oaxaca. Journal of the Washington Academy of Sciences 39(12): 409–416.

Smith, H. M., D. A. Langebartel, and K. L. Williams. 1964. Herpetological type specimens in the University of Illinois Museum of Natural History. Illinois Biological Monographs 32: 1–80.

Smith, H. M., and K. R. Larsen. 1974. The gender of generic names ending in *-ops.* J. Herpetol. 8(4):375.

Smith, H. M., and L. E. Laufe. 1945. Mexican amphibians and reptiles in the Texas Cooperative Wildlife Collections. Trans. Kansas Acad. Sci. 48(3): 325–254.

Smith, H. M., and J. D. Lynch. 1967. A new cryptic lizard (Iguanidae: *Sceloporus*) with comments on other reptiles from Oaxaca, Mexico. Herpetologica 23(1): 18–29.

Smith, H. M., T. P. Maslin, and R. L. Brown. 1965. Summary of the distribution of the herpetofauna of Colorado. University of Colorado Studies, Series in Biology, 15: 1–52.

Smith, H. M., and M. B. Mittleman. 1943. Notes on the Mansfield Museum's Mexican reptiles collected by Wilkinson. Trans. Kansas Acad. Sci. 46: 243–249.

Smith, H. M., and E. O. Moll. 1969. A taxonomic rearrangement of the pit vipers of the *Bothrops nigroviridis* complex of southern Mexico. J. Herpetol. 3(3–4): 151–155.

Smith, H. M., and W. L. Necker. 1944 [dated 1943]. Alfredo Dugès' types of Mexican reptiles and amphibians. Anales de la Escuela Nacional de Ciencias Biológicas, México 3(1–2): 179–233.

Smith, H. M., and G. Pérez-Higareda. 1965. A range extension of the lance-headed rattlesnake, *Crotalus polystictus.* Journal of the Ohio Herpetological Society 5: 56.

Smith, H. M., and R. B. Smith. 1969. Early foundations of Mexican herpetology: an annotated and indexed bibliography of the herpetological publications of Alfredo Dugès, 1826–1910. University of Illinois Press, Urbana. 87 pp.

———. 1976. Synopsis of the herpetofauna of Mexico, vol. 3. Source analysis and index for Mexican amphibians. John Johnson, North Bennington, Vt.

Smith, H. M., R. B. Smith, and H. L. Sawin. 1977. A summary of snake classification (Reptilia, Serpentes). J. Herpetol. 11: 115–122.

Smith, H. M., and E. H. Taylor. 1945. An annotated checklist and key to the snakes of Mexico. Bulletin of the U.S. National Museum 187: 1–239.

———. 1950a. An annotated checklist and key to the reptiles of Mexico exclusive of the snakes. Bulletin of the U.S. National Museum 199: 1–253.

———. 1950b. Type localities of Mexican reptiles and amphibians. Kansas University Science Bulletin 33(8): 313–380.

———. 1966. Preface to the reprint of Herpetology of Mexico, 3 vols. Eric Lundberg, Ashton, Md. 610 pp.

Smith, H. M., and R. Van Gelder. 1955. New and noteworthy amphibians and reptiles from Sinaloa and Puebla, Mexico. Herpetologica 11(2): 145–149.

Smith, H. M., and K. L. Williams. 1963. New and noteworthy amphibians and reptiles from southern Mexico. Herpetologica 19(1): 22–27.

Smith, H. M., K. L. Williams, and E. O. Moll. 1963. Herpetological explorations on the Río Conchos, Chihuahua, Mexico. Herpetologica 19(3): 205–215.

Smith, L. J., A. T. Holycross, C. W. Painter, and M. E. Douglas. 2001. Montane rattlesnakes and prescribed fire. Southwest. Nat. 46(1): 54–61.

Smith, M. A. 1926. Monograph of the sea-snakes (Hydrophiidae). Taylor and Francis, London. 130 pp.

———. 1942. Remarks on the nasal pit in snakes. Copeia 1942(4): 256.

———. 1943. The fauna of British India, Ceylon, and Burma: Reptilia and Amphibia, vol. 3. Serpentes. Taylor and Francis, London. 583 pp.

Smith, M. S., and C. L. Ownby. 1985. Ability of polyvalent (Crotalidae) antivenin to neutralize myonecrosis, hemorrhage, and lethality induced by timber rattlesnake (*Crotalus horridus horridus*) venom. Toxicon 23: 409–424.

Smith, N. 1958. Poisonous snakes of Pennsylvania. Pennsylvania Game News 29(6): 12–17.

Smith, N. G. 1969. Avian predation of coral snakes. Copeia 1969(2): 402–404.

Smith, P. W. 1961. The amphibians and reptiles of Illinois. Illinois Natural History Survey Bulletin 28: 1–298.

Smith, P. W., and W. L. Burger. 1950. Additional noteworthy herpetological records for Illinois. Natural History Miscellanea 56: 1–3.

Smith, P. W., and D. M. Darling. 1952. Results of a herpetological collection from eastern central Mexico. Herpetologica 8(3): 81–86.

Smith, P. W., and M. M. Hensley. 1958. Notes on a small collection of amphibians and reptiles from the vicinity of Pinacate lava cap in northwestern Sonora, Mexico. Trans. Kansas Acad. Sci. 61(1): 64–76.

Smith, P. W., and J. C. List. 1955. Notes on Mississippi amphibians and reptiles. Am. Midl. Nat. 52: 115–125.

Smith, S. M. 1973. A study of prey-attack behaviour in young loggerhead shrikes, *Lanius ludovicianus* L. Behaviour 44: 113–141.

———. 1975. Innate recognition of coral snake pattern by a possible avian predator. Science 187: 759–760.

———. 1976. Predatory behaviour of young turquoise-browed motmots, *Eumomota superciliosa.* Behaviour 56: 309–320.

———. 1977. Coral-snake pattern recognition and stimulus generalisation by naive great kiskadees (Aves: Tyrannidae). Nature 265: 535–536.

———. 1978. Predatory behaviour of young great kiskadees (*Pitangus sulphuratus*). Animal Behaviour 26: 988–995.

———. 1980. Responses of naive temperate birds to warning coloration. Am. Midl. Nat. 103: 346–352.

Smith, S. M., and A. M. Mosdtrom. 1985. "Coral snake" rings: are they helpful in foraging? Copeia 2: 384–387.

Smyth, T. 1949. Notes on the timber rattlesnake at Mountain Lake, Virginia. Copeia 1949(1): 78.

Sneath, P. H. A., and R. R. Sokal. 1973. Numerical taxonomy. W. H. Freeman, San Francisco. 573 pp.

Snellings, E., Jr., and J. T. Collins. 1996. Natural history notes: *Sistrurus miliarius barbouri* (dusky pigmy rattlesnake): maximum size. Herpetol. Rev. 27(2): 84.

———. 1997. Natural history notes: *Sistrurus miliarius barbouri* (dusky pigmy rattlesnake): maximum size. Herpetol. Rev. 28(1): 46.

Snider, A. T., and J. K. Bowler. 1992. Longevity of reptiles and amphibians in North American collections, 2d ed. Society for the Study of Amphibians and Reptiles, Herpetological Circular No. 21. 44 pp.

Snyder, C. C., J. E. Pickins, R. P. Knowles, J. L. Emerson, and W. A. Hines. 1968. A definitive study of snakebite. Journal of the Florida Medical Association 55: 330–337.

Snyder, D. H. 1972. Amphibians and reptiles of Land between the Lakes. Tennessee Valley Authority, Golden Pond, Ky. 90 pp.

Snyder, D. H., D. F. Burchfield, and R. W. Nall. 1967. First records of the pigmy rattlesnake in Kentucky. Herpetologica 23(3): 240–241.

Snyder, G. K., H. W. Ramsey, W. J. Taylor, and C. Y. Chiou. 1973. Neuromuscular blockade of chick biventer cervicis nerve-muscle preparations by a fraction from coral snake venom. Toxicon 11: 505–508.

Snyder, R. C. 1945. Notes on the snakes of southeastern Alabama. Copeia 1945(3): 173–174.

Soini, P. 1973. Notes on an upper Amazonian coral snake, *Micrurus putumayensis* Lancini. J. Herpetol. 7(3): 306–307.

———. 1974a. Polychromatism in a population of *Micrurus langsdorffi*. J. Herpetol. 8(3): 267–269.

———. 1974b. Ofidios venenosos del nor-oriente peruano. Unpublished ms. 93 pp.

Sokal, R. R., and F. J. Rohlf. 1981. Taxonomic congruence in the Leptopodomorpha re-examined. Syst. Zool. 30: 309–325.

Solís, F. 1993 [dated 1991]. Commentarios sobre dos especies de serpientes en Panamá: *Tantilla alticola* (Boulenger) y *Bothrops picadoi* (Dunn). Scientia (Panamá) 6(2): 107–110.

Solís, R. A., R. Ibáñez D., and C. A. Jaramillo. 1996. Estableciendo una uniformidad sobre las especies de serpientes presentes en Panamá. Rev. Biol. Trop. 44(1): 19–22.

Solomon, G. B. 1974. Probable role of the timber rattlesnake, *Crotalus horridus*, in the release of *Capillaria hepatica* (Nematoda) eggs from small mammals. Virginia Journal of Science 25: 182–184.

Solórzano, A. 1989a. Distribución y aspectos reproductivos da la mano de piedra, *Bothrops nummifer* (Serpentes: Viperidae) en Costa Rica. Rev. Biol. Trop. 37: 133–137.

———. 1989b. Social behavior and reproduction in the terrestrial montane pitviper *Bothrops godmani* from Costa Rica (abstract). First World Congress of Herpetology, 11–19 September 1989, University of Kent at Canterbury, U.K.

———. 1990. Reproduction in the pit viper *Porthidium picadoi* (Serpentes: Viperidae) in Costa Rica. Copeia 1990(4): 1154–1157.

———. 1993. Mitos y creencias populares sobre los reptiles en Costa Rica. Imprenta Jiménez y Tanzi, San José. 56 pp.

———. 1995a [dated 1994]. Una nueva especie de serpiente venenosa terrestre del género *Porthidium* (Serpentes: Viperidae), del suroeste de Costa Rica. Rev. Biol. Trop. 42: 695–701.

———. 1995b. A case of human bite by the pelagic sea snake *Pelamis platurus* (Serpentes: Hydrophiidae). Rev. Biol. Trop. 43: 321–322.

———. 1998 [dated 1997]. Reproduction of *Bothriechis nigroviridis* (Serpentes: Viperidae), in Costa Rica. Rev. Biol. Trop. 45(4): 1675–1677.

———. 2004. Serpientes de Costa Rica. Universidad de Costa Rica, San José.

Solórzano, A., and L. Cerdas. 1984. Confirmación de la presencia de *Micrurus clarki* Schmidt (Elapidae) en Costa Rica. Rev. Biol. Trop. 32(2): 317–318.

———. 1986. A new subspecies of the bushmaster, *Lachesis muta*, from southeastern Costa Rica. J. Herpetol. 20(3): 463–466.

———. 1988a. Ciclos reproductivos de la serpiente coral *Micrurus nigrocinctus* (Serpentes: Elapidae) en Costa Rica. Rev. Biol. Trop. 36(2A): 235–239.

———. 1988b. Incubación de los huevos y nacimiento en la coral gargantilla *Micrurus mipartitus hertwigi* (Serpentes: Elapidae) en Costa Rica. Rev. Biol. Trop. 36(2B): 535–536.

———. 1988c. Biología reproductiva de la cascabel centroamericana *Crotalus durissus durissus* (Serpentes: Viperidae) en Costa Rica. Rev. Biol. Trop. 36: 221–226.

———. 1989. Reproductive biology and distribution of the terciopelo, *Bothrops asper* Garman (Serpentes: Viperidae) in Costa Rica. Herpetologica 45(4): 444–450.

Solórzano, A., L. D. Gómez, J. Monge-Nájera, and B. I. Crother. 1998. Redescription and validation of *Bothriechis supraciliaris* (Serpentes: Viperidae). Rev. Biol. Trop. 46: 453–462.

Solórzano, A., J. M. Gutiérrez, and L. Cerdas. 1988. *Botrhops* [sic] *ophryomegas* Bocourt (Serpentes: Viperidae) en Costa Rica: distribución, lepidosis, variación sexual y cariotipo. Rev. Biol. Trop. 36: 187–190.

Solórzano, A., M. Romero, J. M. Gutiérrez, and M. Sasa. 1999. Venom composition and diet of the cantil, *Agkistrodon bilineatus howardgloydi* (Serpentes: Viperidae). Southwest. Nat. 44: 478–483.

Sonderquist, T. R., and N. R. Middlebrook. 1984. New herpetological records from Arizona north of the Grand Canyon. Herpetol. Rev. 15(4): 115.

Sonnini de Manoncourt, C. N. S. 1776. Observations sur les serpens de la Guianne, et sur l'éfficacité de l'Eau de Luce pour en guérir la morsure. Observations sur la Physique, sur l'Histoire Naturelle et les Arts 8: 469–476.

Sonnini de Manoncourt, C. N. S., and P. A. Latreille. 1801–1802. Histoire naturelle des reptiles, avec figures dessinées d'apres nature, 4 vols. Deterville, Paris.

Soto, J. G., J. C. Pérez, M. M. López, M. Martínez, T. B. Quintanilla-Hernández, M. S. Santa-Hernández, K. Turner, J. L. Glenn, R. C. Straight, and S. A. Minton. 1989. Comparative enzymatic study of HPLC-fractionated *Crotalus* venoms. Comp. Biochem. Physiol. B 93: 847–855.

Soto, J. G., J. C. Pérez, and S. A. Minton. 1988. Proteolytic, hemorrhagic, and hemolytic activities of snake venoms. Toxicon 26: 875–882.

Soulé, M., and A. J. Sloan. 1966. Biogeography and distribution of the reptiles and amphibians on islands in the Gulf of California, Mexico. Trans. San Diego Soc. Nat. Hist. 14(11): 137–156.

Souza Campos, J. de, and L. E. de Mello Filho. 1966. Observações biológicas sôbre a Ilha da Queimada Grande. Fôlha Médica 52(5): 343–346.

Spaite, D. W., R. C. Dart, K. Hurlbut, and J. T. McNally. 1988. Skin testing: implications in the management of pit viper envenomation (abstract). Ann. Emerg. Med. 17: 389.

Spawls, S., and B. Branch. 1995. The dangerous snakes of Africa. Ralph Curtis Publishing, Sanibel Island, Fla.

Speed, M. P. 1993. Müllerian mimicry and the psychology of predation. Animal Behaviour 45: 571–580.

Speed, M. P., and J. R. G. Turner. 1999. Learning and memory in mimicry, II. Do we understand the mimicry spectrum? Biological Journal of the Linnean Society 67: 281–312.

Spencer, C. L., M. S. Koo, and J. B. Slowinski. 1999. Natural history notes: *Micrurus browni browni* (Brown's coral snake). Diet. Herpetol. Rev. 30(3): 169

Spencer, C. L., M. M. Tierney, M. S. Koo, and J. V. Vindum. 1998. New county records from Sierra and Nevada Counties, Tahoe National Forest, California, USA. Herpetol. Rev. 29(3): 182–183.

Spengler, J. C., H. M. Smith, D. Chiszar, and G. Casas-Andreu. 1982. Geographic distribution: *Crotalus basiliscus oaxacus*. Herpetol. Rev. 13(1): 25.

Spieth, H. T. 1950. The David Rockefeller Mexican Expedition of the American Museum of Natural History: introductory account. Am. Mus. Novitat. 1454: 1–67.

Spix, J. B. von. 1824. Serpentum brasiliensium species novae. Franc. Seraph. Hübschmanni, Munich.

Spix, J. B. von, and C. F. P. Martius. 1824. Travels in Brazil, in the years 1817–1820. Trans. H. E. Lloyd. Longman, London.

Stabler, R. M. 1948. Prairie rattlesnake eats spadefoot toad. Herpetologica 4(5): 168.

Stadelman, R. 1940. Maize cultivation in northwestern Guatemala. Compiled by the Carnegie Institution of Washington from data collected in the field by Raymond Stadelman. Carnegie Institution of Washington Publication No. 523: 83–263.

Stafford, P. J. 2000. On the status of the coral snake *Micrurus nigrocinctus* (Serpentes, Elapidae) in Belize, and its northernmost distribution in Atlantic Middle America. Herpetol. Rev. 31(2): 78–82.

Stafford, P. J., and J. R. Meyer. 2000. A guide to the reptiles of Belize. Academic Press, San Diego. 356 pp.

Stahnke, H. L. 1950. The food of the Gila monster. Herpetologica 6(4):103–106.

———. 1952. A note on the food of the Gila monster, *Heloderma suspectum* Cope. Herpetologica 8(3): 64–65.

Stahnke, H. L., W. A. Heffron, and D. L. Lewis. 1970. Bite of the Gila monster. Rocky Mountain Medical Journal 67: 25–30.

Starace, F. 1998. Guide des serpents et amphisbènes de Guyane. Ibis Rouge Editions, Guadeloupe, Guyane. 449 pp.

Starbroek News. 1999. Man dies following snakebite. Starbroek News, Georgetown, Guyana, November 9: 14.

Starrett, B. L. 1993. Geographic distribution: *Crotalus viridis helleri* (southern Pacific rattlesnake). Herpetol. Rev. 24(3): 109.

Starrett, B. L., and A. T. Holycross. 2000. Natural history notes: *Crotalus lepidus klauberi* (banded rock rattlesnake). Caudal luring. Herpetol. Rev. 31(4): 245.

Stebbins, R. C. 1943. Diurnal activity of *Crotalus cerastes*. Copeia 1943(2): 128–129.

———. 1954. Amphibians and reptiles of western North America. McGraw-Hill, New York. 536 pp.

———. 1972. Amphibians and reptiles of California. University of California Press, Berkeley. 152 pp.

———. 1985. A field guide to western reptiles and amphibians, 2d ed., revised. Houghton Mifflin, Boston. 336 pp.

Stechert, R. 1980. Observations on northeastern snake dens. Bulletin of the New York Herpetological Society 15: 7–14.

Stedman, J. G. 1796. Narrative, of a five years' expedition, against the revolted negroes of Surinam, in Guiana, on the wild coast of South America; from the year 1772, to 1777. J. Johnson, London.

Steel, M. A., M. D. Hendy, and D. Penny. 1993. Parsimony can be consistent! Syst. Biol. 42: 581–587.

Steindachner, F. 1870. Herpetologische notizen, II. Über einige neue oder seltene Reptilien des Wiener museums. Sitzungsberichten der Akademie der Wissenschaften in Wien. Mathematisch-naturwis-senschaftliche Klasse 61: 11–25.

Stejneger, L. H. 1893. Annotated list of the reptiles and batrachians collected by the Death Valley expedition in 1891, with descriptions of new species. North American Fauna 7: 159–228.

———. 1895 [dated 1893]. The poisonous snakes of North America. Annual Reports of the U.S. National Museum 1893: 337–487.

———. 1899. Reptiles of the Tres Marías and Isabel islands. North American Fauna 14: 63–71.

———. 1902. The reptiles of the Huachuca Mountains, Arizona. Proceedings of the U.S. National Museum 25(1282): 149–158.

———. 1907. Herpetology of Japan and adjacent territory. Bulletin of the U.S. National Museum 58: 1–577.

———. 1910. The batrachians and reptiles of Formosa. Proceedings of the U.S. National Museum 38(1731): 91–114.

———. 1940. "Sonora" as the locality of the Graham–Clark reptile collections of 1851. Copeia 1940(3): 204–205.

Stejneger, L., and T. Barbour. 1917. A check list of North American amphibians and reptiles. Harvard University Press, Cambridge, Mass. 125 pp.

———. 1933. A check list of North American reptiles, 3d ed. Harvard University Press, Cambridge, Mass. 185 pp.

———. 1940. The generic concept. Copeia 1940: 217–218.

———. 1943. A check list of North American amphibians and reptiles. Bulletin of the Museum of Comparative Zoology 93(1): 1–260.

Stephenson, B., and G. R. Pisani. 1991. Notes on early spring parasites and pathologies of Oklahoma *Crotalus atrox*. Herpetol. Rev. 22(3): 88–90.

Sternfeld, R. 1920. Eine neue Schlange der Gattung *Lachesis* aus Sudamerika. Senckenbergiana Biologica 2(6): 179–181.

Stevan, L. J., and E. B. Seligmann Jr. 1970. Agar-gel and acryla-mide-disc electrophoresis of coral snake venom. Toxicon 8: 11–14.

Stewart, B. G. 1984. Natural history notes: *Agkistrodon contortrix laticinc-tus* (broad-banded copperhead). Combat. Herpetol. Rev. 15(1): 17.

Stewart, G. R. 1994. An overview of the Mohave Desert and its herpetofauna. Pp. 55–70 in Herpetology of the North American deserts: proceedings of a symposium. Southwestern Herpetologists' Society, Special Publication No. 5.

Stewart, M. M., G. E. Larson, and T. H. Matthews. 1960. Morphological variation in a litter of timber rattlesnakes. Copeia 1960(4): 366–367.

Stickel, W. H. 1952. Venomous snakes of the United States and treatment of their bites. United Stated Fish and Wildlife Service, leaflet 339. 29 pp.

Stiles, F. G., and A. F. Skutch. 1989. A guide to the birds of Costa Rica. Cornell University Press, Ithaca, N.Y.

Stille, B. 1987. Dorsal scale microdermatoglyphics and rattlesnake (*Crotalus* and *Sistrurus*) phylogeney (Reptilia: Viperidae: Crotalinae). Herpetologica 43(1): 98–104.

Stoddard, H. L., Sr. 1978. Birds of Grady County, Georgia. Bulletin of the Tall Timbers Research Station 21: 1–175.

Storer, T. I. 1931. *Heloderma* poisoning in man. Bull. Antivenin Inst. Am. 5(1): 12–15.

Storer, T. I., and R. L. Usinger. 1966. Sierra Nevada natural history. University of California Press, Berkeley. 374 pp.

Stoud, C. H. Amon, T. Wagner, and J. L. Falk. 1989. Effect of electric shock therapy on local tissue reaction to poisonous snake venom injection in rabbits (abstract). Ann. Emerg. Med. 18: 447.

Straight, R., J. L. Glenn, and C. C. Snyder. 1976. Antivenom activity of rattlesnake blood plasma. Nature 261: 259–260.

Straight, R. C., J. L. Glenn, T. B. Wolt, and M. C. Wolfe. 1991. Regional differences in content of small basic peptide toxins in the venoms of *Crotalus adamanteus* and *Crotalus horridus*. Comp. Biochem. Physiol. B 100: 51–58.

———. 1992. North–south regional variation in the phospholipase A activity in the venom of *Crotalus ruber ruber*. Comp. Biochem. Physiol. B 103: 635–639.

Strange, R. M. 2001. Female preference and the maintenance of male fin ornamentation in three egg-mimic darters (Pisces: Percidae). Journal of Freshwater Ecology 16: 267–271.

Strauch, A. 1873. Die schlangen des Russischen Reichs in systematischer und zoogeographischer Bezeihung. Mémoires de l'Académie Impériale des Sciences de St. Petersbourg, 7th ser., 21(4): 1–287.

Strecker, J. K., Jr. 1902. A preliminary report on the reptiles and batrachians of McLennan County, Texas. Transactions of the Texas Academy 4: 95–101.

———. 1908a. The reptiles and batrachians of Victoria and Refugio Counties, Texas. Proceedings of the Biological Society of Washington 21: 47–52.

———. 1908b. The reptiles and batrachians of McLennan County, Texas. Proceedings of the Biological Society of Washington 21: 68–84.

———. 1909a. Notes on the herpetology of Burnet County, Texas. Baylor University Bulletin 12: 1–9.

———. 1909b. Reptiles and amphibians collected in Brewster County, Texas. Baylor University Bulletin 12: 10–20.

———. 1910. Notes on the fauna of a portion of the canyon region of northwestern Texas. Baylor University Bulletin 13(4–5): 1–31.

———. 1915. Reptiles and amphibians of Texas. Baylor University Bulletin 18(4): 1–82.

———. 1922. An annotated catalogue of the amphibians and reptiles of Bexar County, Texas. Bulletin of the Scientific Society of San Antonio 4: 1–30.

———. 1924. Notes on the herpetology of Hot Springs, Arkansas. Baylor University Bulletin 27(3): 29–47.

———. 1926a. Amphibians and reptiles collected in Somervall County, Texas. Contributions of the Baylor University Museum 2: 1–3.

———. 1926b. Notes on the herpetology of the east Texas timber belt. 1. Liberty County amphibians and reptiles. Contributions of the Baylor University Museum 3: 1–3.

———. 1926c. Notes on the herpetology of the east Texas timber belt. 2. Henderson County amphibians and reptiles. Contributions of the Baylor University Museum 7: 1–7.

———. 1926d. A list of reptiles and amphibians collected by Louis Garni in the vicinity of Boerne, Texas. Contributions from the Baylor University Museum 6: 1–11.

———. 1926e. Reptiles from Lindale, Smith County, Texas. Contributions of the Baylor University Museum 7: 7.

———. 1927. Chapters from the life-histories of Texas reptiles and amphibians. Contributions of the Baylor University Museum 10: 1–14.

———. 1928a. The copperhead west of the Pecos River. Contributions of the Baylor University Museum 15: 9.

———. 1928b. Common English and folk names for Texas amphibians and reptiles. Contributions of the Baylor University Museum 16: 1–21.

———. 1929a. A preliminary list of the amphibians and reptiles of Tarrant Co., Texas. Contributions of the Baylor University Museum 19:1–15.

———. 1929b. Further studies in the folk-lore of reptiles. Baylor University Contributions to Folk-lore 1: 1–16.

——. 1930. A catalogue of the amphibians and reptiles of Travis County, Texas. Contributions of the Baylor University Museum 23: 1–16.

——. 1935a. Notes on the pit-vipers in McLennan County, Texas. Baylor University Bulletin 38: 26–28.

——. 1935b. The reptiles of West Frio Canyon, Real County, Texas. Baylor University Bulletin 38: 32.

——. 1935c. A list of hitherto unpublished localities for Texas amphibians and reptiles. Baylor University Bulletin 38(3): 35–38.

Strecker, J. K., Jr., and L. S. Frierson Jr. 1926. The herpetology of Caddo and DeSoto Parishes, Louisiana. Contributions of the Baylor University Museum 5: 3–10.

Strecker, J. K., Jr., and J. E. Johnson Jr. 1935. Notes on the herpetology of Wilson County, Texas. Baylor University Bulletin 38(3): 17–23.

Strecker, J. K., Jr., and W. J. Williams. 1927. Herpetological records from the vicinity of San Marcos, Texas, with distributional data on the amphibians and reptiles of the Edwards Plateau region and central Texas. Contributions of the Baylor University Museum 12: 1–16.

——. 1928. Field notes on the herpetology of Bowie County, Texas. Contributions of the Baylor University Museum 17: 1–19.

Streets, T. H. 1877. Contributions to the natural history of the Hawaiian and Fanning Islands and Lower California. Bulletin of the U.S. National Museum 7: 1–172.

Streiffer, R. H. 1986. Bite of the venomous lizard, the Gila monster. Postgraduate Medicine 79: 297–302.

Strimple, P. D. 1988. Comments on caudal luring in snakes with observations on this behavior in two subspecies of cantiles, *Agkistrodon bilineatus* spp. Notes from Noah 15(6): 6–10.

——. 1992. Caudal luring: a discussion on definition and application of the term. Greater Cincinnati Herpetological Society Contributions to Herpetology 1992: 49–54.

——. 1996. Geographic distribution: *Agkistrodon contortrix mokasen* (northern copperhead). Herpetol. Rev. 27(1): 33.

Strimple, P. D., A. J. Tomassoni, E. J. Otten, and D. Bahner. 1997. Report on envenomation by a Gila monster (*Heloderma suspectum*) with a discussion of venom apparatus, clinical findings and treatment. Wilderness and Environmental Medicine 8: 111–116.

Stroupe, D. A., and M. E. Dorcas. 2001. The apparent persistence of *Crotalus horridus* in the Western Piedmont of North Carolina. Herpetol. Rev. 32(4): 287–288.

Strussmann, C., and M. André de Carvalho. 1998. New herpetological records for the state of Mato Grosso, Western Brazil. Herpetol. Rev. 29(3): 183–185.

Strussman, C., and I. Sazima. 1993. The snake assemblage of the Pantanal at Poconé, western Brazil: faunal composition and ecological summary. Studies on Neotropical Fauna and Environment 28: 157–168.

Stuart, J. N., and T. L. Brown. 1996. Geographic distribution: *Sistrurus catenatus edwardsi*. Herpetol. Rev. 27(4): 214.

Stuart, L. C. 1934. A contribution to a knowledge of the herpetological fauna of El Petén, Guatemala. Occas. Pap. Mus. Zool. Univ. Michigan 292: 1–18.

——. 1935. A contribution to a knowledge of the herpetology of a portion of the savanna region of central Petén, Guatemala. Miscellaneous Publications of the Museum of Zoology, University of Michigan 29: 1–56.

——. 1937. Some further notes on the amphibians and reptiles of the Petén forest of northern Guatemala. Copeia 1937(1): 67–70.

——. 1943. Comments on the herpetofauna of the Sierra de los Cuchumatanes of Guatemala. Occas. Pap. Mus. Zool. Univ. Michigan 471: 1–28.

——. 1948. The amphibians and reptiles of Alta Verapaz, Guatemala. Miscellaneous Publications of the Museum of Zoology, University of Michigan 69: 1–109.

——. 1950. A geographic study of the herpetofauna of Alta Verapaz, Guatemala. Contributions of the Laboratory of Vertebrate Biology, University of Michigan, 45: 1–77.

——. 1951. The herpetofauna of the Guatemalan Plateau, with special reference to its distribution on the southwestern highlands. Contributions of the Laboratory of Vertebrate Biology, University of Michigan, 49: 1–71.

——. 1954a. A description of subhumid corridor across northern Central America, with comments on its herpetofaunal indicators. Contributions of the Laboratory of Vertebrate Biology, University of Michigan, 65: 1–26.

——. 1954b. Herpetofauna of the southeastern highlands of Guatemala. Contributions of the Laboratory of Vertebrate Biology, University of Michigan, 68: 1–65.

——. 1955. A brief review of the Guatemalan lizards of the genus *Anolis*. Miscellaneous Publications of the Museum of Zoology, University of Michigan, 91: 1–31.

——. 1958. A study of the herpetofauna of the Uaxactun-Tikal area of northern El Petén, Guatemala. Contributions of the Laboratory of Vertebrate Biology, University of Michigan, 75: 1–30.

——. 1963. A checklist of the herpetofauna of Guatemala. Miscellaneous Publications of the Museum of Zoology, University of Michigan, 122: 1–150.

——. 1964. Fauna of Middle America. Pp. 316–362 in R. Wauchope and R. C. West (eds.), Handbook of Middle American Indians, vol. 1. University of Texas Press, Austin.

——. 1966. The environment of the Central American cold-blooded vertebrate fauna. Copeia 1966(4): 684–699.

Stubb, T. H. 1979. Moccasin. Florida Naturalist 52(4): 2–4.

Studenroth, K. R. 1991. Life history notes: *Agkistrodon piscivorus cananti* (Florida cottonmouth). Foraging behavior. Herpetol. Rev. 22(2): 60.

Suckow, G. A. 1798. Anfangsgründe der theoretischen und angewandten Naturgeschichte der Thiere. Dritter teil, von den Amphibien. Weissmann, Leipzig. 298 pp.

Sues, H. D. 1991. Venom-conducting teeth in a Triassic reptile. Nature 351: 141–143.

Sullivan, B. K. 2000. Long-term shifts in snake populations. Biological Conservation 94(3): 321–325.

Sullivan, B. K., G. W. Schuett, and M. A. Kwiatkowski. 2002. Natural history notes: *Heloderma suspectum* (Gila monster). Mortality/predation? Herpetol. Rev. 33(2): 135–136.

Sullivan, J. B., and W. A. Wingert. 1989. Reptile bites. Pp. 479–511 in P. S. Auerbach and E. C. Geehr (eds.), Management of wilderness and environmental emergencies, 2d ed. Mosby, St. Louis.

Sullivan, J. B., W. A. Wingert, and R. L. Norris. 1995. North American venomous reptile bites. Pp. 680–709 in P. S. Auerbach (ed.), Wilderness medicine: management of wilderness and environmental emergencies. Mosby, St. Louis.

Sumichrast, F. 1864a. Notes on the habits of some Mexican reptiles. Ann. Mag. Nat. Hist., 3d ser., 13: 497–507.

——. 1864b. Note sur les moeurs de quelques reptiles du Mexique. Archives de Sciences Physiques et Naturelles. 19: 45–61.

——. 1870. Notas sobre las costumbres de algunos reptiles de Mexico. Familia de los varanideos. Naturaleza 1: 221–223.

——. 1873. Coup d'oeil sur la distribution géographique des reptiles au Mexique. Archives de Sciences Physiques et Naturelles. 46: 233–250.

——. 1875. Observations sur les moeurs de l'*Heloderma horridum*. Comptes Rendus Hebdomadaires des Séances de l'Académie des Sciences, Paris, 80: 676–679.

——. 1880. Contribution a l'histoire naturelle du Mexique. I. Notes sur une collection de reptiles et de batraciens de la partie occidentale de l'Isthme de Tehuantepec. Bulletin de la Société Zoologique de France 5: 162–190.

——. 1881–1882. Contribución a la historia natural de México. I. Notas acerca de una colección de reptiles y batracios de la parte occidental del Istmo de Tehuantepec. Naturaleza 5: 268–293.

——. 1882. Enumeración de las especies de reptiles observados en la parte meridional de la República Méxicana. Naturaleza 6: 31–45.

Surface, H. A. 1906. The serpents of Pennsylvania. Pennsylvania Department of Agriculture Monthly Bulletin 4: 114–208.

Sutcliffe, R. 1952. Notes made by Dr. Edward Hallowell. Copeia 1952(2): 113–114.

Sutherland, I. D. W. 1958. The "combat dance" of the timber rattlesnake. Herpetologica 14(1): 23–24.

Sutherland, S. K. 1995. Pressure immobilization for snakebite in southern Africa remains speculative. South African Medical Journal 85: 1039–1040.

Sutherland, S. K., and A. R. Coulter. 1981. Early management of bites by the eastern diamondback rattlesnake (*Crotalus adamanteus*): studies in monkeys (*Macaca fascicularis*). American Journal of Tropical Medicine and Hygiene 30: 497–500.

Sutherland, S. K., A. R. Coulter, and R. D. Harris. 1979. Rationalisation of first-aid measures for elapid snakebite. Lancet 1: 183–186.

Sutherland, S. K., and J. Tibballs. 2001. Australian animal toxins. The creatures, their toxins, and care of the poisoned patient, 2d ed. Oxford University Press, Melbourne.

Sutton, K. 1987. Arkansas' venomous snakes, the serious six. Arkansas Game and Fish 18(3): 13–21.

Svihla, A., and R. D. Svihla. 1933. Amphibians and reptiles of Whitman County, Washington. Copeia 1933(3): 125–128.

Swan, L. W. 1952. Some environmental conditions influencing life at high altitudes. Ecology 33(1): 109–111.

——. 1963. Ecology of the heights. Natural History (New York) 72(4): 22–29.

Swanson, P. L. 1933. The size of *Sistrurus c. catenatus* at birth. Copeia 1933(1): 37.

——. 1945. Herpetological notes from Panama. Copeia 1945(4): 210–216.

——. 1946. Effects of snake venoms on snakes. Copeia 1946(4): 242–249.

——. 1952. The reptiles of Venango County, Pennsylvania. Am. Midl. Nat. 47: 161–182.

Swaroop, S., and B. Grab. 1954. Snakebite mortality in the world. Bulletin of the World Health Organization 10: 35–76.

Swarth, H. S. 1921. The type locality of *Crotalus willardi* Meek. Copeia 1921(100): 83.

Sweet, S. S. 1985. Geographic variation, convergent crypsis, and mimicry in gopher snakes (*Pituophis melanoleucus*) and western rattlesnakes (*Crotalus viridis*). J. Herpetol. 19: 55–67.

Swift, L. W. 1933. Death of a rattlesnake from continued exposure to direct sunlight. Copeia 1933(3): 150.

Switak, K. H. 1969. First captive hatching of bushmasters, *Lachesis muta*. International Zoo Yearbook 9: 56–57.

Swofford, D. L. 1999. PAUP*. Phylogenetic analysis using parsimony (*and other methods), version 4. Sinauer, Sunderland, Mass.

Swofford, D. L., G. J. Olsen, P. J. Waddell, and D. M. Hillis. 1996. Phylogenetic inference. Pp. 407–514 in D. M. Hillis, C. Moritz, and B. K. Mable (eds.), Molecular systematics, 2d ed. Sinauer, Sunderland, Mass.

Tabor, S. P. 1985. Geographical distribution: *Sistrurus miliarius streckeri* (western pigmy rattlesnake). Herpetol. Rev. 16(4): 116.

Tada, I. di, and J. Villa. 1975. The serpentarium at Córdoba, Argentina. Herpetol. Rev. 6(3): 76–77.

Taggart, T. W. 1992. Geographic distribution: *Crotalus viridis* (western rattlesnake). Herpetol. Rev. 23(3): 91.

Taggart, T. W., B. I. Crother, and M. E. White. 2001. Palm-pitviper (*Bothriechis*) phylogeny, mtDNA, and consilience. Cladistics 17: 355–370.

Talbot, J. J. [no date]. Una nueva lista sistemática de reptiles del Paraguay. Informe Científico 2(1): 88–90.

Tallon, R. W., K. L. Koch, S. G. Barnes, and J. O. Ballard. 1981. Evenomation coagulopathy from snake bites. New England Journal of Medicine 305: 1347.

Tamiya, N. 1985. A comparison of amino acid sequences of neurotoxins and of phospholipases of some Australian elapid snakes with those of other proteroglyphous snakes. Pp. 209–219 in G. Grigg, R. Shine, and H. Ehmann (eds.), Biology of Australasian frogs and reptiles. Royal Zoological Society of New South Wales, Sydney.

Tan, N. H., and G. Ponnudurai. 1990. A comparative study of the biological activities of venoms from snakes of the genus *Agkistrodon* (moccasins and copperheads). Comp. Biochem. Physiol. B 95: 577–582.

——. 1992. The biological properties of venoms of some American coral snakes (genus *Micrurus*). Comp. Biochem. Physiol. B 101: 471–474.

Tanen, D. A., A. M. Ruha, K. A. Graeme, S. C. Curry, and M. A. Fischione. 2001. Rattlesnake envenomations: unusual case presentations. Archives of Internal Medicine 161: 474–479.

Tanner, V. M. 1927. Distributional list of the amphibians and reptiles of Utah. Copeia 1927(163): 54–58.

——. 1930. The amphibians and reptiles of Bryce Canyon National Park, Utah. Copeia 1930(2): 41–43.

Tanner, W. W. 1957. Notes on a collection of amphibians and reptiles from southern Mexico, with a description of a new *Hyla*. Great Basin Naturalist 17(1–2): 52–56.

——. 1960. *Crotalus mitchilli pyrrhus* Cope in Utah. Herpetologica 16(2): 140.

——. 1966a. A new rattlesnake from western Mexico. Herpetologica 22(4): 298–302.

——. 1966b. A systematic review of the Great Basin reptiles in the collections of Brigham Young University and the University of Utah. Great Basin Naturalist 26(3–4): 87–135.

——. 1978. Zoogeography of reptiles and amphibians in the Intermountain Region. Pp. 43–53 in Intermountain biogeography: a symposium. Great Basin Naturalist Memoirs No. 2.

——. 1985. Snakes of western Chihuahua. Great Basin Naturalist 45(4): 615–676.

——. 1986. *Crotalus lannomi*. Catalogue of American Amphibians and Reptiles 384.1.

Tanner, W. W., J. R. Dixon, and H. S. Harris Jr. 1972. A new subspecies of *Crotalus lepidus* from western Mexico. Great Basin Naturalist 32(1): 16–24.

Taub, A. M. 1963. On the longevity and fecundity of *Heloderma horridum horridum*. Herpetologica 19(2): 149.

——. 1966. Ophidian cephalic glands. Journal of Morphology 118(1966): 529–542.

——. 1967. Comparative histological studies on Duvernoy's gland of colubrid snakes. Bull. Am Mus. Nat. Hist. 138: 1–50.

Taylor, E. H. 1929. A revised checklist of the snakes of Kansas. University of Kansas Science Bulletin 19: 53–62.

——. 1938a [dated 1936]. Notes on the herpetological fauna of the Mexican state of Sonora. University of Kansas Science Bulletin 24: 475–503.

——. 1938b [dated 1936]. Notes on the herpetological fauna of the Mexican state of Sinaloa. University of Kansas Science Bulletin 24: 505–537.

——. 1940 [dated 1939]. Some Mexican serpents. University of Kansas Science Bulletin 26: 445–487.

——. 1941. Herpetological miscellany. No. II. University of Kansas Science Bulletin 27(7): 105–139.

——. 1942. "Island" faunas of the Mexican Plateau. Proceedings of the Eighth American Scientific Congress 3: 503–504.

——. 1944. Two new species of crotalid snakes from Mexico. University of Kansas Science Bulletin 30(4): 47–56.

——. 1949. A preliminary account of the herpetology of the state of San Luis Potosí, Mexico. University of Kansas Science Bulletin 33(2): 169–215.

——. 1950. Second contribution to the herpetology of San Luis Potosí. University of Kansas Science Bulletin 33(11): 441–457.

——. 1951. A brief review of the snakes of Costa Rica. University of Kansas Science Bulletin 34(1): 3–188.

——. 1952. Third contribution to the herpetology of the Mexican state of San Luis Potosí. University of Kansas Science Bulletin 34(13): 793–815.

——. 1953a. Early records of the seasnake, *Pelamis platurus*, in Latin America. Copeia 1953(2):124.

——. 1953b. Fourth contribution to the herpetology of San Luis Potosí. University of Kansas Science Bulletin 35(13): 1587–1614.

——. 1954. Further studies on the serpents of Costa Rica. University of Kansas Science Bulletin 36(11): 673–801.

Taylor, E. H., and I. W. Knobloch. 1940. Report on a herpetological collection from the Sierra Madre Mountains of Chihuahua. Proceedings of the Biological Society of Washington 53: 125–130.

Taylor, E. H., and H. M. Smith. 1939. Miscellaneous notes on Mexican snakes. University of Kansas Science Bulletin 25: 239–245.

Taylor, E. N. 2001. Diet of the Baja California rattlesnake, *Crotalus enyo* (Viperidae). Copeia 2001: 553–555.

Taylor, J. 1993. The amphibians and reptiles of New Hampshire. New Hampshire Fish and Game Department, Concord. 71 pp.

Taylor, R. T., A. Flores, G. Flores, and R. Bolaños. 1974. Geographic distribution of Viperidae, Elapidae, and Hydrophidae in Costa Rica. Rev. Biol. Trop. 21(2): 383–397.

Taylor, W. P. 1912. Field notes on amphibians, reptiles, and birds of northern Humboldt County, Nevada. University of California Publications in Zoology 7(10): 319–436.

———. 1935. Notes on *Crotalus atrox* near Tucson, Arizona, with special reference to its breeding habits. Copeia 1935(3): 154–155.

Telford, S. R., Jr. 1955. A description of the eggs of the coral snake *Micrurus f. fulvius*. Copeia 1955(3): 258.

———. 1971. Parasitic diseases of reptiles. Journal of the American Veterinary Medical Association 159: 1644–1652.

Tello V., G. 1998. Herpetofauna de la Zona Reservada de Tumbes. Pp. 81–87 in W. H. Wust (ed.), La Zona Reservada de Tumbes: biodiversidad diagnóstico socioeconómico. Proyecto Conservación de la Biodiversidad en al Zona Reservada de Tumbes. Australis, Lima, Peru.

Tenery, J. H., and R. R. Koefoot. 1955. Snake bite: a case with observations on early and late treatment. Plastic and Reconstructive Surgery 15: 483–488.

Tennant, A. 1984. The snakes of Texas. Texas Monthly Press, Austin. 561 pp.

———. 1985. A field guide to the snakes of Texas. Texas Monthly Press, Austin. 260 pp.

———. 1997. A field guide to snakes of Florida. Gulf Publishing, Houston, Texas. 257 pp.

———. 1998. A field guide to Texas snakes, 2d ed. Gulf Publishing, Houston, Texas. 291 pp.

Tennent, J. E. 1861. Sketches of the natural history of Ceylon with narratives and anecdotes illustrative of the habits and instincts of the mammalia, birds, reptiles, fishes, insects, etc. Longman Green, London. 310 pp.

Test, F. H., O. J. Sexton, and H. Heatwole. 1966. Reptiles of Rancho Grande and vicinity, Estado Aragua, Venezuela. Miscellaneous Publications of the Museum of Zoology, University of Michigan 128: 1–63.

Tevis, L., Jr. 1943. Field notes on a red rattlesnake in Lower Caifornia. Copeia 1943(4): 242–245.

———. 1944. Herpetological notes from Lower California. Copeia 1944(1): 6–18.

Thayer, F. D., Jr. 1988. Life history notes: *Crotalus atrox* (western diamondback rattlesnake). Hunting behavior. Herpetol. Rev. 19(2): 35.

Theakston, R. D. G. 1997. An objective approach to antivenom therapy and assessment of first-aid measures in snake bite. Annals of Tropical Medicine and Parasitology 91: 857–865.

Theakston, R. D. G., G. D. Laing, C. M. Fielding, A. Freire-Lascano, J. M. Touzet, F. Vallejo, R. H. Guderian, S. J. Nelson, W. Wüster, A. M. Richards, et al. 1995. Treatment of snake bites by *Bothrops* species and *Lachesis muta* in Ecuador: laboratory screening of candidate antivenoms. Trans. Roy. Soc. Trop. Med. Hyg. 89: 550–554.

Theakston, R. D. G., M. J. Lloyd-Jones, and H. A. Reid. 1977. Micro-ELISA for detecting and assaying snake venom and venom-antibody. Lancet 2: 639–641.

Theakston, R. D. G., H. A. Reid, J. W. Larrick, J. Kaplan, and J. A. Yost. 1981. Snake venom antibodies in Ecuadorian Indians. Journal of Tropical Medicine and Hygiene 84: 199–202.

Theakston, R. D. G., and D. A. Warrell. 1991. Antivenoms: a list of hyperimmune sera currently available for the treatment of envenoming by bites and stings. Toxicon 29: 1419–1470.

Thireau, M. 1991. Types and historically important specimens in the Muséum National d'Histoire Naturelle (Paris). Smithsonian Herpetological Information Service 87: 1–10.

Thirkhill, L. J., and B. L. Starrett. 1992. Geographic distribution: *Crotalus willardi willardi* (Arizona ridgenose rattlesnake). Herpetol. Rev. 23(4): 124.

Thomas, L., B. Tyburn, B. Bucher, et al. 1995. Prevention of thromboses in human patients with *Bothrops lanceolatus* envenoming in Martinique: failure of anticoagulants and efficacy of a monospecific antivenom. American Journal of Tropical Medicine and Hygiene 52: 419–426.

Thomas, L., B. Tyburn, J. Ketterlé, et al. 1998. Prognostic significance of clinical grading of patients envenomed by *Bothrops lanceolatus* in Martinique. Trans. Roy. Soc. Trop. Med. Hyg. 92: 542–545.

Thomas, L., B. Tyburn, and the Research Group on Snake Bite in Martinique. 1996. *Bothrops lanceolatus* bites in Martinique: clinical aspects and treatment. Pp. 255–265 in C. Bon and M. Goyffon (eds.), Envenomings and their treatments. Fondation Marcel-Mérieux, Lyon.

Thomas, R. G., and F. H. Pough. 1979. The effects of rattlesnake venom on the digestion of prey. Toxicon 17: 221–228.

Thompson, G. A. 1829. Narrative of an official visit to Guatemala from Mexico. London.

Thompson, J. C. 1913. The correct status of *Elaps collaris*. Notes Leyden Mus. 35: 171–175.

Thompson, J. N. 1994. The coevolutionary process. University of Chicago Press, Chicago.

———. 1997. Evaluating the dynamics of coevolution among geographically structured populations. Ecology 78: 1619–1623.

———. 1999a. The evolution of species interactions. Science 284: 2116–2118.

———. 1999b. Specific hypotheses on the geographic mosaic of coevolution. American Naturalist 153: S1–S13.

Thomsen, L. 1971. Behavior and ecology of burrowing owls on the Oakland municipal airport. Condor 73: 177–192.

Thornton, O. W., Jr., and J. R. Smith. 1993. New county records of amphibians and reptiles from west-central Texas. Herpetol. Rev. 24(1): 35–36.

Thwaites, R. G. (ed.). 1904–1905. Original journals of the Lewis and Clark Expedition. Dodd, Mead, New York.

Tiebout, H. M., III. 1997. Caudal luring by a temperature colubrid snake, *Elaphe obsoleta*, and its implications for the evolution of the rattle among rattlesnakes. J. Herpetol. 31: 290–292.

Tiedemann, F., and M. Haupl. 1980. Typenkatalog der herpetologischen Sammlung. Part II: Reptilia. Kataloge der Wissenschaftlichen Sammlung des Naturhistorischen Museums in Wien 4 (Vertebrata 2): 1–80.

Timmerman, W. W. 1995. Home range, habitat use, and behavior of the eastern diamondback rattlesnake (*Crotalus adamanteus*) on the Ordway. Bulletin of the Florida Museum of Natural History 38(1–9): 127–158.

Timmerman, W. W., and M. P. Hayes. 1981. The reptiles and amphibians of Monteverde: an annotated check list to the herpetofauna of Monteverde, Costa Rica. Pensión Quetzal, Monteverde. 32 pp.

Tinkham, E. R. 1971a. The biology of the Gila monster. Pp. 387–413 in W. Bucherl and E. E. Buckley (eds.), Venomous animals and their venoms, vol. 2. Venomous vertebrates. Academic Press, New York.

———. 1971b. The venom of the Gila monster. Pp. 415–422 in W. Bucherl and E. E. Buckley (eds.), Venomous animals and their venoms, vol. 2. Venomous vertebrates. Academic Press, New York.

Tinkle, D. W. 1959. Observations of reptiles and amphibians in a Louisiana swamp. Am. Midl. Nat. 62: 189–205.

———. 1962. Reproductive potential and cycles in female *Crotalus atrox* from northwestern Texas. Copeia 1962(2): 306–313.

Tinoco-V., R. A. 1978. Las serpientes de Colombia: ciencia, mitos y leyendas. Ediciones Editorial Mejoras, Barranquilla, Colombia. 105 pp.

Tipton, R. 2004. Snakes of the Americas: lexicon. Krieger, Melbourne, Florida.

Tiranti, S. I., and L. J. Avila. 1997. Reptiles of La Pampa Province, Argentina: an annotated checklist. Bull. Maryland Herpetol. Soc. 33(3): 97–117.

Tobey, F. J. 1985. Virginia's amphibians and reptiles: a distributional survey. Privately printed, Virginia Herpetological Society, Purcellville. 114 pp.

Tobiasz, E. C. 1941. Birth of two broods of massasaugas. Copeia 1941(4): 269.

Tomer, J. S., and M. J. Brodhead (eds.). 1992. A naturalist in Indian Territory: the journals of S. W. Woodhouse, 1849–50. University of Oklahoma Press, Norman. 304 pp.

Torres R., J. R., M. A. Torres A., and M. A. Arroyo-Parejo. 1995. Coagulation disorders in bushmaster envenomation [letter]. Lancet 346: 449–450.

Touzet, J. M. 1983. Los ofidios de la región lojana según las relaciones de 1808. Cultura Rev Banco Central (Ecuador) 5(15): 481–488.

——. 1986. Mordeduras de ofidios venenosos en la comunidad de los indigenas Siona-Secoya de San Pablo de Kantesyia y datos sobre la fauna de reptiles y anfibios locales. Publicaciones Museo Ecuatoriano de Ciencias Naturales 5: 163–190.

Tovar-Tovar, H., and F. Mendoza-Quijano. 2001. Geographic distribution: *Agkistrodon taylori* (Taylor's cantil). Herpetol. Rev. 32(4): 276–277.

Townsend, C. H. T. 1916. Voyage of the *Albatross* to the Gulf of California in 1911. Bull. Am. Mus. Nat. Hist. 35(24): 399–476.

Transeau, E. N. 1948. General ranges of the principal vegetation types of North America [map]. Adapted version printed in H. J. Oosting, The study of plant communities. W. H. Freeman, San Francisco.

Trape, J. F., G. Pison, E. Guyavarch, and Y. Mane. 2001. High mortality from snakebite in southeastern Senegal. Trans. Roy. Soc. Trop. Med. Hyg. 95: 420–423.

Trapido, H. 1937. A guide to the snakes of New Jersey. Newark Museum, Newark. 60 pp.

——. 1939. Parturition in the timber rattlesnake, *Crotalus horridus horridus* Linné. Copeia 1939(4): 230.

——. 1941. The timber rattlesnake in Vermont. New England Naturalist 10: 26–27.

Trauth, S. E. 1986. Geographic distribution: *Crotalus atrox* (western diamondback rattlesnake). Herpetol. Rev. 17(3): 67.

——. 1987. Geographic distribution: *Sistrurus miliarius streckeri* (western pygmy rattlesnake). Herpetol. Rev. 18(1): 21.

——. 1988. Geographic distribution: *Sistrurus miliarius streckeri* (western pigmy rattlesnake). Herpetol. Rev. 19(1): 21.

Trauth, S. E., and B. G. Cochran. 1992. In search of western diamondback rattlesnakes (*Crotalus atrox*) in Arkansas. Bull. Chicago Herpetol. Soc. 27(4): 89–94.

Trauth, S. E., R. L. Cox, W. E. Meshaka Jr., B. P. Butterfield, and A. Holt. 1994. Female reproductive traits in selected Arkansas snakes. Proceedings of the Arkansas Academy of Science 48: 196–209.

Trejos, J. F. 1937. Geografía de Costa Rica, física, política, y económica. Imprenta Universal, San José. 346 pp.

Tremper, R. L. 1982. Captive propagation and husbandry of *Crotalus catalinensis* at the Fresno Zoo. Annual Report of the Symposium on Captive Propagation and Husbandry 5: 70–75.

Triplehorn, C. A. 1955. Notes on the young of some North American reptiles. Copeia 1955(3): 248–249.

Triplett, J. R. 1991. Geographic distribution: *Agkistrodon piscivorus leucostoma* (western cottonmouth). Herpetol. Rev. 22(4): 135.

Troost, G. 1836. On a new genus of serpents, and two new species of the genus *Heterodon*, inhabiting Tennessee. Annals of the Lyceum of Natural History, New York, 3: 174–190.

Troschel, F. H. 1853. Über *Heloderma horridum* Wiegm. Archiv für Naturgeschichte 19(1): 294–315.

——. 1855. Bericht über die Leistungen in der Herpetologie wahrend des Jahres 1854. Archiv für Naturgeschichte 21: 411–425.

——. 1860. Bericht über die Leistungen in der Herpetologie wahrend des Jahres 1859. Archiv für Naturgeschichte 26(2): 265–278.

——. 1866. Bericht über die Leistungen in der Herpetologie wahrend des Jahres 1865. Archiv für Naturgeschichte 32(2): 180–192.

——. 1874. Bericht über die Leistungen in der Herpetologie wahrend des Jahres 1873. Archiv für Naturgeschichte 40(2): 146–170.

Trowbridge, A. H. 1937. Ecological observations on amphibians and reptiles collected in southeastern Oklahoma during the summer of 1934. Am. Midl. Nat. 18: 285–303.

True, F. W. 1883. Bite of North American coral snakes. American Naturalist 17: 26–31.

Trutnau, L. 1970. Die Skorpion-Krustenechse *Heloderma horridum* (Wiegmann). Aquarien Terrarien 17(7): 228–231.

Tryon, B. W. 1977. Reproduction in captive Lower California rattlesnakes, *Crotalus enyo enyo* (Cope). Herpetol. Rev. 8(2): 34–36.

——. 1978. Reproduction in a pair of captive Arizona ridge-nosed rattlesnakes, *Crotalus willardi willardi* (Reptilia, Serpentes, Crotalidae). Bull. Maryland Herpetol. Soc. 14: 83–88.

——. 1985a. *Bothrops asper* (Terciopelo). Caudal luring. Herpetol. Rev. 16: 28.

——. 1985b. *Bothrops asper* (Terciopelo). Reproduction. Herpetol. Rev. 16: 28.

——. 1986. The island, the rattlesnake, and the species survival plan. Bulletin of the British Herpetological Society 16: 20–24.

Tryon, B. W., and H. K. McCrystal. 1982. Natural history notes: *Micrurus fulvius tenere* (Texas coral snake). Reproduction. Herpetol. Rev. 13(2): 47–48.

Tryon, B. W., and C. W. Radcliffe. 1977. Reproduction in captive Lower California rattlesnakes, *Crotalus enyo enyo* (Cope). Herpetol. Rev. 8(2): 34–36.

Tschudi, J. J. von. 1845. Reptilium conspectum quae in Republica Peruana reperiuntur et pleraque observata vel collecta sunt in itinere a Dr. J. J. de Tschudi. Archiv für Naturgeschichte 11(1): 150–170.

——. 1980. Viagem às Províncias do Rio de Janeiro e São Paulo (1857–1859). Universidade de São Paulo, São Paulo. 218 pp.

Tu, A. T. 1976. Investigation of the sea snake, *Pelamis platurus* (Reptilia, Serpentes, Hydrophiidae), on the Pacific coast of Costa Rica, Central America. J. Herpetol. 10: 13–18.

——. 1977. Venoms: chemistry and molecular biology. Wiley, New York. 560 pp.

Tu, A. T., and B. L. Adams. 1968. Phylogenetic relationships among venomous snakes of the genus *Agkistrodon* from Asia and the North American continent. Nature 217: 760–762.

Turk, F. A. 1947. Studies of acari. IV. A review of the lung mites of snakes. Parasitology 38: 17–26.

Turner, F. B. 1955. Reptiles and amphibians of Yellowstone National Park. Yellowstone Library and Museum Association, Yellowstone Park, Wyoming. 40 pp.

Turner, J. R. G. 1967. On supergenes. I. The evolution of supergenes. American Naturalist 101: 195–221.

——. 1977. Butterfly mimicry: the genetical evolution of an adaptation. Evolutionary Biology 10: 163–206.

——. 1984. The palatability spectrum and its consequences. Pp. 141–161 in R. I. Vane-Wright and P. R. Ackery (eds.), The biology of butterflies. Academic Press, London.

——. 1985. Fisher's evolutionary faith and the challenge of mimicry. Oxf. Surv. Evol. Biol. 2: 159–196.

Turnipseed, G. 1993. Geographic distribution: *Crotalus atrox* (western diamondback rattlesnake). Herpetol. Rev. 24(4): 155.

Tyler, M. J., T. Burton, and A. M. Bauer. 2001. Parotoid or parotid: on the nomenclature of an amphibian skin gland. Herp. Rev. 32(2): 79–81.

Tyler, R. E. 1849. Notes on the serpents of St. Lucia. Proc. Zool. Soc. London 1849: 100–104.

Uddman, R., P. J. Goadsby, I. Jansen-Olesen, and L. Edvinsson. 1999. Helospectin-like peptides: immunochemical localization and effects on isolated cerebral arteries and on local cerebral blood flow in the cat. Journal of Cerebral Blood Flow and Metabolism 19: 61–67.

Uhler, F. M., C. Cottam, and T. E. Clarke. 1939. Food of snakes of the George Washington National Forest, Virginia. Pp. 605–622 in Transactions of the Fourth North American Wildlife Conference.

Ulber, T. M. 1995–1997. Catalogue of valid species and synonyms, vol. 3: Elapinae. Herprint International, Bredell, South Africa. 274 pp.

Underwood, G. 1962. Reptiles of the eastern Caribbean. Dept. of Extra-mural Stud., Univ. West Indies, Port-of-Spain, Caribbean Affairs, n.s., 1: 1–192.

——. 1967. A contribution to the classification of snakes. British Museum of Natural History, London.

——. 1993. A new snake from St. Lucia, West Indies. Bulletin of the Natural History Museum, Zoology Ser. 59(1): 1–9.

——. 1995. A tale of old serpents. Saint Lucia National Trust, Castries, Saint Lucia, West Indies. 29 pp.

Underwood, G., and E. Kochva. 1993. On the affinities of the burrowing asps Atractaspis (Serpentes: Atractaspidae). Zoological Journal of the Linnean Society 107: 3–64.

UNESCO. 1980. Vegetation map of South America. UNESCO, Paris.

United States Fish and Wildlife Service. 1978. Listing of the New Mexican ridge-nosed rattlesnake as a threatened species with critical habitat. Federal Register 43: 34476–34480.

Uribe-Peña, Z., A. Ramírez-Bautista, and G. Casas-Andreu. 1999. Anfibios y reptiles de las Serranías del Distrito Federal, México. Institudo de Biología, Universidad Nacional Autónoma de México, Cuadernos 32: 1–119.

Uzzell, T. M., Jr., and P. Starrett. 1958. Snakes from El Salvador. Copeia 1958(4): 339–342.

Valdujo, P. H., and C. Nogueira. 2000. Natural history notes: Bothrops neuwiedi pauloensis (jararaca robo-de-osso). Predation. Herpetol. Rev. 31(1): 45.

Valdujo, P. H., C. Nogueira, and M. Martins. 2002. Ecology of Bothrops neuwiedi pauloensis (Serpentes: Viperidae: Crotalinae) in the Brazilian Cerrado. J. Herpetol. 36(2): 169–176.

Vallarino, O., and P. J. Weldon. 1996. Reproduction in the yellow-bellied sea snake (Pelamis platurus) from Panama: field and laboratory observations. Zoo Biology 15: 309–314.

Valls-Moraes, F., and T. de Lema. 1997. Envenomation by Phalotris trilineatus in Rio Grande do Sul State, Brazil: a case report. Journal of Venomous Animals and Toxins 3(1): 255.

Van Bourgondien, T. M., and R. C. Bothner. 1969. A comparative study of the arterial systems of some New World Crotalinae (Reptilia: Ophidia). Am. Mid. Nat. 81: 107–147.

Vance, T. 1981. Geographic distribution: Agkistrodon contortrix contortrix (southern copperhead). Herpetol. Rev. 12(1): 13.

Van den Brule, B. 1982. Los ofidios veneosos de Guatemala. Centro de Estudios Conservacionistas, Serie Documentos Ocasionales No. 2. 73 pp.

Van Denburgh, J. 1894. Notes on Crotalus mitchelli and "Crotalus pyrrhus." Proc. California Acad. Sci., 2d ser., 4: 450–455.

——. 1895a. A review of the herpetology of Lower California. Part I. Reptiles. Proc. California Acad. Sci., 2d ser., 5: 77–163.

——. 1895b. Description of a new rattlesnake (Crotalus pricei) from Arizona. Proc. California Acad. Sci., 2d ser., 5: 856–857.

——. 1896. Additional notes on the herpetology of Lower California. Proc. California Acad. Sci., 2d ser., 5: 1004–1008.

——. 1897. The reptiles of the Pacific coast and Great Basin. An account of the species known to inhabit California, and Oregon, Washington, Idaho, and Nevada. Occasional Papers of the California Academy of Sciences 5: 1–236.

——. 1898. Some experiments with the saliva of the Gila monster (Heloderma suspectum). American Philosophical Society Transactions, n.s., 19: 201–220.

——. 1905. The reptiles and amphibians of the islands of the Pacific Coast of North America from the Farallons to Cape San Lucas and the Revilla Gigedos. Proc. California Acad. Sci., 3d ser., 4(1): 1–40.

——. 1912. Notes on a collection of reptiles from southern California and Arizona. Proceedings of the California Academy of Science, 4th ser., 3: 147–154.

——. 1920. Description of a new species of rattlesnake (Crotalus lucasensis) from Lower California. Proc. California Acad. Sci., 4th ser., 10(2): 29–30.

——. 1922a. The reptiles of western North America. Part I. Lizards. Occasional Papers of the California Academy of Sciences 10: 1–611.

——. 1922b. The reptiles of western North America. Part II. Snakes and turtles. Occasional Papers of the California Academy of Sciences 10: 617–1028.

——. 1924. Notes on the herpetology of New Mexico, with a list of species known from that state. Proc. California Acad. Sci., 4th ser., 8(12): 189–230.

Van Denburgh, J., and J. R. Slevin. 1914. Reptiles and amphibians of the islands of the west coast of North America. Proc. California Acad. Sci., 4th ser., 4(5): 129–152.

——. 1915. A list of the amphibians and reptiles of Utah, with notes on the species in the collection of the Academy. Proc. California Acad. Sci., 4th ser., 5(4): 99–110.

——. 1921a. A list of the amphibians and reptiles of Nevada, with notes on the species in the collection of the Academy. Proc. California Acad. Sci., 4th ser., 11(1): 27–38.

——. 1921b. A list of amphibians and reptiles of the peninsula of Lower California, with notes on the species in the collection of the Academy. Proc. California Acad. Sci., 4th ser., 11(4): 49–72.

——. 1921c. Preliminary diagnoses of more new species of reptiles from islands in the Gulf of California, Mexico. Proc. California Acad. Sci., 4th ser., 11(17): 395–398.

Van Devender, R. W. 1980. Preliminary checklist of the herpetofauna of Monteverde, Puntarenas Province, Costa Rica and vicinity. Brenesia 17: 319–326.

Van Devender, T. R. 1977. Observations on the Argentine iguanid lizard Leiosaurus bellii Duméril and Bibron (Reptilia, Lacertilia, Iguanidae). J. Herpetol. 11(2): 238–241.

Van Devender, T. R., and R. Conant. 1990. Pleistocene forests and copperheads in the eastern United States, and the historical biogeography of New World Agkistrodon. Pp. 601–614 in H. K. Gloyd and R. Conant (eds.), Snakes of the Agkistrodon complex: a monographic review. Contributions to Herpetology 6. Society for the Study of Amphibians and Reptiles, Ithaca, N.Y. 614 pp.

Van Devender, T. R., and C. H. Lowe Jr. 1977. Amphibians and reptiles of Yepómera, Chihuahua, Mexico. J. Herpetol. 11(1): 41–50.

Vane-Wright, R. I. 1976. A unified classification of mimetic resemblances. Biological Journal of the Linnean Society 8: 25–56.

Van Hyning, O. C. 1931. Reproduction of some Florida snakes. Copeia 1931(2): 59–60.

——. 1933. Batrachia and reptilia of Alachua County, Florida. Copeia 1933(1): 3–7.

Van Mierop, L. H. S. 1976a. Poisonous snakebite: a review—snakes and their venom. Journal of the Florida Medical Association 63: 191–200.

——. 1976b. Poisonous snakebite: a review. 2. Symptomatology and treatment. Journal of the Florida Medical Association 63: 201–210.

Van Mierop, L. H., and C. S. Kitchens. 1980. Defibrination syndrome following bites by the eastern diamondback rattlesnake. Journal of the Florida Medical Association 67: 21–27.

Vanzolini, P. E. 1946. Regressão do peso sôbre o comprimento em Bothrops jararaca e sua variação sexual e estacional. Papéis Avulsos do Departamento de Zoologia, São Paulo 7(25): 271–292.

——. 1947. Notas sôbre um deródimo de Crotalus durissus (Laur.). Papéis Avulsos do Departamento de Zoologia, São Paulo 8: 273–283.

——. 1948. Notas sôbre os ofídios e lagartos da Cachoeira de Emas, no município de Pirassununga, estado de São Paulo. Revista Brasileira de Biologia 8(3): 377–400.

——. 1953. On the type locality of some Brazilian reptiles and amphibians collected by H. H. Smith and described by E. D. Cope. Copeia 1953(2): 124–125.

——. 1981a. A quasi-historical approach to the natural history of the differentiation of reptiles in tropical geographic isolates. Papéis Avulsos do Departamento de Zoologia, São Paulo 34(19): 189–204.

——. 1981b. Introduction. Pp. ix–xxix in J. B. von Spix and J. G. Wagler, Herpetology of Brazil, 1824–1825. Reprint, Society for the Study of Amphibians and Reptiles, [Athens, Ohio].

———. 1985. *Micrurus averyi* Schmidt, 1939, in central Amazonia (Serpentes, Elapidae). Papéis Avulsos do Departamento de Zoologia, São Paulo 36(8): 77–85.

———. 1986a. Levantamento herpetológico da área estado de Rondônia sob a influéncia da Rondonia BR 363. Progr. Polonoroeste, Relat. de Pesq. 1: 1–50.

———. 1986b. Addenda and corrigenda to the catalogue of Neotropical Squamata. Smithsonian Herpetological Information Service 70: 1–25.

———. 1991. A biometrical note on *Bothrops moojeni* Hoge, 1966 (Serpentes, Viperidae). Anais da Academia Brasileira de Ciências 63(4): 389–401.

Vanzolini, P. E., and M. E. V. Calleffo. 2002a. On some aspects of the reproductive biology of Brasilian *Crotalus* (Serpentes, Viperidae). Biologia Geral e Experimental 3(1): 1–35.

———. 2002b. A taxonomic bibliography of the South American snakes of the *Crotalus durissus* complex (Serpentes, Viperidae). Anais da Academia Brasileira de Ciências 74(1): 37–83.

Vanzolini, P. E., and J. H. Ferreira Brandão. 1946 [dated 1944–1945]. Notas sôbre algumas diferencas sexuais na folidose de *Bothrops alternata* D. & B., 1854, e sua variação geográfica. Mem. Inst. Butantan 18: 251–258.

Vanzolini, P. E., and W. R. Heyer. 1985. The American herpetofauna and the interchange. Pp. 475–487 in F. G. Stehli and S. D. Webb (eds.), The great American biotic interchange. Plenum Press, New York.

Vanzolini, P. E., A. M. M. Ramos-Costa, and L. J. Vitt. 1980. Repteis das Caatingas. Anais da Academia Brasileira de Ciências, Rio de Janeiro. 161 pp.

Vargas-Baldares, M. 1978. Renal lesions in snakebite in Costa Rica. P. 497 in P. Rosenberg (ed.), Toxins: animal, plant, and microbial. Pergamon Press, Oxford.

Vaz, Z. 1938. Nova especie do genero *Ophidascaris* parasita da cascavel (*Crotalus terrificus*). Livro Jubilar Prof. Lauro Travassos, pp. 495–500.

Vaz-Ferreira, R., F. Achaval, and M. Meneghel. 1980. Relaciones entre progenitores y cria en reptiles de la Rep. O. del Uruguay. Res. Jorn. C. Nat. (Montevideo), 1: 121–122.

Vaz-Ferreira, R., L. C. de Zolesi, and F. Achaval. 1970. Oviposición y desarrollo de ofidios y lacertilios en hormigueros de *Acromyrmex*. Physis 29(79): 431–459.

———. 1973. Oviposición y desarrollo de ofidios y lacertilios en hormigueros de *Acromyrmex*. II. Trabajos del V Congreso Latinoamericano de Zoología, Montevideo, 18–23 October 1971 1: 232–234.

Vaz-Ferreira, R., and B. Sierra de Soriano. 1960. Notas sobre reptiles del Uruguay. Rev. Fac. Human. Ci. (Montevideo) 18: 1–55.

Vázquez de Kartzow, A. R. 1995. Mordedura de serpientes venenosas. Ediciones Rosaristas, Bogotá, Colombia. 114 pp.

Vázquez-Días, J., and G. E. Quintero-Díaz. 1997. Anfibios y reptiles de Aguascalientes. Centro de Investigaciones y Estudios Multidisciplinarios de Aguascalientes, Gobierno del Estado de Aguascalientes, CIEMA. 145 pp.

Velasco, A. L. 1890a. Geografía y estadística del estado de Guanajuato. Geografía y estadística de la República Mexicana, vol. 5. Secretaria de Fomento, México, D.F. 300 pp.

———. 1890b. Geografía y estadística del estado de Morelos. Geografía y estadística de la República Mexicana, vol. 7. Secretaria de Fomento, México, D.F. 140 pp.

———. 1892. Geografía y estadística del estado de Tamaulipas. Geografía y estadística de la República Mexicana, vol. 12. Secretaria de Fomento, México, D.F. 240 pp.

———. 1895. Geografía y estadística del estado de Campeche. Geografía y estadística de la República Mexicana, vol. 16. Secretaria de Fomento, México, D.F. 140 pp.

Velasco-Torres, J. J. 1970. Contribución al conocimiento de la herpetología del norte de Nuevo León, México. Ph.D. dissertation, Universidad de Nuevo León, Monterrey. 69 pp.

Vellard, J. A. 1938a. Une *Lachesis* peu connue du nord-est du Brésil, *L. erythromelas*: étude de son venin. Comptes Rendus de la Société Biologique 127: 38.

———. 1938b. Variations géographiques du venin de *Crotalus terrificus*. Travaux de la Station Zoologique de Wimereux 8: 699–711.

———. 1941. Serpents venimeux du Venezuela. Annales des Sciences Naturelles 3: 193–225.

———. 1943. Diferenciación biológica de la cascabel sudamericana. Acta Zoológica Lilloana 1(1): 55–88.

———. 1946. Morfología del hemipenis y evolución de los ofidios. Acta Zoológica Lilloana 3: 263–288.

———. 1948. El veneno de *Lachesis muta* (L.). Publicaciones del Museu de Historia Natural "Javier Prado," Serie A, Zoología, 1(1): 1–55.

———. 1955. Propriétés venimeuses de "*Tachymenis peruviana*" Wiegmann. Folia Biológica Andina., Serie 2, Zoología (Lima), 1: 1–14.

Velloso Calleffo, M. E. 1997. Geographic distribution: *Micrurus averyi* (coral snake). Herpetol. Rev. 28(4): 210.

Vêncio, D., and D. A. de Oliveira. 1980. Ofidismo no estado de Goiás. 1. Epidemiologia. Revista Goiana de Medicina 26(3–4): 125–130.

Verhoeven, K. 1994. Snakes of Rara Avis, Costa Rica. Privately published. 19 pp.

Verrill, A. E. 1870. The biter bitten. American Naturalist 3: 158–159.

Vest, D. K. 1981a. Envenomation following the bite of a wandering garter snake (*Thamnophis elegans vagrans*). Clinical Toxicology 18(5): 573–579.

———. 1981b. The toxic secretion of the wandering garter snake, *Thamnophis elegans vagrans*. Toxicon 19: 831–839.

———. 1988. Some effects and properties of Duvernoy's gland secretions from *Hypsiglena torquata texana* (Texas night snake). Toxicon 26: 417–419.

Vetencourt-Finol., H. 1960 [dated 1959–1960]. Ofidios venenosos de Venezuela. Revista de Medicina Veterinaria y Parasitolgía, Maracay, 18(1–8): 161–192.

Vial, J. L., T. J. Berger, and W. T. McWilliams Jr. 1977. Quantitative demography of copperheads, *Agkistrodon contortrix* (Serpentes, Viperidae). Researches on Population Ecology 18(2): 223–234.

Vial, J. L., and J. M. Jimenez-Porras. 1967. The ecogeography of the bushmaster, *Lachesis muta*, in Central America. Am. Midl. Nat. 78: 182–187.

Vidal, N., S. G. Kindl, A. Wong, and S. B. Hedges. 2000. Phylogenetic relationships of Xenodontine snakes inferred from 12S and 16S ribosomal RNA sequences. Molecular Phylogenetics and Evolution 14: 389–402.

Vidal, N., and G. Lecointre. 1998. Weighting and congruence: a case study based on three mitochondrial genes in pitvipers. Molecular Phylogenetics and Evolution 9(3): 366–374.

Vidal, N., G. Lecointre, J. C. Vié, and J. P. Gasc. 1997. Molecular systematics of pitvipers: paraphyly of the *Bothrops* complex. Comptes Rendus de l'Académie des Sciences, Paris, Sciences de la vie 320: 95–101.

———. 1999. What can mitochondrial sequences tell us about intergeneric relationships of pitvipers? Kaupia 8: 107–112.

Villa, J. 1962. Las serpientes venenosas de Nicaragua. Editorial Novedades, Managua. 93 pp.

———. 1969. Notes on *Conophis nevermanni*, an addition to the Nicaraguan herpetofauna. J. Herpetol. 3(3–4): 169–171.

———. 1971. Notes on some Nicaraguan reptiles. J. Herpetol. 5(1–2): 45–48.

———. 1972a. Un coral (*Micrurus*) blanco y negro de Costa Rica. Brenesia 1: 10–13.

———. 1972b. Snakes of the Corn Islands, Caribbean Nicaragua. Brenesia 1: 14–18.

———. 1981. Three albino snakes from Nicaragua: an update. Herpetol. Rev. 12(3): 81.

———. 1983. Nicaraguan fishes, amphibians, and reptiles: checklist and bibliography. Universidad Centroamericana, Managua. 53 pp.

———. 1984. The venomous snakes of Nicaragua: a synopsis. Milwaukee Public Museum, Contributions in Biology and Geology 59: 1–41.

Villa, J., and A. Rivas. 1972 [dated 1971]. Tres serpientes albinas de Nicaragua. Rev. Biol. Trop. 19: 159–163.

Villa, J., L. D. Wilson, and J. D. Johnson. 1988. Middle American herpetology: a bibliographic checklist. University of Missouri Press, Columbia. 132 pp.

Villanueva Forero, M. J. 2002. Evaluación de 170 casos de pacientos hospitalizados por ofidismo en el Hospital de Apoyo de La Merced entre Enero de 1998 y Diciembre del 2000. Tesis Médico Cirujano, Universidad Peruana Cayetano Heredia, Lima, Peru.

Vincent, J. W. 1982. Color pattern variation in *Crotalus lepidus lepidus* (Viperidae) in southwestern Texas (USA). Southwest. Nat. 27(3): 263–272.

Viosca, P. 1933. Louisiana out-of-doors, a handbook and guide. Self-published, New Orleans. 187 pp.

Víquez, C. 1933. Animales venenosas de Costa Rica. Imprenta Nacional, San José, Costa Rica. 305 pp.

——. 1940. Nuestros animales venenosos. Imprenta Nacional, San José, Costa Rica. 312 pp.

Visinoni, A. 1995. Contribuciones para el conocimiento de la herpetofauna boliviana: *Lachesis muta muta* (Linnaeus, 1766) (Serpentes: Viperidae) en Bolivia. Ecologia en Bolivia 24: 103–112.

Visser, J. 1967. Color varieties, brood size, and food of South African *Pelamis platurus* (Ophidia: Hydrophiidae). Copeia 1967(1): 219.

Vital Brazil, O. 1980. Venenos ofidicos neurotóxicos. Revista da Associação Medica Brasileira 26(6): 212–218.

Vital Brazil, O., and R. J. Vieira. 1990. Neostigmine in the treatment of snake accidents caused by *Micrurus frontalis*: report of two cases. Revista do Instituto de Medicina Tropical de São Paulo 38(1): 61–67.

Vitt, L. J. 1974. Body temperatures of high latitude reptiles. Copeia 1974(1): 255–256.

——. 1992. Lizard mimics millipede. National Geographic Research and Exploration 8: 76–95.

——. 2001. Lizards in the land of El Dorado. Fauna, March–April, pp. 44–55.

Vitt, L. J., and A. C. Hulse. 1973. Observations of feeding habits and tail display of the Sonoran coral snake, *Micruroides euryxanthus*. Herpetologica 29(4): 302–304.

Vitt, L. J., and R. D. Ohmart. 1978. Herpetofauna of the lower Colorado River: Davis Dam to the Mexican border. Proceedings of the Western Foundation of Vertebrate Zoology 2(2): 35–72.

Vitt, L. J., and L. D. Vangilder. 1983. Ecology of snake communities in northeastern Brazil. Amphibia-Reptilia 4: 273–296.

Voge, M. 1953. New host records for *Mesocestoides* (Cestoda: Cyclophyllidea) in California. Am. Midl. Nat. 49: 249–251.

Vogt, R. C. 1981. Natural history of amphibians and reptiles in Wisconsin. Milwaukee Public Museum, Milwaukee. 205 pp.

Vogt, R. C., J. L. Villarreal Benítez, and G. Pérez-Higareda. 1997. Lista anotada de anfibios y reptiles. Pp. 507–532 in E. González Soriano, R. Dirzo, and R. C. Vogt (eds.), Historia natural de Los Tuxtlas. Universidad Nacional Autónoma de México, México, D.F.

Vorhies, C. T. 1929. Feeding of *Micrurus euryxanthus*, the Sonoran coral snake. Bull. Antivenin Inst. Am. 2(4): 98.

——. 1948. Food items of rattlesnakes. Copeia 1948(4): 302–303.

Voris, H. K. 1972. The role of sea snakes (Hydrophiidae) in the trophic structure of coastal ocean communities. Journal of the Marine Biological Association of India 14: 429–442.

——. 1975. Dermal scale–vertebra relationships in sea snakes (Hydrophiidae). Copeia 1975(4): 746–755.

——. 1983. *Pelamis platurus* (culebra del mar, pelagic sea snake). Pp. 411–412 in D. H. Janzen (ed.), Costa Rican natural history, University of Chicago Press, Chicago.

Voris, H. K., and H. H. Voris. 1983. Feeding stategies in marine snakes: an analysis of evolutionary, morphological, behavioral, and ecological relationships. American Zoologist 23: 411–425.

Wacha, R. S., and J. L. Christiansen. 1982a. Development of *Caryospora bigenica*, new species (Apicomplexa, Eimeriidae) in rattlesnakes and laboratory mice. Journal of Protozoology 29(2): 272–278.

——. 1982b. Life cycle pattern of *Caryospora* sp. (Coccidia). Journal of Protozoology 29(2): 289.

Wagler, J. G. 1824. Serpentum Brasiliensium species novae. . . . In J. de Spix (ed.), Animalia nova sive species novae. Monaco. 75 pp.

——. 1830. Natürliches System der Amphibien, mit vorangehender Classification der Säugthiere und Vögel. Ein Beitrag zur vergleichenden Zoologie. J. G. Cotta, München. 354 pp.

Wagner, E., R. Smith, and F. Slavens. 1976. Breeding the Gila monster *Heloderma suspectum* in captivity. International Zoo Yearbook 16: 74–78.

Wagner, V. 1985. Crotoxin: a review of the physiological effects of South American rattlesnake venom. Journal of the Northen Ohio Association of Herpetologists 11(1): 9–28.

Wainberg, R., C. Camp, and J. B. Jensen. 2000. Geographic distribution: *Sistrurus miliarius miliarius* (Carolina pigmy rattlesnake). Herpetol. Rev. 31(1): 57.

Walbaum, J. J. 1792. Petri Artedi Sueci Genera piscium. In quibus systema totum ichthyologiae proponitur cum classibus, ordinibus, generum characteribus, specierum differentiis, observationibus plurimis. Redactis speciebus 242 ad genera 52. Ichthyologiae, pars iii. Artedi Piscium, 1–723.

Waldbauer, G. P. 1971. Phenological relationships of some aculeate Hymenoptera, their dipteran mimics, and insectivorous birds. Evolution 25: 371–382.

——. 1988a. Aposematism and Batesian mimicry. Evolutionary Biology 22: 227–259.

——. 1988b. Asynchrony between Batesian mimics and their models. American Naturalist 131: S103–S121.

Walker, C. F. 1931. Notes on reptiles in the collection of the Ohio State Museum. Copeia 1931(1): 9–13.

Walker, E. P. 1938. Eyes that shine at night. Ann. Rep. Smithsonian Institution 1938: 349–361.

Wall, F. 1921. Snakes of Ceylon. H. R. Cottle, Government Printer, Colombo, Ceylon. 581 pp.

Wallace, A. R. 1867. Mimicry and other protective resemblances among animals. Westminster and Foreign Quarterly Review, n.s., 32: 1–43.

——. 1870. Natural selection and tropical nature: essays on descriptive and theoretical biology. Macmillan, London.

Wallace, R. L., and L. V. Diller. 1990. Feeding ecology of the rattlesnake *Crotalus viridis oreganus* in northern Idaho. J. Herpetol. 24(3): 246–253.

Wallach, V., and R. Günther. 1998. Visceral anatomy of the Malaysian snake genus *Xenophidion*, including a cladistic analysis and allocation to a new family (Serpentes: Xenophidiidae). Amphibia-Reptilia 19: 385–404.

Walley, H. D. 1963. The rattlesnake, *Crotalus horridus horridus*, in north-central Illinois. Herpetologica 19(3): 216.

——. 2002. An incident of envenomation from *Heterodon nasicus*. Bull. Chicago Herpetol. Soc. 37: 31.

Walter, F. G., M. C. Fernandez, and L. M. Haddad. 1998. North American venomous snakebite. Pp. 333–352 in L. M. Haddad, M. W. Shannon, and J. F. Winchester (eds.), Clinical management of poisoning and drug overdose, 3d ed. Saunders, Philadelphia.

Walters, A. C., and W. Card. 1996. Natural history notes: *Agkistrodon piscivorus conanti* (Florida cottonmouth). Prey. Herpetol. Rev. 27(4): 203.

Walters, A. C., D. T. Roberts, and C. V. Covell Jr. 1996. Natural history notes: *Agkistrodon contortrix contortrix* (southern copperhead). Prey. Herpetol. Rev. 27(4): 202.

Wang, E. 2002. Natural history notes: *Crotalus durissus* (Neotropical rattlesnake). Predation. Herpetol. Rev. 33(2): 138–139.

Ward, R. 1983. Geographic distribution: *Sistrurus catenatus*. Herpetol. Rev. 14(1): 28.

Warrell, D. A. 1986. Tropical snake bite: clinical studies in south-east Asia. Pp. 25–45 in J. B. Harris (ed.), Natural toxins: animal, plant, and microbial. Clarendon Press, Oxford.

——. 1987. Geographical and intraspecies variation in the clinical manifestations of envenoming by snakes. Symposium Zool. Soc. London 70: 189–203.

——. 1994. Seasnake bites in the Asia-Pacific Region. Pp. 1–36 in P. Gopalakrishnakone (ed.), Seasnake toxinology. Singapore University Press, Singapore.

——. 1996. Venoms, toxins, and poisons of animals and plants. Pp. 1124–1151 in D. J. Weatherall, J. G. G. Ledingham, and D. A. Warrell (eds.), Oxford textbook of medicine, 3d ed. Oxford University Press, Oxford.

Warrell, D. A., N. M. Davidson, B. M. Greenwood, L. D. Ormerod, H. M. Pope, B. J. Watkins, and C. R. Prentice. 1977. Poisoning by bites of the saw-scaled or carpet viper (*Echis carinatus*) in Nigeria. Quarterly Journal of Medicine 46: 33–62.

Warrell, D. A., S. Looareesuwan, R. D. G. Theakston, R. E. Phillips, P. Chanthavanich, C. Viravan, W. Supanaranond, J. Karbwang, M. Ho, R. A. Hutton, et al. 1986. Randomized comparative trial of three monospecific antivenoms for bites by the Malayan pit viper (*Calloselasma rhodostoma*) in southern Thailand: clinical and laboratory correlations. American Journal of Tropical Medicine and Hygiene 35(6): 1235–1247.

Wasserman, G. S. 1988. Wound care of spider and snake envenomations. Ann. Emerg. Med. 17: 1331–1335.

Waterton, C. 1825. Wanderings in South America, the North-west of the United States, and the Antilles in the years 1812, 1816, 1820, and 1824. London. 341 pp.

Watkins-Colwell, G. J. 1995. Natural history notes: *Sistrurus catenatus catenatus* (eastern massasauga): Reproduction. Herpetol. Rev. 26(1): 40.

Watrous, L. E., and Q. D. Wheeler. 1981. The outgroup comparison method of character analysis. Syst. Zool. 30: 1–11.

Watt, C. H. 1978. Poisonous snakebite treatment in the United States. JAMA 240: 654–656.

——. 1985. Treatment of poisonous snakebite with emphasis on digit dermotomy. Southern Medical Journal 78: 694–699.

Watt, C. H., and J. F. Gennaro. 1965. Pit viper bites in south Georgia and north Florida. Transactions of the Southern Surgical Association 77: 378–386.

Watt, H. F., H. M. Parrish, and C. B. Pollard. 1956. Repeated poisonous snakebites in the same patient. North Carolina Medical Journal 17: 174–179.

Watt, H. F., and C. B. Pollard. 1954. Case of serious Florida diamondback rattlesnake (*Crotalus adamanteus*) bite. Journal of the Florida Medical Association 41: 367–370.

Wauer, R. H. 1964. Reptiles and amphibians of Zion National Park. Zion Natural History Association, Zion National Parks, Utah. 55 pp.

Weale, J. P. M. 1871. Protective resemblances. Nature, April 27, pp. 507–508.

Weatherhead, P. J., and K. A. Prior. 1992. Preliminary observations of habitat use and movements of the eastern massasauga rattlesnake (*Sistrurus c. catenatus*). J. Herpetol. 26(4): 447–452.

Webb, R. G. 1966. The lizard *Sceloporus bulleri* in western Mexico. Yearbook of the American Philosophical Society 1965: 356–357.

——. 1970. Reptiles of Oklahoma. University of Oklahoma Press, Norman. 370 pp.

——. 1984. Herpetogeography in the Mazatlán–Durango Region of the Sierra Madre Occidental, Mexico. Pp. 217–241 in R. A. Seigel et al. (eds.), Vertebrate ecology and systematics, Special Publications of the Museum of Natural History, University of Kansas, No. 10.

Webb, R. G., and R. H. Baker. 1962. Terrestrial vertebrates of the Pueblo Nuevo area of southwestern Durango, Mexico. Am. Midl. Nat. 68(2): 325–333.

Webb, R. G., and C. M. Fugler. 1957. Selected comments on amphibians and reptiles from the Mexican state of Puebla. Herpetologica 13(1): 33–36.

Webb, S. D. 1978. A history of savanna vertebrates in the New World. Part II. South America and the Great Interchange. Annual Review of Ecology and Systematics 9: 393–426.

Weber, R. A., and R. R. White. 1993. Crotalidae envenomation in children. Annals of Plastic Surgery 31: 141–145.

Wehekind, L. 1955. Notes on the foods of the Trinidad snakes. British Journal of Herpetology 2: 9–13.

——. 1960. Trinidad snakes. Occasional Papers of the Royal Victoria Institute Museum (Trinidad) 1: 1–8.

Weinstein, S. A., C. F. Dewitt, and L. A. Smith. 1992. Variability of venom-neutralizing properties of serum from snakes of the colubrid genus *Lampropeltis*. J. Herpetol. 26(4): 452–461.

Weinstein, S. A., and K. V. Kardong. 1994. Properties of Duvernoy's secretions from opisthoglyphous and aglyphous colubrid snakes: a critical review. Toxicon 32: 1161–1185.

Weinstein, S. A., P. J. Lafaye, and L. A. Smith. 1991. Observations on a venom neutralizing fraction isolated from serum of the northern copperhead, *Agkistrodon contortrix mokasen*. Copeia 1991(3): 777–786.

Weinstein, S. A., S. A. Minton, and C. E. Wilde. 1985. The distribution among ophidian venoms of a toxin isolated from the venom of the Mojave rattlesnake (*Crotalus scutulatus scutulatus*). Toxicon 23: 825–844.

Weinstein, S. A., and L. A. Smith. 1990. Preliminary fractionation of tiger rattlesnake, *Crotalus tigris*, venom. Toxicon 28(12): 1447–1456.

Weir, J. 1992. The Sweetwater rattlesnake round-up: a case study in environmental ethics. Conservation Biology 6(1): 116–127.

Weis, R., and R. J. McIsaac. 1971. Cardiovascular and muscular effects of venom from coral snake, *Micrurus fulvius*. Toxicon 9: 219–228.

Weiss, H. J. 1970. Rattlesnake bite. Lancet 2: 156.

Weiss, H. J., S. Allan, E. Davidson, and S. Kochwa. 1969. Afibrinogenemia in man following the bite of a rattlesnake (*Crotalus adamanteus*). American Journal of Medicine 47: 625–634.

Weissenberg, S., M. Ovadia, G. Fleminger, and E. Kochva. 1991. Antihemorrhagic factors from the blood serum of the western diamondback rattlesnake *Crotalus atrox*. Toxicon 29: 807–818.

Weissenberg, S., M. Ovadia, and E. Kochva. 1992. Inhibition of the proteolytic activity of hemorrhagin-e from *Crotalus atrox* venom by antihemorrhagins from homologous serum. Toxicon 30: 591–597.

Welch, K. R. G. 1980. On a collection of reptiles from Trinidad. Southwestern Herpetological Society Bulletin (San Diego) 3: 1–6.

——. 1990. Review of The venomous reptiles of Latin America. Litteratura Serpentium 10: 146–147.

Wellman, J. 1963. A review of the snakes of the genus *Conophis* (family Colubridae) from Middle America. Publications of the Museum of Natural History, University of Kansas, 15: 251–295.

Welsh, H. H., and A. J. Lind. 2000. Evidence of lingual-luring by an aquatic garter snake. J. Herpetol. 34: 67–74.

Welsh, J. H. 1967 [dated 1966]. Serotonin and related tryptamine derivatives in snake venoms. Mem. Inst. Butantan 33: 509–518.

Welter, W. A., and K. Carr. 1939. Amphibians and reptiles of northeastern Kentucky. Copeia 1939(3): 128–130.

Werler, J. E. 1951. Miscellaneous notes on the eggs and young of Texan and Mexican reptiles. Zoologica 36(1): 37–48.

——. 1964. Poisonous snakes of Texas and first aid treatment of their bites. Texas Parks and Wildlife Dept. Bull. 31: 1–62. [Originally published 1950.]

——. 1978. Poisonous snakes of Texas. Texas Parks and Wildlife Department Bulletin 31: 1–53.

Werler, J. E., and D. M. Darling. 1950. A case of poisoning from the bite of a coral snake, *Micrurus f. tenere* Baird and Girard. Herpetologica 6(7): 197–199.

Werler, J. E., and J. R. Dixon. 2000. Texas snakes. University of Texas Press, Austin. 544 pp.

Werler, J. E., and J. McCallion. 1951. Notes on a collection of reptiles and amphibians from Princess Anne County, Virginia. Am. Midl. Nat. 45: 245–252.

Werler, J. E., and H. M. Smith. 1952. Notes on a collection of reptiles and amphibians from Mexico, 1951–1952. Texas Journal of Science 4(4): 551–573.

Werman, S. D. 1984a. Natural history notes: *Bothrops schlegelii* (eyelash viper). Coloration. Herpetol. Rev. 15(1): 17–18.

——. 1984b. Taxonomic comments on the Costa Rican pitviper, *Bothrops picadoi* (Dunn). J. Herpetol. 18(2): 207–210.

——. 1984c. The taxonomic status of *Bothrops supraciliaris* Taylor. J. Herpetol. 18(4): 484–486.

——. 1992. Phylogenetic relationships of Central and South American pitvipers of the genus *Bothrops* (sensu latu): cladistic analyses of biochemical and anatomical characters. Pp. 21–40 in J. A. Campbell and E. D. Brodie Jr. (eds.), Biology of pitvipers. Selva, Tyler, Texas.

——. 1997. Systematic implications of lactate dehydrogenase isozyme phenotypes in Neotropical pitvipers (Viperidae: Crotalinae). Pp. 79–88 in R. S. Thorpe, W. Wüster, and A. Malhotra (eds.), Venomous snakes: ecology, evolution and snakebite. Clarendon Press, Oxford.

——. 1999. Molecular phylogenetics and morphological evolution in Neotropical pitvipers: an evaluation of mitochondrial DNA sequence information and comparative morphology of the cranium and palatomaxillary arch. Kauptia 8: 113–126.

Werman, S. D., B. I. Crother, and M. E. White. 1999. Phylogeny of some Middle American pitvipers based on a cladistic analysis of mitochondrial 12S and 16S DNA sequence information. Contemporary Herpetology 3. [On-line publication.]

Werner, F. 1896. Beitrage zur Kenntniss de Reptilien und Batrachier von Centralamerika und Chile, sowie einiger seltenerer Schlangenarten. Verhandlungen der Zoologisch-Botanische Gesellschaft in Wien 46: 344–365.

——. 1897. Über einige neue oder seltene Reptilien und Frosche der zoologischen Sammlung des Staates in München. Sitzungsberichte der Akademie der Wissenschaften zu München 27(2): 203–220.

——. 1900. Über Reptilien und Batrachier aus Columbien und Trinidad. II. Verhandlung der Zoologisch-Botanischen Gesellschaft in Wien 50: 262–272.

——. 1901a. Über Reptilien und Batrachier aus Ecuador und Neu-Guinea. Verhandlungen der Zoologisch-Botanische Gesellschaft in Wien 51: 593–614.

——. 1901b. Reptilien und Batrachier aus Peru und Bolivien. Abhandlungen Berichte Königl. Zoologischen und Anthropolisch-Ethnographischen Museum, Dresden 9(2): 1–14.

——. 1903a. Über Reptilien und Batrachier aus Guatemala und China in der zoologischen Staats-Sammlung in München nebst einem Anhang über seltene Formen aus anderen Gebieten. Abhandlungen Bayerische Akademie der Wissenschaften, Mathematisch-Physikalische Klasse (München) 22(2): 342–384.

——. 1903b. Neue Reptilien und Batrachier aus dem naturhistorischen Museum in Brüssel. Zoologischer Anzeiger (Leipzig) 26(693): 246–253.

——. 1922. Synopsis der Schlangen-Familien der Amblycephalidae und Viperidae nebst Vebersicht über die kleineren Familien und die Colubriden der Acrochordineugruppe. Auf Grund des Boulenger'sehen Schlangenkatalogs (1893–1896). Archiv für Naturgeschichte 88(8): 185–244.

——. 1927 [dated 1926]. Neue oder wenig bekannte Schlangen aus dem Wiener naturhistorischen Staatsmuseum. III. Teil. Sitzungsberichten der Akademie der Wissenschaften in Wien. Mathematisch-naturwissenschaftliche Klasse 135(1): 243–257.

West, L. W. 1981. Notes on captive reproduction and behavior in the Mexican cantil (*Agkistrodon bilineatus*). Herpetol. Rev. 12(3): 86–87.

Wettstein, O. 1934. Ergebnisse der osterreichischen biologischen Costa Rica–Expedition 1930. Die amphibien und reptilien. Sitzungsberichten der Akademie der Wissenschaften in Wien. Mathematisch-naturwissenschaftliche Klasse 143 (1–2): 1–39.

Wharton, C. H. 1960. Birth and behavior of a brood of cottonmouths, *Agkistrodon piscivorus piscivorus*, with notes on tail-luring. Herpetologica 16(2): 125–129.

——. 1966. Reproduction and growth in the cottonmouth, *Agkistrodon piscivorus* Lacépède, of Cedar Keys, Florida. Copeia 1966(2): 149–161.

——. 1969. The cottonmouth moccasin on Sea Horse Key, Florida. Bulletin of the Florida State Museum, Biological Sciences, 14(3): 227–272.

Wharton, C. H., T. French, and C. Ruckdeschel. 1973. Recent range extensions for Georgia amphibians and reptiles. Herpetol. Rev. 1(1): 22.

Wharton, C. H., and J. D. Howard. 1971. Range extensions for Georgia amphibians and reptiles. Herpetol. Rev. 3(4): 73–74.

Wheeler, G. C., and J. Wheeler. 1966. The amphibians and reptiles of North Dakota. University of North Dakota Press, Grand Forks. 104 pp.

Wheeler, G. M. 1875. Report upon the collections of batrachians and reptiles made in portions of Nevada, Utah, California, Colorado, New Mexico, and Arizona, during the years 1871, 1872, 1873, and 1874. Report upon geographical and geological explorations and surveys west of the one hundredth meridian, in charge of First Lieut. Geo. M. Wheeler, Engineer Dept., U.S. Army, Washington, D.C., vol. 5: 509–584.

White, F. N., and R. C. Lasiewski. 1971. Rattlesnake denning: theoretical considerations on winter temperatures. Journal of Theoretical Biology 30: 553–559.

White, J. 1991. Snakebite: an Australian perspective. Journal of Wilderness Medicine 2: 219–244.

White, R. R., and R. A. Weber. 1991. Poisonous snakebite in central Texas. Annals of Surgery 213: 466–472.

Whitley, R. E. 1996. Conservative treatment of copperhead snakebites without antivenin. Journal of Trauma—Injury, Infection, and Critical Care 41: 219–221.

Wickler, W. 1968. Mimicry in plants and animals. McGraw-Hill, New York.

Widmer, E. A. 1970. Development of third-stage *Physaloptera* larvae from *Crotalus viridis* Rafinesque, 1818, in cats with notes on pathology of the larvae in the reptiles (Nematoda, Spiruroidea). Journal of Wildlife Diseases 6(2): 89–93.

Widmer, E. A., P. C. Engen, and G. L. Bradley. 1995. Intracapsular asexual proliferation of *Mesocestoides* sp. tetrathyridia in the gastrointestinal tract and mesentaries of the prairie rattlesnake (*Crotalus viridis viridis*). Journal of Parasitology 81(3): 493–496.

Widmer, E. A., and H. D. Specht. 1992. Isolation of asexually proliferous tetrathyridia (*Mesocestoides* sp.) from the southern Pacific rattlesnake (*Crotalus viridis helleri*), with additional data from two previous isolates from the Great Basin fence lizard (*Sceloporus occidentalis longipes*). Journal of Parasitology 78(5): 921–923.

Wied-Neuwied, M. 1815–1817. Viagem ao Brasil. Translation by Edgar Süssekind and Flavio Poppe. Editora Nacional, São Paulo. 1940. 511 pp.

——. 1820. Über die Cobra Coral oder Cobra Coraes der Brasilianer. Nova Acta Academiae Caesareae Leopoldino-Carolinae Germinicae Naturae Curiosorum, Halle, 10(1): 105–110.

——. 1821. Reise nach Brasilien in den Jahren 1815 bis 1817, vol. 2. 345 pp.

——. 1822–1831. Abbildungen zu Naturgeschichte Brasiliens. Weimar. Isis von Oken 11: 13–14, 17, 21–22, 24. Lieferungen 1–15: 90 unnumbered plates.

——. 1825. Beiträge zu Naturgeschichte von Brasilien, vol. 1. Landes-Industrie-Comptoirs, Weimar. 614 pp.

Wiegmann, A. F. A. 1829a. Über die Gesetzlichkeit in der geographischen Verbreitung der Saurier. Isis von Oken 22(3–4): 418–428.

——. 1829b. Über das Acaltetepan oder Temaculcachua des Hernandez, eine neue Gattung de Saurer, *Heloderma*. Isis von Oken 22(6): 624–629.

——. 1834. Herpetologica Mexicana seu descriptio amphibiorum Novae Hispaniae. Pars prima. Saurorum species. Luderitz, Berlin. 54 pp.

Wiens, J. J. 1993. Phylogenetic systematics of the tree lizards (genus *Urosaurus*). Herpetologica 49(4): 399–420.

——. 1995. Polymorphic characters in phylogenetic systematics. Syst. Biol. 44: 482–500.

——. 2000. Phylogenetic analysis of morphological data. Smithsonian Institution Press, Washington, D.C. 220 pp.

Wiley, E. O. 1981. Phylogenetics. The principles and practice of phylogenetic systematics. Wiley, New York.

Wiley, G. O. 1929. Notes on the Texas rattlesnake in captivity, with special reference to the birth of a litter of young. Bull. Antivenin Inst. Am. 3(1): 8–14.

——. 1930. Notes on the Neotropical rattlesnake (*Crotalus terrificus basiliscus*) in captivity. Bull. Antivenin Inst. Am. 3(4): 100–103.

Wilkinson, J. A., J. L. Glenn, R. G. Straight, and J. W. Sites Jr. 1991. Distribution and genetic variation in venom A and B populations of the Mojave rattlesnake (*Crotalus scutulatus scutulatus*) in Arizona. Herpetologica 47(1): 54–68.

Willard, D. E. 1967. Evidence for toxic saliva in *Rhadinaea flavilata* (the yellow-lipped snake). Herpetologica 23(3): 238.

Williams, A. A. 2002. Geographic distribution: *Crotalus horridus* (timber rattlesnake). Herpetol. Rev. 33(1): 67.

Williams, E. E. and P. E. Vanzolini. 1980. Notes and biogeographic comments on anoles from Brasil. Papéis Avulsos do Departamento de Zoologia, São Paulo 34(6): 99–108.

Williams, H. 1960. Volcanic history of the Guatemalan highlands. University of California Publications in Geological Sciences 38: 1–86.

Williams, J. D. 1988. Las corales. Pp. 1–32 in G. B. Cabral (ed.), Fauna argentina, vol. 2. Anfibios y reptiles. Centro Editor de América Latina, Buenos Aires.

Williams, J. D., and F. Francini. 1991. A checklist of the Argentine snakes. Boll. Mus. Reg. Sci. Nat. Torino 9(1): 55–90.

Williams, K. L. 1960. Taxonomic notes on Arizona herpetozoa. Southwest. Nat. 5(1): 25–36.

Williams, K. L., P. S. Chrapliwy, and H. M. Smith. 1961. Snakes from northern Mexico. Chicago Academy of Sciences, Natural History Miscellanea 177: 1–8.

Williams, P. L., and W. M. Fitch. 1989. Finding the minimal change in a given tree. Pp. 543–470 in B. Fernholm, K. Bremer, and H. Jornvall (eds.), The hierarchy of life. Elsevier, Amsterdam.

——. 1990. Phylogeny determination using dynamically weighted parsimony method. Methods Enzymol. 183: 615–626.

Williamson, G. K., and R. A. Moulis. 1994. Distribution of the amphibians and reptiles in Georgia. Savannah Science Museum Special Publications 3. 912 pp.

Williamson, M. A. 1971. An instance of cannibalism in *Crotalus lepidus* (Serpentes: Crotalidae). Herpetol. Rev. 3(1): 18.

Williamson, M. A., P. W. Hyder, and J. S. Applegarth. 1994. Snakes, lizards, turtles, frogs, toads, and salamanders of New Mexico. Sunstone Press, Santa Fe, N.M. 176 pp.

Willis, F., and W. L. Burger. 1969. Sociability of newborn and mother rattlesnakes. Unpublished ms. on file in Herpetological Library at the University of Texas at Arlington.

Willis, T. W., and A. T. Tu. 1988. Purification and biochemical characterization of *atroxase*, a nonhemorrhagic fibrinolytic protease from western diamondback rattlesnake venom. Biochemistry 27(3): 4769–4777.

Wills, C. A., and S. J. Beaupre. 2000. An application of randomization for detecting evidence of thermoregulation in timber rattlesnakes (*Crotalus horridus*) from northwest Arkansas. Physiological and Biochemical Zoology 73(3): 325–334.

Willson, P. 1908. Snake poisoning in the United States: a study based on an analysis of 740 cases. Archives of Internal Medicine 1(5): 516–570.

Wilson, A. P., and S. A. Minton. 1983. Geographic distribution: *Agkistrodon piscivorus leucostoma* (western cottonmouth). Herpetol. Rev. 14(3): 84.

Wilson, E. O. 1994. Naturalist. Island Books, Washington, D.C. 380 pp.

Wilson, L. D. 1983. Update on the list of amphibians and reptiles known from Honduras. Herpetol. Rev. 14: 125–126.

——. 1984. The status of *Micrurus ruatanus* (Günther), a coral snake endemic to the Bay Islands of Honduras. Herpetol. Rev. 15(3): 67.

Wilson, L. D., and D. E. Hahn. 1973. The herpetofauna of the Islas de la Bahía, Honduras. Bulletin of the Florida State Museum, Biological Sciences, 17(2): 93–150.

Wilson, L. D., and J. R. McCranie. 1979a. Notes on the herpetofauna of two mountain ranges in Mexico (Sierra Fría, Aguascalientes, and Sierra Morones, Zacatecas). J. Herpetol. 13(3): 271–278.

——. 1979b. New departmental records for reptiles and amphibians from Honduras. Herpetol. Rev. 10(1): 25.

——. 1984. *Bothrops nasuta*. Catalogue of American Amphibians and Reptiles 349.1–349.2.

——. 1991. Additional departmental records for the herpetofauna of Honduras. Herpetol. Rev. 22(2): 69–71.

——. 1992a. *Bothriechis marchi* (Barbour and Loveridge), March's palm-pitviper. Catalogue of American Amphibians and Reptiles 544.1–544.2.

——. 1992b. *Micrurus ruatanus* (Günther), babaspul (local dialect), coral (Spanish), Roatan coral snake. Catalogue of American Amphibians and Reptiles 545.1–545.2.

Wilson, L. D., J. R. McCranie, and M. R. Espinal. 1996. Coral snake mimics of the genus *Pliocercus* (family Colubridae) in Honduras and their mimetic relationships with *Micrurus* (family Elapidae). Herpetological Natural History 4(1): 57–63.

——. 2001 [dated 2000]. The ecogeography of the Honduran herpetofauna and the design of biotic reserves. Pp. 109–158 in J. D. Johnson, R. G. Webb, and O. A. Flores-Villela (eds.), Mesoamerican herpetology: systematics, zoogeography, and conservation. Centennial Museum, special publ. University of Texas at El Paso.

Wilson, L. D., J. R. McCranie, and L. Porras. 1978. Two snakes, *Leptophis modestus* and *Pelamis platurus*, new to the herpetofauna of Honduras. Herpetol. Rev. 9(2): 63–64.

Wilson, L. D., and J. R. Meyer. 1972. The coral snake *Micrurus nigrocinctus* in Honduras. Bulletin of the Southern California Academy of Sciences 71: 139–145.

——. 1982. The snakes of Honduras, 1st ed. Milwaukee Public Museum Publications, Biology and Geology 6: 1–150.

——. 1985. The snakes of Honduras, 2d ed. Milwaukee Public Museum, Milwaukee, Wisc. 150 pp.

Wilson, L. D., and L. Porras. 1983. The ecological impact of man on the south Florida herpetofauna. Special Publications of the Museum of Natural History, University of Kansas, No. 7. 89 pp.

Wingert, W. A., and L. Chan. 1988. Rattlesnake bites in southern California and rationale for recommended treatment. Western Journal of Medicine 148: 37–44.

Wingert, W. A., T. R. Pattabhiraman, R. Cleland, P. Meyer, R. Pattabhiraman, and F. E. Russell. 1980. Distribution and pathology of copperhead (*Agkistrodon contortrix*) venom. Toxicon 18: 591–601.

Wingert, W. A., and J. Wainschel. 1975. Diagnosis and management of envenomation by poisonous snakes. Southern Medical Journal 68: 1015–1026.

Witz, B. W., D. S. Wilson, and M. D. Palmer. 1991. Distribution of *Gopherus polyphemus* and its vertebrate symbionts in three burrow categories. Am. Midl. Nat. 126: 152–158.

Wolfenbarger, K. A. 1952. Systematic and biological studies on North American chiggers of the genus *Trombicula*, subgenus *Eutrombicula*. Ann. Entomol. Soc. America 45(4): 645–677.

Wolff, H. 1958. Insuficiência hipofisária anterior por picada de ofídio. Arquivos Brasileiros de Endocrinologia e Metabologia 7: 25–47.

Wolff, N. O., and T. S. Githens. 1939a. Record venom extraction from water moccasin. Copeia 1939(1): 52.

——. 1939b. Yield and toxicity of venom from snakes extracted over a period of two years. Copeia 1939(4): 234.

Wong, H. 1997. Comments on the snake records of *Chilomeniscus cinctus*, *Crotalus exsul*, and *C. mitchellii* from Islas Magdalena and Santa Margarita, Baja California, Mexico. Herpetol. Rev. 28(4): 188–189.

Wood, F. D. 1933. Mating of the prairie rattlesnake, *Crotalus confluentus confluentus* Say. Copeia 1933(2): 84–87.

Wood, J. T. 1954. The distribution of poisonous snakes in Virginia. Virginia Journal of Science 5: 152–167.

Wood, J. T., and W. E. Duellman. 1947. Preliminary herpetological survey of Montgomery County, Ohio. Herpetologica 4(1): 3–6.

Wood, J. T., W. W. Hoback, and T. W. Green. 1955. Treatment of snake venom poisoning with ACTH and cortisone. Virginia Medical Monthly 82: 130–135.

Wood, S. F., and F. D. Wood. 1936. Occurrence of Haematozoa in some California cold-blooded vertebrates. Journal of Parasitology 22: 518–520.

Woodburne, M. O. 1956. Notes on the snake, *Sistrurus catenatus tergeminus*, in southwestern Kansas and northwestern Oklahoma. Copeia 1956(2): 125–126.

Woodbury, A. M. 1929. A new rattlesnake from Utah. Bulletin of the University of Utah 20(6). 2 pp.

——. 1930. *Crotalus confluentus concolor*. Bull. Antivenin Inst. Am. 4: 23.

——. 1931. A descriptive catalogue of the reptiles of Utah. Bulletin of the University of Utah 21(5): 1–129.

——. 1941. Copulation in gopher snakes. Copeia 1941(1): 54.

——. 1947. The Mohave rattlesnake in Utah. Copeia 1947(1): 66.

——. 1958. The name *Crotalus viridis concolor* Woodbury. Copeia 1958(2): 151.

Woodbury, A. M., and R. M. Hansen. 1950. A snake den in Tintic Mountains, Utah. Herpetologica 6(3): 66–70.

Woodbury, A. M., and R. Hardy. 1947. The speckled rattlesnake in NW Arizona. Herpetologica 3(5): 169.

Woodbury, A. M., and D. D. Parker. 1956. A snake den in Cedar Mountains and notes on snakes and parasitic mites. Herpetologica 12(4): 261–268.

Woodbury, A. M., B. Vetas, G. Julian, H. R. Glissmeyer, F. L. Heyrend, A. Call, E. W. Smart, and R. T. Sanders. 1951. Symposium: a snake den in Tooele County, Utah. Herpetologica 7(1): 1–52.

Woodbury, A. M., and D. M. Woodbury. 1944. Notes on Mexican snakes from Oaxaca. Journal of the Washington Academy of Sciences 34(11): 360–373.

Woodin, W. H. 1953. Notes on some reptiles from the Huachuca area of southeastern Arizona. Bulletin of the Chicago Academy of Sciences 9(15): 285–296.

Woodson, W. D. 1943. The Gila monster's bite. Frontiers, October, pp. 19–20.

——. 1944. Gila monster. New Mexico Magazine 8: 19–20.

——. 1947. Toxicity of *Heloderma* venom. Herpetologica 4(1): 31–33.

——. 1949. Gila monster in California? Herpetologica 5(6): 151.

Wozniak, E. J., G. L. McLaughlin, and S. R. Telford Jr. 1994. Description of the vertebrate states of haemogregarine species naturally infecting Mojave Desert sidewinders (*Crotalus cerastes cerastes*). Journal of Zoo and Wildlife Medicine 25(1): 103–110.

Wray, K., and R. Owen. 1999. New records of amphibians and reptiles for Nassau County, Florida. Herpetol. Rev. 30(4): 237–238.

Wright, A. H. 1919. The snakes of Monroe and Orleans County, N.Y. Copeia 1919(67)(March 19): 12.

——. 1950. Common names of the snakes of the United States. Herpetologica 6(6): 141–186.

Wright, A. H., and S. A. Bishop. 1915. A biological reconnaissance of the Okefinokee Swamp in Georgia. II. Snakes. Proc. Acad. Nat. Sci. Philadelphia 1915: 139–192.

Wright, A. H., and A. A. Wright. 1957. Handbook of snakes of the United States and Canada, vol. 2. Comstock Publishing, Ithaca, N.Y. 540 pp.

Wright, B. A. 1941. Habit and habitat studies of the massasauga rattlesnake (*Sistrurus catenatus catenatus* Raf.) in northeastern Illinois. Am. Midl. Nat. 25: 659–672.

Wucherer, O. 1863. On the species of *Craspedocephalus* which occur in the Province of Bahia, Brazil. Proc. Zool. Soc. London 1863: 51–54.

——. 1867. Sôbre a mordedura das cobras venenosas e seu tratamento. Gazeta Médica da Bahia 1(21): 241–243.

Wüster, W. 2000. Precedence of names in wide use over disused synonyms or homonyms in accordance with Article 23.9 of the Code. Reptilia, Serpentes (1) *Trigonocephalus caribbaeus* Garman, 1887. Bulletin of Zoological Nomenclature 57(1): 9.

Wüster, W., P. Golay, and D. A. Warrell. 1997a. Synopsis of recent developments in venomous snake systematics. Toxicon 35(3): 319–340.

——. 1998. Synopsis of recent developments in venomous snake systematics, No. 2. Toxicon 36(2): 299–307.

——. 1999a. Synopsis of recent developments in venomous snake systematics, No. 3. Toxicon 37: 1123–1129.

Wüster, W., and C. J. McCarthy. 1996. Venomous snake systematics: implications for snake bite treatment and toxinology. Pp. 13–23 in C. Bon and M. Boyffon (eds.), Envenomings and their treatments. Fondation Marcel-Mérieux, Lyon, France.

Wüster, W., S. Pierini, and G. Puorto. 1994. Geographic distribution: *Bothrops moojeni* (Brazilian lancehead). Herpetol. Rev. 25(2): 76.

Wüster, W., M. D. Salamão, G. J. Duckett, R. S. Thorpe, and BBBSP. 1999b. Mitochondrial DNA phylogeny of the *Bothrops atrox* species complex (Squamata: Serpentes: Viperidae). Kaupia 8: 135–144.

Wüster, W., M. G. Salamão, J. A. Quijada-Mascareñas, R. S. Thorpe, and BBBSP. 2002a. Origin and evolution of the South American pitviper fauna: evidence from mitochondrial DNA sequence analysis. Pp. 111–128 in G. W. Schuett, M. Höggren, M. E. Douglas, and H. W. Greene (eds.), Biology of the vipers. Eagle Mountain Publishing, Eagle Mountain, Utah.

Wüster, W., M. G. Salomão, R. S. Thorpe, G. Puorto, M. F. D. Furtado, S. A. Hoge, R. D. G. Theakston, and D. A. Warrell. 1997b. Systematics of the *Bothrops atrox* complex: new insights from multivariate analysis and mitochondrial DNA sequence information. Pp. 99–114 in R. S. Thorpe, W. Wüster, and A. Malhotra (eds.), Venomous snakes: ecology, evolution and snakebite. Clarendon Press, Oxford.

Wüster, W., R. S. Thorpe, M. da G. Salomão, L. Thomas, G. Puorto, R. D. G. Theakston, and D. A. Warrell. 2002b. Origin and phylogenetic position of the Lesser Antillean species of *Bothrops* (Serpentes, Viperidae): biogeographical and medical implications. Bulletin of the Natural History Museum London (Zoology) 68(2): 101–106.

Wüster, W., R. S. Thorpe, G. Puorto, and BBBSP. 1996. Systematics of the *Bothrops atrox* complex (Reptilia: Serpentes: Viperidae) in Brazil: a multivariate analysis. Herpetolgica 52(2): 263–271.

Xavier, V. 2002. Variação entre filhotes de representantes do complexo *Bothrops neuwiedi* (Serpentes, Viperidae, Crotalinae). Phyllomedusa 1(1): 11–30.

Ximénez, Francisco. 1615. Quatro libros de la naturaleza, y virtudes de las plantas, y animales que están recevidos en el uso de medicina en al Nueva España, y la methodo, y corrección, y preparación, que para administrarlas se requiere con lo que el Doctor Franciso Hernández escrivío en lengua latina. Mexico. 203 pp.

Yachi, S., and M. Higashi. 1998. The evolution of warning signals. Nature 394: 882–884.

Yamaguti, S. 1961. Systema helminthum III. The nematodes of vertebrates. Interscience Publishers, New York.

Yancey, F. D., II. 1996a. Geographic distribution: *Crotalus atrox* (western diamondback rattlesnake). Herpetol. Rev. 29(3): 154.

——. 1996b. Geographic distribution: *Crotalus viridis viridis* (prairie rattlesnake). Herpetol. Rev. 29(3): 154.

Yanosky, A. A. 1989a. Approche de l'herpetofaune de la réserve écologique El Bagual (Formosa, Argentine). I. Anoures et Ophidiens. Revue Française d'Aquariologie, Herpétologie 16(2): 57–62.

——. 1989b. La ofidiofauna de la reserva ecológica El Bagual, Formosa: abundancia, utilización de los habitats, y estado de situación. Cuadernos de Herpetología 4(3): 11–14.

Yanosky, A. A., and J. M. Chani. 1988. Possible dual mimicry of *Bothrops* and *Micrurus* by the colubrid *Lystrophus dorbignyi*. J. Herpetol. 22(2): 222–224.

Yanosky, A. A., J. R. Dixon, and C. Mercolli. 1996. Ecology of the snake community at El Bagual Ecological Reserve, northeastern Argentina. Herpetological Natural History 4(2): 97–110.

Yarlequé-Chocas, A. 2000. Las serpientes peruanas y sus venenos. Universidad Nacional Mayor de San Marcos Fondo Editorial, Lima, Peru. 78 pp.

Yarrow, H. C. 1875. Report upon the collections of batrachians and reptiles made in portions of Nevada, Utah, California, Colorado, New Mexico, and Arizona, during the years 1871, 1872, 1873 and

1874. Report upon geographical and geological explorations and surveys west of the one hundreth meridian, in charge of First Lieut. Geo. M. Wheeler, Engineer Department, United States Army, Washington, D.C. 5(4): 509–584.

———. 1883 [dated 1882]. Check list of North American Reptilia and Batrachia, with catalogue of specimens in the United States Museum. Bulletin of the U.S. National Museum 24: 1–249.

Yerger, R. W. 1953. Yellow bullhead preyed upon by cottonmouth moccasin. Copeia 1953: 115.

Young, B. A. 1991. Morphological basis of "growling" in the king cobra, Ophiophagus hannah. Journal of Experimental Zoology 260: 275–287.

———. 1997. A review of sound production and hearing in snakes, with a discussion of intraspecific acoustic communication in snakes. Journal of the Pennsylvania Academy of Science 71(1): 39–46.

———. 2001. Direct measurement of venom flow in rattlesnakes. P. 152 in Abstracts for 2001 Joint Annual Meetings of the Herpetologists' League and the Society for the Study of Amphibians and Reptiles, 27–31 July, Indianapolis, Indiana.

Young, B. A., and I. P. Brown. 1993. On the acoustic profile of the rattlesnake rattle. Amphibia-Reptilia 14: 373–380.

———. 1995. The physical basis of the rattling sound in the rattlesnake Crotalus viridis oreganus. J. Herpetol. 29(1): 80–85.

Young, B. A., S. Sheft, and W. Yost. 1995. The morphology of sound production in Pituophis melanoleucus (Serpentes: Reptilia) with the first description of a vocal chord in snakes. Journal of Experimental Zoology 273: 472–481.

Young, B. A., J. Solomon, and G. Abishanin. 1999. How many ways can a snake growl? The morphology of sound production in Ptyas mucosus and its potential mimicry of Ophiophagus. Herpetological Journal 9: 89–94.

Young, B. A., K. Zahn, M. Blair, and J. Lalor. 2000. Functional subdivision of the venom gland musculature and regulation of venom expulsion in rattlesnakes. Journal of Morphology 246: 249–259.

Young, R. A. 1992. Effects of Duvernoy's gland secretions from the eastern hognose snake, Heterodon platyrhinos, on smooth muscle and neuromuscular junction. Toxicon 30: 775–779.

Young, R. A., D. M. Miller, and D. C. Ochsner. 1980. The Grand Canyon rattlesnake (Crotalus viridis abyssus): comparison of venom protein profiles with other viridis subspecies. Comp. Biochem. Physiol. B 66: 601–603.

Yuki, R. N. 1997. Geographic distribution: Bothrops neuwiedi (Neuwied's lancehead). Herpetol. Rev. 28(3): 158.

Yuki, R. N., U. Galatti, and R. A. T. Rocha. 1999. Contribuição ao conhecimento da fauna de Squamata de Rondônia, Brasil, com dois novos registros. Boletim do Museu Paraense Emílio Goeldi, Zoologia 15(2): 181–193.

Zamprogno, C., and M. Das Graças Zamprogno. 1997. Natural history notes: Bothrops jararacussu. Prey. Herpetol. Rev. 28(1): 45.

Zamudio, K. R., and H. W. Greene. 1997. Phylogeography of the bushmaster (Lachesis muta: Viperidae): implications for Neotropi-cal biogeography, systematics, and conservation. Biological Journal of the Linnean Society 62: 421–442.

Zamudio, K. R., D. L. Hardy, Sr., M. Martins, and H. W. Greene. 2000. Fang tip spread, puncture distinace, and suction for snake bite. Toxicon 38(5): 723–728.

Zann, L. P., R. J. Cuffey, and C. Kropach. 1975. Fouling organisms and parasites associated with the skin of sea snakes. Pp. 251–265 in W. A. Dunson (ed.), The biology of sea snakes. University Park Press, Baltimore.

Zarafonetis, C. J. D., and J. P. Kalas. 1962. Serotonin degradation by homogenates of tissues from Heloderma horridum, the Mexican beaded lizard. Nature 195: 707.

Zeiller, W. 1969. Maintenance of the yellow-bellied seasnake, Pelamis platurus, in captivity. Copeia 1969(2) 407–408.

Zhang, F. J. 1992. Division of the genus Trimeresurus (sensu lato) based on the morphology of their skulls. Pp. 48–57 in E. M. Zhao, B. H. Chen, and T. J. Papenfuss (eds.), Proceedings of the First Asian Herpetological Meeting. China Forestry Press, Beijing.

———. 1998. Description of the distinct pit viper of genus Ermia (Serpentes: Viperidae) of China. Russian Journal of Herpetology 5: 83–84.

Ziegler, T., H.-W. Herrmann, P. David, N. L. Orlov, and S. G. Pauwels. 2000. Triceratolepidophis sieversorum, a new genus and species of pitviper (Reptilia: Serpentes: Viperidae: Crotalinae) from Vietnam. Russian Journal of Herpetology 7: 199–214.

Zimmerman, A. A., and C. H. Pope. 1948. Development and growth of the rattle of rattlesnakes. Fieldiana: Zoology 32: 357–413.

Zimmerman, B. L., and M. T. Rodrigues. 1990. Frogs, snakes, and lizards of the INPA–WWF Reserves near Manaus, Brazil. Pp. 426–454 in A. H. Gentry (ed.), Four Neotropical rainforests. Yale University Press, New Haven, Conn.

Zug, G. R., L. J. Vitt, and J. P. Caldwell. 2001. Herpetology, 2nd ed. Academic Press, London. 630 pp.

Zweifel, R. G. 1952. Notes on the lizards of the Coronados Islands, Baja California, Mexico. Herpetologica 8(2): 9–11.

———. 1954. Notes on the distribution of some reptiles in western Mexico. Herpetologica 10(3): 145–149.

———. 1958. Results of the Puritan-American Museum of Natural History expedition to western Mexico. 2. Notes on reptiles and amphibians from the Pacific Coastal islands of Baja California. Am. Mus. Novitat. 1895: 1–17.

———. 1959a. The provenance of reptiles and amphibians collected in Mexico by J. J. Major. Am. Mus. Novitat. 1949: 1–9.

———. 1959b. Additions to the herpetofauna of Nayarit, Mexico. American Museum Novitatates 1953: 1–13.

———. 1960. Results of the Puritan-American Museum of Natural History expedition to western Mexico. 9. Herpetology of the Tres Marías Islands. Bull. Am. Mus. Nat. Hist. 119(2): 77–128.

Zweifel, R. G., and K. S. Norris. 1955. Contributions to the herpetology of Sonora, Mexico: descriptions of new subspecies of snakes (Microides euryxanthus and Lampropeltis getulus) and miscellaneous collecting notes. Am. Midl. Nat. 54: 230–249.

Zwinenberg, A. 1977. Leptophis ahaetulla. Deutsche Aquarien- und Terrarienzeitschrift 30(2): 64–68.

INDEX

Names for genera and species fully treated in this work are in bold, as are page numbers for the main accounts. The letter *f* following a page number indicates figure; *k*, key; *m*, map; *t*, table; pl. indicates color plate number (1–751 are in volume 1; 752–1500 are in volume 2). Page numbers in italics refer to the chapters on snakebite. Common names are alphabetized by the full name (e.g., Ixtlán coralsnake, *not* coralsnake, Ixtlán).

bald cypress, 14
Balsan coralsnake, 199
bamboo, 554
banana di rif, 50
banded gecko, 107, 507
banded rattlesnake, 550
banded rock lizard, 510
banded sand snake, 119
Banisteriopsis, pl. *1497*
barba amarilla, 2, 6, 262, 350, 373, 375, 737
Barbour's montane pitviper, 429
Barisia imbricata, 510, 511
Barisia sp., 105, 451
barnacle, 236
Barnett's lancehead, 381, *740*
barriga morada, 409
bass, 255
Bassariscus astutus, 477
basswood, 12, 14
bastard rattlesnake, 614
bat, 256, 293, 509
Batis maritima, 50
beaded lizard, 2, 6, 8, 96, 99, 100, 101, **103–106**. *See also Heloderma horridum*
bead and coral, 162, 171
beargrass, 16
bec-kara-acá, 304
bee, 244, 625
beech, 12, 14, 550
beech leaf snake, 268
Beechey's jay, 100
beetle, 624
bejuca, *725*
bejuquilla, *725*
bejuquilla mojosa, *725*
benda-gubisi, 464
bergimaka, 378
bergi-owroekoekoe, 382
Betula alleghaniensis, 12
bicho'hi', 537
Bidens graveolens, *754*
big bluestem, 14
big brown bat, 510
bil palka, 263
birch, 550
bird, 348, 349, 425, 440, 458, 624, 628f, 636, 709. *See also names of individual species*
birri, 305
bison, 477
Bitis arietans, 653
Bitis atropos, *730*
Bitis gabonica, 437
Bitis sp., 629, 648f, 651f
black bear, 477, 515
blackbush, 532
black cherry, 14
black-faced lancehead, 418
black-headed bushmaster, 444
black-headed coralsnake, 150
black-headed snake, 119
black iguana, 120, 512
black mangrove, 37
black massasauga, 610
black moccasin, 272
black-necked forest cobra, 108
black racer, 606
black rat, 256
black rattler, 610
black scorpion, *743*
black snake, 272
black snapper, 610
black-speckled palm-pitviper, 302, *734*
black-tailed hairy dwarf porcupine, 440
black-tailed horned pitviper, 452
black-tailed jackrabbit, 512

black-tailed rattlesnake, 562, *700*
black-throated blue warbler, 509
black-throated sparrow, 507, 508
blakka drarasneki, 189
blakka kraka sneki, 189
Blarina brevicauda, 255, 256, 509, 606
Blarina sp., 255, 606
blindsnake, 1, 119, 120, 459
blotched coralsnake, 150
blotched palm-pitviper, 307
blow snake, 620
bluebunch fescue, 14
bluebunch wheatgrass, 14
blue-footed booby, 507
bluegrass, 14
blue spruce, 14
blunt-tail moccasin, 272
boa, 1
Boa constrictor, 265, 278, 283, 317, 384, 439, 448, 462, 463, 465, 466, 469, 472, 475, pl. *1499*
Boa constrictor imperator, pl. 1043
Boa constrictor ortonii, pl. 1044
Boa contortrix, 249, 266, 645
Boa sp., 324, 345, 625t, 645
bobcat, 514
bobwhite, 506, 509, 606
boca-podre, 397
bocaracá, 304, 305, 307
bocaracá de javillo, 448
boca de sapo, 413, 415, 417, 418, 421
bocorám, 159
bocuda, 413, 417, 418
boesi-owroekoekoe, 382
Bogert's coralsnake, 152
bog lemming, 509
boichumbéguaçu, 222, 228, 230
boicinim, 542
boicininga, 542
boiçinininga, *709*
boicinunga, 542
boicoatiara, 365, 385
boicorá, boi-corá, 159, 223
boicoral, 190
boicotiara, 365, 385
boiçuninga, 542
boiçununga, 542
boid, 626, 631
Boidae, 635f
boipeva, 389
boipevussu snake, *724*
boipinima, 206, 209, 217
boiquirá, 542
Boiruna maculata, 723, pls. 1045–1046
Boiruna sp., 625t, 720t, 723
Boletém, 542
Bolitoglossa sp., 425
Bolivian coralsnake, 226
Bolivian lancehead, 408
bolpach, 282
Bolyeriidae, 635f
boomslang, *721*
boquidorá, 373
boquidorada, 373
borot kabí, 433
bosmeester, 446
Bothiochis mammifera, 281
Bothriechis, 4, 241, 242t, 243, 244, 245, 246, 247f, 247k, 248k, 276, **290–296**, 291t, 295k, 297m, 299f, 304, 304f, 320, 400, 425, 433, 452, 625t, 631, 646, 647f, 655, 656, 656t, 658, 659, 670, 670f, 671, 672, 673, 674, 678f, 681, 716, 733
Bothriechis albocarinata, 4, 319, *735*
Bothriechis alticolus, 319
Bothriechis aurifer, 6, 22t, 24t, 29k, 33k, 35t, 36k, 241, 276, 290, 291t, 291f, 292, 293, 295k,

296k, 296f, **296–297**, 297m, 298, 301, 303, 304, 309, 655, 670f, 673, 674, 679f, 681, *733*, pls. 369–372
Bothriechis aurifera, 296
Bothriechis aurifera aurifera, 296, 656t
Bothriechis aurifer marchi, 301, 656t
Bothriechis bernoulii, 297
Bothriechis Bernoullii, 297
Bothriechis bicolor, 7, 22t, 24t, 29k, 33k, 35t, 36k, 40, 246f, 276, 290, 291t, 292, 293, 294, 295k, 296k, 297m, 297, **297–299**, 303, 308, 309, 654f, 655, 656t, 670f, 673, 674, 679f, 681, 733, pls. 373–377, *1415*
Bothriechis bilineata smaragdina, 313
Bothriechis bilineatus bilineatus, 313
Bothriechis bilineatus smaragdinus, 313
Bothriechis brachystoma, 462, 465
Bothriechis godmani, 433
Bothriechis Godmanni, 422, 431
Bothriechis lansbergii, 462, 465, 474
Bothriechis lateralis, 42, 43k, 45t, 46k, 48t, 49k, 245, 290, 291t, 291, 292, 293, 294, 295k, 296k, 299f, **299–301**, 300m, 301, 302, 303, 425, 651f, 654f, 655, 656t, 659t, 670f, 673, 674, 679f, 681, 733, 734, pls. 378–383
Bothriechis mahnerti, 402
Bothriechis marchi, 39t, 40k, 42, 42t, 291t, 293, 294, 295k, 296k, 297m, 298, 299f, 301, **301–302**, 304, 309, 670f, 673, 674, 681, 733, 734, pls. 384–387
Bothriechis mexicanus, 284
Bothriechis nasutus, 467
Bothriechis nigroviridis, 2, 45t, 46k, 48t, 49k, 276, 290, 291t, 291, 292, 293, 294, 295k, 299f, 301, 302m, **302–303**, 304, 309, 646, 651f, 654f, 655, 656t, 659t, 670f, 673, 674, 679f, 681, 734, pls. 388–390
Bothriechis nigroviridis marchi, 301, 733
Bothriechis nummifera, 281, 284, 285
Bothriechis nummifera var. *notata*, 281
Bothriechis oligolepis, 315, 318, 319
Bothriechis oligolepis albocarinatus, 319
Bothriechis oligolepis oligolepis, 316, 318
Bothriechis ophryomegas, 470
Bothriechis ornatus, 4, 298
Bothriechis punctatus, 406
Bothriechis punctatus mahnerti, 402
Bothriechis punctatus punctatus, 406, 407
Bothriechis rowleyi, 22t, 24t, 29k, 33k, 276, 291t, 292, 294, 295k, 296k, 297m, 298, 299f, **303–304**, 309, 658, 670f, 673, 674, 681, pls. 391–394
Bothriechis schlegeli, 304
Bothriechis schlegelii, 5, 6, 22t, 24t, 29k, 33k, 35t, 36k, 37t, 38k, 39t, 40k, 42t, 43k, 45t, 46k, 48t, 49k, 53t, 55k, 57k, 59t, 60k, 76t, 77k, 80t, 81k, 83k, 276, 290, 292t, 291, 292, 293, 294, 295t, 295k, 297, 298, 301, 302, 303, **304–307**, 304f, 305f, 306m, 308, 309, 315, 329, 330, 350, 404, 407, 450, 454, 456, 630, 651f, 653, 654f, 655, 658, 659t, 670f, 672, 673, 674, 679f, 681, 734, pls. 395–414
Bothriechis schlegelii nigroadspersus, 656t
Bothriechis schlegelii schlegelii, 656t
Bothriechis scutigera, 431
Bothriechis supraciliaris, 5, 45t, 46k, 290, 291t, 292, 293, 295k, 306m, 307, **307–308**, 450, 673, 674, 679f, pls. 415–421
Bothriechis taeniata lichenosa, 4, 321
Bothriechis taeniatus, 321
Bothriechis taeniatus lichenosus, 321
Bothriechis taeniatus taeniatus, 320
Bothriechis thalassinus, 5, 35t, 36k, 39t, 40k, 291t, 292, 295k, 296k, 297m, **308–309**, 308f, 634, 674, 679f, pls. 422–426
Bothriechis trianguligera, 431

Elaps Surinamensis, 230
Elaps tener, 195
Elaps tenere, 195
Elaps tristis, 169, 195
Elaps tschudii, 232
Elapsoidea, 639f
Electra angulata, 236
elephant tree, 499
elegant coralsnake, 197
Eleutherodactylus rhodopis, 458
Eleutherodactylus sp., 293, 348, 349, 425
Elgaria kingii, 512
Elgaria sp., 119
elm, 12, 14
Elymus condensatus, 14
Engelmann spruce, 14
Enterobacter sp., 760
Entonyssidae, 515, 516
Entonyssus ewingi, 515
Entonyssus rileyi, 516
é pak-ti, 542
epazote, 284
Epicrates cenchria alvarezi, pl. 1098
Epicrates cenchria cenchria, pl. 1097
Epicrates cenchria crassus, pl. 1099
Epicrates sp., 311, 345, 761
epiphyte, 14, 21, 38, 45
Eptesicus fuscus, 510, 511
equine, 701
equis, 6, 332, 373, 375, 378, 738
equís colorada, 329
equis jergón, 332
equis negra, 373
equis pachona, 373
equis rabo de chucha, 373
equis rabo de hueso, 373
equis rabo fino, 373
equís sapa, 330
equís-veinticuatro, 468
Eremophila alpestris, 507
ericine boa, 620
Ermia, 646, 656
Erythrolamprus aesculapii, 122, 150, 714, 719, 723
Erythrolamprus aesculapii aesculapii, pls. 1100–1109
Erythrolamprus aesculapii venustissimus, pl. 1110
Erythrolamprus bizona, 723, pl. 1111
Erythrolamprus guentheri, 176, pls. 1112–1113
Erythrolamprus mimus micrurus, pl. 1114
Erythrolamprus ocellatus, pl. 1115
Erythrolamprus pseudocorallus, pl. 1116
Erythrolamprus sp., 110, 147, 159, 163, 226, 620, 624, 625t, 719, 719t, 720t, 723
Erythrolamprus venustissimus, 723
Escherichia coli, 735, 737, 739, 747, 760
escorpión, 6, 104, 1006
Esox sp., 255
Estesia, 95
Estesia mongoliensis, 95
estrellita, 321
Euglandina rosacea, 255
Eumeces brevilineatus, 508t
Eumeces copei, 512
Eumeces fasciatus, 118, 254, 255
Eumeces inexpectatus, 117, 118, 255, 606
Eumeces laticeps, 255
Eumeces obsoletus, 254, 605
Eumeces schwartzei, 119
Eumeces skiltonianus, 510, 511
Eumeces sp., 117, 118, 119, 254, 255, 510
Eumeces tetragrammus, 118
Eunectes murinus, pl. 1500
Eunectes sp., 761
Eurheloderma, 95
European starling, 511

Eurycea longicauda, 255
Eurycea lucifuga, 255
Evotomys carolinensis, 509
eye-dee-ah-mo, 313
eyelash palm-pitviper, 305, 734

Fagus grandifolia, 12, 14
Falco sparverius, 122, 515
falsa cascabel, 381
false cobra, 724
false coralsnake, 6, 719, 726
false water cobra, 724
Farancia abacura, 118, 171, 255
Farancia abacura reinwardti, pl. 1117
Farancia sp., 625t, 639f
Fea's viper, 240
Felis pardalis, 514
fence lizard, 255, 512
fer-de-lance, 6, 354, 370, 373, 383, 389, 396, 738, 743
Ferrocactus, 451, 453
fescue, 14
Festuca idahoensis, 14
Ficimia olivacea, 118
Ficimia publia, 119
Ficimia sp., 119, 625t
Ficimia streckeri, pl. 1118
Ficus, 266
filariasis, 728
fir, 21, 535, 567
fish, 253, 255, 256, 745
Fistularia corneta, 235
five-lined skink, 254
flecha, 305, 406
Florida cooter, 256
Florida coralsnake, 169
Florida diamondback rattlesnake, 526
Florida gopher mouse, 604
Florida leopard frog, 254
Florida softshelled turtle, 256
Florida worm lizard, 117
flying squirrel, 509
Fonseca's lancehead, 388
forest-pitviper, 4, 309–313, 383, 400. See also Bothriopsis; names of individual species
forest rat, 311
Formica, 514
Fouquieria splendens, 16
four-eyed opossum, 348
fox, 514, 607
foxsnake, 630
fox squirrel, 507, 509
Franseria dumosa, 15
Franseria sp., 107
Fraxinus americana, 12
Fraxinus sp., 14
free-tailed bat, 255
Fregata magnificens, 235, 348, 364
frigatebird, 235, 364
frog, 255, 293, 311, 347, 348, 349, 425, 439, 458, 459, 605, 606, 626. See also names of individual species
furta-cor, 389

Galbulidae, 122
Galictis vittatus, 122
galleta grass, 538
galwemma, 104
gamarrilla, 263
Gambel's quail, 99, 100
gapper, 272
Gapper's red-backed mouse, 255
gargantilla, 6, 158, 162, 180, 194, 201, 202, 208
gartersnake, 169, 256, 618, 631, 726
Gastrophryne carolinensis, 255, 606
Gastrophryne olivacea, 254

Gastrophryne sp., 254
gata, 373
gecko, 348, 439
gekkonid, 120, 348
Geococcyx californicus, 515
geometrid, 626
Geomys, 512
Geomys bursarius, 507, 508t
Geophis brachycephalus, pl. 1119
Geophis carinosus, 119
Geophis damiani, pl. 1120
Geophis dubius, 119, 120
Geophis duellmani, pl. 1121
Geophis dunni, 120
Geophis laticinctus, pl. 1122
Geophis nasalis, 119, 120
Geophis sallei, 119
Geophis semidoliatus, 119, pl. 1123
Geophis sp., 110, 425, 625t
Gerrhonotus, 105
ghost crab, 256
giant armadillo, 441
giant chinkapin, 15
giant sequoia, 15
giant wild rye, 14
Gila monster, 2, 6, 8, 95, 96, 99, 100, 101, **106–107**, 510. See also Heloderma suspectum
glass lizard, 117, 254
Glaucomys sp., 509
Glaucomys volans, 509
Glossophaga soricina, 293
glossy crayfish snake, 256
glossy ibis, 256
Gloydius blomhoffii, 647f, 647, 648f, 650, 653, 654f, 655, 660, 679
Gloydius blomhoffii blomhoffii, 649
Gloydius blomhoffii brevicaudus, 649
Gloydius caliginosus, 649
Gloydius halys, 648f, 650, 651f
Gloydius halys caraganus, 649
Gloydius halys halys, 649
Gloydius halys monticola, 649
Gloydius himalayanus, 648f, 649
Gloydius intermedius, 648f, 650
Gloydius intermedius caucasicus, 649
Gloydius intermedius intermedius, 649
Gloydius intermedius stejnegeri, 649
Gloydius monticola, 648f
Gloydius saxatilis, 649
Gloydius shedaoensis, 648f, 651f
Gloydius sp., 245, 249, 646, 647, 648, 649, 650, 651, 652, 654, 655, 656, 660, 671, 673, 757t
Gloydius strauchi, 240, 648f, 649, 651f
Gloydius ussuriensis, 648f, 649, 651f, 665
Glyphorhynchus spirurus, 459
goat, 514
Gobiderma, 95
Godman's montane pitviper, 433, 746
golden lancehead, 389, 741
golden mouse, 510
goldfinch, 510
Gomesophis brasiliensis, pl. 1124
Gomesophis sp., 345
Gonatodes fuscus [albogularis], 348
Gonatodes humeralis, 348
Gonatodes sp., 311
gopher, 506, 571, 581
gophersnake, 630
gopher tortoise, 106, 500, 521, 526, 604
Gopherus agassizii, 100
Gopherus polyphemus, 500, 521, 604
Gracilinanus agilis, 349
grage à grand carreaux, 750
grama grass, 14, 15, 556, 562, 567, 581, 596
grand fir, 15
grasshopper, 254, 278, 510

loblolly pine, 14, 615
loco, *754*
locust, 254
lodgepole pine, 15
loggerhead shrike, 122, 256, 515, 607
Lojan lancehead, 399, *744*
longleaf pine, 14, 615
longnosed snake, 254
long-ringed coralsnake, 174
long-tailed rattlesnake, 586
longtailed salamander, 255
long-tailed shrew, 606
Lophocereus schottii, 16
Lophortyx californica, 511
Lophortyx gambeli, 99, 100
lora, 300, 301, 302, 305, 313
lorita, 313
loro, 313, *734*
loro machaco, 313, 316, *735*
loro machacuy, 313
loro mashaco, 313, 318, 319
Louisiana waterthrush, 254
Lowesaurus, 95
lowland moccasin, 272
Loxocemidae, 635f
lucerito, 305
luna moth, 254
lung mite, 515, 516
lung worm, 349, 440
lyresnake, 727
Lystrophis dorbignyi, 626, pl. 1190
Lystrophis hystricus, pl. 1191
Lystrophis mattogrossensis, pl. 1192
Lystrophis pulcher, pl. 1193
Lystrophis semicinctus, pls. 1194–1195
Lystrophis sp., 115, 345, 620, 625t, *720t*, 725

Mabuya mabouya, 348
Mabuya macrorhyncha, 348
Mabuya nigropunctatus, 348
Mabuya sp., 118, 120, 349
Mabuya unimarginata, 254
ma ára, 542
macabrel, 321, 373
macagua, 373, 446
Macambira, 347, 386
macanch, 381
macanche, 404, *740*
macanchi, 378, 399
macanchillo, 319
macao, 373
macapé, 446
macaucho, 399
macaurel, 321, 373, 446
maccourracourra, 223
machacú, 378
macubuleru, 378
Magaera, 646
Magnolia acuminata, 14
mahogany, 21, 37
maikir, 542
maitre de la brousse, 446
makanch, 332
makasneki, 446
makha mil, 542
makkaslang, 446
Malacoptila panamensis, 122
male coral, 157
malha de sapo, 391, 397
mamba, 108
mammal, 349, 425, 440, 459. *See also names of
    individual species*
Mammalia, 425t, 426f, 427f
Manabí hognosed piviper, 461, *753*
mandrill, 630
mangrove, 14, 50, 64, 75

mangrove rattler, 272
Manodistomum sp., 516
mano de metate, 282, 284
mano de piedra, 281, 284, 286, 287, 288
manti, 624
mantis, 254
many-banded coralsnake, 202
manzanilla, 50
manzanita, 15, 21, 573
mapaná, 329, 332, 373, 378, 448, 465, *738,
    753*
mapaná barriga del moncholo, 465
mapaná blanca, 373
mapaná de uña, 373
mapaná prieta, 373
mapaná rabo seco, 373
mapaná rayo, 443, 446
mapanare, mapanaré, 6, 305, 321, 373, 378,
    382, 446
mapanaré cejuda, 305
mapanaré de Amazonas, 382
mapanaré de carabobo, 378
mapanaré del monte, 465
mapanaré guayanesa, 378
mapanaré liquenosa, 321
mapanaré mariposa, 305
mapanaré rabiseca, 406
mapanaré rabo frito, 465
mapanare rayada, 313
mapanaré terciopelo, 373, 378
mapanare tigrito, 313
mapanaré verde, 313
mapaná tigre, 373
mapapero, 373
mapepire, 446
mapepire ananas, *750*
mapepire balcin/balsain/balsín, 373, *737*
mapepire gallé, 446
mapepire valsin/valsin, 373, *737*
mapepire z'ananna, 446, *750*
mapipi, 446
maple, 550
maracá, 542
maracábóia, 542
Marajó lancehead, 400
marashar, 321, 378
marauá-boi, 313
marine toad, 122
Marmota flaviventris, 511
Marmota sp., 510
marsh rabbit, 256, 506
marsh rat, 348
marsupial, 348, 440
martiguaja, 443, 446
Martinique lancehead, 396, *743*
masacoatl, 284
masked shrew, 255, 509, 606
massasauga, 603, 604, 605, 606, 607, 608, *698*
Masticophis, 100, 514
Masticophis flagellum, 118, 253, 508, 515
Masticophis taeniatus, 254, 481
Mastigodryas bifossatus, 725
Mastigodryas bifossatus triseriatus, pl. 1196
Mastigodryas heathi, 120
Mastigodryas pulchriceps, pl. 1197
Mastigodryas sp., 345, 625t, *719t, 720t*, 725
matabuey, 444, 448
matacaballo, 378, 465
mataganado, 201
matagatos, 201
Maticora, 639f, 640, 642, 644
Mato Grosso lancehead, 417
Mauritia flexuosa, 346, 438
Mayan coralsnake, 171
mazacóatl, 284, 454, 455
mazacuata, 448

mba'echiniva, 542
mbaraka, 542
mbói, 6
mbói-chiní, mboi chi-ni, 542
mbói-chumbé, 6, 159, 217, 226
mbói-chumbé-guazú, 226
mboí/mbói cuatía, 365, 366
mboí-hobú, 313
mboí-kwatiara, 366, 385
mboi-mbaraka, 542
mbói-yvyvovó, 159, 217
meadow jumping mouse, 255
meadow vole, 255, 511, 606
Medem's coralsnake, 176
mejiya, 542
Meleagris, 506
Melospiza melodia, 508t, 511, 606
Membranipora tuberculata, 236
meokárima, 316
Mephitis, 243
Merendón palm-pitviper, 309, 634
Mérida pygmy coralsnake, 224
Merriam pocket mouse, 606
Merrill's song sparrow, 510
Merten's coralsnake, 177
Mesaspis, 105, 425
Mesaspis gadovii, 425, 451
Mesocestoides sp., 515, 516
Mesocestoides variabilis, 516
Mesopotamian coralsnake, 209
mesquite, 16, 20, 107, 117, 266, 455, 521, 528,
    532, 556, 563, 581, 588, 599, 612
metapil, 265
metapilcoate, metapilcuate, 284
metlapilocóatl, 284
Mexican dusky rattlesnake, 593
Mexican ground squirrel, 506
Mexican horned pitviper, 4, **449–452**, 455. *See
    also Ophryacus; names of individual species*
Mexican jumping pitviper, 284
Mexican palm-pitviper, 303
Mexican pygmy rattlesnake, 431, 576
Mexican small-headed rattlesnake, 553
Mexican spotted owl, 514
Mexican vole, 451
Mexican west coast rattlesnake, 534
Microcaecilia sp., 119
microfilarian, 101
Micropechis, 639f
Micropterus dolomiuei, 255
Micropterus sp., 255
microteiid, 119, 120
Microtus californicus, 511
Microtus chrotorrhinus, 255, 509
Microtus longicaudus, 511
Microtus mexicanus, 451, 508t, 510
Microtus montanus, 511, 512
Microtus ochrogaster, 255, 507, 606
Microtus pennsylvanicus, 255, 511, 606
Microtus pinetorum, 255
Microtus sp., 255, 509, 510, 512, 606
Micruridae, 124
Micruroides, 108–125, 110t, 125k, 126, 127,
    132–133, 134, 136, 625t, 626, 639f, 641f, 644,
    687
Micruroides euryxanthus, 12t, 13t, 16k, 17k,
    22t, 24t, 26k, 30k, 116, 117, 119, 121, 122,
    132, 133f, 133m, **133–135**, 620, 628, 641f, *685,
    686, 687, 688, 755, 757*, pls. 23–25
Micruroides euryxanthus australis, 133, 133m,
    134, 135
Micruroides euryxanthus euryxanthus, 132f, 133,
    133m, 134, 135
Micruroides euryxanthus neglectus, 133, 133m,
    135
Micruroides fulvius, 169

tamagás verde, tamagá verde, 6, 296, 298, 301
Tambo coralsnake, 183
Tamias amoenus, 511
Tamias sp., 100, 510
Tamias striatus, 509, 510
Tamiasciurus hudsonicus, 511
Tamiasciurus sp., 509
tanbark oak, 15
Tancitaran dusky rattlesnake, 574
Tantilla atriceps, 118
Tantilla coronata, 118, 254
Tantilla gracilis, 118, 196
Tantilla melanocephala, 120, 349
Tantilla nigriceps, 606
Tantilla planiceps, 118
Tantilla relicta, 118
Tantilla rubra, 118, 119, 458
Tantilla sp., 115, 118, 119, 120, 147, 159, 625t
Tantilla supracincta, pl. 1313
Tantillita canula, 119
tapeworm, 119, 515
Taxidea, 500
taxinchan, 373, *709*
Taxodium distichum, 14
taya, 332, 373, 378
taya del Cauca, 334
taya equis, 373, 378
Taylor's cantil, 265, 266
t'dadema, 218
tecuhtlacozauqui, 583
tecutlacotzauhqui, 562
tegu lizard, 325, 348
teiid lizard, 508
tejeraia, 467
Teleuraspis, 646, 658
Teleuraspis birrí, 304
Teleuraspis castelnaudi var. *brachystoma*, 465
Teleuraspis Castelnaui, 320
Teleuraspis Castelnaui var. *brachystoma*, 465
Teleuraspis Lansbergi, 465
Teleuraspis nigroadspersus, 304
Teleuraspis nitida, 304
Teleuraspis nummifer, 281, 284
Teleuraspis Schlegelii, 304
Teleuraspis schlegelii, 304
Teleuraspis undulatus, 454
temacuil, 104
temacuilcahuya, 95, 104
ten pace snake, *685*
teotlacozauhqui, 584
tepecolcóatl, 562
tepemechín, 468
tepocho, 284, 373
tepocolcóatl, 534, 584
tepotzo, 284, 373
tepoxo, 284, 373
Teratoscincus sp., 630
terciopelo, 6, 370, 373, 409, 634, *737, 738*
terciopelo de pestaña, 305, 307
termite, 502
térotero, 378
Terranova caballaeroi, 256
Terrapene carolina, 254, 256
Tetrathyridia, 515, 516
teuhtlacotzauhqui, 562
teuhtlacozauhqui, 534, 562, 584
Texas coralsnake, 196
Texas earless lizard, *725*
Texas horned lizard, 605
Texas ratsnake, 118
Texas spiny lizard, 605
Texas spotted whiptail, 100, 605
Thamnocenchris aurifer, 296
Thamnodynastes chaquensis, pl. 1314
Thamnodynastes gambotensis
Thamnodynastes hypoconia, pl. 1315

Thamnodynastes nattereri, 726
Thamnodynastes rutilus, pl. 1316
Thamnodynastes sp., 345, 625t, 720t, 726, 726f, 727, pls. 1319–1320
Thamnodynastes strigatus, 726, pl. 1317
Thamnodynastes strigilis, 726, pl. 1318
Thamnophis atratus, 631
Thamnophis couchi, 727
Thamnophis elegans, 726
Thamnophis elegans terrestris, 727
Thamnophis elegans vagrans, 481, 727, pl. 1321
Thamnophis marcianus, 118, 727
Thamnophis marcianus marcianus, pl. 1322
Thamnophis ordinoides, 481
Thamnophis proximus, 118, 254, 727, pl. 1323
Thamnophis sirtalis, 254, 256, 606, 621, 727
Thamnophis sp., 118, 256, 719t, 726
Thanathos montanus, 407
Thanatophis Boussingaultii, 461
Thanatophis Castelnaudi, 320
Thanatophis colgadora, 304
Thanatophis Lansbergi, 465
Thanatophis montanus, 406, 407
Thanatophis nummifer, 281, 284
Thanatophis Schlegelii, 304
Thanatophis sutus, 467
Thanatophis torvus, 304
Thanatos Boussingaultii, 461
Thanatos Castelnaudi, 320
Thanatos Lansbergii, 465
Thanatos montanus, 406, 407
Thanatos nummifer, 281
Thanatos Schlegelii, 304
Thanatos sutus, 467
Thanatos torvus, 304
Thecadactylus rapicauda, 439
Thecadactylus sp., 6
Theraphosa blondi, 349
thirteen-lined ground squirrel, 510
Thomomys bottae, 508, 509, 511
Thomomys sp., 512
Thomomys talpoides, 511
Thomomys umbrinus, 512
threeawn grass, 14
thrush, 254
Thryothorus modestus, 425
Thubunacea cnemidophorus, 515, 516
Thuja plicata, 15
thunder-and-lightning snake, 169
thunder snake, 196, 268
Thunnus albacares, 235
Tibicen canicularis, 252
Tibicen sp., 254
tick, 101, 516
tigra, 373
tigra mariposa, 316, 409
tigra-veinticuatro, 316
tiger rattlesnake, 588
Tigre, 373
Tilia americana, 12
Tillandsia sp., 266
timber rattlesnake, 256, 550, *696*
timbo, timbó, 281, 282, 288
timbo chingo, 433
tira peia, 411, 415, 421
tiro, 305
Tisiphone, 646
Tisiphone cuprea, 267
Tityus trinitatis, 743
tiznada, *738*
tlehua, 562, 571
Tleua, 562
tl'iish, 537
toad, 254, 348, 349
toad-headed pitviper, 4, **322–326**. *See also*
  Bothrocophias; names of individual species

toboa oscura, 433
toboa real, 448
toboba, 262, 282, 288, 300, 305, 307, 468, 473, *753*
toboba chinga, 282, 468
toboba de altura, 433, 746
toboba de árbol, 302
toboba de pestaña/pestañas, 305, 307
toboba rabo amarillo, 373
toboba real, 373
toboba tiznada, 373
toboíta, 433
tobosas grass, 567, 581, 596, 612
tole-chini, 104
Tomes's spiny rat, 440
tommygoff, 6, 468
Tomodon dorsatus, 727, 727f, pl. 1324
Tomodon sp., 345, 625t, 720t, 727
tongue worm, 515
torito, 452, 455
Tortuga Island diamond rattlesnake, 589
Tournefortia gnaphaloides, 50
towhee, 506, 509
Townsend ground squirrel, 511
Townsend's solitaire, 512
Toxicocalamus, 639f
Toxicophas atrofuscus, 267
Toxicophis leucostoma, 271
Toxicophis piscivorus, 271
Toxicophis pugnax, 271
Toxicophis sp., 249
trabichuri, 465
Trachemys scripta, 256
Trachipogon, 585
Trachyboa boulengeri, pl. 1325
Trachyboa gularis, pl. 1326
Trachyboa sp., 324, 345, 625t
Trachyderma, 95
Trachyderma horridum, 95, 103
trapjaw, 272
Travassosascaris araujoi, 349
tree fern, 21, 303
treefrog, 255, 292, 293, 311, 325, 606
tree viper, 290
Triceratolepidophis, 646, 656, 657
trichomonad, 349, 459
tricolor heron, 256
Trigalus, 436
trigonocephale, le, 396
Trigonocephali, 646
Trigonocephalus, 245, 368, 436, 646, 652
Trigonocephalus alternatus, 365
Trigonocephalus ammodytes, 445
Trigonocephalus asper, 373
Trigonocephalus atro-fuscus, 267
Trigonocephalus (Atropos) undulatus, 449, 454
Trigonocephalus atrox, 377
Trigonocephalus bilineatus, 262, 313
Trigonocephalus (Bothrops) arboreus, 313
Trigonocephalus (Bothrops) pubescens, 419
Trigonocephalus caribbaeus, 383
Trigonocephalus Castelnaudi, 320
Trigonocephalus cenchris, 267
Trigonocephalus Colombiensis, 371
Trigonocephalus Contortirx, 267
Trigonocephalus crotalinus, 445
Trigonocephalus histrionicus, 267
Trigonocephalus holosericeus, 377
Trigonocephalus jararaca, 390
Trigonocephalus (Lachesis) brasiliensis, 446
Trigonocephalus lanceolatus, 371, 396
Trigonocephalus Lansbergii, 465
Trigonocephalus lansbergii, 465
Trigonocephalus nummifer, 281, 284
Trigonocephalus piscivorus, 271
Trigonocephalus pulcher, 4, 319, 320